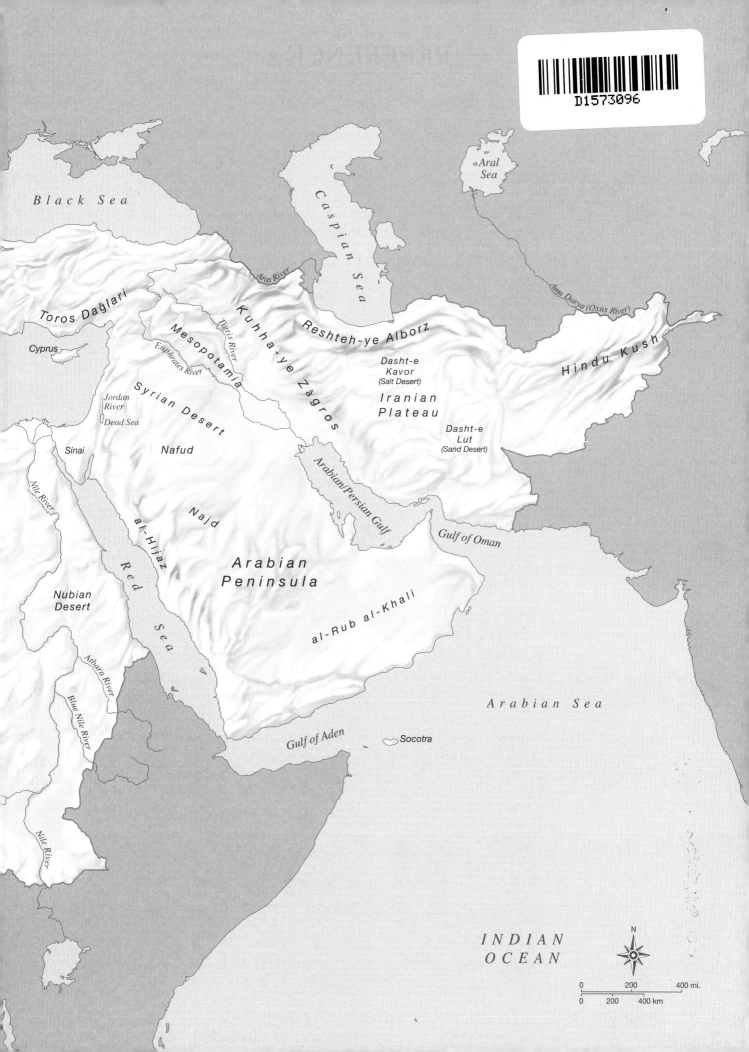

REFERENCE

TOURO COLLEGE LIBRARY
Boro Park 53rd Street

WITHDRAWN

*Biographical Encyclopedia of the Modern
Middle East and North Africa*

Editorial Board

EDITOR IN CHIEF

Michael R. Fischbach
Randolph-Macon College

ASSOCIATE EDITORS

Aida Bamia
University of Florida

Mine Eren
Randolph-Macon College

Geremy Forman
Tel Aviv University and University of Haifa

Eric Hooglund
Bates College

J. E. Peterson
Independent scholar

REFERENCE

Biographical Encyclopedia of the Modern Middle East and North Africa

VOLUME II
L-Z

TOURO COLLEGE LIBRARY
Boro Park 53rd Street

WITHDRAWN

Michael R. Fischbach
EDITOR IN CHIEF

THOMSON
━━━━━★━━━━━ ™
GALE

Detroit • New York • San Francisco • New Haven, Conn. • Waterville, Maine • London

BP53

Biographical Encyclopedia of the Modern Middle East and North Africa

Michael R. Fischbach

© 2008 Gale Group

Thomson and Star Logo are trademarks and Gale is a registered trademark used herein under license.

For more information, contact:
Gale Group
27500 Drake Rd.
Farmington Hills, MI 48331-3535
Or you can visit our Internet site at
http://www.gale.com

ALL RIGHTS RESERVED
No part of this work covered by the copyright herein may be reproduced or used in any form or by any means—graphic, electronic, or mechanical, including photocopying, recording, taping, Web distribution, or information storage retrieval systems—without the written permission of the publisher.

For permission to use material from the product, submit your request via the Web at

http://www.gale-edit.com/permissions, or you may download our Permissions Request form and submit your request by fax or mail to:

Permissions Department
Gale Group
27500 Drake Rd.
Farmington Hills, MI 48331-3535
Permissions Hotline:
248-699-8006 or 800-877-4253, ext. 8006
Fax 248-699-8074 or 800-762-4058

Cover photographs reproduced by permission of AP Images (portraits of Mohamed ElBaradei and Orhan Pamuk), © Reuters/Corbis (portrait of Hanan Mikha'il Ashrawi), © Francois Lenoir/Reuters/Corbis (portrait of Shirin Ebadi), and Jack Guez/AFP/Getty Images (portrait of Yossi Benayoun).

Since this page cannot legibly accommodate all copyright notices, the acknowledgements constitute an extension of the copyright notice.

While every effort has been made to secure permission to reprint material and to ensure the reliability of the information presented in this publication, Gale Group neither guarantees the accuracy of the data contained herein nor assumes any responsibility for errors, omissions, or discrepancies. Gale Group accepts no payment for listing; and inclusion in the publication of any organization, agency, institution, publication, service, or individual does not imply endorsement of the editors or publisher. Errors brought to the attention of the publisher and verified to the satisfaction of the publisher will be corrected in future editions.

EDITORIAL DATA PRIVACY POLICY
Does this publication contain information about you as an individual? If so, for more information about our editorial data privacy policies, please see our Privacy Statement at www.gale.com.

LIBRARY OF CONGRESS CATALOGING-IN-PUBLICATION DATA

Biographical Encyclopedia of the Modern Middle East and North Africa / Michael R. Fischbach, editor in chief.
    v. cm.
    Includes bibliographical references and index.
    Contents: v.1. A-K
    ISBN 978-1-4144-1889-6 (set hardcover)—ISBN 978-1-4144-1890-2 (v. 1)—
    ISBN 978-1-4144-1891-9 (v. 2)
    1. Arab countries–Biography 2. Middle East–Biography 3. Africa, North-Biography
    I. Fischbach, Michael R.
    CT1866.B56 2008
    920.056—dc22

            2007028169

5/26/09

LAABI, ABDELLATIF
(1942–)

Moroccan writer Abdellatif Laabi is a French-language poet, playwright, translator, essayist, novelist, raconteur, and activist whose works reveal his engagement with social and political issues and a strong commitment against oppression, injustice, and human rights abuses. He played a key role in the cultural renewal of Morocco in the mid-1960s, restating the complex issue of developing nations nationalism and decolonization.

PERSONAL HISTORY

Laabi was born in Fez, Morocco (presumably in 1942), to a Muslim family of craftsmen, into an illiterate environment. He has pointed out that one of the reasons he started to write was to allow people who are not able to express themselves to speak. His mother, Ghita, was in constant crisis about her condition as a woman, and in a way was a feminist without knowing, Laabi has said; he made her the central character in one of his novels, *La fond de la jarre* (The bottom of the jug, 2002).

Laabi attended the French-Muslim School. At school, children were taught only in French. At that time, he realized his condition of colonization, and this situation generated internal conflict: when he began to write, the only language that he really knew was French, even though his birth language was Arabic. When he was fourteen years old, Morocco declared its independence from France. He entered the University of Rabat where he earned his B.A. in French literature in 1963. After graduation he worked as a French literature teacher at the Lycée Mulay Idris, also in Rabat.

In 1963 he and a number of other writers and artists founded the Théâtre universitaire marocain, where he met his wife, Jocelyne. They staged plays by Fernando Arrabal and Bertolt Brecht, and after only one season they were censored and the theater was closed down. He also founded an important literary review, the journal *Souffles* (Breaths), in 1966; the Arabic version of this journal was called *Anfas*. He founded it with the poets Mohammed Khair-Eddine, a major poet and novelist who died in 1995 in total poverty, and Mostafa Nissaboury, who continues to write and publish. Later on, other artists and writers participated in the project, from Morocco, Algeria, other parts of Africa, France, and one from Germany. *Souffles/Anfas* was considered a meeting point for poets who felt the need for a poetic revival, but soon it was a focus for all Moroccan creative and intellectual actors: painters, filmmakers, theater people, researchers, and thinkers. The magazine lasted for six years and published twenty-three issues in French and eight in Arabic before it was banned in 1972. The magazine allowed an avant-garde movement to be born

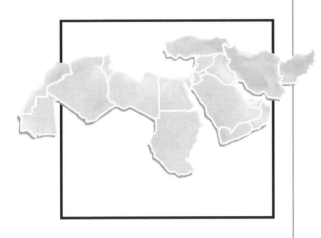

BIOGRAPHICAL HIGHLIGHTS

Name: Abdellatif Laabi

Birth: 1942?, Fez, Morocco

Family: Wife, Jocelyne; two sons, Yacine and Qods; one daughter, Hind

Nationality: Moroccan

Education: B.A., French literature, University of Rabat, 1963

PERSONAL CHRONOLOGY:

- **1958:** French-Muslim school; teaches in French
- **1963:** Founding member, Théâtre universitaire marocain
- **1964:** Teaches French literature at Lycée Mulay Idris, Rabat
- **1965:** Massacre of children and parents at a peaceful demonstration in Casablanca, 23 March, a turning point in professional and political life
- **1966:** Founding member, director, Souffles/Anfas (Breaths); founds with Abraham Serfaty Association de Recherche Culturelle (ARC); joins Parti pour la liberation et le socialism (PLS), former Moroccan Communist Party
- **1972:** Sentenced to ten years in prison
- **1980:** Released from prison
- **1985:** Exiled to Paris with family
- **1988:** Elected to Académie Mallarmé

and express itself, and therefore encouraged the literature of all Arab countries, as well as opening Morocco to cultures of the other countries of the Maghreb and of developing nations.

This group of writers rebelled against French literature. Growing up under colonialism, they were not allowed to learn the language of their country and were forced to live culturally dependent; consequently they wanted to be finished with colonial history. They thought that not only the economy and the government had to be decolonized, but people's minds as well.

At the same time, Laabi involved himself in national politics. In 1966, he joined the Parti pour la libération et le socialism (PLS) and founded, with Abraham Serfaty, the Association de Recherche Culturelle (ARC). Both of them were imprisoned in 1972 and tortured. Laabi, editor-in-chief of *Souffles/Anfas*, was charged with con-

spiracy against the state and sentenced to ten years in prison for "crimes of opinion" (for his political beliefs and his writings against the regime of King HASSAN II) and served a sentence from 1972 to 1980. While in prison, Laabi received strong support from friends and intellectuals all over the world. In 1979 an international committee for his freedom was created with the participation of many intellectuals and the support of numerous foreign journals. He continued to write poetry during this period and received numerous literary prizes (such as the Liberty Prize awarded by the French PEN Club). He describes his prison years in a series of poems and letters titled *Chroniques de la citadelle d'exil* (Chronicles of the citadel of banishment, 1983). In 1985 he was forced into exile in France, as was his friend and fellow contributor to *Souffles/Anfas*, Serfaty, in 1991 after seventeen years in jail. Laabi tried to return to his homeland several times, but since 1995 has lived definitively in Paris. In 1985 Laabi was nominated as commander of the Ordre des Arts et des Lettres by Jack Lang, French minister of culture; since 1988 he has been a member of the Académie Mallarmé.

INFLUENCES AND CONTRIBUTIONS

One of Laabi's early influences was the work of Frantz Fanon, among others; Aimé Césaire and the Moroccan writer Driss Chraibi were very important to him. He was also deeply influenced by non-French or non-Arab writers such as Fedor Dostoevski. But most important was his awareness of what was happening in the Maghreb during the 1950s and 1960s. Like many of his generation, he thought with Fanon that colonized countries had to break free of the West. As a writer, he believed that there were moments in history—in the history of literature too—when individuals are the instruments for the articulation of social needs.

Laabi was particularly influenced by the 23 March 1965 massacre in Casablanca of children and parents at a peaceful demonstration in opposition to Hassan II's suspension of the constitution. This tragic event was a turning point in Laabi's professional and political life, and Laabi went on to write a poem about the massacre.

Laabi's other contribution has been the extensive translation into French of a large number of Arabic poets. He has translated the poems of the Moroccan Abdallah Zrika in *Rires de l'arbre à palabre*; (1982; Laughter of the palaver tree); an anthology of Palestinian poetry, *La poésie palestinienne de combat* (1970; Palestinian poetry of struggle); MAHMUD DARWISH, in *Rien qu'une autre année* (1983; It is only another year); the Syrian novelist Hanna Mina, in *Soleil en instance* (1986; Sun in process); a collection of poetry by the Iraqi ABD AL-WAHHAB AL-BAYATI, *Autobiographie du voleur de feu* (1987; Autobiography of the fire thief); and a collection of poems by

WHAT IS LIFE IF NOT DIGNITY?

Writing is still a risk in many countries. This was the case in Morocco when I was still living there—I was put in prison.... There are equally serious but different atrocities which occur in countries which we call democracies [in Western countries]. There is the numbing of consciousness, an indifference which is gradually settling in, there are unacceptable things that happen every day, and pass as normal. I am implicated in this, because I am aware that the West is a part of me. It's my humanity as well. To me there is a single human condition, within which there are different situations. And I don't understand how one could think that the intellectual should be absent from all that—do your work and leave the world behind the door. If this satisfies certain intellectuals, that's their prerogative. But for me, poetry is too closely connected to life and what it stands for. What is life if not dignity, liberty, the ability to express oneself freely?

INTERVIEW WITH KRISTIN PREVALLET *DOUBLE CHANGE* 3 (2002). AVAILABLE FROM HTTP://WWW.DOUBLECHANGE.COM/ISSUE3/LAABI.HTM.

the Palestinian Samih al-Qasim, *Je t'aime au gré de la mort* (1988; I love you at the pleasure of death).

He has written an impressive amount of poetry himself, including the collections *Le règne de barbarie, et d'autres poèmes* (1980; The reign of barbarism and other poems), which marks the beginning of his poetic and literary writings; *Le spleen de Casablanca* (1997; Casablanca spleen); and the illustrated collection *Petit musé portatif* (2002; A small portable museum). Laabi has also written plays, including *Le baptême chacaliste* (1987; Jackalian baptism), *Exercices de tolérance* (1993; Exercises in tolerance), *Rimbaud et Shéhérazade* (2000; Rimbaud and Scheherazade), and *Écris la vie* (2005; Writing life). He has also published four novels: *L'oeil de la nuit* (1969; The eye of the night), *Les rides du lion* (1989; The wrinkles of the lion), and *Le chemin des ordalies* (1982; The road of ordeals, published in English as *Rue de Retour*, 1989), reedited in 2000 as *Le fou d'espoir* (Crazy with hope), in which he relates his painful years in prison. *Le fond de la jarre* (2002; The bottom of the jug) evokes traditional life in Fez during the colonial period. He has written three books for children as well.

THE WORLD'S PERSPECTIVE

Even though Laabi is a celebrated intellectual in Europe, there is still a marked tendency for Western and Moroccan critics alike to minimize or dismiss the political commitment of Maghrebi writers who receive literary prizes, reside outside their home countries, and choose to participate in official dialogues concerning nationalist sore points such as francophony. Moreover, his work and that of other francophone writers has not been very well represented in American literary magazines, although that may be changing.

LEGACY

Laabi seeks to eliminate the dividing lines between literary genres. He refuses to be constrained by blind adherence to any particular literary register or ideology. He is above all a poet with an impressive number of published collections, who has sought renewal through the elimination of antiquated and unsuitable traditions. His work as a translator has contributed to make Maghrebi and Arab writers known in Europe; but mostly he has developed a work that exhorts readers to commit and that always reminds them that the fight for freedom is endless.

BIBLIOGRAPHY

WORKS BY LAABI

Rue du Retour [Le Chemin des ordalies, 1982]. Translated by Jacqueline Kaye. London: Readers Intenational, 1989.
"Interview with Kristin Prevallet." *Double Change* 3 (2002). Available from http://www.doublechange.com/issue3/laabi.htm.
The World's Embrace: Selected Poems. Translated by Anne George, Pierre Joris, Edris Makward, et al. San Francisco: City Lights Books, 2003.
Abdellatif Laâbi's Official Web site. Available from http://www.laabi.net.

OTHER SOURCES

Hitchcott, Nicki, and Laila Ibnlfassi. *African Francophone Writing: A Critical Introduction.* Oxford and Washington, DC: Berg, 1996.
Wolf, Mary Ellen. "Textual Politics in Contemporary Moroccan Francophone Literature." *Journal of the Midwest Modern Language Association* 25, no. 1 (Spring 1992): 32–40.

Laura Ruiz

LAHHAM, DURAID
(1934–)

The Syrian comedian Duraid (Durayd, Dureid) Lahham is one of the most popular and recognized Arab comedians of the second half of the twentieth century and the start of the twenty-first century. He is particularly remembered for his iconic television and film character, Ghawwar al-Tawsha, and for the not-so-veiled political jabs in his plays and films directed at the Arab world and its leaders.

PERSONAL HISTORY

Lahham was born in 1934 into a Shi'ite Muslim family in the Hayy al-Amin district of Damascus, Syria. His father was Syrian, his mother came from south Lebanon, and the family lived in modest circumstances. While in secondary school, Lahham performed in several plays, as well as when he attended Damascus University where he studied chemistry. After graduation, Lahham started out on a career as a chemistry professor at the university. Because of dance lessons he gave at the time, he became acquainted with actors and the artistic scene in Damascus. These connections helped land him his first television role in 1960. That year marked the beginning of Syrian state television under the direction of Sabah Qabbani. He brought in Lahham to act in a television miniseries called *Sahrat Dimashq* (Damascus evening) along with stage actor Nihad Qal'i. Thereafter Lahham quit teaching to devote himself full time to acting, even though this was considered a bad career move in a society that viewed a government job such as a university professor to be a secure and prestigious source of income.

Lahham teamed up with Qal'i in a television show called *Aqd al-Lu'lu* (The pearl necklace), which later was made into a film featuring the Lebanese starlet, Sabah. The comedic duo went on to make more than a dozen films in the 1960s. Surely their biggest successes at that time, however, were the hugely popular Syrian television series *Maqalib Ghawwar* (Ghawwar's pranks), which first aired in 1966, and *Sahh al-Nawm* (Good morning), which aired in 1971. Both were comedies in the style of Abbott and Costello and Laurel and Hardy. Lahham's character, Ghawwar al-Tawsha, was a naive, clownlike figure who always wore a fez (Arabic: tarbush), *shirwal* (baggy peasant trousers), and wooden clogs, and who embodied many traditional Syrian stereotypes. He also played off the straight-man character in the series, Husni al-Burazan, played by Qal'i. Wildly popular, *Sahh al-Nawm* spawned a television sequel in 1973 and a film by the same name.

Ghawwar also was a notable character at the time because he spoke with a Syrian accent. Lahham was aware that most prominent actors in the Arab world at the time were Egyptians, and that the Egyptian dialect and accent of Arabic had become dominant in Arabic film and television. But he refused to mimic an Egyptian dialect and remained true to his origins. His massive popularity around the Arab world thus ensured that more and more

BIOGRAPHICAL HIGHLIGHTS

Name: Duraid (also Durayd, Dureid) Lahham

Birth: 1934, Damascus, Syria

Family: First wife, May al-Husayni; son, Tha'ir; daughter, Abir; second wife, Hala al-Bitar; daughter, Dina.

Education: Studied chemistry at Damascus University

PERSONAL CHRONOLOGY:
- **1960:** Appears in first television show *Sahrat Dimashq* (Damascus evening)
- **1966:** *Maqalib Ghawwar* (Ghawwar's pranks) first airs
- **1971:** Appears in *Sahh al-Nawm* (Good morning)
- **1974:** Acts in *Day'at Tishrin* (October village)
- **1976:** Performs in *Ghurba* (Exile)
- **1978:** Acts in *Kasak Ya Watan* (Cheers to you, O homeland)
- **1981:** Film *Imbaraturiyyat Ghawwar* (Ghawwar's empire) debuts
- **1987:** Films *al-Hudud* (The border) and *al-Taqrir* (The report) debut
- **1990:** Film *Kafrun* debuts
- **1992:** Children's play *al-Asfura al-Sa'ida* (The happy bird) opens
- **1997:** Appointed UNICEF ambassador for children's affairs in Syria
- **1998:** *Awdat Ghawwar* (The return of Ghawwar) airs
- **1999:** Appointed UNICEF ambassador for childhood in the Middle East and North Africa
- **2004:** Resigns from UNICEF position
- **2006:** Film *al-Aba al-Sighar* (The young parents) debuts in Cairo

Arabs became familiar with a Syrian accent that until then largely was unknown to Arab television audiences.

After he began branching out into films, Lahham kept the character Ghawwar, although the character became less of a clown and more of an Arab Everyman dealing with the oppression and challenges facing the Arab world. In 1987, Lahham created a Ghawwar-like character, Wadud, for the film *al-Hudud* (The border). In 1990, Wadud appeared in the children's film *Kafrun*, as well. Lahham brought Ghawwar back onto Syrian television in 1998 in the series *Awdat Ghawwar* (The return of Ghawwar). After a short hiatus starting in the late 1990s, Lahham resumed making films. By 2006, he had appeared in twenty-six films, the latest being *al-Aba al-Sighar* (The young parents) in 2006.

INFLUENCES AND CONTRIBUTIONS

Surely Lahham's greatest contribution to popular Arab culture was his iconic character, Ghawwar al-Tawsha. Ghawwar was an easy character with whom ordinary Syrians and Arabs could identify: He was not rich, he was not attractive, and he did not live a life drastically different from their own. Similar to Palestinian cartoonist Naji al-Ali's famous child character, Hanzala—the simple spectator in al-Ali's political cartoons—Ghawwar became an artistic vehicle for drawing ordinary persons into Lahham's artistic works and political perspectives.

Another of Lahham's contributions to Arab television and film is his political commentary. After the Arab world's disastrous defeat at the hands of Israel in the June 1967 Arab-Israel War, Lahham's work took on more of a political tone. Similar to other intellectuals and artists, Lahham searched for the reasons and meanings behind the catastrophic defeat, which contrasted so sharply with the bellicose, patriotic prewar verbiage that Arabs had been hearing from their leaders. The humility of Ghawwar was the perfect vehicle for Lahham to pillory the powerful forces that he perceived running roughshod over ordinary Arabs' lives. It has been claimed that one reason why his political sarcasm and irony was tolerated in Syria was because President HAFIZ AL-ASAD was a fan.

Lahham's political works stemmed from his conviction that art could make a difference in the Arab world, where open political dissent rarely was tolerated. Sly, comedic attacks on all that was wrong could, as he later said, shock and make change. He collaborated with others in producing these works, particularly with the sharp-penned Syrian playwright Muhammad al-Maghut, who helped Lahham write political plays attacking corruption, inefficiency, and national weakness in the Arab world. The Israeli defeat of Syria and Egypt in the October 1973 Arab-Israeli War produced a new spurt of political energy in Lahham, as did Egypt's unpopular peace treaty with Israel in 1979. Among Lahham's noted political plays were three that he staged within five years after the 1973 defeat: *Day'at Tishrin* (October village, 1974), *Ghurba* (Exile, 1976), and *Kasak Ya Watan* (Cheers to you, O homeland, 1978). Lahham described *Kasak Ya Watan* as a play about the death of relations between a citizen and his country.

CONTEMPORARIES

■

Muhammad al-Maghut (1934–2006). Writer, poet, and playwright Muhammad al-Maghut was born in Salamiyya, Syria, in 1934. Al-Maghut was noted for his satirical, pointed look at modern Arab life and Arab leaders. In one of his plays he noted bitterly, "Policemen, Interpol men everywhere; you search for the perfect crime. . . . There is only one perfect crime; to be born an Arab." Al-Maghut is particularly remembered for working with Duraid Lahham in writing plays such as *Kasak Ya Watan* (Cheers to you, O homeland) and *Ghurba* (Exile). He died in Damascus in 2006.

In addition to his plays, Lahham also made several notable films with political themes. In 1981, the Ghawwar character appeared in the film *Imbaraturiyyat Ghawwar* (Ghawwar's empire) where he saves his neighborhood from the rivalry between two powerful men that threatens to destroy it. However, in the process Ghawwar himself ends up creating an oppressive dictatorship even as he pledges to support freedom and justice. Two other particularly noteworthy examples of political films were collaborations with al-Maghut: *al-Hudud* (The Border, 1987) and *al-Taqrir* (The Report, 1987). In the former, the unfortunate protagonist finds himself stuck along the border between two Arab states, and is resigned to live a life in no-man's-land between the two because he somehow lost his passport. It was a biting commentary on the bankruptcy of the Arab regimes' talk of Arab unity. *Al-Taqrir* features an honest government employee who loses his job as a result of his honesty, and then devotes his life to collecting evidence of official corruption in order to make a public presentation of his findings. He never gets the opportunity, however, because he is trampled to death as he enters the arena in which he intends to present his report.

Lahham later abandoned his hope that art could affect politics after an encounter with an important Arab leader left him politically and artistically defeated; years later, Looking back years later, he said in a brief 2003 interview for the *London Review of Books*, "A major leader in an Arab country said to me, 'You say what you want, and I'll do what I want.'" Lahham could ridicule the rulers all he wanted, and his audience could laugh, but at the end of the day, the rulers would still be in power. His art was toothless; its value lay only in its ability to entertain. Lahham reflected on his epiphany in a 19 August 2006 interview with the *New York Times*: "Yeah, I felt

THE ARAB RULERS LIED TO US

There is no doubt that the 1967 [Arab-Israeli] war which was dubbed al-Naksa [The Defeat] was very hard on us, as we were dreaming of achieving something. In four hours this dream evaporated, and we discovered that the Arab rulers lied to us, and that the victories they claimed were nothing but words. This defeat made us feel that art should have a say in what happens. Therefore I offered the plays "Kasak Ya Watan," "Day'at Tishrin," "Ghurba," and Sani al-Matar... [but] theater requires physical, psychological and daily efforts. My age as a grandfather has not left me any of these capabilities. But the more painstaking reason is that my theater is committed to national issues. National issues have become small in comparison to the Arab citizen's daily concerns. In the past, when we mentioned a statement about Arab unity, the hall used to be filled with enthusiasm and applause, but these days everybody is concerned about his bread, which has become more important.

DURAID LAHHAM, 2002 INTERVIEW WITH *AN NAHAR* NEWSPAPER.

disappointed. We had thought that artwork could shock and make change. But no, artwork, at the end of the day, even if it is critical, is entertainment."

THE WORLD'S PERSPECTIVE

Lahham and his comedic personas were loved throughout the Arab world by ordinary people and leaders alike, the latter of whom gave Lahham many awards and decorations over the decades. Even though he helped Arabs laugh at their leaders, several of them gave him medals. In 1976, Syrian president Hafiz al-Asad awarded him the Medal of the Syrian Republic. Other Arab leaders bestowed decorations on him as well, including Tunisia's Habib Bourguiba in 1979, Libya's MU'AMMAR AL-QADDAFI in 1991, and Lebanon's EMILE LAHOUD in 2000.

The United Nations recognized Lahham, as well. In 1997, UNICEF—the United Nations Children's Fund—chose him to be its ambassador for children's affairs in Syria in recognition of the 1990 children's film *Kafrun* and the 1992 children's play *al-Asfura al-Sa'ida* (The happy bird). Two years later, he became UNICEF's ambassador for childhood for the Middle East and North Africa. Not everyone appreciated him, however. In 2004, Lahham resigned from his position with UNICEF following a diplomatic incident involving Israel. When

visiting areas of southern Lebanon that formerly had been occupied by Israel from 1982 to 2000, Lahham gave a press conference near the Lebanese-Israeli border in which he sharply criticized Israeli prime minister ARIEL SHARON and U.S. president George W. Bush, comparing both to the Nazi dictator Adolf Hitler. After his remarks appeared in the Lebanese and Israeli press, Israel lodged a complaint with UNICEF about the political nature of Lahham's comments. After UNICEF probed the matter, Lahham resigned from his position.

LEGACY

Duraid Lahham will be remembered as a comedic giant in Arab film, television, and stage, as well as a person who masterfully articulated the hardships and frustrations of the average Arab during a critical and turbulent period in their history. He also was one of the most important figures in the early years of Syrian television and film production.

BIBLIOGRAPHY

Duraid Lahham's Official Web site. Available from www.duraidlahham.com.

Glass, Charles. "Is Syria Next?" *London Review of Books* 25, no. 14 (24 July 2003). Available from http://www.lrb.co.uk/v25/n14/glas01_.html.

Hamdan, Mas'ud. *Poetics, Politics, and Protest in Arab Theatre: The Bitter Cup and the Holy Rain.* Brighton, U.K.: Sussex Academic Press, 2006.

Slackman, Michael. "An Arab Artist Says All the World Really Isn't a Stage." *New York Times* (19 August 2006). Available from http://www.nytimes.com/2006/08/19/.

Michael R. Fischbach

LAHOUD, EMILE
(1936–)

Lebanese general and politician Emile Geamil Lahoud is the eleventh president of the Republic of Lebanon. He has long played a key role in Lebanese politics, especially since becoming head of state in 1998. It was under his leadership that Israel was pushed out of Lebanon in May 2000 after twenty-two years of occupation. Lahoud brought an end to sectarianism and rebuilt and rearmed the Lebanese army. However, he has ruled over a nation divided. His own policies mimic the divide, in which he silences the anti-Syrian opposition and allows the neighboring country to infiltrate Lebanese military and security agencies.

Emile Lahoud. AP IMAGES.

PERSONAL HISTORY

Lahoud was born on 12 January 1936 in Baadat, Lebanon. His parents, General Jamil Lahoud and Adrinee Badjakian, raised Emile in the military way, with thought first for duty to country. Lahoud attended La Sagesse elementary school in Beirut, and then went to Bumana high school in north Metn. After his mandatory schooling, Lahoud decided to attend the military academy. In 1959 he graduated and became a lieutenant, serving on the ship *Tyre* as a commander. Earlier he had served as a naval engineer. Lahoud attained the prestigious role of commander of the second fleet from 1966 to 1968, and then of the first fleet for the next two years. He transferred into the army through the influence of his cousin, General Jean Njeim. After Njeim's death, and not long after Lahoud's transfer, Lahoud decided to stay on in the army, gaining rank and popularity. During his time in the army, he trained from 1972 to 1973, and again from 1979 to 1980 at the U.S. Naval Command College. As of 1980, Lahoud was positioned in the army command as the director of personnel, and in three years time managed to gain a position at the Defense Ministry. President Amine Gemayyel, in the fall of 1988 was exiting the presidency with no successor, as the parliament was unable to convene to elect one. As a last resort, President Gemayel appointed General MICHEL AOUN to serve as interim prime minister. This created some obvious tension and problems between Aoun and the parliamentary

BIOGRAPHICAL HIGHLIGHTS

Name: Emile Geamil Lahoud

Birth: 1936, Baadat, Lebanon

Family: Wife, Andree Amadouny; children, Karine, Emile Jr., and Ralph

Nationality: Lebanese

Education: La Sagesse School, Beirut; Bumana High School, Metn; the military academy, 1956–1959. Studied maritime engineering and rescue operations during the 1960s in Great Britain, and attended the U.S. Naval Command College in Rhode Island from 1972 to 1973 and 1979 to 1980

PERSONAL CHRONOLOGY:

- **1950s:** Attends military academy; navy engineer and commander of the landing ship, *Tyre*

- **1960s:** Named commander of the second and first fleets

- **1970s:** Studies maritime engineering and rescue operations in Britain and the U.S. Naval Command College

- **1980s:** Appointed director of personnel and commander of the Lebanese army

- **1998:** President of Lebanon

body. Lahoud tried to wrangle with him to gain the presidency for himself, as well as concessions with Syria, but was unsuccessful. In September 1989, after months of supposed incompetence, Aoun fired Lahoud. Then in November, Lahoud was appointed commander of the armed forces. This led him to his most important role to that date. Lahoud would play a major role in the ending restabilization of Lebanon after its civil war. After the war ended, with the Lebanese army severely weakened, Lahoud took the leading role in rebuilding the all-important army. He sought, and gained, equipment to rebuild from the United States, and made military service mandatory for all able-bodied males. The only negative concession he made was that he allowed Syria the right to control the army through the highest channels possible. This was a major set back for Lebanese independence, as Syria now had an open door and powerful controlling influence within Lebanon. In October 1998, Lahoud was elected unanimously by those seated in the national assembly to the presidency. Those not wanting to participate were WALID JUMBLATT and his followers. They protested by having no part of the vote, and by walking out on the election. RAFIQ HARIRI was also a vocal opponent of Lahoud's election to such a lofty position. Hariri saw Lahoud as being a Syrian puppet. Unfortunately, there is evidence that he may have been, as he had definitely used his command of the army to help quash opposition to the post–civil war dominance of Lebanon by the Syrians. In 1993 Syria and the Lebanese government, headed by Lahoud, signed the Defense and Security Pact. This pact gave unprecedented access to the Syrians to all functions of Lebanese government and military. In the two years from 1994 to 1996, many demonstrations and protests broke out, but were quelled and outlawed. Lahoud did try to clean up and do away with abuses upon his gaining the presidency, but was prevented by Syrian officials due to their complicity in those abuses. Around this time public support for Lahoud dipped, and his popularity was low on the street. He ran a heavy-handed regime, where any opponents were quieted and suppressed. There was hope that a military man, and one perceived to be fiercely loyal to Lebanon, would assert Lebanese independence. Instead critics accused Lahoud of leading the country further and further under the yoke of Syria. In March 2000, Lahoud, seemingly making a misstep, threatened Israel with guerrilla attacks from Palestinians within Lebanon if it pulled out of Lebanon before a peace treaty could be enacted. In 2004 Syria pressured the national assembly to grant Lahoud another presidential term. After the late 2006 conflict with Israel and their incursions into the south of Lebanon with claims of attacks by guerrillas from the Lebanese side, Lahoud and Israel went back to the armistice of 1949.

INFLUENCES AND CONTRIBUTIONS

From an early age Lahoud was heavily influenced by his father and his military service. He was raised with military values, and a duty and honor before anything else attitude. He has also, in recent years been influenced heavily by Syria and Syrian politics. Lahoud has contributed much to Lebanon; he has rebuilt the army and opened diplomatic connections with other nations. He has spent virtually his whole life in the service of, in one way or another, Lebanon.

THE WORLD'S PERSPECTIVE

Global perceptions of Lahoud are mixed. In the West, the president is seen as a puppet of Syria, and as having allowed that country open access to all functions of Lebanese politics. In a *U.S. News and World Report* article written by Fouad Ajami, he called Lahoud a supplicant of Syria, doing Syria's bidding. Many Lebanese tend to agree that President Lahoud has allowed the Syrians free and unfettered access to Lebanese politics, and disagree with

his appointment of pro-Syrian figures to head sensitive military and security positions. Also, Lahoud has been criticized heavily for silencing any opposition with force. However, the rest of the Lebanese population and other Arab leaders believe that Lahoud is a real patriot who dramatically transformed the Lebanese army and instituted the flag service, requiring all Lebanese males to give a full year of military service, reequipping the army with new arms, weapons, and uniforms. President Lahoud ensured that all military units were thoroughly integrated across sectarian and regional lines and were frequently rotated around the country stamping out sectarianism, a problem the Lebanese have faced in the past. However, the crackdown against dissidents and assassinations of former prime minister Hariri and other prominent Lebanese politicians and thinkers has largely been blamed on President Lahoud's Syrian allies. Support for the embattled president, even among his Maronite community, has plummeted and the call for his resignation become louder and stronger.

LEGACY

It remains too early to assess Lahoud's ultimate legacy, as he is the sitting president. His legacy seemingly will not be one of all happiness and accomplishments. There is some extreme anger directed toward him, especially regarding his conciliatory nature with Syria. He will leave behind a good legacy in the rebuilding and rearming of the army, as well as his ending sectarianism in the military service. However, again this is a double-edged sword, because he also allowed Syria to become intricately involved in the military, its workings, and those of the government. In the end, his military service seems to be his strongest legacy, as most, if not all, Lebanese are certainly proud of his over forty years of service.

BIBLIOGRAPHY

Gambill, Gary C., Ziad K. Abdelnour, and Bassam Endrawos. *Middle East Intelligence Bulletin* 3, no. 11 (November 2001).

"Lebanese President Emile Lahoud: Address to the Arab Summit in Cairo." 21 October 2000. Available from http://www.meib.org/articles/0011_ldoc1021.htm.

"U.S. Is Lebanese Army's Patron." *Washington Post* (5 December 1998).

Khodr M. Zaarour

LAKHDAR-HAMINA, MUHAMMAD
(1943–)

An Algerian film director, Muhammad Lakhdar-Hamina is best known for his 1975 film *Chronicle of the Years of*

BIOGRAPHICAL HIGHLIGHTS

Name: Muhammad Lakhdar-Hamina

Birth: 1943, M'Sila, Algeria

Family: Two sons, Malik and Tariq

Nationality: Algerian

Education: Studied law and agriculture in France (incomplete); film studies at the Fakulta Akademie Múzických umĕní (FAMU), Prague (incomplete)

PERSONAL CHRONOLOGY:

- **1958:** Deserts the French army and joins the Algerian resistance

- **1959:** Begins cinematography studies at the FAMU, Prague

- **1961:** Collaborates with film director Djamel Chanderli in his film *Yasmina*

- **1962:** Returns to Algeria and founds Office des actualités algériennes

- **1965:** Releases his first long film, *Le Vent des Aurès*

- **1975:** Receives Golden Palm at the Cannes Film Festival for *Chronicle of the Years of Embers*

- **1981–1984:** Becomes director of the Office National pour le Commerce et l'Industrie Cinématographique

- **1986:** His film *The Last Image* is featured as the Official Selection of the Cannes Film Festival

- **2003:** *Chronicle of the Years of Embers* is featured in the retrospectives section at the Cannes Film Festival

Embers. He is one of the most prominent figures in contemporary Arabic cinema.

PERSONAL HISTORY

Born on 23 February 1943 at M'Sila, Algeria, Lakhdar-Hamina began his studies in his native country. He first became interested in the world of cinema at the Lycée Carnot in Cannes, France. After beginning studies of agriculture and law at French universities, he deserted the French army in 1958 and joined the anti-French Algerian resistance in Tunisia, where he worked for the provisional Algerian government in exile. His film career

began as he joined the Algerian Maquis (guerrillas). In 1959, the Algerian National Liberation Front (FLN) sent him to Prague, where he pursued his cinematography studies at the cinema school, Fakulta Akademie Múzických umĕní (FAMU) the Czech academy for cinema and television. However, he quit his studies in order to work for the Barrandov Studios. In 1960 he joined the Service Cinema, created by the Algerian government in exile. In 1959, the Algerian ministry of information in exile commissioned Lakhdar-Hamina, together with Djamel Chanderli and Pierre Chaulet, to produce a movie about Algeria's predicament under French colonialism. The documentary film, titled *Djazzaïrouna* (Our Algeria), aimed at portraying the goals pursued by the Algerian nationalist guerrilla movement, the Maquis. In 1961, Lakhdar-Hamina collaborated with Chanderli in the movie *Yasmina*, which tells the story of a refugee girl who must flee her village following its destruction. Lakhdar-Hamina collaborated again with Chanderli in *La Voix du People* (1962; The people's voice) and *Les Fusils de la Liberté* (1961; The guns of freedom). Upon Algerian independence in 1962, he returned to his homeland where, together with his colleagues from Tunisian exile, he founded the Office des actualités algériennes, of which he was director from 1963 until its dissolution in 1974. From 1981 until 1984 he acted as director of the Office National pour le Commerce et l'Industrie Cinématographique.

INFLUENCES AND CONTRIBUTIONS

From its inception, Algerian cinema was intertwined with the ideological and existential debates that surrounded the Algerian war of independence and the postcolonial nation-building stage. In this context, Lakhdar-Hamina's cinematographic career has significantly contributed to the development of a new filmic language characteristic of contemporary Maghrebi cinema in general and Algerian in particular, notably distinct from the filmic experiences of other Arab countries and most particularly of the Egyptian cinematic industry.

Following Algeria's independence, Algerian cinema focused on new artistic forms concerned with the search for national identity, but financial difficulties and the lack of an Algerian industry made this task all the more challenging. North American audiences have remained for the most part unaware of Algeria's cinematographic experience. Following the nationalization of Algeria's film industry in June 1969, the American Motion Pictures Export Association of America (MPEAA) called for a boycott of all Algerian productions. Since its inception, Algerian cinema developed a clearly anti-imperialistic stance. In this regard, Algerian cinematographers in general and Lakhdar-Hamina in particular have remained deeply committed to the ideological tenets of the nonaligned movement and Third Worldism.

PERSONAL DRAMA WITHOUT ORNAMENTATION

I wanted to reconstitute on the screen their personal drama without ornamentation, without demagogy, and through the tragedy of two beings thrown in turmoil, and to denounce the war and the violence. I do not like, however, to linger on the description of violence.

MUHAMMAD LAKHDAR-HAMINA, ON *WIND OF THE AURÈS,* CITED IN BOUDJEDRA, RACHID. "THE BIRTH OF ALGERIAN CINEMA: THE ANTI-HERO." *ALIF: JOURNAL OF COMPARATIVE POETICS* NO. 15 (1995): 260–266.

In December 1973, African, Latin American, and Asian filmmakers gathered in Algiers for the first meeting of the Third World Cinema Committee, which became an effort to build an independent Third World cinematographic movement.

Lakhdar-Hamina's first films explore issues of national identity and the search for the Self in the context of postcolonial emancipation. In 1963, he wrote the script and dialogue for the film *Sour le signe de Neptune* (Under Neptune's sign). In 1965 he released his first long movie, *Le Vent des Aurès* (Wind of the Aurès). The movie portrayed the story of an Algerian woman in search of her imprisoned sons during the Algerian war of independence. *Le Vent des Aurès* received the Best First Work Award at the 1966 Cannes Film Festival and was nominated for the Golden Palm. It was also nominated for the Grand Prix at the 1967 Moscow International Film Festival. It may be considered in its own right the foundational stone of contemporary Algeria cinema. In *Le Vent des Aurés,* Lakhdar-Hamina portrays with painstaking detail the disintegration of a peasant society marred by the structural violence of colonial occupation. The movie is clearly influenced by Soviet cinema and aesthetics, particularly that of Soviet Ukrainian director Alexandre Dovjenko. The director adeptly translated this influence to an Algerian scenario. *Le Vent des Aurès* consecrated Algerian cinema in the international scene. Lakhdar-Hamina's following movie, *Hassan Terro,* explored in a comical manner the tragedy of Algeria's war of independence by portraying the misadventures of its main character, a bourgeois character trapped in the midst of the Algerian revolution. His third movie *Décembre* (December), released in 1972, explores the issue of torture. The movie narrated the case of a French officer troubled by the violent acts of torture perpetrated by the French army against members of the FLN.

Chronique des années de braise (*Chronicle of the Years of Embers,* 1974), however, is Lakhdar-Hamina's most important work. In 1975, he achieved worldwide recognition when the movie was awarded the Golden Palm at Cannes. The film, which offers a personal vision of the Algerian revolution, traces the evolution of the revolutionary movement from 1939 until the beginnings of the 1954 insurrection against the French. To this day, *Chronicle of the Years of Embers* remains the only African film to have been awarded the Golden Palm at Cannes. The movie is divided into six sections: "The Years of Ashes," "The Years of Embers," "The Years of Fire," "The Year of the Cart," "The Year of the Massacre," and "1 November 1954," a date that marks the beginning of the Algerian revolution and of the war of independence. It tells the story of an Algerian peasant, Ahmad, who flees his village to escape famine and drought. The film presents violence as an unavoidable stage in the conflict between colonizer and colonized; in this regard, Lakhdar-Hamina chose to focus on the predicament of Algerian peasant communities and emphasized the gap that separated the rural Algerian peasantry from the wealthy French colonists. One of the movie's main message appears to be that, just as violence begets more violence, so colonialism can only be fought through a violent uprising. The transformation of Ahmad from illiterate peasant to revolutionary leader symbolizes the maturation of an independent national consciousness aimed at national liberation. From a cinematographic point of view, *Chronicle* makes use of camera techniques that emphasize feelings of uprootedness, deprivation, and suffering caused by a colonial system of exploitation. Characteristically, Lakhdar-Hamina has consistently chosen to portray the ideological debates surrounding the construction of a national identity amidst the violent struggle against colonial domination through the representation of a national collective represented by single heroic characters, such as Ahmad, or typical antiheroes such as Hassan Terro. Equally, the prominence of the peasant world in Lakhdar-Hamina's filmography seems to consecrate rural life as one of the most important scenarios in the construction of national identity. This mythification of the Algerian peasantry as a repository of national pride and resistance would eventually be transformed during the 1980s, when Algerian cinema became more concerned with urban characters and focused on the crisis of postcolonial conflicts.

In *Vent de sable* (Sand storm), released in 1982, Lakhdar-Hamina portrays the life of an isolated rural community fragmented by violence. It tells the story of Amara, a man whose wife gives birth to their eighth daughter; unable to withstand the dishonor of not fathering a son, Amara plans a revenge. The plot allows Lakhdar-Hamina to explore the difficult terrain of gender relations and gender violence. His most recent movie, *La Dernière Image* (The last image), was part of the Official Selection at Cannes Film Festival in 1986 and was nominated for the Golden Palm. Lakhdar-Hamina's son, Malik Lakhdar-Hamina, became well known after the release of his first long film, *Autumn: October in Algiers* (1992), a film that explores the riots of October 1988 through the microcosm of an Algerian family split by a Westernized versus Islamicized view of contemporary Algeria. His other son, Tariq Lakhdar-Hamina, is a film producer. A polemic figure, Lakhdar-Hamina has been occasionally accused of mismanagement and nepotism in his filmic productions.

THE WORLD'S PERSPECTIVE

A true son of the Algerian revolution, Lakhdar-Hamina is one of the foremost representatives of contemporary Arabic cinema and is widely recognized as one of its most prominent figures abroad. His cinematographic work has received worldwide recognition at the Cannes Film Festival, where it remains the only African film to have been awarded the Golden Palm as of 2007.

LEGACY

Despite ceasing his cinematographic production in 1986, Lakhdar-Hamina will be remembered as one of the most important contemporary Arab cinematographers of our time.

BIBLIOGRAPHY

Boudjedra, Rachid. *Naissance du Cinéma Algérien*. Paris: François Maspero, 1971.

———. "The Birth of Algerian Cinema: The Anti-Hero." *Alif: Journal of Comparative Poetics*, no. 15 (1995): 260–266.

Hafez, Sabry. "Shifting Identities in Maghrebi Cinema: The Algerian Paradigm." *Alif: Journal of Comparative Poetics*, no. 15 (1995): 39–80.

Pearson, Lyle. "Four Years of North African Film." *Film Quarterly* 26, no. 4 (Summer, 1973): 18–26.

Vanesa Casanova-Fernandez

LARIJANI, ALI ARDASHIR
(1958–)

A powerful Iranian politician, Ali Ardashir Larijani is head of the Supreme National Security Council and a key figure in Iran's nuclear program.

Ali Ardashir Larijani. AP IMAGES.

PERSONAL HISTORY

Larijani was born in 1958 in al-Najaf, Iraq, the son of a senior Shi'ite Muslim cleric from Iran, Ayatollah Mirza-Hashem Amoli. He also is the son-in-law of another senior cleric, Ayatollah Morteza Motahari, who was killed in a 1979 bombing attack. Larijani's brother, Sadegh Larijani, is also a cleric who currently sits on Iran's powerful Council of Guardians.

Ali Larijani obtained a B.S. in computer science from Sharif University of Technology, and both an M.A. and Ph.D. in Western philosophy from Tehran University. During the 1980s he was an acting commander of the revolutionary guard corps. Larijani served as minister of culture and Islamic guidance under President Ali Akbar Hashemi Rafsanjani. Thereafter, from 1994 to 2004, he was head of Iranian national television and radio. In May 2004, Supreme Leader Ayatollah ALI KHAMENEHI appointed Larijani as his adviser and one of his representatives to the Supreme National Security Council, and President MAHMOUD AHMADINEJAD appointed Larijani as the council's head in 2005 after Larijani's failed presidential bid.

BIOGRAPHICAL HIGHLIGHTS

Name: Ali Ardashir Larijani

Birth: 1958, al-Najaf, Iraq

Nationality: Iranian

Education: B.S. (computer science), Sharif University of Technology, Tehran; M.A. and Ph.D. (Western philosophy), Tehran University

PERSONAL CHRONOLOGY:

- **1980:** Acting commander, Revolutionary Guard Corps
- **1994:** Head of Iranian national television and radio
- **2004:** Appointed to Supreme National Security Council
- **2005:** Designated head of the Supreme National Security Council

INFLUENCES AND CONTRIBUTIONS

As head of Iranian state television in the 1990s, Larijani began removing television shows he deemed objectionable on Islamic grounds, and broadcasting instead ones that he believed would instill Islamic values in Iranian citizens. In 2003, he set up two 24-hour television broadcasts in Arabic, which reportedly are popular in neighboring Iraq. As head of the Supreme National Security Council, he is one of the most powerful figures in Iran today. His power on the council stems from the fact that he is Khamenehi's adviser, and he is reportedly taking his orders directly from the ayatollah and not from President Ahmadinejad.

THE WORLD'S PERSPECTIVE

Larijani is known inside Iran and abroad as a conservative who has risen to power along with the wave that brought Ahmadinejad to the presidency, and already has become a powerful force within the government. The outside world's first true glimpse of Larijani has come by virtue of his acting as the chief negotiator and spokesman for Iran's nuclear program. While meeting with Western and United Nations (UN) officials (including head of the International Atomic Energy Agency, MOHAMED ELBARADEI), who expressed grave concern about Iran's intentions, Larijani steadfastly insisted that Iran has the right to develop nuclear power, and is

allowed under the Nuclear Non-Proliferation Treaty to enrich uranium.

LEGACY

It is too early to assess Larijani's legacy, but he remains a key conservative in the country who has been tasked with a major assignment, dealing with the West and the UN over Iran's ambitions to develop a nuclear program.

BIBLIOGRAPHY
"Profile: Ali Larijani." BBC News. 7 April 2007. Available from http://news.bbc.co.uk/.

Michael R. Fischbach

LAROUI, ABDALLAH
(1933–)

Abdallah (Abdullah) Laroui (the French rendering of his name; an Arabic-English transliteration is 'Abd Allah 'Arawi) is a Moroccan historian and philosopher. He has published extensively in French, Arabic, and English on contemporary Arab ideologies, Islam, modernity, and Maghrebi history. He taught at Muhammad V University in Rabat from 1963 until his retirement in 2000 and remains active in the Royal Society of Morocco.

PERSONAL HISTORY

Laroui was born in Azemmour, Morocco, in 1933 into an educated Arabic-speaking family that was engaged in government service. He briefly attended Qur'an school and then public school. After World War II, when the French authorities were more accommodating to talented Moroccan students, he won a scholarship to the Collège Sidi Mohammed in Marrakesh. He then studied for the *baccalauréat* at the Lycée Lyautey in Casablanca and the Lycée Gourand in Rabat and in 1953 entered the Institut d'Études Politiques in Paris, where he studied history and economics. Laroui learned from Charles Morazé, the author of *Les bourgeois conquérants*, that history was not facts but rather the development of social structures. He studied the ideas of Karl Marx as a historian and a theoretician but not as a prophet. He became interested in the history of the Islamic world and studied contemporary Arabic thought as an independent scholar.

In 1958, Laroui completed a *diplôme d'études superieurs* on the commercial relations between Morocco and Europe in the Middle Ages. He then returned to Morocco where he worked in the Ministry of Foreign Affairs. After serving as cultural attaché in Cairo and Paris he resigned from the Foreign Service for political and personal reasons. He then returned to Paris to study

BIOGRAPHICAL HIGHLIGHTS

Name: Abdallah Laroui (Abdullah, 'Abd Allah 'Arawi)

Birth: 1933, Azemmour, Morocco

Family: Wife, Latifa Benjelloun-Laroui; son, Isam

Nationality: Moroccan

Education: Qur'an school, public school, Collège Sidi Mohammed, Marrakesh, and Lycée Lyautey, Casablanca, 1938–1950; *baccalauréat*, Lycée Gourand, Rabat, 1952; *diplôme d'études superieurs*, Institut d'Études Politiques, Paris, 1958; *agrégation*, Paris, 1963; doctorate, Paris, 1976

PERSONAL CHRONOLOGY:

- **1958–1963:** Serves in Ministry of Foreign Affairs; cultural attaché in Cairo and Paris

- **1963–2000:** Teaches history, Muhammad V University, Rabat

- **1969–1970:** Lectures as visiting associate professor, University of California, Los Angeles

- **1996:** Delivers lecture as Fulbright 50th Anniversary Distinguished Fellow, Middle East Studies Association, Providence, Rhode Island

- **2000:** Retires as university professor emeritus, Muhammad V University, Rabat; active member, Royal Academy of Morocco

for the *agrégation* (a teacher's exam) in Islamic studies. In 1963 he completed the *agrégation* and was appointed assistant professor of history at Muhammad V University in Rabat. He taught the history of North Africa as a visiting professor at the University of California, Los Angeles in 1969–1970, then returned to Rabat, where he taught methods of historical research until he retired as university professor emeritus in 2000. He has for many years been an active member of the Royal Society of Morocco.

INFLUENCES AND CONTRIBUTIONS

Laroui's book, *Idéologie arabe contemporaine: essai critique* (Contemporary Arab ideology: a critical essay), was published just before the Arab-Israeli War of June 1967. He argued that Arab intellectuals and leaders should under-

stand that the underlying processes of history govern all societies and are not specific to any region or civilization. It was not enough to call for scientific or technological advance without a better understanding of history. His ideas inspired many Arab intellectuals seeking to understand the weakness of Arab societies manifested during the

LAROUI SPEAKS

Whoever affirms categorically that such and such Western value-system, be it liberalism, rationalism, humanism, etc., is incompatible with Islam is talking theology and therefore, while he may well be right in his domain—I mean theology—he is in no way entitled to translate his idiom into sociology or political science. His assertion means no more than that the West, as he defines it, is never to be found in the non-West. I see the same tautology behind the so-called uniqueness of Islam, and during the last two decades my main concern was to unveil it to Muslim audiences. I continue then the same battle, in different circumstances, using the same language, the same logic....

The collapse of the Berlin wall was not due to the policy of containment, blockade, propaganda as much as to a wise policy of easy term loans, free trade and enhanced cultural exchanges. The same strategy should secure the same results elsewhere. Sooner or later a developing society frees itself from ideas and ideals that do no longer correspond to its new aspirations.

For reasons I need not detail here such an evolution will probably occur more easily in the "Ajam" countries of Asia than in the Arab Middle East and North Africa, not because the former are less religious but simply because the latter are on the whole less fortunate. Seeing that happening some time in the future, somewhere in the vast Islamic world, seeing that the law of society has at last prevailed over the orders of tradition or the commands of ideology, many will, I am sure, cry out, as they do now, facing the staggering performances of some Asian nations: Well, the seeds were always there; we failed to see them before, but now we take notice and we cheer.

ABDALLAH LAROUI, "WESTERN ORIENTALISM AND LIBERAL ISLAM: MUTUAL DISTRUST?" *MIDDLE EAST STUDIES ASSOCIATION BULLETIN* 31, NO. 1 (JULY 1997). AVAILABLE FROM HTTP://FP .ARIZONA.EDU/MESASSOC/BULLETIN/LAROUI.HTM.

June 1967 war, and impressed Gustave von Grunebaum, a leading scholar at the University of California, Los Angeles (UCLA), who invited him to teach at UCLA for the academic year 1969–1970. His book *L'Histoire du Maghreb: un essai de synthèse* (1975; *The History of the Maghrib: An Interpretive Essay*, 1977) grew out of his lectures at UCLA. He returned to Morocco to write his doctoral dissertation, which he defended in 1976 and published in 1977 as *Les Origines sociales et culturelles du nationalisme marocain, 1830–1912* (The social and cultural origins of Moroccan nationalism, 1830–1912). In this work he analyzed Moroccan nationalism as a case of delayed consciousness and argued that nationalists prefer to hold on to their traditions rather than to see historical reality as it is.

He developed his ideas in *La crise des intellectuels arabes: traditionalisme ou historicisme?* (1974; *The Crisis of the Arab Intellectual: Traditionalism or Historicism?*, 1976), a collection of articles arguing that historicism can facilitate the modernization of Arab ideology. Arab intellectuals must break with traditionalism and work out—with the tools of historicism—new approaches to language reform and social policy. An historicist analysis can lead to the reform of the Arabic script, to women's liberation, and to urban planning. For Laroui, intellectual Marxism is the easiest and clearest way to grasp the analytical logic of historicism or the workings of history. In *Islam et Modernité* (1987; Islam and modernity), he explains that to understand the present situation in Muslim countries it is necessary for Islam to be analyzed as a process and not as an idea. "Islam" is not a dogma that can explain current problems.

Laroui disagreed with those who took critiques of Orientalism to mean that only Arabs or Muslims could write about themselves. He was, however, sympathetic to the view that the study of the "Orient" should be understood in the context of European imperial political interests, just as Arab cultural output should be understood in the context of Arab nationalism. He criticized the Orientalists who tended to stop with linguistic analysis. He believed that it was possible to work toward an objective science of society, whether it is called sociology, anthropology, or history. Insiders and outsiders should struggle for objectivity, though absolute objectivity was not possible. Western scholars may have a better understanding of comparative history, while Muslim scholars may understand the language or culture. For Laroui, contemporary Arab thought is more concerned with the Western world than it is with Islamic ideas. He disagreed with those who argued that Islamic culture was different from others in essential ways; he consistently argued that history is a science and that the laws of history can be applied everywhere. Islamists, on the other hand, believe

that historical laws were given from the beginning in a well-guarded book (*kitab mahfuz*).

Laroui urges scholars to study the role of polygamy and the relation between family structure and war in Islamic history, and has argued that historians should specialize not only in history but also in literature, economics, linguistics, philosophy—anything but just history. Laroui himself has written several novels, and in recent years has been publishing his memoirs, *Khawatir al-Sabah* (Recollections). Volume three, covering the years 1982 to 1999, was published in 2005. His most recent book is the magisterial *Le Maroc et Hassan II: un temoignage* (2005; Morocco and Hassan II: testimony).

THE WORLD'S PERSPECTIVE

Laroui is widely recognized for his contributions to the international debate on Western and Islamic modernity. He is best known for his advocacy of historicism in a framework of Hegelian and Marxist humanism. For Islamic modernists who struggle to reclaim a sense of authenticity, Laroui's insistence that the tools of history apply equally and inexorably to Islamic and to all other religious and cultural traditions has been enormously influential. He has placed Islamic philosophy in a universal context. In the post-1967 era, his critique of Arab culture encouraged Arab intellectuals to question the nature of the Arab nation-state and to find it parochial and inauthentic.

LEGACY

Laroui's most important legacy may be his critique of the "Islamic" state. He has argued that this state, with its authoritarian and reactionary tendencies and rejection of open dialogue with the West, is a manifestation of the class interests of the petit bourgeoisie rather than of inherently Islamic or Arab values. He calls for a liberal bourgeois state that opposes the authoritarian Islamic state and that allows for academic and artistic freedom.

BIBLIOGRAPHY

WORKS BY LAROUI

Idéologie arabe contemporaine: essai critique [Contemporary Arab ideology: a critical essay]. Paris: Maspéro, 1967.

L'Algérie et le Sahara marocain [Algeria and the Moroccan Sahara]. Casablanca: Serar, 1976.

La crise des intellectuels arabes: traditionalisme ou historicisme? Paris: Maspéro, 1974. (English: *The Crisis of the Arab Intellectual: Traditionalism or Historicism?* Translated by Diarmid Cammell. Berkeley: University of California Press, 1976.)

Les origines sociales et culturelles du nationalisme marocain, 1830–1912 [The social and cultural origins of Moroccan nationalism, 1830–1912]. Paris: Maspéro, 1977.

L'Histoire du Maghreb: un essai de synthèse. Paris: Maspéro, 1970. (English: *The History of the Maghrib: An Interpretive Essay*. Princeton, NJ: Princeton University Press, 1977.)

Islam et modernité [Islam and modernity]. Paris: La Découverte, 1987.

"Western Orientalism and Liberal Islam: Mutual Distrust?" *Middle East Studies Association Bulletin* 31, no. 1 (July 1997). Available from http://fp.arizona.edu/mesassoc/Bulletin/laroui.htm.

Khawatir al-Sabah [Recollections]. Volume One, 1967–1973; Volume Two, 1974–1981; Volume Three, 1982–1999. Casablanca: Arab Cultural Center, 2001, 2003, 2005.

Le Maroc et Hassan II: un temoignage [Morocco and Hassan II: testimony]. Quebec: Les Presses Inter Universitaires, and Casablanca: Arab Cultural Center, 2005.

Al-Afah: riwaya. Casablanca: Arab Cultural Center, 2006.

OTHER SOURCES

El Kurdi, Bassam. *Autour de la pensee de Abdallah Laroui* [Debating Laroui's theory]. Casablanca: Le Contre Culturel Arabe, 2000.

Gallagher, Nancy. "The Life and Times of Abdallah Laroui, a Moroccan Intellectual." *Journal of North African Studies* 3, no. 1 (1998): 132–151.

Nancy Gallagher

LIVNI, TZIPI
(1958–)

Tzipora ("Tzipi") Livni is an Israeli politician and minister of foreign affairs and vice prime minister in the

Tzipi Livni. © HOPI MEDIA/BERNHARD J. HOLZNER/EPA/CORBIS.

Kadima-led government of EHUD OLMERT. She was only the second woman to become foreign minister of Israel, following Golda Meir decades earlier. Livni was also one of the founding members of the Kadima Party. Before joining Kadima, she was a member of the center-right Likud Party.

PERSONAL HISTORY

Livni was born 8 July 1958 in Tel Aviv, into a prominent political family. Both her parents were members of the Irgun, a right-wing Jewish nationalist underground organization that fought against the British mandate in Palestine before the establishment of the State of Israel. Her father, Eitan Livni, was a right-wing hero who was operations chief of the Irgun; he later became a Knesset member for Menachem Begin's Herut Party.

Livni grew up in Tel Aviv. After finishing high school, she completed her compulsory military service in the Israel Defense Forces (IDF), attaining the rank of lieutenant. She then went on to study for a law degree at Bar-Ilan University.

Livni worked for the Israeli intelligence agency Mossad for four years, from 1980 to 1984. Following that, she practiced law in a private firm for ten years, specializing in public and commercial law. From 1996 to 1999, Livni worked as the director general of the Government Companies Authority, which was responsible for the privatization of government corporations and monopolies.

Livni entered national politics in 1999 when she was elected to the fifteenth Knesset as a member of the Likud. She quickly rose through party ranks. From 1999 to 2001, she was a member of the Likud opposition to the Labor-led coalition government of Ehud Barak. Following the Likud's victory in the February 2001 general elections, Livni was appointed minister of regional cooperation in Prime Minister ARIEL SHARON's government. She went on to hold various positions in Sharon's governments (2001–2003, 2003–2006), including minister of agriculture and rural development, minister of immigrant absorption, minister of housing and construction, and minister of justice.

Livni became known to the Israeli public during this time, and gained a reputation as one of the more centrist and dovish members of the Likud Party. On 12 November 2005, she became the first politician from the Israeli right to speak at the official annual commemoration of the assassination of YITZHAK RABIN. Livni was a strong supporter of then–prime minister Sharon, and backed his controversial plan for a unilateral Israeli disengagement from Gaza. She was instrumental in getting the Knesset to approve this plan, against the objections of other Likud Knesset members.

BIOGRAPHICAL HIGHLIGHTS

Name: Tzipora ("Tzipi") Livni

Birth: 1958, Tel Aviv, Israel

Family: Husband; two children

Nationality: Israeli

Education: LL.B., Bar-Ilan University

PERSONAL CHRONOLOGY:

- **1980–1984:** Works for Israeli intelligence agency, Mossad

- **1996–1999:** Director general, Government Companies Authority

- **1999:** Elected member of Knesset for Likud

- **2001:** Appointed minister of regional cooperation

- **2002:** Appointed minister of agriculture and rural development

- **2003:** Appointed minister of immigrant absorption

- **2004:** Appointed minister of housing and construction; receives Champion of Good Government Award

- **2005:** Appointed minister of justice

- **2006–present:** Minister of foreign affairs, vice prime minister

After Sharon left the Likud in November 2005 and established a new centrist party, Kadima, Livni resigned from the Likud and joined Sharon in the new party. In January 2006, she was appointed acting foreign minister by acting Prime Minister Olmert following the resignation of Silvan Shalom. She also continued to serve as justice minister. In the March 2006 election for the seventeenth Knesset, she was placed third on the party's list of candidates, which effectively guaranteed her reelection to the Knesset.

After Kadima won the March 2006 election, Olmert formed a new coalition government and appointed Livni as foreign minister. She was also given the title of vice prime minister.

During Israel's monthlong war with Hizbullah in July 2006, Livni staunchly defended Israel's actions to the world and engaged in intensive diplomacy to gain international support for Israel. She favored a quick end to the conflict, but was overruled by the prime minister, who wanted more time for Israel to degrade Hizbullah's military capabilities. Livni's domestic popularity increased as a result of her

efforts during the war, while Olmert's popularity greatly declined, due to the IDF's failure to decisively win the war.

As Livni became one of the most popular politicians in Israel, she emerged as a possible contender to replace the beleaguered Olmert in the leadership of Kadima. Livni herself expressed an interest in one day becoming prime minister, fueling the Israeli media's speculation of a growing rivalry between Livni and Olmert. Relations between them were also strained by Livni's public calls for Israel to conduct immediate negotiations with moderate Palestinians on the borders of an interim Palestinian state, a diplomatic move opposed by Olmert. In May 2007 Livni publicly called for Olmert's resignation following the publication of a highly critical interim report by the Winograd Committee, which was established to investigate the government's handling of the conflict with Hizbullah the previous summer. Olmert refused to resign, and Livni's attempt to oust him failed, as she did not gain the support of most Kadima members of the Knesset. Nevertheless, Livni continued to remain in the government.

INFLUENCES AND CONTRIBUTIONS

Livni grew up in a well-known right-wing nationalist family. Ideologically, her parents were followers of Revisionist

EVERY INNOCENT CASUALTY IN THIS CONFLICT IS A TRAGEDY

In many parts of the world, we are seen mainly through the lens of the Arab-Israeli conflict. And too often, that lens is distorted. To many, this conflict is portrayed as a clash of David and Goliath, with Israel perceived unjustly as Goliath. But this simplistic image ignores the fact that Israel remains a threatened democracy in a hostile region.

We have, of necessity, the capacity to defend ourselves but we will always be constrained in its use by our values. And yet, we face an enemy willing to use all the means at its disposal, to kill without restraint and without distinction.

Every innocent casualty in this conflict is a tragedy. There is no difference between the tears of a grieving Israeli mother and a grieving Palestinian mother. But there is a critical moral difference between the terrorists that hunt down civilians, and the soldiers that target terrorists, while trying to avoid civilian casualties.

TZIPI LIVNI, ADDRESS TO THE 61ST UN GENERAL ASSEMBLY, 20 SEPTEMBER 2006.

Zionism, the movement established by Vladimir Jabotinsky that championed Jewish possession over the entire "Land of Israel"—which, it was claimed, included all of present-day Israel, the West Bank, Gaza, and Jordan (the claim to the latter territory was dropped by the late 1960s). A map of this territory ("Greater Israel") was even carved on her father's gravestone.

Livni initially adopted this Revisionist ideology and supported Israel's permanent control over the West Bank and Gaza, areas captured by Israel in the 1967 Arab-Israeli war. Later, however, Livni came to the conclusion that Israel could not remain a Jewish and democratic state if it continued to rule over the Palestinians in these areas. She therefore abandoned her commitment to Greater Israel, in favor of maintaining a secure Jewish majority within a smaller Israel. This stance led her to support Sharon's disengagement plan and then Olmert's "convergence" plan. She also publicly accepted the future creation of a Palestinian state.

Livni's moderate political positions were especially significant and influential because of her Revisionist family background. Like Olmert, another scion of a prominent Revisionist family, Livni's acceptance of the need for an Israeli withdrawal from Gaza and large parts of the West Bank helped move some of the ideological right in Israel in a more pragmatic and centrist direction.

THE WORLD'S PERSPECTIVE

Livni came to international attention when she became the second woman to serve as Israel's foreign minister, following Golda Meir decades earlier. She is seen as a rising star in Israeli politics and even a possible future contender for prime minister. As foreign minister, she has received favorable international assessments and is considered to be an articulate and effective advocate for Israel on the world stage.

LEGACY

While Livni's legacy cannot yet be known, she made headlines when she became the first cabinet minister in Israel's history to explicitly differentiate between Palestinian attacks against Israeli soldiers and attacks against civilians. In an interview on 28 March 2006 on the American television news program *ABC Nightline*, Livni stated: "Somebody who is fighting against Israeli soldiers is an enemy and we will fight back, but I believe that this is not under the definition of terrorism, if the target is a soldier." In making this important distinction, Livni challenged the prevailing tendency in Israel to describe all Palestinian violence against Israelis—soldiers and civilians—as terrorism.

BIBLIOGRAPHY

Livni, Tzipi. "Address." United Nations, 61st General Assembly. New York, 20 September 2006. Available from http://www.un.org/webcast/ga/61/pdfs/israel-e.pdf.

Shavit, Ari. "The Livni Plan." *Ha'aretz* (9 January 2007). Available from http://www.haaretz.com/hasen/spages/806887.html.

Dov Waxman

MADANI, ABBASSI
(1931–)

Abbassi Madani (also known as Abbas Madani, or Shaykh Abbas Madani) is a leader in the Islamist political movement in Algeria. After 2003, living in exile in the Persian Gulf state of Qatar, Madani was one of the key leaders of the Islamic Salvation Front (in French, Front Islamique du Salut, or FIS). As a legal political party in 1990, it won half of the vote in local Algerian elections, the first held in that country after thirty years of one party rule by the National Liberation Front (in French, Front de Libération National, or FLN). These electoral victories, however, led to the intervention of the Algerian army, the invalidation of the elections, the banning of the FIS and other Islamic parties, and the arrest of the two main FIS leaders, Ali Belhadj and Madani. Even from exile, and despite ill health, Madani continues to be considered by many as the main political and intellectual leader of the FIS, and a significant figure for political Islamists both within and outside of Algeria.

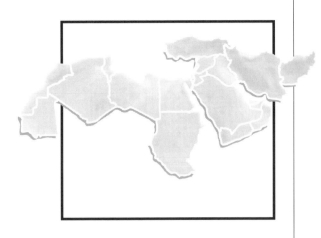

PERSONAL HISTORY

Madani was born in 1931 in the Algerian town of Sidi Okba, southeast of Algiers, near the city of Biskra, where his family moved when he was ten. His father was an imam (Islamic religious teacher/leader), and Madani had a traditional religious education in Arabic with only two years in a French high school. After that he attended an *école normale* (normal school/institution of higher education that trains teachers) in Algiers from which he graduated with a diploma qualifying him to be a teacher.

It was in Algiers that he became involved in the resistance against French occupation and colonization, which was coalescing into a coherent insurgency by the 1950s. As a member of one of the insurgent groups, Madani was put in charge of planting bombs at Radio Algiers. He was caught and arrested by French authorities on 17 November 1954, and put in jail where he remained for the next seven years. He was released in 1961, one year before Algerian independence was won. After independence Madani was not involved in politics except to denounce the perceived anti-Islamic tendencies of the secular and socialist FLN that now had control of the government. He also had ties to the organization Al Qyam (Values), founded in 1964 to protest the secularism of the FLN government.

After independence Madani returned to the University of Algiers where he had been studying before his arrest and pursued studies in educational psychology. From 1975 to 1978 he went to the United Kingdom to complete a doctorate in education. Madani returned as a professor to the University of Algiers, teaching in the faculty of education. It was in the early 1980s when

Abbassi Madani. AP IMAGES.

BIOGRAPHICAL HIGHLIGHTS

Name: Abbassi Madani (Abbas Madani)

Birth: 1931, Sidi Okba, Algeria

Education: Teaching diploma, Normal School, Algiers; 3rd cycle in psychology, University of Algiers; doctorate in education, University of London, 1978

Family: Married; six children

Nationality: Algerian

PERSONAL CHRONOLOGY:

- **1954:** Arrested by the French authorities for insurgency against colonial rule

- **1978:** Receives doctoral degree and begins teaching at the University of Algiers

- **1982:** Arrested for demanding that the FLN make changes toward Islamic values and tenets

- **1989:** Invited to form a new Islamist political party and cofounds FIS with Ali Belhadj

- **1991:** Arrested for allegedly endangering security of Algeria, sentenced to twelve years in prison

- **1997:** Released to house arrest

- **2003:** Released from house arrest, leaves country for Qatar

- **2005:** Ill and living in Qatar, issues statement supporting Algerian president's call for amnesty for combatants of civil war

economic problems were leading to discontent with the FLN leadership that Madani returned to political activism, this time with the growing Islamist movement that was seeking an alternative to the FLN government, and advocating a more central role for religion in the governing of Algeria. He was arrested in 1982 after taking part in the largest Islamist demonstration in the country to date at the University of Algiers, when five thousand turned out to hear Shaykhs Abdellatif Soltani and Ahmed Sahnoun. At this meeting a petition was written and endorsed by these two shaykhs, plus Madani, and was sent to the Algerian president Chadli Bendjedid. The petition requested that the government undertake various reforms to bring Islamic values to bear on political and economic development; it did not, however, demand an end to FLN rule, nor a transformation to theocracy.

Madani was kept in prison, this time with no trial, until 1984. Upon his release he returned to teaching. Instead of the University of Algiers, he was employed at the Institute of Educational Sciences. During the fall of 1988, antigovernment demonstrations, fomented from a wide political spectrum (not just the Islamists), resulted in a harsh government crackdown on dissent. Soon after-

ward, however, the Bendjedid government, in a dramatic reversal, opened the political system and legalized opposition parties, including those with an Islamist platform. Madani took on a leading role in organizing an Islamist party, at first attempting to make a single party that would include everyone in the movement. This proved difficult, however, and several Islamist political parties resulted, including the FIS, cofounded in 1989 by Madani and Ali Belhadj, a young teacher and imam.

The FIS was successful as a new political party and, in 1990 and 1991, captured nearly half of the vote in local elections, especially in urban areas. However, in 1992 the Algerian military reacted against the Islamist electoral victories, deposed Bendjedid, canceled and voided the election results, and outlawed the FIS. The military had intervened, arresting and jailing Madani and Belhadj, even before the FIS had been disbanded. In

1992 the two men were judged by a military tribunal, convicted of endangering national security, and sentenced to twelve years in prison. It is said that during this time Madani was suffering from ill health and was often confined in isolation, with no visitors allowed, and in austere conditions. Madani remained in prison until 1997, when he was placed under house arrest in Algiers, guarded by military security personnel. His house arrest continued until 2003, when the policy was lifted. He soon left the country, first for medical treatment in Malaysia, and then to live in exile in Qatar.

INFLUENCES AND CONTRIBUTIONS

Madani's early experiences growing up in a religiously observant family, with a father who was an imam, and his grounding in Islamic education, had a profound impact on his outlook. Thus although he was not a religious scholar, nor did he become a member of the Islamic *ulama* (religious leaders or Islamic clergy), his background contributed to his later conviction that Islam provides the guidelines for political, social, and economic development and governance, and these beliefs eventually became part of the FIS platform. It was becoming a young adult during the early days of the burgeoning revolution against French control that would mobilize Madani politically: first to oppose French, and later to criticize the secular, Western-influenced FLN government.

The indigenous mobilization against French rule in Algeria would play an important role in the formation of Madani's political thinking. Islamic identity was a key element in the Algerian revolution, due to an alliance between the country's *ulama* and Western secular revolutionaries, as well as a lack of any popular Algerian nationalist feeling. The Association of Algerian *Ulama* (AUMA), founded by Shaykh Abdelhamid Ben Badis in 1931 and influenced by Salafism, had, by the 1950s, cultivated among their followers the awareness of Islamic identity as a counter to French secular and cultural domination. Salafism, from the Arabic word for pious ancestors, was a movement to return to the basic values and ideals of Islam. Particularly in North Africa there was an emphasis on discouraging the worship of marabouts (Islamic holy men, whose tombs would become places of worship and pilgrimage) and other practices deemed heretical. The Salafis in Algeria also sought to return to the fundamentals of Islam in order to reconcile and make relevant Islamic practices with modern societies. This reconciliation would influence Madani in his scholarly work on education and society in Algeria, and later in his development of an Islamist agenda for the Algerian political scene.

Although there was not a strong sense of an Algerian nation, which had never existed in the past, there was strong resentment against the French colonial policies that sought to remove Islamic and Arabic influences from

CONTEMPORARIES

Ali Belhadj (1956–; or Benhadj), a Tunisian by birth, cofounded the Islamic Salvation Front (FIS) with Abbassi Madani. Belhadj received a religious education and became a teacher and an imam, preaching at mosques in Algiers. He was arrested in 1982 for opposing the ruling FLN government and in 1991 for being a leader of the FIS, which was alarming secular and military forces in Algeria with its electoral wins and antidemocratic rhetoric. Released from jail in 2003, Belhadj was arrested again in 2005. Often called in the media the fiery orator or firebrand imam of the FIS, he has expressed more radical Islamist views, such as declaring Islam incompatible with democracy because it is God who must rule, not the people. His views on democracy, though contradicted by his colleague Madani who insisted that FIS would not undermine Algerian democracy, became official components of the FIS platform. Some say that the two founders of FIS made an effective team, with Belhadj being the more charismatic, impassioned leader, and Madani offering the voice of reason and rationality.

the public sphere. These religious leaders who made up the AUMA, although not advocating revolution in the beginning, would lend their support to the secular nationalists in mobilizing Algerians to revolt against the colonial power. Thus, in the early 1950s when Madani joined the insurgency against the French, preserving and promoting Islamic identity, Islamic values, and Islamic institutions for Algeria was well established. Madani, however, was not a member of the *ulama,* and although he advocated for the infusion of Islamic values and law into the political process, he would not call for rule by the *ulama,* or for a theocracy.

Madani was disillusioned with the political process after independence, as the FLN leadership moved toward a socialist and Western model of governance and economic development, with little incorporation of Islamic ideals, other than to declare Islam the official religion of the country. Islamic law did continue to cover areas of family law and inheritance, however there were reforms to modify and in effect Westernize these sets of laws (called the Family Code), a move countered by the *ulama,* and in particular Al Qyam. Thus the secular and the Islamist tendencies became polarized after independence, but the religious leaders did not actively resist the uncontested control of the single-party FLN rule. So whereas Madani was sympathetic to the ideas promulgated by Al Qyam and was associated with the group, during the 1960s and 1970s he concentrated his energies on academic and teaching pursuits, and neither he nor Al Qyam openly challenged FLN control of Algeria.

His interest in education was apparent early on with his training as a secondary school teacher, and then with his graduate work in education and psychology. He would later blend his religious beliefs with his professional training, writing essays on educational issues in Islamic countries, and in particular Algeria. With his doctorate from the United Kingdom, and his fluency in English, French, and Arabic, Madani was also exposed to Western history and economic and political ideas, which also influenced his approach to Islam as a political and socioeconomic system for Algeria. This diverse background may have resulted in his more moderate stance on Islam and politics, especially in comparison with his colleague, Belhadj. Whereas the latter has often been portrayed as the radical face of the FIS, Madani is viewed as being a thoughtful and rational communicator, and has described the compatibility of Western models such as democracy and capitalism with Islam.

Whereas Madani's experiences growing up in French colonial Algeria provided the foundation for his vision of an Islamic alternative to a secular Western nation-state, the civil war that ensued in Algeria after the disruption of the democratic process in 1991 influenced Madani's preoccupation with resolving the conflict in Algeria. From his exile in Qatar, Madani has often issued statements and plans for political reconciliation and peace in his home country. The terrible violence in Algeria that began in 1991, which after a decade had killed hundreds of thousands of Algerians, has been blamed on the government and the military, as well as on the radicalization of the Islamist movement. Madani called in 2005 for national reconciliation in which all political prisoners would receive amnesty, including those from the more radical factions.

Madani's continued visibility in the context of Algerian politics, even from exile, is due to the key role he played in the unprecedented democratization of the Algerian political system from 1989 to 1991. Although short-lived, it was a response to the calls for political change in the 1980s, in which Madani was central. By the time of Bendjedid's policy change that legalized other political parties, Madani had succeeded in achieving, along with Belhadj, the coalescence of the Algerian Islamist movement into one of the first Islamist parties in Algeria. Madani is credited with lending to the FIS a more moderate tone. Whereas Belhadj was known for giving

impassioned speeches and declaring Islam incompatible with democracy, Madani had a less radical demeanor.

Even by his critics, Madani was perceived as being a moderate Islamist. He insisted upon participating in the democratic process, stating that the FIS would work within the principles of a pluralistic system that allowed the expression of different political viewpoints. Madani's intellectual approach, which incorporated Western ideas and allowed for modern science and technological development, could partially explain the large constituency of middle-class, urban Algerians who voted for the FIS. During the 1990 elections Madani declared that one should retain "the Qur'an in one hand, and knowledge and science in the other, never separating the two, for with one you achieve your spiritual life, and with the other your material life" (Abderrahim, 1990, p. xi).

THE WORLD'S PERSPECTIVE

Madani's influence on the Algerian political scene might be considerably less from exile, but his symbolic leadership of an Islamic alternative to Western secularism and his pronouncements for national reconciliation and a return to the democratic process in Algeria have kept him in the Algerian and Middle Eastern media. He is recognized as the leader of the "ex-FIS." Madani has been viewed, overall, favorably in the Middle East and other parts of the Muslim world, as an Islamist leader, but also as an Algerian nationalist seeking a peaceful settlement to the Algerian political tragedy. In 2005 he declared his support for the government of ABDELAZIZ BOUTEFLIKA. He particularly favored Bouteflika's intention to grant amnesty for the combatants of the civil war.

In the Western world there is less understanding of Madani and his role in the Algerian conflict, with some considering Madani a terrorist simply by virtue of being a leader of a banned Islamist group. There was also some ambiguity immediately after the elections were shut down as to the FIS's stance on violence, and Madani's stance in particular. However, he has since distanced himself from the radicalized factions of the Algerian Islamic movement, particularly the Armed Islamic Group (GIA) which took up arms after 1991, and has stated that the FIS is committed to participation in a nonviolent political process.

Human rights groups such as Amnesty International consider Madani a victim of a repressive government crackdown on democracy and of an unjust judicial system that serves the government. In 2001 the United Nations Working Group on Arbitrary Detention concluded that both Madani and Belhadj were arrested arbitrarily and subsequently held without a fair trial by the Algerian military.

EXPLORING

Is Islam compatible with democracy? The Western notion of democracy carries with it the assumption that secularism must accompany democratization, with religion removed from the public sphere. This separation of religion and state has its basis in the Western European experience of political domination by religious institutions. In Algeria, however, as throughout the Middle East, the experience of religion and politics was different. In those regions, religion was infused throughout society, lending rules of social, political, and economic organization, but without theocratic rule (or rule by religious leaders). In Algeria the French attempt to remove Islam from the public sphere (following the French separation of church and state) caused many Algerians to seek out and promote their Islamic identity and beliefs. Thus the rise of Islamism in the 1980s must be seen within this context, as Algerians were seeking political and economic alternatives. Islamic scholars have argued that Islam is not antithetical to democracy, and there are institutions within Islam that allow for participation and shared decision making. It is argued that there could be different forms of democracy, with Islamic democracy being one of them.

LEGACY

Madani is an Algerian leader who bridges the span of the country's history from the time of the revolution through the end of FLN control and the country's tragic struggle to develop more democratically. Having fought in the revolution, being imprisoned by the French and later by his own nationalist government for opposing its secular policies, Madani has been a central figure in the process of decolonization and political development in Algeria. He will be remembered as a key leader in Algeria's transformation from a nation state ruled by a single party to a much more diverse and pluralistic state. Following the tragic events that ensued during the 1990s, the country has not returned to single-party rule. Madani will be associated with the civil strife as a victim because he was imprisoned during much of that time. As an educator and as an Islamist, he leaves behind many writings that suggest avenues for reconciling the role of Islam in political life with the tenets of modern society, such as democracy and scientific advances. It seems that religion continues to be a major avenue for political expression in

Algeria. However, the balance has yet to be found on how to incorporate the secular with the religious in the political sphere.

BIBLIOGRAPHY

"Abassi Madani and Ali Benhadj v. Algeria." Working Group on Arbitrary Detention, United Nations Document E/CN.4/ 2003/8/Add.1 at 32 (2001). Available from http://www .umn.edu/humanrts/wgad/28-2001.html.

Abderrahim, Abdel Kader. "D'une main le Coran, du l'autre le fusil." *Les Cahiers de l'Orient* 18 (1990): 11.

"Algerie." Amnesty International. Available from http://web .amnesty.org/report2004/dza-summary-fra.

Burgat, Francois, and William Dowell. *The Islamic Movement in North Africa.* Austin: University of Texas, Center for Middle Eastern Studies, 1993.

Takeyh, Ray. "Islamism in Algeria: A Struggle between Hope and Agony." *Middle East Policy* 10, no. 2 (Summer 2003): 62–75.

Mary Jane C. Parmentier

MADINI, AHMAD AL-
(1948–)

Moroccan novelist, short-story writer, and literary critic, Ahmad al-Madini ushered in a new epoch of Moroccan Arabic literature by introducing a new tradition of writing and literary criticism at the end of the 1970s. Al-Madini is a member of the modern school of Arabic literature that prefers experimentation to the prioritization of a writer's faithfulness to traditional literary patterns and reluctance to challenge the classical realist text. His contribution consists of his emphasis on a new literary discourse that called for the creative practice of the novelist. Throughout his writings and literary criticisms, al-Madini advocated a divorce from the simplistic and naive understanding of realism in Moroccan Arabic literature. He supported a new literary practice that parts from the shallow understanding of the theory of reflection, the concept of mimesis, and the notion of realism. Al-Madini also abandoned classical interpretations of linear plots and character development in favor of monologues and a mixture of poetic and prose styles. Overall, al-Madini launched a spirit of literary rebellion similar to Driss Chraibi in French Moroccan literature.

PERSONAL HISTORY

Al-Madini was born in 1948 in Casablanca, Morocco, and he pursued his primary and secondary education there. He was influenced by Marxist ideas that prevailed among students in the Moroccan university. After independence, university students played a major role in the national political debate. Al-Madini was largely influenced by this

BIOGRAPHICAL HIGHLIGHTS

Name: Ahmad al-Madini

Birth: 1948, Casablanca, Morocco

Nationality: Moroccan

Education: B.A. (Arabic language and literature), University of Sidi Mohammed Ben Abdallah, 1986; post-graduate diploma, Muhammad University, 1978; Ph.D., Sorbonne, Paris, 1990

PERSONAL CHRONOLOGY:

- **1971:** *al-Unfu fi'l-Dimagh* (short stories)
- **1976:** *Zamanun bayna al-Wilada wa'l-Hulm* (novel)
- **1980:** *Fann al-Qissa al-Qasira fi'l-Maghrib* (literary criticism)
- **1988:** *al-Tariq ila al-Manafî* (short stories)
- **1993:** *Hikayat Wahm* (novel)
- **1998:** *Madinat Baraqish* (novel)
- **2003:** *Fas law Adat Ilayhi* (novel)

Dimagh (short stories, 1971), *Zamanun bayna al-Wilada wa'al-Hulm* (novel, 1976), *Fann al-Qissa al-Qasira fi'l-Maghrib* (literary criticism, 1980), *al-Tariq ila al-Manafî* (short stories, 1988), *Hikayat Wahm* (novel, 1993), *Madinat Baraqish* (novel, 1998), and *Fas law Adat Ilayhi* (novel, 2003). Al-Madini is still an active member at the Faculty of Letters, Muhammad V University in Rabat. He is also politically affiliated with the USFP.

INFLUENCES AND CONTRIBUTIONS

Unlike French Moroccan literature, Arabic literature in Morocco has been directly influenced by the literary tradition of the Mashriq (eastern Arab world) and Egypt. The development of Arabic literature witnessed dramatic

CONTEMPORARIES

Born in Ben Ahmed, Morocco, El Miloudi Chaghmoum (1947–) is a professor in the Faculty of Letters, University of Moulay Ismail in Meknes. He earned his doctorate in philosophy from the Faculty of Letters and Humanities in Rabat. A member of the Union of Moroccan Writers, Chaghmoum published his first collection of short stories titled *Ashya Tataharak* in 1972. Similar to al-Madini, he challenged the literary tradition of the early Moroccan writers and called for leaving the conventions of the classical period, especially in terms of the role for narration. His novels and short stories are modernist in terms of their narrative discourse and storyline. Chaghmoum introduced a multiplicity of narrative levels in his fiction. In his novel *Ayn al-Faras*, the narrative consists of diegetic, extradiegetic, and metadiegetic levels. These narrative transgressions defy the logical expectation of the traditional reader. His characters rebel against the unitary voice of the Godlike narrator and break away from the conventional rule of the novel of the 1960s. Chaghmoum calls for a new literary vision that transcends reality and frees the characters from the daily shackles of realism in order to be able to innovate and create new imaginary and futuristic worlds. His fictional world searches for a new image of Moroccan characters. His main works include *al-Dhal'u wa al-Jazira* (1980), *Safar al-Ta'a* (1981), *al-Ablah wa'l-Mansiyyat wa Yasmin* (1982), *Ayn al-Faras* (1988), *Masalik al-Zaytun* (1990), *Shajar al-khallata* (1995), *Khamil al-Madaji* (1995), *Nisa ali al-Rindi* (2000), and *al-Anaqa* (2001).

political culture that was dominated by Marxist ideologies. In 1968, al-Madini earned his bachelor's degree in Arabic language and literature from the University of Sidi Mohammed Ben Abdallah in Fez. He wrote his thesis on the art of the short story in Morocco under the supervision of Mohammed Serghini. In 1978, he earned his postgraduate diploma in Arabic literature from Muhammad V University. He finished his educational training by attending the Sorbonne in France, where he defended his doctorate on the realist vision in the Moroccan contemporary novel in 1990. After finishing his higher education, al-Madini worked as a lecturer at the Sorbonne before he joined the University of Paris-VIII, and later University of Muhammad V in Rabat as an assistant professor.

Al-Madini's literary career started as a writer for the Moroccan publication *al-Alam* (The banner), the voice of the Istiqlal Party. In the political division within the Socialist Union of Popular Forces (USFP), he contributed to *al-Muharrir*, which was directed by Omar Benjelloun; later he wrote for *al-Ittihad al-Ishtiraki*. Al-Madini is one of the most prolific writers and members of the Union of Moroccan Writers (UEM). His literary works include short stories, novels, and works on literary criticism and theory. His works include *al-Unfu fi'l-*

changes in terms of the thematic and technical aspects of the literary text. These periodical transformations are the outcome of the writers' direct responses to the political and social realities of Morocco. Therefore, three periods of literary production in Morocco can be distinguished. The early period was characterized by a naïve understanding of artistic production where the literary world was built around the worldview of the narrator. These works tended to be autobiographical, such as Abd al-Majid Ben Jalloun's *Fi'l-Tufula* (1957). The second period started in the early 1970s and produced only a wave of literary criticisms, characterized by a Marxist perspective. The third period began at the end of the 1970s and saw a drastic change at the level of the writer's understanding of modern and new techniques of literary writing. Among the key figures of this period is al-Madini, whose contribution was reflected both at the level of literary production and critical theorization of the novel and the short story in the Morocco.

Al-Madini argued that the short story was late to reach the Arab Maghreb (western Arab world, that is, North Africa) because of the socioeconomic condition of Morocco during the colonial period. He contended that the Moroccan short story did not emerge until the 1940s, and that it was influenced by the Egyptian short story, which set a model of literary and critical writing in the Arab world. Equally important, al-Madini believed that the traditionalist Islamic salafiyya movement limited any artistic expression by encouraging respect for Islamic education and a strong adherence to traditional cultural heritage instead of celebrating new forms of expression that transcend the quotidian. Therefore, instead of using classical artistic expressions to describe existing patriarchal traditions norms as Ben Jalloun (1919–1981) did, al-Madini sought a new stylistic approach to the Moroccan novel, and inaugurated a phase of experimentation in the postcolonial literary tradition. Beginning in the 1970s, literary experimentation began with al-Madini (*Zamanun bayna al-Wilada wa'l-Hulm*, 1976), ABDALLAH LAROUI (*al-Ghurba*, 1971; *al-Yatim*, 1978), Mohammad Azzedine Tazi (*Abraj al-Madina*, 1978), and Said Allouch (*Hajiz al-Thalj*, 1974). In these narrative works, there was an overlapping of time and narrators, which was absent in the early works. The polyphonic nature of the narrative was also characterized by the limitation of descriptive scenes. This new period reached maturation during the 1990s.

Al-Madini's contribution to Moroccan Arabic literature should also be seen within the context of his interest in literary criticism as the guiding principle for scientific literary production. Al-Madini argued that the new Moroccan literary text should move beyond Gustave Flaubert's concept of the absolute power of the narrator and deconstruct the chronological nature of the plot. This revolt against classical artistic

AL-MADINI SPEAKS

I want to write about reality, but without writing a realist narrative. Al-Madini Ahmad. *Madinat Baraqish*. Mashurat al-Rabita, 1998.

techniques and patterns was triggered by the political, social, economic, and cultural transformations in the Arab world, especially after the Arab armies were defeated in the 1967 War. The new French novelists such as Claude Simon, Michel Butor, and Alain Robbe-Grillet influenced al-Madini. The monologue novel of James Joyce, Virginia Woolf, Ernest Hemingway, Franz Kafka, and Marcel Proust also influenced his writing techniques. Finally, Arab novelists such as Haidar Haidar, Ghalib Halsa, Ghassan Kanafani, and Abdul-Rahman Mounif also molded the modern novel in Morocco. Accordingly, al-Madini argued, life is too complex to be seen from the perspective of a single narrative eye.

The political failures of the progressive forces (leftist Marxist-Leninist) and the beginning of a new political era in modern Morocco ushered in by the Green March of 1975, when Morocco laid claim to the region of Western Sahara, initiated the beginning of experimentation in the writings of al-Madini. In 1967, he wrote *Zamanun bayna al-Wilada wa'l-Hulm* where he shook the rules of traditional writings. In fact, al-Madini argued that his purpose was to write about reality, but without writing a realist narrative. The Moroccan reality of his novels and short stories is a context where political and ideological themes are discussed without the dominance of a sole hero in the narrative. In *Madinat Baraqish* (1998), al-Madini revisited the political events of the 1960s from a polyphonic perspective where a variety of voices merge to counter the official silence.

THE WORLD'S PERSPECTIVE

Al-Madini is celebrated for his groundbreaking literary novels and his ability to theorize new styles of artistic forms by critiquing schools of literary production in postindependence Morocco. His literary experimentation has been positively viewed for its perceptive use modern European styles of writing without falling into blind imitation of the European modern novel.

LEGACY

Many critics argued that the movement from the classical to the modernist stylistic techniques in the Moroccan novel and short story was unnatural compared to Egypt, Syria, and Iraq. They contended that the Moroccan reader was not prepared for this abrupt shift given its meager knowledge of literary forms of writing. Therefore, the common belief was that the new novel in Morocco was nothing but a fabricated literary fashion that did not emerge as a reaction to the social transformations of Moroccan society.

Al-Madini rejected this critical viewpoint of the conditions that led to the rise of the modern novel in the late 1970s. He believed that this movement is a native literary experience that reacted to the political failures of the national political parties and leaders. Al-Madini claimed that any blind literary representation of the national past heritage without questioning its limitation and problems would reproduce this reality and maintain it. The role of the writer is to create new literary worldviews and picture alternative solutions. In light of this, al-Madini saw literary works as artistic forms of social and political change. He went to the extent of criticizing the works of Ben Salem Himmich as historical novels that encouraged the reproduction of historical periods of failure and cultural heritage. Al-Madini wanted to break all connections with the past and redirect literary toward modern perspectives.

BIBLIOGRAPHY

Genette, Gérard. *Narrative Discourse: An Essay in Method*, translated by Jane E. Lewin. Ithaca, NY: Cornell University Press, 1983.

Jay, Salim. *Dictionnaire des écrivains marocains*. Paris: Eddif, 2005.

Aomar Boum

MAHDAOUI, AHMAD RAFIQ AL-
(1898–1961)

Ahmad Rafiq al-Mahdaoui (Mahdawi) was a Libyan poet called the "Poet of the Homeland" because most of his poetry was dedicated to the cause of liberating his country from Italian colonial rule.

PERSONAL HISTORY

Al-Mahdaoui (sometimes known just as Rafiq al-Mahdaoui) was born in 1898 in the village of Fissatu in the western, mountainous part of Libya, and was thirteen years old when Italian military forces invaded the country in 1911. His father was a civil servant with the Ottoman administration, and had moved from Benghazi, the city of his origins, to western Libya. Subsequently he was transferred to Misrata and to Zawiya, and during this period Ahmad Rafiq obtained his primary school certificate in Turkish primary schools.

In 1910, al-Mahdaoui moved with his family to the city of Alexandria in Egypt, where he stayed until the prime of his youth. He obtained his secondary school certificate and composed his first poems, influenced by Egyptian

---

BIOGRAPHICAL HIGHLIGHTS

Name: Ahmad Rafiq al-Mahdaoui (Mahdawi)

Birth: 1898, Fissatu, Libya

Death: 1961, Athens, Greece

Nationality: Libyan

Education: Secondary school, Alexandria, Egypt

PERSONAL CHRONOLOGY:

- **1910:** Moves to Alexandria
- **1920:** Returns to Benghazi, works in municipal government
- **1922:** Fired from municipal job by Italian Fascist authorities; goes to Turkey and works as merchant
- **1934:** Returns to Libya
- **1946:** Again returns to Libya
- **1951:** Appointed senator in Libyan parliament
- **1961:** Dies in Athens while seeking medical treatment

---

poets of the era such as Ahmad Shawqi and Hafiz Ibrahim. In 1920 he returned to Benghazi where he was granted a post as secretary in the city municipality.

Al-Mahdaoui continued working and writing until the Italians took notice of the patriotic approach in his poetry. The Italian government was taken over by the Fascist Party in 1922, and with the more coercive rule that followed, al-Mahdaoui was fired from his job. He traveled to Turkey where he worked as a merchant before returning to Libya in 1934, a few years after Libyan resistance to Italian rule had been halted and the country pacified. The Italians were not happy with his homecoming, as he was not ready to remain silent. His epic poem "Ghayth al-Saghir" ("Little Ghayth") condemning Italian rule was circulated secretly. The poem depicted a boy named Ghayth expressing his intention of taking revenge upon the Italian official who had killed his father. A decree was issued ordering al-Mahdaoui to leave the country, and he returned to Turkey, joining the Turkish civil service and climbing the career ladder to become mayor of the famous town of Adana in southeastern Anatolia.

In 1946, a year after World War II came to an end and three years after the British defeated Italian forces in Libya and established a military administration there, al-Mahdaoui returned to Benghazi from exile. He remained there for the rest of his life, taking a very active part in the cultural and political life of his country during those formative years of its history. Upon the declaration of the country's independence in 1951, he was appointed a senator in the upper house of parliament and remained there until the end of his life. He died on 6 July 1961 while on a visit to Athens for medical treatment, and his body was brought back to Benghazi for burial.

INFLUENCES AND CONTRIBUTIONS

Al-Mahdaoui's poetry mirrors the destiny of Libya and the lives of its people in the first half of the twentieth century. Although he wrote poetry covering most aspects of life—social, emotional, and otherwise—his main topics were political and patriotic. He also wrote some essays, as well as poems in the local Libyan dialect to be put to music and sung at weddings and other social occasions, thereby adding a modern flavor to the lyrics of oral, traditional, folkloric literature.

In al-Mahdaoui's poetry we see a poet who abides by traditional rules of Arabic poetry as they had been established by his artistic forebears. Although one of his poems shows how fed up he was with these traditional measures and rhymes and rules that imprisoned the soul and talent of the poet within their walls, he never ventured in his poetry to break with, or even deviate from, these rules.

Al-Mahdaoui's long work "Ghayth al-Saghir" was considered one of his best poems and was dramatized by other poets and playwrights, and introduced on stage and screen. One of the most successful dramatizations was done by the Libyan poet and prose writer Muhammad Ahmed Oraieth, and was published in book form. Khalifa al-Tillisi commented in his 1965 biography of al-Mahdaoui, *Rafiq: the Poet of the Homeland*, that he had a very sharp sense of humor, and wrote very satirical political poems. He gave as an example the poem about a watermelon the poet bought from the market, finding to his disappointment when he opened it at home that it was as rotten as the head of a Libyan government minister. Al-Mahdaoui's antigovernment poetry circulated secretly even after independence, attacking the king and the government of the day in very harsh language.

THE WORLD'S PERSPECTIVE

Al-Mahdaoui's poetry was hailed and praised by prominent Egyptian writers, two of whom—the poet Aziz Abaza and the thinker, scholar, and novelist Muhammad Farid Abu Hadid—introduced one of the three volumes of his *Diwan Rafiq* (Rafiq's diwan; in this context, "Diwan" refers to a poetry collection). The first volume was published in 1962, one year after his death, while the other two were issued in 1965 and 1971. A small book about his life with selections of his poems was published

during his lifetime by an Egyptian school teacher, Muhammad Sadiq Afifi. In his introduction to al-Mahdaoui's poetry, Abaza described how al-Mahdaoui was able to unify his personal pain and agony with that of his country and his people, lending his poetry authenticity. In his introduction, Abu Hadid named some of the works of the Libyan poet that had caught his attention as the most remarkable and excellent.

Al-Mahdaoui's poetry was given unlikely praise by the thinker and critic Abbas Aqqad, who had previously attacked the poet Ahmad Shawki for his traditional style and for being a mere servant to old modes and molds who was not keeping up with the times. Aqqad said in an article published on 15 October 1954 in the prestigious Egyptian journal *Akhbar al-Yawm* that his duties as a writer compelled him to draw the attention of his readers in Egypt to this greatly talented poet who could express himself in the most powerful poetic terms, communicating with other suffering souls and planting in them a redeeming effect. In later years the Egyptian philosopher Abd al-Rahman Badawi recalled in his memoirs his days in Libya when people used to express their admiration for a poet like Ahmad Rafiq al-Mahdaoui, in whose poetry he found no sense of poetry at all.

Modern-day critics think that the high position al-Mahdaoui enjoyed in the minds of the older generation was due not so much to his merits as a poet—and his talent is modest compared to highly talented poets—as to the content of his poetry and its message at a time of struggle and colonial rule. This view has been expressed in many papers and seminars on modern Libyan poets, and even the major book that hails him as a poet, that of al-Tillisi, indicates that this is so.

LEGACY

Despite the classical form of his poetry, and despite the passage of more than five decades since the end of colonial rule, al-Mahdaoui is remembered as the "Poet of the Nation" in Libya.

BIBLIOGRAPHY
Ward, Philip. "Contemporary Art in Lybia." *African Arts* 4, no. 4 (1971).

Ahmad al-Fagih

MAHFOUZ, NAGUIB
(1911–2006)

An Egyptian novelist, screenwriter, and playwright, Naguib Mahfouz (Najib Mahfuz) became the first Arab writer to receive the Nobel Prize for achievements in literature in 1988. During the seventy years of his professional career,

Naguib Mahfouz. © STR/EPA/CORBIS.

BIOGRAPHICAL HIGHLIGHTS

Name: Naguib Mahfouz (Najib Mahfuz)

Birth: 1911, Gamaliyya district of Cairo, Egypt

Death: 2006, Cairo, Egypt

Family: Wife, Atiyyatullah; two daughters, Fatima and Umm Kulthum

Nationality: Egyptian

Education: B.A. (philosophy), Cairo University 1934

PERSONAL CHRONOLOGY:

- **1930s:** Against his father's will, rejects getting a medical education and chooses instead to study philosophy

- **1930:** Publishes article "The Dying of Old Beliefs and the Birth of New Beliefs"

- **1936:** Decides to pursue career in literature and abandons study of philosophy

- **1939:** Publishes first novel, *Abath al-Qadr* (Irony of Fate)

- **1939–1954:** Civil servant at Ministry of Islamic Affairs

- **1954–1969:** Director of Foundation for Support of the Cinema

- **1956–1957:** Publication of *al-Thulathiyya (The Cairo Trilogy)*

- **1969–1971:** Consultant for cinema affairs in Ministry of Culture

- **1988:** Becomes first Arab writer to receive the Nobel Prize in Literature

- **1994:** Attacked by Islamic fundamentalists, who stab him several times in the neck intending to kill him for the alleged heresy in his books; survives attack, but is left with permanent injuries to nervous system

Mahfouz published 34 novels, more than 350 short stories, dozens of movie scripts, and 5 plays. Mahfouz was the author of the script of several famous movies produced in Egypt, such as *Saladdin* (1964) and *Adrift on the Nile* (1971). Mahfouz also pursued a career as a civil servant, holding different positions in the Ministry for Islamic Affairs (1939–1954), working at the State Cinema Organization (1954–1969), and serving as consultant for cinema affairs in the Ministry of Culture (1969–1971) and director of the Foundation for Support of the Cinema.

PERSONAL HISTORY

Mahfouz was born into the family of a Muslim civil servant in the Gamaliyya district of Cairo, Egypt, on 11 December 1911. He was the youngest of seven children in the family and was named after the doctor who delivered him, Naguib Pasha Mahfouz, professor of medicine, who is credited as the father of Egyptian obstetrics and gynecology. Mahfouz remembered his father as a conservative civil servant, who prepared his son to follow his

footsteps in career. Naguib's mother often took him to museums and this may have had an influence on him as Egyptian history, especially the history of ancient Egypt, became one of the dominant themes in his prose.

Having finished his secondary education, Mahfouz rejected his father's suggestion to study medicine and entered Cairo University where he studied philosophy and obtained his bachelor's degree in 1934. Having spent a year toward his master's degree in philosophy, Mahfouz chose to pursue a career as a professional writer.

In 1936 he started working at the newspaper *al-Risala* and contributed to the newspapers *al-Hilal* and *al-Ahram*. Mahfouz started his writing career by publishing short stories and essays. During these years the ideas of Musa Salama, an Egyptian intellectual of Coptic Orthodox Christian origins, had a fundamental influence over Mahfouz's thoughts. Salama was introduced to the ideas of socialism and social-democratic values while he was studying in France and Britain, where he got to know and was influenced by George Bernard Shaw and Herbert George Wells, the prominent members of the Fabian Society, which gave birth to the Labour Party in the U.K.

Mahfouz's first published book was a translation of James Baikie's work on ancient Egypt titled *Misr al-Qadima* (*History of Ancient Egypt*). It was published in the magazine *al-Majalla al-Jadida* in 1932. In the meantime Mahfouz continued publishing series of short stories in different literary newspapers and magazines.

In 1939 Mahfouz accepted the position of civil servant at the Ministry of Islamic Affairs where he worked until 1954. In 1939 Mahfouz published his first novel, *Abath al-Qadr* (Irony of fate). Initially, the novel was titled *Hikmat Khufu* (Wisdom of Cheops). The plot was based on the ideas of fatalism. The pharaoh, who lived about 2680 BCE, was told by an oracle that his son would not be able to inherit the throne, and that it would fall into the hands of Dedef, the son of the high priest of the temple Ra. Despite all the efforts of the pharaoh, nothing stops the realization of the oracle's prophesy.

Two other novels, *Radubis* (1943) and *Kifah Tibah* (1944; Struggle of Thebes), were also based on historical events that took place in ancient Egypt. The main character of *Radubis* is a courtesan named Radubis, who was the lover of the pharaoh Mernere, the last king of the ancient Sixth dynasty in Egypt. Mahfouz used the love story between these two characters to describe the complex human, emotional, and social relations in ancient Egypt.

Kifah Tibah describes the Hyksos wars, the decline and fall of the Middle Kingdom in 1785–1575 BCE. The novel portrays the struggle of Egypt as it strove to keep control against a foreign Asian power. With the fall of Hyksos, Egypt gained its independence and started flourishing. This book resonated with the decline of colonialism and the rise of independent statehood in Egypt in the twentieth century.

These books were part of a large and incomplete project of thirty historical novels. Inspired by Sir Walter Scott, a British writer of the late eighteenth to early nineteenth centuries, Mahfouz intended to cover the whole history of Egypt in a series of historical novels. The project remained unfinished, because Mahfouz shifted his interest

toward writing about the lives of ordinary people in rural Egypt and in Cairo, where he grew up.

In 1948 Mahfouz wrote *al-Sarab* (Mirage), which became a turning point in his development as an author. Mahfouz based the plot of this novel on Sigmund Freud's method of psychoanalysis. He used the same writing style in another novel he wrote one year later, *Bidaya wa Nahaya* (*The Beginning and the End*).

In 1950s Naguib Mahfouz wrote *al-Thulathiyya* (*The Cairo Trilogy*), which earned him fame as a writer in Egypt and other Arab countries. The trilogy of fifteen hundred pages included three novels: *Bayn al-Qasrayn* (1956; *Palace Walk*), *Qasr al-Shawq* (1957; *Palace of Desire*), and *al-Sukkariyya* (1957; *Sugar Street*). The plots of the novels unfolded in Cairo.

The trilogy covered the life of al-Sayyid Ahmad Abd al-Jawwad and his family across three generations, from World War I to the overthrow of King Faruq in 1952. Al-Sayyid Ahmad Abd al-Jawwad is a tyrannical head of a family who demands unconditional obedience from his wife Amina, his sons Yasin, Fahmi, and Kamal, and his daughters Khadija and A'isha. *Bayn al-Qasrayn* describes the influences of the nationalist ideas on Fahmi, the middle son of the al-Jawwad family. A law student, Fahmi starts participating in anti-British nationalist demonstrations, growing increasingly hostile toward the British military forces, located directly in front of the place where the al-Jawwad family lives. The youngest brother of the family, Kamal, is not into any political struggle, and has even befriended some of the British soldiers. Fahmi continues his political activities despite orders from his father to stop. The oldest brother, Yasin, is described as a hedonist, who, similar to his father, enjoys spending his time with courtesans and wine. The daughters of the family, Khadija and A'isha, have different personalities; Khadija is rude and opinionated, whereas A'isha is quiet and conciliatory. These different characters and their attitudes toward the changes unfolding in their society depicts the spread of different sociopolitical ideas in Egypt during this period, including the ideas of nationalism, socialism, and Islamic fundamentalism, as well as the intellectual environment and the moral code of the traditional Egyptian society in a period of three generations.

In 1954 Mahfouz was appointed director of the Foundation for Support of the Cinema, the State Cinema Organization. Mahfouz worked in this capacity for the next fifteen years.

In 1959 Mahfouz published the novel *Awlad Haratina* (*Children of Gebelawi*). It was published in a serialized version by the *al-Ahram* newspaper. The novel's plot was closely related to religious themes, with an allegorical family representing God (Gebelawi) and his children Moses (Gabal), Jesus (Rifa'a), and Muhammad (Qasim), who settle in different quarters of the valley after their father Gebelawi banishes them from the house. The symbol of modern science, Arafa, comes after all prophets while they all claim him to be one of their own. The person representing each religion claims a closer affiliation with science than any of the other religions.

As the events in the novel unfold, Mahfouz freely interprets the stories reflected in the Qur'an, the Bible, and the Torah. The leading figures in the Islamic al-Azhar University vehemently protested against what they called a blasphemy and heresy against religion and God. Crowds demonstrated in front of the al-Ahram office and demanded that the the novel be banned. Although it was never officially outlawed, it was not published in Egypt. The novel *Awlad Haratina* was first published in Lebanon in 1961. Although it was translated into several foreign languages and brought fame to Mahfouz abroad, in Egypt he was haunted by the controversy surrounding the novel long after having written it.

Mahfouz wrote *Tharthara Fawq al-Nil* (*Adrift on the Nile*) in 1966. In 1971 this novel was made into a film and immediately created controversy in Egypt for its depiction of decadence in Egyptian society under the rule of the late president Gamal Abdel Nasser. According to the novel's plot, Anis, who hates the hypocrisy in the Egyptian government, the illiteracy of the Egyptian public, and the many unsolved problems of society, decides to escape from reality by smoking a *shisha* (also called a hookah, *nargila* or *argila;* a waterpipe used for consuming tobacco and sometimes drugs). Soon Anis finds out that he is not alone; the majority of the people in the government elite, middle, and even lower classes do the same thing themselves to escape. Anis stops smoking drugs, but immediately transforms into a lone madman in a society of drugged individuals who do not see, and do not want to see, the realities surrounding them. The government of Anwar Sadat, fearful of being associated with this novel and movie, banned it under the protests of still-strong Nasser supporters in Egypt.

In 1966, Mahfouz's novel *Midaq Alley* (1947) became the first of his works to be translated into English. After his introduction to foreign audiences, he has been widely read abroad ever since, and many of his novels and short stories have been translated into different foreign languages. In 1969 Mahfouz brought out a collection of short stories titled *Taht al-Mizalla* (Under the shelter), the central themes of which were violence and public indifference toward the fate of others. In the 1970s Mahfouz published several novels, including *Al Hubbu Tahta-al-Matar* (1973; Love under the Rain), *Al Jarima* (1973; Crime), and *al-Karnak* (1974). While all of these works were well-received, the novel *Harafish* (1977) gained the most popularity. Despite his popular-

ity, however, Mahfouz continued to court controversy. After the Framework for Peace in the Middle East (Camp David Accord) was adopted by Egypt and Israel in 1978, Mahfouz defended Sadat's stance, which led to restrictions being imposed on the publication of his novels in a majority of Arab countries beyond Egypt. The constraints on his publications continued throughout the 1980s.

Mahfouz published in 1983 a fundamental novel titled *Amam al-Arsh* (In front of the throne). The plot developed around the gathering of all Egyptian leaders from the ancient pharaohs to President Sadat. All the presidents, kings, and pharaohs had to justify their policies before the court of Osiris, the ancient Egyptian god of life, death, and fertility. Aside from tackling the interesting political and social issues from different periods of the Egyptian history, the work gained significance in that it looked at Egypt not just as a modern Arab country with Islamic heritage, but also as a region with a profound and unique ancient history. The last point was conveyed through the accusations of the pharaoh Rameses II on Nasser. Ramses blames Nasser for reducing Egypt to an insignificant state, having let the features of majestic Egypt dissolve into the vague outlines of Arabism. Nasser in his turn blames Sadat for not being tough enough against the foreign influence. Sadat gets support from the pharaoh Akhenaten, who was dethroned because of his unsuccessful attempts to bring monotheism into ancient Egypt. Akhenaten's support for Sadat allowed Mahfouz to show the similarities in the fates of reformer-rulers in ancient and modern Egypt. He further developed the theme of Akhenaten in a separate novel titled *al-A'ish fi'l-Haqiqa* (1985; The dweller of the truth). That same year Mahfouz wrote another novel titled *The Day the Leader Was Killed*, this time about Sadat.

In 1988 Mahfouz became the first Arab writer to win the Nobel Prize in Literature. Mahfouz, who never traveled abroad, sent his daughters to collect the prize. Yet, at the peak of his career as a writer, Mahfouz had to live though yet another controversy related to *Awlad Haratina* (*Children of Gebelawi*). In 1988, the religious leader of Iran, Ayatollah Ruhollah Khomeini issued a *fatwa* (Islamic religious ruling) calling for the execution of British author Salman Rushdie for his book *The Satanic Verses* and its controversial statements about the Islamic religion. This in turn caused Egyptian theologian Umar Abd al-Rahman to publicly state that if Mahfouz had been punished for writing *Awlad Haratina*, Rushdie would not have dared publish *The Satanic Verses*. In 1994 a religious radical acted on those thoughts and stabbed the eighty-two-year-old writer in the neck, leaving him with permanent injuries to his nervous system.

CONTEMPORARIES

Taha Husayn (1889–1973; also Hussein) was one of the most influential Egyptian writers and intellectuals. He was a figurehead for the modernist movement in Egypt. He earned the title of Amid al-Adab al-Arabi (Dean of Arabic Literature). Having contracted an eye disease in childhood, Husayn became blind for the rest of his life. Despite his physical disability, Husayn graduated from al-Azhar University, entered the secular Cairo University upon its establishment and earned a Ph.D. in literature. Husayn earned his second Ph.D. from the Sorbonne in France. Husayn became the founding rector of the University of Alexandria.

Husayn was a proponent of the idea of pharaonism, which maintained that Egypt comprised in itself the diametrically opposite civilizations of the ancient Egypt and the Arab/Eastern culture, and that Egypt's progress depended upon returning the country to its ancient roots. He published a number of novels, stories, criticisms, and social and political essays, some of which were translated into foreign languages.

Despite this attack, Mahfouz continued writing, creating new novels and short stories until his death in 2006. In 2005, he wrote the novel *The Seventh Heaven*. Mahfouz later died in a Cairo hospital on 30 August 2006.

INFLUENCES AND CONTRIBUTIONS

Mahfouz spent his childhood and youth in the period when Egypt first struggled for independence from the British, then searched for national identity and the optimal sociopolitical system, all of which were accompanied by intense political and occasionally military struggles. Mahfouz stated that the events of the anti-British revolution of 1919, which took place when he was only eight years old, influenced his life in a tremendous way. That was the year when the British military used force in an attempt to suppress the independence movement in Egypt.

During the early period of his activity as a writer, Mahfouz became interested in different political theories. Nationalism, socialism, as well as liberal democratic values were in the scope of his interest and were reflected in his stories and novels. Mahfouz used different characters in his writings as mediators between issues of local and wider scope, describing history and politics with human life in its center.

The early stages of Mahfouz's writing were heavily influenced by the themes of ancient history of Egypt. He was looking for a link between the civilization of ancient Egypt, its Islamic heritage, and the modern nationalist ideas. Mahfouz opposed pan-Arabism in the sense that he did not want to have ancient Egyptian heritage be deluded with and limited to the period of history when Egypt got acquainted with the Arabic and Islamic civilization.

LEGACY

Mahfouz permanently drew parallels between the developments in ancient Egypt and the developments of his time. His novels *Abath al-Qadr*, *Radubis*, and *Kifah Tibah*, at the early stages of his writing career, as well as *Amam al-Arsh* and *al-A'ish fi'-l-Haqiqa*, reflecting the later stage of his development, and many other novels and short stories written in the interim period addressed the issue of communication between these two civilizations of Egypt.

In the late 1940s, Mahfouz introduced another technique into his writing style, focusing on the daily life of ordinary people, with the interpretation of huge sociopolitical processes developing in Egypt from their viewpoints. The culmination of this style was the *Cairo Trilogy*, after which a number of literary critiques called him the "Arab Balzac" (after French writer Honoré de Balzac). A portion of his novels and stories written in this style were sharply critical of the political situation in his country, which put him under significant pressure.

Another turning point in Mahfouz's prose was *Awlad Haratina*. The mystic forces of the world affecting human life, the attempts to understand God, and experimenting with free interpretations of religious books constituted the new direction in his writing. This path of his prose with some shifts in focus reflected itself in his *Leyali Alf Leyla* (1981; The Arabian nights), *The Thief and the Dogs* (1982; *Al-Lyssu va al-Kilabi*), *Amam al-Arsh* (1983; In front of the throne) and many other novels and stories he wrote in his late stage of literary development.

Mahfouz continued experimenting with the new themes, topics, and techniques until the latest days of his prose.

BIBLIOGRAPHY

Beard, Michael, and Adnan Haydar. *Naguib Mahfouz: From Regional Fame to Global Recognition*. Syracuse, NY: Syracuse University Press, 1993.

Ghitani, Gamal al-, and Britta Le Va. *The Cairo of Naguib Mahfouz*. Cairo: American University in Cairo Press, 1999.

Gordon, Hayim. *Naguib Mahfouz's Egypt: Existential Themes in His Writings*. New York: Greenwood Press, 1990.

Moosa, Matti. *The Early Novels of Naguib Mahfouz: Images of Modern Egypt*. Gainesville: University Press of Florida, 1994.

ENGLISH TRANSLATIONS OF WORKS BY MAHFOUZ

Palace Walk, Book 1 of *The Cairo Trilogy* (published in Arabic, 1956)

Palace of Desire (Book 2 of *The Cairo Trilogy*; originally published in Arabic, 1957)

Sugar Street (Book 3 of *The Cairo Trilogy*; originally published in Arabic, 1957)

Children of Gebelawi (originally published in Arabic, 1959)

The Beginning and the End (originally published in Arabic, 1956)

Adrift on the Nile (originally published in Arabic, 1966)

The Journey of Ibn Fattuma (originally published in Arabic, 1983)

Midaq Alley (originally published in Arabic, 1947)

The Harafish (originally published in Arabic, 1977)

The Beggar (originally published in Arabic, 1965)

The Thief and the Dogs (originally published in Arabic, 1961)

Autumn Quail (originally published in Arabic, 1962)

Adil M. Asgarov

MAHIEDDINE, BAYA
(1931–1998)

Algerian artist Baya Mahieddine (Madiedine, Mehiedine; born Fatma Haddad), known simply as Baya, illustrates an imaginative world of fantasy through her semifigurative, semiabstract approach to painting. Using gouache (a medium resembling watercolor) Baya portrays women, animals, and floral motifs with decorative patterns and vivid colors that seem to blend ancient Islamic art with modern occidental abstractionism. Her distinctive style has attracted the attention and inspired the commentary of such figures as Pablo Picasso, André Breton, ASSIA DJEBAR, and Jean Pélégri.

PERSONAL HISTORY

Born on 12 December 1931 in Bordj-el-Kifan near Algiers, Baya was orphaned five years later. Her grandmother cared for her until 1942, after which Marguerite Caminat Benhoura became her adoptive parent. Raising Baya in Algiers, this French surrogate mother encouraged Baya to pursue art as a means of developing her imagination and self-expression. In her gouaches of persons, animals, and landscapes, Baya demonstrated an original talent.

While visiting Algiers, the Parisian gallery owner Aimé Maeght perceived Baya's gift for art and decided to show her work in his gallery in 1947 in Paris. The following year, Baya traveled to the French pottery center Vallauris, on the Riviera, in order to study Madoura-style ceramics. During this time, she found herself in a studio next to Picasso, who noticed her ability and spoke with her. After returning to Algeria, however, Baya chose to work exclusively in painting.

BIOGRAPHICAL HIGHLIGHTS

Name: Baya Mahieddine (Mahiedine, Mehiedine)

Birth: 1931, Bordj el-Kifan, Algeria

Death: 1998, Blida, Algeria

Family: Husband, El Hadj Mahfoud Mahieddine (dec.); six children

Nationality: Algerian

PERSONAL CHRONOLOGY:

- **1947:** First show, Galerie Maeght, Paris
- **1953:** "Traditional" marriage to El Hadj Mahfoud Mahieddine, thirty years her senior
- **1953–1963:** Bears six children, abandons painting
- **1963:** Exhibition of early work, Musée National de Beaux Arts, Algiers; resumes painting
- **1960s–1990s:** Successful exhibitions in several countries
- **1970s:** Husband dies

After marrying the musician El Hadj Mahfoud Mahieddine in 1953, Baya adopted a more "traditional" Algerian Muslim lifestyle (Pélégri, 1987, p. 12). She moved to Blida with her husband and raised six children. During these initial years of marriage and motherhood, Baya temporarily abandoned her art. Although critics can only speculate on the significance of this detail, the decade of Baya's break from painting corresponds with the years of the Algerian war for independence (Khanna, 2003, p. 261). The Algerian author Assia Djebar observed that Baya appreciated the "protected" environment of her "sanctuary-home" (Djebar, 1990, pp. 17–18; author's translation for all quotes).

Shortly after the "euphoric days" that followed the independence of Algeria in 1962, the artist Jean de Maisonseuil found a way to get Baya to recommence her art. The Musée National de Beaux-Arts of Algiers, where he was a curator, put together a show of her older work in 1963, inspiring her to pick up her brushes and paint once again. She resumed her work at home, where she listened to her husband playing his lute every evening (Djebar, 1990, pp. 17–18). In her postmarriage work, she displayed the same youthful imagination and talent as she had initially.

In the mid-1970s, Baya faced an overwhelming hardship rivaling that of her orphanhood: the death of her husband, who was of a "mature age" when he married Baya (Djebar, 1990, p. 17). In despair, she exclaimed, "I thought I might die!" Yet for the sake of her children and her "friends from all over who fill up their eyes with [her] watercolors," she perseveres (Djebar, 1990, p. 18). Almost twenty-five years after her husband's passing, Baya joined him on 11 November 1998 in Blida, following a long illness.

INFLUENCES AND CONTRIBUTIONS

The premature death of Baya's biological parents undoubtedly left a deep mark on her. With regard to her orphanhood, she admitted, "When I was little, I was always sad. I lost my parents when I was five" (Djebar, 1990, p. 17). Although she barely elaborated on her bereavement, she discovered comfort through her art. In describing the exhilaration that she felt while painting, she explained that she entered "another" world and discovered happiness by "forget[ting] everything" (Ferhani, 1990, p. 19).

Specific works such as "Femme et enfant en bleu," "Personnage et oiseau rouge," and "Femme et oiseau bleu," shed light on how Baya's painting brought her joy. In these three works of 1947, the same subjects reappear: a woman, a child and a bird. Each picture portrays the woman cuddling the child in her arms with an exotic, feathered creature looking on from the side. "Femme et enfant en bleu" differs slightly from the other two by showing the mother affectionately peering into the face of the baby cradled in her arms. In "Personnage et oiseau rouge" and "Femme et oiseau bleu" the maternal figure has the infant tightly clasped against her breast. In these scenes, Baya re-created an ideal world in which the infant would never fear leaving the secure embrace of the parent: a peaceful depiction that compensates for the traumatic loss that Baya remembered from her childhood.

While Baya owed her survival of loss to her artwork, she blazed a unique trail of North African feminine creativity through her paintings. She demonstrated creative sensitivity that surpassed the social boundaries of her cultural background by removing the veil of invisibility that typically shrouds women in her country. Experiencing the world of Baya resembles crossing through a "feminine Algerian desert," in the words of Djebar (p. 17). Moreover, by illustrating a feminine perspective and ingenuity, Baya unintentionally led a fight: a "woman's battle." For her women contemporaries, she modeled a way of building a name and an identity (Djebar, p. 18).

Baya became an inspiration not only in her homeland, but also around the world. From her first show at Galerie Maeght, her art has circulated internationally. Institutions in Cuba, France, and Japan own her work. Regarding the allure of her art, Pélégri asks, "What therefore is the secret of Baya?" (Pélégri, p. 12). This open-ended question indicates something of her perpetual fascination.

WHEN I PAINT, I AM HAPPY

■

When asked why she prefers certain subjects for her works, she explains that she simply paints what she feels: "Why birds?", they ask me. Well, I like birds. Why butterflies? Well, because I like butterflies. For all this, I do not give a theme. I feel it and I put it onto paper. I take pleasure in that, but I cannot say why my painting is like this or like that. When I paint, I am happy, I am in another world, I forget everything. People tell me: "Why [do you paint] the same thing?" I find that if I change, I will no longer be Baya.

(FERHANI, AMÉZIANE. "INTERVIEW DE BAYA." IN
TROIS FEMMES PEINTRES. PARIS: INSTITUT DU MONDE ARABE
ET EDIFRA [1990]: 19.)

THE WORLD'S PERSPECTIVE

The issue of *Derrière le miroir* (the Galerie Maeght's own magazine, which served as a catalog of its exhibitions) devoted to Baya's 1947 show contained commentaries on her work by André Breton, Émile Dermenghem, and Jean Périssac. Breton shared his admiration of Baya's innovation and her consequent impact on the public. "I speak, not like so many others in order to lament an end, but to promote a beginning, and of this beginning, Baya is queen." Baya represents the start of an "age of emancipation and harmony" that breaks away from the "systematic" condition of convention. Breton believes that Baya characterizes the spontaneity and "revolutionary" freedom with which art should be pursued (Breton, 1990, p. 16).

Baya introduces newness through her artwork by her unique approach to painting. Throughout her career as an artist, she incorporates shapes and designs with "pure" form and bold colors that evoke the tones of Fauvism, the short-lived early twentieth-century art movement. At the same time, she maintains figurative distinctiveness as she depicts scenes ranging from outdoor landscapes to ornate interiors, where each picture is filled with women, exotic vegetation, or imaginary creatures in harmonious camaraderie. Although Baya never completely dissociates herself from such concrete imagery, her art shifts toward abstraction in the mid-1970s, coincidentally around the time of her husband's death. In "Les poissons" (1976), undulating shapes and lines combine with a striking array of circular forms that vaguely resemble the outlines of fish. From a Eurocentric perspective, this use of pure color, geometric representation, asymmetry, decorative lines, circles, and dots, bring to mind compositions of contemporary occidental artists such as Henri Matisse, as Pélégri suggests (Pélégri, p. 10).

In addition to exemplifying these technical artistic qualities, the paintings of Baya also reflect her sociocultural context. Breton famously refers to her imagery, with its nostalgic content, as "happy Arabia" (Breton, p. 16). Based on her birthplace and the decorative Kabyle designs that she incorporates, Baya most likely came from an Arab-Kabyle background (Pélégri, p. 12; Maisonseuil, 1987, p. 14). Through representations of imaginary animals, Baya visually narrates fictional tales like those told by Scheherazade in *Arabian Nights*, according to Pélégri (p. 10). Moreover, her use of detailed vegetal ornamentation suggests "arabesque" motifs of a kind visible in ceramics, tiles, textiles, and miniatures typical of Islamic art (*Arabesques et jardins*, 1989, p. 26). For this reason Frank Maubert finds that these paintings evoke "North African folklore" while preserving a "Muslim aesthetic" (1998, p. 8).

Rather than simply admiring the gouaches of Baya in the way that they illustrate an idyllic image of Arabia, Djebar identifies a "frail and strong" woman behind the scenes. Baya prevails against the "grayness of the foggy halftones of daily life"—the monotonies of household chores—and faces the difficult loss of her husband with the resilience of her creative spirit. "[Y]ou are there: [T]he original eye of your liberated women smiles at the sky of birds, at the guitar, at the repopulated world of your heart," declares Djebar (p. 18). Instead of mourning her misfortune, Baya overcomes her tribulations by joining the people, animals, and instruments that she paints in her multicolored cosmos.

LEGACY

Combining characteristics of ancient Islamic art with the dynamic form and color of modern occidental painting, Baya demonstrates creativity that establishes her place among Algerian painters. For the people of Algeria, she preserves a nostalgic "happy Arabia" while for her international public she depicts an equally captivating and magical haven (Breton, p. 16). The imaginative stories that she tells through the vibrant scenes of her works will continue to mystify and attract individuals globally. Finally, by securing a lasting name for herself—a major accomplishment for an Algerian woman—she has made a path for others to follow.

BIBLIOGRAPHY

Arabesques et jardins de paradis: collections françaises d'art islamique. Musée du Louvre. Paris: Éditions de la Réunion des musées nationaux, 1989.

Bouabdellah, Malika. "Baya." In *La peinture par les mots*. Algiers: Musée National des Beaux-Arts D'Alger, 1994.

Breton, André. "Baya." In *Trois femmes peintres: Baya, Chaibia, Fahrelnissa*. Paris: Institut du Monde Arabe: EDIFRA, 1990.

Djebar, Assia. "Le combat de Baya." In *Trois femmes peintres: Baya, Chaibia, Fahrelnissa*. Paris: Institut du Monde Arabe: EDIFRA, 1990.

Ferhani, Améziane. "Interview de Baya." In *Trois femmes peintres: Baya, Chaibia, Fahrelnissa*. Paris: Institut du Monde Arabe: EDIFRA, 1990.

Khanna, Ranjana. "Latent Ghosts and the Manifesto Baya, Breton and Reading for the Future." *Art History* 26, no. 2 (2003): 238–280.

Maisonseuil, Jean de. "Afterword." In *Baya, Issiakhem, Khadda: Algérie, expressions multiples*, edited by Michel-Georges Bernard, Benamar Mediène, Jean Pélégri, et al. Paris: ADEIAO, 1987.

Maubert, Frank. "Lumineuse Baya." In *Baya: Gouaches 1947*. Paris: Galerie Maeght, 1998.

Pélégri, Jean. "Baya l'oiseau mauve." In *Baya, Issiakhem, Khadda: Algérie, expressions multiples*, edited by Michel-George Bernard, Benamar Mediène, Jean Pélégri, et al. Paris: ADEIAO, 1987.

Sénac, Jean. *Visages d'Algérie*. Paris: Paris-Méditerranée, 2002.

C. Wakaba Futamura

MAJID, ALI HASAN AL-
(1941–)

Ali Hasan al-Majid (also Ali Hassan al-Majeed) was one of the top Iraqi military and Ba'th Party officials during the rule of dictator SADDAM HUSSEIN. The new post-Saddam Iraqi government put him on trial for supervising the genocide against Iraq's Kurdish population in 1988, among other crimes. In June 2007 al-Majid was found guilty and sentenced to death by hanging.

PERSONAL HISTORY

Al-Majid was born in either 1941 or 1943. He is a first cousin of former Iraqi dictator Saddam Hussein, whose father, Husayn al-Majid, was the brother of Ali's father, Hasan al-Majid. Both Saddam and Ali Hasan al-Majid were born in al-Awja, Iraq, a village near the city of Takrit. They both hail from Sunni Arab families from the al-Bejat clan, which is part of the larger al-Bu Nasir tribe.

Unlike his cousin, al-Majid served in the Iraqi army. By the late 1960s, he was a motorcycle messenger and member of the Ba'th Party. When a 17 July 1968 coup toppled the government and brought the Ba'th into power in Iraq, a distant relative of al-Majid, General Ahmad Hasan al-Bakr, became the new president. However, real power in the new regime lay in the hands of Saddam and the Ba'th Party security services that he oversaw. In 1980, Saddam appointed al-Majid, who had been promoted to general in the army, as the head

Ali Hasan al-Majid. AP IMAGES.

BIOGRAPHICAL HIGHLIGHTS

Name: Ali Hasan al-Majid (also Ali Hassan al-Majeed, as well as "Chemical Ali")

Birth: 1941 or 1943, al-Awja, Iraq

Family: Married; children

Nationality: Iraqi

PERSONAL CHRONOLOGY:

• **1980:** Named head of General Security Service

• **1987:** Appointed general secretary of Ba'th Party's Northern Bureau

• **1988:** Oversees Anfal campaign against the Kurds

• **1990:** Becomes military governor of Kuwait

• **1991:** Named minister of the interior; crushes Shi'ite uprising in southern Iraq; made defense minister

• **1996:** Becomes member, Committee of the Four

• **1998:** Appointed military commander, Southern Region

• **2003:** Invasion of Iraq; captured by U.S. forces

• **2006:** Put on trial for genocide, war crimes, and crimes against humanity

• **2007:** Found guilty, given death sentence

of the General Security Service—thus making him one of the most powerful men in Iraq. He eventually was chosen as the director of the Revolutionary Command Council, the regime's top consultative body.

It was his close family ties to Saddam that underlay al-Majid's power and position in Iraq. This was in keeping with Saddam's policy of placing family members, members of his extended tribe, and other Sunni Arabs from the Takrit area in the regime's most important positions. Al-Majid retained the post of head of the General Security Service until 1987, one of the few individuals Saddam allowed to head that or any other sensitive agency for a long period of time. Despite this, al-Majid later confessed that he still feared Saddam, who had done away with close relatives before when he distrusted them.

Al-Majid was notorious for his brutality in carrying out the wishes of Saddam. In March 1987, Saddam made him general secretary of the Ba'th Party's Northern Bureau, which encompassed the Kurdish regions of Iraq. In this capacity, al-Majid directly supervised the notorious 1988 Anfal campaign of genocide against the Kurds. He later served as the military governor of Kuwait during

the harsh Iraqi occupation of the country from August 1990 until February 1991. He was appointed minister of the interior in March 1991, in time to take charge of the ferocious government crackdown on the Shi'ite rebellion that flared up that month in the wake of Iraq's defeat in the Gulf War. Thereafter, al-Majid served as Iraq's defense minister from 1991 to 1995, although Saddam dismissed him in 1995 after he discovered that he had been smuggling grain to Iran.

In February 1996, al-Majid was back in Saddam's favor. He led the notorious attack that killed his nephews, Lieutenant-General Husayn Kamil Hasan al-Majid and Colonel Saddam Kamil Hasan al-Majid, who had just returned to Iraq after defecting to Jordan the year before. Shortly after their defection, Saddam—who was both their second cousin and father-in-law—dispatched Ali Hasan al-Majid to Jordan to persuade them to return. He failed when Jordan's King HUSSEIN BIN TALAL refused to allow him to see them. After several months, the two men decided to return to Iraq. Although they had been promised clemency from Saddam if they returned, both men were killed almost immediately after returning home during a thirteen-hour gun battle with al-Majid and other family members. Some reports state that al-Majid himself fired the coup de grâce shot into Husayn Kamil's head.

Al-Majid continued to be given sensitive and important positions by Saddam. In 1996, he became a member of the Committee of the Four, or the Quartet, Saddam's senior foreign policy advisory group. In December 1998, Saddam appointed al-Majid commander of the Southern Region, one of four military regions established to confront a possible American attack. In this capacity he was responsible for harshly suppressing the Shi'ite uprising in the south in 1999 known as the al-Sadr intifada.

The U.S.-led coalition forces invasion of Iraq in March 2003 led to the downfall of al-Majid and the entire Ba'th regime. Shortly before the invasion, in September 2002, he traveled to several North African Arab states. It was the first time that he had left Iraq since 1988. American intelligence officials surmised that he might have been trying to locate a sanctuary to which Saddam could flee into exile. During the invasion, his death or capture was a major American goal. American aircraft bombed al-Majid's home in Basra on 4 April 2003, and British forces in the city initially reported that he had died in the attack. These reports were erroneous, however, and American forces later captured al-Majid on or about 19 August 2003.

The new Iraqi government established the Iraqi High Tribunal to try members of Saddam's government for various crimes. Al-Majid was charged with genocide, crimes against humanity, and war crimes. His trial on the charges of genocide against the Kurds began on 21 August 2006. He was found guilty on 24 June 2007, and was sentenced to death by hanging.

INFLUENCES AND CONTRIBUTIONS

Al-Majid was one of Saddam Hussein's most loyal lieutenants after the latter took power in Iraq in 1979, and the most notoriously brutal. His three most infamous acts were supervising the genocidal Anfal campaign against the Kurds in 1988; serving as military governor of Iraqi-occupied Kuwait (what the Iraqis called the new, nineteenth province of Iraq) in 1990 to 1991; and directing the regime's crushing of the Shi'ite uprising in southern Iraq in March 1991.

The 1988 Anfal campaign came on the heels of a similar program the year before. On 29 March 1987, during the Iran-Iraq War, Decree No. 160 put all state, Ba'th Party, and military apparatuses in northern Iraq under al-Majid, who had been made the party's secretary general of the Northern Command. Under his command were the Iraqi military, military intelligence, general intelligence, the Popular Army, and the pro-regime Kurdish *jahsh* militia. With these forces at his disposal, al-Majid carried out a large counterinsurgency program against

CONTEMPORARIES

Born in al-Dawr (also al-Dur), Izzat Ibrahim al-Duri (1942–) long served as one of Saddam Hussein's most senior and loyal lieutenants. Along with Saddam and Taha Yasin Ramadan al-Jazrawi (1938–2007), he was the only other surviving member of the July 1968 Ba'th Party coup in Iraq by the time of the party's overthrow in 2003. By that time, al-Duri was vice chairman of the Revolutionary Command Council, deputy commander of the armed forces, and a member of the Committee of the Four (the Quartet), Saddam's senior foreign policy advisory group. Trusted by Saddam in part because he had no independent power base from which to mount a challenge to the Iraqi dictator, al-Duri was the only one of the Quartet who was allowed to drive himself to meetings with Saddam. Saddam had the other three chauffeured to meetings as a security precaution.

Al-Duri was in charge of the defense of northern Iraq during the 2003 U.S.-led coalition forces invasion. He went into hiding after the fall of Baghdad in early April 2003, and became the sixth-highest person on the American most-wanted list. He appears to have played a leading role in coordinating some of the anti-American resistance activities in the country after the war ended. Known to have suffered from leukemia, conflicting reports about him and his whereabouts have emerged, ranging from claims that al-Duri has died to those saying he is still alive and in hiding in Syria. There also have been reports that al-Duri was declared head of the underground Iraqi Ba'th Party after Saddam's execution in December 2006.

antiregime Kurdish fighters. The Kurds had risen up in armed insurrection against the central Iraqi government in 1961, and again in the early and mid-1970s. With the Iran-Iraq War of 1980 to 1988 waning, al-Majid ordered a renewed government offensive against the Kurds. Forbidden areas were declared in order to deny sanctuary to Kurdish *peshmerga* (Kurdish: those who face death) fighters. Large-scale deportations removed thousands of villagers from these areas. At least seven hundred villages were demolished. Any human or even animal remaining in the forbidden areas was subject to being killed on sight.

Al-Majid was personally responsible for such killings. He issued directive SF/4008 on 20 June 1987, which stated that "all persons captured in those villages [in 'forbidden areas'] shall be detained and interrogated by the security services and those between the ages of fifteen and seventy [in practice it meant just males] shall be executed after any useful information has been obtained from them, of which we should be duly notified." It was during the 1987 campaign that the first documented Iraqi government uses of chemical weapons inside Iraq occurred. The first incident was an attack on a Kurdish political party headquarters in Zewa Shkan on 15 April 1987. The next day, chemical strikes were launched against the villages of Balisan and Shaykh Wasan as well.

In 1988, the regime renewed its counterinsurgency program through an even more massive program called the Anfal (Arabic: spoils) campaign, which was named after a chapter in the Qur'an by that name. Once again, forces under al-Majid's command tried to deny large portions of Iraqi Kurdistan as sanctuary to the *peshmergas* by deporting and/or killing the areas' inhabitants and destroying their villages. Anfal consisted of eight separate military offensives launched between 23 February and 8 September 1988. By the time the government declared an amnesty on 8 September 1988, an estimated 2,000 Kurdish villages had been depopulated and destroyed during that time, although some figures are higher. Conservative estimates place the Kurdish death toll at 50,000, but most put the count higher, in the range of 100,000 to 182,000. Al-Majid himself later suggested that no more than 100,000 Kurds were killed. The organization Middle East Watch later determined that Iraqi forces attacked at least 60 villages with chemical weapons during Anfal. The worst and most famous of these attacks took place in a town, not a village: the 16 March 1988 chemical attack on Halabja. Somewhere between 3,200 and 5,000 Kurds were killed with mustard gas (a blistering agent) and Sarin gas (a nerve agent).

Two years later, al-Majid was made military governor of Kuwait after Iraq invaded the small emirate in August 1990. Under his rule, Iraqi forces and agents were guilty of torture, rape, killings, looting, theft of cultural property, and disappearances. An estimated 1,000 Kuwaitis were killed during the occupation, and an additional 600 remain unaccounted for after having been taken away by retreating Iraqi forces during the Gulf War. A 1992 U.S. Defense Department study found Iraq guilty of sixteen violations of the laws of war during its occupation of Kuwait. The Kuwaiti government also compiled extensive documentation on Iraqi war crimes.

Finally, al-Majid was minister of the interior at the time that government forces crushed the March 1991 Shi'ite uprising in southern Iraq. The uprising broke out as the Iraqi army was retreating into Iraq from Kuwait when the Gulf War ended. After initial successes,

---

AL-MAJID SPEAKS

■

I will kill them [Kurds] all with chemical weapons! Who is going to say anything? The international community? F*** them! The international community and those who listen to them.

1987 MEETING WITH BA'TH PARTY OFFICIALS IN NORTHERN IRAQ.

From now on I won't give the [Kurdish] villagers flour, sugar, kerosene, water or electricity as long as they continue living there... Why should I let them live there like donkeys who don't know anything?... What if we prohibit the whole basin from Qara Dagh to Kifri to Diyala to Darbandikhan to Sulaymaniyya? What good is this basin? What did we ever get from them?... For five years I won't allow any human existence there.... In the summer nothing will be left.

15 APRIL 1988 MEETING WITH BA'TH PARTY AND GOVERNMENT OFFICIALS IN NORTHERN IRAQ.

---

the rebels were viciously beaten back by army forces, which used indiscriminate violence against civilian populations in their attacks. Tens of thousands of Shi'ites were killed in the fighting or executed, and religious shrines and institutions destroyed. Numerous mass graves have since been discovered. United Nations Security Council Resolution 688 condemned these attacks, as well as those the army launched against the Kurdish uprising that broke out at the same time.

THE WORLD'S PERSPECTIVE

Inside Iraq, Ali Hasan al-Majid was greatly feared, particularly in the Kurdish regions. He also was famous for the coarse, Takriti-accented language that he used. Al-Majid was also well-known internationally for being one of Saddam Hussein's top henchmen, and the one with arguably the most blood on his hands outside of Saddam himself. Groups such as Human Rights Watch have meticulously documented his involvement in the Anfal campaign in particular, and prepared a criminal case against him for future use based on millions of internal Iraqi documents captured by Kurdish forces during their March 1991 uprising in northern Iraq. He also was one of the top officials sought by American forces during the 2003 invasion of Iraq. Al-Majid was the fifth most senior Iraqi on the American most wanted list, and was the king of spades in the famous deck of cards that depicted these wanted individuals.

LEGACY

Al-Majid will go down in history as the executor of some of Saddam Hussein's worst crimes during the last two decades of the twentieth century. In particular, he will have the infamous distinction of having orchestrated the 1988 Kurdish genocide, the worst case of ethnic genocide perpetrated in the Middle East since the extermination of the Armenians in 1915.

BIBLIOGRAPHY

Burns, John F, "With Hussein Gone, Other Iraqi Trials Lose Impact," *New York Times*, 17 May 2007.

"Chemical Ali in U.S. Custody." CNN. Updated 21 August 2003. Available from http://www.cnn.com.

Meiselas, Susan, and Andrew Whitley. "Photo Essay: The Remains of Anfal." *Middle East Report*, no. 189 (July 1994): 8-11.

Michael R. Fischbach

MAKTUM, MUHAMMAD BIN RASHID AL-
(1949–)

Muhammad bin Rashid al-Maktum (Maktoum) is the emir of Dubai and prime minister, defense minister, and vice president of the United Arab Emirates.

PERSONAL HISTORY

Shaykh Muhammad bin Rashid al-Maktum was born in Dubai in 1949, the third son of Shaykh Rashid bin Sa'id al-Maktum, who ruled Dubai from 1958 to 1990. The al-Maktum family is from the Al Bu Falasa section of the powerful Bani Yas tribe, which also includes (in its Al Bu Falah section) the Nahyan family, rulers of neighboring Abu Dhabi. In 1833 the Al Bu Falasa section left the broader Al Bu Falah group to make its home east of Abu Dhabi in the coastal village of Dubai, and Shaykh Muhammad's family and the people of Dubai have ever since been known for their urban, maritime, and commercial identity, often contrasted with the Al Bu Falah's desert and tribal character.

Shaykh Muhammad's eldest brother, Maktum bin Rashid al-Maktum, became the ruler of Dubai from 1990 until his death in 2006. His other older brother, Hamdan bin Rashid al-Maktum, United Arab Emirates (U.A.E.) Minister of Finance and Industry since the U.A.E.'s inception on 2 December 1971, has served as crown prince of Dubai from 1971 to 1990, as deputy ruler from

Muhammad bin Rashid al-Maktum. AP IMAGES.

1990 to 2006, and again as crown prince from 2006 to the present. His younger brother is Major General Ahmad bin Rashid al-Maktum, deputy chairman of Dubai Police and Public Security, as well as the head of Emirates Airways and the Dubai Department of Civil Aviation.

Shaykh Muhammad received his early education in Dubai, first by way of private lessons in Arabic and religious studies, and then, beginning in 1955, successively at al-Ahmadiyya School, al-Sha'b School, and Dubai Secondary School. In 1966, he attended the Bell School of Languages at Cambridge University. Shaykh Muhammad is also a 1971 graduate of the Mons Officer Cadet School in Aldershot, United Kingdom.

INFLUENCES AND CONTRIBUTIONS

In late December 1967, Britain announced that it intended to abrogate its more than a century-old series of treaties by which it conducted the defense and foreign relations of nine east Arabian principalities (emirates and shaykhdoms) in the Persian Gulf region. This decision to

BIOGRAPHICAL HIGHLIGHTS

Name: Muhammad bin Rashid al-Maktum (Maktoum)

Birth: 1949, Dubai

Family: Wives, Shaykha Hind bint Maktum bin Juma' al-Maktum and Princess Haya bint al-Hussein of Jordan; seven sons; nine daughters

Nationality: Emirati

Education: Private tutoring; al-Ahmadiyya School; al-Sha'b School; Dubai Secondary School; Bell School of Languages, Cambridge University, 1966; Mons Officer Cadet School, Aldershot, U.K., 1971

PERSONAL CHRONOLOGY:
- **1968:** Receives first public appointments: head of Dubai Police and Public Security; director of Department of Oil
- **1971:** Appointed United Arab Emirates minister of defense
- **1995:** Appointed crown prince
- **2006:** Succeeds as emir, Dubai, vice president and prime minister, United Arab Emirates

In February 1972, the Emirate of Ra's al-Khaymah also joined, thereby expanding the U.A.E. to the seven-state union that exists today. The other two states, Bahrain and Qatar, chose to become independent.

"TO THE SOUL OF THE CHILD MARTYR, MUHAMMAD AL-DURRA"

Pressed back, without supporter
A child defenseless, confronting aggression
Hiding, the bullets of tyrants
Have no mercy for a child, so young
Seeking shelter, slaughter him the criminals
Savages, whose tyranny never waned
Oh Muhammad, in Paradise of the eternal
Oh Muhammad, your voice reverberates
  throughout
Oh Muhammad, with you, the God of the
  Worlds
Whose mercy enfolds you forever
Oh Muhammad, who saw you grieved
And all, if we could, would sacrifice
A thousand million, the Muslims
All for you, Muhammad, fathers
Alas, where is the peace of the just?
The peace you seek is futile
Lost it, without doubt, the usurpers
When allowed their hatred to renew
And boiled the blood of Arabs, East and West
When Sharon visited the mosque
Oh Arabs, comrades for years
Bury that which passed, as became
Our greatest concern, to defend against
  aggressors
Who against al-Aqsa their aggression began
My nation, would that you unite
In lines, terrified then the enemies
Follow Zayid, the leader of the wise
Who called for unity and initiated
Oh Saladin, oh the greatest conquerors
Oh Umar, oh the dignified and the generous
The state of the nation allures the greedy
We seek naught but unity to satisfy

MUHAMMAD BIN RASHID AL-MAKTUM. "TO THE SOUL OF THE CHILD MARTYR, MUHAMMAD AL-DURRA"

transform these polities from protected-state status to independence had a profound impact on Dubai and the other emirates. They were thus presented two challenges: the first was to determine what if any changes might be required to the existing systems of governance; the second was to reach agreement on the configuration of any new state or states: whether the nine shaykhdoms would become a single entity or two or more states seeking admission to such international organizations as the United Nations and the League of Arab States.

Regarding the first, the rulers decided to maintain the governmental and political status quo as far as their individual emirates were concerned. Resolving the second proved more difficult. The rulers of Abu Dhabi and Dubai declared in February 1968 that they had agreed to establish a bipartite federation and invited the seven other shaykhdoms to join them.

Soon thereafter, a series of meetings among all nine of the emirates' rulers began to lay in earnest the groundwork for what would become, in 1971, the six-state U.A.E., comprised of Abu Dhabi, Ajman, Dubai, Fujayrah, Sharjah (ash-Shariqah), and Umm al-Qaywayn.

In 1968, near the beginning of this three-year process of transition from imperial rule to national sovereignty and independence, Shaykh Muhammad received his first two public appointments. He became head of Dubai Police and Public Security as well as director of the Department of Oil. The latter assignment entailed close cooperation with the main concessionaire, the American firm Continental Oil Company (Conoco). The nature of the work in each of these institutions, combined with the then small size of Dubai's population, required that Shaykh Muhammad work with numerous expatriate advisers as well as foreign workers; the latter comprised thousands from numerous developing countries, the Indian subcontinent in particular. A consequence of Shaykh Muhammad's holding these two portfolios was that he became familiar early on with the increasingly vital strategic role that Dubai and virtually the entire Gulf would play in terms of regional and global economic growth, together with the necessity of developing a long-term strategy for expanding the emirate's human resource capabilities and the concomitant vital role that the maintenance of peace, prosperity, and political stability locally, nationally, and internationally would play in enhancing Dubai, its fellow Gulf countries, and their allies' prospects for success.

Military Matters In late 1971, one of the outcomes of the negotiations between his father, Shaykh Rashid bin Sa'id al-Maktum, Dubai's emir, and the emir of Abu Dhabi, Shaykh Zayid bin Sultan Al Nahyan, was that Shaykh Muhammad was appointed minister of defense for the newly created U.A.E. His younger brother, Shaykh Ahmad bin Rashid al-Maktum, was appointed commander of the Dubai Defense Force (DDF), which was essentially synonymous with the Central Command of the U.A.E.'s armed forces. This command initially assumed responsibility for the defense of Dubai and adjacent emirates immediately to the north. It would continue to do so until the command was eventually and fully integrated into the U.A.E. Defense Forces. This occurred in stages, beginning in 1976 and ending in the 1980s when the last of the force's seconded British commanders retired, the DDF ceased to exist, and the U.A.E. government assumed its expenses. As minister of defense, Shaykh Muhammad had earlier worked extensively with leaders of the Abu Dhabi Defense Force to forge a national defense force, subsequently known as the U.A.E. Armed Forces, with the latter effectively subsuming the DDF and Abu Dhabi Defense Force, together with the far smaller defense force of the Emirate of Ra's al-Khaymah. In the process, Shaykh Muhammad developed a multifaceted and ongoing professional relationship with Shaykh MUHAMMAD BIN ZAYID AL NAHYAN, third eldest son of the emir of Abu Dhabi and the Abu Dhabi ruling family's most prominent military leader. During

the 1980s, Muhammad bin Zayid became a lieutenant general and deputy supreme commander of the U.A.E. Armed Forces, the first commander having been Zayid himself, followed by his other son, KHALIFA BIN ZAYID AL NAHYAN, who, upon Zayid's passing in 2004, became emir of Abu Dhabi and U.A.E. president.

The U.A.E. military's earliest deployment was to Lebanon in 1976 as part of the Arab Deterrent Force seeking to end the Lebanese Civil War that had erupted the year before. It was subsequently one of the first Arab armies to provide logistical, operational, and humanitarian assistance to Iraq in the aftermath of the 1980–1988 Iran-Iraq War and, again, to both Kuwait and Iraq in 1991 following the reversal of Iraq's aggression against Kuwait. In the weeks immediately prior to Iraq's 2 August 1990, attack against Kuwait, the U.A.E. was one of the first Arab countries to call for foreign military action opposing Iraq's invasion. When this failed, it joined Saudi Arabia and Iran in replacing the 4.5 million barrels a day of Iraqi and Kuwaiti oil that the United Nations Security Council forbade anyone to purchase. Simultaneously, the U.A.E. advocated that concerted international military action should restore Kuwaiti sovereignty.

The U.A.E.'s armed forces were also deployed to Somalia in 1993 and to Kosovo in 1999 as part of the multinational forces in those two conflicts. In the latter operation, the U.A.E. contributed 1,450 troops, mechanized infantry, and an Apache helicopter. In the 1990s, the U.A.E. military engaged in a program of expansion, purchasing new weapons and equipment, and the process of "emiratization," increasing the number of U.A.E. citizens to replace officers and soldiers from other countries, especially Oman and Pakistan.

Dubai as a Commercial Center Shaykh Muhammad remained involved in domestic developments in Dubai, especially in its booming commercial sector. In 1977, he was tasked by his father, Shaykh Rashid, with administrative responsibility for Dubai's international airport. In keeping with the al-Maktum family's interest in international trade, Shaykh Muhammad quickly grasped the potential business opportunities represented by a state-of-the-art facility that would provide world-class shopping and other amenities to passengers transiting Dubai on international aircraft. He also saw that it would further the Dubaian merchant community's aspirations for the emirate to become an Arabian variant of Singapore or Hong Kong.

In 1985, Shaykh Muhammad decided to create a Dubai-based airline, Emirates Air. Many questioned the need for it, given that a Gulf-based airline, Gulf Air, already existed, albeit with ownership, and therefore decision making, dispersed among four non-Dubaian co-owners, Abu Dhabi, Bahrain, Oman, and Qatar. That same year, Shaykh Muhammad was appointed to supervise the Jabal

'Ali Free Zone, associated with Jabal 'Ali Port, one of the world's largest. In assuming responsibilities for the success of such a vast infrastructural undertaking, Shaykh Muhammad was following in the footsteps of his father, who was known for his commitment to long-range planning and decision making.

The combination of mega-investments in the emirate's airport, seaport, and ship repair facilities, together with the practically nonstop expansion and modernization of its wholesale and retail merchandising, importing, and reexporting activities, proved to be extremely profitable, and made Dubai a logical location for foreign companies seeking a site for their regional headquarters, as well as a center for cost-effective distribution of goods and services to markets in Arabia, the Gulf, the Indian subcontinent, and parts of Central Asia as well as East Africa. Moreover, the end of the Cold War and the implosion of the Soviet Union in the early 1990s spurred expansion of Dubai's economic and commercial activities beyond what anyone had earlier foreseen as possible. Dubai became a hub for chartered and regularly scheduled commercial flights to and from such consumer goods-deprived countries as Azerbaijan, Kazakhstan, Kyrgyzstan, Uzbekistan, and Tajikistan. Passengers from those places returned home laden with every consumer good and luxury item imaginable for themselves and their friends and relatives, and Dubai reaped the benefits.

The success of Shaykh Muhammad's business-driven vision for Dubai did not come cost-free. Among other effects was a massive influx of foreigners who flocked to the emirate in search of business or employment opportunities. Inevitably among them were tens of thousands of non-Muslims who neither spoke Arabic nor had more than the most rudimentary knowledge, understanding, or respect for the traditional culture and mores of Dubai's citizens. Compounding the complexity of accommodating the needs of so many newcomers was the fact that, but a few decades earlier, the emirate's indigenous inhabitants had lived a far more simple life. Indeed, the lives of many if not most people who were born and raised in Dubai from as recently as the early 1960s was one in which there were few instances of social dislocation and almost no political unrest. Similarly, the earlier era could hardly have differed more in terms of the nature and extent of economic and commercial development. Indeed, apart from only a dozen or so of the emirate's older and more well-established merchant families, there was little likelihood of most Dubaians' prospering financially, let alone becoming business tycoons with the ability to guarantee their children a life of material abundance.

Another mixed blessing was almost complete lack of import duties levied by Dubai or the U.A.E. on goods entering the emirate, either for local consumption or for reexport. Dubai's leaders, and the merchant class that supported them, grew ever more certain over time that the emirate's commercial success was inextricably linked to this low level of taxation. The same fact, however, was and is the chief obstacle to the goal of achieving the common market among the six Gulf Cooperation Council (GCC) countries (Bahrain, Kuwait, Oman, Qatar, Saudi Arabia, and the U.A.E.) envisioned in June 1981 shortly after the GCC's establishment. In Dubai's defense, Shaykh Muhammad and his fellow decision makers argue that the emirate's prosperity overwhelmingly depends on its successful pursuit of three main interests, facetiously but factually cited as business, business, and business. More specifically, they stress that the emirate's commercial prowess turns directly on the extent to which it operates, as do rival commercial entrepôts Colombo, Gibraltar, Hong Kong, and Singapore, on the principle of importing massive volumes of goods with very slim margins of profit per item. Viewed from this perspective, anything that would raise the level of taxes on imports runs the certain risk that Dubai's profit-conscious business partners, both the producers of incoming goods as well as foreign customers, would switch to its competitors.

The Future Emir In 1995, Shaykh Muhammad's eldest brother, Shaykh Maktum bin Rashid, who had become emir on the death of their father in 1990, appointed Muhammad crown prince, or heir apparent (Wali al-Ahad). With the economic boom sustained by conspicuous consumption unleashed by the collapse of the Soviet Union, Shaykh Muhammad was persuaded that the promotion of tourism should become one of the emirate's major economic objectives. Accordingly, that same year he announced the creation of the Dubai Shopping Festival, an annual event designed to extend the emirate's economic development far into the future. To this end, Shaykh Muhammad lent his support to such major undertakings as the expansion of Dubai's airport; construction of the Burj al-'Arab (Arab Tower), the world's tallest hotel; and the ambitious Palm Islands project, the creation of a group of artificial islands in the shape of a palm tree in the shallow waters of the Gulf, on which would be built a set of luxury resorts. These and other such endeavors aimed at the international carriage trade highlighted Shaykh Muhammad's business-driven ambitions for Dubai and his powerful influence in guiding a substantial segment of the U.A.E.'s overall economic and commercial growth throughout the 1990s and beyond.

In 2004, Shaykh Muhammad married Princess Haya bint al-Hussein, daughter of King HUSSEIN BIN TALAL of Jordan and half-sister of the current king, ABDULLAH II BIN HUSSEIN. The marriage was viewed as having the potential for enhancing the existing strategic and geopolitical cooperation between two of the Arab world's most important subregions.

TOURO COLLEGE LIBRARY

On 4 January 2006, on the death of his elder brother the emir, who in addition to ruling Dubai served as the U.A.E.'s vice president (since 1990) and prime minister (since 1971), Shaykh Muhammad succeeded him in all three positions while retaining the portfolio of U.A.E. minister of defense.

In 2006 and 2007, Shaykh Muhammad and his fellow leaders in Dubai and the other U.A.E. emirates found themselves in a quandary not of their making. Future prospects for continued stability and economic success had grown cloudy, as a result of the mounting international opposition to Iran's nuclear development programs and quest for expanded regional power and influence. Iran remains not only Dubai's largest and most militarily powerful maritime neighbor but also one of its perennially most important customers for reexported goods.

Shaykh Muhammad recognizes that Dubai and the U.A.E. are incapable of defending themselves unaided against the possibility of an Iranian attack. Further, it is uncertain whether, and if so for how long, the emirate could withstand a sustained campaign of internal subversion and sabotage by Iranian agents, supporters, and sympathizers among the tens of thousands of overseas Iranians in the midst of Dubai. The uncertainty is compounded by its appearing to be out of the question that Dubai could, or indeed would ever want to, expel this particular group of foreigners who are essential to the ongoing success of Dubai's economy and its citizens' standard of living. No one can predict with assurance what might be the likely consequences were Iran to wage a covert campaign to undermine stability and security in Dubai, whether or not in reaction to an American and/or Israeli military attack against the Islamic Republic.

THE WORLD'S PERSPECTIVE

Shaykh Muhammad is known internationally for having been largely responsible for the development of the Arab world's most successful business-minded city-state, as well as having helped to forge and sustain the developing world's longest-lasting and most successful confederation of sovereign states.

Beside his reputation as a business-friendly modernizer who deeply respects many of the traditions and customs of his forebears, Shaykh Muhammad is known for his fondness for some of the more romanticized aspects of Bedouin life, among them falconry and horses as well as camel riding, breeding, and racing. Shaykh Muhammad's renowned love of horses and horse racing led him in 1994 to establish Godolphin Stables, Inc., which further enhanced his reputation as a world-class horse owner. Since 1996, his sponsorship of the Dubai World Cup has annually drawn an elite assembly of equestrians from around the world. Adding to his long string of successes in backing championship horses in

prominent competitions in Britain, the United States, and elsewhere, he is the owner of Bernardini, the winner of the 2006 Preakness Stakes.

Shaykh Muhammad is also known for his skill in writing and reciting poetry. His poems are in the *nabati* style traditionally associated with the tribes of Arabia and their local Arabic dialect. Shaykh Muhammad has written poems on subjects ranging from the personal and intimate to the public and national, as in one poem extolling the legendary virtues of U.A.E. founding president Shaykh Zayid, which Shaykh Muhammad recited live on national television for nearly an hour to the accompaniment of stirring music and film clips portraying many of the highlights of Shaykh Zayid's extraordinary life and accomplishments. Another such poem was an elegy for the young Muhammad al-Durra, who in 2000 during the second Palestinian intifada was seen on news footage aired on television worldwide being killed by Israeli soldiers as he crouched against a wall with his father in Gaza City as they tried to protect themselves. Other examples include Shaykh Muhammad's odes to his father and meditations on the life and creatures of the desert.

LEGACY

Shaykh Muhammad has been a major driving force behind Dubai's long-lasting economic boom. His interest in economic development has consistently been manifested in his strong pro-business policies and numerous projects designed to encourage the emirate's rapid and ongoing economic development. Well before becoming ruler of Dubai in 2006, Shaykh Muhammad was heavily involved in promoting the emirate as a business and tourism hub; his activities have made Dubai a brand name identified with luxury tourism and shopping. Along with Dubai Development and Investment Authority Board Chairman Muhammad al-Jirgawi, with whom he launched the Dubai Shopping Festival, Shaykh Muhammad also pioneered telecommunications and electronic information services in such projects as Dubai Internet City and Dubai Media City.

BIBLIOGRAPHY

Abdullah, Muhammad Morsy. *The United Arab Emirates: A Modern History.* London: Croom Helm; New York: Barnes & Noble Books, 1994.

Al Abed, Ibrahim and Peter Hellyer, eds. *United Arab Emirates: A New Perspective.* London: Trident Press, 2001.

Anthony, John Duke. *Arab States of the Lower Gulf: People, Politics, Petroleum.* Washington, D.C.: Middle East Institute, 1975.

———. *Dynamics of State Formation: The United Arab Emirates.* Abu Dhabi: Emirates Center for Strategic Studies and Research, 2002.

Emirates Centre for Strategic Studies and Research (ECSSR) Web site. Available from http://www.ecssr.ac.ae/ECSSR_Index_en/.

Heard-Bey, Frauke. *From Trucial States to United Arab Emirates: A Society in Transition.* 2nd ed. London and New York: Longman, 1996.

Peck, Malcolm C. *The United Arab Emirates: A Venture in Unity.* Boulder, CO: Westview Press; London: Croom Helm, 1986.

Rugh, Andrea B. *The Political Culture of Leadership in the United Arab Emirates.* London and New York: Palgrave Macmillan, 2007.

Wilson, Graeme. *Rashid's Legacy: The Genesis of the Maktoum Family and the History of Dubai.* London: Media Prima, 2006.

John Duke Anthony

MALA'IKA, NAZIK AL-
(1923–2007)

An Iraqi poet and literary critic, Nazik Sadiq al-Mala'ika played a leading role in the genesis and rise of modern Arabic poetry. Her poetry and literary criticism marked a radical break with and revolt against traditional and neo-classical forms of Arabic poetry, and charted the early course of the Arabic free verse movement.

PERSONAL HISTORY

Al-Mala'ika was born in Baghdad in 1923 to a well-to-do literary family. Her maternal grandfather was a famous poet and jurisprudent of nineteenth-century Iraq. Both of her parents were published poets. Her mother had published anti-British colonial political poetry under a pseudonym and her father was the editor of a twenty-volume encyclopedia. The family home provided a rich and fertile space for cultural development with much traffic and visits from famous cultural figures.

Al-Mala'ika was a precocious child and started to compose poetry in the spoken Iraqi dialect when she was still seven years old, and in classical Arabic by the age of ten. Recognizing her gifts, her father, who was a grammar teacher, encouraged her and took a special interest in cultivating her talents by providing her with his own extracurricular education in Arabic poetics and grammar at home. She finished high school in 1939 and enrolled at the High Teachers Training College in Baghdad, which later became the College of Education. Al-Mala'ika majored in Arabic language and literature, but was also interested in studying other European languages and arts. While at the Teachers College, she also registered to study the *ud* (or oud; a type of lute) and acting at the Institute of Fine Arts. She had been interested in music since her early years and college provided her with a great opportunity to pursue this interest in a methodical way with renowned specialists. Through acting, al-Mala'ika had hoped to improve her performance and

BIOGRAPHICAL HIGHLIGHTS

Name: Nazik al-Mala'ika

Birth: 1923, Baghdad, Iraq

Death: 2007, Cairo, Egypt

Nationality: Iraqi

Education: B.A in Arabic with higher distinction, High Teachers, college in Baghdad, 1944; Rockefeller scholarship to study literary criticism at Princeton, University, 1950–1951; M.A in comparative literature, University of Wisconsin, 1956

Family: Husband, Abd al-Hadi Mahbuba

PERSONAL CHRONOLOGY:

- **1947:** Publishes her first collection, *Night Lover*
- **1949:** Publishes her second collection, *Splinters and Ashes*
- **1957:** Starts teaching at the College of Education in Baghdad and publishes third collection, *The Depth of the Wave*
- **1962:** Publishes first work of literary criticism, *Issues of Contemporary Poetry*
- **1964–1968:** Moves to Basra to help establish the University of Basra; elected chair of the department of Arabic
- **1970:** Moves to Kuwait to lecture at the University of Kuwait
- **1978:** Publishes *For Prayer and the Revolution*
- **1979:** Publishes *The Psychology of Poetry*
- **1982:** Retires and returns to live in Iraq
- **1985:** Volume of critical essays by major Arab literary critics and scholars in honor of al-Mala'ika is published by the University of Kuwait
- **1996:** Moves to Cairo, Egypt
- **1999:** Publishes *The Sea Changes Its Colors*
- **2002:** *Complete Works of Prose and Poetry* is published in Cairo

ability to recite poetry. In addition to Arabic language and literature and English, she also studied Latin as soon as it was introduced to the Teachers College in 1941–1942 and became interested in Latin poetry, especially the Roman poet Catullus (84–54 BCE). In 1949 al-Mala'ika started studying French at home together with her brother and developed a good reading knowledge after studying it formally in 1953. She composed and recited poetry in her college years and started establishing her name by publishing in local journals and newspapers. The 1941 nationalist revolt against the pro-British monarchy in Iraq had a significant influence on al-Mala'ika's political leanings and accentuated her strong nationalist sentiments.

In 1947, al-Mala'ika published her first collection, titled *Night Lover*. Its themes were dominated by despair, disillusionment, and alienation. This could be attributed to both subjective and objective reasons. In addition to the influence of English romantic poetry and the romanticism of Arabic poetry of the preceding decades, the debilitating effects of World War II, and colonization in much of the Arab world intensified the poet's sadness and despair. It was also in 1947 that al-Mala'ika composed her famous poem "Cholera." She was greatly moved by the news of the death and suffering caused by the cholera epidemic that had spread in Egypt. This prompted her to write the poem that many consider to be the first free-verse poem written in Arabic. In it she broke the two-hemistich monorhyme of traditional Arabic poetry by introducing multiple rhyme endings and mixing meters in novel ways. At first, her family, especially her father, dismissed the poem as unmetrical and bizarre, but al-Mala'ika persisted and predicted that it would be revolutionary and would change the map of Arabic poetry. She continued to write and experiment in this new form. Her second collection, *Splinters and Ashes*, was published in Baghdad in 1949. It was prefaced with an introduction in which al-Mala'ika theorized about her new form of composition. Although there had been earlier experiments with form and structure, they were never presented in an acceptable and sound mode, as al-Mala'ika finally did. This book marked an event, par excellence, in the history of modern Arabic poetry as it launched the movement of free verse and established al-Mala'ika as one of its pioneers. Al-Mala'ika argued that the traditional monorhyme was a serious obstacle and a hindrance to the development of Arabic poetry and its potential, and must be abandoned. The collection included poems written in the old traditional form and nine in what came to be known as free verse. Hundreds of articles and essays were written in response to al-Mala'ika's new poetry, many rejecting its premise, but many others welcoming this radical break and praising her for opening new horizons for modern Arabic poetry. Her fame and influence quickly spread throughout the Arab world and poets started to write in the form she introduced.

Her knowledge and mastery of English helped her earn a Rockefeller scholarship to study literary criticism at Princeton University in the United States in 1950.

Princeton was still a men-only school at that time. She studied literary criticism with some famous American scholars and literary critics, including the leading poet, critic, and exponent of New Criticism, Allen Tate (1899–1979). Upon returning to Iraq in 1951, al-Mala'ika began writing more prose and literary criticism.

In addition to poetry and literary criticism, al-Mala'ika was critical of patriarchy and called for more freedoms for women. In 1953, she delivered a lecture at the Women's Union in Baghdad titled "Women between Negativism and Morality." In 1954 she delivered another lecture, titled "Fragmentation in Arab Society."

Personal tragedy struck al-Mala'ika in 1953 when her mother fell ill and she had to accompany her to London for surgery. She did not survive the surgery and al-Mala'ika witnessed her mother's death. Upon her return to Baghdad with the coffin, al-Mala'ika had a nervous breakdown and underwent medical treatment.

A scholarship to study comparative literature at the University of Wisconsin in the United States in 1954 helped al-Mala'ika cope and move on. She spent two rich years immersed in the Anglo-American critical tradition. Al-Mala'ika credits her studies at Wisconsin with sharpening her critical sensibilities and enriching her both existentially and intellectually. Some of her impressions and memoirs of her time in Wisconsin were later published in the Egyptian daily *al-Ahram* in 1966.

Al-Mala'ika returned to Iraq in 1956 and published her third collection, *The Depth of the Wave*, in Beirut in the following year. Her poems displayed a departure from intense romanticism toward a philosophical acceptance of life's hardships. She was initially supportive of the July 1958 coup d'état that ended the pro-British monarchy and ushered in the Republican era in Iraq. She even wrote a poem celebrating this change and saluting the nascent Iraqi republic. However, she soon came to see the communist leanings of the Republican regime as a deviation from the Arab nationalist path she favored. She moved to Beirut and lived there for a year (1959–1960), as she had been appointed to teach literary criticism at the College of Education in 1957. After her return from Beirut in 1960, she befriended her colleague in the department of Arabic, Abd al-Hadi Mahbuba, and they married in mid-1961.

In 1962 al-Mala'ika published her most important work of literary criticism, *Issues of Contemporary Poetry*. As a sign of her political leanings, the book was dedicated to Egyptian president Gamal Abdel Nasser, an archenemy of Abd al-Karim Qasim (1914–1963), Iraq's prime minister at the time.

The book attempted to provide the theoretical premise for the free verse movement and posited the foundations of what al-Mala'ika perceived to be the most productive approach to composing, as well as evaluating, this new poetry. In contrast to the calls for engagement in literature that were gaining currency in the Arab world, al-Mala'ika was vehemently opposed to privileging the social and political message in poetry—calling such approaches naive and unacceptable—and believed that that would weaken other technical aspects of the poem that are essential to its success. For her, the subject matter was merely raw material and the least important aspect of the poem itself. What mattered, first and foremost, was the skeleton. This overemphasis on form was the target of much criticism later, especially since many poets adopted the new forms but maintained a traditional perspective and vision, and thus problematized form as the sole measure of radicalism and modernism. The book also included a solid critique of Arab critics themselves who were faulted for being in awe of European approaches and not focusing on the particulars of Arabic poetry itself. Al-Mala'ika also lamented the lack of mastery, methodological chaos, and the loosening of linguistic standards and artistic criteria. The book was a radical break with traditional forms, but it restricted the scope of experimentation to the examples al-Mala'ika had culled from her contemporaries and deemed other experiments unacceptable. Moreover, al-Mala'ika still considered meter and rhythm to be essential pillars of poetry. This stance was soon to clash with the revolutionary call for total abandonment of both by the pioneers of the prose poem.

In 1964 al-Mala'ika's husband was appointed the president of the University of Basra, and the couple moved to Basra to help establish the university. Al-Mala'ika taught in the department of Arabic and was later elected to be its chairperson. In 1968 they both returned to Baghdad and in 1970, the couple moved to Kuwait to teach at Kuwait University where they continued to live until their retirement in 1982. Both al-Mala'ika and her husband lived in Iraq until 1996 when she moved to Cairo, Egypt.

Al-Mala'ika kept a low profile in her last decades and suffered from serious health problems. She declined invitations to conferences and festivals and did not grant interviews or make any public statements about political and cultural events. She was admitted to the hospital in early 2007, and died on 20 June 2007.

INFLUENCES AND CONTRIBUTIONS

Al-Mala'ika had a somewhat unique opportunity in that she received solid training, personal and institutional, in both the classical tradition of Arabic literature and poetics and a solid grounding in English language and literature that was further enriched by her graduate studies in the United States. Moreover, her exceptional lin-

---

CONTEMPORARIES

■

Badr Shakir al-Sayyab (1926–1964) was born in Jaykur, near Basra, in southern Iraq. Together with al-Mala'ika and ABD AL-WAHHAB AL-BAYATI (1926–1999), he is considered one of the pioneers of the free verse movement in the Arab world. He studied at the High Teachers' Training College in Baghdad in 1948 and was al-Mala'ika's classmate. He worked as a teacher first, then a civil servant and journalist. Al-Sayyab was first drawn to communism and then leaned more toward Arab nationalism. His political activism led to arrests and self-imposed exile. He suffered a degenerative disease toward the end of his life and died at a hospital in Kuwait in 1964. He was greatly influenced by the English poets and later by T. S. Eliot. His later, more mature poetry incorporated Mesopotamian mythology. Similar to al-Mala'ika, al-Sayyab, around the same time, experimented with metrical feet and with new rhyme patterns, contributing to what came to be known as free verse.

---

guistic and poetic gifts and voracious reading, coupled with access to Western languages and traditions, allowed her to make a monumental contribution as a poet and critic. Her exposure to and readings of English poetry inspired her to experiment with the Arabic meters and to liberate the Arabic poem from the shackles of monorhyme and fixed meters. Having an intimate knowledge of Arabic meters and prosody, al-Mala'ika reconfigured the form of the Arabic poem in an entirely new way. The traditional classical poem had a fixed form using a fixed number of feet from one meter in a every line. Each line was equally divided into two hemistiches and maintained the same rhyme throughout the poem. Al-Mala'ika broke the unity and uniformity of the poetic line by writing lines of various length, including different numbers of feet and using poly-rhyme. This was a radical break with a tradition that predominated for centuries. However, al-Mala'ika was against doing away altogether with both rhyme and meter, as is the case in what came to be known as the prose poem—the form that has now become the most popular and pervasive.

THE WORLD'S PERSPECTIVE

There is a consensus that al-Mala'ika was a pioneering figure in the history of modern Arabic poetry. Her name and her contributions appear in every major study of modern

> ## "STRANGERS"
>
> ■
>
> Put out the candle and leave us two strangers here
> / We are parts of the night, so why the flame? /
> Light falls on two illusions in the night's eyelid /
> It falls on splinters of hope called "we" and I call
> them: boredom / Like light, we are strangers here
> / The pale and cold meeting on a rainy day / was a
> death to my songs and a grave to me feelings /
> The clock chimed in the dark: nine, then ten /
> And I, in my pain, listen and count / I was
> perplexed, asking the clock / of what uses is my
> joy / If we spend our evenings as / Strangers /
> Hours passed, covered with withering / like an
> unknown tomorrow / Is it dawn or dusk? / Hours
> passed and silence was like winter / I thought it
> strangled my breaths and floated in my blood / I
> thought it was saying under the evenings whirl-
> wind: / You are strangers / Put out the candle for
> the two souls are in a thick night / Light falls on
> two faces the color of autumn / Can't you see that
> our eyes are cold and withering? / Can't you hear
> our still and silent hearts? / Our silence is the echo
> of a dangerous siren / warning us that we will be /
> Strangers / Who brought us here today and where
> did we start? / Yesterday we were not compan-
> ions, so let us / jump over the memory As if it
> never was / some flighty love that entertained us /
> Oh if we were to return to where we were / before
> we were when we are still / Strangers
>
> "STRANGERS." A POEM BY NAZIK AL-MALA'IKA.

Arabic poetry. Tens of dissertations have been written about her poetry and criticism, and a number of her poems and essays have appeared in translation. Although there are hundreds of works on her career in Arabic, a volume in English or another European language has yet to appear. Nevertheless, it seems that she has secured her position in the history of Arabic literature as one of the architects of its modernity. The main critique that has been raised in retrospect is that al-Mala'ika's approach focused solely on form to the detriment of the content or the poetic vision, both of which are considered equally important to construct a truly modern and radical poetics.

LEGACY

Al-Mala'ika is considered by the great majority of critics and scholars to be one of the most important Arab poets and critics in the second half of the twentieth century.

She was one of the first few, if not the first poet, to break away from the traditional form of the two-hemistich monorhyme and write in a new form that came to dominate the Arab literary scene until it was eclipsed by the prose poem, which abandons both meter and rhyme. The predominantly romantic themes of her poetry might have lost some of their appeal with time, but her foundational role in establishing a new poetic form is still preserved half a century after her debut. Her work as a literary critic defined the parameters of this new form of poetry and helped to launch and institutionalize it, as well as enrich the debates and the vocabulary around it.

BIBLIOGRAPHY

al-Musawi, Muhsin Jasim. *Arabic Poetry: Trajectories of Modernity and Tradition.* London: Routledge, 2006.

Jayyusi, Salma Khadra. *Trends and Movements in Modern Arabic Poetry.* Leiden, Netherlands: Brill, 1977.

Moreh, Shmuel. *Modern Arabic Poetry 1800–1970: The Development of its Forms and Themes under the Influence of Western Literature.* Leiden, Netherlands: Brill, 1976.

Sinan Antoon

MALEH, HAYTHAM AL-
(1931–)

Haytham al-Maleh (Haitham al-Mala) is a Syrian lawyer and human rights advocate.

PERSONAL HISTORY

Born in Syria in 1931, little is publicly known about the early life of al-Maleh, which is not surprising for a human rights advocate in authoritarian Syria who has had to operate clandestinely for much of his activist career. A lawyer and former judge, al-Maleh began his human rights activities in 1978 by helping to form a human rights group within the official Syrian Bar Association. In early 1980, he and others carried out a one-day work stoppage as a protest against war. The regime of the ruling Ba'th Party, in power in Syria since 1963, imprisoned al-Maleh from 1980 until 1986.

INFLUENCES AND CONTRIBUTIONS

Out of prison, al-Maleh went on to become one of Syria's most prominent human rights advocates, critical of the government and the emergency powers under which it has operated ever since the Ba'th Party took power. In July 2001, forty human rights advocates met at al-Maleh's office in Damascus and formed the Human Rights Association in Syria (HRAS). Al-Maleh was

BIOGRAPHICAL HIGHLIGHTS

Name: Haytham al-Maleh (Haitham al-Mala)

Birth: 1931, Syria

Family: Two sons, Ilyas Maleh and Anas

Nationality: Syrian

PERSONAL CHRONOLOGY:

• **1978:** Helps form human rights group within Syrian Bar Association; participates in one-day work stoppage

• **1980:** Imprisoned

• **1986:** Released from prison

• **2001:** Helps form Human Rights Association in Syria; disbarred; tried for establishing a human rights organization and distributing its magazine without permission; pardoned

• **2004:** Signs Damascus Declaration for Democratic National Change

• **2006:** Convicted of insulting the president and other charges; is pardoned without having served jail time

chosen to be its director. This bold step occurred during the relatively short liberalization felt in Syria after the death of the country's longtime leader, HAFIZ AL-ASAD, in June 2000. However, Asad's son and successor, BASHAR AL-ASAD, soon clamped down on the country much as his father had. In April 2002, the Damascus Lawyers Disciplinary Council disbarred al-Maleh for three months. This came after he complained about the lack of fairness of the trial of political prisoner Ma'mun al-Humsi, whom he had been defending. Shortly thereafter in June 2002, the Damascus Bar Association disbarred him for three years.

Al-Maleh soon faced more serious legal problems. In September 2002, when he was in Jordan seeking medical treatment, Syria's deputy military prosecutor filed charges against him for establishing a human rights organization without the approval of the ministry of social affairs and labor, and for distributing HRAS's magazine, *Tayyarat* (Currents), in the country without permission. A military court eventually tried him in July 2003, but he was pardoned four days after the trial began when the court ruled that a 9 July presidential decree from President Asad applied to his case. In December 2003 the government allowed al-Maleh, who had been subject to a ban on foreign travel, to leave for Germany, whereupon he delivered a speech on human rights in Syria before the Human Rights Committee of the German parliament. The following February, Syrian authorities prohibited him from leaving Syria for the United Arab Emirates, in an act that many believe stemmed from its displeasure over his speech in Germany.

During his own legal troubles, al-Maleh served as the lawyer in Syria for the high-profile case of Maher Arar. Arar was a Canadian Syrian who was seized by U.S. authorities at John F. Kennedy Airport in New York in September 2002 during a stopover on his flight from Tunisia to Canada, and forcibly flown to Syria. Arar was imprisoned and tortured there for nearly a year until his release and return to Canada in October 2003. The case developed into a major scandal in Canada after it was revealed that American authorities may have acted in response to information given to them by Canadian police officials to the effect that Arar had links to terrorism.

Al-Maleh has continued his human rights work in Syria despite both government harassment and his own advancing age. He was one of the signers of the Damascus Declaration for Democratic National Change in October 2004. In May 2006, he was convicted for insulting the president and defaming military officials. The court sentenced him to only ten days' imprisonment based on his age and his profession as a lawyer, but he appealed the conviction. While the case was still on appeal, al-Maleh was granted presidential amnesty at the end of the year.

THE WORLD'S PERSPECTIVE

Al-Maleh's activities have been recognized around the world. He has received an award from the Egyptian Human Rights Association, and in March 2006, was awarded the Geuzen Medal by the Geuzen Resistance 1940–1945 Foundation in the Netherlands. However, a government-imposed travel ban prohibited him from traveling to receive it, so his sons Ilyas Maleh and Anas al-Maleh accepted it on his behalf.

LEGACY

Haytham al-Maleh will be remembered as a pioneer in the legal and human rights struggle against authoritarian rule in Syria.

BIBLIOGRAPHY

"Once-Jailed Syrian Father and Son Warn U.S. Attack Would Destroy 'Not Only the Regime but the Country Itself.'" Democracy Now. Updated 4 March 2005. Available from http://www.democracynow.org.

Michael R. Fischbach

MALIKI, NURI KAMIL AL-
(1950–)

Nuri Kamil Muhammad Hasan al-Muhasin al-Maliki is Iraq's prime minister. He is a longtime member of the Shi'ite Islamic Da'wa Party, which was banned in Iraq until 2003. Fearing persecution by the Ba'th regime of SADDAM HUSSEIN, he left Iraq in 1979 for Jordan, Syria, Iran, and again Syria, where he engaged in opposition activities against the Iraqi regime. After the fall of the regime, he returned to Iraq and became involved in politics. He has been a member of the Iraqi National Assembly since 2004. He was chosen prime minister in late April 2006 and sworn in on 20 May.

PERSONAL HISTORY

Al-Maliki was born in July 1950 in Abi Sharq near Hilla in Babil province to a well-known, middle-class family. His grandfather, Hasan Abu'l-Muhasin, was a religious cleric and a noted poet who actively participated in the 1920 anti-British revolt and later became a member of parliament and minister of education in 1926.

Al-Maliki finished high school in Hindiyya and then attended the College of Usul al-Din (Principles of Reli-

Nuri Kamil al-Maliki. AP IMAGES.

BIOGRAPHICAL HIGHLIGHTS

Name: Nuri Kamal Muhammad Hasan al-Muhasin al-Maliki

Birth: 1950, Abi Sharq, near Hilla, Babil province, Iraq

Family: Wife, Fariha Khalil; four daughters, one son.

Nationality: Iraqi

Education: B.A., College of Usul al-Din, Baghdad, 1973; M.A., Arabic literature, University of Salah al-Din, Irbil, 1992

PERSONAL CHRONOLOGY:

- **1968:** Joins al-Da'wa, Shi'ite religious party
- **1979:** Leaves Iraq to live in exile
- **1980:** Condemned to death by Saddam Hussein's regime
- **1980–1989:** Lives in exile in Tehran during Iran-Iraq War
- **1989–2003:** Settles in Damascus, becomes head of Da'wa Party office for Syria and Lebanon; Publishes *al-Mawqif*, the party journal
- **2003:** Returns to Iraq, becomes deputy chairman of De-Ba'thification Committee
- **2005:** January, elected member, transitional National Assembly; becomes senior Shi'ite figure on National Assembly committee to draft permanent constitution; 15 December, elected member, National Assembly 2006: April, nominated as prime minister; 20 May, government sworn in

gion) in Baghdad. This college was established by Ayatullah Murtada'l-Askari, one of the leaders of the Da'wa Party. Both Muhammad Baqir al-Hakim, who was killed in Najaf in 2003 and Shaykh Arif al-Basri, executed by the Ba'th regime in 1974, were teachers at this college. He obtained a B.A. degree in 1973. In 1995, while in exile in Syria, al-Maliki obtained a master's degree in Arabic language and literature from the University of Salah al-Din in Irbil, then in Iraqi Kurdish territory free of Saddam's control. He wrote his dissertation on his grandfather, a study of his life and the political trends in his poetry, under the supervision of the well-known

Kurdish politician, Dr. Fu'ad Ma'sum. While in Irbil, al-Maliki established ties with members of the Kurdistan Democratic Party (KDP).

After graduation from the College of Usul al-Din in 1973 al-Maliki was employed at the Department of Education in Hilla until he left Iraq in 1979. More importantly, he became involved with the Da'wa Party. Like most members of al-Da'wa, al-Maliki joined the party while he was in college, in 1968. Soon after it came to power in 1968, the Ba'th began to crack down on Shi'ite Islamist groups, chief among them the Da'wa, an underground group. During the 1970s, the Da'wa Party, a main opponent of the Ba'th regime, committed several acts of violence against the regime, such as placing bombs in public places and undertaking assassination attempts on Ba'th officials. During these years, al-Maliki remained an active member of the party. In 1979 when Hussein became president of the republic, he issued an order that membership in the Da'wa Party would be punished with execution. Faced with the threat of execution as an active Da'wa member, al-Maliki fled Iraq, first to Jordan, then to Syria and from there to southwest Iran (al-Ahwaz) before finally settling in Tehran. (In exile, al-Maliki was sentenced to death in 1980.) In Tehran, al-Maliki was joined by other Iraqi Da'wa members also fleeing Iraq, such as Ibrahim al-Ja'fari, prime minister of Iraq in 2005. In 1980, these two leaders joined forces with other Iraqi exiles and continued their anti-Hussein activities. In Iran, al-Maliki assumed the names Jawad al-Maliki and Abu Isra' al-Maliki, fearing the long arm of Hussein's police able to strike opponents anywhere. He retained these names until he became prime minister–designate in April 2006. On 26 April his office stated that he would use his original name.

Exile in Syria and Return to Iraq Al-Maliki stayed in Iran until around 1989 when he left for Damascus. In Syria, he became very active in the Da'wa Party's anti-Hussein activities and soon became head of its office in Syria and Lebanon. Most of his work during his years in Syria was underground, dealing with Da'wa Party activities where he was responsible, among other things, for jihadist members who crossed into Iraq to accomplish "missions," some of them paramilitary operations. Al-Maliki also published and wrote for *al-Mawqif* (The position), the official journal of the Da'wa Party in Syria. *Al-Mawqif* was competing with the *al-Jihad* newspaper issued by the same party in Iran. *Al-Mawqif* had a pro-Arab orientation; therefore some considered al-Maliki the Arab face of the Da'wa Party. In Damascus, al-Maliki became the Da'wa Party representative in the Joint Action Committee, a Damascus-based opposition coalition that led to the founding of the Iraq National Congress, a U.S.-backed opposition coalition. As an exile in

Syria, al-Maliki participated in several opposition conferences. He was the organizer of the important Iraqi opposition conference held in Beirut in 1991.

After the fall of Baghdad on 9 April 2003 at the hands of U.S.-led coalition forces, almost all Iraqi opposition politicians returned to Iraq, among them the leaders of the Da'wa, chief among them al-Maliki and al-Ja'fari. Among the other Shi'ite religious parties that returned was the Supreme Council for the Islamic Revolution in Iraq (SCIRI; now the Supreme Iraqi Islamic Council [SIIC]), with its militia, the Badr Brigade. Not long after this, Iraq saw the rise to prominence of MUQTADA AL-SADR, son of the Grand Ayatollah Muhammad Sadiq al-Sadr, killed by Hussein's regime in 1999, who gathered around him a large part of the Shi'ite community, particularly the poor and downtrodden. In general, the Sunni community did not welcome the U.S.-led invasion and Sunnis began to oppose the Americans. After 2004 ill feeling increased slowly between Sunnis and Shi'ites, and underground groups in each community began killing members of the other. By the end of 2006, intercommunal strife between Sunnis and Shi'ites became a fact of daily life, especially in mixed areas in and around Baghdad.

After returning to Iraq, al-Maliki was very active in Da'wa Party activities. In 2003, he assumed the post of vice president of the De-Ba'thification Committee, charged with cleaning the civil service of noted Ba'thists. On 18 August 2003, a semiappointed "parliament" of one hundred people was chosen by caucuses. Al-Maliki became a member and assumed the functions of its vice president. In January 2005, Iraq had its first general election for a new "transitional" National Assembly, elected for the purpose of drafting a new permanent constitution for Iraq. The Shi'ite bloc won a majority of seats (Sunnis generally boycotted the election), and al-Ja'fari of the Da'wa Party was chosen to be prime minister. Al-Maliki won a seat in the assembly and was appointed a member of the committee charged with drafting the new constitution. He performed this function with great zeal and interest. He was also appointed a member of the assembly's National Security Committee and Sovereignty Committee.

Elections for a Permanent Government In the December 2005 election for a permanent government, although the Sunnis participated massively, the Shi'ite United Iraqi Alliance (UIA) won the plurality of seats. The election results closely mirrored the ethnic and sectarian distribution of the population. Shi'ites make up between 55 and 60 percent of the population; Sunnis about 20 percent; Kurds 20 percent, and others (Christians, Turkmen, etc.) about 3–5 percent. The winning bloc nominated al-Ja'fari to be Iraq's first full-term prime minister of the post-Hussein era. However, al-Ja'fari faced opposition from Kurds and Arab Sunnis in the parliament. Because there was a need to find a person who could pass a vote of confidence in the assembly, al-Maliki was presented as an alternative candidate acceptable to all parties. Finally, after a contentious behind-the-scenes struggle, al-Ja'fari's name was removed and in late April 2006, al-Maliki was nominated as prime minister by Iraq's president, JALAL TALABANI.

As a veteran of the Da'wa Party who had fought the Ba'th regime for more than thirty years and was sentenced to death by it, al-Maliki was a promising candidate to the country's Shi'ite majority. His nomination brought relief to many Iraqis who had waited for more than four months to get an acceptable prime minister.

Al-Maliki began his new functions by demonstrating that he is both tough and at the same time flexible enough to reach the compromises needed under the circumstances. He stressed that he wanted to build bridges to the Sunnis and to rebuild the country. The twenty-four-point plan of national reconciliation he presented to parliament and the nation at the end of June 2006 followed these lines. In April 2006, even before he was sworn in as prime minister, al-Maliki traveled to Najaf to meet with Ayatollah ALI HUSAYNI AL-SISTANI, the chief religious authority for the Shi'ites. Sistani reportedly told al-Maliki that he had to put an end to bombings, drive-by shootings, and other killing; to fight corruption and to restore services. Sistani also urged al-Maliki to form a government of leaders who would put national interest above their personal interests or those of their party or sect. It took al-Maliki more than three weeks to negotiate the formation of a cabinet with all of the parties and factions in the assembly; it was finally sworn in on 20 May 2006. The cabinet obtained parliamentary approval despite the reservations of deputies of the Sunni National Dialogue Party, who complained about the manner in which cabinet appointments had been made. The cabinet took office despite the failure to fill three seats—the critical sovereignty ministries of defense, interior, and national security. These were later filled by individuals officially not affiliated with parties, a move aimed at calming the Sunnis, who had accused the former minister of interior, a Shi'ite, of sectarianism and allowing "death squads" to operate freely against Sunnis in his ministry.

According to al-Maliki's statements to the press and visiting scholars, he advocates a dialogue among those with different ideas, including minorities. He believes that people should be free to hold various views, and that people should have the right to work and to succeed in their endeavors, but that some limits should be put on freedoms; freedom in Iraq cannot be practiced exactly as it is in the United States, because Iraq is different. Al-Maliki says he believes in some form of federalism, but does not want to see Iraq divided or split up. To prevent the return of authoritarianism, he believes in a high degree of decentralization in Iraq. His aspiration is that Iraq should be free, live in peace, and have positive relations with the Arab world, the United States, and others. Al-Maliki has some understanding of the United States since he has visited his married daughter who lives there. Politically, he is not considered to be tied to Iran, although he lived in that country during most of the 1980s. Several sources have reported that one reason for his state visit to Iran in the summer of 2006 was to tell the Iranians to stop interfering in Iraq's internal affairs. Although al-Maliki speaks only Arabic, his Arabic is excellent and he is an articulate speaker.

INFLUENCES AND CONTRIBUTIONS

Three influences have been paramount in al-Maliki's life: his involvement with the Da'wa Party; his opposition to the Ba'th regime; and his exile in Iran and Syria. The three are intertwined.

Al-Maliki was in his teens when he joined the Da'wa Party in 1968 as a college student. Iraqi universities and schools were the hub of the Iraqi Islamic movement during the 1960s and 1970s. At that time, the Da'wa Party was the most important Shi'ite political organization in opposition to the Ba'th. The origins of the Da'wa Party go back to the late 1950s. The real founder of the party was a young cleric, Muhammad Baqir al-Sadr, who advocated the renewal of Shi'ite theology and its teaching in Shi'ite establishments. He also advocated the establishment of an Islamic government in Iraq. Al-Sadr was arrested by Hussein and executed in 1980.

Throughout its history, the Da'wa Party has suffered from division. One division occurred around 1972, when one of its leaders in Baghdad, Sayyid Sami al-Badri, left the party to establish what he called the Islamic Movement, which later became the Jund al-Imam (Army of the Imam) movement. In 1979, some other Da'wa leaders, headed by Abd al-Zahra Uthman, also known as Izz al-Din Salim, left the party to set up the Da'wa Islamic Movement. In 2003, Salim was selected as a member of the Iraq Governing Council, which ruled Iraq after the fall of Hussein. He was the temporary president of the council in June 2004 when he was killed by a suicide car bomb. Another division of the party came at the end of the 1990s or early in the 2000s when leaders such as Sayyid Hashim al-Musawi (also known as Abu Aqil), Dr. Falah al-Sudani, and Abd al-Karim al-'Anazi left the party to establish Da'wa Tanzim (the Da'wa Organization).

During all of these divisions, al-Maliki remained loyal to the original branch of the party, whose spokesman was Shaykh Muhammad Mahdi al-Asifi. Al-Asifi left the party in the 1990s, to be replaced by al-Ja'fari. Da'wa leaders, such as al-Maliki, assert that the party had collective leadership and that there was no single leader at any time. During all of these divisions, especially that between the Da'wa and the Da'wa Tanzim, al-Maliki chose the middle ground, attempting to be a connecting link between competing elements.

Most of al-Maliki's adult life has been directed toward opposition to the Ba'th regime. He was involved with the Da'wa Party during a period in which it engaged in violent opposition to the regime. Islamic underground groups, for example, were responsible for an attack on Tariq Aziz, then deputy prime minister, in April 1980, while he was visiting al-Mustansiriyya University in Baghdad. Da'wa members participated in a major Shi'ite demonstration and other acts of resistance to the Ba'th regime. As a result of the crackdown by the regime on Da'wa members, many fled to neighboring Iran, which had undergone a Shi'ite Islamic revolution in 1979. Iran gave refuge to the fleeing Iraqi Arab Shi'ites. Faced with increasing Shi'ite opposition in Iraq and what he considered a threat from the revolutionary regime in Iran to spread its Islamic revolution to Iraq, Hussein ordered the expulsion of several hundred thousand Iraqis of Persian origin from Iraq. Finally, Hussein staged a surprising military attack against Iran on 23 September 1980 that resulted in Iranian retaliation, beginning a bloody war that lasted eight years, from 1980 to 1988. With so many Iraqi Shi'ites in exile in Iran, Iraqi Shi'ite parties there gained strength and increased their activities during the war. Al-Maliki was involved in these activities.

Divisions among Shi'ite Political Groups Although he spent some time in Iran, al-Maliki never lost his sense of Arab and Iraqi identity. The main Shi'ite groups at that time were the Da'wa Party and the SCIRI, headed by Muhammad Baqir al-Hakim and sponsored by Iran. While the two parties worked against Hussein's regime, their positions toward the ongoing war deviated. On the one hand, SCIRI declared total support for Iran in the war and formed a special brigade, the Badr Brigade, composed of Iraqi Shi'ite refugees, to fight alongside the Iranian army. The Da'wa Party, on the other hand, saw a split in its ranks over the war and the Iranian Islamic regime. While one group in the Da'wa gave its total support to Iran, al-Maliki and al-Ja'fari, with their followers, took a more nuanced position. They advocated keeping their distance from Iran in the war against Iraq, as well as from the ruling principles of the Iranian regime, based on the concept of *wilayat al-faqih* (rule of the Islamic jurist), which gives the rule of the state to clerics, not laypeople. Al-Ja'fari left Iran for Britain in the mid-1980s; al-Maliki, however, stayed in Iran until around 1989 when he went to Syria.

Syria at that time was under the firm control of President HAFIZ AL-ASAD, leader of the Syrian Ba'th Party, which was a rival to the Iraqi Ba'th of Hussein. Asad thus gave refuge and support to Iraqi Shi'ite Islamists who opposed Hussein, among them the Da'wa and pro-Syrian Iraqi Ba'thists. In Syria, al-Maliki became the "Arab face" of the Da'wa, while continuing to oppose the Hussein regime. He played a major role after the 1991 rebellion in Iraq in organizing an Arab opposition coalition against the Ba'th regime, which eventually led to the founding of the Iraq National Congress, backed by the United States. The Da'wa participated in that coalition between 1992 and 1995. On at least one occasion, al-Maliki disagreed with the party leadership. He supported the idea of participating in the London opposition conference with other anti-Ba'th groups in December 2002; he and his supporters were opposed by the faction headed by al-Ja'fari, who refused to attend. This indicates a pragmatic willingness in al-Maliki to search for middle ground.

This search for middle ground may be al-Maliki's most important contribution to post-Hussein Iraq, although it is too soon to evaluate its effectiveness. While the Kurds welcomed his twenty-four-point plan, the Arab Sunnis were divided among themselves. Some gave measured approval, but Sunni insurgents, fighting the Iraqi government and U.S. forces, rejected it, demanding a scheduled withdrawal of American and other troops from Iraq before negotiating any reconciliation. They insisted, at the same time, that there should also be a general amnesty for everyone, including those who have killed American and Iraqi government forces. By summer 2007, reconciliation efforts were still ongoing with no noticeable results. Al-Maliki's contributions will be evaluated on the basis of how well this succeeds.

THE WORLD'S PERSPECTIVE

Al-Maliki has been prime minister for too short a time for there to have developed a foreign consensus on his leadership. In the West, especially the United States, he is regarded as well-meaning but weak. The nomination of al-Maliki was welcomed by the United States. The U.S. ambassador to Iraq, Zalmay Khalilzad, stated that al-Maliki has a "reputation as someone who is independent of Iran and that he sees himself as an Arab and an Iraqi nationalist" (*Washington Post*, 26 April 2006). For the rest of the world, al-Maliki is a new figure on the Iraqi scene. He has yet to produce real positive changes and is being watched to see how effective he will be in solving the major problems Iraq faces.

LEGACY

Al-Maliki will be remembered as Iraq's first permanent prime minister in the post-Hussein era. His legacy is uncertain since his time in office has been short. He assumed his post in a difficult time, with the country facing a civil war between Shi'ites and Sunnis. Moreover, he has had to accommodate two different forces, the Americans who want to shape Iraq in a direction that satisfies their interests and a Shi'ite base that includes, among others, the anti-American movement of MUQTADA AL-SADR. Without much party organization or his own militia, al-Maliki has to balance these forces. He put together a plan of reconciliation, but faced with opposition from Sunnis and even some Shi'ites, has been unable to achieve much. Al-Maliki also faces the dilemma of reconciling his desire to put an end to the U.S.-led occupation and the need for foreign troops to maintain his government in existence.

BIBLIOGRAPHY

Allawi, Ali A. *The Occupation of Iraq: Winning the War, Losing the Peace.* New Haven, CT: Yale University Press, 2007.

Bozarslan, Hamit, and Hosham Dawod, eds. *La Société Irakienne: Communautés, Pouvoirs et Violences.* Paris: Éditions Karthala, 2003.

Ignatius, David. "In Iraq's Choice, A Chance For Unity," *Washington Post,* 26 April 2006.

Jabar, Faleh A., ed. *Ayatollahs, Sufis and Ideologues: State, Religion and Social Movements in Iraq.* London: Saqi, 2002.

———. *The Shi'ite Movement in Iraq.* London: Saqi, 2003.

Luizard, Jean-Pierre. *La Question Irakienne.* Paris: Librairie Artheme Fayard, 2004.

Marr, Phebe. *The Modern History of Iraq.* 2nd ed. Boulder, CO: Westview Press, 2004.

Sakai, Keiko. "Modernity and Tradition in the Islamic Movements in Iraq: Continuity and Discontinuity in the Role of the Ulama." *Arab Studies Quarterly* (Winter 2001).

Louay Bahry

MARDIN, ŞERIF
(1927–)

Şerif Mardin is a prominent Turkish sociologist and political scientist. Mardin's influence can mainly be found in the analysis of state and societal relationships. His analyses are characterized by a center-periphery model that provides an excellent conceptual tool for understanding the social and cultural features of Turkish politics. Mardin's articulations of state theory with historical sociology overcome the limitations of many current varieties of state and society examinations, and his writings provide a viable starting-point for theoretical and political concerns of the early twenty-first century.

PERSONAL HISTORY

Mardin was born in 1927 in Istanbul, Turkey. He belongs to a well-known scholarly family. Many members of Mardin family taught in Turkish Medrese (a college for Islamic studies) and Turkish universities for years. Mardin started his education in Galatasaray Lycée in Istanbul and then went to the United States to complete his B.A. in political science at Stanford University in 1948. After com-

pleting his B.A., he went to the School of International Relations at Johns Hopkins University to obtain his M.A. degree. Then, he returned to Turkey to join the Faculty

BIOGRAPHICAL HIGHLIGHTS

Name: Şerif Mardin

Birth: 1927, Istanbul, Turkey

Family: Divorced; one son, Osman

Nationality: Turkish

Education: B.A., political science, Stanford University; M.A., international relations, Johns Hopkins University; Ph.D., political science, Stanford University, 1958

PERSONAL CHRONOLOGY:

- **1954–1956, 1961–1972:** Professor, Faculty of Political Science, Ankara University
- **1958–1961:** Research associate, Princeton University, Department of Oriental Studies
- **1958–1959, 1970–1971:** Visiting professor, Princeton University
- **1959–1961:** Visiting professor, Harvard University
- **1960–1961:** Research fellow, Middle East Institute, Harvard University
- **1965–1966, 1970, 1971–1973, 1986:** Visiting professor, Columbia University, Middle East Institute
- **1973–1991:** Professor, Department of Political Science, Boğaziçi University, Istanbul
- **1975:** Visiting professor, University of California, Los Angeles
- **1980–1982:** Visiting research fellow, St. Antony College, Oxford University
- **1985:** Visiting professor, University of California, Berkeley
- **1985:** Visiting professor, École des Hautes Études en Sciences Sociales (Paris)
- **1989–1999:** Visiting professor then tenured professor, American University, Washington, D.C.
- **1999–present:** Professor, Faculty of Arts and Social Sciences, Sabancı University, Istanbul

of Political Sciences in Ankara University as a teaching assistant from 1954 to 1956. At Ankara University, Mardin studied with Yavuz Abadan, who was perhaps the best-known academician of his time for his studies on philosophy of law and state. Undoubtedly, when Mardin associated with Abadan, he had already been exposed to other ideas in political theory, but it was Abadan's benign influence as the scion of a tradition of openness to new ideas at the Faculty of Political Sciences of Ankara University that seems to have held a significant role in Mardin's development as a political thinker.

In 1958, Mardin returned to the United States once more, this time to complete his Ph.D. in political science at Princeton University. He also worked as a research associate there, and wrote his dissertation, titled "The Genesis of Young Ottoman Thought." After completing his Ph.D., he began to work on the political ideas of the Young Turks during a stay at the Middle East Center of Stanford University. Then between the years 1961 and 1972 he was a full-time, tenured professor of political science at Ankara University. In 1973, Mardin moved to Istanbul where he joined the department of political science at Boğaziçi University as a professor. He kept this position until 1991. Throughout his academic career he taught political science as a visiting professor at several other leading universities. He was offered a research associate position in the Department of Oriental Studies at Princeton University from 1958 to 1961. He participated in research projects in the Middle East Institute at Harvard University as a research fellow in 1961 and taught in the Middle East Institute at Columbia University in 1965, 1966, 1970, 1971 to 1973, and 1986. He was a visiting research fellow at St. Antony's College at Oxford University from 1980 to 1982, and a visiting professor at École des Hautes Études en Sciences Sociales in 1985. He also visited the University of California, Los Angeles, in 1975, the University of California, Berkeley in 1985, and Syracuse University from 2005 to 2006. He served as the chair of Islamic studies in the School of International Service at the American University in Washington, D.C., between 1989 and 1999. Since 1999, he has been a professor of political science at the Faculty of Arts and Social Sciences at Sabanci University in Istanbul.

INFLUENCES AND CONTRIBUTIONS

One of the distinguished contributions of Mardin is his effort to examine in a detailed and inquisitive manner social and political developments of the Turkish state and society by applying historical and methodological principles of interpretation. Mardin's work offers a depiction of the distinctive characteristics of the social and political developments of Turkish society that can be defined in relation to both Islamic societies and Western political institutions. His studies approach social and political development of Turkey as an exceptional case, exception-

CONTEMPORARIES

Halil İnalcık (1916-) has published widely on Ottoman history. He has brought into light a new understanding of demographic, social, and political changes in Ottoman society, and his perspective has made highly acknowledged contributions to the histography of Ottoman state and society. İnalcık argued that studying the Turkish social formation within a Western methodological framework may mislead historians because it does not squarely fit in any ideal type that has been abstracted from major cases in both the West and the East. He thinks it is important for historians to have a clear view of their subjects and to contribute toward an ideographic explanation and understanding.

ality of which requires using not only a comparative perspective, but also a particular ontological and epistemological positioning congruent with the case at hand.

In his 2005 "Turkish Islamic Exceptionalism Yesterday and Today," Mardin suggests that that his treatment of Turkish social and political development processes as exceptional is based on the recognition of the unique ability of actors in regard to political organization that the other Islamic societies were not able to develop. With the term *unique ability*, Mardin refers to the concordant relationship between the secular state as the locus of legitimate power and Islam as a religion mobilizing individuals for political causes within and through its symbolic order. The studies of Mardin focus on analysis of the historical development of the relationship between Islam and state in Turkey, Islam's influence on the social and cultural structure, the process in which it is reflected in the people's worldview, its associations, and the political and cultural forms of its expression. Mardin formulated his framework for understanding the structural characteristics of state-society relation in both the Ottoman society and modern Turkey with a unique interpretation of the structures of strong state and weak civil society as center, which he calls periphery problematique. With reference to the strong state and weak civil society model, he sought to give an account of the extension of the polity by locating the sources of change in the asymmetric relationship between the ruling elite and the ruled people.

Mardin, in his 1973 "Center Periphery Relations: A Key to Turkish Politics?," places the state, rulers, and intellectuals in the center, and places society, people, and religious institutions in the periphery. The relationship between the state and society through religious institutions, which was a distinct feature of the Ottoman Empire, changed to a large extent during the process of Turkish modernization. With the disintegration of the Ottoman Empire, bureaucratic elite who were highly influenced by the positivist understanding of French secularization and aimed to transform the Turkish society toward modernity saw the control of Islamic practices and institutions as essential for the continuation of the transformation of society.

Nevertheless, the emphasis on Islam as the unifying source of national identity on the one hand and the secularization process on the other created tensions between the state and society in various forms and at different periods. This tension often represents a confrontation between the center represented by the bureaucratic elite that controls the state and tries to separate the state and religious affairs in order to transform both institutions of the state and the society toward modernity, and the periphery represented by the people who preserve the traditional ways of life. The confrontation between the center and the periphery reveals itself explicitly in the tension between the aspirations of the ruling bureaucratic elite who are not willing to share sovereignty and the desire of traditional societal forces who would like to have shares in the state capacity yet preserve their customary lifestyles and hence cling to the status quo. This also means that discordance between the center and the periphery not only leads to a struggle over power within and through the legitimate political process, but also involves a contest over core values and identities. As the formally constructed national identity imposed by the bureaucratic elite could not diffuse into the whole of society and consequently in the polity, the center could not resist some of the religious demands made by the people.

THE WORLD'S PERSPECTIVE

Mardin made major contributions to history, sociology of religion, and political theory. The significance of his work that lays out a comprehensive framework for sociological and political analysis of the Turkish development process can be attested to by the emergence of a genre of research that takes his problematique as its departure point. In particular, Mardin's articulations of politics with sociology, political theory, and history constitute a lasting effect. Whereas mainstream academic divisions of labor attempt to isolate politics from sociology, history, and other disciplines, Mardin introduced a robust sociological dimension and historical criticism to political theory and developed his theoretical perspective in interaction with concrete analyses of society, politics, and culture in the present age. This multidimensional approach thus assigns sociology an important role within political theory, providing critical theory with strong normative and historical perspectives. His attempt to get at the multidimensional

---

MARDIN'S THOUGHTS

■

For the population at large religion was a moral prop, something to lean on, a source of consolation, a patterning of life; for the ruling elite it was addition, and probably much more, a matter related to the legitimacy of the state. Both groups could at times neglect religion or by-pass it, but the form of this by-passing was different: for the masses it consisted of breaking religious taboos and then atoning for it later; for the ruling it consisted in pushing religion into the background when required by secular political purposes. "Religion and the state are twins" was the way in which this close association was expressed, but in the Ottoman Empire one of the twins could often become more equal.

MARDIN, ŞERIF. "IDEOLOGY AND RELIGION IN THE TURKISH REVOLUTION." *INTERNATIONAL JOURNAL OF MIDDLE EAST STUDIES* 2, NO. 3 (1971): 197.

---

view allows him to theorize deep-seated transformations, developments, challenges, and conflicts.

LEGACY

Mardin's studies are characterized by a broad critical and pluralist perspective that attempts to capture the major sociohistorical, political, and cultural features of the historical development of Turkey, its influence on the social and political structures, the process in which it was reflected in the people's worldview, its organization, and the political and economic manifestation of Islam. Such a perspective profoundly tries to highlight the ways in which people think about, classify, and categorize social experiences as influenced by wider social and political processes, and that these reflect fundamental changes, development, contradictions, and struggles of the day, and continuously reproduce different forms of power within different contexts. Mardin's perspective thus continues to be relevant because it not only reflects the importance of accepting pluralism and rejecting confrontational exclusivism but it also provides a mode of general theoretical analysis and addresses issues that continue to be of relevance to contemporary theory and politics in Turkey. It does not represent a fixed position but continuously opens itself to admitting new ideas, or it evaluates ideas for correspondence to the truths and realities of everyday life. Hence, it takes an inclusive position for evaluating the diversity of possible meanings that are active in social and political life. Mardin's perspective endorses these meanings with an understanding that is historical, social, and political, and that avoids historical determinism. It seeks out self-knowledge within understanding of differences seen as a process of being produced in political contexts and formed within wider discourses of knowledge and power. It does not simply accept things for integration into a social political theory without any deliberate scrutiny. It encapsulates pluralistic, multivocal, and multifaceted discourses with avoidance of determinism and reductionism.

BIBLIOGRAPHY

WORKS BY MARDIN

"Opposition and Control in Turkey." *Government and Opposition* 1, no. 3 (1966): 375–387.

"The Mind of the Turkish Reformer: 1700–1900." In *Arab Socialism: A Documentary Survey*, edited by Sami A. Hanna and George H. Gardner. Leiden, Netherlands: E.J. Brill, 1969.

"Power, Civil Society and Culture in the Ottoman Empire." *Comparative Studies in Society and History,* no. 11 (1969): 258–281.

"Ideology and Religion in the Turkish Revolution." *International Journal of Middle Eastern Studies* 2, no. 3 (1971): 197–211.

"Center Periphery Relations: A Key to Turkish Politics?" *Daedalus,* no. 102 (1973): 169–190.

"Religion in Modern Turkey." *International Social Science Journal* 29, no. 2 (1977): 279–297.

"Religion and Politics in Modern Turkey." In *Islam in the Political Process*, edited by J. P. Piscatori. Cambridge, U.K.: Cambridge University Press, 1983.

"A Note on the Transformation of Religious Symbols in Turkey." *Turcica,* no. 16 (1984): 115–127.

Religion and Social Change in Modern Turkey: The Case of Bediuzzaman Said Nursi. Albany: State University of New York Press, 1990.

"The Just and the Unjust." *Daedalus,* no. 120, (1991): 113–129.

Cultural Transitions in the Middle East. Leiden, Netherlands: E.J. Brill, 1994.

"Religion and Secularism in Turkey." In *Atatürk: Founder of a Modern State*, edited by Ali Kazancıgil and Ergun Özbudun. London: Hurst & Company, 1997.

The Genesis of Young Ottoman Thought: A Study in the Modernization of Turkish Political Ideas. Syracuse, NY: Syracuse University Press, 2000.

"Turkish Islamic Exceptionalism Yesterday and Today: Continuity, Rupture and Reconstruction in Operational Codes." *Turkish Studies* 6, no. 2 (2005): 145–165.

Religion, Society, and Modernity in Turkey. Syracuse, NY: Syracuse University Press, 2006.

Gürcan Koçan

MARGALIT, DAN
(1938–)

Dan Margalit is a prominent Israeli journalist, veteran commentator on Israeli affairs, and political talk show host. He is best known for his columns in the *Haaretz* and *Maariv* newspapers, and for his role hosting *Erev Hadash* (New evening) and other political debate programs.

PERSONAL HISTORY

Margalit was born in Tel Aviv, mandatory Palestine in 1938. His maternal grandparents arrived with the second *aliyah* (wave of Jewish immigration into Palestine) that took place between 1904 and 1914. His mother was born in Ottoman-controlled Palestine, and his father was born in Warsaw, Poland. His parents met in 1935 when they were studying in Switzerland. His mother, Ora Aharovich, was a psychologist and his father, Israel, was a doctor.

From childhood, Margalit aspired to be a journalist and began to write in children's newspapers. He was a leader in the Scout movement and he attended Herzliyah Gymnasium high school. After graduation he was inducted into the kibbutz unit of the Israeli army. After finishing his army service, he completed a bachelor's degree in international relations at the Hebrew University of Jerusalem and later completed a master's degree in modern Jewish history.

Margalit's professional experience began in 1960 when he got a job at the weekly paper, *ha-Olam ha-Zeh* (This world), a satirical political news magazine under the leadership of Uri Avneri. In 1965 he began writing on criminal and employment issues for the weekly insert of *Haaretz*, one of Israel's major newspapers. In 1969 Margalit began to cover government affairs for the newspaper in Jerusalem.

In 1971 Margalit published his first book, *Sheder me'ha-Bayit ha-Lavan* (Broadcast from the White House), which described the War of Attrition that began after the 1967 War and lasted until August 1970. He became *Haaretz*'s Washington correspondent in 1974, but returned to Israel in 1977 to continue his professional writing on political and national issues.

Margalit also developed a career in television broadcasting. At the outbreak of the Lebanon war in 1982, Margalit became a regular host of the daily current affairs interview program *Erev Hadash* (New evening) on Israel's Educational TV. In 1993, he became the host and founding moderator of a new television program on Channel 1, *Popolitika*, a round-table political debate in front of a live studio audience. The show received high ratings, perhaps in part due to the drama of participant shouting matches. After several moves between Israel Television's Channel 1 and Channel 2, the program eventually changed names to *Kemoatzet ha-Hahamim* (Council of Sages) and moved to Channel 10.

BIOGRAPHICAL HIGHLIGHTS

Name: Dan Margalit

Birth: 1938, Tel Aviv, mandatory Palestine

Family: Married twice; three daughters

Nationality: Israeli

Education: Hebrew University of Jerusalem, B.A. in international relations, M.A. in modern Jewish history

PERSONAL CHRONOLOGY:

- **1960:** First job at *ha-Olam ha-Zeh*
- **1965:** New job writing for *Haaretz*'s weekly insert
- **1969:** Moves to Jerusalem to cover government affairs
- **1971:** Publishes his first book, *Sheder me'ha-Bayit ha-Lavan*
- **1974–1977:** Becomes *Haaretz*'s Washington correspondent
- **1982:** Becomes a regular host of *Erev Hadash* on Israel's Educational TV
- **1992:** Appointed editor of *Maariv*, but returns to *Haaretz* several months later after conflict with the publisher, Ofer Nimrodi
- **1997:** Publishes *Raiti Otam*
- **1992–2001:** Political columnist for *Haaretz*
- **1993:** Becomes host of *Popolitika*
- **2001:** Returns to write for *Maariv*'s weekly insert

In the early 1990s, Margalit moved from *Haaretz* to *Maariv*, the Israeli newspaper with the second-largest circulation after *Yediot Aharonot*. In 1992, he was appointed editor of the paper by its publisher Ofer Nimrodi. However, he resigned his editorship about eight months later, accusing the publisher of being too involved in the editorial content and trying to influence his decisions. He returned to *Haaretz* where he wrote a column on politics until 2001, when he resigned and went back to *Maariv* to write a column for the paper's weekly Friday insert.

INFLUENCES AND CONTRIBUTIONS

Margalit's views are characterized as moderate but security-oriented left, and he self-identifies strongly as a Zionist. Concern for the state of the country and its security shape Margalit's articles, and are regular themes in his columns. For instance, regarding Zionism and Israel's well-being, Margalit has written about the role of education in instilling Zionist values, teaching Hebrew, educating students on Jewish cultural and religious history, and encouraging Israel to view the immigration of Jews to the country as the ingathering of the exiles. He frequently speaks about Jewish unity and the need for Israelis to set aside personal interests and act first and foremost out of concern for the Jewish people and Israel. Margalit has expressed opposition to post-Zionism, which he believes denies the Jewish people's right to self-definition. He also criticizes what he sees as the extreme left's ongoing justification of Palestinian terrorism, its noncritical stance on Palestinian rejectionism, and its inability to differentiate between Palestinians' intentional targeting of Israeli civilians through rocket attacks and Israeli military responses that accidentally result in the deaths of Palestinian civilians.

EXPLORING

Post-Zionism refers to a broad trend of critical thought about Israel's past, but the concept is ambiguous and not all scholars whose works are identified as post-Zionist accept the label, which is often associated with being anti-Zionist. The post-Zionist debate encompasses diverse disciplines such as sociology, history, and archaeology, and finds popular expression in the arts and literature.

In a first attempt to provide a comprehensive look at post-Zionism, Laurence Silberstein proposes that *post-Zionism* is a term applied to a current set of critical positions that problematize Zionist discourse, and the historical narratives and social and cultural representations that it produced. Silberstein notes the activist nature of post-Zionism, referring to it as a space-clearing enterprise. Post-Zionist histories question basic postulates of Jewish and Israeli identity, such as the Jews as a nation and Israel as a democracy, and paint a more negative picture of the origins and nature of Zionism and the nascent Jewish state. Contradictory positions within post-Zionist writings have led to a number of criticisms. For example, although post-Zionists claim to recognize diversity, they tend to discuss Zionism in singular, monolithic terms.

Margalit has maintained a strong interest in the events of the Holocaust. He was particularly influenced by two major Holocaust-related trials. The first was the controversial Kastner trial that shook up Israeli society in the 1950s and continues to be a subject of heated debate. Rudolf (later known as Israel) Kastner was the lay leader of the Jewish Relief and Rescue Committee during the Nazi occupation of Hungary during World War II. As the head of this organization, Kastner led the negotiations with the Nazis, including S.S. officer Adolf Eichmann, to save the lives of Hungarian Jews. After the war, Kastner moved to Israel. In 1954, the Israeli government sued Malchiel Gruenwald on behalf of Kastner for libel after Gruenwald published a pamphlet accusing Kastner of collaboration with the Nazis. The court accepted this accusation and acquitted Gruenwald. In 1958 the Israeli High Court of Justice overturned most of the ruling, but not before Kastner was assassinated. The second case that captivated Margalit was the trial of Eichmann in Israel in 1961. He was indicted on fifteen criminal charges, including charges of crimes against humanity. Eichmann was hanged on 1 June 1962 in the only civil execution ever carried out in Israel.

Margalit is a strong supporter of the liberal High Court of Justice, particularly under the presidencies of AHARON BARAK and Dorit Beinisch (r. 2006–), who he feels have protected the country against the influence of the extreme right and ultra-Orthodox religious Jews.

Since the start of the second Palestinian intifada, Margalit's writings have been focused primarily on two topics. The first is the need for building a separation fence between Israel and the Palestinian territories. Margalit supports the construction of the barrier between Israel and the West Bank. His security orientation is also reflected in his opposition to security budget cuts. Furthermore, since the 2005 Israeli withdrawal from Gaza, which Margalit believes was in Israel's best interest, he has supported a strong Israeli response to indiscriminate Palestinian firing of missiles into Israel's southern cities. He also favors withdrawal from most of the West Bank so that Palestinians can have territorial continuity and Israel can retain major border settlement blocs such as Ma'aleh Adumim and Ariel, in line with then-Israeli prime minister Ehud Barak's final status proposal at the Camp David II summit in July 2000. Although Margalit has suggested Israel might compromise by giving some parts of Jerusalem to the Palestinians, he has been adamant that Israel not compromise over the Palestinian demand for the return of the Palestinian refugees from the 1948 Arab-Israeli War. According to Margalit, blame for the refugees' plight does not lie with Israel, and acquiescence to this demand would result in the destruction of Israel as a Jewish state by admitting hundreds of thousands of non-Jews into the country.

The second topic on which Margalit has focused more recently is corruption among the Israeli government, especially since ARIEL SHARON's election as prime minister in 2001. However, in 1997, Margalit published the political memoir, *Raiti Otam* (I saw them), which provided an inside perspective on corruption among the political leadership and media, based on his personal relationships. This book remained near the top of the best-seller list in Israel for twenty-five weeks, mostly in the number one place.

THE WORLD'S PERSPECTIVE AND LEGACY

Margalit is an iconic media personality in Israel, having written for major Israeli newspapers since the 1960s and hosted shows on several channels on Israeli television. His book, *Sheder me'ha-Bayit ha-Lavan* (1971; Broadcast from the White House), attracted considerable attention and criticism in Israel. Among other things, it drove Chaim Herzog, the future president of Israel, to investigate how so many state secrets were leaked from the government to the book's author. Margalit was also the moderator of the pre-1996 elections debate between candidates BINYAMIN NETANYAHU and SHIMON PERES, which was widely seen as a critical moment that ended Peres's chance of reelection.

During his time in Washington, D.C., in the late 1970s, Margalit famously exposed Leah and YITZHAK RABIN's illegal American bank account. This disclosure resulted in Rabin's resignation from his post as prime minister and in the prosecution of Leah Rabin. It also led to the election of the Likud Party for the first time in Israeli history in 1977. Margalit has long been dedicated to fighting corruption. Nevertheless, he has sometimes been seen as hypocritical for his close friendships with the Israeli political elite including EHUD OLMERT, detailed in his 1997 best seller, *Raiti Otam*. Margalit has been criticized from the Left for his defense of Olmert against corruption in light of evidence to the contrary. Margalit is also sometimes seen as insensitive to religious Jews and has been criticized by the religious right for not having their views represented on his debate programs and for his comment that religious Israelis in the army should expel Jews from Gaza during the withdrawal or face a quota limiting their numbers in the army. The inclusion of the former Shas Party leader and interior minister, Aryeh Deri, as a regular panelist on the *Council of the Sages* despite his imprisonment on corruption charges has also garnered criticism for Margalit.

As a veteran commentator on Israeli affairs, Margalit is widely cited by other Israeli newspapers, as well as the international media, including the United Kingdom's national broadcaster, the British Broadcasting Corporation (BBC).

BIBLIOGRAPHY

Doron, Daniel. "Top Pundit Tells All," *Jerusalem Post* (22 February 2007). Available from http://www.jpost.com.

Glick, Caroline. "Scorched-Earth Kulturkamp." *Jerusalem Post* (11 July 2005).

Margalit, Dan. "Out of the Closet." Israel21c. Available from http://www.israel21c.org.

———. "Oust Peretz from the Defense Ministry." *Maariv* (13 February 2007).

Shavit, Ari. "Media Malfunction." *Haaretz.* Available from http://www.haaretz.com.

Tzvi, Dorit Keren. "The End of a Beautiful Friendship." *Haaretz Friday Magazine* (16 February 2007).

Aliza Craimer

MAS'ADI, MAHMOUD AL-
(1911–2004)

Mahmoud al-Mas'adi (Mahmud Messad, Masadi) was an important Tunisian literary and political figure. As minister responsible for public education, he oversaw the creation of a public school system open to all in his newly independent country, and helped to establish the first Tunisian university. As a writer, Mas'adi was a member of a group of Tunisian writers with whom Tunisian literature moved into modernity. His best-known work, *Haddatha Abu Hurayra, Qala* (Abu Hurayra said, 1973), is considered a modern classic.

PERSONAL HISTORY

Mas'adi was born in Tazerka, Cap Bon, Tunisia, in 1911. He studied in the Sadiqiyya school, where he received a bilingual education. He studied in Paris in the 1930s and obtained his doctorate in Arabic literature from the Sorbonne in 1947. He taught in high schools from 1936 to 1948 before moving to the Institute of Higher Education in Tunis, where he held the post of professor of Arabic literature from 1948 to 1953.

Under the French Protectorate, he joined the pro-independence Neo-Destour Party in 1934 and later became secretary general of the General Union of Tunisian Workers (1948–1953). He was imprisoned by the French colonial authorities for almost a year (1952–1953), and was afterward placed under house arrest.

In independent Tunisia, after 1956, Mas'adi became minister for national education (1958–1968), inspector general of teaching (1969–1970), minister of cultural affairs (1973–1976), and finally, president (speaker) of Parliament (1981–1987; he had been a member since 1959). Mas'adi was named Tunisia's representative at UNESCO, where he was a member of the Executive Council (1974–1978 and 1980–1985). As minister of

---

BIOGRAPHICAL HIGHLIGHTS

∎

Name: Mahmoud al-Mas'adi (Mahmud Messadi, Masadi)

Birth: 1911, Tazerka, Cap Bon, Tunisia

Death: 2004

Family: Married

Nationality: Tunisian

Education: Ph.D., Arabic literature, Sorbonne, Paris, 1947

PERSONAL CHRONOLOGY:

• **1936–1948:** High school teacher

• **1944–1947:** Editor of *al-Mabahith*

• **1948–1953:** Professor, Institute of Higher Education, Tunis; secretary general, General Union of Tunisian Workers

• **1952–1953:** Imprisoned by French colonial authorities for pro-independence political activity

• **1958–1968:** Minister for national education

• **1969–1970:** Inspector general of teaching

• **1973–1976:** Minister of cultural affairs

• **1981–1987:** President of Parliament

• **1974–1978, 1980–1985:** Member of Executive Council, UNESCO

---

education Mas'adi reorganized and expanded public education in Tunisia, and presided over the foundation of the University of Tunis in 1960.

INFLUENCES AND CONTRIBUTIONS

Mas'adi had a deep command of both Arabic and French. In his literary writing he used only Arabic. His bilingual education allowed him to create a unique and what to many might appear an impossible hybrid style, a hermetic one that often defies easy comprehension, strongly influenced by Qur'anic Arabic, with a rigorous sentence structure and a vocabulary suitable for philosophical themes. This last is exemplified in his play *Al-Sudd* (The dam, 1955). In this work (which despite its intellectual depth has never been performed on stage), a couple, Maymuna and Ghaylan, land among a tribe living in an arid valley. When water comes out of an old spring, Ghaylan decides to build a dam to exploit the water. His wife is skeptical but he perseveres despite numerous failures, encouraged by an invisible force, Mayara. In the end both are swept away by a hurricane.

No one better represents than Mas'adi the trend toward modernism—in which the individual human being becomes the center of interest—in Arabic and specifically Tunisian literature. It is through his writings and the journal *al-Mabahith* (Investigations), founded by Muhammad al-Bachrouch and edited by Mas'adi from 1944 to 1947, that this entered Tunisia. The journal both gave Tunisia's writers access to literary modernism and provided them a literary venue for their work. The essays Mas'adi published in the journal, and his theoretical texts, appeared later in the book *Ta'silan li-Kayan* (1979; The grounding of the human being).

The philosophy embodied in his writings is an existential one of commitment of the individual to a search for significance in the shaping of his role in life. This is, in his view, the factor that determines a person's destiny. While *Al-Sudd* is set in a secular context, his other writings, *Haddatha Abu Hurayra, Qala* and *Min Ayyam Imran wa Ta'ammulat Ukhra* (From the days of Imran and other considerations, 2002) are strongly anchored in Islamic history and philosophy. The author returns to a more secular framework in *Mawlad al-Nisyan* (1974; The birth of forgetfulness) to portray a general theme that preoccupies all humanity, and is at the center of all religions, the struggle between good and evil experienced by every individual. He believes that "only the tragic is literature."

Mas'adi's writings are characterized by their unusual choice of language and style, reminiscent of classical Arabic religious texts such as the Hadith (sayings and actions of the prophet Muhammad) and the use of Isnad (the chain of authorities for the verification of truth of the Hadiths) in his book *Haddatha Abu Hurayra, Qala*. The protagonist of this work, a companion of the Prophet in Islamic history, represents the writer. He is tormented by a fruitless effort to find a meaning for the human existence. He looked for it in adventures, love, and faith but finally finds it in the Truth.

THE WORLD'S PERSPECTIVE

Mas'adi achieved renown in his country as a man of letters, as a journalist, and as a politician. The quality of his writings and his superior culture and knowledge gave him throughout the years a distinction and a place in society that few intellectuals have attained.

On the international level, through his position at UNESCO, Mas'adi was respected among his peers and in francophone literary circles. His choice to represent Tunisia in this United Nations cultural body was a happy one for his country; it placed him in a prominent spot where he was recognized and appreciated. *Al-Sudd* was translated into French and was first published in Canada in 1981, then

---

WHERE IS THE ROAD THAT DOES NOT END IN ORDER TO MEET YOU THERE

∎

She descended and asked,

"How can I meet you after my lean evenings?"

...They stood facing each other and she said,

"Where is the road that does not end in order to meet you there?"

He said,

"It might be to the right."

She said,

"Or it might be to the left."

He said,

"To the left for you and to the right for me, that is the place of encounter. Now, give me your hand before we lose the directions."

She offers her right hand and he offers his right hand, facing each other forward, but they do not reach.

God said,

"This is the tragedy of the impossible encounter between my creatures in life. There is no encounter except by me in the union of annihilation after death."

MAHMOUD MAS'ADI, "THE DAY OF THE IMPOSSIBLE ENCOUNTER," IN **MIN AYYAM 'IMRAN.**

---

in France in 1994. His short stories published in the journal *al-Mabahith* in 1939 were collected in *Mawlid al-Nisyan* (published in French as *La genèse de l'oubli*, 1993). As in his other writings the author uses known figures in Arabic literature to ponder the meaning of life. In "Sindbad and Purity," after a stormy night Sindbad says, "It lasted very long, this farcical struggle between two ogres, the ogre of death and the ogre of life. Won't one finally overcome the other? Won't they finally stop? I do not see spectators here, for whom do they continue to fight?" In search of purity, Sindbad takes his boat and rows alone in the fury of the storm and the darkness of the night. This was his last voyage. "Ever since, the purity of the depths has kept him in its bosom."

LEGACY

It is difficult to talk about Mas'adi's legacy because despite his modernity he stands apart in his country's cultural and literary arena. Critics find it difficult to classify him. His style recalls the language of the Jahiliyya (pre-Islamic) period and the prose of the Qur'an, written in a pure Arabic without the use of foreign words, and his symbols do not often relate to the contemporary world. His message that the human being should assume responsibility for himself and his actions would suit any time period and should consequently have a profound echo in any in which the concept of the freedom of the individual is the ideal. It is possibly the style and the hermetic language used to convey the message that impedes its propagation. Moreover, al-Mas'adi's philosophy is embodied in fictional form; it lacks a plan of action, an indication of a path to follow.

Haddatha Abu Hurayra, Qala has been assigned reading in Tunisia's secondary schools, raising the question of whether one day the author will influence future writers or will remain forever unique in the history of modern Tunisian literature.

BIBLIOGRAPHY

Baccar, Taoufik, and Salah Garmadi, eds. *Ecrivains de Tunisie: anthologie de textes et poèmes.* Paris: Sindbad, 1981.

Fontaine, Jean. *Al-Adab al-Tunisi al-Mu'asir.* Tunisia: al-Dar al-Tunisiyya lil-Nashr, 1989.

———. *Histoire de la Littérature Tunisienne.* Vol. 2, *Du XIIIe siècle à l'indépendance.* Tunis: Ceres, 1999.

WORKS BY MAS'ADI

Al-Sudd (1955; The dam)

Haddatha Abu Hurayra, Qala (1973; Abu Hurayra said)

Mawlid al-Nisyan (1974; The birth of forgetfulness)

Ta'silan li-Kayan (1979; The grounding of the human being)

Essai sur le rythme dans la prose rimée en arabe (1981; An essay on rhythm in Arabic rhymed prose)

Min Ayyam Imran wa Ta'ammulat Ukhra (2002; From the days of Imran and other Considerations)

Aida A. Bamia

MASH'AL, KHALID
(1956–)

Khalid Mash'al (Khaled Mesh'al, Meshaal, Mashal, Mashaal) is a senior leader in the Palestinian movement Hamas.

PERSONAL HISTORY

Mash'al was born in 1956 in the village of Silwad, near Ramallah in the West Bank (then under Jordanian occu-

Khalid Mash'al. AP IMAGES.

pation). His father began working in Kuwait in the 1960s and the rest of the family followed him there after the Israeli occupation of the West Bank (along with the Gaza Strip, the Golan Heights, and the Sinai Peninsula) in 1967. While in school in Kuwait Mash'al became interested in Palestinian and Islamic activism, and some allege that he joined the Muslim Brotherhood in 1971. As a student at Kuwait University studying physics he founded a student bloc called al-Haqq al-Islami (The Islamic Truth) that challenged Fatah (YASIR ARAFAT's group within the Palestine Liberation Organization [PLO]) for leadership of the General Union of Palestinian Students (GUPS). Following his graduation in 1978 he taught physics in Kuwait. He married in 1981 and has seven children.

INFLUENCES AND CONTRIBUTIONS

With the start of the intifada in December 1987 and the creation of Hamas (Harakat al-Muqawama al-Islamiyya

BIOGRAPHICAL HIGHLIGHTS

Name: Khalid Mash'al (Khaled Mesh'al, Meshaal, Mashal, Mashaal)

Birth: Silwad, Jordanian-controlled West Bank, 1956

Family: Wife; four sons; three daughters

Nationality: Palestinian

Education: Kuwait University, physics, 1974–1978

PERSONAL CHRONOLOGY:

- **1988:** Becomes an active member of Hamas
- **1991:** Moves/is expelled to Jordan
- **1997:** Survives assassination attempt against him by Israeli Mossad agents in Jordan
- **1999:** Expelled from Jordan
- **2001:** Takes up residency in Syria, political leader of Hamas bureau in Syria
- **2004:** Likely becomes head of political wing of Hamas after assassinations of Shaykh Ahmad Yasin and Abd al-Aziz al-Rantisi

[the Islamic Resistance Movement]) the following year by the members of the Muslim Brotherhood in Palestine, Mash'al made connections with Hamas. Growing out of the Muslim Brotherhood, Hamas prioritized Islam as a way of life in addition to the struggle on the national front for the liberation of Palestine. Hamas initially was extremely active in providing health care and educational opportunities to Palestinians in the West Bank and Gaza (something it has continued to this day), eventually adopting a more organized and militant platform of resistance that included attacks on soldiers and ultimately suicide bombings, a tactic implemented in 1994. Given the large population of Palestinians who lived in Kuwait, as Hamas grew in reputation (both for its provision of social services and its military resistance) Mash'al was able to draw in Hamas supporters in the diaspora.

Following the Iraqi invasion of Kuwait in August 1990 and the first Gulf War in 1991, hundreds of thousands of Palestinians either fled or were expelled from Kuwait after Arafat cast PLO support for Iraq. From the outset of the invasion, Arafat voted against a resolution calling on Iraq to withdraw from Kuwait in the Arab League, and supported SADDAM HUSSEIN because of promises Hussein made to liberate Palestine. Following the liberation of Kuwait from the Iraqi occupiers, the Kuwai-

tis punished all Palestinians (estimated at 400,000) by expelling them or pressuring them to leave and ending all funding and support for the PLO. Mash'al took up residence in Jordan (as did most of those expelled) and became the head of the Hamas office in Amman. As such, he was in charge of international fund-raising for Hamas and he built relationships in other countries, such as Syria and Iran. Donations and money were sent from this office

RESISTANCE IS A RIGHT WE WILL NOT GIVE UP

We will not recognize the legitimacy of occupation, but that does not mean that we will not deal with reality; we accepted the truce for some time in the past. We will not give up our principles; we are ready to deal with any agreement that does not harm or affect our rights and constants. Oslo Accord is buried and our reference now is the Cairo Agreement with all Palestinian factions and President [Mahmud] Abbas. Hamas knows this phase and believes in transition and moderation and does not impose its ideas on anyone. Christians voted for us and one Christian ran as independent and was supported by us; we will not impose the Shari'a [Islamic law] on anyone. Competence and honesty will be the basis of forming the government. We believe in transition and reality but the map of Palestine does not change. [...] Resistance is a legitimate right; our presence in the PLC [Palestine Legislative Council] will reinforce the legitimacy of resistance. With regards to targeting civilians, we said it before, if they stop targeting our civilians, we will do likewise. Resistance is a right we will not give up. Israel is not offering anything; they even did not negotiate with a government formed by Abu Mazin [Mahmud Abbas]. So let us first rearrange our internal front first. No Israeli official who can guarantee security alongside occupation; so they have to decide: Either occupation or security. the Palestinian people are ready to fight for ages and ages. No peace or security with occupation. I call on the EU [European Union] not to link itself to the U.S. and Israeli positions. Europe knows the region more than them so it can play a bigger role. Calm ended by the end of 2005. Today, the Palestinian people are in the process of reforming and rebuilding the PLO. The calm is part of the tactics but it will stay as part of the resistance.

KHALED MASH'AL IN A PRESS CONFERENCE IN DAMASCUS FOLLOWING THE ELECTION OF HAMAS TO THE MAJORITY OF PALESTINIAN LEGISLATIVE COUNCIL SEATS. 28 JANUARY 2006.

to the West Bank and Gaza for the social welfare programs run by Hamas, although the United States, Israel, and countries in the European Union (EU) believe that such donations were also used to fund the military resistance, including suicide bombings and attacks on Israeli civilians. Undoubtedly both took place. In January 1995 Hamas was declared a terrorist organization by the United States, and President Bill Clinton issued Executive Order No. 12947, making it a felony to raise or transfer funds to designated terrorist groups or their front organizations.

In a notorious incident that brought Mash'al to the attention of the world, Israel tried to assassinate him in September 1997. The government of Israel (under the leadership of Prime Minister BINYAMIN NETANYAHU) described Mash'al as the preeminent figure in Hamas and responsible for the murder of innocent Israeli civilians. Israeli Mossad (secret service) agents carrying Canadian passports entered Jordan and poisoned Mash'al on the street by injecting him in the ear with a toxic substance. Two of the men were captured and Jordan's king, HUSSEIN BIN TALAL, demanded that Israel provide an antidote for the poison, a demand to which initially Netanyahu refused. Because Jordan and Israel had signed a peace agreement in 1994, initiating full diplomatic relations after forty-six years of war and uneasy truces, the Israeli actions on Jordanian soil were considered a serious breach of trust. The peace agreement between them had been brokered by Clinton, who intervened in the Mash'al case and forced Netanyahu to provide the antidote. In the deal, Jordan exchanged the two arrested agents for the imprisoned spiritual leader of Hamas, Shaykh AHMAD YASIN among others.

As part of a crackdown on Hamas in 1999 in Jordan, Mash'al and three other Hamas members were imprisoned and then expelled from Jordan, perhaps because of U.S. pressure in the face of a visit of U.S. secretary of state Madeleine Albright to Jordan. Mash'al moved to Qatar, and then Syria in 2001. The Hamas Political Bureau is now based in Syria, and Mash'al speaks regularly to the press from Damascus. Following the assassination of Yasin in 2004, and then his successor Abd al-Aziz al-Rantisi the following month, Mash'al has been described as the political leader of Hamas and the head of Hamas in Syria.

THE WORLD'S PERSPECTIVE

The United States, Israel, Japan, Canada, and the EU states label Hamas a terrorist organization, and Jordan has banned the movement. Australia and the United Kingdom hold the same position, but only for the Izz al-Din al-Qassam movement, the armed military wing of Hamas. Mash'al is seen certainly as the leader of this movement outside of Palestine and thus is constantly under threat of assassination. The Arab and Muslim world do not share this view of Hamas and Mash'al, and he regularly travels in the Middle East region and speaks publicly.

Following the election of Hamas in the 2006 Palestine Legislative Council elections and their assumption of governmental control in March 2006, funding to the Palestinian Authority (PA) was cut by the United States, Japan, the EU, and Israel (which owes the PA some US$60 million per month that it collects in taxes and customs duties). Hamas has gone to others in states such as Iran and Saudi Arabia for funding for the running of the government, including paying salaries of all government employees, teachers, and health-care workers. Emergency measures were also put in place by United Nations, EU, and U.S. organizations to help pay salaries and alleviate the extreme levels of poverty that have resulted from the economic difficulties and lack of salaries and services.

LEGACY

Mash'al is still fairly new on the Palestinian political scene and is considered a fiery orator. He supports participation in elections while continuing violent struggle for liberation.

> Today we are facing a political structure that used to be based on Oslo—true, it resulted from Oslo—but today this structure represents a new reality in the Palestinian scene. The Palestinian people, with its will, its sacrifice, its Intifada, are creating something new, on which this Legislative Council is based. That's why Hamas and the other forces are joining the Legislative Council on the basis of continued resistance, adhering to the weapons of the resistance, adhering to the Palestinian rights, to rectifying internal Palestinian affairs, to reform, to fighting corruption—this is our platform, and we do not base ourselves on Oslo. Restricting ourselves to the option of negotiations and politics alone, without the resistance, will make the enemy view us with more contempt, rather than with respect. On the other hand, the logic underlying the revolutions of all nations was to maintain a political process alongside resistance. (Interview, "Al-Jazeera TV, 23 January 2006)

BIBLIOGRAPHY
Mash'al, Khalid. Interview by Rashid Khalidi after 2006 elections. Available from http://www.cfr.org.

Rochelle Anne Davis

MASRI, MAI
(1959–)

Masri is a Palestinian filmmaker, director, and producer.

PERSONAL HISTORY

Masri was born in Jordan in 1959 to an American mother from Texas and a father from a noted Muslim

BIOGRAPHICAL HIGHLIGHTS

Name: Mai Masri

Birth: 1959, Jordan

Family: Husband: Jean Khalil Chamoun; two daughters

Nationality: Jordanian, American

Education: B.A. (film), San Francisco State University, 1981

PERSONAL CHRONOLOGY:

• **1983:** Releases *Under the Rubble*

• **1998:** Wins Best Director and Best Camera awards at the Arab Screen Festival in London for *Children of Shatila*

• **2000:** *In the City of Shadows* wins the Cannes Junior Award

• **2002:** *Frontiers of Dreams and Fears* receives fourteen awards

Palestinian family from the West Bank city of Nablus. She developed an interest in film and photography during her high school years in Beirut, traveling to the United States to pursue her university education in 1977, where she received her bachelor's degree in film from San Francisco State University in 1981.

INFLUENCES AND CONTRIBUTIONS

Masri has directed and produced several award-winning films that provide a fine-grained view of women's and children's lives in situations marked by conflict, uncertainty, and crisis, including *Children of Fire* (1990) and *Children of Shatila* (1998). During the later years of the Lebanese Civil War, Masri and her husband, Lebanese filmmaker and producer Jean Khalil Chamoun, filmed Lebanese and Palestinian civilians attempting to live and work under bombardments in Beirut and in South Lebanon, turning their copious footage of the war years into award-winning films such as *Under the Rubble* (1983), *Wild Flowers* (1987), *War Generation–Beirut* (1989), and *Suspended Dreams* (1992). All of these films show the costs of war and displacement, but also the strength of the human spirit and the importance of creative expression in the midst of large-scale destruction. In 1995 Masri directed a portrait of HANAN MIKHA'IL ASHRAWI for BBC television, titled *A Woman of Her Time*. She has

also produced *Hostage of Time* (1994) and the feature film *In the Shadows of the City* (2000).

Masri currently lives in Beirut with her husband and their two daughters. She and Chamoun established Nour Productions.

THE WORLD'S PERSPECTIVE

Masri's films have been broadcast in the Arab world, Europe, the United Kingdom, and North America and have received ten international awards, including Best Documentary at the Institut du Monde Arabe Film Festival in Paris. *Children of Shatila* won Best Director and Best Camera awards at the Arab Screen Festival in London in 1998. *In the City of Shadows* won the Cannes Junior Award in 2000. In 2002, *Frontiers of Dreams and Fears* received fourteen awards including First Prize at the Arab World Academy in Paris; First Prize at the al-Isma'ilyiya International Festival in Egypt; First Prize of Women's Movies festival in Turin; and jury's special award at the Beirut Movie Festival.

LEGACY

While still at work, Masri will be remembered as an important Palestinian filmmaker, particularly in the realm of documentaries.

BIBLIOGRAPHY

Privett, Ray. "The Four Corners of the Earth: Mai Masri on *Children of Shatila*." Facets Multimedia. Available from http://www.facets.org.

Laurie King-Irani
updated by Michael R. Fischbach

MASRI, MUNIB AL-
(1934–)

Palestinian businessman Munib Rashid al-Masri has been described as the wealthiest person in the Palestinian territories. He has played a key role in economic development in the Palestinian Authority and was a close confidant of Palestinian leader YASIR ARAFAT.

PERSONAL HISTORY

Al-Masri was born in Nablus in mandatory Palestine, in 1934. He hailed from a prominent Sunni Muslim family in the city, one whose prominence stemmed from its commercial activities and, during the period of Jordanian control of the West Bank (1948–1967), its positions in government as well. Masri traveled to the United States and graduated from the University of Texas in 1955 with

BIOGRAPHICAL HIGHLIGHTS

∎

Name: Munib al-Masri

Birth: 1934, Nablus, mandatory Palestine

Family: Wife, Angela (American); six children

Nationality: Palestinian

Education: B.S. (petroleum geology), University of Texas, 1955; M.A. (geology and government), Sul Ross State University, Texas, 1956

PERSONAL CHRONOLOGY:

- **1956:** Begins working for Phillips Petroleum Company
- **1963:** Heads Phillips operations in Algeria
- **1965:** Heads Phillips operations throughout the Middle East
- **1970:** Appointed minister of public works for the Jordanian government
- **1971:** Establishes EDGO
- **1994:** Returns to Nablus after establishment of the Palestinian Authority (PA)
- **2003:** Asked by Yasir Arafat to become PA prime minister

a bachelor's degree in petroleum geology, and with an M.A. in geology and government from Sul Ross State University in Texas in 1956.

Masri returned to the Middle East in 1956 and began working with the Phillips Petroleum Company. In 1971 he also established his own engineering and geological services company, which later became known as the Engineering and Development Group (EDGO). In 1963, Masri became head of Phillips operations in Algeria and in 1965 rose to Phillips's chief of operations for the entire Middle East. He also briefly served as minister of public works for the Jordanian government from 1970 to 1971, helping build and repair roads and water infrastructures in Jordan. In 1994 he returned to Nablus from Jordan after the establishment of the Palestinian Authority (PA).

INFLUENCES AND CONTRIBUTIONS

Masri went on to become one of the wealthiest Palestinian businessmen of the second half of the twentieth century, and one who played an important political role within Palestinian politics. He has been particularly

important in the realm of economic development and investment in the PA, the Palestinian government established in parts of Gaza and the West Bank in 1994 as a result of the Israeli-Palestinian peace process. In fact, Masri is the second-largest employer in the PA, after the government itself. His Palestinian Development and Investment Company (PADICO), which he directs, has approximately 35,000 employees, and the Palestine Telecommunications Corporation (PALTEL) employs another 12,000. In 1997 Masri established a Palestinian stock market in Nablus. He also is deputy chairman of the Palestine Investment Fund, and sits on the board of the Amman-based Arab Bank.

He also has wielded an important political role, in large part through his friendship with the late Arafat, the longtime chairman of the Fatah movement and the Palestine Liberation Organization (PLO). Masri first met Arafat in Algeria in 1963 when Masri worked for Phillips Petroleum there. They remained friends for years. While Masri was a Jordanian cabinet minister in September 1970 he tried to arrange for a meeting between Arafat and Jordan's king, HUSSEIN BIN TALAL, during the bitter fighting between the PLO and the Jordanian army. Arafat refused. Masri remained an important friend and sat on the PLO central council. He was so important to Arafat that the Palestinian leader asked him to become prime minister of the PA when he first created the post in 2003. This time it was Masri who refused. Masri also visited Arafat frequently in the months prior to his death, even giving the ailing leader his medicine and flying to the French military hospital near Paris where Arafat spent his final days.

Shortly after Arafat's death in November 2004, various Fatah members approached Masri and asked him to consider running for PA president. There were reports in 2006 that the Jordanian and Egyptians governments favored getting rid of the Hamas-led PA government, and appointing one of two people to become the new prime minister. One of the names suggested was Masri's. He also was a member of the board of directors of the Palestinian National Fund, the PLO's financial arm.

Masri also has involved himself in various philanthropic and other public affairs. He helped establish the college of engineering and technology at al-Najah National University in Nablus, as well as the Nablus Rehabilitation Committee (to help rebuild the city after the destruction wreaked upon it during the al-Aqsa intifada that began in 2000). He sits on the board of trustees of the American University of Beirut, helped establish the al-Quds University Investment Fund, and was the first treasurer of the Geneva-based Palestinian Welfare Association.

THE WORLD'S PERSPECTIVE

Masri is well known in Palestinian and Middle Eastern business circles as one of the wealthiest and most politically important Palestinian businessmen. He also is credited as someone who made his fortunes outside Palestine but returned after the peace process produced a Palestinian government in an attempt to use his wealth and business skills to develop the area's economy. Masri has not always grabbed the headlines in the way that Palestinian political leaders do, and thus remains unknown to many outside the Middle East. But no one can minimize his importance, particularly as a well-connected Palestinian moderate whose name continues to be floated as a possible leader for the PA.

LEGACY

For all his business and philanthropic projects over the decades, Masri likely will be remembered most for the political and economic role he played in the consolidation of Palestinian self-rule in the West Bank and Gaza after the 1993 Oslo Accord signed between Israel and the PLO.

BIBLIOGRAPHY

Orme, William A., Jr. "Big Palestinian Holding Company Dominates Development in the West Bank." *New York Times* (6 May 1999).

Shaked, Ronny. "The Palestinian Rothschild." YnetNews. Updated 27 July 2006. Available from http://www.ynetnews.com.

Urquhard, Conal. "A Man for All Factions." *Guardian* (10 November 2006). Available from http://www.guardian.co.uk.

Michael R. Fischbach

BIOGRAPHICAL HIGHLIGHTS

Name: Salva Kiir Mayardit

Birth: 1951, Qoqrial Town, Bahr al-Ghazzal province, Sudan

Family: Married; children

Nationality: Sudanese

Education: Elementary school

PERSONAL CHRONOLOGY:

- **Late 1960s:** Joins Anyanya rebellion against Sudanese government during first Sudanese civil war
- **1972:** Enters Sudanese army after end of first civil war
- **1983:** Defects from army, helps form Sudan People's Liberation Movement (SPLM)
- **1984:** Leads Sudan People's Liberation Army forces in battle that captures the town of Pashala from government
- **1994:** Elected deputy leader of SPLM
- **2005:** Brokers Comprehensive Peace Agreement between SPLM and Sudanese government in January; becomes vice president of Autonomous Government of South Sudan; takes over as president of South Sudan government upon death of John Garang in July; August, sworn in as first vice president of Sudan

---

MAYARDIT, SALVA KIIR
(1951–)

A founding member of the Sudan People's Liberation Army, Salva Kiir Mayardit (also known simply as Salva Kiir) is the first vice president of Sudan and president of the Autonomous Government of South Sudan.

PERSONAL HISTORY

Mayardit was born in 1951 in Qoqrial (also Gogrial) Town, in southern Sudan's Bahr al-Ghazzal province. He was born to the Awan clan of the main southern Sudanese tribe, the Dinka. He attended the Kojok Primary School and eventually, in the late 1960s, joined the Anyanya movement, the antigovernment rebellion of black African animist and Christian forces in southern Sudan against the Muslim Arab-dominated central Sudanese government in the north during the first Sudanese civil war. After the war ended in 1972, Mayardit joined the Sudanese army as an enlisted man.

INFLUENCES AND CONTRIBUTIONS

In 1983, by which time he had risen to the rank of captain, Mayardit and fellow southern officer, John Garang de Mabior, defected from the Sudanese army and renewed the southern struggle against the government. Together they formed the Sudan People's Liberation Movement (SPLM) along with about a dozen others, and Mayardit ended up heading its military wing, the Sudan People's Liberation Army (SPLA). He acquitted himself well during a battle in which SPLA forces captured the town of Pashala from government forces in 1984, and long was remembered for his actions thereafter. Having been an intelligence officer in the Sudanese army, he became the intelligence chief of the SPLA. At the first SPLM general conference in April 1994, Mayardit was elected Garang's deputy in the movement. Despite their long association with one another, he eventually disagreed with Garang over whether the SPLM should push for total southern independence, or merely autonomy within a federal Sudanese system. He also grew critical of Garang's monopolization of power with the SPLM.

As an SPLM negotiator—he is fluent in Dinka, Arabic, and English, and speaks some Kiswahili—Mayardit represented the movement in a number of important negotiations. He signed the Shagdom Agreement with the northern Umma Party in December 1994, and the Machakos Protocol with the central government in July 2002. He also helped broker the Comprehensive Peace Agreement with the government that ended the second civil war in January 2005. As a result, he was promoted to major general in the SPLA. The charismatic Garang became first vice president of Sudan and president of the newly created Autonomous Government of South Sudan. Mayardit became deputy head of the autonomous government. After only six months in office, Garang died in the crash of a Ugandan government helicopter in southern Sudan on 30 July 2005. The SPLM leadership chose Mayardit to replace him, and he was sworn in as vice president on 11 August 2005.

THE WORLD'S PERSPECTIVE

Mayardit is well known by northern politicians, having served as the SPLM's main negotiator over the years. He is extremely popular among southerners by virtue of his experience, his background as a Dinka from the dominant Qoqrial clan, and because he favors eventual southern independence after the six-year transition period spelled out in the Comprehensive Peace Agreement—in contrast to Garang, who had wanted an autonomous southern government within a federal Sudanese system.

LEGACY

It is too soon to evaluate Mayardit's long-term legacy. But already his contributions to the southern Sudanese movement are many, and his importance to the armed struggle against the central Sudanese government, the peace process, and the consolidation of the post-2005 power-sharing arrangement have earned him a place in the history of southern Sudan.

BIBLIOGRAPHY
Ngala, Joseph. "The Man Expected to Fit into Garang's Shoes." *Standard* (3 August 2005). Available from http://www.eastandard.net/.

"Profile: Salva Kiir." BBC. 2 August 2005. Available from http://news.bbc.co.uk/2/hi/africa/4738295.stm.

Raslan, Hani. "Salva Kiir: From the Battlefield to the Presidential Palace." Center for Strategic and Political Studies. 8 August 2005. Available from http://www.ahram.org.eg/.

Michael R. Fischbach

MEDDEB, ABDELWAHHAB
(1946–)

Abdelwahhab Meddeb is a Tunisian-born French novelist, poet, and essayist. He is the author of about twenty books, including *Matière des oiseaux* (2001; Matter of birds), a collection of poems, for which he received the Max-Jacob Prize in 2002; *La Maladie de l'Islam* (2002; *The Malady of Islam*, 2003) for which he won the François-Mauriac Prize the same year; and *Contre-prêches: Chroniques* (2006; Counter-preaching: chronicles), which earned him the

Abdelwahhab Meddeb. © ERIC FOUGERE/VIP IMAGES/CORBIS.

BIOGRAPHICAL HIGHLIGHTS

Name: Abdelwahhab Meddeb

Birth: 1946, Tunis, Tunisia

Family: Married; one child

Nationality: French (originally Tunisian)

Education: B.A. and M.A., literature and art history, University of Paris IV (Sorbonne); Ph.D, literature and art history, University of Aix-Marseilles

PERSONAL CHRONOLOGY:
- **1973–1974:** Editor, Les Editions du Seuil
- **1974–1988:** Editor, Les Editions Sindbad
- **1989–1990:** Visiting professor, University of Geneva
- **1993–1994:** Visiting professor, Yale University
- **1997–present:** Hosts radio program *Culture d'Islam* (Islamic culture), France Culture network; professor, University Paris X (Nanterre)

Benjamin Fondane International Prize for Francophonie in 2007.

PERSONAL HISTORY

Meddeb was born in Tunis in 1946 and is now a French citizen. After studying literature and art history at the University of Paris IV-La Sorbonne and the University of Aix-Marseilles, he taught francophone literature as a visiting professor at the University of Geneva (1989–1990) and Yale (1993–1994). Currently he teaches comparative literature at the University of Paris X-Nanterre. He has been on the editorial board of Les Editions de Sinbad and Les Editions du Seuil. He has also served as editor of the journals *Dédale* and *Intersignes* (1991–1994). Since 1997 he has hosted a Sunday radio program, *Culture d'Islam* (Islamic culture), on the France Culture network.

INFLUENCES AND CONTRIBUTIONS

The work of Meddeb, like that of most postcolonial Maghrebi writers, crosses genres and disciplines. Meddeb's conception of literature moves beyond the Western cult of self-referentiality and immanence to link the text to the outside world. Literature becomes both a scriptural and a political practice. In *Contre-prêches*, he states that "poetry, like philosophy, like theology, like the artistic gesture at the origin of painting and sculpture, is always

political." Here, political literature has nothing to do with the committed literature of the 1950s and 1960s. It does not adhere to a specific ideology or motto, but rather belongs to what Meddeb calls *archipolitique* (archepolitics): "the closeness of that which is far away, which the poet reaches when he or she breaks the link with events" (*Contre-prêches*, p. 156). According to Meddeb, politics is part of literary representation when narration stops reproducing reality and factual events, when it renders referents opaque, opens itself to alterity, and promotes a dialogue between languages and cultures.

Like ABDEL KEBIR KHATIBI, TAHAR BEN JELLOUN, ASSIA DJEBAR, and many other Maghrebi postcolonial writers, Meddeb writes between genres and disciplines and in form and content exploits the resources of interculturality. *Talismano* and *Phantasia* are polymorphic texts written at the intersection of the novel, the tale, the fable, poetry, autobiography, and the essay. They also mix Western and non-Western generic pratices, include cultural referents specific to Maghrebi and Muslim cultures, and exploit multilinguism. Meddeb even inserts quotations in various languages, including Italian, German, hieroglyphics, Chinese, Japanese, Arabic, Hebrew, and Hindi. In *Phantasia* he states, "The myth of Babel tells how languages multiplied themselves to divide men and pit them against one another. Separation of languages brings war" (p. 82). Meddeb's novels break with linearity and factual events in an ostensible manner. They exploit literary devices that move away from Western classical aesthetics and structural poetics. Borrowing from the French New Novel, they transform its writing by introducing cultural references specific to the Maghreb and by mixing it with parabolic and allegorical Sufi writing as well.

Talismano is a complex nomadic and heterogeneous novel in which a first-person narrator imagines strolling through the Tunisian medina of his childhood. Walking and wandering are metaphors of the quest for identity, of the inscription of the body into writing, and of writing itself. This novel denounces colonial universalism and its continuation through postcolonial regimes that deny the existence of a long tradition of cultural diversity in the Maghreb. It also criticizes the theological notion of Oneness (*l'Un*) that Muslim academic institutions such as al-Azhar, al-Qayrawan, and Zituna emphasize in their teaching. Yet this novel does not exclusively focus on the denunciation of political and religious dogmatism in colonial and postcolonial contexts. Rather, its political dimension appears more in its modes of representation than in its thematics. The discontinuous structure of the novel as well as the broad use of parataxis, agrammatical punctuation, and allegorical representation are a plea for the recognition of the cultural diversity of the Maghreb:

GOD MADE CLEAR... THE PATH THAT LEADS TO FAITH

●

God did not construct the question of faith on force (*ijbar*) and violence (*qasar*), but based on the possibility of persuasion (*tamakun*) and free choice (*ikhtiyar*). God made clear and obvious the path that leads to faith. When all the ways to convince are exhausted in the Book, only coercion remains to lead the hesitant to the truth. But recourse to constraint is unacceptable: the use of violence annuls the testing (*imtihan*) and effort prompted by assiduous application (*taklif*) of the rules.

ABDELWAHHAB MEDDEB, *THE MALADY OF ISLAM*, P. 191.

the latter is part of the West—"Maghreb" literally means "where the sun sets"—and also Arabic and Berber.

Phantasia is another polymorphic novel that explores the relationship between writing and the body. A first-person narrator also strolls in a city, but this time it is Paris. In this text, strolling in the Parisian landscape becomes the pretext for investigating the manipulation of historical and collective memory in colonial and postcolonial contexts, as well as for questioning both Western and Islamic genealogies. In line here with Walter Benjamin's explorations of Paris, in *Phantasia* Meddeb celebrates modernity. He also pays homage to Ibn Arabi and the Sufist tradition. This tradition, in his view, is too often forgotten in the Islamic community due to its praise of free-thinking (*al-ra'y*), love, sensuality, and the body, and whose traces, he argues, could very well resonate as far as the paintings of Henri Matisse, Piet Mondrian, and Kazimir Malevich.

Like most Maghrebi postcolonial writers, postmodern historians, and deconstructionists, Meddeb attests that the writing of history is subject to oblivion and preclusion. One can access historical, collective, and personal memories only as trace and difference. This is even truer in the Maghreb, a region whose history as well as cultural and linguistic diversity have long suffered the stigmas of colonization. Yet literature for Meddeb is always political and functions as a monument that keeps memory traces readable. Thus *Phantasia* aims to reconcile the West and the Maghreb with their past, and their threefold Judeo-Christian-Islamic inheritance.

With the rise of Islamic fundamentalism, Meddeb has become increasingly involved in the denunciation and the study of the origins of Islamic fundamentalism (in French, *Islamisme* [Islamism] or *Intégrisme* [Integ-

rism]) or what the French historian Olivier Roy calls "neofundamentalism", modern religious fanaticism and the call for jihad. His books *La Maladie de l'Islam* and *Contre-prêches* further explore political issues he had previously raised in his literary work, in particular the existence of a link between fanaticism, violence, and historical or cultural amnesia.

In *La Maladie de l'Islam*, Meddeb argues that Islamic fundamentalism, the "malady of Islam," is a product of both Western and Islamic cultural hegemonies and intolerance. By the same token, referring to the West, Voltaire, and Thomas Mann, Meddeb states that intolerance was the "malady" of Catholicism and Nazism that of Germany. He thus presents the conjuncture of two forms of intolerance. The exclusion of Islam from the West as well as literal and deviant readings of the Qur'an have triggered the rise of religious fanaticism within and outside the *umma* (the community of Muslims). Meddeb also agrees with Roy that diaspora, deterritorialization, the media, the Internet, and globalization have contributed to the construction of a mythic and sectarian Islam. As Roy also argues, such an Islam is disconnected from its original territory and has lost its original traditions and cultures. Yet Meddeb does not distinguish between a good and a bad Islam. Where Roy sees in neofundamentalism and present-day Salafism a form of contemporary Westernized militancy, based solely on faith and moral issues yet indifferent to social concerns—akin to that of born-again Christians—Meddeb traces the roots of Islamic fundamentalism far back: Medina in the seventh century, Baghdad in the ninth century and the long reign of the Abbasids (a Sunni Muslim dynasty), the development of Saudi Wahhabism, and the doctrine of Ibn Hanbal, the eight-century founder of the Hanbali school of Islamic law.

Meddeb sees in Ibn Taymiyya, a fourteenth-century radical disciple of Ibn Hanbal, especially in his call for jihad and his manifesto on Divine Law and corporeal punishment (flagellation for wine drinkers, stoning for adulterous women, amputation of hands and feet for robbers), the early symptoms of the "malady of Islam." He holds that the crisis following Crusader and Mongol offensives (twelfth and thirteenth centuries), the "Europeanization" of the world during colonial times, and the present expansion of the "Americanization of the world" have amplified the rise of Islamic fundamentalism. He also contends that without the discovery of oil and without petrodollars, Saudi Arabia Wahhabi ideology would probably have had little impact.

His latest book, *Contre-prêches*, is the compilation of a series of 115 very short essays or chronicles on a variety of topics. Among them are Islam, Iraq, the fall of dictators, religious fanaticism and the reading of natural disasters, the war of images, human sacrifice in Islam, the question of the veil, multiculturalism, and anti-Semitism. Some of these texts began as radio broadcasts in France, Morocco, and Tunisia.

As in *La Maladie de l'Islam*, Meddeb insists on the dangers of cultural amnesia, in particular the illusory attempts of the West to erase traces of cultural exchange between itself and Islamic civilization prior to the development of capitalism. He takes the example of the cities of Seville and Grenada as sites of resistance to cultural amnesia. In his view, the Alcazar and its *mudejar* art demonstrate a will to "adapt Islamic architectural discourse to a Christian destiny" (*Contre-prêches*, p. 100). The Alhambra and the Puerta d'Elvira also testify to the place that Arabic and Islamic memory holds in Western history even though it remains spectral, in a state of trace or haunting as in Louis Aragon's *Fou d'Elsa* or Federico García Lorca's ghostly "Islamic forest" (p. 416). *Contre-prêches* continues Meddeb's critique of Wahhabi Islam and the denunciation of intolerance and fanaticism. Making use of the short text and the radio speech format, Meddeb does not hesitate to take a polemical and provocative tone. Although diversity is part of every culture including that of Europe, Meddeb argues that multiculturalism has opened the door to Islamist fanaticism, that it has led to such events as the murder of the Dutch filmmaker Theo van Gogh.

Meddeb has strong reservations about the role that images play nowadays in our societies, yet he believes in the positive power of images. He condemns the war of images as displayed both by Western and non-Western media, especially regarding the Abu Ghraib prisoner abuse photos and the status of the situation and execution of hostages in Iraq, the display of human sacrifice as contrary to Islam (the sacrifice of Abraham's son is symbolic), and the interpretation of Hurricane Katrina and the 2004 tsunami as proof of God's punishment. Yet he welcomes the way that the Western media exploited SADDAM HUSSEIN's pitiful image and showcased his fall when he was dug out of his dark hole. He also states that Islam does not strictly condemn iconography, but rather its social use: "the image can exist in itself but cannot constitute a socially shared event." In this sense, Ibn Arabi's notion of a "mental icon" that cannot be shared "recuperates Christian iconography" (p. 124).

On the issue of the veil, Meddeb takes a clear and radical stance: He points out that he comes from a country where women took off their veils and that Arabic satellite TV "participates in its [the veil's] diffusion by exploiting a sense of guilt" (p. 265). As he understands it, the veil is a symbol of inequality between men and women; its return as the *hijab* is the sign of "the polemical return of the moral order" (p. 476) and of the "evacuation of Eros from Islamic society" (p. 477).

Meddeb also denounces anti-Semitism in both the Western and the Muslim worlds. He notes that are two kinds of anti-Semitism: Western anti-Semitism, which is rooted in the fantasy of a Jewish conspiracy to take over and rule the world, and Islamic anti-Semitism, which is rooted in the oblivion of the massacre of the Jews in Medina under the leadership of the prophet Muhammad. He finds that the latter should be addressed in order to distinguish it from European anti-Semitism.

THE WORLD'S PERSPECTIVE

Meddeb writes in French and is considered in France to be one of the leading authorities on the culture of Islam. The radio program *Culture d'Islam* aims to demystify the simplistic and caricatural image of an Islam dominated by fundamentalism often displayed in the media. Meddeb's work addresses French and francophone readers of all religious beliefs and cultural origins, and has reached well beyond the Western world and the Maghreb. *La Maladie de l'Islam* has generated a worldwide interest and has been translated into English, Arabic, German, Italian, Portuguese, Spanish, Bosnian, and Turkish. Meddeb's work has garnered mixed reactions. Because he has made efforts to open the Muslim world to classical Europe and the Enlightenment, and criticized Americanization along with Wahhabi and Egyptian fundamentalism, he has been perceived as both pro-Western and anti-American.

LEGACY

It may be too early to speak of Meddeb's legacy. His work has been read as that of a postcolonial writer of great talent in the same vein as Khatibi, Ben Jelloun, or Djebar. His interest in Islam, in Sufism, in the long tradition of cultural diversity in the Maghreb, his gestures at reconciling Europe and the Muslim world with their pasts, and finally his fight against political dogmatism and religious fanaticism in all cultures will continue to have an impact over the years and throughout the world.

BIBLIOGRAPHY

WORKS BY MEDDEB

Talismano (1979)

Phantasia (1987; Fantasia)

Tombeau d'Ibn Arabi (1987; The tomb of Ibn Arabi)

Aya dans les villes (1999; Aya in the cities)

Matière des oiseaux (2001; Matter of birds)

La Maladie de l'Islam (2002; The Malady of Islam, 2003)

Face à l'Islam (2004; Facing Islam)

Contre-prêches: Chroniques (2006; Counter-preaching: chronicles)

OTHER SOURCE

Memmes, Abdallah. *Littérature maghrébine de langue française: Signifiance et Interculturalité*. Rabat: Editions Okad, 1992.

Dominique D. Fisher

MERNISSI, FATIMA
(1940–)

Fatima Mernissi is a world-renowned Moroccan sociologist who has written numerous books on the misogynistic way women are viewed in the Middle East and elsewhere. Mernissi has focused her career on expanding the ideas and general topics broached first in her dissertation. She has gained prominence in part by critiquing key concepts, such as the veil and the seclusion of women from public space and participation in the public sphere, which conservative elements in many Islamic societies consider fundamental to Islamic morality.

PERSONAL HISTORY

Mernissi was born in 1940 in Fez, Morocco. She studied at length in Qur'anic schools as well as at state schools and received a bachelor's degree in political science from Muhammad V University in Rabat. She went on a fellowship to France to study at the Sorbonne but soon moved on to Brandeis University in the United States, where she received a Ph.D. in sociology (1973) with a thesis titled "Effects of Modernization on the Male-Female Dynamics in a Muslim Society." After her dissertation, Mernissi joined the faculty at the University of Rabat, and in 1980 began teaching at Muhammad V University in Rabat. As of 2007, she was a professor there in the Depart-

Fatima Mernissi. © HOUBAIS MUSTAFA/EPA/CORBIS.

BIOGRAPHICAL HIGHLIGHTS

Name: Fatima Mernissi

Birth: 1940, Fez, Morocco

Nationality: Moroccan

Education: B.A. (politics), Muhammad V University, Rabat; Ph.D. (sociology), Brandeis University, 1973

PERSONAL CHRONOLOGY:

- **1973:** Teaches at the University of Rabat
- **1975:** Publishes *Beyond the Veil: Male-Female Dynamics in a Modern Muslim Society*
- **1980:** Begins teaching at Muhammad V University
- **1991:** Publishes *The Veil and the Male Elite: A Feminist Interpretation of Women's Rights in Islam*
- **1992:** Publishes *Islam and Democracy: Fear of the Modern World*
- **1993:** Publishes *The Forgotten Queens of Islam*
- **2000:** Publishes *Scheherezade Goes West*
- **2003:** Receives Prince of Asturias Award in Spain; receives Erasmus Prize in the Netherlands

---

ment of Sociology. Since 1973, she has published numerous books in French, English, and Arabic on women in the Islamic world.

Mernissi is deliberately provocative in the hope of effecting social change. The controversial aspect of her work derives both from a deep critique of received ideas and a polemical approach in her assessment that outrages the more conservative elements in society and even perturbs numerous relatively moderate academics. Mernissi does, however, make an effort to document examples of times and places in which women were held in high regard in the Middle East, in order to argue implicitly for the nonessential character of the chauvinism she critiques (in her *The Forgotten Queens of Islam*, 1993). The charge that she is overly influenced by Western ideas is also hard to support, given her general critique of chauvinism and the critique she makes of both so-called Orientalist misunderstandings of the Middle East and Western misunderstandings of women in particular (see her *Scheherazade Goes West*, 2001).

The conservative Muslim view of the veil and the head covering in general (the *hijab*) is that female dress must contribute to modesty and that modesty is essential to feminine morality. This is combined with a conviction that female hair is intensely erotic by nature, not as culturally constructed; that men, being weak, need to be protected from this severe temptation; and that women must therefore cover their hair. Historians of Europe have amply documented the changing nature of the erotic, as viewed from a male perspective, and although a few Westerners still find female hair intensely erotic those who do are generally thought of as more than a little depraved. This discussion has not resonated in the Islamic world where conservatives essentialize female eroticism and argue for the implementation of countermeasures that would be effective at all times and in all public places. Mernissi's first book, *Beyond the Veil: Male-Female Dynamics in a Modern Muslim Society* (1975; a reworking of her dissertation), argues that the primary goal should be to eliminate the physical and symbolic exploitation of women, and that traditional attitudes need to change both because they damage the solidarity of the husband-wife dyad by focusing, implicitly, on sexuality, and because they divert attention from the need for change. She argues, however, that fragile Islamic states will be easier to influence than entrenched Western ones and that, whereas the latter will allow women's rights, it will be a long time before they do anything to prevent the symbolic exploitation of women's bodies.

This early stance was thus neither wholeheartedly pro-Western nor, in fact, critical of Islamic values promoting modesty over overt sexuality. Mernissi's more subtle position has been focused on critiquing the reduction of women to sexual objects both in the Middle East and in the West. A major strand of feminism in the West has responded to patriarchal notions not by a critique of any attempt to base identity on gender but by promoting a multitude of other gender roles as equal bases for identity construction. This argument for gender equality has an inescapable emphasis on sexuality as important to identity that fits poorly with Mernissi's de-emphasis on the essential sexuality of women and promotion of the concept that women, similar to men, are much more than sexual beings.

INFLUENCES AND CONTRIBUTIONS

One of Mernissi's more analytical works, *The Veil and the Male Elite: A Feminist Interpretation of Women's Rights in Islam* (1991), provides an analysis of a few elements of the Islamic tradition, focusing on misogynistic elements. She attributes this misogyny to biased misinterpretations, fabrication of hadith (an account of the sayings or actions of the prophet Muhammad), and willful reliance on authorities famed for their unreliability (such as Abu Hurayra). She argues that veiling and other female-restrictive practices contradict and go against the true revelation and practice of Muhammad. She claims they are central pieces of a misogynistic tradition reflect-

---

THE TONGUE OF CITIZENS IS MULTIFUNCTIONAL

"Two scenes, two calendars, two identities—sovereign citizens there; submissive, faithful Muslims here. In order to survive, we are forced to learn to dance to the disjointed rhythm of what one might call the 'Medina democracy'... The tongue of the believers is monofunctional; to recite the knowledge of the ancestors is its duty and *raison d'être*. In contrast, the tongue of citizens is multifunctional; it can certainly repeat the learning of the ancestors, but everyone is encouraged to say new things, to imagine not only new knowledge but a new world. Believers do not have the right to say or write whatever they want, and especially what comes into their head, which should contain no thoughts that tradition has not sanctioned."

FROM *THE FORGOTTEN QUEENS OF ISLAM*, 1993 (186).

---

ing a general phobia about women and their sexuality. Her argument is that the Prophet spent much of his time criticizing the preexisting misogynistic ideas in pre-Islamic (Arabic: *jahiliyya*, the Period of Ignorance) Arabia as well as in the Jewish tradition, and that ample evidence is available that he completely opposed these ideas. Thus, he insisted on women's right to inheritance and the unacceptability of prostituting slaves, and opposed violence against women consistently and frequently. Yet misogynistic ideas reasserted themselves in the years after Muhammad's death, according to Mernissi, entirely due to the bias of the times and despite the clear general tenor of Qur'anic revelation and the Prophet's behavior.

A typical misogynistic tradition reported by one of the compilers of the *sunnah* (collection of hadiths), al-Bukhari, was that Muhammad said that three things bring bad luck: house, woman, and horse. This is considered a reliable hadith even though it is well known to scholars that the Prophet's favorite wife, A'isha, claimed that Abu Hurayra misreported this and that actually Muhammad said "May Allah refute the Jews! They say three things bring bad luck, house, woman, and horse" (1991b, p. 75). The misogynistic character of the tradition is further exemplified both by the regular use of this false tradition to cast aspersions on women, even as the reputation of the horse remains unsullied, and because even the notion that a man from the Hijaz region of the Arabian Peninsula or from Arabia more generally would have claimed horses were bad luck is implausible. By contrast, the interposition of woman between house and horse in A'isha's version would seem to be a strong attempt to counter any aspersions on women. Mernissi suggests that if the counterintuitive interpretation has come down as truth, it must be seen as indicative of the strong misogynistic elements that have come to dominate in the Islamic tradition.

Mernissi recounts the tradition of how the first verse (Qur'an 33:53 ff) dealing with the *hijab* was revealed by God and points out that it was initially a verse that came to Muhammad just after he lowered a curtain as he went into a room to be alone with his new bride, Zaynab, in order to separate them from a male companion, Anas ibn Malik. It thus had to do with the right to privacy of a man and wife and was followed by a recommendation for women to avoid harm by dressing modestly in turbulent times. The term *hijab* saw broad use in Islamic history and was the term for the barrier to direct perception of God—something caused by ignorance and something that mystics endeavored to overcome. The term historically had three dimensions: It demarcated what is hidden from sight, what is spatially set apart, and what is ethically forbidden. More generally, Mernissi argues that the term's current, almost exclusive, use to refer to a prescribed covering for women whenever in public is part of an obsession with female sexuality and a reductionism that drains the concept of its true significance.

Positive Exemplars One of Mernissi's other concerns is to write about female exemplars in Islamic history who illustrate alternatives to the wife as veiled, crushed, and silent. In *The Forgotten Queens of Islam*, Mernissi discusses a series of historical women who held positions of significant political power and uses these accounts to discuss the question of sovereignty in Islam and the possibilities for women to step outside the harem or household and assume a public role. Mernissi examines nineteen women at length, including two Shi'ite heads of state in Yemen, Asma bint Shihab al-Sulayhiyya and her daughter-in-law Arwa bint Ahmad al-Sulayhiyya, who coruled the Sulayhi dynasty with their husbands (1036–1138 CE) and who are both mentioned in the Friday prayer (*khutba)*, a key attribute of an Islamic head of state. She also discusses Khayzuran, the power behind the throne for three caliphs of the Abbasid dynasty in Baghdad—al-Mahdi, al-Hadi and Harun al-Rashid—and the brief rule of Sitt al-Mulk in Cairo during the Fatimid dynasty.

These cases are used to problematize the notion of *al-nushuz*, the term for rebellion of a woman against the will of her husband, and to argue that the definition of citizenship in the 1948 Universal Declaration of Human Rights implies the right of an individual to exercise free will and hence is incompatible with claims that women must be subservient to men politically, socially, or sex-

ually. Mernissi goes so far as to claim that the architecture of the Islamic caliphate is doubly threatened by universal suffrage: Removing the segregation of women by the *hijab* legitimizes their right to public action, and the removal of the veil that separated the sultan as the head of state from the public threatens the traditional elitist hierarchy by making heads of state accountable to the public.

THE WORLD'S PERSPECTIVE

By likening the Muslim household to a harem (Arabic: *harim*) on the basis of its traditional division of space between a public or male area and a private female or family space, Mernissi has developed a criticism that offends many. The term *harem* became popular in Europe around 1704 as a word for an exotic feature of Baghdad under the Abbasid Caliph Harun al-Rashid when *A Thousand and One Nights* was translated into French. Mernissi's admitted obsession with the idea both gains her easy popularity, even trendiness, in the West and the condemnation of some in the Islamic world who feel she is exploiting both etymology and history to make the Islamic world look bad even though she applies her analysis to the West as well.

Haram, a closely related noun, means forbidden or off-limits in Arabic and there is clearly a sense in which the private sphere of the household is thought to be off-limits (to the public), yet that household private sphere is not generally viewed by men as filled with concubines or women whose primary purpose is to provide sexual services for a licentious male. Mernissi's feminist perspective, however, implies that equation and justifies it through both argument and examples that suggest that, in the popular mind, women in the Islamic world are primarily valued for their sexual services while their capacities for moral and intellectual agency are devalued. Most Muslims would, instead, view the household as an institution whose purpose is to help women to raise moral children and to provide moral support for the husband. Mernissi implies throughout her work that this is not a sufficient role for women to fill and may often, in practice, not even be the key function of the household.

In *Scheherazade Goes West* (2001), Mernissi develops a series of insights into the harem, taken here metaphorically as a term for summarizing Western men's images of the ideal woman: French male views of ideal women in painting, Immanuel Kant's view that women can choose to be learned or beautiful but cannot be both, or American notions that women should be thin (size 4 to 6) and youthful or they are ugly. Her analysis fits into what has been considered literature about "the gaze": women as objects to look at or even to be observed as they regard themselves but without voice or real agency or interaction with the (male) observer. Under Mernissi's scrutiny, the

Islamic tradition clearly differs from Kant by attributing great intelligence and education to the most beautiful female figures in history, and she ascribes this at least in part to the tradition of intense competition between *jariyat* (female slaves; literally women who run) who used education in every field to excel and command attention. She contrasts this view of intelligent women with the popular misogynistic dismissal of women's intellectual and moral value. Mernissi suggests that whereas Islamic society uses space to segregate women and keep them in their place, the West uses time: Age is declared ugly, as is weight, so women are declared ugly unless they appear youthful and have adolescent figures. Misogyny in the West is expressed in the view that normal maturity for a woman is to be ugly. Mernissi claims this view similarly demeans women, making them feel as bad about being female as Middle Eastern claims that women have no proper role in the public sphere and are so intrinsically, and dangerously, sexual that they should be hidden away.

LEGACY

Mernissi's body of work provides a coherent feminist critique, but not one that fits well with mainstream feminism in the West. She emphasizes the deleterious character of sexual reductionism and holds out an ideal of male-female relations that embraces the value of intelligence, education, and pluralism rather than shaping the other into an erotic or neurotic image. Although most of Mernissi's work takes a deceptively simple essay form, it addresses key issues in the modern world and proposes a well-thought-out radical feminist position. This is enhanced by Mernissi's classical Arabic skills, which allow her to unsettle many less educated advocates of the status quo in the Islamic world. Fortunately for Westerners, her critique cuts just as deeply into the complacencies of both modern business and Western feminist scholarship with their different, yet similar, twentieth-century obsession with sexuality. Mernissi's themes of choice, and her often-acerbic phraseology, have regularly led her to be dismissed or even aggressively attacked. After recounting an incident in Malaysia when she was verbally attacked when she discussed the case of Sukayna, a woman born among the Quraysh tribe in the Hijaz in 671 CE who refused to be subservient and had marriage contracts written specifying she did not have to be, Mernissi writes, "What a strange fate for Muslim memory, to be called upon in order to censure and punish! What a strange memory, where even dead men and women do not escape attempts at assassination, if by chance they threaten to raise the *hijab* that covers the mediocrity and servility that is presented to us as tradition" (Mernissi, 1991b, p. 194).

Much of Mernissi's writing is deliberately provocative, but there is no evidence that it would have had the notoriety or the influence it has had if, instead, it had been written in more understated tones or buried in a greater array of footnotes. Her feminism, just as other attempts to paint the world in broad strokes, suffers from serious oversimplification. The notion that all Muslims obsess over female sexuality or that all Europeans still think as Kant did in the eighteenth century or that all Americans prefer skinny, immature-looking women has little chance of being accurate, but this does not make the caricatures she paints any less intriguing. Her critique of the Middle Eastern overemphasis on female sexuality and the Western overemphasis on sexuality, in general, is unlikely to please traditional Muslims, indoctrinated Western businessmen, or academics focused on the primacy of sexuality, but it remains a coherent perspective in a humanist and pluralist tradition.

Mernissi has been honored by receiving the Prince of Asturias Award in Spain in 2003, and on 4 November 2004 was awarded the Erasmus Prize in the Netherlands for her studies on the living conditions of Muslim women, her role in critiquing male discourse about women, and her support for women's emancipation in the Islamic world.

BIBLIOGRAPHY

WORKS BY MERNISSI

"Effects of Modernization on the Male-Female Dynamics in a Muslim Society." Ph.D. diss., Brandeis University, 1974.

Beyond the Veil: Male-Female Dynamics in a Modern Muslim Society. Cambridge, MA: Schenkman Publishing, 1975.

Women in Moslem Paradise. New Delhi: Kali for Women, 1986.

Can We Women Head a Muslim State? Lahore, Pakistan: Simorgh, Women's Resource and Publications Centre, 1991(a).

The Veil and the Male Elite. A Feminist Interpretation of Women's Rights in Islam. Translated by Mary Jo Lakeland. New York: Addison-Wesley Publishing, 1991(b).

Islam and Democracy: Fear of the Modern World. Translated by Mary Jo Lakeland. Reading, MA: Addison-Wesley Publishing, 1992.

The Forgotten Queens of Islam. Translated by Mary Jo Lakeland. Cambridge, U.K.: Polity Press, 1993.

Dreams of Trespass: Tales of a Harem Girlhood. Reading, MA: Addison-Wesley Publishing, 1994.

Harem Within. New York: Doubleday, 1994.

Women's Rebellion and Islamic Memory. Atlantic Highlands, NJ: Zed Books, 1996.

Scheherazade Goes West. Different Cultures, Different Harems. New York: Washington Square Press, 2001.

OTHER SOURCES

El Saadawi, Nawal. *Woman at Point Zero.* London: Zed Books, 1983.

———. *The Nawal El Saadawi Reader.* London: Zed Books, 1997.

Thomas K. Park

MESBAH YAZDI, MOHAMMAD TAQI
(1934–)

Mohammad Taqi Mesbah Yazdi is a prominent Iranian Shi'ite Muslim cleric.

PERSONAL HISTORY

Ayatollah Mesbah Yazdi was born in the town of Yazd in central Iran in 1934. According to his official autobiographical account he studied in Qom from 1952 to 1960 with some of the most prominent religious scholars of the time. As well as Ayatollah Ruhollah Khomeini (d. 1989), these included Allama Mohammad Hossain Tabataba'i (d. 1981), regarded by many as the most significant Shi'ite thinker and exegete of the twentieth century, and Ayatollah Mohammad Taqi Bahjat, an expert on Shi'ite law. From the outset, Ayatollah Mesbah Yazdi was interested, similar to Khomeini himself, in the transcendental philosophic dimension of Shi'ism as an essential part of a religious curriculum. Some forty years later, he still contributes articles and essays on the history of Shi'ite thought and philosophy. He has served as a member of the powerful Majlis-i Khibrigan (Assembly of Experts) since 1990.

Mesbah Yazdi's political activities began in the 1950s. Among his most lasting contributions to the gradual formation of a structured religious opposition to the Pahlavi regime was his cooperation with the Haqqani school, a seminary founded in Qom in the early 1960s with a twofold purpose: first, to define the role and promote the implementation of religion against the increasingly powerful and aggressively hostile secular trends that appeared to threaten the fabric of Islamic society and marginalize religious institutions as far as possible; and second, to serve as a bridgehead between the range of subjects taught in the universities and the religious sciences of the traditional seminaries. In this latter function, it could be regarded as part of a wider movement spearheaded by Ayatollah Borujerdi (d. 1961), the generally acknowledged supreme religious authority at the time, to reform, standardize, and revitalize the curriculum in religious schools. The project included, for example, the instruction of English and of Sunni law and the training of religious scholars in a rigorous manner so that they would be on a par with academics in the field of Islamic studies in well-established universities and institutions of higher learning. The principal organizer and manager of the Haqqani school was Ayatollah Mohammad Hossain Beheshti (d. 1981), who was, similar to Mesbah Yazdi, committed to the active involvement of religion in all spheres of life and especially the inclusion of the doctrine of the custodianship of the jurist (*velayat-e faqih*) as espoused by Ayatollah Khomeini. However, Beheshti

BIOGRAPHICAL HIGHLIGHTS

Name: Mohammad Taqi Mesbah Yazdi

Birth: 1934, Yazd, Iran

Nationality: Iranian

Education: Islamic education at Qom, Iran, 1952–1960

PERSONAL CHRONOLOGY:

- **1952–1960:** Studies at Qom with prominent religious scholars, including Ayatollah Khomeini
- **1960s:** Serves on board of directors of the Haqqani school in Qom
- **1990–present:** Serves on Majlis-i Khibrigan (Assembly of Experts)
- **2006:** Ahmadinejad elected to presidency, allowing Mesbah Yazdi a more prominent role in politics
- **2007:** Serves as head of the Imam Khomeini Institute for Teaching and Research in Qom

found Mesbah Yazdi an awkward colleague to work with, and consequently Mesbah Yazdi's role was limited to an advisory capacity in the two decades prior to the Iranian Revolution. The fecundity of the activities of the Haqqani school to the revolutionary project is illustrated in the prominent posts assumed by its former teachers and administrators. That circle of clerics included Ayatollah Ahmad Jannati, who was appointed to the Council of Guardians (Shuwra-yi negahban) by Khomeini himself and has been serving as its chairman since 1988; and Ayatollah Ali Qoddusi (d. 1981), Tabataba'i's son-in-law, who headed the Haqqani School from 1968 to 1979.

Mesbah Yazdi has written more than one hundred publications on Islamic philosophy, ethics, exegesis, and theology, several of which have been translated into German, French, Arabic, English, and other languages. Mesbah Yazdi has also embarked on several foreign trips in the past twenty years to give lectures and to visit academic centers for Islamic studies. These included a trip to the United States in 1991, Spain and Latin America in 1997, and Syria and Lebanon in 2004.

As of 2007, Ayatollah Yazdi heads the Imam Khomeini Institute for Teaching and Research in Qom. The institute is vested with a clear ideological mandate to propagate the political philosophy of Khomeini, with special emphasis on Islam as a comprehensive political

ideology centered around the doctrine of the custodianship of the jurist. It publishes in addition to monographs
a weekly news magazine, *Partow-i Sokhan*. Throughout
the presidency of Hojjat al-Islam MOHAMMAD KHATAMI
(president for two terms, from 1998 to 2006), when
reformists advocating a far less monolithic view of an
Islamic society appeared on the ascendancy, *Partow-i
Sokhan* regularly lambasted the government's policies, targeting particularly the social liberalization policies, the
fostering of an open society, pluralism, and the primacy
of popular will over the divine will as embodied in the
office of the leader and its occupant, Ayatollah Sayyid ALI
KHAMENEHI. The more outspoken proponents of reform
outside the government itself, who benefited from the
relative relaxation of political and religious censorship to
expound even more radical ideas, came under even harsher
treatment. For example, Mesbah Yazdi wrote several critical
assessments of the political views of ABDOLKARIM SOROUSH,
a prominent liberal religious philosopher and dissident, and
these prompted equally robust replies in retaliation. In an
interview in January 2006, Soroush described Mesbah
Yazdi as a henchman used by radical right-wing clerics
and politicians to bolster populist support for their cause.
He accused Mesbah Yazdi and his followers of a smear
campaign and as people who rejected democracy, human
rights, women's rights, and freedom under the guise of
anti-West and anti-imperialism slogans, and who maligned
concepts vital for the moral welfare of the society, such as
temperance, accommodation, tolerance, and pragmatism
in politics as compliance, concession, laxity, and surrender.

The election of one of Mesbah Yazdi's disciples, MAH-
MOUD AHMADINEJAD, to the presidency in 2006 brought
Mesbah Yazdi into the limelight of Iranian domestic politics
where he was quickly credited with being the main intellectual force behind the new order. Discussing his speech to the
General Assembly of the United Nations in September
2006, Ahmadinejad made the much-publicized remark that
that he had felt the presence of the twelfth imam, the revered
mahdi of Shi'ite Islam, in the chamber. Political commentators and journalists quickly connected the president's invo-
cation of the twelfth imam to Mesbah Yazdi's own messianic
sentiments and his alleged membership in the past to the
radical Hojjatiyeh Society, with its own fervent advocacy of
the imminent return of the *mahdi*. That Soroush too had
been allegedly a past member of the Hojjatiyeh is indicative
of the often tortuously divergent paths taken by religious
clerics and intellectuals in contemporary Iran.

INFLUENCES AND CONTRIBUTIONS
Occupying the far right of the current Iranian political
spectrum, Mesbah Yazdi has come to define, to a large
extent, the tenor and lexicon of political debate, as well as
its fault lines. Several key issues have emerged to draw the
boundaries of various political platforms, among them are

the status of women in society, the definition of the
powerful office of *velayat-e faqih* and the scope of its
powers, and the boundaries and divisions between religion
and politics. In every instance, the forceful clarity with
which Mesbah Yazdi has stated his own stance has been
instrumental in polarizing the debate and encouraging
those who find his notion of an Islamic state objectionable
and ultimately self-destructive to iron out the differences
between their own ranks to form a united front against
such an unpalatable utopia. Thus, after the ascension of
Ahmadinejad, a largely disparate coalition of important
clerics and influential political actors and strategists has
coalesced in opposition to the policies advocated by
Ahmadinejad's government and theorized by Mesbah
Yazdi. Ali Akbar Hashemi Rafsanjani, who currently heads
the powerful Shuwra-yi tashkhis-i maslahat-i nizam (Expe-
diency Council), and the former president Khatami, lead
this loose alliance. It is worthwhile to bear in mind that
only a few years earlier, Khatami's presidency had witnessed a hugely successful campaign led by several prominent journalists and political players of Khatami's
reformist camp to demonize Rafsanjani, portraying him
as corrupt and ruthless. It was successful enough to land
Rafsanjani a stunning defeat in the presidential elections of
2005. His more recent ballot-box popularity owes much
to the austere pronouncements of Mesbah Yazdi and their
negative impact on large sections of the electorate.

In his essay on the political doctrines of Islam, Mesbah
Yazdi has traced the emergence of secularism in the Islamic
world to the council held upon the death of the prophet
Muhammad in 632 at Saqifah to determine Muhammad's
successor. Those who opposed the ascension of Ali ibn Abi
Talib (d. 661), Muhammad's cousin and son-in-law, argued
that Ali may succeed the Prophet, but only in his role as the
main propagator of Islam and religious dogma. Mu'awiya
ibn Abi Sufyan (d. 679), founder of the Umayyad dynasty
(r. 661–750), is, according to Mesbah Yazdi, the first Muslim theoretician of secularism because he disputed Ali's claim
to leadership and argued that Muhammad was a prophet,
but not an imam in the sense of the community's political
leader, the shepherd of his flock. The Qur'an, it is argued,
distinguishes between prophets and imams, most clearly
when it promotes Abraham to the imamate, but denies it
to those of his progeny who are inclined to tyranny. Arguing
that Muhammad was a messenger of God but not necessarily
designated as imam or leader of the community, Mu'awiya,
according to Mesbah Yazdi, laid the foundation for the
separation of church and state in Islam.

The above debate is closely connected to one of the
perennial arguments that have been reverberating in the
Islamic republic since its early days: the nature and
definition of sovereignty as spelled out in the Iranian
constitution. Although ambivalence and allusive prose are
hallmarks of political theology as a discourse, politicians of

all stripes have exploited the unresolved ambiguities in the Iranian constitution on the source of sovereignty, popular or divine, as catchall phrases and political slogans. In that regard, Mesbah Yazdi's radical and emphatic position, which saw no room for popular sovereignty in an Islamic republic, had variegated implications for political discourse in Iran. In the volatile situation of the 2007 elections for the Majlis-i Khibrigan, the declaration provided much-needed fodder for the reformist camp, which used it well to ensure the triumph of Rafsanjani at the expense of Mesbah Yazdi.

Considered conservative and a puritan and on social issues and a hard-liner in matters of foreign policy, Mesbah Yazdi has issued numerous statements that condemn efforts to modify state laws to guarantee more equality to women and strengthen their position in Iranian society. Efforts to change the habits and customs of Islamic nations, he has often noted, are part of the strategies of cultural imperialism aimed at undermining belief and autonomy in Islamic lands. Against secularism, Mesbah Yazdi has described concepts such as tolerance or pluralism as a Trojan horse for the introduction of secularism and individualism, the main enemies of Islamic government and society. He finds the formation of religious movements for fighting enemies necessary. But in the meantime, he scorns this-worldly affairs and instead encourages the spirit of jihad, fearlessness in the face of death and the seeking of martyrdom, asserting they are the first steps toward fighting the enemies of Islam and the revolution of Iran. In several public lectures, Friday sermons, and published works, Mesbah Yazdi has reiterated his belief in the necessity of violence in the promotion of religio-political objectives.

On certain issues, the publicly stated views of Mesbah Yazdi are curiously resonant of those espoused by Pope Benedict XVI, who is committed to redefining Christianity as submission to canon law and loyalty to its spiritual hierarchy. In his declarations against individualism, secularism, the separation of church and state, and women's rights, Mesbah Yazdi advocates a more literal application of religious dogma and a concomitant effort to expand it to all aspects of public life. On gender equality, for instance, he dismisses the mere questioning of evident disparities in the *shari'a* as heretical and threatening to public peace. Religion, Mesbah Yazdi declares, is a matter of unquestioning love as well as firm belief, which is why reason, science, and philosophy cannot undermine it. Belief is not an intellectual matter alone, but rather one that demands devotion and unflinching obedience: The practice of religion without tinkering with its foundations is essential to piety and the ultimate salvation of the Islamic community.

THE WORLD'S PERSPECTIVE

Mesbah Yazdi's work has been translated into various languages, including German, French, Arabic, and English, and he has made several trips abroad to visit foreign centers for Islamic studies. The Western view of Mesbah Yazdi is generally unfavorable because of his approval of violence in the name of religion. The British *Daily Telegraph* called him "a hardliner to terrify hardliners" and expressed alarm at his powerful position as a major spiritual adviser to Iranian president Ahmadinejad.

LEGACY

Mesbah Yazdi will be remembered particularly for his highly conservative religious views, his advocacy of violence and seeking martyrdom, and his political power, especially under the presidency of Ahmadinejad.

BIBLIOGRAPHY

Abdolkarim Soroush's Official Web site. Available from http://www. drsoroush.com.

Biouki, Kay, and Colin Freeman, "Ayatollah Who Backs Suicide Bombs Aims to Be Iran's Next Spiritual Leader." *Sunday Telegraph* (London) (19 November 2006). Available from http://www.telegraph.co.uk.

Freeman, Colin. "The Rise of Prof. 'Crocodile'—A Hardline to Terrify Hardliners." *Daily Telegraph* (London) (19 November 2005). Available from http://www.telegraph.co.uk.

Mesbah Yazdi, Mohammad Taqi. *Tahajumi-i farhangi* [Culture war]. Edited by 'Abd al-Javad Ebrahimi, pp. 131–141. Qom, Mu'assissa-yi Amuzishi va Pazhuhishi-yi Imam Khomeini, 2002. Available from http://www.mesbahyazdi.org/english/index.htm.

———. "Two Critical Issues in Sadrian Philosophy: Substantive Motion and Its Relation to the Problem of Time, and the Principality of Existence." *Transcendent Philosophy: An International Journal for Comparative Philosophy and Mysticism* 2, no. 2 (2001).

Mohammad Taqi Mesbah Yazdi's Official Web site. Available from http://www.mesbahyazdi.org.

Neguin Yavari

MISNAD, MAWZA BINT NASIR AL-
(c. 1956–)

Mawza bint Nasir al-Misnad was born in Doha, Qatar, in the mid-1950s into a prominent merchant family. She married HAMAD BIN KHALIFA AL THANI, now emir of Qatar, in 1976. After her husband became emir in 1995, Shaykha Mawza devoted herself to serving and promoting social and educational causes in Qatar. She heads several institutions in Qatar to promote these causes. She travels abroad with her husband on official visits and is the nearest thing in the Gulf states to a Western-style "first lady."

PERSONAL HISTORY

Mawza's exact birthdate is not known, but she is believed to have been born in the mid-1950s. Her father, Nasir al-Misnad, attended high school in Doha with the current emir of Qatar, Shaykh Hamad bin Khalifa Al Thani. The two men bonded at school. Both were jailed in the 1960s during some student unrest over the policies of the emir of the time, Shaykh Ahmad bin Ali Al Thani. Misnad took his family to Egypt where they stayed for several years before he reconciled with the Qatari government. Following his return, Misnad worked as a high-level official in the Ministry of Education and later became a businessman in construction and trade.

The young Mawza went to local schools while her family was in Egypt. She was married to Hamad around 1976. She was his second wife. His first was his cousin, Mariam bint Hamad Al Thani, with whom he had his eldest son, Mishail (born 1973). Hamad married a third wife in 1989, Nura bint Khalid Al Thani. (The ruling family does not usually marry outside the Al Thani clan with the exception of certain important families, such as the Attiyah and Misnad families.) Shaykha Mawza now lives in a compound in Doha with the emir's other wives.

After she was married, Mawza returned to college and obtained a B.A. in sociology from the University of Qatar in 1986. She remained out of the public eye until some time after Hamad became emir. During this time she raised her seven children. Her eldest son, Jasim, born in 1978, was nominated by his father in 1996 to be crown prince. Jasim was replaced as crown prince in August 2003 by another of Mawza's sons, Tamim, born in 1980. The reason given was that Shaykh Jasim wanted to follow other pursuits. Mawza's two daughters, al-Mayassa, born in 1982, and Hind, born in 1984, are both graduates of Duke University with B.A. degrees in political science. Al-Mayassa, like her mother, has shown an interest in public affairs.

Mawza's position changed once her husband became emir, an event which occured rather dramatically on 27 June 1995, when her husband, then crown prince, ousted his father in a bloodless coup while the latter was in Europe. The reason given for the coup was the slow pace of economic development in Qatar. Since Hamad has become emir, Qatar, a country rich in oil and gas, has seen fundamental changes in almost every aspect of life, transforming it into a developed country integrated into the global economy.

While Hamad was still crown prince, his wife had no public role. However, it is reported that even then she was closely following education issues in the Middle East and neighboring countries. Shortly after her husband assumed power, she began to get involved publicly in issues concerning women, social development, and education. Traditionally, the wives of rulers in the oil-rich countries of

---

BIOGRAPHICAL HIGHLIGHTS

Name: Mawza bint Nasir al-Misnad Mawza

Birth: c. 1956, Doha, Qatar

Family: Husband, Hamad bin Khalifa Al Thani, emir of Qatar; five sons, Jasim, Tamim (crown prince), Muhammad, Khalifa, Ju'an; two daughters, al-Mayassa, Hind

Nationality: Qatari

Education: B.A., sociology, University of Qatar, 1986

PERSONAL CHRONOLOGY:

- **1995–present:** Head, Qatar Foundation for Education, Science and Community Development
- **2002–present:** Vice president, Supreme Council for Family Affairs
- **2003–present:** UN special envoy for basic and higher education

---

the Gulf (Kuwait, Saudi Arabia, Qatar, Bahrain, the United Arab Emirates, and Oman) have no public roles. They are almost never seen in public, their pictures are never published in the press, they do not accompany their husbands on state visits, nor do they mix with men. None has signed contracts or agreements with foreign countries. These are all things Mawza has done, and other Gulf rulers' wives are following in her footsteps, particularly Sabika bint Ibrahim Al Khalifa, wife of King HAMAD BIN ISA AL KHALIFA of Bahrain.

The emir and his wife are said to be very close. Mawza is, to all intents and purposes, the "first lady" of Qatar. She travels abroad with the emir and sometimes addresses public audiences, as was the case, for example, on 29 September 2004, when both she and Hamad were guests of the Saban Center of the Brookings Institution in Washington, D.C., where she addressed a gathering in excellent English while her husband listened in the audience. In that speech, she talked about the need for social justice in the world, how exchanges between people and goods are transforming our world, and the need for a democratic sociopolitical environment. In another visit on 3 August 2003, she and her husband were interviewed together on the U.S. TV show, *60 Minutes*, by Mike Wallace. This was unprecedented for the wife of a Gulf ruler. The emir and his wife receive and entertain foreign dignitaries, both Arabs and non-Arabs. Sometimes, while visiting foreign countries, the shaykh and his wife mingle, without their entourage, with people in the streets, visiting shops and restaurants.

INFLUENCES AND CONTRIBUTIONS

It is not clear exactly what influences have shaped Mawza's interests and her capacity to forge a new role for women in the Gulf, but her education and her stay in the cosmopolitan environment of Egypt in critical years of her youth probably played a part. It is also likely that her father's position in shaping Qatar's education system when she was growing up gave her an interest in and knowledge about the field with which she is so closely associated.

Even more important is her close and collaborative association with her husband and his own pioneering role in modernizing Qatar. Almost immediately after becoming ruler, the emir took steps to modernize the country. He established the now well-known al-Jazeera satellite TV station, which began broadcasting in 1996. Al-Jazeera was the first uncensored, uncontrolled Arab TV station. It offers a variety of daring and open programs, reports and debates, of a kind unseen in the Arab world before. In 1998 Hamad abolished the Ministry of Information, which then controlled the media, making Qatar the first Arab country to do so. In November 1996 the emir surprised everybody by announcing his intention to hold general elections to elect members of a central municipal council in Doha, the first elected council of its kind in any of the Gulf states. That announcement left ambiguous whether women would be allowed to participate in the elections, but slowly and cautiously the emir came forward to announce that women would be allowed not only to vote but also to be candidates. This announcement was met with resistance from conservative Islamic circles, and some who opposed giving women the right to vote were jailed by the emir. Despite this, the elections took place in March 1999 and Qatari women participated for the first time. The emir also replaced the 1972 temporary constitution with a new permanent constitution that went into effect on 9 June 2005. Qatar is waiting for general elections for a Majlis al-Shura (parliament) where men and women will both participate.

Mawza was active in encouraging Qatari women to participate in the elections for municipal council. In the months before the election, she attended lectures and seminars designed to explain what general elections meant, the meaning of civil rights and the importance of female participation. She was assisted in this campaign by Shaykha A'isha, the emir's sister, who was nominated to head the Women's Information Committee, an organization designed to teach women the virtues of democracy.

THE URGENCY OF GLOBAL DIALOGUE IS EVIDENT

We are passing through a period of change where the urgency of global dialogue is evident. Channels of communication between the Arab world and the West, in particular, need to be fostered. Especially, since the tragic events of September 11th, it is imperative that we nurture genuine dialogue. We must not be deafened by echoes from the discourse of intolerance.

It is sometimes hard to believe that an entire civilization can be judged by the deeds of an erratic few. Yet for some time, this is exactly what has happened. It seemed that the clash of civilizations would possibly become a dismal reality of the 21st century. But luckily, rational voices from political and intellectual circles, both in the Arab East and in the West, are beginning to reshape this discourse and take it in the right direction.

In Qatar, we are committed to objectives of citizen empowerment and positive change. We are working diligently to build a culture of personal responsibility and empowerment. For too long, states in our region have played the role of guardian for their citizens. In doing so, we have deprived them of their individuality and capacity to think and act critically. It is time for educated citizens to be effective participants in the management of their society. They must not be content to play the role of spectators. Qatar is a country with great natural resources, and we are seeking to extend material prosperity to prosperity of mind and habit.

2 OCTOBER 2004, BEFORE THE AMERICAN-ARAB ANTI-DISCRIMINATION COMMITTEE.

But Mawza has not merely been an important associate of her husband. She has made contributions to Qatar—and the Gulf—in her own right, particularly in education, family affairs, and above all the role of women. In the last, Mawza soon became a groundbreaker. One of her first appearances in public, aside from women-only gatherings, was in December 1998 when she led a two-hour women's march in the streets of Doha in support of a local charity, the first event of its kind in the region. Later that same month, Mawza traveled (without her husband) to the United States and visited several cultural and educational institutions, including Yale University and the University of Virginia in Charlottesville. At the latter she attended an official dinner arranged in her honor by the president of the university and the board of trustees and gave a speech appropriate to the occasion. She also signed an agreement of cooperation with the university. As far as is known, this is the first time the wife of any Gulf state ruler has undertaken such activities.

However, the main contribution of Mawza in modernizing Qatar is in education, in which she has shown a keen interest. In the 1990s, while her husband was still crown prince, she was telling Western visitors about her vision for the future of education in Qatar. When she discovered how difficult it would be to reform the existing system, she turned to the idea of creating a second, parallel, system. The core of this idea was to open branches of Western universities in Qatar and to reform elementary and secondary education. By 2006 several American universities operated branches in Doha. The revision of the whole K–12 education system in the country is also underway.

The hub of this education program is the Qatar Foundation for Education, Science and Community Development, which Mawza heads. A private nonprofit organization established by the emir in 1995, it oversees higher education and research, including the establishment of branches of foreign universities. In fall 2003, the Qatar Foundation officially inaugurated Education City, a kind of umbrella university campus shared by the foreign universities, including, currently, Virginia Commonwealth University School of the Arts, Carnegie Mellon University, Cornell Medical College, Texas A&M University, and Georgetown University, as well as the Rand-Qatar Policy Institute. Education City also houses a science and technology park, and operates a leading K–12 institution, the Qatar Academy, which helps prepare students for these institutions. The medical college enrolls Qatari and non-Qatari students. Most of the faculty and staff in these university branches are westerners.

Mawza is also concerned with secondary education. In November 2002 she was appointed vice president of the Supreme Education Council, a government institution that oversees reform efforts in the K–12 system. These reforms are already affecting Qatari schools' teaching methods, curricula, and degree of independence from the Ministry of Education. On the advice of Rand, schools are encouraging innovation, and, at the same time, higher academic standards. They concentrate on four subjects—Arabic, English, math, and science. Students in all public and private schools will eventually be evaluated in these subjects by international standards. All indications are that women will play a major role in this system.

Mawza is also president of the Supreme Council for Family Affairs, a government-sponsored institution established in 1998 with the objective of strengthening the role of the family in society. The council is active in studying family issues and organizing meetings and conferences on children's rights and support for families. It runs high-quality training programs to enable families to be independent and productive members of society.

Mawza is also attempting to be a role model for Qatari women, and they are stepping out in the public domain, although carefully. Women are now employed in the public sector in more jobs with greater responsibility, and their numbers are also increasing in the work force generally. Mawza's activities are clearly understood by young women as an example for them. She attends each year's graduation ceremony for the women's branch of Qatar University and gives an appropriate speech. In 2003 she was behind her husband's move to promote a woman, Dr. Shaykha al-Mahmud, to minister of education. Mahmud was the first female minister in any Gulf state; others followed suit. Mawza's aunt, Dr. Shaykha Abdullah al-Misnad, a university professor of education, has assisted Mawza in her efforts to improve the social and educational situation for women. Al-Misnad, formerly a professor and vice president of the University of Qatar, has been the university's president since August 2003—the first woman to hold that office.

THE WORLD'S PERSPECTIVE

Mawza has stepped onto the international stage with her educational and social projects and for the most part gained favorable attention for the role she is playing. When the U.S.-led invasion of Iraq in March 2003 toppled the Ba'th regime, she showed interest in helping the Iraqi people, and in particular their universities. A special committee was formed by the Qatari government, and with the help of Mawza, the United Nations Educational, Scientific, and Cultural Organization (UNESCO) set up a special fund to revitalize the higher education system in Iraq. Qatar donated $15 million to the fund. UNESCO then appointed Mawza as a special envoy for basic and higher education. In this capacity she actively promotes various international projects to improve the quality and accessibility of education. In 2005, she was selected as a member of a high-level United Nations (UN) group, the Alliance of Civilizations, established by the UN secretary general. This group is responsible for developing creative mechanisms for fighting terrorism. In a climate of rising conservative Islamic opinion in the Middle East, however, she must exercise this role with some caution, lest it backfire at home. Thus far, she has done so.

LEGACY

Shaykha Mawza is the first wife of any Arab ruler in the Persian Gulf to enter public life, and engage in social and educational activities in an open fashion, thus opening avenues for women in the future. She has also been an important force behind the policies of her husband, the emir, in opening up the Qatari political system to women, allowing them to vote and to run in elections for the first time in any Arab Gulf country. The fact that she travels frequently with her husband and sometimes alone, that she gives public speeches, and conducts business abroad has made her a pioneer and a role model in her society. She will be remembered as the first "first lady" in any Arab Gulf country.

BIBLIOGRAPHY

Bahry, Louay. "Elections in Qatar: a Window of Democracy Opens in the Gulf." *Middle East Policy* 6, no. 4 (June 1999).

———. "A Qatari Spring." *Middle East Insight* 15, no. 15 (September/October, 2000).

———. "The New Arab Media Phenonmenon: Qatar's al-Jazeera." *Middle East Policy* 8, no. 3 (June 2001).

Bahry, Louay, with Phebe Marr. "Qatari Women: A New Generation of Leaders." *Middle East Policy* 8, no. 2 (Summer 2005).

Crystal, Jill. *Oil and Politics in the Gulf: Rulers and Merchants in Kuwait and Qatar.* Cambridge, U.K.: Cambridge University Press, 1990.

El-Nawawy, Mohammed, and Adel Iskandar. *Al-Jazeera: How the Free Arab News Network Scooped the World and Changed the Middle East.* Cambridge, MA: Westview Press, 2002.

Peterson, J. E. "Qatar and the World: Branding for a Micro-State." *Middle East Journal* 60, no. 4 (Autumn 2006).

Qatar Ministry of Foreign Affairs. "The Constitution." Available from http://english.mofa.gov.qa/details.cfm?id=80.

Rathmell, Andrew, and Kristen Schulze. "Political Reform in the Gulf: The Case of Qatar." *Middle Eastern Studies* 36, no. 4 (October 2000).

U.S. Library of Congress. "Country Studies: Persian Gulf States: Qatar: Historical Background." Available from http://countrystudies.us/persian-gulf-states/68.htm.

Weaver, Mary Anne. "Letter from Qatar." *New Yorker* (20 November 2000).

Zahlan, Rosemarie Said. *The Creation of Qatar.* London: Barnes and Noble, 1979.

Louay Bahry

MONTAZERI, HOSSEIN ALI
(1922–)

Senior Shi'ite Muslim cleric and theologian Hossein (Hussein) Ali Montazeri is an Iranian political and religious figure who played a pivotal role in the Islamic revolution of 1979 and the establishment of the Islamic Republic of Iran as the first major theocratic government in the modern history of the Middle East. Montazeri was one of the original architects of the Shi'ite theocracy in Iran after the victory of the revolution in 1979 and it was

Hossein Ali Montazeri. AP IMAGES.

he who led the way in drafting a new constitution that assigned a significant role to the clerics in the state. He later became the successor to Ayatollah Ruhollah Khomeini, the founder of the Islamic Republic of Iran. In 1989, however, he was demoted from his position as the designated heir to Khomeini because of his public objections to the revolution and the repressive policies of the state. Later in the 1990s Montazeri became one of the leading dissident figures of the postrevolutionary era and a leading advocate of democracy in Iran. After suffering humiliation, death threats, and a house arrest by the government authorities from 1997 to 2003, he remains one of the major voices of opposition in Iran.

PERSONAL HISTORY

Montazeri was born into a poor peasant family in 1922 in the city of Najafabad in central Iran. He began his formal studies in theology in 1937 at the seminary school of Isfahan, where he was recognized for his intelligence and knowledge of the Qur'anic sciences. In 1944 Montazeri moved to the Islamic seminary (*howzeh-ye elmiyyeh*) in Qom, completing his education in Shi'ite jurisprudence

BIOGRAPHICAL HIGHLIGHTS

Name: Hossein (Hussein) Ali Montazeri

Birth: 1922, Najafabad, Iran

Family: Married; three sons, Ahmad, Sayed, and Mohammad (d. 1981); two daughters, Ashraf and Saideh.

Nationality: Iranian

Education: Shi'ite theological seminary of Isfahan, Iran, 1937–1944; Shi'ite theological seminary, Qom, Iran, 1944–1960

PERSONAL CHRONOLOGY:

- **1960:** Instructor, theologian, and scholar at the Qom theological seminary school
- **1966:** Arrested by the Pahlavi regime for antigovernment activities and sentenced to nineteen months in prison
- **1975:** Imprisoned for his antigovernment activities and sentenced to ten years in prison
- **1978:** Released from prison
- **1979:** Appointed by Ayatollah Ruhollah Khomeini as Friday prayer leader of Qom and a member of the governing Islamic Revolutionary Council
- **1979:** Elected as the chairman of the Association of Combatant Clergy and the Assembly of Experts
- **1985:** Elected by the Assembly of Experts to become the successor of Khomeini
- **1989:** Forced to resign the post of Jurist Consulate due to his objections to the shortcomings of the revolution
- **1989:** After his resignation, he resumes teaching philosophy and theology at Qom, though in the 1990s he is banned from teaching because of his opposition to the government
- **2003:** Iranian authorities lift his house arrest

under the supervision of Ayatollah Ruhollah Khomeini (1902–1989). At Qom, Montazeri became a favorite student of Khomeini and one of his most trusted assistants.

From 1944 to the late 1950s Montazeri experienced turbulent events in the course of Iranian political life. The 1940s and 1950s can be described as a moment in modern Iranian history when many Iranians, including

clerics, became politically active in various religious and secular political parties. After the 1941 abdication of the Reza Shah Pahlavi (1878–1944), who ruled the country in an autocratic style, Iran saw a period of democratic zeal and antigovernment movements. Numerous people, especially the young, engaged in pro-democracy parties and demanded greater freedoms and a larger role for ordinary Iranians to play in the political affairs of the country. Anticolonial sentiments were also a major feature of this antigovernment mood in Iran, especially when Mohammad Reza Shah Pahlavi (1919–1980), the son of Reza Shah, came to power in 1941 with the help of the Allies. For many, especially clerics such as Montazeri, the British involvement in the country's economic and domestic politics was indicative of a colonial ambition to take over the country, and the responsibility of the religious leaders was to voice their opposition to the Pahlavi regime (1925–1979) which was seen to be a mere puppet of foreign colonial powers.

In March 1951, Mohammad Mossadeq (1882–1967), a member of the parliament who later that year was elected to be the prime minister, nationalized the Iranian oil, thus closing the operation of the British-owned-and-operated Anglo-Iranian Oil Company (AIOC). Montazeri, following his mentor Khomeini, voiced his support for the popular movements that demanded Iran's right to control its oil production and end the foreign influence in the country's domestic politics. After a successful Central Intelligence Agency (CIA)-led coup that toppled the government of Mossadeq in 1953, a move mainly aimed at deterring Iran from joining the Soviet bloc, Mohammad Reza Shah returned to power and began to rule the country in an autocratic manner, just as his father had.

Although he mainly kept to his studies at Qom, Montazeri gradually began to get involved in antigovernment movements that were primarily operating underground after the return of the shah to power in 1953. The most significant event that led to the involvement of Montazeri in political activities was the launching of the White Revolution by the shah in 1963, which aimed at reforming Iran's traditional economic, educational, and legal system. The far-reaching project, which sought the complete transformation of Iranian society, angered many Shi'ite clerics. According to these clerics, the reforms were a sinister ploy by the government to westernize the traditional fabric of Iranian society, and deprive Iranians of their national identity that was largely protected by the religious leaders based in Qom.

In the early 1960s, similar to many junior level clerics, Montazeri began to actively participate in a number of antigovernment activities. Montazeri's political activities intensified after Khomeini issued in January 1963 in Qom a major declaration denouncing the shah and his plans. Khomeini's revolutionary rhetoric eventually led to his arrest by the Iranian authorities in June 1963. Montazeri participated in demonstrations against the arrest of his mentor and campaigned for his release. After his release in November 1964, Khomeini was arrested again for his criticism of the shah for granting diplomatic immunity to American military officers in Iran, and later that year was sent to exile in Turkey and, eventually, to Najaf, Iraq. Montazeri immediately visited him in Najaf and upon Montazeri's return to Iran he was detained, though shortly released.

From 1965 to 1975 Montazeri became more involved in antishah movements in Qom. In 1975 he was arrested and imprisoned for conspiring to overthrow the monarchy. With the outbursts of the revolution in the late 1970s, Montazeri was released in November 1978 and joined the revolutionary current. From November 1978 to early 1979, while Khomeini was in France after being forced to leave Iraq by vice president SADDAM HUSSEIN in 1978, Montazeri acted as Khomeini's representative in Iran and was considered Khomeini's potential successor.

The most politically charged stage of Montazeri's life began after the overthrow of shah's regime and the establishment of the Islamic Republic. In 1979 Montazeri became a leading revolutionary figure in drafting a new constitution, which assigned a major political role to the clerics within the state. The most significant idea that Montazeri advocated in the new constitution was the doctrine of the absolute rule of the jurisconsult (*velayat-e faqih*), which recognized a senior Shi'ite cleric as the supreme leader of the country. In 1980 Montazeri was elected as the head of the Assembly of Experts, a body of clerics who elect the supreme leader and monitor his activities, and later in that same year he was addressed by the title of grand ayatollah (Ayatollah Ozma) by Khomeini, which made him one of the highest-ranking Shi'ite clerics in the world. The Assembly of Experts then voted in December 1982 to make Montazeri the supreme leader, designating him the highest status in the regime after Khomeini.

From his base in Qom after the revolution, Montazeri helped Khomeini with the management and administration of a vast religious network in Iran and abroad; his network of organizations exercised political influence in both domestic and foreign policy. For nearly nine years (1980–1989) he was responsible for the academic and personal well-being of foreign students, many of whom were of Afghan and Arab origin, who attended and studied at various places within the Qom seminary center. He was also a member of the Revolutionary Council, the Friday Prayer Imam of Tehran and Qom, and the head of the Prisoner Amnesty Council from 1980 to 1988.

In one of the most dramatic episodes in post-revolutionary era, Montazeri, however, lost his position as the designated heir to the office of the Guardian Jurist after he

was forced out of his position by Khomeini in March 1989. There are several reasons for Khomeini's decision to denounce his successor. The most important reason was Montazeri's outspoken support for his son-in-law, Medhi Hashemi, who had embarrassed the speaker of the parliament, Ali Akbar Hashemi Rafsanjani, by exposing his secret dealings with the Reagan administration during the Iran-Contra affairs. But the main cause behind Khomeini's decision was due to Montazeri's own candid criticisms of the government's domestic and foreign policies, which he increasingly viewed as counter to the ideals of the Islamic political system he helped to create in 1979.

After the death of Khomeini in June 1989 and the election of Ayatollah ALI KHAMENEHI to the office of supreme leader by the Assembly of Experts, Montazeri began to keep a low profile and refused to get involved in political affairs on the governmental level. The period of 1989 to 1994 is known as the quietist stage of Montazeri's life, during which he mainly kept to his studies at Qom. But in 1994 Montazeri returned to political activity, this time, however, not as a member of the government but an opposition figure. In October 1994 Montazeri issued a powerful warning to the regime in a twelve-page letter by stating that the Islamic government that he helped to set up in 1979 was managed by corrupt and selfish officials who were destroying the reputation of Islam for the believers. The letter unleashed a series of public announcements by Montazeri against the regime, making him a major dissident figure since the early years of the revolution when many oppositional groups escaped the country or were eradicated by the regime.

The election of the reformist MOHAMMAD KHATAMI to the presidency in 1997 introduced a new political atmosphere in Iran, allowing many dissidents to voice their opinion against the government. But the hard-liner faction of the government, primarily led by the supreme leader, took appropriate measure to curtail opposition. When in early 1997 Montazeri published his six hundred page memoir on the Web, which provided new insights to the numerous executions by the government, the authorities in Tehran saw him as a major threat to their establishment. In November 1997 he was put under house arrest after making a speech that criticized Ayatollah Khamenehi for leading an authoritarian regime. Throughout the country, his followers were arrested for protesting against his arrest. In July 2001 his son, Sayed Montazeri, and another son-in-law, Hadi Hashemi, were arrested for their alleged antigovernment activities.

Montazeri was finally released in 2003 after a number of religious leaders and Iranian legislators demanded that Khatami pardon him from his house arrest. Since his release, Montazeri, his sons, students, and followers, have been actively involved in the reformist movement. Despite the election of the hard-liner MAHMOUD AHMADINEJAD to power in 2005, Montazeri continues to criticize the government on various economic, political, and social issues.

INFLUENCES AND CONTRIBUTIONS

Montazeri has been a central intellectual figure in developing the idea of Islamic government during the time of Occultation (Ghayba), believed by Shi'ite Muslims as a historical period that began in 874 CE when the twelfth imam, Mohammad al-Mahdi, also known as the Hidden Imam, went into hiding, and ends when the imam reappears at the end of time to bring justice to the world. The main question many Shi'ite theologians have been trying to answer since the ninth century has been: What sort of a government should the Shi'ites support that best anticipates the return of Mahdi.

According to Montazeri, the most ideal government during the period of Occultation is the kind that recognizes the most learned cleric as the spiritual leader who can guide and promote the common good for the community. Although the concept, known as the guardianship of the jurisconsult or *velayat-e faqih*, has been usually attributed to Ayatollah Khomeini, it was Montazeri who first made the most elaborate defense of the doctrine. His four-volume work in Arabic on the general topic of the Guardianship of Jurist, titled *Legal Foundations of the Islamic Government* and published in 1964, explored the relationship between Islam and the state and justified the rule of the Shi'ite jurist as the most legitimate representative of the Hidden Imam on earth. For Montazeri, it is the senior cleric who should have the spiritual and political authority to govern over both religious and political affairs, and any other form of government is either corrupt or tyrannical.

The 1979 Iranian Revolution provided an opportunity for Montazeri to put into practice such a doctrine. Montazeri's first significant contribution was made in the early stages of the revolutionary period when he played a central role in the Assembly of Experts by drafting the November 1979 constitution, which institutionalized the office of the jurisconsult. The constitution, which was finally passed in November 1979, institutionalized a theocratic order that recognized the jurisconsult as the central figure in the country's political and legal system. By definition, Montazeri argued, this new Islamic Republic "entails the implementation of Islamic decrees.... Only an expert in Islamic laws [a *faqih*] and not a Western-educated person can discern the Islamicity of laws" (Moslem, 2002, p. 29). The law, interpreted and sanctioned by the Islamic expert, should then be the source of authority in the new Islamic Republic.

However, since 1989 Montazeri has been revising his conception of the guardianship of the jurisconsult by arguing that "the most important point to be highlighted here is that Islam supports the separation of powers and

CONTEMPORARIES

Mohsen Kadivar (1959–) was a former student of Montazeri and a leading dissident cleric in postrevolutionary Iran. Born in Shiraz, Iran, Kadivar completed his undergraduate education at the Shiraz University where he became politically active in the revolutionary movement in 1978. After the victory of the revolution in 1979, he began to study theology at the Shiraz seminary school (1980) and later moved to the Islamic seminary (*howzeh-ye elmiyyeh*) in Qom (1981) where he studied Shi'ite jurisprudence and philosophy under the supervision of Ayatollah Montazeri. In 1997 he became one of the few students to whom Montazeri handed out a written permission to practice *ijtihad*, or permission to issue religious rulings and teach jurisprudence, and later in 1999 he received a Ph.D. in Islamic philosophy and theology from Tarbiat Modares University in Tehran.

Kadivar's political activities against the theocratic regime of Iran began in 1994 and especially after the election of Mohammad Khatami to the presidency in 1997, when he published lengthy critical writings on the doctrine of the absolute rule of the jurisconsult (*velayat-e faqih*), endorsed by Ayatollah Khomeini as the official ideology of the Iranian state. He was arrested in 1999 for arguing that the doctrine assigns too much power to the senior cleric, because such authority can easily be abused and corrupted in a political system. Despite threats against his life by supporters of the regime, Kadivar continues to be active in the reformist movement in Iran.

does not recognize the concentration of power in the hand of a fallible human being" (Abdo, 2001, p. 19). No one person should have the power to rule; and that state authority should be shared by various branches of the government, which are held accountable to the people. When referring to the Iranian Constitution, he describes the role of the supreme leader as someone who "can never be above the law, and he cannot interfere in all affairs, particularly the affairs that fall outside his area of expertise, such as complex economic issues, or issues of foreign affair and international relations" (Abdo, 2001, p. 17).

In his most recent publication on law and Islam, *Resaleh-ye Hoqouq* (2004; Treaties on law), Montazeri boldly defends a democratic conception of spiritual authority. He endorses the idea of the compatibility of human rights with Islamic law by arguing that Islam not only in principle defends human rights, but also advances the rights of women, the elderly, children, and even animals. According to Montazeri, the Prophet of Islam and the holy imams were the staunchest advocates of the sanctity of human rights that include activities from freedom of expression to holding rulers accountable for their actions. He argues that "every person in a society, including those that are in favor or against the government, have the freedom of expression; they have the right to promote their particular ideals and reform programs or changes in the policies of the ruling regime on the basis of rationality, logic and law, and they can get involve in political participation and organization of parties" (Montazeri, 2004, p. 66). In other words, Islamic law accommodates democratic norms of action practiced by the citizens of a political community.

For Montazeri, there is no room for authoritarian rule in an Islamic political system; all authority rests on the people, who elect rulers and remain the sole sovereigns of the state. Even the infallibles (the Prophet and the imams) never claimed to be above the law, and they were also held accountable and subject to criticism by individual members of the Muslim community. Montazeri's reinterpretation of the doctrine of the guardianship of the jurisconsult is viewed as a major contribution to democratic culture in Iran, and an original contribution in bringing closer together Shi'ite theology and democratic thought.

THE WORLD'S PERSPECTIVE

Global perceptions of Montazeri can be divided into two historical phases. The first phase involves the period when Montazeri was one of the leading political figures in the theocratic government from 1979 to 1989. This is when Montazeri received a negative reaction spanning from world leaders to ordinary people for his association with a government that denied the rights of many Iranians, particularly dissidents, religious minorities, and women. Especially for those in Western Europe and North America, Montazeri was the symbol of an antidemocratic order in a country that was taken over by religious fanaticism. He was, however, seen as a more benign figure for advocating moderate policies and opposing state execution of political prisoners. Montazeri's daring objection to the shortcomings of the revolution while a successor to Khomeini in the 1980s received a positive reaction from major media outlets around the world.

Global perceptions of Montazeri became gradually more positive after he was demoted from the post of supreme leader in 1989. In the late 1990s, when Montazeri was highly outspoken regarding the antidemocratic features of the government, many in media and political

---

I CONSIDER TELLING THE TRUTH MY RELIGIOUS DUTY

■

I am very sad and sorry to see that in the present circumstances there is no tolerance in the Islamic society for hearing anything other than what is coming out of the ruling circles, a condition in which the children of Revolution and those concerned with the fate of the country are being sent to jail on a daily basis under various pretexts, and a situation in which Islam, the Revolution, and its late Leader [Ayatollah Khomeini] are being exploited. I have spent a lifetime fighting for the independence and honor of this country and defending the legitimate rights and freedom of people, and I have taught most of the incumbent rulers as my pupils. In a condition where I am being treated like this, what can others expect? As I have said repeatedly, I have no desire to be the Leader; nor am I interested in the position of *marja'yyat* [religious leadership]. Yes, I consider telling the truth my religious duty. So I will keep voicing what I consider to be in the interest of the Revolution and the nation, and like in the past, I will continue to defend the legitimate rights and freedoms of the people.

MONTAZERI, HOSSEIN ALI. INTERVIEW BY GENEVIVE ABDO.

QOM, IRAN, 2000.

---

circles would refer to him as a key dissident cleric for the promotion of democracy in Iran. In this second stage, roughly from 1994 to 2007, Montazeri began to be described as a leading reformist critique of the hard-liner establishment, and as potentially the greatest threat to the theocratic establishment for demanding a separation between politics and religion.

LEGACY

Although it is still too early to assess his definitive legacy, Montazeri will most likely be remembered for his passionate defense of a more benign, more democratic Islam. His rise in popularity both inside and outside Iran has enabled him to symbolize an alternative form of clerical leadership in defiance of an absolutist religious government. However, for his ability to change, reform, and adhere to the democratic values of accountability and popular sovereignty, as interpreted from an Islamic perspective, Montazeri can be regarded as a living legendary figure for many Shi'ite Muslims in Iran and beyond who seek to democratize and reform their societies against secular and religious autocratic regimes.

BIBLIOGRAPHY

Abdo, Genevive. "Re-Thinking the Islamic Republic: A 'Conversation' with Ayatollah Hussain 'Ali Montazeri." *Middle East Journal* 55, no. 1 (2001): 9–24.

Baqer, Moin. *Khomeini: Life of the Ayatollah.* London: Thomas Dunne Books, 2001.

Montazeri, Hossein Ali. *Resaleh-ye Hoqouq* [Treaties on law]. Tehran: Saraie, 2004.

Moslem, Mehdi. *Factional Politics in Post-Khomeini Iran.* Syracuse, NY: Syracuse University Press, 2002.

Wright, Robin. *The Last Great Revolution: Turmoil and Transformation in Iran.* New York: Vintage, 2000.

Babak Rahimi

MOQADDEM, MALIKA
(1949–)

Trained as a nephrologist, Algerian novelist Malika Moqaddem (Mokeddem) gave up medicine in 1985 to devote herself entirely to writing. A descendant of recently sedentarized nomads from southern Algeria, Moqaddem evokes in her work the varied landscapes of the desert, the traditional lifestyle of Bedouin communities, and the oral rhythms of the stories her grandmother told her as a child. An outspoken critic of the misogyny she suffered from in Algeria, and more recently the racial discrimination she has experienced living and working in France, Moqaddem focuses most of her work on her own biographical experiences.

PERSONAL HISTORY

Moqaddem was born in 1949 in the small, Saharan mining town of Kenadsa on the Algerian-Moroccan border. She grew up at the foot of the great pink sand dune, la Barga, about a kilometer away from the traditional mud *ksar* (village). Her father worked as a gardener and later as a watchman for the Houillères du Sud oranais (Coal Mines of the South Oranais), and the family lived on the site. As the oldest of thirteen children (ten of whom lived) in a traditional Bedouin family, Moqaddem was expected to take care of her younger siblings—a role she rejected early on, immersing herself in schoolwork instead and earning high grades.

At puberty, she managed to stay in school, despite the fact that the high school was in the neighboring town of Béchar, more than 19 kilometers away. She was the only girl in her family or village to continue school and the only girl in a class of forty-five students. Supported by teachers, a

---

BIOGRAPHICAL HIGHLIGHTS

Name: Malika Moqaddem (Mokeddem)

Birth: 1949, Kenadsa, Algeria

Family: Divorced; no children

Nationality: Algerian

Education: Medical school, Oran and Paris; diploma in nephrology, 1985, Montpellier

PERSONAL CHRONOLOGY:

- **1985:** Begins writing
- **1989:** Opens private practice in the immigrant quarter of Montpellier
- **1990:** Publishes *Les Hommes qui marchent*
- **1991:** Wins Prix Littré, Prix Collectif du Festival du Premier Roman de Chambéry, and Prix Algérien de la Fondation Nourredine Aba
- **1992:** Publishes *Le Siècle des sauterelles*; wins Prix Afrique-Méditerranée de l'ADELF for *Le Siècle des sauterelles*
- **1993:** Publishes *L'interdite*
- **1994:** Wins Prix Méditerranée for *L'interdite*
- **1995:** Publishes *Des rêves et des assassins*
- **1998:** Publishes *La nuit de la lézarde*
- **2000:** Publishes *Of Dreams and Assassins*
- **2001:** Publishes *N'zid*
- **2003:** Publishes *La transe des insoumis*
- **2005:** Publishes *Mes homes*
- **2006:** Publishes *Century of Locusts*

---

literate paternal uncle, and her grandmother, Moqaddem persuaded her father to let her attend boarding school. She stubbornly refused her mother's attempts to draw her into overwhelming domestic tasks. She further established her independence from her family by working as a residence hall director during the school year, thus earning her own money and giving her father some of her wages. At home during the long, excruciatingly hot summer months, she erected a wall of books between herself and her family, took over the room set aside for guests, stayed up late reading, and then slept long into the day.

Moqaddem also refused an arranged marriage. When she left for medical school in Oran, she suffered from anorexia and insomnia. She traveled to Paris in

1977 where she finished her medical studies, married a Frenchman in 1978 and moved to Montpellier. There, she left hospital practice because of the race and gender bias she perceived and devoted herself to writing and obtaining a diploma in nephrology in 1985. In 1989, she opened a private practice serving North African clients, among others. She returned to Algeria for the first time in 1991 to receive the Nourredine Aba prize for *Les Hommes qui marchent* (1990; Men on the move). Since 1995 she has been a nephrologist seven days a month and a writer the rest of the time. She divorced in 1995. In 2001, after an absence of twenty-four years, Moqaddem visited her family in Kenadsa.

INFLUENCES AND CONTRIBUTIONS

In addition to the oral stories of her grandmother, Moqaddem was greatly influenced by the life and writing of Isabelle Eberhardt (1877–1904), a radical individualist and romantic who married an Algerian, frequented the French Foreign Legion, and later spent time in the Sufi *zawiya* (mystical lodge) in Kenadsa. Similar to Eberhardt, Moqaddem's life has attracted perhaps more attention than her writing; Moqaddem, however, has won a number of literary prizes including: Prix Littré (1991), the Prix Collectif du Festival du Premier Roman de Chambéry (1991), and the Prix Algérien de la Fondation Nourredine Aba (1991) for *Les Hommes qui marchent*, the Prix Afrique-Méditerranée de l'ADELF for *Le Siècle des sauterelles* (Century of Locusts) (1992) and the Prix Méditerranée (1994) for *L'Interdite* (Forbidden Woman).

THE WORLD'S PERSPECTIVE

Moqaddem's six novels and two memoirs are all highly critical of the misogyny she sees embedded in Algerian customs and institutions. Whereas some Western feminists praise her outspoken critique of gender practices and religion in Algeria, others—both Western and non-Western—find her work too self-centered and uncritically pro-Western. Other readers echo this critical divide.

LEGACY

Although her work is stylistically uneven and focuses mainly on her own life experiences, Moqaddem leaves a legacy of extraordinary accomplishment as a woman from a poor, rural background who became a doctor and a writer. She is a rare novelist whose intimate knowledge of Bedouin life and desert landscapes infuses her work with exquisite cultural specificity.

BIBLIOGRAPHY

Duffin, Jacalyn. Review of *The Forbidden Woman*, by Malika Mokeddem. Literature, Arts and Medicine Database. Available from http://litmed.med.nyu.edu/.

> ## MY MEN
> ■
>
> Father, my first man, through you I learned to measure love by the wounds I felt, by the absences I endured. At what age do words start their ravages? I track the images to earliest infancy. The words spring up in me, sketching out a black and white past. It's very early, too early—before reflection began, before I could even express myself, at that point when language starts to make innocence bleed, and cutting words leave a permanent scar that throbs with pain. Later in life, we live with it or rebel against it.
>
> Talking to my mother you used to say "my sons" when you spoke of my brothers; "your daughters" when the conversation concerned my sisters and me. You always said "my sons" with pride. You had a touch of impatience, irony or resentment, sometimes even anger when saying "your daughters." The anger was when I disobeyed, which was often—rebelling to rebel, and also because it was the only way to reach you.
>
> MOQADDEM, MALIKA. *MY MEN*. TRANSLATED BY KARIM HAMDY AND LAURA RICE. LINCOLN: UNIVERSITY OF NEBRASKA PRESS, 2007.

Elia, Nada. Review of *The Forbidden Woman*, by Malika Mokeddem. *World Literature Today* 72, no. 4 (1998): 879.

Helm, Yolande. "Malika Mokeddem: A New and Resonant Voice in Francophone Algerian Literature." In *Maghrebian Mosaic*, edited by Mildred Mortimer. Boulder, CO: Lynne Rienner Publishers, 2001.

Marcus, K. Melissa. Preface in *The Forbidden Woman*, by Malika Mokeddem. Lincoln: University of Nebraska Press, 1998.

Rice, Laura, and Karim Hamdy. Introduction in *Century of Locusts*, by Malika Mokeddem. Lincoln: University of Nebraska Press, 2006.

Laura Rice

MOUSSA, AMR
(1936–)

Amr Moussa (Amre Moussa, Mousa, Musa) is a former Egyptian foreign minister who has been secretary general of the League of Arab States (Arab League) since 2001.

PERSONAL HISTORY

Moussa was born on 3 October 1936 in Cairo. He received his LL.B. at Cairo University in 1957. After practicing law for one year, he joined the Egyptian foreign service in 1958, eventually serving in several departments, overseas missions, and the Egyptian delegation to the United Nations (UN). From 1974 to 1977, Moussa served as adviser and assistant to the Egyptian foreign minister. He was director of the Department of International Organizations twice, from 1977 to 1981 and 1986 to 1990. In 1990–1991, during the crucial Gulf crisis and subsequent war, Moussa served as Egypt's representative to the UN.

Moussa was appointed foreign minister in 1991, and remained in Egypt's top diplomatic post until his unanimous selection as secretary general by the member states of the Arab League in May 2001.

INFLUENCES AND CONTRIBUTIONS

During his tenure as Egyptian foreign minister, Moussa became famous for his blunt assessments and his sometimes quick temper. He was noted for his sharp criticisms directed at Israeli and American policies in the Middle East. He continued with his characteristic bluntness after becoming Arab League secretary general in 2001. In the midst of the war between Israel and Hizbullah in July 2006, for example, Moussa declared that the Middle East peace process was "dead." When asked to comment about the lavish praise heaped on Israeli prime minister ARIEL SHARON by the Quartet (the United States, Russia, the UN, and the European Union) in the wake of the August 2005 Israeli withdrawal from Gaza and a small part of the West Bank, Moussa responded in pithy fashion: "I have described this excessive exaggeration as an absurd thing that detracts from the Quartet's political sobriety" (Moussa, 2005b). Moussa also has been forthright in his assertions that while the Arab League does not want to see Iran develop nuclear weapons, it would be unfair to demand that Iran give up its nuclear program while not asking the same of Israel, which while never having admitted as much is believed to possess more than two hundred nuclear weapons.

Moussa also did much to change and revitalize the Arab League. Under his leadership, the league endorsed a 2002 Saudi peace plan for resolving the Arab-Israeli conflict. He also vowed to clear out the league's bureaucracy and generally make it a more relevant and energetic body instead of, as some have called it, a retirement club for aged Arab foreign ministers. Under his leadership the league established an Arab free-trade zone in January 2005, and moved from making decisions by consensus to voting on them.

THE WORLD'S PERSPECTIVE

Moussa's forthright attitudes and attempts over the years, particularly his criticism of Israel and the United States—

BIOGRAPHICAL HIGHLIGHTS

Name: Amr Moussa (Amre Moussa, Mousa, Musa)

Birth: 1936, Cairo, Egypt

Family: Married; two children

Nationality: Egyptian

Education: Cairo University, 1957, LL.B.

PERSONAL CHRONOLOGY:

- **1958:** Enters Egyptian foreign service
- **1967:** Named Egyptian ambassador to India
- **1974:** Adviser and assistant to foreign minister
- **1977:** Director, Foreign Ministry Department of International Organizations
- **1990:** Serves as Egyptian representative, United Nations
- **1991:** Becomes foreign minister
- **2001:** Chosen secretary general, Arab League

---

a key Egyptian ally—have earned him many admirers in the Arab world. Nowhere is this felt more than in his native Egypt. Popular Egyptian singer Sha'aban Abd al-Rahim released a hit song that includes the lyrics, "I hate Israel, and I love Amr Moussa." Beyond that, there even is a Web site (http://thankyouamrmoussa.com) that was created to thank him and Arab foreign ministers for Moussa's 15 July 2006 statement that the Arab-Israeli peace process is dead. In fact, some have speculated that Egyptian president HUSNI MUBARAK moved him out of the foreign minister's position in 2001 precisely because his growing popularity was seen as a threat to Mubarak's regime. Moussa's name was also floated as a possible presidential candidate after Mubarak announced that there would be multiparty elections in the future.

LEGACY

Amr Moussa is still writing his own legacy. But it is clear that he will be seen as the diplomatic incarnation of the rising Arab frustration with the policies of Israel and the United States in the Middle East.

BIBLIOGRAPHY

Moussa, Amr. Interview with Amr Moussa. "An Offer That Contains the Issues for Peace with Israel." *Der Spiegel* (13 April 2005a). Available from http://www.spiegel.de/international.

———. "Arab League Chief Amr Mousa: What is the Quartet Thanking Ariel Sharon For?" Interview by Ghida Fakhri.

Al-Sharq al-Awsat (London). (4 October 2005b). Translated by *Occupation Magazine.* Available from http://www.kibush .co.il/show_file.asp?num=9193.

Michael R. Fischbach

MUASHER, MARWAN
(1956–)

Marwan Jamil Muasher (Mu'ashir) is a prominent Jordanian diplomat and politician, deeply involved in Jordanian relations with Israel and the United States.

PERSONAL HISTORY

Muasher was born to a Christian family in Amman, Jordan, in 1956. The Lebanese Civil War interrupted his studies at the American University in Beirut, and he completed his B.A. in electrical engineering in 1977 at Purdue University in the United States. Muasher also obtained a Ph.D. in computer engineering from Purdue in 1981.

Muasher thereafter returned to Jordan to work in the private sector, and began writing columns for Jordan's English-language daily newspaper. In 1985, he entered government service at the Jordanian Ministry of Planning. In 1989, he became press adviser to the prime minister, leading

Marwan Muasher. AP IMAGES.

BIOGRAPHICAL HIGHLIGHTS

■

Name: Marwan Jamil Muasher (also Mu'ashshir)

Birth: 1956, Amman, Jordan

Family: Wife, Lynne; children, Omar and Hana

Nationality: Jordanian

Education: American University of Beirut, 1972–1975; B.A., electrical engineer, Purdue University, 1977; Ph.D., computer engineering, Purdue University, 1981

PERSONAL CHRONOLOGY:

- **1985:** Works at Ministry of Planning
- **1989:** Press adviser to prime minister
- **1991:** Jordan Information Bureau, Washington; spokesperson, Jordanian delegation to Madrid peace talks
- **1995:** Jordanian ambassador to Israel
- **1996:** Minister of information
- **1997:** Ambassador to United States
- **2002:** Minister of foreign affairs
- **2005:** Appointed to Jordanian Senate
- **2006:** Senior vice president, World Bank

---

to his appointment as director of the Jordan Information Bureau, part of the Jordanian embassy, in Washington, D.C. from 1991 to 1994. In that capacity, Muasher entered the diplomatic realm by using his fluent, American-accented English as spokesperson for the Jordanian delegation to the Jordanian-Palestinian-Israeli peace talks that commenced in Madrid in October 1991.

In April 1995, Muasher's experience in diplomacy led to his posting as Jordan's first ambassador to Israel, only the second Arab ambassador ever sent to the Jewish state. He went on to become Jordan's minister of information in 1996, and then its ambassador to the United States in 1997. From 2002 to 2004, he was Jordan's minister of foreign affairs, deputy prime minister in 2004 and 2005, and was appointed to the Jordanian Senate in November 2005.

In December 2006, Muasher was appointed senior vice president for external affairs, communications, and United Nations affairs at the World Bank in Washington.

INFLUENCES AND CONTRIBUTIONS

Muasher was the public face of Jordanian diplomacy during a crucial time in Jordan's history. The renewal of Arab-Israeli peace talks in 1991 led to the second peace treaty between Israel and an Arab state, between Jordan and Israel, in October 1994. As spokesperson for Jordanian negotiators and as Jordan's ambassador to Israel, Muasher carried the burden of expressing Jordan's positions clearly and forthrightly. As ambassador to the United States, he worked hard to ensure completion of the U.S.-Jordanian Free Trade Agreement, and as foreign minister, was in office during a time when Jordan's security ties with the United States increased.

Muasher also has had to shoulder his public tasks during times of considerable domestic difficulty and controversy. The peace treaty with Israel was not universally popular in Jordan. As minister of information, Muasher was responsible for censorship under the 1993 Press and Publications Law, and several leading journalists were arrested during his time in office. In a country where the average citizen harbors decidedly anti-American and pro-Iraqi sentiments, he was publicly urging a peaceful resolution of the Iraq crisis even as Jordan secretly allowed U.S. troops to invade Iraq from its territory in March 2003. Muasher has been the highest-profile Christian in the government of a country in which Islam is the state religion, at a time when Islamic opposition to the government has remained strong.

On 16 March 2007 Muasher was appointed senior vice president for external affairs of the World Bank.

THE WORLD'S PERSPECTIVE

Muasher is known as a very capable diplomat who skillfully represented his country's interests. In 2000 he was given the Diplomat of the Year award by the World Affairs Council of Los Angeles.

LEGACY

Muasher was one of the most important Jordanian diplomats working on the Jordanian-Israeli and Palestinian-Israeli relations after the start of peace talks in 1991, and for a long time was the most articulate and visible spokesperson for Jordanian interests other than the king himself.

BIBLIOGRAPHY

Muasher, Marwan. "The Arab Initiative and the Role of Arab Diplomacy." *Bitterlemons* 43 (25 November 2002). Available from http://www.jordanembassyus.org/hemm10262004.htm.

———. "Ten Years down the Road to Peace." *Jordan Times* (26 October 2004). Available from http://www.jordan embassyus.org/hemm10262004.htm.

"Transcript of Interview of CNN's Wolf Blitzer." Embassy of Jordan–Washington, D.C. Updated 14 March 2004. Available from http://www.jordanembassyus.org/hemm 03142004.htm.

Michael R. Fischbach

MUBARAK, HUSNI
(1928–)

Egyptian military officer and politician Husni (Hosni) Mubarak has been one of the most important Arab leaders of the late twentieth and early twenty-first centuries. Appointed vice president in 1975 by President Anwar Sadat, whom he succeeded as president in 1981, Mubarak has held his office longer than any other Egyptian leader of the twentieth century. Continuing Presidents Gamal Abdel Nasser and Sadat's dominance of the executive, legislative, and judicial branches, Mubarak has maintained the Egyptian government's ties to the United States, relations with Israel, and privatization of the economy. Upper classes and foreigners have prospered more in Egypt than the growing Egyptian population, which has become increasingly urbanized but remains poor. By renewing his emergency powers, Mubarak has used security forces against political and religious opponents.

PERSONAL HISTORY

Husni Mubarak was born on 4 May 1928 to an Egyptian middle-class family in Kafr al-Musayliha, Egypt, a small town in the province of Minufiyya. He was educated at local elementary and secondary schools, where he studied

Husni Mubarak. GERARD JULIEN/AFP/GETTY IMAGES.

mainly Arabic and history. His father, an inspector for the Justice Ministry, wanted his son to go to the Higher Teachers College in Cairo and to become a schoolteacher, but Mubarak chose a military career. He graduated from Egypt's Military Academy in 1947 and from the Air Force Academy in 1950. Trained as a fighter pilot, Mubarak served as an instructor at the Air Force Academy from 1954 to 1961, and spent two academic years in the Soviet Union where he learned to fly the latest Soviet jet fighters. He presided over the Air Force Academy from 1967 to 1969.

From the late 1960s to the mid-1970s, Mubarak held the top posts in the air force. From 1969 to 1972, he was the chief of staff of the air force. Then, as commander-in-chief of the air force and deputy war minister, Mubarak assumed a leadership role in the air war Egypt waged against Israel in October 1973. Based on the performance of Mubarak and the air force, he received Egypt's three highest military medals and became the air marshal in 1974.

Mubarak's rise in government was tied to Sadat who removed all Soviet military advisers from Egypt and, after the good showing of the Egyptian military against Israel in 1973, relied increasingly on the United States to negotiate disengagement agreements with Israel. Sadat also replaced the one-party rule of Nasser's Arab Socialist Union with his own National Democratic Party. He traveled to Jerusalem to address the Israeli Knesset in 1977, reached agreement with Israeli prime minister Menachem Begin at Camp David in 1978, and established Egypt's relations with Israel in 1979. Sadat's engagement with Israel upset many Egyptians and turned most Palestinians and other Arabs against him. Most Arab states severed their relations with Egypt and members of the Arab League abandoned its headquarters in Cairo.

In 1975, Sadat made Mubarak vice president. Mubarak observed how Sadat used his new constitution of 1971 to dominate the executive, legislative, and judicial branches of Egypt's government. Sadat's constitution gave the president the power to appoint and dismiss the prime minister and all members of the cabinet. He and the cabinet dominated the so-called People's Assembly by initiating the vast majority of bills, manipulating the parliamentary schedule to pass controversial bills, and lifting immunity from prosecution for any legislators who refused to do the president's bidding. The president appointed and promoted all judges, including those of the Supreme Constitutional Court, most of whose rulings backed the president. In opposition to the one-party rule of the Arab Socialist Union under Nasser, Sadat declared multiparty rule, but in fact used his Committee for the Affairs of Political Parties Committee (PPC) to ensure that his own party, the National Democratic Party

BIOGRAPHICAL HIGHLIGHTS

Name: Husni Mubarak (Hosni Mubarak)

Birth: 1928, Kafr al-Musayliha, Minufiyya province, Egypt

Family: Wife, Suzanne Thabet Mubarak; two sons, Ala and Gamal

Nationality: Egyptian

Education: Egypt's Military Academy, 1947; Air Force Academy, 1950

PERSONAL CHRONOLOGY:

- **1950s–mid-1970s:** Officer in the Egyptian air force

- **1975–1981:** Made vice president of Egypt

- **1981:** Becomes president of Egypt

(NDP), remained dominant. The PPC has six members: the ministers of interior and justice, the state minister for legislative affairs, and three judicial figures appointed by the president's ministers, all of whom served at the pleasure of the president.

In the years immediately before and after Mubarak became vice president, he observed Sadat's use of Islam to counter lingering leftist support for Nasser, whose secularism and socialism had turned most of Egypt's religious leaders into mere employees of the state. Sadat made public demonstrations of his own religious piety, released some members of the Muslim brotherhood who had been imprisoned by Nasser, and permitted the publication of its periodical, *al-Da'wa* (The call). Impatient with the older members of the brotherhood, Muslim students joined al-Jama'a al-Islamiya, whose associations at Egypt's major universities protested against the crowded conditions on campus and the bleak prospects university graduates faced by taking jobs with the government. By the late 1970s, more young Muslims were influenced by the writings of Sayyid Qutb, a member of the Muslim Brotherhood executed by Nasser's regime in 1966. When the radical Islamic organization al-Takfir wa'al-Hijra sought the release of some of their members from prison by taking a government ministers hostage, Sadat's regime arrested and executed scores of the group's members. Mubarak endorsed the president's crackdown on Islamist opponents. Mubarak agreed that Sadat must not hesitate to censor their hostile publications, or to arrest those who challenged the authority of the Egyptian state. However, Mubarak also saw the risks Sadat ran with Egyptian public opinion by courting the U.S. media and supporting publicly the former shah of Iran, Mohammad Reza Pahlavi, who was ailing in Egypt as Sadat's guest.

Islamist militants had underground cells in Upper Egypt and in the slums of Cairo and crowded cities along the Nile. There were cells also inside Egypt's armed forces. One of them, al-Jihad, claimed responsibility for the assassination of Sadat. On 6 October 1981, several men in uniform were riding in a military parade commemorating the anniversary of Egypt crossing the Suez Canal in 1973 when they fatally shot Sadat in the reviewing stand. Taking office immediately, Mubarak was confirmed as president in a referendum held one week after the assassination. Five of Sadat's assassins would be executed in April 1982. Mubarak ordered the arrest of militant Islamists, hundreds of whom were tried on charges of belonging to al-Jihad, which called for overthrowing the government. In September 1984, 174 of the 302 people arrested in conjunction with Sadat's murder were acquitted of conspiring to overthrow the government; sixteen were sentenced to hard labor for life; and the rest received prison sentences up to fifteen years. Mubarak also released some of the more moderate political and religious opposition whom Sadat had detained.

As the violence of Islamist militancy declined in the early 1980s, Mubarak saw increasing numbers of Egyptians look to the more moderate Muslim Brotherhood. This resilient organization, established in the 1920s, mushroomed by the 1940s into millions of members, some of whom were armed and operated underground. By the 1980s, the brotherhood rejected violence. The Muslim Brotherhood emphasized its efforts to provide for the health, education, and welfare needs of millions unserved by the state. The brotherhood also increased its influence on campuses and within professional organizations. Because the state recognized no religious organization as a political party, some Muslim Brotherhood members ran as independents and formed the largest opposition bloc in parliament during the mid-1980s. Mubarak even made some friendly gestures toward Muslim moderates, such as banning alcohol outside tourist areas.

When Mubarak became president in 1981, his declaration of emergency rule gave him control not only of the state, but more ways to manipulate Egypt's politics. President Mubarak renewed this emergency rule every three years, which enabled him to censor, seize, or confiscate letters, newspapers, publications, and all other means of expression and advertising before they were published. The emergency rule also allowed Mubarak to control political campaigns by requiring that all political meetings must report in advance the date, location, and

estimated size of the gathering to the local police, which in turn forwards this information to the Ministry of Interior for approval. These emergency measures made it possible for Mubarak to avoid declaring martial law, which requires suspension of the constitution and the replacement of civil with military courts. Mubarak's regime has used other means to reduce the influence of parties running candidates for the People's Assembly. The general elections of 1984, 1987, and 1990 gave Mubarak's National Democratic Party a huge majority over all the recognized parties, none of which had much impact on the People's Assembly. In 1987, Mubarak was nominated by the necessary two-thirds majority of the legislature to seek a second six-year term as president. The only candidate, Mubarak won 97 percent of the votes cast.

By the end of the 1980s, Mubarak had improved Egypt's standing with the leaders of other Arab states, most of whom had initially seen Mubarak as Sadat's man and no less of a puppet of the United States. President Mubarak conducted Egypt's inter-Arab diplomacy mostly out of public view, in contrast to the public posturing of the charismatic Nasser and flamboyant Sadat. Mubarak's personal diplomacy helped him improve Egypt's relations first with Jordan, Saudi Arabia, and the oil-rich countries of the Gulf, all of which were tied to the United States. He even eased some strained relations with Sudan and Libya, but he faced problems with Lebanon, Syria, and Iraq. Whenever Israeli-Palestinian tensions flared up and the United States sided with Israel, Mubarak had to use great skill in conducting Egypt's relations with other Arab states. In 1989, Saudi Arabia's King Fahd visited Cairo, the same year that Egypt was readmitted into the Arab League. The sevenfold increase in oil prices during the 1970s had given enormous economic power to Saudi Arabia and the oil-rich states of the Gulf. Egypt sided diplomatically, but not militarily, with SADDAM HUSSEIN's Iraq during his costly eight-year war with Iran in the 1980s. When Iraq invaded Kuwait in 1990, Mubarak stood with the United States, the leader of a large coalition of Arab as well as non-Arab allies. Mubarak even ordered forty thousand Egyptian forces to the Gulf War, the only time he used military force outside the boundaries of Egypt itself. As a result, Washington canceled $14 billion worth of Egypt's accumulated foreign debt, which was about half what Egypt owed the United States, mostly for weaponry.

During the early 1990s, Mubarak faced more Islamist protest and violence. He had little success as a mediator in the Israeli-Palestinian conflict after the Palestinians launched their intifada in late 1987. Palestinian and Muslim rage over Israeli settlements in the occupied territories of the West Bank and Gaza was heightened by political, social, and economic frustrations in Egypt. Outbreaks of Islamist violence in Asyut, one of the poorest provinces of Upper

Egypt, as well as in Imbaba, one of the slums of Cairo, increased. In June 1992, Mubarak ordered five thousand members of the security forces to Asyut for the most extensive military operation against Islamists in years. The People's Assembly duly passed new antiterrorism legislation that imposed the death sentence for more crimes. There was a fall in the number of tourists visiting Egypt and a fall in foreign currency earnings, upon which Egypt heavily depended. Following the bombing of the World Trade Center in New York City in February 1993, U.S. authorities arrested Shaykh Umar Abd al-Rahman, the spiritual leader of al-Jama'a al-Islamiya, who had been exiled from Egypt. Later that year, when there were more attacks on foreign tourists and more attempted assassinations of several members of Egypt's cabinet, Mubarak appointed a general to head the Ministry of Interior. In 1993, Egyptian courts sentenced thirty-eight terrorists to death, the largest number of political executions in Egypt's recent history.

By the mid-1990s, armed Islamists were attacking tourist trains and Nile cruise ships, banks, and foreign institutions. The emergency law having been renewed for another three years in 1994, Mubarak put local elections under the Ministry of Interior and warned foreign journalists that they would be arrested or expelled if they did not follow government press restrictions. Mubarak's party lost some parliamentary seats in the general election of 1995, and received hundreds of complaints about voting irregularities. Members of al-Jama'a al-Islamiya claimed responsibility for the attempted assassination of Mubarak on his way from the Addis Ababa airport to a meeting of the Organization of African Unity in 1995. In September 1997, seven German tourists were killed and even more of them were wounded in Cairo; a few weeks later fifty-eight foreign tourists were killed in Luxor by al-Jama'a al-Islamiya. At this juncture, Mubarak took over three main cabinet posts and demanded the arrest of Muslim Brotherhood members and any publications that encouraged armed Islamists.

Islamist terrorism and state repression peaked at the end of the 1990s, as strikes and labor unrest led some politicians to propose the termination of all employment contracts. Even nongovernmental organizations faced new restrictions from the state, along with more arrests and trials of terrorists. As violence lessened, Mubarak announced the release of thousands of prisoners, provided they stopped associating with illegal organizations and renounced violence. Early in 1999, some leaders of al-Jama'a al-Islamiya agreed to a cease-fire, which the government respected while proceeding with the largest security trial Egypt had held since militant Islamists had launched their campaigns against the state.

Mubarak began his fourth six-year term in office late in 1999 and early in 2000 renewed his emergency powers for yet another three years. Facing much opposition

domestically, Mubarak still tried to assert Egypt's influence regionally by criticizing U.S. air strikes against Iraq and against alleged terrorist sites in Afghanistan and Sudan. He also tried to encourage more U.S. peace efforts with the Israelis and Palestinians. Mubarak appointed his son Gamal (also Jamal) to the general secretariat of the National Democratic Party in the hope of energizing the party with the approach of the general election of 2000. New judicial supervision of elections improved fairness, but Muslim Brotherhood members complained of obstructions and the NDP's old guard remained in control of the People's Assembly. A good deal of Mubarak's fourth term was consumed by controversies surrounding Egypt's judicial system.

To Mubarak, the terrorist attacks of 11 September 2001 in New York City and Washington, D.C., justified Egypt's own war against Islamist terror. He soon had twenty-two members of the Muslim Brotherhood arrested for inciting violence and belonging to an outlawed organization. A military court accused ninety-four Islamists of conspiring to assassinate President Mubarak and overthrow the government. Under Mubarak's emergency rule, those on trial had no right of appeal. In 2002, leaders of al-Jama'a al-Islamiya apologized to the people of Egypt for their violent acts of the past and considered offering their victims compensation. In 2003, when the People's Assembly extended the state of emergency for another three years despite overwhelming Egyptian opposition, Mubarak pointed to Western democracies' tightening of security. However, he soon announced that all the emergency laws that had been in place since the assassination of President Sadat in 1981 were to be abolished except for those necessary to maintain public order and security. A committee of the prime minister withdrew six of the thirteen military orders. Mubarak also set up a new council of thirty-five ministers to comply with Washington's push for reform across the Middle East. Some Egyptians took hope from the release of more than seven hundred alleged Islamist militants in the autumn of 2004, but hundreds more were arrested after car bombs destroyed resorts on the Sinai Peninsula. Early in 2005, Mubarak engaged in a national dialogue about reforming the elections for the People's Assembly and the presidency itself. Reform was still being talked about until July 2005, when almost 100 people were killed and 200 more injured at Sharm al-Shaykh on the Sinai Peninsula. By the end of the month, Mubarak announced his intention to seek a fifth six-year term. Promising further reforms as he campaigned for the presidential election in September 2005, Mubarak received more than 88 percent of the votes. His two main opponents gained less than 10 percent, and the seven other candidates each received less than 0.5 percent of the vote. The turnout was low and no presidential candidates were identified by party. In the general election for the People's Assembly at the end of 2005, some veteran NDP and secular party candidates lost seats, but the independents backed by the Muslim Brotherhood gained almost seventy.

Mubarak managed to maintain Egypt's relations with other Arab countries and the United States despite his unwillingness to support U.S.-led campaigns in Afghanistan and Iraq. Further political reforms in Egypt were unlikely as Mubarak announced yet another reorganization of the NDP'S leadership. Mubarak's son, Gamal, was promoted to a key leadership post in the NDP along with other known supporters of the president. With the United States preoccupied by Iraq and Afghanistan, Mubarak spoke less of reform and clamped down on his opponents, particularly those who criticized the judiciary. In Mubarak's fifth term, domestic reforms languished as Mubarak failed to influence the Israeli cabinet and the Palestinian group Hamas, whose electoral victory led to a boycott and a freeze on international support for the Palestinian Authority and the peace process. Egypt's relations with the United States cooled.

INFLUENCES AND CONTRIBUTIONS

Apart from the influence of his father and family when he was young, Mubarak was shaped most by his military career in the Egyptian air force and by his political apprenticeship with Sadat, to whom he remained loyal as long as he lived and even after Sadat's death. Mubarak has little of the warm personal qualities of successful politicians, but has retained the cool demeanor of the dutiful military commander. Neither an ideologue nor a political visionary, Mubarak dislikes public speaking. A pragmatist, he prefers to meet with small groups of men seated informally around the room or at a conference table, where he is at his best negotiating in Egypt or abroad. Preoccupied with the defense of Egypt, he has less interest in domestic issues and feels uncomfortable with concerns, whether religious or secular, about the dire lot of most Egyptians, the poorest of whom are undereducated, underemployed, and undervalued.

Mubarak's greatest contributions may derive from his keeping a sense of proportion about the limited influence of Egypt, a crowded and poor country, in the region and the world. Unlike the young Nasser, who ambitiously saw Egypt at the center of an Arab circle, an Islamic circle, and an African circle, Mubarak sees Egypt as only one of many countries of the modern Middle East. Egypt is more populous than any other Arab country and has an ancient pre-Islamic tradition along with Muslim connections to the pilgrimage to Mecca and the scholars and students at al-Azhar, Sunni Islam's greatest center of religious learning. Further, Cairo is a center of Arab publishing, movies, and media. Unlike the flamboyant Sadat, who enjoyed public fame and much fortune, Mubarak is impressed by neither. He rules in a region where oil-rich leaders have more

---

DIALOGUE WITH THE ISLAMISTS IS NO LONGER AN OPTION

We opt for peace in order to prevent the continued wastage of funds used for the purchase of arms and ammunition. Such funds could now be spent for the welfare and prosperity of the Egyptian people, who have long suffered from the horrors of war in both psychological and material terms.

Dialogue with the Islamists is no longer an option. The late President Sadat tried this and he got nowhere so he got rid of three-quarters of them. We have tried dialogue with them but as soon as they started to get strong they no longer wanted dialogue so I took the decision in 1993 to have no more of that.

HUSNI MUBARAK IN KASEM, MAY. *IN THE GUISE OF DEMOCRACY: GOVERNANCE IN CONTEMPORARY EGYPT.* READING, U.K.: ITHACA PRESS, 1999.

---

money than most other countries. Recognizing that Egypt's economic and military weaknesses contribute to corruption, he has succeeded in keeping Egypt out of war for quarter of a century. That contribution is significant, no matter how limited his successes have been in achieving greater peace in the region and greater prosperity for Egyptians. Fearing more food riots, as shook Cairo in the late 1970s, and maintaining subsidies for the poorest Egyptians, Mubarak has not lowered subsidies as much as ordered by the International Monetary Fund and other agents of globalization. That he has remained president of Egypt for so long, however, indicates that Mubarak is not indifferent to the poor peoples of Egypt. Politically active Egyptians have tired of him and disagreed with him, but they still respect him as a great military officer and a responsible president with a strong sense of duty toward their country.

THE WORLD'S PERSPECTIVE

Different Egyptians, Arabs, and Muslims have different views of Mubarak's presidency. Critics attack him for being cynical or cautious, yet his supporters see his restraint and caution as necessary. Whereas younger Egyptians, Arabs, and Muslims have expressed impatience with Mubarak, the older ones are more likely to value his decades of service and determination to defend Egypt and maintain law and order. Militants who are strongly attached to their own Islamist agendas feel so frustrated by Mubarak that they wish he were dead.

Non-Egyptians, non-Arabs, and non-Muslims throughout the world have different views of Mubarak, if they have ever heard of him or taken any interest in contemporary Egypt. U.S. leaders respect Mubarak's shrewdness and straightforwardness about the Arab world, and always take Mubarak's views seriously even when he quietly criticizes some U.S. policies. Most Americans pay little attention to Mubarak, who refuses to play media politics. No less than the United States, Europe's leaders respect Mubarak's vulnerabilities in presiding over Egypt, the most populous Arab country in a region that is weak compared with countries with more oil riches and powerful weapons.

LEGACY

A stolid figure with a taciturn manner, Mubarak's legacy has been overshadowed by more ambitious, powerful, and rich leaders on the world stage. Historians should value Mubarak less for what he did in Egypt than for what he did not allow Egypt to do. He did not keep Egypt on war footing, nor lead the country into costly and destructive wars. Instead, he helped keep the Egyptian nation on a steady, if unexciting, course in a region with the richest reserves of oil during a time when the Persian Gulf area became of main economic concern to the rest of the world and strategically the most vital to the greatest powers of the world.

Economically, Mubarak had to find a middle way between the rich and poor, the demands of the International Monetary Fund for restructuring, and the anger of those threatened by economic contraction, between the public and private sectors, and between national self-sufficiency and fuller integration in to the global order by pursuing a policy of export-led growth. Politically, Mubarak had to find a middle way between secularism and theocracy, authoritarian control and liberalization, between those who venerated Nasser and those who venerated the founder of the Muslim Brotherhood, Hasan al-Banna, and the angry Islamist assertions of Qutb.

BIBLIOGRAPHY

Amin, Galal. *Whatever Happened to the Egyptians? Changes in Egyptian Society from 1950 to the Present.* Cairo: American University in Cairo Press, 2000.

Baker, Raymond William. *Islam without Fear: Egypt and the New Islamists.* Cambridge, MA: Harvard University Press, 2003.

Elyachar, Julia. *Markets of Dispossession: NGOs, Economic Development, and the State in Cairo.* Durham, NC: Duke University Press, 2005.

Kassem, Maye. *Egyptian Politics: The Dynamics of Authoritarian Rule.* Boulder, CO: Lynne Rienner Publishers, 2004.

———. *In the Guise of Democracy: Governance in Contemporary Egypt.* Reading, U.K.: Ithaca Press, 1999.

Springborg, Robert. *Mubarak's Egypt: Fragmentation of the Political Order.* Boulder, CO: Westview Press, 1989.

Roger Adelson

MUBARAK, MA'SUMA AL-
(c. 1951–)

Mas'uma (also Massouma, Masouma) bint Salih al-Mubarak is a Kuwaiti academic and minister.

PERSONAL HISTORY

Born around 1951 into a middle-class Kuwaiti Shi'ite Muslim family, Mubarak received her B.S. (political sciences) from the University of Kuwait in 1971, and a diploma of planning from the Arab Planning Institute in Kuwait in 1973. She then traveled to the United States for graduate studies, eventually earned an M.S. in political science from Northern Texas University in 1976, an M.S. in international relations from the University of Denver in 1980, and a Ph.D. in the same field from the University of Denver in 1982. Her husband, a Bahraini, also received his Ph.D. from Denver. On her return to Kuwait University, Mubarak was made chair of the political science department in 1983, one of the first Kuwaiti women to hold such a position, and later held visiting appointments at the University of Denver from 1986 to 1988 and at the University of Bahrain from 1990 to 1992 during the Iraqi occupation of Kuwait. She again served as chair of her department from 2001 to 2002.

INFLUENCES AND CONTRIBUTIONS

In the midst of her academic duties and raising three children, she also found time to write regular columns for the Kuwaiti newspapers *al-Anba*, *al-Qabas*, *al-Siyasa*, *al-Watan*, and the Bahraini paper *Akhbar al-Khalij*. She has also held membership of such civil society organizations in Kuwait as the Graduates Society, the Economists Society, the Journalists Society, and the Kuwaiti Cultural Women's Society, in addition to activities in promoting women's rights and human rights in the developing world.

On 12 June 2005, Mubarak was named Kuwait's first female cabinet minister ever, only a month after women were granted the right to vote and run for office in the elected National Assembly. She was given the positions of minister of planning and minister of state for administrative development affairs and retained those positions in the new cabinet of 9 February 2006, the first under Emir Sabah al-Ahmad Al Sabah, who succeeded his brother Emir SABAH AL-AHMAD AL-JABIR AL SABAH upon the latter's death a few weeks earlier. After she was sworn in, she said, "It's a great day for Kuwaiti women who have struggled and persevered persistently to gain their full political rights" ("Kuwait's First Woman

BIOGRAPHICAL HIGHLIGHTS

Name: Mas'uma al-Mubarak (Massouma, Masouma)

Birth: c. 1951, Kuwait

Family: Married; children

Nationality: Kuwaiti

Education: B.S. (political sciences), University of Kuwait, 1971; diploma of planning, Arab Planning Institute, Kuwait, 1973; M.S. (political science), Northern Texas University, Texas, 1976; M.S. (international relations), University of Denver, Colorado, 1980; Ph.D. (international relations), University of Denver, 1982

PERSONAL CHRONOLOGY:

- **1983:** Appointed chair, political science department, Kuwait University
- **1986:** Visiting professor, University of Denver
- **1990:** Visiting professor, University of Bahrain
- **2005:** Appointed Kuwait's minister of planning and minister of state for administrative development affairs
- **2006:** Appointed Kuwait's minister of communications
- **2007:** Appointed Kuwait's minister of health

Minister Sworn In" [20 June 2005]: http://news.bbc .co.uk/2/hi/middle_east/4111234.stm). A few months later on 10 June 2006, the emir appointed a new cabinet in response to the objection of the opposition in the National Assembly to several ministers. Mubarak was retained but moved to the position of minister of communications. In March 2007 Mubarak was appointed minister of health.

LEGACY

Mas'uma al-Mubarak will be remembered as a respected scholar and political commentator, but will occupy a particular spot in history for being the first-ever female cabinet minister in Kuwait.

BIBLIOGRAPHY

"Person of the Week: Dr. Massouma al-Mubarak." ABC News. 17 June 2005. Available from http://abcnews.go.com/.

J. E. Peterson

MUHAMMAD VI
(1963–)

King Muhammad VI of Morocco ascended to the throne on 23 July 1999, becoming the eighteenth king in the Alaouite dynasty that has ruled Morocco since the mid-seventeenth century. He also receives the title of Emir al-Mu'minin, or commander of the faithful, a title that carries both political and religious connotations. He is known for having initiated a timid process of reforms in Morocco that led to the establishment of a limited constitutional monarchy.

PERSONAL HISTORY

King Muhammad VI was born Prince Muhammad ibn al-Hassan in Rabat, Morocco, on Wednesday, 21 August 1963. He is the eldest son of the late King HASSAN II, who was an Arab descendant of the Islamic prophet Muhammad, and Lalla Latifa Hammou, who descends from a prominent Moroccan Berber family. Prince Muhammad was enrolled at the Qur'anic school at the Royal Palace at the age of four, where he received a traditional religious education. Following the completion of his elementary and secondary studies at the Royal College and the achievement of his baccalaureate in 1981, he studied law at Muhammad V University's law school in Rabat, where he received his B.A. in 1985. His undergraduate thesis was titled "The Arab-African Union and the Strategy of the Kingdom of Morocco in matters of International Relations." In 1987

Muhammad VI. ZOHRA BENSEMRA/AFP/GETTY IMAGES.

BIOGRAPHICAL HIGHLIGHTS

■

Name: Muhammad VI, King of Morocco

Birth: 1963, Rabat, Morocco

Family: Wife, Salma Bennani (Princess Lalla Salma, married 2002); son, Moulay Hasssan; daughter, Princess Lalla Khadija

Nationality: Moroccan

Education: B.A. (law), Muhammad V University, Rabat, 1985; Ph.D. (law), University of Nice Sophia Antipolis, 1993; honorary Ph.D. from George Washington University

PERSONAL CHRONOLOGY:

- **1983:** Chairs Moroccan delegation to the seventh summit of the Non-Aligned Movement in New Delhi; chairs delegation of the Organization of the African Unity (OAU) in Addis Ababa

- **1985:** Appointed coordinator of the Bureaux and Services of the General Staff of the Royal Armed Forces

- **1994:** Promoted to major general in the Moroccan army

- **1999:** Becomes king of Morocco; orders creation of the Indemnity Commission to address abuses during the postindependence period

- **2005:** Launches the National Initiative for Human Development

he obtained his Certificat D'Études Supérieures (CES) in political science, and in July 1988, he was awarded a Diplôme des Études Supérieures du Doctorat in public law. Shortly thereafter, in 1998, he embarked on a short period of practical training under the guidance of the then-president of the European Commission, Jacques Delors. On 29 October 1993 he obtained a doctorate in law from the University of Nice Sophia Antipolis (France), with honorable distinction granted by his dissertation committee. His doctoral dissertation revolved around European Union–Maghreb relations. A year later, on 12 July 1994, he was promoted to the rank of major general in the Moroccan army. He also holds an honorary doctorate from George Washington University in Washington D.C., granted on 22 June 2000 for his efforts in expanding democracy in Morocco. His father's decision to educate his son in Morocco during his early formative years has been hailed by Muhammad VI as representative of his father's wish that he remain close to the

interests of the country. As prince, he was entrusted by his father with numerous missions to several Arab, Islamic, African, and European countries. On 10 March 1983, he chaired the Moroccan delegation to the seventh summit of the Non-Aligned Movement in New Delhi, India, and that same year chaired a delegation of the Organization of African Unity (OAU) in Addis Ababa, Ethiopia. On 11 April 1985 he was appointed coordinator of the Bureaux and Services of the General Staff of the Royal Armed Forces. On 23 February 1989, he represented Hassan II at the funeral of Emperor Hirohito of Japan.

Muhammad VI has one brother (Prince Moulay Rachid) and three sisters (Princesses Lalla Maryam, Lalla Asma, and Lalla Hasna). On 21 March 2002 he married Salma Bennani (currently known as Princess Lalla Salma) and granted her the title of princess. They have two children: Moulay Hasssan, the crown prince, born on 8 May 2003, and Princess Lalla Khadija, born on 28 February 2007.

INFLUENCES AND CONTRIBUTIONS

Ever since his ascension to the throne, Muhammad VI has made an attempt to publicly address the most contentious issues of Moroccan society, namely democracy, poverty, unemployment, and illiteracy, while maintaining his predecessor's stance on the Western Sahara conflict—particularly with a strong stance against Western Saharan and Algerian plans for the region—and trying to resituate European-North African relations to an equal footing while reinforcing Morocco's strategic alliance with the United States. During his first address to the nation following his father's death, Muhammad VI pledged to continue the country's development, reiterated his commitment to the idea of a unified Morocco that included the Moroccan-occupied Western Sahara as part of its territory, and stressed the importance of Morocco's ties with other Arab and Islamic nations.

Political Reform Hailed by Western politicians as a young reformer, Muhammad VI seemed to give credit to these views by initiating a process of reforms upon ascending to the throne. Nevertheless, on the matter of democracy, he has often advocated the singularity of Morocco's situation and has specifically rejected all hints at any parallelisms between Morocco and other neighboring countries that underwent a democratic transition process, such as Spain, arguing that each country has to have its own specific features of democracy. Muhammad VI himself has defined his regime as a democratic executive democracy, reflecting the difficulties of an institution that poses as modern and progressive but hesitates when it comes to relinquishing its executive powers. Critics have argued that Morocco's path toward a greater liberalization was not born of a real democratizing interest on the part of the crown, but was rather forced on the

<table>
<tr><td>

A FRAMEWORK OF
COMPROMISE [AND] RESPECT

∎

[W]e strongly adhere to the system of constitu-
tional monarchy, political pluralism, economic
liberalism, regional and decentralized policy,
the establishment of the state of rights and
law, preserving human rights and individual
and collective liberties, protecting security and
stability for everyone. We reiterated our com-
mitment to complete our territorial integrity, in
which the issue of our Saharan provinces is
central. We look forward to the completion of
the referendum of confirmation [that Western
Sahara belongs to Morocco], sponsored and
implemented by the United Nations. Our reli-
gion is one of moderation, openness and clem-
ency. It calls for peace, co-existence, friendship
and the protection of human rights bestowed
on humans by God, human rights which have
been approved by international conventions,
and which Morocco was in the forefront of
signing. If Morocco belongs the Arab and
Islamic worlds, its geographical position at the
top of the continent of Africa, overlooking
Europe from the north and America from the
west, obliges us to pursue the policy of our
blessed father—characterized by openness and
dialogue—by strengthening relations with our
African brothers and links with our European
and American friends for the benefit of our
region and the whole world, within the frame-
work of compromise, respect and the endeavor
to establish security and peace.

EXCERPTS FROM MUHAMMAD VI'S FIRST NATIONAL ADDRESS
FOLLOWING HIS FATHER'S DEATH, JULY 1999.

</td></tr>
</table>

Human Rights Abuses Muhammad VI's democratic credentials have been blemished by persistent accusations of
human rights abuses, documented by international
organizations such as Amnesty International and Human
Rights Watch, among others. Following in the path of
Hassan II, Muhammad VI has taken steps to address the
decades of political violence and repression that followed
independence. The postindependence years, known as
the black years (in Arabic, *al-sanawat al-sawda*; in
French, *les années de plomb,* or the years of lead), saw
the incarceration, torture, and assassination of thousands
of political opponents to the regime, mostly leftists and
Islamists. In August 1999, Muhammad VI ordered the
Royal Advisory Council on Human Rights (Conseil
Consultatif des Droits de l'Homme, or CCDH) to create
an independent Indemnity Commission (Commission
d'Aribtrage) to indemnify former victims of state violence. On 30 September 1999 former leftist political
prisoner Abraham Serfaty returned to Morocco, and on
27 November the family of Mehdi Ben Barka followed.
The king's initiative found a quick response among former political prisoners, who on October 1999 set up the
Moroccan Forum for Truth and Equity (Forum Marocain pour la Verité et l'Equité; al-Muntada al-Maghribi
min ajl al-Haqiqa wa'l-Insaf). The forum has since
demanded that a more extensive process ensue, resembling truth and reconciliation commissions in other parts
of the world. On 7 January 2004, Muhammad VI appointed
Driss Benzekri, the forum's first president, as head of the
newly formed Justice and Reconciliation Commission. Following the example set by Chile and Argentina, Morocco
eschewed punishment for the perpetrators—the CCDH
eventually granted amnesty to torturers and to all those
responsible for secret detention centers—and instead focused
on the process of uncovering the truth about detention and
torture.

Under Muhammad VI, freedom of the press continues to be restricted through legislation that bars explicit
criticism of Islam, the institution of the monarchy, or
Morocco's territorial integrity. Among the best-known
episodes is that of Moroccan journalist Ali Mrabet, editor
in chief of *Demain.* In 2003 he was found guilty of
insulting the king's person and undermining the monarchy, and was sentenced to four years in prison because
of the publication of several caricatures and interviews in
Spanish newspapers, suggesting that one of the king's
palaces was to be sold to foreign developers. Following
a hunger strike, Muhammad VI officially pardoned Mrabet in 2004. In 2005, Mrabet was found guilty of libel
after having characterized Western Saharans in Tinduf as
refugees instead of using the official term, captives of the
Polisario. The Casablanca bombings on 16 May 2003 led
Morocco's parliament to enact strict antiterrorist measures. Following the bombings, several waves of arrests

monarch by the country's economic predicament first,
and the increasing European Union (EU) refusal to grant
loans because of Morocco's extremely deficient human
rights record. Other critics have depicted Muhammad
VI's reforms as a timid continuation of his father's democratically inclined policies of the early 1990s, rather
than as a break with the past. Political reform, which
had raised hopes among Moroccans as well as many of
Morocco's Western allies upon Muhammad VI's ascension in 1999, has remained fragile and inconsistent
throughout. Currently, it is still the king who exerts
direct control over the Defense Ministry, foreign affairs,
and the Interior Ministry, together with numerous other
commissions.

have targeted members of Islamist organizations not loyal to the royal institutions.

Economy Muhammad VI has to confront myriad socioeconomic problems that revolve around poverty (which affects between 15% and 35% of the Moroccan population at different levels), unemployment, high illiteracy rates—particularly among females and in rural areas—and underdevelopment of rural areas that fuels massive migration to urban centers. On 18 May 2005, King Muhammad VI launched the National Initiative for Human Development (NIHD), which he characterized in his address on the occasion as a "large-scale mobilization . . . in the effort to achieve sustainable development." This initiative initially targeted 360 rural communities and 250 urban districts considered to be most in need. Among its objectives are the extension of basic social services and infrastructures, the creation of jobs and regular income, and the upgrading of social services for the poorest sectors of Moroccan society. In his speech, the king acknowledged that poverty and marginality affected considerably large sectors of Moroccan society and cited the creation of urban bidonvilles (slums), illiteracy, social exclusion, and unemployment as the country's most important challenges. He also admitted to the state's responsibility in carrying out the modernization of society while acknowledging the importance of civil society in establishing social networks that guaranteed the viability of economic reforms. With this initiative, Muhammad VI situated social issues at the forefront of Morocco's political priorities. The initiative is a notable shift from a top-down, single-sector tradition in dealing with poverty to a community-driven approach. Analysts have pointed out that among its most positive aspects is the expressed will to include civil society and local authorities in the process, although critics argue that the lack of specific guidelines regarding the inclusion of the NIHD in the general economy of the nation is one of its weakest points. Similarly, although the initiative could contribute to the dynamization of local networks and the strengthening of local authorities, its top-bottom hierarchical structure might make it difficult for political power to be adequately transferred to the local sphere, thus hurting the chances of reform programs to succeed. The initiative has the blessing of the World Bank, which approved a US$100 million loan to support it on 12 December 2006.

THE WORLD'S PERSPECTIVE

Muhammad VI has endured criticism as well as praise for his efforts to strengthen democracy and human rights in Morocco. The world's perspective on Muhammad's reign may ultimately be determined by the extent of the reforms he institutes, and by the ongoing state of the social problems that afflict his country.

LEGACY

While Muhammad VI will certainly be remembered for the steps toward democracy and social reform that he has already taken, the bulk of his reign as king of Morocco is still before him. Only time will tell what his overarching legacy will be.

BIBLIOGRAPHY
Slyomovics, Susan. *The Performance of Human Rights in Morocco.* Philadelphia: University of Pennsylvania Press, 2005.
"'Whatever I Do, It Will Never Be Good Enough': An Interview with King Mohammed VI of Morocco." *Time Europe* 155, no. 25 (26 June 2000).

Vanesa Casanova-Fernandez

MUSRATI, ALI MUSTAFA AL-
(1926–)

Ali Mustafa al-Musrati is a Libyan writer and cultural pioneer.

PERSONAL HISTORY

Al-Musrati was born in Alexandria, Egypt, on 18 August 1926, to a Libyan family fleeing the atrocities associated with Italian colonial rule in Libya in the early 1920s. While he was still a boy, his family moved to the Bulaj neighborhood of Cairo, where he entered secondary school. Al-Musrati obtained his university degree from the Faculty of Theology at al-Azhar University in Cairo in 1946, having attended the classes of well-known scholars, including Muhammad al-Bahey, Salih Sharaf, al-Khadr Husayn—the Tunisian who became the Shaykh of al-Azhar—and the writer Atiyya al-Abrashi, who taught him the methods of teaching. Al-Musrati qualified as a teacher, and spent two years as a member of the Faculty of Arabic language after graduation.

INFLUENCES AND CONTRIBUTIONS

In 1948, al-Musrati participated in a public demonstration demanding the evacuation of foreign military forces from Egypt. His arrest by the police and subsequent jail sentence was his first experience with being a prisoner of conscience. He would repeat the experience three times, all for longer periods, while campaigning for the freedom of his native Libya. The campaign for Libyan independence was launched in Egypt in 1948 by the prominent Libyan political leader Bashir al-Sa'adawi. Upon his return to Tripoli, al-Sa'adawi joined forces with several

BIOGRAPHICAL HIGHLIGHTS

Name: Ali Mustafa al-Musrati

Birth: 1926, Alexandria, Egypt

Nationality: Libyan

Education: University degree, Faculty of Theology, al-Azhar University, Cairo, 1946

PERSONAL CHRONOLOGY:

• **1948:** Imprisoned for demonstration; begins working as political activist

• **1954:** Serves as editor of Libyan radio's monthly magazine, *Huna Tarabulus al-Gharb*

• **1955:** Publishes first book, *Prominent People from Tripoli*

• **1960:** Wins seat in Libyan parliament

• **1970:** Awarded the Certificate of Merit by the Libyan government

existing political organizations to form the National Congress Party, the new largest party in Libya and the political force that led the people of Libya to independence. Al-Musrati rose to instant fame as the party's fiery public speaker and the voice of his people's yearning for liberation. From 1948 to 1951, he was a full-time political agitator and party activist, working under al-Sa'adawi's leadership and mobilizing the public toward achieving independence from the British military administration that had replaced Italian colonial rule after the defeat of Italian forces in North Africa in 1943. His catch phrases, including "I am here in answer to the call of the homeland," ignited the imagination of the masses.

Libyan independence, and the rule of King Idris I in a constitutional monarchy, were declared in 1951. Shortly afterward, however, political differences between the National Congress Party and the new ruling personalities led to the deportation and denationalization of al-Sa'adawi and his assistant Ahmad Zarim. Al-Musrati and a group of party activists were taken to prison after rioting and public demonstrations, accusing the newly appointed government of rigging the elections for the new house of representatives.

Following his release from prison a few months later, al-Musrati confined his activities to the cultural field. In 1954 he was an editor for Libyan radio's monthly magazine, *Huna Tarabulus al-Gharb* (This is Tripoli), and served for a short period as the head of Tripoli radio. But his main focus was his writing, and he contributed to

most journals of the era, including the daily *Tarabulus al-Gharb, al-Ra'id,* and *al-Masa*. He also continued to write lighthearted programs for radio, such as his morning talk show, and was responsible for several radio dramas, including a series on the fables of Juha, a series on the travels of Ibn Battuta, and the series "al-Bukhari Says."

Coming from Cairo, the cultural capital of the Arab world, to a city like Tripoli, which was shedding the dust of a long colonial rule and still lacking cultural institutions, al-Musrati was able to be a pioneer in establishing the foundations of a cultural base. He saw his role as that of a writer with a mission to awaken the people of his country. Al-Musrati sought to fulfill this mission with his earliest books, such as *Prominent People from Tripoli* (published in 1955) and *LamḤāt adabīyah an Lībiyā* (Literary glimpses of Libya, 1956). His *JūḤā fī Lībīyah* (Juha in Libya, 1958) was a survey of how Libyans used the mythical personality of the comedian Juha in expressing their sense of humor. In the same year, he published his book on the history of the press in Libya from the beginning of the twentieth century. *The Struggle of a Journalist*, published in 1961, developed this subject further, focusing on one of the Libyan freedom fighters.

His 1960 work *Ghūmah, fāris al-saḤrā* (Ghuma, the knight of the desert) was dramatized for the theater by the famous Egyptian writer Mustafa Mahmud, and was performed in Cairo. Al-Musrati also wrote books in social studies, including *Libyan Society through Its Proverbs* (1962). In 1963, he published a book on the literary history of Arabs in Italy through the poet Ibn Hamdis al-Siqilli, followed by a book highlighting the life of Asad ibn Furat, who led the Arab conquest of Sicily.

Al-Musrati continued to mine the wealth of Libyan history, particularly the history of struggle, to refresh the public's memories of historic moments of triumph and heroism. He published books on the freedom fighter Sa'adun, on Ibn Khaldun, the Libyan historian of the Qaramanli era, and on the shaykh of the poets of recent Libyan history, Ahmad al-Sharif. Al-Musrati also wrote on several historical Arab travelers who recorded the events of their journeys to Libya, reviving their work and analyzing some of it; his account of al-Hashayshi was published in 1965. He also republished, with introductions and analyses, the books of the religious poet Ahmad al-Bahlul and the nineteenth-century poet Mustafa bin Zikri.

Al-Musrati did not, however, limit his writing to the arenas of research and history. He also ventured into the realm of creative writing. His book *The Gathering of the Ignorants*, from the earlier phase of his career, includes funny and satirical pieces commenting on various social and political deformities he saw in his society. Al-Musrati moved on to serious literature in the form of short stories, collected in *Mirsal, Handful of Ashes,* and *The Torn Sail,* among others. Al-Musrati's stories have the color and flavor of their author, who is famous for his sarcasm, satire, and sense of humor. His characters are mostly simple folk and inhabitants of run-down areas of the city, but they are full of energy and determination, with strong senses of dignity despite their poverty and destitution. His stories from the 1950s and early 1960s are social critiques of the political and economic systems that rule over the fate of those characters, and they document the social history of Libya in the process. In the later 1960s, however, his stories underwent a transformation, one that ran parallel to the deep changes effected in Libyan society as a result of the production of oil in large quantities. This also coincided with the revolution of 1969, led by MU'AMMAR AL-QADDAFI: a major transformation in Libya's system of government. Al-Musrati was one of the personalities who paved the way for the dawning of the revolutionary era and the collapse of the monarchy.

In 1960 al-Musrati returned to the political arena, fighting a strong battle against a government candidate in the parliamentary elections. He won the battle and joined the opposition, whose first priority was cutting the ties to the colonial era that still remained: namely, the British and American military bases occupying part of the country, which were governed by a political pact imposed on the Libyan government. The second major element of the opposition's national agenda was the unification of Libya, in place of the federal system that divided Libya into three states. During his time with the opposition, Al-Musrati established an antigovernment weekly newspaper called *al-Sha'b* (The people). *Al-Sha'b* was subject to censorship and bans until it was prevented from publication altogether.

A few years before the end of monarchical rule, al-Musrati was appointed secretary-general of the high committee of arts and literature to keep him away from political activities. He returned to writing his stories, which concentrated on the conflict between the old and the new in the human soul, and between traditional ways of behavior and modern modes and styles of living. He did not abandon his trademark satirical and sarcastic approach, which permeates the stories in the collections he issued in his later years, regardless of their subject matter. These include *The General in Victoria Station*, 2003, *The Monkey in the Airport*, and *Abd al-Karim under the Bridge*.

With the advent of the revolution in 1969, Al-Musrati took the opportunity of resuming his political activities, introducing himself as a candidate in the parliamentary elections of the Federation of Arab Republics, the union of Egypt, Syria, and Libya, which lasted only a few years in the 1970s. He also participated in numerous political, cultural, and literary seminars in Libya and abroad. He led the Libyan delegations to most of the meetings held by the Union of Arab Writers and Afro-Asian writers'

associations, and in the mid-1980s, he became the secretary-general of the Union of Libyan Writers.

THE WORLD'S PERSPECTIVE

The high esteem in which the Arab world holds al-Musrati can be seen from the various awards granted to him. In 1970, the Libyan government awarded al-Musrati the Certificate of Merit on the first anniversary of the 1969 revolution, in recognition of his efforts prior to the revolution. He has received many other awards, including the Great al-Fatah Medal, the highest honor Libya has to offer, as well as medals from Tunisia and Yemen. The testimonials of other writers are also telling. From the early stages of his career he was encouraged by prominent Arab writers, including Taha Husay, Muhammad Farid Abu Hadid, Husayn Mu'anis, Anis Mansur, and Mustafa Mahmud, who have introduced his books and commented on them in the press.

Al-Musrati's eightieth birthday in 2006 was an occasion for celebration in literary circles throughout Libya, in recognition of the services he has rendered to Libya, its history, and its culture.

LEGACY

Al-Musrati is the most prolific writer in contemporary Libya. His published works exceed thirty books, with a similar number of expected to appear in book form after being published in journals. He will be remembered as a pioneer and supporter of Libyan history and culture.

BIBLIOGRAPHY

Musrati, Ali Mustafa al-. *The General in Victoria Station and Other Stories*. Translated by Saadun Ismail Suayeh. New York: Global Humanities Press, 2003.

Ahmad al-Fagih

MUSTAGHANMI, AHLAM
(1953–)

Ahlam Mustaghanmi (Ahlem Mosteghanemi), a prominent Algerian author, is probably the world's best-known arabophone woman novelist.

PERSONAL HISTORY

Mustaghanmi was born on 13 April 1953 in Tunis. Her parents were from Constantine, a historic city in eastern Algeria, which they left in 1947, moving to Tunisia following Mustaghanmi's father's release from prison by French colonial authorities. Her father, Mohammed-Cherif Mustaghanmi, was an Algerian nationalist and had been arrested following the Sétif demonstration and

BIOGRAPHICAL HIGHLIGHTS

Name: Ahlam Mustaghanmi (Ahlem Mosteghanemi)

Birth: 1953, Tunis, Tunisia

Family: Husband, George Rassi; three sons

Nationality: Algerian

Education: Primary, Tunis; secondary, Algiers; B.A., Arabic literature, University of Algiers, 1971; Ph.D., social sciences, Sorbonne, Paris, 1982

PERSONAL CHRONOLOGY:

• **1973:** Publishes her first collection of poems, *'Ala Marfa' al-Ayyam* (On the harbor of the days)

• **1993:** Publishes her first novel, *Dhakirat al-Jasad* (*Memory in the Flesh*); wins the Nour Foundation Prize for *Dhakirat al-Jasad*

• **1994:** Moves to Lebanon from France

• **1997:** Publishes her second novel, *Fawda al-Hawas (Chaos of the Senses)*

• **1998:** Wins the Naguib Mahfouz Medal for *Dhakirat al-Jasad*

• **1999:** Wins the Professor Georges Tarabey Prize for *Dhakirat al-Jasad*

• **2002:** Publishes her third novel, *'Abir Sarir (Passer by a Bed)*

massacre of 8 May 1945 (Algerian civilians in the city of Sétif participating in a parade marking the end of World War II in Europe demonstrated for Algerian independence and were set upon by French police and settlers, who killed thousands, including Mohammed-Cherif's brothers). In Tunisia, Mohammed-Cherif resumed his activism, making his home a meeting place for Algerian nationalists before the war of independence (1954–1962) and for freedom fighters during the war years.

After independence in 1962, Mohammed-Cherif took prominent positions in the government of Ahmed Ben Bella. When Ben Bella was ousted in a 1965 military coup that put Houari Boumédienne into the presidency, Mohammed-Cherif became very ill. Suffering from an acute nervous breakdown, he spent most of his time in a psychiatric clinic in Algiers where Ahlam visited him at least three times a week. He was unable to comprehend or accept the political conflicts of postcolonial Algeria, which

turned former comrades into rivals aiming to eliminate each other. Disillusioned and resentful, Mohammed-Cherif died in 1992, as Algeria was embarking on a decade of civil war and terrorist violence.

Ahlam Mustaghanmi attended primary school in Tunis and high school in Algiers. Her love for Arabic literature and language was stimulated by her father, who, despite his vocation as a French teacher, had his children learn Arabic, a language he himself had been unable to acquire under French rule. Because of her father's condition, she helped to support her family while still in high school by working for Algerian radio. Mustaghanmi broadcast a radio program, *Hamasat* (Whispers), on literature and music, and at the University of Algiers, where she studied Arabic literature, she was one of the first Arabized graduates in the country in 1971. Two years later she published her first collection of poems, *'Ala Marfa' al-Ayyam* (On the harbor of the days), dedicated to her father (who was too ill to appreciate it) for whom, in her own words, she writes in Arabic.

In 1982 Mustaghanmi earned a doctorate in the social sciences from the Sorbonne in Paris with a study of "L'Algérie, femme et écriture" (Algeria, woman, and writing). In her thesis she proposes that Algerian men must become liberated and emancipated before women can aspire to such ideals. She harshly criticizes the National Union of Algerian Women (UNFA), and calls its members "a gathering of ugly and frustrated women."

During her student years in Paris Mustaghanmi met George Rassi, a Lebanese journalist, whom she married and with whom she lived in Paris and, after 1994, Lebanon. Marriage and motherhood consumed all her time for some years. Later she made a tentative return to writing through her contributions to *Hiwar* (Dialogue), a magazine edited by her husband, and *al-Tadamun* (Solidarity), an Arabic magazine published in London. In 1993 Mustaghanmi made a forceful return to creative writing as a novelist.

Mustaghanmi the Poet Mustaghanmi's career as a writer is clearly divided into two stages: before and after marriage and motherhood. In the first stage she was a poet who enjoyed the freedom of writing and wholly devoted herself to poetry. In the second she has written fiction, after a gap of fifteen years during which she did no literary writing. This period of motherhood, as she describes it, changed her approach. She testifies that writing has not become everything in her life, but "stolen moments" from her normal life. She steals time to write, she even steals her son's desk to write on. She steals words as others steal moments of joy, because writing is the only women's adventure that deserves the risks, which she takes with the avidity of one whose pleasure is both forbidden and threatened.

Mustaghanmi began her career as a poet. She published her first collection of poems, *'Ala Marfa' al-Ayyam* in 1973 and her second, *Al-Kitaba fi Lahzat 'Uriyy* (Writing at a moment of nudity) in 1976. *Akadhib Samaka* (Lies of a fish) followed in 1993.

Mustaghanmi believes that the birth of the poet takes place when he or she faces the public for the first time. She was born at age seventeen when she faced an enthusiastic and critical audience in Algiers. Half of this audience, she has said, came to support her, the other half to condemn her for her femininity and her love of poetry, which they judged indecent at a time when the wounds of the war of independence had not yet healed.

Although she was the only woman poet on that occasion, Mustaghanmi claims that her main concern was not the women's question but the concerns of Algerian youth during the 1970s. "Poetry and the nation were my main concern," she writes on her Web site. "Femininity was my personal problem. This became more obvious to me once I left Algeria and became a wife and a mother, with all the social obligations that this entailed."

It was because of her marriage and children that Mustaghanmi gave up poetry. She told journalists that it was her decision to leave poetry lest she become a bad poet. For her, to be a poet meant to devote her whole life to poetry and to live outside social norms. She considers poetry a form of leisure that is not available to women in her society, since, according to its norms, their prime role is that of motherhood and housework. She has said that she was not so distressed when she discovered that she could no longer write poetry, but she would be very worried if one day she were not able to write at all.

Mustaghanmi the Novelist As a novelist, Mustaghanmi says that she found herself in territory she had not planned to enter. She claims that through writing her first novel, she discovered her second self, a woman with whom she failed to identify at first. She explains that her journey with this second self resulted in a four hundred-page text, which she called a novel, *Dhakirat al-Jasad* (*Memory in the Flesh*). This book, published simultaneously in Algeria and Lebanon in 1993, at first went unnoticed in Algeria, but later became a best seller in the Arab world, running into twenty-two printings within a few years. In 1993 *Memory in the Flesh* was awarded the Nour Foundation Prize for the best work of literature by an Arab woman; in 1998 it won the NAGUIB MAHFOUZ Medal for Literature; and in 1999 it received the Professor Georges Tarabey Prize for the best work of literature published in Lebanon.

Mustaghanmi published her second novel, *Fawda al-Hawas* (*Chaos of the Senses*) in 1997, which reached seventeen printings, and a third, *'Abir Sarir* (*Passer by a Bed*) in 2002, which sold more than eighty thousand copies. These three novels form a trilogy. Their main protagonist is Khaled, a painter and war veteran who fought in the war of independence, which cost him his left arm. In *Memory in the Flesh* Khaled is portrayed as an embittered and nostalgic exile. At an exhibit of his paintings in Paris he meets Ahlam, the daughter of Si Taher, a famous revolutionary martyr, whom he befriended during the revolution. Although much older than she, Khaled falls instantly in love with Ahlam, who for him is the embodiment of the forsaken nation and the city of his youth, Constantine (Arabic: Casantina), which itself is another character. Khaled tells Ahlam that he has condemned her to be his Casantina, and himself to be *majnun* (insane, alluding here to Majnun Layla, a spiritual lover who died as a result of his love). As the daughter of Si Taher, Ahlam is also a link with the revolution as a part of Khaled's life. To Khaled's disappointment Ahlam does not share his feelings and refuses to carry the burden of all the things he sees in her; she belongs to a new generation of women who refuse to confine themselves in the past and prefer to live in the present, with which Khaled fails to identify.

Khaled's sense of loss is identical to that of the liberated nation, around which the trilogy revolves. Algeria and the challenges of the present are at the core of Mustaghanmi's oeuvre, and the chaos suffered by her characters is equally suffered by the young nation, whose misfortunes only became more acute with the outbreak of civil war in the 1990s—the culmination of an identity crisis suffered by the nation since its independence.

INFLUENCES AND CONTRIBUTIONS

The greatest influence in Mustaghanmi's life and writing is the Algerian war of independence. She was born in exile as a result of her father's resistance activities, and throughout her childhood she was very close to news of the war of liberation, not only through meetings taking place in her parents' home, but through the direct involvement of her relatives in the revolution. Her cousin Badia Mustaghanmi was one of the first female students to join the students' strike and the armed revolution thereafter, and became a martyr to the cause. Mustaghanmi, a self-proclaimed nonfeminist, does not make much of this aspect of the revolution in her fiction, focusing instead on male heroes, one of whom was her cousin Azzeddine Mustaghanmi, a high-ranking army officer in the revolution.

Another major influence on her was the heated debate in early postcolonial Algeria about the country's cultural identity. During the colonial period France waged a fierce war against the teaching of the Arabic

CONTEMPORARIES

Zineb Laouedj (1954-), from Maghnia in western Algeria, like Mustaghanmi is among the first generation of Algerian women authors and poets to rise to prominence during the 1970s, with a corpus of poetry that is committed both to the cause of the emerging youth in the newly independent nation, and the creation of a new wave of literature that celebrates freedom and modernity. In 1990 Laouedj earned her doctorate in Syria with a thesis on "Maghrebi Poetry of the Seventies." Since 1994 her life has been split between Paris and Algiers; at present she teaches literature at the University of Algiers as well as at the University of Paris VIII. She writes both in French and in Arabic. She also translates Arabic literary texts into French.

language and Islam. Instead it offered limited access to French schools whose prime mission was acculturation and "civilization." At independence the illiteracy rate was a staggering 96 percent, according to some sources, while the literate elite was educated only in French. A major question during this period was whether Algeria should continue to use the French language or fully Arabize the country and its institutions. The new state endeavored to give Algeria an Arab-Islamic cultural identity through an Arabization campaign (in which Mustaghanmi's father was directly involved, leading a commission on adult literacy and the preparation of teaching materials). This debate generated hostility sometimes amounting to hatred between francophone and arabophone writers and intellectuals, and resulted in the permanent literary silence of some francophone writers, such as Malek Haddad, the temporary silence of some others, such as ASSIA DJEBAR, and the shifting into Arabic by a few, such as RACHID BOUDJEDRA in 1982.

Algeria had produced a very interesting corpus of francophone literature in the 1950s and 1960s, but in 1971 the first Algerian novel in Arabic, *Rih al-Janub* (Wind from the south) by the late Abd al-Hamid Ben Hadouga, was published. Thereafter many other (male) arabophone novelists reached prominence. Mustaghanmi came to maturity after independence and, as we have seen, strongly advocates the country's Arab identity. It is surprising, therefore, to find that she honors the francophone writers who chose to cease writing rather than write in Arabic (which they may be unable to do), calling them "the martyrs of

silence." The one she most exalts is Haddad, who was known for saying that the French language separated him from his mother more than the Mediterranean Sea.

Mustaghanmi continues to view arabophone writers in Algeria as underprivileged despite the state's continued support for Arabic as the nation's language. She helped establish the Malek Haddad Literary Prize for the best Algerian writer in Arabic in 2001. In a June 2001 interview on Algerian television, she expressed her concern about the status of Arabic literature in Algeria and stated that the Haddad Prize should encourage more writers to write in Arabic. She also disclosed that the members of the jury, all of whom she invited from the Middle East, were surprised by the high level of the work submitted.

Together with her admiration for Haddad, Mustaghanmi exalts unreservedly the historic city they both originate from, Constantine, which she says she wrote about without physically visiting. "There are cities that we inhabit," she said in Algiers' *Al Khabar* newspaper in 2001, "and others that inhabit us." It is clear that Constantine inhabits Mustaghanmi in a nostalgic manner; it is the glorious city of her ancestors, and the city of many famous Algerian writers. Her literary, imagined Constantine is not the same as the one she eventually visited in 2001, however; she was very critical about the desolate state of the city.

The third major source of influence on Mustaghanmi's career was her father, to whom she has dedicated all her works. The father in her novels is an idealized figure, her source of inspiration. Details of his biography are found throughout her novels, though with no direct reference to him. Often the story of the father is so closely identified with that of the nation that his illness must be read as the nation's also.

THE WORLD'S PERSPECTIVE

Although Mustaghanmi started her literary career as a poet, she rose to prominence with the publication of the novel *Dhakirat al-Jasad* in 1993. This unique text resulted in a wave of praise for the author but also stimulated a certain amount of critical polemic doubting that an Algerian woman author could write a work of such eloquence and alleging that she had not in fact written the book herself, which caused her a great deal of anxiety. Such allegations suggest the doubts that many Middle Easterners have about Algeria's Arab identity. These unfounded accusations evaporated eventually, but not without leaving Mustaghanmi somewhat bitter. Her only way forward was to continue to write works of similar strength.

In contrast, perhaps inevitably, Mustaghanmi's success was considered by her supporters as a proof of Algeria's "Arabness." On Mustaghanmi's Web site, former Algerian president Ben Bella is quoted saying, "Ahlam is an Algerian sun that shone upon Arabic literature. We are proud of her Arabic writings as much as we

I HAVE LEARNT TO BECOME A PERSON OF INK

I am a woman of paper; I am used to living among books. I am the kind of person who would love, hate, rejoice, mourn, and commit all the sins in the world on paper. I have learnt to become a person of ink, not scared to see myself naked on paper. I like this type of nudity. I like to see my naked body quivering in front of a lake of ink. I believe that the words that undress us are the only words that resemble us, while the words that wrap up our bodies actually disfigure us.

LECTURE DELIVERED IN PARIS, AT L'INSTITUT DU MONDE ARABE, 1997, AVAILABLE FROM HTTP:WWW.MOSTEGHANEMI.NET.

tered the linguistic exile imposed by French colonialism on Algerian intellectuals." She has been praised as well by prominent Arab writers such as Suhayl Idris, NIZAR QAB-BANI, YOUSSEF CHAHINE, and many others. Mustaghanmi's novels have been translated into many languages, including English, French, Italian, German, Spanish, Chinese, Farsi, and Kurdish, a testimony to her world status as a writer.

LEGACY

Mustaghanmi will be remembered as the Algerian woman who wrote excellent novels in Arabic and whose fame surpassed that of many well-established Arab writers. Her novels are an expression of many taboo subjects and contemporary issues, which made them appealing to young Arab readers.

BIBLIOGRAPHY

Jensen, Kim. "A Literature Born from the Wounds: Ahlam Mostaghanemi's *Memory in the Flesh*." *Aljadid* 8, no. 39 (Spring 2002). Available from http://leb.net/aljadid/reviews/0839jensen.html.

Laouedj, Zineb. "Poétesses d'expression arabe." *CLIO: Histoire, femmes et sociétés* 9 (1999). Available from http://clio.revues.org/document288.html.

Littérature Algérienne. "Ahlem Mosteghanemi." Available from http://dzlit.free.fr/mostegh.html.

Zahia Smail Salhi

are of our Arab identity." In the same vein, the Algerian author AL-TAHER WATTAR wrote, "Algeria as a whole was envied in Ahlam, like it is envied in its martyrs and its grief. The whole Algerian school is being targeted. Arabisation and good Arabic writing were also targeted." The Naguib Mahfouz Medal jury described her as "a beacon of light in the midst of darkness, she is the writer who shat-

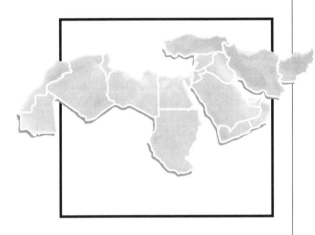

N

NAISSE, AKTHAM
(1951–)

Aktham Naisse (Nuʿaysa) is a noted Syrian lawyer and human rights activist.

PERSONAL HISTORY

Syrian lawyer and human rights activist Naisse was born in Latakia, Syria, on 28 December 1951. Little has been published about his early life other than that he studied in Egypt, not surprising for a human rights advocate in authoritarian Syria who has had to operate clandestinely for much of his activist career. The Baʿth Party government of longtime president HAFIZ AL-ASAD first arrested Naisse in February 1982 and held him for four months, during which time he was tortured. He subsequently was arrested in Syria on numerous occasions.

In December 1989 Naisse created the Committee for the Defense of Democratic Liberties and Human Rights in Syria, which he chairs today. In a state such as Syria that tolerates no dissent whatsoever, this was a remarkably courageous initiative. The committee also formed a clandestine publication that year, *Sawt al-Dimuqratiyya* (The voice of democracy). In 1991 the committee publicly called for free elections, something that led to Naisse's December 1991 arrest and subsequent torture. In 1992 the Supreme State Security Court tried and sentenced him to nine years' imprisonment in the notorious Sayidnaya prison north of Damascus. Naisse had been tortured so badly that he reportedly could not even stand during the trial. Beyond that he suffered eye and kidney problems while in prison. Naisse eventually served seven years until his release in July 1998. Naisse was not permitted to practice law thereafter.

INFLUENCES AND CONTRIBUTIONS

Asad's death in June 2000 allowed the door of political liberties open somewhat in Syria. On 10 December 2000 the Committee for the Defense of Democratic Liberties and Human Rights in Syria was emboldened enough to issue a public declaration. But the climate in Syria under new president BASHAR AL-ASAD (son of Hafiz al-Asad) soon changed. In August 2003 military security personnel questioned Naisse and threatened him and the committee. Undeterred, Naisse's committee posted a public letter on the Internet signed by three thousand and five hundred intellectuals and academics that called for the lifting of the state of emergency still in existence since the military coup of 1963 that brought the Baʿth Party to power. On 8 March 2004 the committee organized a peaceful sit-in demonstration in front of the Syrian parliament building in Damascus—an unprecedented act of public political protest in Syria. Approximately seven hundred demonstrators took part in the action. Naisse

BIOGRAPHICAL HIGHLIGHTS

Name: Aktham Naisse (Nu'aysa)

Birth: 1951, Latakia, Syria

Family: Married with children

Nationality: Syrian

PERSONAL CHRONOLOGY:

- **1982:** Arrested for the first time
- **1989:** Establishes the Committee for the Defense of Democratic Liberties and Human Rights in Syria and distributes the *Sawt al-Dimuqratiyya* (Voice of democracy) publication
- **1992:** Imprisoned
- **1998:** Released from prison
- **2004:** Organizes sit-in in front of Syrian parliament; later arrested; receives Ludovic-Trarieux International Human Rights Award
- **2005:** Acquitted and released; receives Martin Ennals Award for Human Rights Defenders

and one hundred others then presented the parliament with a petition signed by over seven thousand people who again called for an end to the state of emergency. It was a bold act of defiance.

Shortly thereafter, on 13 April 2004, Syrian military security personnel arrested Naisse in Latakia. He was sent once more to Sayidnaya prison, and suffered a stroke there that left him partially paralyzed. He began a hunger strike in prison, and was released on bail on 16 August 2004 pending trial. Human rights groups around the world campaigned for his release, and the court ultimately acquitted him on 26 June 2005.

The regime continues to watch Naisse. For example, on 11 August 2006, he was planning to host a meeting of Arab and Kurdish political groups in Syria at his home in Damascus, when security forces surrounded the house. Those in attendance were searched and sent away.

THE WORLD'S PERSPECTIVE

Naisse's work on behalf of political prisoners and democracy in Syria has earned him considerable international public attention, support, and awards in recent years. His 2004 arrest in particular became the subject of many global human rights groups' efforts to free him. In October 2004, after he had been released from prison on bail, Naisse's efforts were highlighted when he was awarded

the Ninth Ludovic-Trarieux International Human Rights Award (the first award went to the then-imprisoned Nelson Mandela in 1985) in Brussels. That the government lifted the travel ban it had imposed on him and allowed him to travel to Belgium to receive the award is probably indicative of its sensitivity toward how it deals with him now that he has risen to the level of such international attention. In January 2005 a selection committee made up of representatives of eleven major human rights organizations selected Naisse to receive the prestigious Martin Ennals Award for Human Rights Defenders, further testimony of his international fame.

LEGACY

Aktham Naisse will be remembered as one of the most important human rights advocates in modern Syria who publicly defied the Ba'thist state's attempts to stifle him and other dissenters. Particularly noteworthy achievements were his efforts at forming the Committee for the Defense of Democratic Liberties and Human Rights in Syria in 1989, and the 2004 sit-in at the front of the Syrian parliament.

BIBLIOGRAPHY

"Aktham Naisse International Human Rights Prize 'Ludovic Trarieux' 2004." Institut des Droits de l'Homme des Avocats Européens. Available from http://www.idhae.org.

Gershowitz, Suzanne. "Dissident Watch: Aktham Naisse." *Middle East Quarterly* 12, no. 2 (Spring 2005). Available from http://www.meforum.org.

Michael R. Fischbach

NASHER, FARHAD
(1962–)

Farhad Nasher, or Farhad "Darya" Nasher, is a singer and composer from Afghanistan. Nasher has earned wide popularity for his songs and patriotism in Afghanistan and beyond. He sings his songs in various languages, including Persian, Pashtun, Tajik, and Uzbek. His songs about war-torn Afghanistan emphasize the importance of national unity, and his patriotic themes made him a popular singer in Afghanistan and beyond. He won the awards of the Best Singer of the Year in Afghanistan (2003) and Denmark (2005).

PERSONAL HISTORY

Nasher was born on 22 September 1962 in a Kunduz, Gozargah, Kabul province of Afghanistan. His father was an ethnic Pashtun and his mother was a Tajik. His uncle Gholam Servar Nasher was a wealthy businessman and a

Farhad Nasher. AP IMAGES.

BIOGRAPHICAL HIGHLIGHTS

Name: Farhad "Darya" Nasher

Birth: 1962, Kunduz, Gozargah, Kabul province, Afghanistan

Family: Wife, Sultana Emam; one son, Hejran Derya

Nationality: Afghan

Education: Polytechnic Institute of Kabul, University of Kabul

PERSONAL CHRONOLOGY:

• **Late 1970s:** Establishes his first band, called Nayestan, while in high school.

• **Early 1980s:** Establishes his first professional band, called Halgahay Tilayee, later renamed Goroh-e-Baran. Composes songs under the pseudonym Abr (Cloud)

• **1981:** The Afghan National Radio and TV plays his song "Raseed Mojdah" ("The Time of Grief"), resulting in the introduction of an official censorship on the songs of Baran

• **1985:** Baran splits up

• **1988:** Becomes professor of the University of Kabul, teaching western classical music

• **1989:** Emigrates to Europe, later settling down in Virginia, United States

• **1998:** Composes and sings songs for the American-made Afghan movie *In Foreign Land*

• **2001:** Afghanistan Radio broadcasts Farhad Darya's song, "Kabul Jaan," symbolizing the beginning of the post-Taliban era in the country

• **2003:** Wins Best Song of the Year award in Afghanistan for "Salam Afghanistan"

• **2005:** Wins the Best Song of the Year award in Denmark for "Salam Afghanistan"

• **2006:** Composes songs for the Afghan-made film *Through Her Eyes*

well-known philanthropist, founder of the Nasher Gallery and Nasher Library. His grandfather Sher Khan and his great uncle Gholam Nabi Nasher were well-known statesmen until the overthrow of King Zahir Shah.

Nasher spent his childhood in a town called Kunduz, where he lived until the age of seventeen. There he attended the high school named after Sher Khan (Nasher's grandfather). While studying at high school, Farhad Nasher established his first band, which was called Nayestan (Red-bed).

Upon finishing high school in Habibiyya (Kabul), Nasher entered the Polytechnic Institute, later switching to the University of Kabul. During his years in the University of Kabul, Nasher established his first professional band, which was initially called Halgahay Tilayee (Golden Ring), and was later renamed Goroh-e-Baran (Rain Band), a name that was further shortened to just Baran (Rain). Although this band did not make him and his group famous, it played a certain positive role in introducing Nasher to the career of a professional singer. Baran gained a certain popularity among the Afghani people, but due its new genre (folk-pop), the songs of this group could not attract as much of an audience as the traditional music would do in the country. During these years Nasher also wrote songs for other singers under the pseudonym Abr (Cloud).

INFLUENCES AND CONTRIBUTIONS

During the Soviet occupation of Afghanistan that began in December 1979, Nasher became popular as a founder of the Afghan resistance music. In 1981, after the Afghan National Radio and TV played his song "Raseed Mojdah" ("The Time of Grief"), an official censorship was enforced on his songs. In 1985, at the peak of its popularity, Baran split up after its concert in Mezar-e-Sharif. In 1988 Nasher became a professor at the University of Kabul where he started teaching western classical music. In 1989 he immigrated to Europe, later settling down in Virginia in the United States.

It was as an émigré that Farhad Darya Nasher won popularity through a number of his songs and albums that were aimed at describing the fate of his war-torn motherland after the invasion of the Soviets and the nostalgic feelings of love for Afghanistan. In 1998 Nasher composed and sang songs for the American-made Afghan movie *In Foreign Land*, directed by first-time film director Farhad Asefi. In 2006 Nasher composed songs for another film, made in Afghanistan, called *Through Her Eyes*. This film was directed by Mithag Kazimi.

During the reign of the Taliban in Afghanistan, music was restricted as a potential antireligious activity. Nasher's songs started reaching Afghanistan with the fall of this regime. On 13 November 2001 the city of Kabul was awakened with Nasher's song "Kabul Jaan" ("Beloved Kabul"), broadcast by the Radio Afghanistan. This broadcast symbolized the beginning of a new era in Afghanistan and the revival of the music culture in the country, which had a long history before the Taliban's restrictions. In 2003 Nasher's album *Salam Afghanistan*, which emphasized the importance of national unity, became a hit in his home country and earned him the awards Best Singer of the Year in Afghanistan (2003) and in Denmark (2005).

THE WORLD'S PERSPECTIVE

Nasher was strongly influenced by the political cataclysms that took over Afghanistan in 1980s and, at a later period, by his emigrant life. In early 1980s, when Afghanistan was governed by communist rule and occupied by Soviet troops, Nasher's band Baran stood out for its political resistance songs. Despite the official censorship on the songs of this band, Baran successfully performed until 1985 when the group split up. Nasher's "Salam Afghanistan," and other songs with patriotic themes, earned him a wide range of respect and popularity in Afghanistan. Nasher's philanthropy, especially with respect to the disadvantaged people of the Afghan civil war, added to his popularity in the country.

LEGACY

Nasher's style of singing founded a new genre in Afghan music. This genre is currently called folk-pop and consists of adding pop features to the traditional music of Afghanistan. Bringing political and societal motives to songs is yet another novelty introduced by Nasher to modern Afghan music.

CONTEMPORARIES

Asad Badie (1962–) a popular Afghani singer, started his career together with Nasher Darya in the band Baran. After the split of the band in 1985 Asad Badie continued his career as a singer and produced several music albums. Asad Badie immigrated to Europe. Upon receiving his M.D. in Switzerland, he started working as a practicing physician. He continues giving concerts in various cities of Europe and producing music CDs that are popular among the fans of Afghan pop music.

BIBLIOGRAPHY

Lamb, Christina. *The Sewing Circles of Herat: A Personal Voyage through Afghanistan*. New York: HarperCollins, 2002.

"Lyrics—Farhad Darya." AfghanLyrics.com. Available from http://www.virtualafghans.com/afghanlyrics.

Farhad Darya's official Web site. Available from http://www.farhaddarya.info.

Pazira, Nelofer. *A Bed of Red Flowers: In Search of My Afghanistan*. New York: Free Press, 2005.

Adil M. Asgarov

NASR, NA'ILA
(1959–)

A "national treasure" of the People's Democratic Republic of Yemen (South Yemen; PDRY, 1970–1990), Na'ila Nasr Hassan Abbas Nasr was that state's highest ranked table tennis player and was an important national model for the goal of women's equality. She continues to promote women's sports through membership on the Republic of Yemen's Olympic Committee.

PERSONAL HISTORY

Nasr was born in Aden in 1959. Her father, a graduate of the American University in Beirut, was a prominent member of Yemeni Socialist Party. A sportsman, he promoted physical fitness and coached boys' teams in local schools.

Nasr began playing table tennis for fun at home. She began to practice seriously in 1973 while attending intermediate school in Aden. Her talent and potential were soon recognized and she was invited to join the al-Mina' sports club to receive professional coaching. Paradoxically, her father was happy with her success but discouraged her competing at higher levels. In contrast, her mother supported her strongly and continued to do so as her athletic career developed.

Nasr was selected to the first national table tennis team, which trained at the al-Mina' club. In addition to training in Aden with coaches from the PDRY's Soviet-bloc allies, she also trained in the Soviet Union.

As a member of the national team Nasr represented the PDRY from 1976 to 1985. During her career she participated in 161 international tournaments. In these contests, she and her partners achieved a number of high finishes including the gold medal in women's doubles at the Seventh Arab Schools Tournament in Tripoli, Libya. In 1981 she became the PDRY champion, a title she held until 1985. Despite her schedule, Nasr was enrolled in the civil engineering program at Aden University, from which she graduated in 1984.

Following her retirement from competition, Nasr served as deputy chair of the PDRY Table Tennis Association and as a member of the Olympic Committee. In 1989 she was named captain of the national team. Her active involvement in sports lapsed following the unification of the PDRY and the Yemen Arab Republic (North Yemen) in 1990.

For most of the next decade, she focused on her engineering career in the civil aviation ministry. In 2000 she was invited to join the Yemen Olympic Committee where she has served on the executive and administrative committees. When, in July 2003, the Arab Women's table tennis tournament was held in San'a, Nasr was asked to form the Yemen entry; she also coached the team.

INFLUENCES AND CONTRIBUTIONS

From 1970 to 1990 the PDRY followed a Marxist-Leninist form of socialism. A central tenet was the equality of women and men, and this objective became a hallmark of state policy, although its acceptance was more pronounced in cities, especially the more cosmopolitan capital Aden. Legislative efforts were made to promote equality in education, employment, family, and recreation. The state adopted the Soviet model of sports as a means to achieve equality and promote physical well-being, and received support and training from the Soviet bloc.

Although veiling was discouraged, because of social concerns about modesty, girls' sports were organized through schools and overseen by the Ministry of Education. National women's teams in table tennis and volleyball trained at sports clubs which had male and female members.

Nasr's career was influenced by her mother's desire for her success. She credits Salih Sayyid Ahmad, the national team coach, and Fizan Hanbala, an Indian national and an al-Mina' club member, with directing her career. She, like many others, was also influenced by

BIOGRAPHICAL HIGHLIGHTS

Name: Na'ila Nasr Hassan Abbas Nasr

Birth: 1959, Crater, Aden

Family: Single

Nationality: Yemeni

Education: B.S. in civil engineering, College of Technology, University of Aden, 1984

PERSONAL CHRONOLOGY:

• **1975–1986:** Table tennis player, Yemen national women's teams

• **1984–1990:** Civil engineer, Ministry of Civil Aviation, PDRY

• **1989–1990:** Deputy director, PDRY Table Tennis Association

• **1990–present:** Civil engineer, Ministry of Civil Aviation and Meteorology, Republic of Yemen

• **2000–present:** Member, Yemen Olympic Committee

• **2003:** Coach, Yemen Women's National Table Tennis Team

Muhammad Abdullah Far', a journalist nicknamed "father of athletes."

Nasr was the most widely recognized and successful of the PDRY's small corps of women athletes. Even though she was not a member of the party, she was emblematic of official philosophy and the state touted her victories as signs of its success. Her career was heavily covered in the state media: she was frequently interviewed on television and radio and featured in magazines. Twice she was presented awards by PDRY president ALI NASR MUHAMMAD. She was, and remains, widely known.

In the mid-1980s Nasr's performance waned. Following the political turmoil of 1986, the new government was critical of her for not living up to the national goals, and she decided to retire. A public ceremony was held for the occasion on 12 December 1987.

In keeping with the socialist emphasis on physical and mental fitness, Nasr also excelled in school, finishing first in her classes from elementary through college. She is more proud of this accomplishment than of her table tennis prowess. She considers her efforts to make women aware of the importance of sport for health her most important contribution. Nasr also works to improve the social status of women.

THE WORLD'S PERSPECTIVE

Nasr views herself as more than an athlete, but this label best describes how the world thinks of her. The level of respect for her was evident when the Chinese women's table tennis team came to her retirement ceremony.

LEGACY

The two Yemens united in 1990 but waged a brief civil war in 1994. Owing to the declining importance of the socialist perspective in unified Yemen, Nasr's national legacy as an athlete is in doubt. However, her continued active role in sports administration and policy suggests she may still serve as a leader in the promotion of women's sports.

BIBLIOGRAPHY

Alaug, Abdul Karim, and Thomas B. Stevenson. "Football in the Yemens: Integration, Identity, and Nationalism in a Divided Nation." In *Sport in Divided Societies*, edited by A. Bairner and J. Sugden. Aachen, Germany: Meyer & Meyer Sport, 1999.

Clarke, Gill, and Barbara Humberstone. *Researching Women and Sport*. Houndmills, U.K.: Macmillan Publishers, 1997.

Dahlgren, Susanne. "Contesting Realities: Morality, Propriety and the Public Sphere in Aden, Yemen." In *Research Reports*, no. 243. Helsinki: Helsinki University Printing House, 2004.

Fasting, Kari, and Kristin Walseth. "Islam's View of Physical Activity and Sport: Egyptian Women Interpreting Islam." *International Review for the Sociology of Sport* 8, no. 1 (2003): 45–60.

Hargreaves, Jennifer. *Heroines of Sport: The Politics of Difference and Identity*. London: Routledge, 2000.

Pfister, Gertrud. "Women and Sport in Iran: Keeping Goal in the Hijab?" In *Sport and Women: Social Issues and International Perspective*, edited by I. Hartmann-Tews and G. Pfister. London: Routledge, 2003.

Scraton, Sheila, and Anne Flintoff. *Gender and Sport: A Reader*. London: Routledge, 2002.

Thomas B. Stevenson

NASRALLAH, HASAN
(1960–)

Hasan Nasrallah is a major political figure in Lebanon. He is the leader of Hizbullah (Party of God), a mass political party, social service organization, and militia that is the chief political instrument of the poor Shi'ite population of Lebanon. He was the primary strategist of the resistance to the Israeli occupation of South Lebanon in the 1990s and led the war against Israel in the summer of 2006.

Hasan Nasrallah. AP IMAGES.

PERSONAL HISTORY

The ninth of ten children, Nasrallah was born on 31 August 1960 in Qarantina, a shantytown near Burj Hammud, an impoverished suburb of Beirut inhabited predominantly by Armenians and Shi'ite Muslims. Nasrallah's father, Abd al-Karim, had left his vegetable stall in the southern Lebanese village of al-Bazuriyya, near Tyre, to seek his fortune in the capital. He opened a modest grocery store in Burj Hammud that displayed an imposing poster of Imam Musa al-Sadr, then a charismatic leader of Lebanese Shi'ites. By his own account, Nasrallah used to assist his father, but almost always dreamt of the imam as he contemplated the spiritual leader's photograph. Whether his mother's influence or this attachment to the imam—who disappeared on 31 August 1978 on a flight from Libya—was the catalyst for his later activities is debatable. Still, Musa al-Sadr left a deep impact on him, as he did on the vast majority of Lebanese from all religious persuasions.

Like many young men trapped in poverty, Nasrallah became interested in religious studies, even though his father was not particularly pious. In Burj Hammud, Nasrallah attended the al-Najah public school, where he earned a certificate, before switching to another public school in nearby Sin al-Fil. According to Nasrallah, he went to the old Martyrs' Square in downtown Beirut when he was nine to purchase secondhand books from roadside stalls. This visit to Martyrs' Square made an indelible impression on Nasrallah, fostering in him a love

BIOGRAPHICAL HIGHLIGHTS

Name: Hasan Nasrallah

Birth: 1960, near Burj Hammud, Lebanon

Family: Wife, Fatima Yasin; four sons, Muhammad Hadi (d. 1997), Muhammad Jawad, Muhammad Ali, Muhammad Mahdi; one daughter, Zaynab

Nationality: Lebanese

Education: Elementary, al-Kifa' private school, Burj Hammud; intermediate and secondary, al-Thanawiyya al-Tarbawiyya, Sin al-Fil (Beirut) and al-Thanawiyya, al-Bazuriyya, South Lebanon

PERSONAL CHRONOLOGY:

- **1975:** Joins Amal as organization officer, al-Bazuriyya

- **1976–1978:** Studies with Sayyid Muhammad Baqr al-Sadr in Najaf, Iraq

- **1978:** Expelled from Iraq, joins Sayyid Abbas al-Musawi, Ba'albek, Lebanon

- **1979:** Appointed political officer, member of politburo, Amal movement in Biqa region

- **1982:** Withdraws from Amal following disputes in aftermath of Israeli invasion; helps found dissident group later known as Hizbullah

- **1985:** Moves to Beirut

- **1987:** Becomes chief executive officer of Hizbullah, member of its Consultative Council

- **1989:** Travels to Qom, Iran, to pursue religious education

- **1990s:** Leads resistance to Israel in South Lebanon

- **1992:** Elected secretary-general of Hizbullah, succeeding Sayyid Abbas al-Musawi, assassinated by Israelis 16 February

- **1997:** Son Muhammad Hadi killed in South Lebanon by Israeli forces, September

- **2006:** Leads Hizbullah in war against Israel

of his country and reminding him of those who had sacrificed their lives for the land. In 1975 Abd al-Karim Nasrallah moved the family to their ancestral home in al-Bazuriyya to escape the ravages of the civil war that had transformed Qarantina into a slaughterhouse. It was during this period that Hasan Nasrallah opted to pursue serious religious studies. Yet, at fifteen years of age, and even before graduating from a Tyre secondary public school, he joined the Amal Movement, a Shi'ite political organization, which was then known as "the movement of the deprived." This was a natural course for a motivated individual and admirer of Musa al-Sadr.

In the Tyre mosque he attended on a regular basis, Nasrallah met Sayyid Muhammad al-Gharawi, a pious cleric who taught in the name of Imam Musa al-Sadr. Al-Gharawi recommended that Nasrallah consider a serious seminary, which meant travel out of Lebanon. For the first time in his life, Nasrallah thus left Lebanon in 1976 for Iraq, to attend the renowned Shi'ite seminary of Najaf. Al-Gharawi, who knew Sayyid Muhammad Baqr al-Sadr (the cleric who was murdered on 8 April 1980 on direct orders from the Ba'th regime) in Iraq gave Nasrallah a strong letter of recommendation to the erudite al-Sadr.

Hasan earned the honorary informal title of "Sayyid" (a Muslim term of respect meaning, roughly, "master") in Najaf after completing relevant courses in Muslim theology, although he may not have completed a full curriculum. He returned to Lebanon in 1978 after the Iraqi Ba'th regime expelled hundreds of foreign students. In part to fulfill educational requirements, and because he needed a job with a steady income, Nasrallah accepted a teaching position at a school in Ba'albek. The site of ancient Roman ruins set in one of Lebanon's richest and most picturesque places, the Bekáa Valley, Ba'albek was the home of Sayyid Abbas al-Musawi, an up-and-coming Amal leader. Nasrallah completed his religious education under the careful guidance of Musawi, who recruited the charismatic young man into Amal's political wing. Shortly thereafter, Nasrallah became a member of the Amal central political bureau.

Nasrallah married Fatima Yasin, from the southern village of al-Abbasiya; they had five children: Muhammad Hadi (who was killed in 1997), Muhammad Jawad, Zaynab, Muhammad Ali, and Muhammad Mahdi.

INFLUENCES AND CONTRIBUTIONS

Like the Iranian cleric Ayatollah Ruhollah Khomeini, whom the Iraqi government also expelled from Najaf in 1978, Sayyid Hasan Nasrallah was deeply affected by his forced eviction from Iraq. However, the event that changed him was the 1982 Israeli invasion of Lebanon, which turned into an occupation that lasted until 2000. To Nasrallah, the invasion necessitated resistance and it was in 1982 that he and key supporters rebelled against Amal for failing to organize an effective opposition.

CONTEMPORARIES

Abbas al-Musawi (1952–1992) was an influential Shiʻite cleric and early leader of Hizbullah who was assassinated by Israeli commandos in 1992. A native of the Bekáa Valley in eastern Lebanon, Musawi went to Najaf, Iraq, in the 1970s, where he studied in a religious *hawzah* (school). It was in Najaf that he met Ayatollah Ruhollah Khomeini, who instilled a revolutionary zeal in his heart and mind. Back in Lebanon by 1978, Musawi organized the resistance movement in Baʻalbek, as he mounted various guerrilla operations against the Israeli occupation after 1982. His popularity propelled him to the leadership of Hizbullah in 1991, when he replaced the hard-liner Shaykh Subhi al-Tufayli. On 16 February 1992, Musawi, his wife, his son, and four others were killed in an ambush by Israeli forces.

Hizbullah Hizbullah (Party of God) was founded as a faction within Amal in June 1982, and not constituted as a separate body until 1985, when the prominent Shiʻite cleric Shaykh Ibrahim al-Amin officially released its manifesto. The Hizbullah Program, an open letter to all the "Oppressed in Lebanon and the World," was first published as a pamphlet in 1987. It called for the establishment of an Islamic republic in Lebanon, although this was left in abeyance as a future objective. More immediately relevant was the call to fight against imperialism as well as its eradication from Muslim countries and, perhaps even more important, a complete withdrawal of Israeli forces from Lebanon, forces that had occupied parts of southern Lebanon since 1982. During its early stages, Musawi and Nasrallah struggled to give the new organization a semblance of coherence, and quickly embarked on a two-pronged effort: provide the long neglected Shiʻite population of Lebanon with the means to survive, and organize military opposition to occupation. Nasrallah's genuine concerns for the poor coupled with his fiery sermons drew a large Shiʻite following that swelled the ranks. In a largely unexplored chapter of his life, Nasrallah then left Lebanon for Qom, Iran, ostensibly to pursue religious studies. Although details are sketchy, Nasrallah was in Iran between 1987 and 1989. By the late 1980s, Hizbullah had been transformed into an effective guerrilla movement, with an ever-increasing base of support among average Lebanese. In 1991 Musawi became secretary-general of Hizbullah; he was assassinated, along with his wife and child, by Israeli

commandos in 1992. Nasrallah replaced Musawi as Hizbullah leader and vowed revenge for his fallen brethren throughout South Lebanon.

Under Hasan Nasrallah's leadership, Hizbullah was gradually transformed into a movement with formidable military capabilities. Over the course of the 1990s it defended a hapless population largely abandoned by the Lebanese army and all other central authority. Hizbullah took credit for the estimated sixteen hundred Israelis killed in Lebanon between 1982 and 2000, even if its own casualties were probably much higher. Among those casualties was Nasrallah's eldest son, Muhammad Hadi, who was killed by Israeli forces in the Jabal al-Rafi in 1997. Still, Hizbullah's military campaigns were a main factor in the Israeli decision to withdraw from South Lebanon in May 2000, and end an occupation that had lasted over eighteen years. Not surprisingly, Nasrallah was therefore credited, especially among his countrymen—both Christian and Muslim—as well as throughout the Arab and Muslim world, with ending the Israeli occupation. Hizbullah thus significantly bolstered its political standing within Lebanon.

Whether by design or coincidence, Nasrallah came to play a critical role in a complex prisoner exchange with Israel when, in 2004, 400 Palestinian and 30 Hizbullah detainees were freed—and the remains of fifty-nine Lebanese returned to their families—in exchange for businessman and former colonel Elhanan Tannenbaum and the remains of three Israeli soldiers. This agreement was perceived across the Arab world as a great victory for Nasrallah, who was praised for negotiating the deal.

Hizbullah as a Political Force For most of the 1990s but especially after the Israeli withdrawal in 2000, Hizbullah underwent a carefully tailored process of "Lebanization," which led it even to contemplate a rapprochement with a variety of non-Muslim groups. This process entailed Hizbullah's acceptance of a multiconfessional country in the aftermath of the Taʼif Accord, which introduced rough parity between Lebanese Christians and Muslims and re-channeled authority from the president to the prime minister. It was deemed useful to participate in elections, to increase various welfare programs, and expand beyond its Shiʻite constituency. Nasrallah espoused a nationalist, even patriotic, line, although Hizbullah's yellow flag was still quite prominent. Yet, simultaneously, Hizbullah assimilated various other groups, both to improve discipline and enhance its legitimacy. Toward that end, Islamic Jihad, the Organization of the Oppressed on Earth, and the Revolutionary Justice Organization were all incorporated into Hizbullah under Nasrallah's close supervision. The additional manpower and enhanced military capability quickly translated into raw power that, in Lebanon's context, signified an effective "street" presence.

It was at this time that Nasrallah made what was probably a tactical error of some consequence: He continued to back Syria against Prime Minister RAFIQ HARIRI, even though Hariri had stood by Hizbullah for many years and personally supported Nasrallah within the limitations of the Ta'if Accord. When Hariri managed to get international support calling for a withdrawal of the Syrian troops that had been in the country since 1976 (under United Nations [UN] Security Council Resolution 1559), Nasrallah aligned himself with Syria and Iran against a fellow Lebanese leader. Whether Nasrallah actually intended to separate himself from the mainstream is impossible to know, but on 14 February 2005, Hariri was assassinated and a new era in Lebanese history was set in motion.

A week after the assassination, on 21 February a large demonstration in Martyrs' Square called for the removal of Syrian forces from Lebanon. In response, Hizbullah organized an even larger counterdemonstration on 8 March supporting Syria and accusing Israel as well as France and the United States of meddling in internal Lebanese affairs. Nasrallah rejected UN Resolution 1559 calling for the disarming of Hizbullah (and other militias) because, he asserted, Lebanon needed the resistance to defend itself. The pro-Syrian protesters, while flying the Lebanese flag, held pictures of Syrian president BASHAR AL-ASAD along with placards reading "No to the American Intervention." It was unclear whether many of Lebanon's five hundred thousand Syrian expatriate workers participated in the rally, as claimed by the Hariri-owned media, but one thing was crystal clear: Nasrallah was deeply beholden to his Syrian patron. To further display its political muscle, Hizbullah held additional demonstrations in the northern Sunni city of Tripoli as well as the southern city of Nabatiyya.

Less than a week later, on 14 March, one month after the assassination, the Cedar Revolution gathered at an equally large, or possibly larger, demonstration, also at Martyrs' Square. These demonstrations and counterdemonstrations illustrated that Lebanon faced a serious political dilemma.

The 2005 Election To its credit, the outgoing government organized relatively free elections in April 2005 that upset the existing balance of power. The 2005 general elections saw the Current for the Future (Hariri's party, headed after his death by his son, Sa'd) win 36 seats in Parliament (out of 128), while Hizbullah won 14, and Amal gained 15 more for a total of 29 Shi'ite seats. Sa'd Hariri managed to put together a formidable coalition, controlling 72 seats, with the Progressive Socialists, the Lebanese Forces, the Qurnat Shihwan group, and various independents. Even when Nasrallah rallied the Syrian Social Nationalist Party and a few leftist deputies, his

grand total never exceeded 35. There was consequently serious pressure for Nasrallah to align Hizbullah with the Free Patriotic Movement of former General MICHEL AOUN, which controlled a total of 21 seats.

Nasrallah's decision to align himself with Aoun, a former commander of the Lebanese army who fought the Syrians before being exiled to France, could be construed as a second mistake. Aoun, a Maronite Christian, was determined to succeed EMILE LAHOUD as president even if the majority of fellow Maronites rejected his candidacy. Still, Aoun and Nasrallah entered into an unusual national compact, ostensibly to reform the country's confessional electoral system and move in the direction of one man, one vote. Whether Hizbullah would allow its militia to be folded into the Lebanese army in exchange for this new contract was the primary source of disagreement between Hizbullah and the majority. In short, few Lebanese believed that Hizbullah would ever disarm, especially as long as Israel occupied territory— the Shiba Farms—that Hizbullah claimed was Lebanese. Nasrallah donned a non-Shi'ite cover by aligning with the Maronite Aoun, but few Christian, Druze, or Sunni Muslim Lebanese accepted his logic.

War with Israel, 2006 On 12 July 2006, Hizbullah troops kidnapped two Israeli soldiers and killed three others, in a routine border clash similar to previous such exchanges. When Israeli forces attempted to rescue their soldiers, the operation failed with the loss of an additional five, which triggered a massive retaliation. Land, air, and naval strikes continued until 14 August, with devastating consequences for Lebanon and parts of northern Israel. Over 1,100 Lebanese and 165 Israelis were killed; most of the Lebanese were civilians, while 119 of the Israelis were military personnel. An estimated million Lebanese were displaced on a more or less permanent basis. On 11 August 2006, the UN Security Council unanimously approved Resolution 1701 calling for a cease-fire, although much of southern Lebanon remained uninhabitable due to millions of unexploded Israeli cluster bombs.

With his proven military capabilities—lobbing thousands of short- and long-range rockets into Israel—Nasrallah displayed a rare knack for action that, not surprisingly, concerned Lebanese and Arab officialdom. He quickly came under intense criticism from pro-Western Arab regimes, including those of Jordan, Egypt, and Saudi Arabia. Egyptian President HUSNI MUBARAK warned on 14 July 2006 of the risk of "the region being dragged into adventurism that did not serve Arab interests," while Saudi foreign minister Prince Sa'ud called the Hizbullah attacks "unexpected, inappropriate and irresponsible acts."

Although a 26 July 2006 public opinion poll in Lebanon indicated that 87 percent of all Lebanese citizens (80 percent among Christians and Druze and 89 percent among Sunnis) supported Hizbullah in its war with Israel and perceived it as a legitimate resistance organization, Nasrallah came under intense criticism from Lebanese leaders. WALID JUMBLATT, the Druze head of the Progressive Socialist Party, spoke out quite forcefully, challenging Nasrallah's decision to go to war without national consensus. Nasrallah conceded in a 27 August 2006 interview on Lebanon's New TV that he would not have ordered the capture of two Israeli soldiers had he known it would lead to such a war: "We did not think, even 1 percent, that the capture would lead to a war at this time and of this magnitude. You ask me, if I had known on 11 July … that the operation would lead to such a war, would I do it? I say no, absolutely not."

Because Nasrallah grew up in a shantytown partially inhabited by Palestinian refugees, he saw and felt the plight of that hapless population, although he opposed naturalizing them in Lebanon. According to Nasrallah on al-Manar, Hizbullah's television station, on 5 November 2003, "the Lebanese refuse to give the Palestinians residing in Lebanon Lebanese citizenship, and we refuse their resettlement in Lebanon. There is Lebanese consensus on this … we thank God that we all agree on one clear and definite result; namely, that we reject the resettlement of the Palestinians in Lebanon." Still, while he rejected naturalization, Nasrallah was not eager to expel them, as that would increase their burden even more. Nasrallah blamed the Arab states for their overall complaisance, and recommended that Palestinians take up arms and fight the occupation forces. His colorful rhetoric, declaring "death to Israel" or "death to America," stood in stark contrast to his live-and-let-live preferences stated elsewhere. In a 2002 interview with the *New Yorker*, Nasrallah stated that "at the end of the road no one can go to war on behalf of the Palestinians, even if that one is not in agreement with what the Palestinians agreed on." His official Web site carried a starker declaration: "We do not want to kill anyone. We do not want to throw anyone in the sea. Give the houses back to their owners, the fields back to their landlords, and the homes back to the people. Release the prisoners, and leave us alone to live in this region in security, peace and dignity." These pronouncements indicated that Nasrallah was primarily concerned with Lebanese issues and did not necessarily have wider Arab or Muslim regional ambitions. He cared for Palestinians, Syrians, and others, but he cared more about the Lebanese, especially his fellow Shi'ite brethren.

THE WORLD'S PERSPECTIVE

Hizbullah is considered a legitimate resistance movement in the Arab and Muslim worlds while in Lebanon it is an officially recognized political party with elected members of Parliament. Yet, even before the 2006 war with Israel, Hizbullah was designated as a terrorist organization by

DOESN'T THIS ENEMY KNOW WHO WE ARE?

Today on the twenty-second of September you astonish the whole world again, as you verily prove … that you are a great people, a steadfast people, a proud people, a loyal and a brave people … Doesn't this enemy know who we are? We are the children of that Imam, who said: Is it with death you threaten me? Death to us is normalcy and martyrdom is dignity offered from God…. Today, we celebrate the significant historic divine and strategic victory…. That your resistance and steadfastness dealt a severe blow to the New Middle East Project, of which Condoleezza Rice said that the [2006] war was its labor pains, the illegitimate child now aborted…. Just as your resistance provided the victory of the year 2000 as a model of a liberation resistance, in 2006 it has provided a model of steadfastness and legendary endurance—a steadfastness miracle; this … has become a proof against all Arabs and all Muslims, rulers, armies and peoples….

As for saying we are weak. I say the people of Lebanon demonstrated to all peoples of the world, the Lebanese resistance presents the proof against all Arab and Islamic armies. The Arab armies and peoples are not only able to liberate Gaza, the West Bank and East Jerusalem, but simply, and with a little decision coupled with some will, they are able to regain Palestine from the Jordan River to the Mediterranean. However, the problem is when a person places himself between two options: between his people and his throne chooses his throne, between Jerusalem and his throne chooses his throne, between the dignity of his country and his throne chooses his throne.

"TEXT OF HEZBOLLAH LEADER NASRALLAH'S SPEECH DURING 'VICTORY RALLY' IN BEIRUT." CLEVELAND INDY MEDIA CENTER. UPDATED 25 SEPTEMBER 2006. AVAILABLE FROM HTTP:// CLEVELAND.INDYMEDIA.ORG.

Canada, Israel, the Netherlands, and the United States. Australia and the United Kingdom designated the party's "external security organization" as a sponsor of terrorism, differentiating its socioeconomic and political activities from its militia. Importantly, the European Union did not list Hizbullah or any group within it as a terrorist organization, although the European parliament passed a nonbinding resolution on 10 March 2005 that acknowledged "clear evidence" of "terrorist activities by Hizbullah."

Both the powerful council of Europe, made up of European heads of state, as well as the governing body known as the Council of the European Union rejected the recommendation. Both argued that European governments held ultimate responsibility in such designations even if the council designated Imad Mughniyyah, a known Hizbullah operative, as a terrorist. Other countries criticized Hizbullah, citing terrorist activities, without labeling it a terrorist organization.

LEGACY

Hizbullah's military success against Israel in 2006 made it one of the most popular political organizations in the Arab world. Even Sunni and Christian Arabs believed that Nasrallah restored their dignity because Hizbullah fighters did what mighty Arab armies have failed to do. Yet, the perceived heroism associated with inflicting a serious blow to the superior Israeli military force was seriously damaged after Nasrallah turned to divisive tactics in internal Lebanese affairs. First, Nasrallah pulled his five ministers from the government of Prime Minister Fouad Siniora, because of various disputes over the implementation of an international tribunal to determine who was responsible for the assassination of Rafiq Hariri and other Lebanese officials. Second, he authorized the Hizbullah television network, al-Manar, to provide extensive coverage of the execution of former Iraqi president SADDAM HUSSEIN, which angered many, as the footage showed Shi'ite witnesses taunting Hussein as he said his final prayers. The channel's tone seemed gloating and triumphalist and dozens of callers to various talk shows cheered the execution and its manner. And finally, because Nasrallah transformed himself from an effective resistance leader to a politician fighting for power, even some Lebanese Shi'ites resented his following instructions issued by the Iranian spiritual leader, ALI KHAMENEHI.

Nasrallah's legacy is thus two-pronged at this stage of his short career: a national hero for some and, like other Lebanese politicians, an ally much beholden to foreign powers. While the first guarantees him an undeniably important role in Lebanese affairs, the second may hinder this role. It remains to be determined whether Nasrallah can become a player within a group of players or whether he will continue to act the resistance leader. When Nasrallah addressed a crowd in early 2006 gathered to commemorate Ashura, a Shi'ite religious day of atonement, he declared that Hizbullah would not engage in sectarian warfare and that he would not authorize a renewed civil war. "There are figures within the ruling powers who are working to provoke a conflict between Shi'ites and Sunnis in Lebanon," he announced, and "we reject sectarian conflict, civil war [because] we will not aim our weapons at anyone, we will not work in the service of Israel."

BIBLIOGRAPHY

Hamzeh, Ahmad Nizar. *In the Path of Hizbullah*. Syracuse, NY: Syracuse University Press, 2004.

Harik, Judith Palmer. *Hezbollah: The Changing Face of Terrorism*. London: I.B. Tauris, 2005.

Jaber, Hala. *Hezbollah*. New York: Columbia University Press, 1997.

"Nasrallah Regrets Kidnapping of Israeli Soldiers." Ya Libnan. Updated 27 August 2006. Available from http://yalibnan.com.

Noe, Nicholas, ed. *Voice of Hezbollah: The Statements of Sayed Hasan Nasrallah*. London: Verso, 2007.

Passner, Deborah. "Hassan Nasrallah: In His Own Words." Committee for Accuracy in Middle East Reporting in America. Available from http://www.camera.org.

Ranstorp, Magnus. *Hizb'allah in Lebanon: The Politics of the Western Hostage Crisis*. New York: Palgrave Macmillan, 2003.

Saad-Ghorayed, Amal. *Hizbu'llah: Politics and Religion*. London: Pluto Press, 2002.

Sankari, Jamal. *Fadlallah: The Making of a Radical Shi'ite Leader*. London: Saqi Books, 2005.

Selbourne, David. *The Losing Battle with Islam*. New York: Prometheus Books, 2005.

Shanahan, Rodger. *The Shi'a of Lebanon: Clans, Parties and Clerics*. New York: Tauris Academic Studies, 2005.

Tellawi, Karim. "Hezbollah Chief: Lebanon Govt Stirring Conflict between Shia, Sunni." Jafariya News. Updated 27 January 2007. Available from http://www.jafariyanews.com/2k7_news/jan/29nasrallah.htm.

"Text of Hezbollah Leader Nasrallah's Speech during 'Victory Rally' in Beirut." Cleveland Indy Media Center. Updated 25 September 2006. Available from http://cleveland.indymedia.org

Joseph Kechichian

NAZERI, SHAHRAM
(1950–)

A Kurdish Iranian musician, Shahram Nazeri is one of Iran's most acclaimed vocalists.

PERSONAL HISTORY

Nazeri was born to a Kurdish family in Kermanshah, Iran, in 1950. He received traditional music instruction from his father and his uncles. He performed at Sufi (Islamic mystic) ceremonies, began singing at a very early age, and even sang on Iranian national television by age eleven. Nazeri began studying *radif*, the classical Persian repertoire, and worked with some of the masters of modern Persian music, including Abdollah Davami, Nourali Borouman, and Mahmoud Karimi. He also studied to play the tar (a stringed instrument) with Habibollah Salehi. In 1969 he issued his first recording.

In the early twenty-first century he specializes in singing the words of such Sufi writers as Jalal al-Din al-Rumi,

BIOGRAPHICAL HIGHLIGHTS

Name: Shahram Nazeri

Birth: 1950, Kermanshah, Iran

Family: Wife; son, Hafez

Nationality: Iranian Kurd

Education: Independently educated in traditional Iranian music

PERSONAL CHRONOLOGY:

- **1969:** Issues first album
- **1975:** Takes first place at Concours de Musique Traditionnelle
- **2000:** "The Rumi Ensemble" tour in Iran
- **2005:** "The Path of Rumi" tour in North America
- **2007:** Awarded Légion d'honneur by France

Shaykh Attar, and Hafiz of Shiraz. Called the Persian Nightingale and the Pavarotti of Iran, Nazeri sings in both Persian and Kurdish, and has worked with Aref and Sheyda, the leading ensembles in Iran. He currently is working on symphonies featuring the writings of classical Persian writer Hakim Abo'l-Qasim Firdawsi.

INFLUENCES AND CONTRIBUTIONS

Nazeri grew up listening to Sufi religious music and hearing the performances from the classical Iranian tradition. He went on to become a legend in Iran and has recorded over forty albums, including *Gol-e Sad Barg* (The one hundred leaf flower), *Yadegar e Doust* (The friend's memoir), *Sedaye Sokhan e Eshgh* (The sound of love's word), and *Shour Angiz* (Joygiver). He is credited for stimulating an interest in classical Iranian music among the country's younger generations. In 2000, Nazeri went on tour in Iran with a group called the Rumi Ensemble. They held a series of landmark concerts in twenty cities in the country, and introduced Iranian youth to the classical musical genre. In recent years he has performed with his son, Hafez Nazeri, an acclaimed musician in his own right, and has delighted sold-out audiences around the world, including "The Path of Rumi" tour in North America in 2005–2006.

THE WORLD'S PERSPECTIVE

Nazeri is known and acclaimed both at home and abroad, and is one of Iran's best-known musicians outside the country, partially as a result of years of touring

around the world. In 1975 he won first place at the Concours de Musique Traditionnelle. In 2007 France awarded him the prestigious Légion d'honneur medal, and Iran has awarded him its House of Music award.

LEGACY

Nazeri's career is not yet over, but he will surely be remembered for the important role he played in keeping Sufi musical traditions alive in Iran and for promoting Iranian cultural awareness outside Iran at a time when the country's image in the West often was dominated by negative images.

BIBLIOGRAPHY

Curiel, Jonathan. "Iran's Pavarotti: Sharam Nazeri." *Christian Science Monitor*. 11 June 1997.

"Shahram Nazeri." MySpace Music. Available from http://www.myspace.com/shahramnazeri.

"Shahram Nazeri Discography." Shahram Nazeri. Available from http://www.shahramnazeri.org.

"Shahram Nazeri Latest News." Shahram Nazeri. Available from http://www.shahram-nazeri.com.

Michael R. Fischbach

NETANYAHU, BINYAMIN
(1949–)

Binyamin (Benjamin) Netanyahu, popularly nicknamed "Bibi," is an Israeli politician and diplomat who has been a leading member of the conservative Likud Party. He was Israel's prime minister from 1996 to 1999. At the time, he was the country's youngest prime minister and the first to be born after the creation of the State of Israel.

PERSONAL HISTORY

Netanyahu was born on 21 October 1949 in Tel Aviv. He grew up in Jerusalem until his family moved to the United States in 1963 when he was a teenager. His father, Ben-Zion Netanyahu, was a prominent professor of Jewish history and editor of the *Hebrew Encyclopedia*. Netanyahu attended Cheltenham High School, near Philadelphia; after graduating, he returned to Israel in 1967 and enlisted in the Israel Defense Forces (IDF).

During his military service (1967–1972), he served in an elite commando unit and participated in a number of military operations, including the rescue of hostages in a hijacked Sabena airliner at Ben-Gurion Airport near Tel Aviv in 1972. In the same year, he was cited for outstanding operational leadership by Major General Motta Gur. Netanyahu later took part in the 1973 War and reached the rank of captain.

Binyamin Netanyahu. DAVID RUBINGER/TIME LIFE
PICTURES/GETTY IMAGES.

BIOGRAPHICAL HIGHLIGHTS

Name: Binyamin (Benjamin) Netanyahu

Birth: 1949, Tel Aviv, Israel

Family: Wife (third), Sara; three children: Noa, Yair, and Avner

Nationality: Israeli

Education: Massachusetts Institute of Technology (MIT), B.Sc. in architecture, 1974, and M.Sc. in business management, 1976

PERSONAL CHRONOLOGY:

- **1984:** Appointed ambassador to the United Nations

- **1988:** Enters Knesset, becomes deputy minister of foreign affairs

- **1993–1999:** Chair of Likud Party

- **1996–1999:** Prime minister

- **1999:** Resigns Likud leadership following election defeat; temporarily retires from politics

- **2002–2003:** Minister of foreign affairs

- **2003–2005:** Minister of finance

- **2005–present:** Chair of Likud

Netanyahu returned to the United States for his university studies, taking courses at Harvard University and the Massachusetts Institute of Technology (MIT). He attained a B.Sc. in architecture and an M.Sc. in business management from MIT. Following his studies, Netanyahu worked in the private sector from 1976 to 1982, first with the Boston Consulting Group, an international business consultancy, and then in a senior management position at Rim Industries, Inc.

In 1976 Netanyahu's older brother, Yonatan ("Yoni"), was killed leading an IDF commando raid against a hijacked airliner in Entebbe, Uganda. Yoni Netanyahu became a posthumous hero in Israel and the Netanyahu family name became well known. This event deeply affected the younger Netanyahu and led to his lifelong concern with international terrorism. He later organized two international conferences on ways to combat international terrorism, in 1979 in Jerusalem and in 1984 in Washington, D.C., and edited and wrote a number of books on the subject.

In 1982 Netanyahu was appointed deputy chief of mission at the Israeli Embassy in Washington, D.C. He served under Ambassador Moshe Arens, who became his mentor. Two years later, in 1984, he was appointed Israel's ambassador at the United Nations, a position he

held for four years. During this time, he became a familiar face on American television and became known as an articulate and effective advocate of Israel's cause.

In 1988 Netanyahu returned to Israel and began his involvement in domestic politics. He was elected to the Knesset as a Likud member and was appointed deputy foreign minister in the government of Yitzhak Shamir. In this capacity, Netanyahu was Israel's principal international spokesperson during the 1991 Gulf War, for which he became well known to Israelis. Following the war, he was a senior member of the Israeli delegation to the Middle East Peace Conference in Madrid, which initiated the first direct peace negotiations between Israel and Syria, Lebanon, and a joint Jordanian-Palestinian delegation. In the same year, he was appointed deputy prime minister (1991–1992).

Leading Likud Likud leader Shamir retired from politics in the wake of the Likud's electoral defeat to YITZHAK RABIN's Labor Party in the 1992 Knesset elections. In the Likud Party's first primary election to select its leader, held on 25 March 1993, Netanyahu was victorious, defeating Binyamin ("Benny") Begin, son of Prime Minister Menachem

Begin, and veteran politician David Levy. In the course of his campaign, Netanyahu publicly confessed to having had an extramarital affair.

As Likud leader and head of the parliamentary opposition, Netanyahu was a fierce opponent of the Rabin government's policy toward the Palestinians. He sharply criticized the Declaration of Principles adopted at Oslo in 1993 by Israel and the Palestine Liberation Organization (PLO) and the subsequent Oslo 2 ("Interim Agreement") of 1995.

Netanyahu accused the Rabin government of jeopardizing Israel's security by entrusting it to a "terrorist organization"—YASIR ARAFAT's PLO. He also staunchly defended Israel's right to possess the entire historic "Land of Israel" (Eretz Yisrael), including the West Bank (often referred to in Israel as "Judea and Samaria") and Gaza. Netanyahu spoke against Oslo at public rallies attended by right-wing extremists who denounced Prime Minister Rabin and Foreign Minister SHIMON PERES as traitors. After Rabin was assassinated in November 1995 by a right-wing Jewish extremist, Netanyahu was criticized for helping to foster an intensely polarized political climate, which some believe created the conditions for Rabin's assassination.

In the campaign for the May 1996 elections—the first in which Israelis voted directly for prime minister as well as for party—Netanyahu moved to the political center. Despite his earlier rejection of the Oslo Accords, he now accepted them and vowed to continue the peace process with the Palestinians. At the same time, he stated that he would be a tougher negotiator than his opponent, the incumbent prime minister Peres, who had succeeded Rabin. He promised Israelis "peace with security." After a series of suicide bombings inside Israel, this message appealed to many, and Netanyahu won narrowly. He took office on 18 June.

Netanyahu as Prime Minister Netanyahu's three-year premiership represented a major turning point in the Oslo process. Strong international, especially U.S., pressure, coupled with continued domestic support for Oslo, effectively forced Netanyahu to continue it. However, although he could not put an end to it, Netanyahu did his best to stall and drag out negotiations. His government also lifted the freeze on the expansion of Jewish settlements in the West Bank that had been in place under the previous government, allowing for a rapid increase in the number of Jewish settlers in the West Bank.

Despite a deterioration in Israeli-Palestinian relations during Netanyahu's tenure as prime minister, the peace process continued. In January 1997 Netanyahu signed the Hebron Agreement with Palestinian leader Arafat, in which Israel agreed to transfer control of the West Bank town of Hebron to the Palestinian Authority (PA), while keeping 20 percent of the town—the central area where more than 400 Jewish settlers lived among 130,000 Palestinians—under Israeli control. In October 1998 he signed the Wye River Memorandum with Arafat, reluctantly agreeing to carry out a further Israeli withdrawal from the West Bank. These agreements, largely the results of intense U.S. pressure and mediation, caused Netanyahu to lose popularity with the right in Israel.

Although the Israeli-Palestinian peace process dominated Netanyahu's premiership, economic reform was also an important item on his agenda. A proponent of neoliberal economic policies, Netanyahu liberalized Israel's foreign currency regulations, accelerated the privatization of government-owned companies and reduced the budget deficit.

Politically weakened by the loss of right-wing support because of his concessions to the Palestinians and by corruption scandals, Netanyahu called for early elections in May 1999. In the election for prime minister, he lost against his only challenger, One Israel (Labor) Party leader Ehud Barak. Following this defeat, he resigned as leader of the Likud and retired from politics.

Netanyahu's retirement from Israeli politics was only temporary. He returned in 2002 when Likud Party leader and then-prime minister ARIEL SHARON appointed him foreign minister, following Labor's departure from the government coalition. After the 2003 general election, Netanyahu accepted the post of minister of finance in Sharon's new coalition government, after being assured of a free hand in economic policy making.

As finance minister, Netanyahu implemented a controversial program of free-market reforms aimed at stimulating economic growth in Israel, involving privatization of public services and companies, tax cuts, and severe welfare cuts. Due, at least in part, to these measures, the Israeli economy grew by 4.2 percent in 2004.

Netanyahu adamantly opposed Prime Minister Sharon's "disengagement" plan, which called for a complete unilateral civilian and military withdrawal from the Gaza Strip, the dismantling of twenty-one settlements and the evacuation of approximately nine thousand Jewish settlers, as well as the dismantling of four small settlements in the northern West Bank and the evacuation of their residents. Netanyahu was one of the leaders of the Likud "rebels" who fought against the plan, and tried to topple Sharon as party leader. When this failed, Netanyahu resigned in protest from Sharon's cabinet in August 2005.

Leading Likud Again In November, Sharon resigned from the Likud to form a new centrist party, Kadima. Elections for the Likud leadership were held on 20

CONTEMPORARIES

Yonatan ("Yoni") Netanyahu, the older brother of Binyamin Netanyahu, is one of Israel's most famous soldiers. A member of the Israel Defense Forces (IDF) elite Sayeret Matkal unit, he was awarded the IDF's Medal of Distinguished Service for his heroic conduct in the 1973 War. He became a posthumous hero in Israel for leading a commando raid at Entebbe Airport in Uganda, where members of the Popular Front for the Liberation of Palestine (PFLP) and the German Baader-Meinhof Gang were holding Israeli and Jewish hostages after an airline hijacking. The daring nighttime raid, on 4 July 1976, was renamed "Operation Yonatan" in his honor; he was the only Israeli soldier killed during the raid. One hundred hostages were released and three died, while twenty Ugandan soldiers and all seven hijackers were killed in a battle that lasted thirty-five minutes.

December 2005, and Netanyahu won with 47 percent of the vote.

In Likud's campaign for the March 2006 Knesset election, Netanyahu attacked the "convergence" plan presented by new Kadima leader EHUD OLMERT, who succeeded Sharon after the latter's stroke in January 2006, and warned of the dangers to Israel of carrying out another unilateral withdrawal. The Israeli public, however, was unconvinced and Kadima ended up winning the largest number of Knesset seats in the election. Likud managed to win only twelve seats, down from its previous twenty-nine in the 2003 election. As a result, Netanyahu's Likud entered the opposition after the new Kadima-led coalition government was established in May 2006.

INFLUENCES AND CONTRIBUTIONS

As the son of Ben-Zion Netanyahu, who was once a senior aide to Vladimir (Ze'ev) Jabotinsky, founder of Revisionist Zionism, Netanyahu grew up under the influence of that movement's ideology. This right-wing, militant version of Zionism called for establishing a Jewish state with a Jewish majority in all of present-day Israel, the West Bank, Gaza, and Jordan (the claim to the latter territory was dropped by the late 1960s).

In accordance with this ideological background, before becoming prime minister, Netanyahu firmly opposed withdrawing from the West Bank and Gaza,

Palestinian-populated areas captured by Israel in the 1967 War. In addition to believing that these areas rightfully belonged to the Jewish people, Netanyahu also believed that Israel's security requirements necessitated keeping the West Bank to protect Israel's eastern border from Arab attack. He therefore sharply criticized the Oslo agreements signed by the Rabin government with the PLO, which entailed Israel's handing over control of parts of the Occupied Territories to a newly created Palestinian Authority headed by Arafat.

Once in power, however, Netanyahu acted more as a pragmatist than an ideologue. Knowing that he would jeopardize U.S. support for Israel and lose support from many Israelis in the political center if he abandoned Oslo, Netanyahu reluctantly continued it. Instead of championing "greater Israel," he emphasized the need for security and insisted on the principle of reciprocity, meaning that Palestinian gains, such as redeployment of Israeli forces and expansion of autonomy, had to be linked to genuine Palestinian efforts toward peace, especially countering Palestinian terrorist attacks against Israelis (which had escalated in the 1994–1996 period before he entered office).

Netanyahu's intense focus on combating Palestinian terrorism was not only a response to the widespread fears and anxieties of the Israeli public who had suffered from a string of suicide terrorist attacks, but also to his older brother Yonatan's death at the hands of terrorists in the commando raid on Entebbe airport in Uganda in 1976. *Fighting Terrorism* (the title of a book by Netanyahu on the subject) became a personal mission for Netanyahu after that tragic event.

By eschewing revisionist ideology and pragmatically continuing the Oslo process, Netanyahu helped move the Likud Party toward the center of Israel's political spectrum. Under Netanyahu, the Likud became a less ideological, more politically conservative center-right political party. This shift continued under his successor as Likud leader, Sharon.

Another significant contribution that Netanyahu made to Israeli politics was his political style and media strategy, which was heavily influenced by his familiarity with American politics. Netanyahu was the most "American" of Israel's leaders, having been educated in the United States and lived there as a businessperson and a diplomat. Pragmatic, media-savvy, and a great orator, Netanyahu pioneered the use of sound bites, attack ads, focus groups, and constant public opinion polling in Israeli politics. He even hired the American Republican political consultant Arthur Finkelstein to run his 1996 campaign. The success of this campaign led Barak, Netanyahu's challenger in the 1999 election, to use American Democratic political consultants Bob Shrum and Stanley Greenberg in his campaign. Hence, Netanyahu played a large role in bringing about the "Americanization" of Israeli politics.

THE WORLD'S PERSPECTIVE

International attitudes toward Netanyahu, like those of Israelis, tend to be highly positive or highly negative. He was considered to be a skilled diplomat for Israel, popular with Western audiences because of his flawless English and mastery of the Western media. He was especially popular in the United States and among American Jews.

His three-year tenure as prime minister, however, was marked by clashes with the administration of U.S. president Bill Clinton and international criticism of his foot-dragging in negotiations with the Palestinians. As a result, he became deeply unpopular with international supporters of the Oslo peace process. Despite being seen as unprincipled and power-hungry by some, he has always been regarded as an adept politician and a highly articulate defender of Israel's cause.

LEGACY

Netanyahu's principal legacy lies in the historic significance of the two Israeli-Palestinian agreements he signed as prime minister: the 1996 Hebron Agreement and the 1997 Wye River Memorandum. Netanyahu became the first Likud leader to agree to withdraw from parts of the West Bank, thereby effectively abandoning the principle of full Jewish possession of Eretz Yisrael—a principle that had been at the heart of right-wing Zionism since the days of Jabotinsky. Under Netanyahu, the Likud's uncompromising opposition to the partition of Eretz Yisrael was irrevocably undermined. The principle of territorial compromise had been accepted and implemented by Israeli governments on both the right and the left. After Netanyahu, the long-running domestic debate in Israel over the future of the West Bank and Gaza was no longer about whether Israel should withdraw, but by how much, how quickly, and in exchange for what.

BIBLIOGRAPHY

Drake, Laura. "A Netanyahu Primer." *Journal of Palestine Studies* 26, no. 1 (1996): 58–69.

Inbar, Efraim. "Netanyahu Takes Over." In *Israel at the Polls, 1996*, edited by Daniel Elazar and Shmuel Sandler. London and Portland, OR: Frank Cass, 1998.

Lochery, Neill. "Netanyahu Deciphered." *Middle East Quarterly* 6, no. 1 (March 1999): 29–36.

Netanyahu, Binyamin. *A Place among Nations: Israel and the World.* New York: Bantam, 1993.

———. *A Durable Peace: Israel and Its Place among the Nations.* New York: Warner, 2000.

———. *Fighting Terrorism: How Democracies Can Defeat Domestic and International Terrorists*, 2nd ed. New York: Farrar, Straus and Giroux, 2001.

Shindler, Colin. *Israel, Likud and the Zionist Dream.* London: I.B. Tauris, 1995.

Sprinzak, Ehud. "The Politics of Paralysis: Netanyahu's Safety Belt." *Foreign Affairs* 77, no. 4 (July/August 1998): 18–28.

Dov Waxman

NOOR AL-HUSSEIN
(1951–)

Queen Noor al-Hussein (born as Elizabeth [Lisa] Halaby) is the widow of Jordan's long ruling monarch, King Hussein, and a philanthropist and activist.

PERSONAL HISTORY

Noor al-Hussein was born as Elizabeth (Lisa) Halaby on 23 August 1951 in Washington, D.C. Her father, Syrian American Najeeb Elias Halaby, was a former navy test pilot, director of the Federal Aviation Administration in the administration of President John F. Kennedy, and chairman of Pan American World Airways. Her mother, Doris Lundquist, was a homemaker of Swedish descent. Lisa Halaby's childhood was one of privilege. She was

Noor al-Hussein. BRYAN BEDDER/GETTY IMAGES.

BIOGRAPHICAL HIGHLIGHTS

Name: Noor al-Hussein (Nur al-Husayn, Queen Noor; born Elizabeth Halaby)

Birth: 1951, Washington, DC

Family: Husband, King Hussein of Jordan (d. 1999); two sons, Hamzah (b. 1980), Hashim (b. 1981); two daughters: Iman (b. 1983), Raiyah (b. 1986)

Nationality: American, Jordanian

Education: B.A. (architecture and urban planning), Princeton University, 1974

PERSONAL CHRONOLOGY:

• **1974:** Works for British, Australian architectural firms

• **1977:** Works for Royal Jordanian airlines

• **1978:** Marries King Hussein

• **1979:** Works with the National Committee for the International Year of the Child, spearheading an immunization campaign in Jordan

• **1980:** Convenes the Arab Children's Congress

• **1981:** Founds Jerash Festival for Culture and Arts

• **1984:** Helps establish the Jubilee School

• **1985:** Establishes the Noor al-Hussein Foundation

• **1995:** Receives United Nations Environment Program Global 500 Award

• **1998:** Becomes International Patron and Honorary Chair of Landmine Survivors Network

• **1999:** Founding chair of the King Hussein Foundation

haul its airline system. He brought his daughter into the project, and she designed the aviation training facility at Arab Air University in Jordan. Subsequently, she was named director of planning and design projects for Royal Jordanian Airlines.

Jordan's KING HUSSEIN was mourning the death of his third wife, Queen Alia, who had been killed in a helicopter crash in February 1977. He and Halaby first met during a 1977 airport ceremony. The pair became friends and that friendship soon evolved into a romance. Following a courtship of nearly two months, Hussein proposed, and the couple married on 15 June 1978. Hussein immediately announced that he was conferring the title queen upon her, something he had done for Alia but neither of his first two wives. Halaby, who changed her name to Noor al-Hussein (Arabic: The Light of Hussein) and converted to Islam before the marriage, faced some initial problems being accepted in Jordan. She was a non-Arab, non-Jordanian American, originally a non-Muslim, and non-Arabic-speaking woman who was replacing the popular Palestinian Queen Alia. Beyond that, she was required to manage the royal household and raise the king's three youngest children who just had lost their mother. In fact, all of the king's eight children accompanied the royal couple on their honeymoon. She and Hussein later had four children of their own: Hamzah, Hashim, Iman, and Raiyah.

Hussein died in Amman on 7 February 1999. Noor's stepson, Abdullah, became the new king, and her eldest son, Hamzah, became crown prince until relieved of these duties by King Abdullah in November 2004. She continues to reside in Amman.

INFLUENCES AND CONTRIBUTIONS

Queen Noor embarked on a number of philanthropic activities after marrying Hussein. Drawing on her architectural background, she was instrumental in getting the government to adopt the first national professional building code, and spearheaded the movement to preserve Jordan's architectural history by establishing the National Committee for Public Buildings and Architectural Heritage. She also devoted herself to issues concerning child welfare and projects that target maternal and child health care, women's development, environmental protection, and education. In 1979 she worked closely with the National Committee for the International Year of the Child, organizing a national immunization campaign, children's recreation parks and reading programs, and a venture to create Jordan's first children's hospital. The queen convened the Arab Children's Congress in 1980, an annual event that attracts youth from throughout the Arab world with the purpose of enhancing understanding and fellowship through an examination of culture and

educated in exclusive private schools in Washington, D.C., New York City, and Massachusetts, where she attended the Concord Academy. Halaby became a member of the first coeducational class at Princeton University in 1969, graduating in 1974 with a B.A. in architecture and urban planning.

Upon graduation, she accepted a position with an Australian architectural firm that concentrated on urban development. She later worked with a British architectural firm that had been commissioned to modernize the Iranian metropolis of Tehran. In 1976 the Jordanian government contracted with Najeeb Halaby to help over-

MODERATES OF ALL CREEDS MUST EMBRACE THEIR SHARED, UNIVERSAL VALUES

■

Today we have seen how the perverted actions of a violent fringe have hijacked the great faith of the prophet Muhammad for its own ends. Yet Islam has no monopoly on radical fundamentalism. Christianity has carried the banner of "Holy War"—not only at the time of the Crusades, but in recent years, in the bloody execution of "ethnic cleansing" in the Balkans. Tragically there are also Jewish extremists who are willing to use violence to further their vision of a religious utopia—one of them killed YITZHAK RABIN for daring to contemplate peace.... It is convenient for many pundits to describe these affronts as a "clash of civilizations" and promulgate the view that nothing can be changed; that cultural differences are hard-wired; that no amount of dialogue will change the dynamic of conflict; and that geopolitical power politics, bolstered by the threat of force, is the only way to manage these crises. My approach is quite another. Moderates of all creeds must embrace their shared, universal values and defy those who cloak hatred in religious rhetoric.

QUEEN NOOR. "QUEEN NOOR ON CLASHING CIVILIZATIONS." GLOBALIST. UPDATED 14 AUGUST 2006. AVAILABLE FROM HTTP://WWW.THEGLOBALIST.COM.

tory, the National Handicrafts Development Project, the Jordan Design and Trade Center and, in 1985, the Noor al-Hussein Foundation (NHF), to consolidate her diverse and expanding interests. The NHF projects are aimed to develop individual and community self-reliance, and aid in decision making and project implementation, with a strong emphasis on the development of women.

Queen Noor remains active in these endeavors and works in numerous areas of humanitarian aid, stressing education, peace building, and environmental and health initiatives. She served on numerous national committees, from the Royal Society for the Conservation of Nature and the National Federation of Business and Professional Women's Clubs to the SOS Children's Village Association, the Queen Noor Technical College for Civil Aviation, and the Cerebral Palsy Foundation. Beginning in the late 1990s, she advocated an end to so-called honor crimes, in which male relatives following tribal law murder women in the family who have allegedly stained the family honor through sexual impropriety.

After King Hussein's death in 1999, Queen Noor became the founding chair of the King Hussein Foundation International, a nonprofit organization dedicated to peace and security through programs that promote cross-cultural understanding and social, economic, and political opportunities in the Muslim and Arab world.

THE WORLD'S PERSPECTIVE

The Jordanians greeted Noor al-Hussein with some suspicion when she first became their queen. The popular Queen Alia had only died sixteen months before Noor's marriage. Given that approximately one-half of Jordan's population consisted of Palestinians, that Alia was a Palestinian had endeared her to them even more. Although an attractive blond, as Alia was, Noor was an American who initially could not even speak Arabic. By the time of Hussein's death in 1999, much had changed, and her gracious and high-profiled role in Hussein's final days, death, and funeral proceedings earned her considerable support and sympathy in Jordan.

Internationally, Noor al-Hussein was a darling of the international media. Her unlikely rise to royal status garnered her considerable positive media coverage. So, too, did her many charitable activities. She continues to travel widely, and advises and supports many international philanthropic organizations. A testament to her global popularity was that her book, *Leap of Faith: Memoirs of an Unexpected Life*, was a *New York Times* best seller that was translated into fifteen languages.

Noor al-Hussein has received a variety of awards and honorary degrees. In June 1995 she received the United Nations Environment Program Global 500 Award for her activism in environmental protection. In 1998 she became the International Patron and Honorary Chair of Landmine Survivors Network.

history. She was involved in promoting a children's play, *The Kind Chemo*, to raise awareness of cancer detection and treatment in conjunction with her work for the Al Amal Center, Jordan's first comprehensive cancer care center. She was also a participant in the International Children's Hour campaign, where every working person was urged to donate his or her last hour of earnings in 1999 to help make the world better for children in 2000. In 1998 after the death of Diana, Princess of Wales, Queen Noor assumed the leadership position of the Landmine Survivors' Network, an international group of people dedicated to the eradication of the use of landmines.

Noor al-Hussein has been a huge promoter of Arab culture and the arts, and in 1981 founded the Jerash Festival for Culture and Arts. In 1984 the Jubilee School, named in honor of the king's Silver Jubilee, began its planning stages. Queen Noor was at the helm, overseeing the creation of this independent coeducational school for developing outstanding scholarship at the secondary school level. She initiated a National Music Conserva-

LEGACY

Queen Noor will be remembered as the first queen in Jordan who took an active, public role in the life of the nation beyond merely being the consort of the monarch. Her philanthropic contributions to the country have been significant, and she also has done much to humanize the Hashemite monarchy internationally and endear the country to North Americans and Europeans.

BIBLIOGRAPHY

Queen Noor's official Web site. Available from http://www.noor.gov.jo.

Queen Noor. *Leap of Faith: Memoirs of an Unexpected Life.* New York: Miramax, 2003.

———. "Queen Noor on Clashing Civilizations." Globalist. Updated 14 August 2006. Available from http://www.theglobalist.com.

updated by Michael R. Fischbach

ÖCALAN, ABDULLAH
(1948–)

Abdullah Öcalan is a Kurdish militant who, as leader of the Workers' Party of Kurdistan (PKK), led an armed campaign against the Turkish government until his capture and imprisonment in 1999.

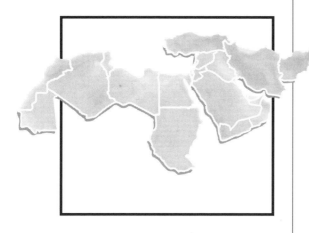

PERSONAL HISTORY

Öcalan was born on 4 April 1948, to a Kurdish father and a Turkish mother in Ömerli, Turkey, a poor village near the Euphrates River in southeastern Turkey in an area sustained by cotton crops. Known to many Kurds by his nickname Apo (uncle), Öcalan has noted that his family took their surname, which means avenger in Turkish, after a relative died in 1925 during a Kurdish uprising against the Turkish government. Öcalan was a religious Muslim as a youth. He attended school in Urfa, then worked in the land registration department in Diyarbakir from 1960 to 1970.

Öcalan entered Ankara University in the Turkish capital in 1971 where he studied political science and became a Marxist. However, he was dismayed that Turkish leftists did not take up the Kurdish cause. During his student years, Öcalan was jailed for seven months in 1972 for involvement in antiregime political activities. After his release and expulsion from the university, Öcalan collected a group of roughly thirty Kurdish and Turkish cohorts in Lice, near Diyarbakir, in southeastern Turkey. In November 1978 they settled on the name Workers' Party of Kurdistan (Turkish acronym: PKK).

INFLUENCES AND CONTRIBUTIONS

Under Öcalan's leadership, the PKK began an armed campaign aimed at Kurdish independence from Turkey. It reportedly began killing members of rival groups as well as Kurdish landlords and pro-government tribesmen, and blew up schools, which the group considered to be aiding the Turkish cause by not allowing Kurds to speak their native language. To help finance their cause, PKK militants robbed banks and jewelry stores, and were suspected of running an international drug ring to raise funds as well. In the midst of an overall atmosphere of upheaval in politics, Turkey declared martial law in the region in 1978. In 1980 about 5,000 people were killed in clashes between the left and right factions that ended in an army coup. Öcalan and his followers fled to Damascus, Syria, allowing President HAFIZ AL-ASAD to use their presence as a way to agitate Turkey, with which Syria had long been embroiled in water and territorial disputes. From there, Öcalan freely traveled around Syria, Lebanon, and northern Iraq, where he was known for dressing in army fatigues as he ran boot-camp-style training for Kurdish guerrillas.

Abdullah Öcalan. JOSEPH BARRAK/AFP/GETTY IMAGES.

BIOGRAPHICAL HIGHLIGHTS

Name: Abdullah Öcalan

Birth: 1948, Ömerli, Turkey

Family: Wife, Kesire Yildirim (divorced)

Nationality: Turkish (Kurdish)

Education: B.A. studies, Ankara University (unfinished)

PERSONAL CHRONOLOGY:

- **1960:** Works at land registration department, Diyarbekir
- **1971:** Enters Ankara University
- **1978:** Forms Workers' Party of Kurdistan (PKK)
- **1984:** PKK launches full-scale war against Turkish government
- **1998:** Declares cease-fire; is expelled from Syria
- **1999:** Captured in Kenya, flown to Turkey, tried, and sentenced to death
- **2002:** Death sentence commuted to life imprisonment
- **2006:** Calls on PKK to observe a cease-fire

In 1984 Öcalan launched a full-scale guerrilla war against Turkey in hopes of establishing an independent, Marxist state for Kurds. Throughout the years, more than thirty-thousand people were killed in the fighting, including PKK guerrillas, Turkish military, political officials, and civilians. The PKK assassinated authorities, kidnapped foreigners, and bombed hospitals and schools. Based on these actions, Turks characterized Öcalan as a ruthless mass murderer while many Kurds revered Öcalan as a brave revolutionary. Support for the Kurds grew around Europe as well, despite Öcalan's tactics, due in no small part to evidence of widespread torture of Kurds by Turkish police, and the forcing of hundreds of thousands of Kurds from their homes, leaving them nowhere to go.

In August 1998 Öcalan declared a cease-fire—not his first—and appeared to be pressing for a new moderation. He insisted that the PKK would no longer use violence and announced that the group no longer sought outright independence from Turkey. Whether he was sincere or not was debated; however, the new stance won him a larger base of support in Europe. At the same time, Turkey for some years had been slowly moving toward acceptance of the Kurds and had relaxed bans on Kurdish language and culture. However, on 20 October 1998 Turkey threatened to invade Syria unless it gave up Öcalan, and Syria subsequently signed an agreement with Turkey saying that it would no longer support the PKK and recognized it as a terrorist organization. Öcalan had to leave Syria and was sent to Athens, Greece, and then Moscow, Russia, where he was refused asylum.

On 12 November Öcalan deplaned in Rome, Italy, and surrendered to authorities at the airport, which surprised Italian officials. They put him under a kind of house arrest, but later that month he was set free as they mulled over his request for refugee status. The situation was complex: Turkey and Italy were close North Atlantic Treaty Organisation allies, but once Öcalan arrived, the mood chilled, since Italian law prevents extradition to countries with the death penalty, which Turkey had at the time. In addition, many Italians supported the plight of the Kurds, and the PKK had ties to some leftists in the Italian parliament. Subsequently, protestors in the Turkish capital burned Italian flags and demonstrated outside of Italian-owned Benetton apparel stores. By late December, Italy ruled that they would not send Öcalan back to Turkey for trial and that he was free to leave, which further incensed Turkey. The United States, meanwhile, supported Turkey's request for extradition and described Öcalan as a terrorist.

Öcalan left Italy in January 1999, after the Italian government, facing pressure from Turkey, sent him back to Russia. Germany could have requested extradition because he was wanted for several murders there as well as some terrorist attacks in 1993, but German prime minister Gerhard Schröder, fearful of unrest among the half-million Kurdish immigrants there, did not press for it. Then, Greek foreign minister Theodoros Pangalos extended aid to Öcalan and he was shuttled to Athens. Once he landed, though, Greece, not officially ready to give him refugee status, had no viable destination for Öcalan, so he was then sent to Nairobi, Kenya, with the understanding that it was a temporary hold for him while Greece attempted to arrange a permanent haven in a different African nation. Greek ambassador to Kenya George Costoulas kept him at his villa, but Öcalan was soon spotted by American Federal Bureau of Investigation agents. The next day, Kenya ordered Öcalan out, and he made plans to be transported to the Netherlands.

However, on 15 February 1999, Öcalan was arrested and whisked away, reportedly by Kenyan police, who then handed him over to Turkish commandos. He was placed on a plane and flown to Turkey, which jubilantly announced his capture. Kurds were outraged at what they saw as a betrayal by Greece, although the Greek government denied cooperation with Turkey. Several reports indicated that American surveillance may have given away Öcalan's whereabouts (although the government officially denied this), and other sources suggested that Israel may have had a hand in the arrest. The exact circumstances were unclear, but Öcalan was blindfolded, handcuffed, and flown to Turkey. Photographs of the shackled, sweating leader were broadcast around the world.

The Turkish government detained Öcalan in a prison on the island of Imrali, about 35 miles off the coast from Istanbul, in the Sea of Marmara. Kurds protested internationally; some rioted and destroyed offices in Europe, others set themselves on fire in various cities across Europe. In March, even though he was in custody, Öcalan was reelected as chairman of the PKK. On 31 May 1999 his trial for treason began, and he immediately apologized for his past and offered an end to the war in exchange for allowing the PKK to function as a political party. The European Court of Human Rights protested Öcalan's trial, stating that the Turkish court system was inherently biased because one of the three judges was appointed by the military. That Turkey was desperate to join the European Union (EU) complicated the trial and sentence. Turkey long was under fire by the EU for its human rights record, its treatment of the Kurds, and that it still maintained the death penalty—something that would bar it from membership in the EU. Still, the case pressed on for four weeks, and he was eventually

found guilty and sentenced to death by hanging. Many Turks rejoiced, whereas Kurds retaliated with escalated violence and killings.

In August 2002 Turkey abolished the death penalty. Öcalan's sentence was commuted to life imprisonment. He remains under heavy guard on Imrali Island, and is the only prisoner remaining there. He has claimed to have abandoned revolutionary Marxism, advocating instead a federal democratic union between Turks and Kurds. The PKK, which had observed a cease-fire from 2000 to 2004, resumed armed attacks. In September 2006 Öcalan called on it to cease such armed activities.

THE WORLD'S PERSPECTIVE

Among some Kurds, Öcalan is seen as a brave freedom fighter who battled for basic civil rights and a homeland for the Kurdish people. He also found support among European leftists and Kurdish communities in Europe. However, Turkey long considered Öcalan a terrorist and claimed that the PKK was responsible for over five-thousand civilian killings, including women and children. The EU and the United States also considered the PKK a terrorist organization.

LEGACY

Öcalan remains an extremely divisive figure in Kurdish and Turkish history. He and the PKK certainly played a major role in Kurdish politics within Turkey. Yet the PKK's war against the Turkish government has not translated into an independent Kurdish state or even a federal solution, and his ideological twists and turns make him a complex figure. The war proved extremely costly and disruptive, and even influenced Turkey's relations with the EU and post–Saddam Hussein Iraq (because of Turkish raids on PKK units operating in Iraqi Kurdistan). Exactly how history will record Öcalan and his impact remains to be seen.

BIBLIOGRAPHY

Öcalan, Abdullah. *Prison Writings: The Roots of Civilization.* Translated by Klaus Happel. Sterling, VA: Pluto Press, 2007.

Özcan, Ali Kemal. *Turkey's Kurds: A Theoretical Analysis of the PKK and Abdullah Öcalan.* London: Routledge, 2005.

updated by Michael R. Fischbach

OLMERT, EHUD
(1945–)

Ehud Olmert is an Israeli politician who became the twelfth prime minister of Israel in 2006. He was a long-time member of Israel's center-right Likud Party before

Ehud Olmert. AP IMAGES.

BIOGRAPHICAL HIGHLIGHTS

Name: Ehud Olmert

Birth: 1945, Nahalat Jabotinsky, mandatory Palestine

Family: Wife, Aliza; four children, Michal, Dana, Shaul, Ariel

Nationality: Israeli

Education: B.A., Hebrew University, 1968; LL.B., Hebrew University, 1973

PERSONAL CHRONOLOGY:

- **1973:** Elected to the Knesset
- **1988–1990:** Minister without portfolio, responsible for minority affairs
- **1990–1992:** Minister of health
- **1993–2003:** Mayor, Jerusalem
- **2003–2005:** Minister of communications
- **2003–2006:** Deputy prime minister, minister of industry, trade and labor
- **2005–2006:** Minister of finance
- **2006–present:** Prime minister, minister of social welfare

joining the newly formed Kadima Party led by then-prime minister ARIEL SHARON. Olmert took over the leadership of Kadima and became acting prime minister after Sharon suffered an incapacitating stroke in January 2006. Following Kadima's electoral victory in March 2006, he became prime minister.

PERSONAL HISTORY

Olmert was born in 1945 in Nahalat Jabotinsky, part of Binyamina, in mandatory Palestine. His parents were among the founders of Nahalat Jabotinsky, named after Ze'ev (Vladimir) Jabotinsky, the leader of the Revisionist Zionist movement that espoused a militant and uncompromising approach in the struggle between Jews and Arabs over possession of Palestine. The third of four sons, Olmert grew up in a staunchly ideological family, whose right-wing nationalist views were widely considered anathema by the majority of Israelis and were thus a cause for social ostracism. His father, Mordechai Olmert, who had emigrated from Harbin, China, in the late 1930s, was a Member of Knesset (MK) from 1955 to 1961 for the Herut Party. This was a right-wing party at the margins of Israeli politics, which at the time was dominated by the center-left Mapai Party under the leadership of David Ben-Gurion, Israel's prime minister for most of the period from 1948 to 1963.

Like most children from Revisionist Zionist homes, as a child Olmert joined the Betar Youth Organization, the highly nationalistic and militaristic youth wing of the Revisionist Zionist movement. For his compulsory military service, Olmert served as an officer in the Golani combat brigade. During his military service he was injured and temporarily released from the army. He later completed his military service in 1971 after working as the military correspondent for the Israel Defense Force's (IDF) magazine *Bamahane*. Between 1965 and 1968, he studied at the Hebrew University of Jerusalem, graduating with a B.A. degree in psychology and philosophy.

Olmert entered right-wing politics at an early age. As a student, he was a member of Herut's student organization. Already actively involved in politics at the age of twenty-one, at the Herut movement's convention in June 1966 Olmert publicly demanded the resignation of Herut Party leader Menachem Begin over the party's losses in six consecutive general elections. In 1968 Olmert became a parliamentary aide in the Free Center Party headed by Shmuel Tamir, a position he held until 1973. From 1970 to 1973 he also studied for a law degree at the Hebrew University. He started working in a private law firm in Jerusalem in 1975 and became a successful lawyer.

In 1973 at the age of only twenty-eight Olmert was elected to the Knesset as part of the Free Center Party, which had then become a faction within the newly formed Likud bloc. At the time, Olmert was the youngest-ever MK. In his early years in the Knesset, Olmert made a name for himself by campaigning against corruption in sports and organized crime. He was reelected in 1977, 1981, and 1984 as part of the Likud list.

In 1985 he officially joined the Likud Party itself and served as a Likud MK until 1998. From 1981 to 1988, he was a member of several Knesset committees: foreign affairs and security, finance, and education. From 1988 to 1990, he served as a minister without portfolio for minority issues in the national unity government led by Yitzhak Shamir. He then became minister of health in Shamir's Likud-led government between 1990 and 1992, during which time he initiated a broad reform of the health-care system.

Mayor of Jerusalem In 1993 Olmert successfully ran for mayor of Jerusalem against incumbent Teddy Kollek, becoming the first member of Likud to hold the position. Olmert rose to public prominence as Jerusalem's mayor, a position he held for ten years, by winning reelection in 1998 (after his reelection he resigned from the Knesset in accordance with a new law forbidding MKs to hold other public offices). During his mayoral term, he focused on making improvements to the city's education system and its transportation infrastructure.

As mayor, Olmert supported politically controversial housing construction projects in the predominantly Palestinian areas of East Jerusalem annexed by Israel in 1981. He helped establish the Jewish neighborhood of Har Homa (formerly Jabal Abu Ghneim), and promoted the creation of a Jewish neighborhood in Ra's al-Amud. He was also involved in the 1996 decision to open an ancient tunnel to the Western Wall, close to the Muslim holy places on the Haram al-Sharif. This prompted large-scale Palestinian demonstrations and fighting between Israeli and Palestinian Authority forces, leaving seventy-nine Palestinians and fourteen Israeli soldiers dead.

During his mayoral tenure, Olmert had to contend with accusations of corruption and cronyism. In 1996 he stood trial on charges of breaking the Party Funding Law as Likud Party treasurer during the 1988 elections. He was eventually cleared of all charges. Through much of his political career, allegations of corruption have been made against Olmert, and numerous investigations have been launched, but he has never been convicted of any crimes.

In September 1999, after BINYAMIN NETANYAHU stepped down as Likud leader after his electoral defeat to Labor leader Ehud Barak, Olmert ran for chair of the Likud Party. Ariel Sharon won the vote by a large margin, with Olmert the runner-up, having received 29 percent of the vote.

Olmert resigned as mayor of Jerusalem in January 2003 and returned to the Knesset after overseeing Likud's successful election campaign. He was appointed deputy prime minister in the Sharon government; and minister of industry, trade, and labor; as well as minister responsible for the Israel Lands Authority, the Israel Broadcasting Authority and the Bedouin Administration in the Negev. He also served as minister of communications in 2003 and 2004.

Although formerly a rival of Sharon within the Likud, Olmert became Sharon's closest ally during his second term in office (2003–2006) and an influential member of his cabinet. He was an early advocate of a unilateral Israeli withdrawal from the Gaza Strip, an idea that was subsequently embraced by Sharon and became the "disengagement" plan of 2004. This controversial plan involved a complete unilateral civilian and military withdrawal from the Gaza Strip, with the dismantling of twenty-one settlements and evacuation of approximately nine thousand Jewish settlers, as well as the dismantling of four small settlements in the northern West Bank and the evacuation of their residents. The plan was strongly opposed by many within Likud and led to a split within the party between its supporters and its opponents. When then–finance minister Netanyahu, a leading opponent, resigned in protest in August 2005, Olmert was appointed acting finance minister. Three months later, the Knesset voted to confirm Olmert in that office.

Following Israel's withdrawal from Gaza in September 2005, Sharon announced in November 2005 that he was leaving the Likud and forming a new centrist party, Kadima. Olmert immediately quit the Likud and together with several other former Likud ministers joined Sharon in Kadima. On 4 January 2006 Sharon suffered a massive stroke and was hospitalized. Olmert became acting prime minister, and a short time later was appointed head of Kadima.

Sharon's Successor In the run-up to the March 2006 general election, Olmert advocated a more extensive unilateral withdrawal from much of the West Bank by 2010, a plan he called "realignment," later renamed the "convergence" plan. Olmert explained that the primary objective of the plan was to preserve Israel's character as a Jewish and democratic state with a large Jewish majority. He indicated that he wanted Israel to retain three large settlement blocs in the West Bank—Ariel, Ma'ale Adumim, and Gush Etzion—where the majority of the settlers lived, while abandoning the smaller and more isolated settlements. The withdrawal would involve the evacuation of somewhere between 20,000 and 80,000 settlers, and leaving between 65 and 90 percent of the West Bank to the Palestinians. He also expressed a willingness to withdraw from outlying Palestinian suburbs of Jerusalem.

In the March 2006 election Kadima won a plurality of the vote and received twenty-nine Knesset seats. Although it received fewer seats than initially expected, it became the largest party in the Knesset and was able to form the new coalition government. In April 2006, one hundred days after being hospitalized, Sharon was declared "permanently incapacitated" and thus unable to continue serving as prime minister. As a result, Olmert became prime minister, although he had already become prime minister–elect. In May 2006, following the conclusion of the coalition negotiations, Olmert's new Kadima-led coalition government was approved by the Knesset, and he was sworn in as prime minister. He also took the job of minister for social welfare.

Olmert presented his new government to the Knesset on 4 May 2006. In his speech to the Knesset, Olmert reiterated his campaign pledge to determine the state's final borders and evacuate more West Bank settlements, with or without the agreement of the Palestinian Authority. Although he announced his intention to try to reach an accord with the Palestinian Authority, it was widely expected that such an agreement would not be reached and that instead the Olmert government would determine Israel's borders by itself and carry out a major unilateral withdrawal from the West Bank.

The convergence plan that was the centerpiece of the Olmert government's agenda, however, soon fell victim to two developments on Israel's northern and southern borders. In the south, on 25 June 2006, armed Palestinian militants from Gaza entered a military base inside Israel via a makeshift tunnel, killed two Israeli soldiers, and abducted a third, Corporal Gilad Shalit. In response, Israel launched a large-scale military operation in Gaza, "Operation Summer Rains," with the goal of stopping Qassam rocket fire from Gaza against its civilian population and securing the release of Corporal Shalit.

Soon afterward, on 12 July 2006, while Israel was engaged in heavy fighting in Gaza, militants from the Lebanese Shi'ite organization Hizbullah crossed the Lebanese-Israeli border, captured two Israeli soldiers, and killed three. Hizbullah also fired Katyusha rockets and mortars at Israeli military positions and border villages. Five more Israeli soldiers were later killed on the Lebanese side of the border while trying to rescue the captured soldiers.

The Lebanon War Prime Minister Olmert characterized the seizure of the soldiers as an act of war by the Lebanese

state. The Israeli cabinet quickly met and authorized a "severe and harsh" retaliation against Lebanon. The IDF then launched heavy artillery and air strikes against targets throughout Lebanon, including Lebanese civilian infrastructure, and imposed an air and naval blockade on Lebanon. Hizbullah responded by launching rockets into northern Israel.

The ensuing conflict between Israel and Hizbullah, sometimes referred to in Israel as the "Second Lebanon War," lasted thirty-four days. When it concluded on 13 August 2006, with a United Nations (UN)-brokered cease-fire—embodied in Security Council Resolution 1701—many people in Israel were bitterly disappointed by the fact that the IDF had not decisively defeated Hizbullah. At best, the war was considered to have been a draw, not the military victory that Israelis were accustomed to.

The Olmert government's conduct of the war was severely criticized in Israel. The most common criticisms were of poor planning, intelligence failures, an overreliance on air power, and deployment of ground troops too late in the conflict. Faced with such criticisms, Olmert admitted to mistakes in the war and appointed a commission of inquiry to examine them, although he resisted appointing a state commission of inquiry with the power to dismiss government ministers, as many of his critics demanded. In the wake of the war, Olmert's domestic popularity plummeted. Politically weakened, Olmert shelved his West Bank convergence plan and concentrated on ensuring his government's survival.

On 30 April 2007, the government-appointed commission of inquiry chaired by retired judge Eliyahu Winograd released its interim report on the 2006 Lebanon War. Focusing on the Olmert government's decision-making process regarding the decision to go to war and during the first five days of the war, the report was harshly critical of Olmert, accusing him of being too hasty in deciding to go to war, proceeding without a detailed military plan, having unrealistic goals, and failing to consult with experts, especially with people outside the IDF. Although the commission did not call for Olmert to resign, Olmert came under intense pressure to do so. Tens of thousands of Israelis gathered in central Tel Aviv demanding his resignation; even his own foreign minister, TZIPI LIVNI, called for him to resign. Olmert, however, refused, and continued to cling to power, despite his massive unpopularity.

INFLUENCES AND CONTRIBUTIONS

Olmert was born into the political tradition known as Revisionist Zionism, founded by Ze'ev Jabotinsky. As the son of Mordechai Olmert, a member of the Irgun, a right-wing Jewish underground militia active in mandatory

EXPLORING

■

The war between Israel and Hizbullah lasted from 12 July to 13 August 2006. More than one thousand people were killed, mostly Lebanese civilians (39 Israeli civilians were killed); and about 900,000 Lebanese and 300,000 Israelis were displaced. Lebanon's infrastructure was also severely damaged. At the conclusion of the war, both sides claimed victory, giving rise to a debate over who won the war. Some claimed that Hizbullah had won because it survived Israel's ferocious air and land assault. Others argued that Israel won because it inflicted heavy losses on Hizbullah, weakening the organization.

Although Israel failed to retrieve its two captured soldiers and destroy Hizbullah's military capability, UN Security Council Resolution 1701, which ended the conflict, was a diplomatic accomplishment for Israel as it led to the dispatch of an enlarged and more robust UN peacekeeping force to southern Lebanon and the deployment of Lebanese army forces to the area, thereby reducing Hizbullah's future freedom of action in its heartland. Hizbullah, however, achieved a propaganda victory by withstanding the might of the IDF.

Palestine and later a Knesset member for the Revisionist Herut Party, Olmert grew up among Herut loyalists. He was a child of the "fighting family," as Irgun veterans called themselves, and like other children from prominent Revisionist families became a member of the Likud Party's dynastic group (Likud's "princes," as they were popularly known). Other members of this group include BINYAMIN NETANYAHU (son of the scholar Ben-Zion Netanyahu), Binyamin Begin (son of Menachem Begin), and Tzipi Livni (daughter of Irgun operative and Herut Party Knesset Member Eitan Livni).

Raised under the influence of Revisionist ideology, Olmert was strongly influenced by its central goal of establishing a Jewish state with a Jewish majority on the whole Land of Israel (Eretz Yisra'el)—which it was claimed included all of present-day Israel, the West Bank, Gaza, and Jordan (the claim to the latter territory was dropped by the late 1960s). This state was to be obtained by force if necessary and secured, in Jabotinsky's famous phrase, by an "Iron Wall."

In accordance with this ideological background, in his early years in politics Olmert's views were firmly on

the right of the political spectrum in Israel. In particular, he opposed withdrawing from land captured by Israel in the 1967 War. Olmert therefore voted against the Camp David Accords with Egypt in 1978 and vocally opposed Israel's withdrawal from the Sinai in 1982.

In later years, however, Olmert's political views changed, and after joining Sharon's government in 2003 he publicly admitted that his earlier stand against the withdrawal from Sinai was wrong. He became a prominent advocate of a unilateral Israeli withdrawal from Gaza as well as from parts of the West Bank. Olmert appeared to have undergone a political conversion from being an ideological right-wing hawk to a pragmatic right-centrist.

It is hard to say when this political shift occurred or what really caused it. Already in the 1980s as a young Likud Knesset member, Olmert began expressing views that differed from the official views of his party. He suggested, for instance, that Israel unilaterally grant autonomy to the Palestinians in the West Bank and Gaza. He also opposed granting pardons to convicted members of Jewish terror organizations, and expressed reservations at extending Israeli law over "Judea and Samaria" (the West Bank).

Nevertheless, during his ten years as mayor of Jerusalem, Olmert was still regarded as one of the most right-wing "Likudniks." He continued to support the goal of a "Greater Israel" and opposed withdrawing from the West Bank and Gaza. He strongly backed the Jewish settler movement and, as mayor, promoted Jewish settlement efforts in Palestinian Arab neighborhoods of East Jerusalem.

It was not until Olmert returned to the Knesset in 2003 and became Sharon's deputy and close ally that his new political orientation became evident. Olmert was among the first Likud politicians to call for a unilateral withdrawal from Gaza. It was only after Olmert publicly floated the idea that Sharon embraced it, and many credit Olmert with persuading Sharon to support it. After Sharon announced his disengagement plan Olmert then became one of its foremost supporters. Olmert's early advocacy of disengagement from Gaza and his central role in the development of Sharon's plan stands out as his most significant contribution to date.

THE WORLD'S PERSPECTIVE

Olmert was little known outside Israel before his swift and dramatic rise to the premiership as a result of Sharon's sudden incapacitation. He was widely considered an unlikely prime minister, lacking his predecessor's charisma and national standing. Moreover, without an impressive military background or much experience in national security, few had previously considered Olmert to be a serious contender for the job.

EVERY HILL IN SAMARIA IS PART OF OUR HISTORIC HOMELAND

∎

We firmly stand by the historic right of the people of Israel to the entire Land of Israel. Every hill in Samaria [northern West Bank] and every valley in Judea [southern West Bank] is part of our historic homeland. We do not forget this, not even for one moment. However, the choice between the desire to allow every Jew to live anywhere in the Land of Israel [and] the existence of the State of Israel as a Jewish country—obligates relinquishing parts of the Land of Israel. This is not a relinquishing of the Zionist idea, rather the essential realization of the Zionist goal—ensuring the existence of a Jewish and democratic state in the Land of Israel. In order to ensure the existence of a Jewish national homeland, we will not be able to continue ruling over the territories in which the majority of the Palestinian population lives. We must create a clear boundary as soon as possible, one which will reflect the demographic reality on the ground.

EHUD OLMERT, AT THE SIXTH HERZLIYA CONFERENCE. ISRAEL NEWS AGENCY. "ISRAEL OLMERT HERZLIYA CONFERENCE SPEECH: DISENGAGEMENT CONTINUES." 24 JANUARY 2006. AVAILABLE FROM HTTP://WWW.ISRAELNEWSAGENCY.COM.

Thrust into the international spotlight almost overnight, Olmert was perceived to be a pragmatic, centrist leader and a canny politician. Early international hopes that he would be the leader to establish Israel's final borders and carry out a major pullback from the West Bank have, however, been dashed by the demise of his much-publicized convergence plan.

LEGACY

While it is too soon to tell what Olmert's legacy will ultimately be, he will be remembered for his important role in bringing about Israel's disengagement from Gaza and subsequently calling for a more extensive withdrawal from the West Bank. Whether or not Olmert eventually succeeds in carrying out his declared goal of determining the borders of Israel and giving up large parts of the West Bank, his own political evolution from right-wing ideologue to pragmatic centrist helped move part of the political right in Israel away from an unyielding commitment to maintaining Israeli control over the Palestinian territories occupied by Israel in the 1967 War.

Olmert's legacy will undoubtedly be tarnished by the perceived failure of Israel's war with Hizbullah in July

2006. Despite Olmert's claim that Israel achieved significant gains, public opinion in Israel and elsewhere has generally regarded the war as a defeat for Israel. Whatever else he does as prime minister, therefore, Olmert will always be remembered—and blamed—for this defeat.

BIBLIOGRAPHY

Halevi, Yossi Klein. "Unwanted Man." *New Republic*, 16 October 2006.

Rubin, Barry. "Israel's New Strategy." *Foreign Affairs* 85 (July/August 2006): 111–125.

Sandler, Shmuel. "Centrism in Israeli Politics and the Olmert Government." *BESA Perspectives on Current Affairs* 17 (June 2006). Available from http://www.biu.ac.il/Besa/perspectives 17.html.

Waxman, Dov. "Between Victory and Defeat: Israel after the War with Hizballah." *Washington Quarterly* 30, no. 1 (Winter 2006–2007): 27–43.

Dov Waxman

OMAR, MULLAH MOHAMMED
(1961–)

A leader of the Taliban in Afghanistan, Mullah Mohammed Omar is currently in hiding.

PERSONAL HISTORY

Described as reclusive, Mullah (a religious title) Mohammed Omar was born in 1961 in the village of Nauda in southern Afghanistan, the son of a Sunni Muslim religious cleric, Mohammed Serwar, who died when his son was just one year old. Omar's father was from the one of the largest of Afghanistan's ethnic Pashtun tribes, the Ghilzai Durrani tribe, and his mother was from the Hottaq Pashtun tribe.

Omar's ambitions were hardly grand. He grew up in Nauda attending a religious school that provided only the basics of education. His study of the Qur'an was without elaboration or depth. Those who knew Omar said he only read the Qur'an, he did not engage in philosophical discussions or understand the intricacies of the Arabic language, the language in which the Qur'an is written.

Omar was teaching at a dilapidated *madrasa* (religious academy) made of sunbaked mud and straw in Sanghesar in southern Afghanistan's Kandahar province when he launched the Taliban movement in 1994. He is married to two wives, and has seven children. One of his wives was married to an uncle of Omar's. When the uncle died, Omar married his widow.

Mullah Mohammad Khaksar, fellow founder of the Taliban movement, and a close friend of Omar's until

BIOGRAPHICAL HIGHLIGHTS

Name: Mullah Mohammed Omar

Birth: 1961, Nauda, Afghanistan

Family: Two wives; seven children

Nationality: Afghan

Education: No formal education

PERSONAL CHRONOLOGY:

• **1980s:** Fights with Mujahideen resistance fighters against Soviet troops

• **1994:** Forms Taliban movement

• **1995:** Becomes ruler of Afghanistan when Taliban take over

• **1996:** Granted title of Amir al-Mu'minin (Commander of the faithful)

• **2001:** Orders giant Buddha statues in Bamiyan destroyed; flees into hiding during United States's invasion of Afghanistan

the Taliban was ousted from power in 2001, said of the hunted Taliban leader: "You could never doubt Mullah Omar's love of the Qur'an, of Islam. He didn't know deep meanings, but he loves Islam, he loves the Qur'an."

INFLUENCES AND CONTRIBUTIONS

Omar's beginnings were humble, but his kingdom, a small mud mosque in Afghanistan's southern Kandahar province, would later become the headquarters of the Taliban movement, which Omar and fifty-nine other clerics would found. Omar would become its head and rule with an iron fist, accepting no challenges to his authority but receiving anyone who professed a belief in Islam.

A devout cleric who adheres to a strict literal interpretation of the Qur'an, Omar joined the fight against the Soviet Union following its invasion of Afghanistan in December 1979. His first battles against the invading soldiers were in Darawood in Uruzgan province, also in southern Afghanistan. He joined Hizb-e-Islami, one of the mujahideen (resistance fighters) movements led by Gulbuddin Hekmatyar. But he soon became disillusioned with Hekmatyar's organization, arguing against the forced collection of money from ordinary Afghans by Hizb-e-Islami.

Omar then joined briefly with Jami'at-e Islami commander Mullah Naqeebullah, fighting alongside him in Argandaub, outside Kandahar city, before joining Harakat-e Islami, led by Maulvi Nabi Mohammed Mohammedi. It was with Harakat-e Islami—considered in the early stages of the war against the Soviet Union to be the strongest of the mujahideen groups, funded by several governments, including the United States—that he remained until the end of the war. The strength of Harakat-e Islami later deteriorated, but its backbone was always the village mullahs (clerics).

Legends have grown up around Omar, among them the tale that the fighting mullah removed his own eye after being hurt in a particularly bitter battle against a military convoy in his native province of Kandahar. According to the legend, a convoy of Soviet and Afghan soldiers was heading south to Kandahar. Omar was among the attacking mujahideen who ambushed the convoy with hand grenades, rocket launchers, and Kalashnikov rifles. Omar's band of mujahideen was hopelessly overpowered and outgunned by the Soviet commandos, who struck back with tank fire and sophisticated heavy weapons. Omar dived for cover as a rocket slammed into the ground nearby, but a piece of shrapnel pierced his eye. According to the legend Omar used the bayonet attached to the barrel of his Kalashnikov rifle to remove the piece of shrapnel, and with it his eye. In reality, Omar did lose his eye in battle, but he was treated at a hospital in Quetta, Pakistan.

The story told about Omar's founding of the Taliban is also a mix of legend, misreporting, and misinformation. Those who began the Taliban with him said the movement was born out of frustration and anger at the lawlessness created by thieving men aligned with the Afghan government, those mujahideen leaders who had taken power when Afghanistan's communist president Mohammed Najibullah was overthrown in 1992.

When the Soviet Union pulled out of Afghanistan in 1989, and Najibullah vacated power in 1992, Omar, like many mujahideen commanders, returned home. Omar resumed his teaching in Sanghesar but said he received his instructions to rise up against the warring mujahideen factions in dreams where Islam's prophet Muhammad came to him and urged him to challenge their lawlessness.

Factional fighting had characterized the rule of the mujahideen government, led by Ahmad Shah Masoud and Burhanuddin Rabbani. Thieves, many of them affiliated with mujahideen leaders, set up checkposts on most major roads throughout the country. The Red Cross estimated that, in the capital of Kabul, fifty thousand people, most of them civilians, died in the four years that Rabbani and Masoud ruled Afghanistan, fighting for power against other leaders such as Gulbuddin Hekmatyar and the ethnic Hazara leader, Abdul Ali Mazari.

The Taliban was formed in 1994, after the mujahideen government had been in power for two years in Kabul. The roads were lawless and anarchy had spread throughout the country. Former mujahideen commanders turned parts of the country into their private fiefdoms. In the capital of Kabul, Masoud and Rabbani battled Hekmatyar's forces, everyone trying to keep or get power. Ordinary Afghans were caught in the cross fire of a bitter and brutal battle. Mullah Mohammed Khaksar recounted the following:

> Let me tell you, the foreign countries got it all wrong about the beginning of the Taliban. It wasn't created by Pakistan, or by the Arabs, or by the Americans. From the beginning the world was wrong about the Taliban.
>
> For example, some people said that the Americans brought the Taliban; and some people said Pakistani intelligence brought the Taliban; and some said the Arabs brought them. But all of these things were wrong. The Taliban came because there was so much corruption, and people were killing each other, and mujahidin commanders had become like thousands of little kings. Then everyone was a commander.

Before launching the Taliban Omar rarely left his village mosque and madrasah, but when he did he went through an endless series of checkposts manned by former mujahideen. Eventually he and a number of like-minded mullahs, all of whom had fought against the former Soviet Union, decided enough was enough. They banded together and attacked one of the checkposts. It was an easy victory. They proceeded through several other checkposts that collapsed quickly and eventually took control of Kandahar.

The Taliban movement was soon hijacked by Pakistan's intelligence, and later by USAMA BIN LADIN's al-Qa'ida movement. Bin Ladin had come to Afghanistan from Sudan in May 1996, before the Taliban took complete control of the country. He was brought to Afghanistan by mujahideen who were part of the government still ruling Afghanistan and waging bitter power struggles. The Taliban took control of Jalalabad in early September and Kabul by late September. Omar had not met Bin Ladin during the war against the former Soviet Union; he met him only after the Taliban took Kabul in late September, when he ordered Bin Ladin to come to Kandahar.

Omar ruled Afghanistan with an iron fist, issuing edicts that his men enforced. He ordered an end to poppy production in Afghanistan, phased over three years; by the final year, 2001, poppy production in Afghanistan had been wiped out. When he was overthrown in December 2001 farmers literally ripped up their wheat and planted poppies, and in 2007 Afghani-

stan is again the world's largest producer of opium, the raw material used to make heroin.

Omar's harsh interpretation of Islam denied schooling to girls and women the ability to work. He ordered all women to wear the all-encompassing burka, a garment most women in the deeply conservative and tribal Afghanistan already wore, with the exception of a small number in the cities. Omar issued an edict in 2000 promising to protect the world's tallest Buddha statues in Bamiyan from destruction, but in March 2001 he reversed his edict and ordered them destroyed. It is believed that Bin Ladin and his austere Wahhabi belief—practiced by most Saudi Arabians—was behind the latter edict. By March 2001 the Taliban had been sanctioned twice by the United Nations, and had no source of income other than Bin Ladin's money.

After the attacks on the United States in September 2001, Omar was issued an ultimatum by the United States: Give up Bin Ladin and close the militant training camps, or be attacked. Omar refused to give him up, but offered instead to have Bin Ladin tried in an Islamic country other than Afghanistan, or in Afghanistan. The United States said that was unacceptable and ordered an assault on Afghanistan that led to Omar's being ousted in December 2001. Since then he has been in hiding, protected by his tribesmen in the south and the east of Afghanistan. There is a US$10 million reward offered by the United States for his capture.

THE WORLD'S PERSPECTIVE

Relatively little is known about Mullah Mohammed Omar. But to many throughout the world, he is inextricably linked to the Taliban and its strict policies toward women, religious minorities, and other policies generally reviled in the West and among many in the Islamic world.

LEGACY

Omar will be remembered as the leader of a movement that, though it ended the factional bloodshed that had beset Afghanistan from 1992 to 1996, came to rule the country harshly and according to a strict version of Sunni Islam. He will also be remembered as the man who prompted the American invasion of the country in 2001 because he refused to hand over Bin Ladin.

BIBLIOGRAPHY

Rashid, Ahmad. *Taliban: Militant Islam, Oil, and Fundamentalism in Central Asia*. New Haven, CT: Yale University Press, 2001.

Kathy Gannon

OZ, AMOS
(1939–)

Born in mandatory Palestine, Amos Oz, born Klauzner, is one of Israel's few major writers whose work and life can be read as embodying the nation, creating a biography that is enjoined to the history of the State of Israel in allegory. He has written over thirty books as of 2007 and continues to publish at an increasing rate; he is a popular speaker on issues of Israel and has gained great success in translation. The recipient of numerous prizes and honors, for some years he has been mentioned as a candidate for the Nobel Prize in Literature.

PERSONAL HISTORY

Oz was born in Jerusalem in 1939 to a family of fervent right-wing Zionists. When Oz was thirteen, his mother committed suicide. After his father's subsequent remarriage, Oz went as an out-child to kibbutz Hulda, a rather isolated settlement in the heart of Judea. At Hulda, he was renamed Oz (Hebrew: "valor" or "courage") in keeping with the kibbutz's tradition of reconceiving old Jews as new Jews.

Oz served in the Israeli army from 1957 until 1960 in the aftermath of the Sinai war. His observations during

Amos Oz. ULF ANDERSEN/GETTY IMAGES.

BIOGRAPHICAL HIGHLIGHTS

Name: Amos Oz (born Klauzner)

Birth: 1939, Jerusalem, mandatory Palestine

Family: Married with children

Nationality: Israeli

Education: Literature and philosophy studies at the Hebrew University of Jerusalem

PERSONAL CHRONOLOGY:

• **Early 1950s:** Mother commits suicide; Oz goes to kibbutz Hulda

• **1957–1960:** Serves in Israeli army

• **1961:** Publishes first story in the magazine *Keshet*

• **1987–present:** Professor at Ben-Gurion University in the Negev

• **2002:** Publishes the autobiographical *A Tale of Love and Darkness*

---

this mandatory military service would greatly affect his work later in life. After his time in the army, Oz studied literature and philosophy in Jerusalem, then returned to the kibbutz to work as a high school teacher.

Oz began his literary career in earnest with the publication of his first story in the innovative journal *Keshet* in 1961, and the public as well as the emerging generation of literary critics readily accepted him. At the same time, Oz developed his serious interest in political activism.

INFLUENCES AND CONTRIBUTIONS

Because Oz's work is so closely intertwined with his personal history and the history of the state of Israel, it is difficult to separate his personal life from his professional life. Having measured in his life the arc of the state of Israel's existence, Oz has always been a writer whose voice, in a self-conscious way, goes beyond textuality and seeks to represent more than himself. Writing about issues that were national even when private in nature, he has created a point of view that lends itself consistently to an allegory of the collective. His style substantiates this voice with his command of Hebrew letters and an uncanny ability to create atmosphere with a few strokes, providing his work grace and unity. Though a self-proclaimed ironist, ever since the publication of *A Tale of Love and Darkness* in 2002, in which Oz lay bare the life of the author, he has become a writer whose biography cannot be told apart from his work.

Oz is related to the famed literary scholar and Zionist thinker, Yossef Klauzner, and he often displays a fine nose for literary celebrity. Childhood encounters with Shmuel Yosef Agnon, Martin Buber, and other literati form major episodes about which much has been written. The details of this childhood in Jerusalem among the British of the mandate, the right wing resistance movements, and the torn and tattered European immigrant Jews have also been retold in many forms, especially in *The Hill of Evil Council* (1978), *Panther in the Basement* (1995), and in *A Tale of Love and Darkness*. Childhood memories of failed dreamers, fervent nationalisms, and a hostile Orient merge into dark and powerful prose, engendering a constant threat of breakdown.

It is difficult to separate Oz's family history from his fiction. His fiction and his novels often deal with a single child among well-meaning, depressive parents. Oz's own father was an underappreciated scholar who worked as a librarian in Jerusalem, and his mother committed suicide when he was thirteen. The tale of their tortured and failed love deeply marks his writing.

During Oz's stay at the kibbutz Hulda after his mother's death, he gained not only a new name but also a socialist humanistic framework to manage the powerful conflicts that his prose and person struggled with. This new worldview helped forge a portrait of the artist as a clear-eyed, brooding, soldierly youth.

During his military service, which took place after the Sinai war, Oz was deeply influenced by war and the reigning, rather foolish, regard to soldierly heroics. In an autobiographical piece from 1975 Oz himself summarizes the experience as informing his peace activism: "Twice, in 1967 with the victorious armored forces in the Sinai desert, and in 1973 among the burning tanks in the Golan Heights, I saw with my own eyes that there is no hope for the weak and the dead, and only partial hopes for the mighty and victorious."

Oz began his literary career in the grand tradition of the pioneer Zionist generation, living in a communal border settlement, mixing menial labor with defense duties, yet finding time for literary reflection and political essay writing. His first story was published in 1961 in the innovative journal *Keshet*, and others followed. Oz's prose and political activism emerged at about the same time and have since merged into a figure of political authority that rests on the reputation of the man of letters. The stories he wrote at the time are collected in *Where the Jackal Howls* (1965; revised 1975) and are among the best work he has ever produced. His early work utilizes the form of the short novella with dexterity in order to expose a world of marginal being within a centralized focal point. The narrator often uses an omniscient voice

that oscillates almost indistinctly between the personal and the collective, allowing the writing to explore the extremes of the human condition in a space constricted by a demanding collective.

Similar to most Israeli culture of the first two decades of independence, Oz's writing was cognizant of the fierce Oedipal battle between the founding pioneer generation and the children born in the land. Oz gives a complex view of this conflict by seeing the founding fathers as pathetic and castrating at once. At the same time he internalizes their view of his generation and of the Jewish state as a disappointing if not failed one, thus his characters are torn by powerful urges that more often than not, result in violence inflected on the self.

After the 1967 War, Oz played an important role in the defining project of *Soldiers Talk*. The book was based on the recordings of numerous encounters the editors held with kibbutz members who were returning from the war. At the time it was seen as a generational portrait sensitive to the suffering of war, but in retrospect one can claim that the book holds the seeds of the narcissism that was to become the main peace movement until the Oslo Accords. Among the editors, Oz was quick to realize the immense distortions of occupation and military might, perhaps because he did not deny the lure of the Jewish past, nor the will to overpower. Having always viewed the east as a threat, Oz rapidly understood how the victory would undo the Zionist attempt to create a model European society in the Jewish land of Israel. In fiction this takes the form of an often-abject dark antagonist that eventually exacts revenge on the ironized self-righteous father figures. This outlook, in a way, also forms the basic rationale of the new peace movement that positioned itself as a belated attempt to stop the flood in order to return to a better more coherent past. Oz has a definite part in ironizing the father figures, yet at the same time he provides the view of peace as a return to a past harmony, to an Israel without an empire, which also happens to be a past in which the kibbutz and the European Jews held a fearsome hegemony.

The prolific two decades that followed the 1967 War were defining for Oz. Moving ably within the forms of narrative, in 1968 he published the successful *My Michael*, a tale of love and female darkness in Jerusalem in the fifties; he then published *Unto Death* (1971) which includes two novellas, one following a failed crusade through Europe and another an elderly émigré. In 1977 he published his first and rather successful attempt at children's literature, *Sumchi*, telling of an eleven-year-old boy in Mandate Jerusalem out for an adventure. In 1978 Oz published the insightful collection of essays *Under the Blazing Light*, mastering the form of the short essay to discuss literary and political matters. These developments were then honed to become what might be Oz's most important work, the ponderous reportage of his travels *In the Land of Israel* (1983). The work is well written and extremely perceptive. Offering the reader even more insight by exposing the assumptions and remissions of the observer. These vary: a compassionate encounter with the settlers in Ofra; a harrowing discussion with a former warrior of 1948, preaching genocide to finally rid the Jews of their Judaizing; a conflicted encounter between embittered and ignorant Mizrahi laymen and a man of letters. *In the Land of Israel* shows Oz is at his best, his eye surveying the land and its inhabitants, binding them with passion and compassion. The draughtsmanship is a fine craft of minute details.

With *A Perfect Peace* published the preceding year, Oz had established himself as a public figure of considerable moral authority with a significant role in the debates over 1982 Lebanon war and its dismal aftermath. As the war began Oz wrote: "Hitler is Already Dead Mr. Prime Minister" trying with little success to convince Menachem Begin that YASIR ARAFAT was no Adolf Hitler. The rightwing sea change in Israel over the next years had helped Oz remain a figure of opposition, sharing with many a view of peace based on a substantial aversion to its surroundings. In 1987, with the publication of *Black Box*, this aversion was explored in a highly allegorical novel mourning the death of a failed generation and fearing the libidinal rise of the abject, religious Mizrahi Jews. As with the problematic attempts at female consciousness, Oz is considerably weaker when he tries to write the other.

During the 1980s, as Oz became increasingly well-known abroad and more involved in academic engagements, the character of his writing changed. Since 1987 he is a full professor at the Ben-Gurion University in the Negev. He has published two literary inquiries that can be attributed to these endeavors. Moderately successful and insightful, they cannot be called major works, and many observers find that in general his work in the 1990s has not developed significantly or reached the level of his former work. Certainly *To Know a Woman* (1989), *Fima* (1991), and *Don't Call it Night* (1994) are well-crafted novels, but even the formally more explorative *The Same Sea* (1999) has not revealed an unknown side of Oz or proved a major development.

A Tale of Love and Darkness appeared in 2002 and seemed to be that long awaited novel, and was perhaps too quickly claimed a classic. Long and elaborate, autobiographical and mythical, it is an almost postmodern text, deconstructing a life in letters in a way reminiscent of Quixote's second part undoing the first: deconstructing fiction with another fiction turning into myth. The tale of Amos finally in first person garnered great success in Israel, and in translation. As it often happens this also launched him into furtive publishing of partial and at times ill-prepared works, including a collection of three almost repetitive essays on German-Jewish relations in *On the Slopes of the Volcano* (2006).

THE WORLD'S PERSPECTIVE

Since the 1980s Oz has become increasingly well-known abroad. His work has been well received in translation, especially his autobiographical *A Tale of Love and Darkness*. Oz had become an international man of letters, publishing often in European journals; his work has appeared in more than 450 editions and has been translated into more than thirty languages.

LEGACY

As of 2007, it is safe to say that Oz has written over the years what might be the most consciously representative body of work Israeli culture has produced. Yet a position that claims moral authority based on literary endeavors is treacherous terrain for a writer, and Oz's position in support of Israel's action in the 2006 war between Israel and Hizbullah seems to prove so. In poetic terms *A Tale of Love and Darkness* might have touched Oz's creative boundary, though he might also turn out to be as prolific and as innovative as his model Shmuel Yosef Agnon was in the latter part of his writing.

BIBLIOGRAPHY

Oz, Amos. "A Tale of Myself." In *Under this Blazing Light*. Tel Aviv: Sifriat Poalim, 1979.

Uri Cohen

PAMUK, ORHAN
(1952–)

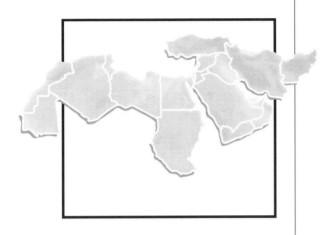

Turkish writer Orhan Pamuk (full name Ferit Orhan Pamuk) is ranked among the outstanding novelists of his country. Often referred to as a postmodern and avant-garde writer, he is mostly praised for his talent in dramatizing local issues, themes, and problematics by masterfully using Western narrative forms and techniques. Although his political statements cause severe public controversies from time to time, he has an immense popularity in his home country, which is accompanied by his growing international reputation. His works have been translated into more than fifty languages and received several national and international literary awards. Orhan Pamuk received the Nobel Prize in Literature in 2006.

PERSONAL HISTORY

Pamuk was born in Istanbul on 7 June 1952, and grew up in a large and prosperous family in Nisantasi, one of the Westernized and wealthy neighborhoods of Istanbul. His grandfather, father, and uncle were engineers, and the family owed its wealth to his grandfather's railway constructions and other industrial enterprises. Nevertheless, from his childhood onward, Pamuk devoted himself to painting, hoping to become an artist. As he tells in his autobiographical work *Istanbul*, the family did not like the idea. They felt that people in Turkey did not value art, and that he would not earn his living by painting. With such convictions, after graduating from the American Robert College in Istanbul, he studied architecture at Istanbul Technical University. However, three years later Pamuk decided to become a novelist, not an architect or artist; and abandoned the architecture school. Afterward he graduated in journalism from Istanbul University in 1976. In 1982 Pamuk married Aylin Türegün. Their daughter Rüya was born in 1991. The couple divorced in 2001.

Becoming a Writer In 1975 Pamuk began to write regularly. His first novel, *Cevdet Bey ve Ogullari* (Cevdet Bey and his sons), is structured around the story of three generations of a wealthy family living in Nisantasi from 1905 to 1970, and is an account of the history of the Turkish Republic, cultural codes of the period, the invention of the Turkish identity, and the lifestyle of upper-middle classes. This family saga was written in the spirit of realist novels of the nineteenth century of Thomas Mann, Leo Tolstoy, and Stendhal. A panoramic historical novel, it was awarded two national prizes and is also significant for marking the beginning of Pamuk's career whose later works were defined as modernist, postmodernist, experimentalist, expressionist, symbolic, and eclectic.

Orban Pamuk. AP IMAGES.

BIOGRAPHICAL HIGHLIGHTS

Name: (Ferit) Orhan Pamuk

Nationality: Turkish

Birth: 1952, Istanbul, Turkey

Family: Married Aylin Türegün in 1982, divorced in 2001; one daughter, Rüya

Education: Studied architecture at Istanbul Technical University for three years; graduated from the Institute of Journalism at the University of Istanbul in 1976

PERSONAL CHRONOLOGY:

- **1979:** Wins Milliyet Unpublished Novel Contest Award (Turkey) for his novel *Cevdet Bey ve Ogullari*

- **1983:** Presented with Orhan Kemal Novel Prize (Turkey) for his novel *Cevdet Bey ve Ogullari*

- **1984:** Awarded Madarali Novel Prize (Turkey) for his novel *Sessiz Ev*

- **1990:** Receives Independent Foreign Fiction Prize (United Kingdom) for his novel *The White Castle*

- **1991:** Wins Prix de la Découverte Européenne (France) for the French edition of *Sessiz Ev*

- **2002:** Awarded Prix du Meilleur Livre Etranger (France) for his novel *My Name Is Red*; presented with Premio Grinzane Cavour (Italy) for his novel *My Name Is Red*

- **2003:** Receives International IMPAC Dublin Literary Award (Ireland) for his novel *My Name Is Red*

- **2005:** Wins Peace Prize of the German Book Trade (Germany); receives Prix Medicis Etranger (France) for his novel *Snow*

- **2006:** Awarded Nobel Prize in Literature (Sweden); presented with Washington University's Distinguished Humanist Award (United States)

Pamuk's second novel, *Sessiz Ev* (The silent house), was published in 1983. This novel was shorter, more symbolic, and more dramatized. It bore the influence of the narrative techniques of modernist writers such as William Faulkner and Virginia Woolf. Just as in his first novel, Pamuk told a story that addresses the present-day cultural and political problems of Turkish society together with their historical roots. However, this time he employed the point of view technique: A narrator did not tell the story, but instead the characters spoke for themselves in each chapter. The author's role was to organize these voices in accordance with the flow of the story. Thus, the technique served to show the multifaceted nature of reality and its diverse perceptions by different characters. The novel received 1984 Madarali Novel Prize in Turkey and its French translation was awarded Prix de la Découverte Européenne in 1991.

A Pioneer in Turkish Literature *Beyaz Kale* (*The White Castle,* 1991) was published in 1985. It constitutes an important turning point both for the author's career and for Turkish novel in general. In *The White Castle* he broke with the realist tradition and attempted something different from his first two novels: Set in the seventeenth century Istanbul, it is an allegorical story of the relationship of two protagonists with reference to the problematic of East and West and the question of identity. The relationship between the Venetian slave and his doppel-gänger, that is, the Ottoman scholar who bought the other as a slave, echoes G. W. F. Hegel's master-slave dialectic. Being the first Turkish novel that launches postmodern narrative techniques such as metafiction and intertextuality, it was first approached with trepidation by reviewers, but later critics positively assessed its multilayered structure and themes regarding the relationships of East and West, tradition and modernity, and us and them.

The novel also marked his international breakthrough. The *New York Times Book Review* honored Pamuk as a new star having risen in the east. The success of *The White Castle*'s English translation brought along success in other languages, winning its author the Independent Foreign Fiction Prize (United Kingdom) in 1990.

Between 1985 and 1988, Pamuk was a visiting scholar at Columbia University in New York where he wrote most of the parts of his fourth novel, *Kara Kitap* (*The Black Book*). In this novel, Pamuk combines the epic approach of his first two novels with mysterious, allegorical, and symbolic imagery and a complicated and interlaced syntax that he first developed in *The White Castle*. Pamuk is generally identified with Istanbul as Marcel Proust with Paris and James Joyce with Dublin. *The Black Book* is the novel in which he is most obviously so. Istanbul is not only the setting of the novel; it is also one of the characters, so to speak. Beyond the mysterious story of a lawyer seeking his missing wife, this encyclopedic novel is an epic of the history of Turkey and Istanbul as well as a narrative of the age-old frictions of Islamism and Westernism, and local and universal.

When it was published in 1990, *The Black Book* became a best seller, a surprising development given the density of Pamuk's style. Due to its complexity as well its unexpected popularity and the reactions toward it made *The Black Book* one of the most controversial novels in Turkish literature. Its translations reinforced Pamuk's international reputation, leading to comparisons with Italo Calvino, Umberto Eco, Jorge Luis Borges, and Gabriel García Márquez. The French translation won the Prix France Culture. In 1991 Pamuk adapted *The Black Book* into a screenplay titled *Hidden Face,* which in turn was made into a film by the famous Turkish director Omer Kavur.

Pamuk's next work, *Yeni Hayat* (*The New Life*), published in 1994, became the fastest-selling book in Turkish history. It is the story of a university student who is heavily influenced by a mysterious book that changes his life. After reading it, he leaves Istanbul and wanders around the countryside on endless bus trips. The story is interwoven with traffic accidents, political assassinations, and paranoid conspiracy theories. Similar to the structure of *The Black Book* but taking place outside

Istanbul, *The New Life* is a symbolic and allegorical journey toward the reasons behind the essential impasses and dilemmas of Turkish culture, structured around a detective story.

Following the publication of *The New Life*, Pamuk took a critical stance in his articles against the violations of human rights and freedom of thought in Turkey. He received furious reactions when he articulated his support for Kurdish political rights.

A World-Famous Writer In 1998, the Turkish state awarded Pamuk the title of state artist, but the author refused it. In the same year, Pamuk's sixth novel, *Benim Adim Kirmiz (My Name Is Red)*, was published. Set in ten winter days in 1591, the novel is about Ottoman artists and their ways of seeing and portraying with references to the Western manners of painting. On another level, it is a love story and a detective story. Pamuk's usual themes, such as identity, the tension between the traditional and the modern, and being caught between the East and the West, are dramatized with the point of view technique, but this time not only living characters but also dead bodies, dogs, trees, horses, colors, and coins spoke for themselves. It is generally accepted to be one of Pamuk's most successful novels as well as the one most widely read and praised abroad. The novel was awarded the French Prix du Meilleur Livre Etranger, the Italian Grinzane Cavour (2002), and the International IMPAC Dublin literary award (2003).

Öteki Renkler (*Other Colors*), a selection of his articles on literature, politics and culture, together with interviews and extracts from his private notebooks, was published in 1999.

In many of his interviews, Pamuk stated his distain for politics and painstakingly kept his political views out of his novels. Nevertheless, in 2002 he published his first and last political novel, *Kar* (*Snow*). The story takes place in the city of Kars in northeastern Turkey, narrating the violence and tension between political Islamists, secularists, and Kurdish and Turkish nationalists. Pamuk was awarded Prix Medicis Etranger (France) in 2005 for this novel.

Finally, in 2003, the author published *Istanbul: Hatiralar ve Sehir* (*Istanbul: Memories and the City*), which was his early memoirs embedded into an essay regarding his perception of Istanbul.

A Controversial Intellectual Pamuk won in 2005 the Peace Prize of the German Book Trade for his literary work. However, Pamuk faced censure in Turkey, where criminal charges of insulting Turkishness had been levied against him for his statements to a Swiss newspaper. Having said that one million Armenians and thirty thousand

Pamuk, Orhan

CONTEMPORARIES

Yaşar Kemal (1923–), also known as Yaşar Kemal Göğçeli, is a leading Turkish novelist. He derives his themes and motifs from Anatolian oral literature legends, folktales, and epics, and combines them with modern-day concerns and problems of villagers. His skillful use of modern narrative techniques from social realism to magical realism, his poetic language, and his creative imagination earned him his national and international prizes and reputation.

Many of his works, some of which are *Iron Earth*; *Copper Sky*; *The Undying Grass*; *The Drumming-Out*; and *Memed, My Hawk*, are translated into several languages. His most famous novel, *Ince Memed*, has appeared in forty languages.

Kurds were killed in Turkey and nobody dares to talk about it, Pamuk became the target of Turkish nationalists' rage and hate campaign, as well as the center of the worldwide debates about the freedom of expression in Turkey. Although the charges were dropped, the case influenced the reception of his being awarded the Nobel Prize in Literature in 2006, being the first Turkish citizen ever to be a Nobel laureate.

INFLUENCES AND CONTRIBUTIONS

Pamuk rejects the role of inspiration in his writing. For him, he made himself an author by reading the masters and examining their ways of writing. Therefore he has an immense range of influences from both Turkish and non-Turkish sources. In *Other Colors*, he says "All my books are made up of the mixture of the methods, habits and histories of the East and the West and I owe the richness of my writing to this mixture."

In the same book, he emphasizes the basic characteristics of the Turkish authors to whom he feels indebted. These authors are, as himself, puzzled about the Republican modernity, the Ottoman legacy, Western lifestyle, and traditional values. That is why the poet Yahya Kemal, the novelist Ahmet Hamdi Tanpinar "who experiences this confusion as a pleasing melancholy," the novelist Oguz Atay "who approaches it with humor," and the novelist Kemal Tahir "who tries to narrate the mystery of this society in Zolaesque manners" are, among many others, the men of letters who have had an influence on him. Besides, as he states in *Istanbul*, the popular historian Resat Ekrem Kocu and the novelist Abdulhak Sinasi Hisar taught him the ways to approach the Ottoman heritage and the soul of Istanbul.

His interviews also make clear that not only modern Turkish writers but also classical Islamic texts and Eastern storytelling tradition have influenced his writing. Especially significant and influential among them are Rumi's *Masnawi* and the *Arabian Nights*.

Pamuk has many influences from Western writers, too. Among them are Leo Tolstoy, Marcel Proust, Vladimir Nabokov, and Thomas Mann. In fact, Pamuk's enduring questions regarding East versus West and his awareness that he lives and writes in a country far away from the center of world literature affects his preferences. He states in *Other Colors* that authors in the center who write as if they were in the periphery like William Faulkner and those in the periphery who write as if they were in the center like Fyodor Dostoyevsky can save us from stifling national demands and cliché international roles.

Pamuk also found certain Western sources methodologically inspiring for him. As he stresses in his Nobel Prize interview, Borges and Calvino taught him to disregard the heavy religious weight of classical Islamic texts and see them as geometrical shapes, as narratives with a certain structure. So he uses them out of their context, in the service of his literary purposes, that is, he uses *Masnawi* not for its religious side, but for its rhetoric and literary games and strategies.

Pamuk is still a prolific writer, therefore one cannot judge his ultimate contribution. Nevertheless, his contributions so far are still noteworthy. The most important contribution would be the fact that he changed the image of a novelist as a militant intellectual. Leaving aside a number of exceptions, the general tendency of Turkish writers had been to use literature as a means of their political goals, be it convincing the masses to modernize, or to adopt the new Republican lifestyle, or to achieve revolution. By structuring his novels by purely literary devices, Pamuk gave literature its autonomy, providing it with new narrative forms and techniques used in world literatures.

Outside Turkey, Pamuk's greatest contribution is to shake any biased judgments against Turkey or Islam or the East. His work has proved a means for his Western audience to achieve an alternative vision of a culture they had previously viewed only through prejudiced clichés.

THE WORLD'S PERSPECTIVE

Worldwide perceptions of Pamuk have generally been positive since his books began to be translated into foreign languages, especially English. Many important critics praise his exceptional talent and vision. In Canadian writer Margaret Atwood's words that appeared in the *Guardian*, "Pamuk gives us what all novelists give us at their best: the truth. Not the truth of statistics, but the truth of human experience at a particular place, in a particular time. And as with all great literature, you feel

600	BIOGRAPHICAL ENCYCLOPEDIA OF THE MODERN MIDDLE EAST AND NORTH AFRICA

> # I'VE ACCEPTED THE CITY INTO WHICH I WAS BORN IN THE SAME WAY I'VE ACCEPTED MY BODY
>
> ■
>
> I sometimes think myself unlucky to have been born in an ageing and impoverished city buried under the ashes of a ruined empire. But a voice inside me always insists this was really a piece of luck. If it were a matter of wealth, then I could certainly count myself fortunate to have been born into an affluent family at a time when the city was at its lowest ebb (though some have ably argued the contrary). Mostly I am disinclined to complain: I've accepted the city into which I was born in the same way I've accepted my body (much as I would have preferred to be more handsome and better built) and my gender (even though I still ask myself, naively, whether I might have been better off had I been born a woman). This is my fate, and there's sense arguing with it. This book is about fate.
>
> (*ISTANBUL: MEMORIES OF A CITY*, TRANSLATED BY MAUREEN FREELY. LONDON: FABER AND FABER, 2006.)

at moments not that you are examining him, but that he is examining you."

Apart from his talent, the international political or sociological developments in the recent decades must have played a role in the growing popularity of Pamuk. When awarding Pamuk the Nobel Prize, the Swedish Academy cited him as an author "who in the quest for the melancholic soul of his native city has discovered new symbols for the clash and interlacing of cultures." According to the Nobel Prize Web site, Horace Engdahl, the permanent secretary of the academy, said Pamuk was selected because he has "enlarged the roots of the contemporary novel" through his links to both Western and Eastern culture. He also stated, "This means that he has stolen the novel, one can say, from us Westerners and transformed it to something different from what we have ever seen before. . . . His roots in two cultures . . . allow him to take our own image and reflect it in a partially unknown and partially recognizable image, and it is incredibly fascinating."

LEGACY

Orhan Pamuk is one of the youngest authors to be awarded the Nobel Prize in Literature. Therefore, his future works and contributions, as well as their perceptions and their contexts, will determine Pamuk's ultimate legacy. However, given such themes as the clash of civilizations, the increasing tension originating from the Western interventions in the Middle Eastern countries, and the rising doubts in the West toward the relationship between Islam and terrorism fill the agenda in international affairs, Pamuk's work will witness that such clashes are not essential but constructed. As he states in his Nobel Lecture, his

> confidence comes from the belief that all human beings resemble each other, that others carry wounds like mine, that they will therefore understand. All true literature rises from this childish, hopeful certainty that all people resemble each other. When a writer shuts himself up in a room for years on end, with this gesture he suggests a single humanity, a world without a centre.

BIBLIOGRAPHY

WORKS BY PAMUK

Cevdet Bey ve Ogullari (Cevdet Bey and his sons). Istanbul: Karacan, 1982.

Sessiz Ev (The silent house). Istanbul: Karacan, 1983.

Beyaz Kale (*The White Castle*). New York: Braziller, 1991.

Gizli Yuz (Secret face). Istanbul: Karacan, 1992.

Benim Adim Kirmizi (*My Name Is Red*). New York: Vintage, 2002.

Yeni Hayat (*The New Life*). New York: Faber and Faber, 2002.

Istanbul: Hatiralar ve Sehir (*Istanbul: Memories and the City*). New York: Knopf, 2005.

Kar (*Snow*). New York: Vintage, 2005.

Kara Kitap (*The Black Book*). New York: Vintage, 2006.

Öteki Renkler (*Other Colors*). New York: Alfred A. Knopf, 2007.

Engin Kiliç

PANAHI, JAFAR
(1960–)

Panahi is a world-famous Iranian filmmaker and part of the Iranian New Wave movement in film.

PERSONAL HISTORY

Panahi was born on 11 July 1960 in Mianeh, Iran. He was attracted to the arts early on, and a book he wrote at age ten won a literary prize. He also became involved in filmmaking as a youth, acting in one 8 millimeter film and codirecting another. While fulfilling his service in the Iranian army during the Iran-Iraq War in the 1980s, Panahi produced a documentary about the war. He later

Jafar Panahi. AP IMAGES.

BIOGRAPHICAL HIGHLIGHTS

■

Name: Jafar Panahi

Birth: 1960, Mianeh, Iran

Family: Wife; children

Nationality: Iranian

Education: College of Cinema and Television, Tehran, Iran

PERSONAL CHRONOLOGY:

• **1994:** Assistant director for Abbas Kiarostami's film *Zir e Darakhtan e Zeyton (Through the Olive Trees);* directs *Badkonake Sefid (The White Balloon)*

• **1997:** Directs *Ayneh (The Mirror)*

• **2000:** Directs *Dayereh (The Circle)*

• **2003:** Directs *Talaye Sorkh (Crimson Gold)*

• **2006:** Directs *Offside*

studied film at the College of Cinema and Television in Tehran. Since then he has remained in Iran working as a filmmaker.

INFLUENCES AND CONTRIBUTIONS

In addition to making films for Iranian television, Panahi was assistant director to legendary Iranian filmmaker ABBAS KIAROSTAMI's production of *Zir e Darakhtan e Zeyton (Through the Olive Trees,* 1994). A protégé of Kiarostami, Panahi's own breakthrough occurred the following year when his first feature film, *Badkonake Sefid (The White Balloon)* burst onto the international cinema world. Written by Kiarostami, it received rave reviews around the world and was awarded the Gold Award at the 1995 Tokyo International Film Festival and the Prix de la Camera d'Or at Cannes. In 2000 he produced *Dayereh (The Circle)*. Whereas *Badkonake Sefid* offered a poignant slice-of-live portrayal of life in modern Iran, *Dayereh,* which consists of three intersecting stories rather than a conventional story line, more openly criticized the treatment of women in the country, and for that reason is banned in his native Iran even though it was highly acclaimed in the West. *Talaye Sorkh (Crimson Gold,* 2003) also was well received worldwide.

Described by one critic as providing a variation of neorealism, Iranian-style, Panahi makes films that plunge into the social fabric of Iran by telling compelling, human stories. Panahi's latest film, *Offside* (2006), is similar to *Dayereh,* another film about women in Iran who run afoul of Iranian authorities. The film is about three Iranian girls who disguise themselves as boys in order to attend a World Cup soccer (football) match that only males are allowed to watch in person. Panahi reportedly was inspired to make the film after the experience of his own daughter, who attended a soccer match despite the ban on female attendees. *Offside* was filmed surreptitiously, with a handheld video camera, using nonprofessional actors. It was edited on a home computer and distributed internationally, although not in Iran.

THE WORLD'S PERSPECTIVE

Even though he is still a relatively new filmmaker, Panahi already has received some top international film awards. In addition to the Prix de la Camera d'Or at Cannes for *The White Balloon,* he received other major awards such as the Golden Leopard Award he garnered for *Ayneh (The Mirror)* at the 1997 Locarno Film Festival. *The Circle* won the Golden Lion at the 2000 Venice Film Festival, a film that also was named Film of the Year by FIPRESCI (Fédération Internationale de la Presse Cinématographique). *Crimson Gold* won the Un Certain Regard Jury

Award at the 2003 Cannes Film Festival. In 2006 *Offside* won the Silver Bear at the Berlin International Film Festival Grand Jury Prize. It also was in the official selection for the 2006 New York Film Festival and the Toronto Film Festival.

At home in Iran, however, several of his films have run afoul of conservative government censors. Described by one critic as the Oliver Stone of Iran, some of his films have been banned.

LEGACY

Already in his young career, Panahi has emerged as one of Iran's most acclaimed filmmakers. As a New Wave Iranian filmmaker, he is destined to go down as one of modern Iran's most accomplished filmmakers, despite the fact that several of his productions are banned in that country.

BIBLIOGRAPHY

Maruf, Maryam. "Offside Rules: An Interview with Jafar Panahi." Open Democracy. Available from http://www.opendemocracy.net/.

Teo, Stephen. "The Case of Jafar Panahi: An Interview with the Iranian Director of *The Circle*." Senses of Cinema. Available from http://www.sensesofcinema.com/.

Michael R. Fischbach

Tassos Papadopoulos. MARK RENDERS/GETTY IMAGES.

PAPADOPOULOS, TASSOS
(1934–)

Tassos Nikolaou Papadopoulos became the fifth president of the Republic of Cyprus in 2003. As president he confirmed his reputation as an uncompromising negotiator when he dealt with two major issues in 2004, Cyprus's entry into the European Union (EU) and a referendum on a United Nations plan to reunify the island, which has been divided since 1974.

PERSONAL HISTORY

Papadopoulos was born on Cyprus in 1934 when it was still a British colony, and was educated at the Pancyprian Gymnasium, the oldest and best-known Greek-language high school on Cyprus. After studying law in London, where he became a barrister, he returned to Cyprus in 1955 and joined the Ethniki Organosis Kyprion Agoniston (EOKA, the National Organization of Cypriot Struggle), which had just launched its struggle for the end of the Cyprus's colonial status and for self-determination and union with Greece.

Papadopoulos served as a senior EOKA official and later on as the head of its political wing, the Pagkypria Epitrope Kypriakou Agona (PEKA, Pancyprian Committee of the Cyprus Struggle), a position akin to chief of propaganda. In 1959 he attended the conference in London, which followed one in Zürich, in which the British, Greek, and Turkish governments, along with representatives from Cyprus, hammered out the logistics of Cyprus's independence and sovereignty. Papadopoulos went on to serve on one of the subcommittees that worked on the draft of the constitution that would determine the power-sharing arrangements between the ethnic Greeks and Turks, roughly 80 and 18 percent of the island population respectively, and which came into effect with independence in 1960. Papadopoulos was appointed minister of interior in a provisional government formed in March 1959 that held office until the island officially became self-governing.

When Cyprus gained independence in August 1960 its first government was formed with the Greek Cypriot Archbishop Makarios as president and the Turkish Cypriot Dr. Fazil Kutchuk as vice president. Papadopoulos was appointed minister of labor and social services. He also served, successively, as minister of finance, minister of health, and minister of agriculture and natural

BIOGRAPHICAL HIGHLIGHTS

Name: Tassos Nikolaou Papadopoulos

Birth: 1934, Nicosia, Cyprus

Family: Wife, Fotini Michaelides; four children, Konstantinos, Maria, Nikolas, Anastasia

Nationality: Cypriot

Education: LL.B. (bachelor of laws), King's College, University of London, 1955

PERSONAL CHRONOLOGY:

• **1955–1959:** Member of Greek-Cypriot EOKA (National Organization of Cypriot Struggle)

• **1959:** Attends London Conference on Cyprus's independence; member of commission drafting constitution

• **1959–1970:** Serves successively as minister of interior, labor and social security, agriculture and natural resources, and health

• **1970:** Elected deputy, Cyprus House of Representatives; establishes law firm, Nicosia

• **2000:** Elected leader, DIKO (Democratic Party)

• **2003:** Elected president

• **2004:** Leads Cyprus into European Union

resources through 1972. In 1971 he was elected to the House of Representatives, standing as a candidate in Nicosia for the center-right conservative Eniaion (Unified) Party, founded by Glafcos Clerides, a future president of Cyprus. In 1971 he established a law firm in Nicosia, Tassos Papadopoulos & Co., which became one of the largest on the island.

Papadopoulos served as chief negotiator Clerides's adviser when the United Nations (UN)–mandated Greek and Turkish intercommunal talks began in 1975, following the tumultuous events of 1974, which began with an attempted coup against President Makarios by Greek Cypriot nationalists and led to the subsequent Turkish invasion and occupation of the northern third of the island. The purpose of the talks was to find a formula that would safeguard the rights and security of both of the island's ethnic groups. The Greek Cypriot government favored a more centralized bicommunal state, while the Turkish Cypriots favored a weaker central government and a two-zone federation. The talks led to a stale-

mate and Clerides resigned in April 1976; he was replaced by Papadopoulos.

Papadopoulos served as Greek Cypriot representative in the intercommunal talks from May 1976 through 1978, when they were suspended. He met his Turkish Cypriot interlocutor, Ümit Süleyman Onan, for several rounds of talks in May 1976, March–April 1977 under the chairmanship of UN Secretary General Kurt Waldheim, and in May–June 1977 in Nicosia. The two sides remained apart. When the talks resumed in the summer of 1978 Papadopoulos had been replaced.

In the next parliamentary elections, in 1981, Papadopoulos ran independently as the leader of the small Center Union Party. He received 7,964 votes or 2.7 percent of the total, which was not enough to earn him a parliamentary seat.

In the 1990s Papadopoulos made a political comeback that led to the leadership of the center-right Dimokratiko Komma (DIKO, Democratic Party). It had been founded in 1976 by Spyros Kyprianou, the man who replaced Makarios as president following the archbishop's death in 1977. Papadopoulos was elected a member of the House of Representatives in the parliamentary elections of 19 May 1991, as a candidate for the Democratic Party in the Nicosia constituency, and was reelected in the next elections on 26 May 1996. Papadopoulos was elected leader of the Democratic Party on 7 October 2000 at a party congress at which the ailing Kyprianou stood down.

Papadopoulos ran for president in 2003 against the incumbent President Clerides, who was seeking a third term, claiming he would be able to secure better deal for the Greek Cypriots in the peace plan being proposed by UN Secretary General Kofi Annan that aimed to bring about Cyprus's reunification. While Clerides was ready to accept the plan and ask the Greek Cypriots to approve it in a referendum, Papadopoulos said he hoped it could undergo major improvements in favor of Greek Cypriot claims. Papadopoulos was backed by, among others, the large communist party, AKEL, an example of how national issues bridge right- and left-wing perspectives in Cyprus. Papadopoulos won the election, held in February 2003, in the first round with a surprising 51.5 percent of the vote, with Clerides receiving a disappointing 38.8 percent.

Following an impasse in the negotiations over the Annan plan, because both leaders of the two communities, Papdopoulos and the Turkish Cypriot Rauf Denktaş rejected it, Annan nonetheless proposed a final settlement in late March 2004. The plan was to be decided upon by a referendum, held separately in the Greek Cypriot Republic and the Turkish Cypriot north, on 24 April 2004. Papadopoulos made an emotional appearance on television urging Greek Cypriots to reject the plan because it did not satisfy Greek Cypriot demands and gave too much to the Turkish Cypriot side. The Greek Cypriots who had fled the north in 1974 objected to the Annan plan because they felt it dispossessed them of their homes in the north by not providing for the return of their properties or even allowing them to seek financial redress. They also believed the plan's clauses on governance made for a very weak central power and would have created a permanent division of Cyprus into two political entities, as well as safeguarded the presence of settlers from mainland Turkey. The voters sided with Papadopoulos; the "no" vote was 75 percent. In the north, 65 percent of Turkish Cypriot voters approved the plan, but without the approval of the Greek Cypriot side, the initiative failed.

The next major event in Papadopoulos's presidency came on 1 May 2004 when Cyprus—the internationally recognized Greek Cypriot part of the island—joined the European Union. Some observers expected that Papadopoulos would use Cyprus's veto powers to block negotiations between the EU and Turkey, especially since Turkey did not recognize the Republic of Cyprus, but that has not been the case.

INFLUENCES AND CONTRIBUTIONS

Papadopoulos demonstrated early in his presidency that he was prepared to take a less conciliatory line toward Turkish Cypriot demands than his predecessors. Considering the significant powers exercised by the office of the president in the Republic of Cyprus, one can speak of a new era in which Greek Cypriot attitudes are hardening and contend that reunification is no longer sought after at any price. The support his party has received in elections and his considerable popularity indicates that Papadopoulos's outlook resonates with the majority of the population.

THE WORLD'S PERSPECTIVE

Papadopoulos's popularity domestically contrasts with his image abroad. His attitude toward the Annan plan drew explicit criticism from Western political observers and implicit criticism from within the UN. When the EU invited Cyprus to join, its officials had assumed that the Clerides administration was committed to the UN plan and that its approval by both communities would pave the way for unification, a development consonant with the principles underpinning European unification. If not, the Turkish Cypriot northern part would remain outside the EU. When Papadopoulos rejected the Annan plan his critics considered that he was operating with double standards, rejecting the Turkish Cypriots but embracing the EU in a self-serving way.

LEGACY

As president, Papadopoulos has transformed Greek Cypriot politics and the political dynamics of the island as a whole by adopting a less conciliatory and more assertive stance than his predecessors toward the Turkish Cypriot community. More than thirty years after the island's division in 1974, reunification appears to be a less urgent goal.

BIBLIOGRAPHY

Anastasiou, Harry. *The Broken Olive Branch: Nationalism, Ethnic Conflict and the Quest for Peace in Cyprus.* Bloomington, IN: Authorhouse, 2006.

Christou, George. *The European Union and Enlargement: The Case of Cyprus.* London and New York: Palgrave Macmillan, 2004.

"Curriculum Vitae." Presidency of the Republic of Cyprus. Available from http://www.presidency.gov.cy/presidency/ presidency.nsf/dmlindex_en/dmlindex_en?OpenDocument.

"Cyprus: A Greek Wreaker." *Economist,* 15 April 2004. Available from http://www.economist.com.

"Cyprus: An Ominous European Beginning." *Economist,* 29 April 2004. Available from http://www.economist.com.

Hannay, David. *Cyprus: The Search for a Solution.* London and New York: I.B. Tauris, 2005.

Hoffmeister, Frank. *Legal Aspects of the Cyprus Problem: Annan Plan and EU Accession.* Leiden, Netherlands, and Boston: Martinus Nijhoff, 2006.

Kerr-Linday, James. *EU Accession and UN Peacemaking in Cyprus.* New York: Palgrave Macmillan, 2006.

Palley, Claire. *An International Relations Debacle: The UN Secretary-General's Mission of Good Offices in Cyprus 1999–2004.* Oxford: Hart Publishing, 2005.

"Profile: Tassos Papadopoulos," BBC News, 17 February 2003. Available from http://news.bbc.co.uk.

Sachs, Susan. "Greek Cypriots Reject a Peace Plan." *New York Times,* 25 April 2004.

Smith, Helen. "Profile: Tassos Papadopoulos," *Guardian,* 17 February 2003. Available from http://www.guardian.co.uk.

Alexander Kitroeff

PARSIPUR, SHAHRNUSH
(1946–)

Shahrnush Parsipur, born in 1946 in Tehran, Iran, is an influential Iranian novelist. She has published eight books of fiction—three of them are translated into English—as well as her prison memoirs. Even though all of her works are currently banned in Iran, her novel *Tuba and the Meaning of Night* became a national best seller. She currently lives in the United States as a political refugee.

Shahrnush Parsipur. AP IMAGES.

PERSONAL HISTORY

Parsipur was born in Tehran, Iran, on 17 February 1946. She is the daughter of an attorney in the Justice Ministry originally from Shiraz (a city in southwest-central Iran). When she was sixteen, she began to write short stories and articles. In 1973 she received her B.A. in sociology from Tehran University.

Her first book was *Tupak-e Qermez* (The little red ball; 1969), a story for young people. Her first short stories were published in the late 1960s. One early story appeared in 1972 in a special short-story issue of a magazine that also featured stories by other Iranian writers. Her novella *Tajrobeh'ha-ye Azad* (*Trial Offers*, 1970; translated into English) was followed by the novel *Sag va Zemestan-e Boland* (The dog and the long winter), published in 1976.

She was a producer and editor of *Rural Women*, a socially inclined weekly show for National Iranian TV. In 1974 she resigned her job in protest against the torture and execution of two journalist-poet activists by SAVAK (the shah of Iran's secret services). She was imprisoned for fifty-four days. In the letter of resignation that she wrote, she indicated that she was not opposing the government or monarchy, but that she believed execution was unjust. After her release, she held a variety of office jobs and in 1976 she moved to Paris to study Chinese language and civilization at the Sorbonne until 1980. She returned to Iran in the wake of the 1979 Iranian Revolution. Parsipur was imprisoned before the 1979 revolu-

BIOGRAPHICAL HIGHLIGHTS

Name: Shahrnush Parsipur

Birth: 1946, Tehran, Iran

Family: Divorced, a son who lives in Iran

Nationality: Iranian

Education: Tehran University, faculty of letters: B.A. in sociology (1973); Sorbonne, Paris: Chinese philosophy and language, 1976–1980

PERSONAL CHRONOLOGY:

- **1967–1974:** Editor and producer Iranian National Television

- **1977:** Publishes *Small and Simple Tales of the Spirit of the Tree*

- **1979:** Returns to Iran in the wake of the Iranian Revolution

- **1981:** Incarcerated for four years and seven months

- **1990:** Spends two periods in jail

- **1994:** Moves to the United States as a political refugee, receives the Lillian Hellman/Dashiell Hammett Award from the Fund for Free Expression

- **2003:** First recipient of Brown University's International Writers Project Fellowship, by the Program in Creative Writing and the Watson Institute for International Studies

tion and again for more than four years in the 1980s for alleged oppositional activities. In 1989 she published her novel *Tuba va ma'na-ye Shab* (published in English as *Tuba and the Meaning of Night*). The publication of her short novel *Women without Men* in 1989 took her to prison twice more in the early 1990s. She was arrested one year after the *fatwa* against Salman Rushdie was issued. Immediately after its publication, *Women without Men* was attacked by fundamentalist journals and media for its references to virginity, and was thus unofficially banned. This also led publishers and booksellers to take her other works out of sale until the early 2000s, when they reappeared in bookstores. The Iranian government banned *Women without Men* in the mid-1990s and put pressure on the author to desist from such writing. Early in the 1990s, Parsipur finished her fourth novel, a story of a female Don Quixote called *Aql-e abi'rang* (*Blue Intellect*), which remained unavailable until 1992.

Translations of Parsipur's stories have appeared in *Stories by Iranian Women since the Revolution* (1991) and in *Stories from Iran: A Chicago Anthology* (1991). English translations of Parsipur's major writings were in print by 1992 when the author traveled around the United States and participated in the International Writer's Program at the University of Iowa. In 1994 Parsipur fled Iran and currently resides in the United States as a political refugee. In the same year she received the Lillian Hellman/Dashiell Hammett Award from the Fund for Free Expression. In 2003 she was also given the first International Writers Project Fellowship from the Program in Creative Writing and the Watson Institute for International Studies at Brown University.

INFLUENCES AND CONTRIBUTIONS

Two writers have greatly affected Parsipur's work: Fyodor Dostoyevsky and Charles Dickens. As a measure of how much she admires Dostoyevsky, Parsipur tells the story of attending an Italian school in Tehran run by Roman Catholic nuns, where every Sunday the nuns would preach to the students. In those moments, she used to think that if she had to become a Christian and marry a Christian, she would marry Dostoyevsky. Regarding Dickens's influence, she pointed out that she read his book *Great Expectations* thirty-three or thirty-four times. When she read it the last time—in prison in the Islamic Republic—she noticed that she still was fascinated by it. Interestingly, however, she has not read anything else by Dickens. Among French writers, Honoré de Balzac has influenced her. Also, two Latin Americans writers have affected her: Gabriel García Márquez from Colombia, and Jorge Luis Borges from Argentina.

Among Iranian authors, Sadeq Hedayat (1903–1951) has deeply influenced Parsipur's writing. She has used Hedayat's book, *Blind Owl*, in two of her works: *Tuba and the Meaning of Night* and *Blue Intellect*. There seems to have been a constant challenge between *Blind Owl* and Parsipur's two books. She was also profoundly swayed by Sumerian myths. One was the myth of Gilgamesh and other was the Sumerian myth of creation, and they are manifest in three of her books: *Women without Men*, in part in *Tuba and the Meaning of Night*, and in a considerable part in *Blue Intellect*.

Both novels, *Women without Men* and *Tuba and the Meaning of Night*, depict the male-dominated culture in harsh terms. Parsipur's other works, such as *Adab-e Sarf-e Chay dar Hozur-e Gorg* (1993, Tea ceremony in the presence of a wolf) and *Khatirat-i Zindan* (1997, Prison memoirs), published while in exile, also reflect her

CERTAIN LIMITED ROLES

From the time I was a young woman I discovered some secrets. And that was that unless you have sexual experiences you cannot enter the domain of public work and social activities. Those in power know this fact and thus transform women to sexual objects. I mean they first and foremost repress and denigrate women, then they direct them to put a wedding gown on and go to their husband's home and come out wearing the shroud. I mean to say that they train women in certain limited roles. So the most important barrier in front of a woman who has ambitions in creative work and wants to do something important is to overcome her fear of sexual taboos and matters. [...] There are some strange fears around which must be overcome. The way to do so is to talk about sexual matters as much as possible openly and honestly. [...] Don't get me wrong, I don't believe in sexual anarchy, not at all. But I completely endorse sexual freedom. This must come to pass so that women can become somebody. Having said all of this I hereby declare in this particular historical juncture that in my judgment the best thing a woman can do is having a husband, live with her children and carry on a quiet and dignified life!

(PARSIPUR IN: BASHI, GOLBARG. "THE PROPER ETIQUETTE OF MEETING SHAHRNUSH PARSIPUR IN THE UNITED STATES." PERSIAN BOOK REVIEW. AVAILABLE FROM HTTP:// PERSIANBOOKREVIEW.NET.)

commitment to the cause of Iranian women. The short stories and articles reunited in *Adab-e Sarf-e Chay dar Hozur-e Gorg* express the author's views on social and cultural issues. These short stories sometimes portray Parsipur's own experience, but also the minds of alienated men and women who seem trapped between two worlds: traditional and modern, old and new, and determined and free.

THE WORLD'S PERSPECTIVE

Parsipur is seen in Western countries primarily as a feminist writer, but she wants to be known not as a feminist but as a free woman. Some of Parsipur's works have been translated into English, French, Italian, and German. Even though Parsipur moved to the United States in 1994 she remains in regular contact with the literary communities in Iran and abroad; because she is deeply respected by the younger generation of writers, she receives numerous manuscripts written by them, especially female authors, who seek her opinion on their work.

LEGACY

By breaking taboos about women's sexuality, Parsipur has contributed to the rise of a feminist discourse after the 1979 Islamic Revolution. Parsipur's narrative, therefore, not only criticizes patriarchal social convention but also attempts to subvert the male-dominated literary style of the prerevolutionary period. The following generations of female writers are nourished by her work.

Her legacy is also informed by her fight to expose the political conditions that Iranian women writers must struggle against in order to continue their literary work. Parsipur's works are among the most successful of writers from Iran. The literary movement to which they belong has produced new forms and creative approaches to social problems and has addressed forbidden topics.

In the 2000s, even pious Muslim women, whether within the ruling elite or from among the oppositional groups, are reinterpreting Islamic ideology to offer a female-favorable reading of the theology. Women's issues have gained a new significance in Iran and can no longer be ignored by politicians. In their campaigns, Iranian candidates have taken the situation of women as a central issue. These developments may be regarded as a way of subverting or a way of appropriating women's discourse, but they do stand in contrast with the state discourse of the Islamic republic and indicate the direction of cultural change. At the center of this process, the works of female authors, mainly inspired by Parsipur's writings, have influenced the course of political development and culture production in Iran.

BIBLIOGRAPHY

Bashi, Golbarg. "Ideological Tyranny in Iranian Women's Studies: A Response to Shahrzad Mojab." Free Thoughts on Iran. Updated 16 November 2005. Available from http://freethoughts.org.

Moayyad, Heshmat, ed. *Stories from Iran: A Chicago Anthology (1921–1991)*. Washington, DC: Mage Publishers, 2002.

Parsipur, Shahrnush. *Women without Men: A Novella*. Translated by Jocelyn Sharlet and Kamran Talattof. New York: Feminist Press, 2004.

———. *Tuba and the Meaning of Night*. Translated by Havva Houshmand and Kamran Talattof. New York: Feminist Press, 2006.

Laura Ruiz

PEER, SHAHAR
(1987–)

Shahar Peer is a promising young Israeli tennis player who is considered one of the best Israeli tennis players ever. She achieved her highest ranking in the Women's Tennis Association (WTA), 15th place, in January 2007, an Israeli record for women players, which Peer shared with another accomplished tennis player, Anna Smashnova. She was also the first Israeli woman to reach the quarterfinals of a Grand Slam tournament.

PERSONAL HISTORY

Peer was born in Jerusalem on 1 May 1987; when she was an infant, her family moved to the nearby town of Maccabim. Her father, Dov, worked in the high-tech electronics industry, and her mother, Aliza, was a physical education teacher. Peer has two older siblings, a brother, Shlomi, and a sister, Shani. Both of them took up tennis as a hobby when they were children. Inspired by her siblings, Shahar started playing tennis when she was only six years old.

In late December 2001, Peer won the girls' title at the American Orange Bowl International Tennis Championships for youth. She turned professional in 2004,

Shahar Peer. AP IMAGES.

BIOGRAPHICAL HIGHLIGHTS

Name: Shahar Peer

Birth: 1987, Jerusalem, Israel

Family: Single

Nationality: Israeli

Education: High school diploma, Maccabim-Re'ut High School, 2005

PERSONAL CHRONOLOGY:

- **2004:** Wins junior championship, Australian Open
- **2005:** Reaches quarterfinals in six Women's Tennis Association tournaments
- **2006:** Wins titles at Pattaya, Prague, and Istanbul tournaments; reaches fourth round, French Open; member of victorious Israeli national women's team, Fed Cup playoffs
- **2007:** Reaches quarterfinals, Australian Open

and her first major achievement followed shortly, when she won the junior championship in the 2004 Australian Open tournament.

In spite of her demanding schedule, Peer attended high school, and graduated in July 2005. Since army service is mandatory in Israel, Peer enlisted in the Israeli Defense Forces (IDF) on 30 October 2005. After completing three weeks of basic training, Peer was assigned to do administrative work as a part of her army service (compulsory service is flexible for professional athletes since they are allowed to travel and practice).

At the age of seventeen, Peer began seeing a clinical psychologist in order to help her develop the emotional capacity required of a professional athlete, especially in regard to dealing with stressful situations. "I didn't want to see a therapist to start with; I assumed that therapy was only good for troubled people, but then I decided to try it out and I realized that it helps me mentally," she explained in an interview.

INFLUENCES AND CONTRIBUTIONS

Although still at the beginning of her career, Peer has already made an impact on professional tennis. In 2005 she reached the quarterfinals of six WTA tournaments. Her major breakthrough came in 2006. In January of that year Peer made her first semifinal appearance at the

Canberra International Tournament, where she lost to Anabel Medina Garrigues of Spain. At the end of January 2006, Peer became the top female Israeli tennis player, after being ranked 43rd by the WTA.

In February 2006, Peer won her first title, at the Pattaya Women's Open tournament in Thailand. In April 2006 she was a member of the Israeli team that played in the Fed Cup playoffs in Bulgaria (the Fed Cup is the most important tennis tournament for national women's teams, organized by the International Tennis Federation). Peer led her team through a series of important wins to an impressive triumph in the finals. She also marked a notable personal milestone when, for the first time in her career, she defeated a top-twenty player, Ana Ivanovic of Serbia.

In the following weeks, Peer kept up her winning streak. In May 2006 she won the Prague Tournament, where she also won the doubles title with the French player Marion Bartoli, and at the end of that month she won the Istanbul Tournament.

In the summer of 2006 she marked another professional highlight, when she defeated a top-ten player, the Russian Elena Dementieva, in the French Open. Peer made it to the fourth round of that tournament, where she lost to the former Swiss champion Martina Hingis. Consequently, she rose in the rankings to 25th place. Peer also reached the fourth round of the 2006 U.S. Open, but lost to Justine Henin Hardenne of Belgium, who was then ranked second in the world.

THE WORLD'S PERSPECTIVE

At the Australian Open in January 2007, Peer made history by becoming the first Israeli woman to reach the quarterfinals of a Grand Slam tournament, after defeating Svetlana Kuznetsova of Russia, who was then ranked 4th. Her victories spurred considerable excitement in Israel. Israeli prime minister EHUD OLMERT even chose to commence the weekly cabinet meeting by applauding her performance. In the quarterfinal she was defeated in a long and exhausting game by eventual champion Serena Williams. In February 2007 Peer made it to the finals of the Memphis Tournament, where she was promptly defeated by Venus Williams.

LEGACY

Peer is a rising talent in the world of professional tennis. She is considered an intense competitor, who covers the court well and changes speeds cleverly. She also received a great deal of international media attention since she competed professionally while still in the army. She was often asked in interviews about her military experience and her first-rate skills as a sniper. "I don't know if it's from tennis or whatever, but I really liked it," she once commented in an interview.

BIBLIOGRAPHY

Clarey, Christopher. "Nadal Clears His Throat and Extends His Streak." *New York Times*, 4 June 2006.

Fed Cup's Official Web site. Available from http://www.fedcup.com.

Passa, Dennis. "Israel's Peer Impresses in Loss to Serena Williams." Associated Press, 23 January 2007.

"Shahar Peer Wins. Her Psychologist Explains How." YNET. Updated 17 February 2007. Available from http://www.ynet.co.il.

Sony Ericsson WTA Tour. Available from http://www.sonyericssonwtatour.com.

Or Rabinowitz

Shimon Peres. ALEX WONG/GETTY IMAGES.

PERES, SHIMON
(1923–)

Shimon Peres (born Perski) is one of Israel's longest-serving politicians and statesmen. For more than half a century, Peres has occupied influential positions in the Israeli Defense Ministry and headed a variety of government ministries, including repeated terms as defense minister and foreign minister. He also served as prime minister between 1984 and 1986, during the Labor-Likud national unity government, and as interim prime minister during the half year following the assassination of Prime Minister YITZHAK RABIN in November 1995. Peres was elected president of Israel in June 2007.

PERSONAL HISTORY

Peres was born in 1923 to a wealthy family in the small Belarussian town of Vishnive, which was then under Polish rule. His father was a lumber merchant, and his mother was a Russian teacher and librarian. Peres attended a Tarbut (Zionist) school that taught classes in modern Hebrew and Yiddish. Socially withdrawn, the young Peres read a great deal and excelled in his studies. As Vishnive was almost completely Jewish in population, Peres grew up in a Jewish bubble, with little significant contact with non-Jewish society.

Zionist enthusiasm motivated the Perski family to move to Palestine well before catastrophe befell the Jews of Europe in the Holocaust. Peres's father left in 1932 to establish a business and a home, and twelve-year-old Shimon and the rest of the family arrived in Tel Aviv in 1935. The young immigrant attended Balfour Primary School and the Ge'ula (Redemption) High School in Tel Aviv. In addition to his studies, Peres joined the Zionist social democratic youth movement Hano'ar Ha'oved V'halomed (Working and Studying Youth), his prestate political base, which he would eventually lead. In 1937, without the permission of his parents, Peres went to study at the Ben Shemen agricultural school near the

Arab town of Lydda. At Ben Shemen, Shimon Perski—who never lost his foreign accent and who spent his entire life trying to fit in with his contemporaries who were born in Palestine—became an Israeli.

During World War II, Peres's father, already in his forties, joined the British army, was taken prisoner by the Germans, and returned to Palestine only after the end of the war. Peres, however, would never serve in the military. In 1940, seventeen-year-old Peres met Berl Katznelson, the spiritual leader of the Zionist labor movement at the time, and David Ben-Gurion, leader not only of Mapai (the Eretz Yisra'el Workers Party) but of the Zionist Organization and the Jewish Agency, the two closely linked organizations which spearheaded the Zionist campaign for a Jewish state in Palestine. This meeting had decisive implications for young Peres's political future.

While still at Ben Shemen, Peres met Sonia Gelman, whom he would marry in May 1945. In 1941 Peres moved to Kibbutz Geva in the Jezreel Valley, where he and a number of friends underwent agricultural training

BIOGRAPHICAL HIGHLIGHTS

Name: Shimon Peres (born Perski)

Birth: 1923, Vishnive, Poland

Family: Wife, Sonia; one daughter, Tzvia; two sons, Nehemia and Yonatan

Nationality: Israeli

Education: Ben Shemen Agricultural School; New York University (1949–1950, not for degree); Harvard University (1950–1951, not for degree)

PERSONAL CHRONOLOGY:

- **1945–1947:** Secretary of the ha-No'ar ha-Oved
- **1947–1948:** Director, human resources and weapons purchase, Hagana, Defense Ministry
- **1948–1950:** Assistant to defense minister, naval affairs
- **1949–1952:** Head, Defense Ministry delegation, New York
- **1952–1953:** Deputy director general, Defense Ministry
- **1953–1959:** Director general, Defense Ministry
- **1959–1965:** Deputy defense minister
- **1959–present:** Member of Knesset for Mapai (1959–1965), Rafi (1965–1968), Labor (1968–2005), Kadima (2006–)
- **1965–1967:** Director general, Rafi

- **1969:** Minister of absorption
- **1974:** Minister of transportation and communication, minister of information
- **1974–1977:** Defense minister
- **1977:** Acting prime minister
- **1977–1984:** Knesset opposition chairman
- **1977–1992:** Labor Party chairman
- **1984–1986:** Prime minister
- **1986–1988:** Foreign minister
- **1988–1990:** Acting prime minister, finance minister
- **1990–1992:** Knesset opposition chairman
- **1992–1995:** Foreign minister
- **1995–1996:** Interim prime minister, defense minister, minister of finance and planning
- **1995–1997:** Labor Party chair, Knesset opposition chair
- **1999–2001:** Minister of regional cooperation
- **2001–2002:** Foreign minister, deputy prime minister
- **2003–2005:** Labor Party chair, Knesset opposition chair
- **2005–2006:** Vice prime minister
- **2006:** Vice prime minister, minister of Negev and Galilee development
- **2007:** President of Israel

in order to eventually establish their own kibbutz. In contrast to his father, his girlfriend Sonia, and many friends who enlisted in the British army during the war, Peres refrained. He also did not join the Hagana, the semilegal military force of Palestine's organized Jewish community. He believed that the task of establishing a Jewish home in Palestine was just as important as fighting the Nazis. In 1942 Peres was one of the founders of Kibbutz Alumot in the Jordan Valley, southwest of Lake Tiberias (the Sea of Galilee). He spent his time working in farming and politics, and before reaching eighteen was recognized as an influential and promising political actor.

Political Ambitions and Weapons Acquisition Although his generation tended to play down individual political ambition, this was not the way of young Peres. His steadfastness and organizational skills brought him success in the internal struggle within the Zionist labor movement over who would control its large youth movement: Peres's mentor and leader Ben-Gurion, or Yitzhak Tabenkin, leader of the United Kibbutz Movement faction, which had just split from Mapai. He thus attracted the attention of the Mapai leadership, which soon became the leadership of the State of Israel. In May 1947 Peres was drafted by the Hagana and, under the supervision and guiding hand of then Jewish Agency treasurer Levi Eshkol, was placed in charge of human resource management and weapons purchasing. Following this assignment, he was charged with acquiring weapons for the newly formed Israeli navy. In this capacity, with Eshkol (a later finance, defense, and prime minister), Peres embarked upon the undertaking that would occupy him for the next two decades: the construction of Israel's military might. While doing so, Peres did not participate in the 1948 War—Israel's "War of Independence"—as a soldier. This biographical detail remained an obstacle throughout his political career, though his work contributed to the Israeli war effort.

Because he did not speak English and had received only a partial education, Peres asked Ben-Gurion to enable him to travel to the United States for academic study. Characteristically, he did not wait for an offer, but rather offered himself. He was appointed as the deputy director of the Israeli Defense Ministry's delegation in New York and quickly took over as its director. In the evenings, he pursued his studies. One important outcome of Peres's work in the United States was Israel Aerospace Industries, which he established with the help of the ideas, people, and budgets he mobilized there. Although only twenty-eight years old when he returned to Israel, Peres was integrated by Ben-Gurion into the senior echelon of the Defense Ministry. This paved Peres's path into Israel's political elite.

In December 1953, just before (temporarily) retiring, Ben-Gurion appointed Moshe Dayan as chief of the General Staff, and Peres as director general of the Defense Ministry. Until the 1967 War, these Ben-Gurion protégés would be Ben-Gurion's most important loyalists in the defense establishment and Israeli politics. This was especially true of Peres, who was younger, lower ranking, and less independent than Dayan. To the dismay of Pinhas Lavon, who replaced Ben-Gurion as defense minister, Peres rapidly became the most powerful force within the defense ministry.

Protégé of Ben-Gurion Peres's loyalty to Ben-Gurion and his evolving alliance with Dayan made him an active participant in contemporary political and diplomatic debates. His personal and political interest in Ben-Gurion's return and his close relationship with Dayan made him an enthusiastic supporter of Dayan's alternatives to the security policies of Prime Minister and Foreign Minister Moshe Sharett. While Sharett strived to maintain the post-1948 status quo to reach a peace agreement with the Arab world, Dayan believed that peace could only be achieved through a second round of warfare, strengthening of Israel's military, modification of the 1949 borders, and "peacemaking" from a position of strength.

With characteristic enthusiasm and thoroughness, Peres worked to bridge the gap between Dayan and Ben-Gurion. He persuaded Ben-Gurion to return from retirement by stressing the importance of Dayan's approach, which contradicted that of Sharett, Ben-Gurion's political rival. In February 1955 Ben-Gurion returned to the defense ministry and in November 1955 to the prime minister's office. From that point on, Peres functioned more as a diplomat than as an official charged with weapons acquisition, in order to promote Dayan's idea

of an Israeli-initiated war. Peres's role in this effort was critical, as Ben-Gurion's precondition for an Israeli-initiated war was a superpower alliance and a substantial arms deal. With the help of his determined mediation, connections, and personal charisma, Peres provided both in the form of a 1956 Israeli-French alliance and arms deal. Sharett was forced to leave the government, and the way was now open for an Israeli-initiated war. When the Suez crisis erupted in July 1956, Israel was ready.

Peres's political influence increased significantly after the Suez-Sinai war of October–November 1956, when Israel joined with France and Britain in attacking Egypt. This was not only due to his role in arming Israel and making the political preparations for the war. Since his first encounter with arms purchases and the weapons industry, Peres had been fascinated by the nuclear option. Ben-Gurion was an important influence on Peres in this realm as well, as was Peres's time in the United States. Peres led Israeli efforts to acquire a functioning nuclear reactor even before the Israeli-French alliance, but these efforts intensified after 1956. Israel's alliance with France and Britain in their joint effort to reimpose their will on a former colonial dependency raised Israel's standing in the eyes of the two European powers. One important outcome of the 1956 war was the construction of the nuclear reactor at Dimona, for which France provided Israel with the knowledge and the means, primarily between 1956 and 1958. Since then, Peres has staunchly supported the view that Israel must possess nuclear weapons and has never deviated from this policy. (It is worth pointing out, however, that Israel has never officially acknowledged possessing nuclear weapons.)

Owing to his political and diplomatic success, Peres was elected to the Knesset in 1959 and appointed as deputy defense minister. He served in this capacity under Ben-Gurion until June 1963 and under Eshkol until 1965, when he and other Ben-Gurion loyalists seceded from Mapai to establish Rafi (List of the Workers of Israel), an alternative party that aimed at replacing Mapai at the helm of government. As Rafi's director general, Peres held significant political influence within the new party, alongside Dayan and Teddy Kollek. From then until the outbreak of war in June 1967, Peres led the opposition to the Eshkol government within the Knesset and the Israeli labor movement. That Eshkol had supervised and supported him when he first entered the Israeli defense establishment in 1947 did not stop Peres, who, like his mentor Ben-Gurion, viewed Eshkol and his government as a disaster to be overcome by all necessary political means. But Rafi won only ten Knesset seats, making Peres's work extremely difficult. The maneuvering of Peres, Dayan, Kollek, and their colleagues, referred to then and for many years to come as "the young ones," against Eshkol, Golda Meir, and Pinhas Sapir, who had established themselves as political leaders in mandatory Palestine, was also very much a generational conflict.

The 1967 War The June 1967 Arab-Israeli War presented Peres with an unprecedented opportunity to strike a blow at Eshkol's power base and to lead the Ben-Gurion loyalists back into power. Peres and his colleagues made effective use of the sense of crisis and fear that seized Israeli society before the war to present Dayan as a miracle cure. On 2 June 1967, Eshkol established a national unity government with Dayan as defense minister. Three days later the war broke out, and although they were not involved in the preparations, Peres and his colleagues were credited with the victory. Peres, however, did make important contributions to the development of the Israel Defense Forces (IDF) between 1948 and 1965, and this made him a legitimate partner in the Israeli victory. Now Peres aimed at taking over the ruling party from within. It was clear that Ben-Gurion, then more than eighty years old, could no longer represent an alternative to Mapai. Peres left his elderly mentor with only a handful of supporters and, with the vast majority of Rafi members, joined the united Israeli Labor Party upon its establishment in January 1968.

After the 1969 elections, won by Labor, Peres served as a government minister for the first time. During the seventh Knesset (1969–1973), Peres served successively as minister of immigrant absorption, minister of transportation, minister of communication, and supervisor of economic development in the occupied West Bank. During the eighth Knesset (1973–1977), he served as minister of information. In 1974, during the political storm that overtook Israeli politics in the aftermath of the 1973 War, Peres replaced Dayan as defense minister. Peres had not occupied a position of central importance in the government or the defense ministry during the war, leaving him untainted by the military failure. When Prime Minister Golda Meir resigned later the same year, Peres ran against YITZHAK RABIN for the position of prime minister, and lost by a small margin. This was the beginning of a long and bitter rivalry between the two men.

Peres continued to serve as defense minister in Rabin's government until 1977. In this capacity, he provided technical and political support for the radical messianic settlers of Gush Emunim in their periodic bids to establish renegade settlements in parts of the West Bank where, according to government policy, settlements were not sanctioned. He also took part in the decision to carry out "Operation Thunderbolt" in July 1976 to free the passengers, mostly Israelis, of a hijacked plane being held at the Entebbe, Uganda airport. When Rabin resigned as prime minister in the midst of a domestic political scandal, Peres took over as acting prime minister and Labor Party chairman, a position he retained until 1992.

In the elections of 1981, as head of the Labor Alignment list, Peres lost again, this time to the right-wing Likud bloc leader Menachem Begin. In the national unity government established after the 1984 elections, Peres served as prime minister for two years, until the power-sharing rotation that replaced him with Likud party chief Yitzhak Shamir. During this period, Peres spearheaded the redeployment of Israeli forces that had invaded Lebanon in 1982 into a "security zone" in southern Lebanon. He also worked closely with Finance Minister Yitzhak Moda'i to reduce the triple-digit inflation then plaguing the Israeli economy.

In 1987, while serving as foreign minister, Peres initiated contacts with King HUSSEIN of Jordan to discuss the possibility of an Israeli return of the West Bank. Prime Minister Shamir, however, rejected the understandings that later came to be known as the London Document. In 1988, during the second unity government, Peres served as finance minister and deputy prime minister. In 1990 he led the vote of no confidence against Shamir's government from within, with support of the Jewish religious parties in the Knesset. But Peres's subsequent attempt to form a new government with himself at the helm, without holding new elections—an act that quickly came to be known as "the dirty trick"—ultimately failed, and he was forced to resign from the government and to lead Labor back into opposition.

Oslo and After In preparation for the 1992 elections, the Labor Party chose Rabin over Peres as party chairman. After Labor's electoral victory, Peres, as foreign minister, oversaw the secret negotiations with the Palestine Liberation Organization (PLO) that ultimately resulted in the 1993 Declaration of Principles, or Oslo Accord. He also played a part in achieving the subsequent peace treaty with Jordan. During the Rabin government of 1992–1995, Peres and Rabin finally managed to overcome their longstanding rivalry and to maintain a fruitful working relationship.

After Rabin's assassination, Peres assumed the posts of prime minister, defense minister, and minister of finance and planning. In 1996, in yet another electoral bid against the Likud, this time as an incumbent in Israel's first direct election for prime minister, Peres lost to BINYAMIN NETANYAHU. The next year, he decided not to run in the Labor primaries for party chairman, and Ehud Barak replaced him in this position. Despite tensions between the two, Barak reserved a seat for Peres in the Labor-led "One Israel" Knesset list in the 1999 national elections. After the Labor victory, Barak appointed Peres to the newly created post of minister for regional cooperation.

EXPLORING

Between September 1993 and September 1995, the Israeli government and the Palestine Liberation Organization (PLO) signed a series of agreements known as the Oslo Accords, named for the location of the secret negotiations unofficially initiated by both parties in late 1992 and mediated by the Norwegian government. As time passed, political figures from both parties signed on to the initiative, making its primary historical significance the mutual recognition of Israel and the PLO.

The basic principles of the agreements were as follows: Israeli retention of its military government and "civil administration" in the West Bank and Gaza Strip, and gradual transfer of various areas of responsibility to Palestinian control; scheduling of final status negotiations, regardless of the status of interim arrangements; commitment by both parties to the spirit of Oslo (a sense of mutual trust and a feeling that both sides are gaining) and the language of Oslo (positive language that offends neither of the opposing parties); the use of economic development as a means of reducing hostility; and the implication that a Palestinian state would be established at the end of the process, conditional upon Israeli agreement.

While the November 1995 assassination of Yitzhak Rabin dealt a mortal blow to the implementation of the Oslo Accords, the mutual recognition they embodied still stands.

In 2000 Peres ran for the primarily ceremonial position of president of Israel, but lost in a Knesset vote to Moshe Katzav. In March 2001 Peres was again appointed as foreign minister in a national unity government formed by Likud leader ARIEL SHARON during the second Palestinian intifada in the Occupied Territories. In June 2003 Peres was elected provisional Labor Party chairman and again led the opposition in the Knesset. In January 2005, the Labor Party joined the Sharon government, and Peres was appointed vice prime minister.

In November 2005 Peres lost to AMIR PERETZ in the elections for Labor Party chairman. A few weeks later, he announced his resignation from the Labor Party and his decision to join Kadima, the party recently established by Sharon to counter the internal Likud rebellion in the wake of his 2005 unilateral withdrawal from the Gaza

Strip and parts of the West Bank. After the 2006 Knesset elections, Peres was appointed minister of Negev and Galilee development. On 13 June 2007 the Knesset elected him president of Israel.

INFLUENCES AND CONTRIBUTIONS

Peres played a decisive role in establishing and developing the Israeli defense establishment, and until the 1980s was closely associated with the security-activist wing of the Labor Party. However, from the 1980s onward, he also emerged as a key leader of the Israeli "peace camp," and in this capacity played an important role in the Oslo Accord and the Israeli-Jordanian peace treaty of 1994. For these activities, Peres received the Nobel Peace Prize in conjunction with Rabin and YASIR ARAFAT in 1994. Perhaps equally important, Peres also helped extricate the Israeli economy from crisis and recession and lead it to growth. As a politician, Peres was repeatedly defeated in Israeli national elections for prime minister. Nonetheless, throughout his generations-spanning career, he never left the political arena. Despite his advanced age, he continues to play an important role in Israeli government and politics.

THE WORLD'S PERSPECTIVE

Despite Peres's central role in building Israel's military might and nuclear capabilities during the formative decades of Israeli statehood, Peres is best known in the international realm for the Arab-Israeli peace activism that has characterized his career since the mid-1980s.

THERE NEED TO BE BORDERS BETWEEN COUNTRIES, BUT NOT THE KIND BUILT ON MINEFIELDS

I am 100% convinced that there will be peace, as, no matter what we do, it is impossible to exist in the global world in a provincial manner.

There need to be borders between countries, but not the kind built on minefields. Instead of placing minefields around Jericho, we need to make sure it [the city] thrives and develops. Then, no one will have a reason to come here.

PERES, SHIMON. "INTERVIEW WITH ISRAELI MEDIA." ISRAEL NEWS: YNETNEWS. UPDATED JUNE 2005. AVAILABLE FROM HTTP://WWW.YNETNEWS.COM/HOME/0,7340,L-3083,00.HTML.

Today, with personal connections with dozens of heads of government, diplomats, politicians, and intellectuals around the world, he is by far the most well-respected international Israeli statesman.

LEGACY

Peres and his policies reflect the constant Israeli efforts—which have been underway since the establishment of the state—to find an effective balance between leaders' desire for both "security" as a Jewish state and peace. Since the 1980s he has promoted the approach that Israel's military and economic power must be focused on signing treaties with its Arab neighbors and with the Palestinians. In 1997 he established the Peres Center for Peace, which supports implementation of his vision of "a new Middle East." He has published a number of books, including *The Next Step* (1965), *David's Sling* (1970), *Entebbe Diary* (1991), and *The New Middle East* (1993).

BIBLIOGRAPHY

Bar-On, Mordechai. *In Pursuit of Peace: A History of the Israeli Peace Movement.* Washington, DC: U.S. Institute of Peace, 1996.

Golani, Motti. *The Road to Peace: A Biography of Shimon Peres.* New York: Warner Books, 1989.

Golani, Motti. *Israel in Search of a War: The Sinai Campaign, 1955–1956.* Brighton, U.K.: Sussex Academic Press, 1998.

Makovsky, David. *Making Peace with the PLO: The Rabin Government's Road to the Oslo Accord.* Boulder, CO: Westview Press, 1996.

Peres, Shimon. *David's Sling.* London: Weidenfeld and Nicolson, 1970.

———. *Battling for Peace: A Memoir.* New York: Random House, 1995.

———. "Interview with Israeli Media." Israel News: Ynetnews .Updated June 2005. Available from http://www.ynetnews .com/home/0,7340,L-3083,00.html.

Peres, Shimon, and Arye Naor. *The New Middle East.* New York: Henry Holt, 1993.

Motti Golani

PERETZ, AMIR
(1952–)

Amir Peretz is an Israeli politician who was deputy prime minister and defense minister in the coalition government of EHUD OLMERT from 200? to 2007. He spent much of his political career fighting for worker's rights and social welfare. He was a trade union activist and served as the head of the Histadrut, Israel's trade union federation, for ten years. He became the leader of the Labor Party in Israel in an upset victory over SHIMON PERES in the

Amir Peretz. AP IMAGES.

leadership contest of November 2005. The party ousted him as leader in May 2007, and he resigned as Olmert's defense minister the following month.

PERSONAL HISTORY

Peretz was born 9 March 1952 in Boujad, Morocco, in the Middle Atlas mountain region. His given name was Armand, which was later changed to Amiram and then to the more modern Amir. He was born into a prominent Moroccan Jewish family and his father was the head of the Jewish community in Boujad.

In 1956, when he was four, his family immigrated to Israel, part of the first wave of emigration from Morocco to the recently established State of Israel. His family settled in Sderot, a new "development" town in the Negev region in the south of the country, close to the Gaza Strip. Like other development towns that were established for the settlement of new immigrants, mostly Jews from North Africa and the Middle East (known as

BIOGRAPHICAL HIGHLIGHTS

Name: Amir Peretz

Birth: 1952, Boujad, Morocco

Family: Wife, Ahlama; four children, Ohad, Shani, Iftah, Matan

Nationality: Israeli

Education: Sderot High School

PERSONAL CHRONOLOGY:

- **1983:** Elected head of Sderot Local Council
- **1988:** Elected to Knesset for the Labor Party
- **1995–2005:** Chair, Histadrut Trade Union Federation
- **1999:** Resigns from Labor Party, founds Am Ehad (One Nation) Party
- **2004:** Merges Am Ehad with Labor Party
- **2005–2007:** Chair, Labor Party
- **2006–2007:** Deputy prime minister, minister of defense

Sephardim or Mizrahim [Easterners]), Sderot was poor, located on Israel's periphery, away from the country's economic and population centers.

Peretz grew up in Sderot and attended the local high school. His father worked in a factory on a kibbutz and his mother in a laundry. After graduating high school, he carried out his compulsory military service in the paratroopers division, attaining the rank of captain. In 1974 he was badly injured when a military vehicle he was repairing crushed his leg. For the next two years, he underwent a long process of rehabilitation, was bedridden for a year and then confined to a wheelchair. Despite his doctors' prediction, he was able to walk again.

While still in a wheelchair, Peretz bought a farm in Moshav Nir Akiva near his hometown of Sderot and grew vegetables for export. It was there that he met his wife Ahlama Zarhiani. During this time, Peretz started to become actively involved in the labor movement. He began campaigning for workers' rights, as well as for peace—issues that would remain at the top of his political agenda for years to come. As Peretz became involved in local politics in Sderot, he returned to live there, and has lived there ever since.

In 1983, at age thirty, on the advice of a friend, Peretz ran as candidate of the Labor Party for head of

Sderot Local Council. Peretz won an upset victory ending the town's long domination by the right-wing Likud bloc. As mayor of Sderot, Peretz promoted urban investment, improvements in local education, and increasing employment. He also took stands on national issues, campaigning against settlement building in the Palestinian territories, and supporting the establishment of a Palestinian state. These were highly controversial positions at that time.

Entry into National Politics Peretz entered national politics in 1988 when he was elected to the twelfth Knesset as a member of the Labor Party. He became a member of "the eight," a group of eight young Labor Knesset members led by Yossi Beilin, and which also included Avraham Burg and Haim Ramon, who advocated a more dovish Labor policy toward Israel's conflict with the Palestinians. They favored a complete Israeli withdrawal from the West Bank and Gaza and a negotiated two-state solution to the conflict.

In 1994, together with Ramon, Peretz challenged the Labor Party's longtime control over the Histadrut, Israel's powerful trade union federation. Running against the Labor Party in the Histadrut leadership elections, their independent list won, and Ramon became chair of the Histadrut and Peretz his deputy. Ramon, however, stepped down from the position the following year when he joined the Labor government after the assassination of Prime Minister YITZHAK RABIN. In December 1995 Peretz was chosen to replace Ramon as chair of the Histadrut and he was twice reelected to the position, in 1998 and 2002.

As head of the Histadrut, Peretz became a well-known public figure in Israel. He gained the image of a leader for the working class. In his first term as Histadrut chair, he was an outspoken and combative leader who frequently clashed with the government over its neoliberal economic agenda involving privatization and cuts in public sector employment. He fiercely defended the deficit-ridden public sector in Israel and supported many strikes by local trade unions. He led numerous general strikes and long-term sanctions ("go-slow" strikes) to protest things such as the failure to pay municipal workers' salaries for months. Peretz also attempted to reform the Histadrut itself, which over the years had become increasingly unwieldy and inefficient.

Later in his tenure, Peretz became more moderate. The number and frequency of strikes decreased, and Peretz focused more on trying to win over public opinion and policy makers. He campaigned for a number of disadvantaged and underprivileged groups, such as the disabled and single mothers. He also campaigned, without success, for a higher minimum wage.

In 1999 Peretz left the Labor Party to form a new party, Am Ehad (One Nation) with a social democratic platform focusing on social welfare issues. The party won two seats in the Knesset elections of 1999, and three seats in the elections of 2003. The party remained outside the government following both elections. Peretz nevertheless gained popularity with the poor and working class as an opponent of free-market economic reform policies, especially those pursued by BINYAMIN NETANYAHU during his tenure as Israel's finance minister (2003–2005), which involved privatization of public services and companies and severe welfare cuts.

Leader of the Labor Party In 2004 Peretz's Am Ehad Party merged with Labor. After the merger, Peretz began campaigning for the leadership of the Labor Party. His platform emphasized social justice, anti-poverty programs, and welfare. He called for Labor to return to its former social democratic, progressive orientation, and to withdraw from the coalition government with ARIEL SHARON's Likud Party. In the contest for party leadership, the incumbent, party stalwart, former prime minister and Nobel Peace Prize–winner Shimon Peres was considered to be the strong favorite. Peretz was seen as an outsider, not part of the Ashkenazi (European Jewish) elite who ran the party.

When the party election occurred in November 2005, however, Peretz scored an upset victory, narrowly beating Peres. As the new leader, he pulled the party out of the government coalition. This move deprived the Sharon government of its Knesset majority and led to a general election in March 2006. Peretz resigned from his position as Histadrut leader and concentrated on his campaign to become prime minister.

In the March 2006 election, the Labor Party won nineteen Knesset seats, coming in second to the new centrist Kadima Party led by Ehud Olmert, who took over the party after Sharon's stroke in January 2006. After coalition negotiations, Labor agreed to join a Kadima-led coalition government with Olmert as prime minister. Peretz tried unsuccessfully for the Ministry of Finance, but instead accepted the job of defense minister, a position that could potentially have improved his credentials in a politically crucial area. He was also made deputy prime minister.

Peretz's appointment as defense minister was a surprise to many, as he was not a former general and was best known for his commitment to social issues. While some worried whether Peretz had the right credentials for this important and prestigious post, others hoped that he would cut the country's large defense budget (as he had promised voters in the run-up to the election), and pursue less aggressive military tactics against the Palestinians in the West Bank and Gaza.

I INTEND TO TRAVEL TOWARDS PEACE

In 1977 Menachem Begin, who then stood at the head of the Likud, created a revolution and removed the Labour Party from power. Begin's revolution was a social revolution, based on promises of social change and on giving a feeling of belonging to the working class, which felt that the Labour Party was alienated from them. Begin carried out a social revolution, but used the "train ticket" he received from the people to travel to the occupied Palestinian territories.

I would like to be the Menachem Begin of the Labour Party, to return to it the social values and the support of the people. If I receive from the people the same "train ticket" that they once gave to Begin, I intend to travel with it towards peace.

AMIR PERETZ, IN LEE, ERIC. "INTERVIEW WITH AMIR PERETZ, LEADER OF THE HISTADRUT AND CANDIDATE FOR HEAD OF THE ISRAEL LABOUR PARTY." *LABOURSTART*, 12 JUNE 2005. AVAILABLE FROM HTTP://WWW.LABOURSTART.ORG.

Defying this hope, however, Peretz, a longtime dove, supported more bellicose actions and policies as defense minister. In particular, he enthusiastically backed Prime Minister Olmert in waging war against the Lebanese guerrilla group Hizbullah in July 2006, in response to Hizbullah's abduction of two Israeli soldiers inside Israel on 12 July 2006.

The monthlong war between Israel and Hizbullah, in which more than one thousand people (mostly Lebanese civilians) were killed and over a million (Lebanese and Israeli civilians) displaced, ended inconclusively. Olmert and Peretz were severely criticized for mishandling the war and many Israelis demanded their resignations. Peretz's domestic popularity greatly declined, and many of his former supporters on the left were bitterly disappointed with him over his role in what they regarded as a costly, misguided war. As a result, in the next election for the leadership of the Labor Party, Peretz was defeated in the first round of voting held on 28 May 2007. Following that, he resigned as defense minister on 15 June 2007.

INFLUENCES AND CONTRIBUTIONS

Peretz was influenced by the progressive social vision of traditional Labor Zionism. Labor Zionist ideology espoused a combination of socialism and Jewish nationalism and sought to create an egalitarian society. The modern Labor Party has its origins in the Labor Zionist movement, but over the decades it has abandoned Labor Zionism's socialist economic program and commitment to egalitarianism. Peretz tried to return the party to its social democratic roots. He wanted to maintain the welfare state in Israel and defend the interests of workers and the poor.

Peretz's opposition to neoliberal economic reforms was also influenced by traditional European social democratic ideas, and the development of a "third way" political-economic approach (pioneered by Tony Blair in the United Kingdom) that attempts to reconcile an expanding free-market economy with social solidarity and the continued provision of public services.

Peretz succeeded in bringing greater public attention to rising social inequality and the plight of the poor and the working class, and thus helped place social issues higher on the Israeli political agenda. He did not, however, bring about a significant change in Israel's socioeconomic policies, which continue to be strongly neoliberal and market-oriented.

THE WORLD'S PERSPECTIVE

Peretz came to international attention only when he became defense minister in the Olmert government. His appointment was greeted with some skepticism abroad because of his lack of military credentials, in contrast to many of Israel's previous defense ministers. He is best known internationally for his role in overseeing Israel's war with Hizbullah in July 2006. Since many people inside and outside Israel were critical of Israel's conduct of this war, international perceptions of Peretz became more negative; he was seen to be a weak, inexperienced, and ineffective defense minister.

LEGACY

Peretz's chief legacy is likely to be his demonstration that it is possible to rise to the top in Israel from a lowly social background. Peretz showed that a Mizrahi Jew from a poor development town on Israel's periphery could become leader of the traditionally Ashkenazi-dominated Labor Party. This helped dispel the party's longstanding image as the party of the Ashkenazi intellectual and economic elite. Under Peretz's leadership, the Labor Party received greater support from working-and lower-middle-class voters, who were attracted by Peretz's emphasis on welfare and social issues.

By attaining the position of defense minister, arguably the second most important political post in Israel, Peretz also challenged the view that only former generals and others with impressive military credentials could lead

the state's powerful defense establishment. The widespread criticisms of his performance in this role, however, renewed the belief of many Israelis that the position should be occupied only by someone with extensive military experience. Peretz's political accomplishments were overshadowed by his poor performance as defense minister and his role in the perceived failure of Israel's 2006 war with Hizbullah.

BIBLIOGRAPHY

Lee, Eric. "Interview with Amir Peretz, Leader of the Histadrut and Candidate for Head of the Israel Labour Party." *LabourStart*, 12 June 2005. Available from http://www.labourstart.org.

Pappe, Ilan. "The Disappointing Trajectory of Amir Peretz." *London Review of Books* 27, no. 24 (15 December 2005). Available from http://www.lrb.co.uk.

Dov Waxman

PORTMAN, NATALIE
(1981–)

Natalie Portman (born Natalie Hershlag) is world famous, Academy Award–nominated Israeli American film actress, and one of the most soughtafter actresses in Hollywood in the early twenty-first century.

PERSONAL HISTORY

Natalie Portman was born on 8 June 1981 in Jerusalem, Israel. She uses her grandmother's maiden name, Portman, as her professional name to protect her privacy. Her father, Avner Hershlag, is an Israeli physician and medical researcher. Her mother, Shelley Stevens, is an American homemaker. The family moved to the United States when Natalie was three years old. They lived in Maryland, Connecticut, and, starting in 1990, on Long Island in New York. A major Hollywood actress, Portman said in *Rolling Stone* that although she loves the United States and lives there, "my heart's in Jerusalem … that's where I feel at home."

At age eleven, she was discovered by a modeling scout at a pizza parlor in New York state, but she was not interested in modeling. She decided to go into acting after spending three summers at the Stagedoor Manor Performing Camp. Still, coming from a well-educated family, Portman always insisted that she wanted to go to college, even after she began acting. When she began attending Harvard University in 1999 she gave up all acting jobs except the *Star Wars* trilogy to which she was

Natalie Portman. EVAN AGOSTINI/GETTY IMAGES.

BIOGRAPHICAL HIGHLIGHTS

Name: Natalie Portman (born Natalie Hershlag)

Birth: 1981, Jerusalem, Israel

Family: Single

Nationality: Israeli, American

Education: B.A. (psychology), Harvard University, 2003. Graduate work at the Hebrew University of Jerusalem, 2004

PERSONAL CHRONOLOGY:

- **1994:** Appears in her first film, *Léon* (also known as *The Professional*)
- **1995:** Appears in *Heat*
- **1996:** Earns Tony Award nomination for Broadway performance of *The Diary of Anne Frank*
- **1999:** Release of *Star Wars: Episode I—The Phantom Menace*
- **2004:** Earns Academy Award nomination and a Golden Globe Award for Best Supporting Actress for *Closer*
- **2006:** Appears in *V for Vendetta* and *Free Zone*

committed, and she graduated from school early in 2003. Portman returned to acting thereafter, although she did pursue graduate coursework in Israel in 2004 when filming in her home country.

INFLUENCES AND CONTRIBUTIONS

Portman grew up in a well-traveled, well-cultured family, and her parents also pushed her to succeed. She began dancing when she was four years old, eventually training in jazz, tap, and ballet. Portman's first film was *Léon* (or *The Professional*; 1994). She was twelve years old at the time. The following year she appeared in *Heat* along with Hollywood heavy hitters Al Pacino and Robert De Niro. In 1996 she acted in *The Diary of Anne Frank on Broadway*, earning a Tony Award nomination in the process. The film that rocketed her to fame was the blockbuster *Star Wars: Episode I—The Phantom Menace* in 1999. She later acted in the two follow-up *Star Wars* films.

The early twenty-first century saw Portman rise to global superstar status. In 2000 she starred in *Where the Heart Is* along with Ashley Judd. Portman appeared with an all-star cast in the 2003 American civil war drama *Cold Mountain*. Her performance in the 2004 film *Closer* earned her an Academy Award nomination and a Golden Globe Award for Best Supporting Actress. In 2006 *V for Vendetta* was released, in which she played the female lead. By mid-2007, she had performed in twenty-two films, including 2006's *Free Zone*, directed by fellow Israeli Amos Gitai.

Portman also has been involved in a variety of off-camera issues and causes. She worked on behalf of Democratic Party presidential candidate John Kerry's 2004 electoral campaign. She cochairs the Foundation for International Community Assistance (FINCA International), which provides small-scale loans to women in developing countries.

THE WORLD'S PERSPECTIVE

Portman's work has been well received internationally, and she already has accumulated awards as testament. In 1996, her Broadway performance off camera in *The Diary of Anne Frank* earned her a Tony Award nomination. Her performance in the 2004 film *Closer* earned her an Academy Award nomination and a Golden Globe Award for Best Supporting Actress.

LEGACY

Natalie Portman is entering her prime as an actress, so it remains to be seen how she will make her mark on the film industry.

BIBLIOGRAPHY

Heath, Chris. "The Private Life of Natalie Portman." *Rolling Stone* (June 2002). Available from http://natalie portman.com.

Levy, Ariel. "Natalie Portman Will Change Your Life." Blender. (November 2005). Available from http://www.blender.com.

Natalie Portman's official Web site. Available from http://www.natalie portman.com.

Michael R. Fischbach

QABBANI, NIZAR
(1923–1998)

Nizar Qabbani was a renowned Syrian poet and diplomat. Known for his progressive thinking, his fame reigned supreme during his lifetime and seems to persist beyond his death.

PERSONAL HISTORY

Qabbani was born on 21 March 1923 in Damascus, Syria, to a middle-class merchant family with a Syrian father and Turkish mother. He was related to the pioneering Arab playwright Abu Khalil al-Qabbani. Nizar Qabbani studied law at the University of Damascus where he graduated in 1945 and subsequently launched a diplomatic career that year which took him to all five continents. He served in the Syrian embassies in Egypt (1945–1948), Turkey (1948), Lebanon, Britain, China, and Spain. His posting in Spain was his favorite; there he wrote some of his most memorable verse. In 1966 he retired as a diplomat and moved to Beirut, Lebanon, where he founded a publishing company called Manshurat. He became one of the Arab world's greatest poets, living the rest of his life outside Syria. He died in London on 30 April 1998.

INFLUENCES AND CONTRIBUTIONS

Qabbani's poetry covers a host of different topics and themes. More than any other modern Arab poet he has become identified with writings about the role and status of Arab women. He has been dubbed in some circles both as women's champion and detractor. He has adopted the feminist cause, defended their usurped rights, and called for them to rebel and take up arms. Yet, at the same time, he has written poetry that adulates women's beauty and bodies in the most traditional vein. Qabbani stands out amongst contemporary Arab poets as one who has written most memorable verses in defense of Arab women very often in a first person narrative:

> My dear sir
> I fear to say what I have to say
> I fear if I do
> The skies will burn
> Your East, dear sir
> Confiscates blue missives, confiscates the dreams
> stored in women's safes
> You may censure our feelings, use knives and
> axes to speak to us
> Slaughter the spring and the desires
> Your East dear sir weaves of women's skulls
> A crown of refined honorability.
> (tr. M. Mikhail)

Nizar Qabbani. AP IMAGES.

He speaks in the voice of untold women when he cries out:

Forgive me sir
If I dared venture into the kingdom of men
Classical literature of course has always been
   men's literature
And love has always been men's prerogative
And sex always the opium sold to men
A myth women's freedom in our land.
   (tr. M. Mikhail)

The suicide of his beloved sister who refused to marry a much older man she did not love had a profound effect on Qabbani's outlook on society and women. He decided to fight the social conditions he saw as leading to her death. His first of four collections, *Qasa'id min Qabbani* (1956), in many ways outlined the trajectory his work would take. His resentment of male chauvinism can be seen in the following:

I AM WOMAN
I am Woman

BIOGRAPHICAL HIGHLIGHTS

Name: Nizar Qabbani

Birth: 1923, Damascus, Syria

Death: 1998, London, United Kingdom

Nationality: Syrian

Education: B.A. (law), Damascus University, 1945

Family: Married twice. First wife: Zahra (died); one son, Tawfiq; one daughter, Hadba; second wife: Balqis al-Rawi (died 1982); one daughter, Zaynab; one son, Umar

PERSONAL CHRONOLOGY:

• **1944:** Publishes first poem, "Qalat li al-Samra"

• **1945:** Enters Syrian diplomatic service

• **1956:** Publishes first *diwan* (collection of poetry), *Qasa'id min Qabbani* (Poems from Qabbani)

• **1966:** Resigns from Syrian diplomatic service, moves to Beirut

• **1975:** Moves to London

• **1998:** Dies in London

The day I came into this world
I found the verdict of my execution ready. (tr.
   M. Mikhail)

He also wrote the collections *Qalat li al-Samra* (The brunette told me, 1942), *Tufulat Nahd* (The childhood of a breast, 1948), *Samba*, 1949, *Anti Li* (You are mine, 1950), *Qasa'id* (Poems, 1956), *Habibati* (My beloved, 1961), and *Rasm bi'l-Kalimat* (Drawing in words, 1966). In addition to his deep concern and love for women, Qabbani was poignantly involved in the politics of his society. Many are his famous poems memorized by the masses and the Literati. "Bread, Hashish, and the Moon" is a harsh assessment of impoverished Arab societies, which inevitably led to their defeat on all fronts. His "Hawamish ala daftar al-naqsa" (Marginalia on the notebook of the disaster, 1967) was an embittered and stinging critique of the bankrupt Arab leadership during the June 1967 debacle when Israel defeated the armies of Jordan, Syria, and Egypt. He also wrote Fath (Palestine Liberation Movement, 1968), Shu'ara al-Ard al-Muhtalla, al-Quds (Poets of the Occupied Land, Jerusalem, 1968), Manshurat Fida'iyya ala Judran Isra'il (Commando graffiti on the walls of Israel, 1970).

In addition to individual poems, Qabbani wrote more than twenty poetry collections (*diwans*). The most famous amongst them are *Habibati* (My beloved, 1961), *Al-Rasm b'il Kalimat* (Drawing with words, 1966), *Qasa'id hubbarabiyya* (Arabian love poems, 1993), and *Mudhakirat Imra'a la mubaliyya* (Memoirs of a carefree woman), which contains perhaps the largest compilation of poems narrated in the first person, as seen in the following:

YOU WANT
You want like all women
Solomon's treasures
Like all women
Pools of perfumes
Combs of ivory
A horde of slaves
You want a lord
Who will sing your glory like a parrot
Who says all day, "I love you" in the morning
Who says I love you in the evening
Who washes your feet in wine
O Shahrazad
Like all women. . . .
I am no prophet
Who throws the rod
And the sea breaks open
O Shahrazad
I am a mere worker from Damascus
I dip my loaf of bread in blood
My feelings are modest, my wages, too
I believe in bread and prophets
And like others dream of love. (tr. M. Mikhail)

THE WORLD'S PERSPECTIVE

Qabbani has been recognized as one of the Arab world's greatest modern poets. Because his language flowed beautifully in free verse form, and often captured the rhythms of everyday Syrian speech, his lyrics also readily lent themselves to song. Some of the best-known Arab singers, both men and women, have immortalized some of his best poems, thus contributing in popularizing his poetry on even a much wider scale. The well-known and beloved Abd al-Halim Hafiz—who dominated the world of song in the sixties, seventies and eighties, and continues to be popular with new generations—sang his poems to adoring crowds, so did Najat al-Saghira and Warda Jaza'iriyya among many others.

This is not to say that everyone loved Qabbani's work. His childhood and youth in Damascus left a deep imprint on his writings, not only the physical realities of minarets, bazaars, food, and accents. He captured the rebelliousness within the conservative city as evidenced in his early poem "Qalit li Al-Samraa" (What the brunette said to me), which he published at his own expense early in 1944. This poem created a controversy that was

---

CONTEMPORARIES

■

Salah Abd al-Sabbur (1931–1981) was born in Egypt and educated at Cairo University. Well versed in English literature, especially T. S. Eliot, he worked in literary journalism, contributing weekly essays on literary criticism to *al-Ahram* newspaper. He was the leading poet in Egypt until his premature death in 1981. He started writing in the romantic vein, quickly moved to socialist realism, and later showed interest in metaphysical issues. His collections include *al-Nas fi Biladi* (The people in my country, 1957), *Aqulu Lakum* (I say unto you, 1961), *Ahlam al-Faris al-Qadim* (The dreams of an ancient knight, 1964), and *Ta'amulat fi Zaman Jarih* (Meditations in a wounded time, 1971). His essays were collected in *Aswat al-Asr* (Voices of the age, 1961) and *Hatta Tabqa al-Kalima* (And the word remains, 1970). His famous poetic drama *Ma'sat al Hallaj* (The tragedy of al-Hallaj) was translated into English as *Murder in Baghdad* by I. Semaan in 1972. His other plays in verse include *Musafir Layl* (Night traveler), *al-Amira Tantazir* (The princess is waiting), *Layla wa'l-Majnun* (Laila and the madman), and *Ba'da an Yamut al-Malik* (After the king dies). He became head of the General Egyptian Book Organization, a prestigious position that also included the Egyptian National Archives at the time.

---

to be the hallmark of his whole career. He subsequently wrote a book *Qissati maa Al-Sh'ir* (My story with poetry) speaking of this specific poem where he denounced his countrymen's torpor and their confined lives, living loving in total oblivion of the world progressing around them. Yet his beloved city remained addicted to his words. When he wrote "Balqis" in honor of his beloved wife who was killed in a bombing at the Iraqi embassy in Beirut in 1982, the poem was smuggled and read widely. "The Autobiography of An Arab Executioner" was celebrated by the Damascenes as they had never celebrated a written text before. In 1988 he read it to huge applause, but also managed to anger the authorities who cut short his visit.

Qabbani is quintessentially a Damascene poet. Damascus had a lasting influence and central place in his life although he lived most of his life away from Syria, and rarely returned. His work was often denounced in political forums, such as the Syrian Parliament where he was publicly chided for his daring political stances. His collection *al-Shi'r Qindil Akhdar* (Poetry is a green lantern, 1963) comprised essays on his poetic art, and his views on literature in general. When his famous poem "Bread Hashish, and the Moon" was published, the Syrian government wanted to prosecute him for his outspoken attacks on religion and Arabism. It was then that he took refuge in Lebanon, and set up his publishing house, before finally settling in England.

LEGACY

Qabbani will be remembered as one of the greatest poets of the twentieth-century Arab world.

BIBLIOGRAPHY

Modern Arab Poets 1950–1975, Three Continents Press, 1976.

Nizar Qabbani's offical Web site. Available from http://www .nizar.net/english.htm.

Paintbrush. Journal of Poetry and Translation, ed. Ben Bennani, Truman State University.

Mona Mikhail

Mu'ammar al-Qaddafi. AP IMAGES.

QADDAFI, MU'AMMAR AL-
(c. 1942–)

Libyan leader Mu'ammar al-Qaddafi (also Moammar Gadhafi) was a junior army officer when he orchestrated a coup d'état in September 1969, ousting the Libyan monarchy and replacing it with a revolutionary government. He soon emerged as the head of the revolutionary government as well as de facto head of state. He is the second longest serving head of state in the world.

PERSONAL HISTORY

Qaddafi was born in central Libya, in the desert south of Sirte near Abou-Hadi, probably in the spring of 1942, although some accounts place his birth in 1943. He was the only surviving son, after three daughters, of a poor Bedouin family and did not attend school until he was nearly ten, when he enrolled in a local mosque school. Qaddafi later attended secondary school in Sebha in southern Libya, where his involvement in political activities eventually resulted in his expulsion. Accounts vary as to exactly why he was expelled; there is considerable evidence he was long active in organizing public protests and distributing subversive literature. Whatever the exact cause, his activities in Sebha demonstrated Qaddafi's early political inclinations and his willingness to challenge established authority.

Qaddafi finished his secondary schooling in the coastal town of Misurata where he renewed contacts with childhood friends and recruited new supporters among like-minded students. Qaddafi enrolled in the Royal Military Academy in 1963, graduating in August 1965. Commissioned as a communications officer, he completed an advanced signals course in the United Kingdom in 1966.

At the time, a career in the Libyan armed forces offered exciting opportunities for higher education and upward socioeconomic mobility, especially for talented and ambitious young men like Qaddafi from the lower levels of Libyan society. The armed forces also represented a potential avenue for political action and rapid change. From the beginning, military service for Qaddafi, with political parties and other political activities banned in Libya, was an instrument, not a goal.

Once he completed the signals course in the United Kingdom, Qaddafi was assigned to a post near Benghazi where he began to organize the network of conspirators that successfully toppled the monarchy on 1 September 1969. The central committee of the Free Unionist Officers, as the young revolutionaries named their movement, formed a ruling Revolutionary Command Council (RCC), appointing more experienced officers and civilians to senior government positions. In theory, the RCC operated as a collegial body, discussing issues and policies

BIOGRAPHICAL HIGHLIGHTS

Name: Mu'ammar al-Qaddafi

Birth: c. 1942, near Abou-Hadi, south of Sirte, Libya

Family: Wife, Safiya Farkash; five sons, Muhammed, Saif al-Islam, Al-Saadi, Al-Muatassim Billah, Khamis; one daughter, Aisha

Nationality: Libyan

Education: Royal Military Academy (graduated 1965); advanced (military) signals courses in United Kingdom

PERSONAL CHRONOLOGY:

- **1969:** Leads Free Unionist Officers in successful coup d'état, ousting King Idris I; promoted to commander-in-chief of Libyan armed forces
- **1969–present:** De facto head of state
- **1973:** Issues Third International Theory, marking commencement of Popular Revolution
- **1975:** Begins publication of *The Green Book*
- **1977:** Declares establishment of People's Authority; named secretary general of newly formed General People's Congress
- **1979:** Adopts title Leader of the Revolution

until consensus was reached. In practice, Qaddafi, who had been appointed commander-in-chief of the armed forces, was able to impose his will through a combination of personality and argument, to the extent that all major domestic and foreign policies reflected his thinking. It soon became evident that he was directing the RCC and was de facto head of state.

The initial policies of the revolutionary government reflected Qaddafi's Islamist roots, together with his support for Arab nationalism. Consumption of alcohol was prohibited, churches and nightclubs were closed, foreign-owned banks were seized, and Arabic was decreed the only acceptable language for use in official and public communications. Later, the American and British military bases in Libya were evacuated, the few remaining Italian residents expelled, and the oil companies subjected to increasingly stringent operating conditions.

The Revolution In 1975 Qaddafi began to summarize the ideological tenets of the revolution, what he termed

his Third International (or Universal) Theory, in a series of three short volumes, known collectively as *The Green Book*. The first part, titled "The Solution of the Problem of Democracy: The Authority of the People," developed the theoretical foundations for direct democracy, the unique system of congresses and committees he later implemented throughout Libya. The second part, "The Solution of the Economic Problem: Socialism," examined the economic dimensions of the Third International Theory, espousing socialism as an alternative to capitalism and communism. The third part, "The Social Basis of the Third International Theory," explored selected social aspects of the Third International Theory, focusing on the family, tribe, and nation.

Over the next decade, Qaddafi progressively implemented a socialist command economy in which the state took over all import, export, and distribution functions. Trumpeting socialism as the solution to mankind's economic problems, his variant of Arab socialism was doctrinal as opposed to pragmatic. It was also highly nationalistic in a region where nationalism and socialism have often been found together. Early statements stressed the indigenous nature of Libyan socialism, portraying it as both an integral part of Libyan political culture and a necessary corrective action. In arguing that socialism stemmed from the heritage of the Libyan people and the heart of the Libyan nation, his approach mirrored what has happened elsewhere in the Arab world where the character of socialism has often been discussed in the context of local history and custom.

In September 1976 Qaddafi announced a plan to create a new national-level representative body, called the General People's Congress (GPC) with an executive body, the General People's Committee, to replace the RCC as the supreme instrument of government. In March 1977 he issued the "Declaration of the Establishment of the People's Authority," stating that direct popular authority would henceforth be the basis for the political system in Libya. At the same time, he changed the official name of the country to the Socialist People's Libyan Arab Jamahiriya. *Jamahiriya* was a newly coined Arabic word with no official meaning, but is generally translated as "people's power" or "state of the masses."

Qaddafi served as secretary general of the General People's Committee, in effect prime minister, until 1979 when he resigned to concentrate on what he described as "revolutionary activities with the masses." It was at this point that he adopted the title Leader of the Revolution. Since that time, Qaddafi has held no official governmental position; nevertheless, he has remained at the center of power and policy making.

Foreign Relations At the outset, Qaddafi pursued a very aggressive foreign policy, based on his interpretation of

Arab nationalism, neutrality, and Arab unity. A strong and vocal advocate of Arab unity, his many attempts to unite Libya with one or more Arab states all ended in failure. Adamantly opposed to colonialism and capitalism, Qaddafi advocated jihad, broadly defined to include economic, political, and military action, as the solution to the Arab-Israeli dispute. Libya's stance on the Palestinian issue influenced its foreign policy in other areas, especially its posture toward terrorism. In so doing, Qaddafi's foreign policy increasingly brought Libya into conflict with its African and Arab neighbors as well as the United States and other Western governments.

By the late 1970s, the United States, which initially had viewed the 1 September Revolution with tolerance, had branded Libya one of the world's principal sponsors of terrorism. Qaddafi's vitriolic condemnation of the Camp David Accords, large arms purchases, support for national liberation movements, and campaign to assassinate opponents abroad combined to justify a U.S. campaign that culminated in the bombing of Libya in April 1986. In the wake of the attack, Qaddafi appeared to moderate elements of Libyan foreign policy; nevertheless, his regime was later implicated in the bombings of Pan Am 103 in December 1988 and UTA 772 in September 1989.

Severe economic problems in the second half of the 1980s, together with the implosion of the Soviet Union at the end of the decade, contributed to a change in Libyan policy at home as well as abroad. In March 1987 Qaddafi announced the first in a series of reforms, rescinding in part earlier socialist directives. In what was dubbed "green perestroika," he envisioned an expanded role for the private sector in conjunction with limited political reforms. This early attempt to promote economic liberalization, a harbinger of things to come, failed to generate widespread popular support.

Moreover, when Qaddafi refused to cooperate with the investigations of the Pan Am 103 and UTA 772 terrorist attacks, the United Nations (UN) in 1992 imposed multilateral sanctions that contributed to mounting discontent and increased privation in Libya. The deteriorating economic situation, reflected in decreased subsidies, unpaid salaries, and a shortage of basic goods, aggravated a political condition in which Qaddafi faced growing opposition from tribal groups, Islamist forces, and the armed forces.

The UN eventually suspended its sanctions in April 1999 after Libya had remanded the two Libyan suspects in the Pan Am 103 bombing. Qaddafi responded by initiating significant changes in the tone and direction of Libyan foreign policy. He championed several new initiatives in Africa, signaling a major shift in emphasis from the Arab world to the African continent, at the same time that he strengthened long-standing diplomatic and commercial ties with key European states. In the wake of the 11 September 2001 terrorist attacks on the United States, he was an enthusiastic, early recruit to the War on Terror, condemning the attacks and expressing sympathy for the victims. Libya had long been a target of Islamist radicals, and Qaddafi's cooperation in the War on Terror was motivated in large part by his recognition of a common threat from Islamist fundamentalists.

After agreeing to pay $2.7 billion in compensation to the families of the victims of the Pan Am 103 bombing, Libya in late December 2003 renounced its unconventional weapons programs, together with related delivery systems, agreeing to international inspections to verify compliance. Welcoming this change in policy, the United States in 2004 restored diplomatic relations and lifted most of the bilateral economic sanctions in place. Remaining trade restrictions were lifted in May 2006 after the United States removed Libya from its list of state sponsors of terrorism.

Reform Qaddafi also initiated a major shift in economic policy in June 2003 when he told the GPC that the public sector had failed and should be abolished. In response, Libyan officials began to promote economic liberalization, focused on diversification, privatization, and structural modernization. Unfortunately, real performance seldom approached official rhetoric with economic reforms in the oil and gas industry proceeding much faster than reforms in other sectors of the economy. In regard to the speed and direction of reform policy, Qaddafi contributed to the prevailing confusion when he stated in July 2006 that Libya should curb the role of foreigners to ensure its wealth remained at home, a statement hardly reassuring to potential investors. One month later, he scolded the nation for its overreliance on oil and gas revenues, foreigners, and imports, telling Libyans they should manufacture the things they needed.

Whatever the speed and scope of economic reform, it is not expected to be followed by significant political liberalization. A wide range of outside organizations and individuals, from the International Monetary Fund to Freedom House to the National Democratic Institute for International Affairs, have suggested that broader governance issues must be addressed before economic reforms can prosper. The issues requiring attention include, but are not limited to, a weak rule of law, an immature legal and court system, and recurrent conflict between municipalities and the central government. In the face of these recommendations, Qaddafi has championed his direct democracy system of congresses and committees, adamantly rejecting any meaningful change in the current political system. Instead, he has made vague references to what he terms "popular capitalism,"

EXPLORING

In June 1988, the General People's Congress adopted the Great Green Charter on Human Rights in the Era of the Masses. Intended to open the way for increased economic and political liberalization, the twenty-seven articles comprising the document addressed a variety of personal rights and guarantees. Largely drawn from earlier statements by Qaddafi, the charter had been foreshadowed in the three parts of *The Green Book*. It guaranteed Libyans some freedom of movement and respect for personal liberty; however, it failed to grant them all the civil and political rights traditionally assumed under domestic and international law. For example, there remained no room for a free press on the false assumption that the Libyan people were free to express themselves in the Congress and committee system. There was no right to strike because Libyans were in theory the owners of the factories where they worked. There was no place for organized opposition because Libyans theoretically were free to express their opposition within the existing political system. Consequently, elementary civil rights continued to be denied to Libyans citizens after 1988.

envisioning a hybrid economic system that would be compatible with unchanged direct democracy.

INFLUENCES AND CONTRIBUTIONS

During his formative years, decisive political events in the Middle East, including the 1948 Arab defeat by Israel in Palestine, the 1952 Egyptian revolution, the 1956 Suez crisis, and the 1958 Egypt-Syria union, strongly influenced Qaddafi's world outlook. His studies in Sebha gave him for the first time regular access to Arab newspapers and radio broadcasts, especially the *Voice of the Arabs* news program from Cairo. From that time forward, he was a fervent admirer of Egyptian President Gamal Abdel Nasser. The anti-imperialist, Arab nationalist foreign policies, and egalitarian, socialist domestic reforms of the Egyptian revolution were wildly popular throughout the region; Qaddafi separated himself from most other Arab youth in his determination to bring the revolution to his own country.

Borrowed from the organization of the Egyptian revolution, the Free Unionist Officers movement and the RCC were outward signs of Egyptian influence. In addition, the

three goals of the 1969 Libyan revolution, freedom, socialism, and (pan-Arab) unity, were the same three goals proclaimed by Nasser at the outset of the Egyptian revolution. The ideological similarities between the two revolutions were doubly significant because Qaddafi in late 1969 was speaking almost two decades after Nasser came to power in 1952 and long after selected policies associated with the revolutionary trinity had been discredited elsewhere in the Arab world. As a result, Qaddafi's early attempts to promote them, especially Arab unity, were widely considered anachronistic and generally rejected.

Disenchanted with Nasser's successor, Anwar Sadat, Qaddafi by the mid-1970s had become his own political visionary and theorist, promoting the Third International Theory. The first part, "The Solution of the Problem of Democracy: The Authority of the People," proved the most enduring. The congress-committee political system in place since the mid-1970s has experienced little change, and Qaddafi has continued to reject any suggestion of political reform, arguing that the Libyan form of direct democracy is superior to the representative democracy found in the United States and elsewhere. In contrast, Qaddafi in the late 1980s began to move Libya away from the socialist command economy outlined in "The Solution of the Economic Problem: Socialism," and the breadth and depth of economic reform broadened after 2003. The third part of *The Green Book*, "The Social Basis of the Third International Theory," proved the most controversial with Qaddafi's often insular, sometimes contradictory, and occasionally reactionary views on a variety of subjects, like women, education, minorities, and the arts, an endless source of debate.

THE WORLD'S PERSPECTIVE

Few world leaders in modern times have stirred as much controversy as the charismatic Qaddafi. In the early years of the 1 September Revolution, he was celebrated as a hero by the revolutionaries and liberation movements of the world. At the same time, he was roundly condemned as a meddling, destabilizing, and dangerous influence, if not a terrorist, by many governments in and out of the region. After a prolonged period of international isolation, Qaddafi, following Libya's renunciation of weapons of mass destruction, took a more positive approach to many of the world's problems. He also remained highly unpredictable and often irascible, enhancing and not diminishing the controversial reputation that has marked his career.

LEGACY

Facing no obvious rival and not old for a head of state, Qaddafi has demonstrated the political skills necessary to remain in power. On the one hand, he is a master of the political system he created, containing potential rivals and managing issues that might unite large numbers of

TERRORISM IS AN AWFUL THING

■

The first part concerns America as an aggressed over [state], whatever are justifications of those who committed it. America, as any other states and individuals, has the right to defend itself, either in accordance with article 51 of the UN Charter, that is actually inoperative or with else. [The] right of self defense is a legitimate matter. And America possesses the power enabling it to [do so]. In this regard, America does not need anybody to defend itself, strike its enemy or even get assistance to justify that. It is a kind of flattering to show readiness to assist America in a matter concerning her and capable of [her]. The second part, terrorism, this matter does not concern America alone. It concerns all the world. This needs an international cooperation and international procedure. America could not fight it alone. And it is illogic and useless to charge America with this mission. What a pity! mingling has appeared, as well as indistinctment, and confusion in perception. Proceeding and cooperation in this matter (terrorism) is not a service to America like flatterers have shown. It is a self defense for each of us. Either America was hit on 9/11 or not, America should not reward who fight terrorism inasmuch as fighting terrorism is not a service to America as those show. It is rather a service to yourself, who among us likes terrorism … who among us likes to live with his children, people and state in a world where terrorism prevails. Terrorism is an awful thing.

AL-GATHAFI SPEAKS… "BROTHER LEADER OF THE REVOLUTION MOAMMAR GHADHAFI PRESENTS AN ANALYSIS ABOUT THE ACTUAL CRISIS THE WORLD IS PASSING THROUGH ABOUT TERRORISM." AVAILABLE FROM HTTP://WWW.ALGATHAFI .ORG/EN/TERRORISM_EN.HTM.

BIBLIOGRAPHY

El-Kikhia, Mansour O. *Libya's Qaddafi: The Politics of Contradiction.* Gainesville: University Press of Florida, 1997.

Joffé, George. "Libya and Europe." *Journal of North African Studies* 6, no. 4 (Winter 2001): 75–92.

Matar, Khalil I., and Robert W. Thabit. *Lockerbie and Libya.* Jefferson, NC, and London: McFarland, 2004.

Obeidi, Amal. *Political Culture in Libya.* Richmond, U.K.: Curzon, 2001.

Qaddafi, Muammar. *Escape to Hell and Other Stories.* Montreal and New York: Stanké, 1998.

————. *My Vision.* London: John Blake, 2005.

St John, Ronald Bruce. *Libya and the United States: Two Centuries of Strife.* Philadelphia: University of Pennsylvania Press, 2002.

————. "Libyan Foreign Policy: Newfound Flexibility." *Orbis* 47, no. 3 (Summer 2003): 463–477.

————. "Round Up the Usual Suspects: Prospects for Regime Change in Libya." *Journal of Libyan Studies* 4, no. 1 (Summer 2003): 5–21.

————. "'Libya Is Not Iraq': Preemptive Strikes, WMD and Diplomacy." *Middle East Journal* 58, no. 3 (Summer 2004): 386–402.

————. *Historical Dictionary of Libya.* 4th ed. Lanham, MD: Scarecrow Press, 2006.

Vandewalle, Dirk. *Libya since Independence: Oil and State-Building.* Ithaca, NY: Cornell University Press, 1998.

————. *A History of Modern Libya.* New York: Cambridge University Press, 2006.

————, ed. *Qadhafi's Libya, 1969–1994.* New York: St. Martin's Press, 1995.

Zoubir, Yahia H. "The United States and Libya: From Confrontation to Normalization." *Middle East Policy* 13, no. 2 (Summer 2006): 48–70.

Ronald Bruce St John

QADDAFI, SAIF AL-ISLAM AL- (1972–)

Saif (Sayf, Seif) al-Islam al-Qaddafi MUʿAMMAR AL-QADDAFI is the eldest son of Libyan leader.

PERSONAL HISTORY

Saif al-Islam Muʿammar al-Qaddafi was born in Tripoli, Libya, on 25 June 1972. He is the eldest son of Libyan leader Muʿammar al-Qaddafi by Muʿammar's second wife, Safiya Farkash. Saif graduated with a B.Sc. in engineering science from al-Fatah University in Tripoli in 1994. From November 1994 until November 1995, he fulfilled his service in the Libyan military. Qaddafi received his M.B.A. from IMADEC University in Vienna, Austria, in 2000. Thereafter he returned to Libya and worked with the National Engineering Service and

Libyans in opposition. On the other hand, no clear rules exist to name his successor; and with no formal mechanism in place to ensure a smooth transition of power, the post-Qaddafi era could well be a time of tension and uncertainty with a wide variety of groups vying for power. As for the political institutions created by Qaddafi, they offer elements of participation and representation, as well as fulfilling important distributive and security functions. Consequently, they could prove valuable to his successor and might well be maintained for some time without major overhaul.

BIOGRAPHICAL HIGHLIGHTS

Name: Saif al-Islam al-Qaddafi (Sayf al-Islam, Seif al-Islam)

Birth: 1972, Tripoli, Libya

Family: Unmarried

Nationality: Libyan

Education: B.Sc. (engineering science), al-Fatah University, Tripoli, 1994; M.B.A., IMADEC University, Vienna, Austria, 2000; Ph.D. studies (international governance), London School of Economics

PERSONAL CHRONOLOGY:

- **1994:** Enters service in the Libyan military
- **1997:** Founds Qaddafi International Charity Foundation
- **2000:** Helps free hostages held by the Abu Sayyaf group in the Philippines
- **2003:** Helps negotiate compensation settlement with families of victims of the 1988 bombing of Pan Am 103 over Scotland

1988 bombing of a Pan American Airways jet over Lockerbie, Scotland. The result was that the United Nations lifted the sanctions it had imposed on Libya less than one month later.

THE WORLD'S PERSPECTIVE

Qaddafi is widely viewed in international circles as the possible successor to his father, even though neither of them holds official positions in the Libyan government. Urbane and multilingual, he cuts a dramatically different image than that of his father, and is seen by some as the symbol of the new Libya.

LEGACY

It is too early to assess Qaddafi's legacy, but it already appears as if he will be remembered as a key player in Libya's early twenty-first-century attempts to end its diplomatic isolation and pariah status and return to the international community.

BIBLIOGRAPHY

Ronen, Yehudit. "Libya's Rising Star: Saif al-Islam and Succession." *Middle East Policy* 12, no. 3 (Fall 2005). Available from http://www.mepc.org.

Michael R. Fischbach

Supplies Company, of which he was a co-owner. Qaddafi began Ph.D. studies in international governance at the London School of Economics in 2002.

He heads the Qaddafi International Charity Foundation, which he founded in 1997. Qaddafi also is president of the Libyan National Association for Drugs and Narcotics Control. He speaks Arabic, French, German, and English.

INFLUENCES AND CONTRIBUTIONS

Qaddafi has served as his father's envoy and has been the key player in several dramatic changes in Libyan policy in the first years of the twenty-first century, including Libya's 2003 announcement that it had abandoned its weapons of mass destruction programs and aspirations, and that it no longer considered Israel a threat. He also articulated the policy that Libya would compensate its former Jewish citizens for property seized from them.

His charity is seen as the vehicle by which he pursues policy around the world. In 2000 Qaddafi and his charity helped free Western hostages being held by the militant Abu Sayyaf group in the southern Philippines. The charity also negotiated the August 2003 compensation deal with the relatives of passengers killed in the December

QANUNI, YUNUS
(1957–)

Mohammad Yunus Qanuni (Qanouni, Qanooni) is a central figure in the political history of modern Afghanistan. A Tajik by ethnicity, Qanuni was the main opposition candidate to President HAMID KARZAI in the Afghan elections of 2005. Qanuni is the most well-known protégé of the famous Tajik leader and resistance fighter Ahmad Shah Masoud. Qanuni actively served in Masoud's resistance militia operating from the Panjsher valley, first against the Soviets and then against the Taliban forces. Since Masoud's assassination in September 2001, Qanuni has remained the most influential and well-known Tajik politician in Afghanistan.

PERSONAL HISTORY

Qanuni was born in 1957 in the Panjsher Valley in Northern Afghanistan. After completing his basic schooling, he ventured to the capital city Kabul to pursue his higher education. One key variable in understanding Qanuni's role and influence in Afghanistan is ethnicity, which arguably represents the most pivotal factor in making sense of the power dynamics in Afghanistan at any particular

Yunus Qanuni. ROBERT NICKELSBERG/GETTY IMAGES.

BIOGRAPHICAL HIGHLIGHTS

Name: Yunus Qanuni (Qanouni, Qanooni)

Birth: 1957, Panjshir Valley, Afghanistan

Nationality: Afghan (ethnic Tajik)

Education: Graduated from the Faculty of Islamic Law, Kabul University, 1980

PERSONAL CHRONOLOGY:

- **1993:** Appointed minister of the Interior of the government headed by Burhanuddin Rabbani
- **2001:** Head of the party delegation at the UN Talks on Afghanistan held in Bonn, Germany; confirmed as Interior minister of the Afghan Interim Administration
- **2002:** Named education minister and adviser on internal security to the presidency in the cabinet of the Transitional Administration
- **2004:** Comes in second in the Afghan presidential elections, losing to Hamid Karzai

moment in history. Qanuni belongs to the Tajik ethnic group which composes roughly 20 percent of the Afghan population. The majority of the population is Pashtun (also Pakhtun, around 70%), with the rest being Uzbeks, Hazaras, and other ethnicities. Situated in close proximity to the Central Asian countries of Tajikistan and Uzbekistan, Afghanistan's narrative of nationhood has always been wrapped in the politics of ethnicity. Moreover, the story of Afghanistan's political history has been most impacted by the continuous tussle for political and cultural authority between the Tajiks and the Pashtuns. The formation, development, and evolution of Qanuni's political career each represent a direct product of this ethnocentric struggle for power, which has dominated the political and indeed the cultural landscape of Afghanistan for at least the past five decades.

The other key variable in understanding Qanuni's contribution to Afghan society relates to his close association with the late Tajik leader and resistance fighter Masoud. Masoud was the biggest influence on Qanuni's development as a politician, soldier, and social critic. The Lion of the Panjshir, as he was popularly called, Masoud was a resistance fighter against the Soviets in the 1980s and again against the Taliban in the mid- and late 1990s. Masoud trained and groomed a new generation of Tajik

leaders and resistance fighters who were charged with the mission of advancing the interests of the Tajik population in Afghanistan both politically and militarily.

Qanuni's Political Journey: From 1979 until September 2001 The conditions of political and ethnic relations that have allowed Qanuni to rise in stature both as a politician and as a social activist can reasonably be dated back to the Soviet invasion of Afghanistan in December 1979. It was following this invasion that Qanuni returned to the Panjhir Valley from Kabul and joined Masoud's resistance forces. The next most important juncture in Qanuni's career came in 1993 when the Mojahedin (Resistance Fighters) forces came to power in Afghanistan. As a result, Qanuni became joint defense minister in the government led by his fellow Tajik Burhanuddin Rabbani. The ensuing civil war between Afghan's warring factions (mostly along ethnic lines) directly affected Qanuni when his car was blown up near Kabul in 1993 and he was seriously wounded. After the fall of Kabul to the Taliban three years later, Qanuni helped found the Supreme Council for the Defense of the Motherland, and later the United Islamic and National Front for the Salvation of Afghanistan. He headed several Afghan delegations for talks with exiled leaders in Europe, including former king Zahir Shah in an attempt to unite all anti-Taliban factions.

Ahmad Shah Masoud's Assassination and the Impact of 9/11 The most transformative event in Qanuni's career was the sudden assassination of his longtime mentor Masoud in September 2001. Because Qanuni's political life was so strongly influenced by his close relationship with Masoud, the latter's sudden death naturally represented a major turning point in the former's career. Masoud was assassinated by suicide bombers disguised as journalists, just a few days before the 11 September 2001 attacks on the United States. After the attacks and the ensuing U.S. war on the Taliban, Qanuni's political prominence rose exponentially as he emerged as the obvious political and military heir to the late Masoud, and was widely recognized as the new leader of the Tajik community in Afghanistan.

The Fall of the Taliban and the Bonn Conference Qanuni was a major player in the U.S.-backed Northern Alliance that helped depose the Taliban in late 2001. After the fall of the Taliban and the subsequent severe power vacuum in Afghanistan, Qanuni's position in the political milieu of the country again rose significantly. The United States and United Nations were keen to address this political vacuum by facilitating the creation of an immediate interim Afghan government. In late November, various Afghan factions assembled in Bonn, Germany, to discuss the formation of this new government. Qanuni is said to have impressed several attendees (both Afghan and non-Afghan) at the conference by his skills of argumentation and political maneuvering, and more importantly, he also managed to secure a major position in the newly formed Afghan cabinet, that of the interior minister. The achievement of this cabinet position has been Qanuni's biggest political victory to date.

In a major setback to his political career, however, Qanuni resigned as interior minister during the emergency Loya Jirga (consultative assembly) in 2003, a move he hoped would win him an even higher position in the cabinet. Exactly the opposite happened, as President Karzai offered him only the ministry of education. Agitated by this treatment at the hands of a Pashtun leader, Qanuni threatened to resign altogether but was persuaded to stay in the cabinet after he was appointed special presidential adviser on security issues. In the 2004 elections, Qanuni ran against Karzai for the presidency of Afghanistan but was heavily defeated. Following this defeat, Qanuni was elected in the 2005 Afghan parliamentary elections, placing second in the Kabul province. In addition to establishing a political party of his own, Mehez-e-Milli (Afghan National Party), Qanuni has formed an alliance of several parties opposed to the current government called the Jabahai Tafahim Milli (National Understanding Front).

THE WORLD'S PERSPECTIVE

Qanuni is seen by the world as Karzai's main political rival in Afghanistan. More generally, he is regarded as a moderate, intelligent, and battle-hardened politician. Qanuni's global stock has somewhat fallen since his unsuccessful campaign for the presidency, but he nonetheless remains a major figure in the political whirlpool of Afghanistan, primarily because of his loyal following in a large section of the Tajik community who regard him as the heir apparent to their political and military hero, Masoud. Countries directly invested in the future of Afghanistan—the United States, Russia, and the Central Asian Republics—are mindful of Qanuni's importance when determining the ethnopolitical climate of the country. From their long and often tumultuous engagement with Afghan society, these foreign countries are well aware of the central role that ethnicity plays in shaping and sustaining the contours of Afghanistan's social, political, and cultural structures.

Qanuni's image in the eyes of the world, however, varies considerably from country to country. Because Qanuni is ethnically a Tajik, he is looked upon most favorably by Tajikistan. Uzbekistan, on the other hand, does not hold a very positive image of Qanuni because its vested interest lies in supporting the most influential Uzbek leader in Afghanistan, Rashid Ahmad Dostum. Pakistan has traditionally harbored the most hostile attitude toward Qanuni and toward Afghan Tajik politicians in general. All Tajik leaders, including Qanuni, his mentor Masoud, and his close associate Rabbani, have been staunch opponents of Pakistan's involvement in Afghan politics. Pakistan's consistent support and preference for rival Pashtun leaders such as Gulbaddin Hekmatyar is the main reason for this strong opposition. Moreover, Pakistan's central role in the creation and training of the Taliban further exacerbated these sentiments. Naturally then, Qanuni is not seen in a positive light by Pakistan. The United States and Russia have adopted a more fluid attitude toward Qanuni and other Afghan politicians, as self-interest, more than anything else, has determined these two countries' stance. For example, although Qanuni was generously supported by the United States immediately after the fall of the Taliban, U.S. support for him dwindled significantly in the 2005 Afghan elections when the trusted U.S. ally Karzai was favored to hold on to the presidency. Although all countries of the world with a vested interest in Afghanistan regard Qanuni as an important and indispensable figure in the geopolitics of Afghanistan, their individual attitude toward him varies considerably according to their specific foreign policy goals.

LEGACY

Qanuni's legacy will invariably be connected to his ethnicity. He will be remembered as a major Tajik leader who resisted both internal and external hostile forces and who doggedly fought for the political and social advancement of his community at a critical juncture in Afghanistan's history. Though his political career is far from over, the contours of Qanuni's legacy will be most strongly influenced by three major periods of his life: the period of armed resistance against the Soviets that saw Qanuni's military and political training at the hands of his mentor Masoud; the period immediately following the fall of the Taliban that included Qanuni's sterling performance at the Bonn Conference and during which a new Afghan government was established; and the Afghan elections of 2004 when Qanuni ran unsuccessfully against his former boss Karzai.

The direction of Qanuni's legacy in the future depends most heavily on the success of the current Karzai government in curbing the influence of the Taliban and in fulfilling Karzai's promises of economic growth and development in this war-torn nation. Intense dissatisfaction with the current government may lead to a political opening for Qanuni. But given the current state of affairs, with strong U.S. backing for Karzai and a general desire for stable government pervading the country, the possibility of such a development is slim. Due to his strong standing among the Tajik community of Afghanistan, however, Qanuni is likely to remain a major player in the political sphere of Afghanistan for a considerable amount of time.

BIBLIOGRAPHY

Entekhabi-Fard, Camelia. "Qanooni's Rejection Ends Afghan Council on a Bumpy Note." *Eurasianet.* Updated 20 June 2002. Available from http://www.eurasianet.org.

Ewans, Martin. *Afghanistan: A Short History of Its People and Politics.* New York: HarperCollins, 2002.

"In 'Mostly Fair' Afghan Election, Karzai Appears Likely Winner." *Online Newshour Update.* Updated 11 October 2004. Available from http://www.pbs.org/newshour.

Qanooni, Yunus. "Departing Afghan Interior Minister Won't Seek New Government Post." Interview by Camelia Entekhabi-Fard. *Eurasianet.* Updated 13 June 2002. Available from http://www.eurasianet.org.

SherAli Tareen

QARADAWI, YUSUF
(1926–)

The Egyptian cleric Yusuf Qaradawi is one of the world's most influential Sunni Muslim scholars. Extremely popular in the Middle East, his weekly television show, *al-Shari'a wa'l-Haya* (*shari'a* [Islamic law] *and Life*), is watched by some 40 million people via the Arab satellite

Yusuf Qaradawi. GRAEME ROBERTSON/GETTY IMAGES.

station, al-Jazeera. Through the Web site IslamOnline.com, Qaradawi has issued over 150 *fatwas* (Islamic legal rulings) on how to merge Islamic law with modern life. Seen as a radical extremist by some, others claim Qaradawi is a progressive voice of moderation in troubled times.

PERSONAL HISTORY

Qaradawi was born in the village of Saft Turab, Egypt, on 9 September 1926, the only child of a poor peasant family of devout Sunni Muslims. His father died before he was born, and his mother died when he was just a year old. Without parents, Qaradawi's aunts and uncles raised him, and they encouraged him to obtain a local profession such as shopkeeping or carpentry. However, Qaradawi chose to pursue a religious education, one of the few opportunities available to boys of humble backgrounds. He memorized the Qur'an before his tenth birthday and, after completing his secondary education, he enrolled at al-Azhar University in Cairo, one of the world's oldest continuously functioning universities and the most important center for Sunni Islamic scholarship.

In 1953 Qaradawi graduated from al-Azhar University's department of basics of religion and, in 1954, he earned a degree from the Arabic language department, finishing at the top of his class of five hundred students. Following his graduation, Qaradawi worked at the Institute of Imams at the Waqf Ministry of Egypt (Ministry

BIOGRAPHICAL HIGHLIGHTS

Name: Yusuf Qaradawi

Birth: 1926, Saft Turab, Egypt

Family: Wife; four daughters; three sons

Nationality: Egyptian

Education: al-Azhar University, Cairo, earned degrees in 1953 and 1954; Ph.D., 1973

PERSONAL CHRONOLOGY:

• **1954–1961:** Attends Institute of Imams, Waqf Ministry of Egypt, and Department of Islamic Culture, al-Azhar University

• **1960:** Publishes *The Lawful and the Prohibited in Islam*

• **1961:** Director, Religious Institute, Doha, Qatar

• **1973:** Founds and chairs Department of Islamic Research, University of Qatar

• **1989:** Founds and chairs Research Center of Sunna and Biography of the Prophet, University of Qatar

• **1997:** Chairs IslamOnline Committee; started IslamOnline.com; founder and president, European Council on Fatwa and Research, Dublin, Ireland

• **2000s:** Hosts *al-Shari'a wa'l-Haya* (*Shari'a and Life*), weekly television show, al-Jazeera

• **2002:** Chairs International Union for Muslim Scholars, Dublin, Ireland

of Religious Endowments) and then at the Department of Islamic Culture at al-Azhar. It was during this time that Qaradawi began his career as a writer, teacher, and scholar, and often preached at mosques in Cairo. During the late 1940s and early 1950s, he was detained in an Egyptian prison several times because of his membership in the Muslim Brotherhood organization, which was noted for antiregime activities and which eventually was banned in 1954.

In 1961, in an exchange of scholars, al-Azhar sent him to Gulf State of Qatar to run the state's Religious Institute in the capital city of Doha, where he has remained in self-imposed exile for more than four decades. In 1973 he established and became chair of the Department of Islamic Research at the University of

Qatar. In the same year, he was awarded his doctoral degree. In 1989 Qaradawi founded the Research Center of Sunna and Biography of the Prophet at the University of Qatar, which he continues to head.

In 1997 Qaradawi helped create and lead the Dublin-based European Council on Fatwa and Research, a group of Islamic scholars who consider the moral, religious, political, and social issues facing Muslims and issue *fatwas* to help Muslims live within Islamic law. In 2002 Qaradawi became head of the newly created International Union for Muslim Scholars, also based in Dublin. (The headquarters are in Ireland because Arab countries refused to allow these groups to form, whereas Irish law permits them.)

Qaradawi is the author of more than fifty books. His *The Lawful and the Prohibited in Islam*, first published in 1960, became a classic text for its practical application of Islamic law to modern life. However, he is best known for his popular Sunday evening television show *al-Shari'a wa'l-Haya*. A strong proponent of using media to education and unite the Muslim world, Qaradawi also serves as chairman of IslamOnline.com, an extensive Web site supported by the Qatar government. Approximately 150 of Qaradawi's *fatwas* appear on the site.

Far from his humble beginnings, the elderly Qaradawi, who has long enjoyed the support of the Qatar royal family, lives in a comfortable, well-adorned home in Qatar. He is married and has seven children. He remains one of the most influential Islamic scholars in the Arab world.

INFLUENCES AND CONTRIBUTIONS

Qaradawi came under the influence Hasan al-Banna and the Muslim Brotherhood during his teenage years. Al-Banna, who founded the Muslim Brotherhood in Egypt in 1928, preached religious renewal, strict discipline and prayer, fierce nationalism, and a violent rejection of the Western infiltration into the Muslim world. By the end of World War II, it had become one of the region's largest and most influential Islamic organizations. Qaradawi's association with the Muslim Brotherhood, historically known for its use of violence, resulted in several detentions in Egyptian jails. He was first imprisoned in 1949 and three times following the 1952 Egyptian revolution that brought Gamal Abdel Nasser to power. Nasser subsequently outlawed the Muslim Brotherhood in 1954. Although Qaradawi remains a member of the Muslim Brotherhood (which, since the 1980s, has toned down its violent rhetoric and has been legalized), he has refused several offers to take over leadership of the organization.

CONTEMPORARIES

Magda Amer (also Majda Amr) (c. 1951–) is a well-known female Islamic preacher in Egypt who teaches *shari'a*, *fiqh* (Islamic jurisprudence), and women's rights in Islam at the Sidiqi Mosque in Cairo's middle class Heliopolis neighborhood. In addition to more strictly religious topics, she also counsels women on how to deal with their husbands, even including material she takes from popular Western books such as *Men Are from Mars, Women Are from Venus*. Amer also is a biochemist, a lecturer in immunology at Ayn Shams University, and runs Egypt's only health food shop in Heliopolis.

Heba Kotb (also Hiba Qutb) (c. 1967–) is a medical doctor who obtained a Ph.D. in clinical sexology from Maimonides University in Florida in 2004. She runs a sex therapy clinic in Cairo's Muhandisin district, and her weekly satellite television show *Big Talk* is broadcast from Cairo throughout the Arab world, offering frank discussions about sexuality. Kotb insists that Islamic teachings encourage sexual pleasure for married couples and decries the ignorance about sexuality that pervades Arab society, particularly among women.

THE WORLD'S PERSPECTIVE

Opinions of Qaradawi range widely. Considered by many in the Arab world as a voice of moderation, he is often branded as a violent extremist in the West. He also incurs the wrath of some fundamentalist Muslims who believe that Qaradawi concedes too much to the infiltration of Western ideals, such as women's rights and democracy. Qaradawi's *fatwas* have sparked significant controversy across the board, especially his rulings regarding women's rights, homosexuality, and condoning of the Palestinian use of suicide bombers.

Qaradawi's ideas regarding women draw mixed reviews. Breaking with fundamentalist Islamic scholars, he believes strongly that education should be available to all Arabs—men and women alike—and he supports women's right to work outside the home. He has also called for more women to serve as jurists and even as judges. In fact, three of Qaradawi's four daughters hold doctoral degrees from a British university, and the fourth earned her master's degree at the University of Texas. All of them work and drive. However, Qaradawi

has also supported the rights of a husband to beat his wife—as a last resort and only to do so lightly—as well as the compulsory wearing of the *hijab* (women's head covering).

On the issue of homosexuality, Qaradawi's *fatwas* are decisive: Homosexuality is a perversion and a corruption of human sexuality and should be punished. According to a television interview with the Middle East Media Research Institute (MEMRI), which aired on al-Jazeera on 6 June 2006, Qaradawi said that homosexuals should receive "the same punishment as any sexual pervert—the same as the fornicator." In the Arab region, where homosexuality is commonly treated as a crime punishable by fines or incarceration—less severe than the punishment for fornication—Qaradawi's teachings on the subject are seldom questioned. However, many Westerners and Europeans, who are outraged by his implied approval of extreme punishment, consider his views extremely homophobic. His acknowledgement that Islamic scholars disagree on the terms of punishment has done little to assuage the anger of the human rights community. According to MEMRI, Qaradawi commented: "Some [scholars] say we should throw them from a high place, like God did with the people of Sodom. Some say we should burn them, and so on. There is disagreement."

For his part, Qaradawi appears genuinely baffled by the West's tolerance of gays and lesbians. "One wonders if the West has given up on Christianity," he told British newspaper the *Guardian* in 2005. "We supposed that the West's history and roots were in Christianity and the latter objects to homosexuality. The Torah also says sodomy is punished by God. We shouldn't give the impression that Muslims are alone on this" (Bunting, p. 31).

Qaradawi has received significant attention because of his fatwa that the Palestinian use of suicide bombers—including women and children—is an acceptable form of jihad (holy war). According to BBC Monitoring, Qaradawi told his al-Jazeera television audience in 2002, "The Israelis might have nuclear bombs but we have the 'children bomb' and these human bombs must continue until liberation" (Abdelhandi, 2004). He also condoned targeting Israeli civilians. Although the United States revoked his ten-year visa in 1999, Britain—on the invitation of London's mayor, Ken Livingstone—issued Qaradawi a visa in 2004, and his visit to participate in a conference sparked considerable controversy in the country.

Qaradawi's call to violence is not indiscriminate, however. Although he declares that Palestinian suicide bombers are martyrs because Israel is a militarized occupying force (thus making all Israelis the enemy because almost all Jewish Israelis must serve in the military), he firmly condemned the terrorist attacks on the United States on 11 September 2001, and urged Muslims to give blood to help the injured. He also condemned the 7 July 2005 subway bombings in London that left fifty two dead and seven hundred injured, as well as the 19 March 2005 car bombing that occurred in Doha, Qatar, killing one British citizen and injuring numerous others.

LEGACY

There will likely be multiple and conflicting legacies related to Qaradawi. To some, he will be remembered as a violent extremist who condoned killing Israeli civilians, including women and children. He will be remembered as an instigator who encouraged terrorists and terrorist organizations such as Hamas and al-Qa'ida. Others will remember him as homophobic, pointing to his *fatwas* that condone physically punishing and perhaps even putting to death homosexuals. His secular critics will also note his rulings on the allowance of wife beating and compulsory wearing of the *hijab*.

Whereas his rulings on women's rights—including the right to an education, the right to work, and the right to participate in civil affairs—make him a man of compromise and moderation to some, Islamic fundamentalists see him as giving away too much to the West and non-Islamic culture. Likewise, Qaradawi's allowance that photography and pictures, as well as some music and art, are lawful has drawn sharp criticism as un-Islamic teachings.

Despite the complexities that will likely be reflected in Qaradawi's legacy, to millions of Muslims around the globe, Qaradawi will be remembered as an influential and authoritative voice that attempted to merge Islamic law with the modern world.

BIBLIOGRAPHY

Abdelhadi, Magdi. "Controversial Preacher with Star Status." BBC. Updated 7 July 2004. Available from http://news.bbc.co.uk.

Bunting, Madeleine. "Friendly Fire: Madeleine Bunting Meets Sheikh Yusuf al-Qaradawi in Qatar." *Guardian* (London) (29 October 2005): 31.

Miles, Hugh. "Two Faces of One of Islam's Most Important Clerics: Hugh Miles on the Man Some Call a Fanatic and Others a Moderate." *Daily Telegraph* (London) (20 July 2005).

"Muslim World Needs Democracy, Says Qaradawi." Muslim News. Updated 8 July 2006. Available from http://www.muslimnews.co.uk/.

Pearl, Judea. "Another Perspective, or Jihad TV?" *New York Times* (17 January 2007): A19.

"Qaradawi Deplores Algiers Bombings." IslamOnline. Updated 11 April 2007. Available from http://www.islamonline.com.

"The Qaradawi *Fatwas*." *Middle East Quarterly* 11, no. 3 (2004): 78–80.

Shadid, Anthony. "Maverick Cleric Is a Hit on Arab TV: Al-Jazeera Star Mixes Tough Talk with Calls for Tolerance." *Washington Post* (14 February 2003): A01.

"Sheik Yousuf Al-Qaradhawi: Homosexuals Should Be Punished Like Fornicators" [Television interview transcript]. al-Jazeera TV, 5 June 2006. Available from http://www.memritv.org/Transcript.asp?P1=1170.

Alisa Larson

QASIM, AWN AL-SHARIF
(1933–2006)

Awn al-Sharif Qasim was a leading scholar in Sudan for the last thirty years of the twentieth century. An expert on Arabic and Islamic culture and language, Qasim took a special interest in the history and people of Sudan. He was a professor and lecturer at the university level and a prolific author, writing over seventy books. He also served as his country's minister of religious affairs from 1971 to 1981.

PERSONAL HISTORY

Qasim was born in the ancient city of Khartoum, the capital of Sudan, on 13 June 1933. He was raised in Khartoum North, where his father, who emigrated from Yemen in 1925, was a local religious authority and educator in Islamic studies.

Qasim attended the College of Liberal Arts at the University of Khartoum, the country's most prestigious and selective university, and earned his bachelor's degree in 1957. Following his graduation, he entered the University of London's School of Oriental and African Studies and was awarded a master's degree in Arabic and Islamic studies in 1960. He remained at the University of London for another year, serving as a lecturer, before returning to Sudan in 1961 to take an academic post at the University of Khartoum, where he remained until 1971. He received a doctoral degree from the University of Edinburgh in Scotland in 1967.

In 1971 Qasim left the University of Khartoum to become Sudan's minister of religious affairs, a position he held for the next ten years. During that time, in 1975, he founded the Institute for Islamic Studies in Khartoum. In 1982, Qasim returned to the University of Khartoum as a professor for two years. From 1984 to 1995, he lectured at the Khartoum International Institute for Arabic Language, serving as the institute's director in 1988. In 1990 Qasim once again returned to the University of Khartoum, this time as the university's president, where he remained until 1994. In 1996 he was named president of Omdurman Ahlia University.

BIOGRAPHICAL HIHGLIGHTS

Name: Awn al-Sharif Qasim

Birth: 1933, Khartoum, Sudan

Death: 2006

Nationality: Sudanese

Education: B.A., College of Liberal Arts, University of Khartoum, 1957; M.A., School of Oriental and African Studies, University of London, 1960; Ph.D., University of Edinburgh, 1967

PERSONAL CHRONOLOGY:

- **1960–1961:** Lecturer, University of London
- **1961–1971:** Lecturer, University of Khartoum, Sudan
- **1971–1981:** Minister of religious affairs, Sudan
- **1982–1984:** Professor, University of Khartoum, Sudan
- **1984–1995:** Lecturer, Khartoum International Institute for Arabic Language
- **1990–1994:** President, University of Khartoum, Sudan
- **1996:** President, Omdurman Ahlia University, Sudan

Qasim earned numerous awards, including the Presidential Award for Scientific Achievements in 1981; the First Honor Golden Science Award for Excellence in Writing, presented by Egyptian president HUSNI MUBARAK, in 1993; and the Az-Zubair Prize for Innovation and Scientific Excellence in 2000.

Qasim died on 19 January 2006.

INFLUENCES AND CONTRIBUTIONS

During his career as one of his country's top academics and most prolific writers, Qasim wrote more than sev-enty books. Titles include *Doblmaciyat Muhammad* (1972; The diplomacy of Mohammed), *Fi ma'rakat al-turath* (1972; In war of culture), *Qamus al-lahjah al-Ammiyah fi'l-Sudan* (1972; Dictionary of Sudanese Arabic), *Risalat al-khatima* (1977; The final message), *Half-ayat al-Muluk* (1988; Dictionary of the region of Halfayat), and *Mawsu'at al-qaba'il wa'l-ansab fi'l-Sudan wa ashhar asma al-a'lam wa'l-amakin* (1996; Encyclopedia of tribes and families in Sudan).

Several of Qasim's works were major undertakings that required years of research. For example, his dictionary of Sudanese dialects, *Qamus al-lahjah al-Ammiyah fi'l-Sudan*, spans over one thousand pages. His most ambitious work, the encyclopedia *Mawsu'at al-qaba'il wa'l-ansab fi'l-Sudan wa ashhar asma al-a'lam wa'l-amakin*, was the result of over ten years of research and encompasses 2,628 pages.

THE WORLD'S PERSPECTIVE

Qasim's encyclopedic works remain some of the leading authorities in the world. For example, *Qamus al-lahjah al-Ammiyah fi'l-Sudan*, his work on Sudanese dialects, has undergone numerous reprints, including a new edition published in 2002. Similarly, the six-volume *Mawsu'at al-qaba'il wa'l-ansab fi'l-Sudan wa ashhar asma al-a'lam wa'l-amakin* is considered one of the best compilations of information on Sudanese culture, people, and history available.

LEGACY

Qasim was a leading scholar and academic in Sudan for over thirty years. During that time, he contributed to the advancement of the Sudanese culture and affirmed Islamic and Arabic culture. His work continues to provide accessible ways to encounter the history and language of Sudan.

BIBLIOGRAPHY

Karrar, 'Ali Salih. "Recent Books: A Sudanese Encyclopedia of Tribes and Genealogies." *Sudanic Africa* 8 (1997). Available from http://www.smi.uib.no/sa/8Awn.html.

Alisa Larson

RABI, MUBARAK
(1940–)

Moroccan novelist and short-story writer Mubarak Rabi (also Rabia, Rabi'a, Rabi') is a psychologist by profession. He teaches psychology at Muhammad V University in Rabat and is the dean of the College of Arts and Sciences at the University of Ben Msik, in Casablanca. He is a member of the Union of Arab writers. His fiction works are influenced by his specialty and it is clear that he considers life and assesses various human situations with the tools of a psychologist.

PERSONAL HISTORY

Rabi was born in 1935 in Sidi Ma'ashu, near Casablanca, Morocco. His undergraduate degree is in philosophy from the Faculty of Arts in Rabat. He later received a master's degree in psychology in 1975. He received his Ph.D. in 1988. He started teaching in 1952 in elementary schools while pursuing his higher education.

He experimented with poetry at the beginning of his literary career but he soon abandoned it to concentrate on fiction, writing short stories and novels. Rabi is a prolific, gifted fiction writer. He was recognized as an outstanding author and awarded the Maghribi Prize for the novel and the short story in 1971.

INFLUENCES AND CONTRIBUTIONS

Rabi is primarily concerned with the human being in his writings. His interest in them begins at childhood, and he stresses the importance of education for children, a point he makes in his novel *Badr Zamanihi* (*The Full Moon of his Time*; 1983) and the essays he wrote in "Awatif al-Tifl" (The child's emotions), 1984, and "Makhawif al-Atfal wa alaqatuha bi'l-Wasat al-Ijtima'i" (Children's fears and their connection with the social environment), 1991.

He considers creative writing an activity without boundaries or restrictions, similar to scientific research. In his view, the novel is the history of the people, especially that aspect of their life not covered by historians. Despite the impressive number of books he wrote, Rabi feels that reality is more eloquent than fiction and he does not feel that he translates this aspect of life in his novels well enough to reflect it. He derives pleasure from writing, which is an exercise that provides him with joy even when he writes about a sad topic. He does not write to fulfill a mission, or to take a stand, or to defend a certain ideology. Some of his stories are rather a gallery of portrait for real-life situations.

Rabi is interested in studying the role of magic and traditional beliefs in the lives of the Moroccans as a common and widespread tendency in his society. This is best illustrated in his collection of short stories,

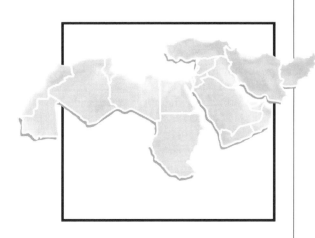

R

BIOGRAPHICAL HIGHLIGHTS

∎

Name: Mubarak Rabi (Rabia, Rabiʿa)

Birth: 1935, Sidi Maʿashu, Morocco

Nationality: Moroccan

Education: Undergraduate degree in philosophy, Faculty of Arts, Rabat; 1975, master's degree in psychology; 1988, Ph.D.

PERSONAL CHRONOLOGY:
- **1952:** Teaches elementary school
- **1969:** Publishes *Sayyidna Qadr*
- **1971:** Receives Maghribi Prize
- **1983:** Publishes *Badr Zamanihi*

Sayyidna Qadr (1969; *Saint Qadr*). One of the most touching stories in the collection is "Sayyidna Qadr"; it presents the case of a bold young woman whose dearest wish in life is to see hair grow. She prays to Sayyidna Qadr hoping for a miracle.

The writer is constantly trying to understand the motivations behind people's actions and the factors that control their good and evil tendencies. He deplores the loss of values in modern societies, which lead to conflicts between people. His fiction remains detached from the political turmoil in Morocco. This in no way means that the author lacks patriotism and did not champion the national cause when his country was under French control. His book, *Min Jibalina* (*From Our Mountains*; 1998), subtitled "Nida al-Hurriyya aw Urs al-Shahid" (The call of freedom or the wedding celebration of a martyr), celebrates the life and struggle of the Moroccan national hero, Muhammad al-Zarqtuni, one of the leaders in the struggle against French colonialism. The story of al-Zarqtuni's struggle offers an opportunity for the writer to describe Moroccan society in that time and the efforts made by many to recuperate their independence and end the exile of King Muhammad V.

A prolific writer, Rabi continues to write fiction. His latest works include a novel *Burj al Suʿud* (*The Lucky Zodiac*; 1990), a collection of short stories, *al-Balluri al-Maksur* (*The Broken Crystalline*; 1996), and a trilogy, *Darb al-Sultan* (*The Sultan's Way*; 1999–2000). His concern remains the human being and the good and evil tendencies that determine a person's actions, all seen with the eyes of a psychologist. As other writers of his generation, he sheds light on human greed, especially in rural areas where some acquire land through illegal means, as portrayed in *al-Tayyibun* (*The Good Hearted*; 1972).

Rabi's novels are anchored in Moroccan society and offer a panorama of its diverse population. His trilogy, *Darb al-Sultan* (*Al-Sultan Street*; 1999–2000), shed light on the changes that occur in his society. Most of his novels are related against the background of love stories that reflect the complexity of gender relations, especially in conservative societies.

THE WORLD'S PERSPECTIVE

Rabi is well known in the Arab world. His fiction works were published mainly outside Morocco, in Lebanon, Tunisia, and Libya. It is not clear whether the Western reader is familiar with his work. There are few translations of Rabi's work in a Western language. For those who meet him in international conferences he is primarily known for his specialty as a psychologist.

LEGACY

Through his involvement in teaching, Rabi has the opportunity to impact generations of Moroccans. As an administrator, he interacts with faculty members who are certainly touched by the message in his writings. In combining the two activities, writing and teaching psy-

---

ALL THINGS INTERACT

∎

One of many tours that the vendor takes, beginning in the farthest corner of the alley and ends the day at the farthest other end. Every day has its gain and its salability. No day goes by without some old and worn out merchandise, it is endlessly renewed and never dries up. It is incessantly renewed. Or is it the result of the call of an experienced caller.... It is a mobile *suq*, active, trade consisting like all trades, of exchange and quarrels in selling and buying. Its unsettling nature and its fluidity are the result of the smile of hesitation and the fear of greed. All things interact ... all contrast and oppose. This does not deny the fact that the master of the mobile suq is the guest of his male and female clients, at the same time. Everyone is willing to accept, with a great spirit of dedication an invitation from a customer, to eat the left over breakfast that she hands him. He accepts it gratefully, uttering the most wonderful wishes to her intention like any holy man, as the customer turns into a benefactor, he reinforces his invocations and repeats Amen, Amen.

FROM DARB AL-SULTAN, DHIL AL-AHBAS, PP. 7–8.

---

chology, Rabi adds his name to an impressive list of Arab writers whose literary activities existed and flourished side by side with their careers. For example, NAGUIB MAHFOUZ, the Nobel Prize winner (1988), refused an offer from the Egyptian government to leave his work and devote all his time to writing, and Ala al-Aswani, the well-known author of *Imarat Ya'qubian* (2002; *The Yacoubian Building*, 2004), continues to practice dental medicine.

BIBLIOGRAPHY

Williams, Malcolm, and Watterson Gavin, trans. *An Anthology of Moroccan Short Stories*. Tangier, Morocco: King Fahd School of Translation, 1995.

Aida A. Bamia

Yitzhak Rabin. FRANCK FIFE/AFP/GETTY IMAGES.

RABIN, YITZHAK
(1922–1995)

Yitzhak Rabin was an Israeli general, politician, and statesman. During his twenty-seven years as an officer in the defense establishment of the Jewish state, Rabin participated in the Palestine Jewish community's military struggle for statehood during the mid-to-late-1940s and in all the Arab-Israeli military confrontations until the 1967 War, in which he served as the chief of general staff (CGS) of the Israel Defense Forces (IDF). During his two terms as prime minister, Rabin laid the foundations for peace between Israel and its Arab neighbors, and between Israel and the Palestinians. In 1995, in the midst of the Israeli-Palestinian peace process he was leading at the time, Rabin was assassinated by a Jewish Israeli religious right-wing extremist.

PERSONAL HISTORY

Rabin, the eldest child of Rosa ("Red Rosa") Cohen and Nehemia Rabin, was born in Jerusalem and raised in Tel Aviv. His parents immigrated separately during and after World War I to mandatory Palestine. There they became active in Zionist socialist settlement organizations such as the General Federation of Jewish Workers and the Hagana (the semi-underground military force of Palestine's Zionist Jewish community). Rabin was educated in the School for Workers' Children and in a Zionist social democratic youth movement called Hano'ar Ha'Oved V'Halomed (Working and Studying Youth).

In 1935, at age thirteen, Rabin was sent to study at Kibbutz Giv'at ha-Shlosha near the Jewish town of Petah Tikva. In 1937 he began studying at the Kaddoorie agricultural school in the lower Galilee. This school produced prominent members of the political and military leadership of the country's Zionist left. There, Rabin

met Yigal Allon, who would be his commander, friend, and source of inspiration. And like most of the other youth there, Rabin was recruited into Jewish underground military activity.

Upon graduating from high school in 1940, Rabin planned to pursue studies in the field of water engineering. But as World War II approached Palestine, he decided instead to make security his primary occupation. In order to prepare for kibbutz life and integrate himself into the military operations of the Hagana with no financial constraints, he joined an agricultural training program at Kibbutz Ramat Yohanan near Haifa. During this period, Rabin spent most of his time in Hagana commanders' courses. As one of the first recruits to the Palmah, an elite Hagana fighting force established in May 1941 to prepare for the possibility of a Nazi invasion of Palestine, Rabin immediately assumed command and instruction responsibilities within the new unit.

During the 1940s, the political organizations to which Rabin belonged were radical activist Zionist-socialist groupings critical of Great Britain's anti-Zionist policies of the time. They cooperated with Britain during the war against Germany but did so reluctantly. At the end of the

BIOGRAPHICAL HIGHLIGHTS

Name: Yitzhak Rabin

Birth: 1922, Jerusalem, Mandatory Palestine

Death: 1995, Tel Aviv, Israel

Family: Wife, Leah (d. 2000); one daughter, Dahlia; one son, Yuval

Nationality: Israeli

Education: School for Workers' Children, Tel Aviv; Kibbutz Giv'at ha-Shlosha, near Petah Tikva; Kaddoorie agricultural school, lower Galilee, 1937–1940; Royal Staff College, Camberley, U.K., 1952–1953

PERSONAL CHRONOLOGY:

- **1946:** Commanding officer (CO), second Regiment, Palmah
- **1947:** Operations officer, Palmah
- **1948:** CO, Harel Brigade
- **1949:** Acting southern front commander, deputy CO, IDF
- **1950:** CO, Operations Department, GHQ Operations Branch
- **1953:** General; head, IDF Training Branch
- **1956:** CO, Northern Command
- **1959:** Head, GHQ Operations Branch
- **1961:** Head, GHQ Operations Branch, deputy CGS
- **1964:** CGS
- **1968:** Ambassador to United States
- **1974:** Minister of labor; prime minister
- **1984:** Minister of defense
- **1992:** Prime minister

arrested Zionist leaders and Palmah commanders in Palestine, including Rabin, in an effort to end the rebellion. The few months Rabin spent in a Rafah prison helped shape his image as a commander and a leader.

In 1947 Rabin and his Palmah colleagues prepared for the decisive phase in the Zionist struggle for a Jewish state. Immediately following the United Nation's (UN) historic 29 November 1947 decision to partition Palestine, the first Arab-Israeli war began, with Rabin on the front lines. At twenty five, he was the commander of the Harel Brigade, charged with the secure passage of Jewish supply convoys to Jerusalem and the campaign for the city. Rabin also participated in the battles for Latrun and the Lydda-Ramla road in May–July 1948. During this period, he experienced the horrors of war, as every third soldier in his brigade was injured or killed. According to his own testimony, this was the most difficult experience of his life.

In the summer of 1948, Rabin became the chief operations officer and deputy commander on the southern front and helped plan the October 1948–January 1949 campaign against Egyptian forces in the Negev desert. As he had neither served in a regular army nor participated in a major war, Rabin's professional military background—like that of many of his contemporaries in the new IDF—was limited. Nonetheless, he emerged as a professional, meticulous, and levelheaded military planner who made critical contributions to IDF successes toward the end of the war. Colonel Rabin participated in the Israeli-Egyptian armistice talks in Rhodes in early 1949. During this formative diplomatic experience, he proved to be an analytical thinker and a skilled negotiator.

Despite his talents, Rabin's rise through the ranks was impeded by his participation in a September 1948 demonstration against Prime Minister and Defense Minister David Ben-Gurion's decision to dismantle the Palmah, due to the unit's strong ties with a political party (Ahdut ha-Avoda [Unity of Labor]). As Rabin's act violated explicit orders, Ben-Gurion prevented him from attaining the position of CGS as long as he remained in office.

Rabin married long-time girlfriend Leah Schlossberg in August 1948 at the height of the war, and they eventually established their home in Tzahala, a Tel Aviv suburb populated by Israel's military and security elite. Between 1952 and 1964, Rabin filled a number of key positions on the IDF general staff. In January 1964, just seven months after Ben-Gurion's final resignation, Rabin was appointed CGS.

Rabin's role as CGS during the June 1967 war occupies an important place in Israeli collective memory. Due to changes in the deployment of Egyptian forces in the Sinai desert in mid-May 1967, Rabin called for a large-scale mobilization of the Israeli reserves. Israel's

war, Rabin and his comrades participated in the Zionist struggle against the British. The Palmah carried out military operations during the rebellion, which also had political and settlement-oriented components, and a wing occupied solely with facilitating illegal Jewish immigration. On 10 October 1945, during on operation to free immigrants jailed in a British camp south of Haifa, Rabin, then a Palmah regiment commander, led the force that penetrated the compound. This was his first meeting with Holocaust survivors. In the summer of 1946, the British authorities

political leadership was split over whether Israel should go to war immediately or first exhaust all diplomatic efforts. All eyes turned to Rabin, who was considered not only a military man but a political authority as well. Rabin was torn between the advantages of a pre-emptive strike and the importance of the diplomatic process. After Ben-Gurion accused him of leading Israel to war, Rabin crumbled under the pressure, suffering a physical and psychological breakdown; he resumed his duties 36 hours later. The army was tense and ready for war. Until the outbreak of hostilities, Rabin mediated between the still hesitant government and the war-ready General Staff. When the decision was finally made to go to war, Israel quickly defeated the surrounding Arab armies and conquered vast territory from Egypt, Syria, and Jordan. Rabin emerged a hero. In January 1968, he left the military and was appointed ambassador in Washington, D.C. In 1973 Rabin returned to Israel and joined the Labor Party.

In October 1973, surprise attacks by Syria and Egypt plunged the region into war again. Due to the unfavorable conditions in which Israel went to war and the high price it paid until the IDF gained the upper hand, the war was a watershed in Israeli history. The widespread public protests following the war resulted in the resignation of Prime Minister Golda Meir, which meant the resignation of the government as a whole. In June 1974, still revered as a hero and untainted by the recent war, a relatively young (50) and politically inexperienced Rabin became Israel's first native-born prime minister.

In the midst of a coalition crisis with the National Religious Party in late 1976, Rabin resigned on the assumption that new elections would stabilize the government. But as the elections drew near, the Israeli media revealed that Leah Rabin held an American bank account, which was illegal at the time. Rabin assumed equal responsibility for the offense, and immediately withdrew his candidacy for prime minister. Although no longer leading his party, Rabin was closely associated with its historic defeat in the May 1977 elections, after almost three decades in power. The dramatic reversal brought Menachem Begin and the Israeli right to power and sent Rabin into opposition. In 1979 he published his autobiography *Pinkas Sherut* (literally, "service notebook;" published in English as *The Rabin Memoirs,* 1996), in which he leveled scathing criticism at his political archrival at the time, SHIMON PERES.

When peace-seeking Egyptian President Anwar Sadat visited Jerusalem in November 1977, Rabin greeted him eagerly. Despite his objection to a few details of the evolving Israeli-Egyptian peace treaty and the opposition of some members of the Zionist activist left, Rabin supported the agreement unwaveringly, regarding it as the continuation of his earlier interim-agreement policies. But Rabin also supported the government's 1982 deci-

sion to go to war against the Palestine Liberation Organization (PLO) in Lebanon, although he spoke out sharply against the war when it deviated from the original plan. (Israel's direct involvement in southern Lebanon began in 1976, when Rabin was still prime minister.)

In 1984 Rabin was appointed defense minister as part of a national unity government. Although he regarded another war with the Arab countries as the greatest threat facing Israel, it was the routine security operations involved with the occupation of the West Bank that came to occupy him most. The eruption of the first intifada in 1987 faced Rabin and the IDF with a new type of popular resistance to Israeli occupation, based not on guns and bombs but on mass demonstrations, stone throwing, and Molotov cocktails. Rabin employed harsh measures against the uprising, reportedly ordering troops to "break the bones" of violent Palestinian demonstrators (instead of shooting them, as a method of controlling them). At the same time, he attempted to improve Palestinian living conditions. He also began trying to extract Israel from Lebanon by gradually redeploying IDF forces into a "security zone" adjacent to the Israeli-Lebanese border.

The Labor Party was voted back into power in 1992. Upon returning to the prime minister's office with a large camp of supporters, Rabin was faced with the challenge of integrating Israel into the post–Cold War international reconciliation process then underway. He immediately renewed the stalled multilateral talks between Israel and its Arab neighbors that had started with the Madrid conference in October 1991. Although he saw the Palestinian issue as the heart of the conflict, he also worked on the Syrian track in hope that this would reinvigorate the Palestinian track. But Rabin also continued his aggressive policies aimed at curbing hostile acts against Israel. In the Occupied Territories, he applied closures and expelled hundreds of suspected terrorists. In Lebanon, he ordered a wide-scale military operation in retaliation for a cross-border missile attack.

On 13 September 1993, Rabin and PLO chairman YASIR ARAFAT signed a "Declaration of Principles on Interim Self Government Arrangements" on the White House lawn. The highlight of the event was an historic handshake between Rabin and Arafat. In Israel, the agreement sharpened divisions between supporters and opponents of the Oslo process. A massacre carried out in February 1994 by a Jewish settler in a Hebron mosque at the Cave of the Patriarchs further heightened tensions, and Palestinian groups began a campaign of suicide bombings in Israel. Although initially in favor of removing all Jewish settlers from Hebron in light of this escalation, Rabin, concerned about sharpening divisions among Jewish Israelis even further, ultimately refrained from this course of action. In this way, he legitimized the continuation of "political settlements" in the West Bank which he himself was fighting.

Rabin received the Nobel Peace Prize in December 1994 together with Arafat and Foreign Minister Shimon Peres. Rabin regarded this international gesture toward those leading the way to peace as extremely significant. The ceremony took place before the completion of a final status agreement, in the shadow of increasing Palestinian terrorist attacks and the intensifying anti-Oslo campaign of the Israeli right. Rabin returned to Israel with the support of the international community, determined to begin solving the tough issues that remained. The signing of the Oslo II agreement in May 1994 and the signing of an Israeli-Jordanian peace treaty that October again intensified political divisions among Palestinians and Israelis alike. Convinced of the justness of his approach and aware of the dangers involved, Rabin now faced a personal smear campaign the likes of which he had never known. Cries of incitement were voiced at demonstrations organized by Oslo opponents, and rabbis legitimized the attacks by making similar pronouncements. Lost in the storm of incitement, voices of supporters could not stop the assassin who awaited Rabin as he descended from the stage of a 4 November 1995 peace demonstration at Kings of Israel Square in Tel Aviv. "Violence erodes the basis of Israeli democracy," he had warned in his final speech, delivered less than an hour before his assassination. Rabin was shot three times at point-blank range by Yigal Amir, a Jewish Israeli from the religious right wing, which since 1967 had been working to make Israeli control of the "whole Land of Israel" (Israel plus the West Bank and Gaza) permanent.

INFLUENCES AND CONTRIBUTIONS

Rabin's most important contribution to Israel's defense establishment was his role in shaping the IDF's doctrine of warfare. Rabin saw the IDF as a people's army and an educational framework, responsible not only for military tasks but a partner in civilian tasks as well. As head of the Education Branch during the early 1950s, he worked to integrate the army into national undertakings of the time. His main focus was overseeing the military's role in absorbing the more than 1 million Jewish immigrants who had recently arrived in the war-torn country, more than doubling its population. Rabin saw this work as a mission with critical security importance.

As CGS from 1964 to 1968), Rabin was faced with Egyptian and Syrian acquisition of advanced Soviet weaponry, Syrian attempts to divert the sources of Israel's water supply, and the Arab states' expanding patronage of terrorism. In this context, Rabin labored over the quantitative and qualitative development of the IDF as a formidable reserve-based military force and a deterrent

to war. He also worked on preparing an operational plan in case of escalation.

Rabin was more than just a general, and this found clear expression in his performance as CGS and the Israeli government's senior military adviser. Prime Minister Levi Eshkol, who also served as defense minister from 1963 to 1967, was interested primarily in the economic side of the military, leaving to Rabin the development of warfare doctrine, from the tactical to the strategic. In this way, Israel had two defense ministers on the eve of the 1967 war: Eshkol and Rabin.

When Jordan joined the war in June 1967, Rabin saw it as an historic opportunity to finish the battle for Jerusalem he had started in 1948. His conquest of East Jerusalem's Old City and the Western Wall, the holiest site in Judaism, in 1967 was one of the high points of his life, and the Hebrew University's decision to award him an honorary doctoral degree following the war reflected

EXPLORING

■

The Oslo peace initiative that Rabin adopted during his second term as prime minister was a product of the Israeli peace movement. This movement, which existed on the fringe of Israeli politics until 1978, consisted of a number of uncoordinated groups working independently and in an unfocused manner. Until 1967, some aimed at creating a counterbalance to Israel's close relations with the West, while others promoted Israeli integration into the Arab Middle East at the expense of the state's Jewish character. The conquests of 1967 refocused debate on geopolitics, as Israel now had territorial assets with which to bargain. The 1973 War, the Israeli settlement movement, and Israel's peace talks with Egypt resulted in the emergence of an extraparliamentary political movement known as Peace Now. From its establishment in 1978, Peace Now worked in conjunction with other groups to secure three primary goals: peace, the Jewish character of Israel, and a solution to the Palestinian refugee problem through the creation of a Palestinian state. Its strategy was territorial compromise, or "land for peace." Due to the failure of the Oslo peace process and the renewed violent confrontations between Israel and the Palestinians in 2000, the Israeli peace movement lost much of the public support it had enjoyed during the previous decade.

Israeli society's respect for his achievements. His speech on the occasion expressed pride, modesty, and concern about how Israel would make use of its victory, and revealed signs of a future supporter of peace.

During his first term as prime minister, Rabin opposed what were then referred to as "political settlements," or ideologically motivated settlements in parts of the West Bank that the Israeli government was still willing to consider giving up as part of a future peace plan. Nonetheless, he refrained from forcefully removing a group of radical settlers who occupied a military camp near Nablus against government orders in 1975, thereby establishing a precedent for the future settlements to come. Although his revitalization of the Israeli economy and the 1976 Israeli commando rescue mission at Uganda's Entebbe airport earned him additional respect in Israel, he was unable to overcome the government corruption that plagued Israel's political and economic leadership.

During the 1980s, Rabin was seen as Israel's top defense authority and enjoyed immense influence throughout the military. The Palestinians' new method of resistance, steadfastness, and willingness to incur losses convinced him that the intifada could not be defeated by force. The struggle's continuing impact on Israeli society made him regard a peace initiative as urgent. In 1989, as he began to recognize the need for a peace treaty with the Palestinians, he promoted a peace initiative that called for elections in the occupied territories and the commencement of final status negotiations with the elected leadership.

When Rabin was returned to office in 1992, he changed Israel's priorities as he had promised. To the dismay of Israeli settlers, he cut settlement budgets and increased government investment in education, welfare, infrastructure, the Arab sector, and the Israeli periphery. Many resources were allocated to the creation of new jobs and the integration of the flood of new immigrants arriving from the former Soviet Union. When Rabin was killed, a large portion of the Israeli public felt that a great opportunity had been lost.

THE WORLD'S PERSPECTIVE

Rabin's political initiatives took place in a post–Cold War context. The high point of his first term as prime minister was the conclusion of interim agreements with Egypt and Syria in 1974 and 1975. This, it would later become clear, was the first step toward what would evolve into the Egyptian-Israeli peace treaty of 1979. Rabin also strived for a peace treaty with Jordan and the establishment of final borders with Syria. His policies strengthened Israel's ties with the United States and Israel's status in the Middle East. Rabin saw the collapse of the USSR as an opportunity for an historic change in the region.

> # VIOLENCE ERODES THE BASIS OF ISRAELI DEMOCRACY
>
> I have always believed that the majority of the people want peace and are ready to take risks for peace. In coming here today, you demonstrate, together with many others who did not come, that the people truly desire peace and oppose violence. Violence erodes the basis of Israeli democracy. It must be condemned and isolated. This is not the way of the State of Israel. In a democracy there can be differences, but the final decision will be taken in democratic elections, as the 1992 elections which gave us the mandate to do what we are doing, and to continue on this course.
>
> RABIN, YITZHAK. "YITZHAK RABIN'S LAST SPEECH." HAGSHAMA. AVAILABLE FROM HTTP://WWW.WZO.ORG.IL/EN/RESOURCES/VIEW.ASP?ID=171.

Rabin regarded the efforts of Islamic terrorists to operate in the west as disastrous for Israel and the world. The reaction of Israel's home front to the 1991 Gulf War strengthened his conviction that Israelis were ready to pay the price of peace. Israel needed to advance the peace process, Rabin reasoned, due to the very real possibility that Israel's enemies in the Middle East could acquire unconventional weapons as well. Israel has never officially acknowledged possessing nuclear weapons itself. The Oslo Accords made relations with Arab and Muslim countries possible and offered a chance for a new era in the region.

Rabin's funeral in Jerusalem was the largest in Israeli history. It was attended by leaders of many countries around the world, including the presidents of the United States, France, and Egypt, the prime minister of Britain and the king of Jordan.

LEGACY

Rabin's main focus during his second term as prime minister was peacemaking. It was not true, he believed, that the world was against the Jewish people, and he maintained that Israel must join the international campaign for peace. He therefore resolved that his government would do everything possible to avoid war and bloodshed. He was the first prime minister since Ben-Gurion to move beyond diplomatic responses to actual initiatives. Israel's agreement to include the PLO in multilateral talks paved the way for progress in negotiations. Despite his misgivings, he approved the secret Oslo negotiating track, thereby providing official Israeli support for the creation of a Palestinian national entity alongside Israel for the first time since the beginning of the occupation. Aware of the dangers involved but convinced of the great opportunity at hand, he recognized the PLO as the representative of the Palestinian people. The longtime military man who just a few years earlier had sanctioned the breaking of bones now adopted the approach that "peace is made with enemies."

Rabin's legacy continues to be contested in Israel, due to the deep divisions among those who support retaining the West Bank and those who call for a Jewish state in only part of historic Palestine/Israel, living in peace alongside an independent Palestinian state.

BIBLIOGRAPHY

Bar-On, Mordechai. *In Pursuit of Peace: A History of the Israeli Peace Movement.* Washington, DC: U.S. Institute of Peace, 1996.

Hammel, Eric. *Six Days in June: How Israel Won the 1967 Arab-Israeli War.* New York: Scribners, 1992.

Inbar, Efraim. *Rabin and Israel's National Security.* Washington, DC: Woodrow Wilson Center, 1999.

Kurtzman, Dan. *Soldier of Peace: The Life of Yitzhak Rabin, 1922–1995.* New York: HarperCollins, 1998.

Parker, Richard B., ed. *The Six-Day War: A Retrospective.* Gainesville: University Press of Florida, 1997.

Peri, Yoram, ed. *The Assassination of Yitzhak Rabin.* Stanford, CA: Stanford University Press, 2000.

Rabin, Yitzhak. *The Rabin Memoirs.* Berkeley: University of California Press, 1996.

———. "Yitzhak Rabin's Last Speech." Hagshama. Available from http://www.wzo.org.il/en/resources/view.asp?id=171.

Ross, Dennis. *The Missing Peace: The Inside Story of the Fight for Middle East Peace.* New York: Farrar, Straus and Giroux, 2004.

Slater, Robert. *Rabin of Israel: A Biography.* New York: St. Martin's Press, 1993.

Watson, Geoffrey. *The Oslo Accords, International Law and the Israeli-Palestinian Peace Agreements.* Oxford: Oxford University Press, 2000.

Motti Golani

RACIM, MUHAMMAD
(1896–1975)

Muhammad Racim (also Mohammed Rasim, and "the Cantor of Algier") was a prominent Algerian artist whose career revived and reawakened the Arab, Islamic, and Oriental arts of his people. His dream was to revitalize the self-esteem and cultural patrimony of the Algiers that had been colonized by the French. His artwork formed part of the cultural renaissance that culminated in the Algerian revolution and independence. He significantly contributed to the documentation of Algerian history that the colonizers had distorted.

PERSONAL HISTORY

Racim was born in 1896 in Algeria, which formed part of the French colonized territories in the Maghreb (North Africa). He was born into a family of famous artists, illuminators, engravers, and woodcarvers. His grandfather and father had large art workshops that enjoyed unquestionable popularity in precolonial Algeria. As a young boy, he was initiated into the art of the miniature, of which he perfected the control of the technique. His entire life was devoted to the art that made him famous throughout the Middle East and the Western worlds. At the age of fourteen, after obtaining a certificate of studies, he joined the Cabinet of Drawing Professional Teaching. He further studied graphics. In 1914 he met the great Orientalist painter Nasreddine Dinet, who greatly influenced his professional life. Racim's first miniature in 1917 was titled "Dream of a Poet." With the scholarship of Casa Velasquez, he visited Andalusia, Spain, where he observed mosques, palaces, gardens, ceramics, music, and manuscripts. He also visited London, where he studied manuscripts and Arabo-Moslems miniatures of Bezhad and al-Wasiti. He visited the Museum of the Navy where he studied naval architecture. At the end of World War I in 1919, Racim's first exhibition took place in Spain and Algiers. In 1922 he settled in Paris. He became the editor of *Art Piazza* and illustrated twelve volumes of *A Thousand and One Nights*. After barely two years in Paris, the Company of the Painters French Orientalists awarded him a gold medal. In 1932, at the age of thirty-six, he married Karine Bondeson, a Swede, and returned with his wife to Algiers. In 1937 his works were shown at an international exhibition in Algeria. By 1950, he was elected honorary member of the Royal Company of the painters and miniaturists of England.

INFLUENCES AND CONTRIBUTIONS

Racim was highly influenced by his family and the rich cultural heritage of Algeria, as well as the Islamic world. In addition, historically, Algerians have exhibited artistic skills in their rendering of images, famous persons, religious icons, and coin inscriptions. The origins of Algerian art history became closely associated with the rebirth of the miniature under the tutelage of Racim. He utilized his skills and professionalism to promote Muslim civilization and Islamic arts. He was proud of the rich Algerian tradition that he seemingly revived through his miniatures. His works were of high colors, such as the *galere barbaresque* sailing off Algiers, that evoked the glorious epoch of the Algerian corsairs. Another remarkable work was the splendid Arab rider and cavalry of the

agents in the complex, fluid interaction of colonized and colonizer. Racim was among the first painters and artists to be recognized by the French from the 1920s. He was highly applauded by both the French and Algerians. Along with other artists, Racim claimed the aesthetics of a synthesis between the heritage of Arab-Muslim calligraphy and Western abstraction. The emergence of Racim as a renowned artist coincided with the period of French global imperialism and empire building in the Maghreb. In the nineteenth and early twentieth centuries, Racim had noted the representation of Arabs, Muslims, and Orientals in the Western visual and nonvisual culture. The Islamic or Oriental's image was a fantasy-based image and was highly stereotypical, and Racim set to rectify this image. Non-Western peoples, especially in the Middle East, were perceived to be exotic, erotic, pagan, lazy, dirty, and above all, the Other. Many Westerners were (and are still) ignorant of the Arab world and held misconceptions about Islam in the Middle East. Racim activated Algerian memory and history by bringing the past back to the present. He adapted the style of the Persian and Ottoman miniature to reflect his historical and figurative paintings. Racim

BIOGRAPHICAL HIGHLIGHTS

Name: Muhammad Racim (Mohammed Rasim, also known as The Cantor of Algiers)

Birth: 1896, Kasbah, Algeria

Death: 1975

Family: Wife, Karine Bondeson (m.1932)

Nationality: Algeria

Education: Algeria, Spain, London

PERSONAL CHRONOLOGY:

- **1910:** Begins teaching at Cabinet of Drawing Professional Teaching
- **1914:** Meets with Orientaliste painter Nasreddine Dinet who entrusts the ornamentation of his book, *The Life of Mahomet*, to him
- **1917:** Creates first miniature, "Dream of a Poet"; visits Spain and the United Kingdom
- **1919:** Has first exhibition in Algiers
- **1922:** Named editor of *Art Piazza*, Paris
- **1924:** Presented with gold medal award by the Company of the Painters French Orientalists
- **1933:** Receives greatest artistic prize of Algeria award
- **1934:** Becomes professor at the School of the Art Schools of Algiers
- **1937:** International exhibition, Algeria
- **1950:** Named honorary member of the Royal Company of Painters and Miniaturists of England
- **1960:** Edits *Moslem Life of Yesterday*
- **1972:** Edits *Mohammed Racim Miniaturiste Algerien*
- **1975:** Dies along with his wife

CONTEMPORARIES

Azouaou Mammeri (1890–1954) was another influential Algerian artist. Mammeri adopted the French traditions in painting and used them to create scenes in his own cultural environment without falling into the Orientalist trope of exploiting his subjects. Mammeri produced landscapes of Moroccan cities. He was promoted by the French colonial regime under Hubert Lyautey. The art critics in the French metropole equally glorified him. In the postcolonial period, however, Mammeri fell from the public eye. According to Benjamin Roger, Mammeri represents the grit of nascent resistance in the Maghreb. Mammeri's renderings of scenes from Muslim religious life, especially, his "Interior of Qur'anic School" in 1921, belied widely held European representations of Islam and Muslims at the period as fanatic, ignorant, and dangerous. Despite Mammeri's emulation of Western arts and co-optation by the French colonial regimes, he was among the subversive indigenous painters and artists. Mammeri's realist representation of Algerian subjects differs markedly from Racim's unique Persian and Ottoman miniature traditions.

amir Abdelkadir that served as a reminiscence of customs and habits of the past. His works of arts profoundly contributed to the Algerian revolution and war of independence. He revived the passion and consciousness of nationalism in Algeria that helped in dispelling stereotypes of monolithic Orientalism. Racism contributed significantly to the revitalization of Algerian historiography that had been suppressed and distorted during the French occupation. In his formative stage, Racim interacted with the Orientalist artist, Étienne Dinet, whose life and work focused on Algeria. Racim and Dinet were active

developed indigenous neotraditionalism by forging his own unique genre of artistic representation. Even though the colonial authorities appreciated his works, they represented precolonial Algerian history and ancient Islamic art.

Beyond his art, Racim was a great Algerian intellectual. In 1930 the French established the National Museums of Fine Arts in Algiers that marked a period of artistic development in Algeria.

One of Racim's most famous works was his 1931 piece, "The Rais," designed in oil and gold leaf. In 1934 he was appointed professor at the National School of Arts, Algiers. He wrote several books, including *Moslem Life of Yesterday* and *Mohammed Racim Miniaturiste Algerien*. By and large, Racim could be regarded as the founder of the Algerian School of Miniature. He built a large following and his disciples further promoted his works. Racim remains the greatest miniaturist of the twentieth century. In many of the art schools located in the Middle East where Western artists taught the history of Western Art, students were also taught the styles of Racim. In the early twenty-first century, compared to other countries in the Middle East, there may not be many art galleries in Algeria but there are a prominent few that focus on contemporary art and museums. Algerian art now takes the form sculpture, graphic works, painting, and craftwork that may be found in markets and tourist centers.

THE WORLD'S PERSPECTIVE

Since 1917 when Racim launched himself into the world of art, he was considered to be a genius and an erudite researcher. In many of his works, he was perceived to have preserved in their entirety the aesthetic techniques specific to the miniature and also to have added value to them without undermining their authenticity. He was assessed to be meticulous, patient, and poetic. His skills are reflected in the directions of the decoration, his steadiness of hand, and his nuanced choices. According to Roger Benjamin in *Orientalist Aesthetics: Art, Colonialism, and French North Africa, 1880–1930*, "Muhammad Racim melded the Persian miniature with Western perspective." Additionally, Benjamin, in "Colonial Tutelage to Nationalist Affirmation: Mammeri and Racim, Painters of the Maghreb", Racim's work "provides a cultural focus that might outlast the reality of colonial occupation" (p. 74).

LEGACY

The legacy of Racim has endured for several decades. He was noted to have engendered artworks in the style of the Islamic miniature with Western arts. By the time he passed away at the age seventy-nine, Racim had left a lasting legacy in the world of art. Barely sixteen years into

his career in 1933, Racim was presented the greatest artistic award of Algeria in 1933, and the medal of the Orientalists. In his fifty-eight-year career as an artist, his works were exhibited in all continents of the world. Some of his works are in the early twenty-first century part of the acquisition of several prominent museums. The National Gallery of Fine Arts in Jordan displays some of his brilliant masterpieces. His numerous paintings led to the flowering of Oriental art in France and the promotion of indigenous arts in the colonies. His artistic career brought interaction between the metropole and the Algerian colony. In 1992 the Musée de l'Institut du Monde Arabe Paris published *Mohammed Racim, Miniaturiste Algerien: du 3 au 29 Mars 1992* in his honor.

BIBLIOGRAPHY

Bellido, Ramon Tio. "The Twentieth Century in Algerian Art." Available from http://universes-in-universe.org/.

Benjamin, Roger. "Colonial Tutelage to Nationalist Affirmation: Mammeri and Racim, Painters of the Maghreb." In *Orientalism's Interlocutors: Painting, Architecture, Photography*, edited by Jill Beaulieu and Mary Roberts, et al. Durham, NC: Duke University, 2002.

Clancy-Smith, Julia. Review of *Orientalist Aesthetics: Art, Colonialism and French North Africa, 1880–1930* by Roger Benjamin. *H-France Review* 3, no. 94 (September 2003).

Makhoul, Sana. "Baya Mahieddine: An Arab Woman Artist." Available from http://www.sbawca.org/.

"Mohammed Racim Miniaturiste Algerien." Available from http://members.aol.com/mracim/racimbio.htm.

Zarobell, John. Review of *Orientalist Aesthetics: Art, Colonialism and French North Africa, 1880–1930* by Roger Benjamin. *African Studies Review* 46, no. 3 (December 2003): 172–174.

Rasheed Olaniyi

RADHI, AHMAD
(1964–)

Considered by many to be Iraq's greatest football (soccer) star, Ahmad Radhi (Amaiesh) had a fourteen-year playing career whose highlights include being named 1988 Asian Footballer of the Year. As a forward on Iraq's national team from 1983 to 1997, he scored forty-two goals.

PERSONAL HISTORY

Soccer was well established in Iraq by the 1950s and a national league was formed in the 1960s. If soccer had not already been a source of pride and center of entertainment, Iraq's success in international play during the 1970s made it so.

Radhi was born on 21 March 1964, and grew up in a poor working-class neighborhood in Baghdad. While

BIOGRAPHICAL HIGHLIGHTS
■

Name: Ahmad Radhi (Amaiesh)

Birth: 1964, Baghdad, Iraq

Family: Married; three daughters

Nationality: Iraqi

PERSONAL CHRONOLOGY:

- **1982–1985:** Plays for al-Zawra team, Baghdad
- **1983–1997:** Plays for Iraqi national team
- **1985–1989:** Plays for al-Rashid, Baghdad
- **1988:** Selected Asian Footballer of the Year
- **1989–1993:** Plays for al-Zawra, Baghdad
- **1993–1994:** Plays for al-Wakra, Doha, Qatar
- **1997–1999:** Plays for al-Zawra, Baghdad
- **1999–present:** President, al-Zawra Football Club; coach of Iraqi under-17 team

nothing has been published about his family or his childhood, it is reasonable to assume that like most boys he spent a lot of time playing soccer in the streets. He probably competed on school teams as well.

A talented youth, at age eighteen he attracted the attention of Uday Saddam Hussein, son of the Iraqi president. Uday was a dominant presence in Iraqi sports, heading the Olympic Committee, directing the national football team, and serving as president of al-Rashid Football Club. In 1983, Radhi was selected to play for the Iraqi national team.

His career blossomed and it may be assumed his talents expanded. In the 1985–1986 season Radhi was a top scorer in the Iraqi league and in 1986, as a player on the national team, he scored Iraq's only world cup goal in a match against Belgium. In the mid-1980s he was a standout for al-Rashid, the dominant team in the Iraqi league.

Some have accused Radhi of being complicit with Uday's political oppression and other crimes, but these claims are unsubstantiated, and there is contradictory evidence. As was common for players who displeased Uday, Radhi was jailed briefly in 1985, 1989, and 1996, when he was beaten, had his head shaved, and was forced to stand in sewage.

In different circumstances, Radhi would almost certainly have enjoyed success playing for European clubs.

However, under Uday's control, player options were limited. In 1990 Radhi signed a transfer agreement to play in Qatar but although he collected his salary, which may have been passed to Uday, he did not compete there. Toward the end of his career he did play in Qatar. Even in Iraq, however, he attained the status and accoutrements of an athletic superstar, including nice cars and houses.

At the end of his playing days, Radhi held positions in the Iraqi Football Association (IFA). In May 2004, he was alleged to have thrown hand grenades at the house of IFA president Husayn Sa'id after the latter fired him. Apparently nothing came of the charges. He is currently president of al-Zawra Football Club and the coach of Iraq's under-17 team. In national elections in 2005, Radhi publicly supported the slate of the Sunni Iraqi Islamic Party.

INFLUENCES AND CONTRIBUTIONS

Radhi's career was almost certainly influenced by his predecessors, Ammo Baba and Basil Gorgis, and his contemporaries, Husayn Sa'id, Falah Hasan, and Thamir Yusif. Athletes' contributions are commonly measured by recognition; in 1988 Radhi was selected Asian Footballer of the Year. In the 1990 World Cup qualifying match against Jordan, he scored four goals. Equally significant, in seventy-three international matches, he scored forty-two goals. He is ranked ninth greatest Asian Footballer by the International Federation of Football History and Statistics.

THE WORLD'S PERSPECTIVE

Radhi's career spanned some of the worst years in Iraq's history. The International Federation of Association Football (known by its French acronym, FIFA) banned international matches in Iraq during the Iraq-Iran War of 1980–1988. Football competitions were interrupted by the 1991 war. Throughout the 1980s and 1990s Uday Saddam Hussein resorted to imprisonment, torture, and extortion in an effort to control athletes. That Radhi not only survived but in many matches played at an exceptional level is testament to his skill and drive. His status as a stellar footballer seems ensured.

LEGACY

At least from an Iraqi perspective, Ahmad Radhi is a monumental football star. In a world where even top athletes fade rapidly from the public mind, Radhi has not. Indicative of his continuing status is that his 1986 World Cup goal is available for viewing on the YouTube Internet Web site.

BIBLIOGRAPHY

Freeman, Simon. *Baghdad FC: Iraq's Football Story.* London: John Murray, 2005.

Joshi, Vijay. "Passion for soccer survives sanctions in Iraq." Associated Press (29 January 1999).

Kaplow, Larry. "For Iraqi Soccer Star, Missed Goals Meant torture." Cox News Service (24 April 2003). Available from http://www.aliraqi.com/forums/archive/index.php/t-18815.html.

Thomas B. Stevenson

RAFEQ, ABDUL-KARIM
(1931–)

Abdul-Karim Rafeq (also Abd al-Karim Rafiq) is a Syrian-American historian who pioneered the use of Islamic court records (*sijillat*) as sources for social and especially urban history. Long affiliated with the University of Damascus, since 1990 he has held the William and Annie Bickers Professorship in Arab Middle Eastern Studies in the Department of History at the College of William and Mary, Williamsburg, Virginia (United States).

PERSONAL HISTORY

Rafeq was born 21 April 1931 in Idlib, Syria, then under French mandatory rule and the chief marketing center of the cotton-growing districts of northern Syria. His mother a Presbyterian; Rafeq attended the British School in Idlib, operated by Presbyterian missionaries from Northern Ireland, from 1937 to 1947. He completed high school and the first two years of his university training at the American College in Aleppo, also a Presbyterian institution (1947–1951).

Rafeq wished to complete his university education by obtaining an American bachelor's degree from the American University in Beirut. His family's financial resources did not permit this, so instead he went to the Syrian University in Damascus (later the University of Damascus). At independence in 1946 the Syrian government sought to expand its pool of secondary-school teachers by covering tuition and living expenses for selected meritorious students. Rafeq was one of the students so chosen, and he enrolled in the Department of History of the Faculty of Letters, earning his *license* in 1955. Rafeq continued for another year in the Higher Institute for Teachers (al-Ma'had al-Ali li'l-Mu'allimin), obtaining his *diplome* in 1956.

Because of his outstanding academic performance, Rafeq was named an instructor in the Department of History at his university, where he taught for two years before being awarded a scholarship for graduate study abroad. Several of Rafeq's colleagues in the department also obtained similar scholarships, notably Khairieh Kasmieh and Ahmad Badr.

Rafeq pursued his graduate studies at the School of Oriental and African Studies at the University of London, studying with, among others, Eric Hobsbawm, Bernard Lewis, and P. M. Holt, the last serving as Rafeq's dissertation adviser. His 1963 doctoral thesis, "The Province of Damascus from 1723 to 1783, with special reference to the 'Azm pashas," which was published by Khayats publishers in Beirut in 1966 under a slightly different title, explores the emergence of local power brokers, both urban and rural, during a transitional period in Ottoman Syria. In its subject matter and general approach, the thesis and book point to Rafeq's main interests during his long scholarly career.

Returning to Damascus, Rafeq joined the faculty of the University of Damascus Department of History as a lecturer in 1964 and rose through the academic ranks, becoming an associate professor in 1969 and a full professor in 1974. He served twice as department chair (1975–1977 and 1988–1990), and was vice-dean for Academic Affairs of the Faculty of Letters (1980–1981). During his tenure at Damascus, Rafeq held visiting positions at the University of Jordan, the Lebanese University, the University of Pennsylvania, the University of Chicago, and the University of California at Los Angeles.

BIOGRAPHICAL HIGHLIGHTS

Name: Abdul-Karim Rafeq (also Abd al-Karim Rafiq)

Birth: 1931, Idlib, Syria

Nationality: Syrian, American

Education: Studies at the American College in Aleppo; *License* (Department of History of the Faculty of Letters), Syrian University in Damascus, 1955; *Diplome,* Higher Institute for Teachers,1956; Ph.D. (history), School of Oriental and African Studies, University of London, 1963

PERSONAL CHRONOLOGY:

• **1964:** Begins teaching at Damascus University

• **1980:** Vice-dean for Academic Affairs, Faculty of Letters, Damascus University

• **1990:** Begins teaching at the College of William and Mary

Rafeq left Damascus in 1990 for the College of William and Mary in Williamsburg, Virginia (United States), where he offers several courses in Middle Eastern history. Rafeq serves or has has served on the editorial boards of several American, British, French, Japanese, Lebanese, and Syrian journals of Middle Eastern studies. He has evaluated for tenure and promotion purposes the work of his colleagues at several American and Arab universities, and has also served on the dissertation committees of several recent Ph.D.s in Syrian history.

INFLUENCES AND CONTRIBUTIONS

Rafeq cites among his principal influences his parents, whose sacrifices made his education and career possible. An early intellectual influence was George Haddad of the Syrian University, who introduced Rafeq to the discipline of history. During his studies in London, Rafeq was influenced by several professors, notably Holt and Lewis, but Rafeq credits Hobsbawm, under whom he studied for a year, with opening his mind to the interpretation of European history and for providing him with a methodology he could apply to Arab history. Rafeq's experiences in London gave him a firm understanding of the importance of archival documents as primary sources for history.

Rafeq's specific focus on the Islamic court records grew out of an encounter after his return to Damascus with Jon Mandaville, who had examined the *shariʿa* (Islamic law) court records of Syria and Jordan for his own research ("The Ottoman Court Records of Syria and Jordan," *JAOS* 86 (1966): 311–319). Rafeq wished to study the socioeconomic structure of Ottoman Syria and its political impact, and the court records appeared to be promising sources. Rafeq's first publication based on these documents was his article "The Local Forces in Syria during the Seventeenth and Eighteenth Centuries" (in M.E. Yapp and V.J. Parry, eds., *War, Technology, and Society in the Middle East*, Oxford, 1975). From the mid-1970s onward Rafeq published numerous articles focusing on the social history of Ottoman Syria as reflected in the Islamic court registers (*sijillat*).

Rafeq's principal contribution has been to develop a corpus of social, economic, and urban history whose distinguishing characteristic is an emphasis on internal developments. Prior to the pioneering work of Rafeq and his French colleague, André Raymond, whose work focuses on Egypt as well as Greater Syria, economic and social historians of the Middle East relied almost exclusively on foreign consular reports and travelers' narratives rather than indigenous documents. Such a reliance had resulted in a historiography that, in addition to being dependent on necessarily incomplete and partial sources, viewed the region as largely passive in the determination of its own fate.

Rafeq's and Raymond's creative use of the Ottoman *shariʿa* court registers, together with the contemporary paradigm shift occasioned by the publication of Albert Hourani's influential "Ottoman Reform and the Politics of Notables," had several results. A new appreciation of the social forces at play in the Ottoman provinces was made possible both by Hourani's emphasis on the notables as the crucial intermediaries between the central Ottoman state and the provincial populace and by Rafeq's exploration of the archival collections in which the notables' actual behavior was detailed. As well, the seventeenth and eighteenth centuries, previously seen as dormant periods of decline between the heyday of Ottoman power in the sixteenth century and the restructuring of the region under European influence in the nineteenth century, were now reassessed as complex periods of continuity and change. Finally, Rafeq's opening up of the court registers made these sources available to new generations of social and cultural historians whose interests went beyond the traditional concerns of political, social, and economic historians.

THE WORLD'S PERSPECTIVE

Rafeq is highly regarded among scholars throughout the world for his pioneering work in Syrian urban history and use of Islamic court records. In May–June 2004, an entire conference was held in Beirut and Syria to commemorate his work titled "Homage to Abdel-Karim Rafeq: Recent Research on Bilad al-Sham under Ottoman Rule (1517–1918)." Also, in recognition of his contributions, as a scholar, a teacher, and an inspiration for other researchers, in 2002 the Syrian Studies Association recognized Rafeq as its first honorary member.

LEGACY

Rafeq's legacy extends well beyond his own work—much of which has been published in Arabic but not yet in Western languages—and its detailed explication of Ottoman Syrian social life, especially in the Damascus province, and of the nature of the *sijillat*. Perhaps most significant is that a new generation of historians has used his method to explore a range of themes and issues in Middle Eastern history. For instance, Abraham Marcus adopted Rafeq's approach in his detailed portrait of eighteenth-century Aleppo (*The Middle East on the Eve of Modernity*, 1989), while Dina Rizk Khoury has similarly approached Mosul (*State and Provincial Society in the Ottoman Empire*, 1997) and Beshara Doumani has made use of the same methods for nineteenth-century Nablus (*Rediscovering Palestine*, 1995). Islamic court records have also been used to go beyond local histories to explore Muslim-Christian relations (the work of Najwa al-Qattan) and, significantly, as prisms through which to examine gender relations (Leslie Peirce's work on Aintab).

BIBLIOGRAPHY

Doumani, Beshara. *Rediscovering Palestine: Merchants and Peasants of Jabal Nablus, 1700–1900.* Berkeley: University of California Press, 1995.

Khoury, Dina Rizk. *State and Provincial Society in the Ottoman Empire: Mosul, 1540–1834.* Cambridge, U.K.: Cambridge University Press, 1997.

Marcus, Abraham. *The Middle East on the Eve of Modernity: Aleppo in the Eighteenth Century.* New York: Columbia University Press, 1989.

Peirce, Leslie. *Morality Tales: Law and Gender in the Ottoman Court of Aintab.* Berkeley: University of California Press, 2003.

Rafeq, Abdul-Karim. "The Law-Court Registers and Their Importance for a Socio-economic and Urban Study of Ottoman Syria." In *L'Espace Social de la Ville Arabe*, edited by Dominique Chevallier. Paris: CNRS, 1979.

———. *The Province of Damascus, 1723–1783.* Beirut: Khayats, 1966.

Sluglett, Peter, ed. *The Urban Social History of the Arab Middle East c. 1750–1950.* Syracuse, Syracuse University Press, 2008.

Geoffrey Schad

RAMON, ILAN
(1954–2003)

Ilan Ramon was the first Israeli, and the fourth Middle Easterner, to fly in space.

PERSONAL HISTORY

Ilan Ramon was born as Ilan Wolferman on 20 June 1954, in Ramat Gan, Israel. After finishing secondary school in 1972, he went into the Israeli military, as is required of most young Israelis. When the October 1973 Arab-Israeli War broke out, Ramon was serving in the Israeli Air Force. The year after the war, he completed flight school and became a fighter pilot. He eventually was qualified to fly the F-4 Phantom and Mirage III-C, and, starting in 1980, the new F-16 Falcons that Israel received from the United States. In June 1981, Ramon was one of the Israeli pilots who bombed and heavily damaged the Osirak nuclear reactor in al-Tuwaytha, Iraq, during a preemptive Israeli attack that was condemned by United Nations Security Council Resolution 487. He served in a number of capacities in the air force, and by August 1994 had been promoted to the rank of colonel.

Ramon was selected to become an astronaut in 1997, and reported for training in Houston, Texas, in July

---

BIOGRAPHICAL HIGHLIGHTS

Name: Ilan Ramon, (born Ilan Wolferman)

Birth: 1954, Ramat Gan, Israel

Death: 2003, over Texas

Family: Wife, Rona; three sons, Asaf, Tal, Yiftah; one daughter, Noa

Nationality: Israeli

Education: B.S., Tel Aviv University, 1987

PERSONAL CHRONOLOGY:

- **1972:** Enters Israeli Air Force
- **1974:** Completes flight school
- **1981:** Participates in bombing raid on Iraq's Osirak nuclear reactor
- **1997:** Selected as astronaut
- **1998:** Begins astronaut training
- **2003:** Flies into space; dies upon reentry

1998. He flew into space, becoming the first Israeli (and the fourth Middle Easterner) to do so, several years later when he served as a payload specialist aboard the American space shuttle *Columbia*'s STS-107 mission from 16 January through 1 February 2003. He spent 15 days, 22 hours, and 20 minutes in space, longer than any other Middle Eastern astronaut or cosmonaut. As a payload specialist, he worked on several experiments during the flight, including the Mediterranean Israeli Dust Experiment.

Ramon, whose mother was a survivor of the Nazi death camp at Auschwitz, was not an observant Jew. However, he was conscious of the symbolism of being the first Israeli in space (he was not the first Jewish astronaut; that distinction belongs to Judith Resnick, an American who died in the *Challenger* disaster in January 1986). Because the flight might mean so much to Jews around the world, including religious ones, Ramon took with him certain items of religious significance: kosher meals; a microfilmed copy of the Torah given to him by Israeli president Moshe Katzav; and a small Torah scroll from the Nazi concentration camp at Bergen-Belsen. He also consulted with rabbis prior to the mission about how to observe the Sabbath properly—the Jewish Sabbath begins at sundown on Friday evening, but determining when "sundown" occurs while in space presents special problems. Ramon also took along a drawing titled "Moon Landscape," a vision of what the moon must look like from space drawn by a fourteen-year-old Jewish boy named Peter Ginz, who died at Auschwitz.

Ramon and the other shuttle astronauts died on 1 February 2003, when the ship broke up during reentry into the atmosphere over Texas. Parts of his body were recovered and identified later amid crash debris, and buried in Nahalal, Israel. Part of an Israeli Air Force flag that he took into space with him also was recovered.

INFLUENCES AND CONTRIBUTIONS

Israelis were jubilant during Ramon's time in space. The flight represented more than just another space journey: For many Israelis, his feat was deeply symbolic. Prior to his mission, Ramon himself spoke openly about the significance of his being the first Israeli in space, and pointed out that he was the son of a mother who survived the Nazi Holocaust, and a father who fought in Israel's war of independence. Both then and during his flight, he was conscious of the symbolism of his feat: An Israeli Jewish phoenix rising into a new day from the dark ashes of the past.

The space flight also came as a joyous and proud moment for Israel, which at that point had been locked in over one and one-half years of bitter fighting with the Palestinians during the al-Aqsa intifada.

THE WORLD'S PERSPECTIVE

Ramon's space journey garnered considerable media attention. His tragic death along with those of the other *Columbia* astronauts immortalized him, and press accounts generally lauded him as a man of humor and stoicism.

LEGACY

Ramon largely will be remembered as the first Israeli in space. His role in the 1981 bombing of the Osirak reactor in Iraq tends to be overlooked compared to his achievement in space, although in a historical sense, the Osirak attack was much more important to Middle Eastern and global history. Had the reactor not been bombed, Iraq would have been much closer than it was to developing nuclear weapons by the time of Iraq's 1990 invasion of Kuwait. It is even conceivable that it might have possessed nuclear weapons by that time, with the result that the United States might not have attacked Iraq in 1991 and 2003.

BIBLIOGRAPHY

Abbey, Allen D. *Journey of Hope: The Story of Ilan Ramon, Israel's First Astronaut.* Jerusalem: Gefen Publishing House, 2003.

"Preflight Interview: Ilan Ramon." National Aeronautics and Space Administration. Available from http://spaceflight.nasa .gov/shuttle/archives/sts-107/crew/intramon.html.

Stone, Tanya Lee. *Ilan Ramon: Israel's First Astronaut.* Minneapolis, MN: Millbrook Press, 2003.

Michael R. Fischbach

RASHID, UDAY
(1973–)

Uday Rashid, Iraq's premier filmmaker of the post–SADDAM HUSSEIN era, has emerged to play an unprecedented role in the Iraqi film industry that was censored and suppressed for two decades. His films depict the dark side of life and humanitarian tragedy in Iraq after the fall of Saddam during the 2003 U.S. military invasion. The films produced amid social decay, hopelessness, and insecurity have reconnected isolated young generations of Iraqis with the outside world. Uday's career rekindles hope and development in the Iraqi film industry, especially for young Iraqis.

PERSONAL HISTORY

Rashid was born in Baghdad, Iraq, in 1973, and today is a documentary filmmaker and musician. He served as the director and screenwriter of 2005's *Underexposure*, a film about Baghdad. After the American attack on Iraq, Rashid and Majed Rasheed produced the film on social life and destruction of Baghdad. The film also shows the response of the people to the new situation. The co-producer was Tom Tykwer. In the main roles were Samar Qahtan (Hassan), Yousif aluminium-Ani (Abu Shaker), Auwatif Salman (Futha), Hayder Helo (Wetter), Hajed Rasheed (Ziyad), and Meriam Abbas (Maysoon). The film was produced in both Iraq and Germany by the Enlil and Creative Pool companies. Rashid's film explores the bleak life of refugee children in Iraqi Kurdistan on the eve of the U.S. invasion in 2003. The post-Saddam Iraq has been characterized by instabilities and social chaos which also affected Rashid. He was living in Europe as an artist but was prompted to return to Iraq after the brutal assassination of a friend who was a television broadcaster. Due to insecurity and perhaps, targets on his life, Rashid could not stay in his own house but had to join his family in Syria. According to Rashid, artists must choose between "personal safety and artistic freedom and honesty." He posited that the resulting double vision, within and above reality, is a precondition for the progress of Iraqi artists. Rashid pointed out that his triple identities of being a Muslim, Arab, and Iraqi cannot be easily divorced from his life and by extension, artwork.

BIOGRAPHICAL HIGHLIGHTS

Name: Uday Rashid

Birth: 1973, Baghdad, Iraq

Nationality: Iraqi

PERSONAL CHRONOLOGY:

• **1992:** Founding member, "Survivors"

• Director of documentary film on Iraqi children

• Director of documentary film on artists' impression of Iraq

• Director of documentary film on the siege of Iraq

• **2005:** Director and screenwriter of *Underexposure*

This is centrally because the ultimate call of the artist is to represent the spiritual core of every person in a way that challenges them to express their religious heritage instead of promoting the destructive aspect.

INFLUENCES AND CONTRIBUTIONS

In 1992 Rashid was the founding member of a group of thirty five young Iraqis called the "Survivors." The group was multi-ethnic, multireligious, and included two women. The central objective of the group included making films and writing screenplays. It acted as an underground culture club which staged closed-showings of plays and poetry readings. Twenty days after the fall of Baghdad in April 2003, the Survivors group published its founding statement. Shortly after the U.S. forces entered Iraq, the culture club staged a free performance of a play titled, "They Dropped by Here." Rashid made two self-sponsored documentaries, *UN Sanctions–Iraqi Children* and *Artists' Impressions of Baghdad*. He was sponsored by the former Iraqi Ministry of Culture to work on a film of the siege of Baghdad, but the original was destroyed during a coalition air raid.

Rashid's *Underexposure* was the 2004 Cannes submission from Iraq. The documentary film is semi-autobiographical, and has a cast of characters that includes a filmmaker, artists, a dying soldier, and an autistic child. Rashid shot and directed the film amidst insurgent attacks and American patrols. The title of the documentary film depicts the large amount of expired film stock that was central to the film's plot whereby the lead character was disturbed that his work may not see the light of the day. Actually, Rashid used expired Kodak film which was the only material he could purchase on the postinvasion black

market to shoot *Underexposure*. The shooting of the film was carried out under state collapse, economic paralysis, political insecurity and socioeconomic breakdown. Rashid chose an old Baghdad house on the island shores of the Tigris to shoot the film. This was perhaps to represent the peace and tranquility of Iraq before the American invasion. While Rashid's team was shooting the film, there was a power outage and the streets of Baghdad were quite unsafe at night. *Underexposure* shows the lives of six characters who wander in Baghdad after the war in search of solace and relief.

THE WORLD'S PERSPECTIVE

Rashid's film has been described as having powerfully addressed the uncertainties, tragedy, and crisis in Iraq in the post-Saddam era. His dexterity and expertise have been hailed as well. Rashid presented a cast that was riddled with both hopelessness and promise. Rashid is a highly skilled director and determined filmmaker who worked successfully with expired film and obsolete technology. His film reconnected generations of isolated Iraqis with the outside world. *Underexposure* weaves together the complexities of a new reality for families, friends, lovers, and strangers. The film "blends reality and fiction to create a lyrical and textured work that captures the dizzying atmosphere of life during war and fiercely illuminates a part of the world long left in the dark." ("Underexposure," Art East, available from http://www.arteeast.org/pages/cinemaeast/series/fall-series-06/).

Rashid already has garnered international exposure and awards. *Underexposure* was the 2004 Cannes submission from Iraq, and won the Best Film Award from the International Film Festival–Singapore.

LEGACY

Rashid's film was Iraq's first postwar feature film. *Underexposure* was shown at the international film festival–Rotterdam, international film festival–Singapore, and in Munich, Germany. Indeed, Rashid's film marked the first uncensored Iraqi film in fifteen years. His film helped to debunk both the personal mythology of Sadam Hussein while in power and the myths of the liberating impact of the U.S. invasion of Iraq. Following the Iraqi invasion by the United States, several museums, galleries, libraries and artworks were either destroyed or looted. In this way, Rashid film represents an enduring documentation of modern trajectories of Iraq. The film combines real footage of the war with fictional scenes. The documentary aspect of the film was shot in the districts of Baghdad where U.S. soldiers operated. Rashid's generation had suffered from Saddam's dictatorship, war, and American occupation with devastating consequences on the "old-fashioned aesthetic sensibilities." His film brought to life and to the global limelight the image of political chaos and social paralysis of contemporary Iraq.

BIBLIOGRAPHY

"Film Club Berlin Baghdad." News from the DVD World. Available from www.filmclub-berlin-baghdad.de.

Hometown Baghdad. Available from http://www.hometownbaghdad.com/.

Kurzen, Benedicte. "Here and There." May 2004. Available from http://digitljournalist.org/issue0405/dis_kurzen.html.

Levine, Mark. "Life before Wartime." OC Weekly. Available from http://www.ocweekly.com/film/film/life-before-wartime/19062.

"World." *Tribune*. Available from http://www.tribuneindia.com/2003/20031108/world.htm.

Rasheed Olaniyi

RAUF EZZAT, HEBA
(1965–)

Heba Rauf Ezzat (also Hiba Ra'uf Izzat) is an Egyptian political scientist and Islamic thinker and activist.

PERSONAL HISTORY

Rauf Ezzat was born in Cairo, Egypt, in 1965. She was educated in German Catholic schools and received a Ph.D. in political science from Cairo University, where she now teaches. In 1995–1996, she was visiting researcher at the University of Westminster in the United Kingdom, and at the Oxford Centre for Islamic Studies in 1998.

INFLUENCES AND CONTRIBUTIONS

Rauf Ezzat has become a prominent spokesperson on gender issues in Egypt and on the Internet. From 1992 to 1997 she wrote a weekly column, "Women's Voice," for *al-Sha'b*, the Islamist-leaning newspaper of the Egyptian Labor Party. She supports change from within to counter what she sees as secularization of the (Muslim) family. Conceptualizing the Muslim family as outside of history, she criticizes Western feminists for analyzing it within the framework of the rise of bourgeois and patriarchal social structures. Yet she gives more centrality to gender than do many Islamic activists, such as her mentors, Zaynab al-Ghazali and Safinaz Kazim. Arguing from central texts of Islamic jurisprudence, she finds strong precedent for women's participation as leaders in public life as long as they are Islamically qualified.

   She has written *Women in Politics: An Islamic Perspective* (1995) and *Religion, Women and Ethics* (2001). In May 2005, she called on Egyptians to wear black to protest the assault on women protesters a week earlier

---

BIOGRAPHICAL HIGHLIGHTS

Name: Heba Rauf Ezzat (Hiba Ra'uf Izzat)

Birth: 1965, Cairo, Egypt

Family: Married, three children

Nationality: Egyptian

Education: Ph.D., political-science, Cairo University

PERSONAL CHRONOLOGY:

• **1992–1997:** Writes weekly column for *al-Sha'b*

• **1995:** Visiting researcher, University of Westminster; writes *Women in Politics: An Islamic Perspective*

• **1998:** Visiting researcher, Oxford Centre for Islamic Studies

• **2001:** *Religion, Women and Ethics* is published

---

while they were protesting during a national constitutional referendum.

THE WORLD'S PERSPECTIVE

Although knowledgeable about Western political philosophy, in her polemics Rauf Ezzat nevertheless expresses common misperceptions about European and American society. She tends to support monolithic notions of "Islamic" and "Western" societies as inevitably dichotomized. She rejects the label of "feminist" and sees feminism as a diversionary and unnecessary practice, irrelevant to those who work within an Islamic framework.

LEGACY

Still active on the Egyptian scene, it is too early to assess Rauf Ezzat's ultimate legacy, but she is sure to play a continued role in Egyptian women's dialogues about gender issues.

BIBLIOGRAPHY

Gawhary, Karim, el-. "An Interview with Heba Ra'uf Ezzat." *Middle East Report* 191 (November–December 1994): 26–27.

Karam, Azza. *Women, Islamisms and the State: Contemporary Feminisms in Egypt*. London: Macmillan, 1998.

Rauf Ezzat, Heba. "Women and the Interpretation of Islamic Sources." In *Islam 21*. Available at http://www.islam21.net/pages/keyissues/key2-6.htm.

Marilyn Booth
updated by Michael R. Fischbach

Ravikovitch, Dalia

RAVIKOVITCH, DALIA
(1936–2005)

Dalia Ravikovitch was one of the most influential Hebrew poets of her generation and, at the time of her death, perhaps the most acclaimed poet writing in Israel. Her work has appeared in translation in twenty-three languages, and she remains an abiding presence in contemporary Israeli culture.

PERSONAL HISTORY

Ravikovitch was born on 17 November 1936, in Ramat Gan, Palestine, a suburb of Tel Aviv. Her father was killed by a drunk driver when she was four, an event whose traumatic impact often appeared in her work. She spent the rest of her childhood on a kibbutz, and afterwards studied at the Hebrew University of Jerusalem. She lived mostly in Tel Aviv, where she worked as a teacher and journalist, and published ten volumes of poetry, three short-story collections and five children's books; she also translated Edgar Allan Poe, T. S. Eliot, and W. B. Yeats into Hebrew. She was awarded numerous prizes including the prestigious Israel Prize in 1998. She died in Tel Aviv on 21 August 2005, and is survived by a son. A major English-language edition of her work is forthcoming.

INFLUENCES AND CONTRIBUTIONS

Ravikovitch belongs to a generation of Israeli poets who began publishing in the 1960s; their work is generally viewed as a rebellion against an earlier generation's thematic and stylistic concerns. Whereas much poetry of the pre-state and early state period was characterized by more collective, even overtly nationalistic themes, the poems of Ravikovitch and her contemporaries Natan Zach and Yehuda Amichai seemed to embrace a more individual and independent sense of poetic voice. Their work focused on the private lives of private individuals, often in the face of public "noise" or interference. Furthermore, both the tone and language of their work were generally more colloquial than their predecessors, in keeping with the growing use of Hebrew as the vernacular language. However, Ravikovitch's earliest work is also marked by a more formal, almost baroque style, a poetics that appeared at odds with the more overtly free verse of her contemporaries; in fact, her early work often hearkens back to an earlier generation of Hebrew poetry marked by more regular verse forms. The uniqueness of Ravikovitch's work was thus clear from the start.

Her first volume, *Ahavat Tapuah Ha-Zahav* (1959; The love of an orange), was embraced by readers and critics alike, and hailed for its fine use of traditional forms and Jewish sources. The oft-anthologized

BIOGRAPHICAL HIGHLIGHTS

Name: Dalia (Dahlia) Ravikovitch

Birth: 1936, Ramat Gan, mandatory Palestine

Death: 2005, Tel Aviv, Israel

Family: Divorced; one son

Nationality: Israeli

Education: Studied at the Hebrew University, Jerusalem

PERSONAL CHRONOLOGY:

- **1959:** Publishes first volume of poetry, *Ahavat Tapuah Ha-Zahav*
- **1976:** The first English-language edition of *Dress of Fire* is published in London
- **1987:** Awarded the Bialik Prize; publishes the poetry collection *Ahavah Amitit* which expressly treats the Israeli war in Lebanon
- **1998:** Awarded the Israel Prize
- **2005:** Dies in Tel Aviv

"Mechanical Doll" touches on themes of gender, society and power that strongly inform Ravikovitch's later work:

> That night, I was a clockwork doll
> And I whirled around, this way and that,
> And I fell on my face and shattered to bits
> And they tried to fix me with all their skill
> Then I was a proper doll once again
> And I did what they told me, poised and polite.
> (*Kaufman, et al.,* p. 143)

Within the confines of this sonnet—a verse form with regular meter and rhyme—Ravikovitch's poetic speaker strains against stereotypical expectations of femininity. This tension between a tightly wrought form and a more unexpected, even audacious poetic voice is typical of Ravikovitch's early work.

A sense of personal responsibility and obligation emerges in the poet's earliest poems, expressly tied to the sudden childhood loss of her father:

> Standing by the side of the road at night this man
> Who was long ago my father.
> And I must go to him in the place where he stands
> Because I was his eldest daughter.

I'M ABOVE THOSE JAGGED MOUNTAIN RANGES

Originally published in 1987, this poem remains one of Ravikovitch's most powerful statements about the poet's obligation to witness.

HOVERING AT LOW ALTITUDE
I am not here.
I am on those craggy eastern hills
streaked with ice,
where grass doesn't grow
and a wide shadow lies over the slope.
A shepherd girl appears
from an invisible tent,
leading a herd of black goats to pasture.
She won't live out the day,
that girl.
I am not here.
From the deep mountain gorge
a red globe floats up,
not yet a sun.
A patch of frost, reddish, inflamed,
flickers inside the gorge.
The girl gets up early to go the pasture.
She doesn't walk with neck outstretched
and wanton glances.
She doesn't ask, Whence cometh my help.
I am not here.
I've been in the mountains many days now.
The light will not burn me, the frost
won't touch me.
Why be astonished now?
I've seen worse things in my life.
I gather my skirt and hover
very close to the ground.
What is she thinking, that girl?
Wild to look at, unwashed.
For a moment she crouches down,

her cheeks flushed,
frostbite on the back of her hands.
She seems distracted, but no,
she's alert.
She still has a few hours left.
But that's not what I'm thinking about.
My thoughts cushion me gently, comfortably.
I've found a very simple method,
not with my feet on the ground, and not flying—
hovering
at a low altitude.
Then at noon,
many hours after sunrise,
that man goes up the mountain.
He looks innocent enough.
The girl is right there,
no one else around.
And if she runs for cover, or cries out—
there's no place to hide in the mountains.
I am not here.
I'm above those jagged mountain ranges
in the farthest reaches of the east.
No need to elaborate.
With one strong push I can hover and
　　whirl around
with the speed of the wind.
I can get away and say to myself:
I haven't seen a thing.
And the girl, her palate dry as a posterd,
her eyes bulge,
when that hand closes over her hair, grasping it
without a shred of pity.

TRANSLATION BY CHANA BLOCH AND ARIEL BLOCH. IN *THE DEFIANT MUSE: HEBREW FEMINIST POEMS FROM ANTIQUITY TO THE PRESENT*, EDITED BY SHIRLEY KAUFMAN, GALIT HASAN-ROKEM, AND TAMAR S. HESS.

And each and every night he stands alone in his place
And I must go down and come to his place.
And I wanted to ask the man until when must I.
And I knew beforehand that always must I.
(*Ravikovitch*, 1995, p. 24 [translation by Barbara Mann])

The necessity, even obligation, to metaphorically revisit the site of her father's death prefigures one of the essential motifs in Ravikovitch's subsequent work—an obligation to witness events both large and small.

Language and Persona Ravikovitch's poetry is characterized by a variety of linguistic registers, blending biblical Hebrew with contemporary diction and slang, often to startling effect. As is generally true of modern Hebrew poetry, her poems often rely on traditional Jewish sources, such as the liturgy or the biblical psalms, to create a subtext and background against which the poem unfolds. Her work also draws extensively on images and motifs from world literature and ancient culture such as *Hamlet* and the Greek figure of Medea who, in "The Burning Dress" (1969) is rewritten to serve as a figure who debunks both conventional depictions of women as scheming, and the storytelling tradition responsible for creating those images.

The poetic persona in Ravikovitch's subsequent volumes is often defined by an exotic (in relation to Israel) geographic locale—for example, Zanzibar, Chad, Cameroon, and Hong Kong. In "Tirzeh and the Wide World," the speaker asks to be taken away and left "among other people, / the likes of whom I've never met, / there I will eat a strawberry confection from the forest, / and gallop on the train in Scandinavia." In Australia, the speaker will "teach the kangaroo / reading and writing, Bible and math," the rudiments of Israeli elementary school. This express desire for connection with "strangers" is undercut by a sense that the speaker is also somewhat in need of rescue: as she floats in the "heart of the ocean," she asks that a net and life vest be tossed to her (*Ravikovitch*, 1995, pp. 94–95). The voice that emerges over the course of Ravikovitch's early volumes—at once wounded and wearily resilient—is entirely unique and resists any normative assumptions about "women's poetry" or "a feminine voice." "The End of the Fall" reflects on the almost existential loneliness that underlies all human experience, whether personal or communal, local or global:

> If a person falls out of a plane in the middle of
>   the night
> Only God himself can lift him up ...
> If a person falls out of a place in the middle of
>   the night
> Only God knows the end of the fall
> (*Ravikovitch*, 1995, pp. 128–129 [translation by
>   Barbara Mann])

The loneliness at the poem's conclusion is made only marginally more bearable by the thought that God himself shares in it, that God is also in need of human deeds and companionship.

While it seems the poet herself had an ambivalent relation to feminism per se, many of her poems treat feminist issues such as gender roles, societal power relations, and a focus on the weak or more vulnerable members of society (women, children, minorities). Furthermore, several of Ravikovitch's poems expressly trace a female poetic tradition of sorts, especially in relation to the work of her predecessor Leah Goldberg (1911–1970) and contemporary Yona Wollach (1944–1985). This delineation of what feminist critics call an alternative literary tradition of women's writing is all the more crucial within the sphere of modern Hebrew writing, given Hebrew's normative association with the patrilineal domain of liturgy, tradition, and rabbinic scholarship.

Poetry and Politics Since the 1980s Ravikovitch's work has increasingly been viewed within the context of political poetry. Hebrew poetry has always been intimately connected to national identity, since its inception as a secular poetic idiom in Eastern Europe in the late nineteenth century. Even before that, the biblical prophets historically played a central role in the articulation of an ethical, often oppositional, point of view regarding national concerns. Ravikovitch's volume *Ahavah Amitit* (1987; Real love) appeared after a decade-long poetic silence. Many of the book's poems initially appeared in the early part of the Israeli war in Lebanon, a period marked by the poet's public protest of the war, alongside other Israeli writers such as Natan Zach and AMOS OZ.

Ravikovitch's late work continued to address themes of power and powerlessness, in an increasingly bold and clear poetic idiom. Her work increasingly included images of diasporic Jewish life, with a special focus on women and a matrilineal tradition. For example in "We Had an Understanding" (1986), a poem addressed to her "European grandmother," the poetic speaker says of their shared "story":

> There are details in it better left untold,
> Better to leave patches of forgetfulness on what
>   happened in the past.
> But the definite resemblance
> Between us
> Produced understanding without sympathy
> (*Kaufman, et al.*, p. 151)

The reader should not mistake this poem for a sentimental or nostalgic attempt to connect with an ultimately irretrievable past. Indeed, the cool irony of a pose which is "understanding" but not sympathetic defines the absolute distance, finally, of the speaker from her grandmother. For Ravikovitch, this distance is both crucial to any aesthetic contemplation of the world, as well as morally suspect. Indeed, the difficult responsibility of "witnessing" in the face of suffering emerges as a major theme in Ravikovitch's later work (see Sidebar: "Hovering at Low Altitude"). "Issues in Contemporary Jewry" (1987) includes a portrait of a destitute "exilic Jewish woman," an image that conflates historical notions of Jewish wandering with more contemporary images of Palestinian refugees. The question of place, and of the relation between a people and a place, is paramount in these later poems, as is recorded in her dystopic, affectionate ode to Tel Aviv, "Lying on the Water": "A rotten Mediterranean city—/ how my soul is bound to hers" (*Kaufman, et al.*, p. 152).

THE WORLD'S PERSPECTIVE

The status of Ravikovitch's work abroad has only grown in recent years, as more translations of her work have been produced; her work is featured in academic conferences and regularly taught in university courses on Hebrew literature, and translations of her work have appeared in such prestigious magazines as the *New Yorker*. In 2007 a comprehensive English-language edition of her poems will be published by W.W. Norton, a leading American trade publisher. This publication signifies the high critical regard for Ravikovitch's work; it will also help introduce her poems to future generations of readers.

LEGACY

Ravikovitch was hailed as a major poetic voice within Israeli literature, from the appearance of her very first poems. Her work has been consistently admired both by critics and a wider, popular readership; her poems have appeared in the weekly newspaper literary supplements, and editions of her poems regularly sell out in bookstores. Her influence and stature were enormous in her lifetime, in spite of the poet's relatively low-key lifestyle. It is perhaps too soon to assess Ravikovitch's final legacy, as her passing is still mourned by lovers of Hebrew poetry.

BIBLIOGRAPHY

Gold, Nili, Barbara Mann, and Chana Kronfeld. "'Hovering at Low Altitude' by Dalia Ravikovitch." In *Reading Hebrew Literature: Critical Discussions of Six Modern Texts*. Hanover, NH: University Press of New England, 2003.

Kaufman, Shirley, Galit Hasan-Rokem, and Tamar S. Hess. *The Defiant Muse: Hebrew Feminist Poems from Antiquity to the Present*. New York: Feminist Press at the City University of New York, 1999.

Ravikovitch, Dalia. *Dress of Fire*. Translated by Chana Bloch. London: Menard Press, 1976.

———. *The Window: New and Selected Poems*. Translated by Chana Bloch and Ariel Bloch. Riverdale-on-Hudson, NY: Sheep Meadow Press, 1989.

———. *Kol Ha-Shirim Ad Koh* [The complete poems so far]. Tel Aviv: Hakibbutz Hameuchad, 1995.

Barbara Mann

REZAZADEH, HOSSEIN
(1978–)

Hossein Rezazadeh is an Iranian weightlifter who has won two Olympic gold medals, four world championships, and two Asian championships. He is one of Iran's most popular celebrities.

Hossein Rezazadeh. AP IMAGES.

PERSONAL HISTORY

Rezazadeh was born on 12 May 1978 in Ardabil, the capital of Ardabil province in Iranian Azerbaijan, the northwestern Turkish-speaking region of Iran. He is the third of seven children. At the age of fifteen his physical education teacher encouraged him to take up weightlifting.

Weighing 343 pounds and competing in the super heavyweight (+ 231 lb.) class, Rezazadeh earned his first international success at the 1999 world championships in Athens, when he won a bronze medal. At the 2000 Summer Olympic Games in Sydney, he astonished everyone by first lifting 468 pounds in the snatch category (where the athlete lifts the weight at once) and then 573 pounds in the clean and jerk category (where the athlete lifts the weight up to below his neck and then raises it above his head) to break the world record. He easily won the gold medal at the 2004 Summer Olympic Games in Athens, where his combined total was 39 pounds more than that of the silver medallist, Viktors Scerbatihs of Latvia.

In Iran the city of Ardabil is known for the religious fervor of its inhabitants, and Rezazadeh is no exception. He shouts *Allahu Akbar* (Arabic: God is greatest) before each lift and wears a competition uniform bearing the name Abolfazl (also Abu'l-Fadl), a major Shi'ite saint

BIOGRAPHICAL HIGHLIGHTS

Name: Hossein Rezazadeh

Birth: 1978, Ardabil, Iran

Family: Married

Nationality: Iranian

Education: Iran

PERSONAL CHRONOLOGY:

- **2000:** Breaks world record in two events at Summer Olympic Games in Sydney; wins gold medal

- **2003:** Sets world record at World Championships in Vancouver

- **2004:** Wins gold medal at Summer Olympic Games in Athens

known for his valor. His international successes and his religious demeanor have combined to make him a major celebrity in Iran. In 2002 he was voted champion of champions in Iran, and in February 2003 his wedding in the Saudi Arabian city of Mecca was broadcast live on television in Iran. As a reward for setting yet another world record at the world championships in Vancouver, Iranian president MOHAMMAD KHATAMI awarded him 600 million rials (about US$60,000) to buy a house in Tehran.

INFLUENCES AND CONTRIBUTIONS

Weightlifting is a discipline in which Iranians had excelled until the 1970s. Iran's first Olympic medallist, Moham-mad-Ja'far Salmasi, was a weightlifter who won a bronze medal at the 1948 London Summer Olympic Games. Throughout the 1950s and 1960s Iranians won international medals in this discipline, always in the lighter weight categories. By the 1970s athletes from the Soviet bloc, benefiting from more scientific training methods, came to dominate the sport. Rezazadeh's contribution is thus remarkable for two reasons: one, he reconnected with Iran's past successes and two, he did so as a heavyweight, a category in which Iranians had not shone before.

THE WORLD'S PERSPECTIVE

Rezazadeh's weight class, the super heavyweights, had been dominated since 1960 by Soviet and then Russian athletes, so his earning a gold medal at the Olympic Games in Sydney created a major sensation. The Turkish government report-edly offered him a substantial sum of money if he accepted

Turkish nationality to win a medal for Turkey at the 2004 Olympic Games in Athens, but unlike the former Bulgarian weightlifter and Olympic gold-medallist Naim Süleymanoglu who left Bulgaria to become a Turkish citizen, Rezazadeh refused the offer, which added more to his popularity at home.

LEGACY

Because of his success at the Olympics along with his reli-giousness and Iranian national pride, Rezazadeh will long be remembered as an important athlete in Iran. His records in weightlifting still stand as of 2007, making him one of the most revered athletes in that sport around the world.

BIBLIOGRAPHY

"Hossein Reza Zadeh: The Champion of Champions." Available from http://rezazadeh.hit.bg.

"Hossein Reza Zadeh Olympic Medals and Stats." Database Olympics. Available from http://www.databaseolympics.com.

"Raising the Bar: Iran Sets World Records to Win Gold." *Sports Illustrated.* Available from http://sportsillustrated.cnn.com/olympics/2000.

H. E. Chehabi

RIMITTI, CHEIKHA
(1923–2006)

Algerian singer and performer Cheikha Rimitti (also known as Cheikha Remettez Reliziana), whose career spanned eight decades, is best known for pioneering a form of popular music known as *raï* (also spelled *ray* or *ra'i*). Rimitti's music was enormously popular in her native Algeria and France, with lyrics marked by frank and explicit expressions of feminine sexuality and desire. With the emergence of an independent Algeria in 1962 came denouncement and censorship of Rimitti's songs, forcing her to relocate to France where she continued to record and perform attaining a worldwide audience that continued to grow until her death in 2006.

PERSONAL HISTORY

Rimitti was born Saïda Belief on 8 May 1923 in the city of Tessala in the western part of French-controlled Algeria. Rimitti was orphaned at an early age and spent the rest of her childhood in poverty, later declaring that misfortune was her teacher. At the age of thirteen, Rimitti began earning money performing bawdy fertility songs at wed-dings, which demanded a multifaceted performance requiring her to dance and sing. It was during this time that Rimitti created her stage name, which, according to legend, developed from her mispronunciation of the French term *remotes* (again) as it related to her generosity

BIOGRAPHICAL HIGHLIGHTS

Name: Cheikha Rimitti (Cheikha Remettez Reliziana)

Birth: 1923, Tessala, Algeria

Death: 2006, Paris, France

Family: Four children

Nationality: Algerian

Education: No formal education

PERSONAL CHRONOLOGY:

- **1938:** Joins troupe of musicians known as the Hamadochis

- **1940s:** Begins performing using the stage name Cheikha Rimitti

- **1952:** Signs a record deal with the Pathe Marconi label; releases the single "Er-Raï, Er-Raï"

- **1954:** Denounced by Algerian officials following the release of the album *Charrag Gataa*, an album rife with themes of sexual libertinism

- **1971:** Seriously injured in a car accident in Algeria

- **1976:** Conducts a pilgrimage to Mecca and vows to abandon alcohol and tobacco

- **1978:** Migrates to France amid growing censorship by the Algerian government

- **1994:** Releases *Sidi Mansour*, a pop *raï* album produced by Robert Fripp and featured Flea of the Red Hot Chili Peppers on bass guitar

- **2001:** Performs in concert in the United States for the first time at Central Park in New York City

- **2005:** Returns to Algeria to write and record her final album titled *N'ta Goudami*

- **2006:** Suffers a fatal heart attack two days after a performance in Paris, France

in buying rounds of drinks for her fans. In essence, Rimitti made a career by performing traditional wedding songs in the cabarets of Algeria, and later, France.

During the 1940s, Rimitti began composing her own words for songs that were sung on Algerian radio stations. Although she was illiterate, Rimitti's lyrics featured clever wordplay, as well as expressions of anxiety and fear in regard to the political situation in Algeria. Rimitti made her first record in 1952 and attained her first hit with the song "Charrag Gataa," a song that

resulted in widespread denunciations for its lyrical content. In addition to sexually charged lyrics, Rimitti's ruminations on Algerian politics drew increased irritation from the colonial government.

Exile Rimitti's music was banned from the airwaves following Algeria's independence in 1962 and the concurrent rise of an Islamic government. Despite the ban, Rimitti was able to perform at private functions and weddings, and her music was spread via a semiunderground system of cassette trading. The 1970s found Rimitti undergoing major life changes, when in 1971 she was involved in a near-fatal car accident that left her in a coma for a short time. In 1976 Rimitti went on the hajj (Islamic pilgrimage) to Mecca, which compelled her to quit drinking alcohol and smoking tobacco. In 1978 Rimitti left Algeria and moved her home to France, where she continued to perform, gaining notoriety among the Arab expatriate community. With the 1980s came a period in which *raï* would attain a wider audience as such musicians as Cheb Khaled and Rachis Tara would incorporate electronic beats and synthesizer melodies with traditional instrumentation to create pop raï, thus cementing Rimitti's legacy as the mother of *raï*.

Worldwide Fame In 1994 Rimitti changed her sound with the recording and release of *Sidi Mansour*, an album in which vocals recorded in France were mixed with instrumentals recorded in the United Kingdom and Los Angeles. The album featured Rimitti's abandonment of the instrumentation of traditional *raï* in favor of that heard in pop *raï*. Notably, the album featured brass musicians known for recording with American rock avant-gardism Frank Zappar and the jazz-funk fusion bass of Flea of the American rock band the Red Hot Chili Peppers. Additionally, Briton Robert Fripp, most famous for his work with the rock band King Crimson, produced the album. Rimitti claimed that the album was exploitative in nature because she never met any of the musicians featured on the album. Nonetheless, the album was significant for Rimitti because it fulfilled a desire to distance herself from the traditional *raï* scene that featured artists that she felt were improperly profiting from her sound. Because of this new direction and the popularity of the featured players, *Sidi Mansour* was immensely popular, thus introducing *raï* to thousands of new listeners worldwide.

Rimitti recorded a few more albums in the wake of the successes and international renown of *Sidi Mansour*. One such album was titled *Aux Sources du Raï*, which was an anthology of Rimitti's works including rerecordings of some of her most famous songs. The album was released in 2000 for the French Institut du Monde label and was well received by critics worldwide. In 2001 Rimitti satisfied a lifelong desire to perform in the United States as a show of gratitude for the goodwill and happiness brought by the American military to Algeria during World War II Rimitti's Central Park concert lasted nearly two hours before an enthusiastic and grateful New York audience.

A Return to Algeria Although she had visited her homeland in the years following her exile, Rimitti had neither performed nor recorded in Algeria since 1978. In 2001 Rimitti expressed a longing to return to her native Algeria, a nation for which she had many concerns, stating, "I pray to God that the country finds peace and tranquility." Rimitti fulfilled her dream in 2005 when she wrote and recorded her final album released the following year, *N'ta Goudami*. The album would be her last original recording, as she suffered a fatal heart attack on 15 May 2006, two days after a performance in Paris, France.

INFLUENCES AND CONTRIBUTIONS

The Essence of Raï Similar to many forms of cultural expression, *raï* is reflective of both the history of those who perform it as well the environment in which they live. In this sense, *raï* is the music of the Algeria. The Arabic term rai can be taken to mean either opinion or way of seeing. *Raï* developed as a musical expression that combined the trans-Mediterranean sounds of northern Africa with those of the Berber-Algerian countryside.

EXPLORING

Central to the makeup, and indeed popularity, of *raï* is the synergistic nature of a music that incorporates myriad Mediterranean musical styles supporting lyrics addressing issues both contemporary and timeless. *Raï* developed in the Berber countryside in colonial Algeria and was transcultural from the very beginning, containing themes found in Spanish, French, Arabic, and Berber music. Moreover, raï was notable for lyrics sung in Orani, a dialect of Arabic that incorporates words and inflections from French, Spanish, and Berber. Many of the early raï singers were female, singing in a masculine vocal register that blurred the sexual identity of the singer. Traditional *raï* instrumentation is composed of four elements: the singer, a *gasaba* (reed flute), a *rbaba* (a single-stringed instrument played with a bow), and a drum, either a *gellal* or a *derbouka*. Lyrically, *raï* songs often contained poetry expressing themes of thirst–both sexual and literal–and movement, both reflective of life in the Maghreb.

CONTEMPORARIES

Cheb Khaled (1960–) is often viewed as *raï's* first superstar, earning him the title the king of *raï*. Born on 29 Feburary 1960 in Sidi-El-Houri, in the Oran region of Algeria, Khaled was influenced both by traditional *raï* and such Western musicians as James Brown and the Beatles. As he began his recording career in the early 1980s, Khaled worked with producer Rachid Baba Ahmed who introduced synthesizers and electronic beats to Khaled's traditionalist singing. The term *pop raï* was coined to describe the nexus between traditional and modern music. As Rimitti did, Khaled faced censorship by the Algerian government and moved to Paris in 1986. While in France Khaled continued to record incorporating elements of jazz, hip-hop, and reggae into his recordings, further blurring the definition of *raï* at the same time he was bringing greater notoriety to Algerian music. Khaled continues to record in France, and is one of the genre's most popular and influential artists.

Early forms of *raï* were performed in wedding rituals, serving the function of promoting fertility. Aurally, *raï* incorporated melodies and song structure that mirrored those of the Grawa-Sufi in western Africa, as well as Spanish flamenco music. In its essence, the musicianship of *raï* was largely a synthesis of sounds and instrumentation that could be heard throughout the Mediterranean world.

The uniqueness of *raï* can be found in the lyrics and their thematic expressions. The poetics of *raï* draw heavily from *malhun*, traditional Algerian folk poetry. Similar to *malhun*, *raï* is unconventional in its use of language and rebellious in its subject matter. *Raï* eventually displaced *malhun* poetry, causing some to lament the popularization of what was deemed an unrefined form of artistic expression.

Lyrics filled with sexuality were inherited from the wedding music custom, and it was from this tradition that Rimitti would construct a poetry that was filled with self-expressions of lust and desire. Nevertheless, sexual desire is but one of the myriad themes articulated in *raï*. The following Rimitti lyric embodies the complex and multifaceted rebelliousness of the music she helped popularize. She sang: "People adore God, I adore beer." The first portion is in direct contrast to the growing

Islamism of Algeria where theology was becoming the most widely expressed form of philosophical expression. The second part of the lyric is more nuanced, for the use of the first person singular, I, was considered taboo for singers of the region, and was downright scandalous for a woman. Additionally, that a woman adores beer stands in defiance of Islamic practice and also expresses the importance of liquid as a means of fulfilling a thirst that to desert dwellers may be more urgent than spiritual thirst. It was these lyrics that drew the ire of the Algerian government that ultimately banned Rimitti's music.

Rimitti's importance lay in the fact that she was able to take a localized, if not secretive, form of music and transform it into a nationwide phenomenon. In its earliest manifestations, *raï* was performed in private wedding ceremonies as an expression of love and fertility. It was deemed too risqué to be performed outside of these ceremonies. An oft-overlooked element of *raï* was that it was performed in the multicultural cabarets of Oran, a city that was more permissive than the rest of Algeria. It was in Oran, Algeria's second-largest city with a vital port, that *raï* was performed in clubs that permitted mixed-race and homosexual dancing. Lyrics filled with themes of lust and displacement featuring a sexually ambiguous voice appealed to the patrons of Oran's bars. Rimitti, and in turn *raï*, emerged from this environment as a popular musical expression of transculturation and the voice of the subaltern.

Raï and Femininity Rimitti's music served as an added form of minority expression, most notably as that of the woman in Arabic northern Africa. *Raï's* lyrical themes explored female sexuality and desire amid a largely masculine society that repressed the feminine voice. *Raï* became popularized in public spaces where women were viewed as objects of desire, all but guaranteeing that the music would stand in direct contrast to the growing Islamist sentiments that were becoming more prominent in Algeria. Rimitti, the so-called mother of *raï* would perform on stage as the central figure, demanding the focus of those in attendance. In her performances, Rimitti would perform, unveiled, singing lyrics filled with themes of feminine agency.

Described as unintentionally feminist, Rimitti's lyrics addressed themes of a female sexuality that could be considered illicit even by Western standards. Rimitti's first hit, titled "Charrag Gataa" (tear, lacerate), was denounced as immoral by critics for the song's implicit claim that women should not be burdened by the chains of virginity. Songs such as these are expressions of a woman's desire to maintain ownership and control of her own body and sexuality. Rimitti thus sings about woman as an object of desire through her own perspective, rather than a sexual being filtered through the prism of a man's lust.

THE WORLD'S PERSPECTIVE

The early 1990s featured a spike in the popularity of so-called world or non-Western music in such nations as the United States, Great Britain, and France. Contributing to such popularity was the spread of cable television, the embracement of world music by American college radio, and the popularity of the universal and durable compact disc as the preferred method of listening to music. Moreover, the increased presence of Middle Easterners and North Africans in Europe and the United States widened the potential audience for music such as *raï*. Rock musician Peter Gabriel's World of Music and Dance (WOMAD) tour contributed to the popularization of world music, as the tour featured a collective of musicians from all the around the globe and performed before sold-out audiences worldwide. In the mid-1990s, the Internet provided another point of access for those interested in listening to world music.

It was during this period that Rimitti found her largest audience outside of the Maghreb (North Africa), as well as her greatest levels of fame. In addition to geopolitical realities of the 1990s and early 2000s, Rimitti's embracement of pop *raï* made her music a feature in some of the world's dance clubs. Pop *raï's* incorporation of synthetic beats and melodies and accelerated tempos melded well with Rimitti's rapid delivery and haunting lyricism to create a music that successfully translated to a younger generation of listeners weaned on electronic music. This was the musical environment in which Rimitti attained a larger audience, as evidenced by increased record sales in Europe and the United States, along with her fan base in the Maghreb.

In addition to robust sales, Rimitti's albums were well received critically. Much has been made about the haunting beauty of Rimitti's voice and its crackling tones that convey the spiritual and literal thirsts that make *raï* both unique and reflective of life in the Maghreb. Rimitti's traditional *raï* albums place her voice at the forefront of the musical production, as the sparse instrumentals serve a purely backing purpose. To the chagrin of some critics, Rimitti's turn toward pop *raï* saw her voice become part of a larger cacophony in which the electronic beat—a clear appeal toward the dance club audience—is paramount to each song. Despite this shift in production, Rimitti's lyrics remain unchanged as the spirit of the music that she helped to popularize persisted.

Rimitti's death in 2006 was reported worldwide, speaking to both her importance in the sociocultural landscape of Mediterranean music and to her role within the growing popularization of world music. Obituaries following Rimitti's death were printed throughout the world and all addressed her importance in popularizing *raï* and presenting a dualistic voice of the subaltern—that of the female and the colonized. When discussing her cultural importance, it is easy to neglect the fact that she was a fine performer with a charisma unmatched by many of her contemporaries. Such sentiments are seen in Rimitti's obituary in the *Times* of London, which described her as "one of the most colourful figures in world music."

LEGACY

There are two means by which one can analyze the importance of a performer whose name is synonymous with the music she helped to popularize. First, and perhaps most important, is her legacy within her native country of Algeria. *Raï,* with its transcultural and secular tone, always represented the voice of the subaltern in both colonial and independent Algeria. In regard to pre-independent Algeria, *raï's* instrumentation, lyrical themes, and means of presentation stood in direct contrast to the cultural hegemony faced in the wake of French colonization. Following independence, *raï* then stood in direct contrast to the Islamic-based moral legislation that marked Algeria's government. Although rarely overtly political, *raï* was rebellious but never revolutionary. Rimitti once commented in an interview with Afropop Worldwide, *"Raï* music has always been a music of rebellion, a music that looks ahead." Thus a study of Rimitti's lifetime of rebellious career reads as a cultural and feminist history of Algeria in colonial, anticolonial, and postcolonial periods. In this sense, Rimitti's life is reflective of the essence of life in Algeria.

In terms of her legacy within the realm of world music, Rimitti serves as one of the most important voices from northern Africa. Although other *raï* artists received equal, if not greater, levels of notoriety, Rimitti's presence served as a reminder of the origins of this uniquely Algerian form of music. Moreover, her expressions of feminine—indeed human—desires have a universal appeal that is both timely and timeless. Rimitti's records and their socially conscious lyrics provide insight into the time and place in which they were recorded. Stated another way, Rimitti's albums challenge the listener to understand what was occurring in Algeria at the time they were recorded. Thus, Rimitti's worldwide legacy is that of a singular voice representative of both her gender and her people.

BIBLIOGRAPHY

Afropop Worldwide. "Interview with Cheikha Rimitti." Available from http://www.afropop.org/multi/feature/ID/44/?lang=gb.

Bamia, Aida Adib. *The Graying of the Raven: Cultural and Sociopolitical Significance of Algerian Folk Poetry.* Cairo: American University in Cairo Press, 2001.

Gross, Joan, David McMurray, and Ted Swedenburg. "Arab Noise and Ramadan Nights: Rai, Rap, and Franco-Maghrebi Identities." In *The Anthropology of Globalization, a Reader,* edited by Jonathan Xavier Inda and Renato Rosaldo. Oxford: Blackwell Publishers, 2002.

Marranci, Gabriele. "Pop-*Raï:* From a 'Local' Tradition to Globalization." In *Mediterranean Mosaic: Popular Music and Global Sounds,* edited by Goffredo Plastino. New York: Routledge, 2003.

McMurray, David, and Ted Swedenburg. "Rai Tide Rising." *Middle East Report* 169 (March–April 1991): 39–42.

"Obituary, Cheikha Rimitti." *Times* (London), 17 May 2006. Available from http://www.timesonline.co.uk.

Virolle, Marie. "Representations and Female Roles in the *Raï* Song." In *Music and Gender: Perspectives from the Mediterranean,* edited by Tullia Magrini. Chicago: University of Chicago Press, 2003.

Kenneth Shonk

ROKEN, MOHAMMED AL-
(1962–)

Mohammed Abdullah al-Roken (Muhammad Abdullah Muhammad Al Rukn, al-Rukn) is a leading legal scholar and lawyer in the United Arab Emirates (U.A.E.). His career has included legal representation of public and private sector clients before all the courts of the U.A.E. and he has served as an adviser to the Federal National Council. However, he has become an outspoken critic of the country's justice system and the government has taken legal action against him. Al-Roken has earned wide admiration as a committed teacher, as a serious and often passionate voice on legal and human rights issues, and in his services to the legal profession, both nationally and internationally.

PERSONAL HISTORY

Al-Roken was born in the emirate of Dubai in 1962. In 1971 Dubai joined with several other emirates to form the U.A.E. He earned an LL.B. degree in law and politics from the U.A.E. National University in 1985, and holds both an LL.M. (1985) and a Ph.D. (1992) in constitutional law from the University of Warwick in the United Kingdom. He practices law in several specialties as senior member of the law firm al-Roken & Associates. He served as president of the U.A.E. Bar Association, is currently vice president of the Union Intérnationale des Avocats, representing the U.A.E., and is a member of several leading international legal associations.

Al-Roken had been an associate professor of public law and assistant dean of the Faculty of Shari'a and Law at the U.A.E. National University from 1992 to 2002. He is a noted author of books and articles on a wide range of legal matters. In the past few years, he has spoken and written forcefully on human rights issues, especially with

BIOGRAPHICAL HIGHLIGHTS

Name: Mohammed Abdullah al-Roken
(Muhammad Abdullah Muhammad Al Rukn,
al-Rukn)

Birth: 1962, Emirate of Dubai

Nationality: Emirati

Education: LL.B. (law and politics), U.A.E.
National University, 1985; LL.M.
(constitutional law), University of Warwick,
United Kingdom, 1985; Ph.D. (constitutional
law), University of Warwick, 1992.

PERSONAL CHRONOLOGY:

• **1992:** Assistant professor of law in the Faculty of
Law and Shari'a on the U.A.E. National
University

• **1994:** Assistant dean for student affairs, U.A.E.
National University

• **1998:** Vice dean, U.A.E. National University;
chairman, U.A.E. Jurists Association

• **2002:** Vice president representing the U.A.E.
with the Union Internationale des Avocats
(International Association of Lawyers)

respect to the situation of expatriate workers in the U.A.E. The government has curtailed his teaching, imposed restrictions on his writing and public speaking, and has on two occasions in 2006 detained him for questioning about his human rights activities. In 2007 he was sentenced by a U.A.E. court to a three-month prison sentence for sex out of wedlock, a charge that international rights groups characterized as contrived.

A complex character, al-Roken's seemingly Western-style liberalism in defense of legal and human rights coexists with a strong commitment to the traditions and morals of Islamic society that might otherwise seem to place him in the camp of political Islamists. He views the rapid pace of economic and social development in the U.A.E., and especially in Dubai, with deep misgiving. His reaction to Dubai's loss of its former identity has led him into what he characterizes as internal exile: physical removal of his place of residence to the outskirts of Dubai City.

INFLUENCES AND CONTRIBUTIONS

Al-Roken has been an important figure since the 1990s as a scholar, lawyer, and human rights activist in the U.A.E.

Immediately after earning his Ph.D. in 1992, al-Roken became an associate professor of law in the Faculty of Law and Shari'a of the U.A.E. National University. In 1994 he was made assistant dean for student affairs and in 1998 was elevated to the position of vice dean of the Faculty of Law and Shari'a. His rapid rise as a teacher and university administrator was matched by a large output of books (seven in Arabic) and articles that have appeared in leading Arab and Western law journals and other publications. His writings have ranged widely over legal and other subjects, including the U.A.E. constitution, the U.A.E.-Iran dispute over ownership of three Persian/Arab Gulf islands, and Christian-Muslim dialogue. Even when his high profile human rights activities had drawn the anger of the government, causing him to lose his university position, the Dubai Cultural Council recognized him as one of the emirate's leading academics. In addition, al-Roken has participated in the discussions of international forums, such as the Arab Judicial Forum.

DEMOCRACY IS NOT AN EPIDEMIC

Current U.S. policy is based on the premise that the root of terrorism and hatred of the U.S. in the Middle East are [sic] to be found in the absence of democracy and in the existence of political regimes that have been closed and fossilized for decades. The solution according to the Bush administration is to establish a new model of democracy within the Arab countries.

The present is the best time to rebuild the region because political conditions are favorable, and objections and resistance to change are weak. The U.S. scenario for redrawing the regional map follows the order in which countries surrounding Iraq will be affected by change. They are the Gulf states, followed by Syria, followed by Egypt.

Democracy is not an epidemic that can spread from one state to another. Creating a model by force of arms will not be appealing to people of the region, particularly those that have not suffered greatly from the absence of political freedoms, humiliation and huge economic decline in the way the Iraqi people have.

ROKEN, MUHAMMAD ABDULLAH AL-. "THE DEMOCRATIZATION PIPE DREAM." *DAILY STAR* (BEIRUT), 11 MARCH 2003. AVAILABLE FROM HTTP://WWW.DAILYSTAR.COM.LB.

In the same year that he became an academic vice dean, al-Roken was chosen, at the age of thirty-six, to be chairman of the U.A.E. Jurists Association (Bar Association), reflecting his position with al-Roken & Associates, a leading commercial, corporate, and banking law firm in Dubai. He and the other members of the firm represent private and public U.A.E. clients as well as foreign clients investing in the U.A.E. before both local and federal courts. al-Roken has also acted as an adviser to the Federal National Council on pending draft legislation. Internationally, he is active as a member of the International Association of Constitutional Law and the International Bar Association, and serves as vice president of the International Association of Lawyers.

It is as a human rights advocate that al-Roken has drawn greatest attention, and it seems likely that his most significant contributions and his most lasting influence are to be in this area. He has made his voice heard on this subject in scholarly publications and increasingly in the popular news media, both newspapers and television. As early as 2000 he was banned from writing a column in the local press because of its sharp criticism of the government. Two years later he was forbidden to teach at the U.A.E. National University.

Al-Roken has offered a sober and thoughtful critique of the laws enacted by the U.A.E. and the other Gulf Cooperation Council (GCC) states to counter the terrorist threat.

In 2005 in the Internet journal *openDemocracy.net*, he expressed concern that the U.A.E.'s antiterrorism law was overly broad in its reach. Previously he had been harsh in his criticism of the antiterrorism policies of the U.A.E.'s principal ally, the United States. In the U.A.E. press in 2002, he described the School of the Americas, a U.S. training facility for Latin American military officers, in an article titled "America's School for Torture" and accused the United States of institutionalizing the violation of human rights. In a 2003 *al-Jazeera* editorial, he described the U.S.-led overthrow of the SADDAM HUSSEIN regime as the initial phase of a democratization pipe dream aimed at reshaping the Middle East region to better serve the interests of the United States and its allies.

It is his efforts to influence the U.A.E. government on granting greater political freedom to its citizens and on human rights issues, especially concerning expatriate workers, which have brought al-Roken international attention and a punitive response from the U.A.E. government. On several occasions, the government has forced cancellation of his public lectures, one of which was about the U.S.-led invasion of Iraq and another on the importance of holding popular elections in the U.A.E. In 2000 his newspaper column in the U.A.E. was banned and in 2002 he was no longer permitted to teach at the U.A.E. National University. In 2004, with

twenty-one other U.A.E. nationals, he submitted an application to establish a human rights organization, a request that, as of 2007, has not been acted upon.

Al-Roken has frequently represented expatriate workers in Dubai in their suits against employers who have allegedly failed to pay wages or offer adequate working conditions. Some of those employers are from prominent families in Dubai, and the lawsuits strengthen official antipathy toward him. On 27 July 2006 and on 23 August 2006 officials in Dubai detained him, both times to interrogate him about his human rights activities and his public speeches. On the second occasion he was held for three days on a charge of immoral behavior, and in January 2007 was tried on that charge and sentenced to three months in prison for sex out of wedlock with a German woman. The arrest that led to the trial and conviction came soon after an interview that al-Roken gave on Arab satellite television about the Israeli assault on Lebanon following the Hizbullah killing and kidnapping of Israeli soldiers. Human Rights Watch condemned his prosecution in a letter to U.A.E. president Shaykh KHALIFA BIN ZAYID AL NAHYAN. Al-Roken has appealed his sentence.

THE WORLD'S PERSPECTIVE

Al-Roken is deeply concerned about the future of his society, in particular Dubai where he was born and grew up, and that concern has been reflected in his widely reported efforts to promote human rights, the growth of civil society, and the development of greater political freedoms. He embodies what would appear to be contradictory impulses. Despite his exposure to Western intellectual traditions, his impressive scholarship, and his brilliant practice of law, he is a traditionalist whose defense of religious morals might even be seen as identifying him with proponents of political Islam. His arguments for democratic reform are aimed not so much at endowing Dubai and the U.A.E. with the democratic values of Western societies as they are at enabling his society to defend its traditional values against the onrush of alien values. He has been described as a gadfly, someone who is troubled by the direction the government of his country has taken and who feels compelled to speak out. His views significantly reflect those of many others in the Gulf states, who are also dismayed at the personal and societal disruption resulting from extremely rapid economic and social development. Because of this, al-Roken's views are certain to have an important continuing impact in the U.A.E. and beyond.

LEGACY

The force of his intellect and his astute use of the news media to air his opinions has given al-Roken considerable stature in the Gulf region and in the international community. Widely noted intervention on his behalf by international human rights organizations has helped to give him and his views further prominence.

Al-Roken's high-profile human rights activities have reinforced U.S. government human rights criticisms of the U.A.E. (even though he has taken issue with the way those criticisms have been made) and helped to draw special attention to this issue. He has focused international attention on a major problem for Dubai and the other Gulf states, the increasing restiveness of ill-paid foreign laborers lacking basic rights, which, if not soon effectively addressed, could undercut the glittering edifice of modernization on the Arab side of the Gulf. Whatever the outcome of al-Roken's appeal of his court sentence, his so-called gadfly political and human rights activities are certain to be emulated and carried forward by others, insuring a significant legacy, although the specific shape of that legacy cannot presently be discerned.

BIBLIOGRAPHY

Heine, Peter, and Haitham Aiash, eds. "Gedanken zum Christlich-Muslimischen Dialog." In *Vom 11 September zum 20 Marz, 2006.* Berlin: Verlag fur Integration und Wissenschaft, 2006.

Hellyer, Peter, and Ibrahim Al Abed, eds. "Dimensions of the U.A.E.-Iran Dispute over Three Islands." In *United Arab Emirates: A New Perspective.* London: Trident Press, 2001.

Robbers, Gerhard, ed. "United Arab Emirates Constitution." In *Encyclopedia of World Constitutions.* New York: Facts on File, 2006.

Roken, Muhammad Abdullah al-. "The Democratization Pipe Dream." *Daily Star* (Beirut) (11 March 2003). Available from http://www.dailystar.com.lb.

Malcolm C. Peck

RUBY
(1981–)

Rania Hussein Muhammad Tawfiq, known as Ruby or Rouby, is an Egyptian singer and actress. She started her career as a model, but rose to fame as a singer. Within a very short period she became renowned for her music as well as her beautiful body and sexy dance moves. Egyptian television has banned her music videos for being too sexy and seductive.

PERSONAL HISTORY

Ruby was born on 8 October 1981 in Cairo, Egypt. She started her career as a model. Later on, she decided to expand beyond the modeling world to become a singer and actress. Her big break was courtesy of the Polish singer Marcel Romanoff, who spotted Ruby in front of

Ruby. © ALADIN ABDEL NABY/REUTERS/CORBIS.

his audience at a performance in Cairo; Romanoff used her in the video for his song "Don't Make Me Cry." While she was a law student at Bani Suwayf University, Ruby began to appear in television commercials. She landed a role in the film *Suqut Hansawwar*, where she played a romantic, wealthy girl who falls in love with her driver. Rania got her new name, Ruby, during this stage of her career.

Ruby's first music video for her debut single "Inta arif leih" appeared in 2003, bringing about bitter criticisms concerning her belly dance costume. Nevertheless, the song, which was composed by Egyptian musician Muhammad Rahim, brought her fame. Her second video, titled "Leih Beydary Kadah," was considered by the critics as provocative as the first one. Her third video, "al-Gharam," was considered too erotic to be shown to the public, so it was banned by Egypt, Syria, and many other Arabic countries. The video was taken from Ruby's 2004 movie *Saba Waraqat Kotchina* (7 playing cards).

Later, Ruby released other videos such as "Ana Umri Mastaneat Hadd" and "Ghawi," which also were taken from the movie *Saba Waraqat Kotchina.* This movie, directed by Sherif Sabri, was censored in Egypt due to its sexual content. In 2005, Sabri directed another video for Ruby titled "Ibqaa Qabilni." The clip's storyboard was about an ancient Egyptian dancing seductively and playing with a snake.

Ruby has received support from Melody Hits TV, which always broadcasts her videos' premieres. It is

BIOGRAPHICAL HIGHLIGHTS

Name: Rania Hussein Muhammad Tawfiq, known as Ruby or Rouby

Birth: 1981, Cairo, Egypt

Family: Single

Nationality: Egyptian

Education: Studied at Bani Suwayf University, Egypt

PERSONAL CHRONOLOGY:
- **2001:** Starred in the movie *Suqut Hansawwar*
- **2003:** First music video "Inta arif leih" is released
- **2004:** Second video "Leih Beydary Kadah" is released

believed that this has been a result of Sabri's agreement with this TV channel. It is rumored that Ruby married her mentor Sabri; however, both of them have denied this. Ruby was scheduled to work on the video for her song "Taht al-Dush" (Under the shower). The media in and outside of Egypt has tried to guess what the upcoming video will be like. However, Ruby's style and the name of the upcoming clip are the best clues for this.

INFLUENCES AND CONTRIBUTIONS

Ruby was influenced by Polish singer Romanoff who saw her at his performance in front of an audience at the American University in Cairo. Romanoff found the Arabic beauty he was looking for in Ruby for his video. Appearing in Romanoff's video influenced Ruby deeply, because it spurred her to change her career goals and become a singer and actress. After her work in television commercials, she became known by thousands. As she became more well known, she received offers to play roles in films. However, she became famous immediately after her first music video, 2003's "Inta arif leih," which was directed by Sabri, who is believed to be the most influential person over Ruby. In addition to producing Ruby's songs, Sabri takes every occasion to defend her to the public, arguing that her videos are artistic, tasteful, and rhythmic. In his view, Ruby does not push the social borders and she has started a trend. Egyptian singer Rahim, who composed the majority of Ruby's music at the beginning of her career, was also influential over her career. As a talented, persistent, and decisive artist, Ruby seems destined to become an example for many singers in Egypt and beyond.

THE WORLD'S PERSPECTIVE

Global perceptions of Ruby generally have been positive, and interest in her music videos is great. Her fame as an artist grew very fast. Even though many Arabic countries have banned her videos and films because of her provocative style and suggestive moves, she has become more and more popular in those countries and abroad. It is obvious that star has pushed the borders of Egypt and perhaps will become well known worldwide.

LEGACY

It is believed that Ruby is more popular than any politician or intellectual figure in Egypt. According to a survey held by a Cairo newspaper, Ruby is the most interesting person in Egypt. The censorship committee of the country considers her as one of the top seductive singers, thus deciding to ban the airing of her songs.

BIBLIOGRAPHY

Ruby's official Web site. Available from http://ruby.tv/.

Sharp, Heather. "Sexy Stars Push the Limit in Egypt." BBC News (4 August 2005). Available from http://news.bbc.co.uk/1/hi/world/middle_east/4722945.stm.

Adil M. Asgarov

SAAB, ELIE
(1964–)

Elie Saab is a Lebanese designer best known for the sheer crimson gown that Halle Berry wore when she received an Academy Award for Best Actress in March of 2002. This was a monumental moment for both Berry and Saab. He became the first Lebanese designer to ever dress an Oscar winner. After that his fame expanded from Middle Eastern royalty and Arabian princesses to American celebrities. The Lebanese press nicknamed Saab "Precious Genius" after he debuted his first set of designs, and CNN described his style as "Arabian Nights' fantasy." His fame and power has risen in Lebanon, as well as in Europe, the United States, and rest of the world.

PERSONAL HISTORY

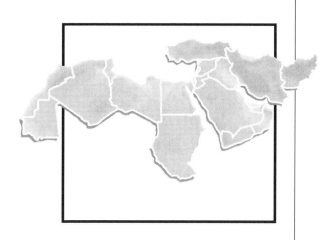

Saab was born on 4 July 1964 in Beirut, Lebanon. By six, he started his career in fashion. Saab is seen as a child prodigy by fashion experts because he is self-trained. A young Saab sewed and designed clothes, but his parents expected him to become a tailor. In 1981 Saab relocated to study fashion in Paris. After one year, however, he returned to Beirut during the Lebanese Civil War. At eighteen, Saab started his own design studio making wedding dresses and evening gowns with a blend of Western and Oriental styles. Saab soon debuted his first collection under his own label at the Casino du Liban. The triumphant event won him the attention of the press. He consequently obtained numerous clients including princesses because of his signature style of making clothing using lace, beading, gems, pearls, crystals, silk threads, rich fabrics like chiffon, and detailed embroidery. His client list grew even stronger in 1990 when Saab acquired a larger studio to handle orders from other countries, including Switzerland and France.

Saab became the first non-Italian designer to become a member of the Italian Camera Nazionale della Moda in 1997. While in Rome at Roma Alta Moda, he showed his first haute couture (a high fashion, exclusive, and trendsetting look) collection outside of Lebanon. The next year he held a fashion show in Monaco attended by Monaco's Princess Stephanie at the plaza of the Monte Carlo Casino. In Milan that year, he also debuted his prêt-a-porter (clothing produced for sale to the general public) collection as, at the time, the only featured non-Italian designer.

After 2000 Saab began doing off-list shows in Paris during the haute couture season, although not scheduled as a featured designer. He became a member of the Chambre Syndicale de la Haute Couture in 2003, making him an invitee and part of the official schedule, a high honor within the design world. Saab showed his first haute couture collection in Paris in 2003, the home of his permanent prêt-a-porter runway.

Elie Saab. AP IMAGES.

INFLUENCES AND CONTRIBUTIONS

The style, elegance, and beauty of his native Beirut, for which it is famous, deeply influenced Saab. He remained true to his culture by blending Middle Eastern cultural style with European styles, especially French and Italian, which in particular have influenced Lebanese fashion. He is recognized for his seductive yet elegant designs that could have been pulled directly from a fantasy. Critics describe his designs as international and modern. Saab's fashions fit women's curves and complement them with elaborate detailing. His main themes are romance and femininity. Saab's accomplishments may result from his bringing the fashion world together through his work. He blends many international styles, while remaining true to the historical and contemporary fashion trends of his native Lebanon.

THE WORLD'S PERSPECTIVE

Global perceptions of Saab have been overwhelmingly positive since his emergence on the international scene in 2002 as the first Lebanese to dress an Oscar winner when he designed Berry's gown. Since then he has designed fashions for many stars including singer Beyoncé Knowles, actresses Marcia Cross, Teri Hatcher, Nicolette Sheridan, Jessica Simpson, Salma Hayek, Patricia Heaton, Debra Messing, and Catherine Zeta-Jones; and Queen Rania of Jordan. Saab has used his design talents to bridge the gaps between East and West, bringing them closer together and reducing cultural misunderstandings.

Featuring elegant evening gowns, Saab has sixty retail outlets and boutiques around the globe. His label is also

BIOGRAPHICAL HIGHLIGHTS

Name: Elie Saab

Birth: 1964, Beirut, Lebanon

Family: Wife, Claudine; three children

Nationality: Lebanese

Education: Fashion studies in Paris, France

PERSONAL CHRONOLOGY:

- **1981:** Moves to Paris to study fashion

- **1982:** Opens design studio producing wedding dresses and evening gowns in Beirut

- **Mid-1980s:** Debuts first collection under his own label at the Casino du Liban

- **1990:** Acquires larger studio to handle growing business and orders from international clients

- **1997:** Becomes first non-Italian member of Camera Nazionale della Moda; shows first haute couture collection in Rome

- **1998:** Holds fashion show in Monaco attended by Monaco's Princess Stephanie; debuts prêt-a-porter collection in Milan

- **2002:** Dresses Halle Berry for her Best Actress Oscar win

- **2003:** Becomes member of the Chambre Syndicale de la Haute Couture; shows first haute couture collection in Paris

known as "ES." ES is headquartered in Beirut, with offices in New York, Paris, and Milan. Saab is known for dazzling clothing that is sexy yet classy. His creations include luxurious fabrics with flourishes and lines.

The international press and colleagues have praised his workmanship and choice of styles that render women beautiful. His fabrication is Middle Eastern, carried out by the one hundred artisans in the Beirut Atelier. His collections featuring rich fabrics and sumptuous embroidery—which have become indispensable to women seeking to show outward signs of prosperity—never cease to amaze.

Using glaciers of silver sequins sparkling on icy gowns, Saab has reached the peak of flashy fashion. No wonder Knowles followed in the high-heeled footsteps of Berry, also selecting Saab as her designer of choice. Having captured the attention of the public, the fashion press, and high-profile celebrities across the world, Saab's

CONTEMPORARIES

Abed Mahfouz (1956-) began his fashion career in the tailoring industry. Mahfouz earned a degree in electrical engineering in 1978, then fell into the garment world through the necessity of helping her sister with her tailoring business in 1985. He became fascinated with design and aspired to create his own fashions. In 1999, Mahfouz was propelled onto the fashion scene with his first collection of wedding dresses premiering at the Royal Plaza Hotel in Beirut. Like Saab, who also has an ongoing passion for creating unique and stunning wedding gowns, Mahfouz has broken into the haute couture world with his premiere collection in 2000.

Güler Sabanci. AP IMAGES.

career likely will continue to flourish and inspire other Lebanese fashion designers.

LEGACY

Although it is too early to assess Saab's ultimate legacy, he has established himself as a capable and talented fashion designer, putting his native Lebanon on the fashion map for the first time. In light of his great achievements, more Lebanese are likely to follow in his footsteps and impact the global fashion industry.

BIBLIOGRAPHY

"Elie Saab Collection Makes it to Paris Despite Protest." Ya Libnan. Updated 23 January 2007. Available from http://yalibnan.com.

Menkes, Suzy. "Elie Saab's flashy fashion." *International Herald Tribune*, 23 January 2007. Available from http://www.iht.com.

Mower, Sarah. "Runway Review: Elie Saab." Style.com. Updated 22 January 2007. Available from http://www.style.com.

Saab, Elie. Interview with the Scene. CNN. Updated 9 October 2006. Available from http://www.cnn.com/2006/TRAVEL/02/03/beirut.qa.

Khodr M. Zaarour

SABANCI, GÜLER
(1955–)

Güler Sabanci is the chairperson of Sabanci Holding, the second largest Turkish industrial and financial conglomerate, with more than sixty companies. In 2006, she was on *Forbes* magazine's list of the world's "100 Most Powerful Women" and ninth on the *Financial Times*' yearly list of the "Top 25 Business Women" of Europe.

PERSONAL HISTORY

Sabanci was born in 1955 in Adana, in southeast Turkey, where her grandfather Haci Ömer Sabanci had established the family's first business, in the textile industry. She was the oldest child of İhsan Sabanci, oldest of Haci Ömer's six sons. Although her very wealthy family was conservative, she was raised in the same way as her brother and male cousins. This was her grandfather's preference. Sabanci told Zeynep Guven at *Hurriyet* that her grandfather said, "My girl will grow up, go to school, learn how to drive, wear pants and go to the factory."

Sabanci attended the TED Ankara High School, where she exhibited an independent and playful character and was a leader of her class. She graduated in 1978 from Boğaziçi (Bosphorus) University in Istanbul with a bachelor's degree in business administration. Eager to go into business, she interned during her free time in factories owned by her family. She has said that she regrets that she did not appreciate her college years enough, because she was always thinking about business.

Immediately after graduation, Sabanci started her career in the Sabanci group's tire manufacturing company, LasSA, as a management trainee. She worked in different functions within the company and was its

BIOGRAPHICAL HIGHLIGHTS

Name: Güler Sabanci

Birth: 1955, Adana, Turkey

Family: Unmarried

Nationality: Turkish

Education: B.A., management, Boğaziçi (Bosphorus) University, Istanbul, 1978

PERSONAL CHRONOLOGY:

- **1978:** Starts as management trainee in Sabanci Holding's tire manufacturing company, LasSA
- **1985-1999:** Manager of KordSA, the group's tire cord manufacturing company
- **1999-2004:** Head of Sabanci Holding's Tire and Reinforcement Materials unit
- **2004-Present:** Chair of Sabanci Holding, head of Sabanci Foundation

general manager for fourteen years. During this period, she managed a series of joint ventures with foreign companies such as Bekaert and Bridgestone, and was later responsible for restructuring separate divisions into a single strategic unit, Tire and Reinforcement Materials, which she oversaw as a member of Sabanci Holding's board. Her work earned her the nickname "the rubber queen." In May 2004, she was elected chairperson of Sabanci Holding, following the death of her uncle Sakip Sabanci, who with his brothers had founded and run the conglomerate for 38 years.

Sabanci also oversees the operations of the Sabanci Foundation (VakSa), Sabanci University, and the Sakip Sabanci Museum. In her spare time, she likes to paint and spend time in the private vineyard she runs with an uncle, where they produce a wide variety of wines.

INFLUENCES AND CONTRIBUTIONS

From early childhood, Sabanci was influenced by her grandfather, Haci Ömer Sabanci, and uncle, Sakip Sabanci, who created and greatly expanded the family business empire. To the surprise of some, her grandfather, a traditional and conservative businessman, took her to his factory even when she was small, and supported her on every front.

Sabanci has been instrumental, both before and after becoming chairperson, in partnering Sabanci Holding with its international counterparts by means of various joint ventures, including those mentioned above. Joint ventures provide financing, access to new markets, and the leverage of the brand names of the partnering companies; they also require robust management to align the business cultures and practices. These ventures have generated productive synergies for Sabanci Holding, giving it access to know-how and technology and allowing it to exploit new industries.

On becoming chairperson, Sabanci initiated a reorganization of Sabanci Holding to reduce and consolidate business units, and to allow them to operate more autonomously. She sought to redefine the company's vision and mission, identify potential new businesses, and develop a new management approach based on delegation and teamwork, an untraditional idea in the conservative Turkish business world. "'Our vision is to triple our revenues to $30bn,'" she has said, "partly through differentiation—'the future of business'—and through investing in the energy sector." She is also a leading advocate of Turkey's entry into the European Union. "In ten years' time Turkey will be a very attractive market … by then its population will be around ninety million, and it'll be a very young population that will bring a great dynamism to Europe" (Smith).

She bought out Dupont's 50 percent share of the joint venture DUSA, making Sabanci Holding the European market leader in polyester manufacturing. By playing in various industries such as polyester, tire and reinforcement materials, cement, textile, energy, and retail, Sabanci Holding provides means for the Turkish economy to grow by exports, foreign investment, and new job opportunities. Akbank, Sabanci Holding's financial institution, received the highest credit ranking in the Turkish banking sector from Moody's, an international credit risk evaluator. Citibank recently purchased 20 percent of Akbank's shares, creating a brand-new partnership. Sabanci Holding achieves risk diversification and business synergies by variety in its business.

In recent years, Sabanci Holding has expanded into Argentina, Brazil, Egypt, Germany, Iran, and the United States, the first Turkish company to expand so far outside its borders. The group's net revenue increased from US$8.6 billion in 2004 to $10.6 billion in 2005; the number of employees increased from 34,000 to 45,000, while Akbank (a Sabanci subsidiary) and Sabanci Holding, at second and fourth place respectively, have become two of the most highly valued companies on the Istanbul Stock Exchange.

Giving Back Sabanci spends considerable time and effort "giving back" to society. "This country made me rich, so it's my duty to give back. I wear two hats. The one is business and increasing my shareholders' value; the other is social responsibility. I believe in the goodness of peo-

CONTEMPORARIES

Sakip Sabanci (1933-2004), Güler Sabanci's uncle, was a businessman, philanthropist, and art collector who, with his brothers, founded Sabanci Holding and led it for thirty-eight years. Under his leadership, the conglomerate grew extensively by expanding into businesses such as textiles, food, tourism, paper and packing, automotives, chemicals, tobacco, cement, insurance, and banking.

Sabanci was not only a very successful businessman and entrepreneur but he was also one of the most colorful and popular personalities in Turkish society. He was listed as the 147th richest person in the world by *Forbes* magazine in 2004. Like his niece, he "gave back" to society by establishing the Sabanci Foundation, through which he exercised the generosity he was famous for, and the museum that was named in his honor after his death.

Sabanci died of cancer at the age of seventy-one. His friendly, humorous, generous character—always smiling, instantly connecting with people, whether poor, rich, famous, or obscure—is remembered fondly by millions. He was, very unusually, given a state funeral.

ple, of trying to be a good person" (Smith). She is president of the Board of Trustees of Sabanci University, near Istanbul, which she helped her uncle Sakip Sabanci establish in 1996 and which she has worked hard to bring to the highest international standards. "Establishing a university is way different from establishing a factory since there is no room for error," she has said (*Capital*). The university is built around the idea of "Creating and Developing Together." During her own university years, she was impatient to go into business and did not spend much time enjoying her life. She therefore supported a system at Sabanci University that allows students to be involved in industry more than they are at other universities so that they know more about business life before they graduate. They can thus get the most out of their academic and campus life while practicing what they learn as early as possible. Sabanci University is also unique in Turkey in the way students determine their major field of study. As in most American universities, they take two years of classes before having to decide on their major. By then, they are more comfortable in their choice, which is reflected in their performance.

Sabanci is also chairperson of the Sakip Sabanci Museum, established by Sakip Sabanci in a former family residence in Istanbul. The museum displays Sakip's extensive collection of Ottoman art and calligraphy, and under the leadership of Güler Sabanci, exhibitions of modern art as well. Art is Sabanci's second passion; at the age of twenty-seven, she came to a crossroad, where she felt she had to make a choice in her professional life, either to keep going in business or become a painter. She decided on the first, but has never abandoned her interest in the second. Through the museum, she introduces the public to the work of internationally famous artists through exhibitions, and through education programs and other activities helps young people and students develop a taste for art.

In addition to these responsibilities, Sabanci is the head of the Sabanci Foundation, a charitable institution founded by Sakip Sabanci and financed by Sabanci Holding. It is the largest of its kind in Turkey. The Sabanci family has always been public-spirited and is known for its generosity. The Sabanci Foundation has more than a hundred education, health, and cultural centers across Turkey and has spent more than $1.1 billion on such projects.

Promoting Women in Business One of Sabanci's biggest contributions is her success as a woman in business, being a role model for her contemporaries and for younger women. She has been successful in a patriarchal, male-dominated business world; she is the first woman ever to be on the board of Turkey's Businessmen's Association, a powerful group that helps shape the Turkish economy. In her interviews with international media, she attempts to correct foreign misperceptions about Turkey, both about the role of women and about other social issues. Her very visibility helps promote the idea of respect for women.

Sabanci believes a society can reach its potential by capitalizing on the abilities of women, by allowing them to participate fully. Her desire is a society in which women are evaluated by their talents and by the tangible results of their efforts. She wants every woman to be given the opportunity to prove her merit and demonstrate what she can accomplish.

THE WORLD'S PERSPECTIVE

As the British journalist Helena Smith put it in 2006, "If Güler Sabanci didn't exist you wouldn't dare to invent her as a realistic fictional character. It's not just her wealth, which is immense. Or that she is a free spirit in a part of the world that is undeniably patriarchal. Or even that she presides over a family-controlled business while, somehow, also being a vintner and Europe's newest, hottest patron of the arts. It is that Güler Sabanci is all these things in Turkey, a country more bound to tradition than most."

PROFESSIONAL WOMEN HAVE ALWAYS BEEN HIGHLY REGARDED IN THIS COUNTRY

The West has the wrong perception about Turkey itself. Since the [foundation of] the [secular] Republic in 1923, professional women have always been highly regarded in this country, whereas I remember going to England in the early Eighties where women were not allowed to lunch in a famous bankers' club in the City.

All over the world there is a gender issue … but in business it is less of a problem because you can be more specific and result-orientated, and measure the results. I was the eldest grandchild of six sons and I must have been three or four when my grandfather took me to the factory.

Sakip [her uncle and the chairperson of Sabanci Holding for thirty-eight years] gave me a lot of moral support. I started off doing standard clerical work, filling out forms in the purchasing department. Then I climbed, step by step. There were times, at some levels, where people may have hesitated, where they may have said "is she going to be able to handle it [managing the company]?" But I did.

SMITH, HELENA. "FIRST LADY OF TURKISH FINANCE." THE OBSERVER (U.K.), 17 SEPTEMBER 2006. AVAILABLE FROM HTTP://OBSERVER.GUARDIAN.CO.UK.

her leadership, the conglomerate has continued to grow its revenue in double digits with new expansions under way such as expansion into the energy sector with potential $3B investment, according to *Forbes*. She has striven hard not only for the sake of business, shareholders, and employees, but has put her time and energy into good works such as the Sabanci Foundation, Sabanci University, and the Sabanci Museum.

BIBLIOGRAPHY

Guven, Zeynep, "I did not appreciate my college years as much." *Hurriyet*, 13 June 1999. Available from http://arsiv2.hurriyet.com.tr/tatilpazar/turk/99/06/13/eklhab/11ekl.htm.

"Evim. Üniversitem. Yüzüğüm (My House, My University, My Ring)." *Capital* (Germany) 20 (14–17 September 2006).

Smith, Helena, "First lady of Turkish finance." *The Observer* (U.K.), 17 September 2006. Available from http://observer.guardian.co.uk.

"The 100 Most Powerful Women: #65 Güler Sabanci." *Forbes*, 31 August 2006. Available from http://www.forbes.com.

Burcu Mercankaya

Sabanci, the most powerful woman in Turkey, with her position in business and society as well as diverse interests that would be hard for anyone to manage, shines as a female leader and, as someone who attracts the attention of the international media, helps Western countries understand Turkey and Turkish women better. She constantly mentions the rights Turkish women gained as early as the 1930s, even before most of their European counterparts, and how they are supported in the Turkish business world. She is a living refutation of common beliefs about Turkey as well as about the power of women.

LEGACY

Sabanci will be remembered as one of the most powerful woman in Turkish business life. As the leader of Turkey's second largest conglomerate, Sabanci Holding, she has demonstrated that women can be as competent and successful as men in management, given the opportunity. She has set the example for future female leaders. Under

SADDIKI, TAYEB
(1938–)

Playwright and director Tayeb Saddiki is considered among the foremost Moroccan dramatists of the twentieth century. Trained in classical Western theater, Saddiki also embraced traditional Moroccan theatrical styles, fusing the two into a path-breaking combination of Western and traditional Moroccan theater. Known for staging spectacles played to large crowds in big arenas, Saddiki developed a style of festive theater that became a popular favorite in the late 1960s and 1970s.

PERSONAL HISTORY

Saddiki was born in 1938 in Essaouaira, a city south of Rabat on Morocco's Atlantic coast. In the early 1950s, when Morocco was still under French colonial control, Saddiki began drama studies at Morocco's official French-directed theater program. Operating under the aegis of Morocco's Department of Youth and Sports, the program was directed by French dramatist André Voisin, who trained Saddiki and many of his contemporaries in classical European-style theater direction and performance.

In 1956, the year Morocco gained formal independence from France, Saddiki left to briefly pursue drama studies in France. Performing with Voisin's company, known as the Troupe du Théâtre Marocain, he participated in the 1956 Festival of Paris. He then worked in Rennes at the Centre Dramatique de l'Ouest with its founder, French dramatist Hubert Gignoux. Saddiki also

BIOGRAPHICAL HIGHLIGHTS

Name: Tayeb Saddiki

Birth: 1938, Essaouaira, Morocco

Nationality: Moroccan

Education: Drama studies at Morocco's official French-directed theater program, early 1950s

PERSONAL CHRONOLOGY:

- **1950s:** Studies theater under André Voisin and the Department of Youth and Sports

- **1956:** Travels to France to perform with the Troupe du Théâtre Marocain

- **1957:** Returns to Morocco; forms the Worker's Theatre troupe

- **1960:** Establishes the Théâtre Municipal de Casablanca

- **1963:** Forms the Saddiki Troupe, a group unaffiliated with official theater

- **1967:** Debuts *Diwan Sidi Abd al-Rahman al-Madjub* at Morocco's Festival of the Throne

- **1971:** Debuts *Maqqamat Badi Zaman al-Hamadani*

- **1974:** Forms the People's Theatre (*Masrah al-Nas*), a traveling company

- **1984:** Directs and releases *Zift*, a film adaptation of his original play *Fi Tariq*

- **1990s:** Becomes artistic director of the Mogador theater in Casablanca

served as stage manager at the Théâtre Nationale Populaire in Paris, which at that time was under the direction of French actor and director Jean Vilar.

Saddiki returned to Morocco in 1957 where, at the urging of the Moroccan workers' union (Union Marocaine du Travail), he formed the Workers' Theatre (Théâtre Travailliste). During the company's short-lived run, Saddiki staged works by French playwright Jean-François Regnard, Russian playwright Nikolai Gogol, Egyptian playwright TAWFIQ AL-HAKIM, and Greek dramatist Aristophanes. It was at this time Saddiki began formulating his own adaptations of Greek and European plays, translating them into formal and colloquial Arabic. His adaptation of Molière's *The Hypochondriac* (*Le Malade Imaginaire*) was Morocco's official entry in the 1958 Festival of the Theatre of Nations in Paris.

Following the 1959 dissolution of the Workers' Theatre, Saddiki returned to the Department of Youth and Sports, where the independent Moroccan government had established the Centre d'Art Dramatique as the new official center of Moroccan theater. Its company, the Troupe du Centre Marocain de Recherches, was headed by Moroccan dramatists Ahmed Tayeb el Alj—another major figure within Moroccan theater and a prolific playwright and translator of Western plays—and Farid Ben M'barek.

Saddiki was invited to Casablanca in 1960 to form a troupe at the Théâtre Municipal de Casablanca. Through this troupe, Saddiki mounted productions of works by Jean Canolle, Sacha Guitry, and other European playwrights. In 1963, Saddiki launched the Saddiki Troupe, which he based in Casablanca in a separate venue from the Théâtre Municipal. In Casablanca, he began exploring traditional forms of Moroccan theater, including the centuries-old *halqa* style of public performance. Saddiki became deeply interested in Moroccan oral traditions, both theatrical and poetic, and over the next few years would use these influences to break away from formal Western-style theater.

His exploration of traditional Moroccan and Arabic art forms, coupled with his Western theatrical training, resulted in his first important original play, *Diwan Sidi Abd al-Rahman al-Majdub*. The play, written in 1965, was based on the poems of sixteenth-century Moroccan poet Abd al-Rahman al-Majdub, and it marked a significant divergence for both Saddiki and Moroccan theater, generally. To stage the play, Saddiki took a particular form of Moroccan performance-in-the-round, the *halqa*, and brought it into a Western-style theater. The play and its physical arrangement engaged the audience in the way of traditional Moroccan public performances, whereas its staging incorporated elements of Western technique.

Morocco's 1967 Festival of the Throne was where Saddiki premiered *Diwan*. It was an enormously popular success, and it ushered in the beginning of Morocco's festive theater movement—a movement that transplanted often boisterous traditional Moroccan performance styles into Western-style theatrical settings. As its name suggests, festive theater used national and local festivals as occasions to present these traditionally inspired plays. Saddiki's signature style was to stage his plays in large arenas at these festivals; this particular format helped him gain widespread popularity in the 1970s. *Diwan* was not Saddiki's first original play to be performed, however. In 1966, the Troupe du Théâtre Municipal de Casablanca staged *Fi Tariq* (On the road), Saddiki's comedic commentary on the imposition of both tradition and modernity on the lives of ordinary Moroccans.

In 1964, Saddiki was named artistic director of the Théâtre National du Mohammad V and became the director of the Théâtre Municipal of Casablanca, a post he held until 1976. In 1971, he staged the grandiose *Maqqamat Badi Zaman al-Hamadani*, which, like *Diwan*, was based on the works of a traditional Moroccan poet (al-Hamadani). Similar to *Diwan*, the play was an outright success, sealing Saddiki's reputation as a master of festive theater. His company went on to perform several works by Moroccan playwrights in the 1970s, including plays by Azzedine Madani, Ahmed Abdeslam Bekkali, and Saddiki's brother, Saïd Saddiki.

Saddiki's troupe was re-formed in 1974 as the *Masrah al-Nas* (The people's theatre) and became a traveling company, performing in cities and villages around Morocco. In the late 1970s and 80s, however, political troubles in Morocco significantly weakened the theater scene, and Saddiki's troupe performed only sporadically after 1976. Saddiki then turned to film and other art forms for a period. In 1984, he adapted *Fi Tariq* into the film *Zift* (Asphalt), in which he played a supporting role.

Masrah al-Nas returned in the 1990s with the production of Saddiki's 1991 play, *Les Sept Grains de Beauté* (The seven seeds of beauty). Saddiki continued experimenting with mobile theater in the late 1990s. Two plays, *Wa-law Kanat Fula* and *Jinan Shiba*, were performed in a moving tent that allowed the plays to be executed in the same physical setting within different locations. Saddiki also began incorporating more fantastical themes into his work. His 1999 play, *Suhur* (Sorcery), is an example of this.

In the late 1990s, Saddiki became artistic director of the Mogador, a theater company in Casablanca whose development he helped finance. It replaced Casablanca's Théâtre Municipal, which authorities had demolished in 1984. The Mogador was designed as a performance arena and art gallery, and in the early twenty-first century has hosted a two-year program for training drama students.

Throughout his career, Saddiki has continued acting in addition to writing and directing, often appearing in his own plays and films. Other film appearances include roles in Omar Chraibi's *L'Homme qui brodait des secrets* (2001) and MOUSTAPHA AKKAD's *al-Risala* (The message; 1976). He writes poetry and practices calligraphic art, and has works published in both fields.

INFLUENCES AND CONTRIBUTIONS

Educated in the Western theatrical tradition, Saddiki's earliest influences include ancient Greek theater and the more modern European playwrights. Early in his career, Saddiki began translating and adapting Greek and European plays for the Arabic stage. He was the first playwright to adapt the works of Irish minimalist Beckett and French absurdist Eugene Ionesco for Arabic-speaking audiences.

Prior to independence, Moroccan dramatists had often—albeit clandestinely—used theater as a forum for

> ## THE WEST WAS INTRODUCED TO GREEK CIVILIZATION THROUGH THE TRANSLATED WRITINGS OF ARAB AUTHORS
>
> I have staged, in adaptation, many plays of the Western theatre.... But I didn't think I could do theatre without dealing with the Greeks. I wanted to render homage to the Greek theatre as the first theatre that has come down to us in written form. I had to start with the Greeks and especially with Aristophanes. Aristophanes is the essence of Greek theatre, a social theatre par excellence that speaks to people in a very direct way. When I read his plays I find myself in a society, in my society. Indeed, we must not forget that the West was introduced to Greek civilization through the translated writings of Arab authors. For five centuries the West knew the Greek plays through Arabic translation. Our culture enabled the West to understand Greek culture.
>
> TAYEB SADDIKI IN KOTZAMANI, MARINA. "TAYEB SADDIKI." *PAJ: A JOURNAL OF PERFORMANCE AND ART* 28, NO. 2 (2006): 38-41.

nationalist and political expression. In the turbulent political climate of the 1960s and 1970s, however, increasing government control over theater and entertainment led (state-supported) dramatists to all but abandon political commentary in their work. As did many of his contemporaries, Saddiki turned instead to social critique. His stage adaptations of Aristophanes' *Lysistrata* and *The Assembly of Women*, for example, were performed as a critique of the situation of Moroccan women. His reworking of Samuel Beckett's *Waiting for Godot*—transformed into *Waiting for Mabrouk*—was also done with Moroccan society in mind.

Saddiki's primary contribution has been carving out a distinct identity for modern Moroccan theater. By the 1950s, French control of official Moroccan theater had led to the establishment and institutionalization of formal French-style theater. After independence, Saddiki and his generation began introducing indigenous and informal Moroccan theatrical styles into their plays and productions. Saddiki and his postindependence contemporaries also reworked European plays into dialectical Moroccan Arabic. Ben Jonson's *Volpone*, which Saddiki adapted in 1960 for the Moroccan national Troupe du Centre Marocain de Recherches Dramatiques, is among the early plays he rewrote in dialect.

In developing his theatrical identity, Saddiki has particularly been influenced by the traditional Moroccan *al-halqa* style of performance. *Al-halqa* (literally, the circle) is a versatile style of public theater that takes place in the round, with actors (and often dancers and acrobats) performing in the center of a circle formed by the audience. Traditionally performed in marketplaces and city gates, the tone of *al-halqa* performances can range from highbrow to vulgar, and the stories portrayed can include mythical and historical narratives as well as tales adapted from the Qu'ran, the Sunna (tradition of the Prophet Muhammad), and local folklore. *Al-halqa* performances involve a great deal of audience participation, something rarely seen in traditional European productions.

Saddiki has also incorporated the *l'basat* tradition of Morocco into his plays. *L'basat*, sometimes known as *bsat*, is more closely related to Western theatrical styles than *al-halqa* and is a relatively more recent development in Moroccan traditional theater, having first appeared in the latter half of the eighteenth century. *L'basat* performances take place on a fixed stage and can incorporate a few dozen themes within a single showing. *Éléphants et Pantalons* (Elephants and trousers), Saddiki's comedic play of 1997, was an adaptation of *l'basat* for the modern Moroccan stage. Saddiki's incorporation of and experimentation with *al-halqa*, *l'basat*, and other Moroccan traditional forms broke with the orthodox practice of writing plays that strictly mirrored Western theater.

In the creation of his original plays, Saddiki has drawn on the poems of Abd al-Rahman al-Majdub and Badi Zaman al-Hamadani, who themselves wrote on Arab and Islamic history and myth. He has also been drawn to the stories of the *Thousand and One Arabian Nights*. These influences reflect an interest in orally transmitted stories and poetry, which Saddiki has stated helped him connect to the traditions of Moroccan performance following his long exposure to Western theater.

Saddiki has also continued to draw on European and classical Greek influences for inspiration, with Aristophanes and Molière among the most significant. Saddiki's attachment to Molière inspired his 1994 play, *Molière, ou l'Amour de l'Humanité* (Molière, or the love of humanity). Molière also appeared as a character in his 1997 *Nous Sommes Fait Pour Nous Entendre* (We are made to understand each other).

THE WORLD'S PERSPECTIVE

Known for writing in Arabic, Moroccan colloquial Arabic, and French—sometimes within the same play—Saddiki has made his work accessible to a wide range of audiences. His plays have been performed in Europe and across North Africa; his first major play, *Diwan Sidi Abd al-Rahman al-Madjub*, has been restaged several dozen times in and around North Africa since its premiere in the late 1960s. More recently, *Nous sommes fait pour nous entendre*, a historical piece about relations between Morocco and France, has been staged in both countries, as has his 1990 play *Le Diner de Gala* (The gala dinner). With a rapidly growing Moroccan diasporic population in Spain and the Netherlands, his plays have also gained popularity and exposure in those nations.

LEGACY

Saddiki was among the first wave of Moroccan dramatists to develop an indigenous Moroccan modern theater independent from formal Western theater. Saddiki institutionalized what had previously been informal Moroccan theater styles, elevating them in status and transforming their use in indoor arenas. His work and the work of others in his generation permanently changed the landscape of Moroccan theater, allowing dramatists more creative (if not political) freedom in their work.

BIBLIOGRAPHY

Amine, Khalid. "Crossing Borders: Al-halqa Performance in Morocco from the Open Space to the Theatre Building." *TDR: The Drama Review* 45, no. 2 (Summer 2001): 55-69.

Kotzamani, Marina. "Tayeb Saddiki." *PAJ: A Journal of Performance and Art* 28, no. 2 (2006): 38-41.

Ouzi, Abdelwahed. *Le Theatre au Maroc: Structures et Tendances.* Casablanca, Morocco: Editions Toubkal, 1997.

Sahli, Kamal. "Morocco, Algeria and Tunisia." In *History of Theatre in Africa*, edited by Martin Banham. West Nyack, New York: Cambridge University Press, 2004.

Nora Achrati

SADI, SAID
(1947–)

Said Sadi is a psychiatrist and leader of the Algerian political party Rally for Culture and Democracy.

PERSONAL HISTORY

Said Sadi was born into a poor Berber family on 26 August 1947 in Aghribs, in Algeria's Kabylia region. He studied medicine at the University of Algiers in the late 1960s. In 1978, he began practicing medicine in Tizi-Ouzou.

INFLUENCES AND CONTRIBUTIONS

A charismatic psychiatrist, he began his militant activities for cultural and workers' rights while a student in 1968 and joined the clandestine opposition party Front des

BIOGRAPHICAL HIGHLIGHTS

Name: Said Sadi

Birth: 1947, Aghribs, Algeria's Kabylia region

Nationality: Algerian Berber

Education: Medical studies, University of Algiers

PERSONAL CHRONOLOGY:

- **1968:** Joins the opposition group Front des Forces Socialistes

- **1974:** Practices medicine in Tizi-Ouzou

- **1980:** A leader of the Berber Spring movement in Algeria; arrested for the first time

- **1985:** Helps form the Human Rights League; arrested, spends two years in prison

- **1989:** Founds Rassemblement pour la Culture et la Démocratie

- **1995:** Runs unsuccessfully in Algerian presidential elections

- **2004:** Again runs unsuccessfully in Algerian presidential elections

Forces Socialistes (FFS; Socialist Forces Front). He strongly opposed single-party rule in Algeria and called for Berber cultural rights. One of the leaders of the 1980 Berber Spring uprising, he demanded recognition of the Berber language and culture within a democratic state. He was arrested that year, and went on to be jailed five times in the 1980s, the last time from 1985-1987.

Said subsequently broke with the FFS and joined a group of militants devoted to human rights and to cultural and women's issues. In 1985 they founded the Human Rights League. In 1989 Sadi founded and headed the Rassemblement pour la Culture et la Démocratie (RCD; Rally for culture and democracy), an outgrowth of the Berber movement. Sadi has been a staunch critic of both the regime and Algeria's Islamists. The RCD boycotted the 1991 legislative elections but participated actively in the November 1995 presidential election and the June 1997 legislative vote. Sadi obtained 10 percent of the votes cast for president in 1995. The RCD obtained nineteen seats at the assembly in 1997.

Sadi has equated Islamism with terrorism, which explains his support for the military against radical Islamism. Although he boycotted the 1999 presidential election, Sadi supported President Abdelaziz Bouteflika's

program to reform the economy, justice and educational systems, and administration. Two members of the RCD served as ministers in the government. Sadi withdrew the RCD from the government because of the Kabylia crisis, triggered in April 2001 following the killing in Tizi-Ouzou of a youngster by the National Gendarmerie. The demonstrations and violence that developed following that incident revealed the regime's inability to provide adequate democratic institutions to represent the nation's diverse interests. Because of the acute crisis, the RCD boycotted the legislative and municipal elections in May and October 2002, respectively. Sadi has sided with the *aruch* (tribal councils) and called repeatedly for the end of repression. In April 2004, Said again ran unsuccessfully for president in the Algerian elections.

THE WORLD'S PERSPECTIVE

Sadi is known internationally for his staunch secularism, his defense of human rights, and his defense of Berber cultural rights in Algeria.

LEGACY

It is too early in Sadi's career and activities to assess his ultimate legacy.

BIBLIOGRAPHY

"Algeria's Presidential Challengers." BBC News (9 April 2004): http://news.bbc.co.uk/1/hi/world/africa/3511120.stm.

Yahia Zoubir
Updated by Michael R. Fischbach

SADR, MUQTADA AL-
(1973–)

Muqtada (Moqtada) al-Sadr, a mid-level Iraqi Shiʿite cleric, has gained political influence in post-SADDAM HUSSEIN Iraq, making him a household name throughout the Muslim world.

PERSONAL HISTORY

Sadr is the heir to a series of leading religious scholars. His uncle and father-in-law, Muhammad Baqir al-Sadr, is considered one of the most respected Shiʿite intellectuals of the past century. Muhammad Baqir al-Sadr was the spiritual leader of the Islamic resistance to the authoritarian rule in Iraq from the 1950s until his execution by Hussein's government in 1980. Muqtada al-Sadr's own father, Sayyid Muhammad Muhammad Sadiq al-Sadr, was an exemplary figure as well. He gained visibility at the height of Hussein's oppressive rule in the late 1990s. He revived the tradition of the Friday prayer and used

Muqtada al-Sadr. AP IMAGES.

BIOGRAPHICAL HIGHLIGHTS

Name: Muqtada al-Sadr

Birth: c. 1973, Najaf, Iraq

Family: Married to the daughter of legendary Shi'ite scholar Muhammad Baqir al-Sadr

Nationality: Iraqi

Education: Iraqi public schools; some traditional religious learning

PERSONAL CHRONOLOGY:

• **2003:** Founded the Mahdi Army; leader of the Sadr Movement

tional elections in December 2005 and gained six ministries in the cabinet.

INFLUENCES AND CONTRIBUTIONS

The first glimpse of Sadr's power involved his decision in 2003 to continue his father's rivalry with the religious establishment in Najaf, the *Hawza.* Ayatullah Muhammad Muhammad Sadiq al-Sadr had criticized the *Hawza* for its decades-long political quietism, branding his style as the 'Vocal *Hawza*,' in a clear contempt of the existing body. In April of that year, Sadr's loyalists surrounded the home of Iraq's leading cleric, Iranian-born Grand Ayatullah ALI AL-SISTANI. For the first time, the issue of clerics' nationality was brought to the fore—the Sadr family is Arab—noting, perhaps accurately, that those Iranian clerics did not feel the pain of the Iraqis or even care enough to take interest in their affairs. What Sadr and his followers failed to estimate was the level of support Sistani had in Iraq, especially among the tribes who sent their fighters to Najaf to protect Sistani and the other grand ayatullahs.

Another problem also faced Sadr that he could never overcome—he is only a junior cleric needing several decades of additional study to advance any claim for replacing Sistani. Ethnic and other prejudices notwithstanding, the sole criterion for acquiring religious authority in the Shi'ite community is knowledge, traditionally acquired by many decades of studying and teaching in the religious seminary, the *Hawza.* In addition to his youth and lack of important credentials, Sadr also failed to receive the backing of his father's disciples who possess the necessary background for such a position, an individual such as Ayatullah Kazim al-Ha'iri.

the sermons as a mobilizing device to create a network that consistenly challenged, and raised the ire of, Hussein's government. After several unheeded warnings, he was assassinated with two of his sons in February 1999. He was survived by one son, Muqtada.

The Sadr network displayed no visible activity between the 1999 assassinations and the U.S. invasion of Iraq in 2003. However, Sadr inherited a network of charities, soup kitchens, and schools as well as the loyalty of his father's disciples. Most importantly, he gained the privilege of representing the Sadr family. To their detriment, policy makers intent on rebuilding Iraq ignored the Sadr movement in the early days of the occupation and instead focused on exile groups, such as the Iraqi National Congress, returning to Iraq from the West or countries in the region. As events unfolded, the Sadr movement proved to be the most formidable political and social group in the new Iraq. As all attempts failed to combat their influence, Sadr and his disenchanted loyalists became the kingmakers of Iraq. With thirty seats in the legislature—the largest faction within the dominant bloc in the parliament—they had the final word on the nomination of the prime minister after the first constitu-

CONTEMPORARIES

Abd al-Aziz al-Hakim (1950-) is the son of the late Grand Ayatullah Muhsin al-Hakim (d. 1970) and the current leader of the family. Following in the footsteps of his father and older brothers, he was educated in the traditional institution of religious education in his Iraqi native city, Najaf. He was imprisoned and persecuted under the regime of Hussein, and he managed to escape to Iran in 1980. He was a founding member of the Supreme Council for Islamic Revolution in Iraq (SCIRI), founded in Iran in 1982 by his older brother, Muhammad Baqir al-Hakim. Hakim became the leader of the Badr Brigade, the military wing of SCIRI.

SCIRI returned to Iraq when Hussein's regime ended in 2003, and it became one of the competing parties for the Shi'ite political leadership. It worked with U.S. officials as a representative of the Shi'ite community in the political process. Unlike the Sadr Movement, SCIRI did establish contacts with U.S. officials before the invasion, which it considered as a necessary evil after all other options to change the regime through national struggle failed. Muhammad Baqir al-Hakim declined to take a political position in 2003 and allowed Hakim to become one of the twenty-five members of the Governing Council appointed by the U.S. Administrator of Iraq, L. Paul Bremer.

Like Sadr, Hakim came to the leadership of the SCIRI after the violent death of his older brother, who had created the power base. On 29 August 2003, a massive bomb exploded near the side of Imam Ali's shrine in Najaf, taking the life of Muhammad Baqir al-Hakim and many other worshipers as they left the shrine following the Friday prayer. Hakim succeeded his brother as the leader of SCIRI. After the Iraqi elections of January 2005, he became the leader of the largest bloc in the Iraqi Parliament.

These setbacks in the religious arena did not end Sadr's ambitions. Thanks to the imprudence of the occupation officials and the key figures in post-Hussein era—both Iraqi and Americans—Sadr became a political leader with a strong power base. He has the loyalty of wide segments of disenchanted Iraqis for whom the regime change did not bring any benefits. In some areas, their lives became worse.

The base of support for Sadr is comprised of a multitude of Iraqi communities both impoverished and politically excluded during Hussein's rule and in the new era. The main stronghold of support is the large section of Baghdad, originally known as al-Thawra City, now renamed as Sadr City—after Sadr's family. Sadr City has a population of more than 1.5 million people, the largest community in Baghdad. Loyalty for Sadr can also be found in Basra and Kufa, the former being the second largest city in today's Iraq and the latter was the capital of Islam (656–661), and he continues to attract the spotlight. Kufa's main mosque was particularly associated with the Sadr Movement because it witnessed the rise of Sadr's father. He gave his famous forty-five Friday sermons in as many weeks before his assassination.

Sadr tested his support by calling for the establishment of a doctrinal army, which he called *Jaysh al-Imam al-Mahdi* (The army of Imam al-Mahdi). The first unit was declared ready on 6 October 2003. There is no precise estimate of this army's troop count, its actual structure, or discipline. Estimates range from 3,000 to 10,000 active participants, as well as large numbers of followers and sympathizers. While they may not pose a real threat for U.S. forces, they are more than a match for any Iraqi force or the militias of the competing factions.

THE WORLD'S PERSPECTIVE

Sadr's image around the world differs depending one's views and attitudes toward the U.S. involvement in Iraq. For opponents of the occupation and the ensuing process, Sadr and his Mahdi Army represent the natural reaction to a heavy-handed occupying force that caused the destruction of Iraq and the death of an untold number of Iraqis. Within the U.S. camp, he is seen as a young, firebrand cleric whose anti-U.S. activities subvert the prospects of democracy in Iraq. In this sense, U.S. officials view Sadr and the Mahdi Army in a manner similar to the Sunni insurgents in Iraq.

In Iraq this binary view becomes a threefold complex. Shi'ites supporting the U.S. position agree about the threat Sadr poses, and they see him as a formidable rival in the fight for the leadership of the Shi'ite community. They do, however, work and negotiate with him. Some Shi'ite leaders find the existence of Sadr as a blessing in disguise, as he makes them appear as moderates to Americans.

The Sunnis of Iraq like Sadr's positions against the U.S. presence in Iraq and appreciate the Arab nationalist flavor of his movement, as opposed to the perceived pro-Iranian positions of the other Shi'ite leaders in Iraq. However, such favorable view of his positions will not lead to full reconciliation of Sunnis and Sadr's efforts. To them, he is a Shi'ite first and foremost, a barrier impossible to overcome.

Even if some form of reconciliation had seemed a possibility in the past, the utterance by Shi'ite onlookers of his name three times prior to the execution of Hussein has destroyed any possibility that existed.

For the Shi'ite masses in Iraq, Sadr and the Mahdi Army are either a menace whose abuse and encroachments on their liberties cause repulsion and misery or a better alternative to everything offered thus far. The latter view is particularly true in areas where Sadr's fighters are the thin line between the Shi'ites and Sunni death squads. The Sadr Movement also operates a very successful charitable network in many areas of Iraq, delivering what the government fails to provide. In this sense, he has made a good name for himself because of the incompetence of his opponents.

LEGACY

In the rapid course of events following the U.S. occupation of Iraq in 2003, Sadr was placed in a position well beyond his previous level of responsibilty. After a few blunders and miscalculations, he learned how to operate more effectively within Iraq's political and military environment. He, however, is far from being secure. His ambition is perhaps more than what the Iraqi circumstances may allow. Sadr aspires to play the role similar to that of Hizbullah's leader, HASAN NASRALLAH, in Lebanon. While possible, the current Iraq is not Lebanon and Sadr is not Nasrallah, making this desire problematic.

To build his legacy, Sadr first must accomplish achievements deemed worthy of his family's heritage. He is seen as merely riding on the coattails of accomplishments of his father and uncle, the legendary scholars and martyrs. He also must survive the murky political conditions of Iraq that always have proved deadly for his type of overconfident leaders.

BIBLIOGRAPHY

Interview with CBC News on 6 April 2004.

Jabar, Faleh. *The Shi'ite Movement in Iraq.* Beruit: Saqi Books, 2003.

Kadhim, Abbas. "Into the Breach." *Al-Ahram Weekly* (August 12, 2004).

Nasr, Vali. *The Shia Revival.* New York: W.W. Norton & Company, 2006.

Rosen, Nir. "America's Unlikely Savior." *Salon.* 3 February 2006.

Sadr, al- Muqtada. A collection of audiotape speeches and interviews given by Muqtada al-Sadr. Available from http://manhajalsadren.com/le8a2at.muqtada.files/index.htm.

Abbas Kadhim

SADR, RABAB AL-
(1946–)

Rabab al-Sadr is a Lebanese social and human rights activist and philanthropist.

PERSONAL HISTORY

Born in 1946 in Iran to a Lebanese Shi'ite Muslim family, Rabab al-Sadr (also Rabab al-Sadr Sharaf al-Din) moved to Lebanon at the age of fifteen. She adopted and promoted the social vision of her brother, Imam Musa al-Sadr, who encouraged her to join the Imam al-Sadr Foundation in Lebanon around 1960 and devote herself to social work and humanitarian aid. Meanwhile, she completed a B.A. in arts and an M.A. in philosophy in Lebanon.

INFLUENCES AND CONTRIBUTIONS

After the disappearance of her brother in 1978 during a visit to Libya, Rabab became the president of the Imam al-Sadr Foundation, which consists in 2007 of six vocational schools and an orphanage. Al-Sadr oversees the girls' section of the foundation, providing much-needed economic assistance and social guidance to orphaned and dependent girls, regardless of their religious background. The foundation faced particular financial and organizational challenges after the dramatic increase in orphans due to the Lebanese war (1975–1991), the Israeli occupation of South Lebanon (1982-2000), and brutal attacks on civilians. She helped obtain a license for the foundation as a nonprofit organization in the U.S. in order to help gather contributions for widows, orphans, and poor children, mostly from South Lebanon. The schools sponsored by

---

BIOGRAPHICAL HIGHLIGHTS

■

Name: Rabab al-Sadr

Birth: 1946, Iran

Family: Husband, Husayn Sharaf al-Din

Nationality: Lebanese

Education: BA in arts and MA in philosophy

PERSONAL CHRONOLOGY:

- **1978:** After the disappearance of her brother, Imam Musa al-Sadr, in Libya, in 1978, becomes president of the Imam al-Sadr Foundation

---

the foundation use modern technology and advanced educational methods and equipment.

Al-Sadr remains critical of the Lebanese government for abandoning South Lebanon and marginalizing it in state development policies. Following the Israeli withdrawal from South Lebanon in May 2000, the foundation launched two mobile medical clinics, which traveled to remote villages with no health facilities in order to offer preventive and curative medical services. Nearly 10,000 people benefited from these services. The foundation works to increase the attendance of orphans at primary schools, trains women for jobs, and runs daylong health centers. Al-Sadr strongly believes in the central role of education for women as a means for social change and personal growth.

THE WORLD'S PERSPECTIVE

During numerous regional and international conferences on women's issues, she called on policymakers to acknowledge the need for gender equality and cooperation between men and women in the pursuit of a harmonious society. Her foundation is known throughout the Middle East, and her admirers and supporters urged her to run in parliamentary elections in Lebanon. However, she has expressed her aversion to politics due to the restrictions it places on social and family life.

LEGACY

Rabab al-Sadr is still active, and it is too early to assess her historical legacy.

BIBLIOGRAPHY

"Exclusive Interviews with Rabab al-Sadr." Al-Sadr Foundation. Available from http://www.sadr-foundation.org.lb/. *Middle East News and World Report* (11 December 2002).

Sadr, Sitt Rabab al-. "Islam and Peace in the Fifteenth/Twenty-first Century." *Center for Global Peace and Nonviolence International*, The American University Center, Washington, D.C., 6–7 February 1998.

"Sadr on Southern Lebanon." *Washington Report on Middle East Affairs* 20, no. 4 (May/June 2001): 90–91.

Rula Jurdi Abisaab
Updated by Michael R. Fischbach

SADR, SHADI
(1974–)

Shadi Sadr is an Iranian women's rights activist who has played an important role in Iran since the 1990s. She is a lawyer, and she began her involvement with Iranian women's rights issues at fifteen. She is an active member of the Stop Stoning to Death Campaign and Iranian Women's Charter. She is the president of Raahi Legal

Shadi Sadr. COURTESY OF SHADI SADR.

Centre for Women and a freelance writer, contributing regularly for *Shargh* (East) newspaper and *Zanan* (Women), a feminist journal. Sadr also is a member of the Iran Bar Association and the Association of Iranian Journalists. She was the editor in chief of the Women in Iran Website http://www.womeninirn.org, and currently she is the editor in chief of *Meydaan* (Women's Field) website, (http://www.meydaan.net). She has written numerous articles and is the author of two books on women and the law.

PERSONAL HISTORY

Sadr was born in 1974 in Tehran, Iran. She has a BA in law and an MA in international law from Tehran University. After she received her law degree in 1996, she became interested in women's issues. She wrote a daily column about women in the *Yase Noo Newspaper*. This was a period when the reform movement associated with President MOHAMMAD KHATAMI's government was expanding. But the judiciary, controlled by the conservative clergy hostile to the reforms, closed many newspapers and journals. The newspapers in which Sadr had published were closed. When she began as a journalist, few journals were interested in women's issues. But her columns on women's rights issues proved so popular that all the journals that published her writings gave her space to write on women's rights issues. In 2002 she set up the Women in Iran Website, among the first communicating through a website in Iran. Her website became popular both within and outside of Iran.

She also has continued to work on women's rights and legal issues. In 2002 she presented at a seminar on the role of women in Islamic countries in Stockholm. She also participated in a panel discussion in Vienna at a conference organized by Women Without Borders in

BIOGRAPHICAL HIGHLIGHTS

Name: Shadi Sadr

Birth: 1974, Tehran, Iran

Family: Husband, Hussein Nilchian; one daughter, Darya

Nationality: Iranian

Education: BA, MA, Tehran University

PERSONAL CHRONOLOGY:

- **2002–2006:** Editor in chief of Women in Iran Website http://www.womeniniran.org

- **2004–present:** President of Raahi Legal Centre for Women

- **2004–present:** Freelance writer

- **2006–present:** Founding member of Stop Stoning to Death Campaign and Women's Charter, http://www.meydaan.net

2003. In 2004 she attended the Fourth World Social Forum in Mumbai, India, and participated in a panel discussion on Feminist Dialogue.

INFLUENCES AND CONTRIBUTIONS

As the president of Raahi Legal Centre for Women, Sadr and her colleagues give free legal advice to women—especially those women subject to domestic and social violence. Through their efforts they succeeded in having the Iranian government suspend in 2003 the laws allowing for stoning to death. This achievement was more than just saving women's lives. They made women's rights issues a public concern to be addressed within Iranian society. Despite these advances, however, Sadr continues to battle the practice. In April 2006 she and her colleagues received information about one case of stoning to death and a few other cases where women and men were sentenced to stoning to death and were awaiting their trials.

Sadr and her colleagues led a campaign to stop this violent act. In a recent interview, Sadr asserted:

> The majority of women and men who are subject to stoning to death are among the poorest section of the society. In some cases, male members of the family force women to become sex workers to pay for their drug addiction. In other cases, women are subject to domestic violence and forced marriages and as the result they kill their

husbands. I believe that Islam is not against gender justice, therefore we can change anti-women laws and regulations.

Sadr and her colleagues have won the support of ordinary people and some government officials through their advocacy on this campaign. Some government officials argue that human rights abuses violate Islam. Others argue that stoning to death can be stopped as it was practiced in pre-Islamic societies. While Islamic peoples have allowed the practice of stoning to death historically, Islam does not require or condone the practice as a matter of moral teaching

Sadr also has been involved in a campaign to enable women to extend their citizenship and nationality rights to their children. In 2007 they succeeded in changing the law to allow Iranian women married to non-Iranian men to pass on their Iranian nationality and citizenship rights to their children under certain circumstances. The children must be born in Iran and live in Iran for eighteen years. On 8 March 2007 (International Women's Day) Sadr and thirty-two women activists were arrested. They were released on bail and await trial that could result in several months of imprisonment.

THE WORLD'S PERSPECTIVE

Although women in Iran have struggled for recognition of their civil rights since the 1979 Iranian Revolution, they have achieved a great deal. Prior to the early 1990s, women were not allowed to be judges and the law gave men the exclusive rights to obtain a divorce and gain custody of the children. Today successful pressure for the reform of family laws and regulations has resulted in women judicial advisors giving advice to the judges on divorce in the Iranian courts. An amendment in Iranian marital law allows women the right to divorce, the right to gain custody of children in the event of a divorce, and the right to refuse the husband to marry a second wife—provided that these rights were reflected on the marriage certificate. All government departments have women's committees, and all newspapers and journals have women's pages. Ninety-four percent of the population is literate and 64 percent of university students are women. Female life expectancy in Iran is 4 percent longer than men, and contraceptive prevalence is 74 percent. Under certain circumstances, mandatory abortion is approved. The number of seats women hold in the Iranian Parliament is the same as in Turkey, and the number of female professionals in Iran is the same as in South Korea. But women activists, who constitute the majority of the students and a large part of the workforce, are not content with these achievements. In a recent interview, Sadr noted:

> These achievements have put us in a special place in the world and in the region. We have become a model for many women in the region. However,

the West still portrays us as passive victims of male and religious oppression. They perceive women in Iran either queuing to burn flags or queuing to do nose beauty operation. They ignore the majority of the women who are engaged in women's rights and democracy issues. Our aim is to reach women and men in the West and change their perception of Muslim women, especially the Iranian women.

Sadr has won a number of awards. She won first prize at the Sixth Press Festival (1999) and the Tenth Press Festival (2003) in Iran. In 2004 she also won the Ida B. Wells Award for Bravery in Journalism from the Women's News Organization.

LEGACY

Shadi Sadr will be recognized as an important Iranian women's rights activist.

BIBLIOGRAPHY

Stop Stoning Forever. Shadi Sadr. Available from http://www.meydaan.net/English/Aboutus.aspx.
Women in Iran. Shadi Sadr. Available from http://www.womeniniran.org.

Elaheh Rostami Povey

Ali Ahmad Sa´id. RALPH ORLOWSKI/GETTY IMAGES.

SA'ID, ALI AHMAD
(1930–)

A noted Syrian modernist poet and essayist, Ali Ahmad Sa'id is arguably the greatest living Arab poet of the early twenty-first century.

PERSONAL HISTORY

Sa'id (known by the pseudonym Adonis) was born in January 1930 in the village of al-Qasabin near the Syrian seaport of Latakia. His family was Alawite, a sect of Shi'ite Islam, and lived in relative poverty in a village with no electricity. At the age of fourteen a great opportunity came his way in 1947 when Syria was celebrating the recently won independence and the newly elected president Shukri al-Quwwatli, who was touring the country. He stopped in the nearby town of Jabla and heard the young Sa'id recite a poem he had written. Sa'id impressed the president, and the poem won him a scholarship to continue his studies in a big city, Latakia.

During Sa'id's time in Latakia he became more politically conscious and was influenced by a Lebanese writer and politician, Antun Sa'aada, the founder of the pan-Syrian political party, the Syrian Social Nationalist Party (SSNP). Sa'aada's writings greatly influenced a

whole generation of young Syrians, and certainly left his imprint on Adonis, a pseudonym Sa'id adopted early on in his life and that has remained with him.

Sa'id soon moved to study at Damascus University around 1950. At the university he studied both literature and philosophy, graduating in 1954. He early on raised serious and controversial questions about old-fashioned Arabic literary conventions. He also raised equally controversial questions about the dire social and political realities in his country, Syria. Later he joined the Syrian army, and during his service his political activism with the SSNP landed him in prison. He sought exile in Beirut, Lebanon, after his release in 1956.

He quickly took to life in Lebanon, and became a naturalized citizen. He also moved away from the SSNP and pan-Syrianism. Sa'id found in Lebanon a nurturing environment for his poetic aspirations. He also got involved in the publishing of literary magazines, especially the seminal modernist poetry publication *Sh'ir* that he established in 1957 with the well-known poet Yusuf al-Khal. *Sh'ir* was a great forum for young poets who

BIOGRAPHICAL HIGHLIGHTS

Name: Al Ahmad Sa'id (known as Adonis)

Birth: 1930, al-Qasabin, Syria

Family: Wife, Khalida Sa'id

Nationality: Syrian, Lebanese citizenship (naturalized)

Education: BA (License), Philosophy, Damascus, Syria, 1954; Ph.D., Sorbonne, Paris, 1973

PERSONAL CHRONOLOGY:

- **1950:** Publishes *Dalila* (his first collection of poetry)
- **1956:** Moves to Lebanon
- **1957:** Co-founds *Shi'r* magazine
- **1960:** Moves to study in Paris
- **1961:** Publishes *Aghani mihyaral-Dimasqi* (*The Songs of Mihyar the Damascene*)
- **1968:** Founds *Mawaqif* (journal)
- **1970:** Visiting professor of Arabic literature, Lebanese University
- **1976:** Visiting professor Damascus University
- **1980:** Professor of Arabic at the Sorbonne, Paris
- **1985:** Visiting professor at Georgetown University
- **1986:** Moves to Paris permanently
- **2001:** Awarded Goethe Medal

experimented with new forms of writing. In 1968 Sa'id founded the influential, avant-garde journal *Mawaqif*, which became widely circulated throughout the Arab world. *Mawaqif* focused on discussing experimental poetry. It proved to be a pivotal venue for aspiring writers who were attempting to break away from the rigid forms of poetry writing that had dominated for centuries.

He early on became an ardent believer that Arab societies had to undergo radical changes if they wished to catch up with the challenges of the twentieth century, and that they needed this change to be able to make their rightful contributions, as they had done so well during the past golden age in medieval times. He firmly believed that this was achievable if Arab heritage was revisited in its positive aspects.

In addition to his prolific poetry, Sa'id is credited for creating a new poetic language, new rhythms that distin-

guish themselves by being deeply rooted in the Arab classical tradition, while at the same time speaking of the contemporary predicaments within society. He is also credited for reviving and modifying an Arab classical form of the short poem (*qit'a*), experimented with widening the scope of the *qasida* (a pre-Islamic poetic form), and cemented the use of the so-called prose poem.

Sa'id has unabashedly criticized his countrymen for their shortcomings. His famous poem "A Mirror for Beirut" ("Mira'at li Beirut"), written in 1967, was celebrated throughout the Arab world. In 1982 when Beirut was under siege, he wrote a long poem that poignantly delineated the dilemma of the Arabs, titled "The Desert" ("Al-Sahara").

INFLUENCES AND CONTRIBUTIONS

Early in his twenties, Sa'id had created a persona and named it Mihyar the Damascene, who embodied his revolutionary vision and creative impulses. In 1961, he published *Aghani Mihyar al-Dimasqhi* (*The Songs of Mihyar the Damascene*), a landmark in modern Arabic poetry He spoke in it of "madness, the intimate friend as well as the ecstasy of madness." Sa'id's madness is by no means insanity, or the triumph of chaos over order. He uses madness more as an intellectual position, a position of rejection. His concept of madness is akin to the power to create a new language to bestow new meanings unto old identities.

Sa'id dedicated all his energies to unmask the oppression of the religious cultures and the corrupt socio-political institutions within the Arab world. He bemoaned the state of backwardness, the conditions of poverty, illiteracy, and the scourge of colonialism. Central among all these was the *nakba* (Arabic: disaster) of the loss of Palestine and the consequences of the creation of the state of Israel in 1948. His poetry is marked by the history of defeats and disasters afflicting the Arab world in the second half of the twentieth century. Similar to most Arab poets, Sa'id has been deeply marked by these historical catastrophes and his poetry resonates with a sense of angst, which is a leitmotif of modern Arabic poetry.

Because of this, Sa'id has become the twentieth-century Arab theorist *par excellence*, in addition to being a leading poet. He has been often compared to the great T. S. Eliot, whose work has profoundly influenced a whole generation of Arab poets, and who, as Sa'id was with Arabic poetry, was the great theoretician of English poetry throughout the twentieth century in addition to being one of the most innovative poets of the Anglo-Saxon world.

Sa'id's poetry is, however, not widely read by the masses within the Arab world, yet he is adored by the intelligentsia and read extensively in translation throughout the world. He has more than once been nominated

IT SEEKS TO VEIL THE MIND

No matter how many points of view there are on the veiling of Muslim women, it is possible to say that they are mere interpretations. For there is no categorical text mandating the veil, as religious fundamentalists would have us believe. There are only interpretations of traditions or proverbs, that have been handed down (mathu'rat).

In summary I am saying that the religious interpretation which calls for imposing the veil upon Muslim women living in a secular country which separates religion and politics and in which men and women are equal in rights and obligations shows a mentality that doesn't only veil women, but seeks to veil humanity, society and life too. It seeks to veil the mind.

ADONIS. "HIJAB FOR THE HEAD OR HIJAB FOR THE MIND?" ARABIC PRESS. AVAILABLE FROM HTTP://WWW.NMHSCHOOL .ORG/TTHORNTON/ADONIS_ON_VEIL.PHP.

for the Nobel Prize for Literature though, as of 2007, was never a finalist. He progressively writes a poetry that is less accessible to the average reader.

He has been compared to the Sufi (mystics) of the ninth and tenth centuries. His poems are microcosms that equate his vision of reality. All manifestations within his universe become themselves manifestations of an essential meaning. Two of the Sufi poets who have especially left their mark on his work are al-Niffari and al-Hallaj, the celebrated martyr of medieval fame. Sa'id has written poetry expressing his admiration and prophetic vision emulating these two great poets.

Modern Arab poets use symbolism extensively, and Sa'id is foremost among them. They have drawn heavily on Western (Greek and Christian) symbols. Sa'id is credited for having assimilated more prominently Sufi and Shi'ite symbolism in his writings, with their mythical, spiritual character, thus introducing a new element into the Arab culture.

Sa'id merges his political beliefs and philosophy of life with his vision of what modern Arabic poetry ought to achieve. He fundamentally believes in an all-encompassing revolution as the only means of destroying the old petrified structures. Unless this takes place then, he believes, all efforts to bring about the long yearned for change will fail. The decades of struggle that only culminated in the shameful Arab defeat in the 1967 War have been a tragic

blow from which the Arabs have not yet recovered. Although Arabs often consider the 1973 War a victory, it is not so much a victory against the traditional enemy Israel, but rather a victory over themselves, their divisions, and their impotence.

Using subversive language, Sa'id continues to write revolutionary poetry. His controversial poem "A Grave for New York" (1971) has been both adulated and vilified. His equally vituperative language against his own people, the subtext being a hope that they wake from their torpor and take action, balances his harsh condemnation of the West. His dream remains an ardent wish to create a new world where peace and harmony will prevail.

Kamal Abu Deeb, a well-known critic, writes extensively about Sa'id. In an article oft-quoted, "The Perplexity of the All-Knowing" (1977), he writes:

"The oppression practiced by the religious culture, the sociopolitical institutions, the conditions of poverty, illiteracy and backwardness, the struggle against colonialism, class struggle, and the desperate search for national identity have not been the only realities which shaped the consciousness of Sa'id's generation...The confrontation with Israel, with defeats for the Arabs in 1948, 1956, and 1967, revealed the depth to which Arab society, political institutions and regimes have sunk: the poetry has embodied the bitterness, frustration and despair eating at the heart of Arab poets in these years. The Palestinian experience has radiated with a new poetic tone, a new symbolism, a new angst which forms a subterranean level of modern poetry."

LEGACY

In all his writings, Sa'id reveals his mastery of language and his power to structure a text as a master builder or architect. Some of his more recent poetry has lost the abstractness of his earlier work of the 1970s. He has displayed a new fondness for the poetry of place, in contrast to his poetry of time. In these texts places such as Cairo, Fez, Marrakech, or San'aa appear with their powerful material presence and distinctive realities.

Sa'id remains bold in his writings. His *al-Kitab* (*The Book*), invoking the name of the Holy Qur'an, has a complex structure of dividing the page into four sections of texts and margins, each representing a different aspect of Arab history and using a different voice, and centered on the persona of the great Arab poet al-Mutanabii. This spirit of daring has kept him in the forefront of the modernist movement and has allowed his poetry to remain an undisputed inspiration to the younger generations of poets.

BIBLIOGRAPHY

Adonis. *The Blood of Adonis: Transpositions of Selected Poems of Adonis.* Translated by Samuel Hazo. Pittsburgh: University of Pittsburgh Press, 1971.

Deeb, Kamal abu-. "The Perplexity of the All-Knowing," *Mundus Artium* 10 (1977): 178-179.

Khouri, Mounah Abdallah. *An Anthology of Modern Arabic Poetry.* Berkeley: University of California Press, 1974.

Mona Mikhail

SAID, EDWARD
(1935–2003)

Edward Wadie (Wadi or William) Said was a literary theorist and Palestinian activist who played a key role in shaping the image of mostly left-wing Western intellectuals concerning the Israeli-Palestinian conflict. With his book *Orientalism* (1978) he provided a major theoretical framework in the twentieth-century humanities to explain Western-Arab relations. His scientific approach was entangled with a pro-Palestinian political bias, making him a controversial figure within the community of scholars on the Middle East. In the last phase of his life, Said broke with the Palestinian leadership when he rejected the Oslo Accords.

Edward Said. JEAN-CHRISTIAN BOURCART/GETTY IMAGES.

BIOGRAPHICAL HIGHLIGHTS

Name: Edward Wadie (Wadi, William) Said

Birth: 1 November 1935, Jerusalem, mandatory Palestine or Cairo, Egypt

Death: 25 September 2003, New York, United States

Family: Wife, Mariam; daughter, Najla; son, Wadie

Nationality: Palestinian

Education: Princeton University, 1957, B.A. English; Harvard University, 1960, M.A., 1964, Ph.D.

PERSONAL CHRONOLOGY:

• **1963:** Becomes instructor at Columbia University, New York

• **1970:** Becomes full professor at Columbia University

• **1977:** Appointed Parr Professor of English and Comparative Literature at Columbia

• **1977-1991:** Member of the Palestinian National Council

• **1999:** President of the Modern Language Association

PERSONAL HISTORY

Said claimed that he was born on 1 November 1935, in Jerusalem, but critics argued that even the statement about his birthplace was propaganda and that Said was born in Egypt, not mandatory Palestine. He came from a Christian Arab background and the choice of his first name, Edward, indicated his father's inclination to Western culture. His father immigrated to the United States before World War I and had returned to the Middle East as a wealthy man.

Most of Said's early life is unclear. In his own descriptions he spent a lot of time in what was then British-mandatory Palestine, while his critics argue that he had a more or less Egyptian upbringing. In any case, he grew up in a still very much British-influenced affluent Arab setting. His early school attendances are also unclear; at times it was claimed that he clashed with the British-style school system and was therefore sent to the United States, which would reinforce his image as an anti-colonial activist even as a schoolboy. It is clear that for some reason or another his father sent Said to the United States for school and academic training, where he succeeded academically, earning a B.A. from Princeton University and an M.A. and a Ph.D. from Harvard University.

Said claimed that the defeat of Arab armies against Israel in the 1948 War first made him politically aware as a Palestinian, but that the real impetus for his political coming-out was the defeat of the Arabs in the 1967 War. Whatever his political ambitions might have been then, he did gain prominence first as a literary scholar and not as an advocate for the Palestinian cause. How much the events of 1948 affected his personal life is another unclear element in his early life. Some of his relatives lost property in 1948 with the establishment of Israel. Said claimed a special relationship to a Jerusalem-based aunt, which to a certain extent was his proof for his strong personal involvement in the Palestinian fate during his adolescence.

Said was a prolific foreign language and music student. After his Ph.D. thesis on British novelist Joseph Conrad, his academic success in the United States led him successively to professorial offices at Columbia University. He became a full professor there in 1970. In 1977, he was appointed to an endowed chair at Columbia as the Parr Professor of English and Comparative Literature. There followed appointments as the Old Dominion Foundation Professor of Humanities and finally University Professor, Columbia's highest honor for a faculty member. He gave the field of comparative literature a new framework when he transferred the anti-colonial intellectual feeling of the 1950s and 1960s into literary theory. He shared the left-wing political leanings of United States and Western students in the 1960s, but because of his Palestinian origins he could somehow argue the anti-colonial sentiment with more individual credibility, despite his strong links with Western academia. His experience of Palestinian, Egyptian, British colonial, and U.S. communities in his youth and adolescence predestined him for a comparative approach. His background and language studies gave him the linguistic background to broaden the field of comparative literature from the comparison of Western literatures with each other to the comparison of Western and non-Western literatures. His celebrity status within the community derived from the fact that he added to the comparison of literatures the question of how one culture is seen by another culture. Though he was probably not the first to ask and explore this question, he was the scholar who examined it the most convincingly.

While his influence in the field of literary theory is undisputed, the 1967 Arab-Israeli War shaped Said into a controversial Palestinian activist. From the 1970s onward, Said was both a literary scholar and a partisan political activist. It is difficult to separate Said's scholarship from his political activism because the object of

Said's research and politics was the same: the problems of the post-colonial Arab world in general and the fate of Palestinians in particular. Because Said was already well known as a scholar in the West by the time of his full political awakening in the late 1960s and 1970s, he became the natural unofficial ambassador for the Palestinian cause in the United States. The Ivy League academic Said could counter the image of Palestinian terrorists responsible for the Munich Olympics massacre and other atrocities. Said became a representative of educated Palestinians and Arabs in the Western media.

As a member of many academic communities both in the United States and Europe, Said became the prototype of the Palestinian or Arab intellectual in the West. He addressed his academic and non-academic audience regularly in important English-language newspapers and journals on both sides of the Atlantic and was at the same time present in quality papers of the Arab world. His election to the Palestinian National Council in 1977 and the publication of his best-known book, *Orientalism*, in 1978 is probably the point in time when Said intellectually left academia for a political career. From that point onward, his public standing was much more dependent on his political views than on his academic achievements.

Said's political role and development were somewhat confusing, though his career includes a consistent opposition to the mainstream political views of the Palestinian leadership at any given time. In the 1970s, when acceptance of the existence of the state of Israel was still a minority view among the Palestinian political elite, Said advocated a two-state solution. He argued for talks between the two sides at a time when YASIR ARAFAT was still contemplating terrorism as the sole approach to the Palestinian problem. When a development that on the surface appeared to be in line with Said's views of the 1970s and early 1980s took place and the Palestinian leadership entered into what appeared to be serious talks with Israel, Said denounced these talks. The Oslo Accords of the early 1990s marked his open split with the Palestinian leadership. Said resigned from the Palestinian National Council in 1991. At a time when the political leadership of the Palestinians openly declared willingness to embrace a two-state solution, Said, as a former advocate of such a solution, denounced it.

In 2000 Said was photographed throwing a stone from the Lebanese side of the Israeli-Lebanese border in the direction of the Israeli frontier installations soon after the Israeli army left southern Lebanon after an eighteen-year presence there. In the photograph, the Ivy League academic and literary theorist represented a symbol of an Intifada activist.

Said's criticism of the leadership of Arafat was not limited to his disapproval of the Oslo Accords. Said became an important critic of the system of bribery and corruption within the Palestinian Authority of Arafat. As a Christian Palestinian, Said did not support the Islamist Hamas and therefore tried to establish a third way between the corrupt system of Arafat and Islamism of Hamas. This effort was cut short by Said's death on 25 September 2003.

INFLUENCES AND CONTRIBUTIONS

For the purpose of a fair representation of Said's influences and contributions, the distinction between his academic and political activities must be recognized, although this distinction may not be possible for the period after the late 1970s. His major contribution as an academic was condensed in his world-famous book *Orientalism* in 1978. The major themes and thesis of this book were elaborated by Said in the remaining twenty-five years of his life, especially in his book *Culture and Imperialism* (1993), and shaped a whole school of literary critics of the anti- and post-colonial movement. Said's work contributed to a transformation and reconstruction of comparative literature that changed the discipline forever.

Said's main political contribution to the Palestinian cause was his role as a culturally acceptable mouthpiece in the form of an Ivy League academic. The image of the Palestinian-American intellectual Said countered the media image of Palestinian terrorists. Maybe this media image was even more important than Said's political message. The influence of his political message is much more difficult to evaluate. It is difficult to determine how much influence Said exerted with his advocacy of a two-state solution in the 1970s and 1980s and with his anti-Oslo approach in the 1990s. At the end of his life his "third way" approach between the corrupt Fatah and the extremist Hamas left him on the fringe of any notable political stream within the Palestinian society. In a way, his political maverick status can be explained by his own academic work: The "Oriental"-born Said had become a Western professor looking back at his roots with all the theoretical and practical problems and deviations outlined in Said's *Orientalism*.

THE WORLD'S PERSPECTIVE

To paraphrase the saying "One man's terrorist is another man's freedom fighter" to apply to Said: One man's brilliant and inspired academic with social consciousness is another man's intellectually corrupt and dishonest sponsor of violence. This marks the range of evaluations of Said. The world started to form an opinion on Said in the late 1970s at exactly the point in time when Said finished his important academic achievements and started his political career as an unofficial intellectual ambassador of the Palestinian cause to the Western world.

Admirers of Said highlight his innovative approach to literary theory. His transformation of comparative literature is presented as a breakthrough in literary theory in the twentieth century and may even be regarded as a new start in literary theory to replace and refute any former theories. Other proponents of Said highlight his social and political activities. Said is portrayed as an Ivy League academic who left his Ivy Tower without concern for what that might cost him in terms of reputation. The Palestinian cause, which he took personally, was more important to him than general appreciation among his academic peers. His followers assert that he was not corrupted by his political opportunities to profit from his involvement with the Palestinian leadership. They stress his early warnings against the corrupt system of the Palestinian Authority. For his admirers Said was an honest man: honest in his academic and political convictions, but also honest and not opportunistic in his political actions.

Said's opponents, on the other hand, highlight his ambiguity with the truth, starting with the possible lie about his birthplace (Jerusalem or Egypt). Even before criticizing his political activities they will contrast his biographical ambiguities with the academic standards expected from an Ivy League academic. The main criticism of his achievements in the field of literary theory is the blurry line between his political opinions and his academic theories. His discovery or deconstruction of the colonialist view of Westerners as outlined in *Orientalism* is contrasted with the theory that his work was a political

---

THE SEDUCTIVE DEGRADATION OF KNOWLEDGE

◼

Positively, I do believe—and in my other work have tried to show—that enough is being done today in the human sciences to provide the contemporary scholar with insights, methods, and ideas that could dispense with racial, ideological, and imperialist stereotypes of the sort provided during its historical ascendancy by Orientalism. I consider Orientalism's failure to have been a human as much as an intellectual one [...] If the knowledge of Orientalism has any meaning, it is in being a reminder of the seductive degradation of knowledge, of any knowledge, anywhere, at any time. Now perhaps more than before.

SAID, EDWARD W. *ORIENTALISM*. NEW YORK: RANDOM HOUSE, 1978, P. 328

---

act by somebody himself deeply biased by his Palestinian background.

Said's political actions are even more controversial. His change of heart concerning Palestinian-Israeli negotiations can be criticized from various viewpoints. His advocacy of a two-state solution in the 1970s and 1980s has been criticized as a sort of treason to the Palestinian cause in what they considered a just war against Israel. His opposition to the Oslo agreement in the 1990s and his infamous border-stone-throwing of 2000 was criticized as a harmful opposition to an ongoing process of Palestinian-Israeli negotiations. The United States's Federal Bureau of Investigation considered him a possible threat and kept him under surveillance from the 1970s until his death.

LEGACY

The academic and the political legacies of Said must be distinguished. His literary theory as outlined especially in *Orientalism* will remain a decisive piece of literary scholarship of the second part of the twentieth century. Although the post-colonial mood is by now history and many of the approaches of *Orientalism* have to be revaluated and possibly redirected in a post-11 September 2001 world, the mark of Said on literary theory from the 1960s and beyond will remain. His political legacy has probably already now evaporated. The contradicting political sides taken by Said were always somehow related to the actual politics of the Palestinian leadership. Said's political actions were mostly reactions against that leadership, so his political views will not easily fit in the new scenery of a post-Arafat Palestinian framework.

Said's reputation suffered after the release of a widely circulated photograph of him throwing a stone across the Lebanese-Israeli border into Israel. The negative effect of this episode on his academic reputation was probably the price Said had to pay for his convictions and for his transformation into a Palestinian icon. He may be longer and more widely remembered as such an icon than as the brilliant literary theorist that he was.

To do justice to Said one has to mention that he restrained from religious extremism and hatred. His efforts with Israeli pianist and conductor Daniel Barenboim to organize joint Israeli-Palestinian youth music education and events may highlight a positive part of Said's legacy and underline the high cultural education of this controversial academic. After his death, Columbia University established the Edward Said Chair in Middle Eastern Studies, and the American University of Beirut established the Edward Said Chair in American Studies.

BIBLIOGRAPHY

Barsamian, David, ed. *Culture and Resistance*. London: Pluto, 2003.

"Edward W. Said and Postcolonial Theory." Political Discourse—Theories of Colonialism and Postcolonialism. Available from http://www.scholars.nus.edu.sg/post/poldiscourse/said/saidov.html.

Hitchens, Christopher, and Edward Said, eds. *Blaming the Victims*, London: Verso, 1988.

Irwin, Robert. *For Lust of Knowing: The Orientalists and Their Enemies*. London: Allen Lane, 2006.

Kramer, Martin S. *Ivory Towers on Sand: The Failure of Middle Eastern Studies in America*. Washington, D.C.: Washington Institute for Near East Policy, 2001.

Lewis, Bernard. *Islam and the West*. New York: Oxford University Press, 1994.

Price, David. "How the FBI Spied on Edward Said." CounterPunch. Updated 13 January 2006. Available from http://www.counterpunch.org.

Said, Edward W. *Beginnings*. New York: Columbia University Press, 1985.

———. *Covering Islam*. New York: Vintage, 1981.

———. *Culture and Imperialism*. New York: Vintage, 1993.

———. *Joseph Conrad and the Fiction of Autobiography*. New York: Columbia University Press, 2007.

———. *Musical Elaborations*. New York: Columbia University Press, 1993.

———. *Orientalism*. New York: Random House, 1978.

———. *Out of Place: A Memoir*. New York: Vintage Books, 2000.

———. *The End of the Peace Process*. London: Penguin, 2002.

———. *The World, the Text, and the Critic*. Cambridge, MA: Harvard University Press, 1983.

Salusinszky, Imre. *Criticism in Society*. New York: Methuen, 1987.

Spikes, Michael P. *Understanding Contemporary American Literary Theory*. Columbia, SC: University of South Carolina Press, 1997.

Sprinker, Michael. *Edward Said: A Critical Reader*. Oxford: Blackwell, 1992.

The Edward Said Archive. Available from http://www.edwardsaid.org.

Viswanathan, Gauri. *Power, Politics and Culture*. London: Bloomsbury, 2004.

Warraq, Ibn. *Defending the West: A Critique of Edward Said's Orientalism*. London: Prometheus, 2007.

Oliver Benjamin Hemmerle

SALAMEH, NADINE
(1979–)

Palestinian-Syrian actor Nadine Salameh is a popular figure in Syrian and other Arab television and cinema. She is perhaps best known for her work in television miniseries and soap operas (*musalsalat*). The daughter of a Palestinian resistance leader, Salameh is prominent as a spokesperson and activist on Palestinian issues.

BIOGRAPHICAL HIGHLIGHTS

Name: Nadine Salameh

Birth: 1979, Beirut, Lebanon

Family: Single

Nationality: Syrian/Palestinian

Education: Damascus's Higher Academy of Theatrical Arts

PERSONAL CHRONOLOGY:

- **1982:** Father detained by Israeli forces during invasion of Lebanon
- **1982:** Relocates to Damascus with family
- **1998:** Begins studying acting at Damascus's Higher Academy of Theatrical Arts
- **1998:** First role in television drama *al-Kawasir*
- **2003:** First cinematic role in *Ru'ya Halima*

PERSONAL HISTORY

Nadine Salameh (also Nadine, Nadeen Salama) was born in Beirut, Lebanon, on 9 August 1979, where her father, Nabil Salameh, was an active member of the Palestine Liberation Organization (PLO). Her family originally came from the port city of Acre in northern Palestine, before becoming refugees during the Arab-Israeli War of 1948. Salameh's early life was affected by the disappearance of her father, apparently captured by Israeli troops during the 1982 invasion of Beirut (as of mid-2007, he has not been seen since). Having spent her early childhood in Palestinian refugee camps in Lebanon, she and her family fled to Syria after the events of 1982. She began her professional career after her secondary education, and during her theater studies at university. She began first with theater work, quickly finding work in television serials that eventually led in 2003 to her first cinematic role.

INFLUENCES AND CONTRIBUTIONS

Salameh's career as an actor began while she was still a student at Damascus's Higher Academy of Theatrical Arts in 1998; she was given her first role at the age of eighteen, acting in the television historical period drama *al-Kawasir* for Syrian television. She gained prominence with Arab audiences across the world through the broadcast of the popular series on satellite television. In the public attention that resulted from this and her subsequent television roles, she distinguished herself from the

mainstream of television stars of her generation by speaking out on political and social issues, in particular those relating to Palestine. Her first film role was in *Ru'ya Halima* (Dreamer's Vision, 2003), directed by Waha al-Rahib; more recent film works have included *al-Batrik* (2005) and *Ratl Kamil min al-Ashjar* (2006).

THE WORLD'S PERSPECTIVE

Across the Arab world, Nadine Salameh has gained fame for her acting, largely for her roles in highly popular television serials. She is perhaps one of the most famous Palestinian actors of her generation across the region. Her work in cinema has also attracted the attention of Arab filmgoers. Her political commitment to Palestinian nationalist issues and other topics has also focused attention upon her, as well as her compelling family history.

LEGACY

Salameh's legacy as an actor has so far been largely defined by her status as a popular star of television programs, although her work is perhaps distinguished by the roles she has chosen—such as that of Zumurruda, the mythical warrior heroine of the television serial *al-Kawasim*, or the role of Jamila, the rebellious protagonist of the film *Ru'ya Halima*, who escapes her patriarchal family in the early 1980s by traveling to Lebanon to join the military resistance against the Israeli invasion of that country. By choosing roles of strong, brave, and politically active women, Salameh has developed a public persona in line with her own political commitments.

BIBLIOGRAPHY

"Nadine Salameh Personal Website." Available from http://www.nadinesalameh.com.

FILMOGRAPHY: TELEVISION

Al-Kawasir (1998).
Masrahi wa Masrahiyya (1999).
Li'l-Amal Awda (1999).
Al-Mizan (1999).
Amir al-Qulub (1999).
Al-Ayyam al-Mutamarrida (1999).
Spotlight (2000).
Al-Basir (2000).
Radm al-Asatir (2001).
Zaman al-Wasl (2001).
Soura (2002).
Unshudat al-Matar (2003).
Zamat al-Samt (2003).
Tarek Ibn Ziyad (2003).
Kuhl al-Ayun (2004).
Hikayat Kharif (2004).
Asr al-Junun (2004).
Faris Bani Marwan (2004).
Al-Taghriba al-Filistiniyya (2004).

Asi al-Dam (2005).
Ashwak Na'ima (2005).
Muluk al-Tawa'if (2005).
Nada al-Ayyam (2006).
Ahl al-Gharam (2006).
Ala Tul al-Ayyam (2006).
Sada al-Ruh (2006).

FILMOGRAPHY: CINEMA
Ru'ya Halima (2003).
Al-Batrik (2005).
Ratl Kamil min al-Ashjar (2006).

Kamran Rastegar

SALAMI, KHADIJA AL-
(1966–)

Independent Yemeni filmmaker Khadija al-Salami is a pioneer both as a documentary filmmaker and as a woman in media. Although employed at the Yemeni embassy in Paris, she makes regular trips to Yemen to film. A number of her films have been featured in international festivals.

PERSONAL HISTORY

Al-Salami was born in 1966 to a family of modest means in the central Yemen highlands town of Ma'bar. Her childhood coincided with North Yemen's civil war (1962–1970), in which her father was a soldier and which created the Yemen Arab Republic. Most of her childhood was spent in the capital, San'a, where she excelled in school.

Following a brief and traumatic arranged marriage at the unusually young age of eleven, Salami resumed her schooling. At fourteen she began working after school, first at the local telephone exchange, but she quickly seized the opportunity to pursue her fascination with broadcasting when she found work at the government radio station. Because she appeared younger than her years she was asked to develop and host a weekly children's television program. This marked a turning point in her life.

While appearing on television, al-Salami continued her secondary school studies. She spent a month in Cambridge studying English, inspiring her desire to continue her studies abroad. At age sixteen she was awarded a U.S. Agency for International Development (USAID) scholarship to study in the U.S. After an intensive English course at Georgetown University in Washington, D.C., she moved briefly to the University of Michigan. She finally settled at Mount Vernon College for Women (now part of George Washington University), from which she received her B.A. in communications in 1985. Additionally, she

---

BIOGRAPHICAL HIGHLIGHTS

Name: Khadija (Khadijah) al-Salami

Birth: 1966, Ma'bar, Yemen

Family: Husband, Charles Hoots

Nationality: Yemeni

Education: B.A., Mount Vernon College for Women, Washington, D.C., 1985; M.A., American University, Washington, D.C., 1990

PERSONAL CHRONOLOGY:

- **1977–1982:** Television broadcaster
- **1984–1990:** Student
- **1990:** First film, *Femmes du Yémen*
- **1993–2005:** Press counselor, Embassy of the Republic of Yemen, Paris
- **2002–2005:** Director of the Yemeni Communication Center, Embassy of the Republic of Yemen, Paris
- **2007:** Awarded France's Medal of Honor at rank of knight by President Jacques Chirac for the role of her documentary films in presenting social and humanitarian issues

---

took courses in filmmaking at the University of Southern California.

Following graduation al-Salami returned briefly to Yemen but soon moved to Paris to escape family pressures. She returned to the U.S. to continue her studies. In 1990 she earned a master's degree in film and video production from American University.

Although filmmaking has been her avocation al-Salami and her American husband, Charles Hoots, live in Paris where she has served as press counselor, and later director of the communication center, at the Yemeni Embassy. With her husband, she has written an autobiography, *The Tears of Sheba* (2003).

INFLUENCES AND CONTRIBUTIONS

Al-Salami's primary stated aim has been to use her films to present the many facets of Yemeni life to a global audience. In pursuit of this objective, she has made films on the remote, culturally unique island of Socotra, among the remaining Jews in the far north, with the culturally unique Munabbih on the Saudi border, and in the eastern deserts of Marib and the Hadramawt.

Al-Salami's life experience underlies her films, which she uses to raise questions about and challenges to Yemeni culture. Although she might not describe herself as a feminist, the theme of gender inequality and the filmmaker's advocacy of social change are clear. She is a strong voice for Yemeni women.

Al-Salami's first film, her master's project, was *Women in Yemen* (1990). It gives insight into her interest in improving the lives of Yemeni women. Based on interviews with five women, the film exposes the challenges faced by rural and urban women.

Women and Democracy in Yemen (2004) was filmed as political parties were selecting candidates to run for parliament in 2003. A few determined Yemeni women confront an array of obstacles, such as gender stereotyping and party politics, as they vie for their parties' nominations for seats in Yemen's parliament. The film follows women on the campaign trail as they try to gain support for their candidacies and contend with officials' obfuscation.

A Stranger in Her Own City (2005) is the story of thirteen-year-old Najima, a girl who refuses to conform to cultural norms. At a time when she is expected to begin wearing the veil, she is happy playing soccer or bicycling like the boys in her neighborhood. Najima's appeal is her outspoken rebellion, which in the end is smothered by local culture.

Amina (2006) tells the story of infamous Amina al-Tuhayf who, at age fifteen, was accused of killing her husband and sentenced to death. She spent nine years in prison where she is filmed. Yemeni president Ali Abdullah Salih, who screened the film, was moved to commute Amina's death sentence. Although this film reveals both positive and negative aspects of women's lives in rural Yemen, the Ministry of Culture has banned it.

Stylistically, al-Salami's films are extremely straightforward—the impression is that the viewer is seeing Yemen exactly as is the filmmaker. This is her goal; she states that her aim is to show people as they really are. Al-Salami often works by herself with a handheld camera, but hers are not home videos. The films exhibit excellent production values characterized by sharp focus and creative framing. More importantly, al-Salami has a clear point of view. By giving voice to her subjects, she expresses herself in a disarming yet forceful manner.

THE WORLD'S PERSPECTIVE

Al-Salami is developing a strong reputation as a filmmaker. This is evident by the inclusion of her films in film festivals. *A Stranger in Her Own City* has been featured in at least ten film festivals in the United States, Europe, and the Middle East and has been broadcast worldwide. Al-Salami's career has been aided by her

WE MUST SPEAK OUT AND ASK QUESTIONS

■

I am trying in my book and in my films to cover sensitive issues. In our Yemeni culture, women are not allowed to express themselves freely, not even about daily life. They are not allowed to speak in public. But if we want our society to change, we must speak out and ask questions.

QUOTED IN CHRIS KUTSCHERA, "YEMEN: A YEMENI WOMAN'S FIGHT FOR FREEDOM." *THE MIDDLE EAST MAGAZINE* (JUNE 2006). AVAILABLE FROM HTTP://WWW.CHRIS-KUTSCHERA.COM/A/KHADIJA.HTM.

connections in French television, which has aired most of her films, but it has been hurt by limited distribution.

LEGACY

While al-Salami has succeeded in bringing Yemen to the wider world, it is too soon to assess her influence, especially in Yemen. Her touristic and historical films have been shown on Yemeni television, but those focusing on women's issues have not.

BIBLIOGRAPHY

Hillauer, Rebecca. *Encyclopedia of Arab Women Filmmakers*. Cairo: American University in Cairo Press, 2005.

Hoots, Charles, and Khadija al-Salami. *The Tears of Sheba*. Chichester, U.K.: Wiley, 2003.

Sakr, Naomi. *Women and Media in the Middle East: Power Through Self-Expression*. London: I.B. Tauris, 2004.

Stevenson, Thomas B. *Visions of Yemen: A Filmography*. Westbury, New York: American Institute for Yemeni Studies, 2003.

FILMOGRAPHY (PRIMARY FILMS)

Femmes du Yémen (Women of Yemen, 1990)

Hadramout, carrefour des civilisations (Hadramawt: Crossroads of Culture, 1991)

Le pays suspendu (A Country in Limbo, 1994)

Terre de Saba (Land of Sheba, 1997)

L'Île de l'homme au pied d'or (The Island of the Man with the Golden Foot, 1998)

Yémen aux mille facettes (Yemen of a Thousand Faces, 2000)

Les Femmes et la démocratie au Yémen (Women and Democracy in Yemen, 2004)

Une Étrangère dans sa ville (A Stranger in Her Own City, 2005)

Amina (2006)

Thomas B. Stevenson

SALIH, ALI ABDULLAH
(1942–)

Ali Abdullah Salih became president of the Yemen Arab Republic (YAR), better known as North Yemen, in 1978 following the assassinations of his two predecessors. Along with Ali Salim al-Bid, he oversaw the unification of the YAR with the People's Democratic Republic of Yemen (PDRY) in 1990. He became president of the newly formed Republic of Yemen (ROY), while al-Bid served as vice president. The delicate balance of power lasted until al-Bid and the former PDRY attempted to secede in 1994. Salih defeated his rival and forced him into exile, subsequently strengthening his position as the head of the country. Salih won re-election in 1999 and again in 2006.

PERSONAL HISTORY

Salih was born on 21 March 1942 in the village of Bayt al-Ahmar in the governorate of San'a. The village is located southeast of the capital in the district of Sanhan, which takes its name from a local tribe. Prior to the revolution of 1962 that overthrew Muhammad al-Badr

Ali Abdullah Salih. AP IMAGES.

BIOGRAPHICAL HIGHLIGHTS

Name: Ali Abdullah Salih

Birth: 1942, Bayt al-Ahmar, North Yemen

Nationality: Yemeni

Education: Primary school in Bayt al-Ahmar, attended military school in 1960 and again in 1964; he received an MA in military science in 1989, and two honorary doctorates from universities in Sudan and South Korea

PERSONAL CHRONOLOGY:

- **1960s:** Corporal in the Republican Army, and a member of a tank crew
- **1970s:** Rises through the ranks of the Yemeni military, eventually achieving the rank of major, and command of the garrison at Ta'izz.
- **1978:** Named president of the Yemen Arab Republic
- **1982:** Convenes the General People's Congress
- **1990:** Oversees unification of the YAR and the DPRY
- **1994:** Preserves unification following a failed seccession attempt by Ali Salim al-Bid
- **1999:** Elected president of the Republic of Yemen in nationwide voting
- **2000:** Successfully amends the constitution, allowing for, among other things, an extension of the president's term of office from six years to seven years
- **2006:** Re-elected president in nationwide elections

Hamid al-Din and the Imamate system of government, the region was known for producing soldiers for the Imam. The Sanhan tribe, of which Salih is a member, is a Zaydi tribe that is part of the Hashid tribal confederation headed by Shaykh Abdullah al-Ahmar. Despite this alliance, different tribal subsections of the confederation have traditionally acted with a great deal of independence.

Salih was raised by his stepfather, a full brother of his deceased father. He was born into a poor family whose members traditionally served in the Imam's army. They filled the lower ranks of the military, and none of his relatives rose to prominence under the Imam. This was partly due to the relative weakness of the Sanhan tribe at the time, as well as the lack of social mobility under the Imamate.

Salih in the Military In 1958 when Salih turned sixteen he traveled to San'a to enlist in the army, following his older brother, Muhammad Abdullah Salih. He attended the military school for noncommissioned officers in San'a in 1960, leaving as a corporal. Both brothers fought in the eight-year civil war following the 1962 overthrow of the Imamate. Along with his stepbrothers and cousins, Salih supported the Republicans against the Royalist forces loyal to the Imam. This largely stemmed from the popular support the revolution gained amongst Salih's peers in the military. Salih spent much of the war as a member of a tank crew. In 1963 he achieved the rank of second lieutenant, the first of many promotions.

His official biography claims that he defended the revolution in numerous battles throughout different governorates in Yemen during the civil war, and that he was wounded while fighting in 1963. His role in the civil war, however, was minimal as he was both young and held a relatively low rank. Both he and his brother were involved in defending San'a during the 70 Day Siege in 1967-68 that broke the back of Royalist resistance. Paul Dresch in *A History of Modern Yemen* writes that as a tank driver, he was remembered as "motoring along Abd al-Mughni Street in San'a, during the fighting of 1968, and shelling point-blank such symbols of leftist progress as the pharmacy and the Bilqis cinema."

The civil war, and particularly the fighting of August 1968, enhanced the power of the military as an institution in its own right. The army now represented a path out of poverty for those lacking traditional connections. Salih made the most of his opportunities, and Dresch and many other observers have noted that he is largely a self-made man. Over the next decade, Salih made his way up the ranks of the Yemeni army, an increasingly more powerful force within the country.

The military's role as the major political power within the country solidified after the 1974 military coup sent President Abd al-Rahman al-Iryani into exile and installed Ibrahim al-Hamdi, a popular military leader, as president. Al-Hamdi and his brother, Abdullah, were murdered in 1977, and Ahmad al-Ghashmi, a tank officer, replaced him as president. Al-Ghashmi was himself assassinated with a briefcase bomb in June 1978 after only eight months in power. Abd al-Karim al-Arashi was appointed interim president. Eventually he declined the job, leaving the way open for Salih.

Salih's YAR Presidency Salih had been close to al-Hamdi and had worked with al-Ghasmi, but he was still a relative unknown when he put himself forward for pres-

ident in July 1978. Prior to becoming president he had risen to the rank of major and headed a large military garrison at Ta'izz since 1975. His political inexperience led many foreign observers to question whether he would survive the year. Salih since has made much of the fact that the international community never had faith in his ability to rule Yemen.

In the immediate aftermath of the assassination of his two predecessors, Salih was wary of suffering the same fate. He took a number of precautionary measures that helped to save his own life. The most important and far-reaching of these was Salih's decision to surround himself with trusted relatives. Important military and intelligence posts were quickly occupied by stepbrothers, cousins, and other family members. This helped to derail an early threat to his rule in October 1978, when an attempted coup failed. Salih survived his early days in power by bringing in former opponents and managing deftly to play one interest group against another. He used a delicate balance of shifting alliances, as well as maintaining and encouraging deep-rooted and personal networks of patronage, to maintain his position of power.

In 1982 Salih opened the General People's Congress (al-Mu'tamar al-Sha'bi al-Amm). This eventually transformed into a general organization that became known as the official government party in the aftermath of unification in 1990. Throughout the 1980s, Salih strongly supported Iraq in its war against Iran. At home, he attempted to limit Saudi influence, while moving skillfully between the different local power blocs in the country and expanding his patronage networks.

Salih's ROY Presidency In November 1989 Salih and Ali Salim al-Bid, the head of the Marxist PDRY, jointly announced that the two countries, the YAR and the PDRY, would unify within the year. Unification took place on 22 March 1990 with Salih as president of the newly formed Republic of Yemen (ROY) and al-Bid as his vice president. The delicate power sharing agreement that the two had worked out lasted until the parliamentary elections in 1993, when al-Bid's Yemeni Socialist Party (YSP) fared worse than expected. Al-Bid retreated to Aden and eventually declared his intention to secede from the union.

Fighting between the two sides broke out in April 1994 and continued until July, when northern forces sacked the city of Aden. Al-Bid and a number of his supporters went into exile, although some have since taken advantage of an amnesty offered by Salih and returned to the country. In the aftermath of the civil war, Salih was reaffirmed as the president of the country.

He ran virtually unopposed for election in 1999, as even his opponent, Najib Qahtan al-Sha'bi, a member of Salih's own GPC party, publicly endorsed Salih for

CONTEMPORARIES

Ali Salim al-Bid (1939-), along with Ali Abdullah Salih, was responsible for bringing about the unification of the YAR and the PDRY in 1990. He was born in the eastern province of Hadramawt to a prominent family that traces its ancestors back to the Prophet Muhammad. Al-Bid played a major role in most of the governments formed following Britain's withdrawal from South Yemen in 1967. He served as secretary general of the Yemeni Socialist Party and head of the PDRY from 1986-1990. In November 1989 Salih and al-Bid jointly announced in Aden that the two countries would unite within the year. Al-Bid became Salih's vice president under the new power-sharing agreement that lasted until the first nationwide elections in 1993. Al-Bid's YSP party fared poorly in those elections, and by 1994 he attempted to secede from the union. The Southern forces were defeated and al-Bid was forced into exile.

president. Not surprisingly, he won with more than 96 percent of the vote. Yemen's major opposition parties including Islah and the YSP failed to nominate a candidate for the country's top office.

Following his overwhelming victory in 1999, Salih submitted a series of constitutional amendments to a popular referendum in 2000. Among the changes were the extension of the presidential term of office from six years to seven years, the right for the president to disband parliament (which as of 2007 has not been used), and expansion to a 111-seat consultative council appointed by the president.

Bowing to international pressure and accusations of rampant government corruption, Salih stepped down as head of Yemen's judiciary in 2006. Later that year, he won re-election against an aging opposition candidate, Faysal bin Shamlan. Despite the outcome never being in doubt, the election was fiercely contested by the opposition. His September 2006 victory cleared Salih to rule Yemen until 2013, giving him thirty-five years as the head of Yeman.

INFLUENCES AND CONTRIBUTIONS

Salih was strongly influenced by both his impoverished youth and his military experiences. His ability to play off rival groups against one another and maintain an ever-

shifting and delicate balance of power stems from his military experiences in mediating conflicts and learning how to lead.

He also has styled himself after other Arab leaders, including Saddam Hussein, who used the military as a path to power. In the aftermath of the Iraq War in 2003 and the subsequent execution of Hussein in 2006, Salih has somewhat tempered this emulation. Numerous pictures and billboards featuring him in various poses and costumes came down shortly after the invasion.

Salih is fiercely loyal to his family, often forgiving shortcomings in their behavior that he would not overlook in others. At times this natural inclination has led to anger and resentment from powerful families, who feel that Salih's networks of patronage are slowly forcing them out of their established positions of power. The influence of his family often pulls Salih away from what is in the best interest of the country in favor of what is in the best interest of his relatives. This is particularly the case with his son and heir-apparent, Ahmad.

In many ways, Salih was viewed as a savior when he first came on the Yemen scene in 1978. He steered the country out of a turbulent time that had witnessed the assassinations of his two predecessors and into a period of relative stability. In addition to his role in stabilizing Yemen during the 1980s, Salih's other major contributions were his role in unifying the country in 1990 and preserving its unification during the 1994 Civil War.

Salih's largest contribution, however, is still ahead of him. He has the choice of either setting a precedent for democracy following the end of his term in 2013 or solidifying his family's rule. If he refuses to stand for president again and actively discourages Ahmad from running for the country's top office, he would chart a new course for contemporary Yemeni politics. This would dwarf all of his previous accomplishments and secure his place in history.

THE WORLD'S PERSPECTIVE

The international community was initially skeptical of Salih's chances for surviving and ruling Yemen when he first came to power in 1978. This early doubt has since given way to admiration and respect for the way that Salih has managed to unify and preserve Yemen throughout the 1990s.

Salih fell out of favor with many in the international community—most notably the United States, Saudi Arabia, and Kuwait—after his support for Saddam Hussein and Iraq during the 1990-91 Gulf War. This was particularly egregious as Yemen then occupied a seat on the UN Security Council. Its consistent abstentions and "no" votes on resolutions aimed at Iraq did not endear it to many in the international community. Unlike other Arab leaders such as King Hussein of Jordan, Salih lacked

HUMAN RIGHTS ARE TIGHTLY CONNECTED TO DEMOCRACY

■

Democracy is the choice of the modern age for all peoples of the world and the rescue ship for political regimes particularly in our third world. It is the way to achieve security, stability, development and better futures for our countries. Human rights are tightly connected to democracy and the state of law and order. Therefore, we should remove anything that contradicts them and stand against all forms of discrimination, oppression and exploitation of the human being and his rights. Ladies and Gentlemen, respect of states' sovereignty, non-intervention in their internal affairs and protection of human rights in the world should be a priority of the international organizations which call for democracy and the bolstering of international law in combating the flagrant violations of human rights. There is no doubt that not all of the world's peoples can enjoy freedom, democracy, and human rights as long as there are gaps that widen everyday in the fields of development, economic growth and knowledge and as long as international justice is absent. Double standards prevail and human rights violations continue in many countries of the world.

DELIVERED AS THE INAUGURAL ADDRESS FOR THE SAN'A INTER-GOVERNMENTAL REGIONAL CONFERENCE ON DEMOCRACY, HUMAN RIGHTS AND THE ROLE OF THE ICC, SAN'A. 11 JANUARY 2004.

the diplomatic chits to restore relations with the United States and other Western powers after miscalculating the ramifications of his decision.

Not until after the September 11, 2001, attacks did Salih truly restore positive relations with the United States and most other Western powers. He was wary of making the same mistakes that had cost Yemen so dearly a decade earlier. Salih made a strong statement of support for the U.S.-led "war on terror" during a visit to the United States in November 2001. Since then he has traveled to the United States on numerous occasions. The United States and other international powers have responded by praising Salih's achievements in leading his country toward full democracy. This response by the international community tacitly acknowledges that Salih's continued rule in Yemen is in the best interest of the stability of the country. For his part, Salih is not shy

about making this clear to his foreign counterparts, often pointing toward Yemen's neighbor Somalia as an example of the chaos that can ensue when a skilled and experienced leader is removed from power.

LEGACY

Salih's ultimate legacy largely will depend on how he prepares Yemen for its future during what he says will be his last term in office, running from 2006-2013. Yemen is facing drastically shrinking oil reserves and sharp decreases in its water table. Revenue from oil exports make up roughly 75 percent of Yemen's budget, and the economy needs to diversify away from oil. The lack of water will also have a negative impact on Yemen's agricultural sector that employs more than half of all Yemenis. Salih has the political capital to deal with these issues, although solving or even managing them will require difficult decisions.

Salih has done a great deal of good for the country. He constructed a stable form of government out of the chaos that followed the assassinations of al-Hamdi and al-Ghashmi. He not only unified the country, but also held it together through a brief but bloody civil war. Since then he has slowly brought the country along a path that he likes to call an "emerging democracy." This stability, however, has been pursued at the expense of building sustainable institutions that could outlast his rule. History will judge Salih as to whether he will be able to fulfill his promise to leave Yemen as a functioning democracy—with free and fair elections, devoid of nepotism, and fully prepared to meet its post-oil future.

BIBLIOGRAPHY

Dresch, Paul. *A History of Modern Yemen*. New York: Cambridge University Press, 2000.

Dresch, Paul, and Haykel, Bernard. "Stereotypes and Political Styles: Islamists and Tribesfolk in Yemen." *International Journal of Middle East Studies*, 27, no. 4 (November 1995): 405-431.

Johnsen, Gregory D. "Salih's Road To Reelection." *Middle East Report Online*, 13 January 2006. Available from: http://www.merip.org/mero/mero011306.html.

Gregory D. Johnsen

SALIH, AL-TAYYIB
(1929–)

Sudanese novelist and short-story writer al-Tayyib Salih won acclaim as a master of style and fictional form early in his career when he published his complex and poetic *Season of Migration to the North*. Although Salih's literary production has been limited—three novels and a series of short stories—his creation of the mythical village Wad

BIOGRAPHICAL HIGHLIGHTS

Name: al-Tayyib Salih (Tayeb Saleh, Taieb Salih)

Birth: 1929, al-Dabba, Merowe district, Sudan

Family: Wife; three daughters, Zeinab, Sara, and Samira

Nationality: Sudanese

Education: Secondary school at the Gordon College, Khartoum; University of Khartoum (agricultural sciences); University of London (economics and political science); University of Exeter (education)

PERSONAL CHRONOLOGY:

• **1950s:** Teacher, Rufah, Sudan

• **1953:** Scriptwriter, British Broadcasting Corporation (BBC) Arabic Section

• **1960:** Head of drama, BBC Arabic Service

• **1968:** Publishes *The Wedding of Zein and Other Stories*

• **1969:** Publishes *Season of Migration to the North*

• **1970s:** Named director-general of Information, Qatar, UNESCO, Paris and Qatar

• **1976:** Kuwaiti filmmaker Khalid Siddiq wins Cannes Film Festival award for *The Wedding of Zein*, film based on Salih's novel

• **1980:** Gives a lecture at the American University in Beirut (May 19)

• **1996:** Publishes *Bandarshah*

• **2001:** Visiting Randolph Distinguished Professor, Vassar College

• **2003:** Re-releases *Season of Migration to the North*

• **2004:** Awarded Third Arab Conference Prize by Egypt

in as head of drama for the British Broadcasting Corporation (BBC), as a journalist for London's Arabic-language weekly magazine *al-Majalla*, and as a cultural envoy working for the Ministry of Information in Qatar and for the United Nations Educational, Scientific, and Cultural Organization (UNESCO).

PERSONAL HISTORY

Al-Tayyib Salih was born in 1929 in a small village on the Nile called al-Dabba in the Merowe district of northern Sudan. Home to a stable agricultural society whose people are a mixture of Arab and Nubian blood, plus nomadic bedouin heritage, the village, Salih notes, is like an archaeological heap where the history of Sudan is condensed in its complex religious history that includes Pharaonic, Pagan, Christian, and then Muslim eras. The collective, unconscious memory of these people is what has continued to occupy a central place in Salih's writing, although he left the village at age ten to go to school in the capital, Khartoum, and has lived and worked much of his adult life in London. He returns to his village often, and sees this village community and his early training at the *Khalwa* (Qur'anic school) as providing the roots of his identity.

After secondary school at the Gordon College in Khartoum, Salih studied agricultural sciences at the University of Khartoum, then political science and economics at the University of London, and education at Exeter. Growing up in the 1930s and 1940s, Salih has explained, he felt his country had a need for doctors and agricultural engineers, not writers. After a brief stint as a teacher, Salih arrived in London at age twenty-four in the winter of 1953 to work for the Arabic section of the BBC. It was at this time that he began to write. Forty years later he would recall:

> When I came to London I felt an inner chill. Having lived the life of the tribe and the extended family of uncles, aunts, grandparents, among people you know and who know you, in spacious houses, under a clear star-studded sky, you come to London to live in an emotionless society, surrounded by the four walls of your room . . . I had an overwhelming feeling that I had left good things behind . . . When I began writing, nostalgia for the homeland and for a world I felt was fast disappearing dominated my work. Nevertheless, I tried not to be carried away by that nostalgia. (Hassan, p. 14)

As Waïl Hassan points out, the cycle of stories from Salih's imaginary village of Wad Hamid cover the turbulent years that saw the fall of the Ottoman Empire and the threat of European imperialism during which time the *Nahda* (Renaissance) movement struggled to meld Arab Islamic heritage with the scientific and technological

Hamid in northern Sudan (akin to Faulkner's Yoknapatawpha county) has made him a major voice in Arabic literature. Salih confessed in his 1980 lecture in Beirut: "When I am writing a sense of futility invades me. I feel I should be doing something else, that I should be somewhere else" (Amyuni, p. 14). Throughout his career, he has been torn between two mutually exclusive worlds: the isolated realm of the creative writer trying to make sense of the chaotic world materializing from his blank sheet of paper, and the chaotic world of real affairs he participated

achievements of European civilization. Salih himself wrote his major works during the decades when the state of Israel was established on Palestinian land, pan-Arabism faltered, and Arab societies struggled with issues of social reform, political legitimacy, and the status of women. "One of the major themes of *Season of Migration to the North*," Salih has explained, "is the East/West confrontation...the confrontation of the Arab Muslim World and the Western European one...I have redefined the so-called East/West relationship as essentially one of conflict, while it had previously been treated in romantic terms" (Amyuni, p. 16). Denys Johnson-Davies, the major translator who can be credited with making Arabic works available to English readers, wrote in *Al-Ahram* that Salih's *Season of Migration to the North* is "one of the few intelligent novels written by a Western or non-Western writer about the East-West conflict."

INFLUENCES AND CONTRIBUTIONS

Salih has struggled, as Hassan's study *Tayeb Salih: Ideology and the Craft of Fiction* explores in detail, with being an active participant in the world and dealing with topical, political events, or being a writer who works in isolation, waiting patiently for reality to become refined through the author's process of dreaming and crafting. Salih greatly respects writers who can manage these two seemingly mutually exclusive realms. In a speech delivered at the American University in Cairo, he commented that he appreciated how Yahya Haqqi from Egypt wrote when the mood took him and that Charles Dickens was able to strike a balance between his career as a novelist and enjoying other aspects of living, whereas Honoré de Balzac was nothing more than a writing machine and that Ernest Hemingway, who was what Salih called a mediocre writer, "died like a failed Gatsby" (Thabet, p. 2). Salih also admires NAGUIB MAHFOUZ, "the pioneer of the novel in the Arab world" (*Tayeb Salih Speaks*, p. 7). He sees Mahfouz as more intellectual and more secular than himself, noting that in his own work he has accepted a magical world, a world that is not secular, a world where miracles can happen. Salih, throughout his life, has battled to balance reality and dream, to balance the pull of tradition and the onslaught of modernity, to balance engagement in contemporary affairs and the withdrawal from the world he feels he requires to write fiction.

Salih's earliest novel, *The Wedding of Zein*, posits a village where miracles happen and the village fool, Zein, can marry the most beautiful girl in town because he is full of heart, compassion, love, and life. This is a village world where people live in harmony and organic unity, and the novella celebrates this harmonious unity. Similarly, the grandfather in *Season of Migration to the North*, Salih comments, "symbolizes our ability as an Arab peo-

---

CONTEMPORARIES

Denys Johnson-Davies (1922-) is the translator of all of al-Tayyib Salih's work that appears in English. Described by EDWARD SAID as the leading Arabic-English translator of our time, Johnson-Davies has translated more than twenty-five volumes of short stories, novels, plays, and poetry, and was the first to translate the work of Nobel laureate Naguib Mahfouz. In *Memories in Translation*, Johnson-Davies explains the difficulty of translating from Arabic. Either the translator hopes to find a publisher after the fact when the English version already has been completed, or finds a press that will simply trust one's judgment from the outset. Johnson-Davies notes that al-Tayyib Salih's famous novel, *Season of Migration to the North*, which he translated three years after it came out in Arabic, might well have remained unpublished had not Johnson-Davies just begun editing the Heinemann Arab Authors series. "It required Naguib Mahfouz to win the Nobel prize," Johnson-Davies reminds us, "for an American publisher of the caliber of Doubleday to take him on" (p. 58).

---

ple to create life and to persist in it despite obstacles and difficult conditions ... not prone to any form of illusion. His is a healthy and germ-free personality. He is unencumbered by complication and disturbance, relying completely on his instinct and his pure simple nature"; Mustafa Sa'eed, on the other hand, embodies all the cultural dissonance and political conflict that have defined the relationship between Europe and Sudan— he is "all mind, meditation, crookedness, and sharp psychological struggles" (*Tayeb Salih Speaks*, p. 17).

Salih aims in his work to transform ordinary, regional Sudanese characters into mythical characters as Homer did in the *Iliad*, raising them above their simple, ordinary lives through art. Unity of place and successive generations of villagers allow Salih to explore in depth the historical sweep of events as they imprint themselves in individual lives. Salih's last novel, *Bandarshah* (two of five planned sections have been published, "Daww al-Bayt" and "Meryud"), is a complicated, nonlinear narrative about struggle over village leadership, and authority on a symbolic level. Allegorically, the takeover of the village by the young, self-interested, and dictatorial bunch called Bakri's boys, from a responsible, balanced, and tolerant older generation group called Majub's gang in *Wedding of Zein* represents the failure of democracy in most Arab and African nations.

The harmony, tolerance, and wicked sense of humor that Salih associates with Wad Hamid is of a piece with his own political beliefs and aesthetic style. Asked about his political beliefs, Salih noted the importance of both appreciating one's origins and of being able to absorb external ideas. Commenting that the Sudan he remembered was a model of tolerance, where people lived in harmony and unity, he says:

> As for myself, I like to believe I am a socialist, in the manner of the great Irish poet Yeats who says: "Justice is a symmetrical thing." ... Social injustice is against harmony.... In my opinion the writer is not capable of establishing his writing upon an immoral foundation. Writing, in essence, is a moral act. Socialism guarantees a basis for a virtuous society and a healthy man. (*Tayeb Salih Speaks*, p. 18-19).

When *Season of Migration to the North* came out in Arabic in 1966, the homegrown military government of General Ibrahim Abbud had been overthrown and a parliamentary system introduced; in the "Introduction" to the 2003 Penguin edition Salih recalls, "the general climate in Khartoum in those days was exhilarating ... For some reason my work became incorporated into this process of intellectual questioning" (Harss). Salih spent a silent decade during the 1980s, but had returned to writing journalism in 1989 at the time Sudan came under the rule of the oppressive Revolutionary Command Council for National Salvation: "Salih emerged as one of the strongest voices denouncing the new regime," Hassan notes; "journalistic writing, with its directness and immediacy, is more effective for dealing with such events than allegory, symbolism or myth making" (*Tayeb Salih* p. 174-75). All of Salih's creative writing has been acknowledged as showing high mastery of the forms of the novel and short story. Long periods of silence have occurred when he has been engaged in other ways of being an agent in the world.

THE WORLD'S PERSPECTIVE

When his novel *Season of Migration to the North* came out in Beirut in the late 1960s, Salih was hailed as the new genius of the Arabic novel; the centrality of this work to contemporary Arabic letters was attested to in 2001, when the Syrian-based Arab Literary Academy in Damascus declared it the most important Arabic novel of the twentieth century. Salih's translator, Johnson-Davies, maintains that this novel is perhaps the most important Arab work of the twentieth century: "No other modern Arabic work of fiction, not even any of the novels of the recent Nobel prize winner, the Egyptian Naguib

---

ILLUSION COLORS OUR SELF-PERCEPTION

◼

In creating *Season of Migration to the North*, Salih was "pondering the idea of the illusory relationship [*alaqa wahamiyya*] between our Arab Islamic world and Western European civilization specifically. This relationship seems to me, from my readings and studies, to be based on illusions [*awham*] on our side and theirs. Illusion colors our self-perception, what we think of our relationship with them, and their view of us as well. Western Europe has imposed itself and its civilization on us ... become part of our cultural makeup whether we like it or not.

To destabilize settled viewpoints, Salih undermined reader security: "Basically, the reader looks for the writer in a work. When the narration begins in the first person, the reader quickly settles down to the view that, here is an autobiography ... [claiming] no responsibility whatsoever. I created therefore a conflicting world in which nothing is certain, and, formalistically, two voices force the reader to make up his/her own mind.

AMYUNI, MONA TAKIEDDINE. SEASON OF MIGRATION TO THE NORTH BY TAYEB SALIH: A CASEBOOK.

Mahfouz, has achieved the literary status of *Season*. Its ability to transcend language and culture barriers is evidenced by the fact that it has been translated into languages as diverse as Norwegian and Japanese" (Johnson-Davies). This novel alone has appeared in more than twenty languages.

In 2004, al-Tayyib Salih was awarded the controversial Third Arab Conference prize for literature by the Egyptian government. The debate surrounding this prize stemmed from the 2003 award ceremony when Egyptian Sonallah Ibrahim, who appeared to have accepted the prize, rejected it at the ceremony on the basis of Israeli rulers being received in Arab capitals with open arms at a time when "Israeli troops are invading whatever remains of the Palestinian land... carrying out a methodical and systematic genocide against the Palestinians" (Anis). Other Egyptian writers such as Gamal El-Ghitani also refused to sign statements that they would not, if awarded the prize, also refuse it. Al-Tayyib Salih, who was the head of the committee that chose Ibrahim for the prize, has commented any writer has the right to turn down an award, but he objected to the manner in which

Ibrahim did so. As for Salih's winning the prize in 2004, many agree that it was an acknowledgment of his stature in the Arab world while at the same time, given his own active participation in struggles of social justice, not excusing governments that undermine human rights.

LEGACY

Similar to William Faulkner's legacy in creating an entire society with all its memorable characters and their foibles, its historical traumas, and its human complexities, Salih's Wad Hamid cycle tells the history of the Arab region and its traumatic entry into modernity from the perspective of the margin. As Johnson-Davies notes, "another important element in Tayeb [sic] Salih's writing, one that is missing in most modern Arabic literature, is his humor and sense of the ridiculous" (2006).

BIBLIOGRAPHY

Amyuni, Mona Takieddine. *Season of Migration to the North by Tayeb Salih: A Casebook.* Beirut: American University of Beirut, 1985.

Anis, Mona. "Speaking Truth to Power." *Al-Ahram.* Available from http://weekly.ahram.org.eg/2003/662/cu5.htm.

Harss, Marina. "Review of *Season of Migration to the North.*" Words without Borders. Available from http://www.wordswithoutborders.org/article.php?lab=SeasonReview.

Hassan, Wail S. *Tayeb Salih: Ideology & the Craft of Fiction.* Syracuse, NY: Syracuse University Press, 2003.

Johnson-Davies, Denys. "Migratory Minds." *Al-Ahram Weekly* no. 665 (20-26 November 2003). Available from http://weekly.ahram.org.eg/2003/665/bo1.htm.

———. *Memories in Translation: A Life between the Lines of Arabic Literature.* Cairo: The American University Press, 2006.

"Lecture by Tayeb Salih, Sudanese Novelist and Visiting Randolph Distinguished Professor, at Vassar November 14." Vassar College. Available from http://collegerelations.vassar.edu/2001/677/.

Thabet, Hanan. "Intellectuals between East and West." *Barqiyya.* Available from http://www.aucegypt.edu/academic/mesc/PDF/Bar%20Vol%205,%20no.%202.pdf.

Laura Rice

SALMAN, ALI
(1965–)

Bahraini politician and cleric Ali Salman Ahmad Salman (also known as Abu Mujtaba) is the secretary-general of Al-Wifaq (Islamic National Accord Society, INAS), the largest Shi'ite organization in the country. Salman helped found Al-Wifaq in 2002, which has become the main opposition group in Bahrain, commanding seventeen of the forty seats in the elected chamber. Salman leads Friday prayers in al-Sadiq Mosque, in Manama, the capital of Bahrain.

Ali Salman. ADAM JAN/AFP/GETTY IMAGES.

PERSONAL HISTORY

Salman was born on 30 October 1965, in Bilad al-Qadim, a Shi'ite village on the outskirts of Manama, the capital of Bahrain. A paternal aunt raised him soon after his parents' separation and his father's demise. While studying at the local schools, Salman developed an interest in sports and became a leading player on one of the village's football teams. His preoccupation with football shielded Salman from engaging in the disturbances that gripped Bahrain after the 1979 Iranian Revolution. Unlike many of his cohorts, Salman did not take part in any of the political protests that engulfed the country and led to the arrest of scores of young people throughout that period.

Reports on that period by Amnesty International and regional human rights watchdog organizations note that the Bahrain government began a consistent pattern of human rights violations after dissolving its parliament in 1975. Those violations amplified after an alleged coup attempt in 1981. Inspired by the success of the Iranian Revolution two years earlier, many young Shi'ite militants sought to reproduce it in Bahrain. Young Shi'ite radicals began for the first time to openly challenge the

BIOGRAPHICAL HIGHLIGHTS

Name: Ali Salman

Birth: 1965, Bilad al-Qadim, Bahrain

Family: Wife, Alia; one son, Mujtaba

Nationality: Bahraini

Education: Secondary school in Bahrain. King Faysal University in Riyadh, Saudi Arabia. Seminary at Qom, Iran; 1992; Shari'a

PERSONAL CHRONOLOGY:
- **1992–1995:** Member of underground Shi'ite networks
- **1996–2002:** Political refugee and activist, United Kingdom
- **2001–present:** Secretary-general of al-Wifaq (Islamic National Accord Society)
- **2006:** Elected member, Bahrain's Chamber of Deputies (December).

"Al Khalifa [the ruling family] conquest" and clamor for the creation of an Islamic republic in the country. The revolutionary rhetoric of the period created a sharp division within the Shi'ite community between those who aspired to reform the regime and those who sought to take it apart. In December 1981, Bahraini authorities announced having foiled a coup attempt planned by the Islamic Front for the Liberation of Bahrain, a radical group with strong links with Iranian revolution leaders. The bungled coup attempt resulted in the arrest of scores of young people. Many of them were held incommunicado under the State Security Measures of 1974 that sanctioned administrative detention without trial for up to three years. Some were convicted and sentenced to long-term imprisonment. Other suspects were forced into exile with their families.

After completing secondary schooling in Bahrain in 1984, Salman received a scholarship to study mathematics at King Faysal University in Riyadh, Saudi Arabia. His outgoing personality and passion for football affected his academic performance. After dropping out in 1987, Salman travelled to Syria and later to Iran. There he settled in the religious town of Qom to study in one of its many seminaries. For the following three years, he led an ordinary life—just like the thousands of young and poor men for whom stipends paid by competing seminaries in Qom provided an opportunity to pursue an

education and secure a vocation. Like dozens of Bahrainis who graduate from Qom every year, Salman was destined for a secure future, earning his living as a freelance preacher, or, with luck and good contacts, as a civil servant. Salman's prospects of gaining government employment were likely to be strengthened by his distaste of politics and by his efforts to distance himself from rival political groups active among young Bahraini seminarians in Qom.

Life for the young Salman took an unexpected turn in 1991 with the arrival in Qom of Shaykh Isa Qasim. Qasim was the senior Bahraini cleric, the leading Shi'ite opposition figure, who also had been a member of parliament in Bahrain from 1973-1975. Qasim headed to Qom for a stint of voluntary exile following the arrest of some of his associates in Bahrain who had been charged with organizing underground Shi'ite networks. Qasim found in the young and politically detached Salman suitable material for a new protégé who would help him overcome his latest setbacks in Bahrain. From that juncture onward, Salman's career would be shaped by his relationship with his mentor.

Once again Salman interrupted his studies to escort his mentor on Qasim's return trip to Bahrain in early 1992. This was a period of relative calm in Bahrain. Reports by human rights watchdog organizations noted a significant improvement in human rights in the country. Many political detainees were released and some exiles were allowed to return home. For most of 1992, Salman stood humbly behind Qasim and attended all his meetings and sermons. While reluctant at first, Qasim's followers began gradually to accept the young cleric Salman as Qasim's emissary and representative. With the personal backing of Qasim, Salman was gradually becoming a leading figure among religious youths in Shi'ite rural areas. Salman's new role was corroborated further through his appointment as Qasim's stand-in in the prestigious role of Friday prayers leader in Qasim's own village. Salman continued to lead Friday prayers after the departure of Qasim to Iran on another self-exile.

In 1991-1992 after Kuwait's liberation from Iraqi occupation, expectations by political activists were boosted by what they made out as a push by the United States and its allies for democratic reforms in the Persian Gulf region. Reports by human rights groups noted a significant improvement in human rights in Bahrain. Encouraged by signs of a political relaxation, intellectuals, human rights lawyers, members of the disbanded parliament, and other political activists were engaged in discussions on ways of moving forward. This was also obvious in the articles published overseas that circulated in the country. The movement culminated in 1992 in what became known as *aridat al-nukhba*, or "the ELITE'S petition." Fourteen prominent Bahrainis—including clerics, businesspeople, and other political activists—drafted and signed the 1992 petition. It appealed to the emir, Shaykh Isa bin Salman Al Khalifa, to reinstate parliament, abrogate the Decree on State Security and other Emergency laws, and revert to constitutional rule. The emir refused to meet with signatories or receive their petition.

On his return to Bahrain in 1992 and with personal backing by Qasim, Salman became actively involved in community affairs and soon assumed a leading role among young religious activists in Shi'ite rural areas. But his political fortunes changed dramatically toward the end of 1994. Salman and other young activists were called on to mobilize popular support for a second petition calling for political reforms in Bahrain. Later events pushed Salman beyond local community politics and helped him carve a national political role for himself.

The 1994 petition, known as *al-arida al-sha'biyya,* or the "Popular Petition," was put together by the same network of prominent Bahrainis who planned to deliver it to the emir as "signed by the masses." Using code words as before, authors of the 1994 petition pressed the government to concede that the country is "facing a crisis resulting from dwindling opportunities and outlets, growing unemployment, mounting inflation, losses in the business sector, problems triggered by the citizenship decrees and preventing many of our children from returning to their homeland."

The task of collecting signatures was entrusted to networks of local youths in various neighborhoods and townships. Salman, a leader of one of the many village-based networks, assumed the task of coordinating the joint activities of these networks, such as organizing demonstrations by mostly unemployed Shi'ite youths who demanded jobs. While his mentor, Qasim, has consistently refused to share in any overt political action—including putting his signature on either the 1992 or the 1994 petitions—Salman was uncharacteristically openly immersed in the signature-collecting campaign.

On 5 December 1994, Salman was arrested with two other young clerics and accused by Bahraini authorities of inciting violence against participants in the annual marathon that passed through Salman's village. Opposition groups charged the arrests were a preemptive move by the security forces. They noted the arrests were made only days before National Day on 16 December, also the date set by the petition committee to deliver its document to the emir.

The arrest of the three clerics sparked a wave of protests culminating in riots. Violent and largely uncoordinated demonstrations erupted in parts of the capital and in most villages, demanding the release of Salman and his colleagues. Within a fortnight—on 17 December—the first death was reported.

Together with Shaykh Hamza al-Dairi and Sayyid Haydar al-Sitri, Salman was deported to Dubai, in the United Arab Emirates, on 15 December 1995. Bahraini authorities may have reasoned the three would travel to Qom where they would remain as hushed and politically harmless as their mentor Qasim. The three clerics, however, decided to move to the United Kingdom where they sought political asylum. Their request was denied, but they were granted leave to stay in the United Kingdom. On arrival in London, Salman associated himself with the London-based Bahrain Freedom Movement (BFM), the most active among Bahraini Shi'ite groups. He became part of the organization's public relations and information sections.

Salman's life in exile was not productive, eventful, or happy. His poor English skills prevented him from fulfilling a plan to continue his academic studies. His relationship with leading BFM people and other Bahraini exiles in London was marred by petty conflicts. He complained that he was sidelined by leading members of BFM and that they limited his access to the Bahraini community in the United Kingdom and to the London-based Arab media. However, his close ties with Qasim in Qom eased his drift toward the more welcoming non-Bahraini Shi'ite community in the United Kingdom.

The sudden death in March 1999 of Shaykh Isa bin Hamad Al Khalifa, the emir of Bahrain, signaled the beginning of a new period in Bahraini politics. Soon after assuming power, his successor, Shaykh Hamad bin Isa Al Khalifa, made several conciliatory gestures towards the opposition, including the release of several of its detained leaders. The new emir also reiterated publicly his commitment to universal suffrage and to a dialogue with representatives of all social forces in the country. Salman was not included in the direct and indirect talks on future reforms between the BFM and emissaries of the new emir. These talks, and parallel ones inside Bahrain proper, encouraged Shaykh Hamad to present to the public the National Charter, his blueprint for the impending political reforms. Supporters of the National Charter hoped it would help transform Bahrain from a tribal autocracy to a modern constitutional monarchy. These hopes—together with the lifting of the State Security Law, the release of political detainees and prisoners, and the return of all exiles—helped convince the skeptical public. This was manifested in the massive turnout, including women, at the plebiscite held to approve them and in the reported 98.4 percent vote in favor.

Salman was among the first batch of London-based exiles to return to Bahrain, where he was united with his mentor Qasim. Soon after his return, Salman joined junior clerics and other Shi'ite political activists to found al-Wifaq in 2002 as an exclusively Shi'ite political organization.

Open backing from Qasim dissuaded other contenders from competing with Salman for the leadership of the organization. He since has been re-elected twice as secretary-general of al-Wifaq.

Three smaller opposition groups—al-Amal (Shi'ite Islamist), Wa'd (leftist), and al-Tajammu al-Qawmi, (Ba'thist)—and al-Wifaq decided to boycott the 2002 elections. Their decision was motivated by their frustration at what they perceived as the king's unwillingness to listen to their views on the substance, pace, and direction of the reform process. The opposition also charged that the monarch reneged on a central component of the proposed reforms when he rewrote the constitution to give himself sweeping powers. Among the controversial amendments were those about the bicameral National Assembly, whose chambers share equal legislative power with the king himself. Organizers of the boycott charged that the forty members of the Shura (Consultative) Council appointed by the monarch would render the forty elected members of the Deputies Council powerless.

Salman and other Bahraini opposition leaders negotiated with royal advisers and finally appealed to the king to postpone the elections. But the king did not concede. Frustrated by the monarch's one-sided decisions, Salman and other opposition figures called for a vote boycott but stopped short of questioning the credibility of reforms or the legitimacy of the emir and the ruling family.

The boycott campaign was only partly successful. While most Shi'ite voters heeded the boycott call, some 53 percent of the electorate went to the ballot box on 24 October 2002. The opposition readily conceded that the government had scored a major success although that figure pales in comparison with the more than 92 percent turnout at the February 2001 plebiscite. Salman, Qasim, and other senior clerics were not in favor of the boycott but had yielded to popular mood and the overpowering sentiment among the rank-and-file members of al-Wifaq.

Salman and other leaders of the opposition, having already accepted that the process of political reforms in the country is a royal privilege—a royal grand gesture toward his people—failed to capitalize on the size of the boycott or keep the momentum. For the next four years, their tactics seemed haphazard—moving from organizing sit-ins and addressing petitions to the monarch to sponsoring seminars and launching regular but small demonstrations. The ad hoc coalition of the four boycotting groups introduced a "Constitutional Conference," holding annual meetings to present and debate opposition demands for a new and consensual constitution. At the same time, opposition leaders continued regular contacts with the king's advisers.

In addition to working in the public space, Salman became fully preoccupied with the tasks of reorganizing al-Wifaq, expanding its membership within the Shi'ite population, and building it up as a potent opposition force. He spent great effort in consolidating personal and organizational ties with other opposition groups, particularly the secular Democratic Action Society and its leftist leaders.

In May 2005 al-Wifaq and its coalition partners decided to engage in the 2006 elections. To overcome protests within al-Wifaq, Salman mobilized the support of nearly all senior Shi'ite clerics in Bahrain. In spite of strong backing, several prominent former members of al-Wifaq called for continuing the boycott. Supporters of Salman also sought "guidance" from the leading Shi'ite authority in Iraq, Grand Ayatullah Ali al-Sistani, who called on people to participate in the vote. Salman and his group won the day. Seventeen candidates on al-Wifaq's ticket, including Salman, were elected to the Chamber of Deputies. A liberal Sunni candidate backed by al-Wifaq also won. Despite their impressive number, the eighteen members of the al-Wifaq bloc can do little without coordinating with the remaining twenty-two members, most of whom are pro-government.

INFLUENCES AND CONTRIBUTIONS

Like most residents of rural areas in Bahrain, Salman's childhood and youth were shaped by poverty and the result of decades of misrule, human rights violations, and ethnic segregation. Like most children in Shi'ite villages, Salman's worldview was colored by folktales of the pillage, rapes, forced labor, and other atrocities allegedly perpetrated two centuries earlier on their Shi'ite ancestors by the ruling Al Khalifa family and its tribal Sunni allies. In 1980-1981, as a young teenager, he witnessed some of the worst violations of human rights in the country following an alleged coup attempt. Hundreds of young people, including teenagers from his village, were arrested or forced to flee the country. This may have led him to shun underground politics and to focus on his studies and football team.

However, the single most important source of influence on the adult Salman is his association with the senior Bahrain cleric Isa Qasim. An ex-member of the Iraqi Da'wa Party since his student days in Najaf, Iraq, Qasim is a devoted follower of the deceased Iranian cleric Ayatullah Ruhollah Khomeini and his concept of *vilayet-e faqih* (or guardianship of the jurisprudent). Salman has, more openly since 2004, followed the path of his mentor in many ways. In a sermon in December 2005, published on his website (http://www.toqa.net), Salman argued that *vilayet-e faqih* is a caring system of governance superior to any other. Democracy, he noted, has many positive aspects, but it also produced Hitler, was responsible for World War II, and is tolerating the death through famine and disease of thousands of African children every day.

WE ARE NOT GOING TO PUSH
PEOPLE TO BECOME MUSLIM

∎

We are not against women becoming (elected)
deputies as they are capable of having similar or
better legislative achievements than men, but
our decision would be determined according
to the public's acceptance of women candidates
as after all we want to win.

We are an Islamic movement and we are looking for Islam to be in society, but the kind of
Islam that does not force itself on people. We
are not going to push people to become Muslim, but we will try to explain the Islamic way
of life and the choice is theirs.

SALMAN, ALI. INTERVIEW. GULF DAILY NEWS. 15 MAY 2006.

Salman also follows Qasim's focus on sermons, short
articles, and fatwas. Unlike other prominent Shi'ite clerics
in Bahrain, Qasim and Salman have until now avoided
publishing a lengthy account of their thoughts on political,
social, or theological matters.

Salman differs from Qasim in an important aspect
that may influence his political career, either negatively or
positively. Unlike his mentor, Salman has developed good
working relations with other members of the Bahrain
opposition. Significantly, he has devoted notable energy
and time to help candidates, including a woman, from the
leftist Wa'ad. Salman's outlook on women's political
rights and public roles is at variance with Qasim's. While
Qasim is conservative, Salman often has expressed his
support for women to share in all spheres of public life.

THE WORLD'S PERSPECTIVE

Salman's public statements and activities since he returned
from exile in 2001 have defined him as a moderate among
Shia clerics in Bahrain. He maintains a close relation with
several leading figures within the secular opposition
groups and networks. This and his views on women's
rights have cost him support among more conservative
clerics. Salman's nonconfrontational approach has earned
him public praise from both the king and prime minister
of Bahrain, as well as other government officials, but it
also has led to alienating certain younger followers and
more radical figures within the Bahraini opposition. Both
sides found confirmation of their views of Salman in his
handling of the 2006 parliamentary election campaign.
Before the invasion of Iraq, Salman participated in anti-
war demonstrations in front of the United States embassy

in Bahrain. At the same time he maintained close working
relation with local representatives of the American
National Democratic Institute, NDI, encouraging members of his organization to attend lectures and workshops
organized by the NDI. This may have influenced the
Bahraini government's decision to close the NDI office
in Manama.

LEGACY

Salman's years at the helm of al-Wifaq have not been
trouble-free. His decisions often have been questioned.
At least twice, public discord has led disgruntled factions
to leave the organization. In 2002 several leading members of al-Wifaq fell by the wayside protesting its decision
to boycott the parliamentary elections held that year. In
2005 another group of leading of al-Wifaq members left
the group protesting its decision to participate in 2006
parliamentary elections. Despite these and other serious
challenges to his authority, Salman has managed to hold
his leadership position. He has publicly recognized that
his authority and the legitimacy of al-Wifaq stem from its
adherence to Qasim's guidance and public backing.
However, Salman's open advocacy of *vilayet-e faqih*
may cost him the support of liberal Shi'ite activists and
the increasingly vocal followers of the *Akhbari* school.
The Akhbari school opposes *ijtihad*, or establishing jurisprudence using reasoning based on the Qur'an and
Sunna rather than legal precedent, while the Usuli school
uses *ijtihad*. Because of this difference, there is a deep rift
between the two schools. In Bahrain, whose religious
thinkers are predominantly Akhbari, the Akhbari-Usuli
schism has often led to violent confrontations between
adherents of the two schools. The tension at least partially explains the frequent splits within the ranks of Shi'ite
activists in Bahrain.

The good working relationship Salman has kept
with other opposition figures since his 1995 deportation
shows his penchant for pragmatic politics. As the leader
of the al-Wifaq parliamentary bloc, his ability to search
for the middle ground without angering either his more
fundamentalist seniors or the liberals within al-Wifaq's
constituency will continue to be put to the test.

BIBLIOGRAPHY

Bahrain Tribune. Available from http://www.bahraintribune.com

Bar Human Rights Committee of England & Wales. *Crises of Human Rights in Bahrain: The Rules of Law under Threat.* London, 1998.

Chaise, Christian. "Bahrainis to fight system from within." Middle East Online. Updated 28 June 2006. Available from http://www.middle-east-online.com/english.

Gulf Daily News (Bahrain). Available from http://www.gulf-daily-news.com/home.asp.

Human Rights Watch. "Routine Abuse, Routine Denial – Civil Rights and the Political Crisis in Bahrain." Bahrain Center for Human Rights. Updated June 1997. Available from http://www.bahrainrights.org/node/161.

Khuri, Fouad I. *Tribe and State in Bahrain.* Chicago and London: University of Chicago Press, 1980.

Momen, Moojan. *An Introduction to Shi'ism: The History and Doctrines of Twelver Shi'ism.* New Haven, CT and London: Yale University Press, 1985.

The International Crisis Group. "Bahrain's Sectarian Challenge." *Middle East Report* no. 40 (6 May 2005). Available from http://www.isn.ethz.ch/pubs/ph/details.cfm?lng=en&id=27459.

Wright, Steven. "Generational change and elite-driven reforms in the Kingdom of Bahrain." *Sir William Luce Fellowship Paper no. 7, Middle East and Islamic Studies* (June 2006). Available fromhttp://eprints.dur.ac.uk/archive/00000221/01/wright.pdf.

Abdulhadi Khalaf

SAMAR, SIMA
(1957–)

Sima Samar is a physician, advocate for democracy and women's rights in Afghanistan, and Afghanistan's Minister for Women's Affairs.

PERSONAL HISTORY

Samar was born on 4 February 1957 in Jaghoori, Ghazni, Afghanistan. Her family is from the Shi'ite Muslim Hazara minority. She received a medical degree from Kabul University in 1982, the first Hazara woman ever to do so. After the communist government of Afghanistan arrested her husband in 1984, she went to Quetta, Pakistan, and became a humanitarian relief worker and supporter of the Revolutionary Association of the Women of Afghanistan (RAWA). She never heard from her husband again.

In 1987, she received funding from the Church World Service and several other organizations to establish a women's hospital in Quetta. In 1989, she organized the Shuhada Foundation to provide medical care and education for Afghan women refugees and their children in Pakistan.

INFLUENCES AND CONTRIBUTIONS

In December 2001, she became minister for women's affairs in HAMID KARZAI's interim Afghan government. She resigned in June 2002, when conservatives threatened her with a death penalty for allegedly questioning the relevance of Islamic law in an interview during a visit to Canada. She was acquitted of the charge of blasphemy by the high court of Afghanistan and given a new position as chair of Afghanistan's Independent Human Rights Commission.

She has criticized the practice of forcing Afghan women to wear the burqah, and has cited the negative health effects on women of restricting the amount of sunlight upon their bodies. Samar currently serves as the chair of the Afghan Independent Human Rights Commission.

THE WORLD'S PERSPECTIVE

She received many awards for her human rights work, including The Ramon Magsaysay Award for Community Leadership, 1994; The John Humphrey Freedom Award in 2001; The Paul Grunninger Human Rights Award from the Paul Grunninger Foundation in Switzerland, 2001; Freedom Award, Women's Association for Freedom and Democracy, 2002; International Human Rights Award, International Human Rights Law Group, 2002; and the Perdita Huston Human Rights Award, 2003. In 2005, Samar was appointed by the UN to be special envoy to the Darfur region of Sudan.

LEGACY

Samar's work is still ongoing, but she surely will be remembered as one foremost female activists in Afghanistan today.

BIOGRAPHICAL HIGHLIGHTS

Name: Sima Samar

Birth: 1957, Jaghoori, Ghazni, Afghanistan

Family: Married (husband disappeared after his arrest in 1984); one son

Nationality: Afghan

Education: M.D., Kabul University, 1982

PERSONAL CHRONOLOGY:

- **1984:** Flees to Quetta, Pakistan, following the arrest of her husband

- **1987:** Establishes a hospital in Quetta

- **1988:** Organizes the Shuhada Foundation

- **2001:** Becomes minister in Afghan interim government

- **2002:** Resigns position as minister

- **2005:** Appointed UN special envoy to Darfur

BIBLIOGRAPHY
Emadi, Hafizullah. *Repression, Resistance, and Women in Afghanistan.* Westport, CT: Praeger, 2002.

"The Plight of Afghan Women: Interview with Sima Samar, Minister of Women's Affairs." *Afghanistan Online.* Available from http://www.afghan-web.com/woman/samar_interview.html

Senzil Nawid
updated by Michael R. Fischbach

SAMMAN, GHADA
(1942–)

Ghada Samman is a Syrian-Lebanese writer.

PERSONAL HISTORY

Samman was born in 1942 in al-Shamiyya, Syria, and moved to Beirut, Lebanon, in 1964. She obtained a BS from The American University of Beirut and Ph.D. in English literature from Cairo University. Samman was briefly arrested and imprisoned by Syrian authorities for alleged political offenses in 1966, and secretly left the country after she was released three months later. She has been living in France since 1984.

INFLUENCES AND CONTRIBUTIONS

Samman is one of the Arab world's most prolific female authors, having published more than thirty books in a variety of genres. Her work has been translated into many languages. She began her career as a journalist and now writes a weekly column for the London-based *al-Hawadith* magazine. Among her books is *al-Raghif Yanbud ka al-Qalb* (1975), which exposes political corruption in the Arab world and attacks social inequality, especially the mistreatment of women. Her *al-Amal Ghayr al-Kamila* (1979) is a multivolume collection of fiction and nonfiction on her travels to various Arab and European capitals, with insightful comparisons on culture, society, and politics.

Samman is also known for her fiction. Her novel *Beirut '75* (1974) is a gripping urban narrative that touches upon class divisions, gender inequality, and the selfish rich. It prophetically anticipated the outbreak of violence in Lebanon the following year. *Beirut Nightmares* (1976) draws from the author's own experiences during the first year of the civil war, when she was trapped for a week near the Beirut hotel district. This sequence of nightmares ranging from the mundane to the surreal is told in a wrenching first-person voice. One of her collections of short stories, *The Square Moon* (1999), is set mostly in Paris and focuses on cultural conflict and the perspectives of exile.

For decades, she has given voice to Arab women: "The liberated woman is not that modern doll who wears make-up and tasteless clothes. . . . The liberated woman is a person who believes that she is as human as a man. The liberated woman does not insist on her freedom so as to

BIOGRAPHICAL HIGHLIGHTS

Name: Ghada Samman

Birth: 1942, al-Shamiyya, Syria

Nationality: Syrian; lives in France

Education: BS, The American University of Beirut; Ph.D., English literature, Cairo University

PERSONAL CHRONOLOGY:

- **1966:** Arrested by Syrian government
- **1974:** Publishes *Beirut '75*
- **1976:** Publishes *Beirut Nightmares*
- **1984:** Moves to France
- **1999:** Publishes *The Square Moon*

abuse it," she wrote in 1961. In her many works of fiction and nonfiction, Samman has been a staunch supporter of Arab nationalism and has criticized Zionist and imperialist policies, but she has not shied away from critiquing repressive aspects of her own culture.

THE WORLD'S PERSPECTIVE

Samman is well known internationally as a significant and prolific Arab writer.

LEGACY

It is too early to assess Ghada Samman's lasting legacy.

BIBLIOGRAPHY

Cooke, Miriam. *War's Other Voices: Women Writers on the Lebanese Civil War.* Cambridge, U.K.: Cambridge University Press, 1988.

Zeidan, Joseph. *Arab Women Novelists: The Formative Years and Beyond.* Albany: State University of New York Press, 1995.

Elise Salem
updated by Michael R. Fischbach

SAQQAF, ABD AL-AZIZ
(1951–1999)

Abd al-Aziz Saqqaf was a distinguished Yemeni economist, human rights advocate, and the editor and publisher of the *Yemen Times*, a bi-weekly independent English-language

BIOGRAPHICAL HIGHLIGHTS

Name: Abd al-Aziz Saqqaf

Birth: 1951, Hujariyya, Yemen

Death: 1999, San'a, Yemen

Family: Wife, 'Aziza Muhammad al-Saqqaf; sons, Walid, Raidan; daughters, Nadia, Haifa

Nationality: Yemeni

Education: Yemen, Egypt, United States; M.A. in economics, Ohio University; Ph.D. in international business, Harvard University, 1979

PERSONAL CHRONOLOGY:

- **1980:** Professor of economics at San'a University
- **1986:** Co-founder of the Yemeni Organization for Human Rights
- **1994:** Executive director of the Yemeni Institute for Development and Democracy
- **1995:** International Freedom of the Press Award, Washington, D.C.
- **1996:** Queen of Sheba Title for Services to the Nation
- **1999:** Founder of Yemen 21 Forum
- **1990–1999:** Editor-in-chief of the *Yemen Times*

newspaper. A strong defender of the democracy movement and the rule of law, Saqqaf played a prominent role in Yemen's cultural and political life during the republican era—especially during its crucial transformation from an authoritarian state to an embryonic democracy in the early 1990s. He provided the impetus for many non-governmental organizations and was a pioneer in investigative journalism in Yemen.

PERSONAL HISTORY

Saqqaf was born in 1951 in Hadharim village in the Hujariyya (Ta'izz province), one of the coffee-producing areas in the southern highlands known as "Lower Yemen." Originally his family came from the Hadramawt in the southeastern part of the country. The area where Saqqaf grew up was strongly influenced by its close proximity to Aden, which remained British-dominated until 1967. During the reign of Imam Ahmad Hamid al-Din (1948-1962), the supreme leader of the religiously-sanctioned Imamate, the southern city of Ta'izz became the seat of government and de facto capital where the first modern schools were founded and English was taught. At eleven, Saqqaf witnessed the end of the Imamate in 1962 from a part of the country that overwhelmingly supported the republic that was installed thereafter.

The son of a laborer, Saqqaf was highly motivated to pursue an education. After attending elementary school in Ta'izz and Aden, he received his secondary education at the al-Sha'b school in Ta'izz, the best school in the country. After obtaining a BA in English at San'a University, he continued to study economics at universities in Egypt and the United States. He earned an MPA from Harvard University, an MA from Ohio University, and a doctorate in International Business at Harvard University and Fletcher School in 1979. He was also an honorary Fulbright alumnus. Following his appointment as professor of economics at San'a University in 1980, he never neglected non-academic work in his field. During a long sabbatical he worked as vice-dean of the Banking Institute in Amman, Jordan.

Throughout his life Saqqaf had a vision of a prosperous and democratic Yemen, and he worked tirelessly to achieve it. A keen supporter of the "cooperative movement," his home village became a model serving to demonstrate that civic organizations could improve local conditions. He obtained sponsorship from foreign donors for a hospital, electricity, water, and schools. Saqqaf successfully brought people of different views and political affiliations together to encourage implementation of "good governance" and support organizations promoting civic participation.

He was dedicated to the advancement of human rights, specifically those of women, children, and groups subject to discrimination such as the Muwalladin, Yemeni nationals born of African mothers. He supported women's rights through lectures and television talk shows, and he organized and participated in numerous conferences. In 1986 he was a major contributor to the Campaign for the Supply of Vaccines for Children, the Yemeni-Saudi relations symposium, and the symposium for the draft law of local government. Saqqaf dedicated much of his time to media work because of his commitment to creating civic spaces outside the established political arenas. He was the first news anchorman at the Yemen Arab Republic's national television channel, where he also started the first English-language bulletin.

Saqqaf was enthusiastic about the unification between the Yemen Arab Republic and the People's Democratic Republic of Yemen in May 1990, an event that brought about fundamental social and political change. The new constitution of the Republic of Yemen—based on Arab, Western, and socialist legal principles—was ratified in May 1991 and welcomed by Saqqaf. It granted voting and candidacy rights, the right to a fair trial, judicial independence, freedom of expression (protecting speech, writing, and pictures) within the law, and equal treatment under the law. It guaranteed more rights and liberties than most Arab constitutions. The years following unification generated civic activism and political liberalism, as Saqqaf had envisioned. He played a key role in many of the newly formed organizations. Professional syndicates of doctors, pharmacists, attorneys, judges, and journalists constituted a politically-aware professional class interested in liberalization. Lawyers and press syndicates defended journalists in court. In 1992, Saqqaf was among those elected to the Supreme Council of the Organization for the Defence of Democratic Rights and Liberties. Its aim was to observe prison conditions, defend legal rights, and encourage other civil society organizations like the Committee for Free Elections.

New press and party legislation gave rise to a great number of political organizations including political parties, broadcast companies, two daily national newspapers, and one hundred periodicals. Satellite dish access to a variety of broadcasts was available, and national television covered the Persian Gulf Crisis in 1990, parliamentary debates, and street demonstrations in 1992. Saqqaf saw media work as a mission and as instrumental in generating political pluralism. He established the *Yemen Times*, the first and most widely-read English-language Yemeni newspaper, on 28 February 1991. The paper is one of the few not linked to a political party, with a declared mission "to make Yemen a good world citizen." Taking a nonpartisan view, it offers the educated public and non-Arabic speakers insight into Yemeni and regional affairs. Saqqaf's application for a license for an independent radio station was denied. He set high moral standards, introducing a work ethic at his paper centering on discipline, commitment, and truthfulness. In spite of the paper's occasional critical stance, Saqqaf insisted that "we are not out to get the regime or to seek replacement of those in power. It is this stand that differentiates the *Yemen Times* from opposition papers."

An astute political observer, he considered his criticism of the status quo to be constructive for he did not aspire to political positions. He took issue with the government's lack of transparency and its allocation of funds to defense at the expense of the education sector. His reporting of the devastating effects of the war between northern and southern forces that led to the collapse of the unity government in 1994 and allegations about the government's improper handling of oil revenues were not looked at favorably by the regime. When in 1993 a press prosecution office was established to monitor the press and prosecute violators of the press law, private attorneys representing the Journalists' Syndicate and a human rights organization defended the *Yemen Times*.

Saqqaf was awarded the International Freedom of the Press Award in Washington, D.C., in 1995 and the Queen of Sheba Title for Services to the Nation in 1996. That same year Saqqaf organized a seminar in San'a on the promotion of an independent and diverse Arab media sector. The subsequent declaration was adopted by Arab journalists in San'a and endorsed by all Arab countries at the UNESCO General Conference in November 1997. In 1997 the Yemeni president appointed Saqqaf to the newly-established Consultative Council. Shortly before his death in 1999 Saqqaf was the first Arab journalist to be nominated for the UNESCO World Press Freedom Prize. He published many books on economic issues and articles in international newspapers and magazines. He died in a car accident in San'a on 2 June 1999.

INFLUENCES AND CONTRIBUTIONS

Saqqaf's work was closely associated with the social and political developments in post-revolutionary Yemen during the early decades of state transformation—the rapid expansion of state institutions and the economic sector, the establishment of Local Development Associations, unification, and democratization. Like many Hujariyya merchants who had backed the revolution and played a vital role in the development of the private sector, Saqqaf saw the need for fundamental economic reforms. He worked toward implementation by training future economists and publishing detailed and trenchant reports about existing monetary policy and other economic issues. When writing about the deterioration of the riyal (Yemen's unit of currency) exchange rate in May 1999, he asked, "Will the Central Bank of Yemen please wake up?" His analysis of the political economy of the Yemen Arab Republic twenty years after its formation reveals his excitement at the dramatic growth in the financial and economic sectors after 1962, noting that the Yemen Bank for Reconstruction and Development was established just a month after the September revolution. He was keenly aware of the challenges faced by the revolutionary regime during its early years—civil war in the 1960s and the withdrawal of Egypt's budgetary and military support after her defeat in the 1967 War—causing the closure of the Yemeni Ministry of Finance. In the early 1980s, Saqqaf advised the government to pursue a more coherent fiscal policy of guiding investments, savings and consumption, and production.

One of Saqqaf's main contributions was the founding of the *Yemen Times,* which has informed the public and world community on Yemeni issues. Saqqaf provided a medium through which his pleas for democracy and respect for human rights could reach foreign diplomats and members of international organizations. After unification, the paper gave generous coverage to public meetings such as the National Conference in 1992.

Organized by urban professionals, it drew together representatives of twenty-two non-ruling parties, forty-two political organizations, professional unions, and leaders of tribal confederations. The resolutions passed at the conference focused on pluralism, separation of powers, neutrality of the armed forces, union rights, and fair multiparty elections. Saqqaf helped to establish the Arab Organization for Human Rights in Cairo in 1982. He was a co-founder and sponsor of organizations including the Yemeni Organization for Human Rights (1986), the Elections Monitoring Committee (1996), the Committee for the Protection of Journalists (New York 1995), executive director of the Yemeni Institute for Development and Democracy (1994), and the National Committee for the Combat of Torture (1998). He also founded the Yemen 21 Forum, a non-governmental organization dedicated to human rights that encouraged other like organizations to form networks in order to mobilize citizens to stand up for their rights to freedom of information and protection from unlawful treatment by the state. Among its members was Dr. Abu Bakr al-Qirbi, Minister of Foreign Affairs since 2002. Saqqaf was both an advocate of civil liberties and a human rights activist who, in spite of many setbacks, was able to witness the fruits of his efforts during his lifetime. In his capacity as chairman of the Human Rights Committee of the Consultative Council, he negotiated the release of thousands of detainees imprisoned without fair trial and the transfer of several underage prisoners to orphanages.

THE WORLD'S PERSPECTIVE

Saqqaf gained international recognition for his dedicated efforts to promote democracy in his country, and was one of the most influential Arab journalists of his time. He often was invited to contribute to international conferences and to accompany government officials abroad. In February 1999 he was a member of an invited government delegation to Egypt. He submitted lectures on Yemen at the Ahram Strategic Center and at the Arab Organization for Human Rights, and he had an audience with President Husni Mubarak. Saqqaf's work and personality were appreciated by international organizations such as UNESCO, UNICEF, and Amnesty International. Following his death, UNICEF Representative Habib Hammam described him as "a great leader" who was "a window of Yemen to the world." Highlighting Saqqaf's courageous defense of press freedom, *Reporters Sans Frontières* and the Center for Media Forum-Middle East and North Africa promised to maintain his legacy. The Muslim Educational Trust of Great Britain praised his grassroot experience and his "courage to deal with real issues head-on." Gianni Brizzi, Representative of the World Bank Resident Mission in Yemen, referenced Saqqaf's "uncompromising urge to better the political,

---

YEMENIS ARE TRADITION-ORIENTED PEOPLE

■

Yemenis are tradition-oriented people, but they were never dogmatic zealots. Today, their frustrations are making them more dogmatic. While technically puritanical religion is not necessarily a bad thing, if it leads to less tolerance and more fanaticism, it is going to be problematic.

YEMEN TIMES, 10 AUGUST 1998.

Many observers believe Yemen is at crossroads. Either we move forward, or the whole process is jeopardized. 'It is like riding a bicycle. If you stop moving, you fall,' explained a senior diplomat in San'a. Indeed, our transformation towards real political pluralism and economic integration with the world has to continue. Otherwise, we risk major upheavals and we risk being left out of the world's mainstream evolution.

YEMEN TIMES, 30 DECEMBER 1998.

The basic premise for Yemen's joining the world community is that it agrees to live by world rules. These include more tolerance of differences of opinion, and acceptance that rivals can mobilize themselves and their supporters in a bid for a transfer of power in a peaceful and legal way. If the rulers block this possibility, which is a remote one in any case, then they are inviting violence.

YEMEN TIMES, 8 MARCH 1999.

---

social and economic environment of the country through what he could best do: using the powerful voice of the media."

LEGACY

In 1999 Henrikas Yushkiavitshus, Assistant Director-General of Communication and Information at UNESCO, noted that "as a man who possessed so many multi-cultural facets," Saqqaf "leaves behind him a legacy which will be difficult to follow." Partly because of the efforts of people like Saqqaf, Yemenis enjoyed several years of unprecedented civil liberties and the country has remained relatively open—especially in comparison with other states on the Arabian Peninsula. That Yemen was the first state on the peninsula to have parliamentary and presidential elections and that by 1994 it had more Amnesty International groups than any other Arab country were in no small measure due to Saqqaf's work. Thanks to his activities, Saqqaf undermined stereotypes of his country as "backward" and steeped in tribal traditions. His name is irrevocably linked with Yemen's move toward representative government that to some extent evolved from the civic institutions he founded and supported. He fought hard to maintain civil society's resilience and can be credited with encouraging dialogue across the political spectrum and the practice of negotiation in conflict situations. He encouraged links with many Arab and international organizations. Saqqaf's mission and work set an important example for others. Significantly, he taught the younger generation never to abandon its idealism, and that the struggle for democracy is tedious but worthwhile.

Saqqaf's newspaper and the success of his local, nongovernmental initiatives are testimony to Saqqaf's enduring legacy. Referring to Saqqaf's engagement in his native village, in 1999 one of the villagers noted that Saqqaf "provided us with life" and that "his efforts in the Arab world and international arena helped enable projects in education...in [several] villages," including two new schools that were then under construction, one sponsored by Qatar and the other by the World Bank. In 2006 the *Yemen Times* was awarded the Free Media Pioneer Award by the International Press Institute in Vienna. The jury noted that the paper had succeeded in a part of the world where independent media are prohibited from offering a platform for the opposition. That same year Saqqaf's daughter Nadia, editor-in-chief of the *Yemen Times*—and one of the few women holding this position in the Arab world—was honored with the first Gebran Tueni Award. (Tueni, a Lebanese publisher, was killed by a car bomb in Beirut in 2006.) In his laudatory "Poem to My Friend," Muhammad Sharaf al-Din, professor in the Classics department of Georgetown University in the United States, said of Saqqaf, "My dearest friend: you had no ties with me / Nor with those who saw you speak and smile / Except your hand and mouth of piercing truth...What you have done and left behind / Is just too great to see / For you have planted hope in all / And such disturbing fearlessness which you mastered so well."

BIBLIOGRAPHY

Carapico, Sheila. *Civil Society in Yemen: The Political Economy of Activism in Modern Arabia.* Cambridge, U.K.: Cambridge University Press, 1998.

"Daddy, we will miss you..."*Yemen Times.* Available from http://yementimes.com/99/iss23/family.htm.

"Dr. Abdulaziz in Brief: A Man of Ideals and Integrity." *Yemen Times.* Available from http://yementimes.com/99/iss23/bio.htm.

"IPI Names *Yemen Times* 'Free Media Pioneer 2006.'" AME Info. Available fromhttp://www.ameinfo.com/79523.html.

Saqqaf, Abdulaziz Y. "Fiscal and budgetary policies in the Yemen Arab Republic." In *Economy, Society and Culture in Contemporary Yemen*, edited by Brian Pridham. London: Croom Helm, 1985.

"*Yemen Times* View Point." *Yemen Times.* Available from http://www.yementimes.com/98/iss36/view.htm.

Gabriele vom Bruck

SA'UD, ABDULLAH BIN ABD AL-AZIZ AL-
(1924–)

Abdullah bin Abd al-Aziz al Sa'ud is the king of Saudi Arabia. He is the eleventh son (and the fourth to succeed to the throne) of King Abd al-Aziz bin Abd al-Rahman al-Sa'ud, who founded the modern Saudi state in 1932.

PERSONAL HISTORY

Abdullah was born in Riyadh to Abd al-Aziz's eighth wife, Fahda bint Asi al Shuraym, of the Abdu section of

Abdullah bin Abd al-Aziz al-Sa'ud. AP IMAGES.

BIOGRAPHICAL HIGHLIGHTS

Name: Abdullah bin Abd al-aziz al Sa'ud

Birth: 1924, Riyadh

Family: Ten known sons, including Mit'ab and Khalid (both Sandhurst graduates who serve as deputy commanders of the National Guard), Abd al-Aziz, Faysal, Sultan, Turki, Mish'al, Fahd, Sa'ud, and Mansur; ten known daughters, Fahda, Nayifa, Aliyya, 'Adila, Nuf, Sita, Sayfa, 'Abir, Sara, and Hayfa

Nationality: Saudi Arabian

Education: Court and religious education

PERSONAL CHRONOLOGY:

- **1951:** Appointed governor of Mecca by King Abd al-Aziz
- **1962:** Appointed commander of the National Guard by King Faysal
- **1975:** Appointed second deputy prime minister by King Khalid
- **1982:** Designated heir apparent and first deputy prime minister by King Fahd
- **1985:** Establishes al-Janadriyya, the annual National Heritage and Culture Festival
- **1985:** Founds the Equestrian Club in Riyadh
- **1995:** Designated regent after King Fahd suffers a stroke
- **2005:** Becomes king, custodian of the Two Holy Mosques, and prime minister; remains commander of National Guard

after Fahd's incapacitating illness, Abdullah navigated the Byzantine al Sa'ud family politics with rare adroitness, pleasing most members. Ultimately, he managed the al Sa'ud as he managed his own extended families (he married several women who gave him at least ten sons and as many daughters).

INFLUENCES AND CONTRIBUTIONS

The primary source of disagreement between Fahd and Abdullah throughout the 1980s was the question of political reforms. King Fahd repeatedly pushed for the rapid adoption of a Basic Law as well as the establishment of the long-promised Majlis al-Shura. Abdullah, on the other hand, made no public allusions to either before 1990. Of course, promises of basic political reforms were almost always associated with internal events that threatened the stability of the ruling family, including the epoch-making 1979 takeover by Islamic militants of the Grand Mosque in Mecca. These pronouncements may well have been designed to appease internal opposition, but the monarch's endorsement of such reforms appealed to the loyalties of various disenfranchised groups, while Abdullah's lukewarm position alienated others.

Another point of disagreement between Fahd and Abdullah in the 1980s concerned the overall organization of Saudi Arabia's defense and security establishment.

EXPLORING

The seven sons of the Hassah bint Ahmad al-Sudayri, led by the late King Fahd, form a formidable alliance within the al Sa'ud dynasty. In 2007, this sub-clan was led by Sultan, who was also heir apparent and Minister of Defense, and included Abdul Rahman (who reportedly handled family finances), Nayif (Minister of the Interior), Turki (another leading businessman), Salman (governor of Riyadh), and Ahmad (Deputy Minister of the Interior). Whether by luck or by design, the political fortunes of the "Sudayri Six" or, as they are now known, the "al Sultan," have been closely linked. For example, as Minister of Defense, Sultan welcomed—perhaps even encouraged—his younger brother Turki's appointment as his deputy in July 1969. Similarly, when King Fahd was Minister of the Interior (1963–1975), he promoted Nayif as his deputy in June 1970. Not surprisingly, when Nayif became Minister of the Interior in 1975, the youngest of the full brothers, Ahmad, was advanced to the deputy post.

the Shammar tribe. She had earlier been married to the Rashidi ruler, Sa'ud, who was killed in 1920. After primary education at the Princes' School from religious authorities and intellectuals, Abdullah was entrusted with his first official post as governor of Mecca. In August 1962, King Faysal appointed him commander of the National Guard, a post he maintained for several years. King Khalid secured his eventual ascendance to the throne when he named Abdullah second deputy prime minister in March 1975. Even though Khalid's successor, King Fahd, preferred the defense minister, Prince Sultan, as his heir, he conferred the position, along with that of first deputy prime minister, on Abdullah in 1982 to maintain family harmony. Over the years, but especially

King Fahd and Prince Sultan made a number of efforts to undercut Abdullah's institutional base, either with proposals to merge various forces under full army command or restrict the National Guard to light weapons that would reduce it to a police force rather than the paramilitary organization it is. For his part, Sultan frequently advocated the establishment of a national conscription program, which would have deprived Abdullah of bedouin recruits for the Guard. Throughout the 1980s, Abdullah resisted these efforts, and the advance in his political standing in the 1990s corresponded with new plans to increase the size and strength of the Guard. Critical commitments made to the regular military and the Guard took on concrete forms in the aftermath of the 1990 Iraqi invasion of Kuwait and the ensuing 1991 Gulf War.

Following that war, the ruling family became sensitive to both domestic and international pressure for liberalizing reforms. Against a new trend of open challenges and calls for reforms from liberal voices, the monarch nominated sixty leading citizens to a Majlis al-Shura. In this endeavor, Fahd was supported by his heir, who, true to al Sa'ud traditions, rallied behind his ruler to ward off opposition.

The 1992 Edict On 1 March 1992, King Fahd addressed his subjects on television and issued several key documents, including the Basic Law of Government, the statutes governing the newly created Majlis al-Shura, and the Law of the Provinces. The monarch's decision was propelled by the rising tide of internal opposition, as well as the repercussions of the Gulf War; it was meant to appear to be a step toward a process of institutional change. One of Fahd's last decisions was to expand the membership of the Majlis from 120 to 150, indicating its acceptance by Saudi elites.

The Basic Law of Government was divided into nine main sections, dealing with the general principles of the state, the law of government, the values of Saudi society, the country's economic principles, the various rights and duties of citizens, the authority of the state, financial affairs, auditing authorities, and general provisions.

The section of the Basic Law dealing with the succession "was of greatest interest and proved to be a bombshell both within and outside the ruling family," according to Simon Henderson in *After King Fahd: Succession in Saudi Arabia* (p. 21). The most controversial part, which provided that "rulers of the country shall be from amongst the sons of the founder … and their descendants," stated that "the most upright among them shall receive allegiance according to the Holy Qur'an and the Sunna of the Prophet (Peace be upon him)." The last line, imposing a qualification ("the most upright") was telling. One interpretation was that seniority was no longer the primary qualification for succession and that

other considerations strengthened a candidate's eligibility. A further clause stated that "the King shall choose the Heir Apparent and relieve him by a Royal Decree." Without a doubt, this last line threatened the balance of power within the royal family, foreshadowing the authority of the heir apparent, or crown prince.

After Fahd suffered a debilitating stroke in late 1995, Abdullah, the crown prince, was designated regent. Fahd never fully recovered, although he formally resumed his duties in 1996. By the time he died in 2005 and Abdullah succeeded him, Abdullah had effectively been the sole ruler of the country for almost a decade.

National Dialogue The 2003 American war in Iraq sent shock waves throughout the Gulf region as it shifted the regional balance of power. This regional change took on a specific character in Saudi Arabia because of the kingdom's custodianship of the two holy mosques in Mecca and Medina. The presence of these holy sites compelled Riyadh to remain exquisitely conscious of its responsibilities to the Muslim world, especially its Sunni component. The last great regional power shift – the 1979 Iranian Revolution – had precipitated important changes in domestic policies throughout the Muslim world, so there was good reason to anticipate similar changes in 2003. However, the desire for political reforms did not spread through the ultraconservative ruling family. Rather, public discourse took on a new dimension—in the form of petitions calling for a movement toward a constitutional monarchy—which redefined how Saudis accessed authority. Sophisticated supplications, addressed to the monarch and the crown prince, became both frequent and public. From early 2003, prominent Saudi reformers, led by Abdullah al-Hamid, argued that the best way to counter the spread of Muslim extremist ideas was to transform the kingdom into a constitutional monarchy. Hamid, along with MATRUK AL-FALIH, Ali al-Diminni, and thirteen other activists were arrested in March 2004, although only the three named individuals were still in custody by mid-2005 when Abdullah, after acceding to the throne, pardoned them. In general, Saudi reformists adopted pacific steps, bordering on the reverential, toward the ruling family. Although their demands challenged the ruler's absolute power, Abdullah deemed it necessary to meet with leading petition signatories, and authorized a process of dialogue by way of a partial rejoinder. Since December 2003, several rounds of National Dialogue were held to discuss, at times with unabashed frankness, sensitive questions. Saudis from all walks of life debated religious differences, education concerns, some of the causes of extremism, gender matters, and municipal elections.

Municipal elections The National Dialogues set the tone for fundamental changes facing Saudi Arabia. The next step was the unhurried introduction of municipal elections, starting in Riyadh on 10 February 2005 and followed by the Eastern Province and several southern provinces in early March. These concluded following elections in the west and north in April. The elections (75% turnout for registered voters in Riyadh) proved far more popular than anticipated. Yet, and not surprisingly, conservative, pro-clerical candidates won most seats, illustrating the intricacies of democratization. Although holders of half of the 178 municipal posts would eventually be appointed, not elected, a significant precedent was established when ordinary Saudis flocked to polling stations, leading observers to foresee an elected Majlis in the future.

Abdullah was somewhat fortunate during his first year as king because he assumed rulership as the government's treasury was relatively healthy and growing steadily. With new and contemplated massive investments in the oil sector, Riyadh considered its unemployment and poverty problems—priorities identified by the new monarch in his inaugural address—as containable threats to long-term internal stability, even if the economy needed to create several million new jobs over the following two decades. He was also fortunate that the Saudi public turned against terrorists spreading havoc throughout the Kingdom. Several hundred individuals have been killed in Saudi Arabia since 2003, and Saudi citizens have mostly supported the state's enforcement of the country's stringent anti-terrorism laws, even if its methods are drastic and overbearing. Whatever arguments liberal reformers have advanced have paled in comparison with conservative pressure to impose law and order. Abdullah has successfully pushed establishment clergymen against the wall, forcing thousands into "reeducation camps," cajoling others to tone down inflammatory rhetoric, and setting clear limits to acceptable behavior.

Foreign Policy Since 2005 Until the Gulf War, Abdullah maintained a cold attitude toward Western powers in general and the United States in particular. His attitude improved somewhat once he saw Washington make good on its promise to support the monarchy by intervening successfully after Baghdad's 1990 invasion of Kuwait. Once he formally became king in mid-2005, Abdullah's attitude toward the West and the United States underwent significant improvement, but is still no better than lukewarm.

Abdullah is not given to his predecessor's dangerous adventurism. Unlike Fahd, who welcomed over half a million foreign troops into the kingdom in 1990, and later allowed an unpopular long-term U.S. military presence, Abdullah quickly signaled that he would not join George W. Bush's post-9/11 crusade in the Muslim world. Even when a marginal Rand Corporation analyst called on the United States to invade Saudi Arabia and seize its oil

fields in July 2003 as a punishment for its lack of cooperation, Abdullah retained his stoicism. Riyadh would not abandon its pro-Muslim and pro-Arab commitments.

The United States and the West Nevertheless, and despite significant efforts by both sides, Saudi-American ties were in deep crisis by the time Abdullah became king. To be sure, serious cooperation continued in counterterrorism, regional defense concerns, and the security of long-term American access to reasonably priced oil supplies, but the critical trust element was now openly questioned. Abdullah was not concerned about established ties between executive branches but with the disastrous public perceptions fueled by woefully biased attitudes toward Muslims in general and Saudis in particular. Saudi Arabia under Abdullah is perceived by Western elites as a foe that cannot be fully trusted and Abdullah cannot afford to seem pro-American in front of his increasingly awakened population when American policies in Iran, Iraq, Lebanon, and Israel/Palestine are contrary to their sentiments and perceived long-term interests.

China and India It was partly this erosion in Saudi-American contacts that prompted Abdullah to embark on his historic visits to China and India. Chinese president Hu Jintao welcomed him at the Great Hall of the People in Beijing on 23 January 2006, declaring that the trip, the monarch's first foreign journey after his accession to the throne, opened a new chapter in Sino-Saudi relations. The two governments signed five agreements, including a landmark pact for expanding cooperation in oil, natural gas, and minerals exploration. As Foreign Minister Sa'ud al-Faysal underscored, "China is one of the most important markets for oil and Saudi oil is one of the most important sources of energy for China." The dramatic progress in cooperation between these governments is a recent phenomenon, as diplomatic ties were established only in 1990, but it was largely produced by Western antagonisms toward Saudi Arabia and the Sunni world.

If the January voyage inaugurated a new era in Sino-Saudi relations, then the 22 April 2006 visit of President Hu to Riyadh, immediately following a stop in the United States, solidified the relationship even further. Importantly, the Chinese expanded their discussions to include Middle East regional issues, including developments in Iraq and Palestine. President Hu became the second foreign leader, after President Jacques Chirac of France, to address the Majlis al-Shura, when he offered Chinese assistance in resolving regional conflicts. This was a direct challenge to Washington's hegemonic role in the region.

No matter how interpreted, Abdullah recognized that the kingdom's ties with China were now on a different level,

LET US BID FAREWELL TO THE AGE OF DIVISION

From this sacred land, the birthplace of our Prophet, has sprung forth the call to Islam, proclaiming the oneness and unity of the Creator, ending man's enslavement of man, and exhorting the principles of equality, right and justice. Thus was this call able to reach the farthest ends of the globe, East and West, by persuasion through just values and good example, and not by dint of the sword, as those deliberately ignore or fail to apprehend the truth, insist on claiming.

Let us recall what a radiant beacon our Islamic civilization was in lighting the way forth for other civilizations, offering them a fine example of the spirit of tolerance and justice, and leading humanity forward through its singular achievements in jurisprudence, intellectual endeavors, the sciences, and literature. Indeed, it is these major contributions that provided the decisive catalyst in bringing enlightenment to the dark ages.

... It is heartbreaking for us to see how our glorious civilization slipped from the exalted graces of dignity to the ravines of frailty. How painful that the ideology sprouted forth by criminal minds has unleashed wanton evil and corruption on earth, and that the ranks of our one Ummah—united in the lofty heights of its glory—have turned into helplessness.

... Let us bid farewell to the age of division and disintegration in order to usher in a new era of unity and dignity by relying first on Allah and then on patience and hard work.

... Islamic unity will not be achieved by bloodletting as the miscreants—in their misguided waywardness—insist on claiming.

Fanaticism and extremism cannot grow on an earth whose soil is embedded in the spirit of tolerance, moderation, and balance. It is here that the Islamic Fiqh Academy, with its overhauled makeup, comes in to assume its historic role and responsibility in resisting the extremist ideology in all its forms and manifestations.

Furthermore, a gradual approach to this end is the way forward to ensure success, which starts with consultation in all walks of life—political, economic, cultural, and social domains—to reach a stage of solidarity and, God willing, to a true and fortified unity worked through strong institutions so as to restore the Ummah to its rightful place in the balance of power.

... You may agree with me that developing educational curricula, and improving them, is a fundamental prerequisite to building a Muslim personality. Steeped in tolerance, such a personality would lay the foundations for a society that rejects isolationism and turns its back on courting hostility to the other by interacting with all humanity, adopting what is good and rejecting what is bad.

Dear brothers: I look forward to a United Muslim Umma and good governance that eliminate injustice and oppression for the sake of the comprehensive Muslim development that eradicates destitution and poverty. I also look forward to the spread of moderation that embodies the Islamic concept of tolerance. Moreover, I look forward to Muslim inventors and industrialists, to an advanced Muslim technology, and Muslim youth who work for their life just as they work for the Hereafter, without excess or negligence, without any kind of extremism.

SAUDI-US INFORMATION SERVICE, ORGANIZATION OF THE ISLAMIC CONFERENCE, 3RD EXTRAORDINARY SUMMIT (2005). "STATEMENT BY THE CUSTODIAN OF THE TWO HOLY MOSQUES, KING ABDULLAH BIN ADULAZIZ." 7 DECEMBER 2005. AVAILABLE FROM HTTP://WWW.SAUDI-US-RELATIONS.ORG.

evolving dramatically to reflect China's growing economic and political strength and its consequent new relationship toward Arabs, Muslims, Islam, and Middle Eastern oil.

Iran In 2007, Abdullah and the world are faced with a new crisis brewing in the Persian Gulf region as Iran's nuclear aspirations are realized. For Saudis, this crisis potentially allies them with the West against neighboring Muslim Iran. How Abdullah is tackling this dangerous situation may foretell future Saudi-Iranian and Saudi-Western relations.

THE WORLD'S PERSPECTIVE

King Abdullah is perceived as a serious ruler outside Saudi Arabia because he has addressed many challenges and engaged in genuine debates on a slew of key questions, including tolerance, national unity, and reform. In Muslim, Arab, and international forums, he has developed good listening as well as persuasive skills. Abdullah repeatedly insists that Riyadh will combat regional, tribal, and ideological discord and has instituted policies that stand with fellow Muslim, Arab, and international governments against terrorism. A savvy statesman who can work the tribal tent as well as confidently as any politician, Abdullah has always paid careful attention to his people, aware of the source of his legitimacy. A pious individual of personal integrity, he is respected by Saudi elites, among whom he enjoys tremendous personal popularity.

LEGACY

With the full power of the monarchy, Abdullah has instituted mild, incremental political reforms and pursued economic integration into the global capitalist economy, symbolized by its membership in the World Trade Organization (WTO). Emboldened by his relative first-year success, Abdullah was determined to take advantage of opportunities facilitated by the petrodollar windfall of recent years. Toward that end, he has allocated significant resources to infrastructure, building railroads, improving airports, erecting new cities, and encouraging foreign investment, which topped $600 billion by early 2006. These initiatives imply that Saudi Arabia intends to be the center of the Gulf region, and one of the major economic forces in the world, despite political challenges.

In the key area of oil production, Saudi Arabia under King Abdullah has increased capacity to meet demand, especially from China and India. Abdullah has supported a sustained production level precisely to guarantee a Saudi role as the ultimate stabilizer of world petroleum prices.

BIBLIOGRAPHY

AbuKhalil, As'ad. *The Battle for Saudi Arabia: Royalty, Fundamentalism, and Global Power.* New York: Seven Stories Press, 2004.

Bligh, Alexander. *From Prince to King: Royal Succession in the House of Saud in the Twentieth Century.* New York: New York University Press, 1984.

Gause, F. Gregory III. "The FP Memo: How to Save Saudi Arabia." *Foreign Policy* 144 (September/October 2004): 66–70.

Gresh, Alain. "Arabie Saoudite: Les Défis de la Succession." In *Monarchies Arabes: Transitions et Dérives Dynastiques,* edited by Abdellah Hammoudi and Rémy Leveau. Paris: La Documentation Française, 2002.

Henderson, Simon. *After King Fahd: Succession in Saudi Arabia.* Washington, D.C.: Washington Institute for Near East Policy, 1994.

Kechichian, Joseph A. "Saudi Arabia's Will to Power." *Middle East Policy* 7, no. 2 (February 2000): 47–60.

———. *Succession in Saudi Arabia.* New York: Palgrave, 2001.

———. "Testing the Saudi 'Will to Power': Challenges Confronting Prince Abdallah." *Middle East Policy* 10, no. 4 (Winter 2003): 100–115.

Long, David E. *The Kingdom of Saudi Arabia.* Gainesville: University Press of Florida, 1997.

Ménoret, Pascal. "Pouvoirs et Oppositions en Arabie Saoudite: De la Contestation Armée à l'Institutionnalisation de l'Islamisme?" *Maghreb-Machrek* 177 (Autumn 2003): 21-35.

Peterson, J. E. *Adelphia Paper No. 348: Saudi Arabia and the Illusion of Security.* London: The International Institute for Strategic Studies, 2002.

Rodenbeck, Max. "A Long Walk: A Survey of Saudi Arabia." *The Economist* 378, no. 8459 (7 January 2006): 1–12.

"Saudi Arabia: New King, Same Dreadful Job." *The Economist* 376, no. 8438 (6 August 2005): 35.

Joseph Kechichian

SAUDI, MONA
(1945–)

Mona Saudi is a Jordanian sculptor and poet.

PERSONAL HISTORY

Saudi (also Muna Sa'udi) was born in 1945 in Amman, Transjordan (now Jordan). She moved to Beirut in 1969 and worked with the artistic department of the Palestine Liberation Organization (PLO). Saudi graduated from the École Normale Supérieure des Beaux Arts in Paris in 1971, and later worked with marble in Carrara, Italy. She went back to Beirut but returned to Amman in 1982, only to return to Beirut in 1996.

BIOGRAPHICAL HIGHLIGHTS

Name: Mona Saudi

Birth: 1945, Amman, Transjordan

Nationality: Jordanian

Education: École Supérieure des Beaux Arts, Paris, 1971

PERSONAL CHRONOLOGY:

• **1969:** Moves to Beirut; works with artistic department of the Palestine Liberation Organization (PLO)

• **1982:** Returns to Amman

• **1987:** "Spiritual Geometry" installed at the Institut du Monde Arabe, Paris

• **1993:** Receives the National Award for the Arts in Jordan

• **1996:** Returns to Beirut

• **1999:** Publishes *An Ocean of Dreams*

INFLUENCES AND CONTRIBUTIONS

Saudi is one of the few Arab women artists to work primarily in stone, and especially to execute large-scale stone sculptures. Her sculptures have been produced in marble, granite, limestone, and other materials, and she has done etchings to accompany them. Influenced by Constantin Brancusi, her work also reflects an engagement with Islamic and ancient Middle Eastern artistic traditions. For example, many of her works are refined, abstract forms taken from Arabic calligraphy and Arabic words, or are done in the spirit of ancient Egyptian and Sumerian art. Saudi describes her pieces as already formed within the piece of stone and says her work is to draw them out through sculpting. Her work is also inspired by her reading and writing of poetry, and her poems have been translated in her collection *An Ocean of Dreams* (1999).

Saudi is also an arts activist. She has published the drawings of Palestinian refugee children and organized arts exhibitions to support the Palestinian cause. She lives and works in Beirut, and her large-scale public sculptures can be found there, as well as in Jordan and at the Institut du Monde Arabe in Paris.

THE WORLD'S PERSPECTIVE

Saudi is recognized internationally for her works, particularly because she remains one of the few female Arab artists to produce large stone sculptures.

LEGACY

Saudi is still at work, and thus it is too early to assess her lasting legacy.

BIBLIOGRAPHY

"Mona Saudi." Darat al Funun: Khalid Shoman Foundation. Available from http://www.daratalfunun.org/main/resourc/exhibit/saudi/saudi.html.

"Mona Saudi—Jordanian Sculptor." Mona Saudi's website. Available from www.monasaudi.com.

Jessica Winegar
updated by Michael R. Fischbach

SAWARIS, ONSI
(1930–)

Onsi Sawaris is a commercial magnate, titan of industry, and billionaire entrepreneur. The political and economic trajectory of Egypt and the Middle East significantly shaped Sawaris's career in business. After his company was contracted in the socialist onslaught of Egyptian president Jamal Abd al-Nasir (Gamal Abdel Nasser) in 1961, Sawaris migrated to Libya where he rebuilt his lost

BIOGRAPHICAL HIGHLIGHTS

Name: Onsi Sawaris

Birth: 1930, Sohag, Egypt

Family: Wife, Youssriya; three sons, Naguib, Sameeh, and Nassef

Nationality: Egyptian

Education: BS in agricultural engineering, Cairo University

PERSONAL CHRONOLOGY:

• **1950:** Proprietor, Orascom Construction Company

• **1961:** Director, El Nasr Civil Works Company

• **1966–1976:** Self-imposed exile to Libya

• **1976:** Orascom Contracting and Trading Company

• **1985:** Contrack International Inc, Virginia

• **1990s:** Orascom Construction Industries

• **1990s:** Orascom Telecom Holding

fortune. Following Egyptian president Anwar Sadat's *Infitah* (Open Door Policy) of the late 1970s, he returned to Egypt to work with his three sons Naguib, Sameeh, and Nassef and became actively engaged in building of a new business empire for the twenty-first-century Middle East. With the myriads of opportunities offered by globalization, the Sawaris family demonstrated shrewd entrepreneurship in transforming Orascom, a modest company in the 1980s, into a conglomerate a decade later. Sawaris is the 129th richest man in the world with a fortune of $4.8 billion, according to *Forbes* magazine. While Africa has produced many wealthy individuals, Sawaris earned his fortunes from the biggest non-oil and non-political business empire in the Middle East.

PERSONAL HISTORY

Onsi (also Unsi) Sawaris was born in 1930 in Sohag, a Coptic Christian city in Upper Egypt. The Copts are a Christian minority in Egypt but highly represented in financial, government, and intellectual sectors. Sawaris enjoyed an early life in the Upper Egyptian gentry. His father was a lawyer and landowner. After earning a BS in agriculture engineering from Cairo University, Sawaris managed his family's land holdings rather than take a government job. From this family business, Sawaris

CONTEMPORARIES

Sadek El-Sewedy, proprietor of Elsewedy Cables, transformed a local manufacturer into a large Middle East regional supplier of cables. Elsewedy Cables is the largest manufacturer of power cables in Egypt and the second largest in the Middle East. The family business has facilities in Egypt (56% market share), Sudan (70%), and Syria. El-Sewedy's family started its operations as a trader in electrical equipment. By 1986 the company became Egypt's and the Middle East's first private-sector cable producer, operating as Arab Cables. Within a decade Arab Cables' capacity quadrupled from about 6,000 tons of copper cables in 1986, to 23,200 tons in 1996. El-Sewedy is one of the Middle East's leading groups in the field of cables, plastics, lighting, and construction.

developed a keen interest in a construction firm initially located in Upper Egypt but then rapidly expanded its operations to Cairo and the Delta areas. He married Youssriya in 1953. The couple has three sons—Naguib, the eldest, attended the Polytechnic School in Zurich; Sameeh studied engineering in Berlin; and Nassef holds a degree in economics from the University of Chicago. Each works in the family business: Naguib controls a telecommunications subsidiary; Nassef runs the corporation's construction business; and Sameeh controls the tourism and travel subsidiaries of the family business.

INFLUENCES AND CONTRIBUTIONS

By the 1960s Sawaris's contracting firm used patronages from the government to grow into one of the largest construction firms in Egypt and the Middle East. He received several contracts from the Egyptian Ministry of Irrigation to dig waterways and basins. He built canals and ditches that collected overflow from the Nile River, and he completed the Aswan Dam in 1970. He also won road-paving contracts. Nasir's nationalization policy halted the rapid expansion of the construction firm and shattered the business. Egypt nationalized his firm for five years, renamed the construction firm El Nasr Civil Works Company, forced Sawaris to work as an employee of the firm, and seized Sawaris's passport. Sawaris and his family migrated to the oil-rich Libya as the socio-political situation in Egypt deteriorated. Between 1966 and 1977, he was able to revive his

business fortunes by constructing water works and undertaking similar projects. In 1976 he returned to Egypt and established Orascom, a general contracting and trading company with five employees. By the 1990s Orascom had transformed into an international conglomerate with operations in the entire Middle East, Africa, Europe, and the United States. The company won contracts from the U.S. Agency for International Development. In 1985, the family established Contrack International in Arlington, Virginia.

Sawaris eventually transferred management control of the conglomerate to his three sons who have embarked on ambitious diversification. The corporation has invested in cement, building materials, cinema, catering, tourism, telecommunication, and broadcasting. Naguib Sawaris established *Iraqna*, Iraq's first mobile phone network with over 500,000 subscribers. He also established an Iraqi television station, *al-Nahrain* (Two Rivers).

The Sawaris Group is the National Bank of Egypt's largest private borrower, and Orascom Construction Industries (OCI) is a leading cement producer in the region employing more than 40,000 in twenty countries. Orascom is also the largest cement exporter in the Middle East. Orascom's Egyptian Cement Company has an annual capacity production of ten million tons, while Algerian Cement Company has a five million ton capacity per year. Orascom's Egyptian Cement Company is constructing cement plants in the United Arab Emirate, Algeria, Iraq, Nigeria, and Saudi Arabia. It also has expanded to Spain and Turkey. Orascom's construction division has completed landmark infrastructural projects including the world's largest swing bridge over the Suez Canal, railways, water treatment plants, five-star hotels, and the three tallest buildings in Egypt.

In 2004, Orascom purchased the Sheba Telecom Company for $50 million. In 2005, Orascom was the top bidder ($256 million) for a 51 percent stake in the Nigerian telecom firm NITEL. Orascom has more than fifty million customers in its countries of operation and another fifteen million in Italy. The company also acquired Italy's largest telecommunication firm, Wind, in June 2005.

Orascom Telecom Holding has more than $2 billion in annual revenue and 14.5 million subscribers in the Middle East and Africa. Following the company's expansion in the 1990s, a financial crisis began 2001 when global demand for telecommunications plummeted. The company had gone public at the height of the Internet boom, raising $320 million by listing on the Cairo Alexandria Stock Exchanges and the London Stock Exchange in 2000. In 2001, the company lost $95 million. The Sawarises mortgaged their assets, including a valuable franchise in Jordan, to offset the debts. Yasir Arafat, the late Palestinian leader, rescued the business empire. Since then, the Sawarises kept expanding and

Raafat, Samir. "From Suares To Sawiris." *Cairo Times.* 24 December 1998. Available from http://www.egy.com/people/98-12-24.shtml

Rasheed Olaniyi

SAY, FAZIL
(1970–)

Fazil Say is a world-renowned Turkish-born, German-trained pianist and performer whose artistry stretches from chamber music to jazz. Recognized as one of the greatest artists of the twenty-first century, Say is not simply a pianist of genius, but also a master composer and improviser. His virtuosity brings innovation to the music landscape of our time, and he receives much adulation from his worldwide audiences. Say performs both classical music and jazz around the globe and is also known for his unique talent to merge in his compositions West and East.

PERSONAL HISTORY

Say was born on 14 January 1970 in Ankara, Turkey. Say is the only child in his family. His father, Ahmet Say, is a music critic who publishes music encyclopedias, and his mother, Güngür Özsoyeller, is a pharmacist. Say's music career began rather by coincidence. Born with a cleft lip and palate, Say underwent many

---

MY PROBLEM WITH MY SONS IS I AM THEIR FRIEND

■

I can barely give them (his three sons) advice. The new generation has its methods and ideas and I have to practice consummate diplomacy when I want to make them see it my way. That is not to say that I am never overruled. My problem with my sons is that I am their friend, because the generation gap is smaller than usual. We talk frankly about everything and they do not believe that obeying their parents is a sacred duty—unlike us in the past. Every decision is open to discussion.

HASSAN, FAYZA. "ONSI SAWARIS: A CAPITAL IDEA." *AL-AHRAM WEEKLY ONLINE.* 22-28 JULY 1999. AVAILABLE FROM HTTP://WEEKLY.AHRAM.ORG.EG/1999/439/PROFILE.HTM.

taking risks in the Middle East, Africa, and Europe. Orascom Telecom bought a license to operate a mobile network in Algeria in 2001 for $747 million and another mobile network in Tanzania for $454 million in 2002.

THE WORLD'S PERSPECTIVE

Sawaris is regarded as the business patriarch whose entrepreneurship built a business empire that he has entrusted to his sons. While many leaders in Africa amassed wealth at the expense of the poor, Sawaris built his non-oil business empire through his entrepreneurial talents. Sawaris is respected internationally for rebuilding his corporation after it was nationalized by the Egyptian government.

LEGACY

The Sawaris family has impacted the Middle East significantly by its varied entrepreneurial endeavors, especially its construction of projects that developed the infrastructure of the region. It also has contributed generously to higher education in Egypt through the Onsi Sawaris Scholarship for Egyptian nationals.

BIBLIOGRAPHY

Gumbel, Peter. "East Meets West." *Time.* 24 April 2005. Available from http://www.time.com/time/magazine/article/0,9171,1053598-1,00.html

Lofthouse, Richard. "Egypt Rising." *CNBC European Business.* 1 September 2006. Available from http://cnbceb.com/2006/09/01/egypt-rising/

Fazil Say. AP IMAGES.

BIOGRAPHICAL HIGHLIGHTS

Name: Fazil Say

Birth: 1970, Ankara, Turkey

Family: Separated. Former wife, Gülyar; one daughter, Kumru (b. 2000)

Nationality: Turkish

Education: Ankara State Conservatory; Robert Schumann Institute, Düsseldorf, Germany, 1987-1992; Berlin Conservatory, 1992-1995

PERSONAL CHRONOLOGY:

- **1994:** Winner of Young Concert Artists International Auditions
- **1998:** Releases first Mozart disc
- **2001:** Echo-Preis Klassik Award and German Music Critics' Best Recording of the Year Award
- **2005:** Releases first sound track for the film *Ultima Thule* by Swiss director Hans-Ulrich Schlumpf
- **2006:** Signs exclusive and unlimited contract with Shott Music Publishers Mainz

surgeries during his early childhood. To speed up the healing process, doctors recommended to his parents that Say should play a blowing instrument. This would help his palate close properly and improve his speaking ability. Following this recommendation, Say began playing the flute at three.

Say was a child prodigy. The first melody he tried to imitate was the main theme of a symphony that he heard from one of his father's records. At four, he could multiply four-digit numbers and was able to memorize the musical themes that he had heard. His early music education began at three. With Ali Kemal Kaya, he began rhythmic gymnastics and received music drills to refine his hearing abilities. At four, he became a private student of Mithat Fenmen, a famous Turkish pianist, composer, and music teacher who had studied under Nadia Boulanger and Alfred Cortot. Fenmen was the first to be involved in Say's piano education and teach him how to read notes. Say began playing the piano in 1975 at five, the year his parents divorced. At six and seven, he began reading biographies of composers that inspired him to become a composer, a dream that he has followed passionately. (*Zaman*, 10 March 2002)

At twelve, Say joined the Ankara State Conservatory where he began his studies in piano and composition. He finished the conservatory, normally a nine-year program, in five years. During this time, he also developed his improvisational skills, improved his techniques through his studies with Kamuran Gündemir, learned composition from Ilhan Baran, and extended his knowledge on contemporary music through his lessons with Ertuğrul Oğuz Firat. Soon piano became his main passion. Ten to fifteen hours a day, he practiced the music by the classical masters and created his own compositions.

He won a scholarship from the Robert Schumann Institute and went to Düsseldorf, Germany, at seventeen. At this time he also wanted to become a soccer player. At nineteen, he became very depressed when his teacher, David Levine, was hospitalized because of AIDS and could not give lessons for a year. Say did not play the piano for one year. As the musician expressed in an interview:

> Then, one night I heard the *Rite of Spring* on the radio, and it touched me very, very deeply—as Stravinsky himself said, it is about the relationship between humans and the earth. The next morning, I decided to begin piano playing again with that piece, and I found the four-hand version and practiced the bass part. When Mr. Levine came out of the hospital, I told him I was playing the piano again and I asked him to play the piece with me. He agreed, and we actually played it together in a couple of concerts in Germany. (Barnes & Noble, 1 April 2001)

His studies with David Levine ended after five years, and Say went to teach at the Berlin Conservatory for three years. During this time, he also composed a piano concerto, one symphony, fifteen chamber music pieces, and thirty songs.

After winning the Young Concert Artists International Auditions, he moved to New York. This award changed his life, launching his international career and making him a star like Emanuel Ax, Murray Perahia, and Pinchas Zukerman— all past winners of the Young Concert Artists International Audition. In 1996 he toured in Europe and the United States and gave forty concerts within six months.

Since then Say has continued to perform constantly. He gives approximately 120 concerts a year, traveling between Europe, America, and Japan. He performs in the world's leading concert halls including Carnegie Hall and Avery Fischer Hall in New York, the Berlin Philharmonie, the Vienna Musikverein, the Concertgebouw in Amsterdam, and the Suntory Hall in Tokyo. He regularly performs with the New York Philharmonic, the BBC Philharmonic, the Baltimore Symphony, the Israel Philharmonic, the St. Petersburg Philharmonic, the *Orchestre National de France*, and other famous orchestras across the world. He has appeared at many festivals such as the Montpellier Festival, the Ruhr Piano Festival, the Lucerne Festival, the Beethoven Festival Bonn, and the Verbier Festival.

While music plays a major role in his life, his private life has suffered much from this hectic lifestyle. The rapid advance of his career, the commitments to tours and concerts, and the tough competition in the music scene affected his marriage. Say married his childhood love Gülyar at twenty-seven after knowing her for eleven years and studying together at the Ankara Conservatory. Their daughter, Kumru, was born in 2000, and the couple separated after five years of marriage in 2002. Although Say's residence was in New York, he settled in Turkey after his daughter was born. She accompanies her father on his concert tours around the world.

INFLUENCES AND CONTRIBUTIONS

Audiences and music critics applaud Say's extraordinary virtuosity, as well as the freshness and vitality with which he has improvised classical masterpieces and given them different nuances. Most impressive is the way that he has created his own style, tempos, and the versions of classical music that give his work a specific texture. Say has a deep attachment to the music of Bach, Mozart, and Stravinsky. He also is influenced by the Turkish folk songs of Aşik Veysel. The Turkish classical music of composer Dede Efendi inspired Say to connect the old and new world, the West with the East. His admiration for Mozart led Say to write a book on him. In *Uçak Notlari* (Airplane Notes—Gedanken zur Musik) (1999) Say discussed the influences of Turkish elements on Viennese culture and Western music. The so-called "Alla Turca" motifs ultimately inspired the German composer to create his famous sonata *Rondo Alla Turca* and his opera *The Abduction from the Seraglio*.

Similar to Mozart, Say is interested to bend the limiting and restrictive boundaries of music, to break out of compartmentalization. Turkish tunes cannot be played with the piano as it is a tempera instrument consisting of twelve notes, while Turkish music is composed by a system of twenty-four notes. Say has found a solution for this dilemma and argued that although melodies of East and West are separated, they create a harmony when used properly. He weaves motifs from Turkish folk music with Western music, providing a new texture to music and sound. Say also points out that although he is trained in Western classical music, his heart belongs to Anatolia. His Turkish identity and nostalgia about Anatolian culture add emotion into his improvisations that influence Say's repertoire. This experience shapes also the theme of the

'Worldjazz' quartet that Say founded with the Turkish virtuoso, Kudsi Ergüner.

At sixteen he wrote *Black Hymns*. In his twenties, Say had signed a contract with Atlantic Records and his first recording was a dedication to Bach and Mozart; his second featured performances with the New York Philharmonic of Gershwin's *I Got Rhythm Variations* and *Rhapsody in Blue*. There are unlimited recordings of the standard repertory, but what makes Say's music special are his "special effects." He uses overdubbing, a computer-controlled Bösendorfer piano, and special microphone placements as musical devices to add color, texture, and vibrant dimensions to his recordings.

At twenty-one he staged his *Concerto for Piano and Violin* with the Berliner Symphoniker, and he premiered his second concerto, *Silk Road*, five years later in Boston. This music describes exotic caravans and is linked by loud strikes on a large Chinese tam tam. In 2001, he premiered his oratorio, *Nazim*, dedicated to the famous Turkish poet Nazim Hikmet and commissioned by the Turkish Ministry of Culture, to a mesmerized audience. He received great public acclaim when he performed the world premiere of his *Piano Concerto no. 3* in Paris in 2002. At the Istanbul Festival in 2003, he presented in a concert of five thousand people his oratorio, *Requiem for Metin Altiok*. His Fourth Piano Concerto was presented in 2005 in Lucerne. Radio France appointed Say Artist in Residence in 2003. He holds the same position at the Bremen Festival in 2005. A DVD production with the title, *Nazim*, was released in 2005 covering Say's work for chorus and orchestra.

THE WORLD'S PERSPECTIVE

With the release of his first recording of Mozart pieces, Say received high praise in press reviews. He has won many international awards for his recordings and is celebrated in the West. He stands out because of the originality and quality he brings to classical masterpieces. The artist expresses his thoughts regarding his personality as follows:

> Whether in Carnegie Hall or a little Turkish village it's the quality of the music which counts; my wish is to bring the score to life, and whereas my Ottoman heritage certainly influences my own compositions, I sincerely hope I don't play Schumann's trout with overtones of traditional Turkish music! But since I left Turkey many years ago, I don't really know whether I'm a Western musician trying to go from West to East, or a Turkish interpreter trying to make a bridge to Western music. What is important however is to understand the mind of the composer I'm playing. (*Culture Kiosque*, 19 May 2003)

YOUR JOURNEY IS LONG AFTER IT PASSES THE KEYS

Who told you that the key pads of a piano are black and white? The keys do not even represent the first two meters of a two square kilometer long bridge. The key connects to sound, the sound to the ear. From our hearing it connects to our feelings, senses, perception. Your journey is long after it passes the keys. Let the keys remain black and white so that the rest of the journey divides itself into all the possible colors.

ZAMAN, 10 MARCH 2002.

LEGACY

Say's incredible talents as a pianist, composer, and recording artist have won him many prestigious awards and the recognition of international audiences. His style and ideas give well-known arrangements new and exciting sounds and harmonies. Music critics are puzzled to find words to praise Say's talent and achievements. The terminology varies from "brilliant," "magician," to "Protégé," and "Wonderboy," a characterization by the German newspaper, *Die Welt*. Music halls are packed by thousands of fans to listen to Say's new works and his interpretations of the masters. As Brooke Edge notes, "Say likes to play the music that inspires him and play it as he feels it. The way it comes through his fingers has been universally acknowledged as filled with fantastic talent, but his occasional deviances from traditional renditions have sometimes ruffled the feathers and fur coats of classical music purists." (*Prague Post*, 7 February 2007). Say has an obsession to perform live, desiring to present to as many audiences as possible.

In 2005, the Franco-German television station ARTE produced a documentary that provides a portrait of the artist. Gösta Courcamp's *Alla Turca* follows the pianist and composer on a concert tour to Istanbul, Aspendos, Munich, and other cities. The French newspaper *Le Figaro* gave the following description about the artist: "He is not merely a pianist of genious; undoubtedly he will be one of the great artists of the twenty-first century." (*Prague Post*, 7 February 2007).

BIBLIOGRAPHY

Akman, Nuriye. "Fazil Say: *Piyano benim vatanım*." *Zaman* . 10 March 2002. Available at http://arsiv.zaman.com.tr/2002/03/10/roportaj/default.htm.

Boccadoro, Patricia. "Interview: Fazil Say." *Culture Kiosque* . 19 May 2003. Available at http://www.culturekiosque.com/klassik/intervie/fazilsay.htm.

Edge, Brooke. "Steaming up the Keyboard: Fazil Say Takes his Own Approach to the Classics." *Prague Post*. 7 February 2007. Available at http://www.praguepost.com/articles/2007/02/07/steaming-up-the-keyboard.php.

Farach-Colton, Andrew. "Fazil Say's Rite of Passage: The Young Pianist Tackles a Handful of Stravinsky." *Barnes and Noble*. 1 April 2001. Available at http://music.barnesandnoble.com.

Leyla, Umar. "Orhan Pamuk'a haksizlik yapildi." *Vatan*. 12 January 2006. Available at http://www.gazetevatan.com.

Mine Eren

SEBBAR, LEILA
(1941–)

Leila Sebbar is an Algerian-French novelist and essayist.

PERSONAL HISTORY

Sebbar was born 9 November 1941 in Aflou, Algeria, to a French mother and an Algerian father. Both were teachers. She moved to France at age seventeen, and still lives in Paris. She writes in French.

INFLUENCES AND CONTRIBUTIONS

Sebbar deals with a variety of topics, and either adopts a purely fictional approach or uses psychology to make her point. Many of Sebbar's novels express the frustrations of

BIOGRAPHICAL HIGHLIGHTS

Name: Leila Sebbar

Birth: 1941, Aflou, Algeria

Nationality: French, Algerian

PERSONAL CHRONOLOGY:
- **1980:** Publishes *Shérazade, 17 ans, brune, frisée, les yeux verts*
- **1985:** *Les carnets de Shérazade*
- **1986:** *Lettres Parisiennes, autopsie de l'exil*
- **1997:** *Une enfance algérienne*
- **2001:** *Une enfance outremer*
- **2007:** *Métro, Instantanés* and *Le Ravin de la femme*

the *Beur*, the second generation of Maghribi (North African) youth who were born and raised in France and who have not yet integrated into French society. Her book *Parle mon fils, parle à ta mère* (1984; Talk son, talk to your mother), illustrates the absence of dialogue between two generations who do not speak the same language.

The events of several novels center around a young woman called Shérazade, a name very close to Scheherazade, the heroine of the classic collection of Arabian tales, the *Thousand and One Nights*. Shérazade is the protagonist of three novels: *Shérazade, 17 ans, brune, frisée, les yeux verts* (1980; Shérazade, 17, brunette, curly hair, and green eyes); *Les carnets de Shérazade* (1985; Shérazade's notes); and *Le fou de Shérazade* (1991; Crazy about Shérazade). Sebbar uses the implicit connection between Shérazade and Scheherazade to establish the contrast between the old and the new generations of Algerian women, drawing a nonconventional image of the female Beur.

Other themes in Sebbar's writings are the problems of emigration and the torments of life in exile. The latter is central to *Lettres Parisiennes, autopsie de l'exil* (1986; Parisian letters, the autopsy of exile), a correspondence with Canadian novelist and essay writer Nancy Huston. Sebbar's double affiliation to Algeria and France is evoked in two short essays: "They Kill Teachers," published in a collection of autobiographical narratives, *Une enfance algérienne* (1997; An Algerian childhood), and "D'abord, ce n'est pas la guerre" (Primarily, it is not war), in *Une enfance outremer* (2001; A childhood overseas). Her recent works include *Métro, Instantanés* (2007) and *Le Ravin de la femme sauvage* (2007).

THE WORLD'S PERSPECTIVE

Sebbar is well known internationally as a major Francophone Arab writer, noted for her explorations of multiculturalism.

LEGACY

Leila Sebbar is still a prolific writer, and it is too soon to assess her ultimate legacy.

BIBLIOGRAPHY

Bamia, Aida. "The North African Novel: Achievements and Prospects." In *Mundus Arabicus*, vol. 5, edited by Issa Boullata. Cambridge, MA: Dar Mahjar, 1992.

Mortimer, Mildred, ed. *Maghrebian Mosaic*. Boulder, CO, and London: Lynne Rienner, 2001.

Aida A. Bamia
updated by Michael R. Fischbach

SEDDIGH, LALEH
(1977–)

Laleh Seddigh is arguably the best race car driver in Iran. She also became the first woman to compete against men in sports in Iran since the Iranian Revolution in 1979.

PERSONAL HISTORY

Seddigh (also Seddiq) was born in February 1977 in Tehran, Iran, to an upper middle class family. She has a BA in industrial management, an MA in production engineering, and currently is studying for a Ph.D. in industrial management and production, all at Tehran University. She teaches at Tehran Azad University. When not driving, she enjoys horseback riding and target shooting among other pastimes.

INFLUENCES AND CONTRIBUTIONS

Seddigh has always been inspired by her father. Her love of cars began when she started driving her father's car around the yard at eight. By eleven she could drive in the street, and she did so when her father was asleep and she could take his car keys. When Seddigh was eighteen she began seeking entrance into the Iranian Automobile Federation's car races. Not one to wait, she and a female navigator

Laleh Seddigh. © HAMAD MOHAMMED/REUTERS/CORBIS.

BIOGRAPHICAL HIGHLIGHTS

Name: Laleh Seddigh

Birth: 1977, Tehran, Iran

Family: Single

Nationality: Iranian

Education: BA (industrial management), MA (production engineering), Tehran University; studying for Ph.D. (industrial management and production), Tehran University

PERSONAL CHRONOLOGY:

- **2000:** Starts racing career
- **2004:** Allowed to compete with male racers by Iran's Automobile Federation
- **2005:** Iranian national champion racer in the 1600cc engine-size category
- **2006:** Earns her International Racing Driving License

entered three-day, non-Federation cross-country rallies—with Seddigh changing her own tires and fixing her vehicle. She became a member of the Proton Rally Team, competed in twenty-eight rallies by 2004, finished in the top three seven times, and won three times.

In 2004, the Iranian Automobile Federation finally allowed her to compete in circuit races against men—making her the first female to compete against males in Iranian sports since the 1979 revolution installed the Islamic Republic. Seddigh completed five races that season in a Peugeot 206 and both 1500cc and 1600cc Proton cars. By March 2005 she had become the Iranian national champion racer in the 1600cc engine-size category over a season of eight races. Iranian television refused to broadcast her standing on the victory platform, standing above the men that she beat. Although temporarily barred from further competition in 2006, Seddigh qualified for her International Racing Driving License during the BMW School Series at the Bahrain International Circuit in Manama that same year, allowing her to race internationally.

Seddigh insists on achieving what she sets out to do, regardless of the barriers erected against females in Iran. "I'm not a feminist, but why should women be lazy and weak? If you're determined, you've got to push. In this society, women are always like a poor people. They don't believe in themselves. They have to believe in their inside power" (Pohl).

THE WORLD'S PERSPECTIVE

Seddigh has received a huge amount of coverage in the international press, especially for a sports figure from a non-Western country. She has been dubbed "The Little Schumacher," a reference to champion German formula one racer Michael Schumacher. As beautiful and glamorous as she is talented, Seddigh's beauty and image have garnered her much media coverage. She also is notable as a woman competing and winning in a male-dominated sport in a conservative, patriarchal Islamic society. A Hollywood film about her life is reportedly being made, and her story has been told in the leading French magazine, *Paris Match*.

LEGACY

Regardless of how the rest of her young career turns out, Laleh Seddigh already has gained fame in Iran by being the first woman allowed to compete in sports against men since the 1979 revolution. The fact that so few people around the world think of Iran and Iranians in the context of race car driving—let alone a champion female driver (a rarity in the West as well)—will guarantee her a place in Iranian sports history.

BIBLIOGRAPHY

Antelava, Natalia. "Iran Salutes Female 'Schumacher,'" BBC News, March 14, 2005. Available from http://news.bbc.co.uk/2/hi/middle_east/4349341.stm.

Laleh Seddigh's website: http://www.lalehseddigh.net.

"Laleh Seddigh: The Persian Daredevil." *Persian Mirror*. Available from http://www.persianmirror.com/community/2006/sports/LalehSeddigh.cfm.

Pohl, Otto. "On This Race-Car Driver's Track, a New Iran." *New York Times*, May 14, 2005. Available from http://www.iht.com/articles/2005/05/13/news/profile.php.

Tait, Robert. "Iran's Speed Queen." *Observer*, March 4, 2007. Available from http://observer.guardian.co.uk/osm/story/0,,2023234,00.html.

Michael R. Fischbach

SEGEV, TOM
(1945–)

Tom Segev is an Israeli journalist and historian who achieved prominence in both fields by the early twenty-first century. He is best known for his weekly column in *Ha'aretz*, Israel's liberal daily newspaper, and a series of widely read and critically acclaimed books on topics central to Israeli history.

Name: Tom Segev

Birth: 1945, Jerusalem

Family: Unmarried

Nationality: Israeli

Education: Hebrew University of Jerusalem, 1970, BA, history and political science; Boston University, 1975, Ph.D., history

PERSONAL CHRONOLOGY:

• **1963:** Begins journalism career at Israel Radio

• **1963–1966:** Serves in Israel Defense Forces as a librarian

• **1971–1975:** Pursues advanced studies in United States

• **1977–1979:** Serves as political advisor to Jerusalem mayor Teddy Kollek

• **1979–present:** Columnist for *Ha'aretz* newspaper, Tel Aviv

PERSONAL HISTORY

Segev was born in Jerusalem in 1945. His parents were German immigrants who settled in mandatory Palestine after fleeing Nazi Germany ten years earlier. In 1948, when Segev was three years old, his father was killed in the first of many Israeli-Arab wars over Palestine. During the 1948 War, the Zionist Yishuv (pre-state organized Jewish community) established the state of Israel in most of what had been mandatory Palestine.

Segev's experience as a child of immigrants, whose first language was not Hebrew (but rather German) and whose father died in the war, was not wholly uncommon in 1950s Israel. As did thousands of other immigrant children, he quickly learned Hebrew and was rapidly integrated into Jewish-Israeli society. The Israeli-Jordanian border established in 1948-1949 divided Jerusalem, and Segev spent his childhood in the Israeli-controlled section of the city. After graduating from the Hebrew University High School, Segev fulfilled his military service, which is compulsory for Jewish citizens of Israel, as a librarian at the National Defense College between 1963 and 1966. Also in 1963, at the age of eighteen, Segev began his journalism career as a news editor for Israeli national radio.

Upon his discharge from the military, Segev trained his sights on academic pursuits. In 1966, he began study-

ing history and political science at the Hebrew University of Jerusalem, receiving his BA in 1970. In 1971, intrigued by the then-popular subdiscipline of psychohistory, Segev left Israel to undertake graduate work at Boston University. He received his Ph.D. in history in 1975, and his doctoral dissertation, which explored the background and motivations of Nazi concentration camp commanders, served as the basis of one of his earlier and lesser-known books, *Soldiers of Evil: The Commandants of the Nazi Concentration Camps* (1988).

In 1977, Segev began a two-year stint as political advisor to Jerusalem mayor Teddy Kollek, and in 1979 began writing for *Ha'aretz*, which remained his long-term professional home as a journalist. In the decades that followed, Segev emerged as a prominent journalist and one of the country's best-known and most influential historians. Despite his success as an historian and his acceptance of a large number of senior fellowships and visiting professorships in the United States and Israel, Segev has chosen to remain an independent scholar.

INFLUENCES AND CONTRIBUTIONS

The subjects about which Segev writes, and the way he writes about them, reflect a deep engagement with his society, a tireless curiosity about its evolution, and a sense of obligation to critically examine its present and past. Similar to many other critical commentators in Israel, Segev is identified with the left wing of Jewish-Israeli politics, which calls for increased democracy, civil rights, and equality for Palestinian citizens of Israel; good governance; Israeli withdrawal from occupied territory; and a land-for-peace negotiating strategy aimed at achieving peace with the Palestinians and the Arab countries that have not yet signed treaties with Israel. Segev's critical approach to Israeli society permeates his weekly column in *Ha'aretz*, which deals primarily with the politics of culture and human rights, and can also be detected in his historical studies.

As an historian, Segev has made important contributions to modern Israeli historiography in content, methodology, and style. Most of his books have been broad in scope and have tackled decisively underexplored issues that are central to Israeli history and identity. *1949: The First Israelis* (1986), one of the first books to make use of declassified archival material relating to the period surrounding the establishment of the state of Israel, offers a sober and relatively unflattering view of the first few years of Israeli statehood. *1949* was one of a handful of archive-based works appearing in the mid- to late 1980s which adopted a much more critical approach to Zionist and Israeli actions than previous Israeli histories had. For this reason, Segev came to be associated with the "new historians," the epithet by which authors of such critical histories quickly came to be known. While, at the time, many Israeli historians considered this "new" or "revisionist" history to be "anti-Zionist" or "pro-Palestinian" propaganda, much of it gradually became accepted by most mainstream scholars of Israeli history and the Arab-Israeli conflict.

Segev's subsequent works also focus on major topics in Israeli history. In *The Seventh Million: The Israelis and the Holocaust* (1991), Segev examines how the Yishuv dealt with the challenges presented by Nazi Germany, the politics of Zionism during the Second World War, and the impact of the Holocaust on Israeli society. *One Palestine, Complete: Jews and Arabs under the British Mandate* (2000) explores the history of the Zionist project during the three-decade period during which the British ruled Palestine (1918-1948). And *1967* provides a fascinating account of the 1967 War—widely considered to be a watershed in the history of Israel and the Arab-Israeli conflict—and the beginning of Israel's occupation of the territories it conquered from Syria, Egypt, and Jordan during the war.

THE WORLD'S PERSPECTIVE

Segev's contributions to Israeli historiography in methodology and style have also been notable. Methodologically, Segev's works have increasingly incorporated broad strokes of social history, a feature which is especially evident in his book on 1967. Stylistically, Segev simply writes like a good journalist, and this makes his books clear, riveting, and difficult to put down. As Segev himself explained in a 2004 interview, "History and journalism are very much the same thing for me. I think the best journalism is historic journalism and the best history is journalistic history" (Kreisler).

LEGACY

Segev's books have been published in Hebrew, English, and a variety of other languages, including Arabic. On an international level, therefore, his work as an historian is better known than his work as a journalist. In Israel, perceptions of Segev's work often depend on readers' ideology regarding the nature of the state of Israel and the politics of the Arab-Israeli conflict. Left-leaning Israelis tend to appreciate his work more, and right-leaning Israelis less. While this dynamic also exists to a certain degree in some circles outside of Israel, most international students and scholars regard Segev as a thorough and insightful historian whose writing has greatly expanded their knowledge and understanding of the complex history of Israel, Zionism, and the Arab-Israeli conflict.

BIBLIOGRAPHY

Kreisler, Harry. "Israeli National Identity: Conversation with Tom Segev, Columnist, *Ha'aretz*, April 8, 2004." Institute of International Studies, University of California, Berkeley. Available from http://globetrotter.berkeley.edu/people4/Segev/segev-con0.html.

Segev, Tom. *1949: The First Israelis*. New York: Metropolitan Books, 1986.

———. *Soldiers of Evil: The Commandants of the Nazi Concentration Camps*. New York: McGraw-Hill, 1987.

———. *The Seventh Million: The Israelis and the Holocaust*. New York: Metropolitan Books, 1991.

———. *One Palestine, Complete: Jews and Arabs under the British Mandate*. New York: Metropolitan Books, 2000.

———. *Elvis in Jerusalem: Post-Zionism and the Americanization of Israel*. New York: Metropolitan Books, 2002.

———. *1967*. New York: Metropolitan Books, 2007.

Geremy Forman

SEZER, AHMET NECDET
(1941–)

Ahmet Necdet Sezer is the tenth president of the Republic of Turkey. The Grand National Assembly of Turkey (TBMM) elected Sezer president in 2000 after Süleyman Demirel's seven-year term expired. Sezer pledged to protect Turkey's secular institutions, social peace, and territorial integrity at all costs.

Ahmet Necdet Sezer. AP IMAGES.

BIOGRAPHICAL HIGHLIGHTS

Name: Ahmet Necdet Sezer

Birth: 1941, Afyonkarahisar, Turkey

Family: Wife, Semra (m. 1964); two daughters, Zeynep and Ebru; one son, Levent

Nationality: Turkish

Education: BA (law), Ankara University, 1962; 1978, LL.M.

PERSONAL CHRONOLOGY:

- **1963–1978:** Served first as a judge in Dicle and Yerköy towns; served as a supervisory judge in the High Court of Appeals in Ankara
- **1983:** Elected as a member to the High Court of Appeals
- **1988:** Appointed by the president as member of the Constitutional Court
- **1998:** Elected chief justice of the Constitutional Court
- **2000:** Elected as the tenth president of Turkish Republic

PERSONAL HISTORY

Ahmet Necdet Sezer was born on 13 September 1941 in Afyonkarahisar, a city in western Turkey. After his graduation from Afyonkarahisar High School, he obtained a BA from the Ankara University Faculty of Law in 1962. He began his career as a candidate judge in Ankara and later served as a reserve officer in the Military Academy. Upon completing his military service, he became a judge in DicleYerköy, a district of the Diyarbakır Province in Turkey. He worked as a district judge for many years and returned to Ankara as a supervisory judge in the Supreme Court. During this period, he also obtained his MA in civil law from the Ankara University Faculty of Law.

In 1983 he was elected to the Supreme Court. In 1988 while serving in the Division Two of the Supreme Court, he was appointed by Turkey's president Kenan Evren to the Court of Constitution as a primary member, Turkey's highest court. Sezer's work ethic was well respected and his decisions so critical that he became the chief justice of the Constitutional Court in 1998.

In May 2000, after Turkey's political parties failed to reach a consensus on a candidate for presidency, Sezer,

the head of the Constitutional Court, received the backing of leaders from all five parties in the parliament. The political leaders—Bülent Ecevit, Devlet Bahçeli, Mesut Yılmaz, Recai Kutan, and Tansu Çiller—all agreed to nominate Sezer to replace outgoing president Suleyman Demirel. Following this, he was elected by the parliament as the tenth president of the Turkish Republic. He was sworn in and the coalition ruling the government appeared stable under his presidency. The government led by Prime Minister Bulent Ecevit began to concentrate on legislating vital economic reforms demanded by the International Monetary Fund (IMF).

President Sezer accomplished much during his seven-year term of presidency, which officially ended in April 2007. He gained vast support from the public because of his protection of secularism in Turkey. He promoted the supremacy of the law and democratization and fought corruption. At his swearing-in cermony, he said, "Unless we abandon elements which resemble a police state, we can't meet the demands of being a modern society" (Morris). He has urged stronger efforts for the country to join the European Union (EU), saying, "Our country, which cannot remain inward-looking, has to become integrated with the values of civilization embraced by the EU. Our success in the areas of the supremacy of the law and democracy will enhance our respectability in the community of modern nations" (*Southeast European Times*). Nevertheless, there were some issues on which President Sezer was criticized as well. Given his lack of experience in foreign affairs, he did not play a major role on the international stage representing Turkey's interests.

INFLUENCES AND CONTRIBUTIONS

President Sezer is known as a man of great personal integrity who possesses a deep respect for the rule of law. He follows the philosophical path of Atatürk, the founder and first president of the Turkish Republic. With the victory of the Turkish War of Independence in 1923, Atatürk instituted a form of democracy with a parliament (the Grand National Assembly), raising Turkey to a modern civilization. He abolished Islam as the state religion and instructed a secular law structure with secular institutions of justice and education. During Atatürk's presidency (1923-1938), educational, social, and economic reforms were begun and messages about the necessity of a peaceful and mutually respectful co-existence of all nations were given. Ahmet Necdet Sezer, inspired by Atatürk, has followed in his footsteps not only as a judge, but also as president.

President Sezer prohibited any type of Islamic influence in the Turkish state and has promoted secularism in every circumstance. His contributions as the chief justice of Turkey's highest court and as the tenth president of Turkey stem from his support of secularism and freedom of expression. There were, however, times that President Sezer and Prime Minister TAYYIP ERDOGAN disagreed on proposed laws. He vetoed those and asked for improvements on behalf of the secularism.

President Sezer always has been a supporter for free speech and encouraged the government and military to repeal laws that imprison journalists and politicians for voicing allegedly subversive views. He has called for an end to the ban on teaching and broadcasting in the Kurdish language.

Overall his election helped to maintain stability throughout the nation. On the international stage, however, President Sezer has not had an active profile due to his lack of experience in foreign affairs. He has supported peace initiatives in Middle East. He met with the presidents of Middle Eastern countries and emphasized the possible consequences of ethnic and sectarian clashes in the Middle East extending beyond the region, adding, "initiatives with common sense should be undertaken to strengthen a peaceful solution" (*Washington Post*). In a joint news conference with Pakistani president General Pervez Musharraf, Ahmet Necdet Sezer said "We are aiming to contribute to efforts to bring peace to our region, to the world and the Muslim world" (*Washington Post*).

THE WORLD'S PERSPECTIVE

When President Sezer was the chief judge in Turkey, his messages were well received in the world. Stephen Kinzer, a *New York Times* correspondent, wrote in 1999, "Ahmet Necdet Sezer, Turkey's highest-ranking judge, surprises country by sharply condemning restrictions on freedom of speech; urges Parliament to repeal series of laws and constitutional provisions; also calls for lifting ban on teaching Kurdish language, which he contends violates international agreements."

His democratic profile and presidential election in 2000 are highly respected internationally. Europeans regarded President Sezer as a leader who could supervise Turkey's reform attempts and change its laws as required for membership in the European Union (EU).

LEGACY

Ahmet Necdet Sezer, a reformist judge with a profound respect for the rule of law, became Turkey's tenth president in 2000. He is the first Turkish president without prior service as either an active politician or a senior military officer. Turkish presidents have vital meanings for Turkey in many aspects. As indicated in its constitution, the president has many critical powers including appointing the chief of General Staff, choosing the members of the Constitutional Court, selecting the justices of the Court of Appeals and the Chief Public Prosecutor's

Office, and also members of the Board of Higher Education (YOK) and university rectors. President Sezer has fullfilled these critical duties and maintained stability during times of conflict between the political power and the state system.

BIBLIOGRAPHY

"Ahmed Necdet Sezer: President of the Republic of Turkey." *Southeast European Times.* Available from http://www.setimes.com.

Kinzer, Stephen. "Chief Judge in Turkey Urges Lifting of Curbs on Free Speech." *New York Times*, 30 April 1999. Available from http://www.nytimes.com.

Morris, Chris. "Turkey's New President Takes Office." BBC News. Updated 16 May 2000. Available from http://news.bbc.co.uk.

"Pakistan, Turkey in Mideast Peace Effort." *Washington Post*, 6 February 2007. Available from http://www.washingtonpost.com.

Presidency of the Republic of Turkey. Available from http://www.cankaya.gov.tr.

Gunes Aygok

SFEIR, NASRALLAH
(1920–)

Mar Nasrallah Boutros Sfeir is the seventy-sixth patriarch of the Maronite Catholic Church, the largest Christian denomination in Lebanon. He has served as the patriarch since 1986, succeeding Cardinal Anthony Peter Khoraish. Pope John Paul II selected Sfeir to become a cardinal in the Catholic Church in 1994. Sfeir has served in Lebanon during a turbulent time, and he is a controversial figure in light of his high profile and outspoken nature within Lebanese religious and political circles and his influence over everyday life in Lebanon.

PERSONAL HISTORY

Sfeir (also Butrus Sfayr) was born in the popular vacation town of Rayfun, on the slopes of the Kisrawan-Kisrawan Mountains. He was born on 15 May 1920 to Marun Sfeir and Hanni Fahid, the only son of their six children. His birth preceded by only four months the formation of the "Greater State of Lebanon." This state formed under the French Mandate after the First World War to afford the Maronite Catholic minority some form of protection and status. The National Pact was an oral agreement formed in 1943 by Lebanon's first president, Bishara al-Khuri (a Maronite), and Riyad al Solh (a Sunni), Lebanon's first prime minister. They reached this agreement on the balance of power in government between the Muslim and Christian factions. To help ease the Christian fear of Muslim domination, they would divide the

Nasrallah Sfeir. AP IMAGES.

BIOGRAPHICAL HIGHLIGHTS

Name: Nasrallah Sfeir

Birth: 1920, Rayfun, Lebanon

Family: Single

Nationality: Lebanese

Education: Maronite Patriarchal Seminary in Ghazir, Kisrawan, Lebanon; BA in philosophy and theology, Oriental Seminary; Institute of Saint Joseph University, 1950

PERSONAL CHRONOLOGY:

- **1950s:** Ordained a priest and appointed pastor of the Diocese of Damascus; taught Arabic literature and the history of philosophy and Translation; appointed General Secretary of the Maronite Patriarchate

- **1960s:** Ordained bishop and appointed patriarchal vicar

- **1970s:** Patriarchal administrator

- **1980s:** President of the Executive Committee of the Assembly of the Catholic Patriarch and Bishops in Lebanon; representative of the President of the Assembly of the Catholic Patriarchs and Bishops in Lebanon at Caritas-Lebanon; spiritual director to the Knights of Malta; elected patriarch by the Synod of Bishops; installed in the See of Antioch and All the East as the seventy-sixth Maronite patriarch; president of the Assembly of the Catholic Patriarchs and Bishops in Lebanon

- **1994:** Founding member of the Assembly of the Catholic Patriarchs in the East; became Cardinal and member of the Pontifical Council for legislative interpretation and the Pastoral Health Service

majority of high-level posts between both religious groups, including the presidency. A 1932 census determined what groups received certain roles, based on the group's status in the country. The president was to be a Maronite Christian, the prime minister a Sunni Muslim, and the speaker of the Chamber of Deputies would thus be a Shii'a Muslim. A Maronite also would serve as chief of staff of the army. Thus the Maronites were guaranteed not to be overwhelmed by the Muslim masses, as they held two very powerful positions. The Maronites agreed to accept an "Arab face" for Lebanon. In return the Muslim citizenry would give up their hopes for unification with Syria and recognize the legitimacy and importance of an "independent" Lebanese state. This government was the predecessor to the modern Lebanese state, and the agreement was very important in the formation of Lebanon. The agreement would have played a central role in the lives of the Sfeir family, and it had a lasting effect on Nasrallah Boutros Sfeir and his views on the autonomous nature of the future Lebanese state.

Sfeir grew up in a time when independence and autonomy were frequently discussed, likely creating in him a strong feeling of nationalism. He also grew up in a Maronite home, in a Maronite region, creating in him a fierce devotion for the Maronite faith, his country, and for the people around him. Many Maronites had been marginalized because of their minority religious status.

The future patriarch studied, in his early years, at Saint Abda- Harharya School, a Catholic school founded by a past Maronite patriarch. From 1937 until 1939 Sfeir attended the Maronite Patriarchal Seminary in Ghazir, Kisrawan, run by the Society of Jesus (Jesuits). He continued his studies and religious formation at the Oriental

Seminary Institute of Saint Joseph University in Beirut from 1940 to 1943 and again from 1944 to 1950, focusing on theology and philosophy. Along the way, he became well versed in many languages. Patriarch Sfeir is fluent in Arabic, both classical and Lebanese, Aramaic, French, English, Latin, and Syriac. This demonstrates his deep passion for the gospel and learning, deeply important to all Maronite patriarchs He has written several books, addressing liturgical and theological topics.

Sfeir was ordained a priest on 7 May 1950 at the age of twenty-nine. He was appointed to the Rayfun parish, a pastor in the church where he had been raised. At this time, he also began his service as secretary to the Diocese of Damascus. This Syrian diocese leads the approximately four thousand Maronites in Syria. Sfeir gained valuable insight into diocesan affairs and Syrian politics while serving in this role. This almost certainly would have affected his later views on Syria and its occupation and control over Lebanon.

Sfeir also spent ten years teaching at the Marianist College. At the college, located in Jounieh, Lebanon, Sfeir taught Arabic literature, the history of philosophy, and translation. During this time, he was very busy serving as a professor, pastor, and secretary to an important diocese, as well as the secretary to the Maronite patriarch. This coveted spot gained him access to the brilliance of his predecessor, and a view into the inner workings of this position. In 1961 he was ordained as a bishop, as well as being appointed patriarchal vicar. This was a rapid progression to a bishop and vicar in just ten years. Before his election to patriarch, Sfeir held various positions of importance within the church, being groomed for a prominent role and attracting attention.

On 19 April 1986 the Synod of Bishops elected Nasrallah Boutros Sfeir to be the seventy-sixth patriarch of the Maronite Church. This made him the spiritual leader of the influential Maronite Church in Lebanon and millions of Maronites around the world. As head of the Maronite Church, he must provide spiritual and literal leadership to his flock. He was installed as the seventy-sixth Maronite patriarch on 27 April 1986. On that day he took over control of the See of Antioch and the Entire East. From that day forward he has been addressed as His Holiness the Seventy-Sixth Patriarch of Antioch and the Whole Levant. Sfeir also has championed liturgical reform, culminating in the issuance of a new Maronite missal, the official document that defines the Divine Liturgy (Mass) for Maronite Catholics. The reform represented a return to the original form of the Maronite Divine Liturgy.

The Maronite patriarch holds a powerful position, requiring close contact with the Roman Rite (the rite of the large majority of Catholics worldwide), other Eastern Rite patriarchs within the Catholic Church, and the pope. The Maronite patriarch has full spiritual authority over all members of the Maronite Rite. The Maronite Church is a part of the Catholic Church and in full communion with the pope, the bishop of Rome. He was selected to be a cardinal by Pope John Paul II in 1994— only the third Maronite patriarch to serve in this capacity. Sfeir is well respected and holds considerable influence within the Catholic Church worldwide.

INFLUENCES AND CONTRIBUTIONS

Sfeir was deeply influenced first and foremost by his Maronite Catholic faith. He also was influenced by the Lebanese nationalism that swept the Levant (Eastern Mediterranean) in the 1930s and 1940s. In 1943 Lebanon achieved independence from France. Sfeir also became a tireless activist for equality and for the future of Lebanon after fifteen years of bloody civil war (1975-1990) and occupations by both Israel and Syria. Not only has Sfeir campaigned for freedom from what he terms "Syria's hegemony" and its puppet government in Lebanon, he also has called for social changes within Lebanon, within his own church, as well as within the Lebanese society as a whole. Sfeir, ever vocal and controversial, has continually sought what he believes best for Lebanon. Some praise him for this, but he has also been accused of promoting his church's betterment and putting the good of his people before the good of the country.

During the Lebanese Civil War, lasting a devastating fifteen years, the patriarch had the difficult task of balancing the political and religious ambitions that surrounded him. After the intervention of Syria in the fighting that broke out among several factions in 1976, Sfeir welcomed Syria's influence in helping his Phalange/Lebanese forces as they were about to be overwhelmed by the more dominant Muslim factions. The Syrian help was less about helping the Maronite forces and more about being concerned with the government of its neighbor and its consequences. Originally Syria was hailed for stopping the intense and damaging fighting, but that praise turned to anger when the Syrians did not leave Lebanon and started to exert control over the settling nation. The interference of Syria, Israel, and the Palestinian Liberation Organization destabilized the country and led to Syrian control of the government.

However, due in large part to machinations behind the scenes and with implications too covert to be directly or easily understood, he changed positions. It appears that the Vatican heavily influenced Sfeir into accepting the 1989 Ta'if Agreement. The Ta'if Agreement was a blow to the powerful political realm of the Maronite community. It delegated Maronite privileges to others, with accountability transferred as well. The governmental structure shifted to allow for an even distribution of

CONTEMPORARIES

Upon the death of Lebanon's Patriarch Meouchi in 1975, the Archbishop of Saida Anthony Khoraiche (1907-1994), was elected to succeed him. The newly elected Patriarch Khoraiche was confronted with the outbreak of the Lebanese Civil War that tore the country apart. A man of the land and of the people, Anthony tried valiantly to restore harmony among all Lebanese. During his tenure the Maronite Seminary of Ghazir was restored, but the war would continue for another fifteen years with interferences by foreign nations including Israel, Syria, and the United States. It was these interferences and the support these countries provided to the warring factions that prolonged the war, increased the bloodshed, and made national reconciliation more difficult.

Due to the political turmoil and security situation in the country, Patriarch Khoraiche resigned his office in 1985 and was succeeded by Nasrallah Sfeir in April 1986. Having been the Vicar for two previous Patriarchs, Patriarch Sfeir was well experienced in the role of Bkerke, in both the ecclesiastical and civil spheres. Bkerke is the seat of the "See of the Maronite Church," located near the bay of Jounieh; Lebanon. Sfeir became a strong voice for reason and sanity in the latter years of the Lebanese conflict.

Christian and Muslim officials. It was an unpopular choice among his followers, and riots ensued.

Considering Sfeir was so vocal in expressing his views of the Syrian occupation, it seems odd that he would be silent on the Israeli occupation in the 1990s, probably owing to his somewhat strained ties with Israel at that time. The twenty-two-year Israeli "occupation" was a result of Israel's interference in the Muslim/Christian conflict, in which they aided the Maronite militias against their Muslim counterparts. It would seem that the Vatican may have had some influence over this "silence" on that topic as well. In more recent conflicts Sfeir been very critical of Israel.

Patriarch Sfeir reached his breaking point with Syria in 2000 after a noticeable silence on the topic for some time. When Syria reneged on a promise not to compromise on free elections, Sfeir responded, "Lebanon isn't governed by its own sons, but by the Syrians who impose their hegemony"(Gamble 2003). He also strongly sug-gested that Syria should stop meddling and trying to control all aspects of Lebanese government. This was strong language, more consistent with his past rhetoric.

The patriarch has had an uneven relationship with the United States. He requested an audience with President George W. Bush and senior administration officials to plead for help in ousting the Syrians from Lebanon in 2001. In 2002 the United States, however, decided to introduce the Syria Accountability Act. This would impose sanctions on Syria if it did not retreat from Lebanon. The patriarch used this pressure to gain concessions from Syria in return for his support. Thus Sfeir publicly denounced the Act, hoping to gain more connections and places within the Syrian-controlled government. It was a means to an end, not necessarily intended as a slap in the political face of the United States.

Recently Patriarch Sfeir again reversed his public acceptance and support for Syria. Most likely this is because he had expected Syria to hold true to its word and allow for more Maronite involvement in governing and influence over Lebanese affairs. Sfeir stated after a meeting with some other Christian oppositionists that he would demand the withdrawal of Syrian troops, noting that the Lebanese government "is wrecking the founda-tions of democracy" and "muzzling freedoms." In 2005 Sfeir's constant demands for the end of Lebanon's occu-pation by Syrian forces and influence came true. The last remaining 250 Syrian troops withdrew from Lebanon on 26 April 2005.

In a show of the influence of the patriarch, the pope mentioned the situation in Lebanon in his Angelus address on 10 December 2006. Pope Benedict XVI stated, "I share the strong concerns expressed by the Patriarch, His Beatitude, Cardinal Nasrallah Boutros Sfeir. Together with them, I ask the Lebanese govern-ment and the political leaders to have exclusively at heart the good of the Country" (Pope Benedict XVI 2006). This is a public and powerful statement by the pope, but the influence of Nasrallah Boutros Sfeir is clearly evident.

THE WORLD'S PERSPECTIVE

Global perceptions of Sfeir have generally been positive. Interested observers feel that Sfeir is usually controversial, but assessments of Sfeir have been negative at times—especially when he has addressed Syria's presence and interference in Lebanon's internal affairs. Although he has taken himself largely out of the public spotlight by maintaining a reduced role in Lebanese affairs, he is still a dominant and influential source of inspiration, hope, spiritual guidance, and political leadership. If history is any indicator of the future, Sfeir will continue to be a strong voice in all Lebanese affairs. He has always tried to do what he felt was the right thing for his beloved

> ## ENDING DIVISION IN LEBANON
>
> I am concerned that all factions in Lebanon are competing to arm themselves as we have returned twenty years to the past. What we need is to end the anti-government protests and clear the streets of demonstrators and allow the streets to reopen in the hopes of ending divisions in Lebanon.
>
> SPOKEN TO HIS CONGREGATION ON THE LEBANESE BROADCASTING SERVICE, LEBANON, FEBRUARY 25, 2007.

Lebanon. His first and most binding love is for the Maronite Catholic Church and his God, and he remains passionate about the course he feels is right for Lebanon.

LEGACY

Although Sfeir has made some controversial statements with regard to foreign interference in Lebanese affairs, he certainly will go down in history as the Lebanese patriarch most associated with the intricacies of Lebanese social and political life. Born in a country that has seen many wars, occupations, invasions, and much political turmoil during his lifetime, Sfeir will long be remembered as the Lebanese who has championed Lebanese independence and equality, as well as social and political harmony for his fellow countrymen. Since the end of the Lebanese Civil War in 1990, Sfeir has faced difficulties maintaining unity within his church and proved to be less successful in keeping the Maronites under one banner of leadership. The most recent conflict with Israel in 2006 has caused Sfeir to come out against Israel, saying that they will only make peace with Israel when "all other Arab nations" do so. The current political division in Lebanon has led the patriarch to become more concerned and vocal about foreign interference in his country. Even with the polarization of that tiny but diverse nation, Mar Nasrallah Sfeir continues to voice his opinions on unity in Lebanon. At the present time, he has become the conscience of the country, pointing to the injustices that exist in the social and political spheres, speaking for the poor and disenfranchised. In his writings and sermons, he has presented an agenda of how Lebanon can achieve a future based on freedom, as well as human rights.

BIBLIOGRAPHY

BBC News. "Lebanese Christian leader wants Syrians out." BBC News Online, February 25, 2007. Available from http://news.bbc.co.uk/2/low/middle_east/1275156.stm.

"Cardinal Mar Nasrallah Boutros Sfeir." Answers.com. Available from http://www.answers.com/topic/cardinal-mar-nasralah-boutros-sfeir.

Gambill, Gary. "*Dossier:* Nasrallah Boutros Sfeir." *Middle East Intelligence Bulletin,* May 2003. Available from http://www.meib.org/articles/0305_ld.htm#_ftn35.

"Lebanon: The National Pact." *Country Studies.* Available from http://country-studies.com/lebanon/the-national-pact.html.

Pope Benedict XVI. "Angelus Message for the Second Sunday of Advent." Public comments for general address following the recitation of the Angelus, Vatican City, December 10, 2006. Available from http://www.vatican.va/holy_father/benedict_xvi/angelus/2006/documents/hf_ben-xvi_ang_20061210_en.html.

"The Biography of Nasrallah Peter Cardinal Sfeir, Patriarch of Antioch and All The East." *St. Maron Publications,* available from http://www.stmaron.org/patriarch_bio.html.

Khodr M. Zaarour

SHAHEEN, SIMON
(1955–)

An internationally known virtuosic musician, composer, and teacher with wide-ranging interests, Simon Shaheen is probably the most famous and accomplished Arab-American musician of the twentieth century.

Simon Shaheen. © DAVID H. WELLS/CORBIS.

PERSONAL HISTORY

Shaheen (also Shahin) was born to a Christian Palestinian musical family in Tarshiha, in Israel's northern Galilee region in 1955. The family moved to Haifa in 1957. Simon's father, Hikmat Shaheen, was an accomplished composer, performer, and teacher, whose musical work profoundly influenced the young Simon. Hikmat's children learned to play instruments early in their lives. At the age of five, Simon started playing the ud (also oud; English: lute) and then violin along with his brothers Najib and William, whose musical lives remain intertwined.

As a young man, he attended the Academy of Music in Jerusalem where, in 1978, he earned degrees in Arabic literature and musical performance, focused not only on Arab musical traditions but also those of the West. He became a virtuosic violin player in both arenas. He was appointed to teach in the Academy and then, in 1980, went to New York for doctoral study in music performance and education at the Manhattan School of Music and at Columbia University. New York has been Shaheen's base ever since.

In New York in 1982, Shaheen established the Near East Ensemble, which he continues to lead, composed of some of the best musicians from Lebanon, Syria, and Palestine who are currently residents of New York. Formed along the lines of the larger instrumental ensembles that became popular in the Middle East in the mid-twentieth century—consisting of multiple violins, sometimes cellos and string basses, and running to ten to twenty members—the group played classical Arab music and emerging classics from the twentieth-century Arab world. Shaheen also wrote his own compositions for himself and the group.

A voracious musician, Shaheen pursued interests beyond Arab music, contributing to soundtracks for *The Sheltering Sky* and *Malcolm X*, and the entire score for the United Nations-sponsored documentary *For Everyone Everywhere*. He established a second ensemble, Qantara, designed to draw jazz, Latin American, Western, and Arab classical musicians into the domain of Arab music. His commercial recordings bespeak his eclectic interests, including a duo performance with vina player Vishwa Mohan Bhatt (*Saltanah*, Water Lily Acoustics, 1997) and Blue Flame (*ARK21*, 2001), perhaps Qantara's most successful work that garnered eleven Grammy nominations.

In addition to concerts, Shaheen also offered private lessons and, eventually, lectures, lecture-demonstrations, and classes about Arab music. His influence and effectiveness within the larger community grew steadily. Working in the New York Arab American community, Shaheen created New York's Mahrajan al-Fann (Festival of [Arab] Arts), held annually since 1994.

In 1996 Shaheen established the Arab Music Retreat, which is held for one week in August in Holyoke, Mas-

---

BIOGRAPHICAL HIGHLIGHTS

Name: Simon Shaheen

Birth: 1955, Tarshiha, Galilee, Israel

Family: Single

Nationality: Palestinian; American citizen

Education: Private music lessons with father Hikmat Shaheen; B.A. (Arabic literature and musical performance), Academy of Music in Jerusalem, 1978; graduate study, Manhattan College of Music, Columbia University

PERSONAL CHRONOLOGY:

- **1980:** Immigrates to New York City
- **1982:** Founds the Near East Ensemble
- **1994:** Receives National Heritage Award, National Endowment for the Arts, Washington D.C.
- **1994:** Founds the annual Mahrajan al-Fann (Festival of Arts) in New York
- **1996:** Founds the Arab Music Retreat
- **1999:** Founds Qantara

---

sachusetts, and is an annual event that remains ongoing. Working with long-time friends and colleagues Dr. Ali Jihad Racy (a professor of ethnomusicology and a well-known musician and composer at the University of California, Los Angeles) and Dr. George Sawa (an award-winning artist and teacher in Toronto, Canada), Shaheen conceived a teaching and performing experience that would select and encourage emerging students of Arab music through intensive study with established and expert artists. This event, now much a part of the Arab musical landscape, in fact draws many accomplished professionals together as well, who learn from each other and teach the less-experienced members.

INFLUENCES AND CONTRIBUTIONS

Without fail, Shaheen identifies his father, Hikmat, as his most important influence. While acknowledging the value of his academic degrees, Shaheen says his real education was working with his father.

The virtuosity he developed in both European and Arab classical music clearly informs much of his work. More than simply applying virtuosic gestures, Shaheen's understanding of the theoretical bases of the two systems

THINK WITH YOUR VOICE

◼

Think with your voice when you listen to Arab music. It has a linear quality like the voice. Concentrate on its melodies and listen to how they interact with the rhythm. Arab music is characterized by the use of quarter-tones, which lie between the half-steps of western music. They have a quality that you may not be able to hear at first. Don't think of them as out-of-tune notes. They are deliberate. The more you listen, the more you will begin to hear them and come to love them, for it is the quarter-tones which distinguish many beautiful maqams [melodic modes] in Arabic music.

CAMPBELL, KAY HARDY. "A HERITAGE WITHOUT BOUNDARIES" *SAUD ARAMCO WORLD MAGAZINE* (MAY/JUNE 1996).

and his extensive repertoire allow him to tack back and forth between the systems and to create an informed and intelligent fusion of the two that is musically interesting and well worth attention.

The results of his efforts within broader communities, with the Mahrajan al-Fann in New York, the Retreat in Holyoke, Massachusetts, and his willingness to work on the projects of others, have already rippled throughout American society in unpredictable ways. Shaheen has modeled self-respecting artistic accomplishment for ever-growing American audiences.

THE WORLD'S PERSPECTIVE

Shaheen attained world recognition relatively early in his career with invitations to perform in highly visible venues including Carnegie Hall, the Cairo Opera House, and the Palais des Arts in Belgium. Qantara has appeared at two World of Music, Arts & Dance (WOMAD) festivals, the Newport Jazz Festival, the Monterrey Jazz Festival, and many others worldwide. In 2000, a group led by Shaheen backed up Sting and Cheb Mami at the Grammy Awards, and Qantara opened for Sting at a Jones Beach, California, performance. Major grants have supported some of his work. In 1994, he won the prestigious National Heritage Award from the U.S. National Endowment for the Arts.

LEGACY

It is not too much to claim that North American understanding of Arab music proceeds from the concerts and teaching of Simon Shaheen, his colleagues Ali Jihad Racy and George Sawa, and their students. Shaheen's

prodigious work within the North American community in concert halls, at music festivals, at college campuses, and within his community have established the musical style and repertory of Syria, Lebanon, Palestine, and Egypt as the model of Arab music familiar, to the extent that any Arab music is familiar, to the ears of American listeners. Students in college Middle Eastern music ensembles play the repertoire that he and his colleagues have advanced and Shaheen himself, through his personal appearances and recordings, serves as a model of virtuosity and musical accomplishment in the domain of Arab music.

Part of this legacy derives from Shaheen's talent and the visibility he and his ensembles have attained. Another part rises from his consummate skill as a teacher and his devotion to the musical enterprise. He has paid close attention to students at many levels of experience and has given generously of his time and skill, regardless of the prestige of the venue.

His work beyond the domain of Arab music—in particular his infusions of Arab music into syncretic styles—may be less well recognized as such, which will be unfair to Shaheen and unfortunate for musical culture if it persists in this way. For Shaheen's creativity, personal learning, and musical curiosity have ranged widely, and they advance musical thinking and virtuosity internationally in a way that merits continued attention.

Working as he has in an environment that can be inhospitable to Arabs, Shaheen's teaching and other educational efforts have helped sustain Arab art in a foreign land and encourage Arab and non-Arab artists to draw from its resources. The results of this effort will outlive Shaheen and form an important aspect of his legacy, as well.

BIBLIOGRAPHY

Campbell, Kay Hardy. "A Heritage without Boundaries." *Saudi Aramco World Magazine*, May/June 1996. Available from http://www.saudiaramcoworld.com/issue/199603/a.heritage.without.boundaries.htm.

Shaheen, Simon. "Beyond the Performance." In *Images of Enchantment: Visual and Performing Arts of the Middle East* (Cairo, Egypt 1998).

Virginia Danielson

SHAHRANI, NEMATULLAH
(1941–)

A religious scholar trained in Afghanistan and Egypt, Nematullah Shahrani has spent much of his life as an apolitical educator, author, and translator of important Islamic literature from Arabic. He lived about twenty

Nematullah Shahrani. AP IMAGES.

BIOGRAPHICAL HIGHLIGHTS

Name: Nematullah Shahrani

Birth: 1941, Shahran, Jerm district of Badakhshan province

Family: Wife, Aaliya Muslih; sons, Waheedullah, Junaidullah, Ahmad; daughters, Maliha, Manizha, Madina.

Nationality: Afghanistan

Education: BA, Kabul University (1965); MA, al-Azhar University, Cairo (1971); legal training, George Washington University, 1976-1977

PERSONAL CHRONOLOGY:

- **1960-70s:** Faculty member and writer, Department of Islamic Studies, Kabul University

- **1981-1990:** Refugee in Pakistan, educator, author in support of Afghan mujahidin

- **1990-1996:** President of Abdullah Ibn Mas'ud University in Takhar province

- **1996-2002:** Returns to Pakistan, member of the "Rome Process" negotiations

- **2002:** Member of Emergency Loya Jergah

- **2003-2005:** Vice president and chair of Constitutional Drafting Commission

- **2005-present:** Minister of Ershad, Hajj and Awqaf (Religious Guidance, Pilgrimage and Religious Endowments)

years as a refugee in Peshawar, Pakistan, supporting the Afghanistan Mujahidin resistance against Soviet occupation and communist regimes. After the fall of Taliban regime, he became one of four vice presidents to Hamid Karzai's transitional administration (2003-2005). Nematullah has also served as chairman of the Constitutional Drafting Commission, a member of the Constitutional Loyah Jergah (Grand Assembly), and as minister of Hajj and Religious Affairs since the election of Karzai as president of the Islamic Republic of Afghanistan in 2005.

PERSONAL HISTORY

Shahrani was born in 1941 in a small Uzbek village, in the Jerm District of the remote mountainous province of Badakhshan, Afghanistan. His father, Mullah Ebaadullah Shahrani, was a village religious functionary who was instrumental in the establishment of the first elementary school in his village, becoming a teacher and a strong advocate of modern education. After completing primary and middle school in Badakhshan, Nematullah—one of thirteen children and the second eldest son in the family—entered Madrassa-yi Abu-Hanifa (an Islamic studies high school) in Paghman, near the capital Kabul. He completed his studies at the Faculty of Islamic Studies (Shari'ayat) at

Kabul University in 1965 and was recruited to the teaching staff of the same unit upon graduation. In 1968 he accepted a scholarship to al-Azhar University in Cairo, the most prestigious institution for the study of Sunni Islam. He earned an MA in tafsir studies (the study of Qur'an Commentaries). Upon his return to Afghanistan in 1971 he rejoined the academic staff of the Faculty of Islamic Studies and became the editor of its official publication, the *Shari'ayat* (Islamic Studies Journal). In 1976-1977, Shahrani was sent to George Washington University in the United States for legal training. The program focused on the administration of justice in the United States and a comparative examination of the Islamic and American court systems.

Although remaining consciously apolitical, unlike other scholars trained in Egypt's al-Azhar University during the same era, Shahrani was imprisoned for a period of time after the Communist coup of April 1978. Upon his release, he left Afghanistan in 1981 with his family for the safety of Pakistan. He spent the next two decades working tirelessly in support of the Afghan Islamic resistance through publications and teaching in various mujahidin educational institutions in and around Peshawar, Pakistan. When the Afghan mujahidin-established Abdullah Ibn Mas'ud University relocated from Peshawar to Taliqan in Takhar province in northeastern Afghanistan in 1990, he became its president and built that institution until the city fell to the Taliban in 1996.

INFLUENCES AND CONTRIBUTIONS

Shahrani's most important contribution has been his phenomenal productivity as an author, translator, and contributor in important national, provincial, and local publications in virtually all parts of Afghanistan. Two of his most celebrated works, published by Kabul University before the onset of the Communist coup and the war of resistance, are *Qur'an Shinaasi* (Studies of the Qur'an or Qur'anology, 1973) and *Fiqh-i Islam wa Qanuni Gharb* (A Comparison of Islamic and Western Law). During the years of exile and jihad resistance, he has authored and translated more than forty books and more than 1,500 published articles on diverse topics, including spiritual, ritual, ethical, legal, and gender relations; health; and socioeconomic and political responsibilities of Muslims in general, and Afghan youth in particular. *Tafsir-i Sura-i Hujurat* (Commentary on "the Inner Apartments," Chapter 49 of the Qur'an) is one of his most significant books published while in exile. Because of his devotion to research and writing he was promoted to the rank of pohand (full professor) in Qur'anic Studies at the Faculty of Shar'iyat. In addition to his vice presidency and ministerial portfolios in post-Taliban governments, he has taught at Kabul University regularly on a part-time basis. Shahrani is multi-lingual, with competency in Dari, Persian, Tajik, Uzbek, Pashto, Arabic, and English. He has traveled extensively and attended many conferences and seminars across the globe.

THE WORLD'S PERSPECTIVE

Shahrani did not join any of the seven established Afghan mujahidin political parties. He has maintained, however, close supportive relations with all of them by contributing articles to their publications, regardless of party affiliation. By emphasizing his role as a nonpartisan Muslim educator and preacher, he gained respect and popularity among the ordinary people and some criticism from a segment of his admirers for not leading a political movement of his own.

LEGACY

His political independence has ultimately served him and the country well. Nematullah became an active member of the Rome Process, which attempted to resolve the vicious civil war after the fall of the Communist regime and the rise of Taliban. After the Emergency Loya Jergah meeting held in 2002 following the American overthrow of the Taliban, he was appointed as a vice president in Hamid Karzai's transitional government. His reputation as a fine scholar and impartial arbiter led to his position as chair of the post-Taliban Constitutional Drafting Commission. He and his colleagues presented President Karzai with a draft constitution, proposing a mixed parliamentary and presidential system with considerable checks and balances for a transparent governance system. The draft presented to the Constitutional Loya Jergah in December 2004, however, had been considerably revised by Karzai's international and domestic advisors in favor of a strong presidential system. Despite much opposition the revised constitution was approved in a tumultuous, extended session of the Loya Jergah. To the dismay of many in Afghanistan, Nematullah and members of the commission have never addressed what happened to their version of the draft constitution. Since the election of Karzai as president, Nematullah has served in the cabinet as the minister of religious guidance, pilgrimage, and religious endowments.

BIBLIOGRAPHY

Dupree, Louis. *Afghanistan.* Oxford and New York: Oxford University Press, 1997.

M. Nazif Shahrani

SHAIR, KAMAL
(1930–)

As a prominent Jordanian business entrepreneur, a frontline politician, diplomat, and philanthropist, Kamal Shair emerged from a modest background to play a leading role in the politics of Jordan, the Middle East, and the global economy. While teaching at The American University of Beirut, he had business in mind. He set up Dar Al-Handasah (House of Engineers), a multinational corporate empire that engaged in trade, construction, and manufacturing. From a small and obscure flat in Beirut, Dar Al-Handasah expanded to have offices in thirty-seven countries and competed with Western consultancies to win contracts throughout the Middle East. He lived through and experienced some of the most dramatic events of the modern Middle East. From Nigeria, Lebanon, Iraq, and Angola, Shair has helped in rebuilding broken communities by taking active parts in post-civil war reconstruction programs.

BIOGRAPHICAL HIGHLIGHTS

Name: Kamal Shair

Birth: 1930, al-Salt, Jordan

Nationality: Jordanian

Education: 1949: B.S., University of Michigan, 1949; M.S., University of Michigan, 1950; Ph.D., Yale University, 1955

PERSONAL CHRONOLOGY:

- **1956–present:** Founding senior partner and managing director, Dar Al-Handasah Consultants (Shair and Partners)
- **1956–1958:** Assistant professor of engineering, The American University of Beirut
- **1958–1962:** Associate professor of engineering, The American University of Beirut (on leave)
- **1962:** Vice president, Jordan Development Board
- **1962:** Governor of the World Bank on behalf of Jordan
- **1967:** Chairman, Board of Directors, Jordan Phosphate Mines Co.
- **1968:** Recipient of First Order of Independence Medal, Jordan
- **1983:** Awarded National Cedar Medal, Lebanon
- **1985:** Controller of Strategic and Operating Plans, Perkins & Will of Chicago; T.Y. Lin of San Francisco; and Penspen of London, U.K.

- **1986–1992:** Member of the Board of Trustees of Beirut University College, Lebanon
- **1987–present:** Member of the Advisory Council of the department of Near Eastern studies, Princeton University
- **1989–2001:** Member of the Jordan senate
- **1990–present:** Member of the Board of Trustees of The American University of Beirut
- **1993–present:** Head of the Committee for Finance and Economic Affairs
- **1994–1998:** Chairman of the Board of Directors, Palestine Development and Investment Co.
- **1999–present:** Member of the Board of Advisors of the MENA region, World Bank
- **2000–present:** Member of the Board of Advisors of the World Bank
- **2001:** Awarded Lebanese Order of Merit Medal, Lebanon
- Member of American Phi Kappa Phi Society
- Member of Lebanese Order of Engineers and Architects, Beirut
- Member of Engineering Union in Iraq
- Member of Jordanian Syndicate of Engineers
- Member of Arab Thought Forum

PERSONAL HISTORY

Kamal A. Shair (also Sha'ir) was born in 1930 in al-Salt, Jordan. He grew up and went to school in Transjordan under the British rule. After two years at The American University of Beirut (AUB), he proceeded to the University of Michigan, where he earned a BS and an MS in engineering in 1949 and 1950, respectively. He attended Yale University where he earned a Ph.D. in engineering in 1955. He served as an assistant professor (1956-1958) and an associate professor (1958-1962) of engineering at AUB.

Shair's foray into the world of business was in 1956 when he established Dar Al-Handasah, which has expanded from Jordan to Europe, the United States, Africa, and Asia. Dar Al-Handasah, established with U.S.$10,000 is today 4,000 strong and has registered a turnover of U.S.$300 million in 1999. For twelve years

(1989-2001), he served in the Jordan senate. In 2006, Shair published *Out of the Middle East: The Emergence of an Arab Global Business.*

INFLUENCES AND CONTRIBUTIONS

Shair was inspired by the ancient Arab world and his rural upbringing. At Yale University, Shair helped established the Arab Students' Organization and addressed the British Labour Party Conference. In 1962, he was the vice president of the Jordan Development Board and handled the politics of water supply. Between 1968 and 1969, he helped developed a seven-year plan to eliminate Jordan's dependency on foreign aid. But the plan collapsed due to the 1967 War. Billions of dollars flew into Jordan from the oil-rich Arab governments along with U.S.$850 million per year worth of aid for ten years following the Camp David Accords between Egypt and

Israel in 1978. This led to an aid-driven prosperity that culminated in high single-digit growth in the 1970s and mid-1980s. The flow of aid entrenched the dependency mentality and a sense of false prosperity among Jordanians. The economic crisis has persisted with deepening poverty and unemployment among the masses. In December 1999, Shair was appointed as a member of the Economic Consultative Council (EEC) formed by King Abdullah II to monitor the implementation of vital economic, social, educational, and administrative reforms that could lead Jordan into the twenty-first century.

THE WORLD'S PERSPECTIVE

In many parts of the Middle East, Shair has been recognized for his outstanding professional leadership and achievements, excellent public service, and generous support for education. According to a review of Shair's book,

> "By not following the usual pattern of patronage and favours, Shair applied a fresh kind of ethic in an environment with a loosely-structured business ethic.... This is quite an extraordinary tale and a very original prism through which to read the turbulent post-World War II history of the Middle East. At the same time we see the growth, despite all the odds, of one of the world's great engineering and business enterprises in a narrative of epic and inspirational proportions" (*Kisostomus*).

LEGACY

Shair's legacy and generous contributions have been recognized in the field of education and politics. The American University of Beirut's Suliman Olayan School of Business launched the Kamal Shair Strategic Leadership Executive Program, a pioneering program into the world of leadership education in the Middle East. Shair received national honors from Jordan and Lebanon.

BIBLIOGRAPHY

Baharuddin, Zulkafly. "Kamal Shair Predicts Tough Days Ahead, Wishes Jordan Could Eliminate Dependency...," June 15, 2000. Available from http://www.jordanembassyus.org/06152000004.htm.

"Olayan School of Business Launches its Strategic Leadership Executive Program." Available from http://www.aub.edu.lb/news/archive/preview.php.

"Out of the Middle East: The Emergence of an Arab Global Business." *Kisostomus.* Available from http://www.kriso.ee/.

Shair, Kamal. "Engineers and Science Parks." Plenary paper at the American University of Beirut, 2005. Available from http://wwwlb.aub.edu.lb/.

Shair, Kamal. *Out of the Middle East: The Emergence of an Arab Global Business* (London 2006).

Rasheed Olaniyi

SHAJARIAN, MOHAMED REZA
(1940–)

Mohamed Reza Shajarian is an Iranian singer generally acknowledged by critics to be the greatest living male singer in the classical tradition of Persian music. He played a major role in moving the musical policies of the Islamic Republic of Iran in a less hostile direction in the mid-1980s, and regularly gives concerts both inside and outside Iran. He has recorded numerous albums. DVDs of many of his concerts are also available commercially.

PERSONAL HISTORY

Shajarian was born on 23 September 1940, in Mashhad, the capital of the northeastern Iranian province of Khorasan. His personal history illustrates the difficulty of being a musician in a society in which the dominant religion is Twelver Shi'ite Islam.

Twelver Shi'ism and Music Twelver Shi'ism, the religion of most Iranians, frowns on music more than Sunni Islam, as its *ulama* (Islamic clerics) deem the enjoyment of music to be conducive to sinful desires for wine and illicit sex. However, this disapproval did not prevent many Iranians from cultivating a rich musical heritage that reaches back to pre-Islamic times. Before recent changes in interpreting Islamic teachings, twentieth-century musicians had to practice their art discreetly, at court, or in the privacy of their homes. Within Iran's capital, Tehran, attitudes gradually became more liberal beginning with the Constitutional Revolution of 1906, but in many provincial centers hostile attitudes persisted. One such city was Mashhad, the site of Iran's major religious shrine, the mausoleum of Imam Reza, whom Twelver Shi'ites revere as the eighth legitimate successor to the Prophet Muhammad. Mashhad is home to many seminaries, and millions of pilgrims from around the world visit it each year, giving the city an aura of piety in which music cannot thrive in public.

In classical Persian ensembles—typically consisting of a drummer, two or three instrumentalists, and a singer—it is the singer who plays the most important part, the lyrics consisting of the poems of the great medieval Persian poets such as Hafiz, Sa'di, and Jalal al-Din Rumi. The vocal techniques and musical modes used in this tradition are the same as those employed in reciting the Qur'an and in the regular call to prayer (*idhan*). This commonality is one of the factors that has allowed secular music to survive in the face of religious disapproval. Mohamed Reza Shajarian's career is a case in point.

BIOGRAPHICAL HIGHLIGHTS

Name: Mohamed Reza Shajarian

Birth: 1940, Mashhad, Iran

Family: First wife, Farkhondeh Gol-Afshan, divorced; three daughters, Raheleh, Afsaneh, and Mozhgan; one son, Homayun; second wife, Katayun Khonsari; one son, Rayan

Nationality: Iranian

Education: Teacher training college, 1960

PERSONAL CHRONOLOGY:
- **1960:** School teacher in Khorasan province
- **1965:** Moves to Mashhad
- **1967:** Moves to Tehran, becomes employee of National Iranian Radio and Television; begins career as independent musican
- **1977:** Resigns from Iranian national radio
- **1979–1982:** Stops singing publicly because of government opposition
- **1982:** Resumes singing in public, although not at public events
- **1985:** Issues first audiocassette
- **1999:** UNESCO confers upon him the IMC-UNESCO Music Prize

Shajarian's Early Years in Mashhad Shajarian's grandparents on both sides were music lovers. His paternal grandfather was gifted with a beautiful voice and enjoyed singing. By contrast Shajarian's father, a real estate agent, was very pious and frowned on music for religious reasons. Thus he did not allow a radio in the house, as the religious authorities had forbidden owning a radio because music was broadcast over it. But having a good voice too, he cantillated the Qur'an and taught this art to a circle of students, including his son. By the time he was twelve, Mohamed Reza Shajarian was invited to recite the holy book on Radio Khorasan.

After finishing high school in 1958, Shajarian attended a teacher's training college. Upon graduation in 1960 he became an elementary school teacher in a village near Mashhad. Having left the stifling atmosphere of home to live in the college's dormitory, he felt free to pursue classical Persian music, known as the *radif*, helped in this study by the college music teacher. He also learned to read notes and started playing the *santur*, a kind of hammer dulcimer. In the same year he married a fellow student with whom he

was to have four children, three daughters and a son. In 1965 he moved to Mashhad and to Tehran in 1967.

Shajarian's Career in Pre-revolutionary Iran In Tehran Shajarian became an employee of the state radio organization and sang with various ensembles using the *nom d'artiste* (pseudonym) of Siavash Bidkani, but he began using his own name in 1971. He studied the *radif* with various masters, in particular Abdollah Davami, an octogenarian master musician who lived as a recluse and generally did not accept students. Shajarian persuaded him to make an exception for him, in return for which he became the master's personal secretary. Davami taught him, among other things, early-twentieth-century *tasnifs*, composed songs that had played a major political role and that had not been performed in decades. At the radio organization, Shajarian also spent long hours listening to old recording of famous singers of the past to study the subtleties of their art.

The dominant form of classical Persian music played on the radio was a light and superficially modernized genre. To safeguard the classical heritage in its purest form the National Radio and Television Organization established the "Center for Preservation and Propagation of Classical Music" in Tehran in 1967, inviting a number of elderly master musicians to join and transmit their knowledge to a limited number of younger musicians. Shajarian participated in this select group and performed with other musicians at the Shiraz Festival of Art, founded at the initiative of Empress Farah in 1967. These concerts established the presence of classical Persian music in its most traditional form on the serious Iranian concert scene, previously dominated by Western classical music. Gradually Shajarian became a household name among music lovers. In 1977 he resigned his position with Iranian national radio and television agency.

Shajarian in the Islamic Republic Shajarian gave a last concert in the autumn of 1979—after the downfall of the shah's regime in the Iranian Revolution and before the seizure of the U.S. hostages in November. The subsequent fall of the provisional government heralded the ascent of revolutionary hard-liners, who gained total control over the state in the summer of 1981. For the first time in Iranian history, Shi'ite *ulama* were now in control of the country, and state cultural policy henceforth reflected their religious doctrine. Music was banned from the public sphere and for three years Shajarian did not perform. He broke his silence at a private concert at the Italian embassy in 1982, as members of the Revolutionary Guards angrily stood guard outside with weapons in hand. In the first half of the 1980s Shajarian recorded a few audiocassettes but it was in 1985 that one was published. Its title *Bidad* was widely perceived as a punning protest against the puritanical policies of the state: While *Bidad* is a piece in the *radif*, it also means "injustice" and can be interpreted to signify "without (*bi*) voice (*dad*)." This seemed to be a clear reference to the regime's efforts to silence musicians. The publication of the tape gave rise to a heated debate in parliament in which hard-liners demanded that Shajarian, who denied any political intent, be reprimanded. But the taboo was broken. In 1987 Shajarian returned to the international concert scene performing in Europe, and in 1988 he gave his first public concert in Iran.

The clampdown on music had led to unprecedented public interest in classical Persian music on the part of Iranians. Bowing to the inevitable, Ayatollah Ruhollah Khomeini, Iran's head of state and supreme religious leader, issued a *fatwa* (Islamic religious ruling) in 1988 in which he broke with tradition and declared that music was permitted as long as it was of a kind that did not arouse illicit desires. This excluded pop music, whose continued absence from the public sphere provided a boost to the serious music that Shajarian and other classical musicians performed. Since the 1990s Shajarian has performed regularly outside Iran, to the point where he has been criticized for neglecting his fans within Iran. He has admitted that he prefers giving concerts outside Iran, as in Iran each concert is preceded by bureaucratic aggravation.

Shajarian is a multitalented artist. Although he made his mark as a singer, he also plays the santur (although never in public), is a master calligrapher, and builds instruments. His hobbies include canary birds and gardening, and he is widely respected for his knowledge of flower cultivation.

INFLUENCES AND CONTRIBUTIONS

According to Shajarian his parents exerted a major influence on him. His general outlook on life he ascribes to the influence of his father, whereas he credits his mother for having inculcated him with a serious work ethic. Artistically, various master musicians of the preceding generation influenced him greatly—singer Banan, santur player Payvar, and *kamancheh* (spike fiddle) player Ebadi.

Shajarian's decision to remain in Iran after the Islamic Revolution and defy the anti-musical inclinations of the Islamic Republic by continuing to hone his skills and practice his art played a major part in keeping classical Persian music alive. It is thanks to musicians like him that this genre was not only preserved but also actually popularized: By the 1990s more Iranians were playing Iranian instruments than ever before. Thanks to Khomeini's liberalizing *fatwas* of 1988, even young men and women from traditional families joined the trend of a renewed appreciation for Iran's musical heritage.

THE WORLD'S PERSPECTIVE

Since 1974 Shajarian has performed outside of Iran. His tours have taken him not only to Europe and North

---

CONTEMPORARIES

Shajarian's belongs to a generation of musicians who together revived classical Persian music while cautiously introducing innovations into it. These include Hossein Alizadeh (b. 1951), a tar and setar player and composer; Mohammad-Reza Lotfi (b. 1947), a tar player; and Parviz Meshkatian (b. 1955), a santur player who became Shajarian's son-in-law. They started playing together in various ensembles (Aref, Sheyda) before the Iranian Revolution and continue collaborating, both in Iran and abroad.

America, but also to South and Central Asia. Of particular poignancy was a concert he gave at the personal invitation of Tajikistan's minister of culture in 1990 in the capital Dushanbe, a concert that was a major milestone in reestablishing close cultural ties between Tajikistan and Iran made possible by glasnost. In 1999 the secretary general of the United Nations Educational, Scientific, and Cultural Organization (UNESCO) conferred upon Shajarian the IMC-UNESCO Music Prize, given since 1975 to individuals and institutions whose activities have contributed to an enrichment and further development of music and served understanding between peoples.

LEGACY

Shajarian has taught and trained a number of pupils who are now enriching the country's musical scene. With his perfectionism, seriousness of purpose, and sober lifestyle, he completed the work of earlier musicians who endeavored to confer dignity and respectability on musicians, traditionally a low-status group. For the music lover, his legacy consists of his recordings, some containing pieces and modes unheard in decades and that would have been lost forever had he not taken an interest in them.

BIBLIOGRAPHY

DeBano, Wendy. "Introduction: Music and Society in Iran, A Look at the Past and Present Century." *Iranian Studies* 38, no. 3 (September 2005): 367-372.

During, Jean, Zia Mirabdolbaghi, and Dariush Safvat. *The Art of Persian Music*. Washington, DC: Mage Publishers, 1991.

Youssefzadeh, Ameneh. "The Situation of Music in Iran Since the Revolution: the Role of Official Organizations." *British Journal of Ethnomusicology* 9, no. 2 (2000): 35-62.

H. E. Chehabi

SHAMMA, NASEER
(1963–)

Naseer Shamma is a world-renowned Iraqi ud (also oud, an Arabic lute) musician and composer. Known for both his virtuosic technique and expressive lyricism, he is regarded as an innovative composer of Arab music, as well as an expert teacher and composer.

PERSONAL HISTORY

Born in al-Kut, Iraq in 1963 Naseer Shamma (also Nasir) has spoken frequently of his attraction to the ud at a young age, although he was a teenager before he began playing the instrument. He enrolled in the Baghdad Academy of Music, run at the time by famous ud master Jamil Bashir (brother of the even more famous Munir Bashir). Shamma received a Diploma in Musical Arts in 1987.

Shamma served in the Iraqi army during the 1991 Gulf War. In 1993 he decided to leave Iraq to pursue his career. From 1993 to 1998 he taught ud performance at the Higher Institute for Music in Tunis.

Naseer Shamma. AP IMAGES.

In 1998 he was invited to Cairo to realize his dream of establishing an institute specifically to train soloists on the ud. *Bayt al-Ud al-Arabi* (The Arab Ud House), as it was named, started under the auspices of the Cairo Opera House in 1998. Students at this institute receive vigorous and intensive training on the ud, culminating in a diploma certifying each as an "ud soloist." *Bayt al-Ud al-Arabi* moved in 2003 to a fourteenth-century house in Islamic Cairo, and it has continued to grow and to attract students from throughout the Arab world and Europe. The institute since has opened various campuses in other countries, including Jordan, Tunisia, and Spain.

Shamma has been based in Cairo since 1998, and he travels frequently for performances. In 1999 he established the nine-person instrumental ensemble *Uyun* (Eyes). It is based upon the model of the Arab *takht*, a small ensemble typically including one player of each of the Arab instruments (ud, qanun, nay, and percussion). Shamma's group also includes two violins, cello, and a string bass. The group places a high premium on technical dexterity and plays a repertoire largely consisting of Shamma's compositions.

INFLUENCES AND CONTRIBUTIONS

Shamma's technical virtuosity is indicative of his position in the lineage of Iraqi masters of the ud, including Sharif Muhi al-Din Haydar, and Jamil and Munir Bashir. However, Shamma consciously has cultivated a unique approach to composition that departs from Iraqi tradition as represented by the Bashirs. Shamma also emphasizes his admiration for European classical music and draws inspiration for his compositions from this repertoire.

Shamma's compositions tend to be lyrical vignettes with titles that evoke an image or idea. He eschews the structured compositional and rhythmic forms of traditional Arab instrumental music, instead creating musical sketches with multiple contrasting sections and imagistic titles such as "Light of the Soul" and "Amidst the Palm Trees."

Shamma also has researched historical treatises on Arab music theory and bases many of his innovations on historical precedent. He stresses the ancient Mesopotamian origins of the ud. Shamma has developed an instrument—based upon a manuscript by the ninth-century music theorist al-Farabi—that uses extra courses of strings to expand the capacity of the ud. Responding to what critics have called "Western-sounding" harmony in his work, Shamma references the historical basis of this harmony in the work of ninth-century scholar al-Kindi. His explorations into history, philosophy, and music theory, along with his self-conscious association with classicism, have earned him the nickname "the little Ziryab" after the ninth-century musician, composer, scholar, and renaissance man of Cordoba who introduced Persian music to the Western world.

BIOGRAPHICAL HIGHLIGHTS

Name: Naseer Shamma

Birth: 1963, al-Kut, Iraq

Family: Wife, Lina al-Teeby (also al-Tibi), a Syrian poet; one daughter

Nationality: Iraqi

Education: Baghdad Academy of Music, Diploma in Musical Arts, 1987

PERSONAL CHRONOLOGY:

• **1988:** Receives "Best (Performer of) Arabic Music" award at the Jarash Festival (Jordan)

• **1993–1998:** Teaches at Higher Institute of Music, Tunis

• **1996:** Moves to Cairo, Egypt, established *Bayt al-Ud al-Arabi* (The Arab Ud House)

THE WORLD'S PERSPECTIVE

Due in part to his émigré status, Shamma's audience is highly transnational. Throughout the Middle East he is known among connoisseurs of instrumental Arab music as a renowned modern ud player, having earned prizes and awards in Iraq, Jordan, Tunisia, Morocco, and Portugal. He has performed throughout Europe, North America, and Japan, and he has released several compact discs on European recording labels.

Although he advocates the separation of art from politics, the humanitarian consequences of political turmoil have inspired several of Shamma's best-known compositions. Perhaps his most famous work, "It Happened at al-Amiriyya" musically portrays the Allied bombing of an Iraqi shelter during the 1991 Gulf War that killed over 400 Iraqis, most of them children. This work has drawn great praise from audiences throughout the world.

LEGACY

Shamma will be remembered as a fine ud player who has generated a great deal of enthusiasm for the instrument among his students and admirers. Shamma has devoted tremendous effort to developing the ud as a solo rather than as a supporting instrument within the vocally oriented Arab music tradition. Shamma's impact on Arab music and musicians throughout the Middle East has been profound. Greater exposure in other parts of the

world surely will secure his status as a consummate musician and representative of Iraqi artistic culture.

BIBLIOGRAPHY

Colla, Elliott. Review of *Le lute de Baghdad. Middle East Report* 215. Summer 2000. Available from http://www.merip.org/mer/mer215/215_colla.html.

Naseer Shamma's official Web site. Available from http://www.naseershamma.com.

SELECTED DISCOGRAPHY

1994: *Le lute de Baghdad.* [The Baghdad Lute] Paris: *Institut du Monde Arabe*

1996: *Ishraq* [Illuminations]. (Italy)

1999: *Rahil al-Qamr* [The Moon Fades]. (London: Gebhard)

2003: *Maqamat Ziryab* [Modes of Ziryab]. (Madrid: Pneuma)

2005: *Hilal* [Crescent Moon] with Oyoun ensemble. (Madrid: Pneuma)

Anne Elise Thomas

SHAMMA, SARA
(1975–)

Syrian painter Sara Shamma, best known for portraiture, was born in Damascus, Syria, to a Syrian father and Lebanese mother. By nineteen, she was working as a full-time artist and graduated by 1995 from Adham Isma'il Fine Arts Institute in Damascus. In addition, she earned a bachelor of arts degree in painting from the Faculty of Fine Arts at Damascus University in 1998. She also taught from 1997 to 2000 at Adham Isma'il. A member of the Fine Arts Syndicate in Damascus, she actively exhibits in Syria and abroad. Shamma has shown all over the United Kingdom as well as throughout Europe, the Middle East, and Canada, and in 2004 was short-listed for the BP Portrait Award. She has work in private collections around the world, continues producing portrait commissions, and regularly updates a website of work and activities.

PERSONAL HISTORY

Shamma (also Shama) was born in Damascus, Syria on 26 November 1975 to a family steeped in arts appreciation, as her mother was the owner of a private art gallery. By the age of four, Shamma was painting. From 1982 to 1985 she attended children's drawing classes at Adham Isma'il Fine Arts Institute. She graduated from the same institution in 1995. By 1998, she also received a B.A. in painting from the Faculty of Fine Arts at Damascus University, ranking first among her fellow graduates. During her last year in school and for two years afterward, she returned to Adham Isma'il to teach.

BIOGRAPHICAL HIGHLIGHTS

Name: Sara Shamma

Born: 1975, Damascus, Syria

Nationality: Syrian

Education: BA, Adham Isma'il Fine Arts Institute
    and Damascus University Faculty of Fine Arts,
    Damascus, Syria, 1998

PERSONAL CHRONOLOGY:
- **1994:** Begins working as full-time artist
- **1997–2000:** Teaches at Adham Isma'il
- **2004:** Short-listed for the BP Portrait Award

One technique for which Shamma has become renown involves scoring the canvas with a blade-cutter, a signature gesture with which she finalizes numerous paintings. These scarifications dramatically underscore myriad tensions with which her work engages. Her phantasms look back at viewers in a manner not unlike Sumerian temple figurines, representing some of the oldest examples of Western civilization's cultural heritage, on view in Damascus. Equally disconcerting, her surrogate human forms with exaggerated eyes and bodily gestures are designed not just for being seen, but also for looking.

As the votives once veiled by ziggurat temples yet now voyeuristically on view in museums, Shamma's humanist tributes are continually interrupted by such startling tactics as razor-blading the canvas. Each incision exposes unmarked white cotton in stark lines that tangle with the illusionistic surface. In later works, she continues to explore the lie of material transparencies, as when simulating Plexiglas barriers between viewers and protagonists, the latter encased within painted realities whose inscriptions nevertheless mark and render visible the transparent plane.

INFLUENCES AND CONTRIBUTIONS

Although a predominantly Islamic country, Syria has nevertheless served as a site for multiple religions, ethnicities, and dynastic empires, clearly on view at such cultural institutions as the National Museum. Most Syrian artists consciously regard this rich and ancient cultural legacy as personal, whether drawing upon Mesopotamian, African, Greek, Roman, Judeo-Christian, Byzantine, or Islamic roots. For example, Eastern Orthodox icon-painting and Mesopotamian forms of art have come to be regarded as peculiarly Syrian, with deeply embedded forms, abiding

traditions, and ritual practices, often reliant upon portraiture. Sara Shamma's lifelong attempt to particularize human figures builds around these and other regional legacies that include Sufi (Islamic mystic) figure Jalal al-Din Rumi, Sufism, and whirling dervishes, the sources for yet another body of work. Her seemingly traditional formal choices in medium are always wed to radical distortions, instigating viewer reflection on the modernist and perhaps contemporary challenges, whether in painting or sculpture, of seeing, being seen, and becoming self-aware, if not divinely engaged.

THE WORLD'S PERSPECTIVE

From the mid-1990s, Shamma has actively pursued opportunities to exhibit work throughout the world, winning several awards since 1998. Syria's steady and undeniable patronage emerges in not only Damascus, where she was honored in 2004 by the Presidential Palace, but also in Aleppo and Lattakia, where she received top honors at the 2001 Biennale. The considerable support from home has nevertheless been eclipsed by the international recognition she has received abroad, as exemplified by the British reception of her work. In 2004, she was short-listed for the prestigious and competitive BP Portrait Award presented by the National Portrait Gallery (NPG) in London, her work subsequently touring the United Kingdom (Exeter, Bristol, Wales, and Aberdeen). That year, the NPG received nearly a thousand submissions (955) for the painted portraiture exhibition. Exhibiting alongside fifty-three others, Shamma won fourth place.

LEGACY

Given the scant visibility of Syrian artists, much less those of female gender, Sara Shamma's successes online and abroad (especially the United Kingdom) may well break ground for expanded appreciation of her homeland's multifarious roots. Damascus has yet to join international contemporary art biennale ranks but if and when it does, Shamma will have forged paths for future cultural exchange.

BIBLIOGRAPHY

Agha, Alia Ayoud. "Sara Shamma: An Explosive Phenomenon." *What's On Magazine* (July, 2005).

Rizk, Mysoon. "Neutralized Disclosure: Deflecting the Gaze in Contemporary Syrian Art." *N.Paradoxa: International Feminist Art Journal* 14, (July 2004): 34-43.

Sara Shamma's official Web site. Available from www.sarashamma.com.

Shamma, Sara. *The Art of Sara Shamma*. Seattle, WA: CUNE Press, 2007.

Mysoon Rizk

SHAMSOLVAEZIN, MASHALLAH

Mashallah Shamsolvaezin is an Iranian journalist, freedom of press activist, and a former editor-in-chief of several banned reformist newspapers. He also was the editor of the influential monthly journal *Kiyan* and is part of a circle of intellectuals including and centered on the work of Iranian philosopher ABDOLKARIM SOROUSH. Shamsolvaezin's bold activities in pursuit of promoting a free and lively press gained him recognition as an important reformist figure and resulted in his imprisonment in Iran for more than a year.

PERSONAL HISTORY

During the early years of his career in post-Revolution Iran, Shamsolvaezin was a reporter for the conservative *Kayhan* daily newspaper. His work then focused on articles concerning Middle East issues. In the early 1990s before he gained prominence as the persecuted editor-in-chief of several popular dailies, Shamsolvaezin served as the editor of *Kiyan,* an influential monthly journal on philosophy, literature, and religion.

In the wake of the surprise presidential victory of reformist MOHAMMAD KHATAMI in 1997, Iran witnessed a proliferation of dynamic daily newspapers and journals. Shamsolvaezin edited several of the most popular and

BIOGRAPHICAL HIGHLIGHTS

∎

Name: Mashallah Shamsolvaezin

Birth: Iran

Family: Wife, Fariba Abbas-Qolizade

Nationality: Iranian

PERSONAL CHRONOLOGY:

• **1980s:** Reporter for *Kayhan* daily newspaper, Middle East Affairs Editor, *Kayhan* daily newspaper

• **1991-98:** Editor-in-chief of *Kiyan* journal of philosophy, religion, and literature

• **1998-99:** Editor-in-chief of consecutively banned *Jam'eh, Tus, Neshat,* and *Asr-e Azadegan* Dailies

• **2000-2001:** Imprisoned as part of a crackdown on reformist journalists

• **2001:** Press activist, journalist, political analyst

influential of these papers, including *Jame'eh, Tus, Neshat,* and *Asr-e Azadegan.* As conservative factions of the government mobilized the judiciary and its forces toward curtailing the expanding pro-reformist public sphere, both Shamsolvaezin and the publications he edited came under fire.

During the period immediately following the election of Khatami, Shamsolvaezin was the editor-in-chief of *Jame'eh* newspaper. The publication advertised itself as the paper of civil society and played an important role in promoting examinations of topics relating to civil society and liberties. Under the direction of conservatives, the paper had its license suspended in June of 1998, about a year after publishing its first issue. Within a month of being shut down, however, the paper reopened with the same staff under a new name, *Tus.* In August, the judiciary ordered the suspension of *Tus* on the grounds that it had "printed lies" and "disturbed the public order." In response to these charges, *Ansar-e Hezbollah,* a militant group considered a vigilante organization and linked to officially sanctioned militias, physically attacked Shamsolvaezin. *Tus* permanently closed in September 1998 after Shamsolvaezin irked authorities by publishing an article critical of the government's harsh stance toward the Taliban. After the closure of *Tus,* the process of obtaining new publication licenses continued with the paper *Neshat* and the weekly *Asre-Azadegan.*

Mashallah Shamsolvaezin. BEHROUZ MEHRI/AFP/GETTY IMAGES.

In October of 1999, during his tenure as the editor of *Asre-Azadegan*, the Tehran Press Court summoned Shamsolvaezin several times to answer charges related to the banning of his previous paper, *Neshat*. The following month he was detained and sentenced to thirty months on charges of insulting Islamic principles for publishing an article critical of the death penalty in Iran. His imprisonment coincided with that of other well-known reform-oriented journalists including Akbar Ganji, Emadeddin Baqi, Masoud Behnoud, and Ebrahim Nabavi. Shamsolvaezin had served seventeen months of his thirty-month sentence in *Evin* prison before his release in April 2001.

Since his release from prison, Shamsolvaezin has continued to promote press freedoms. He has worked as the vice president and spokesperson for the *Anjoman-e Defa Az Matbooat* (Association for the Defense of the Freedom of Press). In August 2006, he was elected to the managerial board of the Iranian Journalists Union.

INFLUENCES AND CONTRIBUTIONS

Leading Iranian philosopher Abdol-Karim Soroush, a central figure in what has become known as the Iranian religious intellectual movement, strongly influenced Shamsolvaezin's intellectual formation. Shamsolvaezin was editor of *Kiyan* at its inception in 1991, and the journal turned into a key forum for Soroush to explore and rework Islamic concepts. Soroush's ideas and similar discourses as printed in *Kiyan* attracted enthusiastic attention, particularly among women and the younger population. *Kiyan* also published the works of several other important figures, including former revolutionary guard soldier-turned-dissident Akbar Ganji. Letters of protest Ganji wrote when jailed on charges of "disturbing the public order" were printed in the pages of the journal. As a result of his activities with *Kiyan*, Shamsolvaezin gained a reputation as both a producer and disseminator of influential ideas.

Shamsolvaezin's significant role in shaping the nature and direction of public discourses about Iranian society and politics were evident during his tenure with Jam'eh, *Tus*, *Neshat*, and *Asr-e Azadegan*. These papers fostered and contributed to debates on critical issues concerning the nature and structure of the state and the laws on which it is based.

THE WORLD'S PERSPECTIVE

Shamsolvaezin's contributions to Iranian journalism and the development of intellectual and political discourses have not been widely considered outside Iran. However, after his arrest in 1999 for his work as a publisher and an advocate of press freedoms in Iran, he did garner international attention. While in prison, the U.S.-based Committee to Protect Journalists honored Shamsolvaezin with an International Press Freedom Award in 2000.

LEGACY

Shamsolvaezin's contributions to dynamic intellectual and political debates about the nature and basis of the Iranian state and society opened new spaces for tackling the most sensitive and significant issues facing Iran. His influence remains despite the persecution and subsequent closure of his newspapers and journals. While his work at *Kiyan* was instrumental in fostering discourses within Iran's intellectual religious movement, the ultimate impact and legacy of Shamsolvaezin's work to champion press freedoms in Iran remains to be determined.

BIBLIOGRAPHY

Jahanbakhsh, Forough. *Islam, Democracy and Religious Modernism in Iran, 1953-2000: From Bazargan to Soroush.* Leiden, Netherlands: Brill, 2001.

Khiabany, Gholam, and Annabelle Sreberny. "The Iranian Press and the Continuing Struggle Over Civil Society 1998-2000." *International Communication Gazette*, 63(2-3) (2001), 203-223.

Niki Akhavan

SHAPIRA, ANITA
(1940–)

Anita Shapira is an Israeli historian who has pioneered the academic study of the origins and development of the state of Israel.

PERSONAL HISTORY

Anita Shapira was born in Warsaw, Poland, in 1940. In 1946 she went with her family to Paris, and the following year they came to Palestine via illegal immigration. Although not ideologically Zionist, Shapira's family felt a deep psychological need to live among Jews as Holocaust survivors. Shapira grew up in Yad Eliyahu, a lower middle class and ethnically mixed town near Tel Aviv. While attending high school in Tel Aviv, Shapira developed a serious interest in history. After briefly studying sociology and history at the University of Haifa, she enrolled at Tel Aviv University, where she went on to complete her BA, MA and Ph.D. studies.

Although raised speaking Polish, Yiddish, and Russian as well as Hebrew, Shapira considered doing her MA thesis on Chartism, a radical reforming movement in mid-nineteenth-century England. She was fascinated by the clash between human idealism and revolutionary enthusiasm on the one hand, and the political and material constraints on human freedom on the other. Shapira decided to switch her focus to the early years of the Zionist labor movement in Palestine. She wrote her MA thesis on the Labor Brigade—a socialist-Zionist faction of the 1920s whose Bolshevik revolutionary values clashed with the more pragmatic and eclectic views of what would become the Labor Zionist leadership, headed by David Ben-Gurion. She continued to study the struggle between ideology and material forces in her doctoral thesis, making a study of Labor-Zionist attempts to fend off inexpensive Arab labor and promote the growth of a Jewish laboring class in Palestine under the British Mandate. This thesis became her first book, *Ha'Ma'avak ha'Nechzav: Avoda Ivrit, 1929-1939* (The Futile Struggle: The Hebrew Labor Controversy, 1929-1939, 1977).

INFLUENCES AND CONTRIBUTIONS

Shapira is the youngest member of the founding generation of professional historians examining the origins and development of the state of Israel. This generation carried out its research through institutions like Tel Aviv University's Institute for Zionist Research, which Shapira directed for a number of years. Shapira, Yosef Gorny, Israel Kolatt, and other pioneering Israeli historians were closely tied, both personally and professionally, to Labor Zionism. From the 1920s through 1970s Labor Zionism was the hegemonic political and cultural force in the Yishuv and state of Israel, and it retained considerable influence within the Israeli intelligentsia for many years thereafter. Thus Shapira served for many years on the board of directors of the Israeli national trade union's prestigious publishing house Am Oved, and she was the initiator and first director of the Yitzhak Rabin Center for Israel Studies.

Shapira has written or edited some twenty books and has published more than fifty scholarly articles. She entered public prominence with her second book, a biography of the Labor-Zionist thinker and leader Berl Katznelson. In Israel the two-volume book sold 26,000 cloth-bound copies. The book's popularity can be attributed to a number of factors: Katznelson's iconic status in the Zionist labor movement; Shapira's engaging style; and, not least, the book's appearance three years after the venerable Labor Zionist parties had finally gone into eclipse—defeated by Menachem Begin's hawkish Likud in the 1977 elections. Many readers believed Katznelson to have epitomized the humanist and socialist values of Labor Zionism, and so the book served as an eulogy for a bygone era.

In 1992, Shapira published *Herev ha-yonah* (Land and Power), a historical analysis of Zionist concepts of force, from the beginnings of Zionist settlement in Palestine to the eve of the 1948 War. The book, now a standard work, argued for a transition in Zionist sensibility from a "defen-

BIOGRAPHICAL HIGHLIGHTS

■

Name: Anita Shapira

Birth: 1940, Warsaw, Poland

Family: Husband, Shmaryahu Shapira; three children

Nationality: Israeli

Education: BA, MA, and Ph.D., Tel Aviv University (1964, 1968, 1974)

PERSONAL CHRONOLOGY:

• **1947:** Family emigrates illegally to Palestine

• **1977:** Publishes first book, *The Futile Struggle*

• **1984:** Publishes biography of Berl Katznelson; sells 26,000 copies in hardcover

• **1992:** Publishes *Land and Power*

• **1997:** Establishes Yitzhak Rabin Center for Israel Studies and serves as first director

• **2004:** Publishes *Yigal Alon: The Spring of his Life*

sive ethos" of force, emphasizing settlement and labor over military organization, to a more "offensive ethos" that emerged in the 1930s as a reaction to violent Arab opposition to the Zionist enterprise. In this book as in much of her other work, Shapira blended literature and poetry with the more conventional sources of political history. Also typical of her style is this book's emphasis on generational divisions between the immigrant fathers and their native-born sons. The former were steeped in both cosmopolitan and Jewish values, committed to ideology and thus wracked by contradictions between universalistic humanism and romantic nationalism. The latter were tougher, more pragmatic, and open to devising military solutions to political problems. The former was the generation of Berl Katznelson, whose biography Shapira had already written; the latter included the likes of Yigal Alon, a Zionist military commander whose life story is the subject of Shapira's later book, *Yigal Alon: aviv eldo* (Yigal Alon: The Spring of his Life, 2004).

While attracted to the highest circles of power, the subjects of Shapira's books are more likely than not to be failed leaders who fall short of realizing greatness. Katznelson was a man of ideas and Alon a man of action, yet neither was able to rise to the summit of political leadership. Shapira's abiding awareness of the chasm separating human aspiration and achievement may account for a later project, a study of the troubled, brilliant early-twentieth-century Hebrew author Y. H. Brenner.

THE WORLD'S PERSPECTIVE

Much of Shapira's work has been translated into English, French, German, and Russian, yet it is particularly attuned to the Israeli political-cultural context and the rhythms of the Hebrew language. Shapira's nuanced stance toward the Zionist enterprise, portrayed by her with deep sympathy as well as profound understanding of its flaws, is seen by some as overly apologetic—constrained, they argue, by an ideological framework that the "new historians" of the late 1980s and afterward have claimed to transcend. Yet even Shapira's critics acknowledge her intellectual acumen and stylistic grace. Her work is essential for understanding the mental universe of Israel's founders and the political ideologies that dominated the state for many decades.

LEGACY

Anita Shapira's work in her field has opened the doors for successive generations of scholars of Israeli history. In addition to being a prolific author, Shapira has directed multiple major academic institutions devoted to the study of Israel, and has mentored many doctoral students who have gone on to careers teaching Israeli history. She is respected and will be remembered as a pioneer in her field.

BIBLIOGRAPHY

Shapira, Anita. *Berl Katznelson: A Biography of a Socialist Zionist.* Cambridge, UK: Cambridge University Press, 1984.

————. *Land and Power: The Zionist Resort to Force, 1881-1948.* New York: Oxford University Press, 1992.

————. "Historiography and Politics: The Debate of the 'New Historians' in Israel." *History & Memory* 7 (1995): 9-40.

————. "Historiography and Memory: Latrun, 1948." *Jewish Social Studies* 3, no. 1 (October 1996): 20-61.

————. "The Bible and Israeli Identity." *Association for Jewish Studies Review* 28, no. 1 (2004): 11-42.

————. *Yigal Alon: The Spring of his Life. A Biography.* Philadelphia: University of Pennsylvania Press, 2007.

Shapira, Anita, and Jehuda Reinharz, eds. *Essential Papers on Zionism.* New York: New York University Press, 1996.

Derek J. Penslar

SHARAA, FAROUK AL-
(1938–)

Farouk al-Sharaa is a Syrian diplomat and foreign minister.

Farouk al-Sharaa. AP IMAGES.

PERSONAL HISTORY

Al-Sharaa (also Faruq al-Shara) was born in 1938 in Dar'a, in the southern Hawran region of Syria. He received a B.A in English from Damascus University, and then worked for Syrian Air in London beginning in 1968. While there he graduated from the University of London in 1972 with a degree in international law. Back in Syria, al-Sharaa worked as the commercial director for Syrian Air from 1972-1976.

Al-Sharaa then became a Syrian diplomat, serving as Syria's ambassador to Italy from 1976-1980. In 1980, he was chosen to become minister of state for foreign affairs. His rise in the diplomatic establishment was matched with his rise in the bureaucracy of the ruling Ba'th Party, and in 1985 he was promoted to the party's central committee. In March 1984, Syrian President HAFIZ AL-ASAD appointed him foreign minister, a position he held until February 2006. Al-Sharaa was one of the few old guard leftovers from his father's inner circle that Syrian president BASHAR AL-ASAD retained after shakeups in the government and party after he assumed the presidency in 2000. However, Bashar took the foreign ministry portfolio away from him and gave al-Sharaa the mostly ceremonial title of vice president.

BIOGRAPHICAL HIGHLIGHTS

Name: Farouk al-Sharaa

Birth: 1938, Dar'a, Syria

Nationality: Syrian

Education: BA (English), Damascus University; degree in international law from the University of London, 1972

PERSONAL CHRONOLOGY:

- **1968:** Works for Syrian Air in London
- **1972:** Commercial director for Syrian Air in Damascus
- **1976:** Syrian ambassador to Italy
- **1980:** Minister of state for foreign affairs
- **1984:** Foreign minister
- **1985:** Ba'th Party central committee
- **1991:** Represents Syria at Madrid peace conference
- **1999:** Meets Israeli prime minister Ehud Barak
- **2000:** Leads Syrian delegation in Syrian-Israeli talks in Shepherdstown, West Virginia
- **2006:** Syrian vice president

INFLUENCES AND CONTRIBUTIONS

As one of the longest-serving foreign ministers in the world, and certainly in the Middle East, al-Sharaa played an integral role in many of the major diplomatic and political developments that affected Syria in the last quarter of the twentieth century. Certainly four of the major foreign policy challenges Syria faced during that time were its decision to support the American-led military coalition that attacked Iraq during the January-March 1991 Gulf War, the Arab-Israeli peace talks that began with the Madrid peace conference of October 1991, the American invasion of Iraq in March 2003, and the Syrian withdrawal from Lebanon prompted by the February 2005 assassination of former Lebanese prime minister RAFIQ HARIRI.

THE WORLD'S PERSPECTIVE

Al-Sharaa was known as an effective and, in many quarters, tough advocate of the positions of Syrian president Hafiz al-Asad, and largely was seen by the world in his role as Syrian negotiator and spokesperson regarding Arab-Israeli peace talks. One of the first instances where the world became acquainted with al-Sharaa was at the October 1991 Madrid peace conference. During the opening remarks, Israeli prime minister Yitzhak Shamir attacked Syria as being "one of the most tyrannical regimes in the world." Nonplussed, al-Sharaa changed his own opening speech at the minute, and caused a stir when, during his speech, he held up an old British "wanted" poster of Shamir and accused him of having had a hand in the September 1948 assassination of UN peace mediator Folke Bernadotte. Al-Sharaa later carried out direct talks with Israeli prime minister Ehud Barak. The two met in Washington in December 1999, and al-Sharaa later led the Syrian delegation at negotiations in Shepherdstown, West Virginia, outside Washington in January 2000.

Al-Sharaa later appeared prominently in the news after the UN decided to launch an investigation into the assassination of Rafiq Hariri. In his October 2005 report to the UN Security Council, UN investigator Detlev Mehler accused al-Sharaa of lying to the UN. UN investigator Serge Brammertz later interviewed al-Sharaa in April 2006.

LEGACY

Al-Sharaa's role in Syrian government and foreign affairs is not yet over, but he will be remembered as a key member of the regime of Hafiz al-Asad and Syria's main public voice during several decades of important foreign policy challenges Syria faced.

BIBLIOGRAPHY

"Farouk al-Sharaa," BBC Profile (22 September 2003): http://news.bbc.co.uk/2/hi/middle_east/3120630.stm.

Michael R. Fischbach

SHARIF, OMAR
(1932–)

An Egyptian film star, Omar Sharif is the only Arab and Middle Eastern actor to rise to Hollywood superstar status.

PERSONAL HISTORY

Omar (also Umar) Sharif was born Michel Demitri Shalhoub (also Shalhub) on 10 April 1932 in Alexandria, Egypt. His father, Joseph Shalhoub, was a wealthy Egyptian merchant of Lebanese Christian descent. His mother, Claire Shalhoub (née Sa'ada) was of Lebanese and Syrian descent. Michel Shalhoub's secondary schooling was at the prestigious Victoria College in Alexandria, after which he reportedly graduated from Cairo University with a degree in math and physics.

BIOGRAPHICAL HIGHLIGHTS

Name: Omar (Umar) Sharif

Birth: 1932, Alexandria, Egypt

Family: Divorced. Former wife, Fatin Hamama (m. 1955); one son, Tarek (b. 1957)

Nationality: Egyptian

Education: Cairo University

PERSONAL CHRONOLOGY:

- **1953:** Appears in his first film in Egypt, *The Blazing Sun*
- **1955:** Converts to Islam, marries Fatin Hamama
- **1962:** Hollywood debut in *Lawrence of Arabia*
- **1963:** Nominated for an Academy Award for his performance in *Lawrence of Arabia*
- **1968:** Appears in *Funny Girl*
- **2003:** *Mr. Ibrahim*; Golden Lion Lifetime Achievement Award at the Biennale Venice Film Festival

INFLUENCES AND CONTRIBUTIONS

Shalhoub made his Egyptian film debut in *The Blazing Sun* in 1953. Between 1953 and 1958, he appeared in twenty-four Arabic-language films, and became a well-known actor in Egypt—the Hollywood of the Arab world. Although Shalhoub was raised as a Catholic Christian, he converted to Islam and changed his name to Omar Sharif in 1955 in order to marry Fatin Hamama, a Muslim who was one of the leading actresses in Egypt.

Sharif became internationally known outside the Arab world after playing a lead role in the famous 1962 film *Lawrence of Arabia,* a part for which he received an Academy Award nomination for best supporting actor. Sharif has appeared in many English-language films, and starred along with many famous actors, including *Doctor Zhivago* (1965, starring with Julie Christie) and *Funny Girl* (1968, with Barbra Streisand). A big star in the 1960s and 1970s, he made a comeback in the 2003 film *Mr. Ibrahim,* in which he played the role of an old Arab man in Paris who adopts a young Jewish boy.

On the set of his first film, Sharif became bored during the long pauses between his scenes and took up the game of bridge to while away the time. He pursued his interest in contract bridge, becoming one of the

world's leading authorities on the game and authoring several books on the subject.

THE WORLD'S PERSPECTIVE

By the mid-1960s, Omar Sharif had become one of the most recognized film stars in the world, hugely popular both in the Arab world and the West. He won the Golden Lion lifetime achievement award for fifty years in films at the 2003 Biennale Venice Film Festival after the film *Mr. Ibrahim*. He also became famous as a contract bridge player and for his passion for casino gambling.

LEGACY

Sharif will be remembered for many things, including his acting skills and his extensive knowledge and writings about bridge, as well as because he was the first—and as of 2007, only—Arab and indeed Middle Eastern actor to transcend his regional stature as an Egyptian actor and rise to superstar status in Hollywood and in Europe.

BIBLIOGRAPHY

"A Tribute to Omar Sharif: Articles and Interviews 2004." Available from http://omarsharif.netfirms.com/articles2004.htm.

Katz, Ephraim. *The Film Encyclopedia.* New York: Crowell, 1979.

David Waldner
updated by Roxanne Varzi
updated by Michael R. Fischbach

SHARON, ARIEL
(1928–)

Ariel Sharon (Ariel Sheinerman) an Israeli general and politician best known for his harsh measures against Palestinians in Lebanon, the West Bank, and Gaza Strip; his disregard for authority; and his dedication to ensuring future Israeli control of the Occupied Territories through civilian settlement. Sharon spent the first half of his career in the military and the second half as a politician, heading a number of government ministries before serving as Israel's prime minister between 2001 and 2006. During his final years in government service, Sharon's policies underwent dramatic changes that led him to unilaterally withdraw Israeli forces and civilian settlements from the Gaza Strip, arousing genuine surprise in supporters and critics alike. Sharon's career ended in early 2006, when he suffered a debilitating stroke that left him comatose and dependent on life support systems. Without a doubt, Sharon was one of the most prominent and controversial political figures in Israeli history.

Ariel Sharon. AP IMAGES.

BIOGRAPHICAL HIGHLIGHTS

Name: Ariel Sharon (Ariel Sheinerman)

Birth: 27 February 1928, Kfar Malal, Palestine

Family: First wife, Margalit (d. 1962); second wife, Lily (d. 2000); three sons, Gur, Omri, and Gilad

Nationality: Israeli

Education: Primary school and high school in Tel-Aviv; Hebrew University of Jerusalem; British Army's Staff College at Camberley

PERSONAL CHRONOLOGY:

- **1942:** Enlists in the Hagana
- **1948:** Company Commander; Battalion Intelligence Officer, Israel Defense Forces
- **1950:** Commander, Golani Reconnaissance Company
- **1951:** Intelligence Officer, IDF Central Command
- **1952:** Intelligence Officer, IDF Northern Command
- **1953:** Commanding Officer, Unit 101
- **1954:** Commanding Officer, 890th Paratroopers Brigade
- **1956:** Commanding Officer, 202nd Paratroopers Brigade
- **1958:** Commanding Officer, IDF Infantry School
- **1964:** Head of IDF Northern Command Staff
- **1966:** General, Head of IDF Training Department
- **1967:** Commanding Officer, Armored Division
- **1970:** Commanding Officer, Southern Command
- **1973:** Resigns from IDF and establishes Likud; Armored Division Commander
- **1975:** Anti-Terrorism Advisor to the Prime Minister
- **1977:** Minister of Agriculture
- **1981:** Defense Minister
- **1983:** Minister without Portfolio
- **1984:** Minister of Commerce and Industry
- **1996:** Minister of National Infrastructures
- **1999:** Foreign Minister; Likud Chair
- **2001–2006:** Prime Minister
- **2005:** Founder and Chair of the Kadima party

PERSONAL HISTORY

Sharon was born on 27 February 1928 in the Jewish settlement of Kfar Malal in mandatory Palestine. His parents, Shmuel and Deborah Sheinerman, immigrated to Palestine from Russia after World War I, settled in Kfar Malal, and established a family farmstead. Sharon went to Ge'ula High School in Tel Aviv.

Sharon's youth was deeply affected by intense disputes between his parents and other members of his settlement. It also was shaped by his involvement from the young age of fourteen in the Hagana—the semi-legal military organization of the organized Zionist community in Palestine—which worked to defend Kfar Malal from nearby Arab villages. This was the beginning of a thirty-year military career during which he would rise to the rank of major general.

In 1947 he became a member of the British-sponsored police force that served in Jewish settlements. At twenty, he served in the 1948 Arab-Israeli War as a platoon commander in the new Israeli army's Alexandroni Brigade and was badly injured in the battle with the Jordanian army for Latrun. After recovering, Sharon served as a battalion intelligence officer and took part in the battle against Egyptian forces for the Faluja pocket in the northern Negev desert. In 1949 Sharon became a company commander and subsequently took command of the reconnaissance company of the Golani Brigade. In 1951 Sharon was appointed as intelligence officer of the Israel Defense Force (IDF) Central Command, and in 1952 he occupied the same position in the Northern Command. He then took a leave of absence and began BA studies in history and Middle East studies at the Hebrew University of Jerusalem.

In 1953, Sharon was called back to active duty to establish Unit 101, a new commando force aimed at carrying out retaliatory raids in response to Palestinian infiltration attacks across Israel's armistice lines with Jordan and the Egyptian-held Gaza Strip. Unit 101 was known for operations that often involved destroying large numbers of homes and exacting civilian casualties in localities believed to be points of origin for cross-border attacks. Under Sharon's command, Unit 101 carried out a number of operations deemed successful by Israeli military commanders. Although the unit's total number of operations was not high, many believe they instilled important principles of warfare in the IDF as a whole. Chief of General Staff (C.G.S.) Moshe Dayan, however, regarded these operations as a significant threat to the moral fiber of the IDF. In October 1953, a retaliatory attack on the West Bank village of Kibya resulted in sixty-nine local casualties, including many women and children. In January 1954 Unit 101 was dismantled after operating for only four and a half months and integrated into an IDF paratroop battalion under Sharon's command.

In 1956 Sharon was placed in command of the 202nd Paratroopers Brigade, with which he fought against Egyptian forces in the 1956 Arab-Israeli War. His brigade took part in the intense fighting over the Mitla pass near the al-Hitan Valley in Egypt's Sinai Peninsula. Thirty-eight soldiers under his command died in the battle. Sharon was severely criticized on charges that the battle was unnecessary and against orders and that he himself had not led his men into battle. As a result Sharon traveled to Britain to study at the British army's Staff College at Camberley, and his advancement in the Israeli military temporarily halted.

Sharon studied law at the Hebrew University between 1958 and 1962, and he also was appointed as the Commanding Officer of the IDF Infantry School. When Rabin became C.G.S. in 1964, Sharon was appointed head of the Northern Command Staff. Two years later he was appointed head of the IDF Training Department, and in this capacity he was promoted to major general.

Sharon fought in the 1967 War as an armored (tank) division commander, earning widespread distinction for his command in the battle of Abu Agayla against the Egyptian defenses at Umm Katif. This battle is still studied in military schools around the world. After the war, Sharon resumed his position as head of the Training Department, and in this capacity he transferred IDF

training bases to the Israeli-occupied West Bank. In 1970, he was appointed head of the Southern Command, assuming primary command of IDF forces in the last months of the Israeli-Egyptian War of Attrition. He leveled harsh criticism against the policies of C.G.S. Haim Bar-Lev in this context, creating tense relations with his colleagues in the General Staff. Toward the end of the hostilities in August 1970 and throughout 1971, Sharon was charged with destroying remaining pockets of Palestinian terrorism and resistance in the Gaza Strip, which Israel had occupied in 1967. During the same period he expelled the bedouin population from the northern part of the Israeli-occupied Sinai desert, and the C.G.S censured Sharon for this act.

In June 1973 Sharon retired from the military, ending three decades of military service and beginning his long political career. He now set his eyes on winning a Knesset (parliament) seat in the upcoming elections as part of the Liberal Party slate, and he worked between June and October 1973 to establish the coordinated alliance of right-wing factions known as the Likud. With the outbreak of the 1973 War, Sharon returned to active military duty as an armored division commander. True to character, he quickly reached disagreements with his superiors and crossed the Suez Canal against orders—an operation which his supporters viewed as the turning point of the war in Israel's favor.

In the post-war Knesset elections of December 1973, Sharon was elected on the Likud Party slate. Between 1975 and 1976, he served as anti-terrorism advisor to Prime Minister and Labor Party Chairman YITZHAK RABIN. Despite his advisory position, he nonetheless encouraged and provided support for the radical messianic settlers of Gush Emunim in their bids to establish renegade settlements in parts of the West Bank. According to government policy and the policy of Rabin himself, such settlements were not sanctioned. In the 1977 Knesset elections, Sharon established and headed a party slate called Shlomtziyon that won only two seats. After the elections, Sharon merged the short-lived party with Likud, and was appointed minister of agriculture under Likud leader and Prime Minister Menachem Begin. From his position within the government, Sharon spearheaded efforts to expand Jewish settlement throughout the territories occupied in the 1967 War in order to perpetuate Israeli control.

When Ezer Weitzman resigned as defense minister in 1980 amid growing tensions within the Begin government surrounding Israeli policies toward the peace process, Sharon aspired to replace him. Begin, however, refused to offer Sharon the post due to what he regarded as Sharon's anti-democratic tendencies. After the Knesset elections of 1981, however, Begin appointed Sharon as defense minister. In this capacity, Sharon instigated an Israeli invasion of Lebanon premised on destroying militant

Palestinian bases of operation in Lebanon and stopping cross-border attacks. The invasion, officially named "Operation Oranim" and publicly referred to by Israeli authorities as "Operation Peace for the Galilee," began on 6 June 1982.

The real motivation behind the Israeli invasion was Sharon's policy of attempting to seize control of Lebanon. Cooperating with the country's Maronite Christian bloc, Sharon desired to install a government that would sign a peace treaty with Israel. Sharon was involved in every phase of the invasion. According to his critics, he undertook some decisive actions without informing Prime Minister Begin or acquiring government authorization. The operation evolved into the Lebanon War and resulted in a long-term Israeli occupation of southern Lebanon lasting until May 2000, when Prime Minister Ehud Barak withdrew all Israeli forces from the country.

Sharon's wartime involvement in the 1982 massacres of civilians at Sabra and Shatila, two Palestinian refugee camps on the outskirts of Beirut, were widely denounced both within Israel and throughout the international community. In September 1982 after the assassination of Lebanese Maronite Christian president-elect Bashir Gemayyel, Christian Phalange militia forces massacred residents of the two camps as retribution. The Kahan Commission, established by the Israeli government to investigate Israel's role in the incident, found Sharon responsible for ignoring the possibility that Phalange forces might carry out a massacre as retribution, for facilitating their entrance into the camps, and for failing to take precautionary measures. In accordance with the commission's recommendation that Sharon should be prohibited from serving as defense minister, Begin removed Sharon from his post in 1983, but kept him on as minister without portfolio.

Sharon served as minister of industry and commerce in the national unity government established after the 1984 elections, but resigned from this position in 1990 in protest of the government's decision to hold elections in the Occupied Territories. After the government's fall in March 1990, the Likud leader, Prime Minister Yitzhak Shamir, appointed Sharon minister of building and housing. In this capacity Sharon greatly intensified Israeli construction projects in the Occupied Territories. Leading up to the 1992 Knesset elections, Sharon competed for the Likud leadership, but placed third behind Shamir and David Levy. Although Likud's fall from power in 1992 sparked Shamir's resignation as party chief, Sharon refrained from running against Binyamin Netanyahu in the internal elections that followed. When Likud returned to power in 1996, Prime Minister Netanyahu at first excluded Sharon from his government, but for political reasons subsequently established a national infrastructures ministry especially for him. In Netanyahu's government, Sharon was a member of the political-security cabinet and eventually served as foreign minister. When Netanyahu resigned from party leader after Likud's 1999 electoral defeat, Sharon was chosen to lead the party.

As Israeli-Palestinian tensions mounted surrounding the lack of progress toward a final status agreement for the West Bank and Gaza Strip in September 2000, Sharon paid a high profile visit to the Temple Mount (in Arabic, al-Haram al-Sharif). In Jerusalem's Old City, it is the location of the sacred Al-Aqsa mosque and a hotly contested holy site between Muslims and Jews. As Sharon had been warned, his visit had tremendous ramifications—sparking a wave of violent protests among Palestinians in the Occupied Territories and within Israel. Some view Sharon's visit as the opening shot of the al-Aqsa Intifada, the second popular Palestinian uprising against Israel. Other analysts regard Sharon's visit not as the cause of the violence, but rather as simply providing a pretext for Palestinians to renew their inevitable, violent struggle against Israel. In the Knesset elections of February 2001, in the midst of an armed Palestinian rebellion in the Occupied Territories and a wave of Palestinian suicide bombings within Israel, hawkish Sharon easily defeated incumbent Labor prime minister Ehud Barak and quickly established a national unity government.

In March 2002 after a Passover-eve terrorist attack at the Park Hotel in the Israeli coastal city of Netanya, Sharon ordered the IDF to commence "Operation Defensive Shield," aimed at extinguishing the uprising with one swift military blow. In addition to renewing full-scale war against the Palestinians, Sharon also reversed some of the achievements of the Oslo Accords by redeploying Israeli forces in large West Bank towns. Troops conquered Ramallah and placed Arafat's compound under siege. During the conquest of Jenin, the city's Palestinian refugee camp was destroyed, sparking accusations of another massacre similar to Sabra and Shatila. An international commission of inquiry, however, cleared Sharon and the IDF of these charges, but nonetheless concluded that the conquest had been carried out with excessive force. Operation Defensive Shield increased Sharon's popularity in Israel. Among segments of the public, it also revived the negative image that he acquired in the aftermath of Israel's invasion of Lebanon in 1982.

In January 2003 Sharon consolidated his power with a sweeping electoral victory. Eleven months later, three years after the outbreak of the al-Aqsa Intifada and one and a half years after "Operation Defensive Shield," Sharon surprised the Israeli public—particularly the settlement movement—by launching a campaign for unilateral Israeli withdrawal from the Gaza Strip. He subsequently announced that the withdrawal would include evacuation of all Jewish settlements in the Gaza Strip, as well as a number of settlements in the northern West

EXPLORING

In August 2005, Israel unilaterally withdrew all military forces and civilian settlements from the Gaza Strip. This move, termed by Israeli government officials as the "Disengagement Plan," included the evacuation of 8,000 Israeli settlers from eighteen settlements in Gush Katif and a number of isolated settlements in the midst of large Palestinian population centers. Preparation and implementation of the plan presented Israeli society with serious challenges. In the clearest manner since 1967, tensions between Israeli democratic governance and its dedication to the ideological imperative of "The Whole Land of Israel" were placed on the table and put to a practical test. In this context, the critical question was how the Israeli democratic system would function if Israel were to declare sovereignty over the Occupied Territories. In such a situation, it is doubtful that the state would function as a democracy.

Although nationalist-religious settlers tended to see themselves as pioneers of future Israeli sovereignty over the territories, it became clear that most Israelis were fed up with the settlers' arrogant and violent behavior, illegal actions, anti-democratic tactics, and strategies. The determination with which the IDF and the Israeli police force carried out the withdrawal was widely but quietly supported by the Israeli left, center, and moderate right. The Disengagement Plan did not decrease violence between Palestinians and Israeli forces and civilians. This would require Israeli-Palestinian joint actions and not unilateral moves. Nonetheless, Sharon's government established a precedent for the future. Until 2005 Israel's 1982 evacuation of the Yamit settlements, for the sake of Israeli-Egyptian peace, appeared as a single, uncharacteristic episode in Israeli history. After the Israeli disengagement of 2005, however, withdrawal from the Occupied Territories and the evacuation of civilian settlements—in certain circumstances—appear to have become legitimate Israeli policy options.

Bank. Despite many difficulties and a rebellion brewing within his own party, Sharon succeeded in maintaining government stability long enough to execute the plan successfully. The withdrawal, referred to by government sources as "disengagement," resulted in high tensions and deep divisions within Likud, the ruling party, and vocal opposition from the far right. After Labor's resignation from the government in November 2005 and the announcement of new elections, Sharon dropped another political bombshell, announcing his resignation from Likud and his establishment of a new party, Kadima.

One month later, Sharon was hospitalized for a mild stroke and on 4 January 2006, days after returning to his prime minister duties, he suffered a second, debilitating stroke. His duties were transferred to Vice Prime Minister EHUD OLMERT, who was elected prime minister in the March 2006 elections. After one hundred days in a coma, Sharon was classified as permanently incapacitated, marking the official end of his term and his career.

INFLUENCES AND CONTRIBUTIONS

Given the controversial nature of his actions and personality, it is important to emphasize that in many ways Sharon was typical of the middle generation of the pre-state Zionist Jewish community in Palestine. His parents' generation built the Zionist enterprise through settlement, agriculture, education, political and military organization, and work in other realms. The next generation—Sharon's

generation—assumed the task of preserving their parents' enterprise that was under constant existential threat from its perspective. Sharon's youth revolved around this theme.

In contrast to their parents, Sharon and his generation did not understand "defense" in tactical terms. From the Palestinian Arab Revolt of 1936-1939 onward, they abandoned their parents' "defensive ethos" and adopted a new "offensive" one. Their use of the term "defense" reflected a worldview of a Zionist enterprise constantly threatened by its Arab surroundings. Their use of the term "defense" was not just semantic; it reflected their conviction that, even when unleashing the first blow, the Jews in Palestine and subsequently Israel were responding to external attacks and not initiating them.

This worldview shaped Sharon's approach throughout his career as a military officer and politician. For this reason Sharon was a symbolic product of the pre-state and early-state social and political consensus. Sharon's uniqueness stemmed from several factors—his overriding personal ambition and audacity; his ability to proceed on the edge of truth, loyalty and discipline; and his ruthless yet captivating personality.

THE WORLD'S PERSPECTIVE

Sharon's name became well known around the world for his controversial methods of battling Palestinian resistance and ensuring permanent Israeli control of the Occupied Territories. When Sharon was elected prime minister in

THE 'DISENGAGEMENT PLAN' HOLDS MANY ADVANTAGES FOR THE STATE OF ISRAEL

■

I am the only Mapainik in this government. I am not talking here so that I can record my voice in a protocol. Consider it carefully. Because once this is approved, I am going to do it.

DURING AN ISRAELI CABINET MEETING, REGARDING HIS PLAN FOR ISRAELI SETTLEMENT IN THE OCCUPIED TERRITORIES, 1977. QUOTED IN SHARON, ARIEL, AND DAVID CHANOFF. *WARRIOR—THE AUTOBIOGRAPHY OF ARIEL SHARON.* NEW YORK: SIMON AND SCHUSTER, 2001.

These are people who I have known for many years, some of the best we have. They are people who built exemplary settlements. These attacks, this incitement is uncalled for. Ultimately, they will do damage. They will not prevent, through force, the government from implementing its decision. This issue is painful for me as well. But as Prime Minister, I am responsible not only for the feelings of these people, but first and foremost for the success of the people. The 'disengagement plan' holds many advantages for the state of Israel.

ON THE SETTLERS, AFTER A LARGE DEMONSTRATION OF ANTI-DISENGAGEMENT PROTESTERS, SEPTEMBER 2004.

2001, it was the first time he had full responsibility for navigating Israel through the Arab-Israeli conflict.

At first he began negotiating this new challenge in his customary fashion—with tactical skill and no strategy. He conformed to President Bush's vision of a Palestinian state and accepted the American "Road Map," ignoring principles of the scheme that might be unfavorable to Israeli interests. He did this based on his confidence that the Palestinians would never fulfill their part in the deal. In this context, however, Sharon also began considering what steps Israel could take unilaterally to improve its situation without Palestinian consent.

To Sharon, deadlock with the Palestinians was a threat. An agreed-upon solution with the Palestinians was impossible in his eyes because he was convinced that they sought neither compromise nor co-existence but rather justice. And as he understood it, their idea of justice—particularly their insistence on the right of return of Palestinian refugees to their former homes in Israel—was incompatible with the continuing existence

of Israel as a Jewish state. But Sharon was also becoming aware of Israel's waning international legitimacy and the radicalization of parts of the Israeli left, the growing importance of Europe, and the fatigue of once-active sectors within Israeli society. Above all, as a true activist, he was incapable of sitting idly by and watching developments from the sidelines, especially as prime minister. He had to do something to reshape Israel, if not the entire Middle East, as he had tried to do twenty-five years earlier in Lebanon. In this context, he came up with the disengagement plan.

LEGACY

Despite the severe criticism of Sharon's military service, his image as a warrior remains etched in Israeli memory. It was precisely his controversial wartime actions—such as the Israeli reprisal operations of the mid-1950s, the battle for Mitla in 1956, and the crossing of the Suez Canal in 1973—that bolstered his reputation not only among his supporters, but throughout the Israeli public.

Until late 2003, Sharon was best known domestically and internationally for his staunch and effective support for broad Jewish settlement in the Occupied West Bank and Gaza Strip and permanent Israeli control of the Occupied Territories. He regarded both territories as essential for Israel's existence and non-negotiable security imperatives. For Sharon, settlements and settlers were tools for achieving this goal and obstructing future territorial compromise.

Sharon's political alliance with the settlers was upset twice. The first time was when Sharon, as defense minister, implemented the evacuation of Israeli settlements in the Yamit district of the Sinai desert in 1982 as part of an Israeli-Egyptian peace treaty. The second time was the disengagement plan of 2005. Until Gaza disengagement, Sharon was the settlers' most effective, influential, and consistent ally within the Israeli political system. Sharon regarded settlers primarily as "soldiers" fulfilling a mission, and this helps explains his ability to completely abandon them the moment the mission changed both in 1982 and 2005.

As with many prominent Israeli political figures, Sharon's legacy is understood very differently within Israel. Many of Israel's Left remember him as the cruel figure responsible for intensifying the oppression of Palestinians in the West Bank and Gaza, for hoodwinking the Israeli government and Israeli society in an irresponsible war in Lebanon that dragged on for decades, and for building the Israeli settlements that would later constitute one of the greatest obstacles to Israeli-Palestinian peace and long-term stability in the region. Many in Israel's Right remember him as a dedicated and insightful activist and leader who worked to ensure Israeli security and the future of the Jewish state. Sharon's legacy, however, has been complicated by his policy reversals of the last years of his career. Sharon's true intentions for making these policy changes remain shrouded in uncertainty.

BIBLIOGRAPHY

Miller, Anita, Jordan Miller, and Sigalit Zetouni. *Sharon: Israel's Warrior Politician*. Chicago: Academy Chicago Publishers & Olive Publishing, 2002.

Morris, Benny. *Israel's Border Wars, 1949-1956*. Oxford: Clarendon Press, 1997.

Schiff, Ze'ev, and Ehud Ya'ari. *Israel's Lebanon War*. New York: Simon and Schuster, 1984.

Sharon, Ariel, and David Chanoff. *Warrior—The Autobiography of Ariel Sharon*. New York: Simon and Schuster, 2001.

Motti Golani

SHARQAWI, AHMAD
(1934–1967)

Moroccan painter Ahmad Sharqawi is one of the leading figures of modern Moroccan art. His work shadowed the first generation of self-taught, unschooled Moroccan artists whose paintings were typically described as naïve and undisciplined. Sharqawi's artistic upbringing within the French school of art influenced his choice to combine Western artistic concepts, Islamic art, Arabic calligraphy, and Berber symbolism. After independence, Sharqawi, André El Baz, and Mohammed Bellal, among other artists, urged the national agencies to establish museums throughout the country as a means of exposing the general public to modern art. For Sharqawi, art was an expression of national identity and he believed it should reflect its multiple dimensions. His use of Muslim, Arab, Berber, and modern Western tokens reflected his attempt to expose his viewers to the complex Moroccan identity.

PERSONAL HISTORY

Sharqawi (also Ahmed Cherkaoui) was born on 2 October 1934 in Boujad, east of Khouribga, Morocco. Boujad houses the Sufi (Islamic mystic) religious brotherhood of al-Shaykh Sidi Muhammad bin al-Arabi bin al-Ma'ti bin al-Salih al-Sharqawi (d. 1601). Ahmad Sharqawi was a descendant of the Sharqawiyya religious brotherhood that emerged as an influential political player in the seventeenth century by supporting the Alawite Sultan Moulay al-Rashid against the al-Dilaiyya brotherhood. At the end of the eighteenth century, the Sharqawiyya brotherhood of Boujad was one of the most prestigious religious and economic centers of Morocco.

Sharqawi attended the local Qur'anic school of his hometown. His passion for Arabic calligraphy was nurtured at an early stage of his Qur'anic and primary

education. He moved to Casablanca to pursue his secondary education. The loss of his mother at a young age, combined with his inability to adjust to urban life, led to a feeling of loneliness he was able to fulfill with his artistic vocation. In 1956, Sharqawi was admitted to the École des Métiers d'Art, where he earned his diploma in 1959. During this period, Sharqawi was able to master modern artistic techniques while contributing intuitive personal sensibilities to his artistic paintings.

In 1959, Sharqawi was hired by Pathé Marconi in order to draw cover models for musical discs in the Oriental department and carry out preliminary research in the field of painting. He produced a number of paintings that departed from traditional styles in Morocco at the time. Later, Sharqawi shifted his style from figurative compositions of Moroccan sceneries to abstract art. This dramatic shift was propelled by the influence of Paul Klee and Roger Bissière. Klee's combined use of oil paint, watercolor, and ink affected Sharqawi's abstract nonrepresentational style. Bissière's influence on Sharqawi was also important, especially in terms of his use of oil paint. Monique de Gouvenain, the director of Galerie Solstice, encouraged Sharqawi to exhibit his canvas works for the first time at the Ateliers de l'Imprimerie Lucienne Thalheimer.

In 1960, after he attended the École des Beaux Art of Paris and joined Aujame's workshop, Sharqawi's career would forge the way for the modern Moroccan school of abstract art. During that year, he became the first Moroccan to inject Arabic calligraphy and Berber signs into his abstract art. The influence of his Berber cultural origin was reflected through geometric patterns and signs that

BIOGRAPHICAL HIGHLIGHTS

Name: Ahmad Sharqawi (Ahmed Cherkaoui)

Birth: 2 October 1934, Boujad, Morocco

Death: 17 August 1967, Casablanca, Morocco

Nationality: Moroccan

Education: École des Métiers d'Art (Paris); École des Beaux-Arts (Paris); College of Fine Arts (Warsaw)

PERSONAL CHRONOLOGY:

• **1961:** Wins bronze medal, Tenth Interdepartmental Meeting, Paris

• **1962–1967:** Exhibits in Paris, Rabat, Casablanca, Tangiers, Tokyo, and European cities

CONTEMPORARIES

Jilali Gharbaoui (1930–1971) was born in Jorf El Melh (near Sidi Kacem), Morocco. Unlike Ahmad Sharqawi, Gharbaoui did not come from a prestigious family background, as he was born to a humble family. At the age of ten, he lost his parents and was adopted by his uncle. After he finished his secondary education, he attended a school of painting in Fez in 1950, working as a newspaper vendor in order to pay for his evening classes. In 1952, Gharbaoui was awarded a scholarship to study at the École des Beaux-Arts in Paris. In 1957, he joined the Académie Julian. After this French experience, he moved to Rome when he received a fellowship between 1958 and 1959. He returned to Morocco in 1960, settling in Rabat. Gharbaoui's work was influenced by French impressionism, the Dutch school of painting, and German expressionism. In 1952, Gharbaoui became interested in abstract painting and became the first Moroccan artist to use geometric expressions in his compositions. After his return from Europe, he emerged, with Sharqawi, as one of the leading national figures to call for a new interpretation of the traditional forms of expressions. He emphasized the use of light in his painting in order to create an aura of sensitivity in his paintings. Gharbaoui also shared with Sharqawi a feeling of loneliness that was usually reflected in their work. However, unlike Sharqawi, Gharbaoui experienced moments of neuroses which led him to commit suicide on 8 April 1971 in Paris.

as he began to combine both French and Polish teachings into his style. In June 1961, he exhibited a series of paintings at the gallery of Krzwe-Kolo. However, despite the intense artistic training, Sharqawi's style had not yet reached its stage of maturity by his Warsaw experience.

He returned to Morocco in August 1961 and began a phase of internal questioning about his style. As he reflected on some of his earlier paintings bought by the Goethe Institute of Casablanca, he noticed the dominance of signs in his old works. At that point, he decided to conduct fieldwork on Berber tattoos and geometric signs in the Atlas Region to gain a better understanding of them. After this ethnographic journey in Berber areas, he departed from the figurative allusions to Berber signs by allowing himself the freedom to give the signs other meanings within paintings. This break from the reproduction of the sign was complemented by new personal use of light and colors (namely green and red). In October 1961, Sharqawi, along with Gharbaoui and Mohammed Melehi, represented the Moroccan school of abstract art during the second annual meeting of young artists in Paris. Here, he stayed on to prepare another exhibition that was organized at the gallery of Ursula Girardon in Paris in March 1962. After this success, Sharqawi held a number of exhibitions in Morocco and France.

In 1963, Sharqawi spurred artistic discussions after he presented a number of paintings that were dominated by a gloomy background and three colors (blue, red, and green). Sharqawi continued to travel back and forth between Morocco and Paris as his exhibitions reflecting his artistic stature flourished in France. In early 1967, he decided to leave his growing fame in Paris and go back to Morocco to train a new generation of modern artists. His return reflected the beginning of a national consciousness among many artists to introduce new expressions of modern art into the national public sphere. Unfortunately, Sharqawi was not able to achieve his dream, dying from a simple appendicitis complication on 17 August 1967 in Casablanca. He was only thirty-three years old.

copy Berber tattoos. This artistic synthesis of Berber traditional forms, Arabic calligraphic forms, and modern Western artistic styles summarized Sharqawi's personal style which inaugurated, along with Jilali Gharbaoui's work, the school of abstract art in Morocco at the beginning of the 1960s. In order to expose the common Moroccan viewer to this new style, Sharqawi organized his first exhibition in Rabat at the Salon de la jeune Peinture.

In 1961, Sharqawi began living in Warsaw for a year after obtaining a fellowship from the Académie des Beaux-Arts of Warsaw (Poland) to study under the supervision of the painter Stajewski, a leading figure of geometric abstraction in modern art. This Polish avant-garde school significantly influenced Sharqawi's later paintings,

INFLUENCES AND CONTRIBUTIONS

Sharqawi's family background and his Western education influenced his art. His childhood upbringing in one of the most influential religious centers of Morocco left within him an intuitive knowledge of Islamic calligraphic symbols that he encountered during his religious education. These calligraphic signs were replicated throughout his works as he became engrossed in painting. His encounters with European schools of art provided him with an artistic discipline that gave his artistic techniques a personal touch. On a personal level, Sharqawi's relationship with his mother's Berber culture also influenced his works, as Berber signs and symbols were often reflected in his paintings. These forms of stylistic repre-

INCARNATED BEAUTY

When I saw Bissière for the first time, I was so moved that I cried. I felt a terrible shock as I stood in front of his paintings. I have in front of me incarnated beauty.

EL MALEH, E. A., ET AL. *LA PEINTURE DE AHMED CHERKAOUI.* CASABLANCA, MOROCCO: SHOOF, 1976.

sentation were personalized as Sharqawi added emotive feelings and expressions that he reflected through color and light in nonrepresentational forms.

THE WORLD'S PERSPECTIVE

Sharqawi is still acclaimed in Europe as one of the most innovative artists in the history of postindependence Morocco. After his death, his paintings continued to be exhibited in museums in Europe and Morocco. The stature of Sharqawi is celebrated worldwide because of his peculiar ability to understand modern European styles of cubism and abstract art and reinterpret them from his indigenous Moroccan perspectives.

LEGACY

During his short life, Sharqawi organized about thirty-two exhibitions in Rabat, Casablanca, Madrid, Tangiers, Warsaw, Tokyo, Paris, and Algiers. These exhibitions became means to encourage and promote modern abstract art in Morocco. Sharqawi's legacy is a combination of his ability to introduce a new form of artistic expression that veered away from representational art, while managing to institutionalize it on the eve of Moroccan independence. In fact, he played a major role in demanding the creation of modern museums in Rabat and Casablanca. In addition, Sharqawi was able to merge Western techniques of paintings with Moroccan traditional styles without a blind imitation of Western art.

BIBLIOGRAPHY

Boutaleb, Abdeslam. *La peinture naïve au Maroc.* Paris: Les Éditions du Jaguar, 1985.

El Maleh, E. A., et al. *La peinture de Ahmed Cherkaoui.* Casablanca, Morocco: Shoof, 1976.

Flamand, Alain. *Regard sur la peinture contemporaine au Maroc.* Casablanca, Morocco: Société d'Edition et de Diffusion Al-Madariss, 1983.

Menfalout, Salifa. "La creation contemporaine au Maroc l'exemple d'Ahmed Cherkaoui." Ph.D. diss. Université de Paris I (Sorbonne), 1997.

M'Rabet, Khalil. *Peinture et identité: l'expérience marocaine.* Paris: L'Harmattan, 1987.

Sijelmassi, Mohamed. *La peinture marocaine.* Paris: Arthaud, 1972.

———. *L'art contemporain au Maroc.* Paris: ACR Édition, 1989.

Aomar Boum

SHAWA, LAILA
(1940–)

Laila Shawa is a Palestinian artist and illustrator.

PERSONAL HISTORY

Laila Shawa (also Layla Shawwa) was born in 1940 in Gaza City, British-controlled Palestine, to a distinguished Muslim Palestinian family. After graduating from the Cairo Fine Arts School and the Leonardo da Vinci School of Art in Cairo (1957–1958), she traveled to Italy and studied at the Accademia di Belle Arte (1958–1964; BA in fine arts), and the Accademia St. Giaccomo (1960–1964; diploma in plastic and decorative arts). In 1960, 1962, and 1964, she studied at the Oskar Kokoschka School of Seeing in

BIOGRAPHICAL HIGHLIGHTS

Name: Leila Shawa

Birth: 1940, Gaza City, British-controlled Palestine

Nationality: Palestinian; resident in Britain

Education: Cairo Fine Arts School; Leonardo da Vinci School of Art in Cairo (1957–1958); Accademia di Belle Arte (1958–1964; BA in fine arts); Accademia St. Giaccomo (1960–1964; diploma in plastic and decorative arts); Oskar Kokoschka School of Seeing, Salzburg, Austria, 1960, 1962, 1964

PERSONAL CHRONOLOGY:

• **1987:** Moves to London

• **1994:** Her work is exhibited at the Washington Museum of Women in the Arts

• **1995:** Finishes *Walls of Gaza*

• **1997:** Exhibits at the Institut du Monde Arabe, Paris

Salzburg, Austria, with renowned expressionist artist Oskar Kokoschka. She has also worked on United Nations Relief and Works Agency for Palestine Refugees in the Near East (UNRWA) children's art programs in Gaza. She later moved to Beirut, and since 1987 has been based in London.

INFLUENCES AND CONTRIBUTIONS

Shawa is an oil painter, a silk-screen artist, and an illustrator of children's books who has also done sculpture. Her famous silk-screen installation *Walls of Gaza* (1992-1995) exemplifies her ongoing interest in political struggle and oppression, and in children who live with war and deprivation. Her photographs of children and graffiti-laden walls in Gaza are juxtaposed on large panels to make the viewer confront the effects of conflict and violence on generations of children. Other works examine breast cancer as a metaphor for other eruptions and invasions, such as the 1991 Gulf War, and atomic bombs, linking the body with the land—a strategy adopted by other Palestinian artists. Shawa's paintings on a variety of subjects, including the restrictions on Middle Eastern women, are reminiscent of Henri Rousseau in style and color.

THE WORLD'S PERSPECTIVE

Shawa's works have been exhibited throughout the Middle East, Europe, and in the United States, including in 1994 at the Washington Museum of Women in the Arts and the Institut du Monde Arabe in Paris in 1997.

LEGACY

Shawa is still active, but clearly already has made her mark as a significant Palestinian artist of the latter decades of the twentieth century.

BIBLIOGRAPHY

Ali, Wijdan. *Modern Islamic Art: Development and Continuity.* Gainesville: University Press of Florida, 1997.

Lloyd, Fran, ed. *Contemporary Arab Women's Art: Dialogues of the Present.* London: Women's Art Library, 1999.

Shawa, Laila. Available at http://www.lailashawa.com.

Shawa, Laila. *Laila Shawa Works 1964-1996.* Cyprus: MCS Publications, 1997.

Jessica Winegar
updated by Michael R. Fischbach

SHAYKH, HANAN AL-
(1945–)

Hanan al-Shaykh is considered one of the most important Arab women writers at the beginning of the twenty-first century.

BIOGRAPHICAL HIGHLIGHTS

Name: Hanan al-Shaykh

Birth: 1945, Beirut, Lebanon

Family: Married with children

Nationality: Lebanese; resides in London

Education: Graduated from the American Girls College in Cairo, 1966

PERSONAL CHRONOLOGY:

- **1966:** Works as a television and print journalist in Beirut
- **1976:** Leaves Lebanon for Saudi Arabia
- **1980:** Publishes *Hikayat Zahra* (The Story of Zahra)
- **1984:** Moves to London
- **1992:** Publishes *Barid Bayrut* (Beirut Blues)
- **2001:** Publishes *Only in London*

PERSONAL HISTORY

Al-Shaykh was born in 1945 in Beirut, Lebanon, to a family of Shi'ite Muslims. She graduated from the American Girls College in Cairo in 1966. She then worked in Beirut as a journalist in television and for the women's magazine *al-Hasna* and later for the prestigious newspaper *al-Nahar.* She left Lebanon for Saudi Arabia in 1976 because of the Lebanese civil war, and lived in Saudi Arabia until 1982. Eventually she moved to London in 1984, where she resides today.

INFLUENCES AND CONTRIBUTIONS

Al-Shaykh first distinguished herself by writing prose fiction that exposed some of the repressive patriarchal traditions of her society. She did so by introducing characters, often women, who unabashedly explored themselves, their families, and their communities. She faced brief periods of censorship and occasional negative reviews. Although some of her fiction is set in the broader Arab world, two of her most prominent novels are situated in Lebanon during the Civil War of 1975 through 1990. Al-Shaykh has become an important voice in critical studies of the war itself. The renowned *Hikayat Zahra* (The Story of Zahra, 1980) is a relentless psychosexual drama that manages, primarily through its complex protagonist, to narrate an insane society in violent civil disarray. Al-Shaykh's stark imagery and gripping plot mesmerized readers. Her follow-up novel, *Barid Bayrut* (Beirut Blues, 1992), structured as a series of letters by another memorable female protagonist, extends the depiction of the Lebanese wars and fortifies the ideology of nonpartisanship, as every militia, army, confessional (religious/ethnic), and national group is subject to critique and to ridicule. Al-Shaykh's focus is on nuanced reactions, complex relationships, and multiple points of view. Her war novels offered new ways of imagining Lebanon in this destructive era.

Since living in London, al-Shaykh has participated in local productions of her experimental plays. One of her publications, *Only in London* (2001), explores some of the issues of Arab émigrés in Europe.

THE WORLD'S PERSPECTIVE

With a keen sense of humor and a fresh Arabic writing style, al-Shaykh's works have extended the possibilities for Arab women writers. Because of good translations into English and other languages, Al-Shaykh's readership is growing outside the Arab world, where she is regarded as one of the major Arab writers of the second half of the twentieth century.

LEGACY

Al-Shaykh is still writing, but it is clear that history will record her as one of the most important Arab novelists of the last few decades of the twentieth century.

BIBLIOGRAPHY

Cooke, Miriam. *War's Other Voices: Women Writers on the Lebanese Civil War.* Cambridge, U.K.: Cambridge University Press, 1988.

"Previously Featured: Life of a Woman." Lebanese Women's Association: http://www.lebwa.org/life/shaykh.php.

Salem, Elise. *Constructing Lebanon: A Century of Literary Narratives.* Gainesville: University Press of Florida, 2003.

Zeidan, Joseph. *Arab Women Novelists: The Formative Years and Beyond.* New York: New York University Press, 1995.

Elise Salem
updated by Michael R. Fischbach

SHEHADEH, RAJA
(1951–)

A Palestinian lawyer, Raja Shehadeh is also an author. Raja Shehadeh was born on 6 July 1951 in Ramallah, Palestine, into a family of sharp intellect with a strong and a long established tradition in the practice of law. His father, Aziz, began his legal practice in the city of Jaffa in 1935 when Palestine had not been partitioned yet. The 1948 War forced Shehadeh to leave his home in

Raja Shehadeh. DAVID RUBINGER/TIME LIFE PICTURES/GETTY IMAGES.

Jaffa on the Mediterranean coast and retreat with his family, similar to scores of other Palestinian families, to a summer house in the West Bank hills of Ramallah. Because Israel had gained control of Jaffa along with many other coastal cities, they had no access to their home and could not return, so the temporary home in Ramallah became permanent in the aftermath of the 1948 War, and the family became refugees along with approximately 750,000 other Palestinians.

PERSONAL HISTORY

As a youngster, Raja Aziz Shehadeh (also Shihada) attended the Quaker school in Ramallah and later graduated from The American University of Beirut in 1973 with a BA in literature and philosophy. In 1976 he was called to English Bar and became a member of the Lincoln's Inn. Since 1978 he has been in private practice in Ramallah and also began writing. Today, he practices law along with his cousins and Fouad Shehadeh, his uncle. Together, they have one of the most prestigious law practices in Palestine. Shehadeh and his uncle have over the years made significant contributions to shaping the legal profession and system in Palestine. At the same time, Shehadeh fell naturally into a writing career; he is

BIOGRAPHICAL HIGHLIGHTS

Name: Raja Shehadeh

Birth: 6 July 1951, Ramallah, West Bank

Family: Wife: Penny Johnson; no children

Nationality: Palestinian

Education: American University of Beirut, 1973, graduated with honors in literature and philosophy, called to the English Bar as member of Lincoln's Inn, 1976

PERSONAL CHRONOLOGY:

- **1978:** Joins Shehadeh law firm, becomes senior partner in 1985
- **1979–1991:** Founds and co-directs Al Haq, the West Bank affiliate of the International Commission of Jurists
- **1979–1995:** Lectures extensively and attends many international conferences on the legal and human rights aspects of the Israeli-Palestinian conflict
- **1983:** Receives the Issam Sartwai Peace Prize
- **1986:** Receives the Rothko Chapel Award for Commitment to Truth and Freedom, presented by President Jimmy Carter
- **1991–1992:** Acts as legal advisor to the Palestinian Delegation to the Israeli-Palestinian peace talks in Washington D.C.
- **1995:** Full-time writer and legal consultant

the author of several books and anthologies about human rights, the Israeli occupation of Palestine, Palestine's status under international law, the Palestinian-Israeli peace accords, and the Middle East. He has also published his personal diaries and a memoir.

Following his return to Ramallah from England as a promising barrister with great vision, Shehadeh established *Al Haq* (Law in the Service of Man) in 1979, a non-partisan, West Bank-affiliate of the Geneva-based International Commission of Jurists which he co-directed until 1991. *Al Haq* was one of the first politically independent Palestinian human rights organizations and became an important group under his strong leadership. He led *Al Haq* into producing a solid number of reference books and publications on the Israeli occupation

and the ensuing violations of international law. It gained repute as a powerful and credible research center, and a cogent critic of Israeli legal and military practices and abuses in the West Bank. After leaving *Al Haq*, Shehadeh served as an advisor to the Palestinian peace negotiating team in Washington, D.C., from November 1991 to September 1992. He is a member of the International Advisory Council of the Netherlands Institute of Human Rights and of the Human Rights Advisory Group of the Commission of the Churches on International Affairs of the World Council of Churches, Geneva.

INFLUENCES AND CONTRIBUTIONS

Shehadeh's early years were colored by the tragic impact of the 1948 and 1967 wars that led, respectively, to the partition of Palestine and the subsequent Israeli occupation of the West Bank, East Jerusalem, and Gaza. These were difficult periods for Arabs in general and Palestinians in particular; he found himself growing up in the midst of a wounded Palestinian population existing within a complex web of politics, conspiracies, and a quagmire of tragedies and externalities—the story of every Palestinian.

In 1985, Shehadeh experienced a great loss with the murder of his father that occurred as Raja was on a speaking tour abroad. Some accounts record this as a politically motivated crime. However, Shehadeh's own account is rooted in a conviction that his father's murder was unrelated to the politics of the time. He made every attempt conceivable to find out the truth and even anointed himself a criminal prosecutor where he probed the murder. He challenged the Israeli police and pushed them to engage more effectively in the investigation. The murderers remained at large and the file was never closed. Shehadeh's relationship with his father and subsequent murder occupied a large part of his psyche and eventually culminated in the writing of a personal memoir titled: *Strangers in the House: Coming of Age in Occupied Palestine*.

Before his father's murder, Shehadeh had the opportunity to work as a lawyer in Ramallah. Israelis occupied the city, so his introduction to the practice of law was under challenging circumstances, especially because Israel ruled the Occupied Territories with a strong hand, issuing military orders that were never published. These orders affected every facet of Palestinians' lives and dealt a strong blow to their ownership of land and property, impacted their water rights, and denied their right to reside and return to their homes in the Occupied Territories. Under his father's tutelage, Shehadeh began to survey and catalog every military occupation law and order in the West Bank. He noted the meticulous way in which Israeli military lawyers had canceled, amended, and supplemented all existing West Bank laws as they saw fit. He also understood how, under the Fourth Geneva Convention, those moves contravened international law.

CONTEMPORARIES

Raji Sourani (1953–) was elected to the International Commission of Jurists (ICJ) in April 2003 and to ICJ's executive committee in April 2006. Sourani is an international board member of the International Federation of Human Rights and an expert member of the International Council of the International Human Rights Law Group. He has received numerous awards for his work, including the Bruno Kreisky Prize for Human Rights in 2002, a human rights prize awarded by the Republic of France in 1996, and a joint laureate of the Robert F. Kennedy Memorial for Human Rights Award in 1991. Sourani studied law at Beirut and Alexandria Universities.

The legal practice of Anis Fawzi Kassim (also Qasim) (1939–) has crossed much of the Arab world. He has an LL.M. degree from George Washington University in Washington, and worked in Kuwait for fifteen years prior moving to Amman in 1993. Operating out of Amman, Anis Kassim is an internationally recognized authority on Palestinian law and issues. He founded and is the editor in chief of the *Palestinian Yearbook of International Law,* has advised the Palestinian Authority on numerous matters relating to new legislation, and was in charge of training the Palestinian Authority's legal department from 1998 to 1999.

However, this was during a period most Palestinian lawyers refused to engage with the occupation and so no one was protesting. Shehadeh's father, by contrast, did protest. He was able to recognize that he could use the Israeli legal system and court to speak out against the occupation. Other Palestinian lawyers chose to boycott the Israeli legal system and went on a long strike from 1967 until 1994, when the Palestinian Authority (PA) was established and along with it came a Palestinian judiciary. Shehadeh's father paid dearly for seeing differently and for working within the Israeli legal system itself by defending Palestinians against land seizures and arbitrary treatment at the hands of the military. For his efforts, his own union disbarred him for life. Shehadeh felt torn at this injustice against both his father and the Israeli violations. His contribution to make amends was the establishment of *Al Haq*.

THE WORLD'S PERSPECTIVE

At this juncture in Palestinian political history and as a consequence of the occupation, Shehadeh became a leader in developing legal means to assert Palestinian rights. He utilized his legal skills and writing abilities as a tool directed against the occupation. His first public legal study was an examination of the impact of unpublished Israeli military orders on Palestinian rights, especially with respect to land and property. These articles and legal studies appeared in *The New York Times, Harper's,* the *Review of International Commission of Jurists, Journal of Palestine Studies,* and *Middle East International.* As a result he earned international recognition for trying to stop the disintegration of Palestinian law and its legal system, and also was recognized for his human rights work. The hardships of the occupation continued to play a major factor in his early to mid-career. His first book of diaries covered the 1980s. During this period, he was fascinated by the notion of *sumud*—perseverance. Palestinians persevered and the 1967 War made them more determined to stay on the land and never repeat the mistake of 1948—where they took refuge elsewhere, thinking that they could return home when the war was over—only to face the refugee problem that now lies at the core of the conflict between Palestinians and Israelis. Shehadeh saw Palestinian determination not to leave their homes and land as the best antidote to Israeli policies aimed at ridding the country of its Palestinian inhabitants. Sumud was the way he felt he was challenging the Israeli occupier. He also became involved in human rights work and believed that, by documenting and exposing the Israeli government's violations of human rights, he would help bring an end to them. In later years, he turned to narrating the history of Palestine and the Palestinian tragedy as a whole through his own personal story.

Another factor that compelled Shehadeh's writing was the eyewitness accounts of how, soon after Israel occupied the Palestinian Territories, Israel began to confiscate large areas of Palestinian land to build Jewish settlements. This led him to write his seminal book *Occupier's Law* in 1988. Since then Israeli governments of both the left and right have gone on building these settlements and the number of settlers has doubled since 1993 when the first peace accord was signed between the Palestine Liberation Organization and Israel—the Declaration of Principles. Slowly, he saw how this country was no longer his. He always commented with deep disappointment how everybody who was able to was leaving Palestine for other countries. He often pondered that maybe this was another purpose behind the Israeli settlements.

LEGACY

As peace initiatives commenced between Palestinians and Israelis, Shehadeh was initially a supporter of the talks that took place in Madrid and Washington in the early 1990s, and he worked on the Palestinian negotiating team as a legal adviser. He left after a year, recognizing that the talks stood no chance of establishing a meaningful peace.

Upon reading the Oslo Accords, in which the Israeli settlements in Gaza and the West Bank remained in place, he became despondent and for a while gave up his human rights work. The course of negotiations left the issues of the settlements, among other issues such as Jerusalem refugees and international borders, to final status determinations. He felt that the Palestinian leadership had abandoned many of the issues on which he had worked for years in their attempt to strike a deal with the Zionist state.

In 1997, Shehadeh wrote a book titled *From Occupation to Interim Accords: Israel and the Palestinian Territories*. In this book he analyzed the overall context for the negotiations process. The late Edward Said wrote the foreword and noted that Shehadeh was the only one to point out how the negotiations were conducted in a manner that allowed Israel to consolidate its legal, strategic, and political hold over the Palestinian territories. Said noted that Shehadeh understood Israel's negotiating strategy that caught the Palestinian leadership unaware and led to an irreversible situation.

In 1991, Shehadeh published *The Sealed Room*, a diary that contains many vivid accounts of what Israeli soldiers did in the West Bank, such as the shooting of a journalist by an Israeli sniper for reporting the Israeli army's atrocities; Palestinian homes bulldozed with their inhabitants still inside; and family homes invaded by rampaging Israeli soldiers.

Yet, Shehadeh has always been a longtime advocate of peace between the Palestinians and Israelis, and for having a state of Palestine in the West Bank and Gaza. He often expressed his support for a two-state solution and believed that the Palestinians and Israelis could have learned to coexist in two separate states side by side. However, he understood and expressed in writing that a Palestinian state that is impoverished, unviable, and without borders or access to markets will have no chance to survive.

Shehadeh went back again, in 2002, to chronicling the pains and experiences he saw around him in another diary titled *When the Bulbul Stopped Singing*. It is the diary of Ramallah during the Israeli military re-occupation of the city in 2002 following the eruption of the second Palestinian Intifada. Shehadeh's account offered more than a simple description of a litany of tragic events. The diary sought to explore why things have come to such a point and analyzed the motives of the Israelis and the shortcomings of the failing strategies of the Palestinian leaderships. The reader is able to gain a sense of what it must have been like to live under foreign occupation, with its murderous and dehumanizing consequences. He

captured Palestinians' human endurance and relied on black humor to communicate his message.

He also described his anger at the Palestinian Authority (PA) for allowing Palestinian civilians, officials, police, and militia to be killed as it continued to pursue failed methods. He pointed out that the leaders never appealed to the existing huge international support and sympathy for the Palestinians. The diary also states that no effort was made to appeal to the antigovernment sentiments in Israel itself, despite the expansionist colonialist policy of the government causing suffering to Israelis and to Palestinians. The diary was recently adapted for stage and premiered at the Traverse Theatre during the Edinburgh Fringe Festival. David Greig, the book's adapter, did not alter the original text—he only edited it into monologues for the solo protagonist. Greig, who has written a number of plays for theatre and radio, stated in the program notes that he wanted to present Shehadeh's story because it "cut through the forest of newsprint" about the conflict in Palestine. He felt that the diary offered a richer, more complex view than that of "the stone throwing rioter, the bereaved mother, the angry crowd, the martyr, the terrorist"—the usual media images of the Palestinians.

In his memoir *Strangers in the House: Coming of Age in Occupied Palestine*, Shehadeh writes about the conflict between father and son. The memoir is suffused with the tumultuous politics of the Middle East and the Palestinian issue forms much of the fabric of the relationships that Shehadeh describes. This contributes to the multiple meanings of the title, which echoes his feelings about his family as well as the situation in Palestine in general. *Strangers in the House* is personal and political. The personal relationship is a photo developer for a portrait of the Palestinian tragedy as a whole. It is filled with metaphors for what was wrong with Palestinian political culture. Instead of picking themselves up and rebuilding after 1948, instead of analyzing their defeat and understanding their adversaries, they have spent the decades whining and pining, composing poetry to a lost world, believing that a rejection of compromise was evidence of virtue and wisdom.

"All that remained was a shadow life," Shehadeh writes, "'a life of dreams and anticipation and memory.'" His memoir derives its power from his willingness, rare among Palestinian writers, to probe the emotional and political limits of his own society. The story of Shehadeh's father and himself, the son, is a rare tale of principle, conviction, and kindness operating in harsh circumstances. But it is also an exceptionally sad one, as Shehadeh shows how his efforts and the efforts of his father had minimal impact—the Israeli military walked all over them, ransacked their offices, threatened their staff, and repeatedly delayed their court dates. Meanwhile, his father was ignored and condemned by the Palestinians.

BIBLIOGRAPHY

Mahdi, Abdul Hadi, ed. *Palestinian Personalities—A Biographic Dictionary.* Jerusalem: Palestinian Academic Society for the Study of International Affairs, Jerusalem, 2006

Hiba Husseini

SHENOUDA III
(1923–)

Shenouda III is the patriarch of the Coptic Orthodox Church in Egypt

PERSONAL HISTORY

Few Coptic patriarchs have had as much experience in both secular and ecclesiastical affairs prior to their election as Shenouda III. Born Nazir Jayyid (in Egyptian Arabic dialect, Gayyid) near Asyut, Egypt, on 3 August 1923, he graduated from Cairo University with a BA in history in 1947 and fought with the Egyptian army in the 1948 War. He earned a bachelor of divinity degree in 1950 from the Coptic Orthodox Theological Seminary, and became a leader in the lay-dominated Sunday School movement, editing its monthly magazine. He took holy orders and became a monk in 1954 at the Syrian Monastery in Wadi Latrun, Egypt. Taking the name Father Antonios the Syrian, from 1956 to 1962 he lived an ascetic life in seclusion in a cave several miles from the monastery.

Within the church, he was a secretary to Cyril VI, and a bishop. Jayyid also was a professor of Old Testament studies at the Coptic Seminary, the editor of its journal, and dean beginning in 1962, whereupon he took the name Shenouda. Elected patriarch in 1971 as Shenouda III, he is the highest-ranking cleric of the Coptic Orthodox Church, the Middle East's largest Christian denomination. His formal title is Pope of Alexandria and the Patriarch of All Africa on the Holy Apostolic See of Saint Mark the Evangelist. He has traveled frequently to North America, Europe, and Australia in order to maintain contact with expatriate Copts worldwide.

INFLUENCES AND CONTRIBUTIONS

Shenouda was among the more than 1,500 Egyptians who were accused by President Anwar al Sadat in September 1981 of extremist religious activity. Exiled and replaced by a council of five bishops, Shenouda fled to the desert monastery of Anba Bishoi in Wadi Natrun, northwest of Cairo. The reasons for his arrest and exile were unclear. Although religious turmoil had increased in the late 1970s and early 1980s (mainly instigated by Muslims opposed to Sadat's peace treaty with Israel),

---

BIOGRAPHICAL HIGHLIGHTS

Name: Shenouda III (born Nazir Jayyid)

Birth: 3 August 1923, near Asyut, Egypt

Nationality: Egyptian

Education: Cairo University, 1947, BA in history, the Coptic Orthodox Theological Seminary, 1950, bachelor of divinity

PERSONAL CHRONOLOGY:

- **1954:** Becomes a monk at the Syrian Monastery in Wadi Latrun, Egypt; changes name to Father Antonios the Syrian

- **1956:** Begins six years of living in isolation in a cave several miles from the monastery

- **1962:** Begins teaching at the Coptic Seminary; becomes known as Shenouda

- **1967:** Writes *al-Khalas fi'l-Mafhum al-Urthuduksi* (Salvation in Orthodox Understanding)

- **1971:** Becomes Coptic Patriarch Shenouda III

- **1973:** Meets Roman Catholic pope Paul VI, the first time a Coptic pope met with a Roman Catholic pope in 1,500 years

- **1981:** Arrested, exiled by Egyptian government

- **1985:** Allowed to return from exile

- **2000:** Receives UNESCO's Madanjeet Singh Prize for the Promotion of Tolerance and Nonviolence

---

the president's charges, including those against Shenouda, could not be proven. Some Copts and Muslims punished by Sadat were active in religious professions and thus superficially gave credence to his allegations, but others had secular occupations—lawyers, writers, journalists, broadcasters, politicians—and appear to have been guilty only of disagreeing with the president.

Sadat's actions may have been a delayed response to Shenouda's September 1977 protest against the proposed imposition of Islamic law (*shari'a*) in Egypt. The proposal would have made apostasy—in this case, conversion from Islam—a capital offense. Shenouda had feared that the law would discriminate against Egyptian Christians and other non-Muslims. He succeeded temporarily, for Sadat's recommendation was withdrawn, only to be reintroduced in 1980. Because armed Muslim militants then unleashed a

CONTEMPORARIES

Michel Sabbah (1933–) was born to a Palestinian Roman Catholic Christian family in Nazareth, British-controlled Palestine. He began his studies for the priesthood at the Latin Patriarchal Seminary in Bayt Jala in 1949, and in 1955 was ordained a priest in the Latin Patriarchate of Jerusalem. In 1987, Pope John Paul II chose Sabbah to become the Latin Patriarch of Jerusalem, the first time that a Palestinian Arab has held the post, making him the highest-ranking Roman Catholic church official in Israel and the Palestinian territories. In 1999, Sabbah served as international president of the Catholic peace organization Pax Christi.

Mar Dinkha IV is the current Catholicos-Patriarch of the Assyrian Church of the East. Born on 15 September 1935 in Darbandokeh, northern Iraq, he was given the name Khananya upon baptism. He became a priest in the Assyrian Church of the East in 1957 and assigned to a church in Iran. He was elevated to bishop in 1968, and in 1976, was selected to head the entire church—which includes congregations in Iran, Iraq, Iran, and elsewhere in the world—under the honorific title Mar Dinkha IV. He resides in Chicago, Illinois.

Ignatius Zaka II is the current Syriac Orthodox (also known as the Syrian Orthodox) Patriarch of Antioch. Born on 21 April 1932 in Mosul, Iraq, as Sanharib Iwas, he became a monk in the Syriac Orthodox church in 1954 and a priest in 1957. In 1980, he became the patriarch of the church. He is based in Damascus, Syria.

Emmanuel III Delly is Patriarch of Babylon for the Chaldeans, and thus head of the Chaldean Catholic church. The Chaldean church has been part of the worldwide Catholic communion headed by the pope in Rome since 1830. He was born on 6 October 1927 in Tel Keppe, northern Iraq. He became a priest in 1952 and a bishop in 1962. In 2003, after the United States invasion of Iraq, he became the patriarch.

Aram I (1947–) is Catholicos of Cilicia for the Armenian Orthodox Apostolic Church's Holy See of Cilicia. Based in Antilias, Lebanon, he oversees Armenian Orthodox churches in the Middle East. Born Pedros Keshishian in Beirut, Lebanon, in 1947, he was ordained a priest in 1968, and a bishop in 1980. From 1980-1995, he served as Bishop of Beirut for the Armenian Orthodox Apostolic Church, after which he was elevated to Catholicos of Cilicia with the name Aram I. He also has held leadership positions in the Middle East Council of Churches and the World Council of Churches.

Torkom Manoogian is Patriarch of Jerusalem of the Armenian Orthodox Apostolic Church. Born 16 February 1919 in an Armenian refugee camp near Ba'quba, Iraq, he became a priest in 1939. In 1990, he was chosen as the Armenian church's Patriarch of Jerusalem, and is partially responsible (along with other churches like the Roman Catholic Church) for the Christian holy sites in Jerusalem.

Born Ilias Giannopoulos in Messinia, Greece, Theophilus III (1952–) is the Patriarch of Jerusalem and head of the Orthodox Church of Jerusalem. He formerly was a priest in the Galilee region of Israel, and later Archbishop of Tabor. He was made patriarch in 2005. Although, as has traditionally been the case, he is Greek, his congregants are Palestinian Christians. Theophilus III is custodian (sometimes jointly with other churches like the Roman Catholic Church) of major Christian holy sites in Jerusalem.

Given the name Hazim at birth in 1921 in Mharday, Syria, Ignatius IV is the Patriarch of Antioch of the Eastern Orthodox Church, and responsible for Orthodox Christians in much of the Middle East. He became patriarch of Antioch in 1979, and along with the patriarchs of Constantinople and Alexandria, is one of the three most important clerics in the Eastern Orthodox Church.

murderous round of terror against the Copts, Shenouda ordered a series of demonstrations that enraged many Muslims and caused them to accuse the patriarch of engaging in politics. Sadat turned down Shenouda's repeated requests for a meeting, and so in 1981 the patriarch refused to accept the government's Easter greeting, humiliating Sadat, who may have taken revenge by the September arrest. Some Copts believed that Shenouda's

dismissal was a political move to balance Sadat's incarceration of many Muslims. Another possible explanation is that, during a 1980 meeting between Sadat and U.S. president Ronald Reagan in Washington, D.C., a group of Coptic expatriates staged a protest, which Sadat wrongly blamed on Shenouda.

The censure of Shenouda for sectarian sedition was both ironic and unfortunate. Although he had vigorously defended the Coptic Church and struck back against Muslim fundamentalists, he has never been antagonistic toward Islam per se. Throughout his career, Shenouda has been sympathetic to Muslim causes and to Egyptian national interests. Some of his theological writings, particularly his major 1967 work *al-Khalas fi'l-Mafhum al-Urthuduksi* (*Salvation in Orthodox Understanding*), are as critical of aspects of Protestantism as of Islamic fundamentalism. Shenouda has specifically denounced the intrusion of religion as a divisive force in political affairs. One result of his historic meeting with the Roman Catholic pope Paul VI in May 1973 (the first visit by an Egyptian pope to his Roman counterpart since 325 C.E.) was a joint statement of concern about the Palestinian problem. In May 1986 Shenouda sent a representative to the funeral of a leader of the Muslim Brotherhood.

After Sadat's assassination in October 1981, Shenouda's plight improved slowly. However, in 1983 an administrative court upheld Sadat's actions against Shenouda and ordered the Coptic Orthodox Church to hold a new papal election; only in January 1985 did a decree from President HUSNI MUBARAK allow Shenouda to regain his office.

Shenouda reaffirmed his policy against politicizing religion by opposing an initiative by the Ibn Khaldun Center in Cairo to host a conference in 1994 on minorities in the Arab world and efforts by the U.S. Congress in 1997 to pass legislation that would have barred aid to Egypt as long as it allowed discrimination against Copts. He attacked Israel's administration of Christian holy places and vowed not to visit Jerusalem until it was freed from Jewish control. He also condemned U.S. policy toward Iraq. Generally, his strategy has been to align Egypt's Copts closely with their Muslim counterparts in the interest of preserving national unity.

THE WORLD'S PERSPECTIVE

The United Nations Educational, Scientific, and Cultural Organization (UNESCO) awarded Shenouda III its Madanjeet Singh Prize for the Promotion of Tolerance and Nonviolence in 2000. Shenouda is a past president of the World Council of Churches and headed for many years the Middle Eastern Council of Churches.

LEGACY

Shenouda will be remembered as an active Coptic pope, who served Egypt's Copts during a difficult period in the last decades of the twentieth century. He also oversaw a tremendous expansion of the Coptic church in North and South America. Shenouda also will be remembered for his commitment to Christian unity, as demonstrated by his meeting Roman Catholic pope Paul VI in 1973. In May 2000, he established the Office for Ecumenical Affairs in the Coptic Archdiocese of North America.

BIBLIOGRAPHY

Biographical Dictionary of Modern Egypt, Arthur Goldschmidt, Jr., ed. Boulder, CO: Lynne Rienner, 2000.

Coptic Encyclopedia. New York: Macmillan, 1991.

Fernandez, Alberto M. "The Coptic Orthodox Salvation Theology of Anba Shenouda III." MA thesis, University of Arizona, 1983.

Hirst, David, and Irene Beeson. *Sadat.* London: Faber and Faber, 1981.

Pennington, J. D. "The Copts in Modern Egypt." *Middle Eastern Studies* 18 (1982): 158-179.

Saif, Leila abu-. *Middle East Journal: A Woman's Journey into the Heart of the Arab World.* New York: Scribner, 1990.

"The Official Site of H. H. Pope Shenouda III." 18 June 2007. http://www.copticpope.org/index.php

Tincq, Henri. "Siege Mentality Grips the Copts of Egypt." *Guardian.* 21 February 1988.

Donald Spanel
updated by Arthur Goldschmidt
updated by Michael R. Fischbach

SHIKAKI, KHALIL
(1953–)

Khalil Shikaki was born in Rafah, Gaza in 1953. Dr. Shikaki has held various academic and research positions, best known among them the position of director of the Palestinian Center for Policy and Survey Research (PSR) in Ramallah. His center is a leading source of information on Palestinian social trends, public opinion on key issues in Palestinian politics, and the Israeli-Palestinian peace process.

PERSONAL HISTORY

Khalil Ibrahim Shikaki (also Shiqaqi) was born in September 1953 in Rafah, Gaza, into a Palestinian family of refugees who left the village of Zarnuqa as a result of the 1948 War. Zarnuqa is located in what is presently the outskirts of the Israeli city of Rehovot. The Shikakis had lived for generations in Zarnuqa, where they owned land and cultivated wheat, apricots, oranges, and cucumbers. Shikaki's grandfather was an imam (Islamic prayer leader) and his father, Ibrahim, used to call for prayer from the local mosque. In May 1948 the family fled the fighting and was never allowed to return by the Israeli government

Shikaki's family history and his childhood as a refugee in Gaza had a profound effect on him. In many ways, the story of the Shikaki family is emblematic of that of the Palestinian people. The traumatic events the family witnessed, intertwined with the more general Palestinian history and national struggle, had divergent effects on Shikaki and his siblings and influenced them to choose different paths in their lives. Shikaki is the second oldest of

Khalil Shikaki. AP IMAGES.

BIOGRAPHICAL HIGHLIGHTS

Name: Khalil Shikaki

Birth: 1953, Rafah, Gaza

Family: Wife, Wafa; two daughters, Muna and Leila; one son, Ibrahim

Nationality: Palestinian

Education: Birzeit University, 1971; BA, international relations and Middle East studies, The American University of Beirut, 1975; MA, international relations and Middle East studies, The American University of Beirut, 1977; Ph.D, Columbia University, 1985.

PERSONAL CHRONOLOGY:

• **1985–1993:** Professor/lecturer at various universities in the United States and the West Bank (al-Najah, University of Wisconsin-Milwaukee, University of South Florida-Tampa)

• **1993–present:** Director of the Palestine Center for Policy and Survey Research (PSR).

• **1995–1999:** Editor of PSR's Quarterly Journal of Palestine Policy, *al-Siyasa al-Filastiniyya*

• **2002:** Visiting scholar, the Brookings Institution, Washington, D.C.

eight children. His siblings include a pharmacist, a businessman, and unskilled workers.

In 1971 Khalil began his studies at Birzeit University in the West Bank. In 1975 and 1977 he completed a BA and MA in international relations and Middle East studies from the American University of Beirut. Between 1977 and 1980 Shikaki worked for General Motors in Kuwait. He then went on to his Ph.D. studies at Columbia University, graduating in 1985. After teaching for one year at Columbia, he returned to the West Bank to teach at al-Najah University in Nablus.

During the first intifada, Khalil returned to the United States and from 1989 through 1990 taught at the University of Wisconsin-Milwaukee. In 1990 he became the director and research associate of a newly created think tank, World & Islam Studies Enterprise (WISE). In 1991, he became a professor at the University of South Florida in Tampa.

In March 1993 after returning to the West Bank, Shikaki established the Center for Palestine Research and Studies in Nablus. Between 1995 and 1999 Shikaki was editor of the center's Quarterly Journal of Palestine Policy, *al-Siyasa al-Filastiniyya*. Since 1993 he has conducted numerous public opinion polls and published many articles (some jointly with Israeli and other Palestinian scholars) about Palestinian politics and the Israeli-Palestinian peace process. Shikaki also served as a member of the Independent Palestinian Election Group formed to prepare for the January 1996 elections in the Palestinian Authority.

In 2002 Shikaki was a visiting scholar at the Brookings Institution in Washington D.C., and since then has been one of the institute's nonresident scholars. He contributes regularly to different forums in the Occupied Territories, the United States, and Israel.

INFLUENCES AND CONTRIBUTIONS

Shikaki's work, publications, surveys, and polls have contributed greatly to understanding political and social trends within Palestinian society. While his academic training and analytical skills are instrumental, his personal life experiences as a refugee in Gaza have undoubtedly contributed to his insights into the Palestinian national struggle and other key political issues, such as the refugee issue and the right of return.

Shikaki's work concerning the refugee issue and the right of return has contributed to the understanding of Palestinian discourse and preferred courses of action on this matter. He has participated in joint Palestinian-Israeli study groups on the refugee issue, worked with Palestinian and Israeli non-governmental organizations (NGOs) and research centers, and conducted important polls and surveys among Palestinian refugees. The results of his surveys have raised some controversy, especially among some Palestinian refugees. They indicated that while Palestinians still demand the right of return as a matter of principle, only 10 percent of refugees actually indicated a preference for returning to live in Israel when selecting among the various alternatives. Upon the release of this survey's results some Palestinians protested them violently by assaulting Shikaki and damaging his office. When asked for his reaction to the violence, Shikaki claimed that often those advocating for the rights of Palestinian refugees are the ones who attempt to silence the refugees' voices when their choices do not fit the advocates' agenda.

THE WORLD'S PERSPECTIVE

Shikaki has studied and taught extensively in the United States and been a visiting scholar at the Brookings Institution, one of the premier think tanks in the U.S. His work in the United States has given him a unique and valuable perspective on the West's academic and political attitudes toward the Middle East in general and Palestine in particular. Khalil's work is generally well respected among Palestinians and Israelis as well as in the West. It is controversial in some circles, mainly because it touches upon core issues and it is at times self-critical when Palestinians are still engaged in their national struggle.

The starkly disparate choices of how to engage in and contribute to the Palestinian national struggle are perhaps best exemplified in the approaches taken by Khalil Shikaki and by his older brother, Fathi. While Khalil is known for his outspoken yet moderate and pragmatic views and his willingness to work with Israeli and American academics and policy makers in search of peaceful solutions to the core issues of the conflict, his older brother had chosen a very different path. Fathi, a physician by profession, was one of the founders of the Islamic Jihad movement. He orchestrated and participated in a number of violent attacks against Israelis and was deported by Israel from the Occupied Territories in 1988. In 1995 Fathi Shikaki was killed in Malta. While Israel has never taken responsibility for the act, it is widely believed that Israeli agents were behind the operation.

LEGACY

Although it is too early to assess Shikaki's ultimate legacy, he will almost certainly be remembered as an important Palestinian thinker and a well-respected voice in the discussion of the Palestinian-Israeli problem.

BIBLIOGRAPHY

Brookings Institution. *Building a State, Building a Peace: How to Make a Roadmap That Works for Palestinians and Israelis.* Washington, DC: The Saban Center at the Brookings Institution, 2003.

Council on Foreign Relations. *Strengthening Palestinian Public Institutions.* New York: Council on Foreign Relations, 1999.

Shikaki, Khalil. "How Palestinians View the Oslo Process." *Internationale Politik Transatlantic Edition* 2, no. 4 (Winter 2001): 45-55. Available from http://en.internationalepolitik.de.

———. "Palestinians Divided." *Foreign Affairs* 81, no. 1 (January-February 2002). Available from http://www.foreignaffairs.org.

Shamir, Jacob, and Khalil Shikaki. "Determinants of Reconciliation and Compromise among Israelis and Palestinians." *Journal of Peace Research* 39 (March 2002): 185-202.

———. "Self-Serving Perception of Terrorism Among Israelis and Palestinians." *Political Psychology* 23, no. 3 (September 2002): 537-557.

Shikaki, Khalil, Robert Rothstein, and Moshe Ma'oz, eds. *The Israeli-Palestinian Peace Process: Oslo and the Lessons of Failure.* East Sussex, U.K.: Sussex Academic Press, 2002.

Adina Friedman

SHIMONI, KOBI
(1979–)

Known by his stage name Subliminal, Shimoni is a hip-hop artist and top-selling recording artist in Israel.

PERSONAL HISTORY

Subliminal was born Ya'akov "Kobi" Shimoni on November 13, 1979, in Tel Aviv, Israel. His parents were immigrant Jews from Islamic countries: His mother was from Mashhad, Iran, and his father came from Tunisia. Shimoni began performing at age twelve, and by age fifteen had met his musical collaborator, Yoav Eliasi (who became known as The Shadow). After a visit to a recording studio in Los Angeles, Shimoni decided to try his luck with hip-hop music in Israel. Together, Subliminal and The Shadow began performing hip-hop music in Israeli clubs in 1995, mimicking American hip-hop artists both in style and dress (wearing baggy pants and gold chains). In 1997, Shimoni helped produce a project titled "Yisra'elim Atzbanim, Ahad Ahad" ("Stressed-Out Israelis, Every One"), his first venture into the recording business in Israel.

After his obligatory army service, Shimoni began devoting himself full-time to music. He released his first album in 2001, *ha-Or me'Tzion* (*Light from Zion*). It was a big hit, and soon was followed by *ha-Or ve ha-Tzal* (*The Light and the Shadow*; a reference to Eliasi) in 2002. Rapping in Hebrew, Arabic, French, and English, Shimoni went on to become extremely popular in Israel. He issued the album *TACT All Stars* with his collaborators in TACT (Tel Aviv City Team) Records in 2004. His most recent solo album was *Bediuk Kshe'Kheshavtem she'ha-Kol*

BIOGRAPHICAL HIGHLIGHTS

Name: Kobi Shimoni (Subliminal)

Birth: 13 November 1979, Tel Aviv, Israel

Nationality: Israeli

PERSONAL CHRONOLOGY:

- **1995:** Begins performing hip-hop
- **1997:** Helps produce "Yisra'elim Atzbanim, Ahad Ahad" ("Stressed-Out Israelis, Every One")
- **2001:** Releases first album, *ha-Or me'Tzion* (*Light from Zion*)
- **2002:** Releases album *ha-Or ve ha-Tzal* (*The Light and the Shadow*)
- **2004:** Releases album *TACT All Stars*
- **2006:** Releases album *Bediuk Kshe'Kheshavtem she'ha-Kol Nigmar* (*Just When You Thought it was Over*)

Nigmar (*Just When You Thought it was Over*) in 2006, and his most recent single was "Adon Olam Ad Matai?" ("God Almighty, When Will it End?"), released in 2007.

INFLUENCES AND CONTRIBUTIONS

One of Shimoni's defining characteristics has been his strongly nationalistic lyrics. When the violence of second Palestinian Intifada broke out in 2000, Shimoni's music began reflecting the frustration he and other Israelis felt toward the Palestinians. Citing his parents' own persecution as Jews living among Muslims, Shimoni sometimes responds to Palestinian critics of Israel in blunt fashion. In a 2005 interview, he noted:

> "When we talk politics with Arabs in Israel, they say, 'My grandfather used to live in Tel Aviv, and now it's owned by Jewish people—we want to come back.' I respond, 'My parents came from Iran and Tunisia, but nobody is going to give our property back to us. It's all been confiscated... We have this little sandbox we call Israel. We give our hearts and lives to make it a proud country. Every one serves in the Israeli Defense Force in order for Israel to survive. You have half of the globe. What the f**k do you want from us? Go live in Saudi Arabia'" (Khazzoom 2005).

A line from his hit song "Divide and Conquer" says, "Dear God, I wish you could come down, because I'm being persecuted. My enemies are united. They want to

destroy me. We're nurturing and arming those who hate us. Enough!"

One of Shimoni's impacts has been to help popularize hip-hop music in Israel. Another major contribution was when he and Eliasi formed TACT Records, which has gone on to become Israel's biggest record label. He even has his own line of clothing. Shimoni also helped discover the Israeli-born Palestinian hip-hop artist Tamer Nafar, who went on to form the group DAM. Eventually, however, the political tensions generated in the heated atmosphere of the Palestinian-Israeli violence of the Intifada led to their estrangement. Their relationship and its demise was documented in the 2003 film *Arotzim shel Za'am* (*Channels of Rage*), directed by Israeli filmmaker Anat Halachmi.

CONTEMPORARIES

Tamer Nafar (1979–; also Tamir al-Nafar) is a Palestinian Arab citizen of Israel who was born on 6 June 1979 in Lod (Arabic: al-Lidd), Israel. His family originally was from Jaffa, but was dislocated during the 1948 War. In 1999, Nafar formed the hip-hop group DAM along with his brother, Suhell Nafar, and with Mahmud Jreri. The music of DAM, which means both blood in Arabic (and Hebrew) as well as Da Arabic MCs, combines traditional Arabic rhythms and instruments with a hip-hop beat and often political lyrics. In 1998, DAM issued its first song "Stop Selling Drugs," a reference to Nafar's drug-infested hometown of Lod, followed in 2001 by "Who's the Terrorist?" In the song, DAM sings:

> You grew up in indulgence, / We grew up in poverty. / You grew up in spacious homes, / We grew up in burrows. / And he, who lost his way, / You turned into a criminal. / Then you, the terrorist, have / The nerve to call me a terrorist?

"Who's the Terrorist" has been downloaded from the Internet over one million times, and an issue of *Rolling Stone* magazine in France featured a free CD copy of it. In November 2006, DAM released its first album, *Dedication*. Although DAM sings mostly in Arabic and English, the group's 2004 song "Born Here" was in both Arabic and Hebrew, in order to appeal to Israeli Jews as well as to Palestinians. DAM has performed in Israel, the Palestinian territories, Germany, Italy, Britain, and the United States.

THE WORLD'S PERSPECTIVE

Subliminal and his collaborators at TACT largely are an Israeli phenomenon, although they have toured elsewhere, including France, Canada, and the United States, and opened for American rapper 50 Cent during his concert in Israel. But they have become one of the biggest selling—if not the biggest selling—musical acts in Israeli history.

LEGACY

Although it is much too early to discuss Shimoni's ultimate legacy, his impact on Israeli music and the Israeli music industry already has been profound.

BIBLIOGRAPHY

"Hip Hop in the Holy Land." *British Broadcasting Corporation.* Available from http://www.bbc.co.uk/.

Khazzoom, Loolwa. "Israeli Rapper Takes U.S.: Subliminal Kicks Off Tour, Kicks Up Controversy." *Rolling Stone*, March 2, 2005. Available from http://www.rollingstone.com/.

Khazzoom, Loolwa. "Israeli Rappers Prove Hip-Hop Will Translate to Any Language." *Boston Globe*, January 4, 2004. Available from http://www.boston.com/.

TACT Records website. Available from http://tact-records.com/.

Michael R. Fischbach

SHOMAN, ABDUL MAJEED
(1912–2005)

As chairman and chief operating officer of the Arab Bank, Palestinian banker Abdul Majeed Shoman was a major figure in the financial world and a force in the Jordanian economy. Shoman also served as the first director of the Palestinian National Fund (PNF) established by the Palestinian Liberation Organization (PLO) and played a key role Palestinian politics, finances, and philanthropic causes.

PERSONAL HISTORY

Abdul Majeed Abdul Hameed Shoman (also Abd al-Majid Abd al-Hamid Shawman) was born in 1912 in Bayt Hanina, Palestine, north of Jerusalem, to a Muslim Arab family. His father, Abdul Hameed Shoman (1890–1974), had left Bayt Hanina for the United States in 1911, shortly before Abdul Majeed's birth. The boy did not meet his father until over a decade later, when he traveled to New York to be with his father after his mother's death. In the United States, Shoman's father established several successful businesses in New York City and Baltimore before returning to Palestine in 1929. A year later, the elder

BIOGRAPHICAL HIGHLIGHTS

Name: Abdul Majeed Shoman

Birth: 1912, Bayt Hanina, Ottoman Palestine

Death: 2005, Amman, Jordan

Family: Married with children

Nationality: Palestinian; Jordanian citizenship

Education: B.A., M.A. (economics and banking), New York University, 1936

PERSONAL CHRONOLOGY:

- **1936:** Begins working with the Arab Bank
- **1949:** Deputy chairman of the Arab Bank
- **1964:** First chairman of the Palestinian National Fund; serves on the first executive committee of the Palestine Liberation Organization
- **1974:** Chairman and general manager of the Arab Bank
- **1978:** Establishes Abdul Hameed Shoman Foundation
- **1983:** First chairman of the Welfare Association
- **1987:** Appointed to Jordanian senate
- **1993:** Appointed to Jordanian senate
- **2001:** Steps down as chief executive officer of the Arab Bank (but retains position of chairman of the board)

Shoman used $70,000 he had generated in the United States to establish the Arab Bank in 1930.

Shoman followed in his father's footsteps. He received his BA and MA in economics and banking from New York University in 1936. After returning to Palestine, he began working at the Arab Bank in 1936. When the Second World War broke out in 1939, he helped stop a run on the bank by methodically paying out nervous depositors' withdrawals with one-Palestine pound banknotes, slowing down the mad rush to withdraw cash and effectively halting the run. The family staved off another major crisis in 1948, when the first Arab-Israeli war left the bank inside Israeli lines. They managed to smuggle out bank records, safe deposit boxes, and other assets across the cease-fire lines into Jordanian-controlled territory, and reestablished the Arab Bank's operations in Amman, Jordan.

From 1949–1974, Shoman assisted his father as deputy chairman as the bank grew. Upon his father's death in 1974, he became its chairman and general manager. Shoman stepped down as chief executive officer of the bank in May 2001, although he retained the position of chairman of the board. He also became an important figure in the Palestinian national movement, serving on the first executive committee of the PLO and as the first director of the Palestinian National Fund.

Shoman also has excelled in philanthropic and cultural projects. He established the Abdul Hameed Shoman Foundation in 1978. A portion of the Arab Bank's profits were put into the foundation, which has been responsible for sponsoring a number of cultural and scientific ventures over the years. In 1983, Shoman also established the Welfare Association to serve Palestinians in the occupied territories. He also served as chairman of the board for the Diana Tamari Sabbagh Foundation, the Medical Care Society, and Jordan Medical Aid for Palestinians. Shoman died in Amman on 5 July 2005.

INFLUENCES AND CONTRIBUTIONS

Shoman was clearly influenced by the example of his father, Abdul Hameed Shoman, and inherited his father's intense commitment to the Palestinian people. A stone-mason from a village near Jerusalem, the elder Shoman traveled to the United States in 1911 where he became a successful businessman. However, he decided to return to the Middle East to use his wealth for the good of Palestine and Palestinian economic development. The Arab Bank that he established was also known to serve its clientele even under difficult circumstances. After the 1948 Arab-Israeli War and the creation of Israel, for example, the Arab Bank had over £500,000 of its funds blocked in Israel by Israeli laws governing the assets of Palestinian refugees. However, it still managed to pay out funds to its refugee depositors who fled during the war after it reestablished its operations in Amman, Jordan.

Under Shoman's direction after 1974, the Arab Bank grew from a large bank in Jordan to become the largest privately owned bank in the Arab world, and one of its major financial institutions. He expanded Arab Bank operations, which in mid-2007 comprised 378 branches in twenty-seven countries in the Middle East, North America, South America, Europe, and Asia. At the time of 2003-2004 fiscal year, the bank's assets totaled more than $34 billion. In November 2003, Oger Saudi Oger, Ltd.—a company owned by Lebanese billionaire businessman and politician Rafiq Hariri—acquired 11 percent of the company. In 1992, when *Forbes* magazine listed Shoman and his family (who at that point owned about 20 percent of the Arab Bank) among its list of world billionaires, it estimated the family's fortune at about $1 billion.

Shoman was also involved in Palestinian politics and financial matters. In 1964, the conference that established the PLO also created the Palestinian National Fund (PNF)

CONTEMPORARIES

Khalid Shoman (1931–2001), half-brother of Abdul Majeed Shoman, was born in New York City. His maternal grandfather, Ahmad Hilmi Abd al-Baqi, was a major Palestinian banker. Shoman received a BA in economics from Cambridge University in Britain in 1955, and an MA from the same institution in 1959. He started working with the Arab Bank in 1956, and became deputy chairman and deputy general manager in 1974. He and his wife, artist Suha Shoman (1944–), established the Darat el Funun artistic complex in 1993.

Abdul Hamid Shoman (1947–), son of Abdul Majeed Shoman, received a BBA from The American University of Beirut. He began working with the Arab Bank in 1972. In May 2001, he became vice chairman of the board and chief executive officer of the bank, and assumed the chairmanship of the board in July 2005 after his father's death. In November 2005, King Abdullah II of Jordan appointed Shoman to the Jordanian senate. He is married with three children.

to finance its operations. Shoman was selected to be the PNF's first director, concurrently sitting on the PLO's executive committee. He soon played a key role in PLO politics. After the discrediting of PLO Chairman Ahmad Shuqayri in the fallout after the disastrous Arab defeat in the June 1967 Arab-Israeli War, Shoman was one of the first members of the PLO executive committee to threaten to resign—and cut off the PLO's funding from the PNF—if Shuqayri did not step down. Shuqayri did resign in December 1967, paving the way for Yasir Arafat to assume the post of PLO chairman in February 1969 after the brief rule of Shuqayri's successor, Yahya Hammuda.

THE WORLD'S PERSPECTIVE

Shoman's financial clout in the Middle East can be seen in the number of financial institutions for which he served as chairman, including the Arab Palestinian Investment Bank, the Commercial Building Company, the Arab Computing Company, the Jerusalem Development & Investment Co, the Arab Real Estate Company for Administration and Investment, the Arab National Leasing Company, and the Arab Finance & Consultancy Services. Shoman also sat on the board of directors of the Arab National Bank in Saudi Arabia. He also received several awards over his career. For example, the Union of Arab

Banks honored him with the title Banker of the Year in 1995, as did the Arab Bankers Association of North America in 1996. King Hussein twice appointed Shoman to the Jordanian senate, first from 1987-1990 and then again from 1993-1997. As a symbol of his great importance to Jordan and its economy, King ABDULLAH II BIN HUSSEIN allowed Shoman to be buried in the royal cemetery in Amman.

On the other hand, the Arab Bank was not above becoming embroiled in controversy in the West. In July 2004 of that year, six families of Americans who were killed or injured in Palestinian attacks in Israel and the Israeli-occupied West Bank and Gaza sued the Arab Bank in a New York court for $875 million. They claimed that the bank's New York branch laundered Saudi-donated funds, eventually sending them to its branches in the Palestinian territories where they were distributed to family members of Hamas and Islamic Jihad members who had carried out suicide bombings. In February 2005, the United States Treasury Department ordered the bank to stop accepting new accounts or transferring funds. Earlier that month, the Arab Bank announced that it would close the New York branch because "the climate of operating in the United States at present is not expedient with the bank's strategy and vision."

LEGACY

Shoman will be remembered as a giant in Palestinian, Jordanian, and Arab banking, and Palestinian politics, as well as a major philanthropist. He was central to the robust success of the Arab Bank and a pillar in the Jordanian economy.

BIBLIOGRAPHY

Abdul Hameed Shoman Foundation website. Available from http://www.shoman.org.

Abdul Majeed Shoman's obituary. *Times* (London). Available from http://www.timesonline.co.uk/tol/comment/obituaries/article543270.ece.

Michael R. Fischbach

SHOUAA, GHADA
(1973–)

Ghada Shouaa is a retired Syrian female athlete who won the gold medal in the heptathalon at the 1996 Olympic Summer Games. She is the holder of the fifth-best heptathlon score of all time.

PERSONAL HISTORY

Shouaa (also Shu'a) was born on 10 September 1973 in the Syrian town of Maharda, northwest of Hama. Standing at six feet, two inches, she played on the Syrian women's national basketball team from 1989-1991. It

Ghada Shouaa. AP IMAGES.

was not until 1991 that she competed in her first heptathlon, a grueling two-day outdoor track-and-field contest consisting of seven individual events—100-meter hurdles, high jump, shot put, 200-meter dash, long jump, javelin throw, and the 800-meter dash. Heptathletes accumulate points for performance based on predetermined formulas for each event.

Shouaa quickly went on to compete in her first major international competition at the August 1991 World Championships in Tokyo, where she placed last in the event. Shouaa won the silver medal in the event at the Asian Games in November 1991, but came in eighteenth at the July 1992 Olympic Summer Games in Barcelona. She continued to acquit herself well in regional events, taking the silver at the Mediterranean Games in June 1993 and the gold at both the October 1993 and October 1994 Asian Games.

For the next four years, Shouaa was one of the world's premier heptathletes. In May 1995 she won the heptathlon at the famous Götzis competition in Austria, and took gold at the World Championships in Göteborg in August. Shouaa won the 1996 Götzis event as well.

Her moment of crowning glory came during the 1996 Summer Olympics in Atlanta. Her main rival at the games, veteran American heptathlete Jackie Joyner-Kersee, withdrew from the competition after the first event. Shouaa went on to win the heptathlon with 6,780

BIOGRAPHICAL HIGHLIGHTS

Name: Ghada Shouaa

Birth: 1973, Maharda, Syria

Nationality: Syrian

PERSONAL CHRONOLOGY:

- **1989-1991:** Member of the Syrian women's national basketball team
- **1991:** Competes her first heptathlon; later wins silver medal in the heptathlon at the Asian Games
- **1992:** Places eighteenth in the heptathletes at the Barcelona Olympic games
- **1993:** Wins a gold medal at the Asian Games
- **1994:** Wins a gold medal at the Asian Games
- **1995:** Wins a gold medal at Götzis; wins a gold medal at the World Championships
- **1996:** Wins a gold medal at Götzis; wins a gold medal at the Atlanta Olympics
- **1997:** Sustains an injury that sidelines her for two seasons
- **1999:** Wins a bronze medal at the World Championships
- **2000:** Drops out of the Sydney Olympics due to injury
- **2001:** Retires from competition

advance the cause of women's athletics within the Arab and Islamic worlds. With the exception of North African Arab countries such as Morocco and Algeria, the Arab world generally has not produced many world-class athletes, male or female, competing and winning international championships. The record for women has been especially meager: Only Shouaa and three other Arab women have ever won an Olympic gold medal.

Recent decades have witnessed more and more female Arab athletes like Shouaa competing in international events, despite the objections of Islamic religious conservatives. To be sure, Shouaa was a partial exception as a Christian competing for a country with an officially secular government. Like all Arab countries Syria is still socially conservative, and a woman wearing shorts and a tank-top in front of both male and female spectators is considered immodest and even immoral by some conservatives. Her performances set an example of a determined Arab woman willing to compete in the international arena according to global standards.

THE WORLD'S PERSPECTIVE

Shouaa's accomplishments were hailed throughout the Arab world, especially in her native Syria. Her gold medal at the 1996 Olympics was the first Olympic gold medal ever for the country, a country that as of 2007 has won only two previous Olympic medals (one silver, one bronze). Yet in the United States in particular, her 1996 Olympic victory in Atlanta—winning the title of "the world's greatest female athlete" in America—went largely unnoticed after American superstar Jackie Joyner-Kersee had dropped out of the heptathlon. American television stopped devoting much coverage to the remaining six heptathlon events after Joyner-Kersee left the competition. American viewers and sports fans thus did not grasp the full magnitude of Shouaa's victory, and how it was hailed in the Arab world and globally.

For her part, Joyner-Kersee complimented Shouaa on the grace that she displayed when Joyner-Kersee was injured, even though the injury left the field wide open for the lanky Syrian. In her 2001 autobiography, Joyner-Kersee wrote that when she dropped out after the first heptathlon event at Atlanta, "Ghada Shouaa, a Syrian heptathlete, came over and hugged me. Then she kissed me on both cheeks. She also kissed Bobby [her husband and coach]. That was the greatest compliment a competitor could have paid me." From the Prologue to Jackie Joyner-Kersee and Sonia Steptoe, *A Kind of Grace: The Autobiography of the World's Greatest Female Athlete* (Grand Central Publishing: 1997).

LEGACY

Shouaa's achievements were not just impressive for their time. Her score of 6,942 points, set in the heptathlon on

points on 28 July 1996—earning her the title "the world's greatest female athlete." It was Syria's first and only Olympic gold medal, and both Syria and the wider Arab world were delirious with joy. She returned to a hero's welcome in Syria.

A serious injury in 1997 kept her out of competition until August 1999, when she placed third at the World Championships in Seville. At the September 2000 Summer Olympics in Sydney, she sustained another injury during the first event, could not even finish the race, and dropped out of further competition. Shouaa retired in July 2001. She later moved to Simmern, Germany, and formed the Ghada Shouaa German-Technio-Trade, an international luxury car sales company.

INFLUENCES AND CONTRIBUTIONS

Shouaa's career as a heptathlete only spanned a decade. But during that period, her athletic talent rocketed her to global stardom. Her legendary performances also helped

26 May 1996 at Götzis, still stands as the all-time Asian record for the event. Shouaa still holds the fifth-best heptathlon score ever achieved by a female heptathlete. Among the women achieving the top ten all-time heptathlete scores, she remains the only one to come from a country outside Europe and the United States. Finally, she still is the only Syrian to have won Olympic gold and one of only four Arab women ever to have done so.

BIBLIOGRAPHY

Downes, Steven. "Cautious Olympic Champion Wants to Wait and See," AFP (19 August 1999). Available from http://news.bbc.co.uk/sport1/hi/athletics/1434109.stm.

Ghada Shouaa's webpage (in German). Available from http://www.shouaa.com/start.html.

International Association of Athletics Federation profile of Ghada Shouaa. Available from http://www.iaaf.org/athletes/athlete%3D67124/.

"Shouaa Calls Time." BBC (11 July 2001). Available from http://news.bbc.co.uk/sport1/hi/athletics/1434109.stm.

Michael R. Fischbach

BIOGRAPHICAL HIGHLIGHTS

Name: Zineb Sidera

Birth: 1963, near Paris, France

Nationality: French, of Algerian origin

Education: Slade School of Art, London; the Central Saint Martin's School of Art and Design, London; and the Royal College of Art, London

PERSONAL CHRONOLOGY:

• **2001:** Completes *Don't Do to Her What You Did to Me*

• **2003:** *Retelling Histories: My Mother Told Me...*

• **2005:** *And The Road Goes On*

• **2006:** *Saphir*

SIDERA, ZINEB
(1963–)

A London-based multimedia artist, Zineb Sidera is of Algerian origin.

PERSONAL HISTORY

Sidera was born in a suburb of Paris, France, in 1963 to Algerian immigrant parents. She later moved to Britain and trained at the Slade School of Art, the Central Saint Martin's School of Art, and the Royal College of Art. Sidera currently is based in London.

INFLUENCES AND CONTRIBUTIONS

Sidera's video installations and photographic work center on displacement and exile; they draw on her own experience of being born in France to immigrant Algerian parents and moving to Britain. Women, the veil, the gaze, and memory are some of the themes that emerge in her artistic exploration of the shifting subject positions that are part of the immigrant and exile experience, especially among Muslim and Arab women living in the West. Similar to many other artists from Arab countries living in exile, Sidera is particularly concerned with capturing the personal and political paradoxes and contradictions of living within and between cultures and finds the veil a useful way to do so. In many of her works, she examines the ways in which veiling has carried multiple meanings—from the history and legacy of the Algerian encounter with French colonialism to its place within individual and family life.

Sidera also explores what she has called the veiling of the mind—the process of censorship and self-censorship within individuals and societies. Through photographs of herself veiled and veiling, or photographs of her own gaze (marked off by obscuring the edges of the work as if it were being seen by a veiled viewer), she challenges stereotypes of the submissive veiled woman while at the same time showing how the veil becomes a sign of backwardness and a vehicle of submission. The ambiguous meanings of visible and invisible veiling are a metaphor for her own restless experience of migration and exile, and for the complicated questions she has encountered therein.

Some of her recent works include *Don't Do to Her What You Did to Me* (1998-2001), *Retelling Histories: My Mother Told Me...* (2003), *And The Road Goes On* (2005), and *Saphir* (2006).

THE WORLD'S PERSPECTIVE

Zineb Sidera is still establishing herself and her reputation. Her first major exhibition in London took place in 2006.

LEGACY

Zineb Sidera is still active, and it thus is too early to assess her legacy.

BIBLIOGRAPHY

Lloyd, Fran, ed. *Contemporary Arab Women's Art: Dialogues of the Present.* London: WAL, 1999.

Lloyd, Fran, ed. *Displacement and Difference: Contemporary Arab Visual Culture in the Diaspora.* London: Saffron Books, 2001.

Jessica Winegar
updated by Michael R. Fischbach

SIRRY, GAZBIA
(1925–)

Gazbia Sirry is one of the most prominent and influential painters in Egypt.

PERSONAL HISTORY

Sirry (also Jadhbiya Sirri) was born in 1925 in Cairo, Egypt, to a family of Turkish origin. She completed training at the High Institute of Fine Arts for Girls in Cairo in 1948 and received additional tutelage in Paris under Marcel Gromaire, as well as at the Slade School of Art in London in the 1950s. She taught at Helwan University from 1955 to 1981 and at The American University in Cairo from 1980 to 1981.

INFLUENCES AND CONTRIBUTIONS

A prolific painter and an art educator who also established a fund in her name to support young Egyptian artists, Sirry's first exhibition was in 1951. Throughout her career, she has been concerned with the fusion of the personal with the social or political, describing her work as embodying her sensual relationship with color and her obsession with the human condition. Sirry was a member of the Group of Modern Art in the 1950s, which adopted the ideology of modernization. Sirry's contribution was to portray nationalist subjects (such as martyrdom against British occupation and peasant mothers) in a figurative style inspired by pharaonic representation and also international Expressionism.

   With the increasing problems of the regime of Egyptian president Jamal Abd al-Nasir (Gamal Abdel Nasser) and the Arab defeat in the 1967 War, Sirry took on grim subjects such as imprisonment, grief, and racial discrimination. In the 1970s and 1980s, her concerns shifted to crowded urban environments and, in contrast, the sparse landscapes of the desert and the sea. The changes in Sirry's subjects and styles parallel the ebbs and flows in the general outlook of Egyptian intellectuals toward politics and society during her career.

THE WORLD'S PERSPECTIVE

Sirry is recognized as one of the Arab world's most significant modern art painters. Between 1953 and 1988, she held eighty-eight solo exhibitions of her work in the Middle East, Europe, and North America. She has received many awards, including the Prize of Rome in Painting in 1952, First Place at the Salon de Caire (Cairo) in 1960, Honorary Prize at the 1956 Venice Biennale, Fourth

---

BIOGRAPHICAL HIGHLIGHTS

Name: Gazbia Sirry

Birth: 1925, Cairo, Egypt

Nationality: Egyptian

Education: High Institute of Fine Arts for Girls in Cairo, 1948; training at the Slade School of Art in London

PERSONAL CHRONOLOGY:

- **1951:** Holds first exhibition
- **1952:** Receives Prize of Rome in Painting
- **1955:** Begins teaching at Helwan University
- **1956:** Honorary Prize at the 1956 Venice Biennale
- **1960:** First Place at the Salon de Caire (Cairo)
- **1968:** Fourth Great Prize of International Art in Monaco
- **1980:** Begins one-year teaching position at The American University in Cairo
- **2000:** Receives State Merit Prize from the Egyptian government

---

Great Prize of International Art in Monaco in 1968, and the Egyptian government's State Merit Prize in 2000.

LEGACY

Gazbia Sirry will be remembered as one of the most well known Egyptian artists of the twentieth century.

BIBLIOGRAPHY

El-Din, Mursi Saad. *Gazbia Sirry: Lust for Color.* Cairo, Egypt: American University in Cairo Press, 1998.

Karnouk, Liliane. *Contemporary Egyptian Art.* Cairo, Egypt: American University in Cairo Press, 1995.

Jessica Winegar
updated by Michael R. Fischbach

SISTANI, ALI HUSSEINI AL-
(1930–)

Iranian-born theologian and jurist Ali al-Sistani is the head of the Shi'ite school of Najaf (Iraq), also known as the Hawza. He is the supreme figure among his peers, the

Ali Husseini al-Sistani. © EPA/CORBIS.

BIOGRAPHICAL HIGHLIGHTS

Name: Ali Husseini Sistani

Birth: 1930, Mashhad, Iran

Family: Married with children

Nationality: Iranian (resident in Iraq)

Education: Iran (Mashhad and Qom), Iraq (Najaf); reached the level of *ijtihad* (independent deduction of legal and religious rulings) and became a grand ayatollah, the highest level of Shi'ite scholarship.

PERSONAL CHRONOLOGY:

• **1960:** Reaches the level of *ijtihad* (becomes an ayatollah)

• **1990:** Completes the third series of graduate courses in jurisprudence (*fiqh*) and principles of jurisprudence (*usul*)

• **1991:** Endorses the Shi'ite uprising in the South and is imprisoned and tortured by Saddam's security police

• **1992:** Succeeds al-Kho'i as the chief Shi'ite scholar in Iraq

• **2003–present:** After the collapse of Saddam's regime, becomes the unrivaled leader of the Iraqi Shi'ite community

three other major clerics in the country, each of whom also carries the title "Grand Ayatollah." He came to the fore of the religious scene in Najaf after the death of his mentor and predecessor, Grand Ayatollah Abu'l-Qasim al-Kho'i, in 1992, being the most prominent scholar among al-Kho'i's students. After spending more than twelve years under virtual house arrest in his residence in Najaf, the U.S. invasion of the country and the removal of Saddam Hussein's regime placed Sistani at the top of Iraq's power pyramid. Immediately after 2003 he became the highest source of political legitimacy in the country in spite of not being an Iraqi citizen. Except for the Americans and other coalition officials, he was visited by almost all national and international figures working on the Iraqi issue. As a matter of tradition, he refused to meet with any official associated with the coalition that occupied Iraq. Nevertheless, he was essential in keeping the majority of the Shi'ites from open revolt.

PERSONAL HISTORY

Grand Ayatollah Ali Husseini al-Sistani was born in 1930 in the holy city of Mashhad, northeastern Iran. Mashhad is a major Shi'ite religious and educational center where the eighth Shi'ite imam, Ali al-Rida (also Riza or Reza) was buried in 817 C.E. The city has been a major pilgrimage place where millions of Muslims arrive from many countries to visit the imam's shrine. Sistani's last name is derived from Sistan, an eastern Iranian city, where his great-grandfather, Sayyid Muhammad al-Husseini, established a new residence after being appointed as Shaykh al-Islam in the province by Hussein al-Safavi, the last shah of the Safavid dynasty (1692-1722). However, Sistani's lineage is better traced by his alternative last name, al-Husseini. The al-Husseini family goes back to the family of the Prophet Muhammad, making Sistani an Arab by ethnicity and an Iranian by nationality. Sistani's family consisted of several prominent religious scholars, the most important of whom was his aforementioned great-grandfather and his father, Sayyid Muhammad Baqir, a student of the legendary scholar Mirza Hasan al-Shirazi of Samarra from Iraq.

Following the custom of most religious families, Sistani began learning the Qur'an at age five. After some early learning, he entered the religious seminary to receive a formal education on the basics. He began his journey with religious science at ten, studying the fundamental Hawza lessons, known as the *muqaddimat*. He finished reading a number of books, including all of the classic books illustrating Arabic grammar and several other books on the basics of logic and mathematics. He then studied *Sharh al-Luma*, a major work on Shi'ite jurisprudence, and the book of Qawanin (Laws) with the late Sayyid Ahmad Yazdi. After finishing the *sutuh* texts (the second level of Hawza studies after which a student qualifies for graduate studies), with Shaykh Hashim al-Qazwini, one of the leading scholars of his time, he also read a number of books on philosophy, including the works of Mulla Sadra, and attended the required lessons on divine teachings. Meanwhile, he attended the Kharij lectures (the level preparing the student for *ijtihad*) of the late Mirza Mahdi Ashtiani and the late Mirza Hashim Qazwini.

At this point, he needed a more prestigious seminary. In 1949 he traveled to Qom, the best learning center in Iran, to begin another round of studies in *fiqh* (jurisprudence) and *usul* (principles of jurisprudence) with two prominent scholars, Sayyid Hussein Tabataba'i and Grand Ayatollah Kuhkamari—the first lectured on *fiqh* and *usul* and the second gave lectures in *fiqh* only.

In early 1951 Sistani left Qom for Najaf, Iraq. Upon his arrival in Najaf, he began attending Ayatollah Kho'i and Shaykh Hussein Hilli's lectures on jurisprudence and principles of jurisprudence. Meanwhile, he attended lectures of other prominent scholars like Ayatollah Hakim and Ayatollah Shahrudi.

Sistani rose in religious ranks to be named a *marje* (religious reference) in 1960, while on a trip to visit his native city, Mashhad, apparently with the intention to settle there. He received a certificate (*ijaza*) from Grand Ayatollah Kho'i and another from Shaykh Hilli, acknowledging that he had attained the level of *ijtihad* (possessing the ability to deduce legal and religious judgments). He also received a similar acknowledgment from the distinguished traditionalist and scholar, Shaykh Agha Buzurg Tehrani, testifying to his skill in the science of Rijal (biographies of the narrators of prophetic traditions).

Upon receiving this good news, he was encouraged to return to Najaf the following year and immerse himself further in the research and teaching of jurisprudence. He started giving a series of lectures at the graduate level on the principles of jurisprudence between 1964 and 1990.

Grand Ayatollah Kho'i decided in his late years to prepare a successor for the position of the supreme religious authority and the leadership of the Najaf Seminary. The choice fell on Grand Ayatollah Sistani for his merits, eligibility, knowledge, and character. Accordingly, he

started leading the prayer in 1986 at Ayatollah al-Kho'i's mosque, al-Khadra, and continued leading prayers there until the mosque was closed in 1993, a year after al-Kho'i's death. His rise to the supreme position in the Shi'ite scholarship and authority in Iraq in 1992 presented him with tremendous challenges, especially because the government considered him an adversary ever since he supported the uprising of 1991. He remained under house arrest until the U.S. invasion of Iraq in 2003, when a new era of reserved activism began.

INFLUENCES AND CONTRIBUTIONS

Sistani presides over the Najaf seminary, known as the Hawza, an institution whose existence has continued for more than a thousand years. In this capacity he is the guardian of a firmly held tradition of learning at the same time as he is expected to make his own contribution to this tradition, mainly through *ijtihad*.

In addition to his teaching, Sistani has written forty-two books and treatises on various religious sciences. Since the fall of Saddam's regime the Sistani leadership has emerged as the most influential religious institution in Iraq. In addition to his dominance in Iraq, he also has representatives (*wakils*) and offices in every country with a Shi'ite community, including major representations in the United Kingdom, India, Iran, Lebanon, Pakistan, Afghanistan, Azerbaijan, Saudi Arabia, Bahrain, Kuwait, Syria, Turkey, and the United States. However, Sistani's most impressive success has been in Iran, whose citizens traditionally follow local ayatollahs. According to Vali Nasr, "many Iranians have begun giving their religious taxes and donations to Sistani's representative in Qom, where Sistani enjoys great popularity and influence among the city's merchants and its teeming bazaars" (*The Shia Revival*, 2006).

The Najaf Hawza continues to grow in size and prestige, becoming the most influential seminary in the Shi'ite world since the collapse of Saddam's regime. Saddam's thirty-five-year tyrannical reign suffocated the school and eliminated its most illustrious scholarly figures either by execution, deportation or—as in the case of Sistani—by placing them under a very strict house arrest. This practice gave rise to the rival seminary in the Iranian city of Qom, especially following the Iranian Revolution in 1979. With Saddam gone from the scene and the ensuing extraordinary level of religious freedom in Najaf, the seminary under Sistani's leadership has recovered almost fully in less than four years and has begun attracting the best and the brightest scholars and students alike. Taking lessons from the Lebanese experience, many centers in Iraq were established and managed by the representatives of Sistani, providing what the Iraqi state has failed to deliver. They built educational and information facilities, including Internet and media outlets in most Iraqi cities.

CONTEMPORARIES

∎

Grand Ayatollah Abu'l-Qasim al-Kho'i (1899–1992) is considered one of the most prolific Shi'ite scholars of the twentieth century. He was born in the Iranian province of Azerbaijan and traveled with his family to Najaf, Iraq, at thirteen to continue his religious studies. His legacy and contribution can be measured by more than thirty books, in addition to his twenty-four volumes on the biographies of the transmitters of prophetic traditions, *Mu'jam Rijal al-Hadith*. Furthermore, few scholars in modern Shi'ite history trained eighteen grand ayatollahs as al-Kho'i did. Among his students are Grand Ayatollahs Ali Sistani, Muhammad Hussein Fadlullah, Muhammad Baqir al-Sadr, and Muhammad Ishaq al-Fayyad. Al-Kho'i took the responsibility of the Shi'ite leadership in the harshest times in centuries, as he had to successfully maintain the neutrality and independence of the school during thirty-five years of the Ba'thist rule in Iraq, especially the reign of terror under Saddam Hussein between 1979 and al-Kho'i's death in 1992.

Al-Kho'i was the main teacher and mentor of Ayatollah Sistani. Prior to his death, he prepared Sistani to take his position as the chief Shi'ite scholar in Iraq and the head of the Najaf school (the Hawza). Sistani said about him, "He, may Allah elevate his status, was an exemplar of the caliber of the early righteous generations, with his unique genius, his many gifts and honorable intellect that qualified him to be at the vanguard among the Shi'ite scholars, who devoted their lives to support the religion and the sect."

In addition to receiving religious guidance, Iraqis can also receive financial support from the well-funded charitable organization of Sistani. Sistani is the best-financed ayatollah in Iraq and one of the best-financed Muslim scholars worldwide. The money comes from the religious duties of the Sistani constituency (*muqallidun*) worldwide. This patronage inevitably translates into more loyalty and popularity for the Grand Ayatollah and the institutions under his guidance.

Sistani has been one of the first ayatollahs to use the Internet and the technological revolution of the current era. The Internet has helped Sistani increase his social and religious network on a worldwide scale. Sistani's website provides religious advice and disseminates his works and religious rulings (*fatwas*) in Arabic, Persian, Urdu, Turkish, French, and English. It receives 15,000 visits and up to 1,200 e-mail messages each day.

After the fall of Saddam in 2003, many Shi'ites who disapproved of the quietist position of the *Hawza* on matters of politics in the previous eighty years surrounded Sistani's home and attempted to force him to leave Iraq. Sistani's popularity among the Iraq tribes helped him survive this challenge to his authority. Having skillfully discerned the situation, Sistani made major modifications to his political position. He began his major political involvement in the post-Saddam era in June 2003, when his office in Najaf issued a communiqué that challenged the American-created Coalition Provisional Authority (CPA)'s decision to form an interim government for the transfer of sovereignty. Sistani demanded an immediate general election, through which all eligible Iraqi voters (men and women) had to vote for their representatives of choice to form a constitutional assembly.

When the CPA announced on 15 November 2003 a plan for the Iraqi political process, Sistani's office responded with a categorical rejection of the plan because, as quoted in Andrew Arato's article, "Sistani v. Bush: Constitutional Politics in Iraq,"

> the instrumentality envisaged in this plan for the election of the members of the transitional legislature does not guarantee the formation of an assembly that truly represents the Iraqi people. It must be changed to another process that would so guarantee, that is, to elections. In this way, the parliament would spring from the will of the Iraqis and would represent them in a just manner and would prevent any diminution of Islamic law.

Since 2003 Sistani has always supported the elections and popular participation in the political process, although he strongly recommended that religious figures keep an advisory role rather than actively holding office, and has led by example. However, he did not keep a mere advisory role when he saw the country at a close range from a catastrophe during the battle between the Multi-National Forces and the fighters of MUQTADA AL-SADR when the battle was coming to the shrine of Imam Ali in Najaf. He returned from London and scored a historical triumph for himself while steering the country away from an imminent bloodbath.

Another strong involvement by Sistani was his personal interference to prevent the United Nations Security Council from including any language referring to the Transitional Administrative Law (TAL) that was governing Iraq before the permanent constitution was ratified. Sistani argued that the TAL was problematic on the basis of its genesis and its content, which would hinder efforts to reach an agreement on a constitution that would secure the interests of all Iraqis.

Following these and many other successful intercessions, Sistani became the most powerful figure in Iraq despite his Iranian citizenship. His humble office in Najaf became the site of pilgrimage for Iraq's officials who seek legitimacy or popular support for their agendas or political aspirations. The man who was thought to be a quietist ayatollah used a remarkable skill to gain the upper hand in every situation, thanks to his incredible self-restraint and immense wisdom that has allowed him to resist the temptations of power and the spotlights.

The Shi'ites have been accustomed to many centuries of giving full allegiance to a hidden imam. Sistani managed to make use of this tendency and successfully keep himself invisible to the people, while simultaneously maintaining a presence in every moment of their lives.

THE WORLD'S PERSPECTIVE

World perceptions of Sistani are prejudiced by the conventional wisdom that ayatollahs are anti-West radicals whose worldviews are still trapped in a seventh-century theological mindset. This opinion was shaped by a long history of negative experience Western officials had in dealing with traditional Shi'ite religious scholars. Major media coverage of everything Shi'ite reinforced this negative image. However, this perception changed very rapidly as Sistani handled his responsibilities in a very admirable way so that the most skeptical of his observers turned quickly to praise him. Additionally, his status was helped by the fact that the other key figures within the Iraqi political process were the corrupt Iraqi politicians and the eccentric neo-conservative Americans, none of whom could compete with an insightful personality like Sistani. They possessed none of his wisdom, self-restraint, or lack of desire for attention.

At every turn Sistani outperformed his rivals. Perhaps the starkest example of his symbolic triumph was his call for national elections in Iraq while the Americans, whose rationale for invading Iraq had been reduced to the single claim of democratizing Iraq, opposed holding elections on the pretense that Iraq was not ready.

LEGACY

Sistani's greatest legacy will perhaps be his triumphant effort to spare the city of Najaf from destruction during the showdown between the U.S. forces and the loyalists of Muqtada al-Sadr. His return from London just in time to prevent the bloodbath and the procession that accompanied his motorcade from Basra to Najaf was an event not experienced by any Shi'ite scholar in the past sixty years. His most memorable trait will be his skill in facing the greatest challenge to Iranian Shi'ite scholars in Iraq—maintaining a pivotal role in the social and political current of events without alienating the author-

> ## SISTANI SPEAKS
>
> It is neither permissible to steal from the private as well as the public property of non-Muslims, nor vandalize it, even if that stealing or vandalizing does not tarnish the image of Islam and Muslims. Such an act is counted as perfidy and violation of the guarantee given to non-Muslims indirectly when one asked permission to enter or reside in that country. And it is forbidden to breach the trust and violate the guarantee in regard to every person irrespective of his religion, citizenship, and beliefs.
>
> SISTANI, GRAND AYATOLLAH ALI. *A CODE OF PRACTICE FOR MUSLIMS IN THE WEST.* LONDON: IMAM ALI FOUNDATION, 1999. AVAILABLE FROM HTTP://WWW.SISTANI.ORG.

ities. He ably overturned an eighty-year-long tradition of quietism and stepped into the political arena to play a constructive role that often has spared many Iraqi and non-Iraqi lives. He will also be remembered for his remarkable resistance to the spotlights that made him more effective and revered by the Shi'ites and the world at large.

BIBLIOGRAPHY

Arato, Andrew. "Sistani v. Bush: Constitutional Politics in Iraq." *Constellations* 11, no. 2 (2004): 174-192.

Kadhim, Abbas. "Al-Sistani's Triumph." *Al-Ahram Weekly.* 2-8 September 2004.

Nasr, Vali. *The Shia Revival.* New York: W.W. Norton & Company, 2006.

Sistani, Grand Ayatollah Ali. *Minhaj al-Salihin* (Path of the Righteous), Vols. 1-3. Beirut: Dar al-Mu'arrikh al-Arabi, 1998.

———. *A Code of Practice for Muslims in the West.* London: Imam Ali Foundation, 1999. Available from http://www.sistani.org.

The Official Website of Grand Ayatollah Sistani. Available from http://www.sistani.org.

Abbas Kadhim

SOROUSH, ABDOLKARIM
(1945–)

Abdolkarim Soroush is a prominent Iranian philosopher, reformer, and scholar. He has come to symbolize a secularizing strain in Iran's contemporary discourse on Islamic reformation. Initially a supporter of the regime of

Abdolkarim Soroush. AP IMAGES.

BIOGRAPHICAL HIGHLIGHTS

■

Name: Abdolkarim Soroush; born Husayn Haj Farajullah Dabbagh

Birth: 1945, Tehran, Iran

Family: Married; two sons, Abdolkarim and Soroush

Nationality: Iranian

Education: Degrees from Tehran University in pharmacology; M.Sc. in analytical chemistry from University of London; extended studies in the philosophy of sciences at Chelsea College, London.

PERSONAL CHRONOLOGY:

- **1980:** Director of Islamic Culture Group at Tehran's Teacher Training College

- **1983:** Research Member at the Institute for Cultural Research and Studies

- **1990:** Cofounder of monthly magazine *Kiyan*

- **1991:** Professor and lecturer at Tehran Academy of Philosophy

- **2000:** Visiting professor at Harvard University

- **2002:** Scholar in residence at Yale University; visiting professor at Princeton University

- **2003:** Visiting scholar at Wissenschaftskolleg Berlin, Germany

- **2006:** Visiting professor at the Free University of Amsterdam ISIM (International Institute for the Study of Islam in the Modern World-Leiden)

Ayatollah Ruhollah Khomeini, Soroush became increasingly critical of the Iranian clerical establishment in the 1990s. His various lectures and publications have become subject to censorship and he has been living and working in exile since 2000.

PERSONAL HISTORY

Abdolkarim Soroush, born Husayn Haj Farajullah Dabbagh, was born in 1945 in southern Tehran, Iran, to a lower middle class family. Soroush underwent his primary schooling in the Qa'imiyyeh School. After spending six years there, he continued his secondary education at Mortazavi High School and a year later transferred to the newly inaugurated Alavi High School. After completing his high school education, Soroush took part in the universities' nationwide entrance examinations in both physics and pharmacy. He successfully passed both exams and decided to focus on pharmacy. Once he completed his degree at Tehran University he served in the army for two years, fulfilling the national compulsory service, after which he moved to Bushehr to render part of his medical service. In Bushehr he was the director of the Laboratory for Food Products, Toiletries, and Sanitary Materials. After one year and three months he returned to Tehran where he was briefly employed at the Laboratory for Medicine Control.

In 1973 he left for London where he studied analytical chemistry at the University of London (MSc). He then continued his studies at Chelsea College and specialized in history and philosophy of sciences. Prior to and during the revolutionary period sweeping Iran, Soroush became politically active by giving speeches that were then transcribed and produced into pamphlets and books. In those years Soroush emerged as an ideologue of the regime and took part in public debates with its

critics, most commonly Marxists whom Soroush would adamantly confront, charging them with dogmatism and historical determinism.

After returning to Iran, Soroush affiliated himself with Tehran's Teacher Training College where he was appointed the director of the newly established Islamic Culture Group. In the aftermath of the 1979 Iranian Revolution, Iran's universities closed and brought the educational system to a halt. A new body was formed, named the Cultural Revolution Institute, which was composed of seven members including Abdolkarim Soroush. Ayatollah Ruhollah Khomeini, revolutionary Iran's new spiritual leader, had personally appointed all members. The main task of this body was to reform and revise the basic curriculum and accelerate the reopening of the universities.

In 1983 Soroush secured a transfer to the Institute for Cultural Research and Studies from his previous post at the Teacher Training College. That same year the Cultural Revolution Institute changed its name to the Cultural Revolution Council and increased its membership to a total of seventeen. Soon thereafter Soroush disassociated himself with the Council and handed Khomeini his official resignation. Since then he has no longer held any official position within the ruling system of Iran, besides occasional advisory functions to specific government bodies.

In the late 1980s and early 1990s, Soroush started developing a more critical perspective toward the ruling Iranian regime. In 1991 he cofounded the monthly magazine, *Kiyan*, which at one point became the most visible forum of religious intellectualism. In this magazine he published his most controversial articles on religious pluralism, hermeneutics, tolerance, and clericalism. The magazine was shut down in 1998 along with other magazines and newspapers under the direct order of the supreme leader of the Islamic Republic, Ayatollah Ali Khamenei. In 1996 Soroush left Iran for an extended tour of lectures in Europe, the United States, and Canada.

In 1997 Soroush returned to Iran after the landslide win of reformist candidate Mohammad Khatemi in the presidential elections. This electoral victory was widely believed to have signaled the emergence of a more open and tolerant Islamic government. Although Soroush managed to establish a new Institute for Wisdom and Research and the promising conducive political environment allowed for various new and old journals to reemerge, Soroush was increasingly subjected to harassment and ultimately lost his job. His public lectures at various universities in Iran were frequently disrupted by hardline Ansar-e-Hizbollah vigilante groups, and he was physically attacked on various occasions.

At the turn of the century he took temporary residence in the West. From the year 2000 onward, Abdolkarim Soroush has been a visiting professor at Harvard University where he taught various classes on Islam and Democracy, Qur'anic Studies, and the Philosophy of Islamic Law. The following year he was a scholar in residence at Yale, and in 2002 to 2003 taught Islamic Political Philosophy at Princeton University. In 2003 to 2004 he took on a visiting scholar position at the Wissenschaftskolleg in Berlin. For the academic year 2006 to 2007 Soroush was the International Institute for the Study of Islam in the Modern World – Leiden (ISIM) visiting professor at the Free University of Amsterdam.

INFLUENCES AND CONTRIBUTIONS

Soroush has attempted to develop an ambitious philosophical framework for the project of reconciling revelation and reason, religious duties, and human rights. His

---

FORCE IS NOT THE BEST WAY TO PRESENT FAITH

■

The Iranian state may be the first ever case of a state that intends to make society religious. But the fact of the matter is that it is neither desirable nor possible for a state to make a society religious, because faith is not amenable to force and because the use of force is not the best way to present faith.

THE IDEAL ISLAMIC STATE: AN UNATTAINABLE QUEST, JANUARY 8, 2006.

I'd noticed this problem in Mr. Khatemi, a problem which I'd previously spoken about in more general terms: lack of vision theoretically leads to lack of courage in action. If you are committed to a line of thinking clearly and decisively, you'll also find the courage to act.

FROM TRANSCRIPT OF TV INTERVIEW WITH SOROUSH BY DARIOUS SAJJADI, BROADCAST ON HOMA TV ON 9 MARCH 2006.

---

overarching endeavor is to combine and synthesize ideas he gathered from his traditional Islamic learning with his intricate knowledge of Western sciences and philosophy.

His body of work is ambitious and consists of a variety of rhetorical and didactic themes that make it hard for the lay reader to fully comprehend the particulars of his arguments. It is only in the last few years that his work has gained notoriety in the West, because most of his work was originally published in Persian and was limited to readers in Iran and the diaspora community.

Soroush is inspired by the fusion of mysticism with the rationalist trend of Islamic philosophy dating back to the medieval Mu'tazilite school of Islamic thought. Soroush's work displays strong mystical tendencies that can be detected in the conceptual structure of his various arguments. He frequently refers to the great mystic poet Jalal al-Din Rumi in his writings and lectures. But he is also familiar and often draws from Western intellectuals such as Juergen Habermas, Michel Foucault, Thomas Kuhn, Paul Feyerabend, and others.

His most notable publication is a compilation of articles that originally appeared in the pages of *Kayhan-i-Farhangi* as a series of articles under the title "The Theoretical Contraction and Expansion of Religion." One key tenet of Soroush's philosophy is drawing a crucial distinction between religion and religious understanding by emphasizing that religious understanding is merely a variety of human understanding. For him, religion remains constant, whereas religious understanding evolves as time passes.

Soroush posits that human interpretations of sacred texts are always in a state of flux because of the influence of the changing times and conditions that believers live in. No interpretation is absolute and fixed for all time, and he points out that religious knowledge is the product of scholars engaged in the study of the unchanging core of Shi'ite Islamic texts. Various scholars interpret the texts differently, depending on their methodology, which may range from the rules of Arabic grammar, to inferential logic, to Aristotelian philosophy. In addition to the particular methods for the study of religion, successive scholars will also be influenced in their interpretations by the advances that have been made in the natural and social sciences. So, the presuppositions of a scholar's intellectual worldview are time-bound. Discerning between correct and incorrect interpretations of religion is an issue of methodology, but because knowledge is a public good, the criteria for distinguishing correct from incorrect knowledge must be open to public scrutiny.

Although there may not be an absolute interpretation of religion, that does not imply that any unsystematic, arbitrary, or haphazard reading of the text should be a valid understanding of religion, or that there is no difference between correct and incorrect understandings.

Another related topic of interest is the role of the clergy in a political system. The clergy's authority, according to Soroush, is based mainly on their expertise in jurisprudence, the technical interpretation of traditional Islamic law. However, as Soroush explains, jurisprudence is only one framework for interpreting the core concepts of Islamic belief, not for conclusively defining them.

The clergy and the centers of power are interconnected in a way that limits the proper development of religious knowledge. Furthermore, structural impediments need to be removed in order for the clerical establishment to reform itself. Seminary students should be encouraged to raise deep and probing questions about the texts they analyze so that the human understanding of religion can be enriched. These students should not be made to feel that a critical reading of religious texts will be perceived as a lapse in faith. Soroush believes that the current system in place only reinforces the ulama's obsession of maintaining their popularity and seeking to expand their audience at the expense of jeopardizing their religious integrity.

Another focus of Soroush's criticism is the income sources of the clergy. The religious establishment has historically been financially supported by the state or by the people. Soroush advocated abolishing both traditions. By relying on external sources for income, the clergy have inherently lost their independence and sense of accountability. Only when the clergy engaged in religious activity are no longer motivated by personal gain but by the genuine desire to understand religion better and cultivate this understanding among the public will they regain their pivotal role in society.

An interrelated current of Soroush's thinking can be found in his writings on ideology, specifically religious ideology. He emphasizes abandoning Islamic ideology as such, because it hinders the growth of religious knowledge. For him, ideologies are meant primarily to fight rival ideologies and to defeat a specific enemy in a specific society. The purpose of an ideology is mass mobilization that is led by the clergy, acting as a class of official interpreters. In an atmosphere of an ideological society, reason and intellectual inquiry are pushed aside and give rise to dictatorships and totalitarian regimes. In order to maintain an official ideological platform that legitimizes the ruling regime, an official class of government-supporter ideologues are imbued with the task of formulation a defense of the ruling ideology.

Soroush's rejection of Islamic ideology as the legitimizing factor in an Islamic state does not amount to his negating the role of religion in politics. Rather he advocates a religious democratic state in which democracy is compatible with religion and an essential to a religious society.

Souroush has enthusiastically embraced key facets of Western development, namely tolerance, freedom of expression, essential oneness of religions, negation of technical domination, preservation of the ecosystem, women's rights, and most importantly, democracy. Although he acknowledges that Western societies have positive features, he is quick to point out that they have defects too. First and foremost on his list of defects is the West's hedonist fetishism with physical gratification.

Considering it both necessary and important to borrow selectively from the West, without succumbing to a blind imitation of Western culture, Soroush has frequently called for a greater dialogue between Iranian and Western cultures. Selective borrowing from Western culture can benefit Iranian culture, provided that this borrowing is the result of free choice.

Commenting on the creation of a state based on Islamic principles, Soroush believes that religiously derived methods of government are insufficient for administering a modern state. Governance methods, according to Soroush, are essentially nonreligious because they are set up to deal with how to plan and administer different aspects of public life. This task necessitates qualified administrative bodies that draw from their expertise in such fields as sociology, economics, and public administration. Religion, per se, offers no specific method or plan of how to govern other than a few legal codes in the *shari'a* (Islamic law) that only cover a limited range of issues.

Soroush has faced a barrage of criticisms over the years. To many in the legalistic spiritual establishment of

Iran, Soroush is at best misguided, and at worst a heretic. He has been viewed by some of his critics as too concerned with pushing religion out of public life and confining it to the private spiritual life of individuals, as is increasingly the case in Western societies. From a theoretical perspective some believe that his concepts are flawed because they do not present an institutional mechanism capable of translating public beliefs into political structures. His response to such accusations has been to the point: It is not Islam per se but the critic's interpretation of Islam that is opposed to democracy.

THE WORLD'S PERSPECTIVES

Abdolkarim Soroush is a leading Iranian philosopher and the embodiment of the Islamic reformation because he uses the dominant religious language of political discourse in Iran. Admirers have referred to him as the Martin Luther of Islam. Others have cautioned attempts at this type of comparison, given the great political, economic, and cultural differences between Luther's Germany and Soroush's Iran.

In recognition of his outstanding intellectual work he was awarded the Erasmus Prize in 2004, and in 2005 *Time* magazine ranked him as among the top hundred men and women whose influence, talent, and exemplary behavior is transforming the world.

His ideas and thoughts have initiated a heated debate and helped create an atmosphere where other reformers could test their ideas and the general public could demand greater participation. Followers in London set up a website under the name Seraj that provides updated information about lectures and interviews he would be giving, and about his publications.

He has a diverse following and it has been noted that Soroush's works have become the subject of many academic dissertations. Many of his books have been reprinted and recently translated into many languages (such as Arabic, Turkish, Indonesian, and English).

LEGACY

At this stage it is too early to assess the legacy of Abdolkarim Soroush's overall volume of work. What make Soroush stand out are his credentials as a devout Muslim and a supporter of the postrevolutionary process.

His major contribution to the debate in contemporary Iran is his contention that Islam is open to different interpretations and therefore cannot and should not be made ideological. Revelation allows for ambiguity of meaning, thus making the same religion adaptable to different societies and historical circumstances. It is his stern belief that no single individual or specific group should claim privileges on holding the true and final interpretation of religion.

The underlying implications of this argument are far-reaching. Namely, it implies that the interpretative work of the clergy (*ulama*) is not definitive, but rather human and historically situated, thus challenging the clergy's self-subscribed exclusive domain of interpretation.

BIBLIOGRAPHY

Ghamari-Tabrizi, Behrooz. "Contentious Public Religion: Two Conceptions of Islam in Revolutionary Iran. Ali Shariati and Abdolkarim Soroush." *International Sociology* 19, no. 4 (2004): 504-523.

Jahanbakhsh, Forough. *Islam, Democracy and Religious Modernism in Iran (1953-2000). From Bazargan to Soroush.* Leiden, The Netherlands: Brill, 2001.

Matin-asgari, Afshin. "'Abdolkarim Soroush and the Secularization of Islamic Thought in Iran." *Iranian Studies* 30, no. 1-2 (1997): 95-115.

Sadri, Mahmoud. "Sacral Defense of Secularism: The Political Theologies of Soroush, Shabestari, and Kadivar." *International Journal of Politics, Culture and Society* 15, no. 2 (2001): 257-270.

Soroush, Abdolkarim. *Reason, Freedom, and Democracy in Islam: Essential Writings of Abdolkarim Soroush.* Translated and edited by Mahmoud Sadri and Ahmad Sadri. New York: Oxford University Press, 2000.

Vakili, Valla. *Debating Religion and Politics in Iran: The Political Thought of Abdolkarim Soroush.* Occasional Papers Series. Washington, DC: Council on Foreign Relations, 1997.

Wright, Robin. *The Last Great Revolution. Turmoil and Transformation in Iran.* New York: Random House, 2000.

Kristian P. Alexander

SOYSAL, MÜMTAZ
(1929–)

Mümtaz Soysal is a professor of constitutional law at Ankara University as well as a columnist in prestigious newspapers in Turkey. He served as a member of Turkish parliament (1991-1998) and minister of foreign affairs (1994). Professor Soysal is the recipient of the first International United Nations Educational, Scientific, and Cultural Organization (UNESCO) Prize for the Teaching of Human Rights (Paris, 1978).

PERSONAL HISTORY

Soysal was born in Zonguldak, Turkey, in 1929. He graduated from Galatasaray high school in 1949 and from Ankara University faculty of political sciences and law in 1954. He worked for two years as an assistant at the Institution of Public Administration for Turkey and the Middle East and later studied at the London School of Economics in England and at Princeton and Berkeley Universities in America. After he returned to Turkey, he received his doctorate from the faculty of social sciences

Mümtaz Soysal. AP IMAGES.

BIOGRAPHICAL HIGHLIGHTS

Name: Mümtaz Soysal

Birth: 1929, Zonguldak, Turkey

Family: Widowed. Wife, Sevgi Soysal (d. 1976); two daughters, Defne and Funda

Nationality: Turkish

Education: BA, Ankara University, 1954; London School of Economics, 1955–1956; Princeton University, 1959–1960; University of California, Berkeley, 1960

PERSONAL CHRONOLOGY:

• **1959–1963:** Administrative law assistant, Ankara University

• **1963–1969:** Constitutional law professor assistant, Ankara University

• **1969–1991:** Constitutional law professor, political sciences faculty, Ankara University

• **1971:** Dean of the political sciences college, Ankara University, arrested during 1971 military coup and serves 14.5 months in prison

• **1974–1978:** Member of the Amnesty International executive board

• **1976–1978:** Vice-chair of the Amnesty International executive board

• **1978–1980, 1988:** Constitutional advisor of Turkish Republic of Northern Cyprus in the Cyprus negotiations

• **1991–1995, 1995–1999:** Member of Turkish Grand National Assembly

where he was later appointed as an assistant (1956). He became an assistant professor in 1959 and an associate professor in 1969. During those years, he was appointed to the Founding Assembly that prepared the 1961 constitution of the Republic of Turkey. He was the founder of the Socialist Culture Society and became the chair of the Mediterranean Social Research Council. He also served as the vice president of Amnesty International.

Soysal became a full professor and was appointed as the dean of his faculty in 1971. However, he resigned after a short period because of his conviction during a 1971 military coup on the basis of a communist propagation he intended to propose in his book. He served 14.5 months in prison. After his sentence, he began to take part in international meetings and many law associations, and has published his work in *Forum*, *Akis*, and *Yön* (one of the founders), *Emek* and *Ortam* reviews, and *Yeni Istanbul*, *Ulus*, *Cumhuriyet*, *Barış*, and *Milliyet* newspapers. He served as a constitutional advisor for the Turkish Republic of northern Cyprus in the Cyprus negotiations between 1978 and 1980, and from 1988 onward.

In the early 1990s, he took an active part in politics and became a member of the Turkish Grand National Assembly between the periods of 1991 to 1995 and 1995 to 1999. He was first elected as deputy of Ankara by joining the Social Democratic People's Party (*Sosyaldemokrat Halk Partisi*, or SHP), which is a Turkish left-wing party established by Murat Karayalçın. However, Soysal gave the government's privatization slate a hard time by trying to stop projects via the courts. He criticized his party for taking a defensive role in the coalition government and suggested offensive approaches. The Social Democratic leader, Deputy Prime Minister Karayalcin, appointed Soysal as the foreign minister of Turkey. Just four days later, Soysal resigned because the government passed a privatization law, earlier opposed by him. While serving in the parliament, his arguments with Çoşkun

Kırca, who had also served as a member of the parliament, put Soysal in front of the spotlight. He took part in accusing the parliament of implanting unconstitutional election laws and disputed some of the parliament's proposals in Turkey's highest court, the Constitutional Court.

Just before 1995 general elections, Soysal decided to continue his political career in another left-wing organization, the Democratic Left Party (*Demokratik Sol Parti*, or DSP). He was elected to the parliament as deputy of Zonguldak. He served as a foreign minister in Bulent Ecevit's cabinet and worked hard to improve relations with Armenia. In 1996, Soysal had applied to the Constitutional Court for cancellation of a law planned to provide privatization of the Turkish Telecom (TT) when he was a deputy of the DSP. The court cancelled the law upon his application. At that time, about U.S.$30 billion was proposed for TT, an amount totaling Turkey's domestic and foreign debts. A year later, he resigned from the cabinet and from Ecevit's Democratic Left Party because of a conflict with the prime minister's wife, Rahsan Ecevit.

Now serving as leader of the newly established Independent Republic Party (*Bagimsiz Cumhuriyet Partisi*, or BCP), he is still opposed to privatization and to higher education being provided in foreign languages. He believes that the recent political approaches do not reflect the needs and expectations of the people. One of his slogans, "Turkey is not governed from Turkey," refers to the control that foreign powers like the United States and the European Union wield over Turkey's economic reforms and foreign policy.

INFLUENCES AND CONTRIBUTIONS

Soysal was influenced by the moral and legal basis of the human rights concept that human beings have universal rights, regardless of legal jurisdiction or ethnicity and nationality. Examples of human rights are the security rights that prohibit crimes, liberty rights that protect freedoms in areas such as belief and religion, political rights that protect the liberty to engage in political activity, due process rights that require a fair trial when charged with a crime, equality rights that guarantee equal citizenship, welfare rights that require the provision of things such as education and protections against severe poverty and starvation, and group rights that provide protection for groups against ethnic genocide and for the ownership by countries of their national territories.

He sincerely believed that these rights exist in morality and in law at the national and international levels, and followed the path of these beliefs through his academic and political career. He received the UNESCO International Human Rights Education Award that was given first in 1979. This UNESCO award was given to him because of his efficient, exemplary, and genuine contribution to the development of the teaching of human rights.

CONTEMPORARIES

Rauf Denktash was born on 27 January 1924 in Paphos, British-controlled Cyprus. After legal studies in Britain, he returned to Cyprus and became a practicing attorney. A member of the Turkish Cypriot community, in 1957 he helped form the Turkish Resistance Organization (TMT) in Cyprus to resist the Greek National Organization of Cypriot Fighters (EOKA) guerrilla organization. After Cypriot independence from Britain in 1960, he became the head of the Turkish Communal Chamber in the new government. After the failed 1974 Greek Cypriot coup that tried to unite Cyprus with Greece, and the subsequent invasion of the northern part of Cyprus by troops from Turkey, the island was divided into two zones: The Republic of Cyprus, which was the power controlling the Greek portion of the island in the south, and the Turkish Federated State of Cyprus, a government headed by Denktash in the north. In 1983, Denktash helped create the new Turkish Republic of Northern Cyprus, although the only nation that recognized the new government was Turkey. He served as the president of the Turkish Republic of Northern Cyprus until 2005.

Soysal lectures as a professor of law on human rights and serves as a deputy in the parliament; he always pays great attention to the Cyprus issue and served as the constitutional adviser to former president of the Turkish Republic of Northern Cyprus, Rauf Denktas; he assumed critical roles during the Annan Plan, which was a proposal by United Nations Secretary-General Kofi Annan to settle the Cyprus dispute of the divided island nation of Cyprus as the United Cyprus Republic. As Soysal had predicted, Greek Cypriots said no to the referendum and were accepted as a member of EU, and Turkish Cypriots are still trying to remove the embargoes that have resulted from this.

As a former foreign minister, Soysal also worked on Kurdish and Armenian issues. He thinks that the United States, and especially Britain, are provoking these issues. As a solution, he proposed a specific economic plan that can be supported by private and state investments for southeastern Anatolia because of the negative economic conditions in the region.

On the political stage, Soysal is known as a strong opponent to many issues, the most famous of which is his opposition to privatization. He believes that a mixed (public-private) economy is still necessary for Turkey's economic progress, especially in the southeast. He says that there should be government policies supporting labor-intensive investments in those regions and that mass migration to other places can be avoided.

When Turkey's attempts at Westernization are the concern, Soysal reminds the Turkish people that the EU says all the time that Turkey will not be a full member, and that the United States is trying to establish an independent Kurdish state just next to Turkey's southeastern region. He believes the Western world is orchestrating the press on the Kemalist republic and is supporting political Islam. Based on these statements, Soysal believes Turkey should get angry, cool off its relationship with these Western countries, be relaxed, and then be in a tough spot with the EU, or try hard to become a stronger and sounder nation.

THE WORLD'S PERSPECTIVE

Soysal is a well-respected human rights activist and his work is highly recognized by Turkish and international authorities. He was the first person to collect the UNESCO International Human Rights Education Award in 1979. Since then, he has continued to work for human rights all over the world.

LEGACY

Soysal is a distinguished professor of law and human rights, and his lectures and work have an influence on the Turkish legal system and political arena. As a former deputy and foreign minister, Soysal had applied to the Constitutional Court for election laws and for the cancellation of a law planned to provide privatization. Even though he has many opponents, he still continues to support the government's role in Turkey's developmental attempts.

BIBLIOGRAPHY

Brown, James. "The Turkish Imbroglio: Its Kurds." *Annals of the American Academy of Political and Social Science* 541 (September 1995): 116-129.

Kushner, David. "Self-Perception and Identity in Contemporary Turkey." *Journal of Contemporary History* 32, no. 2 (April 1997): 219-233

Salem, Norma, ed. *Cyprus: A Regional Conflict and Its Resolution.* London: Macmillan for Canadian Institute for International Peace and Security, 1992.

Soysal, Mümtaz. Speech at United Nations Convention Against Transnational Organized Crime, 13 December 2000. United Nations Office on Drugs and Crime. Available from http://www.unodc.org/palermo/soysal.htm

Erdem Aygok

SUAN, ABBAS
(1976–)

Abbas Suan is an internationally known Palestinian Israeli soccer player, and a leading member of the Israeli national team. He has used his position to raise awareness of the problems of the Palestinian community in Israel and the need for better relations between Arabs and Jews.

PERSONAL HISTORY

Abbas Suan was born on 27 January 1976, in Sakhnin, Israel, a Palestinian Arab village of approximately 24,000 residents in the northern region of Galilee. Before the 1948 War, Suan's father and grandfather owned land and lived in Marsas, Palestine, until they were forced to flee to Sakhnin. Suan is the youngest of seven brothers and two sisters.

Suan began playing soccer at age six. At twelve he joined the youth club, Ha-Po'el Sakhnin, and played intermittently for that organization's professional team. As an adult, he played and later became captain of B'nei Sakhnin, the only Arab team in Israel's first league, from 2003 to 2006. Avraham Grant, coach of the Israeli national team, recruited Suan to his current midfielder postion in 2004. He was one of the national team's top players during the 2005 World Cup qualifying games. In fall 2006, Suan joined Maccabi Haifa, the 2005–2006 champions of the premier league. Suan also has endorsement deals with Subaru, Toto (the Israeli state lottery), and McDonald's.

INFLUENCES AND CONTRIBUTIONS

Suan began playing soccer with his neighborhood friends in Sakhnin. He was influenced by four of his older brothers, who also played soccer for Sakhnin. As Suan matured, he began to look up to players such as Zinedine Zidane and Marcel Desailly of France.

Suan is a soccer icon in Israel, particularly among the Palestinian Israeli community, which comprises about 20 percent of Israel's population. As captain of B'nei Sakhnin he led the team to become the first mainly Arab soccer team to win the Israeli State Cup in May 2004. After Sakhnin won, Suan became not only a focal point for the success of the team, but a hero among the Palestinian community in Israel.

Suan first came to international attention on 27 March 2005 when he kicked the game-tying goal for the Israeli national team during a World Cup qualifying game against Ireland. The goal saved Israel from elimination and allowed the team to continue to compete for an opportunity to play for the World Cup in 2006, for the first time since 1970. Referred to as "the Arab who saved Israel" by *Sports Illustrated* (24 August 2005), Suan, one of only three Arab players on a predominantly Jewish team, became a symbol of peaceful

BIOGRAPHICAL HIGHLIGHTS

Name: Abbas Suan (Abbass Swan, Abbas Souan, 'Abbas Suwwan)

Birth: 1976, Sakhnin, Israel

Family: Wife, Safaa; one son, Muhammad; one daughter, Mabsam

Nationality: Israeli (Palestinian Israeli citizen)

PERSONAL CHRONOLOGY:

- **1993–1994:** Plays for Ha-Po'el Sakhnin youth and professional teams
- **1994–2006:** Plays for B'nei Sakhnin professional team
- **2004:** Leads first Arab team (B'nei Sakhnin) to win Israeli State Cup
- **2004–present:** Plays on Israel National Team
- **2005:** Scores game-tying, last-minute goal against Ireland in World Cup qualifier
- **2006–present:** Plays for Maccabi Haifa professional team

a symbol of the Palestinian Israeli community. Yet he continues to face constant taunts and racism from Jewish fans and players on opposing teams. Opposing fans have chanted "Death to the Arabs," and have held banners saying, "SUAN YOU DON'T REPRESENT US," particularly when Suan played for B'nei Sakhnin.

LEGACY

Abbas Suan will go down in history as the captain of the first Palestinian Israeli team to win the Israeli State Cup and as one of the pioneers of Arab soccer players' participation and success on the Israeli national team.

BIBLIOGRAPHY

Bekker, Vita. "Score One for Tolerance: Arab Israeli Soccer Player Abbas Suan Unites Jews and Arabs through His Game." *Time Europe*, 10 October 2005. Available from http://www.time.com.

Erlanger, Steven. "An Arab star is torn." *The Age*, 24 April 2005. Available from http://www.theage.com.au.

Mitnick, Joshua. "One Big Goal for Soccer, One Small Step for Arab Israelis." *Christian Science Monitor*, 7 April 2005. Available from http://www.csmonitor.com.

Wahl, Grant. "My Sportsman Choice: Abbas Suan." *Sports Illustrated*. (4 November 2005). Available from http://sportsillustrated.cnn.com.

Kenda Stewart

coexistence between the Arab and Jewish communities, as the two groups of fans united to support the national team.

Off the field, Suan has been a relatively outspoken supporter for coexistence and better relations between Jews and Arabs. He also uses his visibility in the media to raise awareness about the social and economic needs of the Palestinian Israeli community. In fact, Suan's 2005 goal has been credited with returning the discussion of the status of Israel's Palestinian citizens to the forefront of public debate in Israel.

THE WORLD'S PERSPECTIVE

Suan held the world's attention in 2005 as the Israeli national team attempted to qualify for the World Cup for the first time in thirty-six years. The international media referred to him as a "national hero." In the 4 November 2005 edition of *Sports Illustrated,* Grant Wahl named Suan as his choice for "Sportsman of the Year." The European edition of *Time* published an article about him in its "European Heroes 2005" issue (10 October 2005). According to Suan in a 4 January 2007 interview with the author in Haifa, he is an "Israeli Arab that does not forget his family in Palestine but respects the rules of his state (Israel)."

In Israel, the perspective is more complicated. Some revere Suan as one of the best soccer players in Israel, and

SULEIMAN, ELIA
(1960–)

Palestinian film director Elia Suleiman (also Sulayman) is perhaps the most prominent Palestinian *auteur* filmmaker, and one of the most acclaimed Arab *auteurs*, having been awarded several of the most prestigious awards from international film festivals for his work. His filmmaking often draws upon autobiographical elements and settings within his hometown of Nazareth, producing a body of work that is strikingly consistent in its use of melancholic humor, its focus on the absurd in the quotidian, and its unflinching engagement with often-unexplored layers of the narratives of tragedy and resistance that define the post-1948 Palestinian experience.

PERSONAL HISTORY

Suleiman was born in 1960 in the Palestinian community of Nazareth in northern Israel. His interest in cinema apparently found a fertile ground only after he moved to New York City in the 1980s, living there for about twelve years. After making a series of short and experimental films in New York, Suleiman returned to Palestine in the mid-1990s, taking a visiting post teaching at

Elia Suleiman. AP IMAGES.

Bir Zeit University in the West Bank while working on his first feature film *Sijl Ikhtifa* (*Chronicle of a Disappearance*, 1996). Living for a period in East Jerusalem, Suleiman left the area around the beginning of the second intifada in 2000, and afterward has largely based himself in France. In 2003, he released his second feature film *Yad Ilahiyya* (*Divine Intervention*, 2002), which won the Jury Prize at the Cannes Film Festival. In addition to filmmaking, Suleiman has produced a small body of film criticism, and has served on film juries such as the main jury for the 2005 Cannes Film Festival.

INFLUENCES AND CONTRIBUTIONS

Suleiman began working in filmmaking during his time in New York, co-directing the feature-length documentary/montage film, *Muqaddima li'l-Nihayat Jidal* (Introduction to the End of an Argument, 1990) with Lebanese-Canadian artist and filmmaker Jayce Salloum. A densely woven, intricately edited montage of news footage, material from classical Hollywood cinema, and documentary video footage from Palestine, this film is one of the finest deconstruc-

BIOGRAPHICAL HIGHLIGHTS

Name: Elia Suleiman

Birth: 1960, Nazareth, Israel

Nationality: Palestinian; citizen of Israel

Education: High school

PERSONAL CHRONOLOGY:

• **1990:** Directs *Muqaddima li'l-Nihayat Jidal* (Introduction to the End of an Argument)

• **1992:** Directs *Homage by Assassination*, a short film in the collection *Harb al Khalij... wa ba'd*

• **1996:** Directs *Sijl Ikhtifa* (*Chronicle of a Disappearance*); awarded Best First Feature Film at Venice International Film Festival

• **2000:** Directs *Hilm Arabi* (The Arab Dream)

• **2002:** *Directs Yad Ilahiyya* (Divine Intervention); awarded Jury Prize at Cannes Film Festival

tions of the representation of the Middle East—in particular the Palestinian-Israeli issue—within Western media. In some ways this work stands in stark contrast to the aesthetic strategies Suleiman was to develop in his later filmmaking. Nonetheless this film presages the particular use of irony and humor developed in his later work.

Suleiman's work is often compared to that of great comedic film talents such as Buster Keaton, Jacques Tati, and even Charlie Chaplin. However, he himself more often cites the work of Robert Bresson as being inspirational, while also noting the influence of East Asian filmmakers such as Hou Hsiao Hsien and Tsai Ming-Liang on his work (Porton, p. 27).

His 1992 short film *Homage by Assassination* sets out many of the aesthetic strategies which would come to define his later cinematic work—elements such as static shots, shots often framed through doorways and windows, the propensity for action to occur at the margins of the frame, as well as the tension developed by awkward silences and inconclusive interruptions. However, critical attention and regard for Suleiman's particular talents as an auteur filmmaker only fully emerged after the release of his first feature *Chronicle of a Disappearance* in 1996. As in *Homage by Assassination*, Suleiman plays the main role in this feature, the character E. S.—a character who never speaks and who most often acts as a passive observer of actions around him. *Chronicle of a Disappearance* is a narrative film only in the most general sense of

CONTEMPORARIES

Elia Suleiman is a member of what may be termed the second generation of Palestinian narrative filmmakers, coming to prominence after the groundbreaking work of Palestinian directors such as the politically committed Mustapha Abu Ali (1938–) ("They Do Not Exist") or the auteur work of Michel Khleifi (1950–) ("Wedding in Galilee"). Suleiman's contemporaries include Hany Abu-Assad (1961–) ("Paradise Now") and Rashid Masharawi (1962–) ("Haifa"), who have brought Palestinian cinema to a higher international prominence as a result of their work during the 1990s. However, Suleiman should also be considered among a group of international filmmakers of Arab or Middle Eastern origin who have achieved a prominence in global cinema in the same period, including figures such as Iran's ABBAS KIAROSTAMI, Turkey's NURI BILGE CEYLAN, and Mauritania's Abderrahmane Sissako.

the term; while purporting to be about the return to Nazareth from a self-imposed exile in New York, most of the action of the film relates to short everyday scenes centered on the mundane lives of a number of Nazerine and Jerusalemite characters who are family, friends, and neighbors (many of them played by Suleiman's actual family, friends, and neighbors). On the surface these disconnected vignettes seem to rarely present a narrative continuity, although the occasional appearance of the character E. S. does allow for a sense of some focus. The camera and Suleiman's protagonist impassively and statically view the scenes with an ironic distance. Many scenes are positively hilarious, albeit with a most intimate kind of melancholic humor, commenting pessimistically on both the status of Palestinians inside Israel as well as on the highly inflated hopes of the "Oslo period" of the 1990s during which the film was made and released.

Chronicle of a Disappearance won several film festival awards and was reviewed favorably by international film critics. Stuart Klawans, writing in *The Nation*, described the film as "thoroughly extraordinary," while also identifying a particular criticism that has also at times been directed at Suleiman's work—an accusation that his work over-intellectualizes the Palestinian-Israeli predicament. Klawans says, "Yes, he's unmasked the absurdity of Jewish nationalism, but without affirming Palestinian nationalism. Such loftiness is possible only for intellectuals, artists, and those

who have never missed a meal; a day-laborer under curfew in Gaza might prefer a political response that fits in the hand." Suleiman has since admitted that he "may have censored" himself somewhat in *Chronicle of a Disappearance*. The film also invited some controversy due to Suleiman's request for payment from Israel for a portion of its production costs (the film was largely produced with French money). Suleiman has responded to this criticism by asserting that, as a citizen of Israel, soliciting these funds was an act of demanding his civil rights rather than an act of political acquiescence.

Suleiman's second feature *Yad Ilahiyya* (*Divine Intervention*) builds upon and continues with the structure and themes developed in *Chronicle of a Disappearance*. The character E. S. returns, and much of the action again takes place in Nazareth with some of the same characters of the first feature. Similarly, the film is constructed around a series of everyday vignettes marked by the same ironic distance and humor. Beneath these similarities, however, the films are distinctly different. *Divine Intervention* has a stronger sense of narrative and pursues a more explicitly political set of issues. The film's narrative follows the failure of E. S.'s father's business, causing his father to suffer a heart attack. While his father is in hospital, E. S. pursues a love affair with a woman who lives in Ramallah; because of the Israeli checkpoint between their homes, they can only meet in a parking lot beside the checkpoint. Eventually his father dies and his lover stops coming to meet him. E. S. continues to act as a silent observer of events around him, in a situation more dire than that of *Chronicle of a Disappearance*. The vignettes are more pointed, more directly engaging with the militarization of Israeli society and the grinding frustration for Palestinians. Also, in *Divine Intervention*, Suleiman pushes the fantasies that result from this frustration into colorful relief, most remarkably in a completely unexpected sequence featuring a Palestinian female ninja-guerilla who fights off a group of Israeli special agents and destroys a helicopter.

Divine Intervention gained a degree of notoriety in 2003 when it was submitted by the Palestinian Authority as the official Palestinian entry to the American Academy Awards. Initially the Academy refused to allow an entry from Palestine, and a public debate ensued. Ironically, only two years later the Academy accepted the Palestinian entry *Paradise Now* (directed by HANY ABU-ASSAD) as a nominee for the 2005 Best Foreign Film award.

THE WORLD'S PERSPECTIVE

Among film scholars and critics, Suleiman is perhaps the most widely acclaimed of the second generation of Palestinian narrative filmmakers. While his contemporaries such as Rashid Masharawi and especially Abu-Assad have themselves attracted significant critical praise and global

> ## THE NORMATIVE PRESSURES OF DAILY LIFE IN THE SPECTACULAR ABSURDITY
>
> ■
>
> Suleiman's film [*Divine Intervention*] makes no claim to documentary reality. What he presents are the normative pressures of daily life in the spectacular absurdity: through involuntary reactions to sight gags, to the over-the-top behavior of checkpoint guards, to the irrational acting-out of people under impossible stress, the viewer is carried beyond whatever didactic political positions he or she came in with.... From this perspective the question of "balance" seems moot. You don't have to be Palestinian to relate to Suleiman's movie in these dark times. It's impossible, on the other hand, to ignore the specific situation *Divine Intervention* addresses. Like any other 'minority' artist, Suleiman finds himself speaking for a whole minority when he basically wants to speak for himself.
>
> GARY INDIANA IN *FILM COMMENT*, 31.

Indiana, Gary. "Minority Report." *Film Comment* 39, no.1 (Jan/ Feb 2003): 28-31.

Klawans, Stuart. Review of *Chronicle of a Disappearance. The Nation* (16 June 1997).

Porton, Richard. "Notes from the Palestinian Diaspora: An Interview with Elia Suleiman." *Cineaste* 28, no. 3 (Summer 2003): 24-27.

Kamran Rastegar

SUSWA, AMAT AL-ALIM AL-
(1958–)

Amat al-Alim al-Suswa is a Yemeni human rights activist.

PERSONAL HISTORY

Al-Suswa was born in 1958 in Ta'izz, Yemen. She started her career early at age seven in Ta'izz as an announcer of children's programs on a local radio station. While working she completed her secondary education in Ta'izz and went on to Cairo University to complete a BA in mass communications in 1980. In 1984, she earned an MA in international communications from The American University, Washington, D.C.

INFLUENCES AND CONTRIBUTIONS

In addition to her long career in Yemeni radio and television as an announcer and program director, al-Suswa has also lectured at San'a University in the faculty of political science and has published reports on women's issues (such as *Yemeni Women in Figures,* San'a 1996). She joined the ruling People's General Congress prior to the unification of North Yemen and South Yemen in 1990 and gained high posts in the party hierarchy, including as member of the Permanent Committee (1986–). She is a long-time activist in Yemen's women's movement and a founding member of the National Women's Committee (NWC). She has chaired both the NWC (1993) and the Yemeni Women's Union (1989-1990). In 1991 she was nominated assistant deputy minister of the ministry of information and in 1997 she became the deputy minister. After leaving the ministry, she served as the country's ambassador to the Netherlands from 2001 to 2003—the first woman in a high foreign ministry position since unification and only the second woman ever to act as a full cabinet member in the Yemeni cabinet. In May 2003 al-Suswa was nominated as the state minister for human rights. She is particularly interested in questions of freedom of opinion and freedom of the press.

audiences, neither has enjoyed the same degree of critical adulation from the highest levels of the film establishments of Europe and the United States. Suleiman himself has maintained a balance between his identification with Palestinian cinema and his position as a largely European-produced filmmaker whose audience is arguably largely outside of Palestine.

LEGACY

Suleiman has already gained prominence among global film experts for his highly developed and very original aesthetic vision. He will most certainly be remembered as one of the most prominent of Palestinian filmmakers, in particular for his use of cinema as a means to raise questions about Palestinian aspirations and identity that are more ambivalent and unresolved than those of prior filmmakers. His film language has already been recognized as influential upon international filmmakers such as Mauritania's Abdelrahman Cissako. It remains to be seen if his work will continue in the same vein as his first two features, or if he will be able to successfully extend his aesthetic vision into new areas.

BIBLIOGRAPHY

"Elia Suleiman." Midnight Sun Film Festival. Available from http://www.msfilmfestival.fi/page.php?p=805.

BIOGRAPHICAL HIGHLIGHTS

Name: Amat al-Amin al-Suswa

Birth: 1958, Ta'izz, Yemen

Family: Married; two children

Nationality: Yemeni

Education: B.A. (mass communications), Cairo University, 1980; M.A. (international communications), The American University, Washington

PERSONAL CHRONOLOGY:

- **1989:** Chair, Yemeni Women's Union
- **1993:** Chair, National Women's Committee in Yemen
- **1996:** Advisor for women and poverty, United Nations Development Programme
- **1997:** Yemeni deputy minister of information
- **2001:** Yemeni ambassador to the Netherlands
- **2003:** Yemeni state minister for human rights

THE WORLD'S PERSPECTIVE

Al-Suswa became a noted figure outside Yemen as well as inside. In 1996, she became the advisor for women and poverty for the United Nations Development Programme, and eventually director of its regional office for Arab countries and deputy director.

LEGACY

Al-Suswa is still leaving her mark, but will be remembered among other things for becoming one of the highest-ranking female politicians in modern Yemen.

BIBLIOGRAPHY

Paluch, Marta, ed. *Yemeni Voices: Women Tell Their Stories.* Sanaa, Yemen: British Council, Yemen, 2001.

Susanne Dahlgren
updated by Michael R. Fischbach

TALABANI, JALAL
(1933–)

Jalal Talabani is the first elected Iraqi head of state since the establishment of modern Iraq in 1921. He is the founder and chairman of the Patriotic Union of Kurdistan, one of the two main parties in Iraq's Kurdistan region.

PERSONAL HISTORY

Talabani was born in 1933 in the village of Kelkan, near Dokan Lake in Iraqi Kurdistan. He received his early education in the town of Koysanjaq and went to secondary school in Kirkuk. Talabani's initiation into politics was at an unusually early age; he joined the Kurdistan Democratic Party (KDP) when he was fourteen years old and moved up in the ranks until becoming a member of its Central Committee when he was barely eighteen years old. He initially tried to enter medical school, but ended up studying law. After three years in the law school, he was compelled to go into hiding in 1956 to avoid persecution for his political activism organizing Kurdish students. The toppling of the monarchy in 1958 enabled him to finish his education; he returned to law school and graduated in 1959. He was drafted into the military, but two years later he was fighting in the Kurdish uprising against the Iraqi government. After serving the Kurdish cause under the banner of the KDP, both as a fighter and as a diplomat and political negotiator, he formed his own views on the best way to achieve his people's objectives. His differences with the KDP leadership led him to form his own party, the Patriotic Union of Kurdistan (PUK) in 1975.

Following his departure from the KDP, Talabani established himself as a leader of a major Kurdish faction that controlled the eastern Iraqi Kurdish territories, mainly with the help of Iran. This relationship with Iran was not free of setbacks and betrayals—the greatest of which took place after the conclusion of the 1975 agreement between the Shah of Iran and the Iraqi government of SADDAM HUSSEIN with the help of Algeria. Under the terms of the agreement, the Shah cut off all military and logistic help to the Iraqi Kurds in exchange for water and territorial concessions.

INFLUENCES AND CONTRIBUTIONS

Talabani was a high-ranking member of the KDP. In this capacity, he participated in many political activities on behalf of the party. He was a member of the delegation that went to Baghdad in 1963 to conduct negotiations with the Iraqi president, Abd al-Salam Arif. However, by 1975, he and fellow KDP members were at odds with the party leader, Mustafa Barzani. They formed their own

Jalal Talabani. AP IMAGES.

BIOGRAPHICAL HIGHLIGHTS

Name: Jalal Talabani

Birth: 1933, Kelkan, Sulaymaniyya, Iraq

Family: Wife; two sons: Qubad and Bavel

Nationality: Iraqi (Kurdish)

Education: Law degree, 1959

PERSONAL CHRONOLOGY:

• **1951:** Elected member of the Central Committee of the Kurdistan Democratic Party (KDP)

• **1959:** Begins practicing law

• **1975:** Founds the Patriotic Union of Kurdistan (PUK), becomes chairman

• **2003:** Appointed member of the (U.S.-controlled) Iraqi Governing Council

• **2005:** Elected president in provisional government

• **2006:** Elected president

party, the PUK, around a group within the KDP known as the Political Bureau, which had existed at least since 1966, when it allied itself with the Baghdad government in a short-lived pact that ended with the 1968 coup that brought the Ba'th to power. The group ended its activities following the announcement of the 11 March 1970 agreement between Barzani and the government.

Throughout the 1980s, Talabani and his PUK engaged the Iraqi government in continuous fighting that ended in the murderous 1988 "al-Anfal" (Spoils of War, a Qur'anic reference) campaign that caused the death of tens of thousands of Kurds, mostly civilians, with conventional and chemical weapons. Talabani and his party were targets of chemical weapons, as the Anfal trial that was held in post-Saddam Iraq revealed. While Saddam Hussein was ultimately responsible for ordering the atrocities, the main figure in charge of executing the campaign was Saddam's cousin, ALI HASAN AL-MAJID, who acquired the nickname "Ali al-Kimawyi" (Chemical Ali). He notoriously bragged about the use of the chemical weapons, but went on to declare, on tape, "I will bomb them [i.e. the Kurds] with chemical weapons. Who is going to object? The international [community]?

F*** the international [community] and those who intercede on their behalf of all God's countries."

Being at a great military disadvantage and feeling abandoned by the international community, which supplied Saddam with conventional and chemical weapons and saw him as a necessary evil, Talabani sought refuge in Iran, saving the fight for another day. This day came in 1991, when Saddam Hussein's regime lost its Western patronage. Following the regime's defeat in Kuwait, popular uprisings—at American urging—started in the Shi'ite cities of southern Iraq and the Kurdish areas of northern Iraq in March 1991. The refusal of the U.S. and its allies to support the rebels caused the collapse of the uprisings and helped the regime crush the southern cities through systematic massacres. Hundreds of thousands fled the area for Iran and Saudi Arabia, while those less fortunate fell into the hands of the Iraqi army.

The fate of Iraqi Kurdistan was comparatively better this time. Painful images in international media of innocent Kurdish civilians leaving their homes in freezing weather in Kurdistan's mountainous terrain aided Talabani in his effort to negotiate the creation of a safe haven in parts of Kurdistan. His mission succeeded, and thousands of lives were saved.

A year later, a parliament and a regional government were founded after fairly democratic elections in the

Kurdish enclave. Having lost contact with their common enemy, the Baghdad government, Talabani's PUK and the KDP, now led by MAS'UD BARZANI, revived their three-decade-long rivalry. A bitter fight ensued between 1994 and 1998. Talabani and Barzani signed a peace agreement in Washington that year, and on 4 October 2002 the Kurdish regional government held a session with both parties represented. Jalal Talabani seized the opportunity and called for a law to ban fighting among Kurdish factions.

In the months prior to the March 2003 U.S. invasion of Iraq, Talabani participated in many conferences held by Iraqi opposition groups in London, Kurdistan, and other places. He secured certain commitments from his Shi'ite counterparts concerning future power- and wealth-sharing arrangements, as well as other outstanding issues between the Kurds and Iraq's Arab governments. Following the collapse of Saddam's regime in April 2003, he was selected by L. Paul Bremer, the U.S. administrator of Iraq, to serve on an Iraqi "Governing Council." He was one of ten members of the Governing Council who took turns serving for a month as president of the Council. For the balance of the year, he was a chief negotiator in the process of writing a transitional law in preparation for drafting a permanent constitution.

Following the two elections held in Iraq after the *de jure* transfer of power to the Iraqis in June 2004, Talabani was elected by the Iraqi parliament to the position of president, making him not only the first elected, but also the first Kurdish Iraqi head of state. The only time a Kurd held substantial power in Iraq was in 1936, when General Bakr al-Sidqi staged a short-lived coup d'état.

THE WORLD'S PERSPECTIVE

Talabani's standing in the international community is excellent. He is generally known for his pleasant personality, apparent humility, and calculated pragmatism. His success in carving a safe enclave for the Kurds in 1991 is a testimony not only to his diplomatic skills, but also to his access to key international policymakers. He is also acknowledged as a moderate Kurdish nationalist. In Europe, he is especially praised for his position against the death penalty.

LEGACY

In spite of his long history of political struggle and his impressive accomplishments, it is too early to discern the ultimate legacy of this still-active politician. In the past he was associated with the effort to secure Kurdish national interests and aspirations, and with intracommunal Kurdish politics. However, since 2003, he has been a major participant in the shaping of the contemporary state of Iraq. Perhaps his greatest legacy—should an Iraqi state

ORDER IS CERTAINLY IMPORTANT, BUT SO IS FREEDOM

You know, before becoming president of Iraq, I always called for Kurdish Arab brotherhood for common struggle, against dictatorship, for having democracy, and democratic federal regime in Iraq. It is some slogans that we struggled for in the past. Nowadays also I can say to the Kurds stay inside democratic federal Iraq, better for you than asking for a kind of independence which is impossible.

JALAL TALABANI, "INTERVIEW WITH RAY SUAREZ." *NEWSHOUR WITH JIM LEHRER*, 15 SEPTEMBER 2005.

There are occasional immoral voices that call for a new dictatorship to be installed in Iraq as, they claim, a less laborious means of imposing order. Order is certainly important, but so is freedom. A restored dictatorship in Iraq will be neither friendly nor benign. Animated by vengeance and fed by oil, a new dictatorship will again seek to make Iraq into the Arab Prussia and the overlord of the Gulf, goals that Iraqi regimes before Saddam aspired to.

Building democracy in Iraq is not a fanciful quest, but a recognition that all other approaches have failed. True stability comes from consent, not from the illusory 'stability' of dictatorships. It is therefore in our mutual interest that we pursue the cause of democracy. We may falter, we may tire, but if we persevere, we shall not be defeated.

JALAL TALABANI, "IRAQ'S MESSAGE TO MR BLAIR." *TIMES* (LONDON), 10 OCTOBER 2005.

that includes Kurdistan survive—will be based on his success in balancing his obligations to his own cause with his constitutional duties as head of the Iraqi state.

BIBLIOGRAPHY

Anderson, Liam, and Gareth Stansfield. *The Future of Iraq.* New York: Palgrave, 2004.

Gunter, Michael. *The Kurds of Iraq.* New York: St. Martin's Press, 1992.

Kadhim, Abbas K. "An Opportunity They Can't Afford to Miss." *Bitterlemons International,* 18 December 2003. Available from http://www.bitterlemons-international.org/inside.php?id=82.

O'Leary, Brendan, et al. (eds). *The Future of Kurdistan in Iraq.* Philadelphia: University of Pennsylvania Press, 2005.

Patriotic Union of Kurdistan (PUK). Official website. Available from http://www.puk.org.

Suarez, Ray. "Newsmaker: Jalal Talabani." Interview, PBS *NewsHour with Jim Lehrer*, 15 September 2005. Available from http://www.pbs.org/newshour/bb/middle_east/july-dec05/talabani_9-15.html.

Talabani, Jalal. "Iraq's Message to Mr. Blair: We Still Need the Troops That Saved Us from Tyranny." *The Times* (London), 10 October 2005. Available from http://www.times online.co.uk/tol/comment/columnists/guest_contributors/article576691.ece.

Abbas Kadhim

TALAT, MEHMET ALI
(1952–)

Mehmet Ali Talat is the current president of the Turkish Republic of Northern Cyprus (TRNC), a government that no country except Turkey has recognized. He was the leader of the left-wing Republican Turkish Party (RTP, *Cumhuriyetçi Türk Partisi*), became prime minister in 2004, and consequently won the presidential election held on 17 April 2005. It was under his leadership that United Nations (UN)-sponsored negotiations between Turkish and Greek Cypriots were continued; however, bi-zonal, bi-communal settlement in Cyprus under the auspices of the UN has not been established yet.

PERSONAL HISTORY

Talat was born on 6 July 1952 in Kyrenia, Cyprus. After his graduation from Kyrenia high school, he began to study electrics at the electronics department of the Middle East Technical University (METU) in Ankara, Turkey. Besides his undergraduate work, he volunteered and became a president in student associations that had been established by Turkish Cypriot students. He was also the founder and the first chairman of Turkish Cypriot Students' Youth Federation (KOGEF). Talat's active role in student associations was translated into his early political career in the youth movement of the Republican Turkish Party. He served on various committees and organs of the RTP for many years.

After graduating from university, he returned to Cyprus and worked as a refrigerator repairer in Kyrenia. He continued his political career and was assigned as the minister of education and culture in the first Democrat Party (DP; *Demokrat Parti*)-RTP coalition government, formed after the parliamentary elections held in December 1993. He continued in the same position during the second DP-RTP coalition government. In the third DP-

BIOGRAPHICAL HIGHLIGHTS

Name: Mehmet Ali Talat

Birth: 1952, Kyrenia, Cyprus

Family: Wife, Oya Talat; one son, one daughter

Nationality: Turkish Cypriot

Education: Middle East Technical University (METU), Ankara, Turkey, 1977, M.Sc. electrical engineering; Eastern Mediterranean University, 2004, M.A. international relations

PERSONAL CHRONOLOGY:

- **1993:** Becomes the minister of education and culture in TRNC
- **1996:** Elected as leader of the RTP
- **2004-2005:** Forms the RTP and DP coalition government
- **2005:** Elected as the second president of TRNC, following president Rauf Denktaş

RTP coalition government, he was assigned as the deputy prime minister and minister of state of the TRNC.

Talat was elected as the leader of the RTP in the fourteenth convention of the Party, which was held on 14 January 1996. This was a turning point in his career, and his political stand began to manifest itself more clearly during these years. He became the leader of the Turkish Cypriots who wanted the unification of the island—the northern, Turkish part of Cyprus controlled by the TRNC and the southern, Greek part controlled by the Republic of Cyprus—and who were prepared to vote yes in the historical referenda of the plan developed by UN Secretary-General Kofi Annan. Talat was elected as a member of parliament from Nicosia in the 1998 and 2003 parliamentary elections, and he formed his first DP-RTP coalition government on 13 January 2004. The same year, he completed his M.A. degree in international relations at the Eastern Mediterranean University, where he submitted his thesis titled "Cyprus Problem and the Annan Plan." After the early elections held on 20 February 2005, he formed the second DP-RTP coalition government on 8 March 2005, which continued until the latest presidential elections.

The presidential journey of Talat begins prior to the 2004 referendum on the Annan Plan. Talat became the opponent of the first president of the Turkish Cypriots,

Rauf Denktaş, who was opposed to the plan. Mehmet Ali Talat initiated a campaign where he instructed Turkish Cypriots about the content of the Annan Plan. A favorable vote (65%) from the Turkish Cypriots was a sign of change in the whole political system of the Turkish Cypriots. Talat, one year after the referendum, was elected president in the first round of elections. On 25 April 2005 Talat became the second president of TRNC, replacing the retiring president Rauf Denktaş. Since then, Talat as the president of the Turkish Cypriots continues to represent a more peaceful and European position.

Talat, who speaks fluent English and German, is married to Oya Talat, and has a son and a daughter.

INFLUENCES AND CONTRIBUTIONS

Talat has dedicated his entire life to clarification of the Cyprus problem. The conflict in Cyprus has influenced and shaped his political views. He has been working on the negotiations for the Cyprus conflict for several years and has been influenced by the idea of bringing a comprehensive, bi-zonal, bi-communal settlement into Cyprus under the auspices of the UN. His policy is toward the unification of the island, thereby having the Turkish part of the island join the European Union (EU). Presently, only the Greek Cypriot side has entered the EU. Since the failure of the Annan Plan, negotiators for reunification continue meeting under the auspices of the UN representatives. On 8 July 2006 Cypriot President Papadopoulos and President Talat met for the first time since 2004.

For more than forty years, the Turkish Cypriot people have been living under embargoes covering all aspects of life. The lifting of embargoes has been made conditional on the settlement of the Cyprus issue. Reaching an end to the Cyprus issue has not materialized due to Greek Cypriots' negative vote for the Annan Plan. Therefore, President Talat believes that the restrictive measures imposed on the Turkish Cypriot people should be lifted. He suggests that the Greek Cypriot stance to squander numerous opportunities no longer be tolerated and the Turkish Cypriot people should not be left in the cold. Among many embargoes imposed on the Turkish Cypriots, the ban of direct flights to North Cyprus is one of the most significant obstacles for Turkish Cypriots seeking to integrate with the world. Mehmet Ali Talat's application to the British Civil Aviation for direct flights to North Cyprus demonstrates one of his numerous contributions.

THE WORLD'S PERSPECTIVE

Success in achieving his political goals and bringing prosperity to the isolated and economically backward north of the island would enable President Talat to shrug off the legacy of the past. Mehmet Ali Talat is a keen pro-European politician who has lobbied hard for the reunification of the island of Cyprus. Unlike his veteran predecessor, Rauf Denktas, who retired after leading the Turkish Cypriot community for three decades, Talat would like to see reunification and membership of the EU for the whole island.

Some local political analysts believe a new era is in store for the north under Talat's pragmatic approach to politics. Compared to Denktas, Talat is more willing to compromise. President Talat urged the EU and UN to revitalize negotiations on the future of Cyprus and end the international isolation of the north.

LEGACY

Talat has dedicated his life to politics, focusing on solving the problems of Cyprus. His efforts, and the success of his campaign (with a 65 percent favorable vote from the Turkish Cypriots) for the Annan Plan, changed the EU's perspective about Turkish Cypriots. The EU understood the desire for a comprehensive solution in Cyprus, and promised Turkish Cypriots it would lift the sanctions imposed upon them. The fate of Cyprus is still unclear but the future will be promising for ultimate peace.

BIBLIOGRAPHY

"Cyprus Politics: 'EU Left Us in the Lurch.'" *EIU ViewsWire* (New York). 25 May 2006. Available from http://www.viewswire.com/article2010505986.html?pubtypeID-930000293&text-euleftusinthelurch.

"Turkish Cypriot Leader Denies He Will Resign Over Dispute with Turkish Army." British Broadcasting Corporation: BBC Monitoring Europe—Political. 8 January 2007.

Gunes Aygok

TALHOUNI, BASSAM AL-
(1964–)

Dr. Bassam al-Talhouni is a Jordanian attorney, academic, and civil rights activist. He is the cofounder and managing partner of MidGlobe (Middle Eastern Advocates and Global Consultants), a law firm based in Amman. He specializes in private commercial law and intellectual property rights in the Middle East.

PERSONAL HISTORY

Al-Talhouni was born in Amman, Jordan in 1964. He undertook his legal studies at the University of Jordan, where he completed a Bachelor of Law (LL.B.) in 1987 and a Master of Law (LL.M.) in 1991. Al-Talhouni worked in the judiciary from 1988 until he was appointed lecturer in private commercial law at Isra University in 1991. In 1992 al-Talhouni co-founded MidGlobe with

BIOGRAPHICAL HIGHLIGHTS

Name: Bassam al-Talhouni

Birth: 1964, Amman, Jordan

Family: Wife, Nadia Mousa; one daughter, Farah, and one son, Samir

Nationality: Jordanian

Education: University of Jordan, LL.B, 1987, and LL.M., 1991; University of Edinburgh, Ph.D., 1996

PERSONAL CHRONOLOGY:

- **1991–1993:** Lecturer at Isra University, Amman
- **1992:** Founded MidGlobe law firm
- **1996–2004:** Professor of commercial law, University of Jordan, Amman
- **2000–2004:** Founds and heads Jordanian Society for the Protection of Intellectual Property Rights
- **2001–2004:** Associate dean of the Faculty of Law, University of Jordan
- **2002–2003:** UNESCO chair for the teaching of intellectual property rights: copyright and neighboring rights
- **2005:** Member of the Committee on Legislation and Justice of Jordan's National Agenda

his brother Dr. Hussam al-Talhouni. In 1993 he joined the Jordanian Bar Association to become a practicing attorney. He continued to lecture at Isra and work for MidGlobe until 1993, when he left to pursue further academic studies at the University of Edinburgh. In 1996, after earning his doctorate with a thesis in commercial law, he returned to Jordan to become professor of commercial law at the University of Jordan, where he was appointed associate dean of the Faculty of Law in 2001. He continued to lecture at the university until 2004.

INFLUENCES AND CONTRIBUTIONS

The protection of intellectual property rights is a novel introduction to the legal systems of developing countries. Jordan agreed to protect intellectual property (IP) rights when it acceded to the World Trade Organization in 1999. This development prompted al-Talhouni to found the Jordanian Society for the Protection of Intellectual Property Rights, a registered nongovernmental organization, in 2000; he headed the organization until 2004. In

addition to his involvement with the Society, al-Talhouni participated in several conferences organized by the World Intellectual Property Organization, a United Nations institution, during which he presented papers on the promotion of IP rights in the Middle East. He writes regularly for local newspapers on issues relating to commercial law and intellectual property rights in Jordan, and has also contributed articles to a variety of academic journals. Al-Talhouni's promotion and efforts to safeguard IP rights in Jordan earned him an award from King ABDULLAH II in 2003.

THE WORLD'S PERSPECTIVE

Al-Talhouni's influence and contributions to the field of commercial law have been recognized beyond Jordan. In 2002–2003, he was designated the United Nations Educational, Scientific and Cultural Organization (UNESCO) Chair for the Teaching of Intellectual Property Rights: Copyright and Neighboring Rights. His appointment was made pursuant to an agreement signed between the University of Jordan and UNESCO that required the university to appoint a chair to oversee the application of UNESCO guidelines on intellectual property rights in Jordan. During his chairmanship, al-Talhouni ensured the enforcement of UNESCO's program on IP and participated in several conferences convened by the World Intellectual Property Organization (WIPO). He also created an LL.M. program at the end of 2002 that offers students at the University of Jordan the opportunity to specialize in the area of intellectual property.

In 2005 Al-Talhouni was selected to participate in the committee on legislation and justice of Jordan's National Agenda initiative, begun by King Abdullah II with the aim of setting guidelines, programs, and strategies to reform Jordan's political, educational, legal, social welfare, and state financial systems over the following decade, outlining policies to which successive governments would be committed. The suggestions of the National Agenda's eight committees were eventually published in 2006.

LEGACY

Al-Talhouni is an influential figure in Jordanian society, where he continues to promote the enforcement of the rule of law, particularly with regard to the protection of intellectual property rights. His efforts in that field may pave the way for Jordan to become a regional hub for foreign investments.

BIBLIOGRAPHY

"Amid Regional Uncertainties, Jordan Continues Its Efforts to Improve Investment Climate." *Middle East Executive Reports* 25, no. 1 (2002): 6.

Nsour, M. "Fundamental Facets of the United States-Jordan Free Trade Agreement: E-Commerce, Dispute Resolution and

Beyond." *Fordham International Law Journal* 27 (2004): 742.

Stovall, H. and H. Ullman. "Middle East Commercial Law Developments." *International Law* 33: 753.

Talhouni, B. al-. "Jordan: Telecommunications—Regulation." *Computer and Telecommunications Law Review* 2, no. 6 (1996): 157.

———. "Jordan—Copyright—New Tougher Copyright Legislation." *European Intellectual Property Law Review* 18, no. 10 (1996): 302.

"U.S. and Jordan Sign Free Trade Agreement." *Middle East Executive Reports* 23, no. 7 (2000): 7.

Lena El-Malak

TAMARI, VERA
(1945–)

Vera Tamari is a Palestinian artist.

PERSONAL HISTORY

Tamari was born in Jerusalem, mandatory Palestine, in 1945, to a family of Palestinian Christians originally from Jaffa. She received a B.A. in fine arts in 1966 from the Beirut College for Women (now the Lebanese American University) in Lebanon. Tamari went on to study ceramics at the Instituto Statale per la Ceramica in Florence, Italy, finishing in 1972. In 1984, she obtained an M.Phil. in Islamic Art and Architecture from Oxford University.

INFLUENCES AND CONTRIBUTIONS

Tamari primarily works with clay, including bas-reliefs, sculptural installations, and what she calls sculpted paintings. In 1975 she became the first artist to establish a ceramics studio in the West Bank when she opened one in al-Bira, near Ramallah. She was a founding member of Al-Wasiti Art Center in Jerusalem, as well as the New Visions Art Group, and is a member of the League of Palestinian Artists and the Khalil Sakakini Cultural Center. Tamari lectures on art at Bir Zeit University, where she founded and directs the Paltel Virtual Gallery. She also created the Founding Committee for the Development of Cultural Heritage. In 1989 she co-authored *The Palestinian Village Home*.

THE WORLD'S PERSPECTIVE

Tamari is recognized as one of the West Bank's leading artists. She has had solo exhibitions in Ramallah and Jerusalem, and took part in international group exhibitions such as Forces of Change: Artists of the Arab World, which was shown at The National Museum of Women in the Arts, Washington, DC, in 1994; New Visions: Art from

---

BIOGRAPHICAL HIGHLIGHTS

Name: Vera Tamari

Birth: 1945, Jerusalem, mandatory Palestine

Nationality: Palestinian

Education: Beirut College for Women (now the Lebanese American University), B.A. fine arts; Instituto Statale per la Ceramica in Florence, Italy, 1972, ceramics studies; Oxford University, 1984, M.Phil. Islamic Art and Architecture

PERSONAL CHRONOLOGY:

- **1975:** Opens first ceramics studio in the West Bank

- **1989:** Takes part in New Visions: Art from the Occupied Territories exhibition that toured Jordan, Italy, and Germany; co-authors *The Palestinian Village Home*

- **1994:** Takes part in Forces of Change: Artists of the Arab World exhibition at The National Gallery of Art, Washington, DC

- **2006:** Participates in Made in Palestine exhibition that toured the United States

---

the Occupied Territories, shown in Amman, Jordan, Salerno, Italy, and both Bonn and Frankfurt, Germany in 1989 and 1990; Tallat: Palestinian Women's Art Exhibition, in Jerusalem in 1986; the Third World Artists Exhibition in London in 1981; and Women Arab Artists, which was shown in Baghdad, Iraq in 1980. More recently, her work was featured in the Made in Palestine exhibition that toured the United States in 2006.

LEGACY

Although her contributions to art are still ongoing, Tamari is likely to be remembered as one of the Palestinian artists who continues to live and work in the West Bank and Gaza under the difficult circumstances of occupation, war, and political upheaval, as well as for her creative use of ceramics.

BIBLIOGRAPHY

Amiry, Suad, and Vera Tamari. *The Palestinian Village Home*. London: British Museum, 1989.

"Interview: Vera Tamari." *Mother Jones*. Updated 11 May 2005. Available from http://www.motherjones.com.

"Made in Palestine: Vera Tamari." Station Museum of Contemporary Art. Available from http://www .stationmuseum.com/Made_in_palestine-Vera_Tamari/ tamari.html.

"Vera Tamari." Occupied Space—Art for Palestine. Available from http://www.occupiedspace.org.uk.

"Visual Arts: Vera Tamari." Khalil Sakakini Cultural Center. Available from http://www.sakakini.org/visualarts/ tamari.htm.

Michael R. Fischbach

TAWFIQ, AHMAD AT-
(1943–)

A Moroccan historian and novelist, Ahmad at-Tawfiq (Tawfiq, al-Taoufik) held various positions before he was appointed Minister of Habous (Religious Endowments) and Religious Affairs in 2003. At-Tawfiq also directs the King Abd al-Aziz Al-Saoud Institute for Islamic Studies and Humanities in Casablanca. He taught history at Muhammad V University in Rabat from 1970 to 1989, and was director of the Center for African Studies at the same university. In 1995 he became director of the National Library. He has published four novels and a collection of historical essays.

PERSONAL HISTORY

At-Tawfiq was born at Mrabda, in the High Atlas mountains near the city of Marrakesh in 1943. In 1976 he earned a Ph.D. from the College of Literature and Humanities in Rabat in the social history of Moroccan rural societies in the nineteenth century. He publishes in the field of social history and works on the verification of manuscripts dealing with the literature of fatwas (religious rulings) and glorious deeds.

At-Tawfiq is the author of four novels written in Arabic. The first to be published, *Jarat Abi Musa* (1997) was made into a film in Morocco a few years later. It was published in English translation under the title *Abu Musa's Women Neighbors* in 2006. The Arabic version of the book received the Morocco Award in 1997. In 1998, at-Tawfiq published his second novel, *al-Sayl* (The Flood); *Shujayrat Hinna' wa Qamar* followed in the same year. It was translated into French as *L'Arbre et la lune* (The Tree and the Moon) in 2002. The latest novel to appear is *Gharibat al-Husayn*, in 2000.

INFLUENCES AND CONTRIBUTIONS

With a bilingual education and an equal command of Arabic and French, at-Tawfiq is well prepared to contribute to his country's strong Franco-Arabic culture. His novels have benefited from his vast knowledge of his

---

BIOGRAPHICAL HIGHLIGHTS

Name: Ahmad at-Tawfiq (Tawfiq, al-Taoufik)

Birth: 1943, near Marrakesh, Morocco

Family: Married with children

Nationality: Moroccan

Education: Ph.D., history, College of Literature and Humanities in Rabat, 1976

PERSONAL CHRONOLOGY:

- **1970:** Teaches at Muhammad V University, Rabat
- **1995:** Director, National Library
- **1997:** Publishes *Jarat Abi Musa*
- **1998:** Publishes *al-Sayl* and *Shujayrat Hinna' wa Qamar*
- **2000:** Appointed minister of Habous and Religious Affairs; publishes *Gharibat al-Husayn*

---

country's history, which gave him a profound understanding of the Moroccan society, especially the rural regions which are often neglected.

A reader of his novels is quite struck by the strength of the feminine characters he depicts. Women are a powerful presence in his works and it is clear that the author has a special affection and respect for them, a feeling that goes back to his childhood. He grew up in a household with a large number of women who cared for him and shaped his outlook. He has a special affection for his mother and he evokes her memory fondly. He is particularly touched by the capacity of mothers to love their children in a way that a father cannot achieve.

There is in at-Tawfiq's novels an underlying Sufi (Islamic mystical) trend that gives his fiction a certain halo of religiosity without it serving as a platform to promote religion. The cause that is clearly dear to his heart is the coexistence of the various ethnic groups in Morocco. Though he is deeply attached to his Berber roots, he sees the future happiness of his country depending on it being a place where the various ethnic groups, Berbers and Arabs, can interact peacefully.

There is an aura of mystery and mysticism that surrounds his characters in three of his novels, *Jarat Abi Musa*, *al-Sayl* and *Shujayrat Hinna' wa Qamar*, leaving them in a poetic haze that strips them of materiality. They seem to oscillate between fiction and reality, their personalities being of an ephemeral nature. At-Tawfiq's most recent novel, *Gharibat al-Husayn*, took a totally different direction, though not perhaps a surprising one for a historian. It is concerned with the Moroccan national struggle for independence.

THE WORLD'S PERSPECTIVE

A late bloomer as a fiction writer, at-Tawfiq was already known as an academician and a respected researcher in his field. His renown led him to a visiting position at Princeton University, where he taught Islamic studies. His message of dialogue and coexistence in Morocco, a country where ethnic divisions between Berbers and Arabs have long torn society, cannot but earn him national and international respect and appreciation. Both his novels and his public speeches as Minister of Habous convey a positive message about the need for a stable and harmonious Morocco.

With his novels, at-Tawfiq has attracted the attention of readers in his own country and beyond. He is invited to international literary conferences, and two of his novels have been translated into Western languages. The production of a film based on *Jarat Abi Musa* reflects the prominent place he holds for Moroccan readers.

LEGACY

At-Tawfiq's greatest message is that of coexistence, dialogue, and appreciation of the diversity of society. His novels are platforms for ideas of reconciliation and an expression of his Sufi inclinations. The reception of his novels testifies to the deep respect and appreciation his readers have for his message.

Few Moroccan writers who write in Arabic have received the warm response he has encountered. Many Moroccan writers in Arabic complain of lack of publicity,

---

FATE ... HITS US WHEN IT WANTS

In his dream, the shepherd saw himself transformed into a woman with Lomy's breasts and his mother's eyelashes. He saw the mountain above his head split into two and let out a huge, naked man carrying a sword and threatening him. As the man hit a big rock with his sword, the shepherd saw springs of water open up and turn into a rapid moving flood that almost drowned him. He cried for help but no one came to his rescue. He woke up at this moment to discover that he was carried away by a real flood pushing him to the bottom of the valley and hitting him against trees and stones. He became quickly aware that this was reality not a dream ... It all happened as he was deep asleep, as he never did before in the forest, but this is fate, it hits us when it wants and surprises us unaware. We only wake up when it is too late.

AHMAD AT-TAWFIQ, *AL-SAYL* (THE FLOOD).

---

even the absence of it, while Francophone novels benefit from the well-organized publicity machine of the French (government-sponsored) cultural centers and generous subventions that their counterparts do not receive. An extreme example is the novelist Ahmad Bou Zfur, who turned down a national fiction award in 2004, to protest the sad state of the Arabic novel in Morocco.

The respect and the consideration that at-Tawfiq has acquired through his academic career, and his services to his country, certainly work in his favor. They provide him with a visibility that other writers do not achieve on their own. However, the interest that readers have shown in his books is motivated by the positive message they provide. At-Tawfiq's choice of Arabic as a language of expression for his novels, despite his knowledge of French, is a significant statement for future generations of Moroccan writers.

BIBLIOGRAPHY

Kalby, Muhammed, Abdelkadir Khatibi, and Muhammed B. Touimi, eds. *Ecrivains marocains du Protectorat à 1965.* Paris: Sindbad, 1974.

WORKS BY AT-TAWFIQ

Tashawauf (Tashawwuf) ila Rijal al-Tasawwuf (1984; *Regard sur le Temps des Soufis* [The Age of the Sufis], 1995).
Jarat Abi Musa (1997; *Abu Musa's Women Neighbors*, 2006).
Al-Sayl (The Flood, 1998).

CONTEMPORARIES

The popularity of Muhammad Shukri (1935–) was first established as a result of a controversy raised by TAHAR BEN JELLOUN, who first published the realistic novel *al-Khubz al-Hafi* in a French translation titled *Le pain nu* (1997), as a slap in the face of Arab publishers who turned it down because of its shocking content, including open references to sexual experiences and crude descriptions of poverty and depravity. This opened the way for Shukri's other publications to find publishers and readers in Morocco. The American writer Paul Bowles translated the novel into English as *For Bread Alone* (1973).

Shujayrat Hinna' wa Qamar (1998; *L'Arbre et la lune* [The Tree and the Moon], 2002).
Gharibat al-Husayn (2000).

Aida A. Bamia

TEKELI, ŞIRIN
(1944–)

Şirin Tekeli is the foremost feminist author and activist of second-wave feminism in Turkey.

PERSONAL HISTORY

Tekeli was born in 1944, the only child of two secondary school philosophy teachers. She received her high school education in Ankara and completed her college education in political science in Lausanne University, Switzerland. She studied the work of David Easton for her Ph.D. in political science in Istanbul University, where she was employed as an assistant professor.

INFLUENCES AND CONTRIBUTIONS

The thesis Tekeli wrote in 1978 for promotion to associate professor was on women's political participation, and prompted her feminist activism. Published in 1982 as a book called *Kadınlar ve Siyasal-Toplumsal Hayat* (Women and political-social life), this study was the first serious and comprehensive discussion of women's marginalization in sociopolitical life written in Turkish and from a predominantly Marxist perspective. Her interviews with Turkish women parliamentarians, which she included in the book, exposed their striking marginality and problems in political life. The book was widely read, moving beyond a narrow academic circle, and had immediate and long-lasting influence in shaping a feminist culture in Turkey.

Tekeli resigned from her position as an associate professor at Istanbul University in 1981 and began her career as a feminist activist, translating and editing books. She engaged in organizing consciousness-raising groups and feminist publication circles in early 1980s and initiated the founding of the Kadın Eserleri Kütüphanesi ve Bilgi Merkezi (Women's Library and Information Center) and Mor Çatı Kadın Sığınağı (Purple Roof Women's Shelter) Foundations with her friends in 1990. She worked as a volunteer in the Women's Library between 1990 and 1996, and helped the institution develop into a vital organ of feminist dialogue. In 1997 she responded to the hunger strikes that were staged in prisons by deciding to work for women's entry into the parliament. She founded KADER, Kadın Adayları Destekleme ve Eğitme Derneği (an association to support and educate

BIOGRAPHICAL HIGHLIGHTS

Name: Şirin Tekeli

Birth: 1940, Ankara, Turkey

Nationality: Turkish

Education: B.A. (political science), Lausanne University, Lausanne, Switzerland; Ph.D. (political science), Istanbul University

PERSONAL CHRONOLOGY:

- **1981:** Resigns from teaching position at Istanbul University
- **1982:** Publishes *Kadınlar ve Siyasal-Toplumsal Hayat* (Women and political-social life)
- **1990:** Helps establish Kadın Eserleri Kütüphanesi ve Bilgi Merkezi (Women's Library and Information Center) and Mor Çatı Kadın Sığınağı (Purple Roof Women's Shelter) Foundations
- **1996:** French government makes her an Officier of l'Ordre des Palmes Académiques
- **1997:** Founds KADER, Kadın Adayları Destekleme ve Eğitme Derneği (an association to support and educate women candidates)

women candidates) in 1997 and served as its president between 1997 and 1999.

THE WORLD'S PERSPECTIVE

Tekeli's activities garnered her attention both in Turkey and abroad. The French government presented her with the award of Officier of l'Ordre des Palmes Académiques in 1996.

LEGACY

It is too early in Tekeli's career and activities to assess her ultimate legacy.

BIBLIOGRAPHY

Tekeli, Şirin, and Nukte Devrim-Bouvard. "Turkish Women and the Welfare Party: An Interview with Şirin Tekeli." *Middle East Report* No. 199 (April-June 1996): 28-29.

Yeşim Arat
updated by Michael R. Fischbach

TERIM, FATIH
(1954–)

Professional soccer coach and former player Fatih Terim is considered the sport's most successful personality in Turkey. Under his leadership, the soccer team Galatasaray won the Union of European Football Association (UEFA) cup in 2000. As of 2007 he is serving as the Turkish national team head coach, and ranks, according to a survey by the International Federation of Soccer History and Statistics (IFSHS), among the best eight soccer coaches in the world. Terim is praised for his ability to motivate his players and use aggressive game strategies. Because of his wide popularity within Turkish society, various political parties approached Terim to place his candidacy in Turkey's 2007 general elections.

PERSONAL HISTORY

Terim was born on 4 September 1954 in Adana, a town in southeastern Turkey. The eldest son of three children, he experienced a difficult childhood as part of an impoverished family. His father, Talat Terim, was physically disabled, and, as a result, Fatih worked a variety of manual-labor jobs to provide for his family from the time he was six. He learned to play soccer on the streets with other kids, and his father, seeing his talent, prayed for his son to become a famous soccer player. Terim's passion for soccer stands out against his disinterest and failure in school. His father's wish to also have his son graduate from the vocational high school ended with disappointment as Terim dropped out of high school during his second year. In 1969, at age fifteen, he joined the local team Adana Demir Spor as a junior player. Because of his financial situation, the club supported Terim with a monthly salary of 150 Turkish liras and kept this agreement a secret, as none of the other players were paid. Within the next three years, Terim achieved the rank of team captain. He played from 1969 to 1973 with Adana Demir Spor and was discovered in 1972 by the Turkish youth national coach, Gündüz Tekin Onay, who watched him play when Adana Demir Spor defeated Galatasaray.

In 1973 Terim signed a contract with Galatasaray, one of the three best known clubs in Istanbul (along with Beşiktas JK and Fenerbahce SK). French scholars founded the Galatasaray Sports Club in 1905 before Turkey was founded as a modern state in 1923. Terim played for eleven years with Galatasaray, proved himself to be a successful soccer player, and also became the team's captain for eight years. His career as a soccer player lasted from 1969 until 1984.

After leaving behind life as a soccer player, Terim took classes in coaching and accepted his first coaching position with Ankaragücü in 1987. This was followed with positions at Göztepe, Galatasaray, ACF Fiorentina, and AC Milan. In 1990, he accepted the position of assistant coach for the

---

BIOGRAPHICAL HIGHLIGHTS

Name: Fatih Terim

Birth: 1954, Adana, Turkey

Family: Wife, Fulya; two daughters, Merve and Buse

Nationality: Turkish

PERSONAL CHRONOLOGY:

- **1969–1973:** Plays for Adana Demir Spor (Team captain in 1973)
- **1969–1984:** Plays for Turkish national teams; National team, team captain; U 21 national team; and U 19 national team
- **1973–1984:** Plays for Galatasaray (Team captain from 1976-1984)
- **1987–1989:** Coaches Ankaragücü
- **1989–1990:** Coaches Göztepe
- **1990–1993:** Turkish National Team Coach; U 21 national team; and Turkish Olympic national team coach
- **1993–1996:** Coaches Turkish national team
- **1996–2000:** Coaches Galatasaray
- **2000–2001:** Coaches Fiorentina
- **2001–2002:** Coaches Milan
- **2002–2004:** Coaches Galatasaray
- **2006–present:** Coaches Turkish national team

Turkish national team under then head coach Sepp Piontek, a German. In 1993 Terim replaced Piontek as the team's head coach and held this position until 1996. Also in 1996 he returned to Galatasaray and served as that team's coach for four years. Under his leadership, Galatasaray became the first Turkish team to win the UEFA Cup in 2000, and to secure a European title. At the same time, Terim took Galatasaray to a new record of four consecutive championships in the Turkish League during the years 1996 to 2000.

Galatasaray's victory was due in large part to Terim's personal involvement in every aspect of the organization, from affecting player morale to improving the team's financial situation. His team's triumph had a great impact on both the team's and Terim's international reputation. Consequently, Terim received an offer to coach ACF Fiorentina, an Italian team from Florence. He accepted and coached from 2000 to 2001. However, due to disagreements between Terim and the chairs of ACF Fiorentina, he resigned in spring 2001. That same year he became manager of the world-class soccer team AC Milan the same year, the second prominent Italian team to hire Terim. However, as Milan did not rank among the top five of the league, Terim was blamed for the team's failure and was fired by the team's board directors for not fulfilling their expectations. He returned to Turkey and became Galatasaray's head coach from 2002 to 2004. Since 2006 Terim has been the Turkish national team head coach and it is speculated that he will resign from this position in 2008, after the European Cup.

INFLUENCES AND CONTRIBUTIONS

Throughout the history of professional soccer, Turkish clubs have struggled to establish themselves among European competitors, importing many foreign players and coaches to help them emerge successfully on the international stage. In this respect, Terim's impact as a home-grown coach is outstanding. He masterminded the Turkish national team's return to top competition and recognition as a member of Europe's soccer elite in the 1990s. The final game between Arsenal, a London club, and Galatasaray at the UEFA Cup in 2000 attracted, according to the *International Herald Tribune*, half a billion viewers across 185 nations. Its description regarding the UEFA Cup final is noteworthy: "Giant video screens have been erected in parks; the Turkish Parliament is in abeyance, and the jailed Kurdish rebel Abdullah Öcalan apparently has put at the top of his wish list a television set in his cell so that he can tune into Galatasaray's attempt to become the first Turkish club to win a European title." In this sense, Terim's accomplishments go beyond sports, achieving a mythic status in Turkish popular culture.

THE WORLD'S PERSPECTIVE

Terim's European successes have changed the status of Turkish soccer forever. His contributions as head coach of the Turkish national team and of Galatasaray have garnered Turkey new respect as a force in international sports.

CONTEMPORARIES

Senol Gunes (1952–), also a former soccer player, became the head coach of the Turkish national team in 2000. Under his leadership, Turkey qualified for the International Federation of Association Football (FIFA) World Cup in 2002 and placed successfully at third position.

FATIH SPEAKS

Some people ask me what system I play. Is it a Dutch system, a French system, or a Brazilian system? They don't understand. It's none of these—it's the Terim system.

AVAILABLE FROM HTTP://WWW.WORLDSOCCER.COM/ FEATURES/MILAN_FEATURES_55676.HTML.

LEGACY

After Galatasaray's triumph at the UEFA cup, Turkey established a new reputation as a formidable soccer team in Europe. With his offensive understanding of soccer, Terim's playing philosophy presents the best Turkish soccer to a European audience. Terim's approach culminates in the idea that one must play positively, attacking soccer for the enjoyment of the fans. His tactics can be seen in his players' offensive approach and slick passing, which are the hallmarks of Turkish soccer. Also, Terim's personality and his insistence on loyalty, honesty, high team morale, and a strong collective team spirit have contributed to the continuous success of his players. Terim's greatest accomplishment is his unique understanding of soccer—as he is able to read and control the game from an outsider's position—his positive dialogue with his players, and his trust in his players to motivate themselves, which all is reflected in the team's success.

BIBLIOGRAPHY

Cakit, Ahmet. *O bir imparator*. Istanbul, Turkey: Altin Kitaplar, 2001.

"Fatih Terim'in Yasamindan kesitler...." Available from http://www.mavilacivert.com/portal.fatihterim.html.

"Fatih Terim." Kim Kimdir. Available from http://www.kimkimdir.gen.tr/.

Hughes, Rob. "European Soccer: After Tragedy, Time for Temperance at UEFA Cup Final." *International Herald Tribune* 17 May 2000. Available from http://www.iht.com/.

Kola, Necati. *Bir syan modeli: Terizm*. Cagaloglu, Turkey: Zaman Kitap, 2000.

"Milan." World Soccer: One World, One Game. Available from http://worldsoccer.com/.

"UEFA/CAF Meridian Cup 2005 Turkey." Confederation Africaine de Football. Available from http://www.cafonline.com/.

Mine Eren

TLAS, MUSTAFA
(1932–)

Mustafa Abd al-Qadir Tlas, a Ba'thist politician and military officer, was a close associate of the late President HAFIZ AL-ASAD and was Syria's defense minister from 1972 to 2005.

Mustafa Tlas. AP IMAGES.

BIOGRAPHICAL HIGHLIGHTS
■

Name: Mustafa Abd al-Qadir Tlas

Birth: 1932, al-Rastan, Syria

Family: Wife: Lamiya al-Jabiri; two sons: Firas and Manaf; two daughters: Nahid and Sariya

Nationality: Syrian

Education: Syrian Military Academy, Hums, 1952–1954; general staff training in Syria; Supreme Institute for Military Studies, Voroshilov Academy, Moscow, 1972; doctoral studies, Sorbonne, Paris, 1980s

PERSONAL CHRONOLOGY:

- **1950–1952:** Schoolteacher
- **1952–1954:** Attends Syrian Military Academy
- **1955–1959:** Tank officer, Syrian army
- **1968:** Becomes member, Ba'th Party Syrian Regional Command, and chief of staff, Syrian army
- **1972–2005:** Defense minister of Syria

PERSONAL HISTORY

Tlas was born to a Sunni Muslim Arab family in al-Rastan, near the large Syrian city of Hums, on 11 May 1932. Tlas worked as a physical education teacher at the al-Kraya School, in the governorate of Suwayda, from 1950 to 1952. He joined the Ba'th Party in 1947.

In 1952 Tlas left teaching and enrolled in Syria's Military Academy in Hums. There he met another young Ba'thist officer, Hafiz al-Asad, and the two men's destinies became permanently intertwined. Tlas was a member of the country's Sunni Muslim majority; Asad was an Alawite, an impoverished minority Islamic sect, but the two had much in common. Both were from modest rural backgrounds, both hoped to advance socially through the opportunities offered by the military, and both were members of the Ba'th Party. Both were posted to the Air Force Academy in Aleppo, although Tlas failed flight training. After leaving the academy in 1954, he became an officer in the armored (tank) corps of the Syrian army in 1955. Tlas later was stationed in Egypt from 1959 to 1961, during the period in which Egypt and Syria were joined as the United Arab Republic (UAR). Asad was stationed there as well. When Syria seceded from the UAR in September 1961,

and Asad was jailed in Egypt, Tlas helped his friend's wife and baby return safely to Syria.

It was Tlas' position in the Ba'th Party, and his friendship with and loyalty to Asad, that led to his prominence in the military and politics from the 1960s on. Asad was a member of the secret Ba'thist Military Committee, which overthrew Syria's government in March 1963. As part of the new ruling elite, Asad brought his friend into its ranks after the coup, and also had Tlas appointed commander of an armored battalion. Tlas was granted other important positions through which he proved his loyalty to the party and its important Military Committee. In 1964 Tlas became deputy commander of an armored brigade and eventually its commander. In August 1965 he was elected to the Ba'th Party's Syrian Regional Command, the local government subordinate to the pan-Arab National Command. Tlas also headed the National Security Court that tried persons accused of plotting against the Syrian regime, including those arrested following the 1964 anti-Ba'thist violence in the city of Hama.

Tlas was dismissed from his positions in the party and military in December 1965 because of growing intra-Ba'thist friction in Syria. However, he was rehabilitated after Asad and other officers staged a coup in February

1966. Asad became defense minister in the new regime, and Tlas soon rose to command the army General Command reserve forces during Syria's disastrous defeat at the hands of Israel in June 1967, when Israel captured the strategic Golan Heights region of Syria. Tlas subsequently was promoted to chief of staff of the army and deputy minister of defense, with the rank of major general, in February 1968. In October 1968, Tlas resumed membership in the Ba'th Party's Syria Regional Command.

Asad later seized power through his own "Correctional Movement" coup in November 1970. As president, Asad rewarded Tlas by appointing him deputy commander-in-chief of the armed forces, and eventually yielded the post of defense minister to him in March 1972. As defense minister, Tlas traveled surreptitiously to Egypt to help plan the joint Egyptian-Syrian attack on Israeli forces in October 1973 that nearly succeeded in recapturing the Golan Heights. He also oversaw the deployment of Syrian forces to Lebanon in March 1976 to help end that country's civil war, the subsequent Syrian occupation of parts of that country, and the modernization of the Syrian military.

Elevated to lieutenant general, Tlas remained defense minister for thirty-three years, and was one of the pillars of the Asad regime. Upon Asad's death in June 2000, Tlas was one of a few senior Ba'thists who oversaw the transition in the presidency from Asad to his son, BASHAR AL-ASAD. The younger Asad replaced many of his father's old Ba'th cronies, but kept Tlas as his defense minister. Tlas finally retired from his post, and from the army, in May 2005.

Outside his official duties, Tlas also founded a publishing house and authored a number of writings on different topics, from military history to poetry.

INFLUENCES AND CONTRIBUTIONS

As a politician, Tlas long remained one of the main pillars of the Ba'thist regime of Hafiz al-Asad. He never really developed an independent power base. Asad in turn bene-

CONTEMPORARIES

Manaf Tlas (1963[?]–), Mustafa Tlas' son, is an officer in the Syrian army and one of the commanders of the powerful Republican Guard. He is a boyhood friend of President Bashar al-Asad, remains close to him, and is considered a prominent member of the younger generation of Syrian politicians. In 2000, Tlas was elected to the Ba'th Party's Central Committee. He is married to Tala Khayr.

I DO NOT WANT A SINGLE TEAR FALLING FROM THE EYES OF GINA LOLLOBRIGIDA

During Israel's invasion of Lebanon [in 1982], and after the deployment of the multinational force, I gathered the Lebanese resistance leaders together and told them: Do whatever you want with the U.S., British, and other forces, but I do not want a single Italian soldier to be hurt … because I do not want a single tear falling from the eyes of Gina Lollobrigida … I admire Gina Lollobrigida. I love it when a woman is beautiful. I've been fond of her ever since my youth. I used to collect her pictures and send her letters from the frontline or any other place in the world.

INTERVIEW IN *AL-BAYAN* NEWSPAPER, DUBAI, 1 JANUARY 1998.

Yasir Arafat, in his concessions to Israel, resembles a strip tease dancer. Whenever she goes on stage, she takes off a piece of clothing. But the difference between Yasir Arafat and a strip tease dancer is that as the dancer strips, her beauty is exposed. But as Yasir Arafat strips, his ugliness is revealed…He has handed over all his cards to the Israeli enemy…Why, you son of 60,000 dogs? You son of 60,000 whores?

TELEVISED SPEECH, 1 AUGUST 1999.

fited from having a Sunni Muslim who was well integrated with the urban Sunni elite occupy a key position in his government alongside many Alawite associates to give the appearance that his regime was not just a bastion of the Alawite sect. As an army officer, Tlas guided the Syrian military during the important period of the 1970s and 1980s, when the armed forces grew significantly in size, strength, and sophistication thanks to growing ties and coordination with the Soviet Union.

THE WORLD'S PERSPECTIVE

For Syria's archenemy, Israel, Tlas is associated with the growth of Syrian military and strategic power after its defeat in 1967. Palestinians recall that Tlas was an outspoken hardliner in Syria's frosty relationship with the Palestine Liberation Organization (PLO) and its longtime chairman, YASIR ARAFAT. Lebanese recall the Syrian army's long occupation of parts of Lebanon, its blatant interference in Lebanon's politics, and the corruption that enriched Syrian officers and their Lebanese collaborators.

Tlas also has received much attention and criticism for his outspoken opinions. In August 1999, he publicly denounced Arafat as a "son of 60,000 dogs and 60,000 whores" for the diplomatic concessions he had made to Israel. In January 1998, he stated in an interview that his admiration for Italian actress Gina Lollobrigida affected orders he gave to pro-Syrian forces in Lebanon. He also outraged Jews because of anti-Semitic books he released through his own publishing house, including the classic anti-Semitic tract *Protocols of the Elders of Zion* and his own book, *The Matzo of Zion*. The latter recounted the 1840 Damascus "blood libel" incident in which Jews were charged with allegedly killing a Christian monk to obtain blood for making matzo bread.

LEGACY

Tlas will go down in history as a key player in the Ba'th Party's lengthy rule in Syria during the twentieth century, a period that saw Syria grow into a significant Middle Eastern political and military power able to project its influence beyond its borders.

BIBLIOGRAPHY

Batatu, Hanna. *Syria's Peasantry, the Descendants of Its Lesser Rural Notables, and Their Politics.* Princeton, NJ: Princeton University Press, 1999.

Seal, Patrick. *Asad: The Struggle for the Middle East.* Berkeley: University of California Press, 1990.

Michael R. Fischbach

TLATLI, MOUFIDA
(1947–)

Tunisian film director Moufida Tlatli is one of the foremost female filmmakers of the Arab world. Trained in Paris at the famous Institut des hautes études cinématographiques (IDHEC) film school, Tlatli became the top film editor in the Middle East, editing over twenty major productions from the 1970s until the 1990s. In 1994 she directed her first feature-length film, *The Silences of the Palace* (*Samt al-Qusur*), and earned international acclaim. She continued her feature filmmaking with *The Season of Men* (2000) and *Nadia et Sarra* (2003), and has received widespread critical attention for her explorations of women's issues in Tunisian society.

PERSONAL HISTORY

Tlatli was born in 1947 in the village of Sidi Bou Said, in the north of Tunisia. While she was brought up in a traditional milieu, she came of age in the era of the Tunisian struggle for independence from France. Tlatli belongs to the generation of president Habib Bourguiba, who upon independence in

Moufida Tlatli. FETHI BELAID/AFP/GETTY IMAGES.

1956 introduced a secular regime and brought about major reforms for women—abolishing polygamy, establishing civil marriage, and granting women divorce, voting, and abortion rights—giving Tunisia the unique status it has in the Arab world today for its advancement of women's rights.

In her adolescence during these early years of Tunisian independence, Tlatli discovered her passion for cinema. In the ciné-club run by her high school philosophy teacher, she was exposed to the films of Ingmar Bergman, Federico Fellini, Roberto Rosellini, and of the existentialist tradition, which opened her eyes to a cinematic world beyond the Egyptian and Hindu films of her youth. She chose to pursue a career in cinema and in 1965 left for Paris to study at the famous IDHEC film school. She had arrived in Paris at a moment often referred to as the golden age of cinema, and her repertoire of viewings included works of Italian neorealist cinema, the French New Wave, Brazilian *cinema novo*, Polish cinema, and films of the Prague Spring. For a young woman in the mid-1960s, however, film directing and production were not considered options of study; women at this time were steered toward training to become either script supervisors, then called script girls, or film editors. Tlatli thus completed her degree in film editing in 1968. Remaining in Paris for four years, she worked as a script supervisor and production director at the former office of French public radio and television, the Office de Radiodiffusion-Télévision Française (ORTF), now divided into seven institutions.

BIOGRAPHICAL HIGHLIGHTS

Name: Moufida Tlatli

Birth: 1947, Sidi Bou Saïd, Tunisia

Family: Married; one daughter, one son

Nationality: Tunisian

Education: Diploma from IDHEC film school, 1968

PERSONAL CHRONOLOGY:

- **1968–1972:** Script supervisor, production director at the former ORTF in Paris

- **1970s–1990s:** Film editor for more than twenty major cinema productions of the Arab world, including Merzak Allouache (*Omar Gatlato, 1976*), Michel Khleifi (*Fertile Memory,* 1980; *Canticle of the Stones,* 1990), Nacer Khemir (*The Wanderer,* 1985), and Férid Boughedir (*Halfaouine, Boy of the Terraces,* 1995)

- **1994:** Directs *The Silences of the Palace* (Samt el qusur)

- **2000:** *The Season of Men* (La saison des hommes)

- **2004:** *Nadia et Sarra*

In 1972 Tlatli returned to Tunisia and started her career as a film editor, a job that spanned twenty-two years and placed her name in the credits of many of the major film productions of the Arab world, including Merzak Allouache's *Omar Gatlato (1976),* Michel Khleifi's *Fertile Memory (1980),* *Canticle of the Stones (1990),* Nacer Khemir's *The Wanderer* (1985), and Férid Boughedir's *Halfaouine, Boy of the Terraces (1995).* A recipient of several prizes at the Festivals of Catharge and Ouagadougou for her editing, she gained prominence in the field and became recognized as one of the most sought-after film editors in the Arab world.

Work as an editor was rewarding for Tlatli. She has stated that she appreciated working alongside a director; she learned and made progress through the films of others. In a 2000 interview in *L'Humanité* with Michòle Levieux, she described it as being in her "temperament to be of service to the universe of an other, to accompany him or her, and to invest [herself] in his or her world." As a film editor, she had the opportunity to work collaboratively with the major Arab filmmakers from the 1970s to 1990s. Director Férid Boughedir commented on the mark Tlatli has made on an entire generation of cinema, stating:

> "When Moufida Tlatli was an editor, she was both big sister and mother to most of the Arab cinema

'young wave.' It is an understatement to say that she adopted our films: she literally poured her heart into them, inspiring the most hesitant with her creative vigor. We were all waiting for this over-abundance of sensitivity, generosity and talent to come to fruition in a film of her own" (Films du Losange, dossier de presse).

Tlatli's passage from editing to directing films of her own followed a period of difficult personal circumstances. Creative and demanding, she traveled across the Arab world and often to Paris for postproduction work. According to custom, after giving birth to her first child she had her mother come to help with childrearing. Soon after, her mother became ill and was diagnosed with Alzheimer's disease. Tlatli took seven years off from her film career to take care of her mother and two children. Witnessing her mother's descent into mutism devastated her, and led her to raise questions about her mother's life and the gap between their generations. Her mother's absolute silence in later life filled Tlatli with the desire to understand all that remained unsaid about her mother's plight—and more generally, the culture of silence that characterizes women's experience in Tunisian society that has been transmitted from one generation to another. These questions took on urgency for Tlatli and compelled her to make her first feature-length film, *The Silences of the Palace,* which was released in 1994.

Though *Silences of the Palace* takes its inspiration from the life of Tlatli's mother, it is not strictly autobiographical. Its setting is a palace of the ruling Bey under the French protectorate at the height of the Tunisian struggle for independence, and it deals with the lives of four generations of women servants. A coming of age story of Alia, the illegitimate daughter of a woman whose life has been spent in domestic—and sexual—servitude to the princes of the palace, it is told in flashbacks and focuses on the years immediately preceding and following Tunisian independence in 1956. Although Alia's departure from the palace with her revolutionary boyfriend and her pursuit of a career as a singer presumably represents an escape from the servitude suffered by the previous generations, her life portrayed ten years later nonetheless raises pertinent questions about the status of women and class in Tunisia, even in the wake of independence and the legal reforms it brought about for women.

Upon its release, Tlatli's film was met with major international acclaim at film festivals throughout the world. It was selected for the Directors Fortnight at the 1994 Cannes Film Festival, and it won a Special Mention for the Caméra d'Or award. In addition, it won the International Critics' Award at the 1994 Toronto International Film Festival, the Satyajit Ray Prize at the 1994 San Francisco Film Festival, and the Golden Tulip at the 1994 Istanbul International Film Festival. Tlatli was also awarded the prize for Best Director at the 1995 All African Film Awards.

Following on the heels of her successful debut feature film, Tlatli continued exploring the nature of oppression still faced by women in Tunisian society in her second feature, *The Season of Men* (*La saison des hommes*), released in 2000. Set on the island of Djerba off the southeast coast of Tunisia, the film focuses on a community of women who wait eleven months of the year for their trader husbands to return from working on the mainland to spend a season with their wives. Tlatli portrays the alienation, solitude, and frustration of the female protagonists for whom the island is similar to a prison, where the male-dominated social structure is perpetuated by custom even in the absence of men. Whereas Tlatli's *Silences of The Palace* was a means of coming to terms with her mother's generation, *The Season of Men* is a film for the generation of her daughter, as the filmmaker expressed in a 2000 interview with Olivier Barlet. The challenges confronting protagonists Aïcha and her companion Zeineb in the face of traditional codes of behavior are just as present for Aïcha's daughters Emna and Meriem, who must still tackle the forces of oppression from within. In this largely male-free space, where solidarity and complicity characterize many of women's relationships, Tlatli aims to raise awareness of the extent to which women are responsible for transmitting patriarchal oppression in spite of themselves, and suggests that women have a share of responsibility for this heritage.

The Season of Men was widely presented at film festivals throughout 2000 and 2001. It was an Official Selection of Un Certain Regard at the 2000 Cannes Film Festival. At the Paris Biennale of Arab Cinema in 2000, it was winner of the Institut du Monde Arabe Grand Prize. It also received awards and nominations at other film festivals including Namur and Cologne.

In 2003, Tlatli completed her third feature-length film, *Nadia et Sarra*. Autobiographical in inspiration, it is the fictive portrayal of the relationship between a forty-seven-year-old literature teacher, Nadia, caught in depression at the approach of menopause, and her eighteen-year-old daughter Sarra. In an interview with ARTE, Tlatli stated her desire to deal with the topic of menopause, which is universal yet so rarely explored. Tlatli's camera plays upon the mirror images of mother and daughter, as Nadia lives this stage of life as a violent shattering of her self-image and the loss of that which constitutes her womanhood. In setting this story within the context of her country, Tlatli aims to unveil the face of modern Tunisia, which has seen the legal emancipation of women but remains under the weight of its traditional past.

INFLUENCES AND CONTRIBUTIONS

Tlatli's first influences can be traced to the social climate in which she was raised, and the period of change which transformed her country and helped shape her education.

THE CONDITION OF ARAB WOMEN

Through my work as an editor, I have close contact with the contemporary preoccupations of Arabic cinema. I've worked with several male and two female directors and I've noticed that they share a common interest in the condition of Arab women. I often wondered why it was that male directors should be so preoccupied with the question of women, until I realized that, for them, woman was the symbol of freedom of expression, and of all types of liberation. It was like a litmus test for Arab society: if one could discuss other freedoms. Most likely there would not be that much freedom of expression, and most likely they could not speak freely about political problems, but the question of women could still be discussed. I think that each country in the Maghreb [i.e. North Africa] tends to take up particular themes and their theme of women's liberation is the one that has been special to Tunisia.

FROM AN INTERVIEW WITH LAURA MULVEY, "MOVING BODIES" 18.

As the eldest child in a family of six children, she was close to her mother and versed in the traditions and values that were espoused by women prior to Tunisian independence. Yet she was also of the first generation to come of age under the presidency of Bourguiba, and the program of women's reforms and social innovation that he launched in the late 1950s. Education was privileged under this administration, and Tlatli's acceptance into the prestigious IDHEC film school in Paris could undoubtedly be seen as a successful realization of doors that were opened at this time.

In interviews, Tlatli has evoked her early exposure to Egyptian and Hindu cinema, yet she cites that her main inspiration can be traced to the European cinematic traditions of the 1950s and 1960s, including Italian neo-realism and the French New Wave. Her studies in Paris—which were concluded at the time of the student protests and events of 1968—and work in Paris until the early 1970s were certainly formative experiences at a radical time for shaping thought on art and social change in an international context. Her French-based training in editing techniques became essential for her work with the new generation of emergent cinema in the Arab world.

Rejecting the stylistic and thematic premises of the escapist industry of Egyptian cinema, Arab directors of this new wave sought to create an original cinema that would represent the social realities of their nations. This social realism offers a countering view to portrayals of Arab locales as exotic sites in Western films, especially in the Hollywood tradition. Directors with whom Tlatli worked, such as Merzak Allouache, Nacer Khemir, and Férid Boughedir, made films that focused on such controversial social themes as urban alienation and gender taboos. Narratives were extremely personal and often took the form of the coming-of-age genre. In the quest for uncovering the experience of truth, documentary techniques were occasionally employed. These directors often sought new ways of storytelling by drawing on Arab traditional sources and bringing innovation to more Western-developed cinematic narrative forms. Stylistically, Arab new wave directors brought technical refinement to their work, privileging the image and sound over words.

Silences of the Palace in many respects is a crowning success of Arab new wave cinema or *Cinema Jedid*, carrying out its ideals thematically, formally, and stylistically. It takes up the issue of anticolonial struggle addressed in the previous generation of Maghribi (North African) cinema, but focuses on its potential impact on several generations of women who live in a cloistered sphere of domestic servitude. News of Tunisian struggle for independence only filters through the walls of the castle through the radio and visitors from the outside, and through scenes depicting the ruling Bey in discussion. The uprising outside the walls—and off scene—seems to barely touch the conditions of women of this class. Tlatli thus forays into issues of feminine experience such as physical violence, slavery, rape, abortion, mental illness, and death that have persisted in silence beyond the passage to independence and the passing of Tunisia's Personal Status Code of 1957. As the coming of age of protagonist Alia is witnessed through flashback scenes that are recollected as she walks through the castle ten years following her departure, the weight of her suffering is palpable, and one wonders whether she has succeeded in leaving behind the past and her nameless origins that bound her to the castle and the community of women who raised her. Tlatli raises the question about whether change in the context of the new Tunisian nation is possible, and whether there are hurdles to still clear with regards to class and gender despite the new reforms that presumably touch the lives of all women.

Tlatli thus succeeds in taking the viewer on a brazenly realistic tour of the cloistered sphere of the Orientalist harem, and this is due to a number of stylistic innovations. While she seems to replicate the palette of color that might evoke Eugène Delacroix's famous 1834 painting of the *Women of Algiers in their Harem*—and she does not refrain from what could be idealized scenes depicting convivial women performing kitchen labor and traditional healing ceremonies—she underscores the silences which traverse the women's joyful songs, and visually captures the silences that reveal the women's complicity in the face of the unspeakable subjugation they must endure. The rule of silence that permeates the visual and dialogic texture of the film is only punctuated by Alia's voice and her performance of songs by Egyptian singer UMM KULTHUM and ultimately the nationalists' anthem that give expression to her aspirations for liberty.

Just as the film uses realism to repudiate Orientalist representations of cloistered North African women, Tlatli also emphasizes ways in which her film resists other Western filmmaking techniques. She uses longer shots to produce a slower pace, to avoid giving in to a Western sense of time. The staging of the film, including decor and settings, are also significant, and work to draw the viewer's attention to distinctively Arabic patterns, colors, and textiles. For Tlatli, rhythm, colors, and gestures all combine to create what she refers to as the poetry of the film that gives a fantastic freedom: in the Arabic tradition the use of symbols and metaphors allows for the expression of the unspoken. These formal and stylistic techniques let Tlatli comment on what is forbidden or unspoken in her culture through signs that nonetheless have meaning within and beyond the Arab world. In this respect, her work touches on the universal, and *Silences of the Palace* can be credited with helping to bring new Arab cinema to a wider international audience.

Tlatli's subsequent films both make use of innovative subject matter and techniques to address a wider audience. In her second film, *The Season of Men,* Tlatli focuses on a distinctive Maghribi cultural space, the communities of women on the island of Djerba that live eleven months of the year without their husbands. Yet this isolated space— similar to the castle in *Silences*—raises larger and even universal questions about the roles women play themselves in perpetuating oppressive traditions: this world portrayed may essentially be free of men, but not of oppression. Tlatli's film thus suggests ways in which women are unable to liberate themselves from mentalities which are nonetheless out of step with the laws and social discourses of the changing times: There are many ways in which the past needs to be continuously confronted in the present. Hence, her most recent film, *Nadia et Sarra*, takes up the universal subject of menopause, as experienced by an urban middle-class Tunisian woman. The change of life that the new woman of modern liberated Tunisia undergoes also requires a coming to terms with the generations of the past. For Tlatli, even today's woman—and ultimately her successive generations—needs to constantly reassess and redress her image of herself in her social context.

THE WORLD'S PERSPECTIVE

Since the release of *Silences of the Palace*, Tlatli has earned prominent international notoriety as a filmmaker and advocate of women's issues in the Islamic Arab world. *Silences of the Palace* has been hailed as a masterpiece and has gone on to become the most widely distributed North African film, and, as pointed out by critic Suzanne Gauch, even was featured in *Time* magazine's list of top ten films of 1994 (though in contrast, *The Season of Men* and *Nadia et Sarra* have as of 2007 not yet had North American distribution). For over a decade, her works have been presented at film festivals throughout the world and have earned awards and recognition, establishing Tlatli as a top Arab filmmaker.

Silences of the Palace is now taught regularly as part of U.S. university curriculum in Arab and Francophone studies, postcolonialism, international film studies, and women's studies. Tlatli has been aligned with such Arab women intellectuals as ASSIA DJEBAR and FATIMA MERNISSI, whose works raise consciousness about the conditions of women in the Arab world and give voice to women's experiences and their quest for agency in the face of male oppression, colonialism, and in the context of the heated social and political issues at stake in the early twenty-first century. Tlatli has thus earned a solid place within the context of international feminism.

Scholarly interest in Tlatli's work straddles three areas. The first preoccupation has largely focused on representations of colonial and postcolonial female subjectivity. Notably, critic Dorit Naaman offers a psychoanalytic-tinted analysis of Alia's complex struggle in *The Silences of the Palace* to gain access to the symbolic—and social— order through not only her voice, but through embracing her body and maternal genealogy.

A second area of scholarship enlists Tlatli's work in a critique of nationhood. Film scholar Ella Shohat has included *Silences of the Palace* in a category of works that she terms post-Third-Worldist, because it contains a feminist critique of the extent to which anticolonial nationalism "disappointed hopes for women's empowerment." The analysis and activism that emerge in Tlatli's work, focusing on the intersection of nation, race, class, and gender, produce "an open-ended narrative far from the euphoric closure of the nation" (Shohat).

Finally, a third focus on Tlatli's work examines the formal strategies she makes use of in her filmmaking. Most recently, a chapter in Gauch's recent book *Liberating Sharazad: Feminism, Postcolonialism, and Islam* looks at how Tlatli deploys non-Western, distinctively Arab formal structures of narrative art from the *Thousand and One Nights* in *The Silences of the Palace*. Drawing on devices from the *Nights* that evoke a potential for change, Gauch argues that the narrative of the film sways its audience and challenges the status quo of the dominant social structures her protagonist and storyteller Alia seeks to exit.

LEGACY

Since Tlatli is still gaining momentum and renown as a filmmaker, it remains too early to assess her ultimate legacy.

Greater international dissemination of her recent feature films will certainly generate more a comprehensive assessment of her body of work on the status of women in modern Tunisian society and her complex exploration of the relationships between the past, present, and future generations of women. The near future will undoubtedly see the emergence of a young generation of filmmakers marked by the passion and vision of her work that brought to cinematic consciousness the hidden corridors of women's silences that certainly are resonant throughout and beyond the Arab world.

BIBLIOGRAPHY

Barbancey, Pierre. "Le Silence des Tunisiennes." *Le Web de L'Humanité.* 20 May 1994. Available from http://www .humanite.fr/.

Barlet, Olivier. "Interview with Moufida Tlatli." *Africultures.* May 2000. Available from http://www.africultures.com/.

"Director Profile: Moufida Tlatli Showcases the Inner World of Women's Emancipation." *Magharebia: The News and Views of the Maghreb.* 3 March 2005. Available from http://www .magharebia.com/.

Films du Losange and Maghrebfilms Carthage. "La Saison des Hommes (The Season of Men): Dossier de Presse." Les Films du Losange. Available from http://www.filmsdulosange.fr/.

Gauch, Suzanne. *Liberating Sharazad: Feminism, Postcolonialism, and Islam.* Minneapolis: University of Minnesota Press, 2007.

Génin, Bernard. "Télérama: Les Silences du Palais." *Film Club de Cannes.* 21 December 2000. Available from http://www .filmclubcannes.com/.

Khannous, Touria. "Strategies of Representation and Postcolonial Identity in North African Women's Cinema." *Journal X: A Journal in Culture and Criticism* 6 (2001): 47-61.

Lennon, Peter. "Sins of the Mothers." *Guardian Unlimited.* 22 June 2001. Available from http://arts.guardian.co.uk/.

Levieux, Michèle. "La Sexualité est le Fondement Même de l'Equilibre Humain." *Le Web de L'Humanité.* 27 December 2000. Available from http://www.humanite.fr/.

Martin, Florence. "Silence and Scream: Moufida Tlatli's Cinematic Suite." *Studies in French Cinema* 4.3 (2004): 175-185.

"Moufida Tlatli: Director Profile." *Festival de Cannes.* 18 June 2007. Available from http://www.festival-cannes.org/.

"Moufida Tlatli-réalisatrice." ARTE. Updated 7 June 2006. 18 June 2007. Available from http://www.arte.tv/fr/.

Mulvey, Laura. "Moving Bodies: Interview with Moufida Tlatli." *Sight and Sound* 5 (1995): 18-20.

Naaman, Dorit. "Woman/Nation: A Postcolonial Look at Female Subjectivity." *Quarterly Review of Film and Video* 17 (2000): 333-342.

Sherzer, Dina. "Remembrance of Things Past: *Les silences du palais* by Moufida Tlatli." *South Central Review* 17 (2000): 50-59.

Shohat, Ella. "Framing Post-Third-Worldist Culture: Gender and Nation in Middle Eastern/North African Film and Video." *Jouvert: Journal of Postcolonial Studies* 1 (1997).

Simarski, Lynn Teo. "Through North African Eyes." *Saudi Aramco World.* 43 (Jan./Feb. 1992): 30-35.

Nadia Sahely

TLILI, MUSTAFA
(1937–)

Mustafa Tlili is a Tunisian novelist, UN official, and scholar.

PERSONAL HISTORY

Tlili was born in 1937 in Fériana, Tunisia. He attended the *madrasa* (traditional school) in his native city and later received a bilingual education at the University of Paris—Sorbonne, where he received a *diplôme d'études supérieurs de philosophie*. He also studied at the UN Institute for Training and Research and worked for almost thirteen years at the UN offices in New York. Tlili moved to France in 1980, and he was made a Knight of the French Order of Arts and Letters. He headed the UN Information Center in Paris; was the director of the UN information center for France, located in Paris; was chief of the Namibia, Anti-Apartheid, Palestine and Decolonization programs at the UN's department of public information in New York; and principal officer/director in charge of communications policy in the same department.

Tlili became a senior fellow at the World Policy Institute at the New School University in New York as well, and an adjunct professor at Columbia University's School of International and Public Affairs. He currently is a senior fellow at the Remarque Institute of New York University (NYU) and an NYU research scholar.

INFLUENCES AND CONTRIBUTIONS

Tlili has published four novels, all written in French. Each reflects in its own way the writer's preoccupation with life's meaning. He is determined to denounce corruption, especially among the aristocracy, whether in the Arabian Peninsula, as revealed in *Gloire des sables* (1982; Glory of the sands); in Paris, as described in *La rage aux tripes* (1975; Visceral anger); or in New York, as in *Le bruit dort* (1978; The noise sleeps). Tlili's fourth and last novel, *La montagne du lion* (1988; Lion mountain), centers on corruption in Tunisia. Tlili's language reflects a playful anger and humorous cynicism toward the upper classes of society.

In spite of Tlili's global outlook and residence outside Tunisia, he remains strongly linked to the Maghrib (North Africa). His multilingual and multicultural background enhances his novels and reflects a new trend among Maghribi writers who write in French: Instead of being confined to two cultures—Arabic and French—as their predecessors were, they are expanding their horizons. With Tlili it is possible to speak of the beginning of the cultural liberation of the French-educated Maghribi writers.

In addition to his literary output, Tlili has been involved in other activities. While at NYU, he has established the well-received program "Dialogues: Islamic World-U.S.-the West."

BIOGRAPHICAL HIGHLIGHTS

Name: Mustafa Tlili

Birth: 1937, Fériana, Tunisia

Nationality: Tunisian

Education: *Diplôme d'études supérieurs de philosophie*, University of Paris—Sorbonne

PERSONAL CHRONOLOGY:

- **1975:** Publishes *La rage aux tripes* (Visceral anger)
- **1978:** *Le bruit dort* (The noise sleeps)
- **1980:** Moves to France
- **1982:** Publishes *Gloire des sables* (Glory of the sands)
- **1988:** *La montagne du lion* (Lion mountain)

He also is a member of Human Rights Watch's Advisory Committee for the Middle East and North Africa.

THE WORLD'S PERSPECTIVE

In addition to his literary work, Tlili is well known internationally for his expertise about foreign policy, and regularly speaks with radio and television journalists.

LEGACY

Still active, Tlili has been influential in the formation of a new, multicultural (rather than merely bicultural) trend among French-educated Maghribi writers.

BIBLIOGRAPHY

Jack, Belinda. *Francophone Literatures. An Introductory Survey.* New York: Oxford University Press, 1996.

Mortimer, Mildred, ed. *Maghrebian Mosaic.* Boulder, CO, and London: Lynne Rienner Publishers, 2001.

Aida A. Bamia
updated by Michael R. Fischbach

TOUMI, KHALIDA
(1958–)

Khalida Toumi is one of the pioneers of the feminist movement in Algeria.

PERSONAL HISTORY

Toumi was known as Khalida Messaoudi before she reclaimed her maiden name. She was born on 13 March 1958 in Ain Bessem, a village in the Berber region of Kabylie in Algeria (although her ancestral village is Sidi Ali Moussa). Her father sent her to school, and she later entered the University of Algiers in 1977 to pursue a degree in mathematics. After graduating from the École Normale Supérieure in 1983, she taught mathematics from 1984 until 1991.

INFLUENCES AND CONTRIBUTIONS

In 1981, Toumi founded the Collectif féminin (Women's Grouping) not only to oppose the ministerial interdiction on Algerian women leaving the country unless accompanied by a male family member, but also to oppose state endorsement of the discriminatory Family Code, which the National Assembly eventually adopted in 1984. Following the adoption of this code, Toumi presided over the Association for Equality between Men and Women, founded by a group of Trotskyite militants. In 1985, she co-founded and became a member of the executive committee of the Algerian League of Human Rights. She later distanced herself from the Trotskyite militants and in 1990 founded the Independent Association for the Triumph of Women's Rights.

Toumi staunchly opposed Islamist ideology and endorsed the government's cancellation of the January 1992 legislative elections, which the Islamic Salvation Front (FIS) was poised to win. During the years of violence and terrorism in Algeria in the 1990s—she herself was publicly threatened with death by FIS Islamic militants in June 1993, and was slightly injured in a June 1994 bomb attack on a secularist demonstration in which she was participating—she traveled to Western countries to provide an anti-Islamist perspective. Toumi also participated in government during that period. She was a member of the National Consultative Council from 1992-1993. A member of the Rassemblement pour la Culture et la Démocratie (RCD), she won a seat in the national assembly in 1997 and served as the RCD's national vice president for human rights and women's issues. From 2000-2001, Toumi was vice president of the National Commission to Reform the Educational System.

After profound disagreements with the RCD's president SAID SADI, she severed relations with the RCD in January 2001, at the peak of the crisis in her native Kabylie; she was subsequently expelled from the RCD. In May 2002, she became minister of culture and communication, as well as the government's spokesperson, the first woman ever to hold that job.

In 1993 Toumi published *Une Algérienne Debout* (*Unbowed: an Algerian woman confronts Islamic fundamentalism*). It appeared in English translation in 1998.

BIOGRAPHICAL HIGHLIGHTS

■

Name: Khalida Toumi

Birth: 1958, Ain Bessem, Kabylie of Algeria

Nationality: Algerian Berber

Education: Studies at University of Algiers; graduated from the École Normale Supérieure, 1983

PERSONAL CHRONOLOGY:

- **1981:** Founded the Women's Grouping
- **1985:** Co-founded Algerian League of Human Rights
- **1990:** Founded the Independent Association for the Triumph of Women's Rights
- **1992:** Member, National Consultative Council
- **1993:** Threatened with death by the Islamic Salvation Front; publishes *Une Algérienne Debout* (*Unbowed: an Algerian woman confronts Islamic fundamentalism*)
- **1997:** Elected to Algeria's National Assembly; receives the Prix International Alexander Langer Pro-europa
- **1998:** Receives the Liberal International Prize for Freedom
- **2000:** Vice president, National Commission to Reform the Educational System
- **2001:** Breaks with the Rassemblement pour la Culture et la Démocratie
- **2002:** Becomes minister of culture and communication and government spokesperson

---

THE WORLD'S PERSPECTIVE

Within Algeria, Toumi has in recent years lost her credibility as a staunch proponent of democracy because of her loyalty to President ABDELAZIZ BOUTEFLIKA, harshly criticized today for his authoritarianism and alliance with Islamists. The independent press and most advocates of democracy did not wish to see Bouteflika re-elected in April 2004.

Internationally she has received various awards for her contributions, including the Prix International Alexander Langer Pro-Europa in 1997, and an honorary doctorate from the Catholic University of Louvain, Belgium, in 1998. In 1998 she also received the Liberal International Prize for Freedom.

LEGACY

Toumi will be remembered as a feminist pioneer in Algeria and a notable Berber politician.

BIBLIOGRAPHY

Messaoudi, Khalida, with Schemla, Elisabeth. *Unbowed: An Algerian Woman Confronts Islamic Fundamentalism,* translated by Anne C. Vila. Philadelphia: University of Pennsylvania Press, 1998.

Yahia Zoubir
updated by Michael R. Fischbach

TUKAN, JAFAR
(1938–)

Jafar Tukan is a Palestinian architect who is the most senior and accomplished architect at work in Jordan and the Middle East in the early twenty-first century.

PERSONAL HISTORY

Jafar Ibrahim Tukan (also Ja'far Tuqan) was born in 1938 in Jerusalem, British-controlled Palestine, to a prominent Muslim Palestinian family from the central Palestinian town of Nablus. His father, Ibrahim Tuqan (1905–1941), was a legendary Palestinian poet. Described as Palestine's poet laureate, he was working at the time of Jafar's birth for the Arabic section of the British administration's radio broadcasting service. Jafar's aunt, Fadwa Tuqan (1917–2003) was a famous poet in her own right as well.

Tukan, who lost his father to illness when he was a small boy, attended the al-Najah National College secondary school in Nablus and graduated with a bachelor's degree in architectural engineering from The American University of Beirut in 1960. Thereafter he worked for the Jordanian ministry of public works as a design architect from 1960 to 1961 before moving to Beirut and joining with Dar Al-Handasah Consulting Engineers. In 1968 Tukan left to start his own architectural firm in Beirut. In 1973 he merged it with another firm to become Rais and Tukan Architects. Its main office was in Beirut, with branches in Abu Dhabi and Dubai. When he moved to Amman in 1976, the firm was renamed Jafar Tukan and Partners Architects and Engineers. The firm merged in 2003 with Consolidated Consultants for Engineering and the Environment, where he works today.

INFLUENCES AND CONTRIBUTIONS

Tukan and his firm are responsible for a number of buildings around the Arab world, especially in Jordan. He designed the Amman municipality building (1997); a prototype kindergarten school in Dubai, United Arab Emirates (1980); the Jubilee High School in Amman

---

BIOGRAPHICAL HIGHLIGHTS

Name: Jafar Tukan (Ja'far Tuqan)

Birth: 1938, Jerusalem, British-controlled Palestine

Nationality: Palestinian; Jordanian citizenship

Education: B.S. (architectural engineering), The American University of Beirut, 1960

PERSONAL CHRONOLOGY:

- **1960:** Design architect, Jordanian ministry of public works
- **1961:** Works for Dar Al-Handasah Consulting Engineers in Beirut
- **1968:** Establishes own architectural practice in Beirut
- **1973:** Establishes Rais and Tukan Architects through a merger with another firm
- **1976:** Moves to Amman, renames company Jafar Tukan and Partners Architects and Engineers
- **2001:** Receives Agha Khan Award for Architecture
- **2003:** Merges firm with Consolidated Consultants for Engineering and the Environment
- **2005:** Selected by Palestinian officials to select a design for Yasir Arafat's mausoleum in the West Bank city of Ramallah

---

(1999); and the SOS Children's Village in Aqaba, Jordan (2001). Tukan also designed the headquarters of the Arab Bank and the Royal Automobile Museum, both in Amman. Shortly after the death of Palestinian leader YASIR ARAFAT in November 2005, Tukan was tasked with the responsibility of selecting a design for Arafat's mausoleum in the West Bank city of Ramallah.

Beyond architecture, Tukan has been involved in other civic activities. He is a member of the board of trustees of the University of Jordan, sits on the executive board of the Jordan National Gallery of Fine Arts, and is a member of the Greater Amman Municipal Council.

THE WORLD'S PERSPECTIVE

Tukan has received a variety of awards and honors over the years that pay tribute to his accomplishments. In both 1993 and 2002 he was given the Architectural Engineer Award from the Arab Cities Organization. His design for the SOS

Children's Village earned him a prestigious Agha Khan Award for Architecture in 2001. The jury citation noted:

> This project has received an Award for creating a pleasant and attractive environment scaled to the needs of children. The aim of the village is to provide care for orphans in family houses rather than in large, impersonal institutions. Its well-defined layout creates generous communal outdoor areas, shaded courtyards and gardens. These spaces serve as safe and calm playgrounds for the children and form a desirable oasis within the arid, desert surroundings. The thoughtful and integrated architecture is a sober, modern interpretation of vernacular traditions, employing locally available building materials. Culturally and aesthetically, it sets a precedent for the creation of a new architecture that looks to the future and acknowledges the past. (Agha Khan Award for Architecture).

Tukan also has worked with prestigious international architects, including the late Japanese architect Kenzo Tange, with whom he collaborated in his design for the campus of the Jordan University for Science and Technology in Irbid.

LEGACY

Tukan will be remembered as the most important Palestinian architect of the second half of the twentieth century, particularly in Jordan.

CONTEMPORARIES

Mohammad al-Asad is a Jordanian architect and architectural historian. He studied architecture at the University of Illinois at Urbana-Champaign, and received his Ph.D. in the history of architecture at Harvard University in 1990. Al-Asad founded the Center for the Study of Built Environment (CSBE) in Amman, and directed it until 2006. He held postdoctoral research positions at Harvard University and the Institute for Advanced Study, Princeton; has taught at the University of Jordan, Princeton University, Massachusetts Institute of Technology, and the University of Illinois at Urbana-Champaign; and currently is adjunct professor at Carleton University in Ottawa, Canada. Al-Asad has served as a reviewer for the Agha Khan Award for Architecture since 1989. He also has been a member of the board of directors for the Jordan Museum, the Royal Society of Fine Arts–Jordan National Gallery of Fine Arts, and the Amman Commission.

BIBLIOGRAPHY

Abu Ghanimeh, Ali, and Marion Pisani. *Jafar Tukan Architecture*. Rome: Libria, 2001.

"Agha Khan Award for Architecture 2001." Available from http://www.akdn.org/.

Michael R. Fischbach

TUMARKIN, IGAEL
(1933–)

Israeli artist Igael Tumarkin was a 2004 Israel Prize laureate. He is best known as a sculptor of monumental public works and autonomous sculptures. He is also a painter and a graphic artist, who works in collaboration with novelists and poets on books for adults and children. Tumarkin is a highly controversial person, renowned for his sometimes blunt public criticism of accepted notions and values.

PERSONAL HISTORY

Tumarkin was born in 1933 in Dresden, Germany, as Peter Martin Gregor Heinrich Hellberg, to a Jewish mother, Berta Gurevitch, and a Gentile father, Martin Hellberg, who were divorced. When the child was two years old his mother immigrated with him to Palestine; later she married Herzl Tumarkin, whose name he bears. As a young man Tumarkin served for two years in the Israeli navy, after which he entered the studio of the sculptor Rudi Lehmann in the artists' village of En Hod on Mount Carmel. In 1955 he traveled to Berlin to meet his father. There he joined Bertolt Brecht's Berliner Ensemble as a set designer and produced his first iron sculptures. From Berlin Tumarkin moved to Amsterdam and then to Paris, where he began working with polyester and industrial and urban waste, the scrap of the First Machine Age, according to the artist. Tumarkin returned to Israel in 1961. He is an extremely prolific artist whose work has been shown in many one-person exhibitions in museums and private galleries in Israel and abroad. He represented Israel at the Venice Biennale (1964), the São Paulo Biennale (1967), and the Tokyo Biennale (1968). His works are in the collections of major museums and in many public spaces in Israel and abroad.

INFLUENCES AND CONTRIBUTIONS

Tumarkin's major contribution to art in Israel lies in his social commitment, his use of materials, and his choice of subject matter. On his return to Israel, Tumarkin pursued his lifelong interest in public, site-specific work. His first sculptures in the desert (*Arad Panorama*, 1962–1968, and *Age of Science*, Dimona, 1962–1969) are built of whitewashed concrete walls of varying heights and forms, straight

BIOGRAPHICAL HIGHLIGHTS

Name: Igael Tumarkin

Birth: 1933, Dresden, Germany

Nationality: Israeli

Education: Informal

PERSONAL CHRONOLOGY:

• **1935:** Taken to Palestine by mother, fleeing Nazi Germany

• **1955–1961:** Lives and works in Berlin (with Brecht's Berliner Ensemble), Amsterdam, and Paris

• **1960s:** Represents Israel, Venice Biennale 1964, São Paulo Biennale 1967, Tokyo Biennale, 1968

• **1974–1976:** Lives and works in United States

• **1970s–1980s:** World travel and study

• **2004:** Awarded Israel Prize

of two parts, and a walk along railroad tracks solved the problem of the base, which the artist made out of railroad cars and signals. In the early 1990s Tumarkin used a computer to enlarge the drawing of a small-scale vertical form, and working in an iron foundry with professionals allowed him to shape tall and narrow or short and wide pillars, reminiscent, according to the artist in his "Autobiographical Andmardk," of "a flame, a fist, a column, a totem, an obelisk." Painted aluminum and wood formed the heads of playwrights, poets, and literary heroes the artist produced in the late 1990s. The heads were often supplemented with paintings incorporating mixed media: photography, computerized prints, acrylic, and markers.

Tumarkin's imagination is often literary, his references cultural, and his subject matter frequently culled from the history of art. Tumarkin has produced new versions of Dürer's *Melancholia*, he has presented modern visions of the crucifixion (*Ecce Homo* and *Agnus Dei*), revisited the images of ancient gods (*Prometheus* and *Astrare*), revised the likenesses of historical heroes (*Cleopatra* and *Jeanne d'Arc*) and paid homage to old and contemporary masters such as Rembrandt, Van Gogh, Picasso, and Brancusi. The only Israeli artist to appear in Tumarkin's pantheon is

and curved; they incorporate sunlight and shade, and invite bodily involvement. The visitor's movement in and around the forms completes the sculpture. Most works in the Tumarkin Garden (1993) at Kokhav 'ha-Yarden (Belvoir) in the Bet She'an Valley are made of local basalt and forged steel, some painted in red, yellow, and blue. The works, some soaring high above the horizon, others lying at ground level, enter into dialogue with the archaeological ruins across the field.

Tumarkin measures time with the use of new materials and with travels that lead to further discoveries. In Japan (1962) he grasped the language of the brush and the use of spraying. In 1964 he incorporated weapon parts that in their new context lose their original function and provoke reflection on militarism and war. The year 1965 marked the time of the human body, first in reliefs and later in three dimensions. At the same time Tumarkin used many materials that to him were new: bronze, nickel, and stainless steel. A prolonged stay in the United States in 1974–1976 introduced him to the use of glass and Cor-Ten steel that mirror the environment. In 1977 the artist's interest in earth architecture took him to India, Iran, Turkey, Egypt, Tunisia, Morocco, Senegal, Mali, Upper Volta (now Burkina Faso), Mexico, Peru, and other places. The travels gave birth to a book of photographs and commentary, *From Earth to Earth Art* (1989), and to Tumarkin's new work, made of earth and scraps of iron, wood, and fabric. A 1984 visit to Berlin and a walk by the Berlin Wall suggested sculptures made

CONTEMPORARIES

Itzhak Danziger (1916–1971), Israeli sculptor, 1968 Israel Prize laureate, was born in Berlin and immigrated to Palestine with his parents in 1925. The family settled in Jerusalem but moved to Tel Aviv after the violence of the 1929 Western Wall Disturbances. Danziger studied art at the Slade School of Art, University of London (1934–1937). In 1938 he returned to Palestine, and after the Second World War traveled among Paris, London and Tel Aviv. Danziger returned to Israel in 1955 to teach at the Technion, Israel Institute of Technology, Haifa. In 1939 Danziger created *Nimrod*, a major masterpiece of Israeli art. The statue, 90 centimeters high and carved out of red Nubian (Nile valley) sandstone, depicts Nimrod, the legendary king of Mesopotamia, as a naked hunter, carrying a bow and with a hawk on his shoulder. Stylistically, the statue is a synthesis of ancient Egyptian, Middle Eastern, and modern idioms. The sheep sculptures, made of iron, evoke desert rocks, canals, and Bedouin tents. Danziger also worked on the conservation of sites, notably the rehabilitation of the quarries of the Nesher cement plant on the western slopes of Mount Carmel. Danziger was killed in a road accident in 1977.

the sculptor Itzhak Danziger, who inspired him to construct his first iron sculpture in 1956. In a large body of work the artist comments on the conditions of war, sacrifice, heroism, and memory. The first sacrifice in Jewish collective memory is the Binding of Isaac, which is daily revived in the continuous offerings on the altar of the century-long Israeli–Palestinian conflict. Tumarkin has presented irreverent and thought-provoking versions of both biblical and contemporary sacrifices.

Behold the Fire and the Wood: But Where is *the Lamb for a Burnt Offering?* (Genesis 22:7), 1962–1983, quotes Isaac's question to his father Abraham. The multipart work consists of a dirty toilet bowl, an open pipe for sewage, a trash altar, a fetish, an old typewriter, two buckets, a chair, and some twigs. To Tumarkin, this accumulation is a shrine without religion or cult, a collection of objects that represent "the fire and the wood," whereas the lamb for the burnt offering is the spectator who chances to sit on the toilet bowl. *Sinai* (1967), a mixed-media triptych the artist produced after the 1967 War, shows the devastation of war and represents its price in human life. The central black wood panel holds disjointed body parts, feet, hands, and bare and helmeted heads, with empty military boots scattered in between. Stains of red paint complete the picture. Tumarkin's best known challenge to the notions of hero and heroism bears the title of a canonical Israeli literary work in order to criticize its assumptions. *He Walked in the Fields* (1967) borrows from the title of Moshe Shamir's novel, which narrates the life and death in battle of the writer's brother, Eli, in the 1948 War. Eli represents the New Jew, the kibbutznik, who lives on the land and dies for it. Tumarkin's hero, a life-size bronze figure, is blind, his teeth are rotten, and his long red tongue hangs out of his gaping mouth. His arms are amputated, his chest is torn open, revealing weapon parts, and his pants are down, with his penis hanging over them. Similarly, in *Hakhnissini Takhat Knafekh* (Let Me Under Your Wing) the artist quotes Haim Nachman Bialik's love poem of that title, only to subvert the lover's longing and change the wing into an iron mantle that conceals rifle barrels.

Rifles, guns, screws, nails, and pipes protrude out of many lacerated bodies in Tumarkin's work, and replace necks, arms, and legs. The subject is the human condition in general, and in a country at war in particular. Tumarkin's first war monument, in the Galilee town of Kiryat Shmona (1969), consists of three battle tanks, each painted in a primary color. Tumarkin's other war monument, in a remote, unfrequented site in the Jordan Valley (1972), is built on the contrast between whitewashed concrete walls of varying widths and heights and a tall black sculpture made of iron. In its sheer size, and in the twenty-meter height of the black sculpture, this monument dwarfs the viewer and contradicts the artist's usual antimilitarist stand. In contrast, the *Monument of the Holocaust and Revival* (1975)

stands in a busy square in the heart of Tel Aviv. This is an iron and glass pyramid that stands on its apex over a large triangle to form a Star of David. To the artist, the upside-down pyramid connotes anguish, and the wide opening upward sends forth shouts of hope and joy. The nation's rebirth is symbolized in the reflections of city life, as the glass panes between the iron bars reflect children, adults, houses, and cars—the triumph of life over death in the concentration camps. Tumarkin's public works engage in dialogue with the viewer and the environment; they reflect sunlight and shade, and change with the time of day and the seasons of the year.

THE WORLD'S PERSPECTIVE

Tumarkin conducts dialogues with the past and the present. He constructs his work out of earth, stone, and bronze, he incorporates urban detritus and uses iron and glass, the quintessentially modern building materials. For Tumarkin, a work of art can never be divorced from its embodiment in matter. To compellingly voice his essentially materialist notion of the artwork and his objection to conceptual art, he showed in the early 1970s mockeries of works that rely on the word alone. The accumulation of objects in reliefs and three-dimensional works is indebted to Dada collages, and the artist's intense social and political engagement follows the tradition of the Dada Berlin artists and Brecht. In this tradition, the work of art is never self-referential, and all formal innovations carry social significance. The site-specific works converse with Danziger's commitment to the landscape and to local conditions, and they parallel similar works by Robert Smithson and Richard Serra, for instance.

Tumarkin is the first Israeli artist to represent the crucifixion theme, which is totally foreign to Jewish culture, and he is among the first to challenge collective values. The artist's opposition to collective values confused a society that in the early 1960s still formed an ideologically cohesive group. Moreover, Tumarkin's return to the human figure contradicted the abstract idiom that had allowed the previous generation of artists to escape the grip of ideologically determined subjects, like life and work on the kibbutz or the depiction of the land.

LEGACY

In his visual work and in his numerous verbal communications Tumarkin repeatedly insists on his dual origin and his divided allegiance. He is firmly committed to Western European culture and art, yet he is from the Middle East, he belongs to the region's open spaces, to the Mediterranean sun and sea; at the same time he carries in him the traditions that were formed in the great cities that lie overseas. In his autobiography, *I Tumarkin* (1981), the artist confesses that he is both from here and from there: "I do not feel a Jew and yet I am from here. Not from there. I feel no bond with Germany—the country, the landscape, the people. Yet my culture is mostly from there, not from here.... I am from the shores of the Mediterranean."

BIBLIOGRAPHY

"Belvoir, Tumarkin Sculpture Garden." *Exhibition catalogue, Tel Aviv Museum of Art* (1996).

Poseq, Avigdor W.G. "'To Be of One's Time': Technology and Inhumanity in Tumarkin." Hebrew University of Jerusalem. Available from http://www.tau.ac.il/arts/projects/PUB/assaph-art/assaph5/articles_assaph5/poseq.pdf.

"Tumarkin, Igael." Israeli Art Center, Israeli Museum, Jerusalem. Available from http://deadseascrolls.tv.

Tumarkin, Igael. *Trees, Stones and Cloth in the Wind.* Tel Aviv: Massada, 1981.

———. *From Earth to Earth Art.* Tel Aviv: Zemora-Bitan, 1989.

"Tumarkin: Sculptures 1957–1992." *Exhibition catalogue, Tel Aviv Museum of Art* (1992).

Esther Levinger

TURABI, HASAN AL-
(1932–)

Hasan al-Turabi is an important Sudanese Islamic thinker and politician.

PERSONAL HISTORY

Hasan (also Hassan) Abdullah al-Turabi was born in 1932 in the city of Kasala, Sudan to a Sunni Muslim family of religious learning and traditions. He earned a B.A. in law from the University of Khartoum in 1955, an M.A. in law from the University of London in 1957, and a doctorate in constitutional law from the Sorbonne in Paris in 1964. He became dean of the University of Khartoum Law School in the same year and a member of the Sudanese parliament in 1965, then attorney general in 1977. In 1979 he became Sudan's minister of justice.

INFLUENCES AND CONTRIBUTIONS

Turabi was the leader of the Islamic Charter Front, the Sudanese branch of the Muslim Brotherhood, becoming secretary-general in 1964. Following the 1969 coup led by General Ja'far Numayri, Turabi was imprisoned. He escaped after six years and fled to Libya, from whence he was allowed to return to Sudan in 1977, becoming part of Numayri's government as part of a compromise with the Sudanese Islamic movements. A few years later, Turabi was imprisoned again, but was released after the overthrow of Numayri in 1985. Under his leadership, the Islamic Charter Front was transformed into the National Islamic Front (NIF) that same year. In 1988 the NIF joined the coalition

---

BIOGRAPHICAL HIGHLIGHTS

Name: Hasan al-Turabi (Hassan al-Turabi)

Birth: 1932, Kasala, Sudan

Family: Wife, Wisal al-Mahdi; son, Isam

Nationality: Sudanese

Education: B.A. University of Khartoum (law, 1955); M.A. University of London (law, 1957); Ph.D. University of Paris—Sorbonne (constitutional law, 1964)

PERSONAL CHRONOLOGY:

• **1964:** Becomes secretary-general, Islamic Charter Front

• **1969:** Imprisoned by Sudanese government

• **1979:** Becomes Sudanese attorney general under Numayri government

• **1988-1989:** Serves as Sudanese minister of justice, minister of foreign affairs in al-Mahdi government

• **1996:** Becomes speaker of Sudanese Parliament

• **2004:** Imprisoned by President Omar al-Bashir

• **2005:** Released from prison

---

government of Sadiq al-Mahdi—Turabi's brother-in-law—and Turabi served first as minister of foreign affairs and later as deputy prime minister. He was the ideological power behind the military regime of OMAR AL-BASHIR that took power from Mahdi in 1989. In 1996 Turabi became the speaker of the Parliament, and his influence spread throughout the state organization and political parties. He eventually fell out of favor with President al-Bashir's regime, and was imprisoned from 2004 to 2005.

Turabi's man influence, however, lies not in his statesmanship, but in his intellectual and ideological developments, as well as his impact on Islamism in North Africa in particular and the Arab world in general. Turabi is a fundamentalist Islamic thinker; he views Islam as the ultimate ideological and political authority for both state and society. He believes that Islam contains all the necessary elements for the creation of a viable and modern civilization and culture. Rather than a return to earlier Islamic social and political practices, Turabi advocates a progressive Islamic revival that incorporates the best of traditional Islam and Western culture. He argues that the state's only purpose is to set rules to enable society to conduct its affairs, and that it must allow society, the primary institution in Islam, to freely pursue its interests. The *shari'a* and the Islamist jurists ensure that the role of the state remains limited. Because any society has the right to exercise *shura* (consultation) and *ijma* (consensus), and because this requires producing *ijtihad* (opinions), pluralism is necessary to enable society to identify which policies best serve its interests. As such, Turabi argues, democracy is simply a Western term identical to Islam's *shura* and *ijma*. Although ultimate sovereignty belongs to God, practical and political sovereignty belong to the people. Society, therefore, always remains free to choose its rulers and representatives. In this fashion, Islam can bring the best of its own civilization along with other civilizations.

Turabi clearly distinguishes the conditions of contemporary life from those present during the rise of Islam in the seventh century. Because Muslims are living in a world much different from the one that Islamic jurisprudence legislated, they must look toward radical social and political reforms in order to bring about the necessary Islamic revival. The historical development of Islamic jurisprudence must be rejected in favor of a process that depends on free thinking, and the state must establish a new circle of *ulama* (Islamic clergy) while continuing to derive its jurisprudence from the people. Any democratic developments in Islam must extend to the institutions of society and the family, each segment of which must work to further Islamic revival in both public and private life. Political freedom is an original part of the creed and nature because freedom is what distinguishes man from animal. This includes the freedom of expression, which is stipulated in the *shari'a*.

As for the individual, Turabi notes that a person is not forced to worship God, but chooses to do so. Individual freedom is essential and cannot be taken away by the state, institutions, or society. This freedom, he argues, must be embodied in a constitution to ensure that the strength of any political leader may be checked by representative councils. Because institutionalization of freedom inevitably leads to its destruction, individual freedoms are bound and protected by Islam.

Turabi's views and writings on Islam seem to place him in the category of moderate Islamist thinkers, but the practice of his authority in Sudan suggests otherwise. Although he has called for freedom of association and multiparty representative bodies, the current Sudanese government has systematically destroyed most civic associations and remains one of the most oppressive regimes and egregious human-rights violators in the Middle East.

CONTEMPORARIES

Sadiq al-Mahdi (1935–) was born on 25 December 1935 in Omdurman, Sudan. He received his M.Sc. in economics from Oxford University in 1957. He became leader of the Ansar al-Mahdi Sufi order, an Islamic mystic order in Sudan which in turn was the pillar of the main political party, the Umma Party. Al-Mahdi was prime minister of Sudan from 1966-1967 and from 1986-1989, when the position was abolished. He is the brother-in-law of Hasan al-Turabi.

THE WORLD'S PERSPECTIVE

Turabi is internationally known as an Islamic thinker and as a key figure in the modern political history of Sudan. He is also known for having given sanctuary in Sudan to Saudi militant USAMA BIN LADIN from 1990-1996. Human Rights Watch has accused Turabi of masterminding the police state and numerous human rights abuses committed between 1989 and 2001.

LEGACY

Hasan al-Turabi will be remembered as the most important Islamic leader in modern Sudanese history, and a key figure in that country's history.

BIBLIOGRAPHY
Burr, J. Millard, and Robert O. Collins. *Revolutionary Sudan: Hassan al-Turabi and the Islamist State, 1989-2000.* Leiden: Brill, 2003.

El-Affendi, Abdelwahab. *Turabi's Revolution: Islam and Power in Sudan.* London: Grey Seal, 1991.

Moussalli, Ahmad. *Moderate and Radical Islamic Fundamentalism: The Quest for Modernity, Legitimacy, and the Islamic State.* Gainesville: University of Florida Press, 1999.

Nkrumah, Gamal. "Hassan al-Turabi: Remaking History." Interview. *al-Ahram Weekly Online* (11-17 May 2006). Available from http://weekly.ahram.org.eg/2006/794/profile.htm.

Turabi, Hasan al-. "Islam, Democracy, the State and the West: Summary of a Lecture and Roundtable Discussion with Hasan al-Turabi." Prepared by Louis Cantori and Arthur Lowrie. *Middle East Policy* 1, no. 3 (1992): 52–54.

Jillian Schwedler
updated by Ahmad S. Moussalli
updated by Michael R. Fischbach

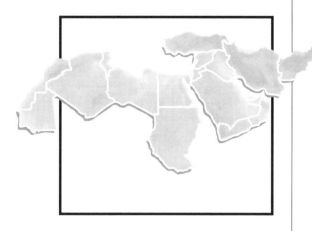

UMM KULTHUM
(c. 1904–1975)

Umm Kulthum (also Om Kultum, Oum Kalsoum, Umm Kaltum, Um Kultum) Ibrahim al-Baltaji was one of the most famous singers of the Arabic-speaking world in the twentieth century. Her eventual role as a cultural icon made her arguably the most important Arab musician of her time.

PERSONAL HISTORY

Umm Kulthum was born in Tammay al-Zuhayra, a village in the Egyptian delta, probably in 1904. Her father, Ibrahim al-Baltaji, was the imam or prayer leader of the local mosque; her mother, Fatima al-Maliji, was a housewife. She had an older brother, Khalid, and sister, Sayyida. The family was poor and its lifestyle not different from most of her Egyptian contemporaries. To make extra money, Umm Kulthum's father sang religious songs for social occasions such as weddings or saints' days and trained his son to accompany him. Umm Kulthum learned these songs by virtue of proximity and surprised her family with her strong voice. Eventually, dressed as a boy, she joined her father's group and performed regularly in the eastern delta. Despite efforts to disguise her gender, she soon was known as the little girl with the powerful voice and became a local curiosity that attracted attention to the family troupe.

She also joined her brother in Qur'an school, or *kuttab*, small local schools designed to teach children to recite the Qur'an properly, to read, write, and sometimes to do some arithmetic. (During Umm Kulthum's childhood, British colonial authorities did not encourage further education for Egyptians.) Although attendance at *kuttab* was more routine for boys than girls, there were other girls in Umm Kulthum's class and, in fact, the lessons of the *kuttab* formed a common fund of knowledge for most Egyptian Muslims of Umm Kulthum's generation. Despite the predictable variability in teaching at these schools, the children tended to absorb a respect for careful pronunciation of Arabic and a sense of the beauty and elegance of the language that remained with many of them throughout their lives. These widely shared sensibilities informed Umm Kulthum's later aesthetic choices and helps explain the strong connections many of her compatriots felt for her art.

The then-new sound recordings—78 rpm gramophone records that circulated all over Egypt in the early years of the twentieth century—provided another means for Umm Kulthum and her family to learn the art of singing and new songs. Because record players often appeared in public spaces—coffeehouses, for example—even people who could not afford the equipment could hear the recordings. The father of one of Umm Kulthum's childhood friends also owned a record player and invited

BIOGRAPHICAL HIGHLIGHTS

Name: Umm Kulthum (Om, Oum Kalsoum, Umm Kaltum, Um Kultum)

Birth: Probably in 1904, Tammay al-Zuhayra, Egypt

Death: 1975, Cairo, Egypt

Family: Married Hasan al-Hifnawi, 1954; no children

Nationality: Egyptian

Education: Village Qur'an school; private teachers in music and literature

PERSONAL CHRONOLOGY:

- **1923:** Moves to Cairo from her village of Tammay al-Zuhayra
- **1924:** First commercial recordings appear on Odeon label
- **1926:** Appears for the first time with instrumental accompanists; signs an extremely lucrative recording contract with Gramophone that establishes her financial base
- **1934:** With her competitor, Muhammad Abd al-Wahhab, opens the first national Egyptian Radio station
- **1936:** Appears in *Widad*, her first musical film
- **1956:** Performs "Wallahi Zaman, ya Silahi," which becomes the Egyptian national anthem
- **1964:** Performs "Inta Umri," Umm Kulthum's first collaboration with Muhammad Abd al-Wahhab
- **1966:** Performs in Paris, her only concert outside the Arab world
- **1967:** Initiates her concerts to benefit Egypt
- **1973:** Performs her last Thursday-night concert
- **1975:** Dies in Cairo

villagers to listen to records in his home. From these, Umm Kulthum learned to love the religious poetry (Arabic: *qasa'id*, singular: *qasida*) performed by al-Shaykh Abu'l-Ila Muhammad who later became her teacher in Cairo.

Following years of traveling the delta, Umm Kulthum came to the attention of musicians from Cairo, themselves traveling to perform at events often sponsored by local wealthy families. They encouraged her father to move the family to Cairo, where increased income and opportunities would be available. After some consideration, the family decided to join the large numbers of villagers migrating to the city in search of work. Similar to many, her family moved into a neighborhood near their new acquaintances and used these contacts to obtain work.

Umm Kulthum appeared in Cairo as a country girl with little urban sophistication, whose repertoire had been performed for years. She seemed initially to be old-fashioned and hopelessly countrified, even though her strong and flexible voice attracted significant attention. An ambitious young woman, she sought through lessons in music and poetry to hone her skills. Al-Shaykh Abu'l-Ila Muhammad, the singer whose work she had admired on recordings, became her main teacher. Her voice attracted a well-known poet, Ahmad Rami, who became her teacher and lifelong mentor. She copied the dress and manners of the elite Muslim women of the city in whose homes she sang; and eventually she replaced her countrified band of male vocalists—whose abilities she now completely outstripped—with an instrumental ensemble of accomplished musicians. Local composers, including Zakariya Ahmad (who had helped her move to Cairo), Muhammad al-Qasabji, Ahmad Sabri al-Najridi, and Da'ud Husni, began to write new songs especially for her.

Similar to many of her colleagues, she also began to make commercial recordings and, largely because of her extensive audience outside of Cairo, these sold extremely well. She accumulated some money and became a desirable commodity for recording companies at the same time that she developed her urban audience. By 1926 she was among the most sought-after singers in Egypt.

The early 1930s brought talkies to Egypt and, with them, musical films became immediately popular. Umm Kulthum made her first musical, *Widad*, in 1936 and subsequently starred in five more films, *Nashid al-Amal, Dananir, A'ida,* and *Sallama,* concluding with *Fatima* in 1946. But the technology that would prove most significant for Umm Kulthum's position in Arab society was radio. Following the success of private radio stations in Egypt in the late 1920s, the Egyptian government opened a national radio station in 1934 and Umm Kulthum, along with her main competitor Muhammad Abd al-Wahhab, became important performers. At the beginning, star singers performed live for as much as twenty minutes, bringing the experience of the wedding or concert hall into homes and coffeehouses. As with record players, radios appeared in public places so that listeners from all walks of life could enjoy the broadcasts. Egyptian Radio also broadcast commercial recordings, supplanting to some extent the popularity of record players.

During the late 1930s and 1940s, Umm Kulthum developed the repertoire that came to represent her "golden age". She established strong collaborations with the composer Zakariya Ahmad and poet Bayram al-Tunisi, both known for their witty and effective use of colloquial language and musical styles. She also cultivated the composition of sophisticated new *qasa'id*, often on religious themes with poetry by such luminaries as Ahmad Shawqi and by the emerging composer Riyad al-Sunbati. These highly successful collaborations produced her well-known songs "Ana fi Intizarak" (I'm waiting for you), "al-Amal" (Hope), and "Huwa Sahih al-Hawa Ghalab" (Is it true that love conquers all). These were written by Zakariya and Bayram. Al-Sunbati and Shawqi wrote "Wulid al-Huda" (The guide [Muhammad] is born) and "Salu Qalbi" (Ask My Heart), and "al-Atlal" (Traces), written by al-Sunbati and Ibrahim Naji, became her signature tune after its first performance in 1966. Whether colloquial or formal, these songs often carried political, historical, and literary undertones that conveyed to listeners the importance of their Arab and Egyptian heritage and the richness of their culture. With her by-then accomplished and virtuosic renderings that brought listeners close to the impact of the words through repeated improvisations, Umm Kulthum and her repertoire brought masses of listeners to the knees with the affect of the music.

In the late 1930s, Umm Kulthum scored an enormous coup in persuading Egyptian Radio to broadcast her concerts live. By then, she had established monthly concerts on Thursday nights in major Cairo theaters that attracted large audiences and lasted throughout the season, that is, from November to June of each year. Friday being the Muslim day of rest, the Thursday-night events occupied what was considered prime time. This concert series lasted for more than thirty-five years and became that by which she was known throughout the Arab world. Eventually, stories were told about life in the Arabic-speaking world coming to a stop for these monthly concerts. Radio remained a critically important patron of musicians throughout World War II, when material for the production of recordings became scarce and communications with European production facilities interrupted. It took on greater social importance than ever following the Egyptian Revolution of 1952 under the government of President Gamal Abdel Nasser who supported the broadcast of entertainment to ameliorate the daily stresses of economic difficulty and who strengthened broadcasting facilities as a means of advancing his political agenda.

Along with many of her compatriots, Umm Kulthum welcomed the Egyptian revolution and sang songs in support of the new regime throughout the 1950s. One of the songs composed for her at the time, "Wallahi Zaman, ya Silahi" (It's been a long time, oh weapon of mine),

was adopted as the Egyptian national anthem and remained so until 1977 when then-President ANWAR SADAT found it too bellicose and replaced it with Sayyid Darwish's "Biladi, Biladi" (My country, my country). She had also, by this time, accepted leadership roles in the world of music. She served as seven-term president of the musician's union in the late 1940s and 1950s, sat on the Listeners' Committee that selected songs suitable for broadcast on Egyptian Radio and, in the 1950s and 1960s, served on governmental committees on the arts.

During the late 1940s and early 1950s, she also suffered from a variety of health issues including a thyroid problem that seems to have originated in the late 1940s, and problems with her vision (prompting her near-constant use of dark glasses). The number of her performances and her production of new songs decreased in the 1950s. In 1954 she married one of her physicians, Hasan al-Hifnawi; their relationship seems to have been important and companionable, although they had no children. As she regained her health in the 1950s, Umm Kulthum took note of the successes of young singers, notably Abd al-Halim Hafiz, and began to seek new songs from younger composers while maintaining her continuing collaboration with al-Sunbati. She and Ahmad had parted ways in a legal dispute and he died in 1961. Baligh Hamdi, Kamal al-Tawil, and Muhammad al-Muji composed for her on texts from popular song lyricists and a new, modern style of song emerged for her, one that was not always valued by her older listeners but that has remained popular nonetheless. In the 1960s, apparently at the behest of President Nasser's government, she and her rival al-Wahhab agreed to a collaboration that produced ten songs, beginning with "Inta Umri" (You are my life) in 1964, a song that has remained wildly popular ever since.

Especially compared to her younger colleague, the Lebanese singer FAYRUZ, in the 1960s, some listeners began to critique Umm Kulthum as insufficiently engaged with the myriad problems with which the Arab world was occupied. Many felt that, with her growing stature as a cultural figure, she should serve as a more outspoken advocate for the rights and plights of Arabs, notably the Palestinians. Perhaps motivated by this view, following Egypt's defeat at the hands of the Israelis in 1967, Umm Kulthum launched one of her most famous endeavors: her concerts for Egypt. Traveling both in Egypt and the Arab world, she launched a series of fund-raising concerts to benefit the Egyptian war treasury, which garnered more than 2 million pounds sterling, an enormous sum at the time. Often, she solicited poetry by local poets, including NIZAR QABBANI from Syria and al-Hadi Adam from Sudan, which were then set to music by al-Sunbati especially for her concerts.

CONTEMPORARIES

Riyad al-Sunbati (1906–1982), a composer, began his life in a village in the Egyptian delta. His father sang at local weddings and special occasions. Later in life, he and Umm Kulthum realized they had met each other as children, their paths crossing in a train station where both families were in transit to performances. He learned to play the *ud* (oud) as a young man and came to Cairo first to study at the new Institute for Arab Music and very soon thereafter to teach there. The young Farid al-Atrash, a nascent *ud* virtuoso and soon-to-be film star, was one of al-Sunbati's early students.

Al-Sunbati's skill at instrumental improvisation soon developed into a prodigious compositional talent. He developed an extraordinary gift for setting poetic texts of all sorts from simple film songs to complex classical *qasa'id*. He wrote for nearly every major singer working in Cairo (the center of Arab music production during al-Sunbati's lifetime). Among his skills was tailoring compositions to the talents of individual voices.

Umm Kulthum and al-Sunbati worked together for the first time for the musical film *Widad* (1936). One of his songs for the film, "'Ala Baladi Mahbub" (For my beloved country), was sung by another actor in the film, but Umm Kulthum liked it so well (as did the audience) that when the recordings from the film were released, she sang the song herself. He also wrote the famous "University Song" for the film *Nashid al-Amal* (*Song of Hope*).

His most magnificent compositions for Umm Kulthum, however, were undoubtedly his *qasa'id*. The first was "Salu Ku'us a-Tila" (Ask the cup of wine) in 1938, a *qasida* written for Umm Kulthum by the poet Ahmad Shawqi after his first meeting with her earlier in the decade. Al-Sunbati composed all of her major poetic works in the 1940s, contributing to a major neoclassical cultural formation. He was a principal author of Umm Kulthum's golden age. He continued to compose work for her until her death, with his "al-Atlal" becoming her signature composition.

The usually contentious Umm Kulthum treated al-Sunbati with great care and respect. She seems to have felt that she could not do without him to provide successful new repertoire. For his part, al-Sunbati, a reserved and taciturn man, never seemed particularly attached to the fame and fortune proximity to Umm Kulthum tended to convey. He seemed happy to compose for a wide variety of performers. Toward the end of his life, al-Sunbati made a studio recording of *ud* improvisations (*taqasim*). As do his vocal compositions, these remain today models of neoclassical invention.

Beginning in about 1972, Umm Kulthum's health began to fail for the final time and she died on 3 February 1975. Her funeral, which was delayed for several days to allow for the arrival of foreign dignitaries, was reported to be larger that that of Nasser's—itself one of the largest funerals in history.

INFLUENCES AND CONTRIBUTIONS

Umm Kulthum brought historically Arabic aesthetics and music into the twentieth century and gave them new life. Working from her prodigious native ability and single-minded devotion to singing and with the help of teachers, she became probably the best singer of Arabic poetry of the century anywhere in the Arabic-speaking world. Arguably, al-Wahhab was equally accomplished in his youth, but his voice began to fade in the 1940s and he turned his attention to composition.

Her position at the pinnacle of Arabic song derived from her command of the language in both its colloquial and sophisticated literary forms; her vocal power and wide range; her command of the complexities of the Arab melodic system of *maqamat* (melodic modes, singular, *maqam*); and, most of all, her ability to fashion one rendition after another of a single line of poetry, each different from the other and each bringing the impact of the meaning of the line to the listener is a slightly different way. This extended the performance of a 10- or 20-minute composition to an hour or more engaging listeners in feeling for poetic sentiment that enveloped them with the rapture called *tarab* (literally, ecstasy) from listening to her. Her Thursday night performances, which began at 9:30 or 10:00 at night, lasted until 3 or 4 in the morning, making this experience the highlight of the month for millions carried by radio waves across the Arab world.

At the same time, Umm Kulthum carefully controlled her public image. She persisted in following the stylish but modest dress of a wealthy Arab woman. Her chignon mimicked the bun in which many working-class women tied their hair. She spoke and acted as a devout Muslim woman of her day. She deflected media attention from her personal life at all times. Thus she enacted a model of feminine respectability in public life that resonated with the widely held mores of modesty in her society and helped instantiate her as a model of cultural accomplishment.

When, in her later years, she spoke about Arab and Egyptian society, she took recourse to her background as a *fallaha* (Arabic: peasant, farmer), a daughter of the country from a poor family and as a good Muslim and patriotic Egyptian. She described herself in terms that would be common to many compatriots of her generation and they often identified her as one of them. With

WE MUST NOT FORGET ... OUR ARTISTIC PERSONALITIES

∎

We must respect our artistic selves.... We must not forget our selves, our artistic personalities, our taste.... Take, for instance, the Indians. They show great respect for themselves in art and in life. Wherever they are, they insist on wearing their own clothes and in their art they are intent on asserting their own independent personality and, due to this, their music is considered one of the best and most successful forms of music in the entire world. This is the way to success for us in music.

AS TOLD TO RAJA AL-NAQQASH IN 1965, REPRINTED IN *LUGHZ UMM KULTHUM* (CAIRO: DAR AL-HILAL, 1978), PP. 48–49.

her artistry and demeanor, she grew to be, as one journalist called her, "the voice and face of Egypt" (*Akhbar al-Yawm*, 19 June 1967).

THE WORLD'S PERSPECTIVE

As a singer devoted to Egyptian and Arabic musical styles and poetic languages, Umm Kulthum came rather late to international attention. A writer in *Look* magazine profiled her in 1966 and his article was among the first actually written for non-Arab listeners. Her only concert outside the Arab world came in Paris in 1967, a performance to which she agreed only because of the number of Arabic speakers likely to be in the audience. Her recordings had been sold internationally since the 1920s but usually in outlets serving the Arab diaspora.

With the interest in world music in the late twentieth century and particularly with the communications available via the Internet, a wider array of audience members have become interested in Umm Kulthum and aware of her remarkable role in the history of Arab music and culture. Her recordings and information about her are now widely available. That said, her art remains perhaps a more deliberately acquired taste, its aesthetics still remote to non-Arab or uninitiated listeners.

LEGACY

Viewed from the standpoint of the early twenty-first century, Umm Kulthum's legacy appears to be musical, first and foremost. Her performances continue to be broadcast and sold using the new media of the compact disc and Internet audio file. Young Arabic speakers listen to her songs, though some of the performances are more than fifty years old. Her impact as an accomplished singer of Arabic poetry has had remarkable staying power. The songs themselves have found their ways into other venues of Arab musical life. Performers ranging from folk musicians to electronic composers and religious singers make reference to her melodies in their own work. Most of the songs themselves have been taken into the turath or heritage of Arab music, which is to say they have been accepted as classics. These are performed by state ensembles of Arabic choruses and orchestras in places such as the Cairo Opera House as statements of Arab classical art.

As a human being, she remains a model of accomplishment and respectability that has served well succeeding generations of young women aspiring to careers in public life, whether in music or in professions such as television news broadcasting. In her own way of life, she articulated a sort of local feminism. Although she is now known worldwide, because her primary medium was Arabic sung poetry her impact will probably always be felt most strongly among Arabic-speaking listeners for whom the art of adding meaning to text using melody is historic cultural value.

BIBLIOGRAPHY

Danielson, Virginia. *"The Voice of Egypt": Umm Kulthum, Arabic Song and Egyptian Society in the 20th Century*. Chicago: University of Chicago Press, 1997.

Goldman, Michael. *Umm Kulthum: A Voice Like Egypt*. Waltham, Massachusetts: Filmmakers Collaborative, 1996.

Gaskill, Gordon. "The Mighty Voice of Um Kalthum." *Life* 52/22 (1 June 1962): 15–16.

When a Woman Sings. Produced by Gabriel Khoury, Marianne Khoury, and Humbert Balsan; a film by Mustapha Hasnaoui. Seattle, WA: Arab Film Distribution, 2004.

Virginia Danielson

WAHBE, HAIFA
(1976–)

Lebanon's top model, designer, pop star, and former Miss South Lebanon, Haifa Wahbe (Wehbe, Wehbi) is a Lebanese singer who has played a major role in the entertainment industry in the Arab world in the last several years.

PERSONAL HISTORY

Wahbe was born on 10 March 1976, to a Lebanese Shi'ite Muslim father and Egyptian Coptic Christian mother in Mahruna, Lebanon. She was a beautiful child, with dreams of stardom, and at sixteen won the title of Miss South Lebanon. From there she went on to compete in the Miss Lebanon Competition in 1995. She was the runner-up, but was stripped of this title after it was learned that she was married and had a child. Undaunted, she modeled and became highly sought after, appearing in 1996 on more than one hundred magazine covers. During her time as a model, she and her husband divorced. Under

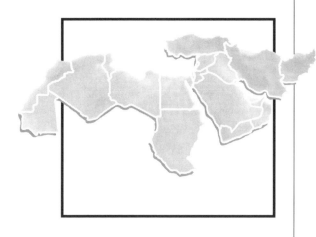

Haifa Wahbe. © JAMAL SAIDI/REUTERS/CORBIS.

BIOGRAPHICAL HIGHLIGHTS

Name: Haifa Wahbe (Wehbe, Wehbi)

Birth: 1976, Mahruna, Lebanon

Family: Divorced; one daughter: Zaynab

Nationality: Lebanese

PERSONAL CHRONOLOGY:

• **1992:** Named Miss South Lebanon

• **1995:** Runner-up for Miss Lebanon, but title was revoked because she was married and had a daughter

• **2002:** Releases first album *Huwa al-Zaman* (It is time)

• **2004:** Voted Best Young Arabic Female Singer by *al-Jumhuriyya* newspaper

• **2005:** Releases second album *Baddi A'ish* (I want to live); participates in pan-Arab reality show *The Valley*; wins Beauty and Arts Award at the International Petra Beauty Festival in Jordan

• **2006:** Releases the single "Bus al-Wawa"; becomes the first Arab artist to introduce and play as an opening act for hip-hop star 50 Cent; ranks 49th of top 99 Most Desirable Women by AskMen.com; appears on an Egyptian Satellite Channel show, *Malakat*

Lebanese divorce and child custody laws, the father is awarded custody, and he decided to keep Haifa from seeing her child. To date she has still not been allowed visitation. In 2005 she was engaged to Saudi businessman Tariq al-Jafali, but the engagement was broken off, many say due to her controversial songs, actions, and dress, making her allegedly an unfit Muslim wife.

INFLUENCES AND CONTRIBUTIONS

Wahbe was influenced by both jazz and Rhythm and Blues, which she listened to growing up. She was also influenced by the death of her only brother, who died at the age of twenty four, due to the Arab-Israeli conflict. She has also stated that she greatly admires HASAN NASRALLAH, the leader of Hizbullah, because he fights for Lebanon. Despite the claims of her critics, she has not forgotten her roots and she uses traditional instruments in many of her songs. Wahbe has contributed to her home state by many

charity works. She additionally has contributed to the rise of sexuality in music being played and being shown on television in Lebanon.

THE WORLD'S PERSPECTIVE

Wahbe has broad appeal. She is well known in the Middle East and apparently was even well liked by the grandsons of SADDAM HUSSEIN. In Egypt there is a movement against her and others that the Egyptian government deems as showing reprehensible behavior, calling hers close to prostitution. Her popularity in other countries outside of the Arab world is mixed and she still is not widely known internationally, except for the many controversies that swirl around her.

LEGACY

She has performed many good works for her community, most notably touring areas of Lebanon damaged during the 2006 fighting between Israel and Hizbullah, as well as trying to raise the nation's morale through benefits and charity work. One tourism student put it perfectly in the *Sunday Telegraph* on 5 November 2006, "Haifa's music offers an escape from the daily tension of Lebanon's politics, and she is certainly easier to dance to than Hizbullah war songs." Wahbe has teamed up with the Red Ribbon Campaign against AIDS. She will be featured in a 2008 calendar and book, with proceeds benefiting the campaign.

CONTEMPORARIES

Lebanese singer Najwa Karam (1966–) is a popular Lebanese pop star who has become a paramount multi-award winner. Karam's rise to fame started with her appearance on the television singing contest Layali Lubnan (Nights of Lebanon) in 1985. Singing her Mowals (traditional Lebanese folklore) with a strong high pitch mountain voice, Najwa gained the warm acceptance and admiration of the audience and walked away with the Gold Medal for a great performance. Since 1985 Karam has released more than a dozen successful albums. Her albums Naghmet Hob (The rhythm of love), Nedmaneh (I have regrets) and Oyoun Qalbi (Eyes of heart) have won her numerous awards including "Best Arabic Artist," "Artist of the Year," "Album of the Year," "Highest Selling Album," and "Best Singer of Traditional Lebanese Song." Karam's career, which spans more than two decades, has made her one of the most popular pop stars in the Arab world.

> ## WAHBE'S WORDS
>
> ■
>
> I believe the whole world knows who started this war (Israeli-Hizbullah conflict in 2006) and who aggressed on whose land. There isn't a war that starts from nothing and he who begins is the unjust one.
>
> HAIFA WAHBE IN HIRST, MICHAEL, "LEBANESE POP DIVA BACKS HEZBOLLAH SHEIKH TO DEFEND COUNTRY'S HONOUR." *SUNDAY TELEGRAPH*, 5 NOVEMBER 2006.

BIBLIOGRAPHY

Bayoumy, Yara. "Hizbullah Chief Wins Unlikely Fan in Sexy Pop Diva." 30 October 2006. Available from http://www.reuters.com.

"Haifa Wahbi Doubts Elissa's World Music Award." Arabic Nights: Arabic Entertainment Directory. Updated 1 January 2007. Available from http://www.arabicnights.com.au/news.

Hirst, Michael, "Lebanese Pop Diva Backs Hezbollah Sheikh to Defend Country's Honour." *Sunday Telegraph*, 5 November 2006.

Sela, Yohai. "Haifa Wehbe—Portrait of a Lebanese Female Vocalist." Omedia.com. Available from http://www.omedia.com.

Khodr M. Zaarour

WATTAR, AL-TAHER
(1936–)

Al-Taher Wattar (also Taher Ouettar, at-Tahar Wattar, al-Tahir Wattar) is a writer and journalist from Algeria. He is one of the most important and highly acclaimed figures in Algerian literature. Wattar writes in Arabic, unlike many Algerian writers who write in French. His first two novels, published in 1974, were among the first novels published in Arabic after Algeria achieved independence from France in 1962. He has written seven more novels as well as plays and short stories. His literary work and his efforts in support of cultural expression have made him a key figure of the politically charged cultural scene in postindependence Algeria.

PERSONAL HISTORY

Wattar was born in 1936 in eastern Algeria, in a village between Annaba and Tebessa called Sedrata. He attended a traditional Arabic primary school and learned the Qur'an. From 1952 to 1954 he studied Islamic jurisprudence at the Ben Badis Institute in Constantine. In 1954 Algeria's National Liberation Front (known by its French acronym FLN) launched a war of independence against French rule. Wattar spent the war years in Tunisia, first attending the Islamic Zaytouna University. He read widely in classical and modern Arabic literature. He also read French and other world literature and began undertaking literary translations. At the same time he was drawn to socialism and the notion of commitment in literature. In 1955 Wattar published his first short stories in newspapers, including "Nuwwa" which he later adapted to a film. He left his studies in 1956 to work for the Civil Organization of the FLN and continued to establish himself as a writer and journalist.

In 1962 he returned to Algeria to take up the post of party controller for the ruling party, the FLN, a role he retained until 1984. As a single party, the FLN brought together a broad range of political perspectives, although power remained firmly in the hands of the army. Wattar stood to the far left of the party, and his writing has expressed a socialist perspective far closer to that of the former communist party. In the early 1960s he founded two cultural weekly newspapers, and in 1973 he founded a further cultural weekly, as a part of the *al-Sha'b* (The people) daily newspaper. He published his first novel,

> ## BIOGRAPHICAL HIGHLIGHTS
>
> ■
>
> **Name:** al-Taher Wattar (Taher Ouettar, at-Tahar Wattar, al-Tahir Wattar)
>
> **Birth:** 1936, Sedrata, Algeria
>
> **Nationality:** Algerian
>
> **Education:** Ben Badis Institute, Algeria; read Arabic, French, and world literatures at Zaytouna University, Tunisia, but took no degree
>
> **PERSONAL CHRONOLOGY:**
>
> - **1955:** Begins writing short stories in Tunis
>
> - **1962:** Returns to Algeria and becomes party controller for FLN; works in cultural journalism
>
> - **1974–present:** Publishes a series of novels, beginning with *al-Laz* (The ace) and *al-Zilzal* (The Earthquake)
>
> - **1989:** Founds al-Jahiziyya cultural association
>
> - **1989–1992:** Works as director of state radio company
>
> - **2004:** Awarded Sharjah Prize by UNESCO for the promotion of Arab culture

al-Laz (The ace), in Algiers in 1974. Since then he has written a further eight novels, the most recent of which, *al-Wali al—Tahir yarfaʻu yadahu bi-duʻa* (Saint Tahar raises his hands in prayer), was published in 2005. In 1989, he founded a cultural association, al-Jahiziyya, and edited its journal *al-Tabyin* (The exposition). He worked as director of state radio between 1989 and 1992.

One aim of al-Jahiziyya was to bring together writers working in Arabic and those writing in French, but political events worked against this. In 1992, the first elections after the end of single-party rule gave a clear lead to the main Islamist opposition party, the Islamic Salvation Front (Front Islamique de salut, FIS). When the military canceled the elections, Algerian opinion was divided. Wattar, along with the former Algerian communist party, opposed the cancellation of elections and the military clampdown against the FIS. As Algeria moved toward open conflict and civil war, Wattar's ambivalent response to the assassination of some French-language writers by the FIS made him a controversial and much-despised figure for many, and undermined his standing. He remained in Algeria during the conflict and continued to write, publishing three novels. In 2004 he was awarded the United Nations Educational, Scientific, and Cultural Organization's (UNESCO) Sharjah Prize in recognition of his contribution to the promotion of Arab culture.

INFLUENCES AND CONTRIBUTIONS

Wattar's early literary work is openly political in its subject matter, themes, and motivation. His later novels move toward greater use of symbolism and allegory, but they remain relevant to key issues confronting Algerian society, including the nature of authority, the role of history and identity, and the place of religion. His work has been influenced above all by Algeria's struggle for independence from French colonial rule, and by the socialist understanding of literary engagement, that is, the understanding that literary writing should play an active role in the struggle of the poor and downtrodden for dignity and justice.

France occupied Algeria in 1830, instituting a period of colonial rule longer and more profound in its impact than that experienced by any other Arab country. During this period French replaced Arabic as the primary written language in education and the affairs of state as part of a wider process of replacing Algerian cultural practices with norms and values supporting the French presence. Opposition to French rule emerged within different sections of Algerian society and was expressed in different ways. Those who had a French education but were denied further advancement or political influence expressed their opposition in French. Those who were educated in Arabic rejected both the French presence and the growing

---

CONTEMPORARIES

Abdelhamid Benhedouga (1925–1996). Abdelhamid Benhedouga (also Abd al-Hamid Bin Haduqa) was born in Eastern Algeria in 1925. He received his primary education in French but learned Arabic from his father. He studied radio production in Marseille before attending Zaytouna University in Tunis to study literature and drama. In 1954 he returned to Algeria as a teacher but left for France after being sought by the police. He later returned to Tunis and worked with the FLN as a writer of short stories and cultural articles. He worked in radio and television broadcasting after his return to Algeria in 1962.

Benhedouga published novels over a period of twenty years from 1972—*Rih al-janub* (The wind from the south)—to 1992. *Rih al-janub* was the first major Arabic novel published in Algeria. Set during the agrarian reform, it depicted the efforts of a young woman to assert her freedom from her father's control. It was highly acclaimed and adapted as a film. Benhedouga's work was primarily within a realist vein and was marked by his socialist commitment. His work was milder than Wattar's in its critique of the Algerian state and the religious classes, aiming to win over rather than condemn opposing views. Benhedouga, Wattar, and RACHID BOUDJEDRA remained the primary figures in Algerian Arabic literature until the emergence of a new generation of writers in the 1990s. He died in October 1996.

---

dominance of the class of Algerians educated in French. Faith in Islam was a factor uniting almost all Algerians, and Arabic remained important as the language of Islam and as a source of identity. The movement of national independence demanded the restoration of Arabic teaching, and during the war of independence Arabic was claimed as the national language of the new state. This was seen as a necessary aspect of independence, and the use of French was associated with foreign domination. The extension of Arabic teaching faced both practical and political difficulties, and language has remained a major source of division within the society.

The issue of language has been reflected in Algerian literature in different ways. Literary writing emerged first in French. By the 1950s the novel was well established and a number of French-language writers gained international prominence during the nationalist struggle. Arabic literary writing emerged later in Algeria than in neighboring Arab countries and initially focused on poetry rather than prose. Arabic novels were published only after independence, the first being Abdelhamid Benhedouga's *Rih al-janub* (The wind from the south) in 1972. Arabic writing was held back by a lack of a readership and faced constraints because of the political role attached to the language by the postindependence state. Within Algeria's cultural revolution, Arabic was charged with promoting an Arab-Islamic cultural identity. A state-owned company controlled publishing, and authors were expected to celebrate the heroic war of independence and the ongoing development effort. Although much Arabic literary writing responded to this command, the work of the most prominent authors has gone beyond such constraints to express a more critical and diverse vision.

Wattar's family was fiercely opposed to French rule and his education in Arabic was a rejection of French influence. He reached adulthood at the point when the nationalist struggle became a bitter war of independence. In Tunis he was exposed to international perspectives of the war. For many on the left and in the developing world, the combat in Algeria symbolized the struggle of the Third World for justice against the dominant nations of Europe and the United States. Wattar became committed to a socialist perspective that viewed the war as the first step in an ongoing revolution to bring education, welfare, and economic justice to all Algerians, and to ensure genuine independence through industrialization.

At the same time Wattar was influenced by socialism in literature and the socialist understanding of a committed literature where writers should seek not only to describe society but also to change it for the benefit of the masses. In addition to his knowledge of the Qur'an and of classical Arabic literature, Wattar was influenced by modern Arabic literature and world literature. He was greatly influenced by the Chilean poet Pablo Neruda whose poetic vision was fused with socialist activism and sacrifice. Other literary influences included Ernest Hemingway and François Mauriac.

Wattar's novels treat political themes, including the struggle against French rule, divisions within the nationalist movement, the agrarian revolution (which aimed to redistribute land to the peasants who worked on it), and the injustices of the postindependence state, including corruption, feudalism, poverty, authoritarian rule, and the treatment of women within the society. His first novel, *al-Laz* (The ace), dramatizes events of the war of independence and portrays the sacrifices made in the fight against French rule. However, it rejects the ruling party's demand that literature should celebrate the nationalist struggle. Instead it records the hidden conflicts within the wartime FLN, and through its symbolism it sounds a critical note with regard to postindependence rule. The novel's central relationship

is between al-Laz—the child of an unmarried mother who has grown into an unruly troublemaker—and Zaydan, the communist fighter who leads the FLN unit near the village. When al-Laz is betrayed and arrested the villagers feel little pity. They view him as a criminal who drinks, takes drugs, and procures prostitutes for the French soldiers in the barracks. However, his actions are a cover for his work helping Algerian soldiers desert from the French army. Al-Laz joins the revolutionary cause when his revolt against the stigma of his birth leads him to approach Zaydan with a plan to kill the French captain. Zaydan guides al-Laz to a more constructive path, and reveals to him that he is his father.

The discovery of his father and the revolutionary cause change al-Laz's behavior from futile and destructive violence to constructive work for the revolution. Al-Laz symbolizes all the dispossessed and the revolution which is their cause, whereas Zaydan represents the revolution's guiding conscience. Following his arrest, al-Laz escapes from the barracks and joins Zaydan's unit. Zaydan hopes to teach his son just as he undertakes the political education of others. But Zaydan is under investigation by the FLN leadership for his membership of the Algerian communist party, accused of blocking the formation of a united front. Zaydan and five European communists fighting for Algerian independence are executed as traitors. The sight of his father's execution makes al-Laz go mad so that he can only repeat the phrase that was a codeword among his comrades: nothing remains in the riverbed except its stones.

The novel's exploration of the past opposes the state's official history of the war of independence. It refuses the state's simplified account of national unity, and refrains from a stereotypical portrayal of good Algerians confronting bad Frenchmen. Its plot offers an alternative understanding, as it depicts the betrayal of the revolution's socialist purpose during the war. As the first major Arabic novel to focus on the war of independence, *al-Laz* occupies an important place within Algerian literature. The hopes and tragedies of its diverse characters offer an insight into the nature of the Algerian revolution, and its portrayal of communist fighters within the nationalist forces challenges the view that communism is a foreign import, opposed to the nation and Islam. This is one element of the novel's exploration of identity, which recurs as a theme throughout Wattar's work, as does his concern with the way the record of history is shaped or distorted by those in power.

Wattar's second novel, *al-Zilzal* (*The Earthquake*), views the agrarian revolution from the perspective of a landholder seeking to safeguard his wealth. Shaykh Bu al-Arwa is an antihero; his view of urban chaos and social upheaval is largely a product of his own prejudice. But his fevered stream of consciousness is ambiguous. The sights he decries—overcrowding, begging, theft, prostitution, black-market trade, and widespread poverty—undermine the much-vaunted progress represented by factories, clinics, and schools. Fleeting voices describe repression or abuses by employers, one voice asks why socialists are imprisoned in a socialist state, another asks why trade unionists need to go underground: overall they associate power with a position in the army or bureaucracy. Bu al-Arwa's Qur'anic injunctions work against him, undermining the association between Arabic and religion. The novel's celebration of agrarian reform and industrialization is modified by its critique of corruption, poverty, and injustice. Its portrayal of class and regional differences counters the state discourse of unity, and Bu al-Arwa's status as a religious teacher exposes the contradiction between the radicalism of the agrarian reform and the conservatism of cultural and language policy. The novel's realism is complemented by its ironic humor.

Wattar's third novel, *Urs baghl* (A mule's wedding), moves away from realism to explore history and identity. Set in a Tunis brothel before the war of independence, it depicts the rivalries between pimps and prostitutes. The novel's meanings are conveyed through allegory and through the drug-induced hallucinations of its main character. Its plot is a suggestive allegory for the way the national leadership employs the same exploitative practices as the former colonial masters, and is drawn into a new relationship with imperialism. Its historical references focus on elements of an Islamic past associated with discontinuity, contestation, and revolutionary movements. These references emphasize that the meaning of Islam has been contested throughout history, and undermine the religious establishment's claim to represent the only true Islam. They show movements of social egalitarianism as part of an Islamic past. The novel aligns itself, and the Arabic language, with socialist policies rejected by the religious and educational establishments. This concern with the past shows how history becomes a battleground of conflicting interpretations as the nation searches for identity and authentic models. Wattar's writing does not challenge the view that the nation should develop according to its own history and heritage, but rather works within this premise to dispute official versions of history.

Although Wattar's writing has remained concerned with themes relevant to his socialist commitment, it has moved away from realism toward allegory, fantasy, and the use of ambiguity and humor. The development of Wattar's work parallels that seen in literary writing in other Arab countries. In terms of its literary qualities, Wattar's language is concise and crafted; he coins new words and uses a language that reflects his Algerian situation and that is clear to readers in other Arab countries. Unlike his contemporary Benhedouga, Wattar assumes a high level

---

EMOTIONAL CHARGE

All my subjects are political. I write from an emotional charge. I am a writer of class and the positions of my class have been shaken and struck.

INTERVIEW, "LE ROMAN SELON OUETTAR," *EL MOUDJAHID* NEWSPAPER, 30 JANUARY 1985.

Algerian literature is at all times committed to the service of the national cause which supported and expressed the revolution, the struggle against colonialism and imperialism. It has made its own the preoccupations of the masses, supported the agrarian revolution, the socialist management of enterprises, free medicine, the democratization of education and it has combated exploitation. We have all been brought up according to this method and a mode of thinking animated by the same preoccupations.

INTERVIEW, "NOUS FAISONS DE LA LITERATURE," *EL DJEICH*, APRIL 1985.

---

of literary awareness in his readers, as well as a knowledge of Arab and Algerian history. The themes of identity and understandings of history have been constant elements of his work along with the portrayal of the divisions within Algerian society. His works have been adapted for film and the theater, and he has used his prominence to criticize the shortcomings of cultural policy in newspaper interviews where he appeared for a long time as an iconic figure with his trademark black beret and moustache. He has also contributed to Algerian culture through his efforts to establish cultural journals offering an outlet for the work of younger writers and through the cultural association he founded.

THE WORLD'S PERSPECTIVE

Wattar's work is known primarily in Algeria, although he is one of the best-known Algerian authors in many other Arab countries along with RACHID BOUDJEDRA and AHLAM MUSTAGHANMI. Book distribution networks between Algeria and the rest of the Arab world are weak, and few Algerian writers, apart from those writing in French and publishing their work in France, are known in other Arab countries. Wattar's work has from the beginning been published and reissued in other Arab countries, with editions in Cyprus, Beirut, Cairo, Jordan, Israel, Tunis, and, more recently, Germany. Most of his novels have also been translated into a range of European and Asian languages, although only one of his novels, *al-Zilzal* (*The Earthquake*), has been translated into English. Wattar is better known in French-speaking countries than in the English-speaking world. This is because his works have appeared in French soon after their original publication, and because there is greater interest in North Africa in France than there is in English-speaking countries. Wattar's work was well received in countries that came within the former Soviet Union as well as in developing nations where Algeria's anticolonial struggle was much admired, lending his works a particular resonance.

LEGACY

Algeria's postindependence state was authoritarian in nature: It suppressed political expression and excluded views other than its own. In this context literary writing has been one of few means for the expression of an alternative vision. Writers using French have evaded state control by publishing their work in France, but this frequently allowed the state to present their work as reflecting a French-influenced perspective at odds with the needs and interests of the new nation. Similarly, works in French have reached a limited readership in Algeria, and have often enjoyed a higher status outside the country than within it. Because Wattar's work is written in the national language and published in Algeria it avoided this charge and reached an audience in Algeria itself. His work is also of key significance because it challenges the association between the Arabic language and Islam, promoted by both the state and the religious establishment. Wattar's works stand as a record of the unresolved tensions within Algerian society. He has been a major player on the Algerian cultural scene through literature, journalism, his role in state radio, and his voluntary efforts to establish cultural groupings and to promote cultural expression and dialogue. The fact that he remains a hate-figure for some Algerians is a reflection of the divisions over language and culture that underlie the importance of his work.

BIBLIOGRAPHY

Al-Taher Wattar's personal Web site. Available from http://www.wattar.cv.dz.

Cox, Debbie. *Politics, Language and Gender in the Algerian Arabic Novel*. New York: Edwin Mellen Press, 2001.

Malley, Robert. *The Call from Algeria: Third Worldism, Revolution and the Turn to Islam*. Berkeley: University of California Press, 1996.

Salhi, Zahia Smail. *Politics, Poetics and the Algerian Novel*. New York: Edwin Mellen Press, 1999.

Wattar, al-Taher. *The Earthquake*. Translated by William Granara. London: al-Saqi, 2000.

Debbie Cox

WIJDAN ALI
(1939–)

A Jordanian art historian, painter and curator, Wijdan Ali (born Wijdan bint Fawwaz Muhana) is also a diplomat.

PERSONAL HISTORY

Wijdan Ali was born in Baghdad, Iraq on 29 August 1939. She was born with the title of *sharifa* (roughly noble) because both her father, Sharif Fawwaz Muhana, and mother, Sharifa Nafi'a bint Jamil Ali, were descendants of the Islamic prophet Muhammad. Descendants of Muhammad are honored throughout the Islamic world, and entitled to carry special titles. On her mother's side Wijdan is the great-granddaughter of Sharif Husayn bin Ali of the Hashemite family of Mecca, who launched the Great Arab Revolt against the Ottoman Empire in 1916. Wijdan also is a first cousin of the late King HUSSEIN BIN TALAL of Jordan.

Raised in Amman, Jordan, Wijdan bint Fawwaz received her B.A. in history from Beirut College for Women (now part of the Lebanese American University) in Beirut in 1961. In 1962 she became the first woman to enter the Jordanian foreign service, although her family did not allow her, as a single woman, to be posted abroad for long periods. As assistant director in the department of international organizations, she represented Jordan at the United Nations (UN) General Assembly in New York, and the General Assembly's Economic and Social Council in Geneva, in 1962. From 1965 to 1966 she worked as program officer for the UN Development Programme in Amman. In April 1966 she married Prince Ali bin Nayif, a distant cousin. Thereafter she became known as Princess Wijdan Ali and left the Jordanian diplomatic service.

INFLUENCES AND CONTRIBUTIONS

Wijdan Ali long has had an interest in art. She took private art lessons in Beirut as an undergraduate, and started painting in 1964. As a member of the Jordanian royal family, Wijdan Ali established the Royal Society of Fine Arts in 1979 and, in 1980, the Jordan National Gallery of Fine Arts, both in Amman. In 1988, she organized the Third International Seminar on Islamic Art, which was held jointly by the Royal Society of Fine Arts and the Islamic Arts Foundation in London. The following year she organized an exhibition on contemporary Islamic art that was held by the same two organizations. From 1989 to 1994, Wijdan Ali also served as editor of Islamic art for the *Encyclopedia of Islamic Culture* that was produced by the Royal Academic for Islamic Civilization Research in Amman. She later traveled to London for graduate studies in Islamic art. She completed an M.A. (1991) and a Ph.D.

BIOGRAPHICAL HIGHLIGHTS

Name: Wijdan Ali (born Wijdan bint Fawwaz Muhana)

Birth: 1939, Baghdad, Iraq

Family: Husband: Prince Ali bin Nayif (married 1966); three daughters: Nafaa (b. 1966), Rajwa (b. 1968), Basma (b. 1970); one son: Muhammad Abbas (b. 1973)

Nationality: Jordanian

Education: B.A. (history), Beirut College for Women, 1961; M.A. (Islamic art), School of Oriental and African Studies, University of London, 1991; Ph.D. (Islamic art), School of Oriental and African Studies, University of London, 1993

PERSONAL CHRONOLOGY:

• **1962:** Enters Jordanian foreign service

• **1964:** Begins painting

• **1979:** Founds Royal Society of Fine Arts

• **1980:** Founds Jordan National Gallery of Fine Arts

• **1988:** Organizes Third International Seminar on Islamic Art in Amman

• **1989:** Editor of Islamic art for the Royal Academic for Islamic Civilization Research's *Encyclopedia of Islamic Culture*

• **1990:** Lectures on Islamic art and aesthetics at Yarmuk University in Irbid, Jordan

• **1994:** Receives an award from the International Council of Women in the Arts

• **2006:** Appointed Jordanian ambassador to Italy

(1993) in that subject from the School of Oriental and African Studies at the University of London.

During 1990 and 1991, Wijdan Ali also lectured on Islamic art and aesthetics at Yarmuk University in Irbid, Jordan, and she has taught at the Higher Institute for Islamic Art and Architecture at Al al-Bayt University. She remains president of the Royal Society of Fine Arts, a member of the Arab Thought Forum and the World Affairs Council of Amman, and a member of the board of governors of the International Centre for Islamic

Studies in London. Having returned to diplomatic service after several decades, Wijdan Ali was appointed Jordan's ambassador to Italy in October 2006.

She has authored several books, including *Modern Islamic Art: Development and Continuity* (1997), and *The Arab Contribution to Islamic Art: From the Seventh to the Fifteenth Centuries* (1999).

THE WORLD'S PERSPECTIVE

Wijdan Ali is recognized internationally as Jordan's leading expert on Islamic art and as an important artist in her own right. In 1994 she received an award from the International Council of Women in the Arts.

LEGACY

Wijdan Ali will be remembered mainly for her contributions to the artistic scene in Jordan, both as a painter and as the founder of the Royal Society of Fine Arts and the Jordan National Gallery of Fine Arts, and as an expert on Islamic art.

BIBLIOGRAPHY

Jordan National Gallery of Fine Arts. Available from http://www.nationalgallery.org/Intro.html.

Wijdan Ali. *Modern Islamic Art: Development and Continuity.* Gainesville: University Press of Florida, 1997.

——— *The Arab Contribution to Islamic Art: From the Seventh to the Fifteenth Centuries.* Cairo, Egypt: American University in Cairo Press, 1999.

"Wijdan Ali, Interview." Nafas. December 2003. Available from http://universes-in-universe.org/eng/islamic_world/articles/2003/princess_wijdan_ali.

Michael R. Fischbach

CONTEMPORARIES

Mona Saudi (1945–) was born in Amman, Jordan, and now lives and works in Beirut. She studied sculpture at the École Supérieure des Beaux Arts in Paris, graduating in 1973. She is one of the few Arab female artists to work primarily on large, modern art stone sculptures. Saudi's works are influenced by the sculptures of Constantin Brancusi, and often are patterned after Arabic calligraphy and ancient Middle Eastern art forms. She is also a poet, and a collection of her poetry titled *An Ocean of Dreams* was published in 1999.

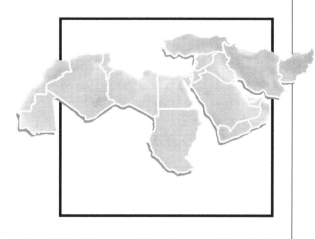

YACOUB, MAGDI
(1935–)

An Egyptian heart surgeon, Magdi Habib Yacoub (Majdi Habib Ya'qub) has performed more heart transplants than any other physician and has been called the leading heart surgeon in the world.

PERSONAL HISTORY

Yacoub was born in Bilbays, Egypt, on 16 November 1935. His family, Coptic Orthodox Christians, was originally from the southern town of Asyut. He began studies at the Cairo University College of Medicine at age fifteen, and was qualified as a doctor in 1957. From 1958 to 1961 he worked at Cairo University Hospital. In 1961, he moved to Denmark and worked at Copenhagen University Hospital.

Yacoub moved to Great Britain in 1962 and began working with the British National Health Service (NHS) at the London Chest Hospital. He began performing pioneering heart surgeries in 1967, and specialized in children with congenital heart problems. Yacoub performed surgery on babies as young as several days old. From 1968 to 1969, he taught at the University of Chicago in the United States. In 1969 he began practicing at Harefield Hospital in London, which went on to become Britain's leading heart hospital. He conducted Britain's first ever heart transplant in 1980, and in that same year, carried out a heart transplant procedure on a man named Derrick Morris, who ended up living until 2005, becoming Europe's longest-surviving heart transplant patient.

In 1986 he became a professor at the National Heart and Lung Institute in London, now part of the Imperial College School of Medicine. While there, he helped develop the procedures involving both heart and lung transplants. Yacoub performed Britain's first live lobe lung transplant in 1984, while performing over twenty-six hundred heart transplants, more than any other surgeon in the world. Yacoub retired from the NHS in September 2001, but he remains a professor at Imperial College, as well as a consultant and global ambassador for transplant surgery.

INFLUENCES AND CONTRIBUTIONS

Yacoub's decision to become a heart surgeon was influenced profoundly by his family. His father, Habib Yacoub, was a surgeon, and young Magdi was drawn to medicine as a result. His youngest aunt died because she suffered from mitral stenosis (a narrowing of the heart valve), which also affected medicine's pull on Yacoub. Years later Yacoub said, "She was very young, in her twenties, and I was left with the impression that she didn't need to die. This motivated me to become a heart surgeon" (Royal Society Web site).

Yacoub always combined research and surgery in his effort to fight human heart failure. He has authored over

Magdi Yacoub. GEMMA LEVINE/HULTON ARCHIVE/GETTY IMAGES.

BIOGRAPHICAL HIGHLIGHTS

Name: Magdi Yacoub (Majdi Habib Ya'qub)

Birth: 1935, Bilbays, Egypt

Family: Married; three children

Nationality: Egyptian; carries British citizenship

Education: M.D., Cairo University College of Medicine, 1957

PERSONAL CHRONOLOGY:

• **1957:** Qualifies as a doctor; works at Cairo University Hospital, Egypt

• **1961:** Works at Copenhagen University Hospital, Denmark; moves to Britain; begins work at London Chest Hospital

• **1968:** Teaches at University of Chicago, United States; begins work at Harefield Hospital, London

• **1980:** Performs first successful heart transplant

• **1984:** Performs first live lobe lung transplant; becomes professor at National Heart and Lung Institute in London

• **1992:** Knighted by Queen Elizabeth II

• **1995:** Establishes Chain of Hope UK charity

• **1999:** Made fellow in Royal Society

• **2001:** Retires from surgery

• **2004:** Receives lifetime achievement award from the International Society for Heart and Lung Transplantation

• **2007:** Announces that his team at Harefield Hospital grew tissue from stem cells that acts like a human heart valve

eight hundred scholarly articles. In the late 1990s, Yacoub embarked upon an ambitious project, one that, if successful, could change the face of medicine: To grow a replacement human heart from stem cells. Assembling a team of over seventy-five biologists, physicists, cellular scientists, engineers, pharmacologists, and others at Harefield Hospital's heart center, he ordered them to study and decipher every aspect of how the human heart works. The aim was to be able to use such information in trying to grow replacement heart parts. In April 2007 his team announced that they successfully grew tissue from stem cells that acts like a human heart valve. If Yacoub's ongoing work proves successful in growing an entire heart valve, it would prove more resilient than artificial heart valves. As Yacoub noted, "The way a living valve functions, it anticipates haemodynamic [*sic*] events and responds and changes its shape and size. It's completely different from an artificial valve which will just open and shut. The heart muscle itself will appreciate something which will make it free to contract properly" (Jha, 2007).

Yacoub also combines medical and charity work. In 1995, he established Chain of Hope UK, a charity that sends doctors around the world to treat patients free of charge and also brings children to Britain for treatment. Chain of Hope also trains doctors in other countries. The group also helped establish the Maputo Heart Center in Mozambique, and hosts Mozambican doctors in Britain for further training. Yacoub also chairs the Royal Society's Role Model project that was established in 2003.

THE WORLD'S PERSPECTIVE

In 1992 Queen Elizabeth II knighted Yacoub. In 1999 he was made a fellow of the Royal Society, Britain's national academy of science. In April 2004 he was given a lifetime achievement award by the International Society for Heart and Lung Transplantation.

LEGACY

Magdi Yacoub will be remembered as the greatest heart surgeon in the world during the time period in which he lived. His contributions to the science of heart and lung transplants and to the study of heart ailments are unparalleled and of tremendous historical importance.

BIBLIOGRAPHY

Jha, Alok. "British Team Grows Human Heart Valve from Stem Cells." *Guardian* (2 April 2007). Available from http://www.guardian.co.uk.

"Sir Magdi Yacoub FRS—King of Hearts." Royal Society. Available from http://www.royalsoc.ac.uk/page.asp?id=1573.

Michael R. Fischbach

YAMANI, MAI
(1957–)

A social anthropologist and researcher, Mai (May) Yamani is the first woman from Saudi Arabia to earn a Ph.D. from Oxford University. Her calls for reform in Saudi Arabia have resulted in her being banned from the country of her birth, where her books are also banned. She lives in London, England, where she is a research fellow at Chatham House.

PERSONAL HISTORY

Yamani, who was born in 1957 in Saudi Arabia, is the daughter of Shaykh Ahmed Zaki Yamani, who served as Saudi Arabia's minister of oil and mineral resources from 1962 to 1986 and as a minister in the Organization of Petroleum Exporting Countries (OPEC) for twenty-five years. Mai Yamani has two full siblings—a younger sister and brother—and five half-siblings from her father's second marriage.

Yamani received her A.B. degree in anthropology in 1979 from Bryn Mawr College, near Philadelphia, graduating with highest honors. She studied social anthropology at Oxford University, becoming the first woman from Saudi Arabia to receive a doctoral degree from Oxford. Following graduation, Yamani continued to study the cultural identity of Saudi Arabia, notably the changing social dynamics related to the influence of younger Arabs, the changing role of women, and the history of the culturally distinct Hijazi Arabs. She works in London at Chatham House (formerly the Royal Institute of Affairs) as a social anthropologist and research fellow.

BIOGRAPHICAL HIGHLIGHTS

Name: Mai Yamani (May Yamani)

Birth: 1957, Saudi Arabia

Family: Daughter of Shaykh Ahmed Zaki Yamani

Nationality: Saudi Arabian

Education: A.B., Bryn Mawr College, Pennsylvania, 1979; Ph.D. Oxford University

PERSONAL CHRONOLOGY:

- **1970s–present:** Social anthropologist; research fellow, Chatham House, London
- **1996:** Edits *Feminism and Islam: Legal and Literary Perspectives*
- **2000:** Writes *Changed Identities: The Challenge of the New Generation in Saudi Arabia*; coedits (with Eugene Cotran), *The Rule of Law in the Middle East and the Islamic World: Human Rights and the Judicial Process*
- **2004:** Writes *Cradle of Islam: The Hijaz and the Quest for an Arabian Identity*

INFLUENCES AND CONTRIBUTIONS

During her time at Oxford, Yamani returned to Saudi Arabia to become the first woman to lecture at King Abd al-Aziz University—albeit to women only within the women's department. She told the audience of the 2005 annual conference of Forum 2000 Foundation: "I arrived with overflowing enthusiasm to introduce ideas of respect and cultural diversity.... Although so many of my female students responded to these exciting, exotic concepts, official censorship was stifling and the compulsory veil became heavier and heavier, both physically and emotionally" ("Our Global Co-Existence," 2005). Ultimately she returned to London to pursue her research, free from the constraints of censorship and the limitations placed on women in her country of birth.

Yamani's first book, *Changed Identities: The Challenge of the New Generation in Saudi Arabia*, was published by the Royal Institute of International Affairs in 2000. *Changed Identities* is based on a series of seventy interviews Yamani conducted over a span of two years with Saudis between the ages of fifteen and thirty. Although her interviewees came from all regions of the state, most were from the middle class, with a few from the royal family or other politically and economically powerful families. According to Yamani, the new generation of younger Saudis now makes up a majority of the country's population and thus is a political and economic force with which to be reckoned.

New opportunities and increased engagement in the outside world through growing access to education, travel, and technological advances have shaped this new generation. "Their views of the world they inhabit," Yamani writes in the book's introduction, "show the notions of tradition and modernity have become contested with no single definition holding common currency. The future of Saudi Arabia will, to a large degree, be decided by which definition triumphs."

In her second book, *Cradle of Islam: The Hijaz and the Quest for an Arabian Identity*, published in 2004, Yamani provides a detailed account of the social and political study of the Hijazi identity within Saudi Arabia. In 1924 the kingdom of Hijaz, which includes the religiously important cities of Mecca and Medina, was conquered by the Najdi tribe of the central region of Arabia and incorporated into what became Saudi Arabia in 1932. Yamani discusses the continuing tensions caused by the state's attempts to assimilate the Hijazi. She argues that the Hijazi's distinct identity has been deliberately suppressed by the state. According to Michael Rubin's 2005 review in *Middle East Quarterly*, "Yamani constructs a convincing argument that the Saudis' 80-year effort to eradicate Hijazi culture and society has failed. Hijazi retain a strong identity, often catalyzed by [the government's] 'saudification' policies."

Yamani has served as editor of several works, including *Feminism and Islam: Legal and Literary Perspectives*, published in 1996, and *The Rule of Law in the Middle East and the Islamic World: Human Rights and the Judicial Process*, published in 2000 and coedited by Eugene Cotran.

THE WORLD'S PERSPECTIVE

Yamani's criticism of her country's government and religious leadership and her ardent calls for reform led her books to be banned from Saudi Arabia, and Yamani herself is prohibited from entering the country. She is also highly critical of British and U.S. policy in the Middle East. In an article appearing in the *Guardian* (Manchester, U.K.) in February 2007, Yamani blasted the U.S. leadership's overuse of the word *moderate* to describe Middle East rulers: "The concept of moderate is merely the latest attempt to market a failed policy, while offering a facile hedge against accusations of Islamophobia and anti-Islamic policies" (p. 28)

LEGACY

As a highly respected researcher from Saudi Arabia, Yamani has already achieved recognition for her work.

As a woman who offers an insider's view into the often opaque world of Saudi women, she provides a unique and welcomed perspective to the discussion of the future of Saudi Arabia. Whether the changes for which she hopes—a more open society, advancements in women's rights, and increased democracy—are realized remains to be determined by history.

BIBLIOGRAPHY

"Our Global Co-Existence: Challenges and Hopes for the 21st Century. Panel 2: Concepts of Co-Existence and Community." Forum 2000 Foundation. Updated October 2005. Available from http://www.forum2000.cz/transcripts/test.

"Propping Up the House of Saud: A Saudi Dissident Speaks." Democracy Now. Updated 24 June 2004. Available from http://www.democracynow.org.

Rubin, Michael. Review of *Cradle of Islam: The Hijaz and the Quest for an Arabian Identity*. *Middle East Quarterly* 12, no. 3 (2005). Available from http://www.meforum.org/article/810.

"Saudi Time Bomb? Interview with Mai Yamani." PBS Frontline. Updated 5 November 2001. Available from http://www.pbs.org/.

Yamani, Mai. *Changed Identities: The Challenge of the New Generation in Saudi Arabia*. London: Royal Institute of International Affairs, 2000.

———. "One More Step on the Road to Collapse." *Independent* (London) (2 August 2005). Available from http://comment.independent.co.uk.

———. "These Moderates Are in Fact Fanatics, Torturers and Killers." *Guardian* (6 February 2007): 28.

Alisa Larson

YASIN, AHMAD
(c. 1936–2004)

Palestinian Ahmad Yasin (known as Shaykh Ahmad Yasin or Yassin) worked for many years as a teacher of Arabic and Islamic studies and as a preacher and social activist, but is best known as a founder and spiritual leader of the Palestinian group Hamas. He was never trained as a formal religious leader, but was called shaykh because of his work preaching and his knowledge of Islam. Yasin eventually embraced the teachings of the Muslim Brotherhood and consequentially became active in promoting the revival of Islam as a complete way of life. He was also active in establishing an influential charitable organization following the Israeli occupation of Gaza in June 1967. As one of the founders of Hamas in 1987–1988, he was seen as the spiritual leader of the movement, guiding its actions. He was known among Palestinians for his simple and humble lifestyle, and was married to a Palestinian woman named Halima with whom he had eleven children. Israelis and many others have vilified him for his

Ahmad Yasin. AP IMAGES.

BIOGRAPHICAL HIGHLIGHTS

Name: Ahmad Yasin (Yassin)

Birth: c. 1936, al-Jura, mandatory Palestine

Death: 2004, Gaza, Palestinian Authority

Family: Wife, Halima; eleven children

Nationality: Palestinian

Education: High school graduate, schoolteacher of Arabic and Islamic studies; University courses in English at Ayn Shams University in Egypt in 1964

PERSONAL CHRONOLOGY:

• **1958–1984:** Teacher

• **1965:** Serves a term in an Egyptian jail

• **1970s:** Founder of al-Mujamma al-Islami, a Muslim charitable group

• **1987:** Founder and spiritual leader of Hamas, the Islamic Resistance Movement

• **1983–1985, 1991–1997:** Serves terms in Israeli jails, where he is released each time in a prisoner exchange

militant stands on Palestinian demands for liberation of Palestine and for encouraging suicide bombings. Upon his release from jail in October 1997 in a prisoner exchange, almost deaf and blind in addition to being in a wheelchair, he became much more well known outside of Hamas as a symbol of the new forms of resistance to the Israeli occupation that were competing with the Palestine Liberation Organization (PLO). He was assassinated by the Israelis in March 2004.

PERSONAL HISTORY

Yasin was born in about 1936 in the fishing village of al-Jura (near the town of Asqalan) on the southern coast of mandatory Palestine. His father died when Yasin was young. Yasin had two brothers and a sister, as well as other siblings from his father's other marriage. He studied in the school in al-Jura until the fifth grade when the village was emptied of its inhabitants in the 1948 War and destroyed; it subsequently was absorbed into the Israeli city of Ashkelon. Yasin became a refugee with his family in the Gaza Strip, in Shati (Beach) camp, and, as did the majority of refugees, lived in extreme poverty. In 1949 to 1950 he worked in a small restaurant in Gaza to

help support his family, and then returned to school. As a child he was called Ahmad Sa'da (after his mother Sa'da Abdullah al-Habil) because there were so many Ahmads in the Yasin family. Active in sports (he participated in soccer, boxing, and gymnastics), he broke his neck at age sixteen while playing with friends. It is said that he was wrestling with his friend Abdullah al-Khatib when the accident happened, something he kept to himself until 1989 out of fear that there would be problems between the families. Despite periods of being able to walk and move, he ultimately wound up confined to a wheelchair for many years of his life.

He participated in the demonstrations in 1956 against the tripartite attack (Britain, France, and Israel) on Egypt, where he discovered his abilities as a speaker and organizer. He finished his secondary studies in 1958 and found work as a teacher, despite his disabilities, and helped support his family, which he did until 1964 when he was accepted as a student at Ayn Shams University in Egypt. He chose to study English. Throughout this period in Gaza, he developed his skills as an orator and preacher, and worked as an imam at mosques.

Yasin's time spent studying in Egypt, his relationship with the underground Muslim Brotherhood (an organization established in Egypt in 1928 that calls for a correct interpretation of Islam and application of this knowledge to one's daily life), and the time he spent in Egyptian jail, are subjects of dispute in the writings about him. He seems to have studied for only one year or part of one year at Ayn Shams University, and he was imprisoned by the Egyptian authorities around the time he was studying in Egypt, or upon his return. He was interrogated and held in solitary confinement for a month. Although accused of having a relationship with the Muslim Brotherhood, he was cleared and released some time around 1965 or 1966. Yasin described the prison experience as "deepening within me my hatred of oppression, and that the legality of any authority has be based in justice and in the right of a person to live a free life" (al Jazeera.net). It is said that he joined the Muslim Brotherhood in 1955, but there is no evidence of that and his release from prison was said to be predicated on the fact that the interrogations revealed that he was not part of the Muslim Brotherhood. He was, however, interested in and perhaps closely studied the ideology and thinking of the Muslim Brotherhood.

Following the Israeli occupation of the Gaza Strip in the 1967 War (along with the West Bank, the Golan Heights, and the Sinai Peninsula), Yasin increased his preaching activities in the al-Abbasi mosque, where he encouraged resistance to the occupation and dedicated himself to social causes by collecting donations and supplies for the families of those killed and imprisoned. While continuing his professional work as a schoolteacher of Arabic and Islamic studies, he also founded al-Mujamma al-Islami (Islamic League) in Gaza in the 1970s, a charitable religious organization that provided health and educational programs and eventually came to control all of the religious institutions in Gaza. At the same time, Yasin embraced the teachings of the Muslim Brotherhood.

Yasin and other sympathizers and members of the Muslim Brotherhood were in opposition to the PLO and they actively worked to combat the secular nature of the PLO's national liberation struggle. He developed a militant group in 1982 (one source names it al-Mujahidun al-Filastiniyyun, or "The Palestinian Warriors," whereas another dubs the group Majd al-Mujahidin, or "The Pride of the Faithful Warriors") with help of Ibrahim al-Muqadima. The group took an anti-PLO position and was largely ignored by the Israelis until they discovered an arms cache in 1983. As a result, the Israeli occupation authorities arrested Yasin and accused him of forming a military organization and illegal possession of weapons, and sentenced him to thirteen years in prison. He was released in a prisoner exchange in May 1985 between the Israeli authorities and Ahmad Jibril's

Popular Front for the Liberation of Palestine–General Command.

Following demonstrations that began in December 1987 over the killing of Palestinian workers by an Israeli truck driver that set off the first intifada, Yasin and a group of Muslim Brotherhood activists and leaders formed an Islamic movement aimed at fighting Zionism and liberating Palestine. They called the movement Harakat al-Muqawama al-Islamiyya (Islamic Resistance Movement), know popularly by the Arabic acronym Hamas (which means zeal in Arabic). The group issued their first leaflet in mid-December 1987, and the group's charter, or covenant, was penned in August 1988.

In August 1988 the Israeli authorities raided and searched Yasin's house and threatened to deport him to Lebanon as part of an attempt to intimidate him into ceasing his activities. He continued his work with Hamas and was active in the intifada. The *Independent*'s obituary of Yasin states that "Hamas was not formally outlawed by the Israeli military authorities until 1989, fuelling the still commonly held belief among secular Arab nationalists that Israel and U.S. intelligence fostered the group as a useful counterweight to Arafat's PLO." In 1989 Yasin is said to have issued a call for the kidnapping and killing of Israeli soldiers so that they (or their bodies) could be used in exchange for Palestinian prisoners, who were being detained in the thousands during the intifada. In addition, Hamas gained a reputation for ruthlessness, especially against fellow Palestinian Muslims suspected of collaborating with Israel. The Israeli authorities arrested Yasin and hundreds of other Hamas members in May 1989. In October 1991 Yasin was sentenced to life in prison plus fifteen years for inciting the kidnapping and killing of Israeli soldiers, a charge he denied, although he admitted in court to being a founder of Hamas. During his time in prison, Yasin's health deteriorated. He lost all sight in his right eye and his sight in his left was weakened, and he suffered from hearing loss and respiratory problems. Two of his sons volunteered to serve his prison term with him in order to take care of him.

Yasin was released from prison again in October 1997 as a result of the botched Israeli assassination attempt of Hamas member KHALID MASH'AL in Jordan. After Jordan released two Mossad intelligence agents who had try to kill Mash'al, Yasin was flown to Jordan for medical treatment and returned to Gaza a few days later to jubilant crowds of tens of thousands of Palestinians. He publicly stated at this time the importance of national unity and his support for the Palestinian Authority (PA) as the authority representing the Palestinian people. Authorities in Israel tried to assassinate Yasin in September 2003 by firing several missiles into his house from an F-16 fighter jet. However, Yasin was only slightly injured. Yet finally, on

EXPLORING

Early in December 1987, during the first days of the demonstrations and strikes that were to become the first intifada, Ahmad Yasin and a group of Muslim Brotherhood activists and leaders formed an Islamic movement aimed at fighting Zionism and liberating Palestine. They called the movement Harakat al-Muqawama al-Islamiyya (Islamic Resistance Movement), know popularly as Hamas. The group issued their first leaflet in mid-December 1987 and the group's charter, or covenant, was penned in August 1988. Initially, Hamas leaflets (leaflets were issued by all of the political factions) called for general strikes, demonstrations, a boycott of Israeli products, and attendance at Friday prayers plus performing an additional prayer for martyrs. Additionally, general resistance to the Israeli occupation forces was called for, such as throwing stones and attacking Israeli soldiers and settlers. It was not until 1994, after the intifada was over and the provisions of the Oslo Accord promising peace between Israelis and Palestinians were being implemented piecemeal, that Hamas began undertaking suicide bombings. Hamas is often criticized for being unwilling to concede to Israel's existence and being unwilling to negotiate with Israelis, although since running in the Palestinian Authority's Palestinian Legislative Council and winning control of the government in 2006, Hamas has made more conciliatory statements. Similar to the Jews who believe that the land of Israel is the land promised to them by God, Hamas believes that "the land of Palestine is an Islamic Waqf consecrated for future Muslim generations until Judgment Day" (Hamas Covenant).

22 March 2004, the Israelis killed him and nine others with missiles fired from a helicopter as he was coming out of a mosque from early morning prayers.

INFLUENCES AND CONTRIBUTIONS

According to a biographer, the lesson that Yasin took from the defeat of the Palestinians and Arabs in 1948 War and the *nakba* (Arabic: disaster; the disaster of the displacement of half of the Palestinian population) was that the Palestinians need to depend on themselves for strength, a lesson that resounded throughout his intellectual and

political life. Yasin said, "the Arab armies that came to fight Israel took the weapons out of our hands and said that it was only appropriate to use the strength of the armies. They tied their destiny to ours with this act, so that when they were defeated, so were we. And during the fear inspired by and the massacres committed by the Zionist gangs, if we had had guns in our hands, we could have changed the course of events" (al Jazeera.net).

Yasin also took on social problems and issues that plagued the Palestinian community. In the 1970s the main focus of his group al-Mujamma al-Islami was to address the lack of health and educational services provided by the occupying Israeli authorities, although the group's religious focus also allowed it to take control of the religious institutions in Gaza. After his release from jail in 1985 he set up a group to curb drug dealing. With the organizations, Yasin and the Islamist activists were able to consolidate their control of religious organizations and to also keep tabs on their opponents through the social networks created. Much of the struggle at this period and up to the present has been against the PLO and the secular national authorities in a struggle to represent Palestinians.

With the founding of Hamas, Islamists entered the mainstream of the political and military arena in Palestine. Yasin was known as the spiritual leader and a key figure of the movement. Hamas was not part of the PLO. Rather, Hamas sees itself as an alternative and competitor to the PLO, although there has been talk recently about it joining the PLO. The members of Hamas drafted a charter or covenant in August 1988, calling themselves a wing of the Muslim Brotherhood in Palestine. They see the movement as both a religious and nationalist one:

> Nationalism, from the point of view of the Islamic Resistance Movement, is part of the religious creed. [...] If other nationalist movements are connected with materialistic, human or regional causes, nationalism of the Islamic Resistance Movement has all these elements as well as the more important elements that give it soul and life. It is connected to the source of spirit and the granter of life, hoisting in the sky of the homeland the heavenly banner that joins earth and heaven with a strong bond. (Hamas Covenant)

After his release from prison in 1997, and then again in 2000 and January 2004, Yasin proposed a truce with Israel if it would withdraw from the West Bank and Gaza Strip and remove all settlements. The proposal in January 2004 was made by Hamas official Abd al-Aziz Rantisi who offered a ten-year truce to Israel in return for complete Israeli withdrawal from the lands occupied in 1967. At this time Yasin stated that Hamas could accept a state in the West Bank and Gaza Strip. Israel has repeatedly refused these offers and Hamas has had trouble making its military wing adhere to them as well, although there were relatively few violent attacks in 2004.

Yasin was in prison during the signing of the Declaration of Principles (Oslo Accords) in 1993, the establishment of the PA, and the period of hope and promise that followed it. After 1997 Yasin was placed under house arrest by the PA a number of times, resulting in anger on the Palestinian street and causing widespread and sometimes violent clashes between PA security forces and Hamas. By all accounts the PA was trying to prove its control over the situation as demanded of it by Israel and the United States. His return in 1997 was during the period of disillusionment and continued Israeli confiscation of land, building of settlements, and decreasing economic possibilities. As were many others, Yasin was against the Oslo Accords although not because, he said, he was against a negotiated settlement, but because the negotiated agreements did not bring about an independent Palestinian state.

THE WORLD'S PERSPECTIVE

Yasin toured Arab and Muslim countries in 1998 and collected millions of dollars in donations to aid the social services that Hamas provides, although the United States and Israel said that the money went to fund terrorism and the military wing of Hamas. Following his release in 1997, he captured world attention and became known worldwide for the first time. Unlike the PA and Fatah, which have been seen as corrupt and extravagant, Hamas, Yasin, and the other Hamas officials are seen by Palestinians as modest and honest, traits that contribute to the success of the movement and its rising popularity.

The assassination of Yasin provoked international condemnation from the United Nations (UN) General Secretary, the UN Commission on Human Rights, the Arab League, and the African Union. Demonstrators filled the streets in the PA and in many other Arab and Muslim countries, and Palestinian president YASIR ARAFAT declared three days of mourning. Palestinian Prime Minister Ahmad Qurei called the killing "one of the biggest crimes that the Israeli government has committed" (*Guardian*, 22 March 2004). British foreign secretary Jack Straw condemned the killing ("All of us understand Israel's need to protect itself [...] but it is not entitled to go in for this kind of unlawful killing and we condemn it" [BBC News, 2004]), whereas the White House expressed that it was "deeply troubled" (BBC News, 2004) while stressing that Israel has the right to defend itself and that Yasin, according to U.S. Secretary of State Condoleezza Rice, had been "personally involved in terrorism." A U.S. State Department spokesman said that the assassination did not help efforts to resume progress toward peace.

LEGACY

The Islamic movement in Palestine prior to the founding of Hamas has been described as more devoted to the

> # WE ARE FOR AN INDEPENDENT PALESTINIAN STATE ON ANY PART OF OUR STOLEN LAND
>
> The difficult decision to make a truce with the Israelis grows out of the need to preserve Palestinian national unity and move the struggle to the arena of the Israeli enemy, who, in implementing the truce would have to do the following: withdraw from the occupied West Bank, stop settlements, stop building the racist separation wall which is devouring Palestinian land, and release political prisoners. [...] We are for an independent Palestinian state on any part of our stolen land. But that does not affect our historic rights to Palestinian land, however long it takes, and whatever the strength and capabilities of the enemy. [...] The Islamic movement in Palestine believes that it is not possible to participate in a Palestinian government while under occupation, without possessing freedom of intentionality or movement on this land. [...] But as regards municipal elections, Hamas has announced that it is ready to participate. On the Legislative and Presidential fronts the decision will be made at that time after studying the situation and conditions of those elections.
>
> YASIN, SHAYKH AHMAD. *AL-BAYAN*. INTERVIEW. AVAILABLE FROM HTTP://SAAID.NET/MKTARAT/FLASTEEN/022.HTM.

revival of Islam than to undertaking actions against the occupation forces. Yasin was part of both of these periods. The *Guardian*'s obituary of Yasin states that, prior to the 1987, Yasin is said to have believed that "the struggle was cultural, moral and educational; it was about combating secularism and the reform and re-Islamicisation of Palestinian society—a preparation for jihad, rather than jihad itself." Led by the Muslim Brotherhood splinter group Islamic Jihad in the early 1980s, the Islamists began armed struggle against the Israeli occupation. Yasin and the other senior leaders of the Muslim Brotherhood in Palestine were close behind with this strategy, and with the founding of Hamas, formed a body that addressed the political realities and new forms of struggle against the occupation, and incorporated them into a Muslim ideological framework.

Yasin never admitted to encouraging this practice, but also never publicly called a halt to it. Notably, a strategic shift in Hamas's policy, after Yasin's death, took place when it decided to run for the Palestinian Legislative

Council (PLC) parliamentary elections in 2006. After a surprise victory in which they won the majority of the seats, they chose ISMAIL HANIYEH as the prime minister. The years 2006 and 2007 were difficult for Palestinians, because of the cutting off of funding to the PA government by the United States, the European Union, Canada, and Japan because of Hamas's presence in the government, and due to internal fighting between Hamas and Fatah that has led to hundreds of deaths.

Because of Yasin's physical limitations and illnesses later in life, he was seen as the spiritual leader of Hamas and its mastermind. In reality, because of the secretive nature of the organization due to constant threats of imprisonment and assassination, both the structure of the organization and the roles of different people are not clear. The *Independent*'s obituary of Yasin read, "He owed much of his fame and popularity among Islamists in Palestine and elsewhere more to luck and the unintended consequences of violent Israeli policies than to his own political cunning."

BIBLIOGRAPHY

Abu-Amr, Ziad. "Hamas: A Historical and Political Background." *Journal of Palestine Studies* 22, no. 4 (Summer 1993): 5–19.

BBC News. Updated 22 March 2004. Available from http://news.bbc.co.uk.

Hirst, David. "Sheikh Ahmad Yassin." Guardian (Manchester, U.K.) (23 March 2004). Available from http://www.guardian.co.uk.

Hroub, Khaled. *Hamas: A Beginner's Guide.* London: Pluto Press, 2006.

Kristianasen, Wendy. "Challenge and Counterchallenge: Hamas's Response to Oslo." *Journal of Palestine Studies* 28, no. 3 (Spring 1999): 19–36.

"Obituary, Sheikh Ahmad Yassin." *Independent* (23 March 2004). Available from http://www.independent.co.uk.

Yasin, Ahmad. *Al-Bayan.* Interview. Available from http://saaid.net/mktarat/flasteen/022.htm.

Rochelle Anne Davis

YERLIKAYA, HAMZA
(1976–)

Turkey's Hamza Yerlikaya is a world- and Olympic champion Greco-Roman style wrestler. A two-time Olympic champion, he is also the only Turkish wrestler ever to win the European championship eight times. Yerlikaya is the third Turkish man after Mithat Bayrak and Mustafa Dagistanli to win wrestling gold at the Olympic Games. In 1996 the International Federation of Associated Wrestling Styles named Yerlikaya Wrestler of the Year.

Hamza Yerlikaya. AP IMAGES.

PERSONAL HISTORY

Yerlikaya's family is originally from Sivas, a town in the Southeast of Turkey, but in 1976 the family moved with three children to Istanbul. Hamza was born in Kadiköy, Istanbul, on 3 June. He was born into a family with six children, in which wrestling was spoken of on a daily basis and even joked about. Yerlikaya's father, Mustafa, was a former wrestler, who had to give up wrestling after the family's move to Istanbul and because of their limited financial situation. Because of his passion for wrestling, Mustafa Yerlikaya signed up his eldest son Muttalip for wrestling at the Istanbul Demirspor Club. A year later, in 1986, Muttalip encouraged Hamza—then eleven years old—to begin wrestling as well.

From 1986 to 1996 Yerlikaya was coached by Salih Bora, joined later by Muzaffer Aydin. Yerlikaya won his first gold medal at the 1992 World Cadets Championship, which was held in Istanbul. He still continues his work for Istanbul Büyükşehir Belediyespor (Istanbul Metropolitan Municipality), a club located in Istanbul, and has been coached by Hakki Basar since 2004. In April 2007 Yerlikaya underwent surgery to correct neck fractures, and was forced to withdraw from international competition.

INFLUENCES AND CONTRIBUTIONS

Yerlikaya placed fourth when he attended his first international competition in 1991, at the World Cadets

Championship held in Alma, Quebec, Canada. In 1993, at the World Wrestling Championship in Stockholm, Sweden, he competed and won a gold medal. Only seventeen years old at that time, Yerlikaya broke the record, becoming the youngest ever wrestling world champion. From 1993 to 1995, Yerlikaya attended various competitions, capturing international attention with his World Championship in 1995. At the 1996 Olympic Games in Atlanta, he won his first Olympic gold medal. He captured his second Olympic title with a gold medal in Sydney, Australia, four years later. To date, Yerlikaya has won three senior World Championships (1993, 1995, 2005), two World Cups (1997, 2006), and is an eight-times winner of the European Seniors Championship (1996–1999, 2001, 2002, 2005, and 2006).

Yerlikaya is currently a parliamentary candidate for the Adalet ve Kalkinma Partisi (AKP; The Justice and Development Party), a right-wing, moderately conservative Turkish party, which has been under the leadership of Recep TAYYIP ERDOGAN, the present prime minister of Turkey, since 2001.

BIOGRAPHICAL HIGHLIGHTS

Name: Hamza Yerlikaya

Birth: 1976, Kadiköy, Istanbul, Turkey

Family: Single

Nationality: Turkish

Education: High school

PERSONAL CHRONOLOGY:

• **1986:** Begins wrestling at age of eleven

• **1991:** Places fourth in first international competition, World Cadets Wrestling Championships in Quebec, Canada

• **1993:** Wins gold medal in World Wrestling Championships in Stockholm, Sweden, at age seventeen; breaks record for youngest champion ever

• **1996:** Wins first Olympic gold medal in Atlanta Olympics

• **2000:** Wins second Olympic gold medal in Sydney, Australia

• **1996–2006:** Wins eight European championships

• **2007:** Withdraws from international competition to undergo neck surgery

STATE ARTISTS EXIST

For sixteen years, no official clerk, no bureaucrat, no worker has worked under the hard conditions that I worked in. Perhaps our jobs may look easy from the outside. During one practice, we lift between 7 to 8 tons of weight, and we have to practices per day. [...] State artists exist. I do not know according to which categories they become recognized as such by the government. I spend my whole life on the mat, achieve many successes, but am not able to receive a reputation as a state athlete. Why does this law not go through, I do not understand. Then one expects success from the athlete. [...] We participate with 40 people to the Olympic Games. But we have a population of 70 Million. A nation with 2 Million populations sends 200 athletes to the Olympics. In Russia, a budget is set aside for the 2008 Olympic Games. We, however, expect success with the help of Allah. If we want to do something, we need to first make an investment.

Hürriyet, 20 February 2007.

THE WORLD'S PERSPECTIVE

Since the 1936 Olympic Games, Turkey has collected 36 Olympic gold medals, the vast majority of them in the wrestling competitions. Yerlikaya has been called the "Wrestler of the Century" and has entered history thanks to his achievements. So far, Yerlikaya has won 22 gold, 4 silver, and 2 bronze medals in international competition and ranks third among the most successful wrestlers in the world.

LEGACY

The idiom "strong as a Turk" is associated with Yerlikaya and his international success in wrestling. His high winning numbers have made Yerlikaya into a national hero, and Turkey celebrates his achievement in 85 kilogram Greco-Roman wrestling.

BIBLIOGRAPHY

"Hamza Yerlikaya: Ömrüm minderde geçiyor." *Hürriyet* (20 February 2007). Available from http://www.hurriyet.com.tr/spor/digersporlar/5984791.asp.

Mine Eren

YOSEF, OVADIA
(1920–)

Rabbi Ovadia Yosef is an ultra-Orthodox Sephardic (also called Mizrahi) rabbi, eminent scholar of Jewish law (Talmud), and powerful figure in Israeli party politics. Yosef's stature derives from his intimate knowledge of the Torah and *halakhah* (Jewish religious law) on the one hand, and the political standing of the Shas Party on the other. Known for his encyclopedic memory and phenomenal knowledge of rabbinical response (religious rulings), Yosef has revolutionized religious observance for many sectors of Israeli society. Lenient in his rulings, Yosef is also notorious for making egregious and at times crude pronouncements about the secular world, secular leaders, Arabs, and Ashkenazic Jews (Jews of European descent, as opposed to those of Sephardic [post-1492 Spanish] or Mizrahi [Middle Eastern/North African] Jewish descent). A comprehensive biography was written on Yosef by Nitzan Chen and Anshel Pfeffer titled *Maran Ovadia Yosef: Ha-Biografia*, although little research of a scholarly nature has been published about him, particularly in English.

PERSONAL HISTORY

Yosef was born Abdullah Yusuf in Baghdad, Iraq, in 1920. In 1924 he moved with his family to Jerusalem, mandatory Palestine, where he was brought up in the traditional Sephardic Jewish day schools. He moved on to Porat Yosef Yeshiva, the only Sephardic Talmudic academy in Jerusalem at that time. He studied under the tutelage of Rabbi Ezra Attia, a distinguished Sephardic Rosh Yeshiva (head of a religious institute for higher education) and Torah scholar. In 1937 Rabbi Attia requested that Yosef teach a class every evening in the Persian synagogue in the marketplace of Jerusalem's Bukharan Quarter. It was there that Yosef began to build lifelong appeal to a growing following of Iraqi Jews who made up the majority of residents in that area, as well as to common people such as market stall owners and manual laborers, who continue to fervently follow his prayers. Later on, the mainstay of his constituency became Moroccan Jews and their descendants, although he succeeded to win a broad base of support from ultra-Orthodox Ashkenazic Jews as well as secular Israelis from different ethnic backgrounds.

Yosef achieved rabbinical ordination (*semiha*) at the age of twenty by Rabbi Ben Zion Meir Ouziel. Yosef married Margalit, a Syrian Jew who, along with their son Rabbi David Yosef and politician Aryeh Deri, was central to administering his affairs until her death in 1994. After 1994 Yosef's other son Rabbi Moshe Yosef and his son's wife Yehudit took over, along with Eli Yishai, the current head of the Shas Party. The Yosefs have eleven children, of which all five boys became rabbis. In 1945 Yosef was

Ovadia Yosef. AP IMAGES.

appointed a *dayyan* (rabbinical judge) in the *bet din* (rabbinical court) of Sephardic Jews in Jerusalem. In 1947 he was invited by Rabbi Aharon Choeka to serve as the deputy chief rabbi of Egypt through Yeshiva A'hava Ve'Ahva and in the Cairo *bet din*. It was during his posting in Egypt that he distinguished himself as a true Zionist by taking a courageous stand against policies that threatened the State of Israel. At a time when Egypt was leading the Arab world's struggle against Israel, Yosef refused to issue anti-Israeli proclamations. He prohibited military contributions by Egyptian Jews to the Egyptian army, and insisted on the right to conduct his services in the Hebrew language.

After three years in Egypt, Yosef returned to Jerusalem and began his meteoric rise up the rabbinical ladder in Israel. He was appointed to the rabbinical court in Petah Tikva and later to the rabbinical court in Jerusalem where he served from 1958 to 1965. In 1965 Yosef was appointed to the Supreme Rabbinical Court of Appeals in Jerusalem. He rose to the position of chief Sephardic rabbi of Tel Aviv–Jaffa in 1968 and then replaced Rabbi Yitshak Nissim as the chief Sephardic rabbi of Israel (called the Rishon le-Zion) and president of the Rabbinical Supreme Court of Israel from 1973 to 1983. The position of chief rabbi of Israel was widely considered to

BIOGRAPHICAL HIGHLIGHTS

Name: Ovadia Yosef

Birth: 1920, Baghdad, Iraq

Family: Wife, Margalit (d. 1994); eleven children (five sons and six daughters)

Nationality: Israeli

Education: Porat Yosef Yeshiva, Jerusalem

PERSONAL CHRONOLOGY:

- **1924:** Immigrates to Jerusalem, mandatory Palestine
- **1940:** Ordained a rabbi
- **1945:** *Dayyan* (rabbinical judge) in the *bet din* (rabbinical court) of Sephardic Jews in Jerusalem
- **1947:** Named deputy chief rabbi of Egypt and member of the Cairo *bet din*
- **1950:** Becomes a member on rabbinical court in Petah Tikva
- **1958–1965:** Becomes a member on rabbinical court in Jerusalem
- **1968:** Named chief Sephardic rabbi of Tel Aviv–Jaffa
- **1973–1983:** Serves as chief Sephardic rabbi of Israel
- **1984:** Becomes spiritual mentor of Shas

East is his support of Sephardic Jewry (also called Mizrahi Jewry) from Middle Eastern and North African countries and success in raising the distinction of Sephardic rabbinical authority in Israel and the world. Yosef is the undisputed chief Sephardic rabbinical authority in Israel and spiritual mentor of the political party Shas, the Hebrew acronym for Sephardic Guardians of the Torah. Yosef has played a key role in ethnic politics in Israel based on the long-standing division in the country between Ashkenazic and Sephardic Jews. Yosef spearheaded a campaign against the Ashkenazid establishment in Israel to reverse the underrepresentation of Sephardic Jewry in Israeli society, religion, and politics.

Through his teachings, Yosef has sought to restore the former eminence of Sephardic religious scholarship and traditions, and particularly those initiated by Rabbi Yosef Caro. This goal is represented in one of his most famous slogans *"le-hakhzir atarah le-yushnah,"* meaning literally, restoring the crown to its rightful place. By this,

CONTEMPORARIES

Elazar Menachem Shach (1898–2001), known also as Rav Leizer Shach and Elazar Menachem Man Shach, was a leading ultra-Orthodox Ashkenazic rabbi in Israel. Shach was recognized as a preeminent Talmudic scholar who served as the head of Ponevezh yeshiva in the religious neighborhood of Bnei Brak in Tel Aviv and as a member of the *Agudat Yisra'el* Council of Torah Sages. Rabbi Shach broke away from the Agudat Yisra'el party to form a new political party, *Degel ha-Torah* (Flag of the Torah) representing ultra-Orthodox, non-Hasidic Lithuanian Jewry. He was instrumental in forging a political alliance between the two parties under the title of United Torah Judaism, which is represented in the seventeenth Israeli parliament, elected in 2006. Shach also helped Rabbi Ovadia Yosef found the Shas party in 1984 but then fell out of favor with Shas after claiming that Sephardic Jews were not ready to hold leadership positions. Rabbi Shach's ideology was characterized by a deep aversion to Zionism, although he functioned within the modern political party system of the State of Israel. He was also highly critical of Rabbi Menachem Mendel Schneerson of the Chabad-Lubavitch Hasidic movement, which he accused of false Messianism.

be a position one held for life until legislation, initiated by Nissim's son Moshe Nissim, who served as justice minister, was passed in the Israeli parliament that limited the post to ten years. The new law forced Yosef to step down in 1983, after which time he was replaced by Rabbi Mordechai Eliahu. However, even after serving as chief Sephardic rabbi, some of the most important and complicated cases of the Rabbinical Supreme Court were still brought to Rabbi Yosef for his advice and guidance. A Sephardic congregation was created for Yosef in the main floor of the Great Jerusalem synagogue, which he led from 1982 to 1994 until moving to the Orthodox Jewish neighborhood of Har Nof in 1994.

INFLUENCES AND CONTRIBUTIONS

Yosef is held in near-saintly regard by hundreds of thousands of Jews of Middle Eastern and North African background. Yosef's most important contribution to the modern Middle

he expresses his goal of restoring the primacy that Sephardic *halakhah* once enjoyed within the biblical world. Yosef is considered the epitome of ethnic pride, which he expresses in his dress and comportment. Whereas other Sephardic rabbis are seen in the black suits and fedora hats common among the ultra-Orthodox Ashkenazi community, Yosef dons traditional Sephardic garb with the blue turbanlike hat; a dark, flowing golden-embroidered robe; and his well-known red tinted eyeglasses, which he uses to correct vision problems that have resulted from diabetes.

Yosef has succeeded in appealing to an audience wider than his core constituency through the compilation of a new *siddur* (prayer book) titled *Yehaveh Da'at* and the codification of his rulings by his son Yitzhak in *Yalkut Yosef*, an authoritative, widely cited, and popular work of *halakhah*, that provides practical guidance for proper religious observance used mostly by Sephardic Jews. *Yalkut Yosef* includes a section on the *Shulkhan Arukh*, a written catalog of Jewish law composed by Rabbi Yosef Caro in the sixteenth century, and *Yoreh De'ah*, which treats aspects of Jewish law, including but not limited to finance, personal status, sexual conduct, and kosher dietary restrictions. Yosef's rulings are followed by virtually all Sephardic rabbis and *dayanim* (rabbinical court judges) in Israel and abroad. He has distinguished himself as a prolific writer with many books to his name, including a detailed commentary on the *Ben Ish Hai*, two sets of *responsa* titled *Yabia Omer* and *Yekhavei Da'ath* and commentaries, *Pirkei Avoth* (Ethics of the fathers) under the title *Anaf Etz Avot*, and *Maor Israel*. Yosef was awarded the Israel Prize for Torah Literature in 1970.

Controversy Yosef's record on the status of women is mixed. Some of Yosef's rulings negate women's equality, such as in 1997 when the rabbi decreed that a man must not walk between two women, just as he should not pass between donkeys, because women are not concerned with the Torah and, similar to other lesser beasts, may contaminate the mind. An article in the *Jerusalem Post* reported Yosef's statement that "a woman without sons is worthless." Nevertheless, Yosef is generally known for leniency, innovation, and flexibility in matters of Jewish law. This is explained by his involvement in the modern elements of Israeli governance as well as his identification with Sephardic scholars of earlier eras that contrasted the harsh and more extreme rulings of Ashkenazic rabbis in Eastern Europe. For example, he supported territorial compromise over the land of Israel during the period of the Oslo Accords (but later retracted) based on the principle of *pikuah nefesh* (the sanctity of life). At a time when the Ashkenazic rabbinical establishment demanded that Ethiopian Jews undergo conversion, Yosef fully recognized their authenticity as Jews, which facilitated their absorption into Israeli society. In relation to women, he pronounced that married women should wear head coverings rather than wigs (*sheitels*), which in his view defeat the purpose of *tzeniut*, modesty-related dress standards. And significantly, he ruled that wives who were married to Israel Defense Forces (IDF) soldiers who went missing in action for a sufficient period should be allowed to remarry.

Alongside veneration for Yosef lies immense controversy surrounding the many incendiary and acrid remarks he has directed at his adversaries, both Jewish and non-Jewish. For example, Yosef stated that it was permissible to kill those who depreciate ultra-Orthodox (*haredi*) yeshiva students (who generally do not serve in the army), saying "anyone who has evil thoughts about the yeshiva students and calls them parasites is a scoundrel, a heretic, and killing him is permitted." In 1999 Yosef pronounced all the justices of Israel's Supreme Court *bo'alei nidot*, meaning literally men who have intercourse with menstruating women. In 2000 Yosef vilified Meretz Party leader Yossi Sarid by comparing him to the biblical villain Amalek. Perhaps the most well-known and egregious controversies from Yosef's weekly sermons pertain to his statement in 2000 that Holocaust victims were the reincarnation of earlier souls who had sinned, his description of Palestinians as vipers brought to Israel's borders, and his theory that Hurricane Katrina in 2005 was God's retribution on the United States for pressuring Israel to relinquish Gaza and parts of the West Bank to the Palestinians in Israeli prime minister ARIEL SHARON's disengagement plan.

Yosef's supporters claim that his sermons are largely misunderstood by the Israeli media and the secular public who do not appreciate the hermeneutic rhetoric of religious speech patterns that he employs to make his points in a strong and lucid manner.

Shas Party In the political sphere, Yosef rose to political prominence as the spiritual mentor of the Shas Party in 1984, which he founded with the encouragement of the Lithuanian Rabbi Elazar Menachem Shach, but without any organizational backing or permanent financial source. Shas is a merger of three electoral lists that broke away from Agudat Yisra'el (National Union) representing the majority of ultra-Orthodox Jewry in Israel. It speaks to Sephardic ethnic pride and is a mandate for social and spiritual renewal. This program is promulgated through an extensive network of organizations spread throughout the country. Particular strength derives from the educational system, El ha-Ma'ayan (To the Wellsprings), which relies on state and Shas Party funding. This network has brought thousands of children into its fold by offering after-school programs, hot lunches, transportation, tutors for Bar Mitzvah, women's support groups, immigrant absorption, and other forms of community service at low or no cost.

Shas rose steadily in popularity from 63,605 votes in the 1984 legislative elections and 4 seats in the Israeli Knesset (parliament), to 107,709 votes in the 1988 elections and 6 seats in the Knesset, to its zenith of 129,347 votes in the 1992 elections and 10 seats in the Knesset. Through its political positioning, Shas achieved the status of a pivotal swing party, exerting disproportionate power by navigating through the traditional margin between Israel's largest parties, Labor and Likud (and now also Kadima and National Union). Shas became the only party that was willing to form a coalition with representatives from either the right or the left of the Israeli political spectrum. In fact, Shas made a pledge during its 1992 electoral campaign to support a Likud government, but with imminent Labor victory, Yosef approved a coalition with the Labor Party instead. This coalition ensured the prime ministerial position of YITZHAK RABIN and his goal of peace negotiations with the Palestinians and the Arab world. In the 1996 elections, Yosef changed again by backing hard-liner Likud candidate BINYAMIN NETANYAHU instead of Labor leader SHIMON PERES.

In exchange for support, Shas has expressed pragmatism in its coalition dealings, consistently claiming choice ministerial portfolios, including the prized Interior Ministry and Ministry of Religious Affairs to ensure unimpeded funding to its network of schools and constituencies. Yosef exerts immense control over Shas Knesset members who obey his orders to vote en bloc on specific matters of policy. This has caused significant resentment on the part of segments of Israeli society who lack equivalent access to state funds. In addition, the reputation of Shas has been stained by accusations of corruption and financial mismanagement. The controversy came to a head when Shas leader Aryeh Deri was convicted on charges of bribery, fraud, and breaching the public trust while serving as interior minister. Although some supporters charge that Deri was singled out for punishment on account of discrimination, he was given a three-year prison sentence and was released after serving two years on 15 July 2002. Yosef was never accused of having been involved in any financial wrongdoing.

THE WORLD'S PERSPECTIVE

Yosef is both revered and scorned by the international community. As an eminent authority on Jewish law, his sermons are taped and broadcast to hundreds of thousands of listeners in Israel and abroad. As such, he is widely adored by Sephardic as well as Ashkenazi Jewry worldwide. Yosef is referred to as *Maran*, an Aramaic word meaning "our master," a title given to particularly respected rabbis, especially among Sephardic Jews. However, Yosef's numerous controversial and derogatory

EXPLORING

Israel has a history of ethnic cleavage as a result of relations of inequality between the Ashkenazic Jews from European descent and Sephardic and Mizrahi Jews from Middle Eastern and North African countries. Although Sephardic/Mizrahi Jews constitute over half the Jewish population of Israel, their socioeconomic and political status is considerably lower than their Ashkenazic counterparts. Ashkenazic Jews were the first to immigrate to prestate Palestine. They filled leadership positions in the State of Israel, which they fashioned on the basis of their Western standards of education, lifestyle, and liberal democratic governance. Sephardic Jews arrived mainly after the state was established and as such, confronted a preexisting Ashkenazic elite with cultural biases against them. Sephardic and Mizrahi Jews from Morocco, Yemen, Iraq, and Iran have long been the victims of discrimination, particularly in areas of their absorption, housing, and education. Over the years, Sephardic Jews protested this unfair treatment and called for social justice, which culminated in the establishment of a protest movement active in the 1970s called the Israeli Black Panthers. However, the issue of ethnic discrimination in Israel continues to fester and is far from being resolved.

statements have diminished his reputation among many sectors and groups. Despite assurances by his supporters that his statements are grossly misunderstood and taken out of context, the international community in general, and the Israel Office of the Anti-Defamation League (ADL) in particular, have repeatedly expressed alarm over the rabbi's remarks, calling them extreme and outrageous. Police investigations were conducted and the Israeli State Attorney's Office has examined his sermons to determine whether or not they amount to incitement of violence.

LEGACY

At the age of eighty-six and without an heir apparent, Rabbi Ovadia Yosef will live out the rest of his life as the sole *halakhic* authority for worldwide Sephardic Jews. He will be remembered as one of the most important *halakhic* sages of the twentieth century and one of the most powerful figures in Israeli politics. Yosef's life is the stuff of legends, having risen from obscurity and a meager background to become one of the world's most renowned religious and political leaders. His cultural war against the Ashkenazic establishment in Israel permanently altered ethnic relations in the country to the advantage of Sephardic pride and achievement. Yosef will be remembered for the thousands of innovative rulings he made in Jewish law and for his style of preaching, which appealed to thousands of admirers, particularly among the common people. But he will also be remembered for the many controversies and public furors his words instigated.

BIBLIOGRAPHY

Chen, Nitzen; Pfeffer, Anshel. *Maran Ovadia Yosef: Ha-Biografia*. New York: Keter, 2004.

Zohar, Zion. "Oriental Jewry Confronts Modernity: The Case of Rabbi Ovadiah Yosef." *Modern Judaism* 24, no. 2 (2004): 120–149.

Tami Amanda Jacoby

ZAHHAR, MAHMUD AL-
(1945–)

Palestinian surgeon Mahmud al-Zahhar was one of the founders of Hamas along with Shaykh AHMAD YASIN in 1987. He is one of the ideological leaders of the movement.

PERSONAL HISTORY

Zahhar was born in the Zaytun district of Gaza City, mandatory Palestine, in 1945. His father was Palestinian and his mother Egyptian. He studied medicine at 'Ayn Shams University in Egypt, graduating in 1971. He spent five more years in Egypt where he specialized in surgery. He returned to Gaza, then under Israeli occupation, where he worked at the newly founded Islamic University of Gaza. One of his colleagues in the Department of Medicine was Dr. Abd al-Aziz al-Rantisi, who was also one of the founding members of Hamas, and who later was assassinated by the Israelis in April 2004. Upon his return to Gaza, Zahhar became active in the Muslim Brotherhood in Palestine, a branch of the banned Egyptian Muslim Brotherhood, which was founded by Hasan al-Banna in 1928. Zahhar is married and has four children.

In addition to practicing medicine and being a political leader of Hamas, Zahhar has written a number of books on the health risks of smoking and the impact of smoking on the residents of the West Bank and Gaza, a study of the Qur'an, a study on media and Islamic discourse, and most recently a novel titled *al-Rasif* (The platform). He has also written a film scenario about a young man named Imad Aql who was killed in 1993 during the first intifada.

INFLUENCES AND CONTRIBUTIONS

Zahhar was one of the founders of Hamas in 1987 along with Yasin and al-Rantisi. When the first demonstrations and actions against the Israeli occupation of the West Bank and Gaza Strip broke out in December 1987 and were labeled the intifada, the Muslim Brotherhood members met and decided to form a more active and political wing to counter the Israeli occupation. They named this group Harakat al-Muqawama al-Islamiyya (Islamic Resistance Movement), or Hamas. It eventually gained followers and supporters as a result of it providing extensive health, education, and social services in the absence of such services due to the occupation, and because of its direct and oftentimes violent resistance to the Israeli occupation military and settlers. The military movement of Hamas is called the Izz al-Din al-Qassam Brigades, named after a Syrian religious activist who set off the Palestinian revolt of 1936–1939. Following the publication of the Hamas charter in August 1988, Israel banned the movement.

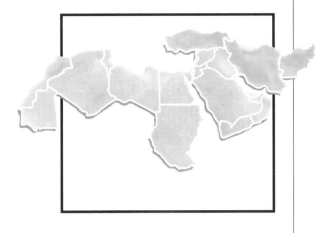

Z

Mahmud al-Zahhar. AP IMAGES.

BIOGRAPHICAL HIGHLIGHTS

■

Name: Mahmud al-Zahhar

Birth: 1945, Gaza City, mandatory Palestine

Family: Wife, Summaya; four children. Eldest son Khalid (b. 1974) killed in Israeli assassination attempt in 2004

Nationality: Palestinian

Education: B.S. in medicine from 'Ayn Shams University in Egypt (1971), M.A. in general surgery (1976)

PERSONAL CHRONOLOGY:

- **1987:** Helps found Hamas

- **1992:** Deported to South Lebanon

- **1994:** Allowed to return to Gaza

- **2004:** Becomes one of Hamas's main leaders; survives Israeli assassination attempt

- **2006:** Minister of foreign affairs in Hamas-led Palestinian Authority government

Yasin was arrested and imprisoned in 1989 and Zahhar and Rantisi are said to have led the group during that period. In December 1992, Zahhar and more than four hundred Islamist activists were deported to southern Lebanon. Among those deported were Rantisi and Zahhar's brother Fadil. The activists camped at a place called Marj al-Zuhur for over a year, and their case was widely covered in the world media. Both Zahhar and Rantisi were eventually allowed to return to Gaza, although Fadil al-Zahhar and seventeen others were not.

Since 1990 Zahhar had been the unofficial representative of Hamas to the Palestine Liberation Organization (PLO) headed by YASIR ARAFAT. But upon Zahhar's return in 1994, he clashed with the newly created Palestinian Authority (PA) that had been put in place in the West Bank and Gaza as a result of the 1993 Declaration of Principles (Oslo Accords). He was arrested several times and spent seven months in a Palestinian jail. In 2004 Israeli aircraft dropped a bomb on his Gaza house in an assassination attempt that resulted in the killing of his oldest son, Khalid, a bodyguard, and wounding his daughter Rima and twenty other people.

THE WORLD'S PERSPECTIVE

As minister of foreign affairs for the newly formed Hamas-led government (March 2006–March 2007), Zahhar sent a letter to the United Nations secretary-general Kofi Annan in which he emphasized the interest of the Palestinian government in starting a serious and constructive dialogue in order to achieve "peace and stability in our region on the basis of a just and comprehensive solution." He urged the international community to "take concrete and urgent measures to put an end to the serious Israeli violations to international law, and to exert pressure on the Israeli government to abide by international law, especially international humanitarian law, and implement the international agreements and the legal decision issued by the International Court of Justice."

Much of the media portrays Zahhar as the leader of Hamas, but following the Israeli assassinations of Yasin and Rantisi in rapid succession in 2004, Hamas has elected leaders but kept their identity and the movement's governing structures secret. He was not included in the Palestinian National Unity government that was established in the PA in March 2007. One of the concerns of many people involves the potential changes to the social fabric of Palestinian society that an Islamist government in power might bring. Following the banning of a book of Palestinian folktales by the Palestinian Ministry of Education, many Palestinians and others have started asking questions about the social agenda of Hamas. In an interview on the al-Arabiyya satellite channel, the host inquired about the banning of movies, songs, and dance. Zahhar replied that such issues are the purview of the clerics, but he stated that people should not be watching or participating in idle things and instead should engage in things that reflect their own realities and serve the nation. He also commented that most Palestinians already do this and that the increased religiosity among people is voluntary and a result of conviction and respect for the self.

LEGACY

Zahhar was part of the shift within Hamas to join the Palestinian government by engaging in the legislative elections of January 2006. Previously, Hamas had boycotted most PA elections, and Zahhar had stated on numerous occasions that Hamas would join a Palestinian government only when Palestinian land was liberated and the government was of a state and not of an autonomy.

Many believed Zahhar would be one of the candidates to be put forth by Hamas to be prime minister following the 2006 legislative elections, but the party chose the lesser-known ISMAIL HANIYEH instead. Zahhar sees the new Palestinian government playing a significant role in restructuring Palestinian internal politics as well as relations with Israelis. "Our government will really need to work on many different things in parallel. We need to get investment from the Middle East. We need to build up many projects here: in the municipalities, in the health

services, in education. And at the same time, we need to speak politically with others, to win the rights of Palestinians both outside and inside Palestine. We are their father." At the same time he is highly critical of Israel. "The Israelis have violated all of the economic agreements from the Paris Agreement to the Rafah Agreement (which was concluded with U.S. secretary of state Condoleezza Rice's intervention in 2005). So we are not obliged to remain within them," he said in an interview with Helena Cobban on 18 March 2006. Zahhar believes that Hamas's clean record and absence of corruption makes the Arab and Muslim countries open to it as a political movement and so they will be willing to fund Hamas. He contrasts Hamas's activities with the PLO, citing the treatment of Arab countries toward the PLO as dismissive because of PLO corruption and bad behavior toward other Arabs.

BIBLIOGRAPHY

Cobban, Helena. "Interview with Zahhar." Just World News. Updated 18 March 2006. Available from http://justworldnews.org/archives/001798.html.

Zahhar, Mahmud. "The Full Text of Zahhar's Letter to Annan." Jerusalem Media and Communication Centre. Updated 4 April 2006. Available from http://www.jmcc.org/new/06/apr/zahharlet.htm.

Zahhar, Mahmud, and Hussein Hijazi. "Hamas: Waiting for Secular Nationalism to Self-Destruct. An Interview with Mahmud Zahhar." *Journal of Palestine Studies* 24, no. 3 (Spring 1995): 81–88.

Rochelle Anne Davis

WE ARE LOOKING FORWARD TO LIVE IN PEACE AND SECURITY

■

We strongly believe in the justice of our cause and in the capabilities of our people to confront and remain steadfast in front of the military occupation of our lands and the illegal measures of the occupation; we also believe that justice and law are the basis of the solution, security and stability in the region and that the logic of force and imposing the status quo is illegal and will be defeated and will only lead to more destruction and instability. We, like all other peoples in the world, are looking forward to live in peace and security and to see that our people enjoy freedom, independence and a dignified life side by side with the rest of our neighbors in this sacred area of the world.

ZAHHAR, MAHMUD. "THE FULL TEXT OF ZAHHAR'S LETTER TO ANNAN." JERUSALEM MEDIA AND COMMUNICATION CENTRE. UPDATED 4 APRIL 2006. AVAILABLE FROM HTTP://WWW.JMCC.ORG/NEW/06/APR/ZAHHARLET.HTM.

ZAKI, MUNA
(1976–)

Muna (also Mona) Muhammad Zaki is one of the top young Egyptian film actresses working in the early twenty-first century.

PERSONAL HISTORY

Zaki was born to a Muslim family on 17 November 1976 in Cairo, Egypt. Her father, Muhammad Ali Zaki, was a college professor, and she grew up in Britain, Kuwait, and the United States. In Egypt, she was recruited somewhat unwittingly into the acting profession when, at age sixteen, she responded to an advertisement in the paper for new actors placed by the famous director Muhammad Subhi. Zaki entered the competition just to meet the famous director, and even though she had not prepared for the audition and did not take it seriously, Subhi liked her and later trained her for eight months in the Studio 2000 program. She eventually performed in a play of his, *Bi'l-Arabi al-Fasih* (In plain Arabic). Thereafter she returned

BIOGRAPHICAL HIGHLIGHTS

Name: Muna (also Mona) Zaki

Birth: 1976, Cairo, Egypt

Family: Husband, Ahmed Helmi (married 2002); daughter, Lily (b. 2003)

Nationality: Egyptian

Education: Studying mass communications at Cairo University. Briefly studied at the Institute for Theatrical Studies

PERSONAL CHRONOLOGY:

- **1997:** Appears in first film, *al-Qatl al-Ladhidh* (The delicious killing)
- **2000:** Wins award for the film *Umar* 2000; wins award for the film *Ayyam al-Sadat* from Egyptian president Husni Mubarak
- **2003:** Receives Best Actress award (along with others) at the Damascus Film Festival; receives Best Actress award (along with others) at the Paris Biennale of Arab Cinema

to the United States, studying at Heritage Academy in Louisiana. Back in Egypt for college, Zaki studied mass communications at Cairo University. While also studying at the Institute for Theatrical Studies she was introduced to director Isma'il Abd al-Hafiz, who had her perform in his television series *al-A'ila* (The family). She went on to star in a number of popular television shows in Egypt.

INFLUENCES AND CONTRIBUTIONS

In 1997 Zaki performed in her first film, *al-Qatl al-Ladhidh* (The delicious killing), with actress Mervat Amin. Zaki went on to perform in over eighteen films. Some of her box-office hits include *Sa'idi fi'l-Jami'a al-Amrikiyya* (A Sa'idi in the American University), *Umar* 2000, *al-Hubb al-Awwal* (First love), and *Leh Khallitni Ahibbak?* (Why did you make me love you?). Perhaps her most famous role was that of Jehan al-Sadat, wife of assassinated Egyptian president Anwar al-Sadat, in the 2001 film *Ayyam al-Sadat* (The days of Sadat). The part of Sadat was played by legendary Egyptian actor Ahmad Zaki (no relation), who gave one of the greatest performances of his career. The film was one of the top-grossing films in Egyptian history. Muna Zaki and the cast were honored by current Egyptian president HUSNI MUBARAK for their performance, and she became the

youngest actress ever to win such an award from the government.

More recently, Zaki has starred with leading Egyptian star Ahmed El Sakka in the films *An al-Ishq wa'l-Hawa* (On love and the wind) and *Taymur wa Shaqiquhu* (Taymur and his brother). She has gone on record criticizing the Egyptian film industry for having women play lead roles whose primary job is to add luster to the male star's role. She has even complained about it to scriptwriters. "I've brought up the subject at every seminar I've ever attended, but to no avail," she noted in 2001. "Perhaps writers don't think we are talented enough. I guess it is also the result of patriarchy. One writer once told me 'what problem do women have that cinema can tackle?' I was too shocked to answer and haven't spoken out since" (http://weekly.ahram.org.eg/2001/562/profile.htm).

THE WORLD'S PERSPECTIVE

Zaki is one of the most sought-after actresses in the Egyptian film industry today. She is popular in her native Egypt. The press even dubbed her Cinderella, a nickname once given to Egyptian actress Su'ad Husni, one of the most popular Egyptian actresses of all time. In 2003 she was one of the Best Actress honorees at the Damascus Film Festival, as well as at the 2004 Paris Biennale of Arab Cinema, both times for her performance in the film *Sahar al-Lalali* (Sleepless nights).

LEGACY

Muna Zaki has just begun her career, but is sure to leave a mark as a talented actress in a country known for the strength of its acting heritage.

BIBLIOGRAPHY

Mona Zaki's official Web site. Available from http://www.mona-zaki.com.

Shahine, Gihan. "Mona Zaki: Expressions of Sympathy." *Al-Ahram Weekly On-Line*. 29 November–5 December 2001. Available from http://weekly.ahram.org.eg/2001/562/profile.htm.

Michael R. Fischbach

ZARQAWI, ABU MUS'AB AL-
(1966–2006)

Abu Mus'ab al-Zarqawi (born Ahmad Fadil Nazzal al-Khalayla) was a Jordanian-born Islamic militant who gained notoriety for leading a group of fighters in Iraq who attacked American troops, Western civilians, and Iraqi Shi'ite Muslims in Iraq in the period after the fall of SADDAM HUSSEIN's government in 2003. Known for videotaping the gruesome beheadings of captives, he aligned himself with Saudi militant USAMA BIN LADIN and the al-Qa'ida network, and eventually topped the list of American forces' most

Abu Mus'ab al-Zarqawi. AP IMAGES.

BIOGRAPHICAL HIGHLIGHTS

Name: Abu Mus'ab al-Zarqawi (name at birth Ahmad Fadil Nazzal al-Khalayla)

Birth: 1966, al-Zarqa, Jordan

Death: 2006, near Ba'quba, Iraq

Family: Two wives, Intisar Baqr al-Umari (Jordanian; m. 1988; two sons, Muhammad and Mus'ab; two daughters, Amina and Ra'ida) and Asra Yasin Muhammad Jarrad (Palestinian; m. 1999; one son, Abd al-Rahman). There are reports of a third wife, an Iraqi (m. 2003)

Nationality: Jordanian

Education: High school dropout

PERSONAL CHRONOLOGY:

• **1989:** Travels from Jordan to Afghanistan to fight Soviet forces

• **1993:** Helps form militant group Bay'at al-Imam in Jordan

• **1994–1999:** Imprisoned in Jordan

• **1999–2001:** Establishes training base near Herat, Afghanistan; renews ties with Usama bin Ladin and al-Qa'ida

• **2001:** Escapes American invasion of Afghanistan

• **2002:** Enters northern Iraq

• **2004:** Establishes militant group Tawhid wa'l-Jihad in Iraq, later called al-Qa'ida in the Land of the Two Rivers

• **2006:** Killed in Iraq

wanted individuals as they battled insurgents in Iraq. Zarqawi was killed by an American airstrike in June 2006.

PERSONAL HISTORY

The infamous Islamic militant known as Abu Mus'ab Al-Zarqawi was born on 20 October 1966 in the large Jordanian industrial city of al-Zarqa. His family was part of the al-Khalayla clan, part of the confederation of settled Jordanian Bedouin clans known as the Bani Hasan tribe.

Zarqawi was known as a hot-tempered troublemaker as a youth. He finished only the ninth grade at al-Zarqa High School in 1982, and worked at several low-paying jobs in 1983 prior to his obligatory service in the Jordanian army from 1984 to 1986. After leaving the military, he ran afoul of the law on several occasions in the late 1980s for shoplifting and assault, among other things. He also was known for his drinking bouts and for his tattoos, both of which are prohibited by Islamic law.

In the late 1980s, however, he became a religious Muslim, and began frequenting the al-Falah mosque in a nearby Palestinian refugee camp. There he was introduced to political Islamic teachings, as well as at the al-Hussein bin Ali mosque in Amman, where he later attended religious education classes. Zarqawi decided to join with other religious groups waging a jihad against the occupying Soviet army in Afghanistan. He did not see combat because of the Soviet withdrawal from the

country, but did participate in the subsequent fighting between Afghan government forces and the guerrillas.

In early 1993 Zarqawi returned to Jordan. He helped establish a militant group called Bay'at al-Imam that sought to attack, among other targets, the Jordanian government. Jordanian authorities arrested him in March 1994. Although sentenced to fifteen years imprisonment, Zarqawi was freed in a general amnesty in March 1999. He soon left for Pakistan, and thence to Afghanistan. He renewed connections there that he had made ten years earlier with the Saudi radical Usama bin Ladin's al-Qa'ida network, and swore an oath of allegiance to Bin Ladin in 2001. However, he established his own training camp for Arab jihadists near Herat.

CONTEMPORARIES

Abu Muhammad al-Maqdisi (1959–; name at birth Isam Muhammad Tahir al-Barqawi) is a Palestinian born in Barqa, near Nablus in the West Bank. He spent most of his early life living and studying in Kuwait, Iraq, Saudi Arabia, and Pakistan, and later became a major, prolific ideologist for Sunni jihadists worldwide in the 1990s. Al-Maqdisi and Zarqawi established the militant group Bay'at al-Imam in Jordan in 1993, although he later broke with Zarqawi while the two were imprisoned in Jordan from 1994–1999. Rearrested in 2000, al-Maqdisi remains in prison in Jordan.

Injured during the American invasion of Afghanistan that began in October 2001, Zarqawi fled the country for Iran in December 2001. He stayed in Iran until April 2002, was arrested briefly, and from there made his way to Syria for several months. By the end of 2002, he operated from the safe haven afforded him by the Ansar al-Islam group in Iraqi Kurdistan. He began to prepare fighters for the anticipated American attack on Iraq. By May 2004, Zarqawi was fighting the Americans (whom he called "crusaders") with his group, Tawhid wa'l-Jihad. He also led attacks on the new Iraqi army and Shi'ite Muslim civilians. In October 2004 Zarqawi changed the group's name to al-Qa'ida in the Land of the Two Rivers, referring to the Tigris and Euphrates.

Zarqawi did not forget his hatred of the Jordanian government and its American and Israeli allies. In October 2002 his militants assassinated an American diplomat in Jordan, and in August 2003 blew up the Jordanian embassy in Baghdad. In November 2005 Iraqi suicide bombers dispatched by Zarqawi detonated themselves in or near three hotels in Amman, killing fifty-nine people.

During the Iraqi insurgency, Zarqawi became notorious for suicide bombings targeting Shi'ite civilians that were carried out mostly by non-Iraqi Arab jihadists, as well as for the brutal murder, often by beheading, of foreigners whom the group captured. Zarqawi's group often videotaped these exploits and posted them on the Internet, adding to his ferocious image, and garnering him media coverage as well as new recruits from across the Arab world. He became the American authorities' most sought-after man after Bin Ladin himself, with a bounty of $25 million placed on his head. On 7 June 2006 American forces finally killed Zarqawi, along with one of his wives and a child of

his, in an air strike on their safe house near Hibhib, not far from the Iraqi town of Ba'quba.

INFLUENCES AND CONTRIBUTIONS

After his thuggish youth, Zarqawi moved toward Islamic fundamentalism (also called Islamic revivalism). Among Sunni Muslims, fundamentalists stress absolute monotheism (Arabic: *tawhid*), and a strict interpretation of Islamic law. They seek to establish Islamic governments run according to *shari'a* (Islamic law), and interpret the Islamic duty of jihad as requiring them to take up arms against perceived enemies of Islam—be they non-Muslims or even Muslims they consider apostates. However, Zarqawi was not a learned ideologue, but someone who employed his charisma and penchant for violence not for petty crime as before, but for jihad.

Zarqawi also owed much to Bin Ladin and al-Qa'ida, although the two did not always see eye to eye. Yet in December 2004 Bin Ladin stated that he personally had selected Zarqawi as his deputy in Iraq. Those with intimate knowledge of Zarqawi cite the prestige and funding available to al-Qa'ida as reasons why Zarqawi, who previously had insisted on maintaining his independence, agreed to join formally with Bin Ladin and al-Qa'ida. For Bin Ladin, Zarqawi's highly publicized exploits in Iraq provided al-Qa'ida with much-needed successes given the setbacks it had suffered in Afghanistan and elsewhere.

THE WORLD'S PERSPECTIVE

Beyond wider global revulsion at his methods, Zarqawi's methods and what has been termed his "battlefield theology" divided the Iraqi insurgency, and led to criticism within jihadist and fundamentalist communities. Yet for all his infamy, some argue that he was not in fact of lasting importance—that his skillful use of the media, and the ruthless nature of his exploits, inflated his importance in Iraq and globally beyond what it actually was. American government documents leaked to the *Washington Post* in 2006 reveal that an American military propaganda campaign also may have had a hand in inflating this image in order to turn the Iraqi population against him, a foreigner on their soil.

LEGACY

Zarqawi was significant for several reasons. His ruthless violence and guerrilla attacks confounded American and Iraqi forces, and helped galvanize wider Arab and Islamic support for the insurgency in Iraq. His methods also divided the insurgents and others (in his native Jordan as well as in Iraq), and added to the ferocious image many around the world had of the resistance and perhaps even of Islam itself. Zarqawi also did much to fuel growing Sunni-

> ## YOU WILL NOT REST PEACEFULLY IN THE LANDS OF ISLAM
>
> ∎
>
> As for the American administration, headed by the bearer of the banner of the cross, Bush—we say to him and to his followers, the Jews, the Crusaders, the Rafidite Shi'ites, the apostates, and others: You will not rest peacefully in the lands of Islam. By God, your life will be unbearable as long as blood flows in our veins and our eyes can see.... And today, with the grace of God, you seek the help of East and West, confused, exhausted, and broken, like someone whom "Satan has prostrated with his touch" (Qur'an 2:275).
>
> "NEW VIDEO BY AL-QAEDA COMMANDER IN IRAQ ABU MUS'AB AL-ZARQAWI: SPECIAL DISPATCH SERIES NO. 1149." MIDDLE EAST MEDIA RESEARCH INSTITUTE. AVAILABLE FROM HTTP://WWW.MEMRI.ORG.
>
> Our [U.S. military's] own focus on Zarqawi has enlarged his caricature, if you will—made him more important than he really is, in some ways.... The long-term threat is not Zarqawi or religious extremists, but these former regime types and their friends.
>
> COL. DEREK HARVEY, UNITED STATES ARMY INTELLIGENCE OFFICER, 2004. IN RICKS, THOMAS. "MILITARY PLAYS UP ROLE OF ZARQAWI," *WASHINGTON POST*, 10 APRIL 2006. AVAILABLE FROM HTTP://WWW.WASHINGTONPOST.COM.

Shi'ite civil strife in Iraq through vicious attacks on Shi'ite civilians. Finally, his fight against the Americans and high-profile association with al-Qa'ida ironically served to stiffen the resolve of the American government to keep its forces in Iraq to prevent it becoming the breeding ground for a new generation of jihadists.

BIBLIOGRAPHY

Brisard, Jean Charles, and Martinez, Damien. *Zarqawi: The New Face of al-Qaeda*. New York: Other Press, 2005.

Gerges, Fawaz A. *The Far Enemy: Why Jihad Went Global*. Cambridge, U.K.: Cambridge University Press, 2005.

Ricks, Thomas E. "Military Plays Up Role of Zarqawi: Jordanian Painted as Foreign Threat to Iraq's Stability." *Washington Post* 10 April 2006.

Michael R. Fischbach

ZAWAWI, OMAR BIN ABD AL-MUNIM
(1930–)

Omani businessman and political consultant Omar (Umar) bin Abd al-Munim Zawawi, one of the wealthiest private individuals in the Middle East, has been a leading figure in the economic development of the Sultanate of Oman since 1970 and a personal adviser on foreign policy matters to Sultan Qaboos bin Sa'id Al 'Bu Sa'id since 1974.

PERSONAL HISTORY

Zawawi was born around 1930 in Karachi, British India (now Pakistan), where his father Abd al-Munim bin Yusuf served as purchasing agent for Sultan Sa'id bin Taymur, ruler of Masqat and Oman. His early education was in Bombay (now Mumbai), and his schooling continued in Beirut and then at Cairo University where he earned his medical degree. Upon graduation he practiced medicine for a time in Saudi Arabia. He later studied medical economics at Harvard University. Zawawi returned to Saudi Arabia where he turned his attention to business, establishing a close association with the prominent Saudi businessman Ghassan Shakir. Meanwhile, his younger brother Qais went to Kuwait, where he worked for the British Bank of the Middle East and then the British embassy before becoming regional manager for Pepsi-Cola in Dubai in the 1960s. Qais returned to Masqat in 1967 to reestablish the family business in Oman. Omar returned to Oman in 1971 to join his brother in the family business. The Zawawis, operating under the umbrella of the Omar Zawawi Establishment (the Omzest Group) holding company, quickly developed a wide range of businesses that played an active role in the economic development of Oman in the wake of the 1970 coup that brought Sultan Qaboos to power.

Zawawi's government service career began officially in 1974 when he became the sultan's special adviser for external liaison, a position that he continues to hold. He has also served on Oman's finance committee.

Despite his many successes, Omar has experienced some tragedy in his life. In July 1992 he overcame colon cancer, following surgery and subsequent chemotherapy at the Mayo Clinic in Rochester, Minnesota. He also survived a September 1995 automobile accident in Dhufar when a car driven by Sultan Qaboos was struck by another vehicle. His brother Qais died in the accident, in which he and the sultan were both injured.

INFLUENCES AND CONTRIBUTIONS

Zawawi's principal influence has been the Zawawi family tradition of commercial activity in combination with service to the Al 'Bu Sa'id royal family of Oman. This

BIOGRAPHICAL HIGHLIGHTS

Name: Omar bin Abd al-Munim Zawawi (Umar)

Birth: c. 1930, Karachi, British India

Family: Wife; one son, Walid; two daughters, Reem and Areej

Nationality: Omani

Education: India; Lebanon; Cairo University (Egypt); Harvard University

PERSONAL CHRONOLOGY:

- Earns medical degree, Cairo University
- Practices medicine in Saudi Arabia
- **1971:** Joins family business with brother
- **1974–present:** Special adviser to the sultan for foreign affairs

association dates perhaps to the early nineteenth century when a Muhammad al-Zawawi took up residence in Masqat, a refugee from the Sa'udi conquest of Hasa in eastern Arabia. Zawawi's grandfather, Yusuf bin Ahmad al-Zawawi, came to Muscat from Mecca in the later nineteenth century. He became one of the principal merchants of that port, a personal adviser to sultans Faysal bin Turki (1888–1913) and Taymur bin Faysal (1913–1932), and a supporter of religious works with the construction of the Zawawi mosque. His international contacts often resulted in his acting as an agent of the government abroad, most notably when he accompanied the Omani delegation under Crown Prince Taymur to the Delhi Durbar in December 1911 to celebrate the accession of King George V of England. Yusuf died in Ta'if, western Arabia, in 1927. Zawawi's father Abd al-Munim continued the Zawawi business interests, settling in India where he served as commercial agent for both sultans Taymur and Sa'id bin Taimur (1932–1970). He often accompanied Sultan Sa'id on his foreign travels.

Zawawi business interests grew rapidly with the economic development of the sultanate following the coup of 1970. During the 1970s and into the 1980s, Zawawi economic activities focused on distribution, construction, and management. Two Zawawi-owned companies, Zawawi Trading Company and Waleed Associates, held exclusive distribution rights for a number of important product lines, including Mercedes-Benz, General Electric, Mobil Oil, Xerox, 3M, IBM, Microsoft, major defense contractors Vosper Thornycroft (shipbuilding) and McDonnell Douglas (aeronautics), and hundreds more.

Zawawi also owned Qurum Contractors, which became one of the largest construction companies in Oman. Zawawi companies built the first schools, hospitals, the color television and the electrical and telephone systems in Oman. Zawawi also played a leading role in the formation of the companies that operated Oman's port and airport.

Zawawi's banking and finance activities date to the formation of the Oman Arab African Bank in January 1979 in partnership with the Cairo-based Arab African Bank (AAB). He served as deputy chairman of the board of that bank. In 1984 he bought out the AAB shares of the Oman Arab African Bank as well as fourteen branches of the British Bank of the Middle East in Oman to form Oman International Bank (OIB), the first wholly Omani-owned bank in the sultanate. He served as chairman of the board of OIB until 1996.

In addition to OIB, Zawawi financial services also included the Muscat Finance Company, which provides consumer loans, and Oman Securities Portfolio Company, founded in 1989 to provide stockbrokerage services. The latter was one of Zawawi's few failures as the company suffered major losses in Oman's stock market in 2001 and ceased operation in early 2002. Another Zawawi financial services company, Oman Insurance Company, founded in 1995, has been far more successful.

Manufacturing has become an increasingly important part of Zawawi business activities. As Oman began developing import replacement industries in the late 1970s, Zawawi's investments included Oman Flour Mills Company and Raysut Cement Company, followed by textile, footwear, glass product, paint, vegetable oil, battery, detergent, agricultural, and paper product factories. In 2003 Omzest undertook a major industrial development projects with the Oman Methanol Company in Suhar.

Zawawi has also been active in the service sector as well. Early activities included Mezoon Travel and Waleed Pharmacy and then expanded to catering and business services. Most recently, he established Waljat College of Applied Sciences to provide technical training to the Omani workforce.

Zawawi business interests became international in 1992 when Omzest opened an office in Beijing to coordinate its business ties with China. The company also has holdings in Egypt in flour mills, in Methanol Holdings (Trinidad), the major producer of methanol in the Caribbean, and in 2006 formed a joint venture with the German electrical engineering and communications company Siemens.

THE WORLD'S PERSPECTIVE

Zawawi's international reputation derives only in part from his business interests. His brother Qais entered the Omani cabinet in December 1973 as minister of state for foreign affairs, and played a prominent role in government economic planning. Zawawi was appointed to the finance committee, but quickly became the principal adviser on foreign affairs to the sultan. Even before becoming special adviser, he was instrumental, as a result of his relationship with Ghassan Shakir, in gaining recognition of Sultan Qaboos's government by the Saudis after the 1970 coup.

As special adviser, Zawawi has continued the family tradition of serving as the sultan's personal envoy when dealing with critical international issues. He accompanied Sultan Qaboos on his first visit to the United States in 1975, was responsible for negotiating diplomatic relations with the People's Republic of China in 1978, and in that same year led talks with the neighboring United Arab Emirates that eventually resulted in the settlement of long-disputed borders. Subsequent missions included trips to Egypt in the wake of President Anwar al-Sadat's peace treaty with Israel in 1979, which resulted in near universal condemnation in the rest of the Arab world; to China in 1990 in the aftermath of the Iraqi invasion of Kuwait; and to Japan and Iran. Zawawi represented the sultan at the Arab foreign ministers' summit in Egypt in 2001 on the second Palestinian intifada. He has often represented Oman in talks with strategically and economically important countries.

LEGACY

Zawawi is a controversial figure. For some he is a primary example of the corruption at the highest levels in the Omani government, where state officials have parlayed their positions into lucrative contracts for their personal business interests. For others he has been the consummate public servant who has served the state well in representing Oman abroad and advising the sultan on international matters, while leading economic development in the country. Zawawi business interests do profit from both Zawawi brothers' connections with the government, and when conflict-of-interest statutes were implemented in the mid-1980s, Zawawi resigned from those positions deemed to be in potential violation. His business interests have brought great wealth. In 2004 the journal *Arabian Business* reported Omar's worth at $415 million, making him the richest private individual in Oman and the forty-third richest man in the Middle East.

Perhaps Zawawi's greatest legacy will be the continuing role that his family will play in Omani affairs, as his three children all continue the family tradition of public service and economic development. His son Walid is a brigadier general in the Omani army and served as director of moral guidance for the armed forces, in addition to his involvement in Omzest's various operations; daughter Reem was the first woman to head a major Omani corporation when she became the chairperson of the board of Oman International Bank in 2002, and she serves on a

number of other boards. His daughter Areej earned a doctorate in education and directs a school in Jordan.

BIBLIOGRAPHY

Allen, Calvin H., Jr., and W. Lynn Rigsbee II. *Oman under Qaboos: From Coup to Constitution, 1970–1996.* London and Portland, OR: Frank Cass, 2000.

Owtram, Francis. *A Modern History of Oman: Formation of the State since 1920.* London and New York: I.B. Taurus, 2004.

Calvin Allen

ZINDANI, ABD AL-MAJID AL-
(1938–)

Abd al-Majid al-Zindani has long been a key religious and political figure in Yemen. He is usually referred to as a "shaykh" in the religious sense of the term, and was instrumental in establishing the Yemeni Reform Grouping (al-Tajammu' al-Yamani li'l-Islah), better known simply as Islah, in 1990. He has also headed the party's Consultative Council since it was established that same year, and from 1993 to 1997 he was a member of the Republic of Yemen's ruling five-man presidential council. In 2004 the United States officially listed him as a terrorist for his alleged role as a terrorist recruiter and financier.

PERSONAL HISTORY

Al-Zindani was born in 1938 near the village of Ba'dan, east of the city of Ibb, 193 kilometers south of San'a, in what was then the Arab Republic of Yemen (North Yemen). Most of Ibb's inhabitants in the 1930s were Sunni Muslims of the Shafi'i school, unlike the Shi'ite Zaydi dynasty that then ruled the country. Al-Zindani claims to be a *naqili*, a scion of the northern Zaydi tribes that moved south with the Qasimi imams in the seventeenth century. This claim is significant in that it allows him superior status in Yemen's social hierarchy.

Al-Zindani spent his primary years in school in Ibb, before moving to the southern port city of Aden, then under British rule, to continue his studies. This was a fairly common practice during the 1940s and 1950s, as a host of Yemeni intellectuals, students, and workers moved back and forth between the two areas. In the mid-1950s he traveled to Cairo to pursue a degree in pharmacology at Ayn Shams University. But like many students at the time, he soon gave that up in favor of Islamic studies at al-Azhar in the late 1950s. He returned to Yemen, before completing his studies, soon after the revolution broke out in 1962. He never pursued another academic degree. This lack of qualifications is sometimes used by his better-credentialed religious colleagues to smear him in the Arabic press.

BIOGRAPHICAL HIGHLIGHTS

Name: Abd al-Majid al-Zindani (Abdelmajid al-Zindani, Abd al-Majeed al-Zindani)

Birth: 1938, Ba'dan, North Yemen

Nationality: Yemeni

Education: Primary schools, Ibb and Aden; attended Ayn Shams and al-Azhar universities, Cairo, failed to complete a degree

PERSONAL CHRONOLOGY:

- **1960s:** Joined al-Zubayri's Hizbullah
- **1974:** Appointed "national guide" by President al-Hamdi
- **1979:** Forced out of Muslim Brotherhood, exiles self to Saudi Arabia
- **1980s:** Works as recruiter and preacher for anti-Soviet jihad in Afghanistan
- **1984:** Establishes Institute for the Scientific Inimitability of the Qur'an and Sunna
- **1990:** Helps establish Islah, is named head of its Consultative Council
- **1993:** Establishes al-Iman University; is named to Yemen's five-man presidential council
- **2004:** Named a "specially designated global terrorist" by the United States

Like many Yemeni students who had studied in Egypt, al-Zindani supported the coalition of army officers, tribesmen, and Egyptians against the Zaydi imam Muhammad al-Badr and his supporting tribes, backed by Saudi Arabia. But in late 1964, under the influence of the Yemeni poet and politician Muhammad Mahmud al-Zubayri, al-Zindani grew tired of Egyptian interference, and joined al-Zubayri's newly formed Hizbullah (Party of God). The party did not survive al-Zubayri's assassination in April 1965.

Al-Zindani, frustrated and angry about the death of his mentor, fled south to Aden, which was involved in its own messy resistance war against Britain that would soon devolve into a civil war. Following the Marxist takeover in the south in 1967, he traveled to Saudi Arabia, where he remained until the end of the civil war in North Yemen in 1970. He was appointed an adviser to the Ministry of Education by President Abd al-Rahman al-Iryani, who had also been close to al-Zubayri during the civil war. But the two soon had a falling out and al-Zindani returned to Saudi Arabia, where he remained until 1974, when al-Iryani was ousted in a coup.

The new president, Ibrahim al-Hamdi, appointed al-Zindani as a national "guide," or *murshid*, a position that allowed him to channel Saudi funding into a number of institutes designed to confront communism. He also renewed his affiliation with the Yemeni branch of the Muslim Brotherhood, which dated from his time with al-Zubayri. Al-Hamdi was assassinated in 1977, and two years later al-Zindani was ousted from the Muslim Brotherhood in what many have termed an internal coup. Jillian Schwedler (2006) has argued, based on numerous interviews, that many of the younger members felt that al-Zindani was developing a cult of personality at the expense of the group's ideals.

Al-Zindani left the country in a rage, into self-enforced exile in Saudi Arabia. In 1984, with Saudi funding, he established and became the first secretary general of the Institute for the Scientific Inimitability of the Qur'an and Sunna at King Abd al-Aziz University in Jidda. This organization produced books and videos arguing that the Qur'an predicted the development and discoveries of modern science. It debated Western scientists as a way of urging them to admit the validity of the Qur'an through scientific proofs. Throughout the 1980s al-Zindani was also active as a recruiter and preacher for the jihad in Afghanistan against the Soviet Union. Al-Zindani was particularly close to the Afghan leader Gulbuddin Hekmatyar, as well as to other Arab participants.

Following unification of North and South Yemen and the establishment of Islah in 1990, al-Zindani returned to live in Yemen, where he was made a member of the five-man presidential council in 1993. That same year, he established al-Iman University in San'a with Saudi and Yemeni funding. The university has often been considered a breeding ground for terrorists, despite al-Zindani's frequent denials. He was also instrumental in providing religious support in the form of a *fatwa* for President ALI ABDULLAH SALIH against an attempted secession in 1994 by the formerly socialist south.

Throughout the 1990s and into the first years of the twenty-first century, al-Zindani sparked a number of controversial court cases by inciting his followers through his weekly sermons, which were widely available on audiocassettes and as CDs, and bringing lawsuits against those he deemed to have insulted Islam. In 2000 he labeled both the publisher of *al-Thaqafiyya*, a weekly cultural newspaper, and the writer Muhammad Abd al-Wali, dead since 1973, as infidels. He based his judgment on a line in al-Wali's book, *San'a: Madina Maftuha* (San'a: an open city), which he deemed to be anti-Islamic. The book was eventually banned. Similar cases involving allegations of defamation of the prophet Muhammad through

CONTEMPORARIES

■

Abdullah al-Ahmar (1933–), known more colloquially as Shaykh Abdullah, is the *shaykh mashaykh* (paramount shaykh) of the Hashid tribal confederation in Yemen. He has headed the Islah Party since it was established in 1990, and has been a constant fixture as the speaker of Yemen's 301-seat parliament. Al-Ahmar was born in Husn Habur, his family's tribal village northeast of San'a, where members of his family have long headed the Hashid. He was selected as shaykh following the assassination of his father Husayn and older brother Hamid by Imam Ahmad in 1960. Shaykh Abdullah was a key republican figure during the 1962–1970 civil war, able to rally numerous tribesmen in support of the fledgling republic. Since that time he has remained one of the most important and powerful players in Yemeni politics. Despite this, he has always supported President Salih in times of crisis. He maintains his own Web site at http://www.alahmar.net.

cartoons, as well as against other writers, have also resulted in lengthy court cases.

In 2004 the U.S. Treasury Department named him a "specially designated global terrorist," a designation adopted by the United Nations (UN) as well. Al-Zindani has steadfastly maintained his innocence, while the Yemeni government has taken no steps to freeze his funds as demanded by the United States and UN. The Yemeni government has maintained that it needs to see proof of al-Zindani's terrorist activities before taking such a step.

INFLUENCES AND CONTRIBUTIONS

Al-Zindani was greatly influenced by the works of Hasan al-Banna, founder of the Muslim Brotherhood, and Sayyid Qutb, which he was exposed to during his time in Cairo in the late 1950s and early 1960s. But it was al-Zubayri who played the largest role in shaping his early thought. Al-Zubayri's fierce anti-imam and anti-Egyptian feelings, as well as his leanings toward the Muslim Brotherhood, had a strong impact on the young al-Zindani.

Al-Zindani himself credits what he has called the "gray pamphlet," published by Communists in Egypt in 1958, as the catalyst for his work on the scientific inimitability of the Qur'an and Sunna. This pamphlet, he has claimed in interviews, attempted to disprove the Qur'an by using modern science. Al-Zindani took this as

a personal challenge, and has spent much of his life attempting to show how the Qur'an prefigured all of modern science. This effort led him, in 2003 and 2004, to attempt to develop cures for such maladies as hepatitis, diabetes, Severe Acute Respiratory Syndrome, and AIDS.

During his numerous stays in Saudi Arabia, he came under the influence of the Saudi cleric Shaykh Abd al-Aziz bin Baz. Al-Zindani was also greatly influenced by the teachings of Muhammad ibn Abd al-Wahhab, the eponymous founder of Wahhabism, particularly his work on *tawhid*, the oneness of God. Along with the study of the scientific inimitability of the Qur'an and Sunna, it is for his teachings on *tawhid* that al-Zindani is best known within the Islamic world. Most of his fourteen books deal with one subject or the other.

Al-Zindani is also famous for his numerous *fatawa*, or nonbinding religious opinions, which are never written down, but issued orally either in a sermon or in response to a direct question from a petitioner. It is through his numerous recorded sermons that al-Zindani has had the greatest impact on Yemeni society and politics.

THE WORLD'S PERSPECTIVE

International perceptions of al-Zindani have largely been negative, even before he was labeled a "specially designated global terrorist." His physical appearance and public posturing fit preconceived ideas of how a Muslim radical should look and act. Al-Zindani's image was also hurt by his close personal relationships with figures such as USAMA BIN LADIN and Hasan al-Turabi, the Sudanese intellectual and ideologue.

Despite these assumptions, however, al-Zindani's thought is much more nuanced and modern than is often assumed. In the political arena he is a frightening man who has inspired violence against those who disagree with him, but intellectually he refuses to accept many of the divisions often placed between Islam and modernity. He has consistently argued that modernity and its inherent technologies are, in fact, part of the heritage of Islam. This inclusiveness, of course, does not spread to Western ideas of morality and secularism.

The negative impressions of al-Zindani in Western countries are, not surprisingly, counterbalanced by a more positive perception of him in the Muslim world. While it is correct, as Paul Dresch (2000) has argued, that many Yemenis of note consider al-Zindani a little divorced from reality, it is also true that he has a sizable following. But while al-Zindani's domestic enemies have a significant amount of power, he has always been protected when it mattered most by President Salih. In March 2006, Salih was quoted in the pan-Arab daily *al-Quds al-Arabi* as telling U.S. Ambassador Thomas Krajeski, "Shaykh al-Zindani is a rational, balanced and moderate man and we know him well, and the Yemeni government guarantees [his actions], and I guarantee his character."

Al-Zindani's following has grown since his inclusion on the terrorist list in 2004, both in Yemen and in the wider Islamic world. This is partly a result of his ideas gaining more traction, as well as the basic idea that the Islamic world tends to believe one of its own over Western allegations.

LEGACY

It is too early to assess al-Zindani's final legacy, but at least a partial picture is available. He will be acknowledged as one of the main guiding forces behind Islah, as well as an important shaper of political opinion in Yemen following the 1962 revolution. It is difficult to tell whether or not the institutions he has created will outlive him, but the continued existence of the Institute for the Scientific Inimitability of the Qur'an and Sunna suggests that al-Iman University will survive him as well. Whether he is ultimately seen as a terrorist or as a more complex religious scholar remains to be seen.

BIBLIOGRAPHY

Dresch, Paul. *A History of Modern Yemen*. New York: Cambridge University Press, 2000.

Dresch, Paul, and Bernard Haykel. "Stereotypes and Political Styles: Islamists and Tribesfolk in Yemen." *International Journal of Middle East Studies* 27, no. 4 (November 1995): 405–431.

Schwedler, Jillian. *Faith in Moderation: Islamist Parties in Jordan and Yemen*. New York: Cambridge University Press, 2006.

Gregory D. Johnsen

ZOGHBI, NAWAL AL-
(1972–)

Nawal al-Zoghbi (Nawwal al-Zughbi) has been a leading Lebanese pop singer since 1991. She has a huge following throughout the Middle East and the Arab-speaking communities of Europe, Australia, and the Americas.

PERSONAL HISTORY

Al-Zoghbi was born in the coastal town of Jubayl (the ancient Byblos), Lebanon, not far from Beirut, on 29 June 1972. She was the first-born of three brothers and a sister. It was noticed early on that she had a passion and gift for singing. Her family supported this as a hobby, but took some convincing when she wanted to make it a career. She was a participant in the Lebanese television show *Studio al-Fan* in 1988, and began singing professionally not long thereafter. Her career truly took off with the release of her

Nawal al-Zoghbi. JOSEPH BARRAK/AFP/GETTY IMAGES.

first album, *Wa Hayati Andak* (I promise on my importance to you), in 1992, after she had toured the Gulf states for two years. She has won numerous awards such as "Best Arabic Singer," "Best Album," and "Overall Best Singer."

In 1998 al-Zoghbi became embroiled in a controversy about song copyrights. She and the famous Syrian singer Huwayda both laid claim to a song titled "Mandam Alayk" (No regrets about you). Huwayda had recorded the song previously, but al-Zoghbi claimed that she had the original, and had been holding onto it. In the end the controversy seemed to cause little fallout for either singer, only giving each a bit more air time and publicity. In fact, it seems to have helped al-Zoghbi, as it is now one of her most popular and most requested songs.

INFLUENCES AND CONTRIBUTIONS

The music of al-Zoghbi, like that of many other Arab singers, was inspired by the legendary Egyptian singers UMM KULTHUM and Samira Sa'id. However, the lyrics al-Zoghbi sings were heavily influenced by the violence of local and regional politics. The star grew up during the Lebanese Civil War of 1975 to 1990. Living near Beirut, she witnessed terrible events, which shaped her outlook. This lengthy and traumatic war instilled in her a deep sense of patriotism and unflinching nationalism, as well as humanitarianism. These attributes can be seen

BIOGRAPHICAL DATA

Name: Nawal al-Zoghbi (Nawwal al-Zughbi)

Birth: 1972, Jubayl, Lebanon

Family: Husband, Elie Deeb; one daughter, Tia; two sons, Georgy, Joey

Nationality: Lebanese (dual Canadian citizenship)

PERSONAL CHRONOLOGY:

- **1988:** Appeared on *Studio al-Fan* TV talent show
- **1992:** Releases first hit album, *Wa Hayati Andak*
- **1997:** Wins Lions Award for best singer in Lebanon and Jordan
- **1998:** Wins award for Best Singer in the United Arab Emirates
- **2004:** Wins awards for Best Lebanese Singer, Best Arabic Singer; Overall Best Song; Best Album
- **2005:** Wins award for Best Arabic Singer
- **2006:** Wins awards for Best Arabic Singer, Album of the Year, Song of the Year, Video Clip of the Year, Best Dancing Song of the Year, Song of the Week (10 times); releases songs dedicated to Palestine, liberation of southern Lebanon from Israeli occupation, and assassinated former Lebanese prime minister Rafiq Hariri; organizes Help Lebanon Campaign in wake of Israel-Hizbullah war

in both her songs and her deeds. She has several songs to her credit, such as "Ya Ummati" (Oh, my people) and "Ya Quds" (Oh, Jerusalem), that are patriotic, as well as others, like "Hikayat Watan" (Story of a nation), that were collaborations with other singers. When asked about her patriotic songs, al-Zoghbi stated that "I have strong feelings towards the relentless violence in the Middle East; I felt the need to do something, so I made this song." "Hikayat Watan" is a call for the liberation of southern Lebanon. She also released a song after former Lebanese prime minister RAFIQ HARIRI'S assassination, titled, "La Ma Khilsit al-Hakaya" (The story has not ended). Along with these songs, she has dedicated her time to the people of Lebanon in times of crisis.

During the Israel-Hizbullah war in mid-2006, when many pop stars fled the country, al-Zoghbi decided to stay and do what she could for her people. In an article

for the English-language monthly *Egypt Today*, she is quoted as saying that it was her "humanitarian and patriotic duty." (She could have easily left the country as so many others did at this time, as she holds a Canadian passport.) She toured the destruction wrought by Israeli bombing, and traveled to schools and colleges as well. She helped to rally her countrymen as well as sympathizers in the region to the cause of getting aid into Lebanon, and to the people. Mainly she did what she is good at, focusing the media's and the public's eye on the plight of the people. In a step that has inspired others, she decided to donate much of her earnings for her most recent album, *Yama Alu* (Oh how much people have said!), and organized a concert that was held in Beirut on 5 October 2006 to raise money for those most desperately in need. The concert was in conjunction with Jordanian Queen Rania's Jordan River Foundation.

To help with the recovery after the war had come to an end and the tanks and soldiers had gone, al-Zoghbi recorded two new songs in the "streets of Beirut." One of them, "Adi" (Normal), is an attempt to stress how life in Lebanon is slowly returning to "normal." Al-Zoghbi was the first Arab singer to call for aid from the larger music world, and to stress the need for all forms of aid for her country. She began, at this time, an organization called the Help Lebanon Campaign to distribute necessities to refugees and to ease their burdens.

THE WORLD'S PERSPECTIVE

Global perception of al-Zoghbi has been very positive. She has a large following in the Middle East, and has also gained in popularity in Europe and in the Americas. She has toured through the United States, Canada, Australia, Britain, France, Sweden, and Germany, and many times in the Middle East and North Africa. She has released ten

FREE AND HAPPY

When I am singing, I feel that I am no more Nawal, I am transformed into a butterfly that is free and happy. When I feel that my audience is happy, I get my greatest reward.... I want to touch the people's hearts, when I am on stage.... I have strong feelings towards the relentless violence in the Middle East, I felt the need to do something, so I made this song ["Ya Quds"].

NAWAL AL-ZOGHBI ON HER OFFICIAL WEB SITE. AVAILABLE FROM HTTP://WWW.NAWALALZOGHBI.NET.

albums so far and has appeared in commercials and promotions for Pepsi-Cola since 2001. Fashion is also important to al-Zoghbi, and she has always tried to be at the forefront. Her patronage has furthered the career of the Lebanese designer ELIE SAAB.

LEGACY

It is too early to assess al-Zoghbi's ultimate legacy, but as a popular singer, an impassioned patriot, and to an extent a role model, she has left a mark not only on pop music but Arab culture in general and Lebanese in particular.

BIBLIOGRAPHY

Nawal al-Zoghbi's official Web site. Available from http://www.nawalalzoghbi.net.

Khodr M. Zaarour

Nationality and Ethnicity Index

Libyan
Mahdaoui, Ahmad Rafiq al-,
484–485
Musrati, Ali Mustafa al-, 556–558
Qaddafi, Mu'ammar al-, 624–628
Qaddafi, Saif al-Islam al-, 628–629

Mauritanian
Abba, Dimi Mint Benaissi, 1–4
Abd al-Qader, Ahmad ben, 10–13
Barra, Mubarkah Bent al-,
156–158
Ebnou, Moussa Ould, 268–270
Hondo, Med, 363–365

Moroccan
Asimi, Malika al-, 127–129
Bannis, Mohammed, 145
Ben Jelloun, Tahar, 185–190
El Moutawakel, Nawal, 274–276
Hassan II, 351–358
Khatibi, Abdel Kebir, 439–441
Laabi, Abdellatif, 459–461
Laroui, Abdallah, 470–473
Madini, Ahmad al-, 481–484
Mernissi, Fatima, 528–531
Muhammad VI, 553–556
Rabi, Mubarak, 637–639
Saddiki, Tayeb, 672–675
Sharqawi, Ahmad, 753–755
Tawfiq, Ahmad at-, 796–798

Omani
Al Bu Sa'id, Badr bin Hamad bin
Hamood, 45–47
Al Bu Sa'id, Qaboos, 48–52
Zawawi, Omar bin Abd al-Munim,
853–855

Palestinian
Abbas, Mahmud, 4–8
Abu-Assad, Hany, 21–23
Arafat, Yasir, 106–112
Ashrawi, Hanan Mikha'il,
125–127
Bakri, Mohamed, 143–145
Barghuthi, Marwan, 150–153
Bishara, Azmi, 196–201
Boullata, Kamal, 208–209
Chacour, Elias, 229–232
Dahlan, Muhammad, 239–242
Darraj, Faisal, 242–244
Darwish, Mahmud, 244–247
El Sarraj, Eyad, 280–282
Habash, George, 313–317
Habibi, Emile, 317–320
Haniyeh, Ismail, 331–334
Hatoum, Mona, 358–362
Jabareen, Hasan, 389–392
Kassir, Samir, 408–411
Khader, Asma, 415–417
Khalidi, Rashid, 421–423
Khalidi, Walid, 423–427
Khouri, Rami, 444–447

Khoury, Makram, 450–452
Mash'al, Khalid, 518–520
Masri, Mai, 520–521
Masri, Munib al-, 521–523
Said, Edward, 685–688
Salameh, Nadine, 688–690
Shaheen, Simon, 730–732
Shawa, Leila, 755–756
Shehadeh, Raja, 757–761
Shikaki, Khalil, 763–765
Shoman, Abdul Majeed, 767–769
Suan, Abbas, 783–784
Suleiman, Elia, 784–787
Tamari, Vera, 795–796
Tukan, Jafar, 810–811
Yasin, Ahmad, 834–839
Zahhar, Mahmud al-, 847–849

Pashtun (Afghanistan)
Karzai, Hamid, 405–408
Nasher, Farhad, 564–566
Omar, Mullah Mohammed,
590–592

Qatari
Al Thani, Hamad bin Jasim bin
Jabr, 84–87
Al Thani, Hamad bin Khalifa,
87–91
Al Thani, Sa'ud bin Muhammad
bin Ali, 91–92
Misnad, Mawza bint Nasir
al-, 534–538

Saharawi (Western Sahara)
Abdelaziz, Mohamed, 13–14

Saudi Arabian
Al Sa'ud, Al-Walid bin Talal,
78–82
Al Sa'ud, Sultan bin Salman,
82–84
Angawi, Sami, 99
Awda, Salman al-, 131–135
Bin Ladin, Usama, 191–195
Faqih, Sa'd al-, 290–292
Jubayr, Adil al-, 392–395
Khashoggi, Jamal, 432–434
Sa'ud, Abdullah bin Abd al-Aziz
al-, 709–714
Yamani, Mai, 833–834

Sudanese
Bashir, Omar al-, 161–163
Ishaaq, Kamala, 385–387
Kabli, Abd al-Karim al-, 399–401
Mayardit, Salva Kiir, 523–524
Qasim, Awn al-Sharif, 635–636
Salih, al-Tayyib, 695–699
Turabi, Hasan al-, 814–815

Syrian
Akkad, Moustapha, 32–34
Al-Azm, Sadik, 40–42
Amiralay, Umar, 97–98
Asad, Bashar al-, 115–119

Asad, Hafiz al-, 120–124
Bayanuni, Ali Sadr al-Din,
166–167
Bayyud, In'am, 171–173
Hamidi, Ibrahim, 329–331
Khaddam, Abd al-Halim,
413–415
Lahham, Duraid, 461–464
Maleh, Haytham al-, 504–505
Naisse, Aktham, 563–564
Qabbani, Nizar, 621–624
Rafeq, Abdul-Karim, 648–650
Sa'id, Ali Ahmad, 682–685
Salameh, Nadine, 688–690
Samman, Ghada, 705
Shamma, Sara, 740–741
Sharaa, Farouk al-, 745–746
Shouaa, Ghada, 769–771
Tlas, Mustafa, 800–803

Tajik (Afghanistan)
Nasher, Farhad, 564–566
Qanuni, Yunus, 629–632

Tunisian
Amari, Raja, 92–93
Béji, Hélé, 176–178
Ben Ali, Zein al-Abidin,
181–183
Bouchnaq, Lotfi, 201–204
Khemir, Sabiha, 441–442
Mas'adi, Mahmoud al-,
516–518
Meddeb, Abdelwahhab,
524–527
Tlatli, Moufida, 803–807
Tlili, Mustafa, 808

Turkish
Ar, Müjde, 103–106
Ayhan, Süreyya, 135–137
Biret, Idil, 195–196
Çetin, Hikmet, 223–225
Ceylan, Nuri Bilge, 226–229
Dündar, Can, 259–261
Erdogan, Tayyip, 283–286
Göle, Nilüfer, 309–311
Karademir, Tuğba, 403–405
Kenter, Yildiz, 411–412
Kulin, Ayşe, 456–458
Mardin, Şerif, 510–513
Öcalan, Abdullah, 583–585
Pamuk, Orhan, 597–601
Qabbani, Nizar, 621–624
Sabanci, Güler, 669–672
Say, Fazil, 717–720
Sezer, Ahmet Necdet,
724–726
Soysal, Mümtaz, 780–783
Tekeli, Şirin, 798
Terim, Fatih, 799–800
Yerlikaya, Hamza, 839–840

Subject Index

Page numbers in boldface refer to the main biography on the individual. Page numbers in italics refer to a photograph of the individual.

A

AA. *See* Architectural Association
AAB. *See* Arab African Bank
Abadan, Yavuz, 511
Abariq Muhashshama (Bayati), 168
Abath al-Qadr (Mahfouz), 487, 489
Abaza, Aziz, 485
Abba, Dimi Mint Benaissa, **1–4**
    music of, 1–3
Abba, Sidaty Ould, 1, 3
Abbas, Ehsan, 169
Abbas, Ferhat, 344
Abbas, Ihsan, 243
Abbas, Mahmud, *4,* **4–8**
    after Arafat's (Yasir) death, 5–6
    Barghuthi (Marwan) and, 151,
      152–153
    Dahlan (Muhammad) in govern-
      ment of, 5, 241
    in Fatah, 5, 6, 108
    Hamas and, 5, 7
    Haniyeh (Ismail) as prime minister
      and, 332
    international recognition of role of,
      7, 8
    in Palestinian national movement,
      4–5, 6
    in peace process, 4–8
    in PLO, 5
    political career of, 5–8
    as president of PA, 6–8, 241
    as prime minister of PA, 5, 7, 241
    Rajub (Jibril) in government of,
      241

Abbasgholizadeh, Mahboubeh, **8–10**, *9*
    NGO activism of, 8–10
    women's rights advocacy by, 8–10
Abd al-Aziz ibn Sa'ud Al Sa'ud (Ibn
    Sa'ud) (ruler of Saudi Arabia), 710
Abd al-Qader, Ahmad ben, **10–13**
    poets influenced by, 12
    in political opposition, 10–11
    writings of, 11–12
Abd al-Rahman, Umar
    arrest of, 550
    on Mahfouz (Naguib), 488
Abd al-Rahman bin Abdul Aziz, 710
Abd al-Sabbur, Salah, 623
Abdelaziz, Mohamed, **13–14**
Abdel-Moati, Mustafa, **14–15**
    art of, 14–15
    influence on Egyptian art, 14–15
Abd Rabbo, Yasser, in DFLP, 315
Abdul Hameed Shoman Foundation, 768
Abdullah (king of Saudi Arabia). *See*
    Sa'ud, Abdullah bin Abd al-Aziz al-
Abdullah I bin Hussein (king of Jordan)
    assassination of, 163, 376–377
    historic preservation relating to, 431
    Hussein bin Talal on, 377, 380
    reign of, 376
Abdullah II bin Hussein (king of
    Jordan), **15–19**, *16*
    accession of, 17, 379
    assassination attempts against, 292
    as crown prince, 16, 17, 377, 379
    domestic agenda of, 17
    Economic Consultative Council
      formed by, 736
    family of, 15–16
    military career of, 16–17
    in peace process, 17–18

    and Talhouni (Bassam al-), 794
    U.S. relations with, 17–19
    in war on terror, 18
Abid, Karim al-, 330
'Abir Sarir (Mustaghanmi), 560
Abla, Mohamed, 15
About Baghdad (film), 100, 101
Abtahi, Hasan, 19, 20
Abtahi, Mohamed Ali, *19,* **19–21**
    blog of, 21
    government career of, 19–21
    in Iranian Revolution, 19–20
    political views of, 20–21
Abtahi, Mohammad Taghi, 20
Abu Ali. *See* Bayati, Abd al-Wahhab al-
Abu Ammar. *See* Arafat, Yasir
Abu-Assad, Hany, *21,* **21–23**
    films of, 21–23
    on suicide bombers, 22–23
    Suleiman (Elia) compared to,
      786–787
Abu Dhabi
    Al Nahyan (Khalifa bin Zayid) as
      emir of, 62–65
    Al Nahyan (Khalifa bin Zayid) as
      prime minister of, 63
    Al Nahyan (Muhammad bin
      Zayid) as crown prince of, 66–72
    Al Nahyan (Zayid bin Sultan) as
      emir of, 62, 64, 65, 66
    domestic policies of, 70
    human rights in, 71–72
    international economic aid from,
      64, 65, 72
    on Iraq, U.S.-led occupation of,
      64–65, 69–70
    line of succession in, 66, 68
    military of, 63

Akat, Asaf Savas, 309
Akbank (financial institution), 670
Akcan, Nihat, 412
Akhar, al- (film), 234
Akhbari school of Shi'ism, 703
Akin, Vedat, 103
Akkad, Malek, 34
Akkad, Moustapha, *32,* **32–34**
    death of, 34
    films of, 32–34
AKP. *See* Adalet ve Kalkinma Partisi
Alaee Taleghani, Azam, **35–37**
    on Iranian Revolution, 35
    as presidential candidate, 35–36
    women's rights advocacy by,
      35–37
Alama, Ragheb, **37–39**
    music of, 37–39
Alam al-Fann Productions, 38
'Ala Marfa' al-Ayyam (Mustaghanmi),
    559, 560
Alami, Musa al-, 424
Al-Ani, Jananne, **39–40**
    photography of, 39
    video installation art of, 39–40
Al-Azm, Sadik, **40–42**
    academic career of, 40–41
    on Arab intellectual history, 40–41
Alberstein, Chava, **42–45**
    music of, 42–45
    political views of, 42, 43, 45
    Yiddish language used by, 42–45
Albright, Madeleine
    on Hussein (Saddam), 374
    on Iran, 437
Al Bu Falasa dynasty (Dubai), 496
Al Bu Nasir tribe (Iraq), 370
Al Bu Sa'id, Badr bin Hamad bin
    Hamood, **45–47**
    foreign policy role of, 46–47
    in peace process, 46–47
Al Bu Sa'id, Hamad bin Hamood, 45
Al Bu Sa'id, Qaboos (sultan of Oman),
    48, **48–52**
    accession of, 45, 48
    Al Bu Sa'id (Badr bin Hamad bin
      Hamood) and, 45
    Al Bu Sa'id (Hamad bin Hamood)
      working for, 45
    cabinet of, 50
    domestic policies of, 49–51
    education of, 48
    environmental policies of, 51, 52
    foreign policy of, 51
    military service of, 48, 49
    modernization under, 49
    Omanization by, 50
    opposition to, 49
    political reform by, 49–51
    successor to, 51

Zawawi (Omar bin Abd al-
    Munim) as adviser to, 853–855
Al Bu Sa'id, Sa'id bin Taymur (sultan of
    Oman)
    coup against (1970), 45, 48
    family of, 48
Al Bu Sa'id, Tariq bin Taymur, 50
Alexandria . . . Why? (film). *See*
    Iskandariyya . . . Leih?
Algeria
    Arabic language in, 561, 826–827,
      828
    art of (*See* Algerian art)
    Berbers in, 218, 252–253, 676
    Berber Spring (1980) in, 676
    censorship in, 658, 659, 660
    civil war of (*See* Algerian civil war)
    education in, 477–478, 480
    feminism in, 808–810
    films of (*See* Algerian films)
    foreign policy of, 215–219
    under France (*See* Algeria, French
      occupation of)
    Francophone influence in, 252, 254
    French language in, 180–181, 561,
      720, 826–827, 828, 829
    French oil concessions to, 216
    French relations with, post-inde-
      pendence, 216, 217–218
    government of (*See* Algerian elec-
      tions; Algerian government)
    history of (*See* Algerian history)
    human rights in, 335, 676
    independence of (*See* Algerian
      independence; Algerian War of
      Independence)
    Islamists in (*See* Algerian Islamist
      groups)
    journalism of Djaout (Taher) in,
      252, 253
    literature of (*See* Algerian literature;
      Algerian poetry)
    medicine in, Moqaddem (Malika)
      in, 543, 544
    military of, Khadra (Yasmina) in,
      417
    Moroccan border dispute with, 216
    music of (*See* Algerian music)
    national identity of (*See* Algerian
      identity; Algerian nationalism)
    psychiatry in, 675
    riots of 1988 in, 217, 335
    Saharawis in, 13–14
    Salafism in, 479
    secularism in, 343, 477–478,
      479–480
    sports in, Boulmerka (Hassiba) in,
      209–212
    theater of, Benaïssa (Slimane) in,
      178–191

translations in, Bayyud (In'am) in
    field of, 171–173
    U.S. relations with, 218
    on Western Sahara, 216–217,
      218, 356
    women of (*See* Algerian women)
Algeria, French occupation of
    (1830–1962), 342, 826
    education during, 826
    film about, 467
    Harbi (Mohamed) influenced
      by, 342
    Madani (Abbassi) opposing, 477, 479
    opposition to, 342, 826
    Racim (Muhammad) on, 645–646
Algerian art
    of Bayyud (In'am), 172
    of Mahieddine (Baya), 490–492
    of Mammeri (Azouaou), 645
    of Racim (Muhammad), 644–645
    of Sidera (Zineb), 771
Algerian Cement Company, 716
Algerian civil war (1990s), 826
    Boudjedra (Rachid) on,
      204–205, 207
    Bouteflika (Abdelaziz) during, 217
    French press coverage of, 205
    Khadra (Yasmina) on, 417–418
    and literature, 114
    reconciliation after, 217–219
    start of, 217
Algerian elections
    cancellation in 1991, 335, 477, 478
    Islamic Salvation Front in, 217,
      253, 335, 477, 478, 480
    presidential, Hannoun (Louisa) in,
      335, 336
Algerian films
    on Algerian War of Independence,
      33, 467–468
    documentaries, 255, 467
    Egyptian involvement in, 234
    Faudel in, 293
    on French colonization, 467
    of Lakhdar-Hamina
      (Muhammad), 466–469
    about women, 468–469
Algerian government and politics
    Bendjedid (Chadli) in, 217, 478, 480
    Benflis (Ali) in, 218, 219
    Boumédienne (Houari) in, 216–217
    Bouteflika (Abdelaziz) in, 215–220
    constitution of, 218, 219
    corruption in, 217
    coup of 1965 in, 216, 343
    coup of 1992 in, 217
    foreign policy of, 215–219
    Hannoun (Louisa) in, 334–337
    Harbi (Mohamed) in, 343
    Harbi (Mohamed) on, 343–344

Algerian government and politics,
continued
in literature, 113–114
opposition parties legalized in, 335,
478, 480
provisional, 343, 344
Zeroual (Liamine) in, 217
Algerian history
A'raj (Wasini al-) on, 114
Djebar (Assia) on, 256, 257–258
government rewriting of, 256
Harbi (Mohamed) on, 343–344
Algerian identity
cultural, 257–259
ethnic, 252–253
French colonization in, 342
Mustaghanmi (Ahlam) on,
560–561
Algerian independence
and education, 826
films about, 33, 467–468
in literature, 113
Racim (Muhammad) on, 644, 645
Wattar (al-Taher) on, 827–828
Algerian Islamist groups. *See also specific
groups*
assassination of critics of, 252
Boudjedra (Rachid) criticizing,
204–205
Boulmerka (Hassiba) on, 210–211
under Bouteflika (Abdelaziz), 217,
218, 219
Djaout (Taher) on, 252, 254
Djebar (Assia) on, 258
Hannoun (Louisa) on, 335
rise of, 253
Algerian League of Human Rights, 809
Algerian literature
Arabic *vs.* French language in, 113,
114, 206–207
by A'raj (Wasini al-), 112–115
by Bayyud (In'am), 172
by Benhedouga (Abdelhamid),
826, 827, 828
by Boudjedra (Rachid), 204–207
by Bouraoui (Nina), 212–214
on civil war (1990s), 204–205,
207, 417–418
by Djaout (Taher), 252–254
by Djebar (Assia), 254–259
after independence, 113
by Khadra (Yasmina), 417–419
by Laouedj (Zineb), 561
by Mustaghanmi (Ahlam),
558–562
by Sebbar (Leila), 720–721
sexuality in, 212–214
by Wattar (al-Taher), 825–829
women as subjects in, 213–214,
256–257, 258

Algerian music
of Faudel, 292–294
of Khaled (Cheb), 660
raï, 292–294
of Rimitti (Cheikha), 658–662
Algerian nationalism
competing groups in, 342–343
Djebar (Assia) on, 256
Madani (Abbassi) on, 479
Algerian People's Party (PPN),
342–343
Algerian poetry
by Bayyud (In'am), 172–173
by Boudjedra (Rachid), 205
by Bouraoui (Nina), 213
by Djaout (Taher), 253
by Laouedj (Zineb), 561
by Mustaghanmi (Ahlam),
559–560
Algerian War of Independence
(1954–1962)
Abbas (Ferhat) in, 344
Algerian writers as critics of,
252–253, 256, 258
Boudjedra (Rachid) in, 204
Bouteflika (Abdelaziz) in, 215
films on, 33, 467–468
French massacre of Algerian immigrants in (1961), 205, 206
French press coverage of, 205
Harbi (Mohamed) in, 343
Lakhdar-Hamina (Muhammad)
on, 467–468
literature about, 113
Madani (Abbassi) in, 477, 481
Mahieddine (Baya) during, 490
Mustaghanmi (Ahlam) on, 560,
561
Wattar (al-Taher) during, 825
Algerian White (Djebar). *See Blanc de
l'Algérie, le* (Djebar)
Algerian women
in Family Code, 219, 335, 809
feminism among, 808–810
films about, 468–469
literature about, 213–214,
256–257, 258
Mahieddine (Baya) on, 491
Moqaddem (Malika) on, 543, 544
Mustaghanmi (Ahlam) on, 560
restrictions on, 257
second-class status of, 335, 336
in sports, obstacles facing, 209–212
Toumi (Khalida) on, 809
Algiers Accords (1965), 216
Algiers Agreement (1975), 159, 372
Ali, Mustapha Abu, 786
Ali, Naji al-, 463
Alimut (Hanoch), 341
Alizadeh, Hossein, 738

Al Khalifa, Hamad bin Isa (king of
Bahrain), *52,* **52–56**
domestic policies of, 53–56
family of, 52, 54–55
as king *vs.* emir, 54
military service of, 52–53
political reforms by, 53–56, 701
Al Khalifa, Isa bin Salman (emir of
Bahrain)
death of, 52, 53, 701
family of, 52
petitions sent to, 701
power of, *vs.* Khalifa bin Salman, 57
Al Khalifa, Khalifa bin Salman, **56–60**
and Al Khalifa (Hamad bin Isa),
53, 55, 60
foreign policy role of, 57–58
government reform by, 57
and National Assembly, 58–59
political power of, 57, 59
as prime minister, 53, 55, 56–60
state security under, 59–60
Al Khalifa Family Council (AFC), 52,
54–55
Alliance of Civilizations, 537
Alliance of Palestinian Forces (APF),
316
Allon, Yigal, 639
All That Remains (Khalidi), 426
Almagor, Gila, **60–62**
in films, 60–62
in theater, 60–62
Al Maktum, Maktum Hashir Maktum,
190
Al Nahyan, Fatima bint Mubarak Al
Qudayra, 66–67
Al Nahyan, Hassa bint Muhammad bin
Khalifa bin Zayid, 62
Al Nahyan, Khalifa bin Zayid (emir of
Abu Dhabi), *62,* **62–66**
economic aid under, 64, 65
family of, 62
Gargash (Anwar) in government of,
301
on Iraq, U.S.-led occupation of,
64–65
and Maktum (Muhammad bin
Rashid al-), 498
military service of, 63
oil resources managed by, 62, 64
as president of UAE, 62, 65
as prime minister of Abu Dhabi, 63
Al Nahyan, Muhammad bin Zayid
(crown prince of Abu Dhabi), *66,*
66–72
as deputy crown prince, selection
of, 66, 68–69
domestic policy role of, 70
family of, 66–67
on human rights, 71–72

on Iraq, U.S.-led occupation of,
69–70
and Maktum (Muhammad bin
Rashid al-), 498
in offsets program, 71
political skills of, 67–68
in UAE military, 68, 70
Al Nahyan, Sultan bin Zayid, 68
Al Nahyan, Zayid bin Sultan (emir of
Abu Dhabi)
death of, 65
economic aid under, 64, 65
in establishment of UAE, 66
family of, 62, 66
legacy of, 65, 71
Alp, Sedat, 260
Al Sabah, Abdullah bin Salim (emir of
Kuwait), 75, 77
Al Sabah, Ahmad (emir of Kuwait), 75
Al Sabah, Hussa bin Sabah Al-Salim,
72–73, 76
Al Sabah, Jabir (emir of Kuwait), 75
Al Sabah, Jabir al-Ahmad al-Jabir (emir
of Kuwait), 75–76
Al Sabah, Jabir Ali al-Salim, 75
Al Sabah, Mubarak al-Kabir (emir of
Kuwait), 74
Al Sabah, Muhammad al-Sabah al-
Salim, 76
Al Sabah, Nasir al-Sabah al-Ahmad,
72–73, *73*
art collection of, 72–73, 76, 91
business career of, 72–73
political career of, 73, 76
Al Sabah, Nasir Muhammad al-
Ahmad, 76
Al Sabah, Nawwaf al-Ahmad al-Jabir,
76
Al Sabah, Sabah al-Ahmad al-Jabir
(emir of Kuwait), **73–78**, *74*
accession of, 74, 76
family of, 72, 73, 74–76
foreign policy role of, 74, 76–77
as prime minister, 74
Al Sabah, Sabah al-Salim (emir of
Kuwait), 75, 76
Al Sabah, Sa'd al-Abdullah (emir of
Kuwait), 74, 75–76, 77
Al Sabah, Salim (emir of Kuwait), 75
Al Sabah family, line of succession in,
74–76
Al Sa'ud, Abdullah bin Abd Al-Aziz. *See*
Sa'ud, Abdullah bin Abd al-Aziz al-
Al Sa'ud, Al-Walid bin Talal, *78,*
78–82
business career of, 78–79, 81–82
family of, 78–79
investments of, 79–82
philanthropy of, 80–82
wealth of, 78, 79, 81

Al Sa'ud, Dalal, 78–79
Al Sa'ud, Fahd bin Abd al-Aziz (king of
Saudi Arabia), 710–711, 712
Al Sa'ud, Faysal bin Abd al-Aziz (king
of Saudi Arabia), 710, 712
Al Sa'ud, Khalid bin Abd al-Aziz (king
of Saudi Arabia), 710
Al Sa'ud, Sultan bin Abd al-Aziz (prince
of Saudi Arabia), 710, 711
Al Sa'ud, Sultan bin Salman, *82,* **82–84**
family of, 82–83
military service of, 83
space flight of, 83–84
Al Sa'ud, Talal bin Abd al-Aziz, 78
Al Sa'ud, Turki bin Faysal bin abd al-
Aziz, 433
Al Sa'ud family
Hariri's (Rafiq) construction work
for, 345
history of, 78–79, 82–83
Al Thani, Ahmad bin Ali (emir of
Qatar), coup against (1972), 87
Al Thani, Hamad bin Jasim bin Jabr
(HBJ), **84–87**, *85*
family of, 84, 86
foreign policy role of, 84–87
on al-Jazeera, 87
oil trust fund managed by, 85
wealth of, 86
Al Thani, Hamad bin Khalifa (emir of
Qatar), *87,* **87–91**
accession of, 88–89
Al Thani's (HBJ) ties with, 85
coup attempt against (1996),
88–89
coup by (1995), 85, 88
as crown prince, 85, 88
domestic policies of, 89–90
family of, 87
al-Jazeera established by, 536
military service of, 87, 88
Ministry of Information abolished
by, 536
reign of, 88–91, 534, 535
religious freedom under, 89
wives of, 90, 534–538
women's rights under, 89–90
Al Thani, Khalifa bin Hamad (emir of
Qatar)
Al Thani (HBJ) under, 85
coup against (1995), 85, 88
coup by (1972), 87
Al Thani, Mariam bint Hamad, 535
Al Thani, Muhammad bin Thani (emir
of Qatar), 87
Al Thani, Nura bint Khalid, 535
Al Thani, Sa'ud bin Muhammad bin
Ali, **91–92**
art collection of, 73, 91–92
wealth of, 91

Alumot (kibbutz), 611
Amal Ghayr al-Kamila, al- (Samman),
705
Amal Movement (Lebanon), 290, 569,
570
Amam al-Arsh (Mahfouz), 488, 489
Amari, Raja, **92–93**
films of, 92–93
Am Ehad Party (Israel)
Labor Party merging with, 617
Peretz (Amir) in, 617
Amer, Ghada, **93–94**
art of, 93–94
on female sexuality, 93–94
Amer, Magda, 634
American University of Beirut (AUB)
Ashrawi (Hanan Mikha'il) at, 126
Habash (George) at, 313–314
Khalidi (Walid) at, 424
Zurayk (Constantine) at, 425
Amichai, Yehuda, 654
Amin, Ahmad, 95
Amin, Galal, **95–97**
academic career of, 95–97
on economics, 95–97
on technology, 96, 97
writings of, 96, 97
Amin, Ibrahim al-, 570
Amina (film), 691
Amiralay, Umar, **97–98**
films of, 97–98
"Amir al-Khalidin" (Abd al-Qader), 12
Amir-Gholi, Parvin, 453
Amman (Jordan)
Arafat's (Yasir) PLO headquarters
in, 108
historic preservation in, 431
hotel bombings (2005) in, 34
Ammar Center for Architectural
Heritage, 99
Amnesty International
on Bahraini human rights, 699
on Madani (Abbassi), 480
on Moroccan human rights, 555
on Yemeni human rights, 708–709
Amour, la fantasia, L' (Djebar). *See*
Fantasia (Djebar)
Amour bilingue (Khatibi), 439, 440
Amour impossible, l' (Ebnou), 268–269
Andalusian culture, music in, 201–203
Andre, Carl, 360
Anfal campaign (1988) (Iraq), 159,
493, 494, 495, 790
Anfas (journal), 186, 459–460
Angawi, Sami, **99**
on historic preservation, 99
social activism of, 99
Angry Arab News Service, 25
Ankara State Conservatory, Kenter
(Yildiz) in, 412

An Nahar (newspaper), Kassir (Samir) writing in, 409, 410
Annan, Kofi, 221
Annan Plan for Cyprus, 604–605, 782, 792–793
Ansar Burney Welfare Trust, 72
Ansar-e Hezbollah (Islamic militant group), 266, 742, 743
Anthem, national, of Egypt, 819
Anthropology, social, Yamani (Mai) in, 833–834
Anti-Semitism
    Islamic, 527
    Khalidi (Rashid) accused of, 422–423
    Meddeb (Abdelwahhab) on, 527
    of Tlas (Mustafa Abd al-Qadir), 803
    Western, 527
Antoon, Sinan, **99–101**
    academic career of, 100
    films of, 100, 101
    poetry of, 100
    on U.S.-led invasion and occupation of Iraq, 100–101
Antun, Farah, 325
Aoun, Michel, *101,* **101–103**
    in exile in France, 101, 102
    Hizbullah supporting, 571
    military career of, 101–102
    and Nasrallah (Hasan), 571
    in National Assembly, 102–103
    political career of, 101–103
    as prime minister, 101–102, 465
APF. *See* Alliance of Palestinian Forces
April Understanding (1996), 346
Aqaba (Jordan), historic preservation in, 431
Aqaba summit (2003)
    Abbas (Mahmud) in, 7
    Abdullah II bin Hussein in, 17–18
    Dahlan (Muhammad) in, 241
Aqd al-Lu'lu (television show), 462
Aqqad, Abbas, 485
Aqsa Intifada, al- (2000–)
    Barghuthi (Marwan) in, 150, 152, 155
    Dahlan (Muhammad) in, 240
    Margalit (Dan) on, 515
    Shimoni (Kobi) on, 766
    start of, 7, 110, 750
Aqsa Martyrs' Brigade, al-, Barghuthi (Marwan) in, 152
Ar, Müjde, **103–106**
    acting career of, 103–106
    activism of, 104, 106
Arab(s)
    in Israel (*See* Palestinian citizens of Israel)
    nationalism of (*See* Arab nationalism)
    women (*See* Arab women)

Arab Afghans, 194, 195
Arab African Bank (AAB), 854
Arab-American music, Shaheen (Simon) in, 730–732
Arab Bank, 767–769
    during Arab–Israel War (1948), 767, 768
    controversy over, 769
    establishment of, 767, 768
    growth of, 768–769
Arab Cables, 716
Arab Children's Congress (1980), 579
Arab Commando Battalions, 314
Arab Cooperation Council, 380
Arab Endowment for Democracy, 384
Arab exceptionalism, 385
Arab Human Development Report, Amin's (Galal) criticism of, 96
Arabian Nights. See One Thousand and One Arabian Nights
Arabian oryx, 51
Arabic calligraphy
    in Boullata's (Kamal) art, 208–209
    Khatibi (Abdel Kebir) on, 439
    in Saudi's (Mona) art, 715
    in Sharqawi's (Ahmad) art, 753, 754
Arabic free verse movement
    Bayati (Abd al-Wahhab al-) in, 168–171, 503
    Mala'ika (Nazik al-) in, 501, 502–504
    Sayyab (Badr Shakir al-) in, 169, 503
Arabic language
    in Algeria, 180–181, 561, 826–827, 828
    in Algerian literature, 113, 114, 206–207
    in Algerian music, 294
    Benaïssa (Slimane) on, 180–181
    in Egyptian theater, 325, 326
    in Khaled's (Amr) preaching, 420
    Khatibi (Abdel Kebir) on, 439, 440
    Khoury's (Makram) acting in, 450, 451
    in Lebanese music, 296, 298, 299
    in Mauritanian literature, 12, 268
    in Moroccan literature, 439
    in Morocco, 460, 675, 796, 797
    in Sudanese music, 400–401
    in Tunisia, 516, 518
Arabic literature. *See also* Arabic free verse movement
    by A'raj (Wasini al-), 112–115
    Darraj (Faisal) on, 242–244
    development of, 482–483
    by Habibi (Emile), 318–320
    isolation of authors of, 113
    literary criticism of, 242–244
    of Madini (Ahmad al-), 481–484

Arabic lute, 739–740
Arabic script, in Boullata's (Kamal) art, 208–209
Arab ideology, Laroui (Abdallah) on, 471–472
Arab intellectual history
    Al-Azm (Sadik) on, 40–41
    self-criticism in, 40–41, 425
    Zurayk (Constantine) on, 425
Arab–Israeli conflict
    Arafat's (Yasir) role in, 108–112
    Aumann (Robert) on, 130
    documentaries on, 144
    films on, 21–23, 97–98, 144
    Hamas in, 834, 835, 836, 837
    intifadas in (*See* Aqsa Intifada; Intifada, first)
    in Jerusalem, 587
    Khalidi (Rashid) on, 421–423
    Kimmerling (Baruch) on, 454–456
    Margalit (Dan) on, 514, 515
    and Operation Summer Rains, 588
    Palestinian literature on, 318–319
    Palestinian poetry on, 244–247
    peace negotiations in (*See* Peace process; *specific events*)
    Qaradawi (Yusuf) on, 634
    right of return in, 244, 333
    Sa'id (Ali Ahmad) on, 683, 684
    Said (Edward) on, 685, 686–688
    Segev (Tom) on, 724
    Shikaki (Khalil) on, 764–765
    two-state solution to (*See* Two-state solution)
    U.S. role in, Habash (George) on, 316
Arab-Israelis. *See* Palestinian citizens of Israel
Arab–Israeli War (1948)
    Abbas (Mahmud) in, 4, 6
    Arab Bank during, 767, 768
    Arafat (Yasir) in, 107
    Chacour (Elias) in, 229
    and democracy in Arab regimes, 385
    films on, 144
    Habash (George) in, 313
    Haniyeh (Ismail) in, 331, 332–333
    Hurvitz (Eli) in, 368
    Khalidi (Walid) on, 424–426
    Rabin (Yitzhak) in, 640
    Sa'id (Ali Ahmad) on, 684
    Said (Edward) on, 686
    Segev (Tom) during, 723
    Sharon (Ariel) in, 748
    Tumarkin (Igael) on, 813
Arab–Israeli War (1956), Sharon (Ariel) in, 749
Arab–Israeli War (1967)
    Al-Azm (Sadik) on, 40–41
    Arab self-criticism after, 40–41

in Israel, of Hamas leaders, 332,
333
Israeli Supreme Court on, 147
in Syria, Jumblatt (Walid) on, 396
Assembly of Experts (Iran), 350, 540,
541
Assia Chemical Labs Ltd., 368
Association de Recherche Culturelle
(ARC) (Morocco), 460
Association for Civil Rights in Israel
(ACRI), 390
Association for Equality between Men
and Women (Algeria), 809
Association for the Support of Women
Voters, 383
Association of Algerian *Ulama*
(AUMA), 479
Association of Combatant Clergy
(MRM), 435
Association of Space Explorers, 83
Association of Women Writers and
Journalists NGO, 9
Assyrian Church of the East, Mar
Dinkha IV as patriarch of, 762
Astromega racing team, 190
Astronauts
Al Sa'ud (Sultan bin Salman),
83–84
Faris (Muhammad Ahmad), 83
Ramon (Ilan), 650–651
Aswan Dam
film about, 233
Sawaris (Onsi) building, 716
Atasi, Nur al-Din al-, coup of 1970
against, 121
Atatürk, Mustafa Kemal
Dündar's (Can) biographical writ-
ings on, 260
in Kulin's (Ayşe) novels, 457
presidency of, 725
Athletics. *See* Sports
Atif, Muhammad, 194
Atiyya, Abdullah bin Hamad al-, 85
Attack, The (Khadra), 418
Attentat, l' (Khadra), 418
Attia, Ezra, 841
Atwood, Margaret, 600–601
Atyaf (Ashour), 125
AU. *See* African Union
AUB. *See* American University of
Beirut
Audeh, Nazek, 344
Au-delá du voile (Benaïssa), 179
AUMA. *See* Association of Algerian
Ulama
Aumann, Robert, *129*, **129–131**
on Arab–Israeli conflict, 130
on game theory, 129–130
Nobel Prize to, 129
Aung San Suu Kyi, 268

Auteur filmmakers, 784, 785
"Autobiographical Andmardk"
(Tumarkin), 812
Autobiography
in Bouraoui's (Nina) novels, 213
of Tumarkin (Igael), 813–814
"Autobiography of An Arab
Executioner, The" (Qabbani), 623
Automobile driving, by women, 134
Auto racing
Beschir (Khalil) in, 190–191
Seddigh (Laleh) in, 721–722
Autumn: October in Algiers (film), 469
Aux Sources du Raï (Rimitti), 659
Avant-garde art, of Amer (Ghada),
93–94
Avant-garde poetry, of Bannis
(Mohammed), 145
Avnery, Uri, Abbas (Mahmud) meeting
with, 6
A'waj, Zeinab al-, 112, 113
Awda, Salman al-, **131–135**
audiotapes of sermons of, 132
bin Ladin (Usama) influenced by,
133
on dialogue with West, 134
on Gulf War (1990–1991),
131–132
on human rights, 132–133
on Iraq insurgency, 134
in Sahwa movement, 131–135
on social justice, 132
on terrorism, 133, 134
Wahhabism of, 131–135
website of, 133–134
on women's rights, 132, 134
Awdat al-ibn al-dhal (film), 234
Awdat al-Ruh (Hakim), 325
Awdat al-Wa'i (Hakim), 325, 326
Awja, al- (Iraq), Hussein (Saddam) in,
370
Awlad Haratina (Mahfouz), 487–488,
489
Awraq al-Zaytun (Darwish), 245
AWSA. *See* Arab Women's Solidarity
Association
"Axis of evil," Iran in, 438
Ayalon, Ami, 153
Ayhan, Süreyya, *135*, **135–137**
athletic career of, 135–137
Ayhan, Yaşar, 135–136
Ayn, al- (Abu Dhabi), 63
Ayn al-Faras (Chaghmoum), 482
Ayneh (film), 602
Ayyam al-Sadat (film), 850
Aziz, Tariq, 509
Azzam, Abdullah al-, 193, 194
Azzawi, Dia al-, **137–139**
art of, 137–139
writings of, 138

Azzawi, Fadhil al-, **139–141**
novels of, 139–141
poetry of, 139–141
political activism of, 139

B

Ba'albek Festival, 296–297
Baba Amin (film), 232
Bab achams (Khoury), 448
Bab al-Hadid (film), 232
Badawi, Abd al-Rahman, 485
Badie, Asad, 566
Badkonake Sefid (film), 602
Badr Brigade (Iraq), 507, 509
Baghdad
Iraq Museum in, 137
Sadr City section of, 678
Baghdad Academy of Music, El Saher
(Kazem) at, 279
Ba'Gilgul Hazeh (Hanoch), 340–341
Bagimsiz Cumhuriyet Partisi (BCP)
(Turkey), 782
Bahrain
Al Khalifa (Isa bin Salman) as emir
of, 52, 53, 57
Al Khalifa (Hamad bin Isa) as king
of, 52–56
Al Khalifa (Khalifa bin Salman) as
prime minister of, 53, 55, 56–60
banking industry in, 59
in border disputes with Qatar,
85–86, 90–91
as constitutional monarchy, 53–54
constitution of, 53, 54, 58
coup attempt of 1981 in, 699, 700,
702
economic development in, 59, 60
elections of 2002 in, 702, 703
elections of 2006 in, 702, 703
foreign policy of, 57–58
government reform in, 57
human rights in, 55, 60, 699, 700,
702
Iranian relations with, 57–58
military of, 52–53
modernization in, 58
National Charter of, 54, 55
parliament of, 53, 54, 59
petitions drafted in, 700–701
political reforms in, 53–56, 701
Qasim (Shaykh Isa) as cleric in, 700
Qatari relations with, 85–86,
90–91
Salman (Ali) as cleric in, 699,
700–702
Shi'ite Muslims in, 699, 700–702,
703
state security apparatus in, 59–60
women's citizenship rights in, 53

Bayanuni, Ali Sadr al-Din, *166,* **166–167**
  in Muslim Brotherhood, 166–167
  political career of, 166–167
Bay'at al-Imam (militant group), 851, 852
Bayati, Abd al-Wahhab al-, *167,* **167–171**
  academic career of, 167–168
  diplomatic career of, 168, 170
  Laabi (Abdellatif) translating works of, 460
  poetry of, 167–171, 503
  political activism of, 168
  travels of, 168–171
Bayn al-Qasrayn (Mahfouz), 487
Bayt al-Ud al-Arabi (Arab Ud House) (Cairo), 739
Bayya al-Khawatim (film), 233
Bayyud, In'am, **171–173**
  art of, 172
  poetry of, 172–173
  translations by, 171–173
BCP. *See* Bagimsiz Cumhuriyet Partisi
BDF. *See* Bahrain Defense Force
Beautiful Creations of Fadhil al-Azzawi, The (Azzawi), 140
Beethoven, Ludwig van, 196
Before Their Diaspora (Khalidi), 426
Begin, Menachem
  Olmert (Ehud) and, 586–587
  Oz (Amos) on, 595
  in peace process, 548
  as prime minister, 613, 641
  Sharon (Ariel) under, 749–750
Behbahani, Hassan, 173
Behbahani, Simin, **173–176**
  family of, 173–174
  Nobel Prize nomination for, 175–176
  poetry of, 173–176
  political activism of, 174–175
  women's rights advocacy by, 174–175
Behesti, Mohammad Hossain, 532
Behold the Fire and the Wood: But Where is the Lamb for a Burnt Offering? (Tumarkin), 813
Beilin, Yossi
  in peace talks with Oman, 46
  and Peretz (Amir), 616
Beinisch, Dorit, 515
  and judicial review, 148
Beirut (Lebanon)
  Arafat's (Yasir) PLO headquarters in, 108
  Israeli siege of (1982), poetry on, 246
  Kassir (Samir) on history of, 409
  reconstruction of, 346
  U.S. Marine barracks bombing in (1983), 289

Beirut '75 (Samman), 705
Beirut Nightmares (Samman), 705
Béji, Hélé, **176–178**
  academic career of, 176–178
  family of, 176–177
  writings of, 176–178
Belhadj, Ali
  on democracy, 479
  in Islamic Salvation Front, 477, 478, 479, 480
Belief, Saïda. *See* Rimitti, Cheikha
Belkhadem, Abdelaziz, 219
Bell, Gertrude, 137
Belloua, Faudel. *See* Faudel
Benaïssa, Slimane, **178–181**
  acting career of, 179–180
  in exile in France, 179, 180
  in theater, 178–181
  writings of, 178–181
Ben Ali, Zein al-Abidin, **181–183**
  coup of 1987 by, 182
  human rights under, 182–183
  military service of, 182
  presidency of, 181–183
  as prime minister, 182
Benayoun, Yossi, *183,* **183–185**
  athletic career of, 183–185
  military service of, 184
Ben Badis, Abdelhamid, 479
Ben Barka, Mehdi, 354, 355, 357
Ben Bella, Ahmad
  Abbas (Ferhat) and, 344
  Boumédienne's (Houari) rivalry with, 216
  Bouteflika (Abdelaziz) in government of, 215–216
  coup against (1965), 216, 343
  Harbi (Mohamed) as aide to, 343
Bendjedid, Chadli
  coup against (1992), 217, 478
  in elections of 1991, 335
  opposition parties legalized by, 478, 480
  presidency of, 217, 478, 480
Benedict XVI (pope), 729
Benflis, Ali, 219
  political career of, 218, 219
  as prime minister, 218, 219
Ben-Gurion, David
  and Peres (Shimon), 610, 611, 612–613
  as prime minister, 612
  and Rabin (Yitzhak), 640, 641
  Rafi Party founded by, 612
Benhedouga, Abdelhamid, 826, 827, 828
Benim Adim Kirmiz (Pamuk), 599
Ben-Itzchak, Baruch, 338
Benjamin, Roger, 645, 646

Ben Jelloun, Tahar, **185–190**
  academic career of, 186
  education of, 185–186
  military service of, 186
  poetry of, 186–187
  Shukri's (Muhammad) book published by, 797
  writings of, 185–189
Benkirane, Abdul Ilah, 354
Benmenni, Abdelhammid, assassination of, 252
Bennis, Mohammed. *See* Bannis, Mohammed
Ben Yosef, Mirit, 184
Berbers
  in Algeria, 218, 252–253, 676
  identity of, 252–253
  Kabyle tribe of, 218
  literature of, 252–253
  in Morocco, 796, 797
  Sadi (Said) on, 676
  in Sharqawi's (Ahmad) art, 753–755
  Tawfiq (Ahmad at-) on, 796, 797
Berber Spring (1980), 676
Berlin Film Festival awards
  to Ceylan (Nuri Bilge), 226
  to Chahine (Youssef), 234
Berry, Halle, 667, 668
Beschir, Khalil, **190–191**
  racing career of, 190–191
Betar Youth Organization (Israel), 586
Beurs (French North Africans), Faudel as, 292–294
Beyaz Kale (Pamuk), 598–599
Beyond the Veil: Male-Female Dynamics in a Modern Muslim Society (Mernissi), 529
Beyond the Walls (film), 248
BFM. *See* Bahrain Freedom Movement
Bible codes research, 130
Bid, Ali Salim al-
  as PDRY president, 692, 693, 694
  as vice president of Yemen, 692, 693, 694
Bidad (Shajarian), 737–738
"Biladi, Biladi" (Egyptian national anthem), 819
Bin Ladin, Muhammad bin Awad, 191
Bin Ladin, Usama, *191,* **191–195**
  Abu Ghayth (Sulayman) working with, 23–24
  in Afghanistan, 192–194
  assassination attempts against, 192, 193
  Awda (Salman al-) influencing, 133
  Azzam (Abdullah al-) influencing, 193, 194
  education of, 192
  family of, 191
  Faqih's (Sa'd al-) links to, 292

and Omani military, 49–50
Palestinian mandate of
(1917–1948), 318, 639–640, 724
Qatar as protectorate of, 88
Salman (Ali) in exile in, 701
Saudi opposition groups in,
291–292
in Suez Crisis (1956–1957), 612
United Arab Emirates controlled
by, 496–497
British School of Archaeology, 137
Brizzi, Gianni, 708
Brookings Institution
Barnea (Nahum) at, 154
Shikaki (Khalil) at, 764, 765
Burg, Avraham, 616
Burney, Ansar, 72
"Burning Dress, The" (Ravikovitch),
656
Burning Sands (film), 60–61
Bush, George H. W., in Gulf War
(1990–1991), 373
Bush, George W.
on Abbas (Mahmud), 7, 8
Abdullah II bin Hussein and,
17–18
Ahmadinejad's open letter to
(2006), 28
on Arafat (Yasir), 110
on "axis of evil," 438
on Dahlan (Muhammad), 241
and ElBaradei (Mohamed), 274
Fadlallah (Muhammad Husayn)
on, 289
and Iran, possible attack on, 70
on Iran as threat, 29, 438
in Iranian art, 306
Iraqi invasion by (2003), 374
Jumblatt (Walid) meeting with,
397
Khouri (Rami) on policies of, 446
Lahham (Duraid) on, 464
Qatari–U.S. relations under, 87
Roadmap to Peace initiative of, 7,
17–18
Syrian–U.S. relations under, 118
Turkey praised by, 286
Turkish–U.S. relations under, 261,
286
Bustani, Lisa al-, 295
Bustani, Nida, 344

C

CAC. *See* Comité Africain de Cinéastes
Cairo Station (film). *See Bab al-Hadid*
Cairo Trilogy, The (Mahfouz). *See*
Thulathiyya, al- (Mahfouz)
Cairo University, Boutros-Ghali
(Boutros) at, 220

Calligraphy, Persian, in Neshat's
(Shirin) art, 94. *See also* Arabic
calligraphy
Camel racing, 72
Campaign to Stop Stoning to Death,
10, 680
Camp David Accords (1978)
Barak (Aharon) in, 146
Begin (Menachem) in, 548
Boutros-Ghali (Boutros) in, 220
and foreign aid to Jordan, 735–736
Hussein bin Talal rejecting, 379
Sadat (Anwar) in, 548
Camp David Summit (2000)
Arafat (Yasir) in, 109–110
Barak (Ehud) in, 110
El Sarraj (Eyad) in, 281
failure of, 109–110
Campus Watch, 422, 456
Cannes Film Festival awards
to Ceylan (Nuri Bilge), 226, 228
to Chahine (Youssef), 234
to Ghobadi (Bahman), 308
to Hondo (Med), 364
Capitalism, Amin's (Galal) criticism of,
95–97
Capital punishment, in Turkey, 584,
585
Çapli, Bülent, 260
Capsi, Mati, 339
Cardiff Bay Opera House (Wales),
architecture of, 322
Car driving, by women, 134
Car racing. *See* Auto racing
Carter, Jimmy, on Barak (Aharon), 146
Carthage Film Festival awards, to
Chahine (Youssef), 234
Casablanca (Morocco)
bombings in (2001), 555
massacre in (1965), 460
Catholic Church
Chaldean, 762
Maronite, 726, 728–730, 750
Melkite, 229–232
Roman, 762
CBS Records, 42
Cedar Revolution (2005), 347, 571
Gemayyel (Amine) in, 397
press coverage of, 25
Çelik, Zeki, 136
Censorship
in Algeria, 658, 659, 660
in Egypt, 277, 488, 665
by Hamas, 848–849
in Iran, 9, 266, 350–351, 436, 443,
470, 606, 680, 742–743, 777,
778
in Iraq, 651
in Jordan, 547
in Lebanon, 756

in Morocco, 459, 555
in Saudi Arabia, 834
self-censorship, 771
Center for Palestine Research and
Studies (Nablus), 764
Center for Strategic Studies (CSS)
(Jordan), 326, 327
Center for the Study of Built
Environment (CSBE) (Jordan), 811
"Center Periphery Relations: A Key to
Turkish Politics?" (Mardin),
511–512
Center Union Party (Cyprus), 604
Central Intelligence Agency (CIA)
in Iraqi coup (1953), 539
Iraqi National Congress supported
by, 235–236
Jordanian cooperation with, 18
Centre d'Art Dramatique (Morocco),
673
Ceramics, by Tamari (Vera), 795
Çetin, Hikmet, **223–225**, *224*
diplomatic career of, 223, 224–225
political career of, 223–224
Cevdet Bey ve Ogullari (Pamuk), 597
Ceylan, Ebru, 226, 228
Ceylan, Emine, 227
Ceylan, Fatma, 226, 227
Ceylan, Mehmet Emin, 226, 227
Ceylan, Nuri Bilge, *226*, **226–229**
films of, 226–229
photography of, 226
Chacour, Elias, **229–232**
Mar Elias Educational Institutions
under, 229–231
writings of, 229, 230, 231
Chaghmoum, El Miloudi, 482
Chahine, Youssef, *232*, **232–235**
in exile in Lebanon, 233
films of, 232–235
political influences on, 234
Chain of Hope UK, 832
Chait, Galit, 405
Chalabi, Abd al-Hadi, 235
Chalabi, Ahmad, **235–236**
influence on U.S. invasion of Iraq,
235–236
in Iraqi National Congress,
235–236
Chaldean Catholic Church, Emmanuel
III Delly as patriarch of, 762
Chamber of Deputies (Jordan), 378
Chamoun, Jean Khalil, 521
Chanderli, Djamel, 467
Changed Identities: The Challenge of the
New Generation in Saudi Arabia
(Yamani), 833
Chaos of the Senses (Mustaghanmi). *See*
Fawda al-Hawas (Mustaghanmi)
Charity work. *See* Philanthropy

Charles (prince of Wales), on Hadid's (Zaha) architecture, 323

"Charrag Gataa" (Rimitti), 659, 661

Charter for Peace and National Reconciliation (Algeria), 218, 219

Chaulet, Pierre, 467

Chavez, Hugo, on Ahmadinejad (Mahmoud), 30

Chebaa, Mohamed, 186

Chehayeb, Akram, 396

Chemical weapons, in Kurdish genocide, 159, 495, 790

Chercheurs d'os, Les (Djaout), 253, 254

Cherkaoui, Ahmed. *See* Sharqawi, Ahmad

"Chess" (Alberstein), 43

Chicago Tribune (newspaper), 396

Chighaly, Aicha Mint, 3

Children
abuse of, in Iran, 265
Alberstein's (Chava) music for, 43–44
in camel racing, 72
Iraqi documentary about, 652
mental health of, 281
rights of, in Iran, 265, 402
welfare of, in Jordan, 579–580

Children of Fire (film), 521

Children of Gebelawi (Mahfouz). *See Awlad Haratina* (Mahfouz)

Children of Shatila (film), 521

China, Saudi relations with, 712–713

Chirac, Jacques, Algerian relations with, 217

Choeka, Aharon, 841

"Cholera" (Mala'ika), 502

CHP. *See* Cumhuriyet Halk Partisi

Chraïbi, Driss, 187, 207

Christian Lebanese Forces (CLF), in Lebanon War (1982), 396

Chronicle of a Disappearance (film), 785–786

Chronicle of the Years of Embers (film), 468

Chronique des années de braise (film), 468

Chroniques de la citadelle d'exil (Laabi), 460

CIA. *See* Central Intelligence Agency

CICONEST construction company, 345

Ciechanover, Aaron, **236–238**, *237*
Hershko's (Avram) work with, 237, 362–363
research on proteins, 236–238, 362

Çiller, Tansu, 224

Cinema Jedid (Arab new wave cinema), 805–806

Circle, The (film). *See Dayereh*

Circumcision, female, 278

Citicorp, Al Sa'ud (Al-Walid bin Talal) in bailout of, 79, 81

Citizenship
in Bahrain, for women, 53
in Israel, Bishara (Azmi) on, 199

Civilian attacks, in jihad, 194–195

Civil liberties, Barak (Aharon) on, 147, 148

Civil rights
Amiralay (Umar) on, 97–98
in Iran, Ebadi (Shirin) advocating, 263–268

Clerides, Glafcos, 604, 605

CLF. *See* Christian Lebanese Forces

Clinton, Bill
Chalabi (Ahmad) supported by, 235–236
on Hamas, 520
Hamidi (Ibrahim) and, 330, 331
at Hussein bin Talal's funeral, 380
Iranian relations with, 437
at Oslo Accords signing, 109
Qatari relations under, 87

Clinton, Hillary Rodham, 380

Clitoridectomy, 278

Clive of India treasures, 91–92

Closer (film), 619, 620

Clothing, women's. *See also*
Headscarves; *Hijab;* Veiling
in sports, 209, 212, 276

Coalition Provisional Authority (CPA) (Iraq), 775

"Coffeeshop Ladies" (exhibition), 306

Cohen, Eli, 61

Cold War
Syria after end of, 122
UN role after, 220–221

Cole, Juan, 34

Colères du silence, les (Benaïssa), 180

Colleges and universities. *See also specific schools*
Al Sa'ud's (Al-Walid bin Talal) donations to, 80
Khalidi (Rashid) on academic freedom at, 423

Colonialism, films about, 364

Colonial paradigm, Kimmerling (Baruch) on, 455

Columbia space shuttle, 650–651

Columbia University, Khalidi (Rashid) at, 421, 423

Comedies (film), Israeli, 248, 249

Comedy, of Lahham (Duraid), 461–464

Comité Africain de Cinéastes (CAC), 364

Commentaries, political
by AbuKhalil (As'ad), 25–26
by Amin (Galal), 96, 97
by Khouri (Rami), 445
by Lahham (Duraid), 463, 464

Commercial law, in Jordan, 793–794

Commission d'Arbitrage (Morocco). *See* Indemnity Commission

Committee for the Defense of Democratic Liberties and Human Rights (Syria), 563–564

Committee for the Defense of Legitimate Rights (CDLR), 290–291

Committee of the Four (Iraq), 494

Communism. *See also specific political parties*
of Bayati (Abd al-Wahhab al-), 168
of Bishara (Azmi), 196–197
in Iraq, 371–372

Communitarianism
Bishara (Azmi) on, 199
Jabarin (Hasan) on, 390

Comprehensive Peace Agreement (2005) (Sudan), 163, 524

Concerts
by Alama (Ragheb), 37–39
by El Saher (Kazem), 279
by Faudel, 293, 294
by Hanoch (Shalom), 340–341
by Umm Kulthum, 819, 820, 821

Congress, U.S., Iraqi Liberation Act passed by (1998), 236

Connery, Sean, 34

Conseil Consultatif des Droits de l'Homme (Morocco). *See* Royal Advisory Council on Human Rights

Conseil de discipline, le (Benaïssa), 179

Conservation, environmental, in Oman, 51

Considérations sur le malheur arabe (Kassir), 409–410

Constitution(s). *See under specific countries*

Constitutional Court (Turkey), 725, 726

Constitutional Democratic Rally (RCD) (Tunisia), 182

Constitutional law, in Israel, 147–148

Construction industry
bin Ladin family in, 191
Hariri (Rafiq) in, 345, 346

Consultative Council (Bahrain), 54, 58

Consultative Council (Morocco), 357

Contract law, in Israel, 148

Contre-prêches: Chroniques (Meddeb), 524–525, 526–527

Convergence plan. *See* Realignment plan

Copaxone, 368

Coptic Orthodox Church, in Egypt, Shenouda III as patriarch of, 761–763

Copts, in Egypt
in business community, 715
terrorism against, 761–763

VOLUME 1: 1–458; VOLUME 2: 459–860

Maktum (Muhammad bin Rashid
al-) as emir of, 496, 500
Maktum (Rashid bin Saʿid al-) as
emir of, 498
military of, 498
poetry of, by Maktum
(Muhammad bin Rashid al-),
497, 500
prosperity of, 499, 500
ruling family of, 496, 498
Salman (Ali) in exile in, 701
tourism in, 499
Dubai Chamber of Commerce and
Industry (DCCI), 301, 302
Dubai Defense Force (DDF), 498
Due process, in Israel, 149
Dujail (Iraq), 1982 massacre in, 374
Dündar, Can, **259–261**
journalism of, 259–261
on Turkish history, 260
on Turkish politics, 259–261
Duras, Marguerite, 213
Duri, Izzat Ibrahim al-, 494

E

Earthquake, The (Wattar). *See Zilzal,
al-* (Wattar)
Eastern Orthodox Church, Ignatius IV
as patriarch of, 762
East of Suez strategy, of Britain, 57
Ebadi, Mohammad-Ali, 263
Ebadi, Shirin, **263–268**, *264*
on coup of 1953, 264–265
family of, 263, 264
feminism of, 265, 267
human rights advocacy by,
263–268
Kar (Mehrangiz) working with,
403
Khorasani (Nushin Ahmadi) and,
443
legal career of, 263–268
Nobel Peace Prize won by, 263,
266, 267, 443, 444
political views of, 264–265
writings of, 264, 265, 267
Ebarahimi, Frashad, 266
Eberhardt, Isabelle, 544
Ebnou, Moussa Ould, **268–270**
isolation of, 270
writings of, 268–270
Ebrahimnezhad, Ezzat, 265–266
Ebtekar, Maʿsumeh, **270–271**
in Iranian hostage crisis, 270–271
political career of, 271, 436
writings of, 270–271
Ecevit, Bülent
Çetin (Hikmet) under, 223
Dündar (Can) on, 260

as prime minister, 725
Soysal (Mümtaz) under, 782
Economic aid
from Abu Dhabi, 64, 65, 72
to Jordan, 735–736
Economic Consultative Council (EEC)
(Jordan), 736
Economic development
Abu Dhabi funding, 64
in Bahrain, 59, 60
in Jordan, 164–165
in Morocco, 355
in Oman, 49, 50
in Qatar, 90
in Tunisia, 182
in Turkey, 285–286
Economics
Amin (Galal) in, 95–97
Aumann (Robert) in, 129–130
Saqqaf (Abd al-Aziz) in, 705,
707
Economic sanctions. *See Sanctions*
Economies
capitalist, criticism of, 95–97
game theory in, 129–130
women's role in, 36–37
Écrivain, l' (Khadra), 417
Eczacibaşi, Nejat F., 260
Eder, Yehuda, 339
Edge, Brooke, 720
EDGO. *See Engineering and
Development Group*
Education
in Algeria, 826
in Iran, 532
in Iraq, 371, 537
in Jordan, 580
in Lebanon, 348
in Morocco, 459, 460
for Palestinian Arabs in Galilee,
229, 230, 231
in Qatar, 89–90, 534, 535, 536,
537
in Saudi Arabia, religion in, 433
for women, 89–90
Educational organizations, Al Saʿud's
(Al-Walid bin Talal) donations to,
80–81
Efendi, Dede, 719
Egypt
in Arab League, 549
Arafat's (Yasir) youth in, 107
art of (*See* Egyptian art)
business community of, Sawaris
(Onsi) in, 715–717
censorship in, 277, 488, 665
Coptic Orthodox Church in,
Shenouda III as patriarch of,
761–763
Copts in, 715, 761–763

economy of, Amin (Galal) on,
95–97
in Federation of Arab Republics,
558
films of (*See* Egyptian films)
foreign policy of, 220, 272
government of (*See* Egyptian
government)
in Gulf War (1990–1991), 549
history of, Mahfouz (Naguib) on,
487, 488, 489
Islamic militants in, 548, 549–550
Islam in, 419–421, 841
Israeli peace negotiations with, 220,
414
Jordanian relations with, 379, 549
Khaled's (Amr) preaching in,
419–421
Libyan relations with, 549
literature of (*See* Egyptian
literature)
medicine in, Yacoub (Magdi) in,
831–833
music of (*See* Egyptian music)
national anthem of, 819
nationalization policy in, 715, 716
political science in, Rauf Ezzat
(Heba) in, 653
psychiatry in, El Saadawi (Nawal)
in, 276–277
Saudi relations with, 549
stem cell research in, 832
Sudanese relations with, 549
Syrian relations with, 121–122
Syrian union with (*See* United Arab
Republic)
terrorism in, 550, 761–763
in UN, Boutros-Ghali (Boutros)
representing, 220–221
U.S. relations with, 549, 550, 551
women of (*See* Egyptian women)
Yosef (Ovadia) as chief rabbi of,
841
Egyptian art
of Abdel-Moati (Mustafa), 14–15
of Amer (Ghada), 93–94
of Sirry (Gazbia), 772
women in, 93–94
Egyptian Cement Company, 716
Egyptian films
by Chahine (Youssef), 232–235
corruption in, 328–329
government restrictions on,
233–234
by Hamed (Marwan), 328–329
historic epics, 233
musicals, 233
private lives in, 328–329
religion in, 234, 235
Sharif (Omar) in, 746–747

Experimental Group, Abdel-Moati (Mustafa) in, 14
Expressionism, of Gershuni (Moshe), 303
ExxonMobil, in Qatar, 90

F

Fadel, al-Amin Weld Muhammad, 12
Fadlallah, Abd al-Ra'uf, 287
Fadlallah, Muhammad Husayn, **287–290,** *288*
    Hizbullah and, 288, 290
    in Lebanese Civil War, 287
    as political leader, 288–290
    as Shi'ite Muslim cleric, 287–290
    on terrorist attacks, 289, 290
Fahd (king of Saudi Arabia). *See* Al Sa'ud, Fahd bin Abd al-Aziz
Faji"at al-Layla al-Sabi'a ba'd al-Alf (A'raj), 114
Falih, Matruk al-, 711
Fall of the Imam, The (El Saadawi), 277
Family Code (Algeria), 219, 335, 809
Fandy, Mamoun, 132–133
Fanon, Frantz, 460
Fantasia (Djebar), 256–257
Faqih, Sa'd al-, **290–292,** *291*
    in Committee for the Defense of Legitimate Rights, 290–291
    influence in Saudi Arabia, 291–292
    links to terrorism, 291, 292
    in Movement for Islamic Reform in Arabia, 291–292
Farah Diba (empress of Iran), 452
Faris, Muhammad Ahmad, 83
Faris, Myriam, 32
Farming. *See* Agriculture
Farokhzad, Forugh, 174
Farsi script, in Iranian art, 306
Farzaneh Women's Studies Journal, 9
Fashion designers, Lebanese
    Mahfouz (Abed), 669
    Saab (Elie), 667–669, 860
Fashion models
    Ruby, 665
    Wahbe (Haifa), 823–824
Fatah
    Abbas (Mahmud) in, 5, 6, 108
    Arafat (Yasir) in, 107–108
    armed wing of (al-Asifa), 6, 108
    Barghuthi (Marwan) in, 150–153
    establishment of, 5, 6, 108
    Hamas' electoral defeat of, 332
    Hamas' rivalry with, 7, 332
    al-Haqq al-Islami challenging, 518
    Khalaf (Salah) in, 108, 110
    PFLP relations with, 316
    in PLO, 5, 108
    Qaddumi (Faruq) in, 6, 108

Rajub (Jibril) in, 241
Said (Edward) on, 687
Wazir (Khalil al-) in, 6, 108
youth movement of (al-Shabiba), 150, 151, 239
Fatima (musical), 201, 203
Fatwa
    against Boudjedra (Rachid), 205
    on music, 738
    by Qaradawi (Yusuf), 632, 633, 634
    against Rushdie (Salman), 488
    Tawfiq (Ahmad at-) on, 796
    by Zindani (Abd al-Majid al-), 856, 857
Faudel (singer), *292,* **292–294**
    acting career of, 293
    music of, 292–294
Fawda al-Hawas (Mustaghanmi), 560
Fayruz (singer), *295,* **295–299**
    family of, 295–296, 297
    musical plays of, 296–297, 298–299
    music of, 295–299
Faysal (king of Saudi Arabia). *See* Al Sa'ud, Faysal bin Abd al-Aziz
Faysal, Toujan al-, 379
Feast to the Eyes (film), 248
Federal National Council (FNC) (UAE)
    under Gargash (Anwar), 301–302
    Roken (Mohammed al-) as adviser to, 662, 664
Federation of Arab Republics, 558
Fédération Panafricaine des Cinéastes (FEPACI), 365
Felicity Party (Turkey), 284
Femininity, in Bouraoui's (Nina) novels, 214
Feminism
    of Abbasgholizadeh (Mahboubeh), 9, 10
    in Algeria, 808–810
    in Amer's (Ghada) art, 93–94
    in Behbahani's (Simin) poetry, 175
    of Ebadi (Shirin), 265, 267
    of Ebtekar (Ma'sumeh), 270–271
    of El Saadawi (Nawal), 276–278
    of Hannoun (Louisa), 335, 336
    of Hashemi (Faezeh), 350
    in Ishaaq's (Kamala) art, 385–386
    of Khorasani (Nushin Ahmadi), 443–444
    of Mernissi (Fatima), 529, 530, 531
    Tekeli (Şirin), 798
    of Parsipur (Shahrnush), 607, 608
    of Qabbani (Nizar), 621–622
    on Qur'an, 9, 36
    Rauf Ezzat (Heba) on, 653

Ravikovitch (Dalia) on, 656
Rimitti (Cheikha) on, 661
of Salami (Khadija al-), 691
of Tlatli (Moufida), 807
of Toumi (Khalida), 808–810
and Turkish films, 105–106
"Femme et enfant en bleu" (Mahieddine), 491
"Femme et oiseau bleu" (Mahieddine), 491
Femmes d'Alger dans leur appartement (Djebar), 257
Fence, separation, in Israel, 148
Fenmen, Mithat, 718
FEPACI. *See* Fédération Panafricaine des Cinéastes
FFS. *See* Front des Forces Socialistes
Fiction. *See* Literature
Fida'iyyin, in Jordan, 108
FIFA. *See* International Federation of Association Football
Fifteenth of Khordad uprising (1963), 427–428
Fifth Castle, The (Azzawi), 139, 140
Figon, Georges, 355
Figure skating, Karademir (Tuğba) in, 403–405
Film(s). *See also under specific countries*
    of Abu-Assad (Hany), 21–23
    of Akkad (Moustapha), 32–34
    on Algerian War of Independence, 33, 467–468
    Almagor (Gila) in, 60–62
    of Amari (Raja), 92–93
    of Amiralay (Umar), 97–98
    of Antoon (Sinan), 100, 101
    on Arab–Israeli conflict, 21–23, 97–98, 144
    Ar (Müjde) in, 103–106
    of Bakri (Mohamed), 143–144
    of Ceylan (Nuri Bilge), 226–229
    of Chahine (Youssef), 232–235
    comedies, 248, 249
    corruption in, 328–329
    of Dayan (Assi), 247–250
    death in, 248–250
    of Demirkubuz (Zeki), 227
    documentaries, 255, 260–261, 467, 521, 651, 652, 690, 691, 785
    Faudel in, 293
    on French colonization, 467
    of Ghobadi (Bahman), 307–309
    government restrictions on, 233–234
    of Hamed (Marwan), 328–329
    historic epics, 233
    of Hondo (Med), 363–365
    on Iraq, U.S.-led invasion and occupation of, 651, 652–653

Film(s), *continued*
Islam depicted in, 33, 34
Kenter (Yildiz) in, 412
Khoury (Makram) in, 450–452
of Kiarostami (Abbas), 307,
452–454
Lahham (Duraid) in, 462–463
of Lakhdar-Hamina
(Muhammad), 466–469
of Masri (Mai), 520–521
musicals, 233, 818, 820
Nasher (Farhad) composing music
for, 566
national values and myths of Israel
in, 247–249
"new wave," 226, 227
of Panahi (Jafar), 601–603
Portman (Natalie) in, 618–620
private lives in, 328–329
of Rashid (Uday), 651–653
religion in, 33, 34, 234, 235
of Saddiki (Tayeb), 674
Salameh (Nadine) in, 689
of Salami (Khadija al-), 690–691
Sharif (Omar) in, 746–747
social problems in, 232–235,
328–329
social realism in, 364–365
of Suleiman (Elia), 784–787
of Tlatli (Moufida), 803–807
on Tunisian independence, 804,
805, 806
Umm Kulthum in, 818, 820
women portrayed in, 103–106,
453, 468–469, 602, 804–805,
806, 807
Zaki (Muna) in, 849–850
Filmco International Productions, 33
Fils de l'amertume, les (Benaïssa), 179,
180
Final Exams (film), 248
Finance Directorate (Bahrain), Al
Khalifa (Khalifa bin Salman) in,
56–57
Fiorentina. *See* ACF Fiorentina
Fiqh (Muslim jurisprudence)
Amer (Magda) teaching, 634
Kar (Mehrangiz) studying, 402
Khamenehi (Ali) on, 429
Fiqh-i Islam wa Qanuni Gharb
(Shahrani), 734
First Light, The (Al Khalifa), 55, 56
FIS. *See* Islamic Salvation Front
FIS de la haine, le (Boudjedra), 205,
207
Fi Tariq (Saddiki), 673
Flag of the Torah. *See* Degel ha-Torah
Flavin, Dan, 360
FLN. *See* National Liberation Front
Flood in Ba'th Country (film), 97, 98

FNC. *See* Federal National Council
Folklore, Sudanese, Kabli (Abd al
Karim al-) on, 399
Folk music, Israeli, 42
Fonda, Jane, 103
Football (soccer)
Benayoun (Yossi) in, 183–185
Gunes (Senol) in, 800
Radhi (Ahmad) in, 646–647
Suan (Abbas) in, 783–784
Terim (Fatih) in, 799–800
Forbes (magazine), 346
Forbidden Vision, The (Bouraoui). *See*
Voyeuse interdite, la (Bouraoui)
Ford Transit (film), 22
Foreign aid. *See* Economic aid
Foreign investments. *See* Investments,
foreign
For Everyone Everywhere (film), 731
Forgotten Queens of Islam, The
(Mernissi), 530
Forouhar, Dariush, 265
Forouhar, Parvaneh Eskanadri, 265
Fortuna (film), 61
Forum Marocain pour la Verité et
l'Equité. *See* Moroccan Forum for
Truth and Equity
Foucault, Michel, 359, 360
France
Algerian occupation by
(1830–1962) (*See* Algeria,
French occupation of)
Algerian relations with, post-inde-
pendence, 216, 217–218
Aoun (Michel) in exile in, 101,
102
Benaïssa (Slimane) in exile in, 179,
180
Chacour (Elias) honored in, 231
Ebnou's (Moussa Ould) novels in,
270
films about, 364–365
Hadid's (Zaha) architecture in,
322
Hakim (Tawfiq al-) studying in, 324
Khatibi's (Abdel Kebir) influence
in, 440
Laabi (Abdellatif) in exile in, 460
Moroccan relations with, 353,
355
in Morocco, power of, 353
oil concessions to Algeria, 216
press coverage of Algeria in, 205
raï music in, 292–294
Rimitti (Cheikha) in exile in, 658,
659
sociology theory in, 243
in Suez Crisis (1956–1957), 612
Free Center Party (Israel), Olmert
(Ehud) in, 587

Free Patriotic Movement Party (Lebanon)
Aoun (Michel) in, 101, 102
platform of, 102
Free Ride (film), 34
Free Unionist Officers (Libya), 624,
627
Free verse movement. *See* Arabic free
verse movement
French language
in Algeria, 180–181, 561, 720,
826–827, 828, 829
in Algerian literature, 113, 114,
206–207
in Algerian music, 294
in Arab literature, 439, 440
Benaïssa (Slimane) on, 180–181
Khatibi (Abdel Kebir) on, 439, 440
in Mauritanian literature, 268
in Morocco, 459, 460, 675, 796,
797
in Tunisia, 527, 808
Frente Popular para la Liberacion de
Saguia el Hamra y Rio de Oro. *See*
POLISARIO
Friedman, Thomas, on Ghandour
(Fadi), 305
Fripp, Robert, 659
From Earth to Earth Art (Tumarkin), 812
From Haven to Conquest (Khalidi), 426
*From Occupation to Interim Accords:
Israel and the Palestinian Territories*
(Shehadeh), 760
From Our Mountains (Rabi). *See Min
Jibalina* (Rabi)
Front de Libération Nationale (FLN).
See National Liberation Front
Front des Forces Socialistes (FFS)
(Algeria), 675–676
Frontiers of Dreams and Fears (film), 521
Front Islamique du Salut (FIS). *See*
Islamic Salvation Front
Frost, Caroline, 323
Fujiwara, Chris, 234
Fulayfil, Muhammad, 295
Füreya (Kulin), 457

G

Gadhafi, Moammar. *See* Qaddafi,
Mu'ammar al-
Galatasaray (Turkish football team),
799, 800
Galilee, Palestinian Arabs in, 229, 230,
231
Gamal, Samia, 92
Game theory, 129–130
Ganji, Akbar, 266, 743
Garang de Mabior, John, 523, 524
Garçon manqué (Bouraoui), 212, 213,
214

Gulf War (1990–1991), *continued*
    start of, 373
    UAE military forces in, 63, 498
    U.S. role in, 373
Gunes, Senol, 800
Güneşe Dön Yüzünü (Kulin), 457
Güngör, Şükran, 412
Gürel, Aysel, 103

H

Haaretz (newspaper), 456, 513, 514,
    722, 723
Habash, George, **313–317**, *314*
    in Arab Nationalist Movement,
        314–315
    in PFLP, 315–317
Habibi, Emile, *317*, **317–320**
    Bakri (Mohamed) and, 143, 144
    in communist parties, 318
    political career of, 318
    writings of, 318–320
Haddad, George, 649
Haddad, Nuhad. *See* Fayruz
Haddad, Wadi (Lebanese typesetter),
    295, 296
Haddad, Wadi (Palestinian doctor),
    314, 315
Haddad Prize. *See* Malek Haddad
    Literary Prize
Haddatha Abu Hurayra, Qala
    (Mas'adi), 517, 518
Hadid, Muhammad al-Hajj Husayn, 320
Hadid, Zaha, **320–323**, *321*
    academic career of, 321
    architecture of, 320–323
Hafiz, Abd al-Halim, 299
Hagana (Jewish paramilitary
    organization)
    Rabin (Yitzhak) in, 639–640
    Sharon (Ariel) in, 748
Haifa (film), 143
Hajj (pilgrimage), Angawi's (Sami)
    involvement in, 99
Hajj Research Center, 99
Hakhmissimi Takhat Knafekh
    (Tumarkin), 813
Hakim, Abd al-Aziz al, 678
Hakim, Muhammad Baqir al-, 678
Hakim, Muhsin al-, 678
Hakim, Tawfiq al-, **323–326**, *324*
    civil service career of, 324–325
    novels of, 324, 325
    plays of, 323–326
    on women, emancipation of, 325
Halaby, Elizabeth. *See* Noor al-Hussein
Halaby, Khalil, 208
Halaby, Najeeb Elias, 578, 579
Halakhah (Jewish religious law), Yosef
    (Ovadia) on, 843

Half Moon (film), 309
Halloween series of films, 33, 34
Halqa style performance, 673, 675
Hamadeh, Marwan, 396
Hamarneh, Mustafa, **326–328**
    academic career of, 326–327
    in Center for Strategic Studies, 326,
        327
    on Jordanian politics, 327
Hamas
    Abbas (Mahmud) and, 5, 7
    assassination of leaders of, 332, 333
    censorship by, 848–849
    charter of, 837, 847
    creation of, 518–519
    electoral success of, 7, 332, 520,
        838–839
    Fatah's rivalry with, 7, 332
    in first Intifada, 836, 837, 847
    fund-raising for, 519–520
    Haniyeh (Ismail) in, 331–334
    in Israeli–Palestinian conflict, 834,
        835, 836, 837
    Izz al-Din Al-Qassam Brigades in,
        520, 847
    Jordan banning, 520
    Mash'al (Khalid) in, 518, 519–520
    Muslim Brotherhood and, 519
    Palestinian Authority clashing
        with, 838, 848
    in Palestinian Legislative Council,
        520, 838–839
    peace proposal by, 837, 838
    Rantisi (Abd al-Aziz) in, 332, 333,
        847
    Said (Edward) on, 687
    social agenda of, 848–849
    suicide bombings by, 519, 520, 837
    as terrorist organization, U.S. on,
        520
    Yasin (Ahmad) as founder of, 834,
        836, 837, 838, 847
    Yasin (Ahmad) as spiritual leader
        of, 834, 837, 839
    Zahhar (Mahmud al-) as founder
        of, 847
    Zahhar (Mahmud al-) as leader of,
        848–849
Hamasat (radio program), 559
Hamdi, Ibrahim al-
    assassination of, 693, 695
    presidency of, 693, 856
Hamed, Marwan, *328*, **328–329**
    films of, 328–329
Hamed, Wahid, 328, 329
Hamid, Abdullah al-, 711
Hamidi, Ibrahim, **329–331**
    journalism of, 329–331
    peace process covered by, 331
Hammam, Habib, 708

Hamzah bin Al Hussein (crown prince
    of Jordan), 17
Hanim, Sitare, 456
Haniyeh, Ismail, **331–334**
    in Hamas, 331–334
    as PA prime minister, 7, 332, 839,
        849
Hannoun, Louisa, **334–337**
    education of, 334–335, 336
    feminism of, 335, 336
    in Parti des Travailleurs, 335
    political career of, 335–337
    as presidential candidate, 335, 336
Hanoch, Lihi, 340, 341
Hanoch, Shalom, **337–341**
    music of, 337–341
    in Tamuz (band), 338, 339–340
    in Tel Aviv, 337–339
Haq, Abdul, 407
Haq, al- (human rights organization),
    758, 759
Haqq al-Islami, al- (Palestinian student
    bloc), 518
Haqqani school (Qom), 532
Harakat al-Shabiba al-Islamiyya
    (Morocco), 354
Harakat-e Islami (Islamic movement),
    589
Harbi, Brahimi, 341–342
Harbi, Mohamed, **341–344**
    academic career of, 343–344
    on Algerian history and politics,
        343–344
    in National Liberation Front,
        342–344
    political views of, 342
Harems
    Djebar (Assia) on, 257
    Mernissi (Fatima) on, 530
    Tlatli (Moufida) on, 806
Hariri, Rafiq, **344–348**, *345*
    Amiralay's (Umar) film about, 98
    assassination of, 98, 118, 346,
        347–348, 396, 414, 415, 571,
        573, 859
    business career of, 344–345, 346
    family of, 344, 345
    Khaddam (Abd al-Halim) and,
        414
    on Lahoud (Emile), 466
    and Nasrallah (Hasan), 571
    political career of, 345–348
    as prime minister, 346–348, 571,
        859
    wealth of, 345, 346
Hariri Foundation, 348
Harisat al-Dhilal (A'raj), 114
Harnik, Meir, 42
Harrouda (Ben Jelloun), 186–187
Harvard Law Review, 149

Hizbullah (Lebanon), *continued*
  Lebanese agreement of understanding with, 102, 103
  military capabilities of, 570
  Nasrallah (Hasan) in, 568, 570–573
  as political force, 570–571
  public opinion on, 571–572
  Syrian support for, 117–118, 414
  as terrorist organization, 572
  Zindani (Abd al-Majid al-) in, 856
Hizbullah Program, 570
Hobsbawm, Eric, 648, 649
Hoda Association, Ibrahim (Saad Eddin) in, 383
Hollywood, Akkad (Moustapha) in, 33–34
Holocaust
  Barak's (Aharon) experience of, 146, 147
  Khoury (Elias) on denial of, 449
  Margalit (Dan) on, 515
  Segev (Tom) on, 724
  Tumarkin (Igael) on, 813
Holt, P. M., 648, 649
Homage by Assassination (film), 785
Homosexuality
  in Hamed's (Marwan) films, 329
  Qaradawi (Yusuf) on, 634, 635
Hondo, Med, **363–365**
  films of, 363–365
  social realism of, 364–365
Hong Kong, Hadid's (Zaha) architecture in, 322
Honor crimes
  in Iran, 403
  in Jordan, 416
Hoots, Charles, 690
Horse racing, in Dubai, 500
Hostage-taking, in Lebanon, 289. *See also* Airplane hijackings; Iranian hostage crisis
Hotel industry, Al Sa'ud's (Al-Walid bin Talal) investments in, 79
Hotoda, Goh, 293
Hot Spot (Hatoum), 359
Hourani, Hani, **366–367**
  art of, 366–367
  political activism of, 366, 367
  writings of, 366, 367
Hourani, Lama, 367
Houston Agreement (1997), 357
HRAS. *See* Human Rights Association in Syria
Hubb al-Kabir, al- (Alama), 38
Hudud, al- (film), 463
Hu Jintao, 713
Hulda (kibbutz), 593, 594
Human body, Khatibi (Abdel Kebir) on, 440

Human development, Basma bint Talal in, 164–165
Human rights
  in Abu Dhabi, 71–72
  in Afghanistan, 704
  in Algeria, 335, 676
  in Bahrain, 55, 60, 699, 700, 702
  Darraj (Faisal) on, 244
  Ebadi (Shirin) advocating, 263–268
  in Egypt, 385
  in Gaza Strip, 280
  Hannoun (Louisa) on, 335
  Ibrahim (Saad Eddin) on, 385
  in Iran, 263–268, 681
  and Islam, compatibility of, 132–133, 542
  in Israel, 390
  Jabarin (Hasan) advocating, 390
  in Jordan, 415–417
  Khader (Asma) advocating, 415–417
  in Kuwait, 552
  in Lebanon, 679–680
  in Libya, 627
  Maleh (Haytham al-) advocating, 504–505
  in Morocco, 357, 555
  Mubarak (Ma'suma al-) on, 552
  Naisse (Aktham) advocating, 563–564
  in Palestinian territories, 280–282, 758, 759
  Roken (Mohammed al-) on, 662, 663, 664, 665
  Sadi (Said) on, 676
  Sadr (Rabab al-) on, 679–680
  Sadr (Shadi) on, 681
  Samar (Sima) on, 704
  Saqqaf (Abd al-Aziz) advocating, 705, 706, 708–709
  Shehadeh (Raja) advocating, 758, 759
  Sourani (Raji) advocating, 759
  Soysal (Mümtaz) on, 782
  Suswa (Amat al- Alim al-) advocating, 787–788
  in Syria, 244, 504–505, 563–564
  in Tunisia, 182–183
  in Turkey, 585, 782
  in UAE, 662, 663, 664, 665
  western ideas of, Awda (Salman al-) criticizing, 132–133
  in Yemen, 705, 706, 708–709, 787–788
Human Rights Association in Syria (HRAS), 504–505
Human Rights Committee of the Consultative Council (Yemen), 708
Human Rights League (Algeria), 676

Human Rights Watch
  on Ebadi (Shirin), 267
  Khader (Asma) in, 416
  on Majid (Ali Hasan al-), 495
  on Morocco, 555
  on Roken (Mohammed al-), 664
  on Tunisia, 183
Humaydi, Ibrahim. *See* Hamidi, Ibrahim
Humor, in Habibi's (Emile) writing, 319
Hurdling, El Moutawakel (Nawal) in, 274–276
Hürriyet (newspaper), 411
Hurvitz, Eli, **367–369**
  in pharmaceutical industry, 367–369
Husari, Sati al-, 314
Husayn, Taha, 489
Hussein, Haya bint al-, 499
Hussein, Saddam, *369,* **369–375**
  in Algiers Agreement (1975), 372
  Antoon (Sinan) as critic of, 100
  Arab nationalism of, 370
  and Azzawi (Fadhil al-), 140
  in Ba'th Party, 370–372
  Bayati (Abd al-Wahhab al-) under, 168
  Chalabi (Ahmad) opposing, 235–236
  coup attempts against, in 1990s, 236
  in coup of 1968, 371
  Da'wa Party members punished by, 507
  Duri (Izzat Ibrahim al-) under, 494
  execution of, 374, 573
  family of, 370, 372
  foreign policy of, 373
  in Gulf War, 373, 378
  Hussein bin Talal and, 379
  in Iran–Iraq War (1980–1988), 372
  Iraqi National Congress opposing, 235–236
  Iraqis killed under, 369, 372, 373
  Majid (Ali Hasan al-) under, 492–496
  Maliki (Nuri Kamil al-) opposing, 506
  PLO supporting, 519
  presidency of, 372–375
  Sadr (Muhammad Baqir al-) executed by, 508, 676
  Salih (Ali Abdullah) influenced by, 694
  supporters of, 374–375
  Syrian relations with, 122
  trial of, 374
  UN inspections and, 374

Sadi (Said) on, 676
of Zarqawi (Abu Mus'ab al-), 851, 852
Islamic Institute, 435
Islamic law. *See Shari'a*
Islamic League. *See* Mujamma al-Islami, al-
Islamic National Accord Society (INAS). *See* Wifaq (Bahrain)
Islamic Republic Party (IRP) (Iran), 428
Islamic Resistance, in Lebanon War (1987), 289
Islamic revivalism. *See* Islamic fundamentalism
Islamic Salvation Front (FIS) (Algeria)
  Belhadj (Ali) in, 477, 478, 479, 480
  Boudjedra (Rachid) opposing, 204–205
  dissolution of, 335, 478
  electoral success of, 217, 253, 335, 477, 478, 480
  Madani (Abbassi) in, 477, 478–479, 480
  Toumi (Khalida) threatened by, 809
  writers killed by, 826
Islamic Shari'a Institute, 287
Islamic Tendency Movement (MTI). *See* Mouvement de Tendance Islamique
Islamic Truth. *See* Haqq al-Islami, al-
Islamic University of Gaza, Haniyeh (Ismail) at, 331, 332
Islamist ideology. *See also specific countries and groups*
  Abu Ghayth (Sulayman) advocating, 23–24
  assassination of Algerian critics of, 252
  under Ben Ali (Zein al-Abidin), 182, 183
  Boudjedra (Rachid) criticizing, 204–205
  Boulmerka (Hassiba) on, 210–211
  under Bouteflika (Abdelaziz), 217, 218, 219
  in democracy, 385
  Djaout (Taher) on, 252, 254
  Djebar (Assia) on, 258
  Erdogan (Tayyip) in, 283–286
  Faqih (Sa'd al-) advocating, 290–292
  Göle (Nilüfer) on, 310
  Hannoun (Louisa) on, 335
  in Iraq during 1970s, 372
  and Khashoggi (Jamal), 432, 433
  modernization and, 310
  in parliamentary elections, 378
  rise of, 253, 354
  and women's rights, 90

Islam Today website, 133–134
ISM. *See* International Solidarity Movement
"Ismi Matar" (Asimi), 128
Israel
  Arab and Palestinian conflict with (*See* Arab–Israeli conflict; Peace process)
  Areas A and B of, 391
  art of (*See* Israeli art)
  Ashkenazic and Sephardic Jews in, inequality between, 842, 844
  biochemistry in, Hershko's (Avram) work in, 362–363
  Bishara's (Azmi) critique of, 198–201
  citizenship in, 199
  as democratic state, 147
  Egyptian peace negotiations with, 220, 414
  elimination of state of, PFLP's position on, 315
  films of (*See* Israeli films)
  government of (*See* Israeli government; Israeli legal system)
  history of state, 722, 723–724, 743–745
  Hizbullah's war with (*See* Lebanon War (2006))
  intelligence agency of (Mossad), 473, 520
  and Iran, possible conflict between, 70
  Iraqi nuclear reactor bombed by (1981), 650, 651
  as Jewish state, 147, 198–200
  Jordanian treaty with (1994), 378, 520, 547
  journalism in (*See* Israeli journalism)
  Lebanese prisoner exchange with (2004), 570
  Lebanese relations with, 346
  Lebanese withdrawal by (2000), 570, 686, 750
  in Lebanon Wars (*See* Lebanon War (1982); Lebanon War (2006))
  literature of (*See* Israeli literature and poetry)
  military of (*See* Israel Defense Forces)
  Moroccan relations with, 357
  Muasher (Marwan) as ambassador of Jordan to, 546, 547
  music of (*See* Israeli music)
  nationalism in, 766 (*See also* Zionism)
  occupied territories in (*See* Occupied Territories)

  Operation Summer Rains by, 588
  Operation Thunderbolt by, 613
  Palestinian citizens of (*See* Palestinian citizens of Israel)
  Palestinian recognition of state of, 333
  pharmaceutical industry in, Hurvitz (Eli) in, 367–368
  Qatari relations with, 86, 90
  separation fence built by, 148
  Sfeir (Nasrallah) on, 729, 730
  society of, Kimmerling (Baruch) on, 454–456
  sociology in, 454–456
  sports in (*See* Israeli sports)
  in Suez Crisis (1956–1957), 612
  Syrian peace talks with, 118, 122, 331
  theater in, 60–62, 450–452
  women of, 654, 656, 843
  Yosef (Ovadia) as chief Sephardic rabbi of, 841–842
Israel, Meir, 339
Israel Defense Forces (IDF)
  Barak (Aharon) in, 146
  Benayoun (Yossi) in, 184
  Fatah leaders assassinated by, 6
  Hamas leaders assassinated by, 332, 333
  Hanoch (Shalom) in, 337–338
  Israeli Supreme Court on assassinations by, 147
  in Jenin camp attack (2002), 144
  Netanyahu (Yonatan) in, 575, 577
  Peres (Shimon) developing, 613
  Rabin (Yitzhak) in, 639, 640–641, 642
  Sharon (Ariel) in, 749
Israeli–Arab conflict. *See* Arab–Israeli conflict
Israeli art
  of Danziger (Itzhak), 812, 813
  expressionism in, 303
  of Gershuni (Moshe), 302–303
  of Tumarkin (Igael), 811–814
Israeli Black Panthers, 844
Israeli Communist Party (ICP), 318
Israeli films
  Almagor (Gila) in, 60–62
  Bakri (Mohamed) in, 143–144
  comedies, 248, 249
  by Dayan (Assi), 247–250
  death in, 248–250
  Khoury (Makram) in, 450–452
  national values and myths in, 247–249
  personal-elitist and political-critical, 249

VOLUME 1: 1–458; VOLUME 2: 459–860

family of, 423, 424
at League of Arab States, 423, 424
writings of, 426
Khalid ibn al-Walid, 423
Khalidi Library (Jerusalem), 424
Khalifa Committee, 64
Khalili, Abbas, 173
Khalilzad, Zalmay, 408, 509
Khamenehi, Ali, *427,* **427–430**
Ahmadinejad (Mahmoud) and, 28
economic policies of, 429
education of, 427
in Fifteenth of Khordad uprising,
427–428
in Iranian Revolution, 428
Khatami (Mohamed) working
with, 429–430, 436–437
Larijani (Ali Ardashir) as adviser to,
469
Montazeri (Hossein Ali) on, 540
and Nasrallah (Hasan), 573
political power of, 28, 427
as president, 428, 429
as religious-political leader,
427–430
religious *vs.* political experience of,
429
Khammash, Ammar, **430–432**
architecture of, 430–432
art of, 430–432
in historic preservation, 430–432
Khan, Riz, 81
Khartoum School, Ishaaq (Kamala) in,
385–386
Khashoggi, Jamal, **432–434**
journalism of, 432–434
on September 11 terrorist attacks,
433
Khatami, Mohamed, *434,* **434–439**
Abtahi (Mohamed Ali) under,
20–21
Ahmadinejad (Mahmoud) and, 27,
438
on dialogue of civilizations, 437,
438
Ebtekar (Ma'sumeh) in government of, 271
economic policies of, 437
education of, 434
family of, 434
free press under, 436
and Hashemi (Faezeh), 349
Khamenehi (Ali) working with,
429–430, 436–437
military service of, 434
political career of, 435–438
presidency of, 429–430,
436–438
under Rafsanjani (Ali Akbar
Hashemi), 435–436

reform movement of 1990s under
(*See* Iranian reform movement)
on Rezazadeh (Hossein), 658
in Society of Combatant Clery,
434–435
Soroush (Abdolkarim) after election of, 778
U.S. relations with, 437–438
women voting for, 36, 350
Khatami, Ruhollah, 434
Khatibi, Abdel Kebir, **439–441**
on calligraphy, 439
education of, 439
literary criticism by, 439
plays of, 439
political analysis of, 439
sociology influenced by, 440–441
writings of, 187, 439–441
Khayrallah, Adnan, 370, 372
Khemir, Sabiha, **441–442**
art of, 441–442
writings of, 442
Khleifi, Michel, 786
Kho'i, Abu'l-Qasim al-
as Shi'ite cleric, 775
as Sistani's (Ali Husseini al-) mentor, 773, 774, 775
writings of, 775
Khomeini, Ruhollah
arrest of, 427–428, 540
Fadlallah (Muhammad Husayn)
supporting, 289
fatwa against Rushdie (Salman)
issued by, 488
fatwa on music issued by, 738
Khamenehi's (Ali) association with,
427–428, 429
Khatami's (Mohamed) association
with, 434, 435
and Mesbah Yazdi (Mohammad
Taqi), 532–533
Montazeri (Hossein Ali) as student
of, 539
Montazeri (Hossein Ali) as successor-designate of, 538, 540
Soroush (Abdolkarim) on, 777,
778
on *vilayet-e faqih,* 702
Khoraiche, Saida Anthony, 729
Khorasani, Javad Mossavi, 443
Khorasani, Nushin Ahmadi, **443–444**
publishing work of, 443
women's rights advocacy by,
443–444
Khouri, George, 444
Khouri, Rami, **444–447**
academic career of, 445–446
on archaeology, 445
journalism of, 444–447
Khouri, Clara, 450–451, 452

Khoury, Dina Rizk, 649
Khoury, Elias, *447,* **447–450**
academic career of, 447
on Antoon's (Sinan) writing, 100
literary criticism by, 448
political activism of, 449
writings of, 447–450
Khoury, Gisele, 410
Khoury, Jamil, 451, 452
Khoury, Makram, *450,* **450–452**
acting career of, 450–452
family of, 450–451, 452
Khubz al-Hafi, al- (Shukri), 797
Khuri, Bishara al-, 726
Kiarostami, Abbas, *452,* **452–454**
films of, 307, 452–454
Ghobadi (Bahman) working with,
307
Panahi (Jafar) working with, 453,
602
Yektapanah (Hassan) influenced
by, 309
Kibbutz. *See also specific kibbutzim*
music at, 337
Kidwa, Nasser al-, 110
Kifah Tibah (Mahfouz), 487, 489
Kimmerling, Baruch, **454–456**
academic career of, 455
on Arab–Israeli conflict, 454–456
sociological work of, 454–456
writings of, 455–456
King Hussein Foundation
International, 580
Kingston, William, 303
Kinzer, Stephen, 726
Kirkuk Group, 139–140
Kirshenbaum, Moti, 156
Kissinger, Henry, on Syria, 118
Kitab, al- (Sa'id), 684
Kitab al-Amir (A'raj), 114
Kitabat Kharij (Asimi), 128–129
Kiyan (journal), 742, 743, 778
Klauzner, Amos. *See* Oz, Amos
Klauzner, Yossef, 594
Klawans, Stuart, 786
Klee, Paul, 753
Knapp, Wilfrid, 46
Knesset (Israel)
Bishara (Azmi) in, 198
Habibi (Emile) in, 318
Israeli Supreme Court on laws of,
148
Knot theory, 130
Knowles, Beyoncé, 668
Koç, Vehbi, 260
Koçali, Filiz, 137
KOGEF. *See* Turkish Cypriot
Students' Youth Federation
Kokar (Iran), films about, 452
Kollek, Teddy, 587, 612, 723

Komisione Banoaan (Iran), 351
Koolhaas, Rem, 322
Kooshyar, Ali, 173
Kop, Yücel, 136
Kotb, Heba, 634
Koza (film), 226–227
Krajeski, Thomas, 857–858
Kseur Platform, 218
Kufic calligraphy, in Boullata's (Kamal) art, 208–209
Kulin, Ayşe, **456–458**
    family of, 456–457
    political activism of, 457
    writings of, 456–458
Kulin, Muhittin, 456
Kunzman, Roman, 43
Kurd(s)
    Barzani (Mas'ud) as president of Iraqi, 158, 160–161
    countries feeling threatened by, 160
    government violence against, 159–160 (*See also* Kurdish genocide)
    in Gulf War (1990–1991), 160, 161
    internal conflict among, 159–160
    Iranian support for, 159
    repression of, 160
    in Turkey, 583–585, 599–600
    in U.S.-led invasion of Iraq (2003), 160
Kurdi, Walid Al, 164
Kurdish culture, 307–309
Kurdish films, by Ghobadi (Bahman), 307–309
Kurdish genocide (1988) (Iraq), 159–160
    Anfal campaign in, 159, 493, 494, 495, 790
    Barzani (Mas'ud) on, 159–160
    chemical weapons used in, 159, 495, 790
    Majid (Ali Hasan al-) in, 159, 492, 493, 494–495, 790
    Talabani (Jalal) targeted in, 790
Kurdish language, 583, 584
Kurdish movement, Hamidi's (Ibrahim) support for, 330
Kurdish music, of Nazeri (Shahram), 573–574
Kurdish rebellions, in Iraq
    of 1974–1975, 159
    after Gulf War (1991), 160, 161
    Talabani (Jalal) in, 789
Kurdish Regional Government (Iraq), establishment of, 160
Kurdistan
    borders of, 307
    Iraqi region of, 158–161
Kurdistan Alliance, 160

Kurdistan Democratic Party (KDP)
    Barzani (Mas'ud) in, 158–161
    establishment of, 158
    Talabani (Jalal) in, 789, 791
Kurdistan Front, establishment of, 160
Kutchuk, Fazil, 604
Kuwait
    Al Sabah (Nasir al-Sabah al-Ahmad) in government of, 73, 76
    Al Sabah (Sabah al-Ahmad al-Jabir) as emir of, 73–77
    Al Sabah (Sabah al-Ahmad al-Jabir) as prime minister of, 74
    Al Sabah (Sa'd al-Abdullah) as emir of, 74, 75–76
    art museums of, 73
    as British protectorate, 74
    business community of, Al Sabah (Nasir al-Sabah al-Ahmad) in, 72–73
    coup of 2006 in, 76
    foreign policy of, 74, 76–77
    human rights in, Mubarak (Ma'suma al-) on, 552
    during Iran–Iraq War, 75
    in Iraq, U.S.-led occupation of, 77
    Iraqi invasion of (*See* Gulf War)
    Islamist ideology in, Abu Ghayth (Sulayman) advocating, 23–24
    line of succession in, 74–76
    Majid (Ali Hasan al-) as governor of, 493, 494, 495
    National Assembly of, 75, 76, 77
    Palestinians in, 519
    political science in, Mubarak (Ma'suma al-) in, 552, 553
    U.S. relations with, 77
    women's rights in, 77, 552
Kyprianou, Spyros, 604

L

Laabi, Abdellatif, **459–461**
    in exile in France, 460
    journal of, 459–460
    poetry of, 460, 461
    translations by, 460–461
    writings of, 187, 460, 461
Labor Party (Israel)
    Am Ehad Party merging with, 617
    on Israeli withdrawal from Gaza and West Bank, 616
    Peres (Shimon) in, 613, 614, 615, 617, 844
    Peretz (Amir) in, 614, 616, 617, 618
    Rabin (Yitzhak) in, 641
    Shas Party in coalition with, 844
Labor rights, in Algeria, Hannoun (Louisa) on, 335, 336

Labor Zionism
    of Peretz (Amir), 617–618
    Shapira (Anita) on, 744, 745
"Ladghat al-Hayya" (El Saher), 279
Lahakat ha-Nahal Entertainment Corps, 337–338
Lahav, Louie, 339–340, 341
Lahham, Duraid, **461–464**
    as comedian, 461–464
    diplomatic career of, 464
    films of, 462–463
    political commentary by, 463, 464
Lahiji, Shahla, 403, 443
Lahoud, Emile, **464–466**, *465*
    as commander of Lebanese army, 465, 466
    image of, 466
    opponents of, 466
    presidency of, 347, 465–466
Laicism, in Turkey, 284, 286
"Laila" (Hanoch), 337, 338
Lakhdar-Hamina, Malik, 469
Lakhdar-Hamina, Muhammad, **466–469**
    on Algerian War of Independence, 467–468
    films of, 466–469
    on French colonization, 467
    on women, 468–469
Lakhdar-Hamina, Tariq, 469
"La Ma Khilsit al-Hakaya" (Zoghbi), 859
Lamara, Jiji, 31, 32
Land, The (film). *See Ard, al-*
Landmine Survivors' Network, 580
Laouedj, Zineb, 561
Larijani, Ali Ardashir, *469*, **469–470**
    Abtahi (Mohamed Ali) under, 20
    in Iranian nuclear program, 470
    Iranian state television headed by, 469, 470
    as Khamenehi's (Ali) adviser, 469
    Supreme National Security Council headed by, 469, 470
Laroui, Abdallah, **470–473**
    education of, 470–471
    in Foreign Service, 470
    as historian, 471–472
    writings of, 471–472
LasSa (tire company), 669–670
Last Summer of Reason, The (Djaout). *See Dernier Été de la raison, Le* (Djaout)
Latin music, Faudel's use of, 293
Laughter and Fun (film). *See Dahahk wa La'ab*
Lavon, Pinhas, 612
Lawful and the Prohibited in Islam, The (Qaradawi), 633
Lawrence of Arabia (film), 747

Leibowitz, Yeshayahu, 362
Leigh, Doug, 404
"Leih Beydary Kadah" (Ruby), 665
Léon (film), 619
Letter of Demands (1991), 132, 290
"Letter to Jesus, A" (Bayyud),
   172–173
"Letter to Noah, A" (Bayyud), 173
Lettres Parisiennes, autopsie de l'exil
   (Sebbar), 721
Levi, Moshe, 340–341
Levieux, Michòle, 804
Levine, David, 718
Levi-Strauss, Claude, 243
Levy, David, 750
Levy, Gideon, 153
Lewis, Bernard, 648, 649
Liberalism, of Bishara (Azmi), 199
Libertarianism, of Harbi (Mohamed),
   342
Liberty, in principle of proportionality,
   149
Libya
   charity work in, 629
   constitutional monarchy in, 557
   coup of 1969 in, 558, 624–625,
      627
   economic reforms in, 626–627
   economic sanctions against, 626,
      629
   Egyptian relations with, 549
   in Federation of Arab Republics,
      558
   films on history of, 33–34
   foreign policy of, 625–626
   history of, 33–34, 557
   human rights in, 627
   independence of, 557
   Italian colonization of, 484
   jamahiriya in, 625
   literature of, by Musrati (Ali
      Mustafa al-), 556–558
   in Pan Am flight 103 bombing
      (Lockerbie), 626, 629
   poetry of, by Mahdaoui (Ahmad
      Rafiq al-), 484–485
   Qaddafi (Mu'ammar al-) regime in,
      624–628
   Sawaris (Onsi) migrating to, 715,
      716
   socialism in, 625
   terrorism sponsored by, 626
   U.S. bombing of (1986), 626
   in UTA flight 772 bombing
      (Niger), 626
Libyan Society through Its Proverbs
   (Musrati), 557
Life according to Agfa (film), 248–249
Life Goes On (film), 452
Life Makers (television show), 420

Light at the End, The (Hatoum), 359,
   360
Likud Party (Israel)
   Begin (Menachem) in, 613
   Livni (Tzipi) in, 473
   Netanyahu (Binyamin) in, 574,
      575–577, 578, 844
   Olmert (Ehud) in, 587, 589
   Sharon (Ariel) in, 576, 577, 587,
      617, 749, 750
Lily (film), 328
Lion of the Desert (film), 33–34
Lire (journal), 270
List of the Workers of Israel. *See* Rafi
   Party
Literacy rates, in Iraq, 371
Literary criticism
   by Ashour (Radwa), 125
   by Azzawi (Fadhil al-), 140
   by Bannis (Mohammed), 145
   by Darraj (Faisal), 242–244
   by Khatibi (Abdel Kebir), 439
   by Khoury (Elias), 448
   by Madini (Ahmad al-), 481, 483
   by Mala'ika (Nazik al-), 501, 502,
      504
Literary theory, of Said (Edward), 685,
   686, 687, 688
Literature. *See also* Poetry; *specific
   countries*
   by Abd al-Qader (Ahmad ben),
      10–12
   on Algerian civil war (1990s),
      204–205, 207, 417–418
   by Antoon (Sinan), 100
   Arabic *vs.* French language in, 113,
      114, 206–207
   by A'raj (Wasini al-), 112–115
   by Ashour (Radwa), 124–125
   by Azzawi (Fadhil al-), 139–141
   by Bayyud (In'am), 172
   by Benhedouga (Abdelhamid),
      826, 827, 828
   by Ben Jelloun (Tahar), 186–189
   by Boudjedra (Rachid), 204–207
   by Bouraoui (Nina), 212–214
   by Kulin (Ayşe), 456–458
   censorship of, 277
   by Chaghmoum (El Miloudi), 482
   Darraj (Faisal) on, 242–244
   by Darwish (Mahmud), 244–247
   by Djaout (Taher), 252–254
   by Djebar (Assia), 254–259
   by Ebnou (Moussa Ould),
      268–270
   by El Saadawi (Nawal), 277–278
   by Habibi (Emile), 318–320
   by Hakim (Tawfiq al-), 323–326
   and history, relationship between,
      256–259

history as subject of, 12, 487, 488,
   489
   by Husayn (Taha), 489
   isolation of authors, 113, 270
   by Khadra (Yasmina), 417–419
   by Khatibi (Abdel Kebir), 439–441
   by Khoury (Elias), 447–450
   by Laouedj (Zineb), 561
   by Madini (Ahmad al-), 481–484
   by Maghut (Muhammad al-), 463
   by Mahfouz (Naguib), 485–490
   by Mas'adi (Mahmoud al-), 516–517
   by Meddeb (Abdelwahhab),
      524–527
   by Musrati (Ali Mustafa al-),
      556–558
   by Mustaghanmi (Ahlam), 558–562
   by Oz (Amos), 593–595
   by Pamuk (Orhan), 597–601
   by Parsipur (Shahrnush), 606–607
   by Rabi (Mubarak), 637–638
   by Salih (al-Tayyib), 695–699
   by Samman (Ghada), 705
   science fiction, 268–270
   by Sebbar (Leila), 720–721
   sexuality in, 212–214
   by Shaykh (Hanan al-), 756–757
   by Shukri (Muhammad), 797
   suicide bombings in, 418
   by Tawfiq (Ahmad at-), 796–797
   by Tlili (Mustafa), 808
   by Wattar (al-Taher), 825–829
   and women, relationship between,
      256–257
   women as subjects in, 213–214,
      256–257, 258, 606, 607, 608
   by Zfur (Ahmad Bou), 797
"Little Ghayth" (Mahdaoui). *See*
   "Ghayth al-Saghir" (Mahdaoui)
Living Spirit, The (Azzawi), 140
Livni, Eitan, 473
Livni, Tzipi, *473,* **473–475**
   diplomatic career of, 474
   disengagement plan supported by,
      473, 475
   as foreign minister, 474, 475
   in Kadima Party, 474
   in Likud Party, 473
   military service of, 473
   in Mossad, 473
   Olmert (Ehud) in rivalry with, 474
   Sharon (Ariel) supported by,
      473–474, 475
   as vice prime minister, 474
Locarno Film Festival, 234
Lollobrigida, Gina, 802, 803
London
   Al-Ani's (Jananne) art in, 40
   Hanoch's (Shalom) music in, 338,
      341

Saudi opposition groups in, 291
7 July 2005 subway bombings in, 635
London (Alberstein), 44
London Document (1987), 613
Lool Group, 338, 339
Lotfi, Mohammad-Reza, 738
Love
    in Bouraoui's (Nina) novels, 213
    in Ebnou's (Moussa Ould) novels, 269
    in Khatibi's (Abdel Kebir) novels, 439
Lover from Palestine, A (Darwish), 246, 247
Loya Jirga (Afghanistan), 408, 631
Lulai, Eli, 338
Lung transplantation, 831
Lu Yehi (Alberstein), 43
"Lu Yehi" (Alberstein), 43
Lyautey, Hubert, 645
"Lying on the Water" (Ravikovitch), 656

M

Ma'ani, Walid al-, 327
Maariv (newspaper), 514
Mabahith, al- (journal), 517
Machakos Protocol (2002), 524
Madaba (Jordan), historic preservation in, 431
Madani, Abbassi, **477–481**, *478*
    in Algerian War of Independence, 477, 481
    Bouteflika (Abdelaziz) supported by, 480
    on education, 477–478, 480
    in exile in Qatar, 477, 479, 480
    in Islamic Salvation Front, 477, 478–479, 480
    National Liberation Front criticized by, 477–478, 479–480
Madinat al-Riyah (Ebnou). See *Barzakh* (Ebnou)
Madinat Baraqish (Madini), 483
Madini, Ahmad al-, **481–484**
    literary criticism by, 481, 483
    Marxism of, 481–482
    writings of, 482–484
Madrid Accords (1975), 216
Madrid Peace Talks (1991)
    Abbas (Mahmud) in, 5, 6
    Asad (Hafiz al-) in, 123
    Ashrawi (Hanan Mikha'il) in, 127
    Khalidi (Walid) in, 426
    PLO excluded from, 109
    Sharaa (Farouk al-) in, 746
    Syrian entry into, 123

Magen, Eli, 338
Maghrib
    A'raj's (Wasini al-) writings in, 113
    definition of, 112
    Khatibi (Abdel Kebir) on novels of, 439
Maghut, Muhammad al-, 463
Mahabad, Kurdish Republic of, 158
Mahdaoui, Ahmad Rafiq al-, **484–485**
    on Italian colonization of Libya, 484
    poetry of, 484–485
Mahdi, Sadiq al-
    coup of 1989 against, 162, 814
    as prime minister, 814, 815
Mahdi Army (Shi'ite military force), 678, 679
Mahfouz, Abed, 669
Mahfouz, Naguib, **485–490**, *486*
    ban on books of, 488
    on Bayati (Abd al-Wahhab al-), 168
    as civil servant, 486, 487
    historical novels by, 487, 488, 489
    Nobel Prize in Literature to, 485, 488
    and Rushdie (Salman), 488
    Salih (al-Tayyib) influenced by, 697, 698
    writings of, 486–490
Mahieddine, Baya, **490–492**
    paintings of, 490–492
    on women, 491
Mahmud, Shaykha al-, 89–90, 537
Maisonseuil, Jean de, 490
Majdub, Abd al-Rahman al-, 673
Majid, Ali Hasan al-, **492–496**, *493*
    in Ba'th Party, 492, 493, 494
    defectors killed by, 493–494
    as defense minister, 493
    as governor of Kuwait, 493, 494, 495
    in Kurdish genocide (1988), 159, 492, 493, 494–495, 790
    as minister of interior, 493, 495
    Shi'ite rebellions suppressed by, 493, 494, 495
    U.S. forces capturing, 494
Majid, Husayn Kamil Hasan al-, 493
Majid, Saddam Kamil Hasan al-, 493
Majles (Iranian parliament)
    on children's rights, 265
    elections for, 437
    Hashemi (Faezeh) in, 348–351
    Khamenehi (Ali) in, 428
    Khatami (Mohamed) and, 20, 435, 436, 437
    Rafsanjani (Ali Akbar Hashemi) in, 349–350

Majles Khobregan (Iran), 350, 540, 541
Majlis al-Nuwwab (Bahrain), 54
Majlis al-Shura (Bahrain), 54
Majlis al-Shura (Oman), 50
Majlis al-Shura (Saudi Arabia), 710, 711
Majma'-ye rohaniyun-e mobarez. See Association of Combatant Clergy
Makarios III (Eastern Orthodox archbishop), presidency of, 604, 605
Makhmalbaf, Mohsen, films of, 453
Makhmalbaf, Samira, films of, 307, 453
Makhtuta al-Sharqiyya, al- (A'raj), 114
Makiya, Kanan, 100
Makramas (royal favors), in Bahrain, 54, 55, 56
Maktoob.com, 304–305
Maktum, Ahmad bin Rashid al-, 496, 498
Maktum, Hamdan bin Rashid al-, 496
Maktum, Maktum bin Rashid al-, 496, 500
Maktum, Muhammad bin Rashid al-, *496*, **496–501**
    as defense minister of UAE, 496, 498, 500
    and economic development, 498–499, 500
    as emir of Dubai, 496, 500
    poetry of, 497, 500
    as prime minister of UAE, 496, 500
Maktum, Rashid bin Sa'id al-, 498
Maktum family, al-, as ruling family of Dubai, 496, 498
Maladie de l'Islam, La (Meddeb), 524, 526, 527
Malady of Islam, The (Meddeb). See *Maladie de l'Islam, La* (Meddeb)
Mala'ika, Nazik al-, **501–504**
    on coup of 1958, 502
    literary criticism by, 501, 502, 504
    poetry of, 501–504
    on women, 502
Male gaze. See Gaze
Maleh, Haytham al-, **504–505**
    human rights advocacy by, 504–505
Malek Haddad Literary Prize, 561
Ma'li, Muhammad An-Anah ben al-, 10
Maliki, Nuri Kamil al-, **505–510**, *506*
    in Da'wa Party, 506, 507, 508–509
    in exile in Iran, 507, 508, 509
    in exile in Syria, 506, 507, 509
    as prime minister, 506, 508, 509–510
Ma'luf (Andalusian music), 201–203
Mami (musician), 293, 294

Mammeri, Azouaou, 645

Mammeri, Mouloud, 252–253

Ma 'na al-Nakba (Zurayk), 425

Manar, al- (television network), 573

Mandaville, Jon, 649

Manoogian, Torkom (Armenian Orthodox patriarch), 762

Manufacturing, in Egyptian economy, 96

Man within Himself, A (Hanoch). *See Adam Betoh Etzmo* (Hanoch)

Man with the Golden Shoes, The (film), 98

Mapai Party (Israel), and Rafi Party, 612

Maqalib Ghawwar (television show), 462

Maqamat (melodic modes), El Saher's (Kazem) use of, 279–280

Maqdisi, Abu Muhammad al-, 852

Maqqamat Badi Zaman al-Hamadani (Saddiki), 674

Maqrizi, al-, 113–114

Marbury v. Madison, 148

March 14 movement (Lebanon), 397

Marconi, Pathé, 753

Marcus, Abraham, 649

Mardam-Bey, Farouk, 408

Mardin, Şerif, 510–513
    education of, 510–511
    on Ottoman Empire, 511, 512
    as political scientist, 510, 511, 512
    on secularism, 511, 512
    as sociologist, 510, 511, 512
    on Turkish identity, 511–512

Mar Dinkha IV (Assyrian Church patriarch), 762

Mar Elias Educational Institutions, 229–231

Mar Elias University, 229, 231

Margalit, Dan, 513–516
    books by, 513, 515
    on Holocaust, 515
    on Israeli–Palestinian conflict, 514, 515
    journalism of, 513–516
    television programs by, 513

Marianne et le marabout (Benaïssa), 179

Marines, U.S., Beirut barracks bombing of (1983), 289

Maronite Catholic Church, in Lebanon
    Khoraiche (Saida Anthony) as patriarch of, 729
    Sfeir (Nasrallah) as patriarch of, 726, 728–730
    Sharon (Ariel) cooperating with, 750

Maronite Catholic Church, in Syria, 728

Marooned in Iraq (film), 308

Marqabi, Najat, 413

Marx, Karl, "The Misery of Philosophy," 244

Marxism
    of Amiralay (Umar), 97
    of Darraj (Faisal), 243, 244
    of Habash (George), 315, 316
    of Hannoun (Louisa), 336
    of Harbi (Mohamed), 342
    Laroui (Abdallah) on, 472
    of Madini (Ahmad al-), 481–482
    of Öcalan (Abdullah), 583, 584, 585
    Tekeli (Şirin), 798
    in South Yemen, 567

Maryama (Ashour), 125

Marzouki, Moncef, 182

Mas'adi, Mahmoud al-, **516–518**
    on Islam, 517
    public school system created by, 516
    style of, 516, 517, 518
    as UNESCO representative, 516, 517
    writings of, 516–517

Masani, Tarek al-, 250

Mas'ari, Muhammad al-, 291

Mas'ari, Muhammad bin Abdullah al-, 290–291

Masculinity, in Bouraoui's (Nina) novels, 214

Mash'al, Khalid, *518,* **518–520**
    attempted assassination of, 520, 836
    in Hamas, 518, 519–520
    Hamidi's (Ibrahim) interview of, 330

Masharawi, Rashid, 786–787

Mashhadi, Muhiy Abd al-Hussein al-, 372

Mashriq
    A'raj's (Wasini al-) writings in, 113
    definition of, 112

Masir, al- (film), 234

Masoud, Ahmad Shah
    assassination of, 631
    political power of, 406–407
    and Qanuni (Yunus), 629, 630, 631

Masrah al-Nas (theater company), 674

Masri, Mai, **520–521**
    films of, 521

Masri, Munib al-, **521–523**
    business activities of, 521–523
    charity work by, 522, 523
    in peace process, 523

Massachusetts Institute of Technology (MIT), Chalabi (Ahmad) at, 235

Masumiyet (film), 227

Mathematics, game theory in, Aumann (Robert) on, 129–130

Matière des oiseaux (Meddeb), 524

Maubert, Frank, 492

Mauritania
    anti-government opposition in, 10–11
    films of Hondo (Med) in, 363–365
    history of, 12
    literature of (*See* Mauritanian literature; Mauritanian poetry)
    music of Abba (Dimi Mint Benaissa) in, 1–3
    Western Sahara claimed by, 13, 356

Mauritanian literature
    by Abd al-Qader (Ahmad ben), 10–12
    by Ebnou (Moussa Ould), 268–270
    history as subject of, 12
    isolation of authors of, 270

Mauritanian poetry
    by Abd al-Qader (Ahmad ben), 10–12
    by Barra (Mubarkah Bent al-), 156–158
    free verse, 11, 156
    modernization of, 12
    narrative style in, 12, 156
    third generation of, 156

Mawaqif (journal), 683

Mawlad al-Nisyan (Mas'adi), 517

Mawqif, al- (journal), 507

Mawsu'at al-qaba'il wa'l-ansab fi'l-Sudan wa ashhar asma al-a'lam wa'l-amakin (Qasim), 636

Mayardit, Salva Kiir, **523–524**
    as president of South Sudan, 523, 524
    in Sudanese army, 523–524
    in Sudanese Civil Wars, 523
    as vice president of Sudan, 523, 524

Mayis Sikintisi (film), 227–228

Mazal G'di (Einstein), 338, 339

M'Barek, Sonia, 202

McMillan, Stephanie, 278

Measures of Distance (Hatoum), 359–360

Mecca (Saudi Arabia)
    historic preservation in, 99
    as holy site, 711

"Mechanical Doll" (Ravikovitch), 654

Meddeb, Abdelwahhab, *524,* **524–527**
    on anti-Semitism, 527
    on Islam, 526–527
    on Islamic fundamentalism, 526
    radio program of, 527
    on women, 527
    writings of, 524–527

Media. *See* Journalism
Medicine
 in Afghanistan, 704
 in Algeria, 543, 544
 in Egypt, 276–277, 831–833
 El Saadawi (Nawal) in, 276–277
 El Sarraj (Eyad) in, 280–282
 Moqaddem (Malika) in, 543, 544
 in Palestinian territories, 280–282, 847
 Samar (Sima) in, 704
 Yacoub (Magdi) in, 831–833
 Zahhar (Mahmud al-) in, 847
Medina (Saudi Arabia), as holy site, 711
Mediterranean music, 251
Mehagrim (Alberstein), 44
Mehakim Le'Mashiah (Hanoch), 340
Mehez-e-Milli (Afghanistan), 631
Mehlis, Detlev, on Hariri's (Rafiq) assassination, 118, 347
Meir, Golda
 and Peres (Shimon), 612–613
 resignation of, 641
Melehi, Mohammed, 754
Melez Desenler (Göle), 310
Melkite Catholic Church, Chacour (Elias) as bishop in, 229–232
Mellion, Stephane, 293
Mémoires à la dérive (Benaïssa), 180
Mémoire tatouée, la (Khatibi), 439
Memoirs of a Country Prosecutor (Hakim). *See Yawmiyat Na'ib fi'l-Aryaf* (Hakim)
Memorandum of Advice (1992), 132, 290
Memory
 in Al-Ani's (Jananne) art, 40
 in Azzawi's (Dia al-) art, 137
 in Benaïssa's (Slimane) plays, 180
Memory in the Flesh (Mustaghanmi). *See Dhakirat al-Jasad* (Mustaghanmi)
"Memory of Forgetfulness" (Darwish), 246
MEMRI. *See* Middle East Media Research Institute
Men, in Bouraoui's (Nina) novels, 213–214
Menderes, Adnan, 260
Menlo College, Al Sa'ud (Al-Walid bin Talal) at, 78
Mental health, El Sarraj's (Eyad) work in, 280–282
Merah-Benida, Nouria, 211–212
Mernissi, Fatima, *528,* 528–531
 feminism of, 529, 530, 531
 on sexuality, 529, 530, 531
 as sociologist, 528–531
 on women, 528–531, 807
 writings of, 187, 528–531

Mesbah Yazdi, Mohammad Taqi, **532–534**
 on Islam, 533–534
 political activities of, 532–534
 on secularism, 532, 533, 534
 as Shi'ite Muslim cleric, 532–534
 on women, 534
 writings of, 532, 533, 534
Me'shirei Eretz Ahavati (Alberstein), 43
Meshkatian, Parviz, 738
Meshkini, Marzieh, 453
Messaoudi, Khalida. *See* Toumi, Khalida
Mestar, Mohamed, 293
Midaq Alley (Mahfouz), 488
Middle Eastern Advocates and Global Consultants. *See* MidGlobe
Middle East Media Research Institute (MEMRI), 634
Middle East Technical University (Ankara), Çetin (Hikmet) at, 223
Middle East Watch, on Kurdish genocide, 495
MidGlobe (Jordan), 793–794
MIFTAH, 127
Migdal, Joel, 455
Mihtajlak (Ajram), 31
Mij Film, 307
Mikha'il, Da'ud, 125–126
Milan (football team). *See* AC Milan
Milani, Hadi, 427, 428
Milhem, Hisham, 154
Military Committee (Syria), 120, 801
Military forces. *See under specific countries*
Milliyet (newspaper), Dündar (Can) writing for, 259–261
Mimar Sinan University (Istanbul), Ceylan (Nuri Bilge) at, 226
Min Ayyam Imran wa Ta'ammulat Ukhra (Mas'adi), 517
Miniatures, by Racim (Muhammad), 644, 645–646
Min Jibalina (Rabi), 638
Min Yawm Ma Ruht (film), 144
MIRA. *See* Movement for Islamic Reform in Arabia
Mirror, The (film). *See Ayneh*
"Mirror for Beirut, A" (Sa'id), 683
"Misery of Philosophy, The" (Marx), 244
Mishmarot (kibbutz), 337
Misnad, Mawza bint Nasir al-, **534–538**
 in Alliance of Civilizations, 537
 on education, 534, 535, 536, 537
 on women, 535, 536–537, 538
 women's rights advocacy by, 90
Misnad, Nasir al-, 535
Misnad, Shaykha Abdullah al-, 537
Misnad, Shaykha al-, 90

Misogyny
 Mernissi (Fatima) on, 529–531
 Moqaddem (Malika) on, 543, 544
MIT. *See* Massachusetts Institute of Technology
MNF. *See* Multinational Force
"Mobile Identity and the Focal Distance of Memory" (Khemir), 442
Mobil oil company, in Qatar, 90
Models, fashion
 Ruby, 665
 Wahbe (Haifa), 823–824
Moderation, Awda (Salman al-) on, 133–134
Modern Forbidden, The (Göle), 310
Modernity
 in Iran, 29
 vs. modernization, 310
Modernization
 Al Bu Sa'id (Badr bin Hamad bin Hamood) on, 47
 in Bahrain, 58
 Göle (Nilüfer) on, 309–311
 in Oman, 47, 49
 in Turkey, 309–311
"Modern Science and the Dangerous Relapse" (Al-Azm), 41
Mofaz, Shaul, 240
Mogador (theater company), 674
Mohammad: The Messenger of God (film), 33, 34
Mohammed, Khalid Shaykh, in September 11 terrorist attacks, 193
Mohteshemi, Ali Akbar, 289
Mojaddidi, Sibgatullah, 406
Monde des livres, le, 417
"Mon Pays" (Faudel), 294
Montazeri, Hossein Ali, *538,* 538–543
 in antigovernment movements, 538, 539–541, 542
 under house arrest, 538, 540
 in Iranian Revolution (1979), 538, 540, 541, 542
 Kadivar (Mohsen) as student of, 541
 as Shi'ite Muslim cleric, 538–539, 540, 541
 as student of Khomeini (Ruhollah), 539
 as successor-designate of Khomeini (Ruhollah), 538, 540
 on *velayat-e faqih* (governance of jurists), 540, 541
 writings of, 541–542
Monument of the Holocaust and Revival (Tumarkin), 813
Moorish Music from Mauritania (Abba), 1–2
Moqaddem, Malika, **543–544**
 in medicine, 543, 544
Morazé, Charles, 470

VOLUME 1: 1–458; VOLUME 2: 459–860

on PLO, 576, 577
    as prime minister, 574, 576, 577,
       578, 613
    and Rabin (Yitzhak), 576
    and Sharon (Ariel), 576, 750
    on terrorism, 575, 576, 577
Netanyahu, Yonatan ("Yoni"), 575, 577
Netherlands, Abu-Assad (Hany) in, 22
Neuer, Hillel, 147
New Communist List. *See* RAKAH
New Life, The (Pamuk). *See Yeni Hayat*
    (Pamuk)
News Hour with Jim Lehrer (television
    show), 394
Newspapers, women's, in Iran,
    350–351. *See also* Journalism; *specific
    papers*
Newsweek (magazine), 32, 273, 305
New Vision art group, 137
"New wave" cinema, in Turkey, 226,
    227
New York Times (newspaper), 101, 134
NGOs. *See* Nongovernmental
    organizations
NGOTC. *See* Non-Governmental
    Organisation Training Centre
NHF. *See* Noor al-Hussein Foundation
Nietzsche, Friedrich, 186
NIF. *See* National Islamic Front
Niger, UTA flight 772 bombing in,
    626
"Night" (Hanoch). *See* "Laila"
    (Hanoch)
Night after Night (Hanoch). *See Erev,
    Erev* (Hanoch)
Night and Fog (film), 185
Nightline (television show), 127
Night Lover (Mala'ika), 502
Nihilism, of Dayan (Assi), 248–249
Nile Boy (film), 232
Nile River, film about, 233
Nimrod (Danziger), 812
1948 (film), 144
1949: The First Israelis (Segev), 723
Nissaboury, Mostefa, 186
Nissim, Moshe, 842
Nissim, Yitshak, 841, 842
Nobel Peace Prize
    to Arafat (Yasir), 111, 614, 642
    Chacour (Elias) nominated for,
       229, 231
    to Ebadi (Shirin), 263, 266, 267,
       443, 444
    to ElBaradei (Mohamed), 274
    to Peres (Shimon), 614
    to Rabin (Yitzhak), 614, 642
Nobel Prize in Chemistry
    to Ciechanover (Aaron), 237–238,
       362
    to Hershko (Avram), 362

Nobel Prize in Economics, to Aumann
    (Robert), 129
Nobel Prize in Literature
    Behbahani (Simin) nominated for,
       175–176
       to Mahfouz (Naguib), 485, 488
       to Pamuk (Orhan), 597, 600,
       601
Nobel Women Initiative for Peace,
    Justice, and Equality (NWI), 268
Non-Governmental Organisation
    Training Centre (NGOTC), 9
Nongovernmental organizations
    (NGOs)
    Abbasgholizadeh's (Mahboubeh)
       involvement in, 8–10
    in Jordan, Basma bint Talal's use
       of, 164–165
Nonproliferation, nuclear, ElBaradei
    (Mohamed) on, 273
Nonviolence
    of Chacour (Elias), 229
    El Sarraj (Eyad) on, 282
Noon (magazine), 277
Noor al-Hussein (queen of Jordan),
    379, *578,* **578–581**
    as architect, 579
    as philanthropist, 578, 579–581
Noor al-Hussein Foundation (NHF)
    (Jordan), 580
North American Treaty Organization
    (NATO)
    in Afghanistan, Çetin (Hikmet)
       working for, 223, 224–225
    in war on terror, 225
North Korea, nuclear program of,
    IAEA inspections of, 273
North Yemen. *See* Yemen Arab
    Republic
Notes on Village Architecture in Jordan
    (Khammash), 431
Nous sommes fait pour nous entendre
    (Saddiki), 675
Novels. *See* Literature
N'ta Goudami (Rimitti), 660
Nu'aymi, Abd al-Rahman bin Umayr,
    90
Nuclear nonproliferation, ElBaradei
    (Mohamed) on, 273
Nuclear programs. *See also* Iranian
    nuclear program; Iraqi weapons of
    mass destruction
    Gulf Cooperation Council
       on, 65
    IAEA inspections of, 273–274
    of North Korea, 273
Nuhawwilu sadd al-Furat (film), 98
Nujum al-Mustaqbal (television
    show), 31

Nur al-Ayn (Diab), 250–251
Nuwwar al-Lawz (A'raj), 113–114
NWC. *See* National Women's
    Committee
NWI. *See* Nobel Women Initiative for
    Peace, Justice, and Equality

O

Obaid, Hasan Ismail, 401
Öcalan, Abdullah, **583–585,** *584*
    extradition of, 584, 585
    as football fan, 800
    Hamidi's (Ibrahim) interview of,
       330
    as leader of Workers' Party of
       Kurdistan, 583–585
Occupied Territories. *See also* Gaza
    Strip; West Bank
    charity work in, 522, 523, 836,
       837, 838
    football in, 783–784
    human rights in, 280–282, 758,
       759
    legal system of, Shehadeh (Raja) in,
       757–760
    medicine in, 280–282
    separation fence in, 148
    sumud (perseverance) in, 759
Occupier's Law (Shehadeh), 759
Ocean of Dreams, An (Saudi), 715
Office for Metropolitan Architecture
    (OMA) (London), 322
Offsets program, of UAE, 71
Offside (film), 602, 603
Oger International, 345
Oger Liban, 346
OIB. *See* Oman International Bank
Oil
    in Abu Dhabi, 62, 64
    in Algeria, 216
    in Bahrain, 57, 59
    French concessions of, 216
    in Gulf War, 373
    in Iran, 539
    in Iraq, 371
    nationalization of, 371
    in Qatar, 85, 88, 90
    in Yemen, 695
Oil du jour, l' (Béji), 177, 178
Ökten, Zeki, 227
Olam ha-Zeh, ha- (newspaper), 513
Olmert, Ehud, **585–590,** *586*
    in Free Center Party, 587
    in Herut Party, 586–587, 589
    as Jerusalem mayor, 587, 589
    journalists in election of, 155–156
    in Kadima Party, 587–588, 617
    in Lebanon War (2006), 588, 589,
       590, 617, 618

Olmert, Ehud, *continued*
  in Likud Party, 587, 589
  Livni (Tzipi) in rivalry with, 474
  military service of, 586
  on Peer (Shahar), 609
  as prime minister, 474, 587–588,
    589–590, 617, 618, 751
  as Sharon's (Ariel) ally, 587,
    589
  on withdrawal from Gaza Strip,
    475, 587, 589, 590
  on withdrawal from West Bank,
    577, 587–588, 590
Olmert, Mordechai, 586, 588–589
Olympic champions
  Ayhan (Süreyya), 136
  Boulmerka (Hassiba), 209–212
  El Moutawakel (Nawal), 274–276
  Merah-Benida (Nouria), 211–212
  Rezazadeh (Hossein), 657, 658
  Shouaa (Ghada), 769–770
  Süleymanoglu (Naim), 658
  Yerlikaya (Hamza), 839, 840
Olympic Games of 1972, Israelis mur-
  dered at, 110
OMA. *See* Office for Metropolitan
  Architecture
Oman
  Al Bu Saʿid (Badr bin Hamad bin
    Hamood) in government of,
    46–47
  Al Bu Saʿid (Qaboos) as sultan of,
    48–52
  Al Bu Saʿid (Saʿid bin Taymur) as
    sultan of, 45, 48
  banking in, Zawawi (Omar bin
    Abd al-Munim) in, 854, 855
  corruption in, 855
  coup of 1970 in, 45, 48
  culture of, preservation of, 50
  economic development in, 49, 50,
    854
  environmental protection in, 51
  foreign policy of, 46–47, 51
  military of, improvements to,
    49–50
  modernization in, 47, 49
  in peace process, 46
  political reform in, 49–51
Oman Arab African Bank, 854
Oman Council, establishment of, 51
Oman International Bank (OIB), 854,
  855
Omar, Mullah Mohammed,
  590–592
  fighting against Soviet invasion,
    591
  legends about, 591
  poppy production stopped by,
    592

  in Taliban, 590–591, 592
  U.S. ultimatum to, 592
Omar Zawawi Establishment, 853
Ombre sultane (Djebar), 256, 257
Om Kultum. *See* Umm Kulthum
Omzest Group, 853, 854
One Dimension art group, 137, 138
One Million Signature Campaign for
  Equal Rights (Iran), 266, 267, 444
One Nation Party (Israel), 617
*One Palestine, Complete: Jews and Arabs
  under the British Mandate* (Segev),
  724
One Thousand and One Arabian Nights,
  11, 114
Only Human (Hanoch). *See Rak Ben
  Adam* (Hanoch)
Operation Defensive Shield (2002),
  750
Operation Summer Rains (2006), 588
Operation Thunderbolt (1976). *See*
  Entebbe incident
Operation Yonatan (1976). *See*
  Entebbe incident
Opium trade, in Afghanistan, 225, 592
Opposition parties. *See also specific
  parties*
  Algerian, legalization of, 335, 478,
    480
  Jordanian, in parliamentary elec-
    tions, 378
  Moroccan, repression of, 355–356
  Tunisian, repression of, 182
Oraieth, Muhammad Ahmed, 485
Oral literature, Barra (Mubarkah Bent
  al-) on, 156
Orascom (Egyptian company), 715,
  716–717
Or Commission of Inquiry, 391
Ordinary, the, Ceylan (Nuri Bilge) on,
  228
Orfanelli, Alvisi, 232
Organisation Socialiste des Travailleurs
  (OST) (Algeria), 335
Organ transplantation, 831
Orghuni, Fakhrazami, 173, 174
Orientalism
  Al-Azm (Sadik) on, 41
  definition of, 41
  Said (Edward) on, 685–688
Orientalism (Said), 685, 686, 687,
  688
Orient express, l' (review), 409
*Origines sociales et culturelles du natio-
  nalisme marocain, 1830–1912, Les*
  (Laroui), 472
Orthodox Church of Jerusalem,
  Theophilus III as patriarch of, 762
Or Yisraʾel (Hanoch), 341
Oryx, Arabian, 51

Osirak nuclear reactor (Iraq), Israeli
  bombing of (1981), 650, 651
Oslo Accords (1993)
  Abbas (Mahmud) in, 5, 6–7, 8
  Arafat (Yasir) in, 109, 641
  Barghuthi (Marwan) on, 152
  failure of, 7
  in Hatoum's (Mona) art, 360, 361
  Hussein bin Talal surprised by,
    378
  Masri (Munib al-) in, 523
  Netanyahu (Binyamin) on, 576,
    577
  Palestinian refugees in, 332–333
  Peres (Shimon) and, 613, 614
  PFLP's rejection of, 316
  PLO in, 109
  principles of, 614
  Rabin (Yitzhak) and, 641–642,
    643, 644
  Said (Edward) on, 686–687, 688
  secret talks leading to, 199
  Sharon (Ariel) reversing, 750
  Shehadeh (Raja) on, 760
  signing of, 5, 8, 109, 614
  Tibi (Ahmad) in, 199
  Yasin (Ahmad) on, 838
Oslo II Interim Agreement (1995),
  Abbas (Mahmud) in, 7
Ososkin, Elisheva, 146
OST. *See* Organisation Socialiste des
  Travailleurs
Öteki Renkler (Pamuk), 599, 600
Other, The (film). *See Akhar, al-*
Other Colors (Pamuk). *See Öteki Renkler*
  (Pamuk)
Ottoman Empire
  İnalck (Halil) on, 511
  in Kulin's (Ayşe) novels, 457
  Mardin (Şerif) on, 511, 512
  Rafeq (Abdul-Karim) on, 648,
    649
Oud (lute), 399, 739–740
Ouettar, Taher. *See* Wattar, al-Taher
Oufkir, Malika, 353
Oufkir, Muhammad, 353
  family of, 353, 356, 357
  under Hassan II, 353, 355–356
  under Muhammad V, 353
Oum Kalsoum. *See* Umm Kulthum
Oz, Amos, *593,* **593–595**
  military service of, 593, 594
  writings of, 593–595
Özgüç, Agah, 104, 105

Ṗ

PA. *See* Palestinian Authority
Pacifism, in Alberstein's (Chava) music,
  43

Palestinian Legislative Council (PLC)
  Abbas (Mahmud) in, 5
  Barghuthi (Marwan) in, 150
  El Sarraj (Eyad) in, 281
  Hamas in, 7, 332, 520, 838–839
Palestinian literature
  Darraj (Faisal) on, 242–244
  by Darwish (Mahmud), 244–247
  by Habibi (Emile), 318–320
  literary criticism of, 242–244
  poetry, 100, 244–247
Palestinian medicine
  El Sarraj (Eyad) in, 280–282
  Zahhar (Mahmud al-) in, 847
Palestinian music
  of Nafat (Tamer), 766
  of Shaheen (Simon), 730–732
Palestinian National Fund (PNF)
  establishment of, 767, 768
  Shoman (Abdul Majeed) as direc-
    tor of, 767, 768
Palestinian nationalist movement
  Abbas (Mahmud) in, 4–5, 6
  Arafat (Yasir) in, 108
  Jabarin (Hasan) in, 389–390
Palestinian right of return
  Darraj's (Faisal) support for, 244
  Haniyeh's (Ismail) support for,
    333
Palestinians: The Making of a People
  (Kimmerling and Migdal), 455
Palestinian state. *See also* Two-state
  solution
  Khalidi (Walid) on, 426
  PFLP's position on, 315
Palestinian territories. *See* Occupied
  Territories
Palmah (Hagana fighting force), Rabin
  (Yitzhak) in, 639–640
PALTEL. *See* Palestine
  Telecommunications Corporation
Pamuk, Orhan, **597–601**, *598*
  as controversial intellectual,
    599–600
  Nobel Prize in Literature to, 597,
    600, 601
  writings of, 597–601
Pan-Africanism, in films, 365
Panahi, Jafar, **601–603**, *602*
  films by, 602–603
  Kiarostami (Abbas) working with,
    453, 602
Pan Am flight 103 bombing
  (Lockerbie)
  and economic sanctions against
    Libya, 626
  Libyan compensation for, 626, 629
  Libyan role in, 626
Pan-Arab nationalism, Khalidi (Walid)
  on, 426

Pancyprian Committee of the Cyprus
  Struggle. *See* Pagkypria Epitrope
  Kypriakou Agona
Pangalos, Theodoros, 585
Papa Amin (film). *See Baba Amin*
Papadopoulos, Tassos, *603*, **603–605**
  in first independent government,
    603–604
  presidency of, 604–605
  and Talat (Mehmet Ali), 793
Paper House (film), 21–22
Papon, Maurice, 205
Paradise Now (film), 22–23
Paris
  Hakim (Tawfiq al-) studying in,
    324
  massacre of Algerian immigrants in
    (1961), 205, 206
Paris I conference (2001), 348
Paris II conference (2002), 347, 348
Parkingallery (Iran), 305–307
Parle mon fils, parle à ta mère (Sebbar),
  721
Parsipur, Shahrnush, **605–608**, *606*
  feminism of, 607, 608
  writings of, 606–607
Parti des Travailleurs (PT) (Algeria),
  335
Parti du Peuple Algerien (PPN),
  342–343
Parti pour la libération et le socialism
  (PLS) (Morocco), 460
Parti Socialiste Destourien (PSD)
  (Tunisia), 182
Party of God. *See* Hizbullah
Pasdaran (Iran). *See* Revolutionary
  Guards
Pashtuns, in Afghanistan, 407, 630,
  631
Passer by a Bed (Mustaghanmi). *See*
  'Abir Sarir (Mustaghanmi)
Patriarchy
  El Saadawi (Nawal) on, 276
  Mala'ika (Nazik al-) on, 502
  Mernissi (Fatima) on, 529
Patriotic Union of Kurdistan (PUK)
  establishment of, 159
  Talabani (Jalal) in, 789, 790, 791
Payame Hajar (periodical), 36
PCP. *See* Palestine Communist Party
Peace movement
  Chacour (Elias) in, 230–231
  Ebadi (Shirin) in, 268
Peace process, Middle East. *See also*
  specific events
  Abbas (Mahmud) in, 4–8
  Abdullah II bin Hussein in, 17–18
  Al Bu Sa'id (Badr bin Hamad bin
    Hamood) in, 46–47
  Arafat (Yasir) in, 108–112, 199

Asad (Bashar al-) in, 117–118
Asad (Hafiz al-) in, 122–123
Ashrawi (Hanan Mikha'il) in, 127
Barghuthi (Marwan) on, 151, 152,
  155
Begin (Menachem) in, 548
Boutros-Ghali (Boutros) in, 220
Dahlan (Muhammad) in, 239–242
Hamidi (Ibrahim) on, 331
Hussein bin Talal in, 378, 379
Jordanian Option in, 109
Khaddam (Abd al-Halim) in, 413,
  414
Khalidi (Walid) in, 426
Masri (Munib al-) in, 523
Moussa (Amr) in, 545
Muasher (Marwan) in, 547
Netanyahu (Binyamin) in,
  575–576, 577, 578
Peres (Shimon) in, 613, 614, 615
press coverage of, 331
Rabin (Yitzhak) in, 639, 641–642,
  643–644
Sadat (Anwar) in, 548, 641
secret talks in, 199
Sharaa (Farouk al-) in, 746
Shehadeh (Raja) in, 758, 759–760
Tibi (Ahmad) in, 199
Yasin (Ahmad) in, 837, 838
Peaks, The (Hong Kong spa), 322
Peckinpah, Sam, 33
Peer, Shahar, *608*, **608–610**
  military service of, 609
  titles won by, 608–609
PEKA. *See* Pagkypria Epitrope
  Kypriakou Agona
Peled, Mattiyahu, 6
Pélégri, Jean, 492
Pella Jordan Valley Renovation, 430–431
People of the Cave (Hakim). *See Ahl al-
  Kahf* (Hakim)
People of the Nile (film). *See Nas fil-Nil,
  al-*
People's Council (Syria), establishment
  of, 121
People's Democratic Republic of
  Yemen (South Yemen)
  Bid (Ali Salim al-) as president of,
    692, 693, 694
  Marxist-Leninist socialism in, 567
  table tennis in, 566–567
  unification of North Yemen and,
    692, 693, 694, 706, 707–708,
    856
  women's rights in, 566, 567
Perah ha-Lilakh (Alberstein), 42
Peres, Shimon, *610*, **610–615**
  in Arab–Israel War (1967), 613
  as defense minister, 613
  as foreign minister, 613, 614

Rabin, Yitzhak, *continued*
    and Ben-Gurion (David), 640, 641
    as defense minister, 641, 642, 643
    fighting British mandate in Palestine, 639–640
    in Labor Party, 641
    military service of, 639–641, 642
    and Netanyahu (Binyamin), 576
    Nobel Peace Prize to, 614, 642
    and Oslo Accords (1993), 641–642, 643, 644
    in peace process, 639, 641–642, 643–644
    on PLO, 641
    as prime minister, 613, 639, 641–642, 643, 844
    resignation of, 146, 641
    Sharon (Ariel) under, 749
Rabin Memoirs, The (Rabin). *See Pinkas Sherut* (Rabin)
Racim, Muhammad, **644–646**
    art of, 644–646
    miniatures of, 644, 645–646
    writings of, 646
Racing. *See* Auto racing; Camel racing; Horse racing
Racy, Ali Jihad, 298, 731
Radhi, Ahmad, **646–648**
    athletic career of, 646–647
Radif (music), 737–738
Radio
    Faqih's (Sa'd al-) stations, 291
    Fayruz performing on, 296
    Lebanese, 296
    Meddeb's (Abdelwahhab) program on, 527
    Musrati's (Ali Mustafa al-) program on, 557
    Mustaghanmi's (Ahlam) program on, 559
    Persian music on, 737
    Umm Kulthum performing on, 818, 819, 820, 821
Radio Iran, 20, 21
Radio Nouakchott, 2–3
Radubis (Mahfouz), 487, 489
Rafeq, Abdul-Karim, **648–650**
    academic career of, 648–649
    as historian, 648–649
Rafi Party (Israel)
    Ben-Gurion (David) founding, 612
    Peres (Shimon) in, 612
Rafiq, Abd al-Karim. *See* Rafeq, Abdul-Karim
Rafsanjani, Ali Akbar Hashemi
    Ahmadinejad (Mahmoud) running against, 27–28

family of, 348–350
in Iran–Contra affair, 540
Khatami (Mohamed) in government of, 435–436
in Majles elections of 2000, 349–350
Mesbah Yazdi (Mohammad Taqi) on, 533, 534
presidency of, 429
Raghif Yanbud ka al-Qalb, al- (Samman), 705
Rahbani, Asi, 296–297, 298
Rahbani, Hanna, 298
Rahbani, Mansur, 296–297, 298
Rahbani, Ziyad, 296, 297
Rahim, Muhammad, 665
Raï music
    by Faudel, 292–294
    instrumentation of, 660, 662
    by Khaled (Cheb), 660
    lyrics of, 658, 660, 661, 662
    by Rimitti (Cheikha), 658, 659–662
"Rais, The" (Racim), 646
Raiti Otam (Margalit), 515
Rajub, Jibril, 241
    Arafat's relationship with, 240, 241
    as national security advisor, 5, 241
RAKAH, Bishara (Azmi) in, 196, 197
Rak Ben Adam (Hanoch), 340
Ramadan, Khaled's (Amr) television shows during, 420
Ramadhan, Taha Yasin, 374
Ramallah (West Bank), Arafat's (Yasir) compound in, Israeli siege of, 110, 240
Ramat Yohanan (kibbutz), 639
Rami, Ahmad, 818
Ramla sound, 339
Ramon, Haim, and Peretz (Amir), 616
Ramon, Ilan, **650–651**
    in Arab–Israeli War (1973), 650
    as astronaut, 650–651
    military service of, 650, 651
Rana's Wedding (film). *See Quds fi Yawm Akhar, al-*
Rand Corporation, 712
Rania (queen of Jordan), 17, 19
Rantisi, Abd al-Aziz, 333, 837
    assassination of, 332, 333, 520, 848
    in Hamas, 332, 333, 847
    and Zahhar (Mahmud al-), 847, 848
"Raseed Mojdah" (Nasher), 565–566
Rasheed, Madawi al-, 131, 134, 135
Rashid, Uday, **651–653**
    documentaries of, 651, 652
    films of, 651–653
Rashidiyya musical ensemble, 201, 202
Rasim, Mohammed. *See* Racim, Muhammad

Rassemblement Constitutionelle Démocratique (RCD) (Tunisia), 182
Rassemblement pour la Culture et al Démocratie (RCD) (Algeria)
    Sadi (Said) in, 675, 676
    Toumi (Khalida) in, 809
Rassi, George, 559
Rauf Ezzat, Heba, **653**
    academic career of, 653
    on feminism, 653
Ravikovitch, Dalia, **654–657**
    academic career of, 654
    journalism of, 654
    poetry of, 654–657
RAWA. *See* Revolutionary Association of the Women of Afghanistan
Rawabida, Abd al-Ra'uf al-, Hamarneh (Mustafa) and, 327
Raymond, André, 649
RCC. *See* Revolutionary Command Council
RCD. *See* Rassemblement Constitutionelle Démocratique; Rassemblement pour la Culture et al Démocratie
Reagan, Ronald
    in Iran–Contra affair, 540
    Moroccan relations with, 357
Real estate, Al Sa'ud's (Al-Walid bin Talal) investments in, 79, 80
Realignment plan (2006)
    Livni (Tzipi) supporting, 475
    Netanyahu (Binyamin) on, 577
    Olmert (Ehud) and, 475, 577, 587–588, 590
Real Time (film), 248
Reasonableness, in government decisions, 148
Refugees, Iraqi
    in Iran, 509
    in Qatar, 86, 90
    Shi'ite, 509
    in Syria, 509
Refugees, Palestinian
    Abbas (Mahmud) as, 4, 6
    of Arab–Israeli War (1948), 4, 6, 229, 331, 332–333, 426
    Chacour (Elias) as, 229
    films about, 144
    Haniyeh (Ismail) as, 331, 332–333
    in Jenin camp, Israeli assault on (2002), 144
    in Jordan, 108, 379, 380, 519
    Khalidi (Walid) on, 426
    in Lebanon, 572
    Oslo Accords on (1993), 332–333
    right of return for, 244, 333
    Shikaki (Khalil) on, 764, 765
Refugees, Saharawi, in Algeria, 13–14

Religion(s)
    diversity of, in Lebanon, 289
    in Egyptian film, 234, 235
    freedom of, in Qatar, 89
    in Israeli art, 303
    patriarchy of, El Saadawi (Nawal)
        on, 276
    Soroush (Abdolkarim) on, 778–779
Religion, Women and Ethics (Rauf
    Ezzat), 653
Religious fundamentalism. *See also*
    Islamic fundamentalism
    in Algeria, Harbi (Mohamed) on,
        343
Renaissance Party (Tunisia). *See* Hizb
    En Nahda
Renditions, extraordinary, Jordan's role
    in, 18
Renewalists, in Turkey, 284
Republican Guard (Iraq), in Gulf War,
    373
Republican's People Party (CHP)
    (Turkey), 223, 224
Republic Turkish Party (RTP), 792
Répudiation, la (Boudjedra), 205–206,
    207
Requim for Metin Altiok (Say), 719
Resaleh-ye Hoqouq (Montazeri), 541–542
Resnais, Alain, 185
Resurrecting Empire (Khalidi), 423
Return of Consciousness, The (Hakim).
    See Awdat al-Wa'i (Hakim)
Return of the Prodigal Son (film). *See
    Awdat al-ibn al-dhal*
Return of the Spirit (Hakim). *See Awdat
    al-Ruh* (Hakim)
Revisionist Zionism
    of Livni (Tzipi), 474–475
    of Netanyahu (Binyamin), 577
    of Olmert (Ehud), 586, 588–589
    Segev (Tom) on, 724
Revolutionary Association of the
    Women of Afghanistan (RAWA), 704
Revolutionary Command Council
    (RCC) (Iraq)
    Duri (Izzat Ibrahim al-) in, 494
    under Hussein (Saddam), 372
    Majid (Ali Hasan al-) in, 493
Revolutionary Command Council
    (RCC) (Libya), 624–625, 627
Revolutionary Command Council
    (RCC) (Sudan)
    Bashir (Omar al-) in, 162
    dissolution of, 163
    establishment of, 162
    Salih (al-Tayyib) against, 698
Revolutionary Council (Iran),
    Khamenehi (Ali) in, 428
Revolutionary Guards (Iran)
    Ahmadinejad (Mahmoud) in, 27

Khamenehi (Ali) in, 428
    in Lebanon, 289
Rezazadeh, Hossein, *657,* **657–658**
    athletic career of, 657–658
    as Olympic champion, 657, 658
Rice, Condoleezza, on U.S.–Turkish
    relations, 261
Rif rebellion (1958), 353
Right of return, Palestinian
    Darraj's (Faisal) support for, 244
    Haniyeh's (Ismail) support for, 333
Right Start Foundation, 420
Rih al-janub (Benhedouga), 826, 827
Rihani, Najib al-, 325
Rim al-Dhahab (film), 233
Rimitti, Cheikha, **658–662**
    in exile in France, 658, 659
    on feminism, 661
    music of, 658–662
    popularity of, 659–660, 661
Ring Seller (film). *See Bayya al-
    Khawatim*
Riots, in Algeria, in 1988, 217, 335
Risalah, al- (film), 33
Riyadh (Saudi Arabia)
    demonstrations in, organized by
        Faqih (Sa'd al-), 291–292
    terrorist attacks in (2003), 134, 433
Roadmap to Peace initiative
    Abbas (Mahmud) in, 7
    Abdullah II bin Hussein in, 17–18
RockFour (band), 338
Rock music, of Hanoch (Shalom),
    337–341
Rogacheva, Lyudmila, 210
Roken, Mohammed al-, **662–665**
    academic career of, 662, 663, 664
    on democracy, 663, 664
    on human rights, 662, 663, 664,
        665
    legal career of, 662–665
Romanoff, Marcel, 665, 666
Rome platform, 205
Romney, Jonathan, 226, 227, 228
Rose, Irvin A., 237, 362
Rosenthal Center for Contemporary
    Art (Cincinnati), architecture of, 322
Rotana, 79–80
Rouby. *See* Ruby
Rouznameh Zan (newspaper), 36
Roy, Olivier, 526
Royal Advisory Council on Human
    Rights (Morocco), 555
RTP. *See* Republic Turkish Party
Ruby, *665,* **665–666**
    music of, 665–666
Ruffieux, François, 211
Rukn, Muhammad al-. *See* Roken,
    Mohammed al-
Rule of law, Barak (Aharon) on, 147

Rumi, Halim al-, 296
Rumi, Jalal al-Din, 778
Rumi, Majda al-, 296
Rumi Ensemble (musical group), 574
Rummah, Ghilan dhi al-, 10
Running
    Ayhan (Süreyya) in, 135–137
    Boulmerka (Hassiba) in, 209–212
Rushdie, Salman, *fatwa* against, 488
Russia. *See* Soviet Union
"Ru'ya" (Asimi), 128
Ru'ya Halima (film), 689

S

Sa'aada, Antun, 682
Saab, Elie, **667–669**, *668,* 860
    fashion designs by, 667–669
Sa'adat, Ahmad, in prisoner exchanges,
    153
Sabanci, Güler, *669,* **669–672**
    business career of, 669–672
    charity work by, 670–671
Sabanci, Haci Ömer, 669, 670
Sabanci, Sakip, 670, 671
Sabanci Foundation, 671
Sabanci Holding, 669, 670, 672
Sabanci University (Turkey), 671
Saba Waraqat Kotchina (Ruby), 665
Sabbah, Michel, 762
Sabbath, observing in space, 650–651
SABCO, 46
Sabra (Israeli Jews)
    definition of, 249
    as myth, 247–249
Sabri, Sherif, 665, 666
Sabuncu, Başar, 105
Sacred Night, The (Ben Jelloun),
    187–188
Sadat, Anwar
    assassination of, 549
    Boutros-Ghali (Boutros) in gov-
        ernment of, 220
    business environment under, 715
    film about, 850
    Islamic militants arrested by,
        548–549
    Mahfouz's (Naguib) books banned
        by, 488
    Muslim Brotherhood members
        released by, 548
    on national anthem of Egypt, 819
    in National Democratic Party,
        548
    in peace process, 548, 641
    presidency of, 548
    Qaddafi (Mu'ammar al-) on, 627
    religious piety of, 548
    and Shenouda III, 761, 763
Sa'dawi, Bashir al-, 556

Saddiki, Tayeb, **672–675**
  films by, 674
  plays written by, 673, 674, 675
  as theater director, 672–675
Saddiki Troupe (theater company), 673
Sadeghi, Zohreh, 434
Sadi, Said, **675–676**
  on Berbers, 676
  as psychiatrist, 675
  and Toumi (Khalida), 809
Sadjadpour, Karim, 438
SADR. *See* Saharawi Arab Democratic Republic
Sadr, Muhammad Baqir al-
  execution of, 507, 508, 676
  as Shi'ite cleric, 508, 676
Sadr, Muhammad Muhammad Sadiq al-, 676–677
Sadr, Muqtada al-, **676–679**, *677*
  religious studies of, 677
  as Shi'ite cleric, 507, 676, 677
  supporters of, 678
Sadr, Musa al-, 568, 569, 679
  disappearance of, 288, 434
  Fadlallah (Muhammad Husayn) and, 288
  Khatami (Mohamed) as son-in-law of, 434
Sadr, Rabab al-, **679–680**
  charity work by, 679–680
  as human rights activist, 679–680
Sadr, Shadi, *680*, **680–682**
  as human rights activist, 681
  journalism of, 680
  women's rights advocacy by, 680–682
Sadr City (section in Baghdad), 678
Sadr intifada, al- (1999), 494
"Safin, al-" (Abd al-Qader), 11, 12
Safqah, al- (Hakim), 326
Sahara. *See also* Western Sahara
  French oil concessions in, 216
"Sahara, Al-" (Sa'id). *See* "Desert, The" (Sa'id)
Saharawi Arab Democratic Republic (SADR), 13–14
  Algeria's support for, 217, 218
Saharawis, 13–14. *See also* Western Sahara
Saharuni al-Layll (Alama), 38
Sahh al-Nawm (television show), 462
Sahnoun, Ahmed, 478
Sahrat Dimashq (television show), 462
Sahwa intellectual movement, Awda (Salman al-) in, 131–135
Sa'id, Ali Ahmad, *682*, **682–685**
  on Arab–Israel conflict, 683, 684
  Bannis (Mohammed) published by, 145
  in exile in Lebanon, 682–683

military service of, 682
poetry of, 682–684
Said, Edward, *685*, **685–688**
  Darraj (Faisal) on, 243, 244
  on Israeli–Palestinian conflict, 685, 686–688
  Khalidi (Rashid) and, 421, 422
  on Khoury's (Elias) writing, 449
  as literary theorist, 685, 686, 687, 688
Said, Shakhir Hassan al-, art of, 137, 138
Saint Qadr (Rabi). *See Sayyidna Qadr* (Rabi)
Saison des hommes, La (film). *See Season of Men, The*
Sakhnovski, Sergei, 405
Sakip Sabanci Museum (Istanbul), 671
Saladdin (Mahfouz), 486
Saladin (film), 34, 233
Saladin (Muslim ruler), film about, 34, 233
Salafism, 479
Salalah (Oman), Al Bu Sa'id family in, 45, 48
Salam, Anbara, 423
Salam, Sa'ib, 426
Salama, Musa, 487
Salam Afghanistan (Nasher), 566
Salameh, Nadine, **688–690**
  acting career of, 688–689
  as Palestinian activist, 688, 689
Salami, Khadija al-, **690–691**
  feminism of, 691
  films of, 690–691
Sales, Sohrab Shahid, 453
Salih, Ahmad, 694
Salih, Ali Abdullah, *692*, **692–695**
  coup attempt against (1978), 693
  family members in power, 693, 694
  on Iran–Iraq War (1980–1988), 693, 694
  military service of, 693
  presidency of, 693–694, 695, 856, 857
  on Tuhayf's (Amina al-) death sentence, 691
  and U.S. relations, 695
  as YAR president, 692, 693
  on Zindani (Abd al-Majid al-), 857–858
Salih, al-Tayyib, **695–699**
  writings of, 695–699
Salih, Muhammad Abdullah, 693
Salloum, Jayce, 785
Salman, Ali, *699*, **699–704**
  in Bahraini Shi'ite opposition, 699, 700–702
  in exile in Britain, 701
  in exile in Dubai, 701

influences on, 702–703
Qasim (Shaykh Isa) as mentor of, 700, 701, 702–703
religious studies of, 700
Salman bin Abd al-Aziz, 710
"Salu Ku'us a-Tila" (Sunbati), 820
Salvation in Orthodox Understanding (Shenouda III). *See Khalas fi'l-Mafhum al-Urthuduksi, al-* (Shenouda III)
Samadzadegan, Behrang, art of, 306
Samak la Yubali, al- (Bayyud), 172
Samar, Sima, **704–705**
  human rights advocacy by, 704
  as physician, 704
  women's rights advocacy by, 704
Samir Kassir Foundation, 449
Samman, Ghada, **705**
  journalism of, 705
  writings of, 705
Samra (Faudel), 293
Samt al-Qusur (film). *See Silences of the Palace, The*
San'a: Madina Maftuha (Wali), 856
Sanctions, UN
  against Iraq, 373–374
  against Libya, 626, 629
Sand Child, The (Ben Jelloun), 187–188
Sands of Gold (film). *See Rim al-Dhahab*
Santur (musical instrument), 737
Sapir, Pinhas, and Peres (Shimon), 612–613
Saqqaf, Abd al-Aziz, **705–709**
  as economist, 705, 707
  human rights advocacy by, 705, 706, 708
  journalism of, 705–706, 707, 709
  women's rights advocacy by, 706
Saqqaf, Nadia, 709
Sarab, al- (Mahfouz), 487
Sarid, Yossi, 843
Sarvath (princess of Jordan), 377
Satanic Verses (Rushdie), 488
Satellites, 83
Satin Rouge (film), 92–93
Satire, in Habibi's (Emile) writing, 319
Sa'ud, Abdullah bin Abd al-Aziz al- (king of Saudi Arabia), *709*, **709–714**
  foreign policy of, 393, 712–713
  Jubayr (Adil al-) under, 393
  and military, 710–711
  and municipal elections (2005), 711–712
Saudi, Mona, **714–715**
  poetry of, 715
  sculptures of, 714–715
Saudi Arabia
  bin Ladin (Usama) criticizing royal family of, 192–193, 194

business community of, Al Saʿud (Al-Walid bin Talal) in, 78–82
censorship in, 834
Chinese relations with, 712–713
diplomatic corps of, Jubayr (Adil al-) in, 393–395
education in, religion in, 433
Egyptian relations with, 549
foreign investment in, 714
government of (*See* Saudi government and politics)
in Gulf War (1990–1991), 131–132, 192
Hariri's (Rafiq) construction business in, 345
Hijazi Arabs in, 833, 834
historic preservation in, 99
holy sites in, 711
Indian relations with, 712–713
Iranian relations with, 713
Islamist ideology in, 290–292, 433
journalism by Khashoggi (Jamal) in, 432–434
military of, 83, 710–711
Qatari border with, 85
Qataris deported to, 89
reforms in, 710, 711
Sahwa intellectual movement in, 131–135
Saʿud (Abdullah bin Abd al-Aziz al-) as king of, 709–714
and September 11 terrorist attacks, 393–394, 433
social anthropology in, Yamani (Mai) in, 833–834
terrorism in, 134, 193, 433, 712
U.S. military in, 192, 193, 712
U.S. press coverage of, 393–394
U.S. relations with, 393–395, 712
Wahhabi Islam in, Awda (Salman al-) in, 131–135
as WTO member, 714
Zindani (Abd al-Majid al-) in exile in, 856, 857
Saudi Binladin Group, 191
Saudi Gazette (newspaper), Khashoggi (Jamal) at, 432
Saudi government and politics
Awda (Salman al-) on, 131–135
Basic Law of, 711
Faqih (Saʿd al-) opposing, 290–292
Jubayr (Adil al-) in diplomatic corps of, 393–395
municipal elections in (2005), 711–712
reforms in, 710, 711
Saʿud (Abdullah bin Abd al-Aziz al-) in, 709–714
Sawa, George, 731

Sawaris, Naguib, 715, 716
Sawaris, Nassef, 715, 716
Sawaris, Onsi, **715–717**
    Aswan Dam built by, 716
    as entrepreneur, 715–717
    in Libya, 715–717
Sawaris, Sameeh, 715, 716
Sawt al-Dimuqratiyya (Naisse), 563
Sawt al-Islah (radio station), 291
Say, Fazil, *717,* **717–720**
    as composer, 718, 719
    musical training of, 718
    as pianist, 717–720
Sayl, al- (Tawfiq), 796, 797
Sayyab, Badr Shakir al-, poetry of, 169, 503
Sayyaf, Abdur Rasul, 408
Sayyid, Ahmad Lufti al-, 324
Sayyid, Jamil al-, 409
Sayyidat al-maqam (Aʿraj), 114
Sayyidna Qadr (Rabi), 638
SCC. *See* State Consultative Council
Scheherazade Goes West (Mernissi), 530–531
Schröder, Gerhard, 585
Schumacher, Michael, 190
Schwedler, Jillian, 856
Science fiction, by Ebnou (Moussa Ould), 268–270
SCIRI. *See* Supreme Council for Islamic Revolution in Iraq
Sculpture
    by Danziger (Itzhak), 812, 813
    by Hatoum (Mona), 358–362
    by Saudi (Mona), 714–715, 830
    by Tumarkin (Igael), 811–813
Sderot (Israel), 615–616
Sealed Room, The (Shehadeh), 760
Season of Men, The (film), 803, 805, 806, 807
Season of Migration to the North (Salih), 695, 697, 698
Sebbar, Leila, **720–721**
    writings of, 720–721
Secularism. *See also specific countries*
    in democracy, 481
    Dündar (Can) advocating, 261
    Erdogan (Tayyip) on, 285, 286
    Harbi (Mohamed) on, 343
    Mardin (Şerif) on, 511, 512
    Mesbah Yazdi (Mohammad Taqi) on, 532, 533, 534
    National Liberation Front and, 477–478, 479–480
    Sezer (Ahmet Necdet) and, 725–726
    Soroush (Abdolkarim) on, 776, 779
Seddigh, Laleh, *721,* **721–722**
    as race car driver, 721–722

Segev, Tom, **722–724**
    as historian, 722, 723–724
    journalism of, 722, 723, 724
    military service of, 723
Self-censorship, 771
Self Criticism After the Defeat (Al-Azam), 40, 41
Senate (Jordan), 378
Sephardic Jews
    and Ashkenazic Jews, 842, 844
    Yosef (Ovadia) as rabbi of, 841–845
September 11 terrorist attacks (2001)
    Al Saʿud's (Al-Walid bin Talal) philanthropy after, 80
    Amin (Galal) on, 97
    Awda (Salman al-) on, 133
    bin Ladin's (Usama) role in, 193
    Jubayr (Adil al-) on, 393–394
    Khashoggi (Jamal) on, 433
    Khatami (Mohamed) on, 438
    Mubarak (Husni) on, 550
    Omar (Mullah Mohammed) receiving U.S. ultimatum after, 592
    Qaddafi (Muʿammar al-) condemning, 626
    al-Qaʿida's role in, Abu Ghayth (Sulayman) on, 23–24
    Qaradawi (Yusuf) condemning, 635
    Salih (Ali Abdullah) on, 695
    Saudi Arabia's response to, 393–394
    Saudi nationals involved in, 393–394, 433
    U.S. press coverage of, 393–394
Sept Grains de Beauté, Les (Saddiki), 674
Serfaty, Abraham, 460, 555
Sessiz Ev (Pamuk), 598
Sétif Revolt (1945), 218
7 July 2005 subway bombings (London), Qaradawi (Yusuf) condemning, 635
Seventh Million, The: The Israelis and the Holocaust (Segev), 724
Sex, Monica, 341
Sexuality
    in Amer's (Ghada) art, 93–94
    in Bouraoui's (Nina) novels, 212–214
    female, 93–94, 104–106
    in Hamed's (Marwan) films, 329
    Kotb (Heba) on, 634
    Mernissi (Fatima) on, 529, 530, 531
    Qaradawi (Yusuf) on, 634, 635
    in Rimitti's (Cheikha) lyrics, 658, 659, 660–661

Sexuality, *continued*
    in Ruby's songs, 665
    in Shukri's (Muhammad) book,
        797
    in Turkish films, 104–106
Seyour, Salman, 398
Sezer, Ahmet Necdet, *724,* **724–726**
    as judge, 725, 726
    military service of, 725
    presidency of, 724, 725–726
    and secularism, 725–726
Sfayr, Butrus. *See* Sfeir, Nasrallah
Sfeir, Nasrallah, **726–730,** *727*
    influences on, 728–729
    on Israel, 729, 730
    in Lebanese Civil War
        (1975–1990), 728, 730
    as Maronite Catholic Church
        patriarch, 726, 728–730
    nationalism of, 727, 728
    religious studies of, 727–728
Sha'b, al- (newspaper), 558, 653
Shabiba, al- (Fatah Youth Movement)
    Barghuthi (Marwan) in, 150,
        151
    Dahlan (Muhammad) in, 239
    establishment of, 150, 151, 239
Shablul (Hanoch and Einstein), 339
Shach, Elazar Menachem, 842, 843
Shaddad, Muhammad Hamid, 386
Shadow, The. *See* Eliasi, Yoav
Shagdom Agreement (1994), 524
Shaheen, Hikmat, 731
Shaheen, Simon, *730,* **730–732**
    as composer, 730, 731, 732
    soundtracks by, 731
    teaching career of, 731, 732
    as violin player, 731
Shahrani, Ebaadullah, 733
Shahrani, Nematullah, **732–734,** *733*
    fighting Soviet occupation, 733
    as religious scholar, 732–734
    religious studies of, 732
    writings of, 734
Shair, Kamal, **734–736**
    as entrepreneur, 734–736
Shajarian, Mohamed Reza, **736–738**
    music of, 736–738
Shakir, Fatina Anin, 99
Shakir, Hani, 251
Shalhub, Michel Demitri Shalhoub. *See*
    Sharif, Omar
Shalit, Gilad, 153
Shalom (Hanoch), 341
Shamir, Moshe, 248
Shamir, Yitzhak
    in Madrid Peace Talks (1991),
        746
    as prime minister, 575, 587, 613
    Sharon (Ariel) under, 750

Shamma, Naseer, *739,* **739–740**
    music of, 739–740
Shamma, Sara, **740–741**
    art of, 740–741
Shamsolvaezin, Mashallah, *742,* **742–743**
    journalism of, 742–743
Shango performance group, 363
Shapira, Anita, **743–745**
    as historian, 743–745
    writings of, 744–745
Sharaa, Farouk al-, *745,* **745–746**
    diplomatic career of, 745–746
    in peace process, 746
Sharabi, Hisham Bashir, 425
Sharett, Moshe, 612
Shari'a (Islamic law)
    Amer (Magda) teaching, 634
    Awda (Salman al-) on, 131–132
    Fadlallah (Muhammad Husayn)
        on, 287
    in historical research, 649
    Kar (Mehrangiz) studying, 402
    Shenouda III against, 761
    in Sudan, 163
    Turabi (Hasan al-) on, 815
    on women's political participation,
        35–36
    Zarqawi (Abu Mus'ab al-) on, 852
Shariati, Ali, 20
Shari'a wa'l-Haya, al- (television show),
    633
Sharif, Omar, **746–747**
    Diab (Amr) and, 250
    discovery by Chahine (Youssef), 232
    films of, 746–747
Sharon, Ariel, **747–753,** *748*
    Barnea (Nahum) on, 155
    under Begin (Menachem),
        749–750
    as defense minister, 749–750, 752
    as foreign minister, 750
    Jerusalem visit of (2000), 750
    in Kadima Party, 576, 587, 751
    Lahham (Duraid) on, 464
    legacy of, 155, 752–753
    in Likud Party, 576, 577, 587, 617,
        749, 750
    Livni (Tzipi) supporting, 473–474,
        475
    and Maronites in Lebanon, 750
    military career of, 747, 748–750,
        751, 752
    and Netanyahu (Binyamin), 576,
        750
    Olmert (Ehud) as ally of, 587,
        589
    and Operation Defensive Shield
        (2002), 750
    Oslo Accords (1993) reversed by,
        750

    as prime minister, 473, 587, 614,
        747, 750–752
    under Rabin (Yitzhak), 749
    under Shamir (Yitzhak), 750
    stroke suffered by, 587, 588, 747,
        751
    and withdrawal from Gaza Strip,
        473, 475, 587, 589, 747,
        750–751, 752
Sharqawi, Ahmad, 187, **753–755**
    art of, 753–755
    influences on, 753, 754–755
Shas Party (Israel)
    Labor Party in coalition with,
        844
    Yosef (Ovadia) in, 842, 843–844
Shawa, Laila, **755–756**
    art of, 755–756
Shawqi, Ahmad, 484, 485, 819, 820
Shaykh, Hanan al-, **756–757**
    writings of, 756–757
Sheba Telecom Company, 716
Sheder me'ha-Bayit ha-Lavan
    (Margalit), 513, 515
Shehadeh, Aziz, 757, 758–759, 760
Shehadeh, Raja, *757,* **757–761**
    as human rights activist, 758, 759
    as lawyer, 757–760
    in peace process, 758, 759–760
    writings of, 757–758, 759, 760
Shell oil company, in Qatar, 90
Shenouda III (Coptic Orthodox patri-
    arch), **761–763**
    religious studies of, 761
    on *shari'a,* 761
    writings of, 763
Shepherdstown (West Virginia),
    Syrian–Israeli peace talks in (2000),
    331
Sher-e Nimai, 174
Sher-e No, 174
Sherkat, Shahla, 350
Sherzai, Gul Aga, 407
Shi'ite Muslims. *See also under specific*
    countries
    Akhbari school of, 703
    Akhbari-Usuli schism of, 703
    attacks on, in Iraq, 852, 853
    Ba'th Party (Iraq) oppressing, 372
    Ba'th Party (Syria) supporting,
        509
    conflict with Sunnis, 507, 508,
        509
    in exile from Iraq, 509
    in exile in Iran, 509
    in exile in Syria, 509
    Fadlallah (Muhammad Husayn) as
        cleric of, 287–290
    in Islamist movement, 372
    leadership of, struggle over, 288

Sultan bin Abd al-Aziz. *See* Al Sa'ud, Sultan bin Abd al-Aziz

Sultan Street, Al- (Rabi). *See Darb al-Sultan* (Rabi)

Summer of Avia, The (Almagor), 61

Sumud (perseverance), 759

Sunbati, Riyad al-, 819, 820

Sunna (record of Prophet), scientific inimitability of, 856, 857

Sunni Islam, scholarship on, by Qaradawi (Yusuf), 632, 633

Sunni Muslims
    on Iran under Ahmadinejad (Mahmoud), 29
    in Iraq, in conflict with Shi'ites, 507, 508, 509
    Wahhabi sect of, 89, 131–135, 433

Sun O (film). *See Soleil O*

Supreme Council for Family Affairs (Qatar), 537

Supreme Council for Islamic Revolution in Iraq (SCIRI), 678

Supreme courts, Barak (Aharon) on role of, 149. *See also specific countries*

Supreme Education Council (Qatar), 537

Supreme National Security Council (Iran), Larijani (Ali Ardashir) as head of, 469, 470

Suq al-Manakh (Kuwaiti stock market), 75

Suqut Hansawwar (film), 665

"Survivors" (Iraqi group of film-makers), 652

Suspended Dreams (film), 521

Suswa, Amat al- Alim al-, **787–788**
    human rights advocacy by, 787–788
    on women, 787

Syracuse University, Maxwell School of Citizenship and Public Affairs, Khouri (Rami) at, 445, 446

Syria
    in Arab–Israeli War (1973), 121–122
    art of Shamma (Sara) in, 740–741
    Defense and Security Pact (1993) signed by, 466
    democracy in, Darraj's (Faisal) support for, 244
    economic reform in, 117, 121, 123
    Egyptian relations with, 121–122
    Egyptian union with (*See* United Arab Republic)
    European relations with, 118
    in Federation of Arab Republics, 558

    films of (*See* Syrian films)
    foreign policy of, 117–119, 121–124, 413–414
    government of (*See* Syrian government)
    history of, Rafeq (Abdul-Karim) on, 648–649
    Hizbullah supported by, 117–118, 414
    human rights in (*See* Syrian human rights)
    Iranian relations with, 122, 414
    on Iran–Iraq War (1980–1988), 122
    Iraqi relations with, 122
    Israeli peace talks with, 118, 122, 331
    journalism of Hamidi (Ibrahim) in, 329–331
    Jumblatt (Walid) and, 395–398
    in Lebanese Civil War (1975–1990), 396
    Lebanese relations with, 346–348, 413–414
    Lebanese withdrawal by (2005), 118, 347, 348
    Lebanon controlled by, 465–466, 571, 728–729
    in Lebanon War (2006), 118
    literature of (*See* Syrian literature; Syrian poetry)
    Maliki (Nuri Kamil al-) in exile in, 506, 507, 509
    Maronite Catholic Church in, 728
    military of, 116–117, 120
    Muslim Brotherhood in, 166–167
    Öcalan (Abdullah) in, 583, 584
    political reform in, 117, 119, 121
    Shi'ite Muslims from Iraq in exile in, 509
    Soviet relations with, 121–122
    sports in, Shouaa (Ghada) in, 769–771
    U.S.-led regime change in, Jumblatt (Walid) on, 397
    U.S. relations with, 117–118, 122–123

Syria Accountability Act (2002), 729

Syriac Orthodox Church, Ignatius Zaka II as patriarch of, 762

Syrian Accountability and Lebanese Sovereignty Restoration Act (U.S., 2003), 118

Syrian Bride, The (film), 451

Syrian films
    by Akkad (Moustapha), 32–34
    by Amiralay (Umar), 97–98
    Lahham (Duraid) in, 462–463
    Salameh (Nadine) in, 689

Syrian government and politics
    Asad (Bashar al-) as president of, 115, 117–119
    Asad (Hafiz al-) as president of, 121–124
    Bayanuni (Ali Sadr al-Din) in, 166–167
    coup of 1963 in, 120
    coup of 1966 in, 801–802
    coup of 1970 in, 121, 802
    democracy in, 244
    foreign policy of, 117–119, 121–124, 413–414
    Hamidi's (Ibrahim) coverage of, 330–331
    Khaddam (Abd al-Halim) in, 413–415
    liberalization of, 117, 119, 121

Syrian human rights
    Darraj's (Faisal) support for, 244
    Maleh (Haytham al-) as advocate of, 504–505
    Naisse (Aktham) as advocate of, 563–564

Syrian legal system
    Maleh (Haytham al-) in, 504–505
    Naisse (Aktham) in, 563–564

Syrian literature
    by Maghut (Muhammad al-), 463
    by Samman (Ghada), 705

Syrian poetry
    by Qabbani (Nizar), 621–624
    by Sa'id (Ali Ahmad), 682–684
    women as subject of, 621–623

Syrian Social Nationalist Party (SSNP), 682

T

"Ta'asa" (Asimi), 128

Tab Leh (Alama), 38

Table tennis, in South Yemen, 566–567

TACT (record label), 765, 766, 767

Tafsir-i Sura-i Hujurat (Shahrani), 734

Taha, Rachid, 293

"Taht al-Dush" (Ruby), 666

Taht al-Mizalla (Mahfouz), 488

Ta'if Accord (1989), 728–729
    Aoun (Michel) against, 102
    Fadlallah (Muhammad Husayn) against, 290
    Hariri (Rafiq) in, 346, 348
    Khaddam (Abd al-Halim) in, 414

Tajammu' al-Yamani li'l-Islah, al-. *See* Islah Party

VOLUME 1: 1–458; VOLUME 2: 459–860

Turkey, *continued*
 economic development in,
  285–286
 in European Union, 261, 286
 films of (*See* Turkish films)
 government of (*See* Turkish
  government)
 Greek relations with, in dispute
  over Cyprus, 604–605, 782,
  792–793
 history of, 260, 511
 human rights in, 585, 782
 Islamists in (*See* Turkish Islamist
  groups)
 journalism in (*See* Turkish
  journalism)
 Kurds in, 583–585, 599–600
 literature of (*See* Turkish literature)
 modernization in, 309–311
 music of (*See* Turkish music)
 national identity in, 310, 511–512
 political parties in, 223, 260 (*See
  also specific parties*)
 political science in, Mardin (Şerif)
  in, 510, 511, 512
 privatization in, 781, 782, 783
 secularism in (*See* Turkish
  secularism)
 sociology in, Mardin (Şerif) in,
  510, 511, 512
 sports in (*See* Turkish sports)
 Supreme Court of, 725
 theater of, Kenter (Yildiz) in,
  411–412
 U.S. relations with, 261, 286
 women of (*See* Turkish women)
Turki bin Abdul Aziz, 710
Turkish Cypriot Students' Youth
 Federation (KOGEF), 792
Turkish films
 Ar (Müjde) in, 103–106
 by Ceylan (Nuri Bilge), 226–229
 decline in, 226
 by Demirkubuz (Zeki), 227
 documentaries, 260–261
 Kenter (Yildiz) in, 412
 "new wave," 226, 227
 revival of, 226–229
 women portrayed in, 103–106
Turkish Foundation of Cinema and
 Audiovisual Culture (TÜRSAK),
 104
Turkish government and politics
 Atatürk (Mustafa Kemal) in, 725
 Çetin (Hikmet) in, 223–224
 corruption in, 725
 coup of 1970 in, 781
 coup of 1980 in, 105
 coup of 1997 in, 284
 Demirel (Süleyman) in, 724, 725

 democracy in, 286, 725
 Dündar (Can) on, 259–261
 Ecevit (Bülent) in, 725
 Erdogan (Tayyip) in, 285–286,
  726, 840
 Evren (Kenan) in, 725
 Sezer (Ahmet Necdet) in, 724,
  725–726
 Supreme Court in, 725
Turkish Grand National Assembly
 (TBMM), Çetin (Hikmet) in, 223,
 224
"Turkish Islamic Exceptionalism
 Yesterday and Today" (Mardin), 511
Turkish Islamist groups
 Erdogan (Tayyip) in, 283–286
 Göle (Nilüfer) on, 310
 modernization and, 310
 political parties of, 283
Turkish journalism
 by Dündar (Can), 259–261
 by Soysal (Mümtaz), 780
Turkish literature
 by Kulin (Ayşe), 456–458
 by Pamuk (Orhan), 597–601
Turkish music
 of Biret (Idil), 195–196
 of Say (Fazil), 717–720
Turkish Parliament. *See* Turkish Grand
 National Assembly
Turkish Republic of Northern Cyprus
 (TRNC)
  Denktas (Rauf) as president of,
   782, 793
  embargoes against, 793
  Talat (Mehmet Ali) as president of,
   792–793
  Talat (Mehmet Ali) as prime min-
   ister of, 792
Turkish Resistance Organization
 (TMT) (Cyprus), 782
Turkish secularism
 in coup of 1997, 284
 Dündar (Can) advocating, 261
 Erdogan (Tayyip) on, 285, 286
 Mardin (Şerif) on, 511, 512
 Sezer (Ahmet Necdet) and,
  725–726
Turkish sports
 Ayhan (Süreyya) in, 135–137
 football, 799–800
 Karademir (Tuğba) in, 403–405
 women's, 136–137
 Yerlikaya (Hamza) in, 839–840
Turkish Telecom (TT), 782
Turkish women
 in business, 671
 headscarves on, Göle (Nilüfer) on,
  309–311
 in sports, 136–137

TÜRSAK. *See* Turkish Foundation of
 Cinema and Audiovisual Culture
Turtles Can Fly (film), 308
Tus (newspaper), 742, 743
Twelver Shi'ism, on music, 736
Twin Tower Fund, Al Sa'ud's (Al-
 Walid bin Talal) donation to, 80
Two-state solution
 Abbas (Mahmud) supporting, 6, 7,
  8
 Barghuthi (Marwan) supporting,
  150, 152
 Hawatma (Nayif) advocating, 315
 Khalidi (Walid) on, 426
 Palestine National Council sug-
  gesting, 316
 PFLP's position on, 315
 in "Principles of Peace" (1977), 6
 U.S. position on, 426
Tykwer, Tom, 651
"Tzel, ha-" (Alberstein), 45

U

UAE. *See* United Arab Emirates
U.A.R. *See* United Arab Republic
Üçüncü Sayfa (film), 227
Ud (musical instrument), 399,
 739–740
UEFA. *See* Union of European Football
 Association
UEM. *See* Union of Moroccan Writers
Uganda, airline hijacking in. *See*
 Entebbe incident
UIA. *See* United Iraqi Alliance
Umma Party (Sudan), 524
Umm Kulthum, **817–821**
 Bouchnaq (Lotfi) compared to, 203
 Bouchnaq (Lotfi) influenced by,
  201
 commercial recordings by, 818,
  821
 concerts by, 819, 820, 821
 Fayruz compared to, 299
 health issues of, 819, 820
 in musicals, 201, 818, 820
 music of, 201, 817–821
 as radio performer, 818, 819, 820,
  821
 style of, 820
 Zoghbi (Nawal al-) influenced by,
  858
Umm Qays, historic restoration in,
 431
Umran, Muhammad, 120
UN. *See* United Nations
Un Autre Soleil (Faudel), 293
Underexposure (film), 651, 652–653
Under the Rubble (film), 521
Under this Blazing Light (Oz), 594

Wattar, al-Taher, **825–829**
 on Algerian independence,
  827–828
 on Khadra (Yasmina), 419
 on Mustaghanmi (Ahlam), 562
 in National Liberation Front, 825,
  827
 writings of, 113, 826, 827–828, 829
Wazir, Khalil al-, 6
 assassination of, 6
 in Fatah, 6, 108
 Rajub (Jibril) as deputy to, 241
Weapons of mass destruction (WMD).
 See Iraqi weapons of mass destruc-
 tion; Nuclear programs
Websites. *See* Internet
Wedding in Galilee (film), 451
Wedding of Zein, The (Salih), 697, 698
"We Had an Understanding"
 (Ravikovitch), 656
Weightlifters
 Rezazadeh (Hossein), 657–658
 Süleymanoglu (Naim), 658
Weitzman, Ezer, 749
Weizman, Ezer, 247
Welfare Association (Palestine), 768
Welfare Party (Turkey), Erdogan
 (Tayyip) in, 283–284
Well, The (Alberstein), 44
West Bank
 art in, of Tamari (Vera), 795
 Israeli occupation of, Khalidi
  (Rashid) criticizing, 422–423
 Israeli retention of, Oslo Accords
  on, 614
 mausoleum of Arafat (Yasir) in,
  810
 separation fence in, Israeli Supreme
  Court on, 148
West Bank, Israeli withdrawal from
 Labor Party on, 616
 Margalit (Dan) on, 515
 Netanyahu (Binyamin) on, 576,
  577
 Olmert (Ehud) on, 577, 587–588,
  590
 Yasin (Ahmad) on, 837, 838
Westernization, *vs.* modernization,
 310
Western Sahara, 13–14
 Algeria's position on, 216–217,
  218, 356
 Mauritania's claim to, 13, 356
 Morocco's claim to, 13, 356–357
Western world
 anti-Semitism in, 527
 Awda (Salman al-) on dialogue
  with, 134
 bin Ladin (Usama) on jihad
  against, 193

human rights ideals in, criticism of,
 132–133
Khaled (Amr) on dialogue with,
 420
Muslim approaches to dealing
 with, 384–385
Turkey as part of, 261
Weymouth, Lally, 333
When the Bulbul Stopped Singing
 (Shehadeh), 760
Where Is the Friend's House? (film), 452
Where the Jackals Howl (Oz), 594
White Balloon, The (film). *See*
 Badkonake Sefid
White Castle, The (Pamuk). *See Beyaz*
 Kale (Pamuk)
White Revolution (1961–1963) (Iran),
 539
White Wedding (Hanoch). *See Hatuna*
 Levana (Hanoch)
WHO. *See* World Health Organization
"Who's the Terrorist?" (DAM), 766
Widad (film), 818, 820
Wiesenberg, Menachem, 44
Wifaq (Bahrain), 699, 700–702
Wijdan Ali, **829–830**
 as art historian, 829–830
 diplomatic career of, 829
Wild Flowers (film), 521
Wildlife preservation, Al Thani (Sa'ud
 bin Muhammad bin Ali) in, 92
Wind Will Carry Us, The (film), 307
Winograd, Eliyahu, 588
WIPO. *See* World Intellectual Property
 Organization
Wiretapping, by U.S., of ElBaradei
 (Mohamed), 274
WISE. *See* World & Islam Studies
 Enterprise
Witt, Katarina, 404
WMD. *See* Iraqi weapons of mass
 destruction; Nuclear programs
Wolferman, Ilan. *See* Ramon, Ilan
Wolfowitz, Paul, 398
Wollach, Yona, 656
Woman of Her Time, A (film), 521
Women. *See also under specific countries*
 in Amer's (Ghada) art, 93–94
 in business, 671
 citizenship for, 53
 clothing of (*See* Hijab; Veiling)
 condition of, 256–257
 in education, 89–90
 in Family Code of Algeria, 219,
  335, 809
 films about, 309, 453, 468–469,
  521, 602, 804–805, 806, 807
 in Ghasemi's (Amir Ali) art, 306
 Hakim (Tawfiq al-) on emancipation of, 325

in Iranian Revolution (1979), 35
Khatami's (Mohamed) policies
 and, 436
in legal careers, 263–264, 401–402
literature about, 213–214,
 256–257, 258, 606, 607, 608
Mahieddine (Baya) on, 491
Mala'ika (Nazik al-) on, 502
Meddeb (Abdelwahhab) on, 527
Mernissi (Fatima) on, 528–531,
 807
Mesbah Yazdi (Mohammad Taqi)
 on, 534
Misnad (Mawza bint Nasir al-)
 and, 535, 536–537, 538
Moqaddem (Malika) on, 543, 544
Mustaghanmi (Ahlam) on, 560
poetry on, 174, 502, 621–623
political participation by, 383, 384
in presidential elections, 35–36
Qabbani (Nizar) on, 621–623
Rauf Ezzat (Heba) on, 653
Ravikovitch (Dalia) on, 654, 656
restrictions on, 225, 257, 592
rights of (*See* Feminism; Suffrage;
 Women's rights)
Sadr (Rabab al-) on, 680
Salami (Khadija al-) on, 691
Samman (Ghada) on, 705
second-class status of, 335, 336
Sidera (Zineb) on, 771
in sports, 136–137, 209–212,
 275–276, 350, 351
sports uniforms for, 209, 212,
 276
stoned to death, 680, 681
Suswa (Amat al-Alim al-) on, 787
Tawfiq (Ahmad at-) on, 796
Tekeli (Şirin) on, 798
Toumi (Khalida) on, 809
and writing, relationship between,
 256–257
Yamani's (Mai) research on, 833
Yosef (Ovadia) on, 843
Zaki (Muna) on, 850
Women and Democracy in Yemen (film),
 691
Women in Iran Website, 680
Women in Politics: An Islamic Perspective
 (Rauf Ezzat), 653
Women in Yemen (film), 691
Women of Algiers in Their Apartment
 (Djebar). *See Femmes d'Alger dans*
 leur appartement (Djebar)
Women's Committees (Iran), 351
Women's Cultural Centre, 443, 444
Women's rights. *See also* Feminism;
 Suffrage; *specific countries*
 Abbasgholizadeh (Mahboubeh)
  advocating, 8–10

REFERENCE

TOURO COLLEGE LIBRARY

3 0000 00077 8534

For Reference

Not to be taken

from this library

TOURO COLLEGE LIBRARY
Boro Park 53rd Street

WITHDRAWN

Middle East, Political

— International boundary
···· Disputed boundary
★ Capital city
• Other city

POLAND

BELGIUM   GERMANY
LUXEMBOURG   CZECH
                                 REPUBLIC   SLOVAKIA

FRANCE   SWITZERLAND   AUSTRIA   HUNGARY   ROMANIA

                              SLOVENIA
                                        CROATIA
                ITALY   BOSNIA AND   SERBIA
                                   HERZEGOVINA   AND   BULGARIA
                                                     MONTENEGRO
PORTUGAL   SPAIN   MACEDONIA
                                                ALBANIA

ATLANTIC   M e d i t e r r a n e a n   S e a   GREECE
OCEAN   Izn

                        ★ Algiers   ★ Tunis
Rabat ★   • Fez   ★ Tripoli   • Benghazi
• Casablanca   TUNISIA
MOROCCO   • Ouargla
• Marrakech
                                                                  • Sabha   L I B Y A
                    A L G E R I A
                          • Adrar
• El Aaiún

Western   • Djanet   • al-Jawf
Sahara

             • Fdérik
                                    MALI   NIGER
     • Atar
                                                                      CHAD
     MAURITANIA
★ Nouakchott

                                                    NIGER

             SENEGAL
GAMBIA   BURKINA FASO

GUINEA-   GUINEA   BENIN
BISSAU
                                    TOGO   NIGERIA
        SIERRA
        LEONE   CENTRAL AFRICAN
                    CÔTE   GHANA   REPUBLIC
        LIBERIA   D'IVOIRE

                                              CAMEROON

                              EQUATORIAL
                              GUINEA   REPUBLIC
                                                          OF THE
                    SÃO TOMÉ   CONGO
ATLANTIC   AND PRÍNCIPE
OCEAN   GABON
                                                         DEMOCRATIC
                                                         REPUBLIC
                                                         OF THE CONGO

                              ANGOLA